ARTIFICIAL WAR

Multiagent-Based
Simulation of Combat

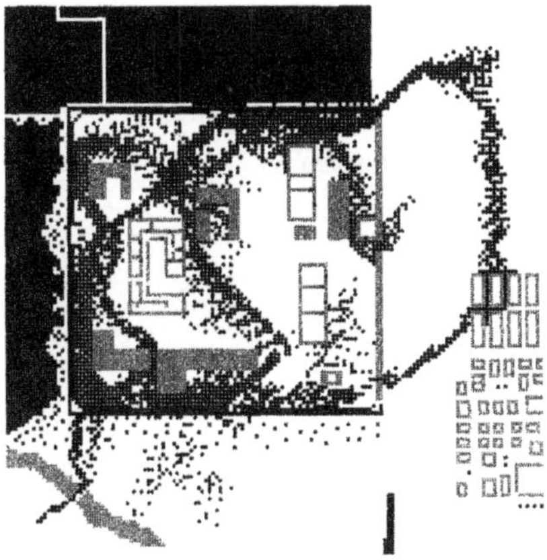

ARTIFICIAL WAR

Multiagent-Based Simulation of Combat

Andrew Ilachinski

Center for Naval Analyses, USA

World Scientific

NEW JERSEY • LONDON • SINGAPORE • BEIJING • SHANGHAI • HONG KONG • TAIPEI • CHENNAI

Published by

World Scientific Publishing Co. Pte. Ltd.
5 Toh Tuck Link, Singapore 596224
USA office: 27 Warren Street, Suite 401-402, Hackensack, NJ 07601
UK office: 57 Shelton Street, Covent Garden, London WC2H 9HE

British Library Cataloguing-in-Publication Data
A catalogue record for this book is available from the British Library.

ARTIFICIAL WAR
Multiagent-Based Simulation of Combat

ISBN-13 978-981-238-834-6
ISBN-10 981-238-834-6

This book is dedicated to four extraordinary individuals who, each in his own way, has shaped much of my professional career as a military operations research analyst: *Richard Bronowitz*, *David W. Kelsey*, *Lieutenant General (Retired) Paul K. van Riper* and *Michael F. Shlesinger*. Without their kind encouragement, gentle guidance and quiet wisdom, the work described herein would not only never have been completed but almost surely would never have gone much beyond being just a faint whisper of a crazy, but interesting, idea.

Foreword

"In war more than in any other subject we must begin by looking at the nature of the whole, for here more than elsewhere the part and whole must always be thought of together."

—Carl von Clausewitz (1780-1831)

In his famous opus, *On War*, the Prussian General Carl von Clausewitz observed that "absolute, so-called mathematical, factors never find a firm basis in military calculations." Yet, today, as in the past, many practitioners and students of war approach it as a discipline founded on scientific principles. They spend considerable intellect, time, and resources in attempts to make war understandable through some system of immutable laws. Theoreticians such as these seem to achieve a measure of satisfaction in presenting papers at professional conferences, writing articles and books, and offering advice to various authorities. In the end, however, their considerable efforts amount to nothing more than *descriptions of what they wish war to be*, not the terrible, brutal, bloody phenomenon that exists in the real world.

The widest and most inappropriate use of such scientific methods for studying and conducting war came during the late-1960s when Secretary of Defense Robert McNamara and his disciples brought systems engineering thinking and tools to the battlefields of Vietnam. Modern military operations they argued needed better quantification. Thus, strict accounting rules dominated much planning and nearly all assessments of how well the war was going. While computers whirling away in Saigon produced numerical "evidence" of success those of us slogging through the rice paddies and jungles came to a very different conclusion. Unfortunately, in the final tally the war-fighters' judgment proved correct and the tragic conflict ended without victory even as it produced a bitterly divided nation.

An intellectual renaissance occurred throughout the American military in the years following the Vietnam War. Officers disillusioned with their recent experience attributed much of the problem to the professional education they received prior to the war. As a result, when they achieved positions of greater authority they eliminated curricula filled with the analytical methods of business administration in favor of ones based on historical case studies and the writings of such philosophers of war as Sun Tzu, Clausewitz, and Mahan. New thinking led to new doctrine rich with the ideas of the classical strategists and replete with examples from history. Eventually leaders at all levels deemed experience, wisdom, and judgment more useful for tackling military problems than checklists, computer printouts, and other mechanistic means. They tagged systems analysts as those who "knew the cost of everything and the value of nothing."

The many reforms implemented by the Vietnam era officers during the late 1970s and the 1980s manifested themselves in *Operation Desert Storm* in 1991, an operation unprecedented in its speed and one-sided results. Not content to rest on their laurels these same officers, now very senior in rank and motivated by recent events and the approaching millennium, intensified their efforts to think about war in the future. Ample evidence existed of the changing character of war—failed states, radical religious movements, terrorists—and of new forms of war brought about by information technologies, precision-guided munitions, and space-based systems. These new dissimilarities from the recent past required attention; nonetheless, the focus of thought remained on the fundamentals of war.

Long recognized as an innovative military service, the *United States Marine Corps* in 1994 undertook a wide review of new discoveries seeking those that showed promise for improving the profession of arms. "Casting their nets widely" and looking far beyond the usual interests of military personnel a handful of Marine officers—of which I was fortunate to be included—learned of the emerging field of nonlinear dynamics, more popularly known as the science of chaos or complexity. Some critics dismissed the nascent theories coming from this new field of study as simply the products of another fad. However, when our group of combat veterans read the reports of researchers associated with the *Santa Fe Institute* we found that their elemental descriptions of activities occurring throughout the natural world matched our own observations of the essentials of actual battles. The more deeply we considered the promising ideas the more convinced we became that war possessed nonlinear characteristics, and thus might be better studied and understood through the lens of complexity theory.

Not surprisingly then, when assigned in summer 1995 as the Commanding General of the *Marine Corps Combat Development Command*—the organization charged with writing concepts for future operations and determining the kinds of organizations and equipment needed for these operations—I established an "Office of New Sciences" to delve into the possibility of employing complexity theory in support of the command's mission. Marines in the office quickly opened an ongoing dialogue with experts in the field. They soon felt confident enough to sponsor a series of workshops and conferences to inform a wider military audience of the potential of this new discipline. About the same time I discovered that a research analyst—Dr. Andrew Ilachinski—employed by the *Center for Naval Analyses*, a federally funded research organization chartered to support the Navy and Marine

Corps, possessed an extensive educational background in nonlinear studies. I immediately sought his assistance.

In an initial discussion Dr. Ilachinski suggested we focus our research on the relevance of complexity theory to land combat because of its unique characteristics, these being hierarchically organized units engaged in multifaceted interactions with each other and the enemy over complicated terrain. I quickly agreed and authorized a six-month exploration of the subject. In July 1996 Dr. Ilachinski published a ground breaking report titled, *Land Warfare and Complexity, Part II: An Assessment of the Applicability of Nonlinear Dynamic and Complex Systems Theory to the Study of Land Warfare.* A separate earlier volume, *Land Warfare and Complexity, Part I: Mathematical Background and Technical Sourcebook* offered material in support of the second volume. The Part II report concluded:

> *"...that the concepts, ideas, theories, tools and general methodologies of nonlinear dynamics and complex systems theory show enormous, almost unlimited, potential for not just providing better solutions for certain existing problems of land combat, but for fundamentally altering our general understanding of the basic processes of war, at all levels."*

Most important, the report suggested specific ways in which an understanding of the properties of complex systems and land warfare might be used, starting with changing the metaphors that elicit images of war and continuing through to developing fundamentally new concepts—or "the universal characteristics"—of land warfare. The report also introduced the possibility of creating an agent-based simulation of combat. Less than three months later in September 1996, Dr. Ilachinski had such a model—*Irreducible Semi-Autonomous Adaptive Combat* (ISAAC)—up and running and a detailed report with source code published. He later introduced an improved Windows version called *Enhanced ISAAC Neural Simulation Tool* (EINSTein).

Combat-experienced Marines who observed the ISAAC program running immediately detected patterns of activity that mimicked those of actual battles and engagements. ISAAC did not generate the statistics and formulas of the traditional military models, it displayed an ebb and flow with the look and feel of real battles.

Complexity theory recognizes that reducing or tearing apart a nonlinear system into its component parts to enable analysis will not work, for the very act of separating the system into lesser elements causes the overall system to lose coherence and meaning. A nonlinear system is not a sum of its parts, but truly more than that sum. Therefore, it must be examined holistically. Clausewitz understood this fact when he wrote that "in war more than in any other subject we must begin by looking at the nature of the whole, for here more than elsewhere the part and whole must always be thought of together." War is not subject to the methods of systems analyses, yet these and other tools of Newtonian physics were the only ones available until Dr. Ilachinski gave us the means to study war as Clausewitz urged.

The more Dr. Ilachinski worked with us the more evident it became that he possessed a combination of qualities seldom found in one person. A brilliant scientist, he also proved to be an exceptionally talented programmer and an accomplished writer able to present material in a style easy for laymen to read and grasp. As a consequence his work very quickly impacted a number of areas. New doctrinal manuals began incorporating ecological vice mechanistic metaphors; Marine Corps professional schools introduced revised courses of instruction into their curricula based on complexity theory; and Marines responsible for modeling and simulation started to explore the possibilities of using agent-based models. An entire new way of thinking soon took hold. Phrases such as "battle management" and "fight like a well-oiled machine" disappeared. Marines recognized that nonlinear phenomena are not subject to the sort of control the term "management" imparts and military units are *complex adaptive systems* not "machines." Officers acknowledging the inherent limitations of nonlinear war-game models no longer accepted uncritically the results their computers churned out.

Within a short time the results of Dr. Ilachinski's work spread widely stimulating and influencing a number of parallel efforts. The following sentences describe but a few of the many spin-off endeavors. Building upon the initial steps of the *Marine Corps University* the *National War College* introduced an entire course based on complexity theory. The *Military Operations Research Society* hosted a workshop on "Warfare Analysis and Complexity" at the *John Hopkins University Applied Physics Laboratory* in September 1997 with the intent of fostering ongoing research in complexity. The Marine Corps used ISAAC software as a basis for *Project Albert*, an enterprise to distill the underlying characteristics of land warfare through a program at the *Maui High Performance Computing Center.* Militaries from Australia, Canada, Germany, New Zealand, and Singapore joined this continuing venture. When histories of this era are written Dr. Andrew Ilachinski is likely to emerge as the "Father of Military Complexity Research."

Publication of *Artificial War: Applying Multiagent-Based Simulation Techniques to the Understanding of Combat* brings the results of eight years of dedicated work to a much wider audience than Dr. Ilachinski's earlier official reports. The timing could not be more fortuitous. Our nation is at war with a tenacious and dangerous enemy and might well be so for years to come. Many of the challenges we face in this war are new and unique. Thus, innovative solutions are called for. Such solutions do not spring full-born; they require research, study and some very profound thinking. Dr. Ilachinski has opened the way for others to follow by providing powerful tools to aid in future explorations while at the same time suggesting ways for present day students to engage in their own deep thinking. Readers whose formal education passed by higher mathematics need not fear this book for Dr. Ilachinski writes in a conversational manner and organizes his work in a way that allows one to move by the more technical sections without losing the overall meaning.

Those in positions with responsibility for planning and conducting the Nation's defense today and into the foreseeable future ignore this book at great peril for it offers deep and meaningful insights into war on land.

Paul K. Van Riper
Lieutenant General
United States Marine Corps (Retired)
Williamsburg, Virginia
December 2003

Preface

This book summarizes the results of a multiyear research program, conducted by me at the *Center for Naval Analyses* (CNA)* between the years 1996-2003, whose charter was to explore applications of complex systems theory to the understanding of the fundamental processes of war. The central thesis of my work, and this book, is that real-world combat between two opposing armies is much less like an inelastic collision between two billiard balls obeying a simple Newtonian-like classical physics—which is essentially how combat has traditionally been described mathematically up until only very recently—than it is a *messy, self-organized ecology of living, viscous fluids consisting of many nonlinearly interacting heterogenous parts, each dynamically adapting to constantly changing conditions* (see figure 0.1). This book represents one particular intellectual thread—as woven and described by the author—of the conceptual and practical consequences that follow from this thesis.

My work on this thesis was originally conceived simply as a broad, high-level—and, so I erroneously thought at the time (in early 1996), *short-term*—examination of possible applications of nonlinear dynamics and complex systems theory to general problems and issues of warfare. However, as one idea led to the next, the project inevitably culminated in the development of a sophisticated multiagent-based model of combat (called EINSTein, and which is now, as I write this preface in November 2003, a mature research-caliber set of computer simulation tools) that uses a suite of artificial-life-like modeling techniques to allow interested students and researchers to explore various aspects of self-organized emergent behavior in combat.

EINSTein is fundamentally different from most conventional models of combat because it represents the first systematic attempt, within the military operations research community, to simulate combat—on a small to medium scale—by using autonomous agents to model *individual behaviors and personalities* rather than specific weapons. EINSTein is the first analytical tool of its kind to have gained widespread use in the military operations research community that focuses its at-

*CNA is a privately owned, nonprofit, federally funded operations research "think tank" that does analyses for the United States *Department of the Navy*. It is headquartered in the state of Virgina, USA. I will have more to say about CNA later in this preface.

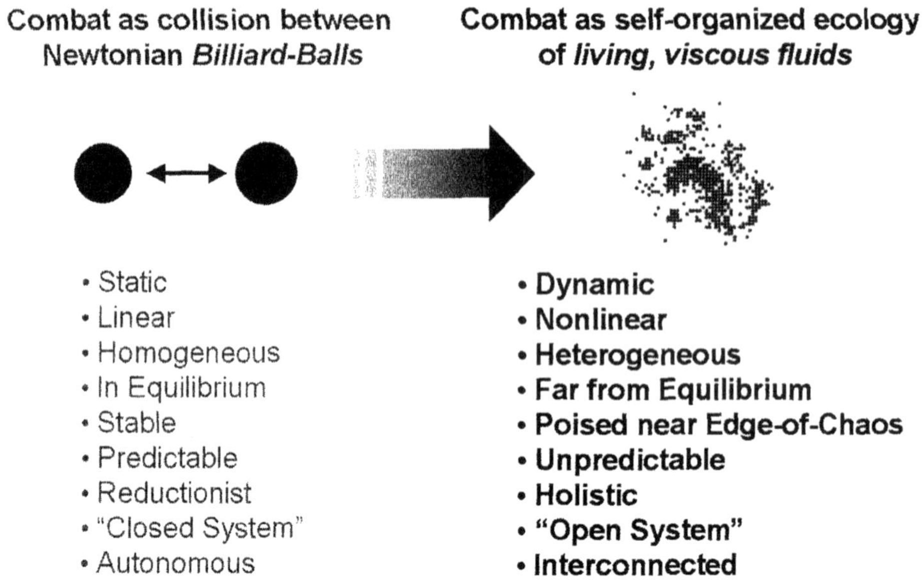

Fig. 0.1 Schematic illustration of the central thesis of this book. Namely, that before one can understand the fundamental processes of war, one must first appreciate that combat is much more like a messy, self-organized ecology of living fluids consisting of many nonlinearly interacting, parts constantly adapting to changing conditions, than it is an inelastic collision of two hard billiard balls.

tention on exploring *emergent patterns and behaviors* (that are mapped over entire scenario spaces) rather than on much simpler, and unrealistically myopic, force-on-force attrition statistics. In addition to introducing this idea of synthesizing high-level behaviors, from the ground up, using low-level agent↔agent interaction rules, EINSTein also takes the important next step of using a genetic algorithm* to essentially *breed entire combat forces* that optimize some set of desirable warfighting characteristics. Finally, on a more conceptual level, EINSTein may be viewed as a prototypical model of future combat simulations that will care less about which side "wins" and more about exploring the regularities (and possibly *universalities*) of the fundamental processes of war.

One of the far-reaching consequences of the work that has led to the design and development of EINSTein—which, remember, is a multiagent-based simulator of *combat*—is evidence that suggests that the same general form of primitive functions

* *Genetic algorithms* (GAs) are a class of heuristic search methods and computational models of adaptation and evolution. GAs mimic the dynamics underlying natural evolution to search for optimal solutions of general combinatorial optimization problems. They have been applied to the traveling salesman problem, VLSI circuit layout, gas pipeline control, the parametric design of aircraft, neural net architecture, models of international security, and strategy formulation. We discuss how genetic algorithms are used by EINSTein to automatically breed multiagent combat forces in chapter 7.

that govern the agent↔agent interactions in EINSTein can be used to describe the emergent behaviors of a variety of other *non*-combat-related (i.e., ecological, social and/or economic) complex systems. I will attempt to show how EINSTein—despite being obviously conceived in, and confined to, the combat arena—may actually be viewed as an exemplar of a vastly larger class of artificial-life simulators of complex adaptive systems. EINSTein thus represents a potentially far more broadly applicable tool for conceptual exploratory modeling than its combat-centric design alone suggests.

It is only relatively recently, during the last decade or so, that the military operations community has made any demonstrable progress in elucidating the fundamental role that nonlinearity plays in combat, beyond that of reciting carefully chosen historical anecdotes or creating suggestive metaphors to illustrate their significance. It is even more recently that a few of the basic lessons learned from the complex adaptive systems theory community have percolated their way into operations research. I would therefore like to use the remaining paragraphs of this preface to share some personal notes about how these two unlikely bedfellows, *complexity science* and *combat operations research,* got together at CNA in the form of the work that is described in this book.

The story begins with my graduate work in theoretical physics in the early 1980s, and about seven years or so before I had ever heard of CNA. Motivated by certain questions having to do with the conceptual foundations of fundamental physics, I had been tinkering with some novel microscopic equations of motion on a discrete dynamic space-time lattice in the hopes of constructing a "toy universe" (i.e., physics jargon for "model") in which the fundamental distinction between *figure* (i.e., particles) and *ground* (i.e., space-time) is blurred (or disappears completely). Though I did not know it at the time, the formalism that I had, out of necessity, created for my own use and was struggling with to understand was something that mathematicians had actually developed decades before, called *cellular automata.** Then—in 1983—just as I was becoming comfortable with using my new formalism for performing computations, a groundbreaking review article by Stephen Wolfram on the *physics* of cellular automata appeared in the journal *Reviews of Modern Physics.*†

*Cellular automata (CA) are a general class of spatially and temporally discrete, deterministic mathematical systems characterized by local interaction and an inherently parallel form of evolution. First introduced by the mathematician John von Neumann in the 1950s as simple models of biological self-reproduction, CA are prototypical models for complex systems and processes consisting of a large number of simple, locally interacting homogenous components. CA are fascinating because very simple rules often yield highly complex emergent behaviors. I will have a *lot more* to say about CA later in the book (see, for example, chapter 2).

†The paper I am referring to is "Statistical mechanics of cellular automata," *Reviews Modern Physics*, Volume 55, 1983, 601-644. The author of this landmark paper is the same Stephen Wolfram who later went on to develop the mathematical software *Mathematica* [Math41], and who, more recently, has published the results of a decades-long solo-research effort into the implications of a cellular-automata-based science, called *A New Kind of Science* [Wolfram02].

This simple (and, as interpreted by me at the time, a preternaturally *meaningful*) synchronicity was too much for a young researcher to ignore; I knew then and there that cellular automata offered a profound new way of looking at the world, and that cellular automata were a subject about which I had to do a lot more thinking. Naturally, cellular automata went on to both play a central role in my graduate work,* and—for reasons that will be made clear below—to also represent an important conceptual cornerstone of the work described in this book.

Upon completing my Ph.D. in 1988, I was eagerly looking forward to making my way westward to New Mexico to take up a post-doc position at the *Los Alamos National Laboratory*'s *T-13* (*Complex Systems*) *Theoretical Division* and the (then still embryonic) *Santa Fe Institute* for complexity research. My joy at being offered this wonderful opportunity (I was told that the dual post-doc position was one of the first of its kind, and I therefore considered it quite an honor) soon turned to dismay as I was informed while packing for my cross-country trip that the funding for these positions would be unavailable for another year. Scrambling to find another position before that summer ended, I was urged by my family and friends to accept one of the other post-graduate offers that I had not yet officially declined. I was soon cajoled to accept an offer that stood firmly in second place on my list of "desired" positions. That offer, which I gratefully—if somewhat reluctantly—accepted, was for the position of research analyst at a prestigious naval think-tank called CNA, a position I have happily held ever since.

Now, CNA and complexity science are not exactly an obvious match...To be sure, CNA was (and still is) a well-known and respected research and development center and has a long, and distinguished history,† but it has certainly never specialized in

*I received my Ph.D. from the *Institute of Theoretical Physics* (ITP) at the *State University of Stony Brook* (New York) in 1988, under the tutelage of Professor Max Dresden, who was then head of ITP. My thesis was entitled *Computer Explorations of Discrete Complex Systems*, and used generalized forms of cellular automata to explore the (classical and quantum) dynamics of self-organized lattice structures. I will be forever indebted to Max for allowing me to pursue interests that seemed—certainly to those making up the intellectual core of ITP at the time—comical, at best, and childishly *pseudo*-physics-like, at worst. Aside from being a well known and respected physicist who specialized in statistical mechanics and the history of physics, Max was a gifted and inspiring teacher. His knowledge, wisdom, humor and grace enchanted all those who knew him, especially his students. For those of you interested in hearing and seeing a master at work doing what he did best, here is a link to some of the (MPEG videos of) lectures he delivered on the history of physics at the *Stanford Linear Accelerator Center* (SLAC) in the early 1990s (Max was Professor Emeritus at SLAC during the last few years of his life): http://www-project.slac.stanford.edu/streaming-media/dresdentalks/dresdentalks.htm. Max, sadly and tragically, died in 1997.

†CNA dates back to World War II (or, more precisely, 1942) when it was known as the *Anti-submarine Warfare Operations Research Group* (ASWORG; see [Tidm84]). ASWORG, or as it was later (and still is) known, OEG (which stands for *Operations Research Group*, and currently one of several other newer divisions within a larger CNA *Corporation*, or CNAC), has the distinction of being the *oldest* military operations analysis group in the Unted States. (RAND, for example, which has a more public profile and about which readers may be more familiar, dates back to 1948.) OEG's analysts pioneered the field of operations research during their ground-

complex systems studies. I knew that by accepting a position at CNA I would forego—perhaps *indefinitely*—the chance to continue the work on complex systems theory that I had started exploring in graduate school. The main reason that this otherwise obviously unwelcome prospect did not hinder me as much as might be expected was that prior to my Ph.D. thesis defense I had signed a contract with a publisher to write a textbook on cellular automata.* That, I thought—and, as it turned out, thankfully, thought *correctly*—would keep the part of my brain interested in complexity occupied and happy while the other part would be free to explore new avenues of research and interests.

In the hindsight of the 15 years that have elapsed since that fateful evaporation of funds I had expected to support my post-doc positions in New Mexico and my initially lukewarm acceptance of CNA's offer to join its research staff—not to mention countless research projects over the ensuing years, reconstructions of naval exercises, a role in assessing the Navy's performance during *Operation Desert Storm*, a multiyear stint as CNA's field representative at the *Whidbey Island Naval Air Station* (located in Washington state),† and a marriage to a wonderful woman I met in Washington, D.C. that has resulted in the births of two healthy and beautiful children—I can honestly say that my tenure at CNA during this time has been by far the most intellectually and personally rewarding period of my life.

Research projects that I was involved with during my early years at CNA included the mathematical and computer modeling of radar processing (such as coherent sidelobe cancellation, adaptive responses to jamming signals, modeling the processing routines of surface surveillance radars), mathematical search theory, an analysis of the Navy's readiness response to reprogramming requirements for airborne electronic warfare systems, a study of the effectiveness of EA-6B electronic jamming effectiveness in SEAD (i.e., *Suppression of Enemy Air Defenses*) missions, the development of a methodology to help assess the relative value of radio spectrum reallocation options, and the modeling of the "soft kill" potential of HARM (i.e., *High Speed Anti-Radiation Missile*). Each of these studies, in its own way, was a "typical" CNA project; which is to say it consisted of a semi-rigorous mathematical analysis of a "problem" that was important to the Navy, and usually involved an

breaking work on mathematical search theory for the Navy (see, for example, Koopman's *Search and Screening* [Koop80] and Morse and Kimball's *Methods of Operations Research* [Morse51]). Throughout its history, CNA has developed, or refined, many important analytical and operational methodologies that have gone on to form the fundamental backbone of modern military operations research.

*How *that* project came to be and unfolded in time, is a story that interested readers are welcome to pursue the details of in the preface to my earlier book, entitled *Cellular Automata: A Discrete Universe*, and published by World Scientific in 2001 [Ilach01b].

†The *Whidbey Island Naval Air Station* in Washington state is where the Navy's *EA-6B Prowler* squadrons are stationed. The *Prowler* is a twin-engine, long-range, all-weather aircraft with advanced electronic countermeasures capability, and is manufactured by *Northrop Grumman Systems Corporation*. I was stationed on Whidbey Island between 1992–1994.

application of some elements of basic physics or engineering. All of them were fun to be a part of. On the other hand, what none of these early projects involved was anything that had anything even remotely to do with complex systems theory, or cellular automata.

That changed, virtually overnight sometime in early 1995, with a short telephone call from US *Marine Corps* Lieutenant General (now retired) Paul van Riper.* LtGen van Riper phoned Rich Bronowitz (who was the director of OEG, which in turn was, and still is, the division within which I work at CNA),† to ask: *"I've been reading a lot about nonlinear dynamics, chaos, and complexity theory. Are there any ideas there that the Marine Corps ought to be interested in?"* With those deceptively simple words, my fate—as it turned out—was effectively sealed.

I had up until that time never met LtGen van Riper, although I certainly knew of his reputation; which was one that engendered great respect as a military thinker, tactician, strategist and visionary (qualities that I would come to know first hand and appreciate deeply in the coming years). Rich, knowing of my long-standing interest in all matters pertaining to complexity, almost immediately passed on LtGen van Riper's "simple" question to me, an act that marked the *de facto* start of my almost decade-long involvement with complexity-related work at CNA.‡

As I look back on this humble origin of CNA's *Complexity & Warfare* project, the only surprising fact about its formative stage is *how long* it took me to convince myself that there was anything of value to be gained by looking into this question (both from the Marine Corps' perspective, and CNA's), beyond simply drawing some "pretty" pictures, conjuring illustrative metaphors, and producing a quick-response memo. Although I immediately saw many obvious—and, as I believed at the time, likely only *shallow*—analogies that could be drawn between, say, chaotic behaviors in nonlinear dynamical systems and combat as it unfolds on

*Lieutenant General (Retired) Paul van Riper was Commanding General, *Marine Corps Combat Development Command* (MCCDC), at Quantico, Virginia during 1994-1996. MCCDC's mission is to develop Marine Corps warfighting concepts and to determine all required capabilities in the areas of doctrine, organization, training and education, equipment, and support facilities to enable the Marine Corps to field combat-ready forces. LtGen van Riper is widely acknowledged as being one of the most forward-thinking and creative military thinkers of the last generation. The research discussed in this book is a direct outgrowth of LtGen van Riper's vision of using the "new sciences" (i.e., *complex systems theory*) to redefine the US Marine Corps *as a mobile, adaptive, wholistic fighting force* (see [vanP97b] and [vanP98]).

†The current director of the *Operations Evaluations Group* (as of September 2003), and one of CNA's Vice Presidents, is Ms. Christine Fox. Christine was appointed head of OEG following Rich's retirement in 2001. Among her many wonderful attributes as director, is Christine's strong penchant for the same kind of creative "out the box" thinking that was so lovingly nurtured by her predecessor. That CNA's *Complexity & Combat* project continued to receive funding and was able to mature in the years following Rich's retirement, is a testament to Christine's own vision, for which the author is profoundly grateful.

‡I am including in this timeline some research I had done while at the *Naval Air Station* on Whidbey Island in the early 1990s. The research involved using neural networks to resolve radar parametric ambiguities as an automated aid for electronic countermeasures.

a real battlefield, I needed to convince myself that these analogies really lived in deeper waters before I committed my time to the project;* i.e., I needed to first convince myself that these "obvious" analogies were only surface-level signposts whose deeper, and more meaningful, roots would point toward a genuinely novel approach to understanding the fundamental dynamics of war. (Rich Bronowitz recognized the importance of looking into this problem well before I did; indeed, it was his eagerness to put together a *Complexity & Warfare* project that prompted him to pass on LtGen van Riper's query over to me. I was very grateful for Rich's patience, as well as his always wise counsel, while I quietly ruminated on the matter for myself.)

The epiphany that finally sparked my realization that there *is* a deep connection between complexity and combat (and that therefore also sparked my realization that LtGen van Riper's query had serious merit), was this (see figure 0.2): if combat—on a real battlefield—is viewed from a "birds-eye" perspective so that only the overall patterns of behavior are observed, and the motions of individual soldiers are indistinguishably blurred into the background (i.e., if combat is viewed wholistically, as a single gestalt-like dynamic pattern), then *combat is essentially equivalent to the cellular automata "toy universes" I had been describing in the book I was busy writing in my spare time at home!*

In cellular automata, simple local rules that are faithfully obeyed at all times by simple agents, often yield amazingly complicated global behaviors (we will see examples of this later in the book). Intricate, self-organized, high-level patterns emerge that are nowhere explicitly scripted by (and that cannot be *predicted* directly from) any of the low-level rules.† An obvious question thus occurred to me: *Might not the same general dynamic template of "Local rules ⟶ Emergent global patterns" apply to the dynamics of combat?*

While a human soldier is, of course, a far more complicated creature than a "simple agent, following simple rules," since we are only interested in the patterns that emerge *on the whole battlefield,* after a large number of human soldiers have interacted, and not in the details of what any one human soldier does, the analogy between emergent patterns in a cellular automata "toy universe" and emergent

*Some of the "obvious" analogies that I had drawn up for myself at this early juncture of the project appear in table 1.3 (see page 13 in chapter 1).

†A well-known example of this is the mathematician John Conway's two-dimensional cellular automata *Life* rule, which is discussed in section 2.2.7.2 (see page 143). This particular rule has been proven to be capable of *universal computation.* This means that with a proper selection of initial conditions, *Life* is equivalent to a general purpose computer, which in turn implies (via a basic theorem from computer science called the *Halting Theorem*) that it is impossible to predict whether a particular initial state of this "toy universe" eventually dies out or grows to infinity. In essence, there are fundamental questions about the behavior of the system, that—despite the fact that we intuitively expect to *be able to answer* them—are actually *un*answerable, even in principle. That this level of fundamental uncertainty about the behavior of a system stems from an almost absurdly simple set of interaction rules (as we will see in chapter 2), renders the whole issue of the relationship between low-level rules and high-level emergent behaviors that much more compelling.

patterns on a real battlefield is actually quite strong. In any event, it was at the instant that this *Cellular-Automata* ↔ *Combat* analogy occurred to me, that—in my mind's eye, at least, if not yet as a formal CNA study—complexity and military operations research had come together at last!

Fig. 0.2 Schematic illustration of the author's self-described epiphany that *combat* "≈" (i.e., mathematically equivalent to) *self-organized, emergent behavior of a complex adaptive system*. The Lanchester equations (shown on the right-hand-side, and introduced in the early 1900s), represent a simple predator-prey-like description of combat attrition. The multiagent-based approch, which is rendered in schematic form on the left-hand-side and which constitutes the conceptual basis of the EINSTein combat simulation introduced in this book, is to endow each notional combatant (i.e., *agent*) with a unique personality, define the rules by which agents may interact, and then allow the whole multiagent system to evolve on its own. Where a Lanchester-equation-based analysis of combat implicitly compels an analyst to build, and rest his understanding of the processes of combat on, a feature-limited, myopic database consisting of simple force-on-force attrition statistics, an artificial-life-inspired multiagent-based approach instead broadens an analyst's attention to *exploring whole spectra of emerging patterns and behaviors*. (This figure contains a slightly altered form of a cartoon that first appeared in the long-defunct *OMNI Magazine*; the original cartoon also appears on page 10 of John Casti's book, *Complexification* [Casti94].)

Having experienced my epiphany, the truth of which I am more convinced of now than ever (particularly in light of the veritable explosion of complexity-related research in the military community in recent years), the next step was obvious. I needed to put together a conceptual roadmap for developing whatever theoretical and practical consequences naturally followed from this provocative vision. This book summarizes the steps that I have taken along this path, as it was conceived by me in 1996.

Assigning credit where it is due, the idea of applying complex systems theoretic ideas to the study of combat is the inspiration of one individual—an individual that it has been my distinct honor of knowing and working with over the years, and a leader whom I have come to regard as a real visionary: *LtGen (Ret) Paul van Riper.*

CNA, as a research organization, would never have committed any of its resources to explore the possible applications of complex systems theory to the fundamental dynamics of warfare—a proposition that, while being a well-defined military operations research initiative, was also undeniably risky because of its inherent novelty—were it not for two unique individuals, both of whom possessed the vision and the firm resolve to nurture creative "out of the box" thinking at CNA: the director of OEG, *Rich Bronowitz*, and the director of research and development, *Dave Kelsey*.

Finally, great credit also goes to *Michael Shlesinger*,, Chief Scientist for *Nonlinear Science* (and managing the *Nonlinear Dynamics* program in the *Physical Science Division* at the *Office of Naval Research* (ONR).* Michael strongly resonated with the complex-systems–theory-based approach to understanding the dynamics of combat from the start, and without his enthusiasm and leadership it would have been impossible to complete the work described in this book.

The last decade has witnessed the development of an entirely new and powerful modeling and simulation paradigm based on the distributed intelligence of swarms of autonomous, but mutually interacting (and sometimes coevolving), agents. The swarm-like simulation of combat introduced in this book—EINSTein—is but one of a growing number of similar artificial-life-like multiagent-based tools that are available to students and researchers for studying a wide variety of physical, social, cultural and economic complex systems.

First applied to natural systems such as ecologies and insect colonies, then later to human population dynamics, and economic evolution, this paradigm has finally entered the mainstream consciousness of military operations research. Ten or more years ago, one only rarely ran across a military research journal article that contained the words "nonlinear," "deterministic chaos," "strange attractor," "complex systems," or "complex adaptive" somewhere in its title. Today, while the appearance of such papers is still far from being commonplace in military journals, when they *do* appear it is no longer surprising.

For example, the journals MOR (*Military Operations Research*), OR (*Operations Research*), and *Naval Research Logistics* have all published papers in recent years the major theme of which is closely related to complex adaptive systems theory. Indeed, journals that are more or less devoted to applying the essential ideas of complexity to problems that were heretofore confined to more traditional opera-

*EINSTein was funded by ONR, with Dr. Shlesinger as sponsor, during the years 2000-2003. The project was called *An Intelligent-Agent-Based "Conceptual Laboratory" for Exploring Self-Organized Emergent Behavior in Land Combat*, and administered under ONR Contract No. N00014-00-D-0700.

tions research domains have also recently appeared (see for example John Wiley & Sons' *Complexity* and The Institute for Operations Research and the Management Sciences' *Organization Science*). Most recently, the *Washington Center for Complexity & Public Policy* has released a landmark survey of the use of complexity science in federal departments and agencies, private foundations, universities, and independent education and research centers [Sanders03]. It is the first sweeping survey of its kind and highlights the fact that complexity-based research has been growing rapidly (especially since the tragic events of 9/11).

Despite the rise in popularity of swarm-like models, however, it is of course always wise to proceed with a bit of caution. The truth is that just as chaos theory was in its infancy in the 1970s—which marked a time of considerable intellectual unrest within the physics and applied mathematics communities as the wheat was slowly disentangled from the chaff—so too is our level of understanding of what multiagent-based simulations *may* (or may *not*) say about the real-world systems they are designed to model also only now beginning to mature into a bona-fide science. There is much we do not yet understand about the behaviors of complex adaptive dynamical systems; there is also much we need to learn about how to design and best use the tools that continue to being developed to help explore those behaviors. Nonetheless, I am convinced that future generations will one day thankfully look back upon the groundbreaking work that is being done today on developing the tools and methodologies to comprehend self-organized emergent behavior in complex adaptive systems, and knowingly appreciate that it is this early work that paved the way to a deeper understanding of how nature really works, *underneath it all.*

And what does the future hold—as far as the mathematical tools and modeling and simulation methodologies borne of nonlinear dynamics and complex adaptive systems theory are concerned—for military operations research in general, and combat analysis in particular? Appreciating that the work described in this book represents only one small, humble step forward on the path to answering this question, I fervently believe that the role such ideas will eventually play in illuminating the fundamental processes of warfare (not to mention their even more important role in helping us understand the universe at large) *will far exceed that of any other military operational research tools that have heretofore been brought to bear on these questions.*

Andy Ilachinski
Center for Naval Analyses
Alexandria, Virginia
November, 2003

Acknowledgments

I would like to thank the many dedicated and visionary pioneers in the fields of physics, biology, computer science, artificial intelligence, simulation and modeling, machine learning, autonomous agent and multiagent systems, robotics, nonlinear dynamics and, especially, complex dynamics systems, who–though I have never met most of them in person–have nonetheless, through their work and creativity, greatly inspired (and continue to inspire) me in my own work.

I wish to extend a particularly deep thanks to the following individuals (listed in alphabetical order) for their encouragement, guidance, and support:

Rosa and Carlos Abraira, Andrew Adamatzky, Gregg Adams, Chris Bassford, Lyntis Beard, Dave Blake, Rich Bronowitz, Alan Brown, Ted Cavin, Admiral Arthur Cebrowski, Julius Chang, Greg Cox, Tom Czerwinski, Phil Depoy, Captain (USN) John Dickman, Karin Duggan, Stu Dunn, Josh Epstein, Christine Fox, Tony Freedman, Matthew Grund, Carol Hawk, John Hiles, Colonel Carl Hunt, Joe Janeczek, Stuart Kauffman, Dave Kelsey, Julia Loughran, Mike Markowitz, Toni Matheny, David Mazel, Ed McGrady, Katherine McGrady, Brian McCue, Barry Messina, Igor Mikolic-Torriera, Captain (USN) Dan Moore, Bob Murray, Jamil Nakleh, Mike Neely, Tom Neuberger, Ron Nickel, Peter Perla, David Rodney, Isaac Saias, Irene Sanders, Dennis Shea, Mike Shlesinger, Mike Shepko, Marcy Stahl, Sarah Stom, Amy Summers, Greg Swider, Dave Taylor, Fred Thompson, Lieutenant General (Retired) Paul van Riper, Chris Weuve and Kuang Wu.

A special thanks goes to Fred Richards, programmer (and physicist) extraordinaire. While the two main programs described in this book (ISAAC and EINSTein) were both conceived and given life to by the author—in their first incarnation as antiquated QuickBasic programs, then in ANSI C and finally in Visual C++—it was only after the formidable (and unenviable) programming chores were put into Fred's capable hands that EINSTein established itself as a professional, fully object-oriented, research-caliber tool.

I would like to acknowledge the research grants that made the work described in this book possible. First, the funding support provided by the *Center for Naval Analyses* (CNA) under its CNA-initiated research program. Second, support by the

US *Marine Corps Combat Development Command* (MCCDC), particularly during the formative years of the project, during which time the *Commanding General* of MCCDC was Lt. Gen. (Ret) Paul van Riper. And third, but not least, the multi-year funding support by the *Office of Naval Research* (ONR), under its *Nonlinear Dynamics* program in the *Physical Science Division* (managed by Dr. Michael Shlesinger). Without CNA's, MCCDC's and ONR's support, none of the work discussed in this book would have been possible.

I extend my heartfelt appreciation to Dr. Jitan Lu of *World Scientific Publishing* for his skillful management of this book project. This is the second book that Dr. Lu has handled for me at *World Scientific*, and his direct involvement has made my two book projects both equally memorable and pleasurable.

Finally, without the love and support of my beautiful wife Irene, my wonderful children Noah and Joshua, and my *wunder*-survivor mom Katie,* I would never have found the strength to complete a book of such scope and length. My only regret is that my dad, Slava, who died a few months before I committed my time to this project, did not live long enough to see the publication of his son's second book. While, as an artist, my dad likely would not have appreciated all of the purely technical aspects of the work described herein, I know he would have resonated deeply on an aesthetic level with the many beautiful "birds-eye" views of agent behaviors and various assorted images of emergent patterns that are sprinkled throughout the book. Were it not for my dad's graceful and humble reminders—through his art and his sage outlook on life—that beauty, in its purest form, is not something that is confined solely to the mathematical equations of physics, *but exists everywhere, all the time, if only we learn how to look*; I would never have opened my eyes widely enough to marvel at just how much of the world remains mysteriously beyond the reach of our intellectual understanding; yet is always open to our joyous wonder and awe.

*My mom, who turned 72 as I started working on this book, miraculously survived *both* terrorist attacks on New York's *World Trade Center*: once in 1993, and again during the tragic events of 9-11; each time she had to make her way down from the 91st floor of the second tower. She was one of the few very lucky survivors of 9-11. That my mom has lived to see her son complete his second book is, for me, a profoundly deep blessing.

Contents

Chapter 1

Introduction

"As we deepen our understanding of how the mental world of meaning is materially supported and represented, an understanding coming from the neurosciences, the cognitive sciences, computer science, biology, mathematics, and anthropology...there will result a new synthesis of science, and a new...worldview will arise. I am convinced that the nations and people who master the new sciences of complexity will become the economic, cultural and political superpowers of the next century."

—Heinz Pagels, *The Dreams of Reason* (1988)

This book summarizes the results of a multiyear research program, conducted by the *Center for Naval Analyses* (CNA),* and sponsored in part by the *Office of Naval Research* (ONR), whose basic charter was to use complex adaptive systems theory to develop tools to help understand the fundamental processes of war. The chapters of this book are mostly self-contained, so that they may be read in any order, and are roughly divided into two parts.† Part one (including this chapter and chapters 2 and 3) introduces the general context for the ensuing discussion, and provides both qualitative and more technical overviews of those elements of nonlinear dynamics, artificial-life, complexity theory and multiagent-based simulation tools that are applied to modeling combat in the second part of the book. Part two consists of a detailed source-code-level discussion of a multiagent-based model of combat called EINSTein, including its design, development, and sample behaviors. The final chapter summarizes the main ideas introduced throughout the book and offers some suggestions for future work. A user's guide, tutorial and links to additional on-line resources appear in the appendices.

*CNA is a federally funded research and development center whose history dates back to World War II when it was known as the *Antisubmarine Warfare Operations Research Group* (ASWORG; see [Tidm84]) and its analysts pioneered the field of operations research during their groundbreaking work on mathematical search theory for the Navy (see, for example, Koopman's *Search and Screening* [Koop80] and Morse and Kimball's *Methods of Operations Research* [Morse51]).

†Readers who want to start learning about EINSTein *immediately* and are already familiar with the basic ideas of nonlinear dynamics, deterministic chaos and complex systems theory, and who are acquainted with multiagent-based simulation techniques, may skip ahead to begin reading at chapter 5.

1.1 Brief History of CNA's *Complexity & Combat* Research Project

CNA's complexity research began with a pioneering exploratory study in 1996, that was originally sponsored by the Commanding General, *Marine Corps Combat Development Command* (MCCDC).* This section provides a brief sketch of the history of this research: the basic "problem," as it was presented to CNA, a summary of various phases of the project, how the project has evolved over the years and how—most recently—it has culminated in the development of one of the first research-caliber artificial-life labs for exploring self-organized emergence on the battlefield. Table 1.1 lists some of the principal documents (and modeling and simulation software) that have been produced during the years 1996-2003.

1.1.1 *The "Problem"*

The initial goal of the project was to assess—in the broadest possible conceptual terms—the general applicability of *nonlinear dynamics* and *complex systems theory* to land warfare. Obviously, in order to fully appreciate the enormous scope of what this goal actually entailed, one must first understand what is meant by the terms "nonlinear dynamics" and "complex systems theory." A self-contained technical primer on both of these disciplines appears in chapter 2; we will here give only a short qualitative introduction to these important fields of study.

1.1.1.1 *Nonlinear Dynamics*

Nonlinear dynamics and complex systems theory entered the research landscape as recognized disciplines roughly 35 years ago and 15 years ago, respectively. In the simplest possible terms, "nonlinear dynamics" refers to the study of dynamical systems that evolve in time according to a nonlinear rule. In a *linear* dynamical system, any external disturbance induces a change in the system that is *proportional to the magnitude of the disturbance.* In other words, small changes to the input result in correspondingly small changes to the output. *Nonlinear* systems are dynamical systems for which this proportionality between input and output does not necessarily hold. In nonlinear systems, therefore, arbitrarily small inputs may lead to arbitrarily large (and, in chaotic systems, exponentially large) output.

*MCCDC's mission is to develop Marine Corps warfighting concepts and to determine associated required capabilities in the areas of doctrine, organization, training and education, equipment, and support facilities to enable the Marine Corps to field combat-ready forces; and to participate in and support other major processes of the combat development system. At the conception of CNA's *Complexity & Combat* project, the Commanding General of MCCDC was (now retired) Lt. Gen. Paul van Riper. Lt. Gen van Riper is widely ackowledged as being one of the most forward-thinking and creative military thinkers of the last generation. The research discussed in this book is a direct outgrowth of Lt. Gen van Riper's vision of using the "new sciences" to redefine the US Marine Corps *as a mobile, adaptive, wholistic fighting force* (see [vanP97b] and [vanP98]).

Document	Year	Description
Land Warfare and Complexity: Part I [Ilach96a]	1996	Provides a self-contained mathematical reference and technical sourcebook for applying nonlinear dynamics and complex systems theory to combat-related issues and problems
Land Warfare and Complexity: Part II [Ilach96b]	1996	Assesses the applicability of nonlinear dynamics and complex adaptive system theory to the study of land warfare.
A Mobile CA Approach to Land Combat [Ilach96c]	1996	Introduces an early version of the DOS-based ISAAC model, and includes a user's guide.
Irreducible Semi-Autonomous Adaptive Combat (ISAAC): An Artificial-Life Approach to Land Warfare [Ilach97]	1997	Describes the design and implementation of the mature ISAAC model (i.e., final version 1.8.6), and introduces companion programs to explore fitness landscapes and to use a genetic algorithm to "breed" agents (tailored to specific missions).
EINSTein's Beta-Test User's Guide [Ilach99a]	1999	Contains a detailed user's guide and tutorial for using a pre-release (beta) version of ISAAC's follow-on, the Windows-based EINSTein.
ISAAC: Agent-Based Warfare [Ilach00b]	2000	Peer-reviewed paper summarizing ISAAC program, published in *Military Operations Research*.
EINSTein: An Artificial-Life Laboratory for Exploring Self-Organized Emergence in Land Combat [Ilach00a]	2000	Summarizes the design, architecture and implementation of an interim version of EINSTein, and an enhanced behavior space, more robust action selection, terrain, command and control, built-in data-collection and data-visualization functions, and a significantly improved embedded genetic algorithm heuristic search utility.
EINSTein v1.0.0.4β [Ilach01a]	2001	CD-ROM containing the install program for the last (pre-release) beta version, along with supporting documents.
Multi-Agent-Based Synthetic Warfare: Toward Developing a General Axiological Ontology of Complex Adaptive Systems [Ilach02]	2002	This CRM describes all changes and additions that have been made to EINSTein's basic design since the previous milestone, including a re-designed, and enhanced, action selection logic, more robust terrain and weapon classes, improved path finding logic and a new class of user-defined paths, along with the many changes that have been made to the user-interface. EINSTein is also placed on a solid theoretical foundation by using EINSTein's design ontology as an exemplar of more general models of complex adaptive systems.
EINSTein v1.1 [ilach03a]	2003	CD-ROM containing the install program release version 1.1, along with all supporting documents.
Exploring Self-Organized Emergence in an Agent-Based Synthetic Warfare Lab	2003	Peer-reviewed paper summarizing EINSTein program, published in special Artificial-Life Software issue of *Kybernetes* journal [ilach03b].

Table 1.1 Partial list of documents and simulation software produced during CNA's *Complexity & Combat* research program.

As we will see later in some detail, one of the characteristic features of *chaos* in nonlinear systems is precisely this kind of extreme sensitivity to initial conditions. Also, in nonlinear systems, the effect of adding two inputs first and then operating on their sum is not, in general, equivalent to operating on two inputs separately and then adding the outputs together; or, more colloquially, *the whole is not necessarily equal to the sum of the parts.*

That there is a natural connection between the general study of nonlinear dynamical systems and warfare may be appreciated, at least conceptually (leaving aside the mathematical details until later in the book), by recalling this old nursery rhyme that is usually taught to small children to emphasize the importance of taking care of small problems so that they do not grow into big ones:

"For the want of a nail, the shoe was lost;
For the want of the shoe, the horse was lost;
For the want of the horse, the rider was lost;
For the want of a rider, the battle was lost;
For the want of the battle, the kingdom was lost;
*All for the want of a nail."**

1.1.1.2 *Complex Systems Theory*

The science of complexity may be regarded as an outgrowth of nonlinear dynamics. Despite being somewhat of a misnomer, because the "science" behind complexity is arguably more a general philosophy of looking at behaviors of complex systems than a rigorous well-defined methodology, this emerging discipline nonetheless has many potentially important new insights to offer into the understanding of the behaviors of complex systems.

A *complex system* can be thought of, generically, as any dynamical system that is composed of many simple, and typically nonlinearly, interacting parts. Gases, fluids, crystals, and lasers are all familiar kinds of complex systems from physics. Chemical reactions, in which a large number of molecules conspire to produce new molecules, are also good examples. In biology, there are DNA molecules built up from amino acids, cells built from molecules, and organisms built from cells. On a larger scale, the national and global economies and human culture as a whole are also complex systems, exhibiting their own brand of global cooperative behavior. One of the most far-reaching ideas of this sort is James Lovelock's speculative "Gaia" hypothesis, which asserts that the entire earth is essentially one huge, complex organism [Love79].

A complex *adaptive* system is a complex system whose parts can also evolve and adapt to a changing environment. *Complex systems theory* is then the study of the behavior of such systems, and is rooted in the fundamental belief that much of the

*This well known rhyme, which I have seen quoted in many similar, though not always exactly the same, forms is usually attributed to Benjamin Franklin.

overall behavior of diverse complex systems—such as natural ecologies, economic markets, the human brain, and patterns of conflict on a battlefield—stems from the same basic set of underlying principles. The rudiments of complex systems theory will be outlined in the next chapter.

Comparing the two disciplines—*nonlinear dynamics* (which includes the analysis of chaotic dynamics) and *complex systems theory*—nonlinear dynamics is unquestionably a significantly more mature science. Complexity theory remains essentially an "infant science," despite frequent claims to the contrary made by some of its more vocal advocates. That is not to say, however, that complexity research has not spawned an impressive repertoire of tools, both conceptual and practical. We will see many examples of the use of such tools throughout this book. Indeed, the increasing popularity of multiagent-based modeling techniques to explore complex systems (not to mention their widespread use in business software and commercial entertainment) is itself a testament to the undeniable value these techniques have shown in pioneering artificial-life studies during the last 15 years.

Very loosely speaking, it can be said that where chaos is the study of how simple systems can generate complicated behavior, complexity is the study of how complicated systems can generate simple behavior. Since both chaos and complex systems theory attempt to describe the behavior of dynamical systems, it should not be surprising to learn that both share many of the same tools, although, properly speaking, complex systems theory ought to be regarded as the superset of the two methodologies.

Together, nonlinear dynamics and complex systems theory form a growing pool of knowledge and conjectures about (1) what tools are best suited for describing the characteristics of real-world complex systems and for describing systems that exhibit an apparently "complicated" dynamics, and (2) what universal behavioral properties many real-world complex systems seem to share. These two fields encompass a remarkably wide variety of subdisciplines, including deterministic chaos, stochastic dynamics, artificial life, ecological and natural evolutionary dynamics, evolutionary and genetic programming, cellular automata, percolation theory, cellular games, agent-based modeling, and neural networks, among many others (see table 1.2). Applications range from biology, to chemistry, to physics, to anthropology, to sociology and economics.

Despite the fact that there is considerable overlap both between nonlinear dynamics and complex systems theory—as well as among the individual research areas, concepts and tools that constitute these two overlapping disciplines—there are nonetheless two deep themes that run through, and summarize the essence of, all complexity research:

- *Surface complexity can emerge out of a deep simplicity*, embodying the idea that what may at first appear to be a complex behavior, or set of behaviors, can in fact stem from a simple underlying dynamics.

Research Area	Concepts	Tools
agent-based simulations	adaptation	agent-based simulations
artificial life	autonomous agents	backpropagation
catastrophe theory	autopoiesis	cellular automata
cellular automata	complexity	cellular games
cellular games	computational irreducibility	chaotic control
chaos	computational universality	entropy
chaotic control theory	criticality	evolutionary prog.
complex adaptive systems	dissipative structures	fuzzy logic
coupled-map lattices	edge-of-chaos	genetic algorithms
discrete dynamical systems	emergence	inductive learning
evolutionary programming	fractals	information theory
genetic algorithms	intermittency	Kolmogorov entropy
lattice-gas models	phase space	lattice-gas models
neural networks	phase transitions	Lyapunov exponents
nonlinear dynamical systems	prisoner's dilemma	maximum entropy
percolation theory	punctuated equilibrium	neural networks
petri nets	self-organization	Poincare maps
relativistic information	self-organized criticality	power spectrum
self-organized criticality	strange attractors	symbolic dynamics
time-series analysis	synergetics	time-series analysis
··· (many others)	··· (many others)	··· (many others)

Table 1.2 A small sampling of research areas, concepts and tools falling under the broad rubric of "complexity " science. Many of the terms and concepts shown here are discussed in the technical primer that appears in chapter 2 of this book.

- *Surface simplicity can emerge out of a deep complexity*, embodying the idea that enormously complicated systems that *a-priori* have very many degrees-of-freedom and therefore are expected to display "complicated" behavior, can, either of their own accord via self-organization, or through selective "tuning" by a set of external control parameters, behave as though they were really low-dimensional systems exhibiting very "simple" behavior.

In this context, MCCDC's original research directive at the start of CNA's *Complexity & Warfare* project was effectively interpreted as a request to address the following basic problem:

> *"What aspects of the general behavior of complex systems, and what specific conceptual, mathematical, modeling and/or simulation tools that have been developed for studying the behavior of complex systems, are likely to provide insight into our general understanding of the fundamental processes of war?"*

Thus, the initial phase of CNA's study, conducted between in the years 1995/96, focused on answering this focused (though obviously still conceptually sweeping question, and culminated in two broad overviews of the "new sciences" and their applicability to combat.

The first report—*Land Warfare and Complexity, Part I* [Ilach96a]—provides a semi-technical review of both nascent and well established disciplines falling under the broad rubric colloquially labeled as complexity science (including nonlinear dynamics, chaos, time-series forecasting and predictability, chaotic control, genetic algorithms, cellular automata, self-organized criticality, and neural networks). Some elements of this report appear in chapter 2. The second report—*Land Warfare and Complexity, Part II* [Ilach96b]—uses the information contained in the first volume to help identify specific applications and assess both their risk (as measured by expected time of conceptual and/or practical development) and potential reward. Together, parts *I* and *II* of *Land Warfare and Complexity* represent the first serious examination of the thesis that two heretofore ostensibly unrelated research disciplines—namely, military operations research and complex systems theory—actually overlap; and that the study of one may provide insight into the study of the other.

1.1.2 *Applying the "New Sciences" to Warfare*

Land Warfare and Complexity, Part II [Ilach96b] introduces a convenient eight-tier-tall "scaffolding" on which to organize the potential applications of complex systems theory to warfare, the main conclusions of which are summarized below (all of the points made here are discussed in greater detail in chapter 3). These tiers range roughly from applications involving the least risk and least potential payoff (at least, as far as a practical applicability is concerned) on Tier-I, to applications involving the greatest risk, but also the greatest potential payoff, on Tier-VIII:

- Tier I: *General Metaphors for complexity in War*
- Tier II: *Policy and General Guidelines for Strategy*
- Tier III: *"Conventional" Warfare Models and Approaches*
- Tier IV: *Description of the Complexity of Combat*
- Tier V: *Combat Technology Enhancement*
- Tier VI: *Combat Aids*
- Tier VII: *Synthetic Combat Environments*
- Tier VIII: *Original Conceptualizations of Combat*

1.1.2.1 *Tier-I: General Metaphors for Complexity in War*

The first tier of applicability consists of constructing and elaborating upon similar sounding words and images that most strongly suggest a philosophical resonance between behaviors of complex systems and certain aspects of what happens on a battlefield. It is on this tier that the well-known Clauswitzian images of "fog of war," "center-of-gravity" and "friction" are supplanted by such metaphors as "nonlinear," "coevolutionary" and "emergent." This first tier is accompanied by words of both encouragement and caution. On the one hand, the act of developing metaphors is arguably an integral part of what complex systems theory itself is all about, and therefore ought to be encouraged. On the other hand, an unbridled, impassioned use of metaphor alone, without taking the time to work out the details of whatever deeper insights the metaphor might be pointing to (i.e., without exploring what the other tiers of applicability might have to offer), runs the risk of both shallowness and loss of objectivity.

1.1.2.2 *Tier-II: Policy and General Guidelines for Strategy*

The second tier of applications takes a step beyond the basic metaphor level of Tier I by using the metaphors and basic lessons learned from complex systems theory to guide and shape how we formulate strategy and general policy. Tier-II thus extends the first tier of application to the military organization as a whole. It consists of using both the imagery of metaphors and the tools and lessons learned from complex systems theory to enhance and/or alter organizational and command and control structures. Potentially useful policy implications of ideas borrowed from the lessons of complexity theory include:

- *Look for Global Patterns.* Search for global patterns in time and/or space scales higher than those on which the dynamics is defined. Systems can appear to be locally disordered but still harbor a global order.
- *Exploit Decentralized Control.* Encourage decentralized control, even if each "patch" attempts to optimize for its own selfish benefit, but maintain interaction among all patches.
- *Find Ways to Adapt Better.* The most successful complex systems do not just continually adapt, they struggle to find ways to continue to adapt better. Move towards a direction that gives you more options.

1.1.2.3 *Tier-III: Conventional Warfare Models and Approaches*

Tier-III consists of applying the tools and methods of nonlinear dynamics to more or less "conventional models" of combat. The idea on this tier is not so much to develop entirely new formulations of combat so much as to extend and generalize existing forms using a new mathematical arsenal of tools. Examples of applications include:

- Using nonlinear dynamics to explore implications of nonlinearities in generalized forms of the Lanchester equations.
- Exploiting an analogy between the form of the Lanchester equations and Lottka-Voltera equations describing predator-prey interactions in natural ecologies to develop new models of combat.

- Using genetic algorithms to perform sensitivity analyses and otherwise "test" the veracity of existing complex simulation models.

1.1.2.4 *Tier-IV: Description of the Complexity of Combat*

This tier consists of using the tools and methodologies of complex systems theory to describe and help look for patterns of real-world combat. The fundamental problem is to find ways to identify, describe and exploit the latent patterns in behavior that appears, on the surface, to be irregular and driven by chance. Examples of applications include:

- Looking for evidence of chaos in historical combat data.
- Using various qualitative and quantitative measures from nonlinear dynamics and complex systems theory to describe the complexity of combat.
- Using phase-space reconstruction techniques from nonlinear dynamics to reconstruct attractors from real-world combat data and make short-term predictions based on underlying patterns.

1.1.2.5 *Tier-V: Combat Technology Enhancement*

Tier V consists of applying complex systems theory tools to enhance existing combat technologies. The objective of this middle tier of applications is to find ways to improve, or provide better methods for applying, specific key technologies. Examples of applications include:

- Using fractals for data compression.
- Using cellular automata and chaotic dynamical systems for cryptography.
- Using genetic algorithms for intelligent manufacturing.
- Using synchronized chaotic circuits to develop cheap IFF (*Identification Friend* or *Foe*).

1.1.2.6 *Tier-VI: Combat Aids for the Battlefield*

Tier-VI consists of using the tools of nonlinear dynamics and complex systems theory to enhance real-world operations. Examples of applications include:

- Using genetic algorithms to "evolve" operational tactics and targeting strategies.
- Developing tactical picture agents to adaptively identify, filter and integrate relevant information in real-time.
- Developing autonomous robotic devices to act as sentries and to help in material transportation and hazardous material handling.

1.1.2.7 *Tier-VII: Synthetic Combat Environments*

Tier-VII consists of developing full system models for training purposes and/or for use as research laboratories from which general (and possibly universal) patterns of behavior can be obtained. Examples of applications, ranging from least to most sophisticated, include:

- Using cellular automata to explore basic behavioral properties of simple local rule-based combat models.
- Using multi-agent based simulations of combat to explore behavioral properties of combat models of mid-level complexity.
- Using SWARM (a general purpose modeling system developed at the *Santa Fe Institute*) to develop a full system-level model of land warfare.

1.1.2.8 *Tier-VIII: Original Conceptualizations of Combat*

Tier VIII represents the potentially most exciting—and certainly most far-reaching—tier of the eight tiers of application. It consists of using complex systems theory inspired ideas and basic research to develop fundamentally new conceptualizations of combat. Examples of applications include:

- Using genetic algorithms to "evolve" possible low-level rules that describe high-level observed combat behavior.
- Using neural nets to "induct" otherwise unseen behavioral "patterns" on a battlefield.
- Developing ways of exploiting the nature of chaos in combat phase-space to selectively "drive" combat to move towards more favorable regions.
- Exploiting the collective intelligence of very many otherwise "simple" autonomous micro-bots to conduct "fire-ant" warfare.

1.1.2.9 *Most Promising Applications*

Leaving a detailed discussion of the many potential applications that populate these tiers to a later chapter (see chapter 3), we here briefly address the obvious question, "*What are the most promising applications of complexity-related methodologies to combat and warfare in general?*" In a roughly ascending order of the probable length of time that an application is likely to require before maturing to a point at which a definitive assessment of its payoff can be made, here are the seven applications that were assessed as being most promising in [Ilach96b]:

(1) *Exploit the general analogy between the form of the Lanchester equations and Lottka-Voltera equations describing predator-prey interactions in natural ecologies to develop a generalized Neo-Lanchesterian approach to land combat.*

(2) *Use phase-space reconstruction techniques from nonlinear dynamics to reconstruct attractors from real-world combat data and make short-term predictions based on underlying patterns. Part of this involves developing an appropriate phase-space description of combat.*
(3) *Develop simple local-rule-based models of combat to explore general behavioral patterns and possible universalities in combat.*
(4) *Use genetic algorithms to "breed" tactics and strategies. Specific applications might include tank tactics, targeting strategies and using genetic algorithms as backbones of real-time adaptive battlefield decision aids.*
(5) *Develop multi-agent-based simulations of land warfare to be used as training tools along the lines of commercial games such as SimCity and SimLife. Explore the possibility of using the Santa Fe Institute's SWARM modeling system.*
(6) *Develop agent-based tactical picture agents to adaptively retrieve, filter, and integrate battlefield and intelligence data.*
(7) *Reexamine existing policy and policy procedures, at the highest levels, in light of the basic lessons learned from complex systems theory.*

Of course, there are many more theoretical avenues to explore in the long-term as well. These include developing measures of complexity of combat, developing general data-collection methods that emphasize "process" instead of more traditional force-on-force attrition "statistics," looking for and exploiting characteristic fractal-like behaviors in combat, using various sophisticated pattern recognition techniques to look for any high-level exploitable patterns on the battlefield and/or information databases that describe the progress of a campaign, and finding ways of exploiting the ability to both "control" and "tame" chaos on the battlefield. These, and other possibilities, are all discussed in [Ilach96b] and chapter 3 of this book.

1.1.2.10 *Why Land Warfare?*

Of the many different kinds of modern warfare that could be chosen as a testbed for applying the ideas and tools of complex systems theory, land warfare, as a whole, is ideally suited for three reasons: (1) *Number of individual dynamical components*—land warfare involves potentially vast numbers of mutually interacting combatants (where "combatant" refers to any irreducible element of combat; for example, it can refer to an infantryman, a tank or transport vehicle, depending on circumstance), so that it can naturally be described as a "complex system." While a natural unit of measure for the size of a naval force, for example, is the number of ships, the natural unit for land warfare is the number of individual soldiers; (2) *Complexity of environment*—land warfare generally takes place within a much more complex environment than do other forms of combat. Air combat, for example, takes place within an almost homogeneous medium and interactions arise mainly within line-of-sight. Likewise, while the ocean is arguably a "complicated" medium, and the maneuvering of combat ships involves complicated dynamics, naval warfare actually represents a relatively simple environment in the context of complex systems modeling. On the other hand, the surface of the earth is strewn with complexities, from its effects on various sensors and communications systems to its profound implications for the composition of combat forces and tactics; and (3) *Psychological factors*—land warfare depends on psychological factors (that range from the morale and courage of the individual soldier to the ineffable effects of group cohesion in combat) to a far greater extent than do other forms of combat.

Having said all this, it remains true that land combat represents only *one level* of activity within a complex nested hierarchy of warfare-related levels existing on many scales, not the least of which is political. To make full use of what complex systems theory has to say about the general dynamics and nature of war, its lessons must be applied not just to land combat alone, but to the entire chain of combat and command & control structures.

1.1.3 *Warfare & Complexity*

The most important lesson to have emerged out of the initial stage of CNA's *Complexity & Combat* study was that the general mechanisms responsible for emerging patterns in complex adaptive systems can be used to gain insight into the patterns of behavior that arise on the real combat battlefield; i.e., that *combat can be modeled as a complex adaptive system.* In other words, land combat may be described—mathematically and physically—as a nonlinear dynamical system composed of many interacting semi-autonomous and hierarchically organized agents continuously adapting to a changing environment.

It is not hard to appreciate that military conflicts, particularly land combat, possess all of the characteristic features of complex adaptive systems (see table 1.3):* combat forces are composed of a large number of nonlinearly interacting parts and are organized in a command and control hierarchy; local action, which often appears disordered, induces long-range order (i.e., combat is self-organized); military conflicts, by their nature, proceed far from equilibrium; military forces, in order to survive, must continually adapt to a changing combat environment; there is no master "voice" that dictates the actions of each and every combatant (i.e., decentralized control); and so on.

There have also recently appeared a number of papers discussing the fundamental role that nonlinearity plays in combat; see Adams [Adams00], Beckerman [Beck99], Beyerchen [Beyer92], Brown, *et.al.* [BrownM00], Czerwinski, *et.al.* [Czer98], Hedgepeth [Hedge93], Ilachinski [Ilach96a, Ilach96b], Miller and Sulcoski [MillerL93, MillerL95], Saperstein [Saper95, Saper99], Schmitt [Schmitt97], and Tagarev and Nicholls [Tagarev96].

*A more complete treatment of each of these properties, beyond the short description that appears in table 1.3, appears in section 2.2.3 (see discussion that starts on page 105).

General Property of Complex Systems	Description of Relevance to Land Combat
Nonlinear Interaction	Combat forces composed of a large number of nonlinearly interacting parts; sources include feedback loops in C2 hierarchy, interpretation of (and adaptation to) enemy actions, decision-making process, and elements of chance
Networks of Agents	Military organizations consist of many agents and meta agents, including individual combatants, squad leaders, company commanders, ..., joint forces, etc.
Nonreductionist	The fighting ability of a combat force cannot be understood as a simple aggregate function of the fighting ability of individual combatants
Bounded Rationality	Individual combatants have neither infinite resources nor operate in an environment with infinite information; they are constrained to choose their actions quickly, locally and use bounded information
Emergent Behavior	The global patterns of behavior on the combat battlefield unfold, or emerge, out of nested sequences of local interaction rules and doctrine
Hierarchical Structure	Combat forces are typically organized in a (fractal-like) command and control hierarchy
Decentralized Control	There is no master "oracle" dictating the actions of individual combatants; the course of a battle is ultimately dictated by the aggregate of local decisions
Self Organization	Combat, which often appears "chaotic" locally, displays long-range order
Nonequilibrium Order	Military conflicts, by their nature, proceed far from equilibrium; understanding how combat unfolds is more important that knowing the "end state"
Adaptation	In order to survive, combat forces must continually adapt to a changing environment, and find better ways of adapting to the adaptation pattern of their enemy
Micro::Macro Feedback Loops	There is a continual feedback between the behavior of (low-level) combatants and the (high-level) command structure
Autopoiesis	While the identity of squads, fire-teams and the entire echelon of authority constantly changes over time, a structured fighting force and C2 structure remains intact; self-organized, autopoietic structures constantly arise in firefights and skirmishes on the battlefield

Table 1.3 Land combat as a complex adaptive system.

This implies that, in principle, land combat ought to be amenable to the same methodological course of study as any other complex adaptive system, such as the stock market, a natural ecology, an immune system, or the human brain [Kelso95]. Implicit in this central thesis is the idea that the *conceptual* links that exist between properties of combat and properties of complex systems can be extended to forge a set of *practical* connections as well. Land warfare does not just look like a complex system on paper, but can be modeled by using the same basic principles that are used for discovering and identifying behaviors in a variety of other (ostensibly unrelated) complex systems. To demonstrate how this can be done, CNA developed two pioneering complexity-based models of combat called ISAAC and EINSTein (introduced below)

These models have been developed to address the basic question: *"To what extent is land combat a self-organized complex adaptive system?"* As such, they are designed to be used as interactive toolboxes—or "conceptual playgrounds"—in which to explore high-level emergent behaviors arising from various low-level (i.e., individual combatant and squad-level) interaction rules, and *not* as detailed system-level models of specific combat hardware (M16 rifle, M101 105mm howitzer, etc.).

ISAAC and EINSTein are simulation tools that sit squarely in the middle ground between two extremes: (1) highly realistic models that provide little insight into basic processes, and (2) ultra-minimalist models that strip away all but the simplest dynamical variables and leave out the most interesting real behavior. By focusing on primitive processes and emergent behaviors, not hardware—while adhering to the multiagent-based "minimalist modeling" philosophy—ISAAC and EINSTein allow users to quickly assess the multidimensional trade-offs among the fundamental characteristics describing combatants in battle.

1.1.4 *ISAAC*

ISAAC, which is an acronym for *Irreducible Semi-Autonomous Adaptive Combat,** is one of the first agent-based simulations of small-unit combat to be widely used by the military operations research community. "Agent-based simulation" refers to a growing suite of modeling and simulation tools developed by the artificial-life community [Lang95] to describe complex adaptive systems [BarY00].†

Introduced in 1997, ISAAC served as a *proof-of-concept* that the theretofore speculative proposition that real combat behaviors may be reproduced by using swarms of software agents, obeying simple local rules, can be turned into a practical reality. Color plate 1 (page 247) shows a screenshot of a typical ISAAC work-session. The red and blue squares represent notional red and blue force agents, respectively, and the various numbers that appear along the left- and right-hand sides of the screenshot represent values of the many parameters the define how agents sense and react to their environment. All of these quantities will be defined in later chapters.

ISAAC was developed for DOS-based computers, and its source code is written in ANSI C. Although ISAAC's functions are, in many respects, primitive, compared

*The acronym ISAAC was suggested to me by a friend (Lyntis Beard; who also coined the acronym EINSTein) as a tongue-in-cheek homage to Isaac Newton. It seemed an appropriate choice to make, since the so-called "new" sciences (i.e. a colloquial way of referring to the study of complex adaptive systems) are usually described as representing a fundamental shift *away from* linear (or "Newtonian") thinking. Newton was, of course, well aware of the prevalence of nonlinearities in nature.

†Many of the most important concepts and mathematical tools used in the nonlinear dynamics and complex system theory research communities, particularly those pertaining to artificial-life studies, are introduced and discussed in chapter 2 of this book.

to functions appearing in its successor simulation, EINSTein (see discussion in next section), the basic design and architecture of the two programs (and certainly the underlying philosophy; see discussion in chapter 4) are essentially the same.

The final version of ISAAC (version 1.8.6) is described in detail in [Ilach97]. Standalone fitness landscape mapping and genetic algorithm "agent breeder" programs, that use ISAAC data files, are also available on the ISAAC/EINSTein CNA website at URL address:

http://www.cna.org/isaac/downsoft.htm .

What sets ISAAC apart from all previous models used by military analysts, is that ISAAC actively takes a *bottom-up*, *synthesist* approach to the modeling of combat, rather than relying on the more conventional *reductionist*, or *top-down*, distillations of combat dynamics. Models based on differential equations homogenize the properties of entire populations and ignore the spatial component altogether. Partial differential equations—by introducing a physical space to account for troop movement—fare somewhat better, but still treat the agent population as a continuum. In contrast, ISAAC consists of a discrete heterogeneous set of spatially distributed individual agents (i.e., combatants), each of which has its own characteristic properties and rules of behavior. These properties can also change (i.e., adapt) as an individual agent evolves in time.

The basic element of ISAAC is an *agent*, which loosely represents a primitive combat unit (infantryman, tank, transport vehicle, etc.) that is equipped with the following characteristics:

- *Doctrine* → a default local-rule set specifying how to act in a generic environment.
- *Mission* → goals directing an agent's behavior.
- *Situational Awareness* → sensors generating an internal map of an agent's local environment.
- *Reaction* → a set of rules that determine how an agent behaves in a given context.

A global rule set determines combat attrition, reconstitution and reinforcement. ISAAC also contains both local and global commanders, each with their own command radii, and obeying an evolving command and control rule hierarchy.

Most traditional models focus on looking for equilibrium "solutions" among some set of (typically, predefined) aggregate variables. For example, the Lanchester equations (see below), which are still being used in many of today's otherwise state-of-the-art military simulations to adjudicate combat attrition, are effectively *mean-field equations* (in the parlance of physics): i.e., certain variables such as attrition rate are assumed to represent an entire force and the outcome of a battle is said to be "understood" when the equilibrium state has been explicitly solved for. In contrast, ISAAC focuses on understanding the kinds of emergent patterns that might arise while the overall system is *out of equilibrium*. In ISAAC, the final outcome of a battle—as defined by, say, measuring the surviving force sizes—takes second stage to exploring how two forces might coevolve during combat. A few examples of the kinds of *non*equilibrium dynamics that characterize much of real combat include: the sudden "flash of insight" of a clever commander that changes the course of a battle; the swift flanking maneuver that surprises the enemy; and the serendipitous confluence of several far-separated (and unorchestrated) events that lead to victory. These are the kinds of behavior that Lanchesterian-based models are in principle incapable of addressing. ISAAC, and its direct successor EINSTein (see below), represents a first step toward being able to explore such questions.

Shortly after ISAAC was developed (for MS-DOS based PCs), MCCDC sponsored a port of its source code to a vectorized, parallel version that can be run by the *Maui High Performance Super Computer* (MHPSC); see [Brand01]. A number of researchers have used this new data to examine specific combat issues. For example, Michael Lauren, with New Zealand's *Defence Operational Technology Support Establishment*, has published a number of interesting findings based on ISAAC/Maui runs in a series of reports ([Lauren99], [Lauren00a] and [Lauren00b]). Lauren has found ISAAC useful for modelling "fluid" situations, such as reconnaissance, patrol through a potentially hostile crowd, ambush or "shock" situations, and for investigating the effects of training levels. Focusing his attention on the statistical distributions of attrition outcomes of battle, Lauren has identified some significant differences between agent-based models of combat that explicitly include rules for maneuver and results derived from Lanchester models.

In particular, Lauren provides strong evidence that the intensity of battles obeys a fractal power-law dependence on frequency, and displays other traits characteristic of high-dimensional chaotic systems, such as fat-tailed probability distributions and intermittency. Lauren has found that the attrition rate depends on the cube root of the kill probability, which stands in marked contrast to results obtained for stochastic variants of Lanchester's model, in which, typically, the attrition rate scales linearly with an increase in kill probability. If the agent-based model is assumed to be a more accurate model of real combat processes, a $1/3$ power-law scaling implies that a relatively "weak" force, with a small kill probability, may actually constitute a much more potent force than a simple Lanchester-based approach would suggest. The potency comes from the ability to maneuver (which is never explicitly modeled by Lanchester-based approaches) and to selectively concentrate fire-power while maneuvering.

Brown [Brown00] has analyzed a very large number of ISAAC runs (numbering over 750K using the MHPSC) to search for an optimal balance between a commander's propensity to move towards the objective and his propensity to maneuver to avoid the enemy in order to minimize time to mission completion and friendly losses. Brown's data suggest that friction can significantly influence the battlefield but that a strong commander-subordinate bond can reduce the effect. In addition, this exploration also demonstrates that fractional factorial designs provide almost as much information from ISAAC as full factorial designs with only a fraction of the runs. Other research that is based, in part, on ISAAC and/or ISAAC's conceptual design, includes that by Hencke [Hencke98], Roddy and Dickson [Roddy00], Sunvold [Sunv99] and West [West99].

1.1.5 *EINSTein*

EINSTein (*Enhanced ISAAC Neural Simulation Toolkit*) was introduced in 1999 and—at the time of writing this book*—is still being actively developed. It is based on ISAAC, but uses entirely new source code and decision algorithms and contains a vastly richer landscape of user-defined primitive functions. The underlying dynamics is patterned after mobile cellular automata rules,† and are somewhat reminiscent of Braitenberg's *Vehicles* [Brait84]. Mobile cellular automata have been used before to model predator-prey interactions in natural ecologies [Bocc94]. They have also been applied to combat modeling [Woodc88], but in a much more limited fashion than the one used by EINSTein.‡

EINSTein is the central focus of this book, and its design and development is discussed in great detail in chapters 4-7. By way of introduction, we here only briefly mention some of EINSTein's major features, which include:

- *Dialog-driven I/O, using a Windows graphical-user-interface front-end, and allowing multiple simultaneous document views*
- *Object-oriented C++ source code base to facilitate end-user/analyst programming enhancements*
- *Over 200+ user-programmable functions on the source code level*
- *Integrated natural terrain maps and terrain-based adaptive decision-dynamics*
- *User-defined waypoints and path*
- *Context-dependent and user-defined agent behaviors*
- *Multiple squads, with inter-squad communication links*
- *Local and global command-agent dynamics*
- *Genetic algorithm toolkit to tailor agent rules to desired force-level behaviors*
- *Data collection and multi-dimensional visualization tools*
- *Mission fitness-landscape profilers*

*October 2003.

†An overview of cellular automata appears in chapter 2. For a more detailed technical discussion, see *Cellular Automata: A Discrete Universe* [Ilach01b].

‡Woodcock's, Cobb's and Dockery's paper, "Cellular Automata: A New Method for Battlefield Simulation," was published by the journal *Signal* in 1988 [Woodc88], and is the earliest reference the author has been able to find to a cellular automata model of combat. Woodcock and Dockery went on to publish a pioneering study of applications of nonlinearity to warfare, called *The Military Landscape: Mathematical Models of Combat* [Dock93b]. Because of its breadth of coverage, and because its authors are equally well versed in technical analysis and military operations, there is no finer way for young researchers wanting to explore these fields than by starting with this reference book.

Color plate 2 (page 248) provides a snapshot of a typical EINSTein work-session; note the significantly improved graphical user-interface over the one embedded within ISAAC (see color plate 1, page 247). The screenshot contains three active windows: *main battlefield view* (which includes passable and impassable terrain elements), *trace view* (which shows color coded territorial occupancy) and *combat view* (which provides a gray-scaled filter of combat intensity). All views are simultaneously updated during a run. Toward the right-hand side of the screenshot appear two data dialogs that summarize red and blue agent parameter values. Appearing on the lower left side and along the bottom of the figure are time-series graphs of red and blue center-of-mass coordinates (as measured from the red flag) and the average number of agents within red and blue agent's sensor ranges, and a dialog that allows the user to define communication relays among individual squads.

During the last several years, EINSTein has evolved into a research-level caliber artificial-life "laboratory" for exploring self-organized emergent behavior in land combat. It is written, and compiled, using Microsoft's *Visual C++* [MSC++], uses Pinnacle Publishing Inc.'s *Graphics Server* [Pinn] for displaying time-series plots and three-dimensional renderings of fitness-landscapes, and currently consists of about 150K lines of code. EINSTein runs under almost all versions of Microsoft's Windows (including 95, 98, Me, NT, 2000, and XP).

EINSTein's source code is divided into three basic parts: (1) the *combat engine*, (2) the *graphical user interface* (GUI), and (3) *data collection* (and *data visualization)* functions. These parts are essentially machine (i.e., CPU and/or operating system) independent and may be compiled separately.

Unlike ISAAC, EINSTein has adhered, from the start, to a rigorously object-oriented (OO) design. This means that everything in EINSTein is an *object*, and every object is an instance of a *class*. A class is a repository of the properties of, and behaviors associated with, objects. On the most basic level, the program proceeds by objects communicating with other objects, by sending and receiving *messages*. Messages are requests made of other objects to perform specific actions, and are parceled out along with whatever information is necessary for those actions to be completed.

Object-oriented code also includes the concept of *inheritance*, which refers to the rooted-tree structure into which the classes are organized. Using inheritance, behaviors associated with instances of a class are automatically available to all classes that descend from that class on the tree.

1.1.5.1 *Portability Across Multiple Platforms*

EINSTein's code base is highly portable and is relatively easy to modify to suit particular problems and interests. For example, an EINSTein-based combat environment may be developed as a standalone program on a CPU platform other than the original Microsoft Windows target machine used for EINSTein's original development.

Any developer/analyst interested in porting EINSTein over to some other machine and/or operating system is tasked only with providing his own machine-specific GUI as a "wraparound" to the standalone combat and data-visualization engines (that may be provided as *Dynamic Link Libraries*, or DLLs). Moreover, it is very easy to add, delete, and/or change the existing source code, including making complicated changes that significantly alter how agents decide their moves.

1.1.5.2 *Availability*

EINSTein's current version (release version 1.1) is available for download on the internet at URL address:

http://www.cna.org/isaac/einstein_install.htm .

Appendixes D and E of this book provide brief, but self-contained, installation instructions, a concise user's guide and tutorial to EINSTein. A comprehensive manual (in Adobe's PDF format) to EINSTein [Ilach99a] is also available on the web at URL address:*

http://www.cna.org/isaac/einstein_users_guide.pdf .

EINSTein (along with its precursor ISAAC) represents the first systematic attempt, within the military operations research community, to simulate combat—on a small to medium scale—by using autonomous agents to model *individual behaviors and personalities* rather than specific weapons. Because agents are all endowed with a rudimentary form of "intelligence," they can respond to a very large class of changing conditions as they evolve during battle. Because of the relative simplicity of the underlying dynamical rules, EINSTein can rapidly provide potential outcomes for a wide spectrum of tunable parameter values defining specific scenarios, and can thus be used to effectively map out the space of possible behaviors.

As we will see in a later chapter that presents sample behaviors, EINSTein possesses an impressive repertoire of emergent behaviors: *forward advance*, *frontal attack*, *local clustering*, *penetration*, *feints*, *retreat*, *attack posturing*, *containment*, *flanking maneuvers*, *"Guerrilla-like" assaults*, among many others; in short, EINSTein's repertoire consist of almost all of the basic kinds of real combat behaviors that are known to emerge on the real-world combat battlefield. Moreover, behaviors frequently arise that appear to involve some form of intelligent division of red and blue forces to deal with local firestorms and skirmishes, particularly those forces whose personalities have been bred (via a genetic algorithm) to perform a specific mission. It is important to point out that such behaviors are not hard-wired but are rather an emergent property of a decentralized, but dynamically interdependent, swarm of agents.

*To view PDF files you will need to install Adobe's free *Acrobat Reader* software, available at URL address http://www.adobe.com/products/acrobat/readermain.html

Color plate 3 (page 249), which shows screen captures of spatial patterns resulting from 16 different rules, illustrates the diversity of behaviors that emerges out of a relatively simple rule base. The sample patterns appearing in this plate are those that arise for red and blue forces consisting of a *single* squad. *Multi-squad* scenarios, in which agents belonging to different squads obey different rules, often result in considerably more complicated emergent behaviors. An important long-term goal in developing EINSTein is that the program can be used as a more general tool—that transcends the specific notional combat environment to which it is obviously tailored—for exploring the very poorly understood relationship between micro-rules and emergent macro-behaviors. We will have much more to say about this important fundamental question later on in the book.

Air Force Studies and Analyses Agency	US Joint Forces Command
American Red Cross	Korea Inst. for Defense Analyses
Athabasca University (Canada)	Lockheed Martin
New York Police Department	Marine Corps Warfighting Lab
Atlantic Southeast Airlines	MITRE Corporation
Bentley College	Mobile Aerospace Engineering
Boeing Company	MYPRO Design Studio
BreakAway Games	Nat. Defense Academy of Japan
CDA/HLS	Nat. University of Singapore
Center for Army Analysis	Naval Postgraduate School
Center for Naval Analyses	Naval Surface Warfare Center
Strategic Studies Group	Naval Undersea Warfare Center
CORDA, BAE Systems	New Mexico State University
Defense Information Systems Agency	RAND Corporation
Defense Sci & Tech Organization (Aus)	Royal Military College of Science
Defence Technology Agency	Saab Dynamics
Dep. of National Defence (Canada)	Tottori University (Japan)
Electronic Arts	University of Alberta, Canada
General Dynamics	University of New South Wales
George Mason University	University of Chile
Hellenic Complex Systems Laboratory	University of Orleans (France)
Institute of Defense Analysis (IDA)	U.S. Army
University of Alberta	U.S. Army Research Laboratory
Indian Institute of Technology	US Army War College
Science Applications International Corp	University of Warsaw
University of Paderborn	Naval Undersea Warfare Center
Northrop Grumman	Wayne State University

Table 1.4 Partial list of affiliations of registered users of EINSTein.

Research Group	**Brief Description of Work**
600+ Registered Users	U.S. Dept. of Defense, Academic, Commercial, Research (see table 1.4)
Air Force Institute of Technology	Strategic Effects of Airpower [Tighe99]
U.S. Marine Corps Combat Development Command (MCCDC)	Project Albert (consortium: MHPCC, Mitre, SAIC, NPGS, GMU, John Hopkins); Hunter Warrior Experiment [West99]
Center for Naval Analyses	USMC Ground Combat Study (Taylor, et.al. [TaylorD00]); Gaming and Adaptive Agents for Command and Control Research (Perla, et. al. [Perla02]; Persian Gulf War Scenario Gamelet (Cox, [Cox02])
Mitre	Combat Analysis Tools [Jacyna01]
United States Military Academy	Adaptive Command and Control [Kewley01]
Naval Postgraduate School (NPGS)/Moves Institute	Human and Organizational Behavior [Roddy00]; Helicopter reconnaissance [Unrath00]; Information and Coordination [Hencke98]; Self-Organization in Theater Ballistic Missile Defense Networks [Sunv99]; Small Unit Combat [Wooda00]; Operational-Level Naval Planning [Ercetin01]; Marine Infantry Squads in an Urban Environment [Aragon01]; Human Dimension of Combat [Brown00]; Modeling Tactical Level Combat [Pawl01]; Modeling Conventional Land Combat [Mert01]; Tactical Land Navigation [Stine00]
Defense Operational Technology Support Establishment (New Zealand)	Fractal Statistics in Combat [Lauren99, Lauren00b]; Peacekeeping [Lauren00c]; Reconnaissance / Counter-Reconnaissance Dynamics [Baigent00]
Defense Science and Technology Organization (Australia)	Impact of Reconnaissance on Battlefield Survivability [Gill01]

Table 1.5 A sampling of research conducted by various organizations and academic institutions that is based (in part or whole) on ISAAC and/or EINSTein

Interim versions of both ISAAC and EINSTein, along with all approved-for-public-release support documentation, have been freely available to the academic and military operations research communities, from the start of CNA's complexity research project. This material is available on-line on the internet at EINSTein's homepage:

http://www.cna.org/isaac .

Following the final pre-release beta version of EINSTein, prospective users have been asked to fill out a registration form before downloading the installation program. This form (along with email-based communication) has made it possible to track (albeit imperfectly) the growing numbers of on-line users of EINSTein.

Table 1.4 contains a partial list of the academic, commercial, research, and/or military affiliations of registered users of the program. The diversity of the entries appearing in this table attests to the very wide-spread interest in EINSTein. The full list, as of this writing (October 2003), contains the registration information for more than 1000 individuals. Table 1.5 lists recent research projects that have either used EINSTein, or—as in the case of thesis studies conducted at the *Naval Post Graduate School* (in Monterey, California)—have been directly inspired by ISAAC, EINSTein and/or EINSTein's agent decision-making architecture.

1.2 Background and Motivations

"We can see how many factors are involved (i.e., in battle) and have to be weighed against each other; the vast, the almost infinite distance there can be between a cause and its effect, and the countless ways in which these elements can be combined. The function of theory is to put all this in systematic order, clearly and comprehensively, and to trace each action to an adequate, compelling cause...theory should show how one thing is related to another."—-Clausewitz, *Prussian military theorist* (1780-1831)

As a background to why the multiagent-based simulation approach (as embodied by both ISAAC and EINSTein) is almost ideally suited for describing combat—and how the methodology differs from traditional warfare modeling techniques—we must first appreciate what has been, for the last century, the conventional wisdom regarding our fundamental understanding of the basic processes of war. This conventional wisdom effectively begins, and ends, with the so-called Lanchester equations of combat.

1.2.1 *Lanchester Equations of Combat*

In 1914, F. W. Lanchester introduced a set of coupled ordinary differential equations–now commonly called the *Lanchester Equations* (LEs)–as models of attrition in modern warfare [Lanch95]. Similar ideas were proposed around that time by Chase [Chase02] and Osipov [Osipov95].

These equations are formally equivalent to the Lottka-Voltera equations used for modeling the dynamics of interacting predator-prey populations [Hofb88]. The LEs have since served as the fundamental mathematical models upon which most modern theories of combat attrition are based, and are to this day embedded in many state-of-the-art military models of combat. Taylor [TaylorG83] provides a thorough mathematical discussion.

LEs are very intuitive and therefore easy to apply. For the simplest case of directed fire, for example, they embody the idea that one side's attrition rate is proportional to the opposing side's size.

In mathematical terms, let $R(t)$ and $B(t)$ represent the numerical strengths of the red and blue forces at time t, respectively, and α_R and α_B represent the constant effective firing rates at which one unit of strength on one side causes attrition of the other side's forces. Then Lanchester's well known directed fire (or "Square law") model of attrition is given by:

$$\begin{cases} \dfrac{dR}{dt} = -\alpha_B B(t), \quad R(0) = R_0 \\ \\ \dfrac{dB}{dt} = -\alpha_R R(t), \quad B(0) = B_0, \end{cases} \tag{1.1}$$

where $R(0)$ and $B(0)$ are the initial red and blue force levels, respectively.

1.2.1.1 *Closed-Form Solutions*

The closed form solution of these equations is given in terms of hyperbolic functions as:

$$\begin{cases} R(t) = R_0 \cosh\left(t\sqrt{\alpha_B\alpha_R}\right) - B_0\sqrt{\alpha_B/\alpha_R}\sinh\left(t\sqrt{\alpha_B\alpha_R}\right) \\ B(t) = B_0 \cosh\left(t\sqrt{\alpha_B\alpha_R}\right) - R_0\sqrt{\alpha_R/\alpha_B}\sinh\left(t\sqrt{\alpha_B\alpha_R}\right), \end{cases} \tag{1.2}$$

and satisfies the simple square-law state equation,

$$\alpha_R\left(R_0^2 - R(t)^2\right) = \alpha_B\left(B_0^2 - B(t)^2\right). \tag{1.3}$$

Despite the simplicity of this equation (which can be found embedded in many large-scale combat models), almost all attempts to correlate LE-based models with historical combat data have proven inconclusive, a result that is in no small part due to the paucity of data. Most data consist only of initial force levels and casualties, and typically for one side only. Moreover, the actual number of casualties is usually uncertain because the definition of *casualty* varies (killed, killed + wounded, killed + missing, etc.).

Two noteworthy battles for which detailed daily attrition data and daily force levels do exist are the battle of Iwo Jima in World War II and Inchon-Seoul campaign in the Korean War. While the battle of Iwo Jima is frequently cited as evidence for the efficacy of the classic LEs, it must be remembered that the conditions under which it was fought were very close to the ideal list of assumptions under which the LEs themselves are derived. A detailed analysis of the Inchon-Seoul campaign [Hartley95] has also proved inconclusive. Weiss [WeissH57], Fain [Fain75], Richardson [RichLF60] and others analyze attrition in battles fought from 200 B.C. to World War II.

1.2.1.2 *Limitations*

While the LEs may be relevant for the kind of static trench warfare and artillery duels that characterized most of World War I, they lack the spatial degrees of freedom, to realistically model modern combat. They are certainly too simple to adequately represent the more modern vision of combat, which depends on small, highly trained, well-armed autonomous teams working in concert, continually adapting to changing conditions and environments. The fundamental problem is that they idealize combat much in the same way as Newton's laws idealize physics.

Strictly speaking, the LEs are valid only under a special set of assumptions: homogeneous forces that are continually engaged in combat, firing rates that are independent of opposing force levels and are constant in time, and units that are always aware of the position and condition of all opposing units, among many others. Because Lanchester's direct-fire equations assume that each side has perfect information about where the opposing side's forces are located and what opposing force units have been hit, they are models of highly organized combat with complete and instantaneous information.

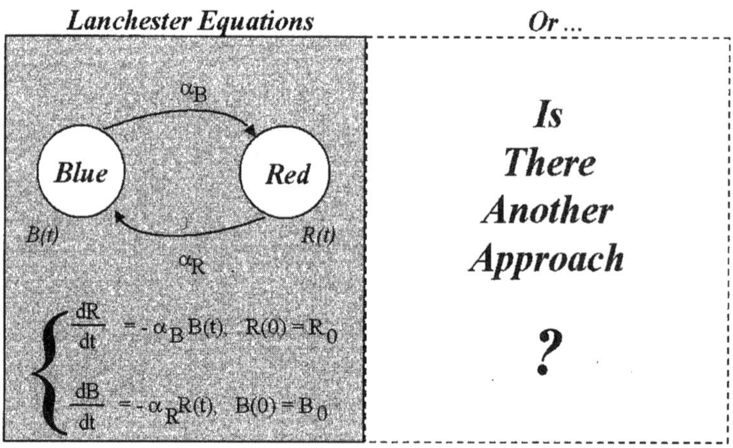

Fig. 1.1 The force-on-force attrition *challenge*.

LEs suffer from other fundamental shortcomings, including modeling combat as a deterministic process, requiring knowledge of attrition-rate coefficients (the values of which are, in practice, very difficult if not impossible to obtain), an inability to account for any suppressive effects of weapons, an inability to account for terrain effects, and the inability to account for any spatial variation of forces. Perhaps their most significant drawback is that they completely ignore the *human element*; i.e., the uniquely individual, often imperfect, psychology and decision-making capability of the human soldier.

When these shortcomings are coupled with the US Marine Corps' *Maneuver-Warfare* land combat doctrine—which is fundamentally based on the art of maneuver and adaptation vice pure force-on-force attrition [Hooker93]—the use of a purely force-on-force-driven analytical methodology to describe modern combat begins not just to strain credibility, but to literally smack of an oxymoron. The question is, "*Is there anything better?*" Is there a way, perhaps that bucks the conventional way of representing land combat? See figure 1.1.

While there have been many extensions to and generalizations of Lanchester's equations over the years, including their reformulations as stochastic differential equations and partial differential equations designed to minimize the inherent deficiencies, very little has really changed in the way we fundamentally view and model combat attrition. However, recent developments in nonlinear dynamics and complex systems theory—particularly those in *artificial life* (see below)—provide a powerful new set of theoretical and practical tools to address many of the deficiencies mentioned above. These developments provide a fundamentally new way of looking at land combat.

1.2.2 *Artificial Life*

Artificial Life, introduced as an interdisciplinary research field by Chris Langton,* is an attempt to understand life as it is by examining a larger context of life as it could be. The underlying supposition is that life owes at least as much to its existence to the way in which information is organized as it does to the physical substance (i.e., matter) that embodies that information. Similarly, ISAAC and EINSTein are both designed to be tools that can help us understand combat as it is by allowing analysts to explore a larger context of combat as it could be.

The fundamental concept of artificial life is *emergence*, or the appearance of higher-level properties and behaviors of a system that—while obviously originating from the collective dynamics of that system's components—are neither to be found in nor are directly deducible from the lower-level properties of that system. Emergent properties are properties of the "whole" that are not possessed by any of the individual parts making up that whole: an air molecule is not a tornado and a neuron is not conscious.

Artificial life studies *real* (that is, *biological*) life by using artificial components (such as computer programs) to capture the behavioral essence of living systems. The underlying supposition is that if the artificial parts are organized correctly, in a way that respects the organization of the living system, then the artificial system will exhibit the same characteristic dynamical behavior as the natural system on higher levels as well. Notice that this bottom-up, synthesist approach stands in marked contrast to more conventional top-down, analytical approaches.

*Chris Langton organized the first international conference on artificial life in 1987 [Lang89] and remains one the field's important conceptual and spiritual leaders.

Artificial life-based computer simulations are characterized by these five general properties [Lang89]:

(1) *They are defined by populations of simple programs or instructions about how individual parts all interact.*
(2) *There is no single "master oracle" program that directs the action of all other programs.*
(3) *Each program defines how simple entities respond to their environment locally.*
(4) *There are no rules that direct the global behavior.*
(5) *Behaviors on levels higher than individual programs are emergent.*

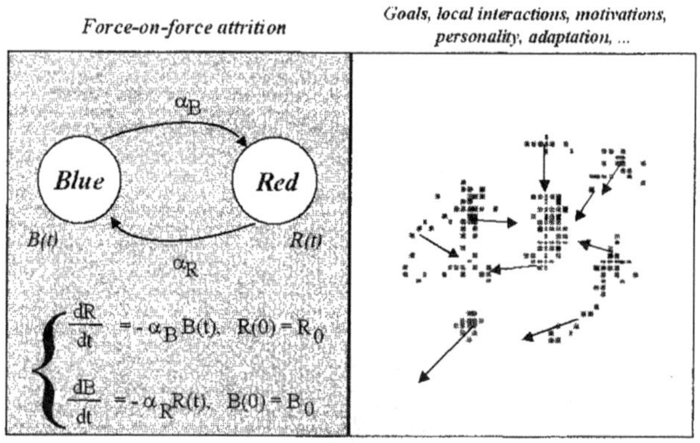

Fig. 1.2 A schematic illustration of how *artificial-life* tools may be used as the basis of an alternative new approach to the classic force-on-force attrition problem; see text.

Figure 1.2 shows, schematically, the form of an artificial-life-based "solution" to the force-on-force attrition challenge posed in figure 1.1. Fundamentally, the artificial-life-based approach represents a shift in focus from "hard-wiring" into a model a sufficient number of (both low- and high-level) details of a system to yield a desired set of "realistic" behaviors; the rallying cry of such models being *"More detail, more detail, we need more detail!"* .....*to*..... Looking for universal patterns of high-level behavior that naturally and spontaneously emerge from an underlying set of low-level interactions and constraints; the rallying cry in this case being *"Allow evolving global patterns to emerge on their own from the local rules!"* As we will see in detail in later chapters, EINSTein is a direct application of artificial-life techniques to modeling the dynamics and self-organized emergent behaviors on the real battlefield. As a gentle first example of how simple rules can unexpectedly generate complex behavior, consider Craig Reynolds' well-known simulation of flocking birds, called *Boids*.*

*Other examples of decentralized-rules and self-organized emergent behaviors are given and discussed on a more technical level in chapter 2).

1.2.2.1 *Boids*

One of the most breathtakingly beautiful displays of nature is the synchronous, fluid-like flocking of birds (see figure 1.3). It is also an excellent example of emergence in complex systems. Large or small, the magic of flocks is the very strong impression they convey of some intentional centralized control directing the overall traffic. Though ornithologists still do not have a complete explanation for this phenomenon, evidence strongly suggests that flocking is a decentralized activity, where each bird acts according to its local perceptions of what nearby birds are doing. Flocking is therefore a group behavior that emerges from collective action.

Fig. 1.3 Are the rhythmic global patterns of flocking birds the result of a centralized control or an example of self-organized *decentralized* emergent order?

Craig Reynolds [Rey87] programmed a set of artificial birds—which he called *Boids*—to follow three simple local rules:

- *Maintain a minimum distance from other objects (including other boids),*
- *Match the velocity of nearby boids, and*
- *Move toward the perceived center of nearby boids.*

Each boid thus "sees" only what its neighbors are doing and acts accordingly. Reynolds found that the collective motion of all the *Boids* was remarkably close to real flocking, despite the fact that there is nothing explicitly describing the flock as a whole. The boids initially move rapidly together to form a flock. The *Boids* at the edges either slow down or speed up to maintain the flock's integrity. If the path bends or zigzags in any way, the *Boids* all make whatever minute adjustments need to be made to maintain the group structure. If the path is strewn with obstacles, the *Boids* flock around whatever is in their way naturally, sometimes temporarily splitting up to pass an obstacle before reassembling beyond it. There is no central command that dictates this action.

Reynolds' *Boids* is a good example of decentralized order not because the *Boids'* behavior is a perfect replica of the flocking of birds that occurs in nature—although it is a close enough match that Reynold's model has attracted the attention of professional ornithologists—but that much of the *Boids'* collective behavior is entirely unanticipated, and cannot be easily derived from the rules defining what each individual *Boid* does.*

1.2.2.2 *Decentralized Sorting*

As a second example of an emergent "group mind" behavior that spontaneously appears without being centrally orchestrated, consider a decentralized sorting algorithm designed by Beckers, et.al. [Beckers94]. Inspired by the self-organized manner in which real ant colonies sort their brood, the algorithm has simple robots move about a fenced-in environment that is randomly littered with objects that can be scooped up. These robots (1) *move randomly*, (2) *do not communicate with each other*, (3) *can perceive only those objects directly in front of them* (but can distinguish between two or more types of objects with some degree of error), and (4) *do not obey any centralized control.* The probability that a robot picks up or puts down an object is a function of the number of the same objects that it has encountered in the past.

Coordinated by the positive feedback these simple rules induce between robots and their environment, the result, over time, is a seemingly intelligent, coordinated sorting activity. Clusters of randomly distributed objects spontaneously and quite naturally emerge out of a simple set of autonomous local actions having nothing at all to do with clustering *per se.*

The authors suggest that this system's simplicity, flexibility, error tolerance, and reliability compensate for their lower efficiency. While one can argue that this collective sorting algorithm is much less efficient than a hierarchical one, the cost of having a hierarchy is that the sorting would no longer be ant-like but would require a god-like oracle analyzing how many objects of what type are where, deciding how best to communicate strategy to the ants. Furthermore, the ants would require some sort of internal map, a rudimentary intelligence to deal with fluctuations and surprises in the environment (what if an object was not where the oracle said it would be?), and so on. In short, a hierarchy, while potentially more efficient, would of necessity have to be considerably more complex as well. The point Beckers, et. al. are making is that a much simpler collective decentralized system can lead to seemingly intelligent behavior while being more flexible, more tolerant of errors, and more reliable than a hierarchical system.

*Craig Reynolds' web site (at URL address http://www.red3d.com/cwr/boids/) contains many *Boids*-related resources, including a JAVA implementation of *Boids*, a video of the original *Boids* movie created in 1986 (in which *Boids* are shown avoiding cylindrical obstacles), and links to other computational models of rule-based group dynamics.

1.3 Models & Simulations: *A Heuristic Discussion*

"We have to remember that what we observe is not nature in itself but nature exposed to our method of questioning."—Werner Heisenberg, *Physicist* (1901-1976)

The fundamental challenge of physics—*physics* is here used as an obvious (but by no means sole) exemplar of the set of conceptual tools our species has evolved to quench its natural curiosity to understand how the universe works—has always been the understanding of the phenomenologically observed complexity in nature using a minimal set of simple principles; i.e., *finding simple models that simulate the world.* Indeed, physics is predicated on the idea that, if we are clever enough to focus our attention on just those parts of nature that are critical for a particular process to exist, and understand how *those* parts alone interact (while ignoring all other parts of the system), that we can then—to a high degree of fidelity—deduce what nature is going to do *before* nature itself actually does it.

An outfielder in baseball takes this fact for granted each time he runs back to catch a ball whose trajectory he is effectively able to "precompute" in his mind's eye—using a mental *model*—the instant he sees the bat hit the ball. He knows where the ball will fall *before the ball actually gets there.** Any good physicist will tell you that you can calculate where the ball will be at all times t—i.e., its position $\vec{x}(t) = (x(t), y(t))$, where $y(t)$ is the ball's height off the ground at time t—by knowing only its initial height ($y(0) = h$), initial velocity ($\vec{v}_0 = (v_x(0), v_y(0))$), and the value of the gravitational acceleration due to Earth's gravity (g):

$$x(t) = v_x(0) \cdot t, \;\; y(t) = h + v_y(0) \cdot t - gt^2/2. \tag{1.4}$$

Of course, this is only the *simplest* such model, and the one that incorporates the fewest abstract components; other, more complicated models of a baseball's trajectory that take into account other physically relevant factors can easily be imagined. For example, we can extend our basic model by including the effects of the spin of the baseball, or the temperature and humidity of the air in the baseball park, or wind effects, along with a host of other such factors.

Some obvious questions one can ask, regardless of what physical system one is trying to model, are: *"How do we know that a particular model or simulation is a 'good' one?"* and *"How do we know that some other model, one that is based perhaps*

*The act of catching a baseball is, of course, in practice, far more complicated than the text above suggests. Whatever the means by which an outfielder really accomplishes this, he almost certainly does *not* "mentally integrate" the equations of motion. One recent suggestion is that outfielders intuitively traverse a curved path that results in a linear optical ball trajectory at all times. By always keeping the ball on a straight line in their visual field as a cue to determine where to go, outfielders thus essentially reduce the complicated three-dimensional problem into a simpler two-dimensional problem (see [McBeath95] and [Abou96]). The book, *The Physics of Baseball* (by Robert Adair, Perennial Press, 2002), contains a wealth of fascinating information on this, and other questions regarding the physics of baseball.

on a different set of principles, is not a 'better' one?" Along with, *"What do we mean by 'better'?"*

It may surprise the reader to learn that these are deceptively hard questions to answer; indeed, a major ingredient of modeling and simulation consists more of art than science. To answer these questions fully, one must first understand the nature of, and the often subtle interrelationships among, such concepts as "reality" (whatever that is), "mathematical and/or physical theory," "conceptual distillation," and what is meant by "predicting" the outcome of an experiment or the evolution of a system. Since we have only a short space here to discuss these issues, if the reader wishes to explore them more deeply, we can recommend any of the following texts: *Handbook of Simulation* [Banks98], *An Introduction to Mathematical Modeling* [Bender00], *Simulation* [Ross01], and *Theory of Modeling and Simulation* [Zieg00].

One of the most thoughtful analyses of the use of multiagent-based simulations, in particular, as generative exploratory tools, is a paper by Epstein [Epstein99] (multiagent-based simulations are discussed later in this chapter).

Finally, John Casti's book, *Would-Be Worlds* [Casti96], while written on a popular level, also contains a cogent philosophical discussion of using models to "simulate" reality that bears directly on the ideas outlined in this section.*

1.3.1 *Definitions*

We begin by noting that there is an unfortunate terminological ambiguity that often arises in discussions regarding modeling and simulation. Sometimes, the terms "model" and "simulation" are used interchangeably; on other occasions they are distinguished as to meaning but in ways that are not always consistent. Even in military operations research, ambiguities persist despite the fact that the *Defense Modeling and Simulation Office* has issued official definitions.† Indeed, the ubiquity of the phrase "modeling and simulation," or its abbreviated form "M&S," which constantly appears throughout the military research literature, symposia and high-level briefings only nurtures the erroneous view that the terms "model" and "simulation" convey the same meaning.

In the discussion that follows, the word "model" is used to refer to a *conceptual representation of some aspect of reality* (such as a physical system). This representation may take the form of a simple diagram, a verbal description or a set of mathematical equations. For example, using this nomenclature, figure 0.1 that ap-

*Readers interested in exploring the relationship between mathematics (as exemplar of "model") and physics (as exemplar of our understanding of "reality") on an even deeper philosophical level, are urged to read the classic paper "On the Unreasonable Effectiveness of Mathematics in the Natural Sciences" by the Hungarian physicist Eugene Wigner [Wigner60].

†See "DoD High Level Architecture for Modeling and Simulation," by Judith Dahmann, December 1996, *Defense Modeling and Simulation Office*; available on-line at URL address http://www.dmso.mil.

pears on page xiv (in the Preface) illustrates—partly diagrammatically and partly verbally—the "Billiard-Ball" and "Artificial-Life" *models* (along the left-hand and right-hand sides of figure 0.1, respectively). Likewise, the Lanchester equations (defined in equation 1.1) constitute a manifestly mathematical form of the Lanchester combat *model.*

The word "simulation" is used to refer to a *dynamical implementation of a model*, and in this sense may be thought of as a generalization, or extension, of what we have just defined as being a "model." A model provides an abstract distillation of a system, and is an implicitly static construct; it is a conceptualization, not a dynamic reproduction. In contrast, a simulation is an explicitly dynamical realization of how a particular system evolves in time (albeit one that may also be abstract and simplified).

For example, where the Lanchester combat attrition *model* is nothing more than the mathematical embodiment of the abstract verbal description, "One side's attrition rate is proportional to the opposing side's force size," we do not have a Lanchester combat attrition *simulation* (in our parlance) until we have programmed a computer to solve the Lanchester model (i.e., integrate the Lanchester equations) and, say, plot a graph for the red and blue force strengths as a function of time. A simulation—as the term is used here and throughout this book—is thus essentially the computational analog of the purely descriptive (i.e., mathematical) model. In short, a simulation entails the *active, synthetic recreation* of the dynamics of either a real physical system, or a model of a real system.

There is, of course, a considerable and unavoidable overlap between these two definitions. Unfortunately, any attempt to fashion a finer distinction between the terms "model" and "simulation" would also convey the false impression that a meaningfully real distinction exists. In truth, the difference is largely semantic, and depends more on the context of a discussion and the backgrounds of the individuals engaged in the discussion, than it does on any objective properties of either term.

A model may include a dynamical component; a simulation may (and usually does) consist, in part, of a detailed mathematical conceptualization. A simulation may, for example, consist of a set of embedded functional relationships among variables in the cells of a numerical spreadsheet. In this case, the act of "running" the simulation—an action that is enabled by a simple click of a mouse button, and whose sole dynamical effect is to instantly update the numerical values that appear in the rows and columns of the spreadsheet—is arguably functionally equivalent to having the spreadsheet itself (i.e., the *model*) displayed on the computer monitor. There is little substantive difference between these two cases (or interpretations).

Just as not all models are implemented as computer programs (or, because they may be conceptually "too simple" to even be *generalizable* to a full-blown simulation), not all simulations are wrapped around an embedded core distillation beyond that (in the case of computer simulations) of the underlying source-code that serves as the *de facto* "model."

1.3.2 *Connection to Reality*

*"...In that empire, the craft of cartography attained such perfection that the map of a single province covered the space of an entire city, and the map of the empire itself an entire province. In the course of time, these extensive maps were found somehow wanting, and so the college of cartographers evolved a map of the empire that was of the same scale as the empire and that coincided with it point for point. Less attentive to the study of cartography, succeeding generations came to judge a map of such magnitude cumbersome, and, not without irreverence, they abandoned it to the rigours of sun and rain. In the western deserts, tattered fragments of the map are still to be found, sheltering an occasional beast or beggar..."**

All models (and all simulations) simplify reality; the best ones strive to distill the essence of a real physical system. Models and simulations are never developed to simultaneously encompass *all aspects* of a physical system; reality is far too complex for that to be possible (or even desirable, in the unlikely event that it is feasible to accomplish for a particular system). Just as the fanciful college of cartographers described in the above quote found, much to their dismay, that a map of their empire that reproduced the details of the empire on the same spatial scale, point by point, was effectively useless *as a map* (such a map is obviously a surrealistic absurdity!), so too we expect any model (thought of as a conceptual "map" of reality) that reproduces all of the details of a physical system—*as a whole, and all at once*—to be equally as inept at providing any meaningful insight into how that physical system really behaves. Indeed, if we could develop a model that faithfully reproduced the details of the system we want to study, down to the system's molecular (or subatomic) level, we would surely find the model to be as difficult to fathom as the original system. If this were the case, what would we have gained in our ability to *understand the system*, beyond that which the real system already provides for us?

Clearly, if a model is to help us genuinely understand a system, then it must confine its focus to a specific feature (or, at most, a few important features) of the physical system we are interested in studying. Otherwise, we face the specter of being so mired in the model's own complexity, that we lose sight of what we are really interested in; namely, the behavior of the real system. A good model, therefore, provides an intelligent *distillation of reality*, and necessarily leaves out all but the essential dynamical components of the system being modeled.

Figure 1.4 summarizes, schematically, the conceptual relationship among *mathematical models*, *computer simulations* and *reality* (in the context of combat). Before building a model of anything, the developer is wise to heed the physicist Werner Heisenberg's admonition to recognize that what we observe—either directly by our senses, or indirectly, via the models we build—is not the reality, but the reality as it is exposed to our method of questioning, or to the assumptions and constraints that underlie our model (see the quote by Heisenberg on page 29).

*From the essay "Of Exactitude in Science" in *A Universal History of Infamy*, by Jorge Luis Borges and Adolfo Bioy Casares (published by Penguin Books, 1975).

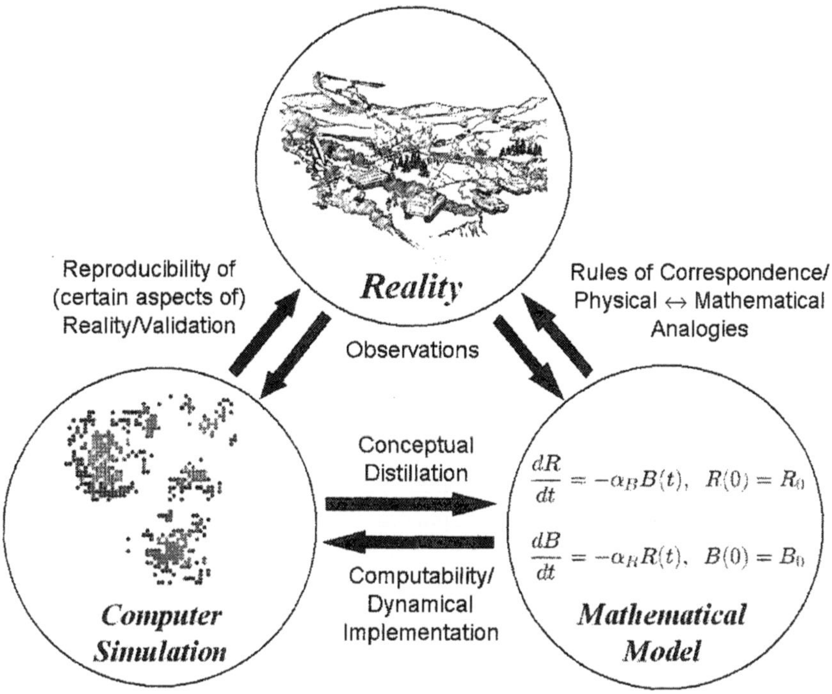

Fig. 1.4 A schematic illustration showing the interrelationship among *mathematical models*, *computer simulations* and *reality* (in the context of combat); see text for discussion.

In general, one finds that the most useful models all tend to share the following basic properties:

1. *The most useful models are developed in a well-defined context.*

A good model starts with the basic question, *"Why is this model being developed?"* A model that is designed without its developer asking and providing at least tentative answers to a set of context-setting questions, *beforehand*, is at best dangerous and at worst useless. Different design goals obviously entail different questions and will yield different models. Is the output of the model to be qualitative or quantitative? Is it to descriptive or predictive? Is the output to be broadly applicable or heavily context-dependent? Is the purpose of the model to explicitly mimic reality, or is it to create a robust, synthetic environment in which a only a limited domain of behaviors will be explored? If the model is a *combat* model (the class of model on which we will soon fully focus our attention), then why is it being developed? Is the combat model to be used as a training tool (if so, then by whom—inexperienced soldiers, operations analysts, officer candidates, or senior decision makers)? Is the combat model to as an automated decision aid? As a synthetic combat environment in which the merits of competing tactics and/or strategies are explored? The kind of model that finally emerges, and the level of detail it eventually encompasses, depends strongly on how these, and other, context-defining questions are all answered. To develop a model without a well-defined context, and without having a good understanding of the kinds of questions that the model will subsequently be asked to address or answer, is a prescription for failure.*

2. *The most useful models are those that respectfully simplify the real system.*

A good model skeletonizes (i.e. reduces) a system down to its most important parts and endogenous drivers without compromising the overall integrity of the system. If a model harbors the same effective order of complexity as the system it is designed to "model," its developer may succeed in canning the system for future study—in the sense that the real system can be studied in *absentia* by using its surrogate model instead—but the challenge of simplifying and understanding the real system's behavior is undiminished (see discussion of the *Tierra* simulation below). Not surprisingly, there is no all-encompassing answer to the question, *"What is the optimal way to distill a real system into its essential parts?"* At best, finding a close-to-optimal distillation involves a bit of science and a bit of art; at worst, there is no "good" way to do it at all, without in some way compromising the integrity of the real system. In the end, how well a model (or simulation) models (or simulates) reality must be judged by direct observation; i.e. we use the model (or simulation), subject to the assumptions and constraints of its design, and compare its output—as best as we can (keeping in mind that this step is not always possible)—to how the "real" system behaves.

3. *The most useful models are those that are both tractable and fast.*

If the purpose of a model is to simulate the evolution of a system, the model must not only be computationally tractable, but must be able to faithfully reproduce the system's essential behavior *quickly enough* so that whatever decisions need to be made based on the model's output are made on time. If the computational cost of obtaining a "solution" for a given input grows exponentially with the size of the problem, the model's usefulness may be limited. If the purpose of the simulation is to provide a real-time decision aid, for example, the model must "predict" the outcome of (possibly very many) sets of different starting conditions in less time than it takes one set of real conditions to evolve. The constraint "quickly enough," of course, means different things in different modeling scenarios. What "quickly enough"

*There is a wonderful modeling-related fable called "Is Peekaboo a Machine?" that appears in a book of logic puzzles written by Raymond Smullyan [Smull80]. Peekaboo is a dog whose behavior the protagonist-modeler wants to *predict* by simulating it. So, after performing dozens of experiments with his pet dog, consulting with the world's leading animal psychologists, spending months of effort distilling his observations into a mathematical model consisting of over 100 coupled partial differential equations, and finally running the world's most powerful supercomputer for weeks to solve the equations, he finds his answer: *Peekaboo will do whatever it wants!*

is interpreted to mean for a particular problem critically affects the assumptions and simplifications that the developer must make to achieve a desired run-time goal. Of course, not every "problem" is amenable to a satisfactory modeling and/or simulation "solution" for a given set of run-time constraints and/or goals. The holy-grail of every system modeler (and one that is unfortunately unlikely to be attained any time soon, at least in a mathematically rigorous sense), is a conceptual map—or a *meta*-model, if you will—of the set of models that *are* achievable for a specific set of assumptions, constraints and design goals. Short of having such a conceptual map, much of real-world modeling consists of hard work, patience and creativity.

1.3.3 *Mathematical Models*

Roughgarden, et.al. [Rough96] partition the set of possible models into the following three basic (and slightly overlapping) classes:

- Class 1: *Minimal Idea Models*
- Class 2: *Minimal System Models*
- Class 3: *Synthetic System Models*

1.3.3.1 *Minimal Idea Models*

A *Minimal Idea Model* (MIM) explores some idea or concept without the inconvenience of specifying the details of the system, the environment in which the system evolves, or much of anything else. The assumption is that the phenomenon of interest is a computational entity whose properties are essentially the same across a wide range of possible universes.

An example of a MIM is a simple cellular automaton model of a complex system.* In its most elementary form, a cellular automaton provides a way of exploring the implications of having a discrete space, discrete time, and a discrete local dynamics, and no more. It can be used as a basic template on top of which more realistic models can be built, but is itself useful primarily for looking for possible universal behaviors that appear in all complex systems obeying a local-rule dynamics.

Because MIM's leave out many of the details of a real-world system, their success ought to be measured less in terms of their "predictive value" and more in terms of their ability to "make a point," demonstrate the plausibility of a concept or simply communicate an idea.† Most of the early models of complex systems in the complex systems theory community reside in this class.

*An overview of cellular automata appears in chapter 2 (pages 137-148). For a more detailed technical discussion, see *Cellular Automata: A Discrete Universe* [Ilach01b].

†See chapter 24 in [Belew96] for a further discussion of this point.

1.3.3.2 *Minimum System Models*

A *Minimal System Model* (MSM) is designed to explore the dynamics of some greatly simplified subset of features of the real system and/or environment. An MSM is essentially a MIM with some attention given to modeling the real-world environment. This class of models respects the details of the real system, but judiciously strips away unnecessary information.

Of course, it may turn out in the end that the omitted information was crucial for understanding how the real system behaves. What to include and what to exclude is always the design choice of the modeler. But if the omissions are carefully and wisely chosen, and the simplified system retains the essential drivers of the real system, an MSM is a useful vehicle from which to abstract basic patterns of behavior.

1.3.3.3 *Synthetic System Models*

A *Synthetic System Model* (SSM) is an expansion of an MSM in which, ideally, all the assumptions about, and known properties of, a real system are treated formally and completely. It is a synthesis of detailed descriptions of all the component parts and processes of the system of interest.

An example of an SSM is *Santa Fe Institute*'s SWARM, with which it is possible to develop full system-level simulations of complex systems [SWARM]. EINSTein also belongs firmly to this class of model, as it is essentially a synthetic combat arena. As alluded to above, however, an inevitable price to be paid for developing an SSM is that the behavior of the SSM often proves to be just as difficult to understand as the behavior of the real system (see discussion of the *Tierra* model below).

1.3.4 ***Computer Simulations***

The Lanchester equations (equation 1.1) of land combat were borne of a rich tradition in the sciences to build abstract, simplified models of natural systems. Such models tended to be analytical in nature, often taking the form of differential equations. The emphasis was on simplicity: such models provided simple descriptions of real processes and were generally simple to solve. With the advent of the computer, of course, modeling became more concerned with incorporating a greater and greater level of detail about a physical system. In fact, computer simulations offer the following important advantages over traditional forms of mathematical modeling:

- *Computer simulations can capture real-world complications better than mathematical models.*

While computer models are all, at heart, algorithmic prescriptions for carrying out the steps of a formal model, formal mathematical models are generally able to capture only the gross aggregate characteristics of a system (such as the number of constituents, average properties, and so on). Computer models, on the other hand, are more adept at capturing the subtle nuances that describe real-world systems. There is no easy way, for example, to use a mathematical model to describe a feedback between a local bit of information and a global variable.

- *Mathematical models can typically be solved only in the limit of infinite-sized populations and/or infinite time.*

Mathematical models thus generally provide simplified idealizations of behavior, while computer models are able to deal with the complications of having finite sized systems evolving for finite times.

- *Mathematical models are generally poor at describing transient behavior.*

As we will see later in this book, one of the most important general lessons of complex systems theory is that complex adaptive systems spend much of their "lifetime" not in equilibrium but in *far-from*-equilibrium states. Indeed, from the standpoint of the overall richness of dynamical behavior, the least interesting systems to study are those that quickly reach an equilibrium. However, it is also notoriously difficult to model far-from-equilibrium systems with traditional mathematical modeling techniques. Computer simulations are powerful computational and/or visualization tools for exploring transient behavior.

- *Computer simulations provide a controlled synthetic environment.*

Computer simulations provide a controlled environment in which to interactively study effects of changing initial conditions, control parameters, boundary conditions, and so on. Mathematical models are obviously much less flexible.

1.3.5 *What Price Complexity?*

We have already alluded to an important set of tradeoffs that the developer of any model (or simulation) must assess throughout the development cycle. The developer must continually adjudicate the relative merits of, on the one hand, *including a threshold number of endogenous variables* so that the model is rich enough to capture the real-world behavior of the system the researcher is interested in studying, and, on the other hand, judiciously *excluding a sufficient number of exogenous variables* so that the model does not become so overwhelmingly complex—by itself—that insights into the model's behavior are as hard to achieve as insights into the real system. As an example of the subtleties that can arise in this regard, even in models that at first appear to be quite simple, consider an early (and now, well-known) artificial-life simulation called *Tierra*.

1.3.5.1 *Tierra*

Tierra, developed by Tom Ray of the *University of Delaware* and the *ATR Human Information Processing Research Laboratories* in Kyoto in the early 1990s, is a model that pioneered the bottom-up approach to simulating the evolution of artificial organisms at the level of the genome [RayT93]. *Tierra* was one of the first synthetic environments in which Darwinian evolution could proceed entirely without any intervention from a human operator.

The organisms of *Tierra* are machine-language computer programs consisting of strings of assembly-language-level code written specifically for *Tierra* (which was itself programmed using the C computer language). A program—i.e., a virtual *Tierran* organism; "virtual" because it "lives" only inside of *Tierra,* and not the main computer within which Tierra itself resides—evolves either by mutation or recombination. A typical evolution of a *Tierran* system starts from a single organism that is capable of self-reproduction. Errors occasionally (and deliberately are made to) creep into the system, rendering some organisms incapable of further self-reproduction and mutating others so that they are able to produce offspring more quickly and efficiently.

The real-world Darwinian "struggle of evolution" within *Tierra* is essentially a struggle for CPU-time and computer memory: CPU-time is the effective "energy" of this virtual world, and memory is the "material" resource. Similarly, "survival-of-the-fittest" translates to mean that the fittest organisms of the population are those that have managed by whatever means (or by whatever strings of code they have been able to find or construct) to capture more of these available time and space resources than other organisms. Organisms that are able to reproduce quickly and use up relatively little computer memory space in doing so, therefore come to dominate the population.

What is remarkable about *Tierra,* is that out of this seemingly simple dynamical substrate, diverse ecological communities spontaneously emerge. Ray, and subsequent *Tierra* researchers, have identified many virtual-world analogues of natural ecological and evolutionary processes: competitive exclusion and coexistence, host and parasite dynamics, parasitic enhancement of ecological diversity, symbiosis, evolutionary arms races, punctuated equilibrium, and the role of probability and historical factors in *Tierra*'s evolutionary growth and adaptation.

We mention this model here for two reasons: (1) To illustrate the difference between *simulation* and *instantiation,* and (2) To provide a concrete example of how difficult it is to understand the behavior of even a "simple" model.

Tierra illustrates the difference between *simulation* and *instantiation.* In a simulation, computer data structures are explicitly designed to represent real biological entities, whether they are predators and prey, cells, or whatever. In contrast, in an instantiation of artificial life, computer data structures do not have to explicitly represent a real organism or process. Rather, data structures must only obey rules that are abstractly related to the rules governing real processes.

The relationship between simulation and instantiation will take on greater importance later on in this book, after we have formally introduced EINSTein. We will see—by way of analogy—that agents are to real soldiers, in EINSTein, as source-code-chunks are to natural organisms in *Tierra*. In neither case is the source code or an "agent" exactly equivalent to its natural counterpart. However, they both embody an analogous set of properties and interact according to an analogous set of rules that are obeyed by natural organisms.

Because *Tierra* evolves according to a rich palette of rules that are intentional analogs of those that govern natural Darwinian evolution (the resulting complexity of which we are all familiar with), it ought not surprise us that *Tierra*—treated as a bona fide complex system—exhibits a similarly high degree of behavioral and evolutionary complexity. In turn, this emergent complexity renders the researcher's ability to understand *Tierra* almost as daunting an experimental task as understanding the behavioral characteristics of a natural ecology!*

The lesson, stated succinctly, is that an unwelcome but likely cost of developing a preternaturally realistic *virtual*-instantiation of a natural complex system is having to cope with just as difficult a task of ascertaining what is "really going on" in the instantiation as ascertaining what the *real* system is doing. While this cost may, for some systems (and their corresponding models), be fundamentally unavoidable and therefore something that the researcher must accept and learn to live with, it is nonetheless worth keeping in mind by those who wish to develop such models, if only to minimize the chances of the "cost of understanding" escalating too high.

To further explore these and other related issues, the reader is urged to consult any of the following thoughtful discussions: Bankes [Bankes94a], Denning [DennP90], Epstein [Epstein96, Epstein99] and Casti [Casti92, Casti96].

1.4 Combat Simulation

Before moving on to discuss the class of simulations to which EINSTein belongs—namely the class of multiagent-based simulations—we first briefly consider the existing state-of-the-art in military simulations of *combat*. Almost all conventional warfare simulations use one, or both, of the following two kinds of computer generated forces: (1) *semi-automated forces* (SAFORs), that require "man in the loop" interactions to make tactical decisions and to control some of the activities of the

*Indeed, as the author learned during a lecture by Tom Ray (delivered at one of the early artificial-life conferences; see [Lang89] and [Lang92]), the experimental method Ray and his colleagues followed during the exploratory stages of understanding *Tierra*'s behavior was—for all practical purposes—identical to what all ecologists do to study the *real world*. Namely, they kept detailed notes on what chunks of code were doing what, where and when; then toiled for endless hours, rummaging through their data, searching for clues and patterns or anything else that might catch their attention. In short, the recognition of emergence of *Tierran* organisms—while remarkable—was *far from obvious*, even to the designers of the program, and required hard work to isolate, identify, and understand. Any researcher who wishes to "understand" their own "simple" model of a complex system will, inevitably, face this same set of issues.

aggregated force, and (2) *automated forces* (AFORs), whose actions are completely specified by the computer software.

AFORs are computer representations of real forces that attempt to mimic pertinent aspects of human reasoning and behavior well enough so that the actions of the forces appear realistic. Usually, these actions are prescribed at the engagement level (i.e., at the level of troop movement, target selection and weapon firing)—though they can include high-level command functions—and are defined either by (1) a scripted (i.e., "hard-wired") series of actions, or (2) via traditional AI modeling techniques, such as expert systems and case-based reasoning. However, the methodology by which human behavior is incorporated into military models in active use today is arguably in its infancy.

Expert systems are developed by first interviewing subject-matter experts to distill a set of rules used to solve problems and then incorporating that information into the source-code. Case-based reasoning is an alternative approach in which SAFORs effectively learn from their experience. The SAFORs add bits of information to their knowledge base as their experience grows and tailor their behavior accordingly in real time.

Depending on the model, and the context in which it used, both AFORs and SAFORs are useful. In training systems, for example, AFORs are used to create virtual opponents for trainees to engage one-on-one in simulated battles; SAFORs are used to represent any aggregated forces (such as tank platoons or army brigades) that require human control at some high level of abstraction. The human operator provides strategic direction, such as to maneuver a platoon across a river; the computer directs the SAFORs to carry out the command. SAFORs have proven to be particularly useful for large networked training simulations, for which it is impractical to have to rely on the availability of human experts, well versed in foreign force doctrine.

1.4.1 *Modeling and Simulation Master Plan*

The degree to which the *Department of Defense* (DoD) modeling and simulation community is becoming increasingly interested in the development of computer-generated forces, is reflected in DoD's recently released *Modeling and Simulation Master Plan* (MSMP) [DoD95], which asserts that:

> *"...the representation of humans in models and simulations is extremely limited, particularly in the representation of opposing forces and their doctrine and tactics. In view of the limited theoretical underpinnings in this area, this issue will require extensive research before human behavior can be modeled authoritatively."*

In particular, *Objective 4* of the MSMP commits DoD to establishing authoritative representations of human behavior. This objective consists of two important sub-objectives: (1) the representation of individual human behavior, and (2) the representation of the behavior of groups and organizations.

The major impact of the MSMP has been on the development of fairly high-level, very-large-entity, models. Since the MSMP's release, for example, DARPA has sponsored the development of SAFORs for the *Synthetic Theater of War* (STOW) program [STOW] – which includes both intelligent forces and command forces – and has started another project called the *Intelligent, Imaginative, Innovative, Interactive What If Simulation System for Advanced Research and Development* (I^4WISSARD), which uses case-based reasoning techniques to improve the realism of its automated forces.

One of the first simulations to include *adaptive* AFORs, though mostly in an air-to-air combat context, is an on-going project called SOAR, developed jointly by Carnegie Mellon University, the University of Southern California, and the University of Michigan [Soar]. SOAR is an ambitious, large-scale, general cognitive architecture for developing systems that exhibit intelligent behavior.

1.4.2 *Modeling Human Behavior and Command Decision-Making*

The *Defense Modeling and Simulation Office* (DMSO) has recently taken an active role in generating interest in developing the policies and procedures outlined in the MSMP. For example, the DMSO requested the *National Research Council* (NRC) to establish a panel on modeling human behavior and command decision-making. This panel was tasked with reviewing the state-of-the-art in representing human behavior in military simulations, emphasizing individual-cognitive, team, and organizational behavior. The panel's report—published in *Modeling Human and Organizational Behavior: Application to Military Simulations* (MHOBAMS) [Pew98]—concluded that future military simulations require much better models of human behavior than has heretofore been available:

> *"...the modeling of cognition and action by individuals and groups is quite possibly the most difficult task humans have yet undertaken. Developments in this area are still in their infancy. Yet important progress has been and will continue to be made. Human behavior representation is critical for the military services as they expand their reliance on the outputs from models and simulations for their activities in management, decision making, and training."*

1.4.3 *Conventional Simulations*

MHOBAMS provides an excellent review of existing models that include some form of computer generated forces. Those that are designed for training, research and development, and/or analysis of advanced concepts include ELAN, JANUS, CASTFOREM, and ModSAF. Additional details about these, and other models, are provided by the *Army Model And Simulation Office* [ArmyMS] and the *Modeling and Simulation Resource Repository* [ModSimR].* A brief description of these models is provided here to give the reader an idea of their scope and depth.

*An excellent resource that summarizes the capabilities and limitations of virtually all modeling and simulation programs sponsored by the *Department of Defense* (in the USA) is [Kuck03].

1.4.3.1 *ELAN*

ELAN [ELAN] is a simple. event-sequenced, land combat model developed by the U.S. *Army Training and Doctrine Command Analysis Center*. It is a medium resolution division (and below) combat model and focuses mainly on terrain and tactics. Modeled features include maneuver, acquisition, direct fire, fire support, mines, smoke, terrain, and weather. All actions can be triggered by combat situation and specifiable doctrine.

Its main virtue is a faster-than-real-time simulation capability and an on-line suite of analysis tools. Combat is adjudicated via a discrete time step approximation to the extended Lanchester equations. Tactical terrain resolution is effectively limited to two kilometers.

1.4.3.2 *JANUS*

The Janus [JANUS] combat model is a high resolution simulation of red and blue forces with resolution down to the individual platform and soldier. Weapon systems have distinct properties, such as dimension, weight, and carrying capacity. Conventional direct fire from both ground and air systems is adjudicated according to predefined probability distributions and are a function of line-of-sight, probability of acquisition, identification and firing criteria, response time, reload rates, range, the ballistic characteristics of the weapon, and the postures of firing soldiers and targets. The model requires manual entry of the capabilities and location of all weapon systems, and human participation is required to make certain other game decisions.

1.4.3.3 *CASTFOREM*

The *Combined Arms and Support Task Force Evaluation Model* (CASTFOREM) is currently the Army's highest resolution, combined arms combat simulation model [CAST]. CASTFOREM is used for weapon systems and tactics evaluation in brigade and below combined arms conflicts. The model uses closed-form mathematical expressions, probability distributions, along with an embedded expert system (which is implemented via decision look-up tables) to perform some elements of command and control. It was designed primarily to simulate intense firefights about 1 to 1-1/2 hours in duration for echelons up to and including brigade. However, because individual scenarios take about as long to run as the firefights the program is simulating, it is difficult to conduct any meaningful exploratory analyses.

1.4.3.4 *ModSAF*

The *Modular Semi-Automated Forces model* (ModSAF) [ModSAF], developed by the US Army's *Simulation, Training, and Instrumentation Command* (STRICOM), is designed mainly for training purposes and runs in real time. However, it does not have an extensive analysis capability.

ModSAF is an interactive, high resolution, entity level simulation that represents combined arms tactical operations up to the battalion level. It consists of a set of software modules and computer generated forces applications that provide a credible representation of the battlefield, including physical, behavioral and environmental models. Notional human behavior currently includes basic movement, sensing, shooting, communications, tactics and situational awareness. However, because ModSAF requires that the representation of all human behavior be hard-wired into the underlying code, it is too restrictive to use as an analytical combat engine to explore general behavioral and/or adaptive learning models.

All of these models are useful, to various degrees, for training purposes and/or the analysis of the performance of specific weapon systems. However, they are also all very complex, are usually tied to a small set of specific computing hardware, are difficult to interface, have limited data collection facilities, and require real-time (or close to real-time) run times (thus making it effectively impossible to conduct meaningfully large exploratory analyses of possible behaviors). As DoD is planning to place even greater emphasis on a few key, large, ultra-high-resolution models – i.e., the so-called J-models, including JWARS [JWARS98] (the joint assessments model), JSIMS [JSim99] (the joint training model), and JMASS [JMASS] (the joint assessment model) – the need for developing smaller, more tightly-focused models, that can help with basic concept development and be used to enhance intuition about fundamental principles and expected behaviors, becomes that much greater.

1.4.4 *Future of Modeling Technology*

The *Chief of Naval operations*, in a memorandum on November 28, 1995, asked the *National Research Council* to examine, through its *Naval Studies Board* (NSB), the impact of advancing technology on the form and capability of the naval forces through the year 2035. One of the eight technical review panels, organized under the committee on *Technology for Future Naval Forces*, was the *Panel on Modeling and Simulation.*

The main objectives of this panel were:* (1) to explain why the *Department of the Navy* (DoN) ought to be concerned about modeling and simulation, (2) to assess what DoN (and DoD) must do to fully benefit from existing, and future, modeling and simulation technology, (3) to clarify the extent to which decisions on technical, force-composition and operations planning issues can benefit from modeling and simulation, and (4) to define priorities for modeling-and-simulation-related research.

The panel's report, which constitutes the ninth volume of the NSB's full series of reports [Tech97], discusses modeling and simulation as a foundation technology for developments that will become central to the DoN and DoD over the next three to four decades.

*The panel made no attempt to conduct a full survey of modeling and simulation relevant to the *Department of the Navy*.

Among the panel's recommendations for research in key warfare areas, is "...the need to take a holistic approach rather than one based exclusively on either top-down or bottom-up ideas." Crediting the Marine Corps for pushing the envelope in this regard (as, for example, in their embrace of alternative concepts in the Hunter/Warrior experiments [HunWar]), the report states that it is "plausible...that cellular-automata models could help illuminate behaviors of dispersed forces with varying command-control concepts ranging from centralized top-down control to decentralized control based on mission orders."

Even more notably, in the context of CNA's *Complexity & Warfare* project, is that among the panel's recommendations for fundamental research in modeling theory and advanced methodologies appear the following two priority areas: (1) *agent-based modeling and generative analysis*, and (2) *exploratory analysis under uncertainty*. The report states:

> *"Some of the most interesting new forms of modeling involve so-called agent-based systems in which low-level entities with relatively simple attributes and behaviors can collectively produce (or generate) complex and realistic emergent system behaviors. This is potentially a powerful approach to understanding complex adaptive systems generally—in fields as diverse as ecology, economics, and military command-control."*

1.5 Multiagent-Based Models and Simulations

Agent-based simulations of complex adaptive systems are becoming an increasingly popular theoretical exploratory tool in the artificial-life community, and are predicated on the basic idea that the (often complicated) global behavior of a real system derives, collectively, from simpler, low-level interactions among its constituent agents. Insights about the real-world system that the agent-based simulation is designed to model can then be gained by looking at the emergent structures induced by the interaction processes taking place within the simulation. Two excellent recent texts on agent-based modeling, as applied to a variety of disciplines, are by Ferber [Ferber99] and Weiss [WeissG99]. Books and collections of papers focusing on applications to social science (and other systems that involve some aspect of "human reasoning") are by Gilbert and Troitzsch [Gilb99], Gilbert and Conte [Gilb95] and Conte, et. al. [Conte97].

The purpose behind building an agent-based simulation of a system is twofold: it is to learn both the *quantitative* and *qualitative* properties of the real system. Multiagent-based simulations are well suited for testing hypotheses about the origin of observed emergent properties in a system. This is done simply by experimenting with sets of initial conditions at the micro-level necessary to yield a set of desired behaviors at the macro-level. Moreover, agent-based models provide a powerful framework within which to integrate the explanatory power of what—*a-priori*—may appear to be unrelated disciplines. For example, while basic agent-agent interactions may be described by simple physics and high-level group dynamics, the internal decision-making capability of a single agent may be derived, in part, from a deeper understanding of the psychology of motivation, fear.

Much of what currently falls under the broad rubrics of either "complex adaptive systems" or "agent-based modeling" actually consists of a hodgepodge of on-the-fly, hand-crafted and tinkered techniques and approaches that say more about the research style of a particular researcher than they do about the how the field is practiced as a whole. The current crop of models, as developed by the artificial-life community, are either specifically tailored to particular problems or are general purpose simulators (like the *Santa Fe Institute*'s SWARM programming language [SWARM]; see below) that must be carefully tuned before they are used to model a specific system.

1.5.1 *Autonomous Agents*

The fundamental building block of most models of complex adaptive systems is the so-called *adaptive autonomous agent.* Adaptive autonomous agents try to satisfy a set of goals (which may be either fixed or time-dependent) in an unpredictable and changing environment. These agents are "adaptive" in the sense that they can use their experience to continually improve their ability to deal with time-dependent goals and motivations. They are "autonomous in that they operate completely autonomously, and do not need to obey instructions issued by a God-like, central, oracle.

An adaptive autonomous agent is characterized by the following general properties:

- *Interaction with Environment:* It senses the (often complex and dynamic) environment through its sensors and reacts accordingly.

- *Goal-Driven Motivations:* It is an entity that, by sensing and acting upon its environment, tries to fulfill a set of goals. The goals can take on diverse forms, including satisfying local states and/or end goals, maximizing intermediate rewards, or by keeping the states of internal needs within desired bounds.

- *Intelligence:* It has an internal information processing and decision-making capability by which it uses local information to select actions.

- *Adaptive Dynamics:* It is able to adapt to changing contexts and environments by learning to associate actions with contexts and/or by anticipating future states and possibilities. Since a major component of an agent's environment consists of other agents, the aggregate behavior of the system typically consists of networks of agents continually adapting to the patterns of adaptation of other agents. The adaptive mechanism is usually some form of heuristic search algorithm such as a genetic algorithm.

An agent's goals can take on diverse forms:

- *Desired local states*
- *Desired end goals*
- *Selective rewards to be maximized*
- *Internal needs (or motivations) that need to be kept within desired bounds*

Since a major component of an agent's environment consists of other agents, agents generally spend a great deal of their time adapting to the adaptation patterns of other agents. The adaptive mechanism of an adaptive autonomous agent is typically based on a genetic algorithm.*

1.5.2 *How is Multiagent-Based Modeling Really Done?*

Most agent-based models are generally developed according to the basic steps outlined in figure 1.5.† The critical steps—steps four and five—are highlighted in yellow. The most important step is step five: *sit back and watch for patterns!* Much of the early work on trying to understand the behavior of a system consists of finding ways to spot overall trends and patterns in a system's behavior, while continually interacting and "playing" with "toy-models" of the system; i.e., it consists of taking part in a dialectic with a conceptual model of the system. If one is serious about applying the "new sciences" to land warfare, one must be ready to rethink some of the conventional strategies and approaches to modeling systems.

Another important element of multiagent-based modeling, as applied to combat, is that the *forward*-problem and *inverse*-problem must both be studied simultaneously (see figure 1.6); the interplay between real-world *experience* (and data) and *theory* must never be overlooked.

The *forward*-problem consists of observing real-world behavior (or, in cases where that is impossible, the behaviors of the agent-based simulation), with the objective being to identify any emergent high-level behavioral patterns that the system might possess. The *inverse*-problem deals with trying to induct a set of low-level rules that describe observed high-level behaviors. Starting with observed data, the goal to find something interesting to say about the properties of the source of the data. Solving the forward problem requires finding the right set of theoretical tools that can be used to identify patterns, while the inverse problem needs tools that can be used to induct low-level rules (or models) that generate the observed high-level behaviors.

* *Genetic algorithms* (GAs) are a class of heuristic search methods and computational models of adaptation and evolution. Genetic algorithms mimic the dynamics underlying natural evolution to search for optimal solutions of general combinatorial optimization problems. A discussion of how genetic algorithms are used by EINSTein to automatically breed multiagent combat forces appears in chapter 7.

†The conceptual, mathematical and programming details of multiagent-based modeling are discussed in chapter 4.

Step 1 -- Think of an interesting question to ask regarding the behavior of a real system (or find a real system to study)

Step 2 -- Simplify the problem as much as possible without losing the "essence" of the system

Step 3 -- Write a program to simulate the individual agents of the system, following simple rules with specified interactions

Step 4 -- "Play" (i.e. interact) with simplified models of the system

Step 5 -- ***Sit back and watch for patterns;*** run the program many times to build up statistics and intuition for patterns of behavior

Step 6 -- Develop theories about how the real system behaves

Step 7 -- Tinker with model, change parameters, identify sources of behavioral changes, simplify it even further!

Step 8 -- *Repeat steps 4-7!*

Fig. 1.5 Typical steps involved in multiagent-based modeling.

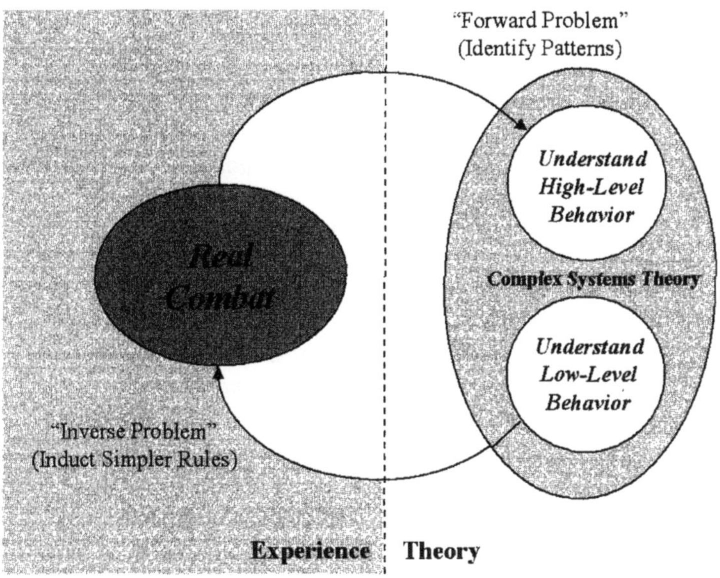

Fig. 1.6 Schematic of the interplay between experience and theory in the *forward-* and *inverse-*problems of simulating combat.

A lengthier discussion of modeling and simulation and how it pertains to land warfare appears in [Ilach96a] and [Ilach96b]. Thoughtful discussions about the general use of models are given by Denning [DennP90], Epstein [Epstein99] and Casti [Casti96].

1.5.3 *Agent-Based Simulations vs. Traditional Mathematical Models*

Agent-based simulations and traditional computer simulations (as well as conventional differential-equation based models) differ in one key respect: while traditional models ignore layers of complexity for the sake of achieving a simplified description of overall behavior of a system, agent-based simulations seek to find the simplest underlying explanation for the observed complexity. Traditional models focus on high-level descriptions because they assume that the behaviors of individual agents must be driven by complicated behavior that itself cannot be modeled. In contrast, agent-based models proceed from the assumption that it is the interaction among agents—all of whom individually behave according to rather simple rules—that leads to the complex behavior that is observed.

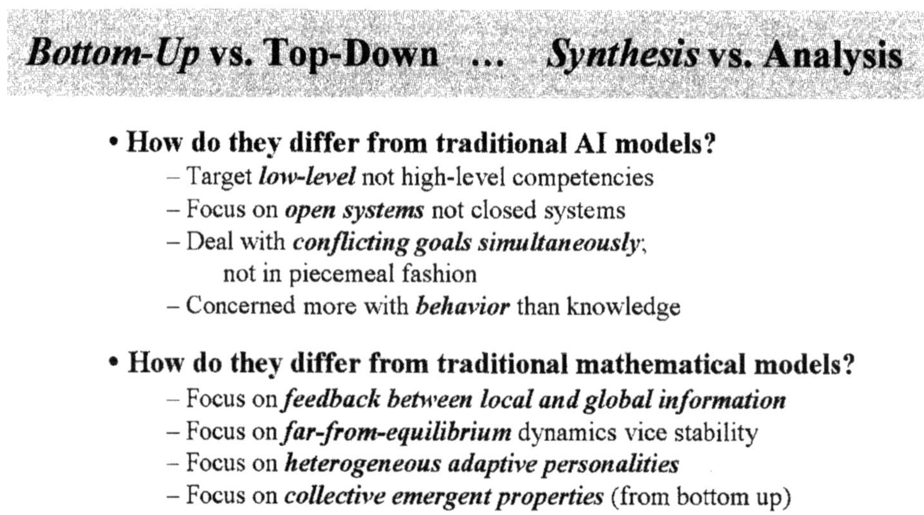

Fig. 1.7 Multiagent-based simulations vs. traditional models

In the context of modeling combat, agent-based simulations represent a fundamental shift from focusing on simple force-on-force attrition calculations to considering how complex, high-level properties and behaviors of combat emerge out of (sometimes evolving) low-level rules of behaviors and interactions. In general, the conceptual focus of agent-based models is on finding a set of low-level rules defining the local behavior of individual agents; the collective action of these agents determines the dynamics of the whole system. Figure 1.7 summarizes some of the major differences between agent-based simulations and conventional models.

1.5.3.1 *Synthesist Approach*

Agent-based models take an actively *generative* (or *synthesist*) approach to understanding a system, *from the bottom up.** This is in contrast to the purely analytical approach that most traditional models take to the same problem, in which a system is regarded as being "understood" when it has been analyzed, and its essential ingredients distilled, from the top down. Where traditional models ask, effectively, *"How can I characterize the system's top-level behavior with a few (equally top-level) variables?,"* agent-based simulations instead ask, *"What low-level rules and what kinds of heterogeneous, autonomous agents do I need to have in order to synthesize the system's observed high-level behavior?"*

While a valid and useful answer to the first question can often be found, there is at least one significant drawback to this approach: so many simplifying assumptions must usually be made about the real system, in order to render the top-level problem a soluble one, that other natural, follow-up questions such as *"Why do specific behaviors arise?"* or *"How would the behavior change if the system were defined a bit differently?"* cannot be meaningfully addressed without first altering the set of assumptions. An analytical, closed-form "solution" may describe a behavior, however, it does not necessarily provide an explanation for that behavior. Indeed, subsequent questions about the behavior of the system must usually be treated as separate problems.

1.5.3.2 *Explanatory Tools*

An important benefit of using an agent-based simulation is that, once the simulation is used to generate the desired behavior, the modeler has immediate and simultaneous access to both the top-level (i.e., generated) behavior of the system and a low-level description of the system's underlying dynamics: i.e., the agent-based simulation thus becomes a powerful methodological tool for not just describing behaviors but *explaining why specific behaviors occur.* While an analytical solution may provide an accurate description of a phenomenon, it is only with an agent-based simulation that one can fine-tune one's understanding of the precise set of conditions under which certain behaviors emerge.

In agent-based-models of combat, the final outcome of a battle—as defined, say, by measuring the surviving force strengths—takes second stage to exploring how two forces might coevolve as a series of firefights and skirmishes unfold. Such models are designed to allow the user to explore the evolving patterns of macroscopic behavior that result from the collective interactions of individual agents, as well as the feedback that these patterns might have on the rules governing the individual agents' behavior.

*Epstein [Epstein99] and Axtel [Axtel00] present cogent arguments for why multiagent-based models are particularly useful as generative, explanatory, tools in social science. They both stress that by effectively decoupling individual rationality from macroscopic equilibrium, multiagent-based models represent a new hybrid theoretical-computational tool.

Any system whose top-level behavior is a consequence of the aggregate behavior of lower-level entities—biological systems, neural systems, social systems, economic systems, among many others—is amenable, in principle, to an agent-based simulation of its behavior.

1.5.4 *Multiagent-Based Simulations vs. Traditional AI*

"It is hard to point at a single component [of an AI program] as the seat of intelligence, there is no homunculus. Rather, intelligence emerges from the interactions of the components of the system. The way in which it emerges, however, is quite different for traditional and behavior-based AI systems."—Luc Steels [Steels95]

While the kinds of problems best suited for agent-based simulations are similar to the kinds of problems for which traditional artificial intelligence (AI) techniques have been developed, there are important differences. Maes [Maes94] lists four critical ways in which using adaptive autonomous agents differs from traditional artificial intelligence:

1. *Target Low-Level Behaviors:* Traditional AI focuses on systems exhibiting isolated "high-level" competencies, such as medical diagnoses, chess playing, and so on; in contrast, agent-based systems target lower-level behaviors, with high-level competencies emerging naturally, and collectively, of their own accord.
2. *Target Open Systems:* Traditional AI has focused on "closed systems" in which the interaction between the problem domain and the external environment is kept to a minimum; in contrast, agent-based systems are "open systems," and agents are directly coupled with their environment.
3. *Target Multi-Objective Goals:* Most traditional AI systems deal with problems in a piecemeal fashion, one at a time; in contrast, the individual agents in an agent-based system must deal with many conflicting goals simultaneously.
4. *Bounded Rationality:* Traditional AI focuses on "knowledge structures" that model aspects of their domain of expertise; in contrast, an agent-based system is more concerned with dynamic "behavior producing" modules. It is less important for an agent to be able to address a specific question within its problem domain (as it is for traditional AI systems) than it is to be flexible enough to adapt to shifting domains.

As agent-based simulation techniques mature, the methodology has the potential to usher in an alternative way to do science; a way that is neither totally deductive nor totally inductive, at least in the conventional sense. While agent-based simulations, like deductive methods, start from a set of primitive rules and assumptions they do not prove theorems; rather, they generate behaviors that must themselves be studied inductively. Unlike traditional induction, however, that uncovers patterns in empirically derived data, agent-based simulations provide the framework for discovering (presumably real-world) high-level patterns that emerge out of the collective interactions of simulated low-level rules.

1.5.5 *Examples of MultiAgent-Based Simulations*

Figure 1.8 lists a few well-known multiagent-based models. Recent examples include ECHO (an agent-based model of natural ecologies [ECHO]), MOAB (the U.S. Geological Survey's model of animal behavior [MOAB]), *Sugarscape* (in which cultural evolution is studied by observing the collective behavior of many interactive agents, each endowed with a notional set of social interaction rules [Epstein96]) and TRANSIM (in which Albuquerque's road-traffic network is meticulously reproduced, boulevard by boulevard, and the simultaneous actions of many agent-drivers are used to explore countless *"What if?"* scenarios [Barrett97]).

(Roughly) Increasing Sophistication →

- **Fluid Dynamics**
  - Lattice gas models
- **Ant Foraging**
  - Decentralized collective sorting (Deneubourg)
- **Animal Behavior**
  - MOAB (U.S. Geological Survey)
- **Natural Evolution**
  - *Tierra* (Ray)
- **Traffic Flow**
  - TRANSIM simulation of traffic patterns in Albuquerque, NM (Barrett)
- **Natural Ecologies**
  - ECHO (Holland)
- **Intelligent Software Agents**
  - *Knobots* (Maes)
- **Urban Dynamics**
  - *SimCity* (Maxis)
- **Artificial Societies**
  - *Sugarscape* (Epstein & Axtell)
- **Meta-Simulation**
  - SWARM (Langton, Santa Fe Institute)

Fig. 1.8 Recent Examples of multiagent-based models and simulations.

The popular series of *SimCity* and *SimCity*–related commercial games (*SimLife*, *SimAnt*, etc.) all make heavy use of agent-based methodologies [Wright89]. More recent examples of commercial games that are also making original contributions to adaptive-agent modeling methodology are Cyberlife's *Creatures** and Activision's

* *Creatures* was created by Steve Grand, who has also written a sophisticated layman's introduction to designing artificial life forms, called *Creation* [Grand00]; see also *Cyberlife Research* homepage, http://www.cyberlife-research.com.

*Shogun Total War.** The latter game, *Shogun*, is a multiagent-based game of Samurai warfare in feudal Japan, and is particularly interesting in the context of this report, in that, according to its developers, it's rule-base embodies a codified form of Sun Tzu's *The Art of War* [Tzu91].

1.5.5.1 *SWARM*

Santa Fe Institute's SWARM, developed by Chris Langton, is a multiagent *meta*-simulation platform for the study of complex adaptive systems [SWARM].† Although EINSTein is a stand-alone program (and consists of independently developed software modules), and is not in any way based on SWARM, EINSTein nonetheless shares many attributes of SWARM's design. With an eye toward providing a background for our discussion of EINSTein in later chapters, it is therefore instructive to first learn about the basics of SWARM.

The goal of the SWARM project was to provide the research community with a general-purpose artificial-life simulator. The system comes with a variety of generic artificial worlds populated with generic agents, a large library of design and analysis tools, and a "kernel" to drive the actual simulation. These artificial worlds can vary widely, from simple 2D worlds in which elementary agents move back and forth, to complex multidimensional graphs representing multidimensional telecommunication networks in which agents can trade messages and commodities, to models of real-world ecologies.

Everything in SWARM is an object with three main characteristics: *Name*, *Data* and *Rules*. An object's Name consists of an ID that is used to send messages to the object, a type and a module name. An object's Data consists of whatever local data (i.e. internal state variables) the user wants an agent to possess. The Rules are functions to handle any messages that are sent to the object. The basic unit of SWARM is a *swarm*: a collection of objects with a schedule of event over those objects. SWARM also supplies the user with an interface and analysis tools.

The most important objects in SWARM, from the standpoint of the user, are *Agents*, which are objects that are written by the user. Agents represent the individual entities making up the model; they may be ants, plants, stock brokers, or combatants on a battlefield. Actions consist of a message to send, an agent or a collection of agents to send the message, and a time to send that message. Upon receiving a message, agents are free to do whatever they wish in response to the message. A typical response consists of the execution of whatever code the user has written to capture the low-level behavior of the system she is interested in. Agents can also insert other actions into the schedule.

*See http://www.totalwar.com/.

†SWARM was originally developed by the *Santa Fe Institute* (http://www.santafe.edu/) but is now under control of the *Swarm Development Group* (http://www.swarm.org/).

Three other properties of SWARM are noteworthy:

- *Hierarchical Structure:* In order to be better able to simulate the hierarchical nature of many real-world complex systems, in which agent behavior can itself be best described as being the result of the collective behavior of some swarm of constituent agents, SWARM is designed so that agents themselves can be swarms of other agents. Moreover, SWARM is designed around a time hierarchy. Thus, SWARM is both a nested hierarchy of swarms and a nested hierarchy of schedules.

- *Parallel Processing:* SWARM has been designed to run efficiently on parallel machine architectures. While messages within one swarm schedule execute sequentially, different swarms can execute their schedules in parallel.

- *Internal Agent Models:* One can argue that agents in a real complex adaptive system (such as the economy) behave and adapt according to some internal model they have constructed for themselves of what they believe their environment is really like. Sometimes, if the environment is simple, such models are fixed and simple; sometimes, if the environment is complex, agents need to actively construct hypothetical models and testing them against a wide variety of assumptions about initial states and rules and so forth. SWARM allows the user to use nested swarms to allow agents to essentially create and manage entire swarm structures which are themselves simulations of the world in which the agents live. Thus, agents can base their behavior on their simulated picture of the world.

Being a general purpose simulator rather than a model of a specific complex system, SWARM can deal with a wide variety of problems and systems, including economic models (with economic agents interacting with each other through a market), the dynamics of social insects, traffic simulation, and ecological modeling.

1.5.5.2 *General Purpose Simulations*

Other simulation tools include *AgentSheets* (http://www.agentsheets.com), *Ascape* (developed by the *Brookings Institute*), MAML (developed by the *Complex Adaptive Systems Laboratory* at the *Central European University* in Hungary), *Repast* (by the *University of Chicago's Social Science Research Computing Laboratory*), *Netlogo* (Developed at *Northwestern University*), and *Starlogo* (developed by MIT). World wide web URL links to these simulation tools and additional resources appear in Appendix A.

1.5.6 *Value of Multiagent-Based Simulations*

Axelrod [Axel97] has argued that there are seven broad uses for simulations, in general. These include *prediction*, *specific task performance* (whereby a simulation is used as a substitute for human experts to perform needed tasks), *training* (wherein a simulation is used a surrogate for the real system to train users), *entertainment* (consider, for example, the commercial games *Creatures* and *Shogun*), *education* (a good example of which is the *SimCity* series of games [Wright89]), *proof* (wherein certain behaviors are proven to exist, by demonstration), and *discovery*.

The most important uses of agent-based simulations of combat—as implemented, for example, in ISAAC and EINSTein—are the last two on Axelrod's list: *proof* and *discovery*. To which a third use may also be added: *explanation*. Lanchester's equations of combat focus on the equilibrium solution to an oversimplified mathematical model that assumes, among other things, homogeneous forces and no spatial maneuvering. While a "solution" can usually be readily found, either analytically or numerically, it possesses little or no explanatory power with respect to observed behavior and—since the most interesting aspects of real combat are typically found in the transient, far-from-equilibrium stages of an engagement—are incapable of discovering, or providing insight into, novel behaviors.

An obvious example of the difference between the informational value of purely *descriptive* models (which is the set of models to which the Lanchester equations belong) and multiagent-based simulations, if they are viewed as *generative* computations, is DNA. An organism's DNA does not contain a full description of the organism, as a whole, but instead contains only the instructions by which an organism is formed.

Another wonderful example appears in Lewis Wolpert's *Principles of Development* [WolpL97]. Wolpert considers *origami*, the art of paper folding, and observes that:

> *"...by folding a piece of paper in various directions, it is quite easy to make a paper hat or a bird from a single sheet. To describe in any detail the final form of the paper with the complex relationships between its parts is really very difficult, and not of much help in explaining how to achieve it. Much more useful and easier to formulate are instructions on how to fold the paper. The reason for this is that simple instructions about folding have complex spatial consequences."*

In the same way, multiagent-based models are most useful when they are applied to complex systems that can be neither wholly described (mathematically or otherwise, due to their innate complexity) nor be "built" by brute force from a model or design. They are best applied to systems that can only be created by a generative process.

With regard to combat, in particular, combat models based on differential equations are essentially *descriptive*. Moreover, they homogenize the properties of entire populations and ignore the spatial component altogether. Partial differential equations–by introducing a physical space to account for troop movement–fare somewhat better, but still treat the agent population as a continuum. In contrast, multiagent-based-models consist of a discrete heterogeneous set of spatially distributed individual agents (i.e., combatants), each of which has its own characteristic properties and rules of behavior. These properties can also change (i.e., adapt) as an individual agent evolves in time. Combat is allowed to unfold naturally, in time, according to the generative rules and processes as prescribed by the model; the multiagent-based model does not try to describe the outcome of combat directly.

In multiagent-based models, the final outcome of a battle—as defined, say, by measuring the surviving force strengths—takes second stage to exploring how two forces might coevolve during combat. Such models are designed to allow the user to explore the evolving patterns of macroscopic behavior that result from the collective interactions of individual agents, as well as the feedback that these patterns might have on the rules governing the individual agents' behavior.

1.5.7 *CA-Based & Other EINSTein-Related Combat Models*

Neither ISAAC nor EINSTein were born in a vacuum, of course, and the design of both of these programs owes much to earlier work. For example, the earliest versions of ISAAC were directly inspired by an even earlier cellular-automata-based "conceptual" model, that was designed by Woodcock, Dockery and Cobb in 1988 [Woodc88] (see *Minimalist Models* below).

Cellular automata (CA), which were briefly mentioned in the *Preface* (see page xv), are a class of spatially and temporally discrete, deterministic mathematical systems characterized by local interaction and an inherently parallel form of evolution [Ilach01b]. First introduced by the mathematician von Neumann in the early 1950s to act as simple models of biological self-reproduction, CA are prototypical models for complex systems and processes consisting of a large number of identical, simple, locally interacting components. The study of these systems has generated great interest over the years because of their ability to generate a rich spectrum of very complex patterns of behavior out of sets of relatively simple underlying rules. Moreover, they appear to capture many essential features of complex self-organizing cooperative behavior observed in real systems. A mathematical survey of CA appears in the next chapter (see pages 137-148).

Below are listed (in *alphabetical*, not chronological order) a few early CA-based models of combat that are either direct precursors of CNA's multiagent models ISAAC and EINSTein, or are based directly or in part on EINSTein's design.

1.5.7.1 *CROCADILE*

CROCADILE (*Conceptual Research Oriented Combat Agent Distillation Implemented in the Littoral Environment*) has recently been developed at the *Australian Defence Force Academy* [Barlow02]. Like EINSTein, CROCADILE is an open, extensible agent-based distillation engine. Among its strengths are a robust weapons class that includes the option of using projectile physics to adjudicate outcomes of combat, and an integrated 3D combat environmental. Typically, multiagent-based models of combat (such as ISAAC and EINSTein and the others listed above) are deliberately kept as "simple" as possible. For example, weapons are modeled essentially as elements that have a certain probability of hitting a target. CROCADILE instead incorporates a more realistic—albeit more complicated— projectile-physics representation of its weapons. Munitions may be fired with specified speed and heading and a 3D collision detection algorithm is employed to detect when agents are hit or where the explosions occur. Target size, speed, and distance, along with certain terrain characteristics, are all weighed to determine whether an individual shot hits its intended target.

1.5.7.2 *DEXES*

The *Deployable Exercise Support* (DEXES) system, developed by Woodcock and Cobb ([Woodc00]), is a mathematical model of societal dynamics (encompassing economic, social, political, and public health variables), and has been used to support exercise and training for multi-national peace and humanitarian operations. Although DEXES is not a combat model, it is included here as an important example of a simple, agent-like, rule-based simulation that – because of its small size and streamlined design – can be rapidly deployed in either analytical or training contexts anywhere in the world, with minimal cost and support overhead. The DEXES simulation package has so far been used in twelve international exercises.

1.5.7.3 *MANA*

MANA (*Map Aware Non-uniform Automata*) is an agent-based combat model developed by New Zealand's *Defence Technology Agency* [Lauren01]. While it is independently developed and shares no source code with either ISAAC or EINSTein, MANA is clearly based on these precursor models. In particular, MANA's use of numerical weights to motivate agents' behaviors, its use of contextual constraints for behavioral tuning, and dialog-driven parameter settings for sensor range, fire range, and so on, are all obviously patterned after how they are implemented in ISAAC and EINSTein.

Nonetheless, MANA exhibits many interesting and unique characteristics, including the ability to provide agents with *memory maps* of the locations of previously sensed enemies. Thus, agent actions at time t are not based solely on the environment as it is perceived by them at time t, but rather on a combination of what they currently perceive and remember. MANA effectively allows agents to build internal "pictures" of their world as the simulation progresses.

1.5.7.4 *Minimalist Models*

Dockery and Woodcock, in their massive treatise *The Military Landscape* [Dock93b], provide a detailed discussion of many different minimalist models from the point of view of catastrophe theory and nonlinear dynamics. Minimalist modeling refers to "the simplest possible description using the most powerful mathematics available and then" adds layers "of complexity as required, permitting structure to emerge from the dynamics." Among many other findings, Dockery and Woodcock report that chaos appears in the solutions to the Lanchester equations when modified by reinforcement. They also discuss how many of the tools of nonlinear dynamics (see chapter 2) can be used to describe combat. Indeed, Dockery and Woodcock also developed what is likely the first CA-based model of combat, with which they were able to show, convincingly, that highly elaborate patterns of military force-like behavior can be generated using only a small set of CA-like rules [Woodc88].

Using generalized predator-prey population models to model interactions between military and insurgent forces, Dockery and Woodcock illustrate (1) the set of conditions that lead to a periodic oscillation of insurgent force sizes, (2) the effects of a limited pool of individuals available for recruitment, (3) various conditions leading to steady state, stable periodic oscillations and chaotic force-size fluctuations, and (4) the sensitivity to small changes in rates of recruitment, disaffection and combat attrition of simulated force strengths.

This kind of analysis can sometimes lead to counter-intuitive implications for the tactical control of insurgents. In one instance, for example, Dockery and Woodcock point out that cyclic oscillations in the relative strengths of national and insurgent forces result in recurring periods of time during which the government forces are weak and the insurgents are at their peak strength. If the government decides to add too many resources to strengthen its forces, the chaotic model suggests that the cyclic behavior will tend to become unstable (because of the possibility that disaffected combatants will join the insurgent camp) and thus weaken the government position. The model instead suggests that the best strategy for the government to follow is to use a moderately low level of military force to contain the insurgents at their peak strength, and attempt to destroy the insurgents only when the insurgents are at their weakest force strength level of the cycle.

1.5.7.5 *SEM*

SEM (*Strategic Effects Model*), and its theater-level extension called HITM (*Hierarchical Interactive Theater Model*) are two recent ISAAC/EINSTein-inspired agent-based models, developed by Hill, et.al. [Hill03]. Both models are implemented in JAVA and are interesting because they are among the first simulations to directly encode Boyd's *Observe Orient Decide Act* (OODA) loop in their dynamics [Boyd87].

Boyd introduced the OODA loop as a conceptual model to describe the dynamics of a fighter pilot's decision processes. However, over the years, the OODA loop concept has both spawned and nurtured many discussions in a variety of combat (and even business-related) contexts.* The OODA loop model, in essence, asserts that—whatever the *detailed rules* are that define how an agent acts—an agent's

*The web site *War, Chaos and Business* (at URL address http://www.belisarius.com/) contains a wealth of OODA-related information and links to additional resources. This site also contains a complete inventory of the writings of John Boyd, including several of his landmark briefing slides.

decision process continually follows the same basic four-step template:

- *Observe the environment,*
- *Internalize and assimilate the environmental stimuli in the proper context,*
- *Decide on one of the possibly large set of viable actions that can be taken,*
- *Implement the desired action.*

An agent that executes its OODA loop faster than another agent has, according to the OODA-loop conceptual model, a tactical advantage over its adversary. By endowing each of their agents with an OODA-loop, both SEM and HITM allow analysts to explore the basic OODA-loop analysis question: *"What can be done to gain an OODA-loop advantage against an opponent?"*

1.5.7.6 *Socrates*

Socrates is another agent-based distillation of combat that is similar in its design, scope and capability to EINSTein [Bent01] (see also [Ching02]). In particular, Socrates use the same instinct-driven attractor/repeller agent action paradigm, takes place in the same notional 2D world and uses an equivalent probability-based weapons model. *Socrates* has been developed by *Emergent Information Technologies Inc.*, under the auspices of the U.S. Marine Corps' *Project Albert* [Albert].

1.5.7.7 *SWarrior*

Science Applications International Corporation's *SWARM Marine Infantry Combat Model* (SWarrior) model [SWarrior] uses the *Santa Fe Institute*'s SWARM [SWARM] meta-modeling and simulation environment to simulate the dynamics of light, dispersed, mobile forces. It is based on the operations and forces deployed by the Marine Corps during its 1997 Hunter Warrior training experiment, exploring as a baseline, red and blue forces whose number, capabilities and behaviors resemble the forces used during Hunter Warrior [HunWar].

SWarrior is written in Objective C, runs in the Unix operating environment and includes a Java front-end interface for web-based access.

1.5.7.8 *THOR*

An improved object-oriented version of Woodcock, Cobb and Dockery's minimalist CA model of combat [Woodc88], called THOR, was developed by Olanders ([Olanders96], [THOR]) for her Masters Thesis at *George Washington University* (and sponsored by the *Swedish Defense Materiel Administration*).* THOR includes a

*The only CA-based combat models to which I have found any reference in the literature—prior to the introduction of ISAAC (the earliest version of which appeared in the fall of 1996; see page 14)—is Woodcock, *et.al.*'s model and THOR. While I was unaware of THOR's existence while developing ISAAC, I certainly knew about Woodcock, *et.al.*'s model [Woodc88]. Indeed, this pioneering paper subsequently proved to be a powerful stimulus for my own work.

hierarchically ordered command and control structure, and consists of entities that are capable of situational assessment, can initiate and coordinate movement, and can engage in combat. The rules operate by an "army" first locating and steering toward the enemy, setting the tactics for engagement and then setting the attrition rules. The decision to advance, engage, or retreat is made by a notional commander. All engagements proceed according to "aimed" fire.

1.6 EINSTein as an Exemplar of More General Models of Complex Adaptive Systems

While EINSTein has been designed, from the ground up, with a focus on combat, EINSTein's underlying design philosophy has from the outset been motivated by trying to achieve a considerably broader applicability. Because EINSTein's behavior depends more on the abstract set of interrelationships among classes than on the details of interpretation regarding any one class, EINSTein arguably transcends its strictly combat-centric origin and interface with the user and represents a much more general programming architecture for developing agent-based simulations.

The fact that EINSTein includes particular agent characteristics and rules of interaction that result in emergent behavior that is consistent with combat does not imply that the core logic that maps local context to action cannot also describe the behavior of other, non-combat-based, complex adaptive systems.

At its core, EINSTein is much more than simply a hard-wired "killing jar" of warring agents (though this is how it is currently, and exclusively, being used). Rather, EINSTein consists of a much more general set of conceptual, logical, and dynamical links among classes of abstract entities. These general links can be used to describe vastly different real-world systems, unrelated to combat, except by vestiges of common or overlapping interpretations of primitive elements.

A combat modeler is obviously interested in exploring ways in which various factors influence how a soldier (or squad, or force) performs an assigned combat mission. The same primitive information that defines, in this combat scenario, what an agent "is" (a combatant), what an agent is able to "see" (other combatants, flags, terrain, etc.), with whom an agent is able to "communicate" (squad mates), how an agent selects an action in a given context (by weighing options according to a "personality"), and so on, can be used to define the corresponding elements of an agent simulation of, say, social interaction in an office environment, or buyer-seller trade relations in a market setting.

As examples of EINSTein's versatility—both on a practical simulation level and on a more conceptual modeling-design level—consider three recent applications that have been made of EINSTein at the *Center for Naval Analyses* (CNA):

- A *Persian Gulf "War Gamelet" Scenario*, which applies EINSTein's built-in rules (for land combat), to maritime ship stationing and combat,

- *SCUDHunt*, in which game-playing agents based on EINSTein's agent architecture are used "play" a (human-based) wargame, and
- *Social Modeling: Riots and Civil Unrest*, in which EINSTein's movement rules are added to an existing social model to create an agent simulation of decentralized social uprisings.

1.6.1 *Persian Gulf Scenario*

EINSTein has been used as the basis of several *Persian Gulf* (PG) scenario-based "war games" played at CNA,* the *Naval Post Graduate School* (NPGS), and, most recently, at a symposium sponsored by the *Military Operations Research Society* (MORS).†

The PG-scenario was developed as an easy-to-use, scalable test-bed for experimenting with maritime cost-effectiveness trade-offs. EINSTein's ostensibly land-based *soldier* "agents" are, in the PG-scenario, interpreted as *naval ships* (cruisers, frigates, carriers, etc.). EINSTein's design is flexible enough so that, with relatively minor tweaking of its built-in parameters (on the *graphical user interface level*, not the source-code level, where considerably deeper changes than those required by the PG-scenario can be made), *soldiers* can be converted to *ships*. In one variant of the game, conducted at a campaign analysis class at NPGS, fifteen students were broken up into five teams. Figure 1.9 shows a screenshot from a typical interactive run.

The teams engage in a round-robin series of mock-battles, taking place over the course of four days. The goal of the exercise is to try to identify the minimum cost of a hypothetical "agent fleet" that decisively defeats the enemy.

The games conducted at NPGS (as well as at CNA and the MORS mini-symposium) were enthusiastically received not only as hands-on general introductions to agent-based modeling, but as a bona-fide source of credible observations and lessons-learned about the problem of cost-effectiveness trade-offs and acquisition. The PG-scenario also demonstrates how a set of agent rules developed for one form of combat (namely, land-based combat) may be made to apply (almost equally as well) to another form of combat, in this case one that is maritime-based.

1.6.2 *SCUDHunt*

As a second example of the relative ease with which EINSTein's design can be applied to an ostensibly very different "problem," consider a recently completed

*The PG-scenario "gamelet" was developed using EINSTein by CNA analyst, Greg Cox [Cox02].

†The symposium *New Techniques: A Better Understanding of Their Application to Analysis* was held in November, 2002 at *John Hopkins University* (Baltimore, Maryland): http://www.mors.org/meetings/new_techniques/new_tech_final.htm. See also the final proceedings of an earlier MORS-sponsored conference (*Warfare Analysis and Complexity*): http://www.mors.org/publications/reports/Warfare_Analysis_Complexity-Final.pdf.

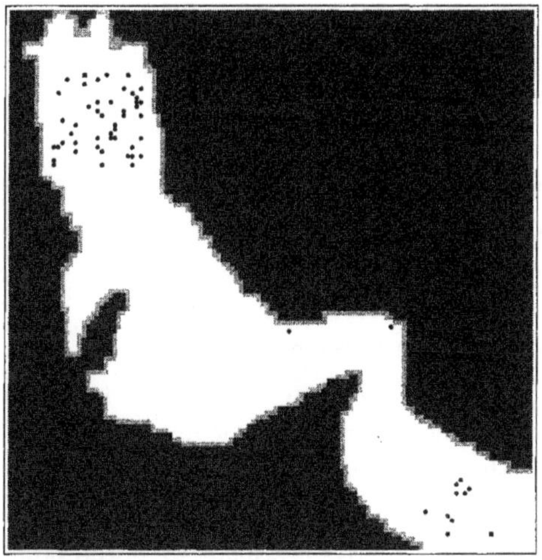

Fig. 1.9 Snapshot of EINSTein's nominally land-combat "battlefield" converted to combined *land* (grey) and *sea* (white) elements for the Persian-Gulf scenario war game.

CNA project called SCUDHunt that uses wargaming agent technology to explore joint command and control (C2) issues [Perla02].

The *Joint C4ISR Decision Support Center* (DSC) in the *Office of the Assistant Secretary of Defense* (C3I) asked CNA to explore how the use of wargames and computer-based agent technology may help advance its C2 research. Toward this end, a board-based wargame called SCUDHunt was developed, in which (human) players assume the roles of sensor asset managers and attempt to deploy their sensors to search a small map for hidden "SCUD" launchers. Each sensor is defined by its coverage ability and reliability. SCUDHunt is played most effectively when players work together, sharing information and developing their shared situational awareness in order to find the SCUDs and make accurate strike recommendations.

One of the practical difficulties associated with "playing" SCUDHunt, is the relatively large number of human players that are required to play the "game," along with the time-consuming task of coordinating the schedules of, and explaining the rules and protocols of the game to all of the participants. A typical SCUDHunt "game" involves 24 human players, broken up into 6 teams of 4, all of whose schedules must be coordinated to ensure the required sequence of games are completed. As a result, it is difficult to play SCUDHunt a sufficient number of times to ensure statistically meaningful results. Thus, an agent-based SCUDHunt human/agent-hybrid wargame was developed.

Artificial agents represent "players" of the original human-only variant of the SCUDHunt game. These agents perform exactly the same functions as the human players (albeit not necessarily in the same fashion, of course): *collect and interpret information from and about the sensors under their control, decide where to place their sensors*, and *exchange various kinds of information*, along with their decisions, with other agents. Agents also decide which locations (on a notional map representing the playing "board") represent the most likely target positions at the end of each turn of the game.

While EINSTein was not used directly to develop the agent-based SCUDHunt, the main ingredients of EINSTein's action selection logic were used to define SCUDHunt agents, the rules by which they interact, and the decision process by which they adjudicate their moves. The greatest challenge, familiar from EINSTein's own design, was to endow agents with a personality-driven artificial intelligence that is simultaneously powerful enough to mimic some important aspects of human decision-making (so that the agents' actions appear to be intelligent actions), and simple enough so that the analyst is not overwhelmed by having too many parametric "knobs" to tweak.

A SCUDHunt-agent's personality consists of parameters that define how an agent obtains, interprets, and uses game-generated information, and includes the interpretation of sensor reports, trust (of other agents), strike-plan logic, and sensor-placement logic. The state of the game is defined by a *belief matrix*, $B(x, y)$, which is a measure of an agent's belief that a SCUD is at location (x, y). Agent decisions (which are equivalent to EINSTein's *actions*) are essentially logic-driven updates of the values of the components of their belief matrix.

The way in which partial beliefs are added to an agent's current belief, using local knowledge, proceeds in exactly the same way as EINSTein's agents combine the value of two or more environmental features to modify a component of their current personality weight vector.*

1.6.3 *Social Modeling: Riots and Civil Unrest*

While social agents will not, typically, be "at war" with one another—so that many of EINSTein's combat adjudication functions can be safely turned off for such a case—almost all of the primitive forms of local information processing (sense, assimilate, act, adapt) remain the same. Only the interpretations of some of the variables might need to be changed, but not their function, nor the way in which the variables are dynamically intertwined. See, for example, the examples given in Gilbert's and Troitzsch's text on applying agent-based techniques to the social sciences [Gilb99].

As an example of how EINSTein-like rules may be to simulate certain aspects of social dynamics, consider a recent CNA study that generalizes Epstein, *et.al.*'s multiagent-based model of *civil disobedience* [Epstein01]. In Epstein's model, "agents" are members of the general population and are either actively rebellious or not. Cops are "authority" agents that wish to minimize (or eliminate) rebellion.

*The mathematical details appear in *Appendix 9: SCUDHunt-agent Architecture* (pages 419-425) of [Ilach02].

Aside from a parameter that defines the range of an agent's *vision* (what in EINSTein is the sensor range), the critical parameters that determine an agent's action are its *grievance* (toward the notional authority) and *risk aversion*. Agents evolve according to a simple rule that defines transitions between quiescent and active states as a function of grievance and net risk (equal to the product of risk aversion and estimated arrest probability). Agents are allowed to move *randomly* to any site within their vision range.

Given its relative simplicity, Epstein, *et.al.*'s model yields remarkably interesting (and plausibly suggestive) behavior. Nonetheless, it is not rich enough to capture any sense of real-world movement. Tony Freedman (a research analyst at CNA) has recently generalized the model to include a finer set of agent states, and has also enhanced this earlier model by using EINSTein's personality weight vectors to help adjudicate agent movement in a more intelligent fashion.

In Freedman's variant, there are four separate classes of agents: *instigators* (I), *reactors* (R), *passives* (P) and *cops* (C). The first two classes are further divided into two and three types, respectively: $I \rightarrow \{I_1, I_2\}$, and $R \rightarrow \{R_1, R_2, R_3\}$. Intuitively, agents of type I_1 spread rumors and propaganda and otherwise actively urge violence against authority; agents of type I_2 are active, violent and recruit others to become active. Similarly, R_1 are angry but inactive (they will listen to, and be drawn to, agitators); R_2 are active and protesting; and R_3 are active and violent. Passives are simple innocent bystanders who typically want to run away from trouble (but who can sometimes join a mob). Freedman uses essentially the same measures of grievance, risk and anger as used by Epstein, *et.al.*, but introduces an agent-specific movement rule: move a site within your vision that best satisfies your weighed desire to be closer-to or farther-away-from agents in specific states. For example, instigators (I_1) may be assigned a much higher weight to move closer to agents of type R_3 than they do to move toward other instigators, and to move away from cops (i.e. they may be assigned a negative weight).

Freedman's variant of Epstein, *et.al.*'s civil unrest model not only offers a crude, but dynamically rich, model of decentralized social uprisings using internal states as action triggers, but also endows agents with a more realistic (semi-"intelligent") movement logic. Although—at the time of this writing (December 2003)—the model is only at an early alpha stage of development, it already demonstrates an impressive range of interesting behaviors.

1.6.4 *General Applications*

As evidenced by the above list of recent applications of EINSTein (and/or EINSTein's core methodology) to problems that are specifically related to land combat, it ought to come as no surprise that EINSTein possesses a broader applicability than to the combat arena alone; of course, the same could be said about *any* multiagent-based simulation, as long as its design adheres carefully to a high-level "blueprint" of a general complex adaptive system.

First, and foremost, EINSTein is a multiagent-based, complex adaptive system simulator. This means that if EINSTein succeeds, by any measure, in modeling combat as a "complex system," it can only have succeeded in doing so because it respects, on a fundamental level, the two most important tenets of complexity theory:

(1) *The observed, high-level, emergent global behaviors of a complex system derive from the collective, low-level, nonlinear interactions among its constituent agents, and*
(2) *There exist universal patterns of behavior that underlie, and describe, widely diverse kinds of complex systems.*

The second tenet is the more far-reaching of the two. It suggests that, analogously to certain universal behaviors appearing in nonlinear iterative maps—such as the existence of Feigembaum's critical parameter convergence rate constant in a family of one-dimensional maps that includes the logistic equation (see page 81 in chapter 2)—there are universal behaviors that describe families of complex systems.

1.6.5 *Universal Patterns of Behavior*

A strong candidate for one such universal pattern may be the recently discovered *fractal power-law scaling* of attrition, which has been observed in both real-world and multiagent-based simulated data. As Bak [Bak96] and others have argued, power-law scalings seem to be ubiquitous in a variety of otherwise unrelated complex systems (see, for example, [Jensen98]).* This suggests that while the details of the dynamics describing different systems may obviously differ, the form of whatever underlying mechanisms are responsible for the emergence of fractal scalings must be essentially the same. One can thus argue that any agent-based model that has successfully captured the underlying forms of agent interactions necessary to generate universal emergent behaviors, has not only demonstrably captured an important driver of the real-world system (in EINSTein's case, the system being "combat"), but by virtue of this can also potentially be used to describe other, at first sight, seemingly unrelated, systems.

A discussion of fractal power-law scaling in EINSTein, as well as other evidence that fractals may play an important role in both EINSTein and real-world combat, appears in section 6.4 (see pages 453-468).

1.7 Goals & Payoffs for Developing EINSTein

EINSTein has been developed for three reasons. First, to demonstrate the efficacy of multiagent-based model alternatives to more conventional combat models whose

*The appearance of power-law scalings in complex systems, in the context of a phenomenon called *self-organized criticality*, is discussed in section 2.2.8 (see page 149).

attrition components have traditionally been based on some form of the Lanchester equations. Second, as a more general prototype artificial-life test bed for exploring self-organized emergent behavior in combat (viewed as a complex adaptive system). The third reason for developing EINSTein is, by far, the most ambitious and far-reaching. It is to provide the military operations research community with an easy-to-use, intuitive combat simulation "laboratory" that—by respecting both the principles of real-world combat and the dynamics of complex adaptive systems—may lead researchers one step closer to a fundamental theory of combat.

The most important immediate payoff to using EINSTein is the radically new way at looking at fundamental issues that it offers the military researcher. However, agent-based models are best used to enhance understanding, not as prediction engines. Specifically, EINSTein is being designed to help researchers...

- Understand how all of the different elements of combat fit together in an overall combat phase space: *"Are there regions that are "sensitive" to small perturbations, and, if so, might there be a way to exploit this in combat (as in selectively driving an opponent into more sensitive regions of phase space)?"*
- Assess the value of information: *"How can I exploit what I know the enemy does not know about me?"*
- Explore trade-offs between centralized and decentralized command-and-control (C2) structures: *"Are some C2 topologies more conducive to information flow and attainment of mission objectives than others?" "What do emergent forms of a self-organized C2 topology look like?"*
- Provide a natural arena in which to explore consequences of various qualitative characteristics of combat (unit cohesion, morale, leadership, etc.)
- Explore emergent properties and/or other "novel" behaviors arising from low-level rules (even combat doctrine if it is well encoded): *"Are there universal patterns of combat behavior?"*
- Provide clues about how near-real-time tactical decision aids may eventually be developed using evolutionary programming techniques
- Address questions such as *"How do two sides of a conflict coevolve with one another?"* and *"Can one side exploit what it knows of this coevolutionary process to compel the other side to remain out of equilibrium?"*

1.7.1 *Command & Control*

EINSTein contains embedded code that hardwires in a specific set of command and control (C2) functions (i.e., both contain a hierarchy of local and global commanders), so that either program can be used to explore the dynamics of a given C2 structure. However, a much more compelling question is, *"What is the best C2 topology for dealing with a specific threat, or set of threats?"* One can imagine using a genetic algorithm, or some other heuristic tool to aid in exploring potentially very large fitness-landscapes, to search for alternative C2 structures. What forms should local and global command take, and what is the optimal communication connectivity pattern among individual combatants, squads and their local and global commanders?

1.7.2 *Pattern Recognition*

An even deeper issue has to do with identifying the primitive forms of information that are relevant on the battlefield. Traditionally, the role of the combat operations research analyst has been to assimilate, and provide useful insights from, certain conventional streams of battlefield data: attrition rate, posture profiles, available and depleted resources, logistics, rate of reinforcement, FEBA location, morale, etc. While all of these measures are obviously important, and will remain so, the availability of an agent-based simulation permits one to ask the following deeper question: *"Are there any other forms of primitive information - perhaps derived from measures commonly used to describe the behavior of nonlinear and complex dynamical systems - that might provide a more thorough understanding of the fundamental dynamical processes of combat?"* For example, we have already alluded to evidence that suggests that the intensity of battles—both in the real world and in agent-based models of combat—obeys a fractal power-law dependence on frequency. and displays other traits characteristic of high-dimensional chaotic systems; we will examine this evidence in some detail in a later section.

1.7.3 *"What If?" Experimentation*

The strength of agent-based models lies not just in their providing a potentially powerful new general approach to computer simulation, but also in their infallible ability to prod researchers into asking a host of interesting new questions. This is particularly apparent when EINSTein is run interactively, with its provision for making quick "on-the-fly" changes to various dynamical parameters. Observations immediately lead to a series of *"What if?"* speculations, which in turn lead to further explorations and further questions. Rather than focusing on a single scenario, and estimating the values of simple attrition-based measures of single outcomes (*"Who won?"*), users of agent-based simulations of combat typically walk away from an interactive session with an enhanced intuition of what the overall combat fitness landscape looks like. Users are also given an opportunity to construct a context for understanding their own conjectures about dynamical combat behavior. The agent-based simulation is therefore a medium in which questions and insights continually feed off of one another.

1.7.4 *Fundamental Grammar of Combat?*

Wolfram [Wolfram94] has conjectured that the macro-level emergent behavior of all cellular automata rules falls into one of only four universality classes, despite the huge number of possible local rules. While EINSTein's rules are obviously more complicated than those of their elementary CA brethren, it is nonetheless tempting to speculate about possible forms for a fundamental grammar of combat.

The rudiments of one approach to developing this grammar are outlined in a later chapter. We conclude this chapter by suggesting that developing a mathematically prescribed combat grammar is—conceptually speaking—equivalent to specifying an *axiological ontology* of combat as a member of a much broader set of complex adaptive systems.

1.8 Toward an *Axiological Ontology* of Complex Systems

While a few general-purpose agent-based simulators are available (such as the *Santa Fe Institute*'s SWARM [SWARM], the *Brooking Institute*'s *Ascape* [ASCAPE], and the University of Chicago's Social Science Research Computing Laboratory's *Repast* [Repast]), and some attempts have been made at abstracting some basic principles that presumably underlie all such models (most recently, and notably, by Holland [Holl99]), no rigorous, mathematical description of the complex adaptive dynamics in agent-based systems has yet emerged.

The long-term goal of the EINSTein project is to develop a formalism—or, more precisely, a *mathematical simulation language*—that is built from primitive notions of agent characteristics and behaviors and uses interaction rules among agents (and between agents and their environment) to describe the fundamental relationship between contexts and action that is believed to underlie the behaviors of all complex adaptive systems. The core of this simulation language is a method for assigning, interpreting, and modifying the "value" of the objects and the relationships among objects that constitute a dynamical environment; i.e., a fundamental *calculus of value.*

1.8.1 *Why "Value"?*

Understanding the dynamics of "value" is central to understanding the basic structure and behavior of complex adaptive systems. The essence of a system may only be gleamed by answering such basic questions as, *"By what objective measure can one part of a system be distinguished from another?,"* or *"Why should a given part pay more, or less, attention to any other part of a system?"* That such questions fundamentally cannot have clearly-defined, *a priori* answers—and what the absence of *a priori* answers implies about the dynamics of complex systems—may be appreciated with the help of a simple, but provocative, result from combinatorics, known as the *Ugly Duckling Theorem* (introduced by Watanabe in 1985 [Watan85]).

Suppose that the number of predicates that are simultaneously satisfied by two nonidentical objects of a system, O_A and O_B, is a fixed constant, P. The theorem asserts that the number of predicates that are simultaneously satisfied by neither O_A nor O_B and the number of predicates that are satisfied by O_A but not by O_B are both also equal to P. While this assertion is easy to prove, and appears innocuous at first, it has rather important consequences.

For example, suppose that there are only three objects in the world, arbitrarily labeled (■,■,◊). An obvious interpretation is that this describes two kinds of objects: two ■'s and one ◊. But there are other ways of partitioning this set. For example, line them up explicitly this way: ■ ■ ◊. An implicit new organizing property seems to emerge: the leftmost ■ and the rightmost ◊ share the property that they *are not in the middle.* We are free to label this property using the symbol ■, and the property of being in the middle, ◊. Now, substituting the new property for each of the original objects, we have ■ ■ ■ → ■ ◊ ■.

Had we sorted these three objects according to the new property (that discriminates according to spatial position), we would again have two kinds of objects, but in this case they would have been different ones. Obviously, we can play this game repeatedly, since there are endless possible properties that can arbitrarily be called ■ and ◊. *That is the point.* Unless there is an objective measure by which one set of properties can be distinguished from any of the others, there is no objective way to assert that any subset of objects is better than, or different from, any other.*

The theorem demonstrates that there is no *a priori* objective way to ascribe a measure of similarity (or dissimilarity) between any two randomly chosen subsets of a given set. Asymmetries within a system (i.e., differences), and thus a *dynamics*, can be induced only either via some externally imposed "aesthetic" measure, or generated from within. In either case, the fundamental driver behind all emergent behaviors of a complex adaptive system is a *self-organized calculus of relative value.* A system, whether it is designed to solve a specific "problem" or evolves in a more open-ended fashion, must decide by itself, and for itself, which parts are more or less important (i.e., have greater or lesser value) than others.

1.8.2 *Why "Axiological Ontology"?*

Axiology–which is a term derived from the Greek words *axios*, meaning worth, and *logos*, meaning science–is the study of value and value judgements. The study of value as a science was pioneered, in the context of philosophical ethics, by Robert Hartman [Hart67] about 40 years ago. Nicholas Smith ([Smith56a], [Smith56b]), in two survey articles published in the early sixties, developed the rudiments of a "calculus of value" in the context of operations research. While Hartman's work deals with broad philosophical issues (morality, aesthetics, etc.) and is relatively well known, Smith's papers are today, inexplicably, forgotten, though they, remarkably, anticipate some basic results of much later developments in what are now called complex systems studies.

A basic aim of the research summarized in this book is to take a step toward extending Hartman's and Smith's concepts of value into a fully realized mathema-

*The *Ugly Duckling Theorem* complements another well-known theorem called the *No Free Lunch Theorem*, proven by Wolpert and Macready in 1996 [Wolp96]. The *No Free Lunch Theorem* asserts that the performance of all search algorithms, when averaged over all possible cost functions (i.e., problems), is *exactly the same.* In other words, no search algorithm is better, or worse, on average than blind guessing. Algorithms must be tailored to specific problems, which therefore effectively serve as the "external aesthetic" by which certain algorithms are identified as being better than others.

tization of the more general class of context-based value judgements, action selections and emergent behaviors in multiagent-based models; as well as to show how such a mathematization can be used to help guide the design and development of multiagent-based models of other kinds of complex systems.

"Ontology," in the context of artificial intelligence (AI) research, means *specification of a conceptualization.** Ontologies are sets of fundamental concept definitions, and can be used to describe the classes, structures and relationships that characterize a complex system of agents. Since complete ontologies must address several closely related epistemological questions (such as knowledge acquisition, knowledge representation, knowledge interpretation, and knowledge sharing), we liken our long-term goal of developing an abstract, multi-agent simulation language, to developing a general axiological ontology of complex adaptive systems.

*The term *ontology*, as used in this book, is not to be confused with the same term that is often used in philosophy, where it denotes a branch of metaphysics that deals with the nature of being. For details on ontology, as it pertains to AI, particularly in the context of knowledge sharing and compositional modeling languages, see [Gruber93] and [Iwasaki96].

Chapter 2

Nonlinear Dynamics, Deterministic Chaos and Complex Adaptive Systems: *A Primer*

"Every system is linked with its environment by circular processes which establish a feedback link between the evolution of both sides. The contours of this paradigm...provide a scientific foundation of a new world-view which emphasizes process over structure, non-equilibrium over equilibrium, evolution over permanence, and individual creativity over collective stabilizations."—Erich Jantsch, *Philosopher* (1929-1980)

This chapter contains a semi-technical primer on nonlinear dynamics, deterministic chaos and complex adaptive systems theory. One must achieve at least a rudimentary understanding of these disciplines—their general features, mathematical vocabulary, and methodology—in order to fully appreciate the material that is presented in later chapters.

Apart from providing a succinct, self-contained introduction to these subjects—which are, of course, important research areas on their own, and about which entire books continue to be written (references are provided throughout our discussion)—chapter 2 introduces the theoretical framework and mathematical background necessary to understand and discuss nonlinear dynamics and complex systems theory *as they apply specifically to land warfare issues*, and as critical components of the conceptual scaffolding on which the multiagent-based model of combat, EINSTein—which is discussed in detail in later chapters (see chapters 5-7)—is directly based.

While the discussion in this chapter is necessarily brief and far-from-complete, it is the author's sincere wish that this chapter also provides a broader value to the reader, and that it is viewed as a general sourcebook of information; one that can be consulted from time to time either for background material and/or for definitions of technical terms, or perused for the simple pleasure of reading.

Appendix A, at the end of the book (see page 561), is a compendium of additional information sources (that are available on the world wide web) that pertain to combat, complexity, nonlinear dynamics, and multiagent-based modeling and simulation. These resources include papers, simulation and modeling tools, visualization aids, pointers to other research groups, and additional links.

2.1 Nonlinear Dynamics and Chaos

"Not only in research, but also in the everyday world of politics and economics, we would all be better off if more people realized that simple dynamical systems do not necessarily lead to simple dynamical behavior."—R. M. May

So concludes Robert May in his well-known 1976 *Nature* review article [May76] of what was then known about the behavior of first-order difference equations of the form $x_{n+1} = F(x_n)$. What was articulated by a relatively few then, is now generally regarded as being the central philosophical tenet of chaos theory: *complex behavior need not stem from a complex underlying dynamics.*

In this section we introduce the basic theory and concepts of nonlinear dynamics and deterministic chaos. The discussion is neither rigorous nor complete; it is intended only to serve as a primer on some important concepts that will be used throughout the book. Interested readers are encouraged to consult one of the many excellent review articles and texts that are available on nonlinear dynamics; for example, the texts by Rasband [Rasb90], Schuster [Schus88], Devaney [Devaney89], Iooss, et al. [Iooss83] and Pietgen, et al. [Peitgen92]. Nonlinear time series analysis is covered in depth by Kantz and Schreiber [Kantz97]. A review of regular and irregular motion in classical Hamiltonian systems is given by Tabor [Tabor89]. There are also several good collections of reprints of landmark papers dealing specifically with chaos: see [Bai84], [Bai87], [Bai88] and [Cvit84].

2.1.1 *Brief History*

Table 2.1 shows a brief chronology of some of the milestone events in the study of nonlinear dynamics and deterministic chaos.

Chaos was born, at least in concept, at the turn of the last century with Henri Poincare's discovery in 1892 that certain orbits of three or more interacting celestial bodies can exhibit unstable and unpredictable behavior. A full proof that Poincare's unstable orbits are chaotic, due to Smale, appeared only 70 years later. E. N. Lorenz's well-known paper in which he showed that a simple set of three coupled, first order, nonlinear differential equations describing a simplified model of the atmosphere can lead to completely chaotic trajectories was published a year after Smale's proof, in 1963. As in Poincare's case, the general significance of Lorenz's paper was not appreciated until many years after its publication. The formal rigorous study of deterministic chaos began in earnest with Mitchell Feigenbaum's discovery in 1978 of the universal properties in the way nonlinear dynamical systems approach chaos.

The term "chaos" was first coined by Li and Yorke in 1975 to denote random output of deterministic mapping. More recently, in 1990, Ott, Grebogi and Yorke suggested that certain properties of chaotic systems can be exploited to control chaos; that is, to redirect the trajectory of a chaotic system into another desired orbit. Ironically, chaos can be "controlled" precisely because of its inherent insta-

Year	Researcher	Discovery
1875	Weierstrass	Constructed everywhere continuous and nowhere differentiable function
1890	King Oscar II of Sweden	Offered prize for 1st person to solve the n-body to determine the orbits on n-celestial bodies and thus prove the stability of the solar system; this problem remains unsolved in 1995
1892	Poincare	In the course of studying celestial motion, discovered that the ("homoclinic") orbit of three or more interacting bodies can exhibit unstable and unpredictable behavior (chaos is born!)
1932	Birkhoff	Observed what he called "remarkable curves" in the dynamics of the plane with itself
1954	Kolmogorov	Discovered that motion in phase space of classical mechanics is niether completely regular nor completely irregular, but that trajectory depends on the initial conditions; KAM theorem
1962	Smale	Produced mathematical proof that Poincare's homoclinic orbits are chaotic
1963	Lorenz	First systematic analysis of chaotic attractors in simplified model of atmospheric air currents; coined the "Butterfly effect"
1970	Mandelbrot	Coined the term "fractal" and suggested applicability to a wide variety of natural phenomena
1971	Ruelle & Takens	Suggest new mechanism for turbulence: strange attractors
1975	Li & Yorke	Use "chaos" to denote random output of deterministic mappings
1976	May	Wrote important review article in Nature on complicated dynamics of population dynamics modelss
1978	Feigenbaum	Discovered universal properties in the way nonlinear systems appraoch chaos
1981	Benzi, Sutera, Vulpiani	Introduced concept of "stochastic resonance"*
1990	Ott, Grebogi, Yorke	Beginning of chaos control theory
1990	Peccora	Beginning of synchronization of chaotic systems

Table 2.1 Some landmark historical developments in the study of nonlinear dynamical systems and chaos.

bilities, and there is no counterpart "control theory" for nonchaotic systems.

Experimentally, deterministic chaos has by now been observed in just about every conceivable physical system that harbors some embedded nonlinearity:† arms races, biological models for population dynamics, chemical reactions, fluids near the onset of turbulence, heart beat rhythms, josephson junctions, lasers, neural networks, nonlinear optical devices, planetary orbits, etc.

* *Stochastic resonance* is a counterintuitive phenomenon in which a weak periodic signal (which, by itself, is essentially undetectable) is rendered detectable by adding stochastic noise to a nonlinear dynamical system. A recent review article appears in *Physics Today* [Buls96].

†Note that nonlinearity is a *necessary*, but not sufficient condition for deterministic chaos. Linear differential or difference equations can be solved exactly and do not lead to chaos.

Fractals—that is, self-similar objects that harbor an effectively infinite number of layers of detail—were (formally) born in 1875, when the mathematician Weierstrass had constructed an everywhere continuous but nowhere differentiable function, though Weierstrass neither coined the term nor was, in his time, able to fully appreciate the complexity of his own creation. A fuller understanding of fractals had to await the arrival of the speed and graphics capability of the modern computer. The term "fractal" was introduced by Mandelbrot about a hundred years after Weierstrass' original construction [MandB82].

2.1.2 *Dynamical Systems*

A dynamical system is any physical system that evolves in time according to some well-defined rule. Its state is completely defined at all times by the values of N variables, $x_1(t), x_2(t), ...x_N(t)$, where $x_i(t)$ represent any physical quantity of interest (position, velocity, temperature, etc.). The abstract space in which these variables "live" is called the phase space Γ. Its temporal evolution is specified by an autonomous system of N, possibly coupled, ordinary first-order differential equations:

$$\begin{cases} \dfrac{dx_1}{dt} & = & F_1\left(x_1, x_2, \ldots, x_N; \alpha_1, \alpha_2, \ldots, \alpha_M\right) \\ \dfrac{dx_2}{dt} & = & F_2\left(x_1, x_2, \ldots, x_N; \alpha_1, \alpha_2, \ldots, \alpha_M\right) \\ \quad\vdots & & \\ \dfrac{dx_N}{dt} & = & F_N\left(x_1, x_2, \ldots, x_N; \alpha_1, \alpha_2, \ldots, \alpha_M\right), \end{cases} \tag{2.1}$$

where $\alpha_1, \alpha_2, ..., \alpha_M$ are a set of M control parameters, representing any external parameters by which the evolution may be modified or driven. The temporal evolution of a point $\vec{x}(t) = (x_1(t), x_2(t), ...x_N(t))$ traces out a trajectory (or *orbit*) of the system in Γ. The system is said to linear or nonlinear depending on whether $\vec{F} = (F_1, F_2, ..., F_N)$ is linear or nonlinear.* Nonlinear systems generally have no explicit solutions.

2.1.2.1 *Poincare Maps*

Once the initial state $\vec{x}(t = 0)$ of the system is specified, future states, $\vec{x}(t)$, are uniquely defined for all times t. Moreover, the uniqueness theorem of the solutions of ordinary differential equations guarantees that trajectories originating from different initial points never intersect. In studying deterministic chaos, one must make a

*If f is a nonlinear function or an operator, and x is a system input (either a function or variable), then the effect of adding two inputs, x_1 and x_2, first and then operating on their sum is, in general, not equivalent to operating on two inputs separately and then adding the outputs together; i.e., $f(x_1 + x_2)$ is, in general, not equal to $f(x_1) + f(x_2)$.

distinction between chaos in *dissipative* systems (such as a forced pendulum with friction) and *conservative* systems (such as planetary motion).

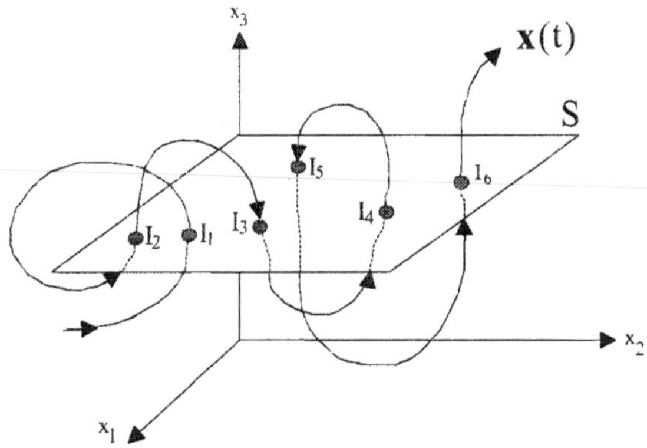

Fig. 2.1 Schematic illustration of a *Poincare map*; see text for details.

A convenient method for visualizing continuous trajectories is to construct an equivalent discrete-time mapping by a periodic "stroboscopic" sampling of points along an orbit. One way of accomplishing this is by the *Poincare map* (or surface-of-section) method. In general, an $(N-1)$–dimensional surface-of-section S in the phase space Γ is chosen, and we consider the sequence of successive intersections—$I_1, I_2, ..., I_n$—of the flow $\vec{x}(t)$ within S. Introducing a system of coordinates, $y_1, ...,$ y_{N-1}, on S and representing the intersections I_i by coordinates $y_{i,1}, y_{i,2}, ..., y_{i,N-1}$, the system of differential equations is replaced by the discrete-time Poincare mapping (see figure 2.1):

$$\begin{cases} y'_{i,1} = G_1(y_{i,1}, y_{i,2}, \ldots, y_{i,N-1}; \alpha_1, \alpha_2, \ldots, \alpha_M), \\ y'_{i,2} = G_2(y_{i,1}, y_{i,2}, \ldots, y_{i,N-1}; \alpha_1, \alpha_2, \ldots, \alpha_M), \\ \vdots \\ y'_{i,N-1} = G_{N-1}(y_{i,1}, y_{i,2}, \ldots, y_{i,N-1}; \alpha_1, \alpha_2, \ldots, \alpha_M). \end{cases} \tag{2.2}$$

Poincare maps of this form have the obvious advantage of being much simpler to study than their differential-equation counterparts, without sacrificing any of the essential behavioral properties. They may also be studied as generic systems to help abstract behaviors of more complicated systems.

2.1.2.2 *Phase Space Volumes*

Consider a small rectangular volume element ΔV around the point $\vec{x}_0$. For discrete-time Poincare maps of the form $\vec{x}_{n+1} = \vec{G}(\vec{x}_n)$, the rate of change of ΔV—say, Λ—is given by the absolute value of the Jacobian of $\vec{G}$:

$$\Lambda = |J| = \left| \det \left(\frac{\partial G_i}{\partial x_j} \right) \right| . \tag{2.3}$$

Since the motion in phase space is typically bounded, we know that volumes do not, on average, expand; i.e., Λ, and therefore the Jacobian J, are not positive. On the other hand, the behavior of systems for which $\Lambda < 0$ (called *dissipative systems*) is very different from the behavior of systems that have $\Lambda = 0$ (called *conservative systems*).

2.1.2.3 *Dissipative Dynamical Systems ($\Lambda < 0$)*

Dissipative systems—whether they are described as continuous flows or Poincare maps—are characterized by the presence of some sort of "internal friction" that tends to contract phase space volume elements. Contraction in phase space allows such systems to approach a subset of the phase space called an *attractor*, $A \subset \Gamma$, as $t \to \infty$.

Although there is no universally accepted definition of an attractor, it is intuitively reasonable to demand that it satisfy the following three properties: (1) *Invariance:* A is invariant under the map F (i.e., $FA = A$); (2) *Attraction:* there is an open neighborhood B containing A such that all points $\vec{x}(t) \in B$ approach A as the set of initial points $\vec{x}_i(t = 0)$ such that $\vec{x}_i(t)$ approaches A is called the *basin of attraction* of A; and (3) *Irreducibility:* A cannot be partitioned into two nonoverlapping invariant and attracting pieces (a more technical demand is that of topological transitivity: there must exist a point $\vec{x}^*$ in A such that for all $\vec{x}$ in A there exists a positive time T such that $\vec{x}^*(T)$ is arbitrarily close to $\vec{x}$).

The simplest possible attractor is a *fixed point*, for which all trajectories starting from the appropriate basin-of-attraction eventually converge onto a single point. For linear dissipative dynamical systems, fixed-point attractors are in fact the only possible type of attractor. Non-linear systems, on the other hand, harbor a much richer spectrum of attractor-types. For example, in addition to fixed-points, there may exist periodic attractors such as *limit cycles* for two-dimensional flows or *doubly periodic orbits* for three-dimensional flows. There is also an intriguing class of attractors that have a very complicated geometric structure called *strange attractors* [ruelle80].

The motion on strange attractors exhibits many of the properties normally associated with completely random or *chaotic* behavior, despite being well-defined at all times and fully deterministic. More formally, a strange attractor S is an attractor (meaning that it satisfies properties 1–3 above) that also displays *sensitivity to initial conditions.* In the case of a one-dimensional map, $x_{n+1} = f(x_n) = f^2(x_{n-1}) = \cdots = f^n(x_1)$, for example, this means that there exists a $\delta > 0$ such that for all $x \in S$ and any open neighborhood U of x, there exists $x^* \in U$ such that $|f^n(x) - f^n(x^*)|$. The basic idea, to which we will return many times, is that initially close points become exponentially separated for sufficiently long times. This has the important consequence that while the behavior of each initial point may be accurately followed for short times, prediction of long time behavior of trajectories lying on strange attractors becomes effectively impossible. Strange attractors also frequently exhibit a self-similar or Cantor-set-like structure, and are characterized by non-integer *Hausdorff* dimension (see page 95).

2.1.2.4 *Conservative Systems* ($\Lambda < 0$)

In contrast to dissipative dynamical systems, conservative systems preserve phase-space volumes and hence cannot display any attracting regions in phase space. Consequently, there can be no fixed points, no limit cycles and no strange attractors. However, there can still be chaotic motion in the sense that points along particular trajectories may show sensitivity to initial conditions.

A familiar example of a conservative system from classical mechanics is that of a *Hamiltonian* system. Although the chaos exhibited by conservative systems often involves fractal-like phase-structures, the fractal character is of an altogether different kind from that arising in dissipative systems.

2.1.3 *Deterministic Chaos*

> *"Chaos is a name for any order that produces confusion in our minds."*
> *—G. Santayana, Philosopher, Poet, Humanist and Critic (1863-1952)*

Deterministic chaos is the irregular or random appearing motion in nonlinear dynamical systems whose dynamical laws uniquely determine the time evolution of the state of the system from a knowledge of its past history. It is *not due* to external noise, to the fact that the system may have an infinite number of degrees-of-freedom or to any "Heisenberg uncertainty"-like relations operating on the quantum level. The source of the observed irregularity in deterministic chaos is an *intrinsic sensitivity to initial conditions.*

A more mathematically rigorous definition of chaos, that holds for both continuous and discrete systems, is due to Devaney [Devan86]. Let V be a set. A map $f : V \to V$ is said to be *chaotic* on V if (1) f has sensitive dependence on initial conditions, (2) f is topologically transitive,* and (3) periodic points are *dense* in V.† More succinctly, f is a chaotic map if it possesses these three characteristics: unpredictability, indecomposability and some degree of regularity. It is unpredictable because of its sensitive dependence on initial conditions; it is indecomposable be-

*A *topologically transitive* orbit is an orbit such that, for all pairs of regions in the phase space, the orbit at some point visits each region of the pair. That is to say, it is always possible to eventually get from one area around a state to an area around any other area by following the orbit.

†A set of points X is *dense* in another set Y if an arbitrarily small area around any point in Y contains a point in X.

cause it cannot be decomposed into two subsystems that do not interact (under f); and, despite generating behavior that appears to be random, a "regularity" persists in the form of a dense set of periodic points. Several examples of deterministic chaos are discussed below.

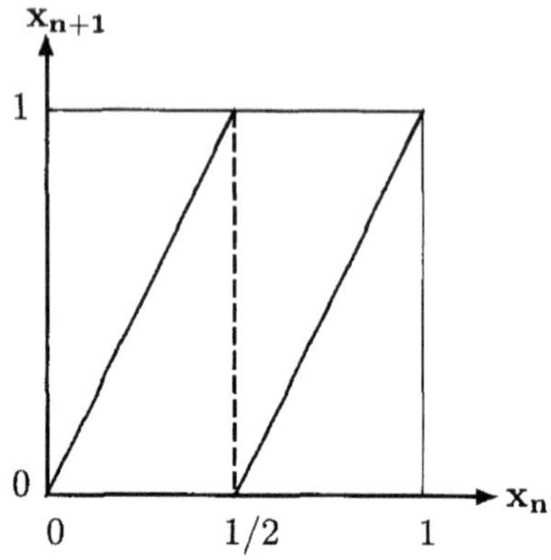

Fig. 2.2 The *Bernoulli Shift* map: $x_{n+1} = f(x_n) \equiv 2x_n \pmod 1$, $0 < x_0 < 1$.

2.1.3.1 *Example #1: The Bernoulli Shift Map*

Despite bearing no direct relation to any physical dynamical system, the one-dimensional discrete-time piecewise linear *Bernoulli Shift* map nonetheless displays many of the key mechanisms leading to deterministic chaos. The map is defined by (see figure 2.2):

$$x_{n+1} = f(x_n) \equiv 2x_n \pmod 1, \quad 0 < x_0 < 1, \tag{2.4}$$

where by (mod 1) we mean that x (mod 1) $= x-$ *Integer*(x), and *Integer*(x) is the "integer part of" of x.

We are interested in the properties of the sequence of values x_0, $x_1 = f(x_0)$, $x_2 = f(x_1) = f^2(x_0)$,... —or the *orbit* of x_0—generated by successive applications of the Bernoulli shift to the initial point, x_0. In turns out that the most convenient representation for the initial point, x_0, is as a binary decimal. That is, we write

$$x_0 = \sum_{i=1}^{\infty} \alpha_i 2^{-i} = \frac{\alpha_1}{2} + \frac{\alpha_2}{4} + \cdots \equiv 0.\alpha_1\alpha_2\alpha_3\cdots, \tag{2.5}$$

where $\alpha_i \in \{0,1\}$ for all i.* For example, the binary expansion of $1/3 = 0/2 + 1/22 + 0/23 + 1/24 + ... = 0.0101$, where 01 means that the sequence "01" is

*It is not difficult to show that such binary expansions—in fact expansions to an arbitrary base $\beta > 1$—are complete in the unit interval. See I. Niven, "Irrational Numbers," *The Carus Mathematical Monographs*, Volume 11, 1956.

repeated *ad infinitum*. Expansions for arbitrary rationals $r = p/q$, where p and q are integers, are relatively easy to calculate. Expansions for irrational numbers may be obtained by first finding a suitably close rational approximation. For example, $\pi - 3 \sim 4703/33215 = 0.001001000011$, which is correct to 12 binary decimal places.

This binary decimal representation of x_0 makes clear why this map is named the Bernoulli *shift*. If $x_0 < 1/2$, then $\alpha_1 = 0$; if $x_0 > 1/2$, then $\alpha_1 = 1$. Thus,

$$x_1 = f(x_0) = \begin{cases} 2x_0 \text{ if } \alpha_1 = 0 \\ 2x_0 - 1 \text{ if } \alpha_1 = 1 \end{cases} \Rightarrow f(x_0) = 0.\alpha_2\alpha_3\alpha_4\cdots \tag{2.6}$$

In other words, a single application of the map f to the point x_0 discards the first digit and shifts to the left all of the remaining digits in the binary decimal expansion of x_0. In this way, the nth iterate is given by $x_n = \alpha_{n+1}\alpha_{n+2}\alpha_{n+3}\cdots$

What are the properties of the actual orbit of x_0? Since f effectively reads off the digits in the binary expansion of x_0, the properties of the orbit depend on whether x_0 is *rational* or *irrational*. For rational x_0, orbits are both periodic and dense in the unit interval; for irrational x_0, orbits are nonperiodic, with the attractor being equal to the entire unit interval. Moreover, the Bernoulli shift is *ergodic*. That is to say, because any finite sequence of digits appears infinitely many times within the binary decimal representation of almost all irrational numbers in $[0, 1]$ (except for a set of measure zero), the orbit of almost all irrationals approaches any x in the unit interval to within an arbitrarily small distance an infinite number of times.*

We now use the Bernoulli shift to illustrate four fundamental concepts that play an important role in deterministic chaos theory:

- *Stability*
- *Predictability*
- *Deterministic randomness*
- *Computability*

Stability. Chaotic attractors may be distinguished from regular, or nonchaotic, attractors by being unstable with respect to small perturbations to the initial conditions; this property is frequently referred to as simply a sensitivity to initial conditions. However, while all Bernoulli shift orbits are generally unstable in this sense, only those originating from irrational x_0 are chaotic. Suppose that two points, x_0 and x_0^*, differ only in the nth place of their respective binary decimal expansions. By the nth iterate, the difference between their evolved values, $|f^n(x_0) - f^n(x_0^*))|$, will be expressed in the first digit; i.e., arbitrarily small initial differences—or *errors*—are exponentially magnified in time. If $|x_0 - x_0^*| \sim 10^{-31}$, for example, their respective orbits would differ by order ~ 1 by the 100th iterate. Physically, we know that any measurement will have an arbitrarily small, but inevitably finite, error associated with it. In systematically magnifying these errors, nonlinear maps such as

*For a simple proof of these assertions, see page 174 in [Ilach01b].

the Bernoulli shift effectively transform the information originating on microscopic length scales to a form that is macroscopically observable.

Predictability. Exponential divergence of orbits places a severe restriction on the predictability of the system. If the initial point x0 is known only to within an error δx_0, for example, we know that this error will grow to $\delta x_n = exp(n \ln 2)\ \delta x_0$ (mod 1) by the nth iteration. The relaxation time, τ, to a statistical equilibrium—which is defined as the number of iterations required before we reach a state of total ignorance as to the location of the orbit point within the unit interval $[0,1]$; i.e., τ is the minimum n such that $\delta x_n \sim 1$—is therefore given by $\tau \sim -\ln|\delta x_0|/\ln 2$. For all times $t > \tau$, the initial and final states of the system are causally disconnected.

Deterministic Randomness. On the one hand, the Bernoulli shift is a linear difference equation that can be trivially solved for each initial point x_0: $x_n = 2^n x_0 \pmod 1$. Once an initial point is chosen, the future iterates are determined uniquely. As such, this simple system is an intrinsically deterministic one. On the other hand, look again at the binary decimal expansion of a randomly selected x_0. This expansion can also be thought of as a particular semi-infinite sequence of coin tosses,

$$\begin{array}{rcccccccc} x_0 & = & . & 0 & 1 & 1 & 0 & 1 & \cdots \\ & & & \downarrow & \downarrow & \downarrow & \downarrow & \downarrow & \\ & = & . & T & H & H & T & H & \cdots \end{array} , \qquad (2.7)$$

in which each 1 represents *heads* and each 0 represents *tails.* In this way, the set of all binary decimal expansions of $0 < x_0 < 1$ can be seen as being identical to the set of all possible sequences of random coin tosses. Put another way, if we are merely reading off a string of digits coming out of some "black-box," there is no way of telling whether this block-box is generating the outcome by flipping a non-biased coin or is in fact implementing the Bernoulli shift for some precisely known initial point. Arbitrarily selected x_0 will therefore generate, in a strictly deterministic manner, a random sequence of iterates, x_0, x_1, x_2, ... Moreover, it is important to point out that while one is always assured of randomly selecting an irrational x_0 (with probability one)—by virtue of the fact that rationals only occupy a space of measure zero—one is at the same time limited in a practical computational sense to working with finite, and therefore rational, approximations of x_0. The consequences of this fact are discussed below.

Computability. While one can formally represent an arbitrary point x by the infinite binary-decimal expansion $x = 0.\alpha_1\alpha_2\alpha_3...$, in practice one works only with the finite expansion, $x = 0.\alpha_1\alpha_2\alpha_3...\alpha_n$. Conversely, any sequence of coin tossings is also necessarily finite in duration and therefore defines only a rational number. Given this restriction, in what sense are chaotic orbits computable? When implemented on a computer, for example, a single iteration of the Bernoulli map is realized by a left shift of one bit followed by an insertion of a zero as the rightmost bit. Since any x_0 is stored as a finite-bit computer word, the result is that all x_0 are eventually mapped to the (stable fixed point) x_0^*:

$$\begin{array}{rcccccccccc} x_0 & = & 0 & . & \alpha_1 & \alpha_2 & \alpha_3 & \cdots & & \alpha_{n-1} & \alpha_n \\ x_1 & = & 0 & . & \alpha_1 & \alpha_3 & \alpha_4 & & & \alpha_n & 0 \\ \vdots & & \vdots & & \vdots & \vdots & \vdots & & & \vdots & \vdots \\ x_n & = & 0 & . & 0 & 0 & 0 & 0 & & 0 & 0 \end{array} \quad (2.8)$$

All of the points of a finite length orbit, $x_0, x_1, ..., x_m$, may therefore be assured of having at least m-bit accuracy by computing x_0 to $n+m$ bits. A number x is said to be *computable* if its expansion coefficients α_i may be algorithmically generated to arbitrarily high order. Thus, so long as the initial point x_0 is itself a computable irrational number, its orbit will be chaotic and computable. One can show, however, that there are many more noncomputable irrationals than computable ones.

2.1.3.2 *Example #2: The Logistic Map*

Just as the *Bernoulli* map provides important insights into some of the fundamental properties of dynamical chaos, the *Logistic* map is one of the simplest (continuous and differentiable) nonlinear dynamical systems that captures most of the key mechanisms that produce dynamical chaos. Indeed, the Logistic map captures much of the essence of a whole class of real-world phenomena, including that of the transition to turbulence in fluid flows.

Although the study of its behavior dates back at least forty years, and includes such distinguished theorists as Ulam and von Neumann [Ulam52], Metropolis and Stein [Metro73], and May [May76], the most profound series of revelations was no doubt obtained by Mitchell Feigenbaum in 1975, culminating in his universality theory ([Feig78], [Feig79]).*

Feigenbaum observed that the "route to chaos" as it appears in the logistic map, actually occurs (apart from a few mild technical restrictions) in *all first-order difference equations* of the form $x_{n+1} = f(x_n)$, where the function $f(x)$, after a suitable rescaling, has a single maximum on the unit interval $[0, 1]$. Moreover, the transition to chaos is characterized by a scaling behavior governed by universal constants whose value depends only on the order of the maximum of $f(x)$. The

*It is ironic that such an intensely computational mathematical science as chaos theory owes much of its modern origin to calculations that were performed not on a large mainframe computer but rather a simple programmable pocket calculator, a Hewlett-Packard HP-65! Feigenbaum would explain years later that had the series of intermediate calculations not been carried out sufficiently *slowly*, it is likely that most of the key observations would have been missed [Feig80]. Anticipating results discussed later in the book, it is amusing to note that with multiagent-based modeling, we have—in a sense—come full-circle computationally! It is only because modern desktop PCs allow researchers to run simulations at tremendously *high speeds* (and usually with tremendously large numbers of agents) that we are finally able to discern interesting emergent behaviors. *That* part of the story will be taken up when we begin our discussion of EINSTein in chapter 4.

subsections below provide an overview of the behavior of this simple, but important, dynamical system.

Definition. The Logistic map is defined by:

$$x_{n+1} = f_\alpha(x_n) = \alpha x_n(1 - x_n), \qquad x_0 \in (0,1),\ 0 < \alpha \leq 4. \tag{2.9}$$

As long as the single control parameter, α, is less than or equal to four, the orbit of any point $x_0 \in (0,1)$ remains bounded on the unit interval. Notice also, that like the Bernoulli map, this map is *noninvertible*; i.e., there are two antecedents, x_n and x_n', for each point x_{n+1}. We now want to study the behavior of orbits as a function of the parameter α. That the behavior of this map strongly depends on the value of α is easily appreciated from figure 2.3, which shows sample evolutions for $\alpha = 0.5, 2.5, 3.3$, and 4.

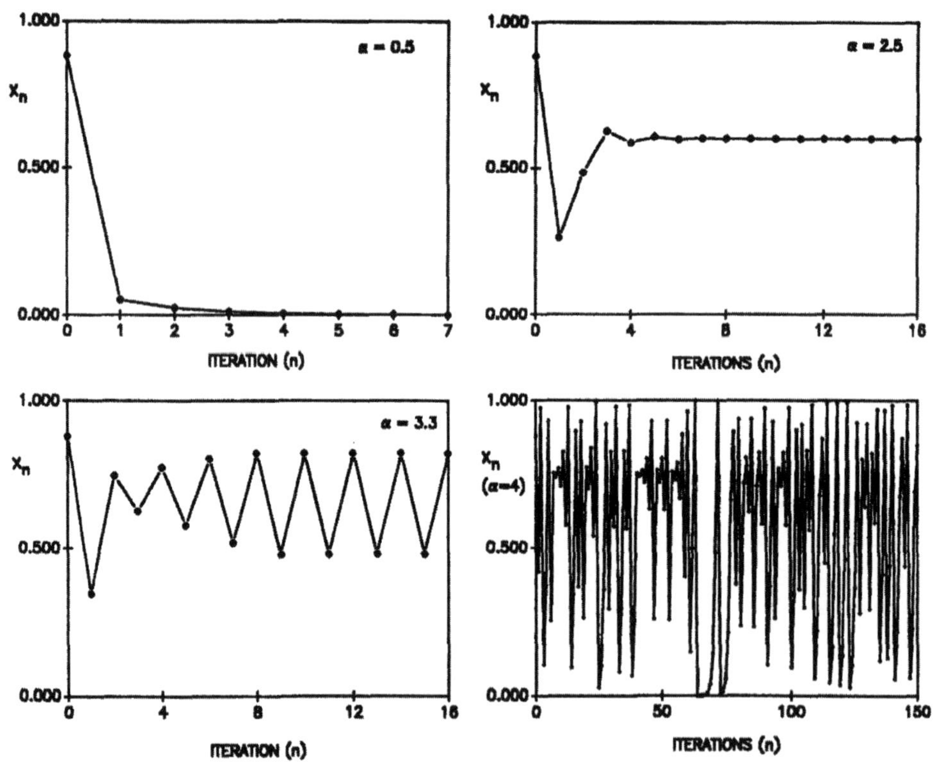

Fig. 2.3 Plots of x_n versus iteration n for four different values of α for the *Logistic* map: (a) $\alpha = 0.5$, (b) $\alpha = 2.5$, (c) $\alpha = 3.3$ and (d) $\alpha = 4$; see text.

Fixed Point Solutions. We begin by asking whether there are any values of α for which the system has fixed points. Solving the fixed-point equation:

$$x^* = f_\alpha(x^*) = \alpha x^*(1 - x^*), \tag{2.10}$$

we indeed find two such points: $x^* = x^*_{(0)} = 0$ and $x^* = x^*_{(1)} = (\alpha - 1)/\alpha$. In order for $x^*_{(1)}$ to be in the unit interval, we must have that $\alpha \geq 1$. What of the stability of these two points? As we have already seen in the case of the Bernoulli map, the divergence of initially close-by points is a crucial issue in the analysis of the dynamical behavior.

Given a fixed point, x^*, the subsequent evolution of a nearby point, $x^{*\prime} = x^* + \epsilon$, where $\epsilon << 1$, may be determined by substituting $x_n = x^* + \epsilon_n$ and $x_{n+1} = x^* + \epsilon_{n+1}$ into equation 2.9 and leaving only the terms that are linear in ϵ_n and ϵ_{n+1}:

$$\epsilon_{n+1} = \alpha(1 - 2x^*)\epsilon_n + \mathcal{O}(\epsilon_n^2). \tag{2.11}$$

We find that, regardless of the initial point x_0, the deviations from the fixed point $x^*_{(0)}$ decrease exponentially fast for all $\alpha < 1$; i.e., all points $x_0 \in (0,1)$ are attracted to the fixed point $x^* = 0$: $\lim_{n\to\infty} x_n = 0$.

At the critical value $\alpha = \alpha_1 = 1$, however, $x^*_{(0)}$ becomes unstable and the α-dependent fixed point $x^*_{(1)}$ becomes stable. This exchange of stability between two fixed points of a map is known as a *transcritical bifurcation*. By using the same linear-stability analysis as above, we see that $x^*_{(1)}$ remains stable if $-1 < \alpha(1 - x^*_{(1)}) < 1$, or for all α such that $1 < \alpha < 3$. Something more interesting happens at $\alpha = 3$.

Period-2 Limit Cycle. At the second critical value, $\alpha = \alpha_2 = 3$, $x^*_{(1)}$ itself becomes unstable and is replaced by a stable attracting period-2 limit cycle, $\{x^1_{(2)}, x^2_{(2)}\}$. This new bifurcation—called the *pitchfork bifurcation*—is shown schematically in figure 2.4 below.

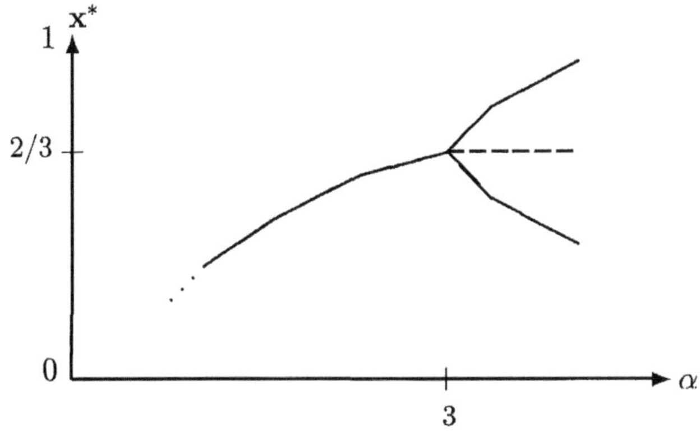

Fig. 2.4 A schematic representation of the *pitchfork bifurcation*: a stable fixed point bifurcates into a period-2 limit cycle plus an unstable fixed point.

The points $x^1_{(2)}$ and $x^2_{(2)}$ are each fixed points of the doubly iterated map, $f^2(x)$:

$$\begin{aligned} x^* &= f(f(x^*)), \\ &= \alpha^2(x^*(1-x^*)\left[1-\alpha x^*(1-x^*)\right], \\ &= \alpha^3 x^*\left(x^*-(1-\frac{1}{\alpha})\right)\left\{x^{*^2}-\left(1+\frac{1}{\alpha}\right)x^*+\frac{1}{\alpha}\left(1+\frac{1}{\alpha}\right)\right\}. \end{aligned} \tag{2.12}$$

Neglecting the two previous, and now unstable, fixed point solutions $x^* = 0$ and $x^* = 1 - 1/\alpha$, the new stable period-2 solution is given by:

$$\begin{aligned} x^1_{(2)} &= \frac{1}{2\alpha}\left(1+\alpha+\sqrt{\alpha^2-2\alpha-3}\right), \\ x^2_{(2)} &= \frac{1}{2\alpha}\left(1+\alpha-\sqrt{\alpha^2-2\alpha-3}\right). \end{aligned} \tag{2.13}$$

Noting that the derivative $f^{2'}(x^i_{(2)}) = f'(x^1_{(2)})f'(x^2_{(2)})$, $i = 1,\ 2$, we find that the period-2 solution is stable as long as $|\alpha^2(1-2x^1_{(2)})(1-2x^2_{(2)})| < 1$, or

$$\alpha_2 = 3 < \alpha < \alpha_3 = 1 + \sqrt{6}. \tag{2.14}$$

At $\alpha_3 = 1 + \sqrt{6}$ we again have a simultaneous loss of stability for the period-2 set $\{x^1_{(2)},\ x^2_{(2)}\}$ and a bifurcation to a 4-cycle.

Period-n Limit Cycles. As α increases, the system undergoes an infinite sequence of successive period-doublings via pitchfork bifurcations. In general,

- A stable period-2^{n-1} limit cycle exists for all α such that 2^{n-1},
- At the nth critical value of α, α_n, all points of the 2^{n-1}-cycle simultaneously become unstable via pitchfork bifurcations in $f^{2^n}_\alpha = [f^{2^{n-1}}_\alpha]^2$, leading to a new stable period-2^n cycle for $\alpha_n < \alpha < \alpha_{n+1}$.

While the period of the limit-cycles approaches infinity as $n \to \infty$, the distance between successive values of the critical α rapidly decreases:

$$\left\{\begin{array}{ll} \alpha_1 = 3.0 & \alpha_6 = 3.56969\cdots \\ \alpha_2 = 3.44949\cdots & \alpha_7 = 3.56989\cdots \\ \alpha_3 = 3.54409\cdots & \alpha_8 = 3.56993\cdots \\ \alpha_4 = 3.56441\cdots & \vdots \\ \alpha_5 = 3.56876\cdots & \alpha_\infty = 3.5699456\cdots. \end{array}\right. \tag{2.15}$$

What does the orbit look like for α_∞? It is an infinite, aperiodic, self-similar point set with a noninteger dimensionality: i.e., it is a *fractal.* Before describing the nature of this orbit in greater detail, we pause briefly to formally introduce the notion of a fractal set; this important concept will arise repeatedly throughout the book.

Fractal Sets and Dimensions. Consider a subset $A \in X$ and an arbitrary metric ∂. Let $N(A,\epsilon)$ be the smallest number of ϵ-balls needed to cover the set A:

$$N(A,\epsilon) = \text{ smallest integer } n \text{ such that } A \subset \bigcup_{i=1}^{n} b(x_i,\epsilon), \tag{2.16}$$

for some distinct set of points $\{x_i,\ i=1,2,\ldots,n\}$. If $N(A,\epsilon)$ increases as $N(a,\epsilon) \sim \epsilon^{-D}$ for $\epsilon \to 0$ then D is called the fractal dimension (sometimes also called the capacity) of the set A. Solving for D, we find that:

$$D_{\text{fractal}} = \lim_{\epsilon\to 0} \frac{\ln\ N(A,\epsilon)}{\ln\ (1/\epsilon)}. \tag{2.17}$$

That D_{fractal} gives the expected result for simple sets in Euclidean space is easy to see. If A consists of a single point, for example, we have $N(A,\epsilon)=1,\ \forall\epsilon$, and thus that $D_{\text{fractal}}=0$. Similarly, if A is a line segment of length L, then $N(A,\epsilon)=L/\epsilon$ so that $D_{\text{fractal}}=1$. In fact, for the usual n-dimensional Euclidean sets, the fractal dimension equals the topological dimension. There are more complicated sets, however, for which the two measures differ.

Consider the triadic Cantor set construction on the real line: let $x_0=[0,1]$ and x_1 be the set obtained from x_0 be deleting the open interval $(\frac{1}{3},\frac{2}{3})$. Let x_2 be the set obtained from x_1 be deleting the middle thirds $(\frac{1}{9},\frac{2}{9})$ and $(\frac{7}{9},\frac{8}{9})$. Continue in this fashion, letting $x_n = x_{n-1} - \bigcup_{i=0}^{\infty}\left(\frac{1+3i}{3^n},\frac{2+3i}{3^n}\right)$ (see figure 2.5). Then the Cantor set is the intersection $C=\bigcap_{n=0}^{\infty} x_n$. It is totally disconnected, compact, and uncountable.

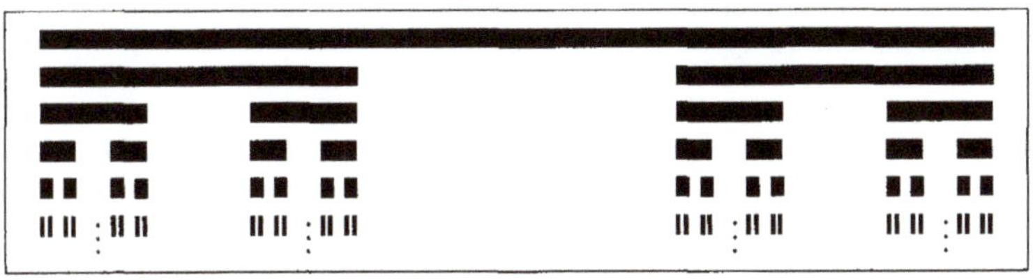

Fig. 2.5 First six steps of the construction of the triadic *Cantor* Set. The infinite-time limit point set has fractal dimension $D_{\text{fractal}} = \ln 2/\ln 3$.

Although the length of the Cantor set is zero—

$$L = 1 - \frac{1}{3} - \frac{2}{9} - \frac{4}{27} - \cdots = 1 - \frac{1}{3}\sum_{i=0}^{\infty}\left(\frac{2}{3}\right)^i = 0, \tag{2.18}$$

—its fractal dimension is *greater* than zero: since at the nth step of the construction $N(\epsilon)=2^n$ balls of size $\epsilon=(1/3)^n$ are needed to cover the set, we see immediately that:

$$D_{\text{fractal}}(Cantor) = \lim_{n\to\infty} \frac{\ln\ 2^n}{\ln\ 3^n} \sim 0.6309. \tag{2.19}$$

Although it is not the only such measure, the fractal dimension quantifies the intuitive belief that the Cantor set is somewhere "in-between" a point and a line. Several useful generalizations of D_{fractal} will be introduced later in this section.

Now that we have at least a passing familiarity with a fractal set, we return to addressing the question, *"What does the orbit for the Logistic map* (equation 2.9) *look like for* α_∞*?"* The answer is that the orbit is a fractal, with fractal dimension $D_{\text{fractal}} \sim 0.5388$ [Grass86]. Figure 2.6 shows the first six stages in the Cantor-set like construction.

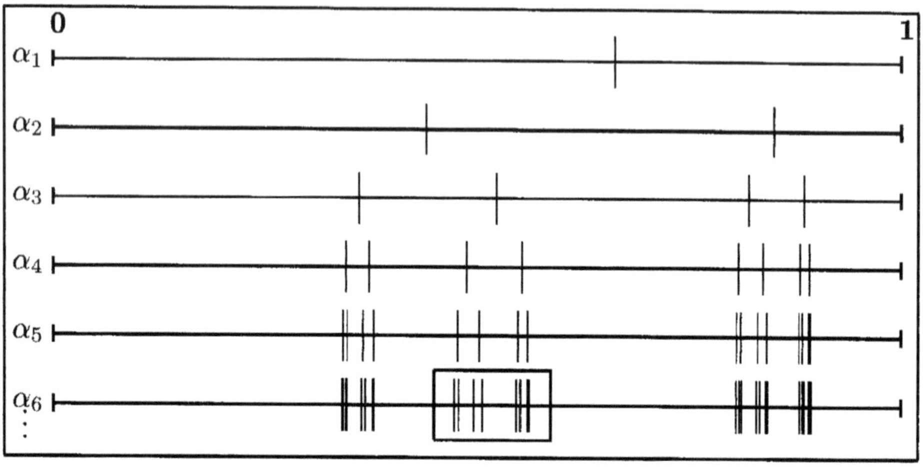

Fig. 2.6 Sets of stable attractors for the first six critical values of α. Note the self-similarity between the boxed subpattern for α_6 and the entire pattern for α_4 appearing two lines above. A Cantor-set-like fractal pattern appears in the limit $\alpha_{n\to\infty}$.

Universality. Feigenbaum's remarkable discovery consisted of the following two quantitative observations (see figure 2.7):

1. *Critical Parameter Convergence:* Feigenbaum's found that the convergence rate of the critical parameters, α_n, is in fact *geometric*; i.e., the α_n scale as $\alpha_n = \alpha_\infty - c\,\delta^{-n}$, where $n >> 1$ and c and δ are constants. A little calculation shows that

$$\delta \equiv \lim_{n\to\infty} \frac{\alpha_n - \alpha_{n-1}}{\alpha_{n+1} - \alpha_n} = 4.6692016091\cdots . \tag{2.20}$$

This first universal *Feigenbaum* constant, δ, describes the geometric convergence of critical parameters, α_n, for all one-dimensional maps $x_{n+1} = f(x_n)$, where $f(x)$ has a single locally quadratic maximum on $[0,1]$.* For example, while the set of critical α's, α'_1, α'_2, $\ldots$, α'_∞, calculated for the system defined by $x_{n+1} = \alpha \sin \pi x_n$, will be distinct from the set of α's computed above for the Logistic equation ($\alpha'_\infty \sim 0.892$), their geometric convergence to α'_∞ is determined by the same constant, δ.

*The technical condition that has to be met is that the so-called *Schwarzian* derivative of $f(x)$, $f'_S \equiv (f'''(x)/f'(x)) - \frac{3}{2}(f''(x)/f'(x))^2$, must be negative on $[0,1]$.

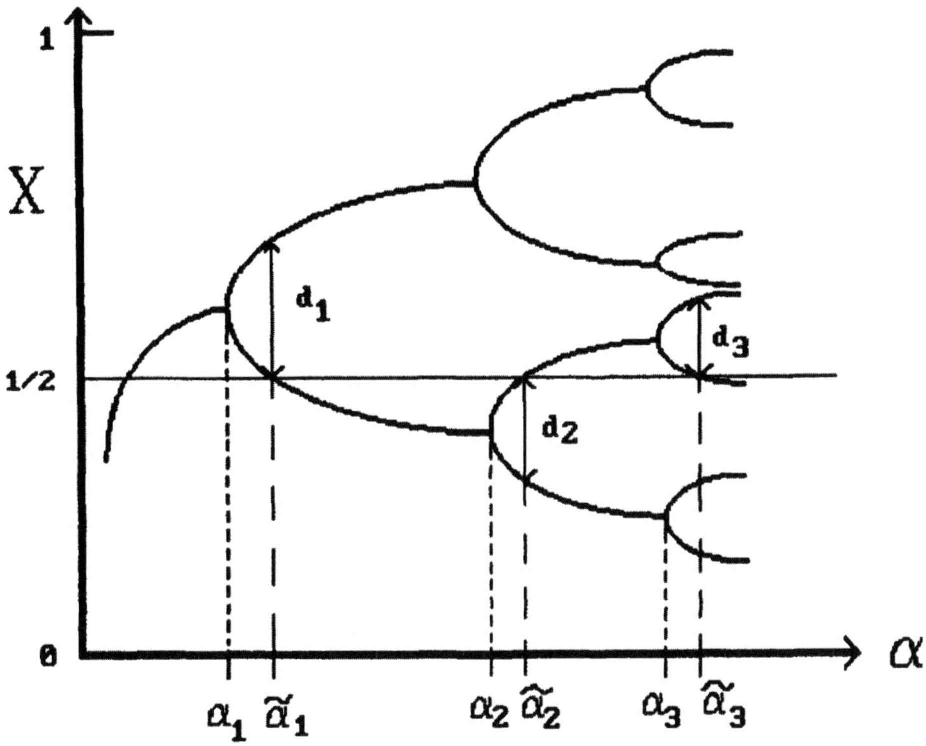

Fig. 2.7 An illustration of some parameters describing pitchfork bifurcations used to define *universality*; see text.

2. *Scaling of Pitchfork-branch Splittings.* We define a *supercycle* to be a cycle, $\{x_i^*\}$, such that $\prod_{i=1}^{2^n} f'(x_i^*) = 0$. In particular, since $f'_\alpha(x) = 0$ only when $x = 1/2$, we know that the point $x = 1/2$ must always be an element of a supercycle. Define d_n to be the smallest distance between $x = 1/2$ and the nearest other point on the same 2^n-supercycle:

$$d_n \equiv f_{\tilde{\alpha}_n}^{2^{n-1}}\left(\frac{1}{2}\right) - \frac{1}{2}, \tag{2.21}$$

where $\tilde{\alpha}_n$ defines the new n^{th} critical value of α, $\alpha_n < \tilde{\alpha}_n < \alpha_{n+1}$, at which $x = 1/2$ becomes an element of the 2^n-cycle. Feigenbaum's second observation was that the relative scale of successive splittings at $\tilde{\alpha}_1$, $\tilde{\alpha}_2$, ... approaches another universal constant, Δ:

$$\Delta \equiv \lim_{n\to\infty} \frac{d_n}{d_{n+1}} = 2.5029078750\cdots. \tag{2.22}$$

Note that the convergence rate of $\tilde{\alpha}$ follows the same form as for α_n: $\tilde{\alpha}_n - \tilde{\alpha}_\infty = c'\delta^{-n}$, where δ is the same as above and $\tilde{\alpha}_\infty = \alpha_\infty$.

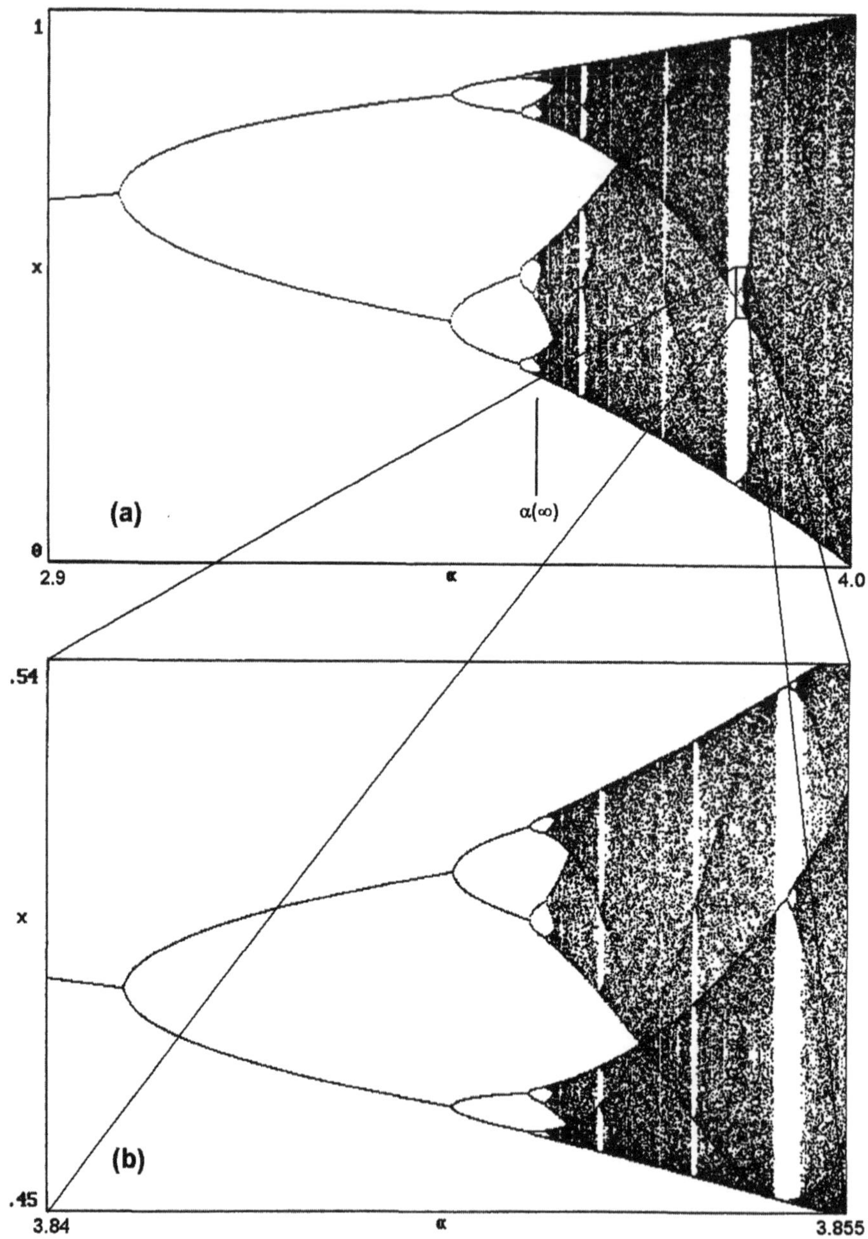

Fig. 2.8 (a) Attractor set of the logistic map for $2.9 < \alpha \leq 4$; (b) Attractor set of the logistic map for $3.840 < \alpha < 3.855$; i.e., a blowup of the boxed region shown on the right hand side in (a); see text for details.

Behavior for $\alpha > \alpha_\infty$. What happens for $\alpha > \alpha_\infty$? The simple answer is that the logistic map exhibits a transition to chaos, with a variety of different attractors for $\alpha_\infty < \alpha \leq 4$ exhibiting exponential divergence of nearby points. To leave it at that, however, would surely be a great disservice to the extraordinarily beautiful manner in which this transition takes place.

An overview is provided by figure 2.8. Figure 2.8-(a) shows the numerically determined attractor sets for all $2.9 < \alpha \leq 4$; figure 2.8-(b)—lest it be thought that the "white" regions in figure 2.8-(a) are artifacts of the printing process—shows a blowup view of the windowed region within one of those wide white bands in figure 2.8-(a).

The general behavior is summarized as follows:

1. The attracting sets for many—but not all—$\alpha > \alpha_\infty$ are aperiodic and chaotic on various subintervals of $[0, 1]$.

2. As α increases, the chaotic intervals merge together by inverse bifurcations obeying the same δ, Δ scalings as in the $\alpha < \alpha_\infty$ region, until the attracting set becomes distributed over the entire unit interval at $\alpha = 4$.

3. There are a large number of windows of finite width within which the attracting set is a stable periodic cycle; chaotic and periodic regions are in fact densely interwoven. The largest window—a snapshot of which is shown in figure 2.8-(b)—corresponds to a stable 3-cycle and spans the width $3.8284\cdots < \alpha < 3.8415\cdots$.

4. The periodic windows harbor m-cycles, $m = 3, 5, 6, \ldots$, that undergo period doubling bifurcations, $m \to 2m \to 4m \to \cdots$, at a set of critical parameters, $\hat{\alpha}_1, \hat{\alpha}_2, \ldots$, that again scale as $\hat{\alpha}_n = \hat{\alpha}_\infty - \hat{c}\,\delta^{-n}$, with the same universal δ that appears in equation 2.20.

5. Other periodic windows harbor period *triplings*, *quadruplings*, etc., occurring at different sets of $\{\hat{\alpha}_i\}$, but all of which scale in the familiar fashion (albeit with different universal $\hat{\delta} \neq \delta$).

6. Although a rigorous mathematical analysis of the $\alpha_\infty < \alpha < 4$ region is at best very difficult to come by, it turns out that we have already discussed much of the most chaotic behavior, which occurs at $\alpha = 4$ and covers the entire unit interval. A simple change of variables suffices to show that the behavior of the logistic equation at $\alpha = 4$ is effectively identical to that of the Bernoulli map, the properties of which were discussed at some length in the preceding section. Define θ_n, $0 < \theta_n < 1$, by $x_n \equiv \frac{1}{2}(1 - \cos 2\pi\theta_n)$, and substitute this expression into equation 2.9:*

*Our earlier discussion of the randomness of the iterates of the Bernoulli map therefore applies equally well to the behavior of the $\alpha = 4$ attractor set of the logistic equation (see page 78).

$$\begin{aligned} x_{n+1} = 4x_n(1-x_n) \quad &\Longrightarrow \\ \frac{1}{2}(1-\cos 2\pi\theta_{n+1}) &= 4\cdot\frac{1}{2}(1-\cos 2\pi\theta_n)\cdot\frac{1}{2}(1+\cos 2\pi\theta_n), \\ \sin^2\pi\theta_{n+1} &= 1-\cos^2 2\pi\theta_n = \sin^2 2\pi\theta_n, \\ \theta_{n+1} &= 2\theta_n \mod 1. \end{aligned} \tag{2.23}$$

2.1.4 *Qualitative Characterization of Chaos*

What are the criteria by which dynamical systems can be judged to be chaotic? Suppose you are given a dynamical system, S, or a set of time-series data of S's behavior of the form:

$$\vec{\varsigma}(t) = \varsigma(t_0), \varsigma(t_1), \varsigma(t_2), \ldots, \varsigma(t_N), \tag{2.24}$$

where $\varsigma(t_i)$ represents the state of S at time t_i and S's state is sampled every $t_{i+1} = t_i + \Delta t$ time steps for some fixed Δt. *How can you tell from this time series of values whether S is chaotic?* In this section we give four qualitative criteria:

- *The time series "looks chaotic"*
- *The Poincare map is space-filling*
- *The power spectrum exhibits broadband noise*
- *The autocorrelation function decays rapidly*

2.1.4.1 *Time Dependence*

Using the time series method is both intuitive and easy. The gross behavior of a system can often be learned merely by studying the temporal behavior of each of its variables. The system is likely to be chaotic if such temporal plots are nonrecurrent and appear jagged and irregular. Moreover, sensitivity to initial conditions can be easily tested by simultaneously plotting two trajectories of the same system but starting from slightly different initial states. Figure 2.9, for example, shows the divergence of two trajectories for the logistic map with $\alpha = 4$ whose initial points—$x_0 = 0.12345$ and $x_0^* = 0.12346$—differ only in the 5th decimal place.

2.1.4.2 *Poincare Maps*

Recall that the Poincare map is a method for visualizing continuous trajectories by constructing an equivalent discrete-time mapping by a periodic "stroboscopic" sampling of points along an orbit. Consider a two-dimensional trajectory in three-dimensional space. The structure of such a trajectory can be readily identified by plotting its intersections with a two-dimensional slice through the three-dimensional space in which it lives. The system is likely to be chaotic if the discrete point set on the resulting Poincare plot is fractal or space-filling.

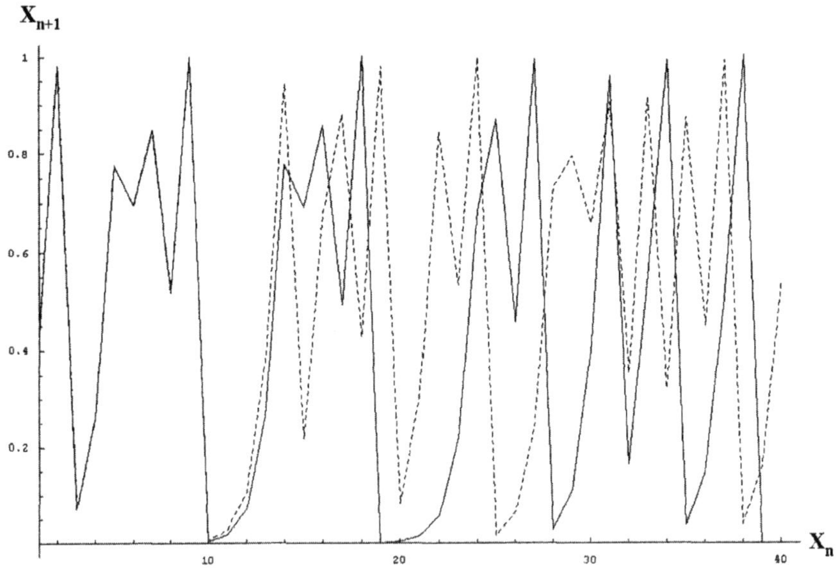

Fig. 2.9 Divergence of trajectories for two nearby initial points (differing by $x_0 - x_0^* = 10^{-4}$) for the logistic equation for $\alpha = 4.0$.

2.1.4.3 *Autocorrelation Function*

The autocorrelation function, $C(\tau)$, of a time series measures the degree to which one part of the trajectory is correlated with itself at another part. If a series is completely random in time, then different parts of the trajectory are completely uncorrelated and the autocorrelation function approaches zero. Put another way, no part of the trajectory harbors any useful information for predicting any later part of the trajectory. As the correlation between parts of a trajectory increases, parts of a trajectory contain an increasing amount of information that can be used to predict later parts and the value of the autocorrelation function thus increases.

For continuous signals, the autocorrelation function $C(\tau)$ is defined by:

$$C(\tau) = \lim_{T\to\infty} \frac{1}{T} \int_0^T c(t)\, c(t+\tau)\, dt, \text{ where } c(t) = \varsigma(t) - \lim_{T\to\infty} \frac{1}{T} \int_0^T \varsigma(t)\, dt. \quad (2.25)$$

For discrete systems, $C(\tau)$ is defined by:

$$C(\tau) = \lim_{N\to\infty} \frac{1}{N} \sum_{i=1}^{N} c(t_i)\, c(t_i+\tau), \text{ where } c(t_i) = \varsigma(t_i) - \lim_{N\to\infty} \frac{1}{N} \sum_{j=1}^{N} \varsigma(t_j). \quad (2.26)$$

A rapid decay (say, with an exponential dropoff) of $C(\tau)$ is a criterion for the presence of chaos.

2.1.4.4 *Power Spectrum*

If a system is chaotic that means its signal is irregular and aperiodic in time. A measure that is often used to distinguish between multiply periodic behavior (that can also appear irregular and complicated) and chaos is the power spectrum of the signal, $P(\omega)$. For continuous systems it is defined by:

$$P(\omega) = |\varsigma(\omega)|^2, \tag{2.27}$$

where $\varsigma(\omega)$ is the Fourier-transform of the signal $\varsigma(t)$:

$$\varsigma(\omega) = \lim_{T\to\infty} \int_0^T \varsigma(t)\, e^{i\omega t}\, dt. \tag{2.28}$$

For discrete systems, the Fourier-transform of the signal $\varsigma(t)$ is defined by:

$$\varsigma_k = \frac{1}{N} \sum_{t=0}^{N-1} \varsigma(t)\, e^{2\pi ikt/N}. \tag{2.29}$$

In either case, for multiply periodic motion the power spectrum consists only of discrete lines of the corresponding frequencies. Chaotic motion, on the other hand, induces broadband noise in $P(\omega)$, that is mostly concentrated in the lower frequencies.

2.1.5 *Quantitative Characterization of Chaos*

The previous section introduced several qualitative criteria for the presence of chaos in a dynamical system. In this section we define a set of quantitative measures of chaos:

- *Lyapunov exponents*
- *Generalized entropies and fractal dimensions*

2.1.5.1 *Lyapunov Exponents*

As we have seen, a fundamental property of chaotic motion is *sensitivity to small changes to initial conditions.* Initially closely separated starting conditions evolving along regular dynamical trajectories diverge only linearly in time; a chaotic evolution, on the other hand, leads to an exponential divergence in time. *Lyapunov characteristic exponents* quantify this divergence—for both conservative and dissipative systems—by measuring the mean rate of exponential divergence of initially neighboring trajectories.

Consider two initial points of a one-dimensional trajectory—x_0 and $x_0^* = x_0+\varepsilon$—separated by some small quantity ε. Suppose each of these points evolves according to the map $x_{n+1} = f(x_n)$, for some function f. Figure 2.10 shows that after N

steps, the Lyapunov exponent $\lambda(x_0)$ measures the exponential separation between the Nth iterates of x_0 and x_0^*, or between $f^N(x_0)$ and $f^N(x_0+\varepsilon)$, respectively.

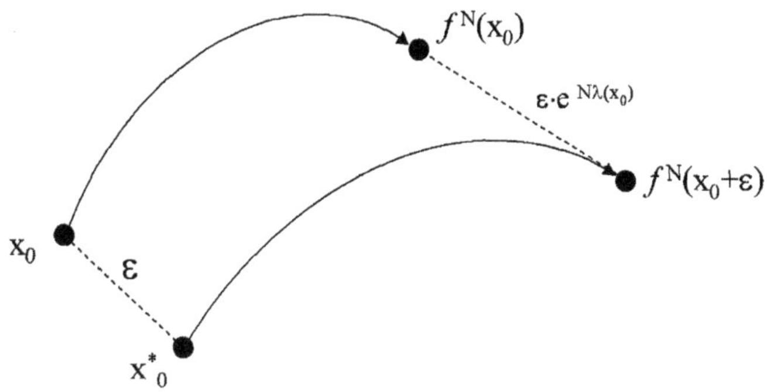

Fig. 2.10 Schematic definition of *Lyapunov exponent*; see text for details.

From figure 2.10, we see that:

$$\varepsilon e^{N\lambda(x_0)} = \left| f^N(x_0+\varepsilon) - f^N(x_0) \right|, \tag{2.30}$$

which in the limit as $N, \varepsilon \to \infty$ yields the following expression for $\lambda(x_0)$:

$$\begin{aligned} \lambda(x_0) &= \lim_{N,\varepsilon\to\infty} \tfrac{1}{N} \log \left| \tfrac{f^N(x_0+\varepsilon)-f^N(x_0)}{\varepsilon} \right|, \\ &= \lim_{N\to\infty} \tfrac{1}{N} \log \left| \prod_{i=0}^{N-1} f'(x_i) \right| = \lim_{N\to\infty} \tfrac{1}{N} \sum_{i=0}^{N-1} \log |f'(x_i)|, \end{aligned} \tag{2.31}$$

where $f'(x_0)$ is the derivative of the function f evaluated at the point x_0. Thus $e^{\lambda(x_0)}$ is the average factor by which the distance between initially closely separated points becomes stretched after one iteration. If $\lambda \le 0$, nearby trajectories tend to converge rather than diverge and the motion is *regular*; if $\lambda > 0$, nearby trajectories tend to diverge from one another and the motion is *chaotic.*

As an example, consider the logistic map (equation 2.9). A straightforward formal application of equation 2.31 gives:

$$\lambda = \lim_{i\to\infty} \frac{\alpha}{i} \sum_{j=0}^{i-1} \ln\ |(1-2x_j)|\,. \tag{2.32}$$

Figure 2.11 shows a numerically obtained plot of λ vs. α for $2.9 \le \alpha \le 4$.* Consistent with our earlier observations of the behavior of this map, we see that (1) $\lambda \le 0$ for all $\alpha < \alpha_\infty$, (2) $\lambda > 0$ for most $\alpha > \alpha_\infty$, and (3) that there are multiple windows in the chaotic regime for which λ dips down below zero and the attractor thus becomes periodic. Finally, we note that Feigenbaum's ubiquitous universal

*This plot is obtained by smoothing over 1100 equally spaced points ($\delta\alpha \sim 0.001$), with each point representing an average over 10,000 iterations.

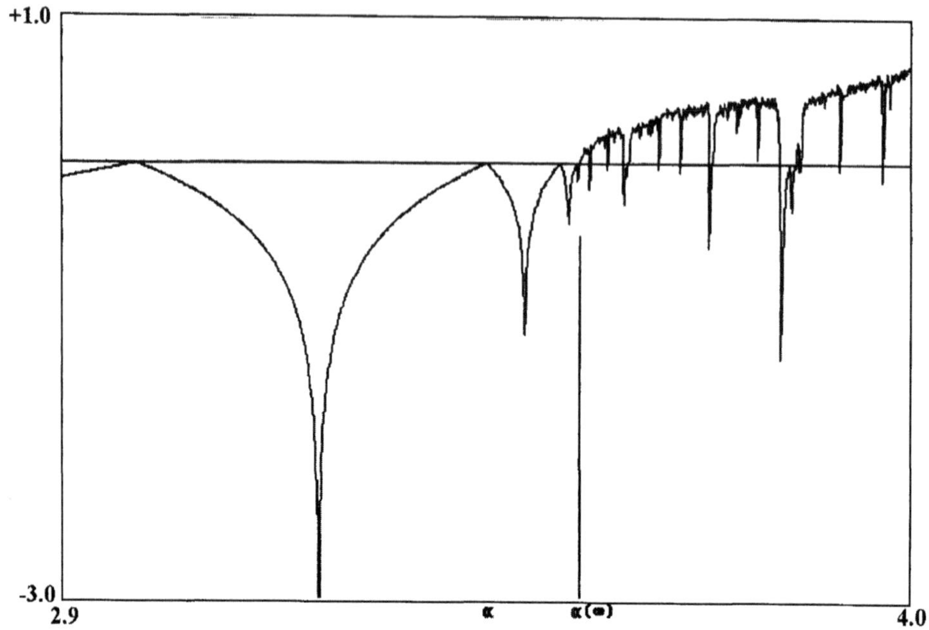

Fig. 2.11 *Lyapunov* exponent versus α for $2.9 \le \alpha \le 4$

constant δ shows up even here: it can be shown that near α_∞, $\lambda \sim |\alpha - \alpha_\infty|^\eta$, where $\eta = \log 2/\log \delta$.

Information–Theoretic Interpretation. As defined above, the Lyapunov exponents effectively determine the degree of "chaos" that exists in a dynamical system by measuring the rate of the exponential divergence of initially closely neighboring trajectories. A suggestive alternative interpretation of their numeric content, is an information-theoretic one. It is not hard to see that Lyapunov exponents are very closely related to the rate of information loss in a dynamical system (this point will be made more precise during our discussion of entropy in the next section).

Consider, for example, a one-dimensional interval $[0,1]$, that is partitioned into n equal sized bins. Assuming that a point x_0 is equally likely to fall into any one of these bins, learning which bin in fact contains x_0 therefore constitutes an *information gain*

$$I_0 = -\sum_{i=1}^{n} \frac{1}{n} \log_2 \frac{1}{n} = \log_2 n, \tag{2.33}$$

where $\log_2$ is the logarithm to the base 2. Now consider a simple linear one-dimensional map $f(x) = \alpha x$, where $x \in [0,1]$ and $\alpha > 1$. By changing the length of the interval, and thereby decreasing the effective resolution, by a factor $\alpha = |f'(0)|$, a single application of the map $f(x)$ results in an effective *information loss:*

$$\begin{aligned}
\delta I &= I_1 - I_0, \\
&= -\sum_{i=1}^{n/\alpha} \frac{\alpha}{n} \log_2 \frac{\alpha}{n} + \sum_{i=1}^{n} \frac{1}{n} \log_2 \frac{1}{n}, \\
&= -\log_2 |f'(0)|.
\end{aligned} \tag{2.34}$$

Generalizing to the case when $|f'(x)|$ depends on position, and averaging over a large number of iterations, we obtain the following expression for the mean information loss:

$$\begin{aligned}
< \delta I > &= -\lim_{N \to \infty} \frac{1}{N} \sum_{i=1}^{N-1} \log_2 |f'(x_i)|, \\
&= \lambda / \log 2,
\end{aligned} \tag{2.35}$$

where the latter expression is obtained by direct comparison with equation 2.31, defining the one-dimensional Lyapunov exponent, λ. We thus see that, in one dimension, λ measures the average loss of information about the position of a point in $[0, 1]$ after one iteration.

2.1.5.2 *Entropies and Dimensions*

While Lyapunov exponents, as discussed in the last section, confirm the presence of chaos by quantifying the magnitude of the exponential divergence of initially neighboring trajectories, they do not provide any useful structural or statistical information about a strange attractor. Such information is instead provided by various *fractal dimensions.*

Recall that fractals are geometric objects characterized by some form of self-similarity; that is, parts of a fractal, when magnified to an appropriate scale, appear similar to the whole. Fractals are thus objects that harbor an effectively infinite amount of detail on all levels. Coastlines of islands and continents and terrain features are approximate fractals. A magnified image of a part of a leaf is similar to an image of the entire leaf. Strange attractors also typically have a fractal structure.

Loosely speaking, a fractal dimension specifies the minimum number of variables that are needed to specify the fractal. For a one-dimensional line, for example, say the x-axis, one piece of information, the x-variable, is needed to specify any position on the line. The fractal dimension of the x-axis is said to be equal to 1. Similarly, two coordinates are needed to specify a position on a two-dimensional plane, so that the fractal dimension of a plane is equal to 2. Genuine (i.e., *interesting*) fractals are objects whose fractal dimension is *noninteger.*

Fractal (or "Box") Dimension. The fractal dimension was introduced earlier in equation 2.17 (on page 85). If the minimum number of d-dimensional boxes of side ϵ needed to cover the attractor $\mathcal{A}$, $N(\epsilon)$, scales as $N(\epsilon) \propto \epsilon^{\alpha}$ for some constant α, that constant is called the *fractal dimension* (sometimes referred to as the *Kolmogorov capacity*, or just *capacity*) of $\mathcal{A}$. In other words,

$$D_F = \lim_{\epsilon \to 0} \frac{\ln[N(\epsilon)]}{\ln(1/\epsilon)}. \tag{2.36}$$

Since $N(\epsilon) \approx D_F \log(1/\epsilon)$, D_F essentially tells us how much information is needed to specify the location of $\mathcal{A}$ to within a specified accuracy, ϵ. In practice, one obtains values of $N(\epsilon)$ for a variety of ϵ's and estimates D_F from the slope of a plot of $\ln(N(\epsilon))$ versus $\ln(1/\epsilon)$.

Notice that while D_F clearly depends on the metric properties of the space in which the attractor, $\mathcal{A}$, is embedded—and thus provides some structural information about $\mathcal{A}$—it does not take into account any structural inhomogeneities in the $\mathcal{A}$. In particular, since the box bookkeeping only keeps track of whether or not an overlap exists between a given box and $\mathcal{A}$, the individual frequencies with which each box is visited are ignored. This oversite is corrected for by the so-called information dimension, which depends on the probability measure on $\mathcal{A}$.

Information Dimension. As above, we partition the d-dimensional phase-space into boxes of volume ϵ^d. The probability of finding a point of an attractor $\mathcal{A}$ in box number i $(i = 1, 2, \ldots, \mathcal{B}(\epsilon))$, is

$$p_i(\epsilon) = \frac{N_i(\epsilon)}{N_{\mathcal{A}}}, \tag{2.37}$$

where $N_i(\epsilon)$ is the number of points in the ith box and $N_{\mathcal{A}}$ is the total number of points in $\mathcal{A}$; $p_i(\epsilon)$ is thus the relative frequency with which the ith box is visited.

The amount of information required to specify the state of the system to within an accuracy ϵ (or, equivalently, the information gain in making a measurement that is uncertain by an amount ϵ), is given by:

$$I(\epsilon) = -\sum_{i=1}^{N(\epsilon)} p_i(\epsilon) \ln p_i(\epsilon). \tag{2.38}$$

The *information dimension*, D_I, of an attractor $\mathcal{A}$ is then defined to be:

$$D_I = \lim_{\epsilon \to 0} \frac{I(\epsilon)}{\ln(1/\epsilon)}. \tag{2.39}$$

Notice that if $\mathcal{A}$ is contained in a *single* box, b_i, then $p_i(\epsilon) = \delta_{ij} \frac{1}{N(\epsilon)} \Longrightarrow I = 0$. On the other hand, if each box is visited equally often—i.e., if $p_i(\epsilon) = 1/N(\epsilon)$, for all i—then $I(\epsilon) = \ln[N(\epsilon)] \Longrightarrow D_I = D_F$. For unequal probabilities, $I(\epsilon) < \ln[N(\epsilon)]$, so that, in general, $D_I \leq D_F$.

Correlation Dimension. Another important measure—called the *correlation dimension*—is based on the correlation integral $C(\varepsilon)$, which measures the probability of finding two points of an attractor in a box of size ε:

$$\begin{aligned}
\sum_{i=1}^{N(\epsilon)} p_i^2(\epsilon) &= \text{probability that two points on } \mathcal{A} \text{ occupy same } \epsilon^d \text{ box} \\
&\sim \text{probability that the distance between two points on} \\
&\quad \text{the attractor is less than or equal to `}\epsilon\text{'} \\
&= \lim_{N\to\infty} \frac{1}{N^2} \{\# \text{ of pairs `}ij\text{' whose distance } |\mathbf{x}_i - \mathbf{y}_j| \le \epsilon\} \\
&= \frac{1}{N^2} \sum_{\substack{i,j=1 \\ i\neq j}}^{N} \theta\left(\epsilon - |\mathbf{x}_i - \mathbf{x}_j|\right), \\
&= C(\epsilon) \text{ (see equation ??)}
\end{aligned} \tag{2.40}$$

where $|\cdots|$ denotes the Euclidean distance, and $\theta(x)$ is the *Heaviside* function:

$$\theta(x) = \begin{cases} 1 & \text{if } x > 0, \\ 0 & \text{if } x \le 0. \end{cases} \tag{2.41}$$

$C(\varepsilon)$ essentially counts the number of pairs of points falling within a hypersphere of radius ε that is centered on each point (and normalizes by a factor $1/N^2$). The correlation dimension, D_{corr}, is then defined as:

$$D_C = \lim_{\epsilon\to 0} \frac{\ln\left(C(\epsilon)\right)}{\ln(\epsilon)}. \tag{2.42}$$

Grassberger and Procaccia [Grass83] show that $0 \le D_C \le D_I$, where D_I is the information dimension defined in equation 2.39. The correlation integral and correlation dimension can be used to determine two additional properties from experimental time series data: (1) the *embedding dimension*, D_E—the dimension D_E in the time series $\vec{x}(t_i) = \{\varsigma(t_i), \varsigma(t_i+\tau), \ldots, \varsigma(t_i + (D_E - 1)\,\tau)\}$ above which D_{corr} no longer changes is the (minimal) embedding dimension of the attractor; (2) a *measure of distinction between deterministic chaos and random noise*: suppose there is a strange attractor embedded in d-dimensional space and an external random noise is added. Each point on the attractor becomes surrounded by a uniform d-dimensional cluster of points. Suppose the radius of this cluster is ε_{noise}. Then for $\varepsilon >>$ enoise, the correlation integral $C(\varepsilon)$ counts these clusters as points and the slope of the $\log[C(\varepsilon)]$ versus $\log(\varepsilon)$ plot yields the correlation dimension of the attractor. For $\varepsilon < \varepsilon_{noise}$, most of the points counted by $C(\varepsilon)$ fall within the uniformly filled d-dimensional clusters and the slope of the $\log[C(\varepsilon)]$ versus $\log(\varepsilon)$ plot crosses over to d.

Generalized Fractal Dimensions. The three dimensions introduced above, D_F, D_I and D_C, are actually three members of an (uncountably infinite) hierarchy of generalized fractal dimensions [Hent83]. The hierarchy is defined by generalizing the information function $I(\epsilon)$ (equation 2.38) used in defining D_I to the νth-order *Renyi information* function, $I_\nu(\epsilon)$:

$$I_\nu(\epsilon) \equiv \frac{1}{1-\nu} \ln \sum_{i=1}^{N(\epsilon)} p_i^\nu(\epsilon), \qquad \nu \geq 0, \tag{2.43}$$

where $p_i(\epsilon)$ is, as above, the probability of finding a point of an attractor, $\mathcal{A}$, in box number i ($i = 1, 2, \ldots, \mathcal{B}(\epsilon)$).

Using this generalized information we get the νth-order generalization of D_I (equation 2.39), D_ν:

$$D_\nu = \lim_{\epsilon \to 0} \frac{I_\nu(\epsilon)}{\ln(1/\epsilon)}. \tag{2.44}$$

It can be shown that D_ν is a non-decreasing function of ν [hent83]; i.e. that $D_\nu \leq D_{\nu'}$ for all ν, ν' such that $\nu \geq \nu'$.

Lyapunov Dimension. An interesting attempt to link a purely *static* property of an attractor, $\mathcal{A}$—as embodied by its fractal dimension, D_F (equation 2.36)—to a *dynamic* property, as expressed by its set of Lyapunov characteristic exponents, λ_i, was first made by Kaplan and Yorke in 1979 [kaplan79]. Defining the *Lyapunov dimension*, D_L to be:

$$D_L = j + \frac{\sum_{i=1}^{j} \lambda_i}{|\lambda_{j+1}|}, \tag{2.45}$$

where j denotes the largest λ such that $\sum_{i=1}^{j} \lambda_i \geq 0$, the *Kaplan-Yorke Conjecture* is that $D_F = D_L$. Although the equality appears to be rigorously true only for completely homogeneous attractors, it is often approximately satisfied by inhomogeneous attractors as well. Because the calculation of λ_i is a relatively easy one, this simple relation has proven to be useful for obtaining quick characterizations of fractal attractors.

2.1.6 *Time-Series Forecasting and Predictability*

As has been repeatedly stressed throughout this discussion, chaos theory tells us that a chaotic dynamical system is sensitive to initial conditions. This, in turn, implies that chaos precludes long-term predictability of the behavior of the system. The essence of chaos, after all, is the unpredictability of individual orbits; thinks of the random sequence of heads and tails from tosses of an unbiased coin or the dripping of a faucet. On the other hand, suppose a system's orbit lies on a strange attractor. If we know something about this attractor—its general shape, for example, perhaps along with an estimate of the visitation frequencies to its different parts—this clearly provides some information about what the deterministic (albeit chaotic) system is doing. This added information, in turn, may be sufficient to allow us to make predictions about certain short-term (and long-term) behavioral trends of the system.

Chaotic dynamics is often misunderstood to mean *random* dynamics. Strictly speaking, since chaos is spawned from a deterministic process, its apparent irregularity stems from an intrinsic magnification of an external uncertainty, such as that due to a measurement of initial conditions. Sensitivity to initial conditions amplifies an initially small uncertainty into an exponentially large one; or, in other words, short-term determinism evolves into long-term randomness. Thus, the important distinction is not between chaos and randomness, but between chaotic dynamical systems that have low-dimensional attractors and those that have high-dimensional attractors [Eub89].

For example, if a time series of evolving states of a system is generated by a very high dimensional attractor (or if the dynamics is modeled in a state space whose dimension is less than that of the attractor), then it will be essentially impossible to gather enough information from the time series to exploit the underlying determinism. In this case, the apparent randomness will in fact have become a very real randomness, at least from a predictability standpoint. On the other hand, if the time series is generated by a relatively low dimensional attractor, it is possible to exploit the underlying determinism to predict certain aspects of the overall behavior. A powerful technique to make the underlying determinism of a chaotic time series stand out is the so-called embedding technique.

Consider some real-world data, tabulated as a time series, $\vec{\varsigma} = \{\varsigma(t_1), \ldots, \varsigma(t_N)\}$. The data may represent observations of the closing prices of the Dow Jones industrials, annual defense expenditures, or combat losses on the battlefield.

The embedding technique is a method of reconstructing a state space from the time series. It assumes that if the embedding dimension is large enough, the behavior of whatever system is responsible for generating the particular series of measurements can be described by a finite dimensional attractor. Its main strength lies in providing detailed information about the behavior of degrees-of-freedom of a system other than the ones that are directly observed. Estimates of the error introduced by extrapolating the data can also be made.

The embedding technique consists of creating the state vectors $\vec{x}_i$ from $\vec{\varsigma}$ according to:

$$\vec{x}_i = (\varsigma(t_i), \varsigma(t_i + \tau), \ldots, \varsigma(t_i + (m-1)\,\tau))\,, \tag{2.46}$$

where τ is a fixed time delay. In principle, the choice of τ is arbitrary, though criteria for its selection exist. If the dynamics takes place on an attractor of dimension d, then a necessary condition for "uncovering" the underlying determinism is $m \geq d$. It can be shown that if r is the dimension of a manifold containing the attractor, than almost any embedding in $d = 2r + 1$ dimensions will preserve the topological properties of the attractor. Of course, the embedding technique does not work for all time series, and the amount of information it uncovers about the underlying determinism for a given time series may be sufficient only to yield very short-term predictions. Nonetheless, the technique has proven to be very powerful in uncovering patterns in data that are not otherwise (obviously) visible. A detailed discussion is given in reference [Kantz97].

2.1.7 *Chaotic Control*

Suppose you have a physical system that exhibits chaos. Is there a way to still use the system—that is, to allow the system to evolve naturally according to its prescribed dynamics—but in such a way as to eliminate that system's chaotic behavior? One way, of course, might be to physically alter the system in some (possibly costly) way. But what if such a restructuring is not an option? What if the only available option is to slightly "tweak" one of the system's control parameters?

It has recently been shown by Ott, et. al. [Ott94] and Romeiras, et. al. [Rome92] that the extreme sensitivity of chaotic systems to small perturbations to initial conditions (the so-called "butterfly effect") can be exploited to stabilize regular dynamic behaviors and to effectively "direct" chaotic trajectories to a desired state. The critical idea is that chaotic attractors typically have embedded within them a dense set of unstable periodic orbits. That is to say, an infinite number of unstable periodic orbits typically co-exist with the chaotic motion. By a periodic orbit, we mean an orbit that repeats itself after some finite time. If the system were precisely on an unstable periodic orbit, it would remain there forever. Such orbits are unstable because the smallest perturbation from the periodic orbit (as might, for example, be due to external random noise) is magnified exponentially in time and the system orbit moves rapidly away from the periodic orbit. The result is that while these unstable periodic orbits are always present, they are not usually seen in practice. Instead, one sees a chaotic orbit that bounces around in an apparently random fashion. Ironically, chaotic control is a capability that has no counterpart in nonchaotic systems The reason is that the trajectories in nonchaotic systems are stable and thus relatively impervious to desired control.

The basic strategy consists of three steps:

(1) *Find some unstable periodic orbits embedded within the chaotic motion*
(2) *Examine these orbits to find an orbit that yields an improved system performance*
(3) *Apply small controlling perturbations to direct the orbit to the desired periodic (or steady state) motion*

Once a desired unstable periodic orbit has been selected, the nature of a chaotic orbit assures us that eventually the random-appearing wanderings of the chaotic orbit will bring it close to the selected unstable periodic orbit. When this happens the controlling perturbations can be applied. Moreover, if there is any noise present, these controlling perturbations can be applied repeatedly to keep the trajectory on the desired orbit.

We make a few general comments:

- Chaotic control is applicable to both continuous and discrete dynamical systems.
- Chaos can be controlled using information from previously observed system behavior. Thus it can be applied to experimental (i.e. real-world) situations in which no model need be available to define the underlying dynamics.
- While chaotic control applies strictly to systems that are described with a relatively few variables, it should be remembered that the behavior of many high (and even infinite) dimensional systems is often described by a low dimensional attractor.
- Before settling into a desired controlled orbit the trajectory goes through a chaotic transient whose duration diverges as the maximum allowed size of the control perturbations approaches zero
- Small noise can result in occasional bursts in which the orbit strays far from the desired orbit
- Any number of different orbits can be stabilized, where the switching from one to another orbit is regulated by corresponding control perturbations

A recent survey article [Shin92] lists applications for communications (in which chaotic fluctuations can be put to use to send controlled, pre-planned signals), for physiology (in which chaos is controlled in heart rhythms), for fluid mechanics (in which chaotic convection currents can be controlled) and chemical reactions. As another recent example, a few years ago NASA used small amounts of residual hydrazine fuel to steer the ISEE-3/ICE spacecraft to its rendezvous with a comet 50 million miles away. This was possible because of the sensitivity of the three-body problem of celestial mechanics to small perturbations. An excellent text on chaotic control is *From Chaos to Order*, by Chen and Dong [ChenG98].

2.2 Complex Adaptive Systems

"There is a constant and intimate contact among the things that coexist and coevolve in the universe, a sharing of bonds and messages that makes reality into a stupendous network of interaction and communication."

—Ervin Laszlo, *Philosopher & Systems Theorist*

While it is difficult to rigorously define a "complex system" or even what is meant by "complexity" without first introducing a few technical concepts (as will be done shortly), there are wonderful examples of complex systems just about everywhere we look in nature, from the turbulence in fluids to global weather patterns to beautifully intricate galactic structures to the complexity of living organisms. All such systems share at least this one property: they all consist of a large assemblage of interconnected, mutually (and typically nonlinearly) interacting parts.

Moreover, their aggregate behavior is *emergent.* That is to say, the properties of the *whole* are not possessed by, nor are they directly derivable from, any of the *parts;* a water molecule is not a vortex, and a neuron is not conscious. A complex system must therefore be understood not just by listing the set of components out of which it is constructed, but by knowing topology of interconnections, knowing the interactions among those components, and—most importantly—by observing how it evolves over time and under different conditions.

Gases, fluids, crystals, and lasers are all familiar kinds of complex systems from physics. Chemical reactions, in which a large number of molecules conspire to produce new molecules, are also good examples. In biology, there are DNA molecules built up from amino acids, cells built from molecules, and organisms built from cells. On a larger scale, the national and global economies and human culture as a whole are also complex systems, exhibiting their own brand of global cooperative behavior. One of the most far-reaching ideas of this sort is James Lovelock's controversial "Gaia" hypothesis, which asserts that the entire earth—molten core, biological ecosystems, atmospheric weather patterns and all—is essentially one huge, complex organism, delicately balanced on the *edge-of-chaos* [Love79].

Perhaps the quintessential example of a complex system is the human brain, which, consisting of something on the order of 10^{10} neurons with 10^3 to 10^4 connections per neuron, is arguably the most *complex* complex system on this planet. Somehow, the cooperative dynamics of this vast web of "interconnected and mutually interacting parts" manages to produce a coherent and complex enough structure for the brain to be able to investigate its own behavior.

The emerging disciplines of complexity and complex adaptive systems explore the important question of whether (and/or to what extent) the behavior of the many seemingly disparate complex systems found in nature—from the very small to the very large—stems from the same fundamental core set of universal principles.

Finally, the most far-reaching consequence of complex adaptive systems theory—as an emerging *science*— is that it engenders a paradigm shift in how the world is viewed: from *reductionism* to *holism.* We will have more to say about this speculative proposition toward the end of this chapter.

2.2.1 *References*

Just as we could only provide a brief outline of nonlinear dynamics in the previous section, so too we can only give a short sketch of complex adaptive systems theory below. Readers interested in learning more about this rapidly growing interdisciplinary field, are urged to consult some of the better references that are available.

These include graduate-level monographs (Auyang [Auyang98], Badii and Politi [Badii97], Flake [Flake98], Kauffman [Kauff93], Holland [Holl95], Mainzer [Main94], and Weisbuch [Weisb91]), popularizations (Lewin [lewin92], Waldrop [wald92], and Gell-Mann [GellM94]), conference proceedings (Cowan [Cowan94], Varela [Varela92], and Yates [Yates87]) and a series of lecture notes from the *Santa Fe Institute* ([Stein89], [Jen90], [Nadel91], [Nadel92], [Nadel93], and [Nadel95]).

Among the most eloquent exegesis' of the complex systems "worldview" are by two of the fields' most intellectually gifted luminaries: Kauffman's *At Home in the Universe* [Kauff95] and *Investigations* [Kauff00], and Wolfram's *A New Kind of Science* [Wolfram02].

Finally, four excellent (and sophisticated) monographs on the general relationship between "part" and "whole" in physics—which is a theme that sits at the very heart of complexity theory—are those by Jantsch [Jantsch80], Kafatos and Nadeau [Kafa90] and Bohm and Hiley ([Bohm93], [Bohm80]).

2.2.2 *Short History*

Whenever a new field emerges, many different individuals contribute to its development. This is of course also true of complex systems theory; but which, unlike some other better-defined fields (if only by their *focus*), required a creative input from researchers in sometimes vastly different fields before finally emerging—in the late 1980s and early 1990s—as a legitimate, albeit strongly interdisciplinary, field of scientific inquiry. Having its origins, in the early 1930s, in Turing's observations of biological pattern formation [Turing36], original contributions of long-lasting fundamental significance came from the mathematician John von Neumann (and his work on self-reproducing automata [vonN51]), von Bertalanffy (and his pioneering work on applying a "system view" to social dynamics [Bert68]), Langton (who virtually single-handedly introduced the field of *artificial-life* [Lang86]), Kauffman (through his application of complex systems theory to the question of the origin of life [Kauff93]), and Axtell's and Epstein's pioneering application of multiagent-based simulations to social systems [Epstein96]. Table 2.2 shows a brief chronology of a few milestone events in the study of complex systems.

Turing, in 1936, published a landmark proof of what has come to be known as the *Halting Theorem.* Turing's theorem fundamentally limits what one is able to know about the running of a program on a computer by asserting that there is in general no way to know in advance if an arbitrary program will ever stop running. In other words, there is, in general, no quick and dirty short-cut way of predicting an arbitrary program's outcome; this is an example of what is called computational irreducibility. About five decades later, Wolfram suggested that computational irreducibility is actually a property not just of computers, but of many real physical systems as well [Wolf85].

Cellular automata were conceived in 1948 by John von Neumann, whose motivation was in finding a reductionist model for biological evolution [vonN51]. His ambitious scheme was to abstract the set of primitive logical interactions necessary for the evolution of the complex forms of organization essential for life. In a seminal work, completed by Burks, von Neumann followed a suggestion by Ulam to use discrete rather than continuous dynamics and constructed a two-dimensional automaton capable of self-reproduction. Although it obeyed a complicated dynamics and had a rather large state space, this was the first discrete parallel computational

Year	Researcher	Discovery/Event
1936	Turing	Formalized concept of computability; introduced concept of a universal computer (i.e., Turing machine) [Turing36]
1948	von Neumann	Abstracted the logical structure of life; introduced self-reproducing automata as a means towards developing a reductionist biology [vonN51]
1950	Ulam	Proposed need for having more realistic models for the behavior of complex extended systems [Ulam52]
1966	Burks	Completed and described von Neumann's work [Burks70]
1967	von Bertalanffy	First application of *systems theory* to human systems [Bert68]
1969	Zuse	Introduced concept of "computing spaces," or digital models of mechanics [Zuse69]
1970	Conway	Introduced two-dimensional cellular automaton *Life* rule [Gard70]
1977	Toffoli	Applied cellular automata directly to modeling physical laws [Toffoli77]
1983	Wolfram	Wrote a landmark review article on properties of cellular automata that effectively legitimized the field as research endeavor for physicists [Wolfram83]
1984	Cowan	*Santa Fe Institute* founded, serving as a pre-eminent center for the interdisciplinary study of complex systems
1984	Toffoli, Wolfram	First cellular automata conference held at MIT, Boston [Farmer84]
1987	Langton	First artificial life conference held at the *Santa Fe Institute* [Lang89]
1992	Varela	First European conference on artificial life [Varela92]
1992	Ray	Introduced the *Tierra* simulator of a digital-organism ecology [RayT93]
1993	Kauffman	Application of complex adaptive system dynamics to biology and evolution [Kauff93]
1996	Axtell & Epstein	Introduced multiagent-based simulation of a notional economy (i.e. *Sugarscape* [Epstein96])
2002	Wolfram	Introduces a new cellular-automata-based computational approach to science [Wolfram02]

Table 2.2 Some landmark historical developments in the study of complex systems.

model formally shown to be a universal computer (which implies, in turn, that it is also computationally irreducible). Twenty years later, the mathematician John Conway introduced his well-known *Life* game, which remains among the simplest known models proven to be computational universal [Berk82].

Other important landmarks include the founding, in 1984, of the *Santa Fe Institute*,* which is one of the leading centers for complex systems theory research; the first conference devoted solely to research in cellular automata (which is a prototypical mathematical model of complex systems), organized by Farmer, Toffoli and Wolfram at MIT in 1984 [Farmer84]; and the first artificial life conference, organized by Langton at Los Alamos National Laboratory in 1987 [Lang89].

*See the *Santa Fe Institute*'s web site at http://www.santafe.edu.

2.2.3 *General Properties: A Heuristic Discussion*

With an eye toward providing a more rigorous description of complex systems and complexity, consider some examples of the dynamics of complex systems:

- *Predator-prey relationships of natural ecologies*
- *Economic dynamics of world financial markets*
- *Chaotic dynamics of global weather patterns*
- *Firing patterns of neurons in a human brain*
- *Information flow on the Internet*
- *Antigen ↔ Antibody interaction in an immune system*
- *Pedestrian and vehicular traffic dynamics*
- *The apparently goal-directed behavior of an ant colony*
- *The spread of infectious disease*

What all of these systems have in common is that they share a significant number of the following list of properties:

1. *Many interconnected, and typically nonlinearly, interacting heterogenous parts*

Each of the systems listed above, as well as countless other examples of complex systems that one can think of, owe their apparent complexity to the fact that they consist not just of isolated parts, but of deeply entwined parts that continually respond to (and change as a function of) changes undergone by other parts to which they are connected. While the parts are usually related in some manner, and may all belong to the same general class of possible system constituents (for example, a predator-prey ecology may include multiple instances of the class "shark," and an urban traffic environment may include many different kinds of "automobile"), how one specific part interacts with another part may also, in general, be a function of the specific part and/or its previous history. How a hungry shark responds to prey its immediate environment may be very different from how another more satiated shark responds.

The most interesting interactions, or those that have the highest probability of producing interesting behaviors, are those that are nonlinear; i.e., the most interesting interactions are those that entail disproportionate responses to (local) information. For example, the magnitude of a single neuron's electrical impulse does not steadily increase with increasing local chemical potential but is triggered, *nonlinearly*, in an all-or-none reaction once it senses a threshold local potential.

Or, consider some site (the "part") on the world wide web (the "system") that languishes for months, attracting few visitors, until, by chance, a word or phrase that appears on the site comes in vogue, is picked up by automated search-spiders and catalogued by websearch engines. Suddenly, and in an unpredictably nonlinear fashion, the site is now besieged by visitors.

2. *Multiple scales of resolution*

Complex systems tend to be organized hierarchically, with complex behavior arising from the interaction among elements at different levels of the hierarchy. A biological organism is, simultaneously, the complex system comprised of DNA, proteins, cells, tissues, and organs; as a whole. Similarly, weather consists of patterns on multiple scales, ranging from the individual molecules of the atmosphere to small dust devils to tornados to full-blown hurricanes than span hundreds of miles across. Typical mathematical tools for studying such systems include fractal analysis, scaling laws, and the renormalization group.

The individual parts of complex systems (which we will henceforth call, generically, *agents*) form groups that then effectively act as higher-level agents that, in turn, also cluster and interact with still other agents; these (still higher-level) groups, in turn, form super-groups than also act as agents, interacting with other agents (on different timescales); and so on.

Koestler observes that an agent on any given level of a complex systems' hierarchy is driven by two opposite tendencies [Koest83]: (1) An *integrative tendency*, compelling it to function as a part of the larger whole (on higher levels of the hierarchy), and (2) A *self-assertive tendency*, compelling it to preserve its individual autonomy. (An early presage, perhaps, of Kauffman's compelling *edge-of-chaos* notion; see below).

3. *Multiple metastable states*

Complex systems generally harbor multiple metastable states. *Multistable* systems have multiple stable fixed points; which particular stable fixed point a system is attracted to depends on the initial configuration of the system. A *metastable* system is a system that is above its minimum-energy state, but requires an energy input if it is to reach a lower-energy state. Metastable *states* are thus states that are in a *pseudo*-equilibrium. Small perturbations to the system lead to recovery, but larger ones can also ignite large changes in the system. A metastable system can act as if it were stable, provided that all energy inputs remain below some threshold.

Because one has to keep track of multiple multistable states, the dynamics of such systems are often difficult to analyze mathematically, a task that is made harder still because it also usually involves dealing with local *frustration* (i.e., conflicting constraints that make it impossible to solve for globally minimal energy states). Examples include protein folding, spin glasses, and memory dynamics of the brain.

The fact that complex systems almost certainly harbor multiple metastable states is important, on the conceptual level, because it compels the researcher to explore as large a volume of a system's ostensibly N-dimensional state space as possible. A moment's thought will show that this deceptively simple assertion radically shifts the way in which complex systems are studied. It is commonly assumed that a system has but one, mathematically well-defined, equilibrium state. Once that state is "solved" for, either in closed-form or by running a simulation, the system is said to be *understood.*

In contrast, because complex systems typically harbor multiple metastable states—none of which are generally "solvable" in closed-form, and the entire set of which depends on where a system "starts" its evolution—one can hope to characterize the "whole system" only by exploring as many attainable states as possible; which therefore also means that one must explore as many evolutions as possible, that start from as many initial configurations as possible. A given state of a system can only be understood by providing a context for its being; i.e., by understanding all of the possible states of a system, and all the possible ways these states can be attained.

4. *Local information processing*

The agents of a complex system typically "see" (and interact with) only a limited portion of the whole system, and act locally; i.e., interagent dynamics is usually *highly decentralized.* There is no God-like "oracle" dictating what each and every agent ought to be doing; no master "neuron" telling each neuron of a brain when and how to "fire." Instead, the parts of the system act locally, using only local information.

The order that emerges on a global scale does so naturally, and does not depend on either a central or external control. Kauffman observes that, "contrary to our deepest intuitions, massively disordered systems can spontaneously 'crystallize' a very high degree of order."[Kauff93] Self-organization takes place as a system reacts and adapts to its external environment, with which it also usually has an open boundary (i.e., energy and/or other system resources are continually exchanged between the *inside* and *outside* of a system).

5. *Self-organization*

Self-organization is a fundamental characteristic of complex systems. It refers to the emergence of macroscopic nonequilibrium organized structures, and is due to the collective interactions of the constituents of a complex system as they react and adapt to their environment. At first sight, self-organization appears to violate the second law of thermodynamics, which asserts that the entropy S of an isolated system never decreases (or, more formally, $dS/dt \geq 0$); see figure 2.12. Since entropy is essentially a measure of the degree of disorder in a system, the second law is usually interpreted to mean that an isolated system will become increasingly more disordered with time. *How, then, can structure emerge after a system has had a chance to evolve?*

Upon closer examination, we see that self-organization in complex system does not really violate the second law. The reason is that the second law requires a

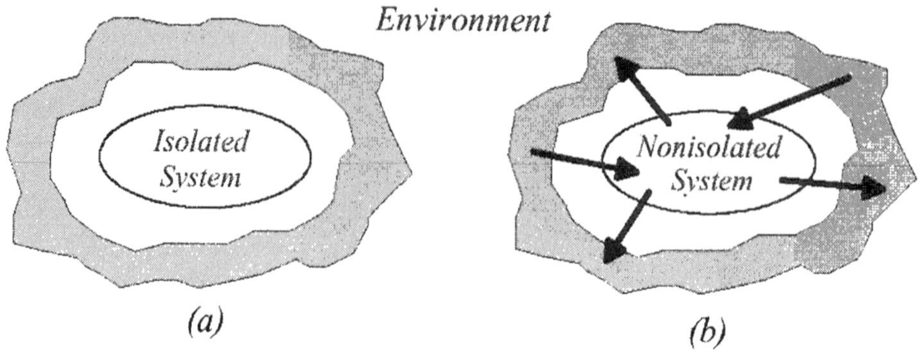

Fig. 2.12 Schematic of *isolated* and *nonisolated* systems; see text.

system to be isolated; that is, it must not exchange energy or matter with its environment. For nonisolated systems consisting of noninteracting or only weakly interacting particles (see figure 2.12-b), S consists of two components: (1) an internal component, S_i, due to the processes taking place within the system itself, and (2) an external component, S_e, due to the exchange of energy and matter between the system and the environment. The rate of change of S with time, dS/dt, now becomes $dS/dt = dS_i/dt + dS_e/dt$. As for an isolated system, dS_i/dt. But there is no such constraint on dS_e/dt. If dS_e/dt is sufficiently less than zero, the overall entropy of the system can itself decrease. Thus, the entropy of a nonisolated system of noninteracting or only weakly interacting particles can decrease due to the exchange of energy and/or matter between the system and its environment.

The situation is more complicated for nonisolated systems consisting of strongly interacting particles and when the system is no longer in equilibrium with the environment. The second law effectively asserts only that a system tends to the maximum disorder possible, *within the constraints due to the dynamics of the system* [Kauff93].

6. *Emergence*

Emergence is one of the central ideas of complex systems theory. Emergence refers to properties of the *whole* that are not possessed by, nor are directly derivable from, any of the system's *parts*. Or, more colloquially, emergence = *novelty*; i.e., complex systems typically surprise us with their behavior. A line of computer code cannot calculate a spreadsheet, an oxygen molecule is not a tornado and (unfortunately) no one can predict a significant gain (or catastrophic crash) of the stock market.

Emergent behaviors, which appear on the macroscale, are typically novel and unanticipated, at least with regard to our ability to predict them from a knowledge of a system's microscale parts and rules alone. Indeed, it is the microscale that induces the macroscale behavior. Some elements of emergent behaviors may be universal, in the sense that more than one set of local rules may induce more or the less same global behavior.

One of the simplest, and ubiquitous, examples of emergence is *temperature*, as read by a thermometer. While temperature is a perfectly well-defined physical quantity on the macroscale, it is a meaningless concept on the level of a single atom or molecule. At the other extreme, we have one of the most provocative examples of emergence in human consciousness, which mysteriously becomes manifest in a cerebral cortex consisting of 100 billion or so interacting neurons.

A superb example of emergence—on a human scale—is due to the physicist David Deutsch, and appears in his book *The Fabric of Reality* [Deut97]. Consider one particular copper atom at the tip of the nose of the statue of Sir Winston Churchill that stands in Parliament Square in London. *How did that copper atom get there?* Is the copper atom's presence merely the consequence of a long (but in principle *computable*) string of interactions with other objects in its environment? Deutsch suggests a deeper answer:

> "It is because Churchill served as Prime Minister in the House of Commons nearby; and because his ideas and leadership contributed to the Allied victory in the Second World War; and because it is customary to honor such people by putting up statues of them; and because bronze is the traditional material for such statues, and so on. Thus we explain a low-level physical observation—the presence of a copper atom at a particular location—through extremely high level theories about emergent phenomena such as ideas, leadership, war and tradition."

Other examples of emergence include (i) the characteristic spirals of the *Belousov-Zhabotinski* chemical reaction [Tyson76],* (ii) the *Navier-Stokes*-like macroscopic behavior of a lattice gas that consists, on the micro-scale, of simple unit-bit billiards moving back and forth between discrete nodes along discrete links [Hass88],† and (iii) the seemingly purposeful task of forming clusters of randomly distributed objects—a behavior common in, say, ant colonies organizing the carcasses of their dead companions—that spontaneously and quite naturally emerges out a simple set of autonomous actions having nothing to do with clustering *per se* (as demonstrated

*The *Belousov-Zhabotinski* reaction is a chemical reaction consisting of simple organic molecules that is characterized by spectacular oscillating temporal and spatial patterns. One variant of the reaction involves the reaction of bromate ions with an organic substrate (typically malonic acid) in a sulfuric acid solution with cerium (or some other metal-ion catalyst). When this mixture is allowed to react exothermally at room temperature, interesting temporal and spatial oscillations (i.e. chemical waves) result. The system oscillates, changing from yellow to colorless and back to yellow about twice a minute, with the oscillations typically lasting for over an hour (until the organic substrate is exhausted).

†The *Navier-Stokes* equations are the fundamental equations describing incompressible fluid flow; see Chapter 9 in [Hach[illegible]b]

by Beckers, Holland and Deneubourg in the context of exploring collective robotics [Beckers94]). The macroscopic behavior in each of these examples is unexpected, *despite* the fact that the details of the microscopic dynamics is well-defined.

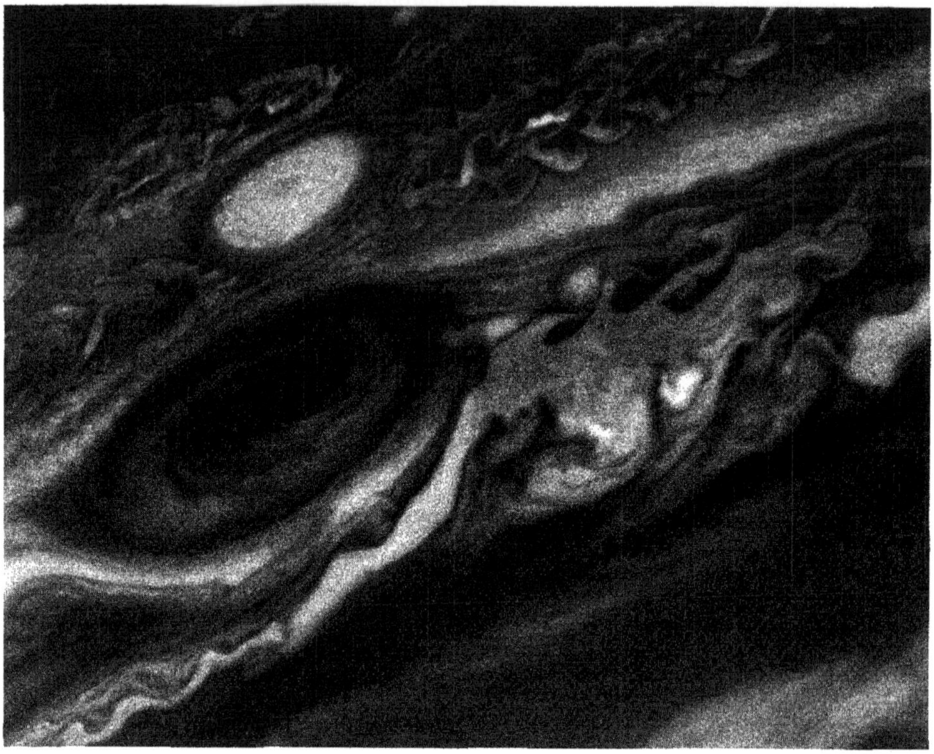

Fig. 2.13 A photograph of the planet Jupiter's *Great Red Spot*, which is a colossal storm that can fit three earth-sized planets within its boundary. The storm rotates in the counterclockwise direction with a period of about 6 days.

7. *Nonequilibrium order*

The long-term behavior of a complex system usually consists of a nonequilibrium order. Nonequilibrium order refers to an organized state that remains stable for long periods of time despite matter and energy continually flowing in and out of the system.*

A vivid example of nonequilibrium order is the *Great Red Spot* on Jupiter (see figure 2.13). This gigantic whirlpool of gases in Jupiter's upper atmosphere—which can fit three earth-sized planets within its boundary—has persisted for a much longer time (at least 400 years) than the average amount of time any one gas

*Nonequilibrium states are also sometimes called either *dissipative structures* [Prig80] or *autopoietic systems* [Varela74].

molecule has spent within it. Despite the millions of individual molecules that have traveled in and out of the *Great Red Spot*, a substantial fraction of which have likely done so repeatedly, some perhaps also circumnavigating Jupiter's entire atmosphere, the *Great Red Spot* itself—as a high-level emergent entity—remains in a stable but *nonequilibrium ordered* state.

8. *Understanding requires both analysis and synthesis*

The traditional Western scientific method is predicated on a fundamentally reductionist philosophy that assumes that the properties of a system may be deduced—and, implicitly, that the system itself may be *understood*—by decomposing the system into progressively smaller and smaller pieces. However, by *analyzing* a system in this way, there is strong chance that the most interesting emergent properties of the system will become lost; the chances of this happening only increases as the complexity of a system's behavior increases. Think of the absurdity of searching for consciousness by stripping a brain down to a few neurons! In meticulously probing the parts, the analytical-reductionist method inevitably loses sight of the whole. The understanding of complex systems also requires that a complementary holistic, or constructionist, approach be undertaken—in parallel with reducing a system down to its essential parts—in which one explores how the system's parts *synthesize* the whole.

Complex systems must be viewed as coherent wholes whose open-ended evolution is continuously fueled by nonlinear feedback between their macroscopic states and microscopic constituents. It is neither completely reductionist, nor completely synthesist.

Consider a natural ecology. Each species that makes up an ecology—which is itself composed of a large number of diverse species—coevolves with other members of the ecology according to a fitness function that is, in part, a function of the evolving ecology as a whole. Individual members of each species collectively define a (part of the)* coevolving ecology; the ecology, in turn, determines the fitness-function according to which its constituent parts evolve. And it is the nonlinear feedback between the information describing individual species (or the system's microscopic level) and the global ecology (or the system's macroscopic level) that those species collectively define that determines the temporal evolution, and identity, of the entire system.

Part of the power, and allure, of using multiagent-based simulations to study complex systems, is that they embody precisely the kind of *generative* tools that a synthetic analysis of a complex system requires. They are designed to be used to build a system, from the bottom up, and allow the analyst to experiment with different ways of putting it together.

*An ecology also includes elements of the environment which the species cohabit. A description of the full ecology must therefore encompass not only the co-evolution among the its constituent species but the complex interactions between those species and the effects they produce in their local environments.

9. *Emphasis on process and adaptation rather than static structure*

A complex adaptive system is almost never stagnant; it continually interacts with, and adapts to changing conditions of, its environment, and always evolves. It can neither be captured, conceptually or mathematically, nor understood, by simply cataloging its parts and the rules according to which they interact. Such static "snapshots" never adequately capture the often latent and subtle patterns that such systems exhibit over long times. It is for this reason that computer simulations of complex systems are indispensable tools for studying them. Mathematical descriptions and/or equations of motion are often rendered tractable *only* if one makes a number of mean-field-like simplifications (such as assuming a strict homogeneity of parts and homogenous interactions); therefore, by *themselves*, they are rarely able to capture any emergent behaviors aside from the simplest.

As strange as it might at first appear, having an explicit "solution" to an equation—particularly one that harbors deterministic chaos (in the mathematical sense discussed earlier in the chapter)—does not necessarily imply that one has gained as deep an insight into the system being modeled as is otherwise possible to achieve by *observing the system (or model) as it unfolds naturally in time.* Consider, for example, Feigenbaum's logistic equation when $\lambda = 4$ (i.e., $x_{n+1} = 4x_n(1-x_n)$; see equation 2.9), which is *solved* by $x_n = \frac{1}{2}\{1-\cos(2^{n+1}\pi y_0)\}$, where $y_0 = \frac{1}{2\pi}\cos^{-1}(1-2x_0)$. One might reasonably wonder about how deep an insight into the behavior of the overall system has been gained by simply writing down this closed-form "solution"? The real depth, and beauty, of the system resides in its *emergent* properties, that are much harder, if not impossible, to embody in a closed-form equation. Think of the fractal nature of the Feigenbaum attractor (figure 2.6) or the intricate structure of the Lyapunov exponent (figure 2.11).

In fact, much of what falls under "complex systems research" consists not so much of writing down and "solving" equations, or recording what state a given system is in at what time, as patiently and systematically observing—and learning to recognize the properties of emergent patterns in—the behaviors that a system exhibits over the course of its (typically open-ended) evolution; and then repeating the process for many different starting conditions. Complex systems theory is, essentially, the art of finding the proper global context in which the local behavior can be understood.

10. *The most interesting behavior is poised between chaos and order*

Chris Langton opens his *Life at the Edge of Chaos* paper at the Artificial Life II conference with the following intriguing question [Lang92]: *"Under what conditions can we expect a dynamics of information to emerge spontaneously and come to dominate the behavior of a physical system?"* While his question was motivated chiefly by an understanding that living organisms may be distinguished from inanimate matter by the fact that their behavior is clearly based on a complex dynamics of information, its roots extend considerably deeper and arguably have much wider applicability.

In his paper, Langton provides a tentative answer to the question by examining the behavior of the entire rule space of elementary one-dimensional cellular automata rules as parameterized by a single parameter λ.* He found that as λ is increased from its minimal to maximal values, a path is effectively traced in the rule space that progresses from fixed point behavior to simple periodicity to evolutions with longer and longer periods with increasing transients, passes through an intermediate transition region at a critical value λ_c, crosses over into a chaotic regime of steadily diminishing complexity until, eventually, the behavior is again completely predictable at the maximal value of λ and complexity falls back to zero. Because the transition region represents the region of greatest complexity and lies between regions in which the behavior is either ordered or chaotic, Langton christened the transition region as the *edge-of-chaos*.

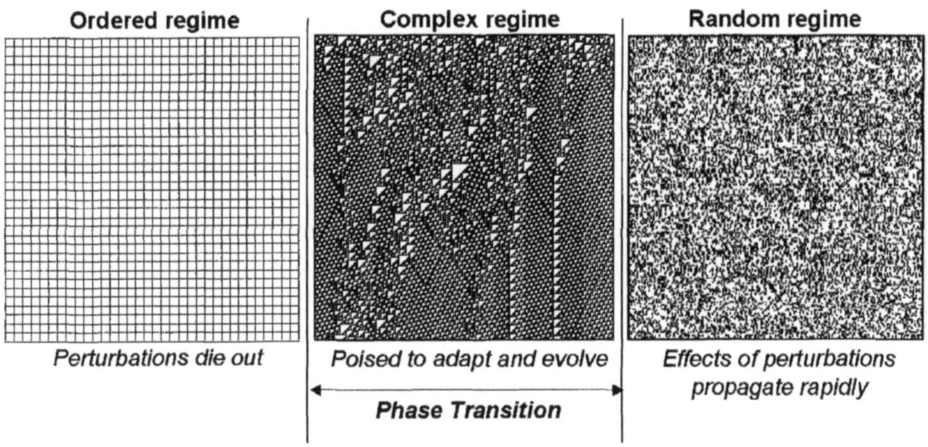

Fig. 2.14 A schematic illustration of the *edge-of-chaos* metaphor; see text.

Langton's complete answer to his question is therefore: *"We expect that information processing can emerge spontaneously and come to dominate the dynamics of a physical system in the vicinity of a critical phase transition."* Langton speculates that the dynamics of phase transitions is fundamentally equivalent to the dynamics of information processing. Strictly speaking, Langton's *edge-of-chaos* idea holds true only for the specific system in which it was discovered. Nonetheless, the idea has frequently been used as a general metaphor for the region in "complexity space" toward which complex adaptive systems appear to naturally evolve (see figure 2.14). Kauffman ([Kauff91], [Kauff95a]) is a staunch advocate of the idea that

*Cellular automata were introduced briefly in the *Preface* (see footnote on page xv), and are discussed at length in the next section (see page 137).

systems poised at the *edge-of-chaos* are optimized, in some sense, to evolve, adapt and process information about their environment.

Effective computation, such as that required by life processes and the maintenance of evolvability and adaptability in complex systems, requires both the storage and transmission of information. If correlations between separated sites (or agents) of a system are too small—as they are in the ordered regime shown in figure 2.14—the sites evolve essentially independently of one another and little or no transmission takes place. On the other hand, if the correlations are too strong—as they are in the chaotic regime—distant sites may cooperate so strongly so as to effectively mimic each other's behavior, or worse yet, whatever ordered behavior is present may be overwhelmed by random noise; this, too, is not conducive to effective computation. It is only within the phase transition region, in the complex regime poised at the *edge-of-chaos,* that information can propagate freely over long distances without appreciable decay. However loosely defined, the behavior of a system in this region is best described as complex; i.e. it neither locks into an ordered pattern nor does it dissolve into an apparent randomness. Systems existing in this region are both stable enough to store information and dynamically amorphous enough to be able to successfully transmit it.*

One of the basic questions to be asked of all complex systems is, *"What are the universal patterns of behavior?"* According to thermodynamics and statistical mechanics, the critical exponents describing the divergence of certain physical measurables (for example, specific heat, magnetization, correlation length, etc.) are universal at a phase transition in that they are essentially independent of the physical substance undergoing the phase transition and depend only on a few fundamental parameters (such as the dimension of the space and the symmetry of the underlying order parameter). Similarly, an important driver fueling the fervor behind the emerging new "sciences of complexity" is the growing belief that high-level behavior of all complex systems can be traced back to essentially the same fundamental set of universal principles. Much of the study of complex systems consists of looking for the low-level underpinnings of universal patterns of high-level behavior.

2.2.4 *Measures of Complexity*

The preceding section provides a list of *properties* that are possessed by almost all complex systems, but does not completely answer the question, *"What is complexity?"* In order to answer this broader question, we must also ask, *"What is complex behavior?"* It is one thing to describe, even qualitatively as we have done, what a

*However intuitive the *edge-of-chaos* idea appears to be, we would be remiss if we did not mention that it has also received a fair amount of criticism in recent years. It is not clear, for example, how to define complexity in more complicated systems like coevolutionary systems, much less imagine a phase transition between different complexity regimes. Even Langton's suggestion that effective computation within the limited domain of cellular automata can take place only in the transition region has been challenged (see [MitchM93a]).

complex system is. It is quite another to quantify the notion of complexity itself, to describe the relationship between complexity and information, and/or to understand the role that complexity plays in various physical and/or computational contexts. In fact, all of these fundamental problems are still open. While we may find it easy enough to distinguish a complex object from a less complex object, it is far from trivial to furnish anything beyond a vague characterization as to how we have done so.

We can appreciate the difficulty in quantifying complexity by once again considering figure 2.14, that appears on page 113. The figure shows three patterns: (a) an area of a regular two-dimensional Euclidean lattice, (b) a space-time view of the evolution of an elementary cellular automata rule,* and (c) a completely random collection of dots. These patterns illustrate the incongruity that exists between mathematically precise notions of entropy, or the amount of disorder in a system, and intuitive notions of complexity. Whereas pattern (b) is intuitively the most complex of the three patterns, it has neither the highest entropy, which belongs to pattern (c), nor the lowest, which belongs to pattern (a). Indeed, were we to roughly plot our intuitive sense of complexity as a function of the amount of order or disorder in a system, it would probably look something like that shown in figure 2.15. The problem is to find an objective measure of the complexity of a system that matches our intuition.

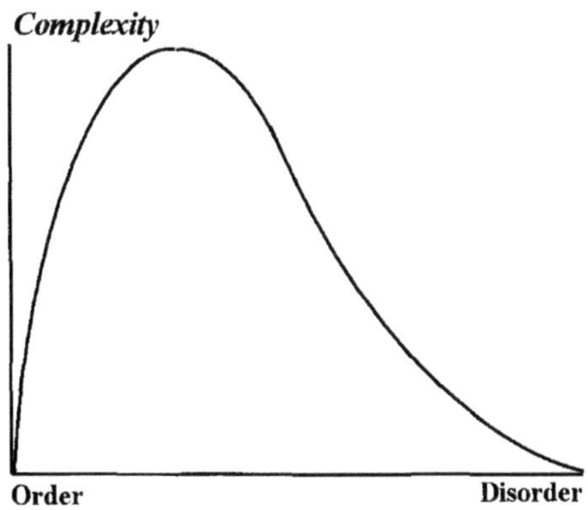

Fig. 2.15 A schematic representation of the "intuitive" relationship between *complexity* and the *degree*

We all have an intuitive feel for complexity. An oil painting by Picasso is obviously more "complex" than the random finger-paint doodles of a three-year-old. The works of Shakespeare are more "complex" than the rambling prose banged out on a typewriter by the proverbial band of monkeys. Our intuition tells us that

*Cellular automata were introduced briefly in the *Preface* (see page xv); they are formally introduced later in this chapter; see page 137.

complexity is usually greatest in systems whose components are arranged in some intricate difficult-to-understand pattern or, in the case of a dynamical system, when the outcome of some process is difficult to predict from its initial state. The problem is to articulate this intuition formally; to define a measure that not only captures our intuitive feel for what distinguishes the complex from the simple but also provides an objective basis for formulating conjectures and theories about complexity.

While a universally applicable measure is unlikely to exist, a number of interesting proposals have been made in recent years. All such measures of complexity fall into two general classes: (1) *Static complexity*—which addresses the question of how an object or system is put together (i.e. only purely structural informational aspects of an object, or the patterns and/or strengths of interactions among its constituent parts), and is independent of the processes by which information is encoded and decoded; and (2) *Dynamic complexity*—which addresses the question of how much dynamical or computational effort is required to describe the information content of an object or state of a system. While a system's static complexity certainly influences its dynamical complexity, the two measures are clearly not equivalent. A system may be structurally rather simple (i.e. have a low static complexity), but have a complex dynamical behavior. For example, think of the chaotic behavior of Feigenbaum's logistic equation.

To glimpse a flavor of the many subtleties that are involved in defining complexity, consider this sampling of eight measures (four are static measures, and are indicated by a boldface '**s**,' and four dynamic, indicated by a boldface '**d**'):*

- (**s**) *Complexity as information*
- (**s**) *Complexity of a graph*
- (**s**) *Complexity of a simplex*
- (**s**) *Complexity of a hierarchical system*
- (**d**) *Computational complexity*
- (**d**) *Algorithmic complexity*
- (**d**) *Logical depth*
- (**d**) *Thermodynamic depth*

2.2.4.1 *Complexity as information*

Given an object composed of N interconnected and interacting "parts," one might at first be tempted to equate the complexity of an object with its "conventional" information content, as defined by Shannon [Shann49]:

*The fact that our discussion is limited to these eight particular measures should in no way be misunderstood to mean that these are the *only* ones possible, as they represent only a small sampling of recent proposals. Discussions of other complexity measures, and of their respective pros and cons relative to given problems, can be obtained by consulting a list references maintained by Bruce Edmonds [Edmonds97].

$$I = -\sum_{i=1}^{N} p_i \log_2 p_i, \tag{2.47}$$

where p_i is the probability of the ith event or part of occurring and $\log_2$ is the base-2 logarithm. The logarithm is used because it is the only function consistent with the reasonable demand that information be additive for independent events. That is to say, if there are two independent sets of outcomes, N_1 and N_2, so that the total number of outcomes is $N = N_1 \cdot N_2$, the information content of N, $\mathcal{I}(N)$, is equal to the sum of the information content of the two independent set of outcomes, $\mathcal{I}(N) = \mathcal{I}(N_1) + \mathcal{I}(N_2)$.

While Shannon's information does give an indication of how much a given object differs from other "like" objects belonging to the same class, there is a drawback to using it as a measure of complexity. Additivity may be a reasonable requirement to have for a measure of "information," it is not an *a priori* reasonable demand to make of a measure of "complexity." The reason is that the complexity of a given system is probably not doubled if two copies of that system are simply merged. If complexity were additive in this way, we could then generate arbitrarily complex objects simply by merging together a desired number of copies of arbitrarily simple objects.

This certainly runs counter to our intuition. Thus, while Shannon information captures some of the flavor of complexity—a DNA molecule, for example, has a large (Shannon) complexity because its parts require a great deal of information to describe, while a crystal has little complexity because relatively little information is required to describe its regular structure—it fails to capture enough of the essence of real complexity to be a useful measure. Complexity cannot be additive; at least not in this simple manner (see **Thermodynamic Depth** below).

Another drawback to using Shannon information as a measure of complexity is the fact that it is based on an ensemble of all possible states of a system and therefore cannot describe the information content of a *single state.* Shannon information thus resembles traditional statistical mechanics—which describes the average or aggregate behavior of, say, a gas, rather than the motion of its constituent molecules—more so than it does a "complexity theory" that must address the complexity of individual objects.

Another way of looking at it is that Shannon information is a formal equivalent of thermodynamic entropy, or the degree of disorder in a physical system. As such it essentially measures how much information is *missing* about the individual constituents of a system. In contrast, a measure of complexity ought to (1) refer to individual states and not ensembles, and (2) reflect how much is *known* about a system rather than what is not. One approach that satisfies both of these requirements is *algorithmic complexity theory.*

2.2.4.2 *Complexity of a Graph*

Perhaps the simplest approach to defining a complexity of graphs is to apply Shannon's information measure to its vertices [Dres74]. Let $\mathcal{P}_V = \{V_1^{(\mathcal{P})}, V_2^{(\mathcal{P})}, \ldots, V_{h(\mathcal{P})}\}$ be a partition of the vertex set $\mathcal{V}$ of G, so that $\sum_{i=1}^{h(\mathcal{P})} V_i^{(\mathcal{P})} = \mathcal{V}$, where $\mid \mathcal{P}_V \mid = h(\mathcal{P})$ depends on the partition. Let $\mid V_i \mid$ be the number of nodes in the set V_i. Then the complexity $\mathcal{I}(G)$ of the graph G is given by minimizing Shannon's information over all possible partitions of this vertex set:

$$\mathcal{I}(G) = \min_{\mathcal{P}} \{-\sum_{i=1}^{h(\mathcal{P})} p_i^{(\mathcal{P})} \log_2 p_i^{(\mathcal{P})}\}, \tag{2.48}$$

Although this measure is occasionally used, it suffers from a serious drawback. Since it is a function only of the vertex set, it ignores all structural information. However, the measure can be improved by including information about a graph's topology. Since a graph is an object that includes both parts (i.e. nodes) and structure (i.e. their interconnectivity pattern), a legitimate measure of complexity of a graph should at least respect sets of topologically equivalent vertices of a graph. One such measure, called *topological complexity*—or *information content*, as it was first called by Rashevsky [Rash55], who introduced a version of this measure for dealing with the complexity of organic molecules—is essentially equal to the entropy of the orbits of a graph's automorphism group. To define it we first need to introduce a few more definitions.

Two graphs, G_1 and G_2 are said to be *isomorphic* if there exists a one-to-one mapping $f : \mathcal{V}(G_1) \to \mathcal{V}(G_2)$ such that $e_{ij} =\in \mathcal{E}(G_1)$ if and only if $f(e_{ij}) = e_{f(i)f(j)} \in \mathcal{E}(G_2)$.

Now, suppose S is a subgroup of $\mathcal{S}_n$. Then $\mathcal{O}(S) = \{f(i) \mid f \in S\}$, $1 \leq i \leq n$ is called the *orbit* of S. Let $s_1, s_2, \ldots, s_h$ be the distinct orbits of S, so that $s_i \cap s_j = 0$ for $i \neq j$ and $\bigcup_{i=1}^{h} s_i = \{1, 2, \ldots, n\}$; that is, the orbits form a partition of the set $\{1, 2, .., \ldots, n\}$.

The *topological complexity*, $\mathcal{C}_T(G)$, of a graph G is then defined by [Mowsh68]:

$$\mathcal{C}_T(G) = -\sum_{i=1}^{h} p_i \log_2 p_i, \tag{2.49}$$

where $p_i = \mid s_i \mid /N$, $1 \leq i \leq h$, and s_i are the orbits of $\mathcal{G}(G)$. Notice that while the topological complexity is formally equivalent to our first attempt at a definition for complexity (see equation 2.48 above)—both are essentially derived from Shannon's information measure—unlike that first attempt, the topological complexity focuses its attention on a particular partition of G; namely, the partition that preserves the graph's topological structure. Despite its being based on Shannon's information, $\mathcal{C}_T$ does not depend on an "ensemble of graphs." Rather, $\mathcal{C}_T$ measures the information content of a particular graph relative to a set of transformations under which the graph's topological structure is invariant.

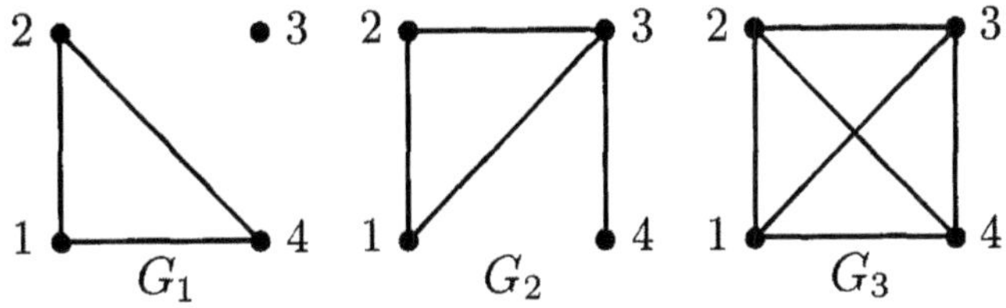

Fig. 2.16 Three sample size-4 graphs for calculating the *topological complexity*, $\mathcal{C}_T$: (a) $\mathcal{C}_T = 0$, (b) $\mathcal{C}_T = 3/2$ and (c) $\mathcal{C}_T = 2 - \frac{3}{4}\log_2 3 \sim 0.811$; see text.

For an example of calculating the topological complexity, consider the three sample size-4 graphs shown in figure 2.16. The automorphism group $\mathcal{G}(G_1)$, for example, is easily found to be $\{\phi, (12), (34), (12)(34), (13)(24), (1423), (1324)\}$, so that $\mid \mathcal{G}(G_1) \mid$ and the orbit $\mathcal{O}(\mathcal{G})$ consists of $\{1, 2, 4\}$ and $\{3\}$. Thus $p_1 = 3/4, p_2 = 1$ and $\mathcal{C}_T(G_1) = 2 - \frac{3}{4}\log_2 3 \sim 0.811$. The complexity of the remaining two graphs may be found in the same manner. Mowshowitz [Mowsh68] develops this concept of a complexity of graphs considerably further in his four papers, which include discussions of its behavior as a function of various graph operations (complement, sum, Cartesian product, etc.), its extension to directed graphs and infinite graphs and the introduction of a graph entropy based on a chromatic decomposition.

We conclude this section by mentioning two older definitions of complexity, each of which also depends on both the size and vertex structure of a graph G: (1) *the number of spanning trees in* G,* and (2) *the average number of independent paths between vertices in* G.

If $\boldsymbol{B} = [b_{ij}]$ is an $N \times N$ matrix in which b_{ii} equals the degree of vertex i, $b_{ij} = -1$ if vertices i and j are adjacent and $b_{ij} = 0$ otherwise, then the number of spanning tree of G is equal to the determinant of any principal minor of $\boldsymbol{B}$ [Har69]. The extremes occur for totally disconnected graphs that have no spanning trees and thus a complexity of zero, and for complete graphs of order N that contain the maximum possible number of distinct trees on N vertices.†

The second measure can be obtained directly from the adjacency matrix $\boldsymbol{A} = [a_{ij}]$ of G. Recalling that $a_{ij} = 1$ if vertices i and j are adjacent and 0 otherwise, it is not hard to show (essentially by using induction on the power k), that $\boldsymbol{A^k} = [a_{ij}^k]$ is equal to the number of paths from i to j containing k edges. Since there are $\binom{N}{2} = \frac{1}{2}N(N-1)$ possible links among N vertices, and the maximal length of a path between two of N vertices is $N-1$, the average number of independent paths between vertices in G is given by $\binom{N}{2}^{-1}\sum_{i,j}\sum_{k<N}[a_{ij}^k]$.

*A *spanning tree* is any tree subgraph of G that connects all the vertices of G.

†The number of spanning trees in the latter case is N^{N-2}, which is a celebrated result due to Cayley [Cay57].

2.2.4.3 *Complexity of a Simplex*

One way of encoding the geometrical structure of a system is to describe it as a *simplicial complex.* That is to say, to piece it together— or form a "complex"—out of a set of elementary building blocks called *simplices.* The system could be either a physical object, such as a rock, in which case a simplicial decomposition is one way of digitizing the object's physical structure, or it could be a complicated set of interrelationships among a set of variables describing the dynamical behavior of the system, in which case a simplicial decomposition gives some geometrical information concerning the dynamics.

An *n-simplex*, $S^{(n)}$, is an n-dimensional generalization of a line. If $x_0, x_2, \ldots, x_n$ are points (not all on the same hyperplane), then $S^{(n)}$ is given by the set of all points X such that $x_0 + \cdots x_n = 1$, $x_i \geq 0$ for all i. A simplex is therefore a convex polyhedron formed by the intersection of $n+1$ half planes. A 0-simplex is simply a point, a 1-simplex is a line, a 2-simplex a triangle, a 3-simplex a tetrahedron, and so on. A set $\mathcal{S}$ of simplices is a *simplicial complex*, denoted by $\mathcal{C}$, if (1) every face of a simplex in $\mathcal{S}$ is also an element of $\mathcal{S}$, (2) the intersection of any two simplices in $\mathcal{S}$ is either empty or a face of each of them, and (3) each point of a simplex in $\mathcal{S}$ has a neighborhood in the n-dimensional Euclidean space that intersects only a finite number of simplices in $\mathcal{S}$.

Casti [Casti92] introduces a (static) measure of complexity, $K(\mathcal{C})$, for a complex $\mathcal{C}$ satisfying the following three complexity axioms: (i) the complexity of a complex consisting of a single simplex is equal to 1, (ii) the complexity of a subcomplex (or subsystem) cannot be greater than the complexity of the entire complex (or system), and (iii) the complexity of the complex formed by combining two complexes cannot be greater than the sum of the complexities of the component complexes.

Casti's complexity measure depends on a quantity called the *structure vector* $\vec{Q}$, which encodes multidimensional information about $\mathcal{C}$. Let the dimension of the highest dimensional simplex in $\mathcal{C}$ be equal to D. Then, for each $0 \leq q \leq D$, two simplices S_i, $S_j \in \mathcal{C}$ are said to be *q-connected* if there exists a sequence of simplices $\{y_{\alpha_i}\} \in \mathcal{C}$, $i = 1, 2, \ldots, r$ such that (1) S_i shares a face of dimension m with y_{α_1}, (2) S_j shares a face of dimension n with y_{α_r}, (3) y_{α_k} and $y_{\alpha_{k+1}}$ share a face of dimension β_k, and (4) $\min\{m, \beta_1, \ldots, \beta_{r-1}, n\}$. In other words, q is the smallest-dimensional link in the chain connecting S_i and S_j. Note that if two simplices are q-connected for some $q > 0$, then they must also be p-connected for all $p < q$.

One can show that the q-connection forms an *equivalence relation* on the complex $\mathcal{C}$. It effectively partitions $\mathcal{C}$ into a set of equivalence classes consisting of simplices that are q-connected to one another. The *structure vector* $\vec{Q} = (Q_D, Q_{D-1}, \ldots, Q_0)$ is defined to be the vector whose Q_q component is equal to the number of q-connected equivalence classes in $\mathcal{C}$. A simple geometrical way of understanding this is to imagine that you are looking at a D-dimensional complex through special glasses that permit you to see only those dimensions greater than or equal to q [Casti92]. You would ee the complex $\mathcal{C}$ broken apart into $\vec{Q}_q$ disjoint pieces.

In terms of the structure vector $\vec{Q}$, Casti [Casti92] shows that the following measure satisfies the three complexity axioms given above:

$$K(\mathcal{C}) = \frac{2}{(D+1)(D+2)} \sum_{i=0}^{D} (i+1) Q_i, \tag{2.50}$$

where D is the dimension of $\mathcal{C}$, Q_i is the ith component of the structure vector $\vec{Q}$ and the constant before the summation is a normalization constant that is inserted to satisfy the first complexity axiom. For a further discussion of K and some interesting applications of this measure, see [Casti88] and [Casti92]. Related material also appears in an earlier book by Casti [Casti79].

2.2.4.4 *Complexity of Hierarchical Systems*

A very natural structure for describing the different "levels" of a complex system, if not the dynamics of their origin, is the *hierarchy*, as first pointed out by Simon* [Simon62] (see figure 2.17). The idea is to cluster the components of a system according to the strength of their mutual interactions by associating the most strongly interacting elements with the topmost of the hierarchy and associating successively weakly interacting components with progressively lower levels. For example, a chunk of condensed matter can be hierarchically parameterized by associating the nodes of the top level of the hierarchy with the atoms that make up the chunk of matter, associating the nodes of the next level of the hierarchy with the molecules that are formed out of atoms, the nodes of the next lower level with the crystals formed out of the molecules, and so on.

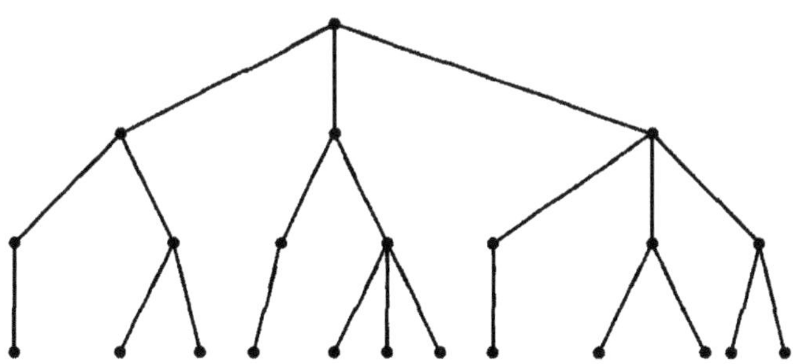

Fig. 2.17 An example of a *hierarchy* composed of three interaction levels and 12 elementary components.

Ceccato, Hogg and Huberman ([HuberB85], [HuberB86], [Cec88]) have defined a measure of complexity of hierarchies that is (1) entirely objective, being based on

* *"My central theme is that complexity frequently takes the form of hierarchy...and hierarchy, I shall argue, is one of the central structural schemes the architect of complexity uses."*

the structure of the hierarchy, and (2) is consistent with the intuitive relationship between the complexity and degree of disorder in a system—namely, it is maximal for systems that are *between* those that are completely ordered or completely disordered. Ceccato, *et.al.*'s measure is determined by examining the diversity of a system, as given by the number of different interactions among the different parts and levels of the hierarchy.

Consider a set of otherwise identical lowest-level components of a system, so that the hierarchy is a *tree* of constant depth. Since we assume that the components are all identical, the only distinction among the various nodes of the hierarchy consists of the structure of the subtrees. Now suppose we have a tree T that consists of β subtrees branching out from the root at the top level. We need to determine the number of different interactions that can occur on each level, independent of the structure of each subtree; i.e. isomorphic copies of trees do not contribute to our count. We therefore need to find the number of nonisomorphic subtrees. We can do this recursively.

The diversity of the tree T, denoted by $\mathcal{D}(T)$, counts the total number of interactions *between* and *within* all subtrees. We therefore proceed in two steps. First count the number of distinct interactions within the clusters represented by the subtrees; i.e. multiply the diversity of all nonisomorphic subtrees. Second, multiply this result by the number of ways, N_k, that k different clusters can themselves interact. Since the total number of possible n-ary interactions among k distinct objects is simply the binomial coefficient $\binom{n}{k}$, N_k is thus given by $N_k = k + \binom{k}{2} + \binom{k}{3} + \cdots + \binom{k}{l} = 2^k - 1$. Combining these two steps, Cecatto's *et.al.*'s suggested measure of complexity of a tree, $\mathcal{C}(T)$ may be expressed as follows:

$$\mathcal{C}(T) = \log_2 \mathcal{D}(T) = \log_2\{f(k_T) \prod_{j=1}^{k} \mathcal{D}(T_j)\}, \tag{2.51}$$

where $\mathcal{D}(T_j)$ is the diversity of the jth subtree, k_T is the number of nonisomorphic subtrees of T and the form factor $f(k_T) = N_k = 2^{k_T} - 1$.* Note that $\mathcal{C}(T)$ gives an absolute measure of complexity, that, in general, grows with the size of the tree. A more convenient relative measure, $c(T)$, that allows one to compare the complexities of different sized hierarchies is defined by $c(T) = \mathcal{C}(T)/\mathcal{C}_{\max}^{(S)}$, where $\mathcal{C}_{\max}$ is the maximum value of $\mathcal{C}(T)$ for trees T of size S. In the case of a *forest*, $\mathcal{F} = \bigcup_i T_i$, composed of n nonisomorphic trees T_i, the complexity is given by:

*The *form factor* f clearly depends on the number of lower levels that must be considered in order to determine whether two subtrees are isomorphic. More generally, it should contain information about the relative importance of a given subtree in T's overall clustered structure—a node that gives birth to a large, diverse subtree should be given greater weight than a node that is at the same level but spawns only a thin subtree. In other words, f is really a function of all of the pertinent gross structural features of the tree at a given level: $f = f(k_T, M_T, N_T, \beta_T)$, where M_T is the total number of levels *below* the given level; N_T is the number of leaves of the given node, and β_T is the number of subtrees emanating from the root.

$$\mathcal{C}(\mathcal{F}) = \sum_{i=1}^{n} \mathcal{C}(T_i) + \log_2 f(\cup_i \mathcal{T}_i). \tag{2.52}$$

For example, consider the two trees shown in figure 2.18. The tree in figure 2.18-a has equal (binary) subtrees, so that its diversity $\mathcal{D} = 1$ and complexity $\mathcal{C} = 0$. The same is true for any tree all of whose nodes have a constant branching ratio. On the other hand, the tree shown in figure 2.18-b has two distinct subtrees, each of which has a diversity of $\mathcal{D} = 1$. The diversity of the entire tree is therefore $\mathcal{D} = 2^2 - 1 = 3$.

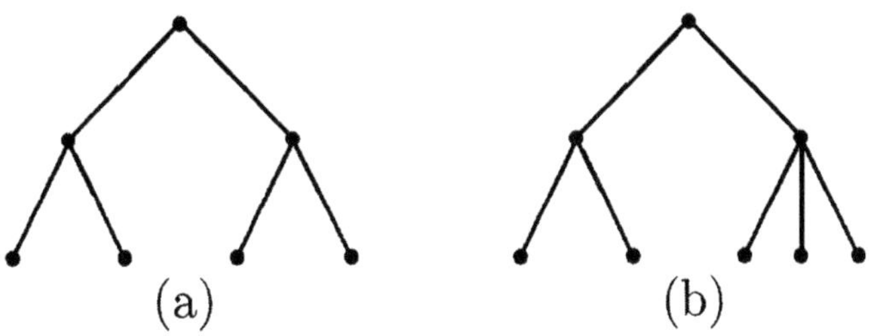

Fig. 2.18 Examples of trees whose subtrees are all identical (a) and different (b).

Huberman and Hogg ([HuberB85b], [HuberB86]) extend this measure to metric trees (where the height of the roots of sub trees from their leaves is an added parameter) and random trees, apply it to adaptation in complex systems and give an illustration of a possible connection between this purely static value and a dynamics of the structure. For other points of view of the role hierarchies play in complex system see Pattee [Pat73], Haken [Haken83], Salthe [Salt85], Nicolis [NicolJ86], and Caianiello [Caian87].

2.2.4.5 *Computational Complexity*

Computational complexity measures the time and memory resources that a computer requires in order to solve a problem. For example, given the "problem" of calculating x^{16} for some real x, one might either choose the most straightforward way to calculate it: $x^{16} = \overbrace{x \times x \times \cdots \times x}^{16}$; or save a little time and instead compute, in turn, $\alpha = x \times x$, $\beta = \alpha \times \alpha$, $\gamma = \beta \times \beta \times \beta$ and $x^{16} = \gamma \times \beta$; or, one might stumble onto a scheme that is easier still in terms of both time and space complexities: $x^{16} = (((x^2)^2)^2)^2$. In general, if we let $\mathcal{N}_{\mathcal{A}}(f)$ represent the number of elementary operations $(+, -, \times, \div)$ required for evaluating the function f, using algorithm $\mathcal{A}$, then we could define a time complexity $\mathcal{C}$ for the evaluation of f as follows:

$$\mathcal{C} = \min_{A \in \mathcal{A}} \mathcal{N}_{\mathcal{A}}(f). \tag{2.53}$$

Of course, the use of such a measure to find the complexity of an *object*, as opposed to the complexity of a *function*, as defined above, presupposes that there exists some natural encoding of that object as a "formula." This is far from obvious.

A somewhat more robust measure may be defined by invoking the *universal Turing machine*. Let $\Sigma_N^{(i)}$ be the initial state of a computation that is designed to solve a size-N problem. If the problem is to find a solution to the *Traveling-Salesman problem*, for example, N would correspond to the number of cities that the salesman must visit.

Let $\Sigma_N^{(f)}$ represent the final state solution of the computation. Then the computational complexity, $H_C[\Sigma_N^{(f)}]$, is defined to be the *time it takes for the fastest program running on a universal computer* U (as measured in number of computing steps, or cycles) *to compute* $\Sigma_N^{(f)}$:

$$H_C[\Sigma_N^{(f)}] = \min_{U(\mathcal{P})=\Sigma_N^{(f)}} \tau_U(\mathcal{P}), \tag{2.54}$$

where $\tau_U(\mathcal{P})$ is the time it takes program $\mathcal{P}$ to run on the universal computer U.

The complexity of an object, thought of as a final state of a formal computational process, is then classified according to how fast H_C grows as a function of the problem size. The first nontrivial class of problems—class **P**—for example, consists of problems for which the computation time increases as some polynomial function of N: $H_C[\Sigma_N^{(f)}] \leq \mathcal{O}(N^\alpha)$ for some $\alpha < \infty$. Problems that can be solved with polynomial-time algorithms are called *tractable*. If they are solvable but are not in the class **P**, they are called *intractable*. If we compare the computation times for the same problem on two different universal computers U_1 and U_2, we might very well find that their respective polynomial-degree growth factors α_1 (for U_1) and α_2 (for U_2) are different; but, because of the ability of universal computers to simulate each other, it will never be the case that we will find another U_i that has a *faster than polynomial-time* growth function. The set of problems in class **P** is therefore effectively independent of the universal computer used in classifying them.

There is another class of problems, known as *nondeterministic polynomial time*—or class **NP**—problems, which may not necessarily be solvable in polynomial time, but the actual solutions to which may be tested for correctness in polynomial time. While it is obvious that $\mathbf{P} \subseteq \mathbf{NP}$, whether $\mathbf{P} \neq \mathbf{NP}$ remains an open question.

Problem classes that are characterized by their *spatial*, rather than temporal, growth requirements may also be defined. Class **PSPACE** problems, for example, require a memory storage space that grows as a polynomial function of the size of the problem size N (but may also require an arbitrary length of time to solve). While there is considerable evidence that $\mathbf{P} \subset \mathbf{PSPACE}$, it too remains an open problem.

Just as there exist universal computers that, given a particular input, can simulate any other computer, there are **NP-complete** (and **PSPACE-complete**) problems that, with that the appropriate input, are effectively equivalent to any **NP** (or **PSPACE**) problem of given size [Garey79]. For example, Boolean satisfiability (i.e. the problem of determining the truth values of the variable's of a Boolean expression so that the expression is true), is known to be an **NP-complete** problem [Garey79]. If, indeed, $\mathbf{P} \neq \mathbf{NP}$, then the time to solve **NP-complete** problems must grow faster than any polynomial in N.

We have only given a cursory look at computational complexity. More detailed discussions appear in the texts by Garey and Johnson [Garey79], Hopcroft and Ullman [Hopc79] and Davis and Weynker [DavisM83].

2.2.4.6 *Algorithmic Complexity*

Algorithmic complexity (sometimes also called "algorithmic randomness," "algorithmic information content," or "Solomonov-Kolmogorov-Chaitin complexity") was first introduced by Solomonov [Solo64], Kolmogorov [Kolm65] and Chaitin ([Chait75], [Chait87]) and has been extended by Zurek [Zurek89]. The algorithmic complexity of a state s, denoted by $K_U(s)$, is defined as *the length of the shortest computer program* $\mathcal{P}_U^*$ (measured in "bits") *such that, when executed on a universal computer* U, *yields the state* s:

$$K_U(s) \equiv | \mathcal{P}_U^* | . \tag{2.55}$$

Its virtue is its ability to assign a measure of complexity to an individual string, without having to resort to ensembles or probabilities. Its main drawback is that it is typically very hard to calculate exactly. Nonetheless it can be estimated for most systems relatively easily.

Suppose a state s is encoded as a binary string of 10^6 0's and 10^6 1's: $s = 10101010\ldots.$ While the number of raw bits defining s is huge, its algorithmic complexity is actually very small because it can be reproduced exactly by the following short program: **<print '10' 10^6 times>**. On the other hand, a completely random string of 0's and 1's—say $s_{\text{rand}} = 01101000110111101\ldots\ldots$—cannot be reproduced by a program that is significantly shorter than the one that simply lists each bit of the string, and therefore cannot be similarly compressed. In this case $K(s_{\text{rand}}) \sim | s_{\text{rand}} |$. Such incompressible strings are called, for obvious reasons, *algorithmically incompressible.*

We make three additional comments concerning algorithmic complexity, as defined by equation 2.55. First, while $K_U(s)$ clearly depends on the universal computer U that is chosen to run the program $\mathcal{P}^*$, *because of the ability of universal computers to simulate one another*, the difference between algorithmic complexities computed for universal computers U_1 and U_2 will be bounded by the $\mathcal{O}(1)$ size of the prefix code $\tau_{U_1 U_2}$ allowing any program $\mathcal{P}$ that is executed on U_1 to be executed on U_2 [Zurek89]:

$$| K_{U_1}(s) - K_{U_2}(s) | < | \tau_{U_1 U_2} | . \tag{2.56}$$

This finite difference obviously becomes increasingly less important in the limit of very long strings. For purposes of mathematical analysis, $K_U(s)$ can be treated as being effectively independent of U.

The second comment is that while $K(s)$ can always be estimated for finite strings, it is in general impossible to tell whether a string of arbitrary length is random; a difficulty that is due to Godel's incompleteness theorem and first pointed out by Chaitin [Chaitin88]. For example, while the binary representations of the decimal parts of π (00100100001111110110 1...), e (1011011111100001010...) or $\sqrt{2}$ (01101010000010011 11...) may all appear to be random—so that their Shannon complexity is large—each string can in fact be represented considerably more compactly using any number of simple (i.e. short) algorithms; i.e. their algorithmic complexity is essentially zero. The final comment is that algorithmic complexity is really a better measure of the degree of randomness in a system rather than its complexity. For example, while we intuitively expect the complexity of a completely random string to vanish, its algorithmic complexity is maximal. Gell-Mann [GellM88] has suggested that the problem is that algorithmic complexity tells us only how much information is required to encode a state; it tells us nothing about how difficult it is to reproduce that state from, say, its bit-string encoding. What is needed is therefore a measure of how much effort is required to deduce a state from its encoded form; i.e. we need a dynamic measure of complexity.

Zurek [Zurek89] has extended the notion of algorithmic complexity to bring it more in line with thermodynamics and conventional statistical mechanics. He proposes that physical entropy consists of the sum of (1) the information missing from available measurements of a system (as determined by Shannon's information), and (2) the information that is already contained in the available data (as measured by the system's algorithmic complexity). In this way, the usual Boltzman-Shannon missing information is generalized to include information about the cost storing information about the system. A detailed discussion of the insights this new notion of physical entropy gives into the whole process of measurement appears in [Zurek90].

2.2.4.7 *Logical Depth*

Bennett ([Benn86], [Benn90]) has recently introduced a measure of dynamic complexity he calls *logical depth*. The logical depth of an object $\mathcal{O}$, denoted by $\mathcal{D}_U^L(\mathcal{O})$, is defined to be *the execution time required by a universal computer U to generate $\mathcal{O}$, while running the minimal-sized program $\mathcal{P}^*$ that does so*:

$$\mathcal{D}_U^L(\mathcal{O}) = \tau_U(\mathcal{P}^*), \qquad \text{where } U(\mathcal{P}^*) = \mathcal{S}(\mathcal{O}), \tag{2.57}$$

where $\mathcal{S}(\mathcal{O})$ is the bit-string representation of object $\mathcal{O}$ and $\tau_U(\mathcal{P}^*)$ is the time it takes the minimal-sized program $\mathcal{P}^*$ to execute on U. As in the case of algorithmic complexity $K_U(s)$ (equation 2.55), because of the ability of universal computers to simulate one another, $\mathcal{D}_U^L(\mathcal{O})$ is roughly independent of the universal computer U used to measure it.

According to equation 2.57, both highly ordered strings (*Ex:* left hand side plot of figure 2.14) and completely random ones (*Ex:* right hand side plot of figure 2.14) are "shallow" since they can both can be computed with "short" programs of the form **<print x>**. On the other hand, a number like π, which we previously saw has a minimal algorithmic complexity, by virtue of the computational effort required to generate N digits even from a simple algorithm, is relatively "deep" when compared to most other length-N numbers. Moreover, logical depth obeys what Bennett calls the "slow-growth law," which suggests that deep objects cannot be produced quickly from shallow ones.

Logical depth is thus consistent with our intuitive understanding of complexity. A "complex" biological organism is deep precisely because it requires a long and complex computation to describe. On the other hand, a regularly arranged crystal is shallow because it can be described by a short algorithm. Likewise, a random state of a physical gas can be reproduced with the simple statement **print** $\boldsymbol{S_G}$, where S_G represents the state of the gas, so that it too, like the crystal, is logically shallow. This last result is also consistent with our intuition: while a gas is certainly a complex system, it lacks organization and therefore contains little innate complexity.

Perhaps the only drawback to using logical depth as a complexity measure in practice is that it is hard to apply to physical systems. One might try to substitute the computational effort required to simulate the evolution of a physical system for execution time to generate a given number, but doing so brings into play another variable: the efficiency and realism with which a mathematical model simulates the actual evolution of the physical system. There are countless examples of relatively "simple" physical processes that computers nonetheless have a very hard time simulating (think of your favorite low-dimensional chaotic system). Would we, in such cases, be measuring the complexity of the physical system or the mathematical model used to describe that system?

2.2.4.8 *Thermodynamic Depth*

Most of the preceding measures of complexity tacitly assume that a state of whatever physical system whose complexity is being measured is amenable to a bit-string representation. Although there are good reasons to make this assumption, it is not unreasonable to search for a measure of complexity that depends solely on the physical properties of the system in question. Lloyd and Pagels have proposed just such a measure, called *thermodynamic depth* ([Lloyd88], [Lloyd90]).

Related to *logical depth* (see above), the thermodynamic depth, $\mathcal{D}_U^T(S)$ of a system $\mathcal{S}$ in state S measures *how much information must be processed in order for* $\mathcal{S}$ *to evolve to* S.

Lloyd and Pagels deduced this measure as the only one that is consistent with the following three properties (that they postulated must be satisfied by any general measure of complexity $\mathcal{C}$): (1) $\mathcal{C}$ must be a continuous function of the probabilities of the experimentally defined trajectories that can result in the $\mathcal{S}$'s given state; (2) If each of N trajectories leading to the given state are equally weighted (i.e. all probabilities $p_i = 1/N$) then $\mathcal{C}$ must be a monotonically increasing function of N (this guarantees that a more accurate experimental determination of the trajectories leading to the given state cannot decrease the state's complexity); and (3) $\mathcal{C}$ must be additive with respect to intermediate processes—i.e., if a process proceeds from state $S_1 \to S_M$ via intermediate states $S_1 \to S_2 \to S_3 \to \cdots \to S_M$, then $\mathcal{C}(S_1 \to S_M) = \sum_{i=1}^{M-1} \mathcal{C}(S_i \to S_{i+1})$.

Lloyd and Pagels show that these three requirements lead uniquely to an average complexity of a state proportional to the Shannon entropy of the set of (experimentally determined) trajectories leading to the given state $(= \sum_i p_i \log_2 p_i)$. The thermodynamic depth of a state S to which the system $\mathcal{S}$ has evolved via the ith possible trajectory is equal to the amount of information required to specify that trajectory, or $\mathcal{D}_U^T(\mathcal{S}) \propto \log_2 p_i$. In the case of Hamiltonian systems, Lloyd and Pagels show that thermodynamic depth is proportional to the difference between the state's thermodynamic entropy (i.e. its coarse grained entropy) and its fine-grained entropy, given by $k_{\mathrm{B}} \times$ *volume of points in phase space corresponding to the system's trajectory*, where k_{B} is Boltzman's constant.

To be more precise, define a trajectory of macroscopic states of a system $\mathcal{S}$ to be an ordered set of macroscopic states $\{S_{i_1}, S_{i_2}, \ldots, S_{i_n}\}$, such that $\mathcal{S}$ was in state S_{i_1} at time t_1, in state S_{i_2} at time $t_2 \geq t_1$, and so on. Let $p(S_{i_1}, S_{i_2}, \ldots, S_{i_n}, S)$ be the experimentally obtained probability for the trajectory $S_{i_1} \to S_{i_2} \to \ldots \to S_{i_n} \to S$ ending with the final state S. The probability that $\mathcal{S}$ evolved to S via the trajectory $S_{i_1} \to S_{i_2} \to \ldots \to S_{i_n} \to S$ is $p(S_{i_1}, S_{i_2}, \ldots, S_{i_n} \mid S) = p(S_{i_1}, S_{i_2}, \ldots, S_{i_n}, S)/p(S)$. Lloyd and Pagels [Lloyd88] prove that the only function that is consistent with their requirements (1)-(3), given above, is:

$$f\left[p\left(S_{i_1}, \ldots, S_{i_n} | S\right)\right] = -k \sum_{i_1, \ldots i_n = 1}^{m_1, \ldots m_n} p\left(S_{i_1}, \ldots, S_{i_n} | S\right) \log_2 p\left(S_{i_1}, \ldots, S_{i_n} | S\right), \quad (2.58)$$

where m_j, $j = i_1, i_2, \ldots, i_n$ is the number of different possible states S_j, and k is an arbitrary constant.

Thermodynamic depth satisfies several welcome properties: (1) it is a purely objective measure in the sense that a different set of measurements using the same experimental data always yield the same depth; (2) it vanishes for both completely ordered and disordered systems; (3) the complexity of merged copies of a given system increases only by the depth of the copying process (which is, by comparison, typically small), and (4) the slightly subtle, but intuitive, property of "revealed probing." By this we mean that it provides the "prober" the ability to tailor depth of the probe to a desired degree of resolution. As finer and finer details of the microscopic state of a gas are revealed by probing the state of the gas to great accuracy, what may initially appear to be shallow may, which successive probing, be discovered to be deep; on the other hand, the fact that successively finer probes of, say, a crystal yield effectively the same (shallow) depth at all levels reveals that the thermodynamic depth of a crystal is indeed shallow.

Zurek [Zurek89] points out the following connection between algorithmic complexity and thermodynamic depth: if Lloyd's and Pagels' notion of thermodynamic depth is used to define a minimal depth—defined by the size of the smallest program that yields a final state $\Sigma^{(f)}$ from initial state $\Sigma^{(i)}$—then it is closely approximated by the difference in the algorithmic complexities of the two states. LLoyd and Pagels [Lloyd88] also note that while the *absolute depth* of a state—which is proportional to the minimum amount of information necessary to identify a trajectory that the system could have followed to reach the desired state—is the obvious analogue of logical depth (see **Logical Depth** above), the two measures are not the same: absolute depth is measured with respect to the most likely trajectory whereas logical depth is measured with respect to the *algorithmically* most likely trajectory. The two measures are the same only if all one-ended input programs have the same probability.

2.2.5 *Complexity as Science: Toward a New Worldview?*

Does complex adaptive systems theory entail a new worldview? While it is much too early in the evolution of this still nascent field to make any definitive assertions regarding how successful a *science* complex system theory represents, if it is viewed purely as a conceptional and methodological vehicle for understanding the dynamics of complex systems, complex systems theory also undeniably represents a radical departure from the traditional scientific worldview. Consider, for example, how physics has traditionally viewed the world (see left-hand-side of figure 2.19).

Traditionally, physics has tended to (and still predisposed to) understand phenomena by first stripping away layers of complexity by isolating the "inside" of a system from an "outside." It then focuses its attention on sets of pairwise interactions $\phi(A, B)$ between separate objects, A and B. Understandably, physics simplifies systems in this way in order to focus on relevant features of a problem and/or to render a problem mathematically tractable, and has unquestionably been successful in doing so (at least within the problem domains to which this conceptual distillation has been heretofore applied).*

At the same time, however, we must also appreciate that this simplification *does not* necessarily reflect a deep philosophical insight into how nature works. Because the universe, *as a whole*, makes no absolute distinctions between objects and their environment, one can hope to understand its behavior, *as a whole*, only by dealing honestly and directly with its irreducible complexity; i.e. in a way that respects its complex intertwined, multilayered webs of many-object interactions.

Objects in the real world possess both an internal structure, consisting of low-level interactions among lower-level constituents, and external interactions within

*Recall our discussion of *conceptual modeling* in chapter 1 (pages 29-39).

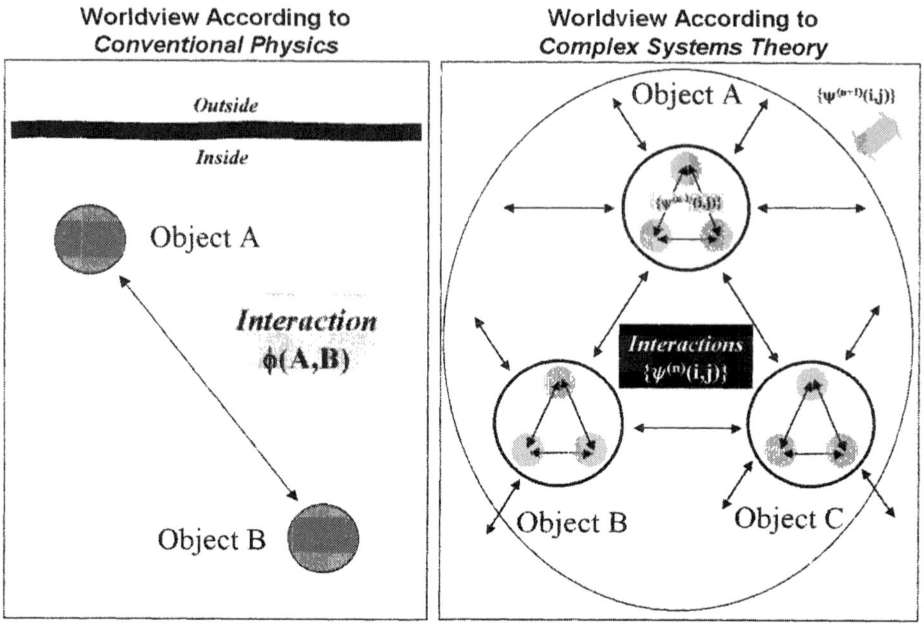

Fig. 2.19 Schematic distinction between two conceptual worldviews: (1) how physics has *traditionally* viewed the world, and (2) the new worldview as expounded by *complex systems theory*; see text.

a context provided for by higher-level constructs. Biological cells, for example, simultaneously harbor an enormously complicated inner world (that consists of enzymes, lipids, DNA, and other structures) and are vital components of a very complicated outer world. Similarly, the viability of human beings as conscious organisms not only depends profoundly on the autopoietic stability of a complicated inner world of highly interconnected cells, but whose mutual interaction, if viewed on a higher level, creates entire cultures.*

Complex adaptive systems theory strongly suggests that (i) most interesting phenomena arise because of an irreducible, coupling between object and environment (so that any distinction between inside and outside is artificial and not representative of how real systems are fundamentally structured [Atman93]), and (ii) "objects" are semantic constructs that are functions of the local context within which their existence, or nonexistence, is assigned meaning, rather than independently, and objectively, existing entities within a system.

Given that, historically, new developments in mathematics and physics have always been closely aligned, we can anticipate a strong need to develop a new "mathematics" in order to effectively deal with these issues. Indeed, the relatively new field

*See H. Bloom's *The Lucifer Principle* (The Atlantic Monthly Press, 1995) for a provocative philosophical examination of cultural evolution as seen through the "eyes" of complexity.

of multiagent-based modeling and simulation—that was borne of the specific need to go beyond traditional methods of describing complex systems and which blends mathematics, computation, biology, sociology and physics—may be a glimpse of this new "mathematics." As an emerging *science*, complex systems theory therefore engenders a conceptual paradigm shift from *reductionism* to a fundamentally *holistic* worldview: a shift away from a long held belief that complex self-organized behavior requires a complex underlying dynamics and/or substructure toward the new notion that complexity is an emergent phenomenon that often arises from the interactions among a large assemblage of otherwise simple parts; i.e. the properties of the *parts* must be understood as a dynamics of *whole.**

Evidence of this shift is nowhere stronger than in the emerging interdisciplinary field of *artificial life.* Artificial life concerns one of the last great frontiers of science: the fundamental principles of life itself.

2.2.6 *Artificial Life*

"Only when we are able to view life-as-we-know-it in the larger context of life-as-it-could-be will we really understand the nature of the beast. Artificial Life (AL) is a relatively new field employing a synthetic approach to the study of life-as-it-could-be. It views life as a property of the organization of matter, rather than a property of the matter which is so organized."–Chris Langton [Lang89]†

Artificial Life (AL) is one of the central research areas in complex adaptive systems theory. Its origin—at least in spirit, if not in name—dates back to the mathematician von Neumann's explorations of self-reproducing automata in the 1950s (see discussion below). AL has recently blossomed, particularly during the last 15 years or so, from being defined by a few toy "worlds" hardly more sophisticated than Conway's *Life*-rule CA universe, to intricately rendered 3D artificial universes populated with interacting creatures undergoing an open-ended evolution. While, in its formative stages, AL could be viewed as being the computational component of complex adaptive systems theory, it is today a mature, focused (albeit still widely

*Fritjof Capra ([Capra86], [Capra97]) has been an eloquent spokesman for an ecological world view, arguing that, ultimately, ecological awareness is a deeply religious awareness in which an individual feels connected with the whole (as in the original root meaning of the Latin word *religare*: "to bind strongly"). Capra believes this world view represents but a small a glimpse of other important paradigm shifts now taking place in how we understand physical reality: (1) from the part to the whole; (2) from structure to process; (3) from objective to "epistemic" science; i.e. a shift from a view in which descriptions of nature are understood as objective and independent of the human observer to a view in which epistemology, or the understanding of the process of knowledge, must be included explicitly in the description of phenomena; (4) from "building" to "network" as metaphor of knowledge; and (5) from truth to approximate descriptions. An excellent closely related monograph on the relationship between "part" and "whole" in physics is *The Conscious Universe* by Kafatos and Nadeau [Kafa90].

†Chris Langton organized the first international conference on artificial life in 1987 [Lang89] and is widely acknowledged as one of the field's founding fathers.

interdisciplinary), research field in its own right. Several conferences dedicated to AL are now held annually.

While even a semi-complete treatment of AL would take us too far afield from the main thread of this book, it is nonetheless instructive to point out how AL derives, in part, from CA theory. AL is mentioned here also for another simple, but ironic, reason. EINSTein—which, because it is a multiagent-based model of *combat*, obviously entails modeling the dynamics of (virtual) *death*—is also, from its conception, design, development, and use, an *artificial-life* model of the dynamics of combat.

References include Adami [Adami98}, Bonabeau [Bona99], Brooks [Brooks99], Emmeche [Emmeche94], Johnson [JohnS95], Langton ([Lang86]-[Lang95]), and Levy [Levy92]. AL-conference proceedings, published by MIT press, are also highly recommended, as they contain many of AL's seminal work (listed in chronological order): [Meyer91], [Meyer93], [Cliff94], [Maes96], [Pfeif98], [Adami98b], [Bedau00], [Meyer00], [Hall01] and [Stand03]. Stand-alone AL systems that can be used both for learning about AL and for research purposes, include *Avida*,[*] *Ecolab*,[†] *Tierra*,[‡] and *SWARM*,[§] coupled with *Evo*,[¶] which is an associated software development framework that allows developers to build complex AL simulations using SWARM.

2.2.6.1 *Self-Reproducing Automata*

John von Neumann originally conceived of cellular automata as abstract models of "self-reproducing machines." He was intrigued by the apparent disparity between how, on the one hand, nature handles reproduction—in which the complexity of the offspring is generally at least as great as its parent—and how, on the other hand, mechanical assembly lines appear to inevitably decrease complexity (i.e. the assembly line is generally a more complex "machine" than the machine (or machines) that it is designed to construct). Von Neumann asked the obvious question of whether there was a way to construct a "self-reproducing machine" capable of

[*] Avida is a joint project of the *Digital Life Laboratory*, headed by Chris Adami, at the *California Institute of Technology* and Richard Lenski's *Microbial Evolution Laboratory* at *Michigan State university:* http://dllab.caltech.edu/avida/.

[†] *Ecolab* is a open source multiagent-based simulation system for studying dynamics of evolution. It is maintained by Russell Standish, Director of the *High Performance Computing Support Unit* of the *University of New South Wales*: http://parallel.hpc.unsw.edu.au/rks/ecolab/.

[‡] *Tierra* was one of the first AL simulations of artificial evolution of digital organisms. It was developed by zoologist Tom Ray, at University of Oklahoma: http://www.isd.atr.co.jp/~ray/tierra/. Tierra is discussed briefly earlier in this chapter (see page 38).

[§] SWARM was originally developed by the *Santa Fe Institute* (http://www.santafe.edu/), but is now under control of the *Swarm Development Group* (http://www.swarm.org/). SWARM is discussed briefly in chapter 1 (see page 52).

[¶] *Evo* is a product of *The Omicron Group*, which is an independent multidisciplinary research group specializing in complex adaptive systems and multiagent simulation: http://omicrongroup.org/evo/.

producing other machines without a concomitant loss of complexity. The following long quote, taken from von Neumann's seminal work, *The Theory of Automata: Construction, Reproduction, Homogeneity* [vonN66], eloquently summarizes his fundamental motivations (note, in particular, his emphasis on self-reproduction):

> We will investigate automata under two important and connected, aspects: those of logics and of construction. We can organize our considerations under the headings of five main questions:
>
> *(A) Logical universality.* When is a class of automata logically universal, i.e. able to perform all those logical operations that are all performable with finite (but arbitrarily extensive) means? Also, with what additional—variable, but in the essential respects standard—attachments is a single automaton logically universal?
>
> *(B) Constructibility.* Can an automaton be constructed, i.e. assembled and built from appropriately defined 'raw materials', by another automaton? Or, starting from the other end and extending the question, what class of automata can be constructed by one, suitably given, automaton? The variable, but essentially standard attachments to the latter, in the sense of the second question of (A), may here be permitted.
>
> *(C) Construction-universality.* Making the second question of (B) more specific, can any one, suitable given, automaton be construction-universal, i.e. be able to construct in the sense of question (B) (with suitable, but essentially standard, attachments) every other automaton?
>
> *(D) Self-reproduction.* Narrowing question (C), can any automaton construct other automata that are exactly like it? Can it be made, in addition, to perform further tasks, e.g. also construct certain other prescribed automata?
>
> *(E) Evolution.* Combining questions (C) and (D), can the construction of automata by automata progress from simpler types to increasingly complicated types? Also, assuming some suitable definition of 'efficiency,' can this evolution go from less efficient to more efficient automata?

Von Neumann approached the problem with the assurance that since self reproduction in nature consists of (albeit highly complex) biochemical machines, the actions of a given biological machine should therefore also be describable by an algorithm. Von Neumann then argued that if such an algorithm exists, then there should also be a *Universal Turing Machine* (UTM) than can perform it; i.e., there should exist a UTM capable of self-reproduction. The fundamental conclusion that von Neumann was really after is actually best expressed in reverse order; namely, that fact that such a self-reproducing UTM exists at all, by itself immediately lends credence to the assertion that the processes by which living organisms reproduce themselves (and, arguably, the mechanisms of life itself) are achievable by machines.

Von Neumann was able to construct a self-reproducing UTM embedded within a 29-state/5-cell neighborhood two-dimensional cellular automaton, composed of several tens of thousands of cells. It was, to say the least, an enormously complex "machine." Its set of 29 states consist largely of various logical building blocks (AND and OR gates, for example), several types of transmission lines, data encoders and recorders, clocks, etc. Von Neumann was unfortunately unable to finish the proof that his machine was a UTM before his death, but the proof was later completed and published by Arthur Burks [vonN66].

Von Neumann's machine is actually an example of a *universal constructor*. It must not only carry out logical operations (i.e. act as a universal computer), but must also be able to identify and manipulate various components. The universal constructor C must be able to both (1) construct the machine whose "blueprint" appears in symbolic form on its input tape and (2) attach a copy of that same blueprint to the machine once it is constructed. Self-reproduction is the special case where C's input tape actually contains the blueprint data for C itself. Alas, there are a few subtleties.

Suppose we start with an automaton A that is given a tape with a blueprint B_A on it. The composite machine will then construct a copy of A but it *is not*, in and of itself, self-reproducing; i.e. the aggregate machine $A+B_A$ creates A, not $A+B_A$. This situation is not remedied by simply adding a description of B_A to B_A, since in this case $A+B_{A+B_A}$ yields $A+B_A$ and not $A+B_{A+B_A}$. Thus, whatever we try seems destined to lead in an infinite regress!

Von Neumann recognized this problem, of course. His solution was to essentially use the cooperative action of several automata to effectively copy a machine's blueprint. He first introduced a 'copier' automaton A' that copies whatever blueprint B it is given. Next, he defined an automaton A'' that inserts a copy of B into the automaton constructed by A. Let us call the composite structure $A + A' + A''$ by $\hat{A}$. Let $B_{\hat{A}}$ be the blueprint of $\hat{A}$ and let $\tilde{A}$ be $\hat{A}$ with $B_{\hat{A}}$ inserted as a tape into A. Then $\tilde{A}$ is self-reproducing and, since $\hat{A}$ exists before the blueprint $B_{\hat{A}}$ is itself defined, no infinite ingress is involved.*

*The reader may be asking, "*Just how 'complex' must a self-reproducing automaton be?*" Consider that Von Neumann's self-reproducing automaton consisted of several *thousand* cells, a five site neighborhood and 29 states per site [vonN66]. A few years later, Thatcher [That62] used the same 29 states but was able to simplify the construction considerably. Codd, in his Doctoral dissertation [Codd70], managed to reduce the number of required states to just *eight* states per cell. Codd's model, however, like that of his predecessor's, unfortunately also involved tens of thousands of cells; a simplified proof was later published by Arbib [Arbib66]. Langton [Lang86], by adopting a somewhat "looser" definition of self-reproduction, managed to construct a self-reproducing structure using the same number of states as Codd's model but requiring an area of just 10×15 sites! The current lower bound on the minimal complexity necessary for self-reproduction belongs to Byl [Byl89], who, using Langton's own "loose" definition, reduced the system requirements to only *six* states per site and an area of just 4×4 sites.

2.2.6.2 General Properties

AL-based computer simulations are characterized by these five general properties [Lang89] (compare this list to our list of general properties of complex adaptive systems, pages 105-114):

(1) *They are defined by populations of simple programs or instructions about how individual parts all interact.*
(2) *There is no single "master oracle" program that directs the action of all other programs.*
(3) *Each program defines how simple entities respond to their environment locally.*
(4) *There are no rules that direct the global behavior.*
(5) *Behaviors on levels higher than individual programs are emergent.*

Looking over this list of properties, it should come as no surprise that multiagent-based modeling techniques—which we discussed earlier in chapter 1 (see pages 44-59)—originated in early AL studies; see for example, our discussion of *Tierra* (page 38), which is one of the first "agent" models of artificial evolution of digital organisms.

AL is an attempt to understand life "as it is" by examining a larger context of *life as it could be.* The underlying supposition is that life owes at least as much to its existence to the way in which information is organized as it does to the physical substance (i.e., matter) that embodies that information. AL thus studies life by using artificial components (such as "agents") to capture the behavioral essence of living systems. The supposition is that if the artificial parts are organized correctly, in a way that respects the organization of the living system, then the artificial system will exhibit the same characteristic dynamical behavior as the natural system on higher levels as well. Notice that this bottom-up, synthesist approach stands in marked contrast to more conventional top-down, analytical approaches.

The fundamental concept of AL is *emergence*, or the appearance of higher-level properties and behaviors of a system that—while obviously originating from the collective dynamics of that system's components—are neither to be found in nor are directly deducible from the lower-level properties of that system. Emergent properties are properties of the "whole" that are not possessed by any of the individual parts making up that whole. Aside from the kinds of emergence that have already been mentioned (see page 108), two excellent examples will be presented below: (1) *Gliders* and other kinds of high-level objects that emerge in an AL-universe known as Conway's *Life* rule (see page 143), and (2) Intricate spatial structures that emerge in another two-dimensional AL-world called *Vants* (page 146). These two cases are particularly interesting because in neither case does there appear any way to predict beforehand—*knowing only the rules that the objects of a given AL "world" obey*—what high-level structures will emerge. In other words, they both display a strongly non-trivial form of emergence; a much stronger form, for example, than, a computer program that can calculate N digits of π, despite the fact that no one line of the program can by itself perform the same function. The calculation, in this example, can only very loosely be called "emergent," as it can be trivially predicted to be the outcome of putting the individual lines of code together to form a complete program.

The concept of emergence that is of interest to the AL-researcher is a far deeper one. Unfortunately, while emergence, as a concept, is central to the study of AL--and to complexity, in general— the reader would be sadly mistaken in assuming that it is anything close to being well-defined. As we have seen already with the idea of complexity itself, and as we will shortly see again with the concept of information, when it comes to defining exactly what we mean by "emergence," the only thing we can honestly assert is that "we know it when we see it" (and even then some of us might choose to call it something else anyway!). Nonetheless, there have been a few recent attempts to erect a more formal framework.

Cariani [Carian92], for example, identifies three major conceptions of emergence: *computational emergence*, *thermodynamic emergence*, and what he calls *emergence relative to a model.* Computational emergence is essentially the view advocated above; namely, that complex global behaviors arise out of a large assemblage of local computational interactions. Cariani criticizes this view on semantic grounds: if an outside observer observes a program whose function he does not know, how can that observer objectively tell if the computations are emergent? Thermodynamic emergence—which is the physical analogue of computational emergence, describing certain behaviors of reaction-diffusion systems, attractor states in dynamics systems and so on—may be said to suffer from the same drawback.

Cariani advocates the view of emergence relative to a model, where the model is introduced to embody the set of an observer's expectations as to how the system in question will behave in the future. If the system behaves in an unexpected way—i.e. in such a way that the model no longer faithfully describes the behavior of the system—the system's behavior can then be formally called "emergent." The modeling framework itself consists of *measurement*, or the semantic operations that relate the formal symbols of the model to the state of an actual system, and *computations*, or the syntactic operations that relate the formal symbols of the model to other symbols. Pragmatic, or intentional, operations, are those that determine an appropriate set of measurements and computations for satisfying the purposes of the observer. The point of these definitions, is that once having set up an epistemological framework for describing operations of modeling relations, the same formal framework can then be used to *"describe the operations of the modeling relations as they appear in organisms, devices, and other observers."*

Another approach, based on tying together the notions of emergence and hierarchy via the generalized *hyperstructure* (see right-hand-side of figure 2.19 on page 130), is suggested by ([Baas93], [Baas94]). Baas also distinguishes between two types of emergence: *deducible* and *observational.* Deducible emergence refers to higher-level processes that can be determined in theory from lower-order structures (ex: phase-transitions in the thermodynamic limit). Observational emergence refers to higher-order processes that cannot be deduced from lower-order structures. An example is Godel's *Incompleteness Theorem*, which asserts that any consistent, finite logical system contains statements that are true but are unprovable within the system [Godel31] (here, observation is the logical "truth" function). Baas [Baas94] ends one of his sections with the provocative question, *"Does emergence in some cases...take the rank among the laws of nature?"*

Let us now turn our attention, briefly, to the prototype of all artificial-life simulations: *cellular automata.* Cellular automata form the conceptual backbone of many, if not all, AL models, and are also direct precursors to multiagent-based simulations, in general, and EINSTein, in particular.

2.2.7 *Cellular Automata*

Cellular automata (CA) are a class of spatially and temporally discrete, deterministic mathematical systems characterized by local interaction and an inherently parallel form of evolution. First introduced by von Neumann in the early 1950s to act as simple models of biological self-reproduction, CA are prototypical models for complex systems and processes consisting of a large number of identical, simple, locally interacting components. The study of these systems has generated great interest over the years because of their ability to generate a rich spectrum of very complex patterns of behavior out of sets of relatively simple underlying rules. Moreover, they appear to capture many essential features of complex self-organizing cooperative behavior observed in real systems.

Although much of the theoretical work with CA has been confined to mathematics and computer science, there have been numerous applications to physics, biology, chemistry, biochemistry, and geology, among other disciplines. Some specific examples of phenomena that have been modeled by CA include fluid and chemical turbulence ([DHum86], [Gerh89]), plant growth [Linde89] and the dendritic growth of crystals [Kess90], ecological theory [Phip92], DNA evolution, the propagation of infectious diseases [Segel99], social dynamics [Epstein96], forest fires [Bak90], and patterns of electrical activity in neural networks [Fran92]. As this book clearly demonstrates, mobile CA are also being used to simulate many aspects of military combat [Woodc88].

The best sources of information on CA are conference proceedings and collections of papers, such as the one's edited by Boccara [Bocc93], Gutowitz [Guto90], Preston [Prest84] and Wolfram ([Wolfram83], [Wolfram94], and [Wolfram03]). An excellent review of how CA can be used to model physical systems is given by Toffoli and Margolus [Toffoli87]. See also *Cellular Automata: A Discrete Universe* [Ilach01b].

While there is an enormous variety of particular CA models—each carefully tailored to fit the requirements of a specific system—most CA models usually possesses these five generic characteristics:

- *Discrete lattice of cells:* the system substrate consists of a one-, two- or three-dimensional lattice of cells.
- *Homogeneity:* all cells are equivalent.
- *Discrete states:* each cell takes on one of a finite number of possible discrete states.
- *Local interactions:* each cell interacts only with cells that are in its local neighborhood.
- *Discrete dynamics:* at each discrete unit time, each cell updates its current state according to a transition rule taking into account the states of cells in its neighborhood.

There is a deceptive simplicity to these characteristics. In fact, as we shall see repeatedly in this book, such systems are capable of extremely complicated behavior. For example, although obeying local rules and having no intrinsic length scales other than the size of the neighborhoods about each site, CA can generate global patterns with very long-range order and correlation. CA are dynamically rich enough to be seriously considered as alternative mathematical models for a variety of physical systems. Indeed, EINSTein (as will see in chapter 4), is essentially nothing more than a basic CA model that has been generalized to allow the individual cells to move; i.e. a *mobile* CA.

While one is free to think of CA as being nothing more than formal idealizations of partial differential equations, their real power lies in the fact that they represent a large class of *exactly computable models*: since everything is fundamentally discrete, one need never worry about truncations or the slow accumulation of round-off error. Therefore, any dynamical properties observed to be true for such models take on the full strength of theorems [Toffoli77].

Exact computability in this sense, however, is achieved only at the cost of being able to obtain approximate solutions. Perturbation analysis, for example, is rendered virtually meaningless in this context. It is not surprising that traditional investigatory methodologies are not very well suited to studies of complex systems. Since the behavior of such models can generally be obtained *only* through explicit simulation, the computer becomes the one absolutely indispensable research tool.

2.2.7.1 *One-dimensional CA*

For a one-dimensional CA, the value of the ith cell at time t—denoted by $\sigma_i(t)$—evolves in time according to a rule F that is a function of $\sigma_i(t)$ and other cells that are within a range r (on the left and right) of $\sigma_i(t)$:

$$\sigma_i(t) = F\left(\sigma_{i-r}(t-1), \sigma_{i-r+1}(t-1), \ldots, \sigma_{i+r}(t-1)\right). \tag{2.59}$$

Since each cell takes on one of k possible values—that is, $\sigma_i(t) \in \{0, 1, 2, ..., k-1\}$ —the rule F is completely defined by specifying the value assigned to each of the k^{2r+1} possible $(2r+1)$–tuple configurations for a given range-r neighborhood:

$$
\begin{array}{cccccc}
\sigma_{i-r}(t-1) & \sigma_{i-r+1}(t-1) & \cdots & \sigma_{i+r}(t-1) & \rightarrow & \sigma_i(t) \\
\hline
0 & 0 & & 0 & \rightarrow & F(0,0,\ldots,0) \\
\vdots & \vdots & & \vdots & & \vdots \\
k-1 & k-1 & \cdots & k-1 & \rightarrow & F(k-1,\ldots,k-1)
\end{array}
\tag{2.60}
$$

Since F itself assigns any of k values to each of the k^{2r+1} possible $(2r+1)$-tuples, there are a total of $k^{k^{2r+1}}$ possible rules, which is an exponentially increasing function of both k and r. For the simplest case of nearest neighbors (range $r = 1$) and $k = 2$ ($\sigma_i = 0$ or 1), for example, there are $2^8 = 256$ possible rules. Increasing the number of values each cell can take on to $k = 3$ (but keeping the radius at $r = 1$) increases the rule-space size to $3^{3^3} \sim 7 \cdot 10^{12}$.

Let $k = 2$ (so that $\sigma_i(t) \in \{0,1\}$) and range $r = 1$, and consider the rule $F : \{0,1\}^3 \rightarrow \{0,1\}$ defined by:

$$
F = \sigma_{i-1}(t-1) \oplus_2 \sigma_{i+1}(t-1), \tag{2.61}
$$

where $\oplus_2$ is addition *modulo* 2. The explicit form of the dynamics is given by listing, for each of the eight possible local states that three adjacent cells can be in at time '$t-1$', the corresponding state at time 't' that is assigned by F to the central cell of this 3-tuple:

$$
\begin{array}{cccccccc}
111 & 110 & 101 & 100 & 011 & 010 & 001 & 000 \\
\downarrow & \downarrow & \downarrow & \downarrow & \downarrow & \downarrow & \downarrow & \downarrow \\
0 & 1 & 0 & 1 & 1 & 0 & 1 & 0
\end{array}
\tag{2.62}
$$

After choosing some specific initial global state,

$$
\vec{\sigma}(t=0) = (\sigma_1(0), \sigma_2(0), \sigma_3(0), \ldots, \sigma_N(0)),
$$

the temporal evolution of this CA is then given by the simultaneous application of F to each of the N lattice cells. For example, if four iterations are applied to a size $N = 17$ lattice with periodic boundary conditions, and the initial state $\vec{\sigma}(t=0) = 01011101011010101$, for example, we find that $\vec{\sigma}(t=0)$ evolves into $\vec{\sigma}(t=4) = 10000011011111000$:

$$
\begin{array}{cc}
\textit{time } (t) & \vec{\sigma}(t) \\
0 & 01011101011010101 \\
1 & 00010100011000000 \\
2 & 00100010111100000 \\
3 & 01010100100110000 \\
4 & 10000011011111000
\end{array}
\tag{2.63}
$$

Space-Time Patterns. Figure 2.20 shows the time evolution of a nearest-neighbor (radius $r = 1$) rule where σ is equal to either 0 or 1.* The row of eight boxes at the top of the figure shows the explicit rule-set, where—for visual clarity—a box has been arbitrarily colored *black* if the value $\sigma = 1$ and *white* if $\sigma = 0$. For each combination of three adjacent cells in generation 0, the rule F assigns a particular value to the next-generation center cell of the triplet.

Beginning from an initial state (at time = 0) consisting of the value zero everywhere except the center site, that is assigned the value 1, F is applied synchronously at each successive time step to each cell of the lattice. Each generation is represented by a row of cells and time is oriented downwards. The first image shows a blowup of the first five generations of the evolution. The second shows 300 generations. The figure illustrates the fact that simple rules can generate considerable complexity.

The space-time pattern generated from a single nonzero cell by this particular rule has a number of interesting properties. For example, it consists of a curious mixture of ordered behavior along the left-hand-side and what appears to be disordered behavior along the right-hand-side, separated by a corrugated boundary moving towards the left at a "speed" of about 1/4 cells per "clock" tick. In fact, it can be shown that, despite starting from an obviously non-random initial state and evolving according to a fixed deterministic rule, the temporal sequence of vertical values is completely random. Systems having the ability to deterministically generate randomness from non-random input are called autoplectic systems.

As another example, consider the rule shown at the top of figure 2.21. Its space-time evolution, starting from a random initial state, is shown at the bottom of the figure. Note that this space-time pattern can be described on two different levels: either on the cell-level, by explicitly reading off the values of the individual cells, or on a higher-level by describing it as a sea of particle-like structures superimposed on a periodic background. In fact, following a small initial transient period, temporal sections of this space-time pattern are always of the form:

...BBBBPBB...BB...BBBPBB...BBBPBBB...,

where "B" is a state of the periodic background consisting of repetitions of the sequence "10011011111000" (with spatial period 14 and temporal period 7), and the P's represent *particles*. The particle pattern P = "11111000," for example, repeats every four steps while being displaced two cells to the left; the particle P = "11101011000" repeats every ten steps while being displaced two cells to the right.

*This rule is usually cited by its *Wolfram code,* which is in this case is equal to *30* (see [Wolfram83]). Consider the $\oplus_2$ rule discussed above. If the bottom eight binary digits of the rule defined in equation 2.62 are interpreted as the binary representation of a decimal number, then the code for this rule, *Code*[$\oplus_2$], is given by its base ten equivalent: Code[$\oplus_2$] = $0 \cdot 2^0 + 1 \cdot 2^1 + 0 \cdot 2^2 + 1 \cdot 2^3 + 1 \cdot 2^4 + 0 \cdot 2^5 + 1 \cdot 2^6 + 0 \cdot 2^7 = 90$. More generally, for an arbitrary rule F of the form given in equation 2.59, its Wolfram code is defined by $\text{Code}[F] \equiv \sum_{\{\sigma_{i-r},\cdots,\sigma_{i+r}\}} F[\sigma_{i-r},\ldots,\sigma_{i+r}]\, k^{\sum_{j=-r}^{r} k^{r-j}\sigma_{i+j}}$.

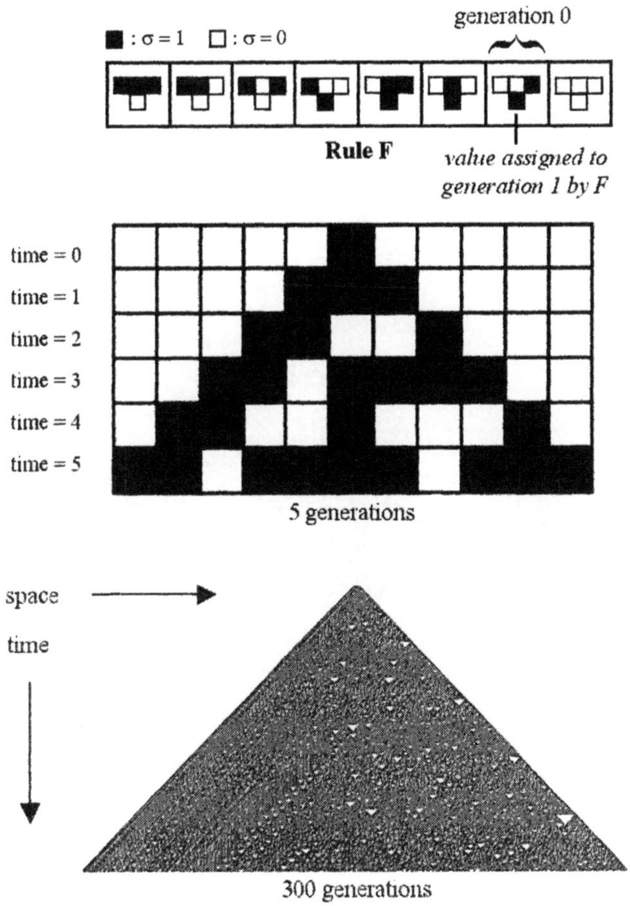

Fig. 2.20 Example of a one-dimensional CA (elementary rule-code 30) starting from a single nonzero seed.

Although the underlying dynamics describing this system is very simple, and entirely deterministic, there is an enormous variety, and complexity, of emergent particle-particle interactions. Such simple systems are powerful reminders that *complex higher-level dynamics need not have a complex underlying origin.* Indeed, suppose that we had been shown such a space-time pattern but were told nothing whatsoever about its origin. How would we make sense of its dynamics? Perhaps the only reasonable course of action would be to follow the lead of any good experimental particle-physicist and begin cataloging the various possible particle states and interactions: there are N particles of size s moving to the left with speed v; when a particle p of type P collides with q of type Q , the result is the set of particles $\{p_1, p_2, \ldots, p_N\}$; and so on. It would take a tremendous leap of intuition to fathom the utter simplicity of the real dynamics.

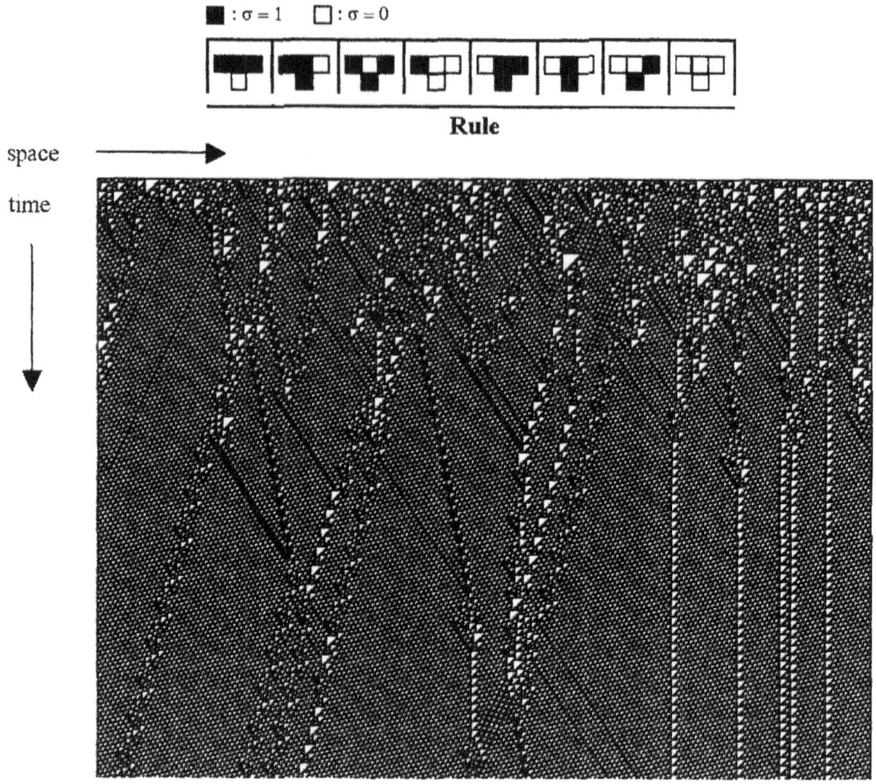

Fig. 2.21 Evolution of a one-dimensional CA starting from a random initial state

Behavioral Classes. In general, the behavior of CA is strongly reminiscent of the kinds of behavior observed in continuum dynamical systems, with simple rules yielding steady-state behaviors consisting of fixed points or limit cycles, and complex rules giving rise to behaviors that are analogous to deterministic chaos.

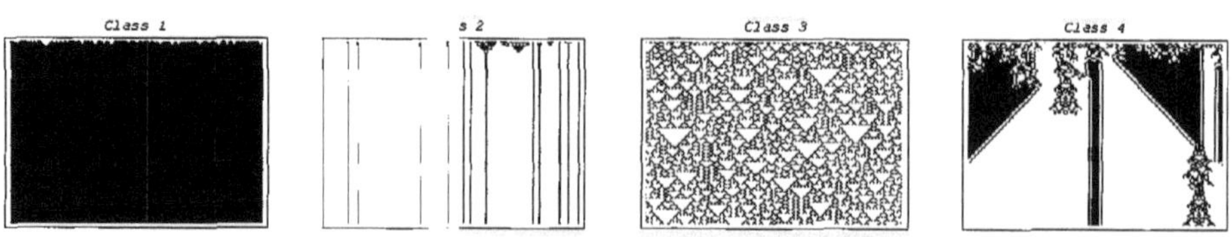

Fig. 2.22 Examples of the four basic *Wolfram* classes of CA behavior, starting from random initial conditions.

In fact, there is extensive empirical evidence suggesting that patterns generated by all (one-dimensional) CA evolving from disordered initial states fall into one of only four basic behavioral classes [Wolfram83] (see figure 2.22):

- *Class 1:* Evolution leads to a homogeneous state, in which all cells eventually attain the same value.
- *Class 2:* Evolution leads to either simple stable states or periodic and separated structures.
- *Class 3:* Evolution leads to chaotic nonperiodic patterns.
- *Class 4:* Evolution leads to complex, localized propagating structures.

All CA within a given class yield qualitatively similar behavior. While the behaviors of rules belonging to the first three rule classes bear a strong resemblance to those observed in continuous systems—the homogeneous states of class 1 rules, for example, are analogous to fixed-point attracting states in continuous systems, the asymptotically periodic states of class 2 rules are analogous to continuous limit cycles and the chaotic states of class 3 rules are analogous to strange attractors—the more complicated localized structures emerging from class 4 rules do not appear to have any obvious continuous analogues (although such structures are well characterized as being soliton-like in their appearance).

2.2.7.2 *Two-dimensional CA*

The formal study of CA really began not, as one might imagine, with the simpler one-dimensional systems discussed in the previous section but with von Neumann's work in the 1940's with self-reproducing two-dimensional CA [vonN66]. Such systems also gained considerable publicity (as well as notoriety!) in the 1970's with Conway's introduction of his *Life* rule [Berk82] and its subsequent popularization by Gardner in the journal *Scientific American* [Gard70].

In one dimension, a given site only has left and right neighbors (albeit neighbors that can be arbitrarily far apart). Thus, there is really only one kind of one-dimensional neighborhood structure that can be used in defining a rule. In two dimensions, however, various neighborhood structures may be used that are related to the symmetries of the underlying lattice. If we restrict ourselves only to lattices that possess both rotational and translational symmetry about each site, for example, we see that we can define CA on *hexagonal* (i.e. 3-neighbor), *square* (i.e. 4-neighbor) or *triangular* (i.e. 6-neighbor) lattices. The most commonly studied square lattice neighborhoods include the *von-Neumann* neighborhood, consisting of the four site horizontally and vertically adjacent to the center site of interest, and the *Moore* neighborhood, consisting of all eight sites immediately adjacent to the center site. Figure 2.23 shows examples of some commonly used neighborhood structures in two dimensions.

Conway's "Life" Rule. *Life* is "played" using the 9-neighbor *Moore* neighborhood (see center graphic in figure 2.23), and consists of (1) seeding a lattice with some pattern of "live" and "dead" cells, and (2) simultaneously—and repeatedly—applying the following three rules to each cell of the lattice at discrete time steps:

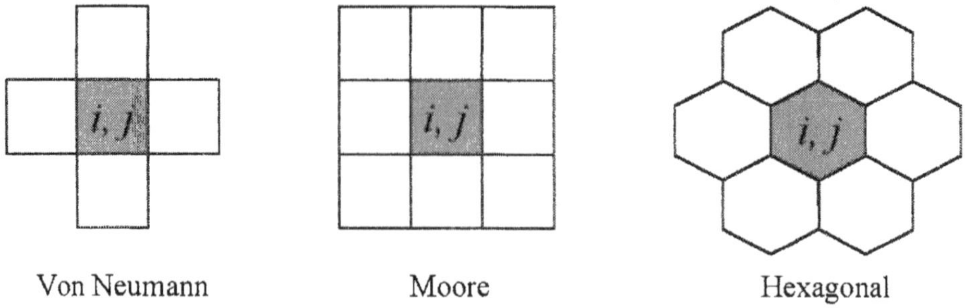

Fig. 2.23 Examples of CA neighborhoods in two dimensions.

- *Birth:* replace a previously dead cell with a live one if exactly 3 of its neighbors are alive.
- *Death:* replace a previously live cell with a dead one if either (1) the living cell has no more than one live neighbor (i.e. it dies of isolation), or (2) the living cell has more than three neighbors (i.e. it dies of overcrowding).
- *Survival:* retain living cells if they have either 2 or 3 neighbors.

One of the most intriguing patterns in Life is an oscillatory propagating pattern known as the "glider." Shown on the left-hand-side of figure 2.24, it consists of 5 "live" cells and reproduces itself in a diagonally displaced position once every four iterations.

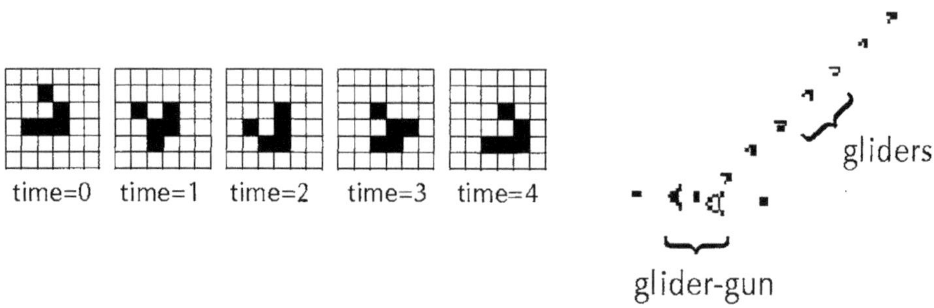

Fig. 2.24 Glider patterns in Conway's two-dimensional *Life* CA rule.

When the states of *Life* are projected onto a screen in quick succession by a fast computer, the glider gives the appearance of "walking" across the screen. The propagation of this pseudo-stable structure can also be seen as a self-organized emergent property of the system. The right-hand-side of figure 2.24 shows a still-frame in the evolution of a pattern known as a "glider-gun," which shoots-out a glider once every 30 iteration steps.

What is remarkable about this very simple appearing rule is that one can show that it is capable of *universal computation.** This means that with a proper selection of initial conditions (i.e. the initial distribution of "live" and "dead" cells), Life can be turned into a general purpose computer. This fact fundamentally limits the overall predictability of *Life*'s behavior.

The well known *Halting Theorem*, for example, asserts that there cannot exist a general algorithm for predicting when a computer will halt its execution of a given program [Garey79]. Given that Life is a universal computer—so that the *Halting Theorem* applies—this means that one cannot, in general, predict whether a particular starting configuration of live and dead cells will eventually die out. No shortcut is possible, even in principle. The best one can do is to sit back and patiently await *Life*'s own final outcome.

Put another way, this means that if you want to predict *Life*'s long-term behavior with another "model" or by using, say, a partial differential equation, you are doomed to fail from the outset because its long-term behavior is effectively unpredictable. *Life*—like all computationally universal systems—defines the most efficient simulation of its own behavior.†

2.2.7.3 *Other Kinds of CA*

There are at least as many variants of the basic CA algorithm as there are ways of generalizing the characteristics of a typical CA system. For example, one can consider *asynchronous* CA (in which the restriction that all sites update their values simultaneously throughout the lattice on each time step is lifted); *coupled-map* CA (which lift the restriction that sites can take on only discrete values by allowing them to take on a range of continuous values); *probabilistic* CA (in which deterministic state-transitions are replaced with specifications of the probabilities of the cell-value assignments); *non-homogeneous* CA (in which the state-transition rules are allowed to vary from cell to cell); *structurally dynamic* CA (in which site values and the network of lattice connections between sites both evolve according to some CA-like rules); and *mobile* CA (in which some, or all, lattice sites are free to move about the lattice).

Since the dynamics embedded within both ISAAC and EINSTein are so closely patterned after mobile CA rules, it is instructive to consider a simple example of such a rule.

*The proof of *Life*'s computational universality, while from simple, is nonetheless conceptually straightforward. It proceeds from the observation that each of the four essential elements for computation—namely, the *storage* (requiring an internal memory), *transmission* (requiring an internal clock and wires), and *processing* (requiring AND, OR, and NOT gates) of information—can all be implemented using a subset of *Life*'s own space-time patterns (such as *gliders*, *glider-guns*, *blocks*, *eaters*, among others). A sketch of the proof appears betwee pages 141-151 in [Ilacha01b].

†For additional details regarding this deceptively "simple" CA rule, and others similar to it, see Berlekamp, et.al. [Berk82], Gardner [Gard70], Poundstone [Pound85], and Wolfram [Wolfram02].

Vants. Introduced by Langton [Lang86], *vants*—which is a contraction of *"virtual ants"*—live on a two-dimensional Euclidean lattice and come in two flavors, *red* and *blue*. Each vant can move in any of four directions (E, W, N, S). Each lattice site is either empty or contains one of two types of food, *green* food or *yellow* food. Vants are fundamentally solitary creatures so that there is a strict conservation of the number of vants.

How a vant moves through the lattice depends on its color. When a red vant enters a site containing green food, for example, it turns to its right, enters the new lattice site, and leaves the previous occupied site colored yellow. When a red vant enters a yellow site, it enters the site on its left and leaves the previously occupied site colored green. A blue vant does exactly the reverse: when it enters a green site it moves into the square on its left and leaves the previously occupied site yellow; when it moves into a yellow site it then moves into the site on its right and leaves the previously occupied site green. If either kind of vant enters an empty site it continues to move straight ahead. If two or more vants enter the same lattice site, they continue with their respective motions—as defined above—as though the site was unoccupied by other vants; i.e. there is no explicit vant-vant interaction at any site.

More formally, let us introduce the "food"-value of lattice site (i, j) at time t, $\zeta_{i,j}(t)$ (= green or yellow); an *occupancy* variable, $\alpha_{i,j}(t)$, which is equal to zero unless the site (i, j) contains at least one vant, in which case $\alpha_{i,j}(t) = 1$; and the vant vector $\vec{\sigma}_n^{(r,b)}(t) = (i, j, d)$, specifying the state of the nth vant at time t, where the superscript labels the vant's color (r = red or b = blue), i and j specify the vant's (i, j) lattice position and $d \in \{E, W, N, S\}$ is its direction.

The food variable at site (i, j) remains unchanged unless the site is occupied, in which case the food type changes from either green $\rightarrow$ yellow, or yellow $\rightarrow$ green:

$$\begin{aligned} \zeta_{i,j}(t+1) &= (\text{green} \cdot \delta_{\zeta_{i,j}(t),\, \text{yellow}} + \text{yellow} \cdot \delta_{\zeta_{i,j}(t),\, \text{green}})\alpha_{i,j}(t) \\ &+ \zeta_{i,j}(t)[1 - \alpha_{i,j}(t)], \end{aligned} \tag{2.64}$$

where $\delta_{x,y}$ is the *Kronecker-Delta* function: $\delta_{x,y} = 1$ if and only if $x = y$, else $\delta_{x,y} = 0$. Table 2.3 shows the rule table for the $\vec{\sigma}_n^{(r,b)}$ transition.*

It is intriguing despite the fundamentally solitary nature of the an individual vant's dynamics—in which each vant effectively moves through the lattice oblivi-

*Langton's *vants* are but a special case of more generalized "ants" [Dewd89]: let the state of each site of the lattice be labeled 1 through n. As an ant moves through a site with state k, its state changes from k to $k + 1$ *modulo* n, and the ant makes either a right or left turn relative to the direction in which it entered the site. In the generalized model, the ant's direction is determined by a deterministic length-n *rule-string*. If R_k is the kth bit of the rule-string, and an ant is leaving a site whose previous value was k, then it makes a right run if $R_k = 1$ and a left turn if $R_k = 0$. In this notation, Langton's vants are defined by the rule-string $\vec{R} = 10$. Although, as one might suspect, it is difficult to prove any general theorems about the behavior of generalized ants, it is easy to prove the following basic theorem [Prop94]: the motion of "ants" moving according to a rule-string that contains at least one '0' and at least one '1' is always unbounded.

	red vants: $\vec{\sigma}_n^{(r)}(t+1)$		blue vants: $\vec{\sigma}_n^{(b)}(t+1)$	
d	$\zeta_{i,j}(t)$ =green	$\zeta_{i,j}(t)$ =yellow	$\zeta_{i,j}(t)$ =green	$\zeta_{i,j}(t)$ =yellow
N	$(i+1, j, E)$	$(i-1, j, W)$	$(i-1, j, W)$	$(i+1, j, E)$
E	$(i, j+1, S)$	$(i, j-1, N)$	$i, j-1, N)$	$(i, j+1, S)$
S	$(i-1, j, W)$	$(i+1, j, E)$	$(i+1, j, E)$	$(i-1, j, W)$
W	$(i, j-1, S)$	$(i, j+1, N)$	$(i, j+1, N)$	$(i, j-1, S)$

Table 2.3 *Vant* rules, $\vec{\sigma}_n^{(r)}(t) \rightarrow \vec{\sigma}_n^{(r)}(t+1)$; see [Lang86].

ous to the motion of any of its cousins—a complex, global, cooperative dynamics nonetheless emerges. This cooperative dynamics results solely from a continual interaction between the sea of vants and an ever-changing collective food pattern. In particular, by coupling two or more vants together—i.e., by allowing each vant to roam freely about, and interact with, a mutual food environment—patterns and structures unattainable by a single vant are able to emerge. Moreover, these patterns and structures are often very obviously *cooperative structures*, requiring the simultaneous cooperative "building efforts" of several vants, working within a localized food area. After watching a typical vant evolution, one is strongly reminded of real ant colonies, in which a global "consciousness" seems to spontaneously emerge out of the mutual interactions among an essentially mindless army of individual ants (see [levy92] and [Gord99]). Langton speculates that such systems provide evidence that an apparent global ordered collective dynamics need not stem from an intrinsically global cooperative dynamics, but may instead be nothing more than an emergent high-level (*phenotype*) construct stemming from an essentially non-cooperative low-level (*genotype*) dynamics [Lang92]: "...such emergent, collective, metastable patterns of dynamical activity must play a role in the distributed dynamics of living and intelligent processes in the real world."*

While a single vant performs little more than a pseudo random-walk, multiple-vant evolutions are ripe with many interesting (Conway *Life*-rule-like; see discussion above) patterns, particularly when the background lattice food color is shown along with the moving vants. Simply by having two or more vants interact within the same environment, the system is able to give rise to essentially static structures, periodic oscillators, orbiting patterns (in which multiple vants appear to "orbit" around one another while weaving a complex food-trail behind them as they slowly move off to one direction), and particle-like states, in which the combined motions of two or more intertwined vants effectively mimics that of a single but larger vant-organism. Some particles are slow moving, some fast, and "new" particles often emerge out of multi-particle collisions. Perhaps the most startling emergent patterns are those involving *diagonal motion*; recall that, *individually*, vants are incapable of any motion except going north, east, south or west.

*Quoted from the video "Self-reproducing loops and virtual ants," by Chris Langton, in *Artificial Life II Video Proceedings*, Addison-Wesley, 1992.

Figures 2.25 and 2.26 show a few snapshot views of vant dynamics. Note that, in both figures, the lattice initially contains only "yellow" food and a site is colored black whenever it contains either green food or a vant of either color.

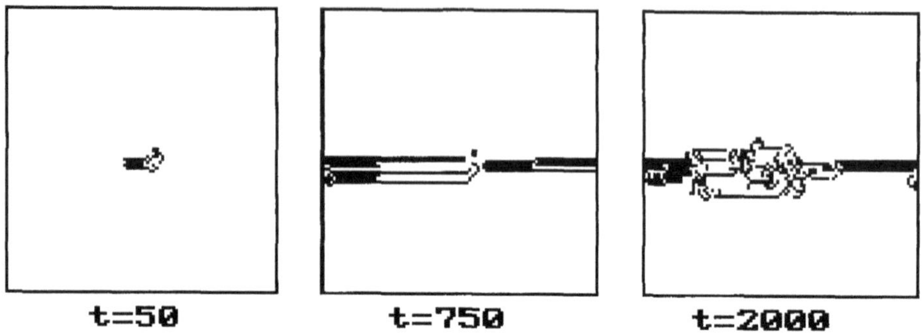

Fig. 2.25 Three snapshots of the evolution of a small colony of *vants*. The initial condition consists of $\vec{\sigma}_1^{(r)}(0) = (0,0,E)$, $\vec{\sigma}_2^{(r)}(0) = (1,1,E)$, $\vec{\sigma}_1^{(b)}(0) = (0,1,W)$, and $\vec{\sigma}_2^{(b)}(0) = (1,0,W)$; rules are defined in table 2.3. See text for details.

Figure 2.25 shows the evolution of two red and two blue vants: $\vec{\sigma}_1^{(r)}(0) = (0,0,E)$, $\vec{\sigma}_2^{(r)}(0) = (1,1,E)$, $\vec{\sigma}_1^{(b)}(0) = (0,1,W)$, and $\vec{\sigma}_2^{(b)}(0) = (1,0,W)$. Notice the appearance of food "bridges," acting as information conduits from one part of a pattern to another; these conduits provide an avenue for vants to make their way quickly across them. Allowed enough "building" time, even a small number of vants are able to construct very complicated conduit networks. Figure 2.26 shows the evolution of a vant system with an initial state consisting of 20 red and 20 blue vants moving in random directions within a 10×10 box at the center of the lattice.

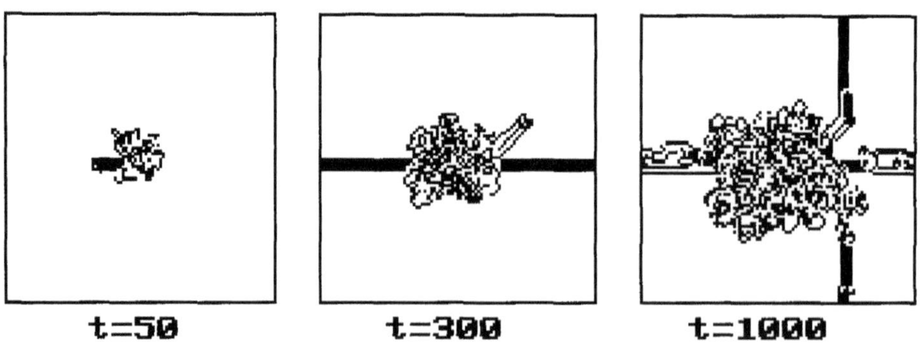

Fig. 2.26 Three snapshots of the evolution of a small colony of *vants*. The initial condition consists of 20 red and 20 blue vants moving in random directions within a 10×10 box at the center of the lattice; rules are defined in table 2.3. See text for details.

2.2.8 *Self-Organized Criticality*

Self-organized criticality (SOC) describes a large body of both phenomenological and theoretical work having to do with a particular class of time-scale invariant and spatial-scale invariant phenomena. As with many of the terms and concepts associated with nonlinear dynamics and complex systems, its meaning has been somewhat diluted and made imprecise since its introduction, in large part due to the veritable explosion of articles on complex systems appearing in the popular literature. Fundamentally, SOC embodies the idea that dynamical systems with many degrees of freedom naturally self-organize into a critical state in which the same events that brought that critical state into being can occur in all sizes, with the sizes being distributed according to a power-law.

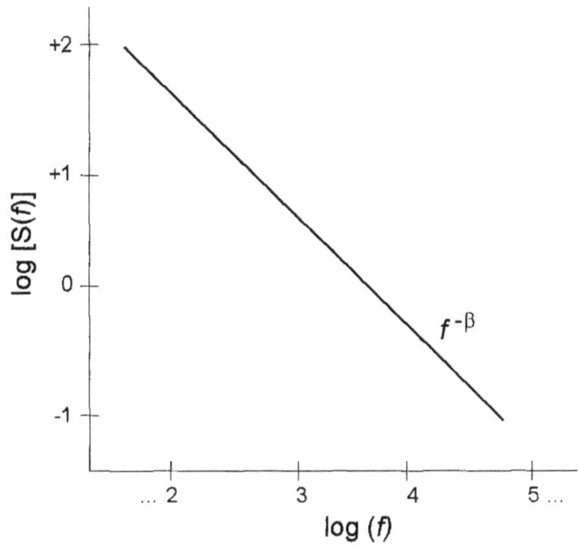

Fig. 2.27 Generic plot of $\log S(f)$ versus $\log(f)$ for a system in a *self-organized critical* state; see text for explanation.

To be more precise, the *power spectra* $S(f)$ (see page 92) for transport phenomena in many diverse physical and social systems—including transistors, superconductors, highway traffic, earthquakes, river overflow, and the distribution of business firm and city sizes ([Axtel01a], [Axtel01a], [Bak88a], [Carl90])—has been experimentally observed to diverge at low frequencies with a power law $f^{-\beta}$, with $0.8 < \beta < 1.4$; i.e. a plot of $\log S(f)$ vs. $\log(f)$ yields a straight line, with slope equal to β (see figure 2.27). Moreover, $S(f)$ obeys this power-law behavior over very large time scales. Commonly referred to as the $1/f$-noise (or *flicker-noise* noise) problem, there is currently no general theory that adequately explains the ubiquitous nature of $1/f$ noise; except for SOC.

SOC seeks to describe the underlying mechanisms for structures in systems that look like equilibrium systems near critical points but *are not near equilibrium.* Instead, they continue interacting with their environment, "tuning themselves" to a point at which critical-like behavior appears. In contrast, thermodynamic phase transitions usually take place under conditions of thermal equilibrium, where an external control parameter such as temperature is used to tune the system.

Introduced in 1987 by Bak, Chen and Wiesenfeld [Bak87], SOC is arguably the only existing holistic mathematical theory of self-organization in complex systems, describing the behavior of many real systems in physics, biology and economics. SOC may provide a fundamental link between such temporal scale invariant phenomena and phenomena exhibiting a spatial scale invariance—familiar examples of which are fractal coastlines, mountain landscapes and cloud formations [MandB82].

Bak, *et. al.*, argue that spatially extended dynamical systems evolve spontaneously into minimally stable critical states and that this self-organized criticality is the common mechanism responsible for a variety of fractal phenomena. They suggest that $1/f$ noise is actually not noise at all, but is instead a manifestation of the intrinsic dynamics of self-organized critical systems.

"Self-organized" refers to the fact that the system, after some initial transient period, naturally evolves into a critical steady state without any tuning of external parameters. This stands in marked contrast with the critical points at phase transitions in thermodynamic systems that can only be reached by a variation of some parameter (temperature, for example).

"Criticality" refers to a concept borrowed from thermodynamics. Thermodynamic systems generally get more ordered as the temperature is lowered, with more and more structure emerging as cohesion wins over thermal motion. Thermodynamic systems can exist in a variety of phases—gas, liquid, solid, crystal, plasma, etc.—and are said to be *critical* if poised at a phase transition. Many phase transitions have a critical point associated with them, that separates one or more phases. As a thermodynamic system approaches a critical point, large structural fluctuations appear despite the fact the system is driven only by local interactions. The disappearance of a characteristic length scale in a system at its critical point, induced by these structural fluctuations, is a characteristic feature of thermodynamic critical phenomena and is universal in the sense that it is independent of the details of the system's dynamics. Other than the absence of any control parameters, the resulting behavior is thus strongly reminiscent of the critical point in thermodynamic systems undergoing a second-order phase transition.

Note that SOC is a *universal* theory in that it predicts that the global properties of complex systems are independent of the microscopic details of their structure, and is therefore consistent with the "the whole is greater than the sum of its parts" approach to complex systems. Put in the simplest possible terms, SOC asserts that complexity is criticality; that is to say, that *SOC is nature's way of driving everything towards a state of maximum complexity.*

2.2.8.1 *Properties*

In general, SOC appears to be prevalent in systems that have the following properties:

- *Many degrees of freedom*
- *Parts undergo strong local interactions*
- *Number of parts is usually conserved*
- *Slowly driven by exogenous "energy" source*
- *Energy is rapidly dissipated within the system*

In systems that have these properties, SOC itself is characterized by:

- *A self-organized drive towards the critical state*
- *Intermittently triggered (i.e.,avalanche-like) release of energy*
- *Sensitivity to initial conditions (i.e. the trigger can be very small)**
- *The critical state is maintained without any external "tuning"*

These ideas will be explained more fully in the examples that follow. For further details, readers are urged to consult any of the following original references: [Bak87], [Bak88], [Bak90], [Bak91], and [Bak93]. Two excellent self-contained book-length summaries of SOC are Bak's *How Nature Works* [Bak96], and Jensen's *Self-Organized Criticality: Emergent Complex Behavior in Physical and Biological Systems* [Jensen98].

2.2.8.2 *Sandpiles*

To better illustrate the concept of SOC, consider a simple model of sand-pile avalanches: a mechanical arm holds a large quantity of sand and sits securely in place some distance above a flat circular table. Slowly—individual grain by individual grain—the arm releases its store of sand. The sand thus begins forming a pile beneath the arm.

At first, the grains all stay relatively close together near where they all fall onto the pile. Then they begin piling up on top of one another, creating a pile with a small slope. Every once and a while the slope becomes too steep somewhere, and a few grains slide down in a small avalanche. Initially, though, additions of sand induces only minor local rearrangements of that pile. However, as the mechanical

*Sensitivity to initial conditions is usually a trademark of chaos in dynamical systems (see discussion on page 76 in this chapter). Unlike fully chaotic systems, however, in which nearby trajectories diverge exponentially, the distance between two trajectories in systems undergoing SOC grows at a much slower (i.e. power-law) rate. Systems undergoing SOC are therefore only *weakly* chaotic. There is an important difference between fully developed chaos and weak chaos: fully developed chaotic systems have a characteristic time scale beyond which it is impossible to make predictions about their behavior; no such time scale exists for weakly chaotic systems, so that long-time predictions may be possible.

arm continues dispensing grains of sand, the average slope of the pile of sand beneath it steepens, and the average size of the resulting avalanches increases.

As the pile grows in size, it gets steeper and steeper, with the added sand sometimes causing minimal restructuring to take place and sometimes causing large avalanches to occur. The avalanches increase as the slope of the pile increases, until, finally, a statistically stationary state is reached for which the sandpile's slope can no longer be increased and any further addition of sand induces rearrangements to take place on all possible length scales and time scales. The size of the pile stops growing at this point, because the amount of sand added to the pile is balanced by the amount of sand that falls off the circular table. This state is the *critical state.* Moreover, the same critical state would be reached if the sandpile is allowed relax after starting with a very large slope.

When a grain of sand is added to a sandpile that is in the self-organized critical state, it may potentially spawn an avalanche of *any size*, from the smallest avalanche consisting of only a few grains to a major "catastrophe" involving very many grains to no avalanche at all. A basic question to ask, is, *"What is the distribution of sandslides that is induced by the addition of a single grain of sand?"*

In the critical state, the *size* of an avalanche does not depend on the grain of sand that triggers it. However, the frequency f of avalanches of a size greater than or equal to a given size s is related to s by a power-law: $f \propto 1/s^{-\beta}$, for some $\beta > 0$; a relationship that, according to Bak, *et. al.*, is the signature characteristic of SOC [Bak87]. There is thus no such thing as an avalanche of average size. An estimate only gets larger as more and more avalanches are averaged together. The critical state is also stable: because even the largest avalanches involve only a small fraction of the total number of grains in the sandpile, once a pile has evolved to its critical state, it stays poised close to that state forever.

There is strong evidence to suggest that just as sandpiles self-organize into a critical state, so do many real complex systems naturally evolve, or "tune themselves," to a critical state, in which a minor event can, via a cascading series of chain-reactions, involve any number of elements of the system. The critical state is an attractor for the dynamics: systems are inexorably driven toward it for a wide variety of initial conditions. Frequently cited examples of SOC include the distribution of earthquake sizes, the magnitude of river flooding, and the distribution of solar flare x-ray bursts, among others. Conway's *Life* CA-rule (see page 143), which is a crude model of social interaction, appears to self-organize to a critical state when driven by random mutations. Another vivid example of SOC is the extinction of species in natural ecologies. In the critical state, individual species interact to form a coherent whole, poised in a state far out of equilibrium. Even the smallest disturbances in the ecology can thus cause species to become extinct. Real data show that there are typically many small extinction events and few large ones, though the relationship does not quite follow the same linear power-law as it does for avalanches. Bak and Chen [Bak91] have also speculated that "throughout history, wars and peaceful interactions might have left the world in a critical state in which conflicts and social unrest spread like avalanches."

2.2.8.3 *Example: One-dimensional CA Sandpile*

It is easy to define a simple one-dimensional CA model of a sandpile. It is defined as follows. Each site of a one dimensional lattice represents a position at which units of sand may be placed. The number of units of sand at site 'i' at time 't' is given by $\sigma_i(t)$. Let $\eta_i(t)$ represent the *local slope*, defined as the difference between the number of units of sand on neighboring sites:

$$\eta_i(t) \equiv \sigma_i(t) - \sigma_{i+1}(t). \tag{2.65}$$

The dynamics, which consists of two operations, is most conveniently expressed in terms of this local slope value. Start with an arbitrary initial pile of sand, $\boldsymbol{\eta}(t{=}0)$. If the local slope at any site i exceeds an arbitrarily chosen threshold value η_c, the system is allowed to relax by continually applying a *relation rule* $\phi_{\rm relax} = \phi_{\rm relax}(\boldsymbol{\eta})$ that effectively slides one unit of sand 'downhill' (i.e. to the right) according to (see figure 2.28):

$$\boldsymbol{\eta}(t+1) = \phi_{\rm relax}(\boldsymbol{\eta}(t)) : \begin{cases} \eta_j(t+1) &= \eta_j(t) \text{ for all } j \neq i-1,\ i,\ i+1, \\ \eta_{i-1}(t+1) &= \eta_{i-1}(t) - 1, \\ \eta_i(t+1) &= \eta_i(t) - 2, \\ \eta_{i+1}(t+1) &= \eta_{i+1}(t) + 1. \end{cases} \tag{2.66}$$

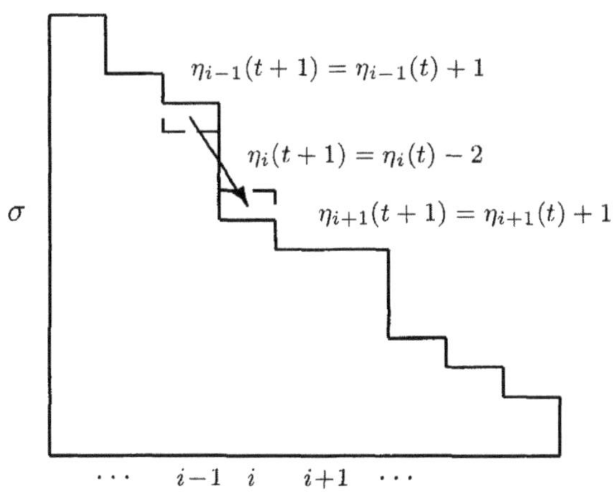

Fig. 2.28 One dimensional sandpile CA; σ_i gives the number of units of sand at site i at time t, $(\ldots, i-1, i, i+1, \ldots)$ label column number, and $\eta_i(t)$ is the difference between the amount of sand on neighboring sites $(= \sigma_i(t) - \sigma_{i+1}(t))$. The figure depicts the rule for the case when the local slope exceeds a specified threshold and causes a grain of sand to slide downhill. See text for complete rule.

After all local slopes of the pile are again less than η_c, one unit of sand is added to a random site i. In terms of the local slope variable, this amounts to applying the *addition rule* ϕ_{add}:

$$\boldsymbol{\eta}(t+1) = \phi_{\text{add}}(\boldsymbol{\eta}(t)) := \begin{cases} \eta_j(t+1) & = & \eta_j(t) \text{ for all } j \neq i-1,\ i,\ i+1, \\ \eta_{i-1}(t+1) & = & \eta_{i-1}(t) + 1 \\ \eta_i(t+1) & = & \eta_i(t) - 1. \end{cases} \tag{2.67}$$

The complete dynamics are then specified by the rule $\Phi = \Phi(\boldsymbol{\eta})$:

$$\boldsymbol{\eta}(t+1) = \Phi(\boldsymbol{\eta}(t)) = \begin{cases} \phi_{\text{relax}}(\boldsymbol{\eta}(t)) & \text{if there exists } i \text{ such that } \eta_i(t) > \eta_c, \\ \phi_{\text{add}}(\boldsymbol{\eta}(t)) & \text{else.} \end{cases} \tag{2.68}$$

Note that equations 2.66 and 2.67 effectively define a simple discrete diffusion process in one dimension; the presence of a threshold condition also makes the diffusion process a *nonlinear* one (see below). Boundary conditions are set by putting a 'wall' on the left hand side of the pile ($\eta_0(t) = 0$ for all t) and allowing sand to fall off an 'edge' on the right hand side ($\eta_N(t+1) = \eta_N(t) - 1$, $\eta_{N+1}(t+1) = \eta_{N+1}(t) + 1$, whenever $\eta_N(t)$ exceeds the threshold η_c). The net effect of these two conditions is to have an overall flow of sand from left to right.

The rather simple dynamics of this one dimensional system can actually be solved exactly. The result is that for any initial configuration the system evolves towards a *minimally stable state* $\boldsymbol{\eta_0}$, all of whose local slope values $\eta_i = \eta_c$. Once this minimally stable state is reached, the addition of a unit of sand to any site results in that one unit sliding from site to site until it finally falls off the 'edge' on the right side, again leaving the pile in the state $\boldsymbol{\eta_0}$. The minimally stable state is thus both sensitive to local perturbation and robust because it is ultimately left unchanged by any perturbation.

If the sand is added completely randomly, the resulting flow is random white noise (i.e. it has a power spectrum equal to $1/f^0$). In order to obtain more interesting dynamics and phenomena—in particular, in order to do away with the robustness of the minimally stable state—we must look at similar systems defined for two or more spatial dimensions. Fortunately, the one dimensional rules given in equations 2.66 and 2.67 are readily generalizable to d (Euclidean) dimensions.

Let $\eta(\mathbf{r}, t)$ be the d dimensional analogue of the one dimensional local slope at lattice point $\boldsymbol{r}$ at time t.* Addition of sand is then generated by the rule:

*The physical meaning of η is not the natural d dimensional analogue of slope. Although the local slope for systems in $d \geq 2$ dimensions is a vector quantity, the model discussed above assumes it to be a scalar. We should point out that despite its name, the sandpile model was originally conceived with a more general purpose in mind; namely, as serving as a simple computational aid in the study of typical behaviors of spatially extended dynamical systems with many degrees of freedom. It is only for its one-dimensional incarnation that the sandpile metaphor is most naturally appropriate. Nonetheless, stricter generalizations of the one-dimensional sandpile model to $d > 1$ dimensions, called *vector avalanche automata* and obeying a threshold relaxation that depends on a (locally conserved) gradient of a scalar field, have also been found to display a self-organized criticality (albeit with different scaling exponents). See [McNam90].

$$\phi_{\text{add}}^{(d)} : \begin{cases} \eta(\mathbf{r}, t+1) &= \eta(\mathbf{r}, t) + d, \\ \eta(\mathbf{r} - \mathbf{x}_i, t+1) &= \eta(\mathbf{r} - \mathbf{x}_i, t) - 1, \end{cases} \tag{2.69}$$

where $\boldsymbol{x}_i$ is a unit vector linking each lattice point to its nearest neighbor in the positive $x_1, x_2, \ldots, x_d$ directions.

If $\eta(bfr) > \eta_c$ then the system relaxes according to:

$$\phi_{\text{relax}}^{(d)} : \begin{cases} \eta(\mathbf{r}, t+1) &= \eta(\mathbf{r}, t) - 2d, \\ \eta(\mathbf{r} \pm \mathbf{x}_i, t+1(&= \eta(\mathbf{r} \pm \mathbf{x}_i, t) + 1. \end{cases} \tag{2.70}$$

In two dimensions, for example, $\phi_{\text{add}}^{(d=2)}$ and $\phi_{\text{relax}}^{(d=2)}$ are given by:

$$\phi_{\text{add}}^{(d=2)} : \begin{cases} \eta(x-1, y, t+1) &= \eta(x-1, y, t) - 1, \\ \eta(x, y-1, t+1) &= \eta(x, y-1, t) - 1, \\ \eta(x, y, t+1) &= \eta(x, y, t) + 2, \end{cases} \tag{2.71}$$

and

$$\phi_{\text{relax}}^{(d=2)} : \begin{cases} \eta(x \pm 1, y, t+1) &= \eta(x \pm 1, y, t) + 1, \\ \eta(x, y \pm 1, t+1) &= \eta(x, y \pm 1, t) + 1, \\ \eta(x, y, t+1) &= \eta(x, y, t) - 4. \end{cases} \tag{2.72}$$

At first sight it might seem as though we should expect the same sort of dynamics as for the one-dimensional case. Namely, that the system will evolve towards a robust least stable state for which $\eta(x, y) = \eta_c$ for all sites x and y. In turns out that this naive expectation is false. Consider a perturbation of an arbitrary site while the system is in the least stable state. The perturbation will cause the neighboring sites to become unstable, which will in turn cause their neighbors to become unstable, and so on, until the entire lattice is made to feel the effects of the initial perturbation. The final state of this avalanche is a statistically stationary, self-organized critical state $\boldsymbol{\eta}^*$, consisting of locally connected domains; it *is not* the least stable state. A perturbation of a single site within a domain leads to a chain reaction affecting all of the sites within that domain.

Spatial Power-Law Distribution. The most important property of the self-organized critical state is the presence of locally connected domains *of all sizes.* Since a given perturbation of the state $\boldsymbol{\eta}^*$ can lead to anything from a trivial one-site shift to a lattice-wide avalanche, there are no characteristic length scales in the system. Bak, *et. al.* [Bak87] have, in fact, found that the distribution function $D(s)$ of domains of size s obeys the power law:

$$D(s) = s^{-\beta}, \tag{2.73}$$

where $\beta \approx 1$ for domains up to size $s = 500$ for a 50×50 two dimensional system and $\beta \simeq 1.35$ for a three dimensional $20 \times 20 \times 20$ lattice.

Note that while the power-law distribution is reminiscent of that observed in equilibrium thermodynamic systems near a second-order phase transition, the mechanism behind it is quite different. Here the critical state is effectively an attractor of the system, and no external fields are involved.

Temporal Power-Law Distribution. The fact that there are no characteristic length scales immediately implies a similar lack of any characteristic time scales for the fluctuations. Consider the effect of a single perturbation of a random site of a system in the critical state. The perturbation will spread to the neighbors of the site, to the next nearest neighbors, and so on, until, after a time τ and a total of $\int$ sand slides, the effects will die out. The distribution of the life-times of the avalanches, $D(t)$, obeys the power law:

$$D(t) \approx t^{-\alpha}, \tag{2.74}$$

where $\alpha \approx 0.43$ in two dimensions and $\alpha \approx 0.90$ in three dimensions.

2.2.8.4 *1/f Noise*

It is not hard to see that, given a power-law distribution of lifetimes (equation 2.74), the power spectrum $S(f)$, defined by:

$$S(f) = \int < F(t_0 + t) F(t_0) >_{t_0} \exp(2\pi i f t)\, dt, \tag{2.75}$$

where $F(t)$ is the instantaneous energy dissipation rate at time 't', and $< \cdots >_{t_0}$ represents an average over all times t_0, also obeys a power law. We follow [Bak87] and [Bak88].

First, to find $F(t)$, let $f(\mathbf{x}, t)$ represent the dissipation of energy at site $\mathbf{x}$ at time 't'. Since the dynamics specified by equations 2.70 yields an energy dissipation of *one unit*, we have that $f(\mathbf{x}, t) = \delta(\mathbf{x}, t)$. The growth rate of a given domain is equal to the instantaneous energy dissipation rate $F(t) = \int f(\mathbf{x}, t)\, dx$. A domain of size $s = \int F(t)\, dt$ (integrated over the duration of a single avalanche) therefore represents *total dissipated energy* resulting from a single perturbation.

Now consider the case where the system is perturbed randomly in space and time and $F(t)$ represents a superposition of many avalanches (occurring simultaneously and independently).* The total power spectrum is the (incoherent) sum of individual contributions for single relaxation event due to single perturbations. Consider the relaxation due to a single perturbation in a given domain. The resulting \index{correlation function}correlation function $C(t) = \frac{s}{\tau} \exp(-\frac{t}{\tau})$ yields a contribution to $S(f)$ equal to $S(f; s, \tau) = s/(1+4\pi f^2 \tau^2)$. The total power spectrum is then given by:

*The notion that $1/f$ noise results from a distribution of relaxation times, operating simultaneously and independently, was first proposed by A. van der Ziel, *Physica*, Volume 16, 1950.

$$
\begin{aligned}
S(f) &= \sum S(f; s, \tau), \\
&\approx \int \frac{s}{1 + 4\pi f^2 \tau^2}\, D(\tau)\, d\tau, \\
&\approx f^{\gamma} = f^{\alpha - 2}.
\end{aligned}
\tag{2.76}
$$

One of the virtues of having such a simple dynamical model (and a major theme of the subject of this book) is the possibility of capturing the truly essential ingredients of certain observed dynamical or physical properties of more complex systems. Flicker noise is a good case in point. The shear breadth of phenomena that purportedly show $1/f$-noise suggests that *if there is a common underlying mechanism responsible for its appearance*, then that mechanism is likely to be independent of the physical details of any given system. Therefore, an extremely useful place to start looking for such a mechanism is in the dynamical behavior of simple dynamical systems that capture the generic properties of a wider classes of more realistic physical systems. (Wiesenfeld, *et. al.* [Wiesen89] compare the simplicity of the 'independent relaxation time' interpretation of $1/f$-noise fluctuations in the sandpile CA model to other recent models yielding $1/f$ noise.)

Chapter 3

Nonlinearity, Complexity, and Warfare: *Eight Tiers of Applicability*

"I propose to consider first the various elements of the subject, next its various (or individual or separate) parts or sections and finally the whole in its internal structure. In other words, I shall proceed from the simple to the complex. But in war more than in any other subject, we must begin by looking at the nature of the whole; for here more than elsewhere, the part and the whole must always be thought of together ... in war as in life generally all parts of a whole are interconnected and thus the effects produced, however small their cause, must influence all subsequent military operations and modify their outcome to some degree, however slight. In the same way, every means must influence even the ultimate purpose."

—Carl von Clausewitz, *Prussian military theorist* (1780-1831)

Recall, from our introductory remarks in chapter 1, that CNA's *Complexity & Combat* study—which eventually culminated in the development of EINSTein (an in-depth discussion of which begins in chapter 4)—was initially focused only on providing a broad overview of possible appliations of the "new sciences" (i.e., nonlinear dynamical system and complex adaptive system theories) to warfare. This early stage of the project produced two main reports: (1) *Land Warfare and Complexity, Part I: Mathematical Background and Technical Sourcebook* [Ilach96a], which provides a semi-technical review of the "new sciences" and many of whose elements are contained in chapter 2, and (2) *Land Warfare and Complexity, Part II: An Assessment of the Applicability of Nonlinear Dynamic and Complex Systems Theory to the Study of Land Warfare* [Ilach96b], which uses the information contained in the first volume to help identify specific applications and assess both their risk (as measured by expected time of conceptual and/or practical development) and potential reward.

Part II starts by examining a need to chage the metaphors that elicit images of war and continues through to developing fundamentally new concepts—or "the universal characteristics"—of land warfare. Before turning our attention in the next chapter to describing the outcome of following through with one of the most important recommendations to emerge from these two reports—namely, the need to develop a multiagent-based simulation of combat—we use this chapter to summarize the main points of *Land Warfare and Complexity, Part II*. Together, parts *I* and *II* of *Land Warfare and Complexity* represent the first serious examination of the thesis that two heretofore ostensibly unrelated research disciplines—namely, military operations research and complex systems theory—actually overlap; and that the study of one may provide insight into the study of the other.

3.1 Approach

There are several useful ways to organize a list of potential applications of complex systems theory to warfare. The simplest, and most direct, way, is to provide a short discussion of how each and every tool and methodology that goes under the broad rubric of "complexity theory"—including cellular automata, evolutionary programming, fuzzy logic, neural networks, and so on—applies to warfare. The drawback to this approach, of course, is that because of the depth and breadth of available tools, one can soon become hopelessly lost in a meaningless sea of technical jargon. Moreover, the specter of having the overall approach be insipidly, and incorrectly, branded a "solution in search of a problem," is unappealing.

An alternative (and complementary) approach is to start with a list of the most pressing problems associated with land combat—going down the list from predictions of battlefield attrition, to command and control, to fire support, to intelligence, and so on—and to provide suggested avenues of exploration using complex systems theory. A drawback to this approach is that because it starts out with a specific list, it is, in principle, capable only of eliciting the most promising applications to existing (i.e. conventional) problems, leaving out what may be the most promising set of applications of complex systems theory to what, in conventional terms, may not (yet!) be recognized as an "issue" or "problem." Indeed, complex systems theory's greatest legacy for defense analysis may prove to be that it is not so much a set of answers to old questions, but rather that it represents an entirely new set of questions to be asked of combat and what really happens on the battlefield. Toward this end, let us introduce a framework for discussing the possible applications of complex systems theory to land warfare that respects both sides of the equation. Consider the following eight separate tiers of applicability, ranging roughly from least risk and least potential payoff (at least, as far as a practical applicability is concerned) for *Tier I*, to greatest risk and greatest potential payoff for *Tier VIII* (see table 3.1):

- *Tier I: General metaphors for complexity in war*
- *Tier II: Policy and General Guidelines for Strategy*
- *Tier III: Conventional warfare models and approaches*
- *Tier IV: Description of the complexity of combat*
- *Tier V: Combat technology enhancement*
- *Tier VI: Combat aids for the battlefield*
- *Tier VII: Synthetic combat environments*
- *Tier VIII: Original conceptualizations of combat*

Tier of Applicability	Description	Examples
I. General Metaphors for Complexity in War	Build and continue to expand base of images to enhance conceptual links between complexity and warfare	nonlinear vice linear, synthesist vice analytical, edge-of-chaos vice equilibrium, process vice structure, holistic vice reductionist
II. Policy and General Guidelines for Strategy	Guide formulation of policy and apply basic principles and metaphors of CST to enhance and/or alter organizational structure	Use general metaphors lessons learned from complex systems theory to guide and shape policy making; Use genetic algorithms to evolve new forms
III. Conventional Warfare Models and Methodological Approaches	Apply tools and methodologies of CST to better understand and/or entend existing models	chaos in Lanchester equations, chaos in arms-race models, analogy with ecological models
IV. Description of the Complexity of Combat	Describe real-world combat from a complex systems theoretic perspective	power-law scaling, Lyapunov exponents, entropic parameters
V. Combat Technology Enhancement	Apply tools and methodologies of complex systems theory to certain limited aspects of combat, such as intelligent manufacturing, cryptography and data dissemination	intelligent manufacturing, data compression, cryptography, IFF, computer viruses, fire ants
VI. Combat Aids	Use complex systems theory tools to enhance real-world combat operations	autonomous robotic devices, tactical picture agents, tactics and/or strategy evolution via genetic and other machine-learning algorithms
VII. Synthetic Combat Environments	Full system models for training and/or to use as research "laboratories"	agent-based models (SimCity), Soar/IFOR, Ascape, SWARM
VIII. Original Conceptualizations of Combat	Use complex-systems-theory-inspired basic research to develop fundamentally new conceptualizations of combat	pattern recognition, controlling and/or exploiting chaos universal behaviors

Table 3.1 Eight tiers of applicability of nonlinear dynamics and complex systems theory to the study of warfare.

Because of the very speculative nature of many of the individual applications making up these eight tiers—applications range from those that are currently undergoing some preliminary form of development to those that currently exist only as vague theoretical possibilities—conventional risk-benefit analysis does not apply.

3.2 Tier I: General Metaphors for Complexity in War

"You don't see something until you have the right metaphor to let you perceive it."
—Thomas Kuhn, *Physicist/Historian* (1922-1996)

The lowest, but certainly not shallowest, tier of applicability of complex systems theory consists of developing a set of metaphors by which war in general, and land combat in particular, can be understood. This set of metaphors represents a new world-view in which the battlefield is seen as a conflict between two self-organizing living-fluid-like organisms consisting of many mutually interacting and coevolving parts.

3.2.1 *What is a Metaphor?*

Etymologically, metaphor (the Greek *metafora*, "carry over") means "transfer" or "convey," the transference of a figurative expression from one area to another. According to the 3rd edition of the American Heritage Dictionary [AmH94], a metaphor is "a figure of speech in which a word or phrase that ordinarily designates one thing is used to designate another, thus making an implicit comparison. One thing conceived as representing another." The Encyclopedia Britannica Online1 adds that metaphor "makes a qualitative leap from a reasonable, perhaps prosaic comparison, to an identification or fusion of two objects, to make one new entity partaking of the characteristics of both. Many critics regard the making of metaphors as a system of thought antedating or bypassing logic." In the present context, we can say that the first tier of applicability of complex systems theory to land warfare represents a reservoir of metaphorical concepts and images with which land warfare can be illuminated and reinterpreted in a new light.

From the standpoint of the amount of "development time" that is required to make use of metaphor, the risk is effectively zero. One either chooses to color one's language with a particular set of metaphors or one does not. The only groundwork that has to be done is to carefully choose the right set of metaphors. Yet, because of the profound relationship that exists between metaphors and the concomitant reality our language and thoughts create for us, incorporating metaphors borne of complex systems theory into our discussions of combat can potentially radically alter our general understanding of warfare. Therefore, the potential "payoff" is great. But one must at the same time be mindful of using a metaphor, or metaphors, on appropriate levels.

A metaphor can apply either to one particular idea or image that is transferred from, or provides a bridge between, one discipline to another, or, more generally, to a symbolic relation that unites the paradigmatic way of viewing an entire field of knowledge. Emmeche and Hoffmeyer [Emmeche91] identify four different levels of metaphorical "signification-transfer" in science as follows:

- *Level-1:* The transfer of single terms to other contexts to create new meaning.
- *Level-2:* Construction of analogies as part of a specific theory or a general and systematic inquiry to elucidate phenomena. The analogy may simply be a heuristic device or a component of an apparently final theory.
- *Level-3:* A unifying view of an entire paradigm, often symbolized by a specific term that refers to the whole frame of understanding under a given paradigm.
- *Level-4:* The most comprehensive level of signification is the level on which science itself is understood as irreducibly metaphorical.

While metaphors can be, and often are, misused, they frequently serve as powerful conceptual vehicles by which a set of tools, models and theories is borrowed from one discipline and meaningfully translated to apply to another discipline. For those that say that metaphors are by their nature somehow "shallow" and not "scientific," one need only be reminded that much of science itself advances first by metaphor. Think of Rutherford's analogy of the solar system for the atom or Faraday's use of magnetized iron filings to think about electric fields, among many other examples. The collection of papers edited by Ortony [Ortony93] has a section devoted to the significance of metaphor in science.

> "Metaphors may be didactic or illustrative devices, models, paradigms, or root images that generate new models. Some metaphors are heuristic, whereas others constitute new meaning...Borrowing is metaphoric in several ways. Theories and models from other disciplines may sensitize scholars to questions not usually asked in their own fields, or they may help interpret and explain, whether that means a framework for integrating diverse elements or hypothetical answers that cannot be obtained from existing disciplinary resources. When a research area is incomplete, borrowing may facilitate an inductive open-endedness. It may function as a probe, facilitating understanding and enlightenment. Or, it may provide insight into another system of observational categories and meanings, juxtaposing the familiar with the unfamiliar while exposing similarities and differences between the literal use of the borrowing and a new area." [Klein90]

One could argue that much of our reality is structured by metaphor, although we may not always be explicitly aware of this. Lakoff and Johnson [Lakoff80] suggest that "many of our activities (arguing, solving problems, budgeting time, etc.) are metaphorical in nature. The metaphorical concepts that characterize those activities structure our present reality. New metaphors have the power to create a new reality... we understand a statement as being true in a given situation when our understanding of the statement fits our understanding of the situation closely enough for our purposes." Sometimes the only way to gain a further, or deeper, understanding of an "accepted" reality is to take a step sideways and reinterpret that reality from an alternative vantage point. Creative metaphors help us take that sideways step.

In speaking about the general role that research centers, such as the Santa Fe Institute, play in helping decide what metaphors are or are not appropriate for given problems, the economist Brian Arthur argues that [Wald92]

> "...the purpose of having a Santa Fe Institute is that it, and places like it, are where the metaphors and a vocabulary are being created in complex systems. So if somebody comes along with a beautiful study on the computer, then you can say 'Here's a new metaphor. Let's call this one the edge of chaos,' or whatever. So what the Santa Fe Institute will do, if it studies enough complex systems, is to show us the kinds of patterns we might observe, and the kinds of metaphor that might be appropriate for systems that are moving and in process and complicated, rather than the metaphor of clockwork."

3.2.2 *Metaphors and War*

Though conventional military thinking has, through history, been arguably dominated by the clockwork precision of the "Newtonian" metaphor—exemplified by the often cited view of combat between two adversaries as "a collision between two billiard-ball"—one can find examples of complexity-ridden metaphors in many important military historical writings.

Consider Sun-Tzu's analogy of a military force to water [Tzu91]:

> "So a military force has no constant formation, water has no constant shape: the ability to gain victory by changing and adapting according to the opponent is called genius."

Here Sun-Tzu likens movement and maneuver on the battlefield to the complex dynamics of fluid flow, which is a very apt metaphor for "combat as a complex system." He also underscores the importance of adaptability on the battlefield, which is the hallmark of any healthily evolving complex adaptive system.

In a recent article in *International Security*, entitled "Nonlinearity and Clausewitz," Beyerchen argues persuasively that much of Clausewitz's military thought was colored by a deep intuitive understanding of nonlinear dynamics [Beyer92]:

> "On War is suffused with the understanding that every war is inherently a nonlinear phenomenon, the conduct of which changes its character in ways that cannot be analytically predicted. I am not arguing that reference to a few of today's 'nonlinear science' concepts would help us clarify confusion in Clausewitz's thinking. My suggestion is more radical: in a profoundly unconfused way, he understands that seeking exact analytical solutions does not fit the nonlinear reality of the problems posed by war, and hence that our ability to predict the course and outcome of any given conflict is severely limited."

Clausewitz's "fog-of-war," "center-of-gravity" and "friction," of course, are well known. In the last section of Chapter 1, Book One, Clausewitz compares war to a "remarkable trinity" composed of (1) the natural force of hatred among the masses, (2) war's inherent element of chance, and (3) war's subordination to governmental policy. He concludes with a wonderful visual metaphor that anticipates one of the prototypical experimental demonstrations of deterministic chaos [Beyer92]: "Our task therefore is to develop a theory that maintains a balance between these three tendencies, like an object suspended between three magnets."

In another section, Clausewitz takes a bold stride beyond the "combat as colliding billiard-balls" metaphor, and anticipates almost directly the core element of the new "combat as complex adaptive systems" view:

> "...war is not an exercise of the will directed at inanimate matter, as in the case with the mechanical arts, or at matter which is animate but passive and yielding as in the case with the human mind and emotion in the fine arts. In war, the will is directed at an animate object that reacts."

It is a great testament to Clausewitz's brilliance and deep insight that he was able to recognize and exploit such provocative imagery to illustrate his ideas, insofar as there was no such field as "nonlinear dynamics" in his day.

In contrast, metaphors of nonlinearity are today much more commonplace, thanks in large part to the popularization of such "new sciences" as nonlinear dynamics, deterministic chaos and complex systems theory. To the extent that Clausewitzian theory itself accurately describes the fundamentals of war, the metaphors borne of nonlinear dynamics and complex systems theory therefore also have much to tell us. However, one should at the same time be cautious of "plumbing the wells of metaphor" too deeply, or of expecting, free-of-charge, a greater clarity or eloquence of expression in return. An unbridled, impassioned use of metaphor alone, without taking the time to work out the details of whatever deeper insights the metaphor might be pointing to, runs the risk of both shallowness and loss of objectivity.

Having said this, it is still true that if, in the end, it turns out that complex systems theory provides no genuinely new insights into war other than to furnish a rich scaffolding of provocative and suggestive metaphors around which an entirely new view of warfare can be woven—i.e. if the "signification-depth" is essentially confined to levels 1 and 2 of Emmeche's and Hoffmeyer's hierarchy (see above)—complex systems theory will have nonetheless fulfilled an enormously important function. Time will certainly tell if the new metaphors are as deep and meaningful as they at first appear or are "just another passing fad" that will soon fade from view. But just the fact alone that these new metaphors are being actively engaged in serious discussion at high levels* is enough to suggest that the consensus reality is already being altered. In a very real sense, the reality of "war as complex adaptive system" did not exist before the discussion started. And the longer a serious discussion continues in earnest, the longer the participants will have to develop a more meaningful complexity-metaphor ridden vocabulary of combat, and the deeper and more compellingly the images and concepts can take root in their minds. Indeed, if these new metaphors capture anything at all that is basic to war, they will, in time, inevitably take just as firm a hold of the language of war for future generations as the Newtonian metaphor of "colliding billiard-balls" has taken hold of the military thinking of past generations.

3.2.3 *Metaphor Shift*

The first tier of applicability of complex systems theory to warfare consists of a set of new metaphors by which war in general, and land combat in particular, can be understood. This set of metaphors represents a shift, away from the old "Newtonian" word-view—that emphasizes equilibrium and sees the battlefield as an arena of colliding objects obeying simple, linear laws and possessing little or no internal structure—to a new (but, ironically, older) "Heraclitian"† world-view, that emphasizes process and sees the battlefield as a conflict between two self-organizing living-fluid-like organisms consisting of many mutually interacting and coevolving parts.

The new "Heraclitian" metaphor is a rich interlacing tapestry of ideas and images, woven of five basic conceptual threads—nonlinearity, deterministic chaos, complexity, self-organization and emergence:

*A number of recent examples may be cited, including conferences sponsored by the United States' Marines Corps *Combat and Development Command* (entitled "Non-Linear Studies and Their Implications for the US Marine Corps"), the *Center for Naval Analyses* ("Complexity and Warfare") and *Ernst and Young* ("Implications of Complexity for Security"). Each of these conferences attracted more than 150 participants, including high-ranking military officers and decision-makers. *The National Defense University* in Washington, D.C. and *Naval Post Graduate School* in Monterey, California are also now offering courses in complex adaptive systems and multiagent-based simulation and modeling.

†The label "Heraclitian," as here used, is patterned after the label used by the geneticist Richard Lewontin to refer to scientists who see the world as a process of flow [Lewontin74]. Heraclitus was an Ionian philosopher who argued that the world is in a constant state of flux. One of his more famous passages is, "You can never step into the same river twice."

3.2.3.1 *Nonlinearity*

In colloquial terms, nonlinearity refers to the property that the whole is not necessarily equal to the sum of its parts. More precisely, if f is a nonlinear function or operator, and x is a system input (either a function or variable), then the effect of adding two inputs, x_1 and x_2, first and then operating on their sum is, in general, not equivalent to operating on two inputs separately and then adding the outputs together; i.e. $f(x+y)$ is, in general, not equal to $f(x)+f(y)$. For example, for the nonlinear function $f(x) = x_2$, $f(x_1+x_2)^2 = (x_1+x_2)^2 = x_1^2+x_2^2+2x_1x_2$, and the last term—$2x_1x_2$—appears as an additional quantity. Nonlinear systems can therefore display a disproportionately small or large output for a given input. Nonlinear systems are also generally very difficult to deal with mathematically, which is the main reason why they are usually replaced by linear approximations. While the act of linearization simplifies the problem, however, most of the interesting behavior of the real nonlinear system is washed away in the process. The "Heraclitian" metaphor reminds us that war is inherently nonlinear, and, as such, ought not be "linearized" away in an attempt to achieve a simplified "solution."

3.2.3.2 *Deterministic Chaos*

Deterministic chaos refers to irregular or chaotic motion that is generated by nonlinear systems evolving according to dynamical laws that uniquely determine the state of the system at all times from a knowledge of the system's previous history. It is important to point out that the chaotic behavior is due neither to external sources of noise nor to an infinite number of degrees-of-freedom nor to quantum-mechanical-like uncertainty. Instead, the source of irregularity is the exponential divergence of initially close trajectories in a bounded region of the system's phase space. This sensitivity to initial conditions is sometimes popularly referred to as the "butterfly effect," alluding to the idea that chaotic weather patterns can be altered by a butterfly flapping its wings. A practical implication of chaos is that its presence makes it essentially impossible to make any long-term predictions about the behavior of a dynamical system: while one can in practice only fix the initial conditions of a system to a finite accuracy, their errors increase exponentially fast. This does not mean, however, that short-term predictability is lost, for deterministic chaos also implies that within what appears to be erratic motion lies an underlying order. This underlying order can potentially be exploited to make short-term predictions.

3.2.3.3 *Complexity*

Complexity is an extremely difficult "I know it when I see it" concept to define, partly because its real meaning consists of two parts, neither of which is easy to quantify: (1) system complexity, which refers to the structural, or organizational, complexity of a system—examples include the interacting molecules in a fluid and the network topology of neurons in a brain; and (2) behavioral complexity, which refers to the complexity of actual behavioral patterns exhibited by complex, or simple, systems, as they evolve—examples include deterministic chaos, multistability, multifractality, and so on. A succinct summary of what nonlinear dynamics and complex systems theory together show, conceptually, is that it is possible to both (a) reduce the system complexity to only a relatively few degrees-of-freedom (i.e. to generate simplicity from complexity), and (b) have simple low-dimensional dynamics exhibit complex behaviors (i.e. to generate complexity from simplicity). Both of these strategies must be used in dealing with, and understanding, the complexities of combat.

3.2.3.4 *Self-Organization*

Self-organization is the spontaneous emergence of macroscopic nonequilibrium organized structure due to the collective interactions among a large assemblage of simple microscopic objects. Patterns emerge spontaneously when, say, certain environmental factors change. It is important to understand that these self-organized patterns arise out of a purely internal dynamics, and not because of any external force. It used to be believed that any kind of order must be due to some "oracle" imposing the order from outside of the system. Self-organization shows that no such oracle is needed. Examples of self-organization abound: convection flows in fluids, morphogenesis in biology, concentration patterns in chemical reactions, atmospheric vortices, etc.

3.2.3.5 *Emergence*

Emergence refers to the appearance of higher-level properties and behaviors of a system that—while obviously originating from the collective dynamics of that system's components—are neither to be found in nor are directly deducible from the lower-level properties of that system. Emergent properties are properties of the "whole" that are not possessed by any of the individual parts making up that whole. Individual lines of computer code, for example, cannot calculate a spreadsheet; an air molecule is not a tornado; and a neuron is not conscious. Emergent behaviors are typically novel and unanticipated.

The metaphor shift, of course, involves many more concepts and images than that to which these five "conceptual threads" alone attest, though these five certainly represent the core set. For example, in general terms, one can say that where the old metaphor stressed analysis, in which a system is understood by being systematically broken down into its parts, the new metaphor stresses synthesis, in which how a system behaves is discovered by building it up from its pieces. Where the old metaphor stressed a mechanistic dynamics, in which combat is viewed as a sequence of strictly materially caused events, the new metaphor stresses an evolutionary dynamics, in which combat is viewed as a coevolutionary process among adapting entities. Where the old metaphor stressed equilibrium and stability, in which "solutions" to combat are found after the system "settles down," the new metaphor stresses the importance of far-from-equilibrium states and the continual quest for perpetual novelty, in which combat never settles down to an equilibrium, and is always in pursuit of the so-called "edge-of-chaos" (see page 112 in section 2.2.3).

Tables 3.2 and 3.3 illustrate the metaphor shift from the old "Newtonian" view of the combat to the new "Heraclitian" view. Table 3.2 compares the old and new metaphors from the standpoint of their respective vocabularies. It is by no means a complete list of relevant words and concepts, and is meant only to capture some of the essential ideas. Table 3.3 extends this list of words by using various contexts within which to compare some of the basic principles underlying the two metaphors.

Old Metaphor ("Newtonian")	**New Metaphor ("Heraclitian")**
Analytical	Synthesist
Basic elements are *Quantities*	Basic elements are *Patterns*
Behavior is Contingent and Knowable	Behavior is Emergent and Unexpected
Being	Becoming
Clockwork Precision	Open-ended Unfolding
Closed System	Open System
Combat as *Colliding Billiard Balls*	Combat as *Coevolving Fluids*
Complexity breeds Complexity	Complexity may breed Simplicity
Deterministic	Deterministically Chaotic
Equilibrium	Out of (or even Far from) Equilibrium
Individualistic	Collective
Linear	Nonlinear
Linear Causal Chains	Feedback Loop/Circular Causality
Mechanistic Dynamics	Coevolutionary Dynamics
Order	Inherent Disorder
Predesigned	Emergent
Predictable	Unpredictable
Quantitative	Qualitative
Reductionist	Holistic
Solution	Process and Adaptation
System is Stable	System Poised on *Edge-of-Chaos*
Top-Down	Bottom-Up *and* Top-Down

Table 3.2 The shift from "Newtonian" to "Heraclitian" metaphors as reflected in their corresponding *vocabularies* of concepts and images.

Further speculations on possible connections between the "new sciences" and war on a metaphor level can found in Beyerchen [Beyer92], Beaumont [Beau94], Hedgepeth [Hedge93], Saperstein [Saper95], and Schmitt [Schmitt95].

Context	"Newtonian" Metaphor	"Heraclitian" Metaphor
Complex Behavior	Complex behavior requires complex models	Simple models often suffice to describe complex systems; *complexity from simplicity and simplicity from complexity*
Patterns of Behavior	Each qualitatively different pattern of behavior requires a different equation	Qualitatively different patterns of behavior can be described by the same underlying equation
Description of Behavior	Each qualitatively different kind of behavior requires new equation or set of equations	One equation harbors a multitude of qualitatively different patterns of behavior
Effects of Small Perturbations	Small perturbations induce small changes	Small perturbations can have large consequences
How to Understand System	A system can be understood by breaking it down into and analyzing its simpler components	Systems can be understood only by respecting the mutual interactions among its components; look at the *whole system*
Origin of Disorder	Disorder stems mainly from unpredictable forces *outside* of system	Disorder can arise from forces entirely *within* the system
Origin of Order	Order must be imposed from *outside* the system	Order can arise in a purely self-organized fashion *within* the system
Nature of Observed Order	Order, once present, is pervasive and appears both locally and globally	A system may appear locally disordered but possess global order
What is the "Goal"?	Goal is to develop "equations" to describe behavior; determined by isolating effect of one variable at a time	Goal is to understand how entire system responds to various contexts, with no one variable dominating
Type of "Solutions"	Goal is to search for "optimal" solution	No optimal solution exists, as the set of problems and constraints continuously changes
Predictability	Assuming that the "correct" model is found and initial conditions are known exactly, everything is predictable and controllable	Long-term predictability may be unattainable even in principle; behavior may be predicted for short-times only
Nature of Causal Flow	Causation flows from the *bottom up*	Causation flows *both from bottom up and from the top down*

Table 3.3 A Comparison Between some of the principles underlying "Newtonian" and "Heraclitian" Metaphors.

3.3 Tier II: Policy and General Guidelines for Strategy

3.3.1 *What Does the New Metaphor Give Us?*

Roger Lewin, in his popular book on complexity [Lewin92], reproduces a fragment of a conversation he once had with Patricia Churchland, a well-known neurobiologist:

"Is it reasonable to think of the human brain as a complex dynamical system?" I asked. "Its obviously true," she replied quickly. "But so what? Then what is your research program? ... What research do you do?"

Notice that if "human brain" is replaced in this fragment by "land combat," the fragment retains the potent sting of Churchland's challenge. Every new research endeavor must begin with at least these two basic steps: (1) a prior justification that the endeavor is a reasonable one to consider undertaking, and (2) a plan of attack. As far as the endeavor of applying complex systems theory to land warfare is concerned, the first step is easy: land combat—on paper—has almost all of the key attributes that any reasonable list of attributes of a complex adaptive system must include (see table 1.3 on page 13 in chapter 1). The second step is by far the more difficult one to take: now that we have established the similarity, what do we do with the connection?

3.3.2 *Policy*

> "If you have a truly complex system, then the exact patterns are not repeatable. And yet there are themes that are recognizable. In history, for example, you can talk about 'revolutions,' even though one revolution might be quite different from another. So we assign metaphors. It turns out that an awful lot of policy-making has to do with finding the appropriate metaphor. Conversely, bad policy-making almost always involves finding inappropriate metaphors. For example, it may not be appropriate to think about a drug 'war,' with guns and assaults."*

The first step to take beyond merely weaving threads of metaphor is to apply the basic lessons learned from the study of complex systems to how we formulate strategy and general policy. This assumes implicitly that political systems and world communities can be just as well described as complex adaptive systems as can be human brains and collections of combat forces. For example, consider that the essence of a (successfully evolving) complex adaptive complex is to exist in a far-from-equilibrium state and to continually search for novelty and new solutions to changing problems. An important lesson learned for a complex systems theoretic approach to policy making is therefore to shift from general policies that emphasize a means to achieve stability to policies that encourage a continual coevolution of all sides.

*Quote attributed to Brian Arthur in reference [Wald92].

General Guideline	Description
Exploit Collective Action	Exploit the synchronous parallel cooperative effort of many low-level agents rather than solving for a global solution all at once
Expect Change	Never take you eyes off, or turn your back on, a system – systems continually evolve and change
Stop looking for "Optimal" Solutions	Forget about optimizing a solution to a problem – the problem is constantly changing
"Guide" Behavior, Do not "Fix It"	Emphasize the process vice solution approach. Instead of focusing on "single points" of a trajectory – or snapshots in time of key events that unfold as a policy is implemented – focus on how to continue to nudge the system in a favorable direction
Look for Global Patterns	Search for global patterns in time and/or space scales higher than those on which the dynamics is defined; systems can appear locally disordered but harbor a global order
Apply Holistic Understanding	Focus more on identifying interdependent behaviors (i.e. how a system responds to different contexts and when interdependent sets of parameters are allowed to change) rather than looking for how a system changes when everything is left constant and one parameter at a time is allowed to change
Focus More "Within" for Understanding Source of Apparent Irregularity	Irregular and random appearing behavior that appears to be due either to outside forces or elements of chance may be due solely to the internal dynamics of a system
Look for Recognizable Themes and Patterns	Exact patterns may not be repeated but the general underlying themes will remain the same
Focus on Process vice Static Measures	Study the logic, dynamics, process, etc. not the material constituents of a system
To "Break Down" Does Not Always Mean to "Get Simpler"	If the behavior of a system is described by a fractal, successively finer views of the fractal reveal successievly finer levels of detail; things do do not necessarily "get simpler"
Exploit Nonlinearity	Focus attack on the nonlinear processes in an enemy's system; these are processes that can potentially induce the greatest effect from least effort
Do not Necessarily Frown on Chaos	A bit of irregularity or "chaos" is not necessarily a bad thing, for it is when a system is at the "edge-of-chaos" that it is potentially best able to adapt and evolve
Exploit Decentralized Controll	Encourage decentralized control, even when patches attempt to optimize their own selfish benefit; maintain interaction among patches
Find Ways to be More Adaptable	The most "successful" complex systems do not just continually adapt, they struggle to find ways to adapt better; move towards a direction that gives you more options

Table 3.4 General behavioral guidelines and strategies for conduct and policy making derived from the "Heraclitian" metaphor.

Similarly, nonlinear dynamics teaches us that it is the nonlinearities embedded in a set of processes that are responsible for instability and irregular appearing behavior. The lesson learned here for dealing with adversaries in a conflict is to focus attention on the nonlinear drivers of an enemy's system, for these are the elements that can potentially induce the greatest effect from the least effort.

Table 3.4 provides general behavioral guidelines and strategies for conduct and policy making derived from the "Heraclitian" metaphor.

3.3.3 *Organizational Structure*

A thorough understanding of complexity and complex adaptive systems can be applied to enhance and/or alter organizational and command structures. Practical techniques can be developed for the military to re-examine their metaphors and beliefs, and to adapt new ones as conditions change. General techniques for building "learning organizations," such as adapted from a systems theory model of management and described in Senge's *Fifth Discipline* [Senge90] can be applied. These techniques include general strategies for dealing with the unexpected and/or accidental, and resolving the dichotomous needs for both stability and creativity. The overall objective is to use the basic lessons of complex systems theory to develop sets of internal organizational "rules" and strategies that are more conducive to adaptation and self-organization. Genetic algorithms, too, can be used to search for better command and control structures (see *Tier-VI*).

3.3.4 *Intelligence Analysis*

Conventional intelligence analysis consists of first assessing the information describing a situation and then predicting its future development. The task is complicated by the fact that the available information is often incomplete, imprecise and/or contradictory. Moreover, the information may be falsified or planted by the adversary as part of a deliberate disinformation campaign. The traditional reductionist approach of dealing with these problems consists of six general steps [Wing95]:

(1) *Data Management:* all collected information is first processed to conform to selected forms of data management (computer data-bases, etc.).
(2) *Reliability Grading:* information is graded for its veracity, which depends on such factors as source of information and existence of collaborative sources.
(3) *Subject Sorting:* information is broken down into more manageable parts, typically by subject.
(4) *Relevance Filtering:* subject sorted information is parsed for degrees of relevance (sorting "wheat from chaff").
(5) *Search for "Trigger Facts":* filtered information is searched for characteristic facts and/or events that are known or suspected as being triggers or indicators of specific future events.
(6) *Search for Patterns:* information is examined for clues of patterns of activity and linkages to assist in making specific predictions.

While there is nothing sacrosanct about any of these six steps, and each intelligence analyst undoubtedly evolves his or her own unique style and approach, the fundamentally reductionist manner in which all such analysis is invariably conducted suffers from a number of significant drawbacks [Wing95]. For example, the process of collating the information often curtails an analyst's ability to respond quickly to important indicators. Adherence to a predefined order (such as requiring that all information be fit into an existing data management system) may also lead to difficulties in assimilating any unexpected or unusual information. In the worst case, information that does not strictly conform to accepted or understood patterns and categories or does not conform to an anticipated course of events, may be ignored and/or discarded. Finally, a predisposition to filtering out and assimilating only "conventional" (i.e. "doctrinal") forms of information makes it hard for an analyst to appreciate (and therefore respond to) other, perhaps unconventional, variables that may in fact play a vital role in determining the future behavior of a system (and without which an accurate prediction may be impossible to obtain).

Complex systems theory, with its emphasis on pattern recognition and its general openness-of-mind when it comes to what variables and/or parameters might be relevant for determining the future evolution of a system, has many potentially useful suggestions to offer the intelligence analyst for his/her analysis of raw intelligence data. For example, complex systems theory persuades an analyst, in general, not to discard information solely on the basis of that information not conforming to a "conventional wisdom" model of an adversary's pattern of activity. Instead, and as has been repeatedly stressed throughout this paper, complex systems theory teaches us to recognize the fact that apparently irrelevant pieces of information may contain vital clues as to an adversary's real intentions.

3.3.5 *Policy Exploitation of Characteristic Time Scales of Combat*

A fundamental property of nonlinear systems is that they generally react most sensitively to a special class of aperiodic forces. Typically, the characteristic time scales of the optimal driving force match at all times the characteristic time scales of the system. In some cases the optimal driving force as well as the resulting dynamics are similar to the transients of the unperturbed system [Hubler92].

The information processing in complex adaptive systems and the general sensitivity of all nonlinear dynamical systems to certain classes of aperiodic driving forces are both potentially exploitable features. Recall that one of the distinguishing characteristics of complex systems is their information processing capability. Agents in complex adaptive systems continually sense and collect information about their environment. They then base their response to this information by using internal models of the system, possibly encoding and storing data about novel situations for use at a later time. According to the *edge-of-chaos* idea (see page 112 in chapter 2), the closer a system is to the edge-of-chaos—neither too ordered nor too chaotic—the better it is able to adapt to changing conditions. In Kauffman's words,

> "Living systems exist in the...regime near the edge of chaos, and natural selection achieves and sustains such a poised state...Such poised systems are also highly evolvable. They can adapt by accumulation of successive useful variations precisely because damage does not propagate widely...It is also plausible that systems poised at the boundary of chaos have the proper structure to interact with and internally represent other entities of their environment. In a phrase, organisms have internal models of their worlds which compress information and allow action...Such action requires that the world be sufficiently stable that the organism is able to adapt to it. Were worlds chaotic on the time scale of practical action, organisms would be hard pressed to cope."*

Now compare this state of affairs with Retired USAF Colonel John Boyd's *Observe Orient Decide Act* (OODA) loop [Boyd87]. In Boyd's model, a system responds to an event (or information) by first observing it, then considering possible ways in which to act on it, deciding on a particular course of action and then acting. From a military standpoint, both friendly and enemy forces continuously cycle through this OODA process. The objective on either side is to do this more rapidly than the enemy; the idea being that if you can beat the enemy to the "punch" you can disrupt the enemy's ability to maintain coherence in a changing environment. One can also imagine exploiting the relative phase relationship between friendly and enemy positions within the OODA loop. For example, by carefully timing certain actions, one can effectively slow an enemy's battle-tempo by locking the enemy into a perpetual Orient-Orient mode.

Cooper [Coop95] has generalized this notion to what he calls "phase- dominance," where the idea is to exploit the natural operating cycles and rhythms of enemy forces and execute appropriate actions exactly when they are needed. In phase-dominance, "time becomes the critical determinant of combat advantage."

3.4 Tier III: "Conventional" Warfare Models and Approaches

Tier III consists of applying the tools and methods of nonlinear dynamics and complex systems theory to more or less "conventional models" of combat. The idea on this tier is not so much to develop entirely new formulations of combat so much as extending and generalizing existing forms using a new mathematical arsenal of tools. Examples include looking for chaos in various generalized forms of Lanchester equations, applying nonlinear dynamics to arms-race models, exploiting common themes between equations describing predator-prey relations in natural ecologies and the equations describing combat, and so on.

*From page 232 of Kauffman's opus, *Origins of Order: Self-Organization and Selection in Evolution* [Kauff93].

3.4.1 *Testing for the Veracity of Conventional Models*

A very practical application of one of the most widely used tools of complex systems theory—namely, genetic algorithms—is to the sensitivity analysis and general testing of conventional models of complex systems. Consider, for example, Miller's *Active Nonlinear Test* (ANT) approach to testing the veracity of complex simulation models [MillerJ96].

As large-scale computational models grow in popularity because of their ability to help analyze critical scientific, military, and policy issues, the same conditions that make them so appealing are also the ones that make testing such models more and more difficult. Such models typically deal with enormously large search, or "solution," spaces and are characterized by a high degree of nonlinearity. Traditional "sensitivity analysis" techniques, which probe for a model's reaction to small perturbations in order to get a feel for how sensitive the model is to variations in values of key control parameters, require simple linear relationships within the model in order to be effective.

This last point is a very important one. If the underlying relationships among a model's key parameters are inherently nonlinear—as they must be in any reasonably realistic model of a real complex system—then information about the effect of systematically perturbing individual parameters may not be useful in determining the effects of perturbing groups of parameters. To see this, suppose that the "model" is given by the functional form $f(x_1, x_2) = x_1 x_2$ (which is obviously nonlinear). Then $f(x_1 + \Delta x_1, x_2) = x_1 x_2 + x_2 \Delta x_1 = f(x_1, x_2) + x_2 \Delta x_1$. Similarly, $f(x_1, x_2 + \Delta x_2) = f(x_1, x_2) + x_1 \Delta x_2$. But $f(x_1 + \Delta x_1, x_2 + \Delta x_2) = f(x_1, x_2) + x_2 \Delta x_1 + x_2 \Delta x_1 + D x_2 \Delta x_1$. Thus the effect of changing both x_1 and x_2 simultaneously differs from the adding the effects of the individual perturbations to x_1 and x_2 by the last term, $D x_2 D x_1$. (The linear approximation works well enough, of course, as long as either the perturbations are kept small or the nonlinearity is small.)

The idea behind Miller's ANT approach is to use a genetic algorithm (or any other nonlinear optimization algorithm) to search the space of sets of reasonable model perturbations. The objective is to maximize the deviation between the original model's prediction and that obtained from the model under the perturbations. Note that while one could, in principle, detect nonlinearities by exhaustively searching through the space of all possible combinations of pertinent parameters, the potentially enormous space that the resulting combinatorical explosion gives rise to makes such an exhaustive search unfeasible even when only a relatively few parameters are involved. Thus, Miller's objective is to use a genetic algorithm to perform a directed search of groups of parameters.

ANTs work essentially by probing for weakness in a model's behavior. The idea is to obtain an estimate of the maximum error that is possible in a model by actively seeking out a model's worst-case scenarios. Miller is quick to point out that this approach has two limitations: (1) it fails to give an estimate of the likelihood that the worst-case scenarios will actually occur (though other techniques, such as Monte Carlo methods, can be used for this), and (2) the inability to "break" a model by probing its worst-case scenarios does not guarantee a model's overall quality (since a not terribly well designed model could simply be insensitive to its parameters).

Variations of the basic ANT technique could prove useful for testing many existing models and simulations of land combat.

3.4.2 *Non-Monoticities and Chaos*

A fundamental lesson of nonlinear dynamics theory is that one can almost always expect to find some manifestation of chaos whenever nonlinearities are present in the underlying dynamics of a model. This fundamental lesson has potentially significant implications for even the simplest combat models.

Miller and Sulcoski, for example, report fractal-like properties and a sensitivity-to-initial conditions in the behavior of a discretized model of the Lanchester equations (augmented by nonlinear auxiliary conditions such as reinforcement and withdrawal/ surrender thresholds) [MillerL93, MillerL95].

A recent RAND study has uncovered chaotic behavior in a certain class of very simple combat models in which reinforcement decisions are based on the state of the battle [Dewar91]. The study looked at nonmonoticity and chaos in combat models, where "monotonic behavior" is taken to mean a behavior in which adding more capabilities to only one side leads to at least as favorable an outcome for that side.

The presence of nonmonoticities has usually been interpreted to mean that there is something wrong in the model that needs to be "fixed" and has been either treated as an anomaly or simply ignored. The main thrust of the RAND report is that, while nonmonoticities often do arise from questionable programming skills, there is a source of considerably more problematic nonmonoticities that has its origins in deterministic chaos .

The RAND study found that "a combat model with a single decision based on the state of the battle, no matter how precisely computed, can produce non-monotonic behavior in the outcomes of the model and chaotic behavior in its underlying dynamics."

The authors of the report draw four basic lessons from their study:

(1) Models may not be predictive, but are useful for understanding changes of outcomes based on incremental adjustments to control parameters.
(2) Scripting the addition of battlefield reinforcement (i.e. basing their input on time only, and not on the state of the battle) generally eliminates chaotic behavior.
(3) One can identify input parameters figuring most importantly in behavior of nonmonoticities—these are the size of reinforcement blocks and the total number of reinforcements available to each side.
(4) Lyapunov exponents are useful to evaluate a model's sensitivity to perturbations.

The RAND report concludes that:

> *"In any combat model that depends for its usefulness on monotonic behavior in its outcomes, modeling combat decision based on the state of the battle must be done very carefully. Such modeled decisions can lead to monotonic behavior and chaotic behavior and the only sure ways (to date) to deal with that behavior are either to remove state dependence of the modeled decisions or to validate that the model is monotonic in the region of interest."*

3.4.3 *Minimalist Modeling*

Dockery and Woodcock, in their massive treatise *The Military Landscape* [Dock93b], provide a detailed discussion of many different "minimalist models" from the point of view of catastrophe theory and nonlinear dynamics. Minimalist modeling refers to "the simplest possible description using the most powerful mathematics available and then" adds layers "of complexity as required, permitting structure to emerge from the dynamics." Among many other findings, Dockery and Woodcock report that chaos appears in the solutions to the Lanchester equations when modified by reinforcement. They also discuss how many of the tools of nonlinear dynamics can be used to describe combat.

Using generalized predator-prey population models to model interactions between military and insurgent forces, Dockery and Woodcock illustrate:

1. *The set of conditions that lead to a periodic oscillation of insurgent force sizes*
2. *The effects of a limited pool of individuals available for recruitment*
3. *Various conditions leading to steady state, stable periodic oscillations and chaotic force-size fluctuations, and*
4. *The sensitivity to small changes in rates of recruitment, disaffection and combat attrition of simulated force strengths.*

This kind of analysis can sometimes lead to counter-intuitive implications for the tactical control of insurgents. In one instance, for example, Dockery and Woodcock point out that cyclic oscillations in the relative strengths of national and insurgent forces result in recurring periods of time during which the government forces are weak and the insurgents are at their peak strength. If the government decides to add too many resources to strengthen its forces, the chaotic model suggests that the cyclic behavior will tend to become unstable (because of the possibility that disaffected combatants will join the insurgent camp) and thus weaken the government position. The model instead suggests that the best strategy for the government to follow is to use a moderately low level of military force to contain the insurgents at their peak strength, and attempt to destroy the insurgents only when the insurgents are at their weakest force strength level of the cycle (pages 137-138 in [Dock93b]).

3.4.4 *Generalizations of Lanchester's equations*

In 1914, Lanchester introduced a set of coupled ordinary differential equations as models of attrition in modern warfare. The basic idea behind these equations is that the loss rate of forces on one side of a battle is proportional to the number of forces on the other. In one form of the equations, known as the directed-fire (or square-law) model, the Lanchester equations are given by the linear equations $dR(t)/dt = -\alpha_B B(t)$ and $dB(t)/dt = -\alpha_R R(t)$, where $R(t)$ and $B(t)$ represent the numerical strengths of the red and blue forces at time t, and α_R and α_B represent the constant effective firing rates at which one unit of strength on one side causes attrition of the other side's forces. An encyclopedic discussion of the many different forms of the Lanchester equations is given by Taylor [Taylor80, Taylor83].

While the Lanchester equations are particularly relevant for the kind of static trench warfare and artillery duels that characterized most of World War I, they are too simple and lack the spatial degrees-of-freedom needed to realistically model modern combat. The fundamental problem is that they idealize combat much in the same way as Newton's laws idealize the real chaos and complexity ridden physics of the world. Likewise, almost all Lanchester equation based attrition models of combat suffer from many basic shortcomings:

- *Determinism, whereby the outcome of a battle is determined solely as a function of the initial conditions, without regard for Clausewitz's "fog of war" and "friction"*
- *Use of effectiveness coefficients that are constant over time*
- *Static forces*
- *Homogeneous forces with no spatial variation*
- *No combat termination conditions*
- *Target acquisition is independent of force levels*
- *No consideration of the suppression effects of weapons*
- *and so on ...*

Perhaps the most important shortcoming of virtually all Lanchester equation based models is that such models rarely, if ever, take into account the human factor; i.e. the psychological and/or decision-making capability of the individual combatant.

3.4.4.1 *Adaptive Dynamic Model of Combat*

The adaptive dynamic model of combat is a simple analytical generalization of Lanchester's equations of combat that adds a basic behavioral dimension by building in a feedback between troop movement and attrition. It is discussed by Epstein [Epstein92b].

Epstein introduces two new parameters: (1) α_a, which is the daily attrition rate the attacker is willing to suffer in order to take territory, and (2) α_d, which is the daily attrition rate the defender is willing to suffer in order to hold territory. He uses these parameters to express some simple expectations of human behavior. If the defender's attrition rate is less than or equal to ad, for example, the defender is assumed to remain in place; otherwise this "pain threshold" is exceeded and he withdraws to restore his attrition rate to more acceptable levels. Similarly, if the attackers "pain threshold" is exceeded, he cuts off the attack. Combat is seen as the interplay of "two adaptive systems, each searching for its equilibrium, that produces the observed dynamics, the actual movement that occurs and the actual attrition suffered by each side." [Epstein92b] Postulating some simple functional forms to express intuitive relationships that must hold true among prosecution, withdrawal and attrition rates, Epstein derives expressions for adaptive prosecution and withdrawal rates for attacking and defending forces. Though we will not go into the details here, Epstein's simple model seems to capture some of the basic behavioral characteristics that are so glaringly missing from Lanchester's equations.

3.4.4.2 *Lotka-Volterra Equations*

Studies in predator-prey interactions in natural ecologies have a rich analytical history dating back to the middle 1920s. Around that time, Lottka and Volterra independently proposed the first mathematical model for the predation of one species by another to explain the oscillatory level of certain fish in the Atlantic. If $N(t)$ is the prey population and $P(t)$ is the predator population at time t then $dN/dt = N(a - bP)$, $dP/dt = P(cN - d)$, where a, b, c, and d are positive constants. The model assumes: (1) prey in absence of predation grows linearly with N; (2) predation reduces prey's growth rate by a term proportional to the prey and predation populations; (3) the predator's death rate, in the absence of prey, decays exponentially; (4) the prey's contribution to the predator's growth rate is proportional to the available prey as well as to the size of the predator population.

What is interesting about these simple Lotka-Volterra equations is that they describe exactly the same model as the one Lanchester used to represent land combat. The same kind of oscillatory behavior found in Lanchester's equations, for example, is exhibited by predator-prey systems. Much work, of course, has been done since Lottka's and Voltera's time to generalize their basic equations, including the addition of nonlinear terms to model real-world interactions better, incorporating the complexities of real-world life-cycles and the immune response of hosts in host-parasite systems, modeling interactions between predator-prey systems and their natural environments, exploring the origins of multistability, and so on. However, despite the many conceptual advances that have been made, which today also include the use of sophisticated computer modeling techniques such as multiagent based simulations, this rich history of analytical insights into the behavior of predator-prey systems has heretofore been largely ignored by conventional operations research "analysis" of combat. Simple Lotka-Volterra-like models of ecologies make up a sizable fraction of the models used in complex systems theory and can potentially be exploited to provide insights into the general behavioral patterns of attacker-versus-defender on the battlefield. One possible approach is discussed in [Dock93b].

Other generalizations of the Lanchester equations include:

- Partial differential equations to include maneuver; primarily work done by Protopopescu at the Oak Ridge National Laboratory [Protop89],
- Fuzzy differential equations to allow for imprecise information, and
- Stochastic differential equations to describe attrition processes under uncertainty.

One can also speculate that there might be a way to generalize the Lanchester equations to include some kind of an internal aesthetic. That is to say, to generalize the description of the individual combatants to include an internal structure and mechanism with which they can adaptively respond to an external environment.* We make precisely this kind of generalization, and discuss important ramifications of doing so from a modeling and simulation standpoint, in our discussion of the ISAAC and EINSTein programs (see chapter 4-7).

3.4.5 *Nonlinear Dynamics and Chaos in Arms-Race Models*

G. Mayer-Kress [MayerK92] has written many papers on nonlinear dynamics and chaos in arms-race models and has suggested approaches to sociopolitical issues. His approach is to analyze computational models of international security problems using nonlinear, stochastic dynamical systems with both discrete and continuous time evolution. Many of Mayer-Kress' arms-race models are based on models of population dynamics first introduced by L. F. Richardson after World War I [RichFC90].

Mayer-Kress finds that, for certain ranges of values of control parameters, some of these models exhibit deterministic chaos. In one generalization of a discrete version of Richardson's equations that models the competition among three nations, for example, Mayer-Kress finds that the two weaker nations will form an alliance against the stronger nation until the balance of power shifts. The alliance formation factor and economical constraints induce nonlinearities into the model that result in multiple stable solutions, bifurcations between fixed point solutions and time-dependent attractors. He has also identified parameter domains for which the attractors are chaotic.

*See, for example, Smith's "Calculus of ethics," [Smith56a, Smith56b]; see, also, the discussion on page 68 in section 1.8.

3.5 Tier IV: Description of the Complexity of Combat

"The aim of science is not things themselves, as the dogmatists in their simplicity imagine, but the relations among things; outside these relations there is no reality knowable."—H. Poincare, *Physicist* (1854-1912)

Tier-IV consists of using the tools and methodologies of complex systems theory to describe and help look for patterns of real-world combat. It is the level on which complexity theory is effectively presented with a "candidate complex system" to study—that system being land combat—and given the opportunity to use its full arsenal of tools to explore in earnest the viability of this candidacy. Thus, this tier asks such basic questions as "What really happens on a battlefield?," "What kinds of complex systems theory inspired measures are appropriate to describe combat?," "Are there any embedded patterns, either in historical data or newly acquired data using sets of new measures, from which one can make short-term predictions of behavior?"

This tier consists of three sub-tiers of applicability:

- *Sub-Tier 1*: Short-term predictability, the objective of which is to exploit techniques such as attractor reconstruction to make short-term predictions about the progress of a battle or series of battles. Note that this does not require knowing the underlying rules governing the behavior of combat and/or having a working model
- *Sub-Tier 2:* Confirmation of chaos from historical evidence, the objective of which is to look for characteristic signs of underlying deterministic chaotic behavior in historical combat records. Some work has already been done in this area, most notably by Tagarev, *et.al.* [Tagarev94], but much more remains.
- *Sub-Tier 3:* Development of measures appropriate for describing combat from a complex systems theoretic point of view. This sub-tier includes using such measures as Lyapunov exponents, power spectra, information dimension, and so on to redefine traditional data-collection requirements and measures-of-effectiveness of combat forces.

3.5.1 *Attractor Reconstruction from Time-Series Data*

Time-series analysis deals with the reconstruction of any underlying attractors, or regularities, of a system from experimental data describing a system's behavior (see section 2.1.4). Techniques developed from the study of nonlinear dynamical systems and complex systems theory provide powerful tools whereby information about any underlying regularities and patterns in data can often be uncovered. Moreover, these techniques do not require knowledge of the actual underlying dynamics; the dynamics can be approximated directly from the data. These techniques provide, among other things, the ability to make short- (and sometimes long-) term predictions of trends in a system's behavior, even in systems that are chaotic.

3.5.2 *Fractals and Combat*

There are several suggestive fractal geometric aspects to land combat. For example, deployed forces are often assembled in a self-similar, or fractal, manner and are organized in a manifestly self-similar fashion: fire teams "look like" squads, which "look like" platoons, which "look like" companies, and so on. The tactics that are appropriate to each of these levels likewise shows the same nested mirroring. While a battalion is engaged in a frontal attack, for example, one of the companies could be conducting a supporting flanking attack that itself consists of two platoons engaged in a smaller-scale version of a frontal attack against two other platoons.

The FEBA (*Forward Edge of the Battle Area*) can also be characterized as a fractal , with greater and greater levels of detail emerging as the resolution is made finer. Woodcock and Dockery [Dock93b], for example, have plotted the FEBA length (in miles) versus the step size used in measuring the length using historical data from the German Summer Offensive of 1941 into Russia during World War II. Figure 3.1 shows three front line traces performed for three selected dates taken from the beginning, middle and end of the offensive. In each case, the log-log plot shows a close fit to the power-law fit characteristic of fractals. The slope yields an estimate of fractal dimension; see discussion starting on page 457 in section 6.4 for a more detailed discussion.

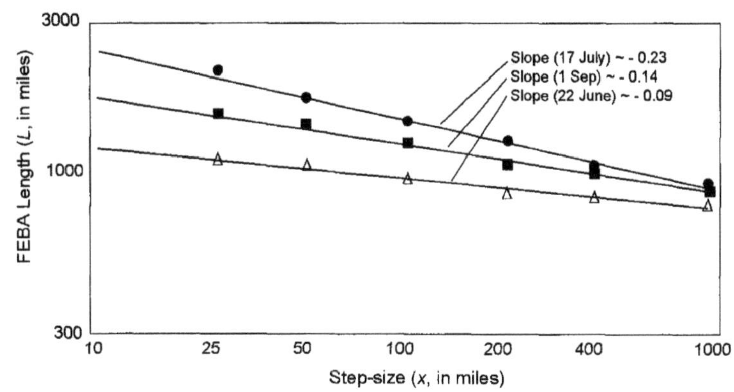

Fig. 3.1 Power-law scaling for FEBA length of German summer offensive of 1941 into Russial; after plot on page 321 in [Dock93b].

What this *does* or *does not* tell us about combat in general is an open question. The largest fractal dimension belongs to the FEBA trace recorded for the most active part of the campaign. Is this suggestive of something fundamental, or—

because fractal dimension depends sensitively on the degree to which a line deviates from "straightness"—is it purely a consequence of the very convoluted nature of this particular trace? As a crude measure of the "complexity" of the evolving FEBA, the fractal dimension might be used to give a feel for the efficacy of a particular advance. Woodcock and Dockery suggest that the most immediate application of the fractal FEBA is to modeling, since it offers the possibility to generate a FEBA directly without detailed modeling. Moreover, a comparison between the daily changes in the fractal dimension of the FEBA calculated from an actual campaign and a computer model can be used to calibrate the model.

More generally, fractals dimensions of a variety of combat related systems (more examples are given below) can be used to quantify both the relevance of large-scaled events to the overall combat process and the subtle interrelationship that exists between small-scale events and large-scale outcomes.

3.5.3 *Evidence of Chaos in War From Historical Data?*

Tagarev, *et.al.* [Tagarev94] provide extensive historical evidence of chaos in tactical, operational and strategic levels of military activity. Tagarev, *et.al.* examine (1) US fixed-wing aircraft losses during the Vietnam war, (2) US Army casualties in western Europe during World War II, and (3) historical trends in US defense spending.

As an example of chaos on the strategic level, Tagarev, *et.al.*, consider time-series plots of US aircraft losses in Vietnam. Recall that, loosely speaking, the fractal dimension of a set specifies the minimum number of variables that are needed to specify the set (see discussion in sections 2.1.4 and 2.1.5). Recall also that the *embedding dimension* is the dimension of the space in which the set of points making up the original time series is embedded.

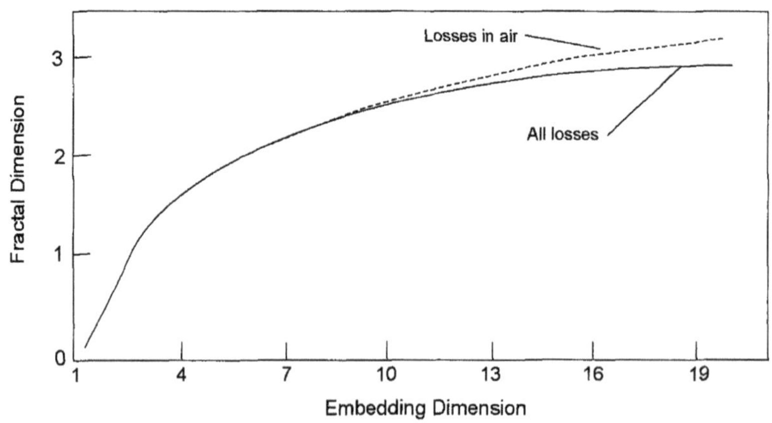

Fig. 3.2 Estimated *fractal dimension* for weekly US aircraft losses in Vietnam (as a whole and in the air); after [Tagarev94].

One essentially constructs d-dimensional data vectors from d points spaced equally in time and determines the correlation dimension* of this d-dimensional point set. Since the set of data points making up Tagarev, *et.al.*'s time-series consists of 443 points, the data points a-priori represent a 443-dimensional space (see [Tagarev96]); see figure 3.2.

If the original data consisted of truly random points, then, as the embedding dimension is increased the calculated correlation dimension should also increase proportionately. The fact that the plot of fractal dimension versus embedding dimension seems to be converging as the embedding dimension increases suggests strongly that despite appearances, the irregular appearing time-series data that was identified by Tagarev, *et.al.*, is not random but is due to a deterministic chaotic process.

3.5.4 *Evidence of Self-Organized Criticality From Historical Data?*

Recall that self-organized criticality is the idea that dynamical systems with many degrees of freedom naturally self-organize into a critical state in which the same events that brought that critical state into being can occur in all sizes, with the sizes being distributed according to a power-law. Introduced in 1988, self-organized criticality is arguably the only existing holistic mathematical theory of self-organization in complex systems, describing the behavior of many real systems in physics, biology and economics. It is also a universal theory in that it predicts that the global properties of complex systems are independent of the microscopic details of their structure, and is therefore consistent with the "the whole is greater than the sum of its parts" approach to complex systems.

3.5.4.1 *Combat Casualties*

Is war, as suggested by Bak and Chen [Bak91,] perhaps a self-organized critical system? A simple way to test for self-organized criticality is to look for the appearance of any characteristic power-law distributions in a system's properties. Richardson [RichLF60] and Dockery and Woodcock [Dock93b] have examined historical land combat attrition data and have both reported the characteristic linear power-law scaling expected of self-organized critical systems. Richardson examined the relationship between the frequency of "deadly quarrels" versus fatalities per deadly quarrel using data from wars ranging from 1820 to 1945. Dockery and Woodcock used casualty data for military operations on the western front after Normandy in World War II and found that the log of the number of battles with casualties greater than a given number C also scales linearly with $log(C)$.

The paucity of historical data, however, coupled with the still controversial notions of self-organized criticality itself, makes it difficult to say whether these

*The *correlation dimension* is discussed on page 96 in section 2.1.5.

suggestive findings are indeed pointing to something deep that underlies all combat or are merely "interesting" but capture little real substance. Even if the results quoted above do capture something fundamental, they apply only to a set of many battles. The problems of determining whether, or to what extent, a power-law scaling applies to an individual battle or to a small series of battles, and—perhaps most importantly—what tactically useful information can de derived from the fact that power-law scaling exists at all, remain open.

3.5.4.2 *Message Traffic*

Woodcock and Dockery [Dock93b] also examine message traffic delays using data collected as part of a military exercise. They find that the number of messages that arrive after a given time delay again follows a linear power-law scaling expected of *self-organized critical* systems.* The authors comment that:

> "The conditional expectation of further delay after waiting a given period actually increases in proportion to the time already waited. Compare this property with the more usual assumption of the Poisson distribution that the delay is independent of the time already waited. The fractal distribution is thus much more in accord with the maxim that 'the worse things get, the more worse they can get.' For the operational commander, the consequence of the hyperbolic fit is that self-initiated action is probably called for after a suitable delay. For the message traffic system designer the implication of the power law fit is to make messages, which are long delayed, candidate for deletion."

3.5.5 *Use of Complex Systems Inspired Measures to Describe Combat*

Sections 2.1.4 and 2.1.5 of chapter 2 of this book discusses several useful qualitative and quantitative characterizations of chaos. Qualitative characterizations include time-plots of the behavior of pertinent variables, Poincare plots, autocorrelation functions and power spectra. Quantitative characterizations include Lyapunov exponents, generalized fractal dimensions (including fractal, correlation and information dimensions), and Kolmogorov-Sinai entropy. A recently introduced idea is to use casualty-based entropy as a predictor of combat.

3.5.5.1 *Casualty-Based Entropy*

Carvalho-Rodriques [Carv89] has recently suggested using entropy, as computed from casualty reports, as a predictor of combat outcomes. Whether or not combat can be described as a complex adaptive system, it may still be possible to describe

*See discussion on *self-organized criticality* in section 2.2.8, page 149.

it as a dissipative dynamical system. As such, it is not unreasonable to expect entropy, and/or entropy production, to act as a predictor of combat evolution. Carvalho-Rodriques defines his casualty-based entropy E by:

$$E_i = \frac{C_i}{N_i} \log \frac{1}{C_i/N_i}, \tag{3.1}$$

where C_i represents the casualty count, in absolute numbers) and N_i represents the force strength of the ith adversary (either red or blue). It is understood that both C_i and N_i can be functions of time.

Figure 3.3 shows a plot of the functional form $E(x) = x \log(1/x)$, where $x = C_i/N_i$. Notice that the curve is asymmetrical and has a peak at about 0.37. One could interpret this to mean that once $x = C_i/N_i$ goes beyond the peak, "it is as if the combat capability of the system ... declines, signifying disintegration of the system itself."*

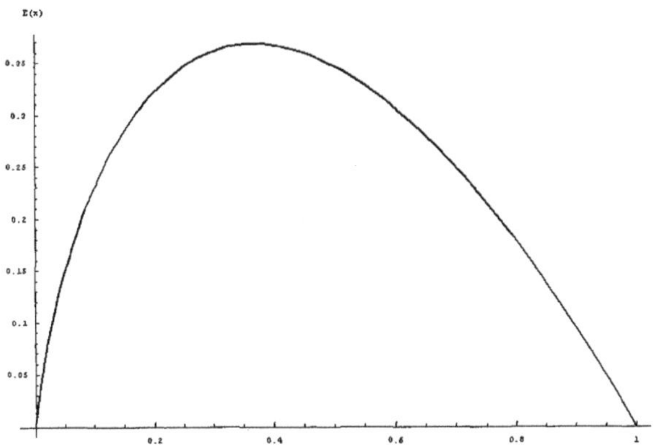

Fig. 3.3 A plot of entropy E(x) = x log (1/x); see text.

Woodcock and Dockery [Dock93b] provide strong evidence that casualty-based entropy is a useful predictor of combat. They base this on analysis on both time-independent and time-dependent combat data derived from detailed historical descriptions of 601 battles from circa 1600 to 1970, exercise training-data obtained from the National Training Center and historical records of the West-Wall campaign in World-War II and Inchon campaign during the Korean war.

They find that plots of E_a (attacker entropy) versus E_d (defender entropy) are particularly useful for illustrating the overall combat process (see figure 3.4):

- *Region I:* a low entropy region corresponding to low casualties and ambiguous outcomes. Initial phases of a battle pass through this region, with the

*See [Dock93], page 197.

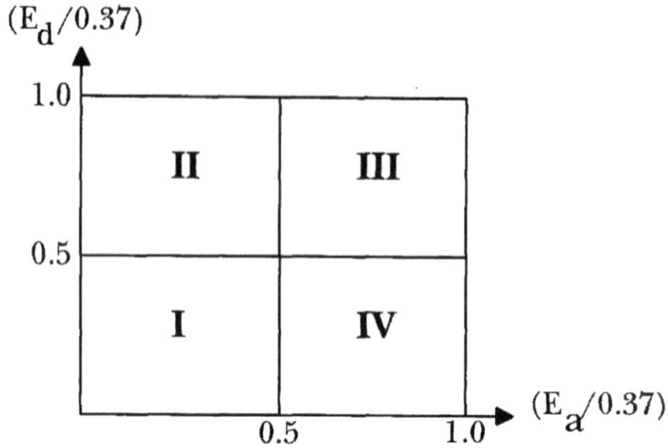

Fig. 3.4 Regions of casualty-based entropy phase space [Carv89].

eventual success or failure for a given side depending on the details of the trajectory in this entropic space

- *Region II:* a region of high entropy for the defender and low entropy for the attacker indicates the attacker wins
- *Region III:* a region of ambiguous outcomes, like region I, region III represents high attrition with outcomes depending on the direction of the trajectory. (Woodcock and Dockery indicate that only simulated combat appears able to reach this region.1)
- *Region IV:* an analogue of region II, where the entropy roles are reversed and the defender wins.

Woodcock and Dockery further suggest that the measurement and display of coupled casualty and reinforcement rates may be a first step towards quantifying the battle tempo. "The tempo is then seen to characterize, not the physical rate of advance (the usual connection), but rather the rate of structural breakdown of the fighting force."*

We note, in closing, that Carvalho-Rodriques's definition of a casualty-based entropy is but one possible definition. One could alternatively use generalizations of the Renyi-entropy, Kolmogorov-Sinai entropy, or topological entropy, among many other definitions (see pages 114-129 in chapter 2). Despite the seeming simplicity of the basic idea, there is strong evidence to suggest that entropy will play a fundamental role in understanding the underlying dynamical processes of war.

*See [Dock93], page 227.

3.5.6 *Use of Relativistic Information to Describe Command and Control Processes*

Relativistic information theory is a concept introduced by Jumarie [Jumarie75] and has been suggested as a possible formalism for describing certain aspects of military command and control processes by Woodcock and Dockery [Dock93b]. Relativistic information may prove to be particularly useful for gaining insight into the interplay among combat, command and control and information.

Generalized entropy is an entropy that is endowed with four components, so that it is equivalent to a four-vector and may be transformed by a Lorentz transformation (as in relativity theory). These four components consists of:

(1) *External entropy* of the environment (H_o), which can be associated with operational and intelligence information
(2) *Internal entropy* of the system (H_i), which can be associated with the readiness of forces information
(3) *System goals*, which can be equated with missing (and planning) information
(4) *Internal transformation potential*, which measures the efficiency of the system's internal information transformation; this can be associated with a measure of the command and control capability information

An additional factor, called organizability, plays the role of "velocity." Woodcock and Dockery show that it is possible to use relativistic information theory to compare the relative command and control system response of two command structures to the world around them. The quantity of interest is dH_i/dH_o, or the rate of change of the internal information environment with respect to changes in the surrounding environment.

> *"Using relativistic information theory it is possible to compare the relative command and control system response of two commanders to the world around them. Their relative perceptions of the change about them is theoretically quantified by relativistic information theory. Because the theory measures changes with respect to the environmental change, we can argue that self-organization is a requirement for a military force. If the internal structure cannot cope with the change in the environment that structure must itself change. The goal of combat must paradoxically be to create a self-organizing structure which nonetheless ensures the destruction of the foes' internal structure."**

*See [Dock93], page 530.

3.6 Tier V: Combat Technology Enhancement

Tier V consists of applying complex systems theory tools to enhance existing combat technologies. This "workhorse" tier is concerned with using specific methods to improve, or provide better methods for applying, specific key technologies. Examples include using computer viruses (a form of "artificial life") as computer countermeasure agents, applying iterated function systems (i.e. fractals) to image compression for data dissemination, using cellular automata for cryptography, using genetic algorithms for intelligent manufacturing, using synchronized chaotic circuits to enhance IFF capability, and "fire-ant" technology.

3.6.1 *Computer Viruses ("computer counter-measures")*

A computer virus can be thought of as an autonomous agent. It is a computer program that tries to fulfill a goal or set of goals without the intervention of a human operator. Typically, of course, viruses have rather simple and sinister goals of tampering with the normal operation of a computer system and/or computer network and then reproducing in order to spread copies of themselves to other computers. Computer viruses are particularly interesting to artificial life researchers because they share many of the properties of biological viruses.

From a military standpoint, computer viruses can be used in two ways: (1) as computer countermeasure agents to infiltrate enemy systems, or (2) as constructive "cyberspace allies" that, for example, can be programmed to maintain the integrity of large databases.

3.6.2 *Fractal Image Compression*

A powerful technique for image compression that is based on fractals—called *Iterated Function Systems* (IFS)—has been developed by Barnsley and his co-workers at the Georgia Institute of Technology [Barn88a, Barn88b]. To appreciate the need for compressing images, consider a typical grey-scale intelligence photograph that need to be disseminated to interested parties. Suppose there are 256 shades of grey and that the image must be scanned and converted into a 1024-by-1024 pixel digitized image. The resulting image can be recorded using a binary string of 1024-by-1024-by-8 binary bits of information. Thus, without compression, one must use close to 10 million bytes of memory to store the image. Image compression involves reducing the required number of bytes to store an image, and can be either *lossless*, so that the original image can be recovered exactly, or *lossy*, so that only an approximate version of the image can be retrieved.

There are, of course, tradeoffs involved among how well the original image can be recovered, what the maximum possible compression rate is, and how fast the actual compression algorithm can be run. Generally speaking, the greater the desired compression, the more CPU-time is required and the greater the risk of some compression loss. Conventional compression schemes, such as Discrete Sin and Cos Transforms, can achieve compression ratios ranging from 2:1 to 10:1, depending on the image. In comparison, while IFS is generally lossy (so that an original image cannot generally be recovered from the compressed image exactly), it is able to achieve extremely high compression ratios, approaching 50:1, 300:1 or better. Microsoft has, in fact, licensed use of this technology to compress images found on its CD-ROM encyclopedia *Encarta*.

IFS uses affine transformations to build a *collage* of an image using smaller copies of the image. An affine transformation is an operation on a set of points that distorts that set by scaling, shifting, rotating and/or skewing. The IFS process involves finding smaller, distorted copies of an image and putting them together in a collage that approximately reproduces the original image. Each distorted copy of the image represents a different affine transformation. Once a collage is formed, the original image can be thrown away. The original image can be recovered by applying the appropriate set of affine transformations to some starting "seed" coordinate and iterating. The trajectory of the points will converge onto an attractor that defines the image. For example, figure 3.5 shows a "recovered" image of a fern using the affine transformation defined by:

$$\begin{cases} x \to s_1 x \cdot \cos(r_1) - s_2 y \cdot \sin(r_2) + t_1, \\ y \to s_1 x \cdot \sin(r_1) - s_2 y \cdot \cos(r_2) + t_2, \end{cases} \tag{3.2}$$

where the parameters r_1, r_2, s_1, s_2, t_1 and t_2 are shown in table 3.5.

Consider what this fern represents. A high resolution digitized image of the original grey-scale image takes up more than a megabyte of memory, Conventional compression schemes might reduce this by a factor of five. But IFS has reduced the image to essentially 28 parameters.

Affine Transformation	r_1	r_2	s_1	s_2	t_1	t_2
1	0	0	0	0.16	0	0
2	-2.5	-2.5	0.85	0.85	0	1.6
3	49	49	0.30	0.34	0	1.6
4	120	-50	0.30	0.37	0	0.44

Table 3.5 Rotation (r_1, r_2), scaling (s_1, s_2) and translation (t_1, t_2) parameters defining the IFS affine transformation of a fern; see figure 3.5.

Of course, not all objects in nature have the manifest self-similarity of a fern. The trick is to find the right group of affine transformations for generating a given image. That a set of affine transformations can be found in general, even for objects that do not exhibit a manifest self-similarity is due to a theorem called the *Collage Theorem*. The collage theorem asserts that given a target image S and a measure of closeness ϵ, a set of IFS affine transformations f can be found such that the "distance" (appropriately measured) between S and $f(S)$ (which is the union of scaled copies of S, called the "collage" of S) is less than ϵ [Barn88a].

Fig. 3.5 An IFS encoded fern using the affine transformation defined in table 3.5.

Applications of IFS compression are wide-ranging and far-reaching. They include more efficient transmission of fax, still imagery and video, more efficient computer data storage and retrieval, and image recognition. There are of course many more details to IFS than there is room to discuss in this paper. An excellent reference is Barnsley's book [Barn88b].

3.6.3 *Cryptography*

In succinct terms, an ideal cryptographic encryption scheme is an operation on a message that renders that message completely meaningless to anyone who does not possess a decryption key, and, at the same time, preserves and reveals the original message exactly to anyone who possess the key. Ideally, the operation is encrypts quickly and decrypts quickly.

All practical cryptographic schemes, of course, are less than ideal, typically because their encryption schemes are less than foolproof (Denning, [DennE82]). Most depend on the presumed computational difficulty of factoring large prime numbers. The effective measure of worth of any cryptographic scheme remains the test of time: the longer a given system is in widespread open use by trained intelligent cryptoanalysts without being "broken," the better the system.

It would take us too far afield of the main subject of this report to go into any great detail about cryptoanalysis. We will only briefly mention some attempts that have been to develop cryptosystems based on nonlinear dynamical system theory and cellular automata [Ilach01]. We follow mainly Gutowitz [Guto93].

The basic idea is to use a nonlinear dynamical system that is known to exhibit deterministic chaos and use it to evolve some initial starting point to some future state. After a certain time has been allowed to elapse, the initial state—which is defined to be the public key—is effectively "forgotten." Because the dynamics is assumed to be strictly deterministic, however, the same initial state always leads to the same final state after a specified number of time steps. Users can thus send messages to one another encoded in some way using some part of the evolved trajectory traced out by the secret initial state. Anyone who does not possess the initial state will not be able to reproduce the trajectory and thus will not be able to decipher the message.

Bianco and Reed [Bianco90] have patented an encryption scheme using the logistic equation as the underlying dynamical system. A drawback to this scheme, however, is that the sequences generated by the logistic map are not truly random, so that an appropriate statistical analysis could identify embedded patterns that could then be exploited to decipher a message. Wolfram [Wolfram84] suggests a discrete dynamical system version of the basic idea that uses the iteration of a cellular automaton to generate a bit string. The cellular automaton chosen is known as rule 30 (see page 137 in chapter 2). What is interesting about this rule is that the temporal sequence of vertical values of its evolving space-time pattern has been shown to satisfy all known tests of randomness. As for the case of a continuous dynamical system, the secret key is the initial state of the cellular automaton system, and a message can be encrypted and decrypted by combining it with the temporal sequences of a given length generated by the rule. Gutowitz [Guto93] has also introduced a much more powerful and sophisticated algorithm based on a cellular automaton model.

3.7 Tier VI: Combat Aids

Tier VI consists of using the tools of complex systems theory to enhance real-world operations. Examples include using genetic algorithms to "evolve" strategy and/or tactics, developing tactical picture agents to adaptively filter and integrate information in real-time, and developing autonomous robotic devices to act as sentries and data collectors.

As will be discussed later in this book (see Chapter 7), genetic algorithms are powerful heuristic tools for finding near-optimal solutions for general combinatorial optimization search problems. One obvious application of genetic algorithms that has found a comfortable home in the artificial life research community, involves their use as sources of the "adaptive intelligence" of adaptive autonomous agents in an agent-based simulation. A related application that is of particular interest to the military strategist, theorist and/or battlefield commander, is that of direct strategy and/or tactics development.

Figure 3.6 shows a schematic representation of what might be called a "strategy landscape." The strategy landscape represents the space of all possible global strategies that can be followed in a given context or scenario. Generally speaking, a genetic-algorithm-based tactics—or strategy—"optimizer" consists of an evolutionary search of this landscape for high-pay-off strategies using whatever local information is available to individual combatants. The shape of the landscape is determined by the fitness measure that is assigned to various tactics and/or strategies. It also changes dynamically in time, as it responds to the actual search path that is being traversed.

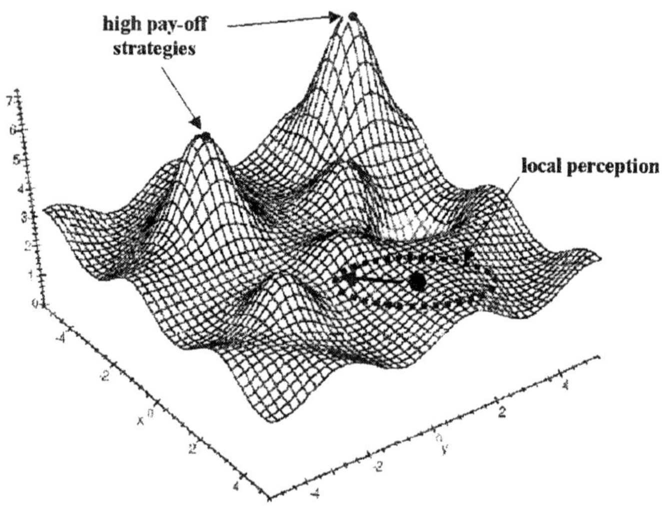

Fig. 3.6 Schematic representation of a *strategy landscape.*

3.7.1 *Using Genetic Algorithms to Evolve Tank Strategies*

Carter, Dean, Pollatz, *et.al.*, [Carter93] suggest using genetic algorithms to "evolve" strategies for the battlefield. While their ultimate goal is to develop a complete architecture for intelligent virtual agents that employ multiple learning strategies, their initial testbed consists of evolving reasoning-strategies for what they call smart tanks. While this testbed is deliberately designed to be as simple as possible, because it involves many of the key elements that make up more realistic models, it is of considerable pedagogical value. For this reason, we discuss the smart-tank testbed briefly below.

Smart tanks live on a simple two-dimensional "battlefield" containing a randomly placed "black-hole" (see figure 3.7). The black-hole represents a lethal area of the battlefield that annihilates any smart tank that encounters it. Smart tanks, generated on one side of the battlefield, must cross over to the other side without encountering the black-hole if they are to be successful and "live." A tank's route is determined by its genotype (see below).

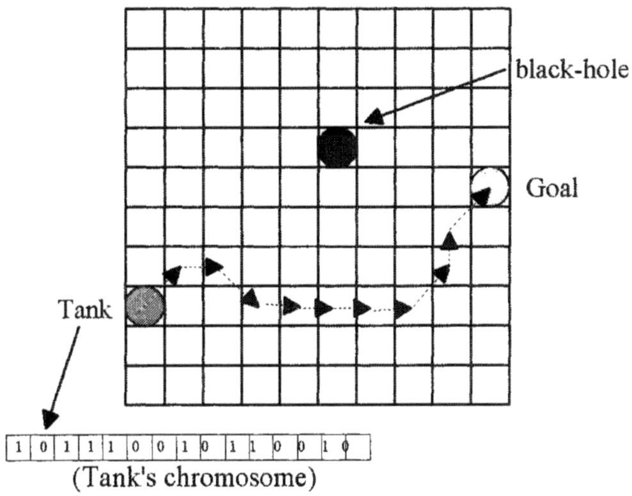

Fig. 3.7 Schematic representation of a genetic-algorithm based *smart tank.*

A smart tank is an artificial organism that consists of three basic components: (1) memory, which is a record of the decisions and fates of three previous smart tanks that have successfully crossed the battlefield, (2) reasoning, which is the internal mechanism by which a tank selects one of several viable strategies, and (3) instinct, which is a basic inference engine common to all tanks, and is included to simulate the basic behaviors that may occur in life threatening or otherwise critical situations. How much weight a given tank assigns to each component—that is, what overall reasoning strategy it chooses to follow—depends on its genetic predisposition.

Smart-tank strategies "evolve" in the following way. First, a population of smart tanks is created. One tank is selected out of this population and crosses the battlefield. It looks ahead a certain number of discrete bins into which the battlefield is decomposed, and gathers information on the destination bin. The exact number of bins that it looks ahead at depends on the tank and its current reasoning strategy. The tank then selects a reasoning strategy upon which to base its next move. After arriving at the destination square this same process repeats itself. If, at any time, the tank encounters a black-hole, it dies and its genetic structure is lost (though a record of it is maintained in a global case-base). If the tank survives—i.e. never encounters—the black-hole, its genes are saved in a "winner's circle." A genetic algorithm then combines the genes in the winner's circle to form a new population of tanks.

Carter, *et.al.*'s initial testbed was designed to use genetic algorithms as a mechanism for creating coordination schemes for three specific learning strategies:

- *Case-based Reasoning.* This strategy consists of using whatever reasoning was the best approach for an identical, or almost identical, situation encountered in the past. Carter, *et.al.*'s actual implementation involved tacking a history of up to 256 previous tank traversals of a 10-by-10 bin battlefield, with a maximum of three histories being accessible by any one tank. The case-based reasoning strategy compares the three histories and selects the closest fit. The suggested move is assigned a confidence level commensurate with the closeness of fit.
- *Rule-based Reasoning.* This strategy consists of using the current information about the local surroundings and determining what rule, out of the current rule set, is best applicable. Rules are of the form "go to bin nearest goal," or "go to bin requiring least amount of energy to get to," and so on. The rule-base also takes into account how well rules have performed in the past.
- *Instinct.* This strategy consists of using one of a set of generic responses. Moves are based on prior determined moves for a given bit pattern in a tank's chromosome. A typical move might consist of going to the adjacent bin that exerts the least amount of pull toward the black-hole (a black-hole's "attraction" for tanks diminishes with distance from black-hole, but its effects are felt in many surrounding bins).

No one of these individual reasoning strategies, of course, works equally as well in all situations. Indeed, one of the main reasons for developing this testbed example was to explore the efficacy of various options and to allow the genetic algorithm to suggest the right "mix" of strategies.

3.7.1.1 *Smart-Tank's Chromosome*

A smart tank's actual chromosome consists of 35 genes. We should immediately emphasize that as is true of almost all other features of this simple testbed, there is nothing sacrosanct about having 35 genes. One could choose to have a greater or lesser number of genes, and to interpret the genes in a different manner from that outlined below. The testbed is here presented in detail for illustrative purposes only, and to suggest only one of many equally as valid approaches that could be used to design a genetic algorithm scheme for evolving strategies for the battlefield.

The functions of a smart tank's 35 binary-valued genes (i.e. each gene takes on either the value 0 or 1) are broken down as follows:

- *Bits 1 - 8:* pointer to the first of 3 accessible histories of previous tank traversals (out of a maximum of 256 stored histories; see "Case-based reasoning" above)

- *Bits 9 - 16:* pointer to the second of 3 accessible histories of previous tank traversals
- *Bits 17 - 24:* pointer to the second of 3 accessible histories of previous tank traversals
- *Bits 25 - 29:* tank characteristics (2 bits for sensitivity, 1 bit for speed, and 2 bits for type and range of look ahead)
- *Bits 30 - 32:* type of reasoning (the 3 bits specify 9 3-bit patterns ranging from 100% rule-based for pattern 111 to 50% rule-based and 50% case-based for pattern 100 to 33% rule-based, 33% case-based and 34 % instincts for pattern 011).
- *Bits 33 - 35:* generic instincts (the 3 bits again specifying 9 possible 3-bit patterns that range from "tank heads toward the goal regardless of forces in the environment" for pattern 000 to "tank moves to square in front of it that has the least force in it" for pattern 010, and so on)

As mentioned above, a greater or fewer number of genes could have been chosen, and all or some of their interpretations altered. What it is hoped the reader will take away from this description of a simple testbed is the general approach to building a genetic algorithm based "strategy evolver."

3.7.2 *Tactical Decision Aids*

Virr, Fairley and Yates [Virr93] have suggested using a genetic algorithm as an integral component of what they call an *Automated Decision Support System* (ADSS).

There are three main phases to any decision making process:

(1) *Data Fusion:* wherein all of the available information is assembled to form a tactical picture of a given situation
(2) *Situational Assessment:* wherein various pertinent aspects of the tactical picture are appraised
(3) *Decision:* wherein the appropriate action, or set of actions, is actually selected

The tactical plan, from which a specific set of condition-contingent actions is selected, can be expressed, in its simplest form, as a sequence of IF-THEN rules of the form

$$\begin{gathered} \dots\dots \\ \textbf{Rule } R_{n-1} \\ \textbf{Rule } R_n\textbf{:} \\ \textbf{IF(condition}_1 \textbf{ AND condition}_2 \textbf{ AND ... AND condition}_N\textbf{)} \\ \textbf{THEN(action}_1 \textbf{ AND action}_2 \textbf{ AND ... AND action}_M\textbf{)} \\ \textbf{Rule } R_{n+1} \\ \dots\dots \end{gathered}$$

Here, condition n_i refers to the ith piece of information assimilated during the data fusion phase (such as speed of target, bearing, etc.) and actionj refers to the jth action that is to be taken (such as turn toward target, engage target, and so on). A Plan P, consisting of a set of rules $\{R_1, \ldots, R_P\}$, forms the rule-base of a *Knowledge Based System* (KBS) for a given tactical situation. Once specified, it can be used for training purposes, to model tactical decisions made by an adversary in simulated combat and/or as a real-time tactical decision aid on the battlefield. The problem, of course, is how to construct P.

Traditionally, P has been constructed by a knowledge engineer; that is, someone who painstakingly elicits from experts the facts and heuristics used by those experts to solve a certain set of problems. Of course, there are two obvious problems with this traditional approach: (1) an expert may not always be able to successfully articulate all of the relevant knowledge required for solving a problem, and (2) there may be enough of a mismatch between the concepts and vocabulary as used by an expert and a knowledge-engineer that though an expert may correctly articulate the relevant knowledge, the knowledge engineer is unable to render that knowledge meaningful within the IF-THEN rule structure of the plan.

One way of circumventing both of these problems—called *Machine Learning* (ML)—is to have the KBS "discover" the required knowledge, and thereby construct the plan P, by itself. Although there are many different techniques that all go under the rubric of ML, they all fall into one of four major categories:

1. *Analytic Learning.* Analytic learning systems require a thorough understanding of the general underlying problem type and must have available a large number of problem-solution exemplars. The technique relies on adapting solutions to problems that it identifies as being "close to" known solutions to known problems.
2. *Inductive Learning.* Inductive learning requires an external "teacher" to produce problem samples. The teacher grades the system's attempts to use its stored knowledge to try to solve each problem in turn. The teacher's grade is then used to update the system's knowledge.
3. *Neural Network Learning.* The neural net (also called the Connectionist) approach consists of applying a learning algorithm (such as back-propagation) to adjust a set of internal weights in order to minimize the "distance" between calculated and desired solutions to selected problems. Given a set of training problem-solution exemplars, the learning algorithm produces a network that, in time, is able to correctly recognize the pattern implicit in all input (i.e. problem) and output (i.e. solution) pairs.
4. *Genetic Algorithm (or Selectionist) Learning.* Selectionist learning systems exploit the learning capability of a genetic algorithm to "evolve" an appropriate knowledge base. Recall that genetic algorithms are a class of heuristic search methods and computational models of adaptation and evolution that mimic and exploit the genetic dynamics underlying natural selection.

Given the basic differences among these four approaches, it is clear that, in general, not all approaches can be expected to be equally appropriate for solving a given kind of problem. Depending on the problem, each approach offers certain unique advantages and disadvantages.

When it comes to the general problem of tactical decision making, a strong case can be made that selectionist learning techniques are the most appropriate. First, there is no complete "domain theory" describing all possible conflicts and scenarios on which to base a general strategy of conflict resolution. This makes it hard to use an analytical learning technique. Second, whatever real-world expertise there is to assist in building a KBS must, of necessity, be both incomplete (because only a small fraction of all possible scenarios can be experienced) and imprecise (because all human experience is fundamentally subjective). Thus, both inductive and connectionist learning techniques, both of which depend critically on having sets of carefully pre-constructed scenario-plan exemplars available for learning, would be difficult to use for this problem. Finally, and most importantly, any tactical plan must be able to continually adapt to changing, and often unanticipated, facts and scenarios. Genetic algorithms, of course, are designed to deal with precisely this kind of open-ended and "changing" problem, as they are particularly adept at discovering new rules.

Now, how specifically can genetic algorithms be used to generate new tactics? The answer depends on how genetic algorithms are incorporated within the parts of a larger class of *Classifier System.*

3.7.3 *Classifier Systems*

Classifier systems were introduced by John Holland [Holl89] as an attempt to apply genetic algorithms to cognitive tasks. A classifier system typically consists of (1) a set of detectors (or input devices) that provide information to the system about the state of the external environment, (2) a set of effectors (or output devices) that transmit the classifier's conclusions to the external environment, (3) a set of rules (or classifiers), consisting of a condition and action, and (4) a list of messages.

Rules are the actual classifiers, and are grouped together to form the classifier's rule-base. Associated with each classifier is a classifier-weight, representing the degree of usefulness of that particular classifier in a given environment. Messages constitute the classifier system's basic means of exchanging information, both internally and at the interface between classifier system and external world.

Although the operation of a real classifier system can be quite complex, their basic operation consists of the following general steps: Information from the world model is first communicated to the classifier at the input interface. The classifier combines this information with rules stored in its rule-base to select an appropriate action, which is, in turn, effected at the output interface, updating the world model. Learning takes place via credit assignment, wherein rules are judged "good" or "bad" in order to teach the system what actions are appropriate in what contexts. The genetic algorithm comes in as the part of the classifier system responsible for deciding how "old" rules in the rule-base are replaced by "new" rules.

3.7.4 *How can Genetic Algorithms be Used?*

Recall that genetic algorithms process a population of "solution-organisms" according to their relative "fitness" (i.e. a figure of merit ostensibly measuring an organism's ability to solve a given problem) so that, over time, as the population evolves, there is an increasing likelihood that some members of the population are able to "solve" the given problem well (or well enough). In the present context, the "problem" is to find new and/or improved rules for a tactical decision knowledge base. The meta-problem, from the point of view of the genetic algorithm, is how to go about ascribing a "fitness" to members of the rule-population. Without a fitness, of course, there is no way for the population to evolve.

Virr, *et.al.* [Virr93] suggest four ways in which a genetic algorithm can be grafted into a classifier system to effectively breed rules:

- *Apply Genetic Algorithm at the Rule Level.* Suppose we take a "population" to consist of rules making up a particular plan. A genetic algorithm can then use the individual rule-strengths as fitnesses guiding their evolution. The major drawback to this approach is that since all of the rules are independent, the genetic algorithm degenerates into a search for a "super-rule" that deals with all situations (which, for typical real problems, does not exist). There are ways, however, of inducing rules to cooperatively link with one another, partially circumventing the drawback to this approach.
- *Apply Genetic Algorithm at the Plan Level.* An alternative is to use a genetic algorithm on a population of plans rather than on a population of rules making up a given plan. Drawbacks to this approach include (1) using a single fitness measure (presumably derived from the fitnesses of the individual rules) to represent the efficacy of an entire plan, and (2) the need for an additional algorithm to generate new rules in the various plans.
- *Apply Genetic Algorithm at the Sub-Plan Level.* Suppose a plan P is partitioned into q subsets, where $1 < q < R$, R is the number of rules in P, and the rules in each subset of the partition are related in some way. Then the rules within a each subset can be viewed as a population, and—since each rule has an associated rule-weight—the population can be subjected to a genetic algorithm. The efficacy of the partitioning scheme itself may also be amenable to a genetic algorithm.
- *Apply Genetic Algorithm at Both the Rule and Plan Levels.* The fourth approach attempts to capitalize on the advantages of the first two approaches by carefully combining them. The idea is to associate one classifier with each plan, and running the set of classifiers in parallel. The genetic algo-

rithm is then applied both at the rule level of each classifier—during which time the plans are allowed to develop independently—and at the plan level, during times in which the operation of the individual classifier systems is periodically suspended.

3.7.5 *Tactical Picture Agents*

Anyone who has spent even a small amount of time "surfing" the World-Wide-Web for information can attest to how difficult it is to find useful information. To be sure, the WWW is filled with untold numbers of glossy pages overflowing with all kinds of information. A quick use of a web search-engine (such as *Google* or *AltaVista*) usually suffices to uncover some useful sites. But what happens when one needs to find some information about a particularly obscure subject area? And what happens when one begins relying on one's web connection for more and more of one's daily workload: e-mail, stock quotes, work scheduling, selection of books, movies, travel arrangements, video conferencing, and so on?

A powerful emerging idea that helps the human "web-surfer" deal with this increasing workload and that is based in part on the methodologies of autonomous agents and genetic algorithms, is that of Intelligent Software Agents.

Software agents are programs that essentially act as sophisticated personal assistants. They act as intermediaries between the interests of the user and the global information pool with which the user has traditionally dealt directly. Software agents engage the user in a cooperative process whereby the human operator inputs interests and preferences and the agent monitors events, performs tasks, and collects and collates useful information. Because software agents come endowed with an adaptive "intelligence," they become gradually more effective at their tasks as they begin learning the interests, habits and preferences of the user.

How does this relate to a military combat environment? Intelligent software agents can be used for adaptive information filtering and integration and as *tactical picture agents*, scouring and ordering the amorphous flood of battlefield and intelligence data. For example, naval commanders must have access to, and have immediate use of, the right information at the right time. They must assimilate and understand all of the relevant information concerning their own situation, including the disposition of the red, blue and white forces, geographical, oceanographic and meteorological characteristics of the surrounding vicinity, status of all weapon systems, and so on. The totality of this information is called the tactical picture.

At the present time, information is disseminated typically via either naval text messages, ship-to-ship communications, radar and sonar tracks, and so on. As technology improves, naval ships and other platforms will have access to a wider range of information, including immediate access to satellite images and weather reports, on-line intelligence analyses, and connectivity to the world-wide-web or some similar globally connected network. It therefore becomes vital to develop intelligent software agent technologies that can automatically perform the data-mining and filtering functions necessary to make effective use of an enormous amount of information.

The development of a tactical picture agent technology to improve the on-board "tactical picture building" ability of all naval platforms must target all three of the following areas:

(1) Modeling of users and tasks so that intelligent software can decide what to search for and how to integrate search results.
(2) Development of intelligent software agents that can locate and filter multimedia information appropriate for a particular task and user.
(3) Develop methods of displaying information that are appropriate for a particular task and environment.

Of course, exactly the same ideas apply to developing a tactical picture agent for air and land combat. Diverse forms of information must be assimilated, filtered, ordered and presented to the field commander.

3.8 Tier VII: Synthetic Combat Environments

Tier VII consists of developing full system models for training purposes and/or for use as research laboratories. Examples include cellular-automata-based and multi-agent-based simulations of combat (along the lines of commercial games like SimCity [Wright89]), cognitive architecture driven simulations such as the one found in Carnegie-Mellon University's SOAR/IFOR [Soar] project, and combat models based on the *Swarm Development Groups*' SWARM [SWARM] general-purpose complex adaptive modeling system. As ISAAC and EINSTein are both examples of synthetic combat environments, and are the main focus of this book, we only briefly touch upon these two models in this overview section.

3.8.1 *Combat Simulation using Cellular Automata*

If one abstracts the essentials of what happens on a battlefield, ignoring the myriad layers of detail that are, of course, required for a complete description, one sees that much of the activity appears to involve the same kind of simple nearest-neighbor interactions that define cellular automata (see pages 137-148 in chapter 2). Woodcock, Cobb and Dockery [Woodc88] in fact show that highly elaborate patterns of military force-like behavior can be generated with a small set of cellular automaton-like rules.

In Woodcock, *et.al.*'s model, each combatant—or *automaton*—is endowed with a set of rules with which it can perform certain tasks. Rules are of four basic varieties:

(1) *Situation Assessment*, such as the determination of whether a given automaton is surrounded by friendly or enemy forces

(2) *Movement*, to define when and how a given automaton can move; certain kinds of movement can only be initiated by threshold and/or constraint criteria
(3) *Combat*, which governs the nature of the interaction between opposing force automata; a typical rule might be for one automaton to "aim fire" at another automaton located within some specified fight radius
(4) *Hierarchical Control*, in which a three-level command hierarchy is established; each lower-level echelon element keys on those in the next higher echelon on each time step of the evolution

These basic rules can then be augmented by additional rules to (1) simulate the impact that terrain barriers such as rivers and mountains have on the movement of military forces; (2) provide a capability for forces to respond to changing combat conditions (for example, a reallocation of firepower among three types of weapons: aimed firepower, area firepower and smart weapons firepower), and (3) replace entities lost through combat attrition. Figure 3.8 shows a schematic of three sample rules. The multiagent-based models ISAAC and EINSTein, which are the main focus of this book, were both motivated strongly by this much earlier, pioneering effort. As we shall see in later chapters, many of ISAAC's and EINSTein's own rules are essentially of the same form as shown here.

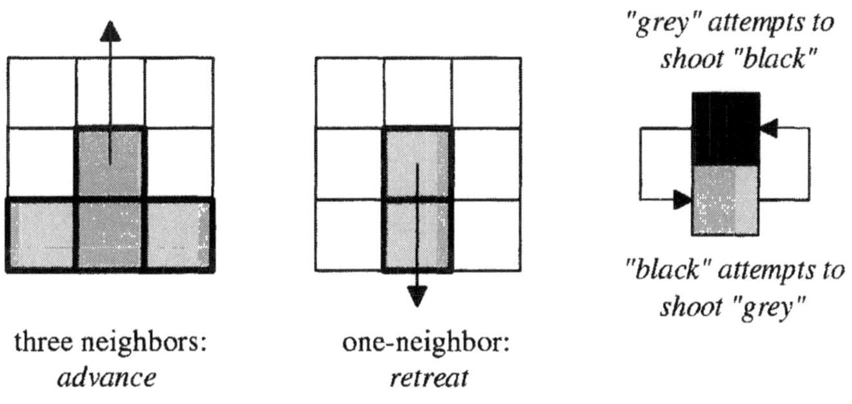

Fig. 3.8 Three sample rules in Woodcock, et. al.'s CA-based combat model.

Woodcock, *et.al.* stress that the goal of CA-based model of combat is not to codify a body of rules that comes as close as possible to the actual behavioral rules obeyed by real combatants; rather, the goal lies in "finding the simplest body of rules that both can generate nontrivial global combat-like phenomena and provide a new understanding of the combat process itself by extracting the maximum amount of behavioral complexity from the least complicated set of rules." Additional details are discussed in chapters 3.1 and 3.2 of *The Military Landscape* [Dock93b].

3.8.2 *Multiagent-Based Simulations*

For many obvious reasons, the most natural application of complexity theory to land warfare is to provide an agent-based simulation of combat. Indeed, the central focus of this book is a detailed look at one of the first comprehensive multiagent-based models of combat ever developed for use by military operations researchers. Relegating the discussion of this model (EINSTein), as well as the discussion of its precursor model (called ISAAC) to later sections of this book, we will limit our discussion here to merely illustrating the salient points.

The basic idea behind using agents to simulate combat is to describe combat as a coevolving ecology of semi-autonomous adaptive combatants: an *Irreducible Semi-Autonomous Adaptive Combat Agent* (ISAACA) represents a primitive combat unit (infantryman, tank, transport vehicle, etc.) that is equipped with the following characteristics:

- *Doctrine:* A default local rule set specifying how to act in a generic environment
- *Mission:* Goals directing behavior
- *Situational Awareness:* Sensors generating an internal map of environment
- *Ability to Adapt:* An internal adaptive mechanism to alter behavior and/or rules.

Adaptation proceeds either immediately, in the sense that agents can tailor behaviors to changing contexts, or may proceed on a longer-time scale by using a genetic algorithm. Ideally, one would hope to find universal patterns of behavior and/or tactics and strategies that are independent of the details of the makeup of individual ISAACAs.

3.9 Tier VIII: Original Conceptualizations of Combat

Tier VIII represents the potentially most exciting—and certainly most far-reaching—tier of the eight tiers of applications. It consists of using complex systems theory inspired ideas and basic research to develop *fundamentally new conceptualizations of combat.* It asks what is simultaneously the most direct and most expansive possible question regarding the complex systems theoretic view of land combat: "*What are the universal characteristics of land combat, thought of as a complex adaptive system?*" Because of the very speculative nature of this question, *Tier-VIII* thus also necessarily takes the longest-term view of expected development time. But while this tier obviously entails the greatest risk, it also promises to yield the greatest potential payoff.

Tier-VIII complements *Tier-IV*, on which the objective is to find complex systems theoretic "measures" that describe combat. *Tier-VIII* is concerned with what to do with those measures once they are found. Ideally, complex systems theory may suggest ways in which battlefields must be configured (or compelled to self-organize) to be maximally adaptable to the most wide-ranging set of environmental circumstances. It would be most interesting, for example, to be able to determine what doctrine, constraints and/or specific rule sets prescribing what local actions can and cannot be taken that are most conducive to pushing a combat force closer to the edge-of-chaos?

In the remainder of this section we discuss briefly a few speculative ideas and technologies that might be used to develop applications lying on this tier of applicability. The discussion is mostly qualitative and is designed to plant seeds for future work. Some more speculative and open questions, whose answers undoubtedly require work to be done on this tier, appear in the concluding section of this paper.

3.9.1 *Dueling Parasites*

Genetic algorithms have thus far figured very prominently on a variety of tiers of applications, ranging from helping design more efficient and robust command and control structures on *Tier-II* to acting as the source of the "adaptive intelligence" of adaptive autonomous agents in a multi-agent simulation of combat on *Tier-VII*. The reason for this, of course, is that genetic algorithms are a mainstay of most complex systems theory models.* Here we outline a potentially powerful generalization of the basic genetic algorithm introduced by Hillis [Hillis90], which may have a natural application to the modeling of combat.†

Conventional genetic algorithms search for "solutions" to problems by "evolving" large populations of approximate solutions, each candidate solution represented by a chromosome. The genetic algorithm evolves one population of chromosomes into another according to their fitness using various genetic operators (such as crossover and mutation), and, eventually, after many generations, the population comes to consist only of the "most-fit" chromosomes.

This basic recipe has, of course, been shown to be useful for finding near-optimal solutions for many kinds of problems. One of the major difficulties that all solution schemes for solving combinatorial optimization problems must contend with, however, is the classical problem of the search space containing local optima: once a search algorithm finds what it "thinks" is the global optimal solution, it is generally difficult for it to find ways to not be "locked into" the local optimum.

Hillis attacks this problem by exploiting host-parasite interactions among two coupled genetic algorithm populations. To illustrate the idea, consider his testbed system, which consists of finding a sorting algorithm for elements of a set of fixed size that requires the smallest number of comparisons and exchanges to be made among the elements. The overall problem is to design an efficient sorting network, which is a sorting algorithm in which the sequence of comparisons and exchanges

*Genetic algorithms are dicussed in chapter 7.

†Dueling parasites have most recently been used for coevolving complex robot behavior [Oster03].

is made in a predetermined order. A candidate sorting network, once defined (by a chromosome), is easy to test.

Now, Hillis' idea is to set up not one but two interacting genetic algorithm populations, one population consisting of "solutions," or sorting programs (the hosts), and the other consisting of "sorting problems" (the parasites). Having the two populations interact effectively sets up an "arms-race" between the two populations. While the hosts are trying to find better and better ways to sort the problems, the parasites are trying to make the hosts less and less adept at sorting the problems by making the problems "harder."

The interaction between the two populations dynamically alters the form of the fitness function. Just as the hosts reach the top of a fitness "hill," the parasites deform the fitness landscape so that the hill becomes a "valley" that the hosts are then forced to find ways to climb out of and start looking for new peaks. When the population of programs finally reaches a hill that the parasites cannot find a way to turn into a valley, the combined efforts of the coevolving hosts and parasites has found a global optimum. Thus, the joint, coupled, population pools are able to find better solutions quicker than the evolutionary dynamics of populations consisting of sorting programs alone.

The application to combat modeling is conceptually straightforward. The idea is to apply genetic algorithms not to just one side of a conflict, or to use genetic algorithms to find "optimal" combat tactics for fixed sets of constraints and environments, but to use joint, coupled, pools of populations, one side of which represents a set of tactics or strategies to deal with specific scenarios, and the other side of which seeks ways to alter the environment in ways that make it harder and harder for those tactics or strategies to work.

3.9.2 *Percolation Theory and Command and Control Processes*

Percolation theory represents the simplest model of a disordered system. Consider a square lattice, where each site is occupied randomly with probability p or empty with probability $1-p$. Occupied and empty sites may stand for very different physical properties. For simplicity, let us assume that the occupied sites are electrical conductors, the empty sites represent insulators, and that electrical current can flow between nearest neighbor conductor sites. At low concentration p, the conductor sites are either isolated or form small clusters of nearest neighbor sites. Two conductor sites belong to the same cluster if they are connected by a path of nearest neighbor conductor sites, and a current can flow between them. At low p values, the mixture is an insulator, since a conducting path connecting opposite edges of the lattice does not exist. At large p values, on the other hand, many conduction paths between opposite edges exist, where electrical current can flow, and the mixture is a conductor. At some concentration in between, therefore, a threshold concentration p_c must exist where for the first time electrical current can percolate from one edge to the other. Below p_c, we have an insulator; above p_c we have a conductor. The threshold concentration is called the percolation threshold, or, since it separates two different phases, the critical concentration. The value of the critical concentration depends on the connectivity pattern of the lattice.

What does this have to do with command and control structures and processes? Conceptually, one can form analogies between conductor sites and information processing and/or data-fusion centers and between electrical current and information. Information can be radar contact reports, commands pumped down echelon or raw intelligence data. The problem of determining the efficacy of a given flow of information can be solved by interpreting it as a percolation problem. Among the intriguing questions that inevitably arise from drawing such an analogy, are *"What command and control architectures are most conducive to information flow?"*, and *"What are the inherent vulnerabilities in the existing command and control structure?"*, and so on.

Woodcock and Dockery also liken percolation through a lattice to the percolation of military forces through an area of obstacles or a combat zone of deployed adversarial forces.*

There is a lot of interesting theoretical work that is being done on random graph theory [Palmer85], which deals with how the global topological properties of a mathematical graph† (such as its overall connectivity, the maximum number of connected clusters of sites that it contains, and so on) change as a function of the number of nodes and links in the graph. Theoretical results such as these provide important information about how the overall efficacy of, say, a command and control communications network depends on quantifiable measures of its topology.

3.9.3 *Exploiting Chaos*

Deterministic chaos seems grounded in paradox: simple equations generate complicated behavior, random appearing trajectories harbor embedded patterns, and so on. Many potential applications depend heavily on apparent paradoxes (if not outright oxymoronic assertions) such as these, seeking to find ways to exploit the inherent regularities that systems exhibiting a deterministic form of chaos are naturally predisposed to possess. Here we mention three such seeming paradoxical properties of chaotic systems that might be exploited on both practical and theoretical levels:

- *Chaotic Control*
- *Chaotic Synchronization*
- *Taming Chaos*

*See page 323 in [Dock93].

†A mathematical graph can be thought of as the network describing an *Integrated Air Defense System*, but where the presence or absence of a given link between nodes is specified by a probability distribution.

3.9.3.1 *Chaotic Control*

Chaotic control refers to using a chaotic system's sensitivity to initial conditions to stabilize regular dynamic behaviors and to effectively "direct" chaotic trajectories to desired states.* It has been amply demonstrated both theoretically and practically for a wide variety of real physical systems. It is interesting to note that this is a capability that has no counterpart in nonchaotic systems for the ironic reason that the trajectories in nonchaotic systems are stable and thus relatively impervious to desired control.

From a theoretical point of view, chaotic control could conceivably be used by decision makers to selectively guide, or "nudge," combat into more desired states. Of course, this presupposes that an appropriate phase-space description of combat has been developed, and all of the relevant control parameters have been identified.

3.9.3.2 *Chaotic Synchronization*

Like chaotic control, the idea of being able to synchronize coupled chaotic systems seems almost an oxymoron, but has its roots in the same basic idea of selectively driving a chaotic dynamical system to restrict its motion to a desired subspace of the total phase space. Chaotic synchronization refers to selectively coupling two identical chaotic systems in such a way that they then evolve with their corresponding dynamical variables exhibiting exactly the same behavior in time.

First introduced by Pecora and Carroll [Pecora90], the underlying principle is to look for a range of parameter settings for which the joint phase space of two chaotic systems is stable to motion on a subspace where the motion is either regular or is of another type of chaotic behavior [Abar96].

Theoretical analysis of the general question of what happens when one chaotic dynamical system is used to "drive" another—which is how, on a conceptual level, one can interpret the selective "nudging" of forces on a battlefield—has potentially enormous implications for our ability to predict how the overall system of ground forces will react. Synchronization also has clear applications to communications and developing a robust and reliable form of IFF. Moreover, the fact that a generalized relationship between driving signals and response system signals exists at all, suggests that this function can in principle be found and used for prediction purposes. Careful attention to the theory behind, and potential practical applications of, synchronized chaos is likely to have a high payoff.

3.9.3.3 *Taming Chaos*

A very recent addition to the list of counterintuitive behaviors of chaotic systems is what can be described as "taming chaos" with chaos. Disorder and noise in physical systems typically tends to destroy any existing spatial or temporal regularities, or

*Chaotic control is discussed, on a slightly more technical level, in chapter 2 (see page 100).

so one's intuition would lead one to expect. Not so! For example, it can be shown that some nonlinear systems are able to transfer information more reliably when noise is present than when operating in a noiseless environment.*

Braiman, Lindner and Ditto [Braim95] have also recently reported an interesting experiment in which an array of periodically forced pendula lapses into spatiotemporal chaos when the pendula are identical, but then snaps into a periodic behavior when disorder is *added* to the system! Braiman, *et.al.*, speculate that disorder can be used to tame spatiotemporal chaos and suggest that "the role of disorder in spatially extended systems may be less of a randomizing influence than an intrinsic mechanism of pattern formation, self-organization and control."† Again, the ability to selectively alter the apparently chaotic patterns of behavior on the spatiotemporal arena of the battlefield has broad implications and potentially an enormously high payoff. Whether, or to what extent, such a "taming" of chaos is possible requires us to first carefully study the general phenomenon for simple models of combat.

3.9.4 *Pattern Recognition*

> "If you see a whole thing—it seems that it's always beautiful. Planets, lives.... But close up a world's all dirt and rocks. And day to day, life's a hard job, you get tired, you lose the pattern." —Ursula K. LeGuin

Battlefield intuition may be likened to an innate ability to perceive (though perhaps not to articulate) underlying patterns in what otherwise seems to be irregular behavior. We compared it to the intuition of the successful stock-broker on wall-street, who has an intuitive "feel" for when certain stocks will rise and fall. Whatever the underlying basis is for battlefield intuition, however, certainly one of the most important fundamental problems facing any commander is the pattern recognition problem.

In order to make sound decisions a commander must know what is really happening on the battlefield. "Knowing what is really happening" does not just mean finding better ways to get at ground truth; it means seeing *patterns of behavior* that others have either not looked for or have simply missed seeing altogether. This is also a fundamental problem faced by any agent in a complex systems theoretic multi-agent based simulation of, say, a natural ecology. In order for an agent to survive and successfully evolve in the ecology, it needs to identify the parts of the environment that are relevant and understand how the relevant parts really fit together, not how they appear to fit. While solving the pattern recognition may, at first, appear to have little in common with "complex systems theory," it is in fact a problem that lies at the core of any complex systems theoretic approach. It is thus also lies at the core of a complex systems theory approach to land warfare.

*This is a phenomenon called *stochastic resonance*; see, for example, [Moss95].

†See [Braim95], page 467.

Now, while this is not to say that complex systems theory has "solved" the pattern recognition problem, it is meant to suggest that some of the tools that complex systems theory has developed for dealing with the general pattern recognition problem can also be applied to discerning patterns on the battlefield.

The "conventional" tool-kit for dealing with patterns embedded in otherwise chaotic dynamics comes from nonlinear dynamics and consists of four basic parts [Abar96]:

(1) *Finding the signal*, in which the signal of interest is first extracted from the raw data; of course, in many instances, the raw data may be the signal, since there is no a-priori way of discerning noise from meaningful information
(2) *Finding the phase space*, which consists of the time-delayed embedding technique of creating a d-dimensional vector out of an a-priori "list" of numbers
(3) *Classifying the signal*, which can be done by using such measures as Lyapunov exponents, various fractal dimensions, and other quantities independent of the initial conditions
(4) *Developing a model* and predicting future behavior, based on the classifications made during the previous step

We will not go into any greater detail about any of these steps, except to say that these are techniques that have by now been fairly well established in the research literature. Of course, as with any general set of tools, each of the tools in this tool-chest has certain advantages and disadvantages and is more or less adept at dealing with specific kinds of data.

In addition to these more or less conventional tools borrowed directly from nonlinear dynamics theory, however, there are other—more theoretical and speculative—methods available. We mention three such methods: (1) high-level rule extraction using genetic algorithms, (2) self-organizing neural nets to sort raw information, and (3) data-base mining for knowledge.

3.9.4.1 *High-Level Rule Extraction*

Richards, Meyer and Packard [RichFC90] have recently suggested a way to extract two-dimensional cellular automaton rules directly from experimental data. Recall that two-dimensional cellular automata are a class of spatially and temporally discrete, deterministic dynamical systems that evolve according to a local evolutionary rule.* Richards, *et.al.*'s idea is to use a genetic algorithm to search through a space of a certain class of cellular automata rules for a local rule that best reproduces the observed behavior of the data. Their learning algorithm (which was applied specifically to sequential patterns of dendrites formed by NH4Br as it solidifies from a supersaturated solution) starts with no a-priori knowledge about the phys-

*Cellular automata are dicussed in chapter 2; see pages 137-148. A thorough technical description appears in [Ilach01].

ical system. It, instead, builds increasingly sophisticated "models" that reproduce the observed behavior.

Though Richards, *et.al.*'s NH4Br testbed has a-priori little to do with combat, it is in principle not that far away. Like combat, dendritic NH4Br data exhibits pattern structure on many different length scales and a dynamics takes place on different time scales. Moreover, there is often very little information available regarding the physical variables describing the dendritic solidification of NH4Br. While one can determine whether a given point is solid or liquid, for example, one typically knows nothing about the solute concentration or temperature field in the liquid. The situation is much the same in combat, where one may know the disposition of one's forces and perhaps something about what individual combatants are doing at what time, but the specifics of their actions and of any internal dynamics they are following are effectively unknown. In the NH4Br, despite this lack of knowledge of what is happening on the micro-level, Richards, *et.al.*'s algorithm is able to find a rule that qualitatively reproduces the observed data.

Richards, *et.al.* comment that while the exact relationship between the rule found by their genetic algorithm and the fundamental equations of motion for the solidification remains unknown, it may still be possible to connect certain features of the learned rule to phenomenological models.

> "We propose that this type of 'derivability gap' is the rule, rather than the exception for most complex spatial patterns observed in nature. For such phenomena, it may be impossible to derive models which explain observed spatiotemporal complexities directly from fundamental equations and 'first principles.' Though perhaps underivable, the dynamical structure extracted by the learning algorithm is undeniable, and represents a new type of progress, perhaps the primary kind of understanding possible for complex patterns."*

It is tempting to speculate what insights a similar approach to extracting "low-level rules" from "high-level observed behavior" on the battlefield might have to offer.

3.9.4.2 *Self-Organizing Maps*

A *Self-Organizing Map* (SOM) is a general unsupervised neural-network.† Introduced by Kohonen in the early 1980s, it is designed to order high-dimensional statistical data so that inputs that are "alike" generally get mapped to each other [Kohon90]. Unlike backpropagating neural nets, that require that the output part of a desired input-output set of pairs is known a-priori, unsupervised learning effectively *informs the trainer* what latent patterns and similarities exist within a block

*[RichFC90], page 201.

†See chapter 10 in [Ilach01b].

of data. Thus, it can be used as a means by which to "self-organize" ostensibly patternless masses of information like raw intelligence data, or existing databases consisting of various unstructured bits of information about an adversary. The idea is literally to allow the raw data to "tell the intelligence analyst" what kinds of innate structural patterns might exist in the data. It is not a cure-all—as it requires behind-the-scenes preprocessing and some assumptions to be made about what kind of structuring and "document-distance" measures are appropriate—but the methodology potentially provides an important first step in helping an analyst, or field commander, intelligently sift through apparently reams of formless information.

An example of how SOMs can be used as "information organizers" is a recent effort called WEBSOM.* WEBSOM is designed to automatically order, or organize, arbitrary free-form textual information into meaningful maps for exploration and search. It automatically organizes documents into a two-dimensional grid so that the closer two documents are "related" to each other the closer they appear together on the grid. More specifically, WEBSOM has been applied to ordering documents on the World-Wide-Web (WWW).

Anyone who has spent even a short time "cruising" the WWW knows that while there is a tremendous amount of information available on the web, desired information is more often than not extremely difficult to find. Typical web search engines are intelligent enough to retrieve useful sites for specific queries, but are next-to-useless when it comes to finding sites or files in cases where the actual subject or object of interest is only vaguely known. Even in those cases where existing search engines are able to find a few useful files, these files are often buried deep in an otherwise lengthy list of files that are only marginally related to a specific query, if at all.

WEBSOM is designed to help such free-form searches by automatically organizing a set of documents so that related documents appear close to each other. An initial testbed for the technique consisted of 4600 full-text documents from the "comp.ai.neural-nets" newsgroup, containing a total 1,200,000 words.†

After being organized by WEBSOM, the newsgroup documents can be viewed on four levels. The top level consists provides an overview of whole document collection. It consists of individual nodes representing the highest-level clusters of documents, arranged by similarity, and uses grey-scales to indicate clustering density. Levels two and three are accessed by clicking the mouse on a desired super-cluster of related documents, and represent successively deeper nestings of documents or-

*The best available inforation on WEBSOM can be found at the URL address http://websom.hut.fi/websom/.

†An interactive demonstration of using WEBSOM for this example appears at the site http://websom.hut.fi/websom/. The discussion follows the paper "Newsgroup exploration with WEBSOM method and browing interface," by T. Honkela, et. al. that can be retrieved from this site.

ganized into mid-level clusters. The fourth, and final, level is accessed by clicking the mouse on a desired cluster on the third level, and consists of actual document listings, now grouped such that all "nearby" documents are closely related. As one proceeds down from the top-most to bottom-most level, one goes from the most general clusters (say, neural nets, fuzzy logic, and forecasting) down to more finely divided clusters (neural nets in plant manufacturing, and fuzzy control of neural nets) down to individual documents. WEBSOM thus effectively maps out the entire "document space" according to what documents actually inhabit that space. "Closeness" is interpreted with respect to semantic content, as approximated by a statistical sampling of word contexts. Other measures could be devised for other applications.

In this specific newsgroup example, WEBSOM provides a display of the similarity relations of the subject matters of the documents. These are reflected in the distances between documents in the document map. The density of documents in different parts of the map are reflected by varying shades of grey on the document display. One can easily imagine suitably generalized versions of this methodology being applied to organizing raw intelligence data. More speculatively, one can imagine using SOMs to provide "unconventional" partitionings of battlefield processes. That is, just as WEBSOM is able to tell us something about the natural ordering in document space, from which we are then able to infer patterns that can be used to more intelligently guide our search for information, so SOMs may be able to tell an analyst or field commander something about the natural ordering in "combat space," from which an analyst or field commander is then able to infer patterns that he can use to make "more informed" decisions.

3.9.4.3 *Data-Base Mining for Knowledge*

Frawley, *et.al.* [Fraw92] define *knowledge discovery* as the "nontrivial extraction of implicit, previously unknown, and potentially useful information from data." Much work has recently been done in the area of database mining, which is essentially an application of the scientific method to database exploration. The basic problem is easy to state: given a data set find a pattern, or patterns, that describes meaningful, consistent relationships among subsets of the database. Ideally, of course, the pattern should be simpler to articulate than merely enumerating all the facts. Knowledge discovery is therefore generally concerned with inducting, from data, possible rules or "laws" that may have been responsible for generating that data. The connection to the basic pattern recognition problem on the battlefield, should again be obvious from a complex systems theory point of view: given that a database D contains a "record" of a land warfare campaign, we are interested in finding the "implicit, previously unknown, and potentially useful information" that can be extracted from D. We do not have the space here to go into the details of the many techniques that are available for addressing the general database mining problem. We briefly mention three recent examples:

(1) *Kepler*, which is a system designed to find functional relationships among quantitative data. Applied to a data base consisting of experimentally derived fluid flow data, for example, Kepler is able to "discover" such basic laws as Bernoulli's theorem for laminar flow.
(2) *Thought*, which is capable of incrementally discovering production rules by classifying and abstracting from given examples, and then finding implications between the descriptions according to the relationships it finds among corresponding clusters of data.
(3) *Posch*, which is an automated artificial intelligence systems designed to discover causal relationships in a medical-record database

Some, though not all, data-mining tools can be thought of as being natural-language equivalents of the more number-intensive techniques developed by nonlinear dynamics for finding underlying patterns in number fields. It would be an interesting exercise to use some of the available data-mining techniques to explore what hidden relationships might exist in historical combat data, for example, not to mention using such techniques for exploring patterns and relationships in data that summarizes combat exercises and /or actual combat.

3.9.5 *Fire-Ant Warfare*

As an example of a potentially far-reaching technology that is clearly inspired by complex system theoretic concepts is the Fire- Ant Warfare idea recently put forth by Libicki [Libicki95]:

> "Today, platforms rule the battlefield. In time, however, the large, the complex, and the few will have to yield to the small and the many. Systems composed of millions of sensors, emitters, microbots and miniprojectiles, will, in concert, be able to detect, track, target, and land a weapon on any military object large enough to carry a human. The advantage of the small and the many will not occur overnight everywhere; tipping points will occur at different times in various arenas. They will be visible only in retrospect."

The idea is to exploit the collective intelligence of a swarm of (perhaps thousands of) tiny intelligence-gathering machines and small smart-weapons. Libicki suggests that systems of millions of sensors, emitters, microbots and miniprojectiles can be used in concert to detect, track, target and land a weapon on military targets.

This approach is reminiscent of Rodney Brooks' [Brooks94] micro-bot artificial-life approach to artificial intelligence.* In contrast to the traditional top-down methods that emphasize abstract symbol manipulations and high-level reasoning skills, Brooks proceeds from the bottom-up by using many small and individually

*A short discussion of Brook's *subsumptive architecture* appears on page 244 in chapter 4.

"simple" micro-bots, or autonomous agents, to assemble a "collective intelligence" that—when the agents act in concert—is capable of performing very sophisticated tasks. We will not say more about this very active school of research, except to suggest that artificial-life-like fire-ant warfare represents not just a conceptual advance in the way we think about warfare, but a significant technological advance in how we conduct it as well.

Chapter 4

EINSTein: *Mathematical Overview*

"A small number of rules or laws can generate systems of surprising complexity. Moreover, this complexity is not just the complexity of random patterns. Recognizable features exist...In addition, the systems are animated; they change over time. Though the laws are invariant, the things they govern change...The rules or laws generate the complexity, and the ever-changing flux of patterns that follow leads to perpetual novelty and emergence."

—John Holland, *Hidden Order* [Holl95]

4.1 Introduction

One of the most important fundamental—and unsolved—problems in artificial-life research is to understand the dynamical relationship between an organism's genotype—or the set of primitive instructions that define an organism (and as encoded by the organism's chromosome)—and its phenotype, or the organism's emergent, macroscopic form (which includes both its morphology and how it interacts with other organisms). In the context of combat, this question assumes the form:

> *What is the relationship between the set of primitive rules that define the actions of individual soldiers (i.e., agents, within a model) and the emergent behavioral characteristics of a large number of soldiers when they are engaged in combat (i.e., agent-agent interactions)?*

The "organism" in this case, is a multiagent *force.* EINSTein—*Enhanced ISAAC Neural Simulation Toolkit** —is a multiagent artificial life "laboratory" whose design and development is predicated on the fundamental belief that the italicized question above is best answered by equating "combat force" with "complex adaptive system," and thereby bringing to bear on the problem the same mathematical and simulation tools that have heretofore been used to explore the dynamics of non-combat-related complex systems.

*Recall that ISAAC (= ***I****rreducible* ***S****emi-****A****utonomous* ***A****daptive* ***C****ombat*) is a DOS-based precursor model (see page 14 in chapter 1). ISAAC's last official version (v1.8.6) can be downloaded from http://www.cna.org/isaac/downsoft.htm.

EINSTein builds upon and extends an earlier model (ISAAC) into a bona-fide research and teaching tool for exploring self-organized emergent behavior in land combat. Figure 4.1 shows several screenshots and a partial list of features. We will examine each of these features, and many more that are not listed here, in the next chapter. EINSTein represents the first systematic attempt, within the military operations research community, to simulate combat - on a small to medium scale - by using autonomous agents to model individual behaviors and personalities rather than specific weapons. Because agents are all endowed with a rudimentary form of "intelligence," they can respond to a very large class of changing conditions as they evolve during battle. Because of the relative simplicity of the underlying dynamical rules, EINSTein can rapidly provide outcomes for a wide spectrum of tunable parameter values defining specific scenarios, and can thus be used to effectively map out the space of possible behaviors.

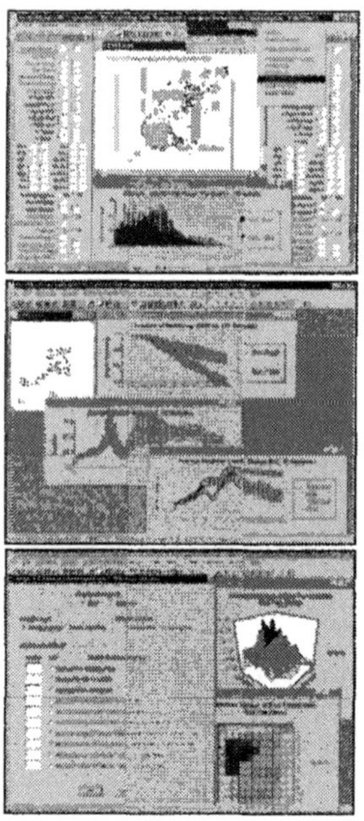

- **"Conceptual laboratory" for exploring self-organized collective behavior in combat**
- **Personality-driven local decisions**
- **Tunable N-dimensional parameter space**
  - *sensor range*
  - *fire range*
  - *movement range*
  - *defense/offense, ... etc. ...*
- **Multiple squads**
- **Communications**
- **Local and global commanders**
- **Passable/impassable terrain**
- **On-line data collection/visualization**
- **Genetic-algorithm force composition**

Fig. 4.1 Some screenshots of EINSTein's run-sessions and a partial listing of the program's features.

ISAAC was originally developed for the US *Marine Corps Combat Development Command* (MCCDC), and is a simple, proof-of-concept model, designed to illustrate how combat can be viewed as an emergent self-organized dynamical process [Ilach97a]. ISAAC introduced the key idea of building combat "from the ground up" by using complex adaptive agents as primitive combatants and focusing on the global coevolutionary patterns of behaviors that emerge from the collective nonlinear local dynamics of these primitive agents. It represents the first systematic attempt, within the military operations research community, to simulate combat by using semi-autonomous agents to model individual behaviors and personalities rather than specific weapons. Because agents are all endowed with a rudimentary form of "intelligence," they can respond to a very large class of changing conditions as they unfold during battle. Because of the relative simplicity of the underlying rule base, the modeler is able to produce outcomes for a wide spectrum of tunable parameter values defining a scenario, and to thus effectively map out the space of possible behavior.

Both ISAAC's and EINSTein's local dynamics are patterned after mobile cellular automata rules, and are somewhat reminiscent of Braitenberg's *Vehicles* [Brait84]. Mobile cellular automata have been used before to model predator-prey interactions in natural ecologies [Bocc94]. They have also been applied to combat modeling [Woodc88],* but in a much more limited fashion than the one used by EINSTein.

Models based on differential equations homogenize the properties of entire populations and ignore the spatial component altogether. Partial differential equations—by introducing a physical space to account for troop movement—fare somewhat better, but still treat the agent population as a continuum. In contrast, EINSTein consists of a discrete heterogeneous set of spatially distributed individual agents (i.e., combatants), each of which has its own characteristic properties and rules of behavior. These properties can also change (i.e., adapt) as an individual agent evolves in time. The model is designed to allow the user to explore the evolving patterns of macroscopic behavior that result from the collective interactions of individual agents, as well as the feedback that these patterns might have on the rules governing the individual agents' behavior.

EINSTein's latest version runs on any personal computer running Microsoft Windows (95/98/···/2000/XP) and may be downloaded on the internet at URL address (see Appendix A):

http://www.cna.org/isaac/einstein_install.htm .

An Adobe PDF-formatted manual to EINSTein [Ilach99a] is also available on the web at URL address:†

http://www.cna.org/isaac/einstein_users_guide.pdf .

Installation instructions, and a short tutorial on how to get started, are given in Appendix B of this report.

EINSTein is a direct outgrowth of ongoing project (sponsored jointly by the *Center for Naval Analyses* and the *Office of Naval Research*) that is looking for

*See section *Tier VII: Synthetic Combat Environments* in Chapter 3 (page 202).

†Appendixes D and E of this book provide self-contained tutorials and a distilled user's guide to EINSTein. Adobe's free Acrobat reader may be downloaded from http://www.adobe.com/products/acrobat/.

possible new forms of a fundamental theory of combat. Some of the current (and planned future) features of EINSTein include:

- *A fully integrated Windows 95/98/NT/2000/XP GUI front-end, including multiple simultaneous battlefield views, and file I/O*
- *An object-oriented C++ source code base to facilitate end-user/analyst programming enhancements (compared to ISAAC's vanilla ANSI-C source)*
- *Integrated natural terrain maps and terrain-based agent decision logic*
- *Multiple squads, with inter-squad communication links*
- *Fast semi-intelligent route planning algorithms for scenarios that include complicated configurations of terrain elements*
- *Context-dependent and user-defined agent behaviors (personality scripts)*
- *Robust class of agent- and squad-based point-to-point and area-dispersed weapons*
- *On-line genetic algorithm toolkit to tailor agent rules to desired force-level behaviors*
- *On-line data collection and multi-dimensional visualization tools*
- *On-line mission-fitness coevolutionary landscape profilers*

Color plate ?? provides a snapshot of a typical EINSTein work-session. The screenshot contains three active windows: *main battlefield view* (which includes passable and impassable terrain elements), *trace view* (which shows color coded territorial occupancy) and *combat view* (which provides a gray-scaled filter of combat intensity). All views are simultaneously updated during a run. Toward the right-hand side of the screenshot appear two data dialogs that summarize red and blue agent parameter values. Appearing on the lower left side and along the bottom of the figure are time-series graphs of red and blue center-of-mass coordinates (as measured from the red flag) and the average number of agents within red and blue agent's sensor ranges, and a dialog that allows the user to define communication relays among individual squads.

4.2 Design Philosophy

"Things should be as simple as possible, but not simpler."—Albert Einstein

Fundamentally, EINSTein addresses the basic question: "*To what extent is land combat a self-organized emergent phenomenon?*" Or, more precisely, "*What are the conditions under which high-level patterns (such as penetration, flanking maneuvers, attack, etc.) emerge from a given set of low-lying dynamical primitive actions (move forward, move backward, approach/retreat-from enemy, etc.).*" As such, EINSTein's intended use is not as a full system-level model of combat but as an interactive toolbox—or "conceptual playground"—in which to explore high-level emergent behaviors arising from various low-level (i.e., individual combatant and squad-level) interaction rules. The idea behind developing this toolbox is emphatically not to model in detail a specific piece of hardware (an M16 rifle or M101 105mm howitzer, for example). Instead, the idea is to explore the middle ground between—at one extreme—highly realistic models that provide little insight into basic processes and—at the other extreme—ultra-minimalist models that strip away all but the simplest dynamical variables and leave out the most interesting real behavior. That is, to explore the fundamental dynamical tradeoffs among a large number of notional variables.

4.2.1 *Agent Hierarchy*

Figure 4.2 shows a schematic of EINSTein's hierarchy of agent and/or information levels. Detailed discussions of each of these levels are given in appropriate sections that follow; here, we describe only those basic aspects of agent hierarchy that are relevant for illustrating EINSTein's overall design philosophy.

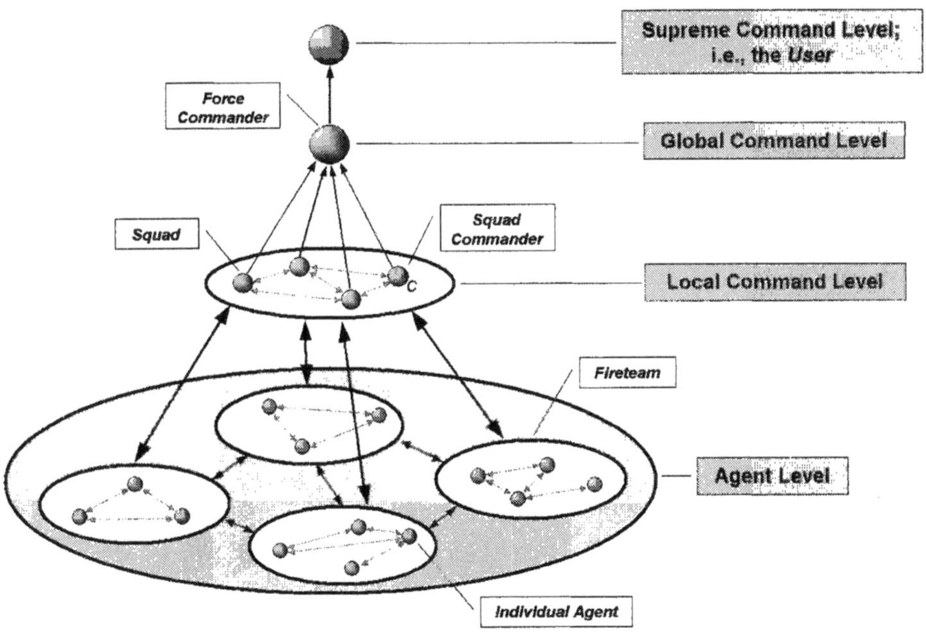

Fig. 4.2 Schematic of EINSTein's hierarchy of information levels; see text.

4.2.1.1 *Combat Agent Level*

The lowest level of the hierarchy is the level of the individual combatant, or agent, and consists of all information contained within the notional battlefield that an individual agent can sense and react to; namely, friendly and enemy agents, and proximity to goals (see below) and/or terrain. This lowest level is the one on which the dynamical interactions between agents occur.

4.2.1.2 *Local Command Level*

The next two levels are command levels that consist of information pertinent to making decisions regarding the behavior on lower levels. Local commanders, for example, assimilate and respond to a "pool" of mid-level information consisting partly of the information contained within their own field-of-view (which typically extends beyond that of a single agent) and partly of the information communicated to them by their subordinate agents. Local commanders use this mid-level information to adjust the movement vectors of the individual agents under their command.

4.2.1.3 *Global Command Level*

Global commanders use global (i.e., battlefield-wide) information to issue movement vectors to local commanders (and, therefore, their subordinate agents) as well as to define how the subordinate agents under the command of one local commander are to interact with the subordinate agents under the command of another local commander.

4.2.1.4 *Supreme Command Level*

Finally, the top-level supreme commander represents the interactive user of the software. The user is responsible for completely defining a given scenario, fixing the size and features of the notional battlefield, setting the initial force dispositions, and specifying any auxiliary combat conditions (such as fratricide, reconstitution, combat termination conditions, and so on). The supreme commander also defines the mission objective required by the genetic algorithm.

4.2.2 *Guiding Principles*

EINSTein's design is predicated upon two guiding principles: (1) To keep all dynamical components and rules as simple as possible (with a view towards optimizing the trade-off between run time and efficiency), and (2) To treat all forms of information (and the way in which all information is locally processed by agents) in a contextually consistent manner. The meaning of this second principle will become clear in the exposition below.

4.2.2.1 *Simplicity*

The first guiding principle is to keep things simple. Specifically, EINSTein is designed to make it as intuitive as possible for the user to program specific agent behaviors. This is done by deliberately keeping the set of combat and movement rules small, and by defining those rules as simply as possible. Thus, the power projection rule is essentially "target and fire upon any enemy agent within a threshold fire range" rather than some other, more complicated (albeit, possibly more physically realistic) prescription. The idea is to qualitatively probe the behavioral consequences of the interaction among a large number of notional variables, not to provide an explicit detailed model of the minutiae of real-world combat.

4.2.2.2 *Consistency*

The second guiding principle is keep things consistent. EINSTein is designed so that almost all dynamical decisions—whether they are made by individual agents, by local or global commanders, or by the user (when scripting a scenario's objectives)—are adjudicated as locally optimal penalty assessments. Decisions are based on an agent's "personality" (see below), which consists of numerical weights that attach greater or lesser degrees of importance to each factor relevant to selecting a particular move in a particular local context (from the point of view of a given agent). It is in this sense that all forms of information, on various levels, are treated on a consistent basis.

Because decisions on different levels necessarily involve different kinds of information - for example, an individual agent's decision to "stay put" in order to survive is quite different, and uses a different form of information, from a global commander's drive to "get to the enemy flag as quickly as possible" - one must be careful to use the information that is important for a decision on a given level in a manner that is appropriate for that particular level.

The decisions taking place on different levels are all mutually consistent in that each decision-maker follows the same general template of probing and responding to his environment. Each decision consists of a personality-weight-mediated "answer" to the following three basic questions:

- *What are my immediate and long-term goals?*
- *What do I currently know about my local environment?*
- *What must I do to attain my goals?*

At the most primitive level, each agent cares only about "moving toward" or "moving away from" all other agents and/or his own and the enemy's flag. An agent's personality prescribes the relative weight that is assigned to each of these immediate "goals." On the other hand, a global commander must weigh such features as overall force strength, casualty rate, rate of advance, and so on in order to attain certain long-term goals. Local and supreme commanders have their own unique concerns. While the actual decisions are different in each case and on each information level, the general manner in which these decisions are made is essentially the same.

4.3 Abstract Agent Architecture

"The division of the perceived universe into parts and wholes is convenient and may be necessary, but no necessity determines how it shall be done."

—Gregory Bateson (Anthropologist, 1904 - 1980) *Mind and Nature*

With an eye toward developing an axiological ontology of multiagent-based models of complex adaptive systems (as mentioned briefly at the end of the last chapter), this section introduces an abstract agent architecture in two parts. The first part defines a symbology that is applicable to a general class of agent-based models. The second part extends this general formalism and applies it to describe the specific agent architecture and dynamics that are embodied in EINSTein. In order to emphasize certain vital aspects of agent-based modeling, a few major themes and elements of EINSTein's architecture are deliberately revisited during the discussion.

4.3.1 *Overview*

Figure 4.3 shows an abstract view of the basic elements of a multiagent-based model, the four main ingredients of which are agents, environment, sensors, and actions.

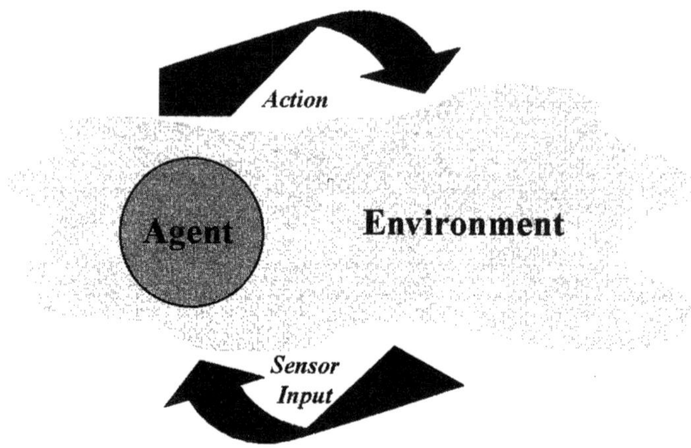

Fig. 4.3 Basic elements of an agent-based model.

Agents are situated in an environment, and are equipped with sensors that provide them with (typically, only limited) information about that environment (of which the agents are also an integral component). After processing this information, agents take some action, which, in turn, usually changes the environment in some way, and thus also alters an agent's perceptions of its immediate surroundings. A run of the model consists of cycling the changing information through this simple feedback loop.

At the heart of the model is an agent's action-selection logic. The logic is used to parse the (usually large) space of possible actions, and select an appropriate subset of actions (which may be as small as a single action or no action at all) that best satisfies an agent's objectives.

Since we usually require that an agent's behavior appear to be intelligent, the problem of designing a robust action-selection logic in agent models is thus essentially a restatement of the paradigmatic problem faced by all artificial intelligence systems:

> *Given an agent $\mathcal{A}$, assigned the task of achieving some goal $\mathcal{G}$, and assuming that $\mathcal{A}$ is allowed to use only the information that its sensors provide about its environment, $\mathcal{I}$, the problem is to find a mapping from the space of all possible interpretations of sensor-derived information to the space of all possible actions such that, for some nontrivial subset of possible initial states, $\mathcal{A}$ achieves its goal $\mathcal{G}$.*

Of course, we are using the word "intelligent" only loosely. In agent-based models, intelligent agent behavior refers to behavior that is...

- *Reactive:* agents "react" to environmental stimuli that consist both of actions by other agents and of fixed features of the battlefield environment.
- *Goal-directed:* agents base their actions on simple goals that they are motivated to fulfill.
- *Boundedly rational:* all actions are derived from a well-defined, logical inference engine applied to localized information, i.e., agents possess, and act upon, only local knowledge, and generally do not know more about their environment than is provided by their limited sensors. Some of the most interesting behaviors of agent-based models result from having agents making local decisions that yield global consequences.
- *Value driven:* the basis of all actions is a set of relative values that are assigned to elements of the dynamical environment. As an agent pursues its goals, over time, different parts of its environment appear more or less important (i.e., appear to require more or less of an agent's "attention") than other parts.
- *Interactive:* arguably the most important element of multiagent-based models (and certainly of EINSTein) is the fact that agents interact with other agents. While an individual agent's problem-solving ability is usually limited, the collective problem-solving ability of many agents, working in concert, may be considerable.

4.3.2 *Dynamics of Value*

The dynamics according to which agents assign *value* to objects in their environment is, as we shall see, the key to generating intelligent behavior. Value judgments consist of weighing estimates of the costs, risks, and benefits of potential actions against an innate attractiveness for (or repulsion from) objects in the environment and/or motivations to attain local goals. Value judgments thus provide dynamic criteria upon which agents base their action selection logic.

An agent's "intelligence" depends largely on the way it partitions its environment and assigns value to different parts of the partition. Its "personality" (which will be quantified more precisely below) consists essentially of the unique set of values that a given agent assigns to parts of its environment, in the context of other agents and value assignments.

Dumb agents effectively live in a homogenous fog of equally valued bits of information. No part of their environment stands out from any other part. All parts are treated equally, and their repertoire of actions, interpreted as intermediate steps toward achieving their goals, is therefore very limited.

Smart agents, on the other hand, are better able to tailor actions to objectives by intelligently partitioning features of their environments according to (possibly changing) perceptions and assessments of the relative values of those features. Agents generally appear "smart" when the information that they value the most consists of precisely those features (i.e., distinctions) of their environment from which further distinctions can be drawn. In other words, if an initial distinction between features does not lead to further distinctions, the information content of the initial distinction is likely to be meaningless, insofar as the action that depends on that information is concerned. As we will see in the next section (when we discuss EINSTein's value-assignment function),* this idea plays a central role in EINSTein's ability to shape intelligent behavior.

We stress that because agent-based models are more abstract than traditional artificial intelligence systems, and are generally designed to be as simple as possible, the phrase "intelligent behavior" does not mean (and ought not be interpreted as referring to) behavior that derives from, or mimics, human intelligent behavior on an agent level. Nonetheless, it is an important, if not explicit, goal of most agent-based models of systems that involve human decision-making to have behaviors that mimic certain aspects of human behavior emerge, naturally, on the *system level.*

4.3.3 *General Formalism*

We now introduce some terms and symbols that will be used throughout our discussion of EINSTein. All multiagent based models consist of some combination of the following basic elements:

*See **Action Selection Logic** beginning on page 230.

- *Environment*
- *Agents*
- *Relations*
- *Actions*
- *Action Selection Rules*

4.3.3.1 *Environment*

The *environment* ($\mathcal{E}$) represents the space in which the entire system evolves. $\mathcal{E}$ consists of a set of

- *Objects* (O), which are distributed throughout that space, and the characteristics of which constitute a set of...
- *Features* ($\mathcal{F}$) that agents use to interpret their environment.

4.3.3.2 *Agents*

Agents ($\mathcal{A} \subseteq O$) are a special—active—subset of objects that are capable of sensing, and reacting to, other (passive) objects in the environment. Although there is no universally accepted definition of a generic agent, all agents share some degree of autonomy. Agents...

- Are defined by a set of *properties* ($\mathcal{A}_P$),
- Generally have an incomplete view of their environment, which we will refer to as their *local environmental context*, ($\mathcal{C}_E$),
- May exist in one of several internal *states* ($\mathcal{A}_S$),
- Base their actions on a set of *motivations* ($\mathcal{M}$) for satisfying certain objectives.

4.3.3.3 *Relations*

Relations (R) describe how objects (both active and passive) are linked to (and/or constrained by) one another. In EINSTein, this includes various environmental bookkeeping functions such as administering how agents are assigned to squads, keeping track of whether one agent is subordinate to, or commands, other agents, and representing how agents communicate with other agents.

4.3.3.4 *Actions*

Actions (A) define the ways in which agents may react to objects in the environment. Agents generally have a repertoire of possible actions to choose from, and select whatever subset of this repertoire they "decide" is appropriate for, and consistent with, their current context.

4.3.3.5 *Action Selection Rules*

Action Selection Rules (Φ), which represent a set of dynamical maps between objects and actions that agents use to react to, and modify, their environment. Φ arguably lies at the heart of agent-based models because the action selection rules codify how agents interact with their environment and each other. These rules are the basis of an individual agent's reactive intelligence and are, collectively, the genotype of any emergent group behavior.

The *global state* of the system at (discrete) time t, $\Sigma(t)$, is a formal "snapshot" of the system at time t that records the identity and location of all objects, agents and their internal states.

A *run*, $\mathcal{R}$, of the model, from time $t = 1$ to $t = T$, consists of the string of global states of the system, $\mathcal{R} = \{\Sigma(1), \Sigma(2), ..., \Sigma(T)\}$, that results from all agent actions starting from initial state $\Sigma(1)$. A basic research challenge is to characterize the set of (and nature of) attainable states, for a given set of agents, initial conditions, and rules.

$\mathcal{A}$'s "decision" to perform an action (which it must select from a larger repertoire of available actions) consists, formally, of applying a map (Φ) from an input space of elements, $\mathcal{I}$ (that is defined, in part, by $\mathcal{A}$'s outer-environmental context, $\mathcal{C}_E \in \mathcal{I}$, and, in part, by $\mathcal{A}$'s internal state, $\mathcal{A}_S \in \mathcal{I}$), to an output space, $\mathcal{O}$, that consists of a set of actions, $A \in \mathcal{O}$:

$$\Phi : (\mathcal{C}_\mathcal{E}, \mathcal{A}_S) \in \mathcal{I} \rightarrow A \in \mathcal{O}. \tag{4.1}$$

The meaning of each of these abstract elements will become clear as their use is illustrated with concrete examples throughout the ensuing discussion.

4.3.4 *Agents in EINSTein*

Agent decisions in EINSTein are consistent with the general form shown in equation 4.1, with one subtle difference. Rather than mapping contexts directly to actions, EINSTein maps the input space to motivations for satisfying certain basic needs (which may change as an agent's context changes).

The virtue of mapping contexts to general motivations rather than specific actions is that an agent's behavior can be shaped in a more robust manner. Rather than focusing, during the design stage, on compiling an exhaustive list of all possible actions that result from all possible contexts, which can quickly lead to a combinatorial explosion and result in "brittle" behavioral logic,* the focus shifts, instead, to providing an agent with a set of general behavioral templates of the form:

> *If an agent $\mathcal{A}$ observes features $f_1, ..., f_N$ of its environment, then $\mathcal{A}$'s motivation to perform an action A will increase (or decrease) according to some function of $f_1, ..., f_N$.*

*See discussion in section **Preventing a Combinatorial Explosion**, beginning on page 242.

This not only allows for smoother transitions to be made between potential actions, resulting in a more robust action selection logic, but also makes it natural to classify agents according to the general pattern of their reaction to environmental stimuli; i.e., agents can be characterized by a unique "personality" (see **Personality** below).

Formally, in EINSTein, Φ is a mapping between an *input space* ($\mathcal{I}$), that defines an agent's local context (as defined for equation 4.1), and an *output space* ($\mathcal{O}$), that now consists of a set of *motivations* for performing actions associated with objects in the environment, $\mathcal{M} \in \mathcal{O}$:

$$\Phi : (\mathcal{C}_{\mathcal{E}}, \mathcal{A}_{\mathcal{S}}) \in \mathcal{I} \rightarrow \mathcal{M} \in \mathcal{O}. \tag{4.2}$$

Agents first scan their local environments, assimilate various forms of information, and then, using their internal value system, select an action (or set of actions) to perform. There is a dynamical feedback loop between agents (which are a part of, and whose decisions are based on, the ambient environment) and the environment (which is continually modified by agent actions).

Figure 4.4 builds upon the general ingredients shown in figure 4.3 to illustrate how they apply to the agent decision process in EINSTein.

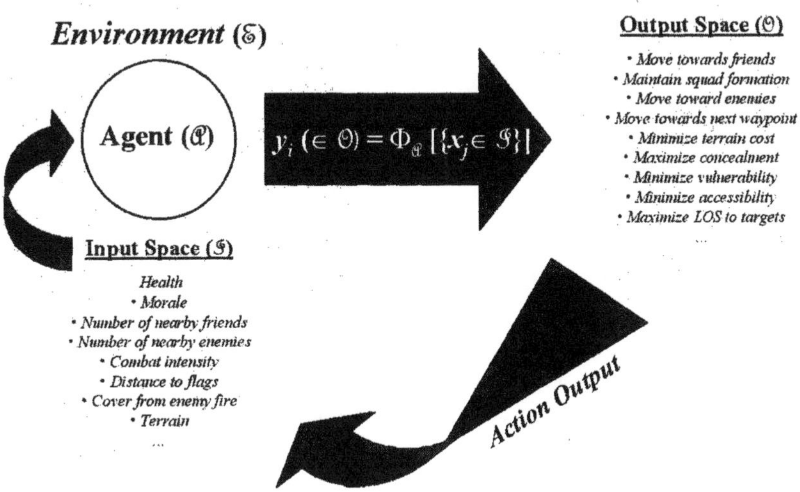

Fig. 4.4 Schematic of agent decisions in EINSTein; see text for details.

4.3.5 *Actions*

EINSTEin's agents are deliberately designed to be very simple. Feedback from users of older versions of EINSTein suggests that users, while observing some interesting behavior emerge on the squad or force levels, are often "fooled" into believing that agents are following a "complicated script." In fact, agents perform only two basic actions:

- *Movement:* agents move from one site to another, constrained by their movement range, r_m (or choose to remain still).
- *Combat:* agents engage enemy agents in combat, which implicitly includes the use of an agent-specific targeting logic.

Complex behaviors, when they arise, emerge naturally from the collective dynamics of these more primitive behavioral characteristics. The actions themselves are kept simple enough so that a typical user is not overwhelmed by having too many primitive options to choose from. If EINSTein provides any insight at all into the fundamental processes of combat, it does so *only* because users are able to quickly develop an intuition about how all of EINSTein's primitives are defined and interact. This is achieved by keeping the number of primitives manageably small.

4.3.5.1 *Action Selection*

How does an agent determine the action it will take? Figuratively speaking, an agent's basic problem, at all times, is to examine all the sites to which it is allowed to move (i.e., that are within an area defined by its movement range), and select the site that represents the optimal value with respect to the "problem" the agent is trying to solve at the current time.

Formally, the problem assumes the form of minimizing the value of a penalty function, $Z_{\mathcal{A}}(x,y)$, that is computed for all sites accessible to $\mathcal{A}$ and the components of which consist of motivations to perform basic tasks. General classes of motivations include:

- *Moving toward, or away from, other agents.*
- *Moving toward, or away from, specific sites or areas on the battlefield.*
- *Minimizing, or maximizing, various local battlefield characteristics* (i.e., static indices of the cost of moving over terrain), *vulnerability* (to possible enemy fire), and *visibility.* Static indices represent default, and unchanging, measures that are calculated once prior to the start of a run and in the absence of agents.
- *Minimizing, or maximizing, various local, dynamic combat characteristics* (such as the projected vulnerability and visibility if moving to site (x,y) as a function of the actual disposition of local forces, relative local firepower concentration, combat intensity, territorial possession,...).

Although the number of terms in $Z_{\mathcal{A}}(x, y)$ is, in practice, quite large, $Z_{\mathcal{A}}(x, y)$ always has the same general form:

$$Z_{\mathcal{A}}(x,y) = \sum_{A} w_{\mathcal{A}}(\text{A}) \cdot \mu(\text{A}; x, y). \tag{4.3}$$

where:

- $-1 \leq w_{\mathcal{A}}(\text{A}) \leq +1$ is a numerical weight value that represents A's motivation for maximizing (if $w > 0$) or minimizing (if $w < 0$) its expected gain from performing the action A. The label "$\mathcal{A}$" appears as a subscript on the motivation w to remind the reader that motivations, which are an integral part of an agent's personality (see below), may be uniquely assigned to individual agents.
- $\mu(\text{A}; x, y)$ represents a measure of how well $\mathcal{A}$ expects it will perform action A in the event that it chooses to move to site (x, y). The lower and upper bounds of $\mu(\text{A}; x, y)$ both depend on A. In simple cases, such as when A = *"move toward squad-mate,"* μ is equal to the distance between a squad mate and a candidate site to which $\mathcal{A}$ may move. For other actions, such as $A =$ *"maximize coverage of assigned patrol area,"* μ is a more complicated function of two or more features.

Because much of EINSTein's behavior, both local and global, depends on how the user defines the penalty function, it is important to understand the subtle conceptual difference between *weights* (w) and *measures* (μ) to which the weights are assigned. Weights represent an agent's motivation to perform a given action, and generally depend on one or more dynamic features of the environment according to functions defined by the user. Only their relative values are meaningful. Informally, we may say that w specifies how strongly $\mathcal{A}$ *either wants, or does not want, to do something* (relative to the set of actions it can perform in a given context).

Measures are also user-defined functions of environmental features (though the features do not have to be exactly the same set as used to define weights), but define how well an agent *expects to perform the action associated with its corresponding weight.* Informally, μ measures how well $\mathcal{A}$ expects to do, assuming that $\mathcal{A}$ has chosen its course of action (consistent with its weights).

Positive weight values are interpreted to mean that an agent is motivated to perform the associated action. Negative values are interpreted to mean that an agent is motivated to *not* perform the associated action (or, more precisely, to perform whatever set of actions are necessary so that the measure associated with performing action A, $\mu(\text{A}; x, y)$, is minimized). If the value of a weight is equal to zero, then the agent effectively *ignores* the action (or actions) that are associated with that weight (and is thus also "blind" to the features that the weight is a function of, for the range on which the weight is zero).

For example, suppose we have a single action,

$$A = \textbf{minimize distance between A and agents friendly to } \mathcal{A}.$$

Then, $w > 0$ means that $\mathcal{A}$ wants to "get closer to" all friendly agents; $w < 0$ means that $\mathcal{A}$ wants to "get farther away from" all friendly agents. In this case, the measure $\mu(\mathrm{A}; x, y)$ = *distance between* $\mathcal{A}$ *and agents that are friendly to* $\mathcal{A}$.*

A point worth emphasizing here, as it becomes an important focus of discussion in the next section, is that $w(A)$ is generally not a fixed value; instead, $w(A)$ takes on a range of values (which is now a higher-level "signature" of an agent's overall personality), and is a function of one or more environmental features, as sensed locally by $\mathcal{A}$.

In general, while $w(A)$ always represents the motivation to perform a single action (and is usually associated with a single feature), the value of $w(A)$ usually depends on several features.

The battlefield site to which $\mathcal{A}$ moves, $(\hat{x}, \hat{y})$, is given by

$$\begin{aligned} (\hat{x}, \hat{y}) &= \mathit{Position}(x, y) \text{ such that } Z_{\mathcal{A}} \text{ is minimum} \\ &= \underset{D[(x_{\mathcal{A}}, y_{\mathcal{A}}), (x,y)] \le r_m}{\text{Minimum}} \{Z_{\mathcal{A}}(x, y)\}, \end{aligned} \tag{4.4}$$

where the search for the minimum value of $Z_{\mathcal{A}}(x, y)$ is conducted over all positions (x, y) whose distance from $(x_{\mathcal{A}}, y_{\mathcal{A}})$, $D[(x_{\mathcal{A}}, y_{\mathcal{A}}), (x, y)]$, is less than or equal to $\mathcal{A}$'s movement range, r_m.

4.3.5.2 *Personality*

According to the *American Heritage Dictionary* [AmH94], "personality" is defined as...

> *"The totality of qualities and traits, as of character or behavior, that are peculiar to a specific person. The pattern of collective character, behavioral, temperamental, emotional, and mental traits of a person."*

In keeping with this definition, but applied to agents rather than humans, an agent $\mathcal{A}$'s personality, $\mathcal{P}_{\mathcal{A}}$, consists of all of $\mathcal{A}$'s internal motivations, behavioral rules, and values (as applied to features of the environment), that are used by $\mathcal{A}$ to select its move or strategy. As explained below, certain features of $\mathcal{P}_{\mathcal{A}}$ may also change as $\mathcal{A}$ evolves during a run.

*Although other functions of distance can also be used; see technical Appendix 6 to chapter 5 (beginning on page 408).

4.3.5.3 *Motivations*

Detailed motivations include:

- *Get closer-to (or farther away from)...*

  —*Other agents* (friends, squad-mates, commander, enemies).
  —*Own flag*
  —*Enemy flag*
  —*User-waypoint-prescribed-path*
  —*Patrol Area*

Implicit in this first basic category is the idea of "tagging" other agents. Tags are used to distinguish among otherwise identical agents. The simplest tag is force color: a friendly agent is trivially distinguished from an enemy agent by allegiance. Other tags include an agent's health, squad, proximity (*"Is an enemy within an agent's close-in lethal zone?"*), and whether an agent has recently fired its weapon. The latter tag is particularly useful in helping adjudicate among targeting options. For example, enemy agents that have just fired their weapons at a particular agent may be singled out for immediate retribution.

- *Maintain minimum distance from other squads (and enemy agents).*
- *Minimize terrain movement cost.* Agents do not want to needlessly expend more energy than they have to.
- *Minimize vulnerability to (i.e., cover from) enemy fire.* Agents want to minimize the number of enemy agents that are in position to fire at them.
- *Maximize concealment.* Agents want to minimize their visibility: i.e., to minimize the number of enemy agents that can "see" them.
- *Minimize accessibility.* Agents want to maximize the difficulty for enemy agents to approach their position.
- *Maximize local health* (i.e., maximize the average health of friendly agents so that $\mathcal{A}$ is surrounded by maximally "capable" friendly support).
- *Minimize local combat intensity.*
- *Maximize line-of-sight to targets* (taking into account fire range, estimated damage, defensive capability, and so on).
- *Minimize blocked line-of-fire by friendly agents*, as well as blocked line-of-fire of other agents.
- *Minimize probability of ambush*, as measured by the probability of being attacked by previously unseen enemy agents (i.e., counting the number of battlefield location potentially within view but obstructed by some form of impassable terrain).
- *Minimize proximity to killed friends.*
- *Maximize coverage of assigned patrol area.* For agents that are assigned to squads under the command of a local commander, the command-agent

needs to weigh the trade-off between keeping his subordinates close enough together for mutual support and having them sufficiently spread out to defend patrol area):

- *Minimize degree of mutual overlap of subordinate sensor fields* (or maximize total nonoverlapping coverage).
- *Maintain (threshold level of) mutual support.* A local commander wants to maximize the number of subordinates that have a threshold level of local support.
- *Maximize robust action selection.* Assuming that their local tactical environment will remain unchanged (as a zeroth order dynamic stability assumption), agents want to maximize the number of action selection options they anticipate having in the future. If the choice, at time t, comes down to moving to a corner site from which the agent anticipates there will be only, say, two likely moves that can be made at time $t+1$, and another currently available move that takes the agent more into the open but from which there are likely to be many possible moves to make at $t+1$, the agent may choose to make the latter move.
- *Maximize territorial possession.* Territorial possession measures the degree to which a given battlefield site "belongs" to either the red or blue force. A site at (x, y) belongs to an agent (*red* or *blue*) according to the following logic: the number of like agents within a territoriality-distance (τ_D) is greater than or equal to territoriality-minimum ($\tau_{\min}$) and is at least territoriality-threshold (τ_T) number of agents greater than the number of enemy agents within the same territoriality-distance. For example, if $(\tau_D, \tau_{\min}, \tau_T) = (2, 3, 2)$, then a battlefield position (x, y) is said to belong to, say, red, if there are at least 3 red agents within a distance 2 of (x, y) and the number of red agents within that distance outnumber blue agents by at least 2.

4.3.6 *Features*

In the most general heuristic sense, agents are both *defined* by and an *integral component of* and a pool of "information" that must be intelligently sifted through if agents are to behave in anything approaching an intelligent manner. Figure 4.5 (which is a more detailed version of figures 4.3 and 4.4) summarizes EINSTein's enhanced action selection logic.

Each agent (a representative agent, labeled $\mathcal{A}$, is shown as a disproportionately large circle at the top left of figure 4.5) has access to the following, partially overlapping, classes of contextual information that it can sense and respond to (table 4.1 provides a summary):*

*Throughout the ensuing discussion, any element that belongs to any of these different classes will be referred to, generically, as a *feature*.

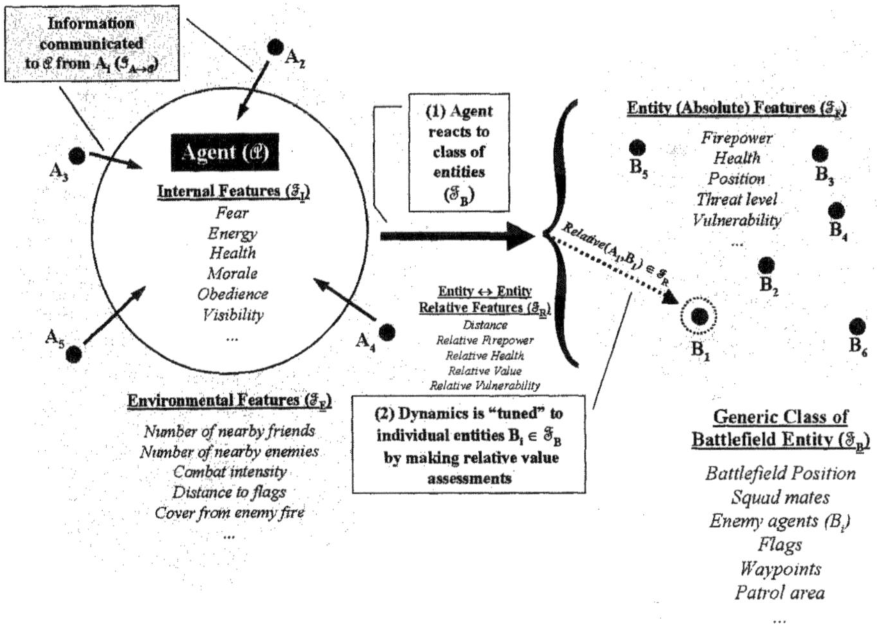

Fig. 4.5 Detailed schematic of the main components of EINSTein's action selection logic.

- *Internal features* ($\mathcal{F}_{\rm I}$). Internal features represent both static and dynamic aspects of an agent's unique personality and experience. Some of these features are "visible" to the outside world (i.e., by other agents); some are not. Internal features include energy level, fear of combat, health, morale, and personality "type" (inexperienced, timid, aggressive, obedient, leader, follower,...). Memory of past states, though not yet included in EINSTein, would also be an internal feature.

- *Environmental features* ($\mathcal{F}_{\rm E}$). Environmental features refer to all forms of information that an agent is able to sense and react to locally. This includes terrain, the nature and intensity of combat, the presence and type of nearby paths and waypoints, and estimates of the tactical utility of specific battlefield positions. It is useful to have symbols for two subclasses of this feature class:

  —*Object feature class* ($= \mathcal{F}_{\mathcal{O}} \subseteq \mathcal{F}_{\rm E}$), that consists of measures pertaining to and assigned to bona-fide objects in the environment (such as agents, flags, waypoints, and tagged terrain elements), and

—*Measure feature class* ($= \mathcal{F}_m \subseteq \mathcal{F}_E$), that consists of various combat-related measures that, while they may be functions of objects, are assigned directly to battlefield sites. Examples of measure features include cover, concealment, and combat intensity (as estimated by an agent to exist) at each of the battlefield locations that are accessible to agents from their current position.

- *Battlefield entity* ($\mathcal{F}_B$). Battlefield entities refer to any member of an object class to which an agent can assign a motivation for either moving toward or away from that member. This class includes, as a subset, the class of (friendly and enemy) agents ($=\mathcal{F}_A \subseteq \mathcal{F}_B$), battles-specific field positions (as fixed by the user or assigned adaptively, during a run, by a fireteam or squad commander), own and enemy flags, waypoints, patrol areas, and so on.
- *Entity (absolute) features* ($\mathcal{F}_F$). An agent responds to individual components of a general battlefield entity class in part by reacting to a set of absolute measures characterizing a given component. For example, if the entity is a specific enemy agent (such as $B_1 \in \mathcal{F}_B$ in figure 4.5), absolute factors include firepower, health, position (near flag, in open, near boundary, etc.), threat level, and vulnerability.
- *Entity↔Entity relative features* ($\mathcal{F}_R$). This class consists of relative measures between a given agent (which is in the process of selecting an action) and a specific agent toward which (or away from) the given agent is deciding to move. These measures include the distance between the two agents, their relative health states, relative firepower, relative vulnerabilities, and relative intrinsic "value" (one may be a young recruit, possessing a low value, the other may be a local commander and have a correspondingly high value).
- *Communicated Information* ($\mathcal{I}_C$). Each agent $\mathcal{A}$ can communicate information to another (friendly) agent, $\mathcal{A}'$ ($=\mathcal{I}_{\mathcal{A}\to\mathcal{A}'}$), and/or receive communicated information from $\mathcal{A}'$ ($=\mathcal{I}_{\mathcal{A}'\to\mathcal{A}}$). While communicated information consists of exactly the same set of features that individual agents are able to discern in their own environment, when it is passed from one agent to another over distances that exceed a receiving agent's sensor range, communication effectively extends the range over which agents are able to probe their local environment.

4.3.7 *Local Context*

The basic ingredient of action selection in all agent-based models is an agent $\mathcal{A}$'s *local context*, which consists of both raw and interpreted forms of information describing $\mathcal{A}$'s (inner and outer) environment at time t.

Feature	Description
Internal ($\mathcal{F}_{\text{I}}$)	Internal features represent both static and dynamic aspects of an agent's unique personality and experience.
Environmental ($\mathcal{F}_{\text{E}}$)	Environmental features refer to all forms of information that an agent is able to sense and react to locally.
Object ($\mathcal{F}_O \subseteq \mathcal{F}_{\text{E}}$)	Object features are measures pertaining to and assigned to bona-fide objects in the environment (such as agents, flags, waypoints and tagged terrain elements).
Measure ($\mathcal{F}_m \subseteq \mathcal{F}_{\text{E}}$)	Measure features are combat-related measures that, while they may be functions of objects, are assigned directly to battlefield sites.
Battlefield ($\mathcal{F}_{\text{B}}$)	Battlefield entities refer to any member of an object class to which an agent can assign a motivation for either moving toward or away from that member.
Entity-Absolute ($\mathcal{F}_{\text{F}}$)	$\mathcal{F}_{\text{F}}$ consists of the set of absolute measures characterizing a given component. For example, if the entity is a specific enemy agent, absolute factors include firepower, health, position (near flag, in open, near boundary, etc.), threat level, and vulnerability.
Entity-Relative ($\mathcal{F}_{\text{R}}$)	This class consists of relative measures between a given agent (which is in the process of selecting an action) and a specific agent toward which (or away from) the given agent is deciding to move.
Communication ($\mathcal{F}_{\text{C}}$)	Each agent can communicate information to—and/or receive information from—other (friendly) agents. While communicated information consists of exactly the same set of features that individual agents are able to discern in their own environment, when it is passed from one agent to another over distances that exceed a receiving agent's sensor range, communication effectively extends the range over which agents are able to probe their local environment.

Table 4.1 A short description of the general classes of contextual information that agents may use to select their actions.

As an example, suppose that we have a simplified version of EINSTein in which only the following five feature primitives are defined: N_E = number of nearby enemy agents, N_F = number of nearby friendly agents, D_{EF} = distance to enemy flag, D_{FF} = distance to friendly flag, and H = health. (N_E, N_F, D_{EF} and D_{FF} are outer environmental features; H represents $\mathcal{A}$'s inner environment.) A "context" $\mathcal{C}$ is simply an explicit list of specific values assigned to each feature. Some possible contexts are:

$$\begin{aligned}
\mathcal{C}_1 &: (N_E = 0, N_F = 0, D_{EF} = 10, D_{FF} = 30, H = 1) \\
\mathcal{C}_2 &: (N_E = 0, N_F = 2, D_{EF} = 15, D_{FF} = 25, H = 1) \\
\mathcal{C}_3 &: (N_E = 5, N_F = 5, D_{EF} = 20, D_{FF} = 10, H = 0.75) \\
\mathcal{C}_4 &: (N_E = 5, N_F = 3, D_{EF} = 40, D_{FF} = 0, H = 0.5)
\end{aligned}$$

Formally, $\mathcal{A}$'s context, $\mathcal{C}_{\mathcal{A}}$, is a time-dependent function of the features that $\mathcal{A}$ uses to select an action. Using EINSTein's feature classes defined above, and labeling the set of *agents* (friendly, enemy or neutral) by $\mathcal{F}_{\text{A}}$, we can write, symbolically:

$$\mathcal{C}_{\mathcal{A}} = C_{\mathcal{E},\mathcal{A}}(\mathcal{F}_{\text{E}}, \mathcal{F}_{\text{B}}, \mathcal{F}_{\text{F}}, \mathcal{F}_{\text{R}}; t) \cup C_{\mathcal{E},(\mathcal{F}_{\text{A}}-\mathcal{A})}(\mathcal{F}_{\text{E}}, \mathcal{F}_{\text{B}}, \mathcal{F}_{\text{F}}, \mathcal{F}_{\text{R}}; t) \cup \mathcal{A}_{\text{S}}(\mathcal{F}_{\text{I}}; t), \tag{4.5}$$

where $C_{\mathcal{E},\mathcal{A}}$ is the part of $\mathcal{A}$'s outer-environmental context that is defined by all features directly accessible by $\mathcal{A}$ (i.e., via $\mathcal{A}$'s own sensors), and includes all feature information other than what is internal to $\mathcal{A}$; $C_{\mathcal{E},(\mathcal{F}_A-\mathcal{A})}$ is the part of $\mathcal{A}$'s outer-environmental context that is defined by information *communicated* to $\mathcal{A}$ (by friendly agents $\in \mathcal{F}_A - \mathcal{A}$); and $\mathcal{A}_S$ is $\mathcal{A}$'s internal state.

Contextual features serve two important, and complementary, dynamical roles:

1. *As components of the input space, contexts are used to determine weight values.*

Since each possible local context is mapped to a specific weight value appearing in $\mathcal{A}$'s penalty function, contexts provide the raw information upon which agents base all their moves. Formally, the weight $w_{\mathcal{A}}(\mathrm{A})$ appearing in equation 4.3, may be written as

$$w_{\mathcal{A}}(\mathrm{A}) = \psi_{\mathcal{A},\mathrm{A}}(\{f_{\mathcal{C}} \in \mathcal{C}_{\mathcal{A}}\}), \tag{4.6}$$

where $\psi_{\mathcal{A},\mathrm{A}}(\{f_{\mathcal{C}} \in \mathcal{C}_{\mathcal{A}}\})$ is an explicit function of $\mathcal{A}$'s context, $\mathcal{C}_{\mathcal{A}}$, is uniquely assigned to $\mathcal{A}$ (and is thus a component of $\mathcal{A}$'s personality) and whose form may depend on action A. Typically, each y depends on several different features, $f_{\mathcal{C}} \in \mathcal{C}_{\mathcal{A}}$. The possible functional forms of ψ, along with the way in which different ψs may be combined to *selectively shape behavior*, are discussed in a later section.

2. *As implicit parts of the output space, since the weights represent motivations to either maximize or minimize measures that are themselves usually defined to be functions of features.*

Since the semantic distinctions among the different feature classes naturally partition otherwise equivalent bits of contextual information (i.e., external features are obviously "different" from an agent's internal states), feature classes can be used, by both the developer and end-user, to impose an ontological structure on the simulation that *mimics the internal order of the real system.** In this sense, we say that the real system is simulated by the agent model.

Loosely speaking, feature classes in the model are ranked according to relative measures of importance as observed in the real system, and individual features are then used by agents in the simulation in a manner that is consistent with that ranking. However, not all features that belong to a given feature class are necessarily assigned an equal weight. Depending on personality differences, some agents may consider one set of features of a given class to be most important for adjudicating their moves, while other agents may rank highest an entirely different set of features. In short, the developer ranks feature classes, agents rank features within a given class, and the way that features are mapped to actions defines the ontological structure of the simulation.

*See page 67 (in chapter 1) for a discussion of our use of the term *ontology*.

4.3.8 *Example*

In EINSTein, environmental features ($e \in \mathcal{F}_{\rm E}$) are ranked highest and typically constitute a first-pass, "coarse-grained" set of features on whose values an agent's default response to other kinds of features (such as battlefield entities, $b \in \mathcal{F}_{\rm B}$) depend. Internal features ($i \in \mathcal{F}_{\rm I}$) are applied afterward and modify, but do not by themselves define, existing weight values. Relative features ($r \in \mathcal{F}_{\rm R}$) are used last, and serve as final "tuning" filters (within the penalty function) to tailor an agent's default behavior to relative contexts between it and other agents.

As an example, suppose an agent $\mathcal{A}$, sensing that it has a sufficient level of nearby fire-support (which is one of $\mathcal{A}$'s environmental features), decides it wants to move toward enemy agent $\mathcal{B}$, with weight w. If no other features are taken into account, this same w applies to *all enemy agents*, regardless of other attributes, absolute and/or relative, that individual enemy agents might possess.

To cite but two ways in which $\mathcal{A}$ may modify w, (1) upon "reflection," $\mathcal{A}$ notes that its *fear of combat* is high and it is currently low on energy (both measures being elements of $\mathcal{A}$'s internal feature space), and decides to decrease its default weight by an amount Δw_1, and (2) noting that $\mathcal{B}$ is already *relatively close* (a measure which is an element of $\mathcal{A}$'s relative feature space), $\mathcal{A}$ decides to decrease its default weight by an additional amount Δw_2. $\mathcal{A}$ thus uses its internal and relative feature spaces to tailor its default weight to specific agents.

4.3.9 *Ontological Partitioning*

In order to make explicit the different dynamical roles that different feature classes play in EINSTein, we first split the full feature space $\mathcal{F}$ into two complementary subspaces, $\mathcal{F} = \mathcal{F}_\mu \cup \mathcal{F}_{\not\mu}$, where $\mathcal{F}_\mu$ consists only of those features to which an agent may assign a weight (i.e., motivation), and $\mathcal{F}_{\not\mu}$ represents the set of features that are used for *determining the values of weights*, but which themselves cannot be meaningfully assigned a weight.

An example of the latter kind of feature is the difference in health values, $\Delta H =$ *health*$(\mathcal{A}_1)$ - *health*$(\mathcal{A}_2)$, between two agents, $\mathcal{A}_1$ and $\mathcal{A}_2$. While ΔH may be used by both $\mathcal{A}_1 1$ and $\mathcal{A}_2$ to help adjudicate their moves, ΔH is not, by itself, a "goal" either agent ever strives to attain.

Next, we partition features belonging to $\mathcal{F}_\mu$ according to:

$$\mathcal{F}_\mu = \mathcal{F}_{\rm A} \cup (\mathcal{F}_{\mathcal{O}} - \mathcal{F}_{\mathcal{A}}) \cup \mathcal{F}_m, \tag{4.7}$$

where:

- $\mathcal{F}_{\rm A}$ is the set of *agents* (friendly, enemy or neutral),
- $\mathcal{F}_{\mathcal{O}} - \mathcal{F}_{\mathcal{A}}$ represents all possible object features that agents can react to, *other than other agents*,and

- $\mathcal{F}_m$, as defined above, is the set of all *measures* that are assigned directly to battlefield sites (but not objects).

Similarly, $\mathcal{F}_\mu$ is decomposed into

$$\mathcal{F}_\mu = \mathcal{F}_\mathrm{F} \cup \mathcal{F}_\mathrm{I} \cup \mathcal{F}_\mathrm{R}, \tag{4.8}$$

where the individual terms are defined in table 4.1.

Finally, we make an important distinction between *local features* that are directly accessible to an agent, via its own sensor, and *communicated features* that the agent cannot detect by itself but which are communicated to it by other (friendly) agents.

4.3.10 *Communication*

We use the subscripts "$\mathrm{L}_\mathcal{A}$" to denote features that are local to $\mathcal{A}$ (for example, agents, $\mathcal{A}\in\mathcal{F}_\mathrm{A}$, that belong to feature class $\mathcal{F}_\mathrm{A}$ and are within $\mathcal{A}$'s sensor range, are denoted symbolically as $\mathcal{A}_{\mathrm{L}_\mathcal{A}}$), and "$\mathrm{C}_\mathcal{A}$" to denote features that are communicated to $\mathcal{A}$ (for example, agents that are beyond $\mathcal{A}$'s sensor range but whose presence is communicated to $\mathcal{A}$ by an agent friendly to $\mathcal{A}$, are denoted symbolically as $\mathcal{A}_{\mathrm{C}_\mathcal{A}}$).

We also introduce an *agent-agent communication weight matrix*, w_C, whose components, $0 \leq (w_\mathrm{C})_{\mathcal{A},\mathcal{A}'} \leq 1$, for agents $\mathcal{A}$ and $\mathcal{A}'$, define, heuristically, the weight that $\mathcal{A}$ assigns to information communicated to it by $\mathcal{A}'$:* $(w_\mathrm{C})_{\mathcal{A},\mathcal{A}'} = 0$ means that $\mathcal{A}$ effectively ignores all information sent by $\mathcal{A}'$; $(w_\mathrm{C})_{\mathcal{A},\mathcal{A}'} = 1$ means that $\mathcal{A}$ treats all information sent by $\mathcal{A}'$ on an equal footing with information obtained via its own sensors.

Using this notation, the general form of EINSTein's penalty function, $Z_\mathcal{A}(x,y)$ (see equation 4.3), becomes...

$$\begin{aligned} Z_\mathcal{A}(x,y) = & \sum_{a_{L_\mathcal{A}}\in\mathcal{F}_\mathrm{A}} w_{\mathcal{A}\to a_{L_\mathcal{A}}}(\mathcal{F}_\mu)\cdot D(\mathcal{A},a_{L_\mathcal{A}}) + \sum_{o_{L_\mathcal{A}}\in(\mathcal{F}_\mathcal{O}-\mathcal{F}_\mathcal{A})} w_{\mathcal{A}\to o_{L_\mathcal{A}}}(\mathcal{F}_\mu)\cdot D(\mathcal{A},o_{L_\mathcal{A}}) \\ & + \sum_{\mu_{L_\mathcal{A}}\in\mathcal{F}_m} w_{\mu_{L_\mathcal{A}}}(\mathcal{F}_\mu)\cdot\mu_{L_\mathcal{A}}(x,y) + \sum_{f_{C_\mathcal{A}}} (w_C)_{\mathcal{A},\mathcal{A}'}\cdot w_{f_{C_\mathcal{A}}}(\mathcal{F}_\mu)\cdot\mu_{C_\mathcal{A}}(f_{C_\mathcal{A}}), \end{aligned} \tag{4.9}$$

where

- The three sums $\sum_{a\in\mathcal{F}_\mathrm{A}}$, $\sum_{o\in(\mathcal{F}_\mathcal{O}-\mathcal{F}_\mathcal{A})}$, and $\sum_{\mu\in\mathcal{F}_m}$ are taken over all *agents*, *objects* (other than agents), and *measures* assigned to position (x,y), and discerned locally by $\mathcal{A}$'s own sensors, respectively,
- $\sum_{f_{C_\mathcal{A}}}$ is taken over all features that are communicated to $\mathcal{A}$,

*The real-valued matrix w_C must not be confused with the binary inter-squad communications link matrix, C_{ij}. C_{ij} fixes the communication channels; w_C, as explained above, determines how information that is communicated via those channels is interpreted.

- $D(O_1, O_2)$is the distance between objects O_1 and O_2,
- $w_{\mathcal{A}\to a_{L_\mathcal{A}}}(\{f \in \mathcal{F}_\mu\})$is $\mathcal{A}$'s weight for moving toward another agent $a_{L_\mathcal{A}} \in \mathcal{F}_\text{A}$, and is a function of features $f \in \mathcal{F}_\mu$,
- $w_{\mathcal{A}\to o}(\{f \in \mathcal{F}_\mu\})$ is $\mathcal{A}$'s weight for moving towards object $o \in (\mathcal{F}_\mathcal{O} - \mathcal{F}_\mathcal{A})$,
- $w_\mu(\{f \in \mathcal{F}_\mu\})$ is $\mathcal{A}$'s weight for minimizing measure $\mu \in \mathcal{F}_m$,

and

- $\mu(x, y)$ is the value of measure μ at position (x, y).

A more precise form of the penalty function reflects EINSTein's internal ranking of the various feature classes and thus incorporates, symbolically, a part of the axiological ontology of combat as embodied in EINSTein. Let $\psi^{(\mathcal{F})} = \psi^{(\mathcal{F})}(\{f \in \mathcal{F}\})$ denote the weight function ψ that is restricted to, and acts only on, features $f \in \mathcal{F}$. We can then rewrite $Z_\mathcal{A}(x, y)$ by making explicit the intermediate steps used in calculating the individual weight terms.

For example, the default value of $w_{\mathcal{A}\to a_{L_\mathcal{A}}}$ is determined by applying

$$\psi_1^{(\mathcal{F}_\mathcal{O},\mathcal{F}_m)}(\{o \in \mathcal{F}_\mathcal{O}\}, \{m \in \mathcal{F}_m\}, \{f \in \mathcal{F}_\mu\})$$

to members of $\mathcal{A}$'s object and measure feature classes. It is then modified by applying a separate function of $\mathcal{A}$'s internal features, $\psi_2^{(\mathcal{F}_\text{I})}(\{i \in \mathcal{F}\text{I}\})$. The final value is determined by tuning the resulting weight value to particular agents, $\mathcal{A} \in \mathcal{F}_\mathcal{A}$, as their individual terms arise in the sum $\sum_{a \in \mathcal{F}_\text{A}}$, according to a function of the relative measures between $\mathcal{A}$ and a, $\psi_3^{(\mathcal{F}_\text{R})}(\{r_{\mathcal{A},a} \in \mathcal{F}_\text{R}\})$. Symbolically,

$$w_{\mathcal{A}\to a} = \psi_3^{(\mathcal{F}_\text{R})}\left[\psi_2^{(\mathcal{F}_\text{I})}\left(\psi_1^{(\mathcal{F}_\text{O},\mathcal{F}_\text{m})}(\text{o,m}), i\right), \text{r}_{\mathcal{A}\text{a}}\right]. \tag{4.10}$$

While it may not be immediately obvious from this general expression, the range of possible weight values, and therefore the dynamic range of contextually appropriate agent actions, is actually quite large and robust. This is because the user has a large palette of functional forms of ψ_1, ψ_2, and ψ_3 to choose from.

4.3.11 *Axiological Ontology*

The basic ingredients needed to develop an axiological ontology of complex adaptive systems have all been introduced. The axiology is contained in the agents' personalities, weights and the rules according to which interacting sets of agents continuously reassess the relative values assigned to features of their environment. The ontology is defined by the dynamical relationship among agents and features, the hierarchical ranking of feature classes, and, implicitly, by the kind of, and order of application of, functions that determine weight and penalty values.

While the details of an ontology must, of course, depend on the characteristics of the specific system being modeled (such as the dynamics of combat in the case of

EINSTein), the essential components of the ontologies of all complex adaptive systems remain fundamentally the same. To understand the global, emergent behavior of a system, one must understand how relative value governs the dynamics of the system: *how value is defined, how value is assigned (to agents by other agents, as well as by agents to features of the environment), and how the perceived value of features changes as the system evolves.*

4.3.12 *Preventing a Combinatorial Explosion*

We conclude this section, and motivate the detailed discussion of EINSTein's action-selection logic that appears in the next section, by mentioning an inevitable "problem" posed by almost all multiagent-based models: *the specter of coping with a combinatorial explosion of possible context-action maps.*

To understand the problem, and appreciate its severity, suppose that $\mathcal{A}$ has movement range r_m, is able to discern N_f features of its environment, where each feature assumes one of n_f different (discrete) values, and selects its move according to a penalty function that depends on N_w weights, each of which takes on one of n_w values. Several obvious, but important, questions immediately come to mind:

1. *How many different contexts can $\mathcal{A}$ be in?*

Since a given context is defined by a list of specific values assigned to each one of the N_f possible features, there are possible contexts.

2. *How many different actions can $\mathcal{A}$ take?*

Since $\mathcal{A}$ can move to any site within a "box" centered on $\mathcal{A}$'s current position and constrained by A's movement range, the number of possible actions (excluding targeting decisions stemming from an agent's combat logic) is equal to $(2r_m + 1)^2$.

3. *How many different personalities can $\mathcal{A}$ have?*

The exact number, of course, depends on how "personalities" are defined in EINSTein (the details of which are discussed in the next section). However, an upper bound can easily be determined by noting that a given personality, once it has been defined, is equivalent to a map (unique to $\mathcal{A}$) that assigns a specific action to a specific context. Since we have just calculated, above, that $\mathcal{A}$ can encounter up to $(n_f)^{N_f}$ different contexts and must select one of $(2r_m + 1)^2$ possible actions for each context, the number of personalities that can be assigned to $\mathcal{A}$ must be $\leq (2r_m + 1)^{2(n_f)^{N_f}}$.

Although, in practice, the actual number of personalities will be significantly less than this, the estimate suggests that we can, in general, expect the number of possible context-action maps to grow exponentially as features are added. Even if we restrict ourselves to only two binary-valued features, we see that—for $r_m = 1$—there are $(2 \cdot 1 + 1)^{2 \cdot 2^2} = 3^8 = 6,561$ possible maps, $(2 \cdot 2 + 1)^{2 \cdot 2^2} = 5^8 = 390,625$ maps for $r_m = 2$, and $5,764,801$ maps for $r_m = 3$. Adding just one other binary-valued feature, we find that there are $(2 \cdot 1 + 1)^{2 \cdot 2^3} = 3^{16} = 43,046,721$ possible maps for $r_m = 1$, and $152,587,890,625\tilde{}10^{11}$ maps for $r_m = 2$. The enormity of the problem becomes acute when it is realized that typical scenarios in EINSTein use a *dozen or more continuous valued features* with (in EINSTein's latest version) effectively unlimited movement range!

The conceptual challenge is therefore twofold: (1) reduce this huge space of possible context-action maps to a manageably small set, and (2) do so without sacrificing the desired level of dynamical richness. It would be easy to design a system composed of only a few hard-wired rules of the form:

IF Context <C> THEN Action <A> ,

(and use only a small set of pre-defined contexts and actions, which is essentially how this problem has been "solved" by earlier versions of EINSTein). However, such a system would certainly be far too brittle and uninteresting, dynamically, to be useful as a research tool.

4.3.12.1 *Finite State Machines*

A common technique for designing an artificial intelligence for autonomous agents is to encode behaviors using a *finite state machine* (FSM) [Hopc79].

FSMs consist of a finite number of states and use a transition function to map an agent's current state, along with whatever other input state information may be appropriate, to an output state (which becomes an agent new current state). FSMs are easy to code, execute quickly (particularly when the transition function is implemented as a fast look-up table), and can be used to describe a wide range of behaviors.

A drawback to using FSMs to design intelligent agents, however, is the same kind of combinatorial explosion illustrated above for context-action maps, except, for FSMs, the explosion is in the number of possible input-output pairs that the FSM must explicitly account for. In practice, it is possible to take into account only a very small fraction of all possible local contexts that an agent can be in. Therefore, FSM-based agent "intelligence" tends to be weak, and is adequate only for relatively simple (mostly static) environments. In light of the exponential growth in states that must be accounted for explicitly by an FSM, as the number of contextual features increases, the usefulness of the traditional FSM approach to designing "reasonably intelligent" combat agents in EINSTein diminishes rapidly.

There are a number of viable alternatives—stemming from basic research in artificial intelligence, robotics, and commercial gaming—that can be used to (at least, partially) circumvent this problem: non-deterministic state transitions, knowledge-based state hierarchies, and the *Combs Method* (as applied to fuzzy-logic states [Combs99]), among others.

4.3.12.2 *Behavior-Based Action Selection*

EINSTein uses an alternative approach that is based on the same kind of input-output maps as used by an FSM, but in which both the input and output spaces are interpreted more loosely as consisting of behaviors, not states.

The distinction, as discussed in the next section, is an important one. Behavior-based intelligence design originated in robotics research, and has been heavily influenced by what is known about the behavior of real animals. Animals, not to mention humans, tend to be simultaneously influenced by many varying factors, and only rarely engage in a "robotic"-like, single-minded behavior. Moreover, an animal must constantly weigh changing environmental conditions with its own internal states to determine which of its motivations should be strengthened, and which weakened (or left alone).

For example, if an animal sees a predator while foraging for food, its motivation to evade the predator will likely overpower its drive to forage, along with all other behaviors. By focusing on the *motivations* for primitive behaviors, and by thus allowing free-form actions to emerge naturally rather than depending on hard-wired, or "scripted" routines, behavior-based action selection is generally more robust at capturing the complexities of natural behavior than are FSMs. And, as a creature's (read: as an agent's) motivations depend almost entirely on how the creature dynamically assigns measures of relative value to different features of its environment, it should come as no surprise to find that the behavior-based action selection logic is essentially a calculus of value.

4.3.12.3 *Layered Architecture*

Parts of EINSTein's action selection logic are patterned loosely on Brook's subsumptive architecture [Brooks99]. Subsumptive architecture, which is consistent with the basic *sense-plan-act* paradigm that underlies EINSTein's design, uses layers of reactive control modules to allow high-level controllers to override lower-level controllers. Each level controls the agent (in Brooks' research, a physical robot) up to a certain level of functional sophistication. In the case of a foraging robot, for example, the top level might be a *homing* module, followed by a *pickup-object* module, followed by an *avoid-collision-with-obstacles* module, followed by, on the lowest level, a module that controls random *wandering*.

EINSTein's action selection logic, as developed in the next section, also borrows elements from Mataric's multiagent generalization of the basic subsumptive architecture [Mata94, Mata95]. Mataric's generalization consists essentially of building reactive controllers on top of a set of learned basis behaviors. The basis behaviors are selected so that (1) they form a complete set with respect to the desired set of goals, and (2) are as simple and robust as possible. The analogue of Mataric's basis behaviors, in EINSTein, are *primitive response-activation functions*, which define a basis set of context-specific behaviors that can be used to "shape" desired agent behaviors. This is an important component of the design of EINSTein's enhanced genetic algorithm, which now can use a complete set of primitive behaviors to conduct its searches.

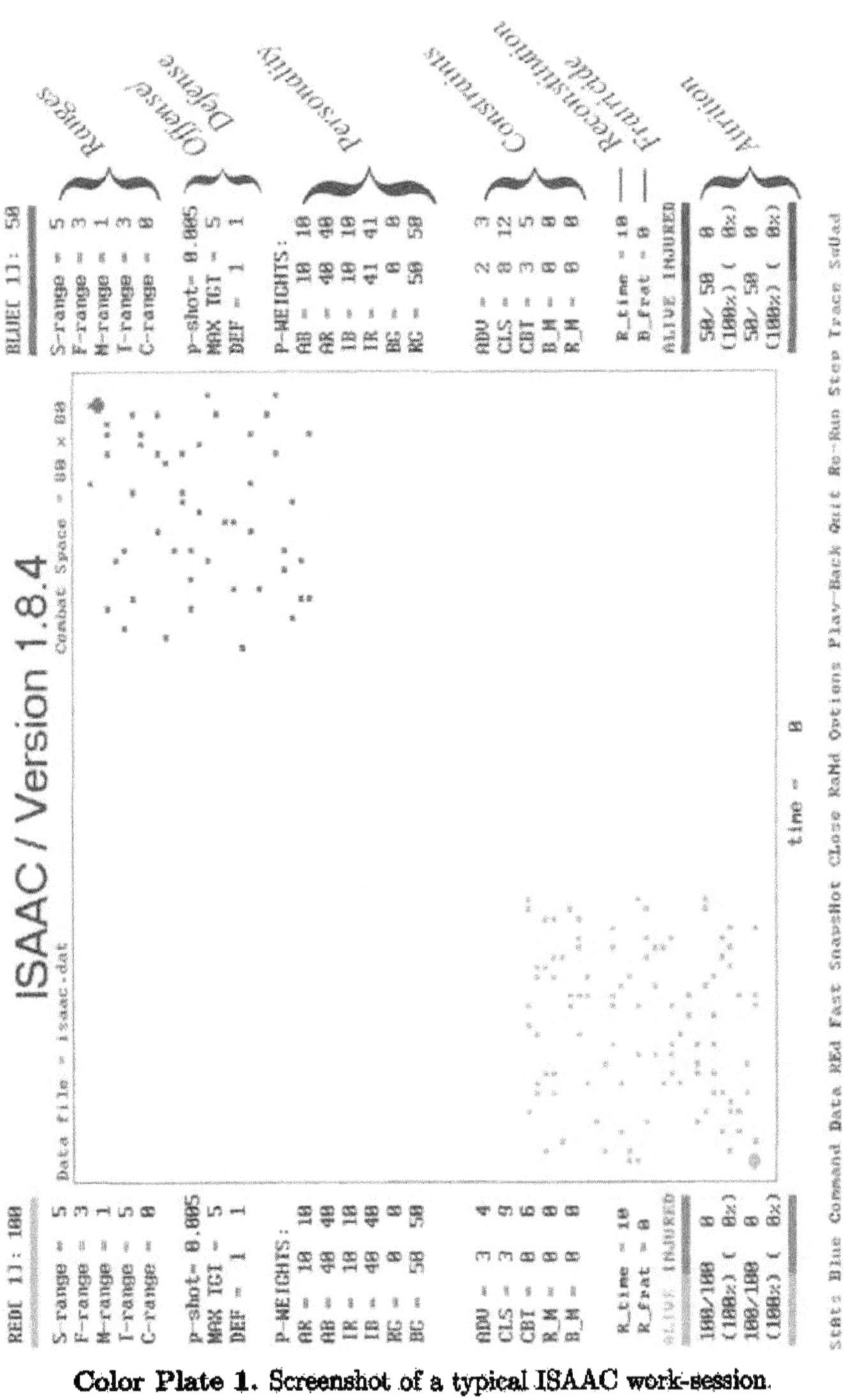

Color Plate 1. Screenshot of a typical ISAAC work-session.

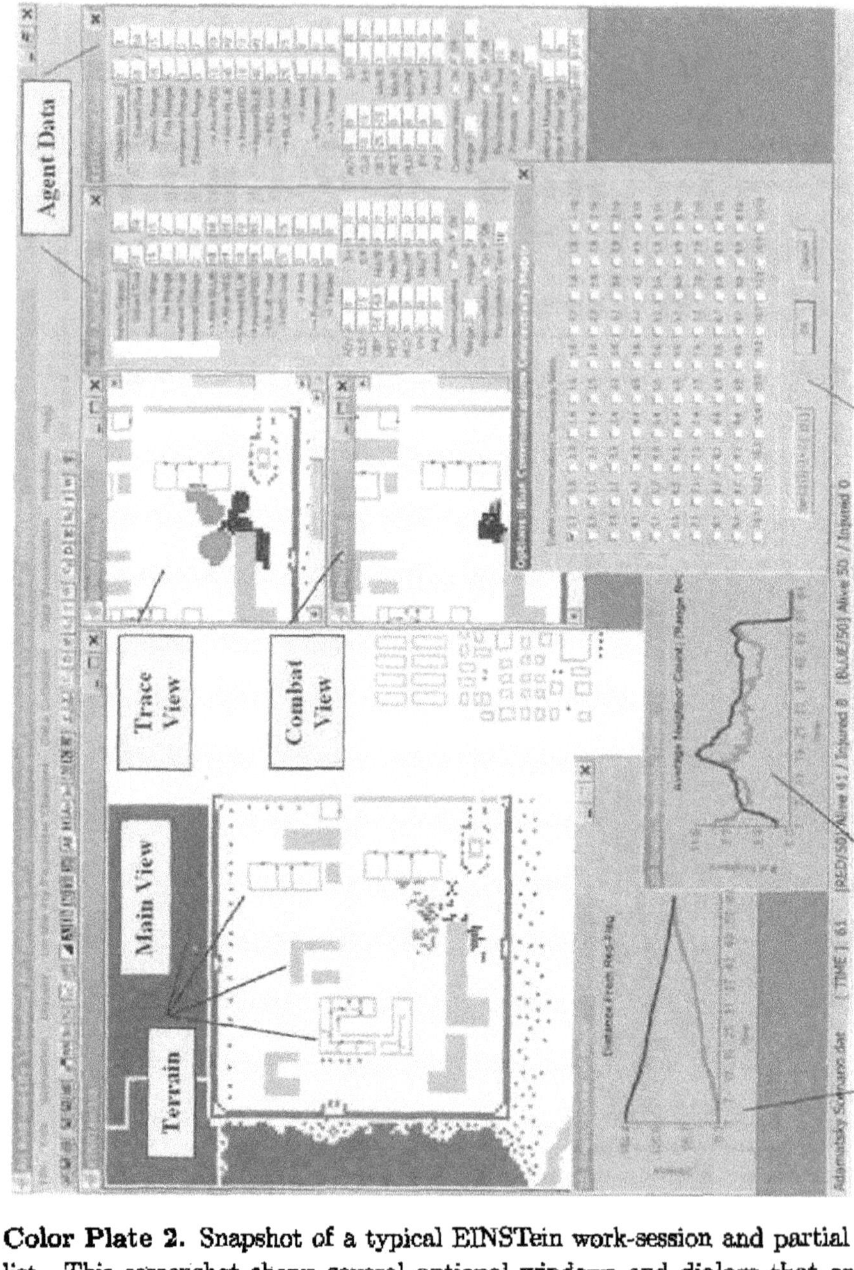

Color Plate 2. Snapshot of a typical EINSTein work-session and partial feature list. This screenshot shows several optional windows and dialogs that are open; EINSTein initially opens up with a single view of the battlefield.

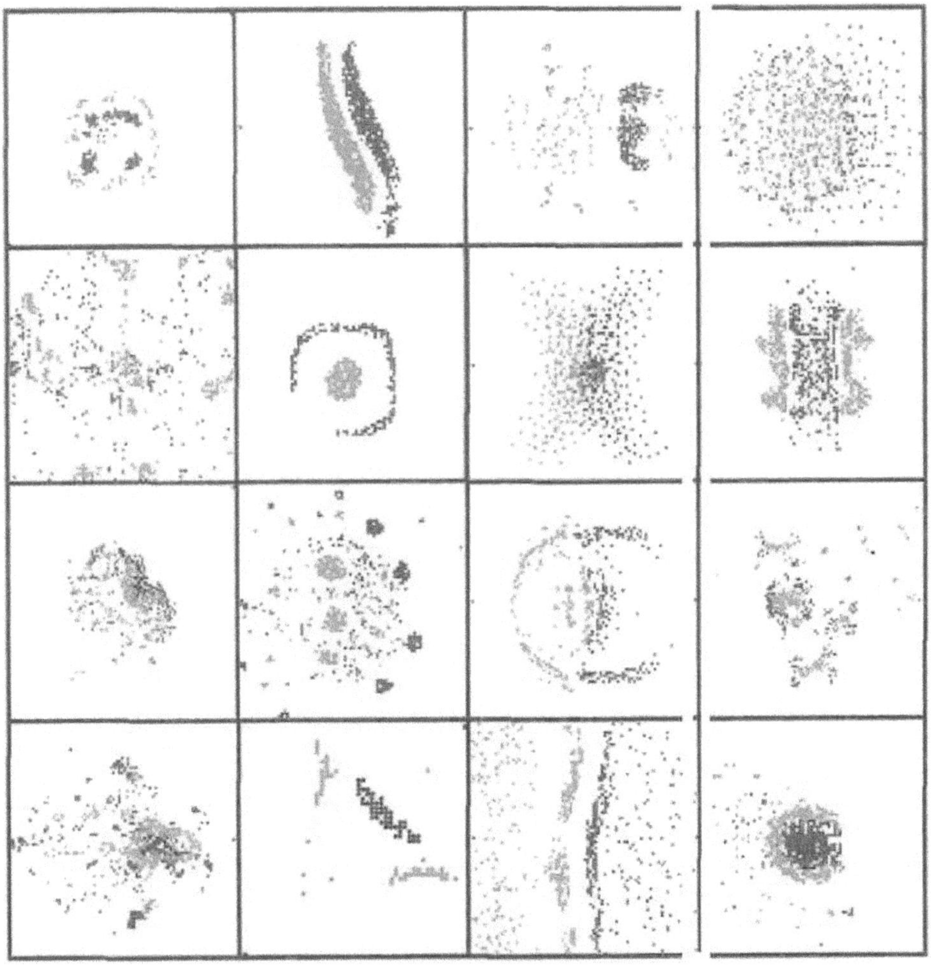

Color Plate 3. A sampling of emergent spatial patterns of opposing red and blue agents obeying some of EINSTein's many possible micro (i.e. local) rules. Each box in this color plate represents one (randomly timed) snapshot of red and blue agents engaged in combat for a single rule. Details regarding agent capabilities and decision logic appear in chapter 5.

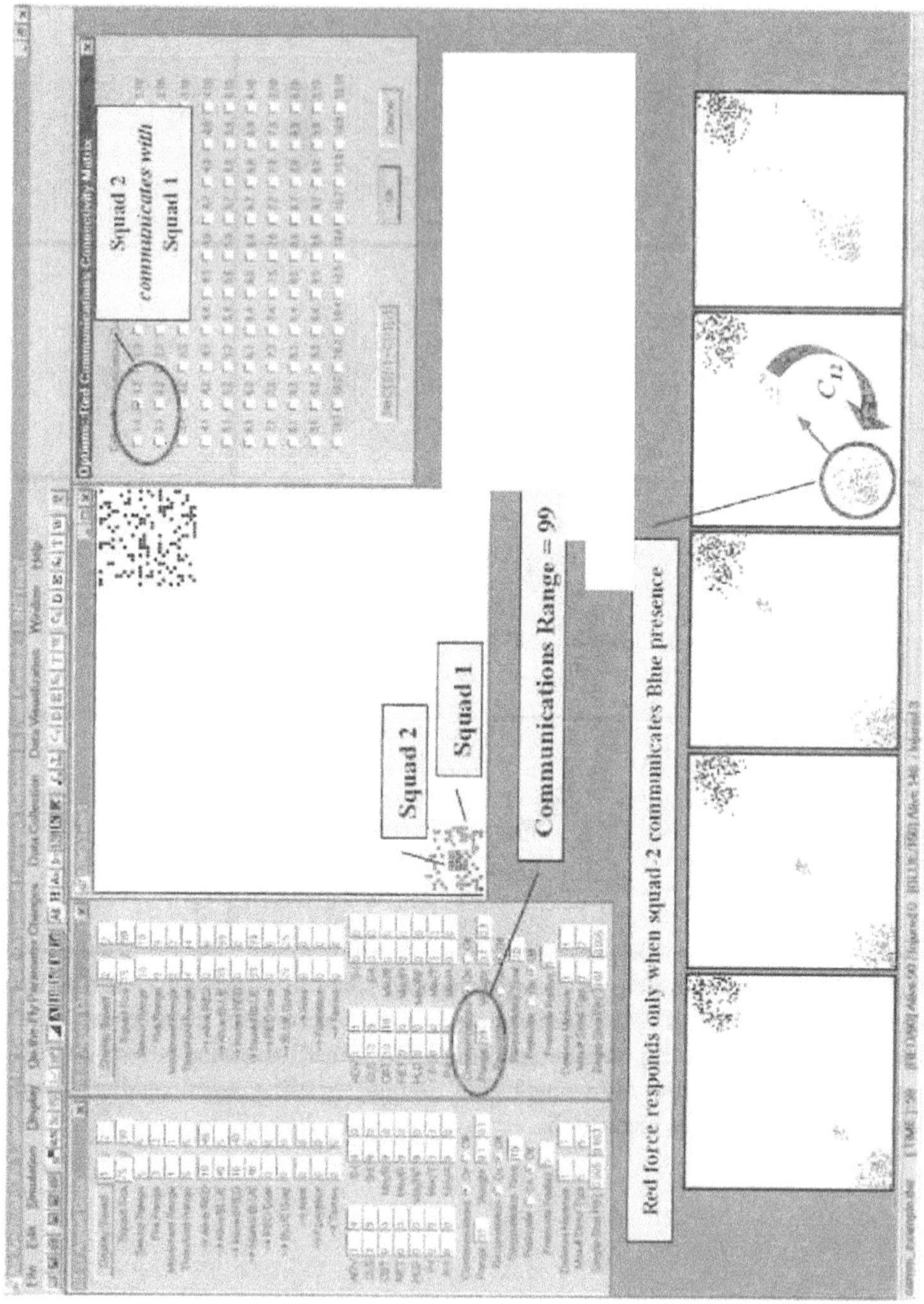

Color Plate 4. Reconnaissance mission scenario using EINSTein's agent-agent communications option (see page 337 in section 5.5.1).

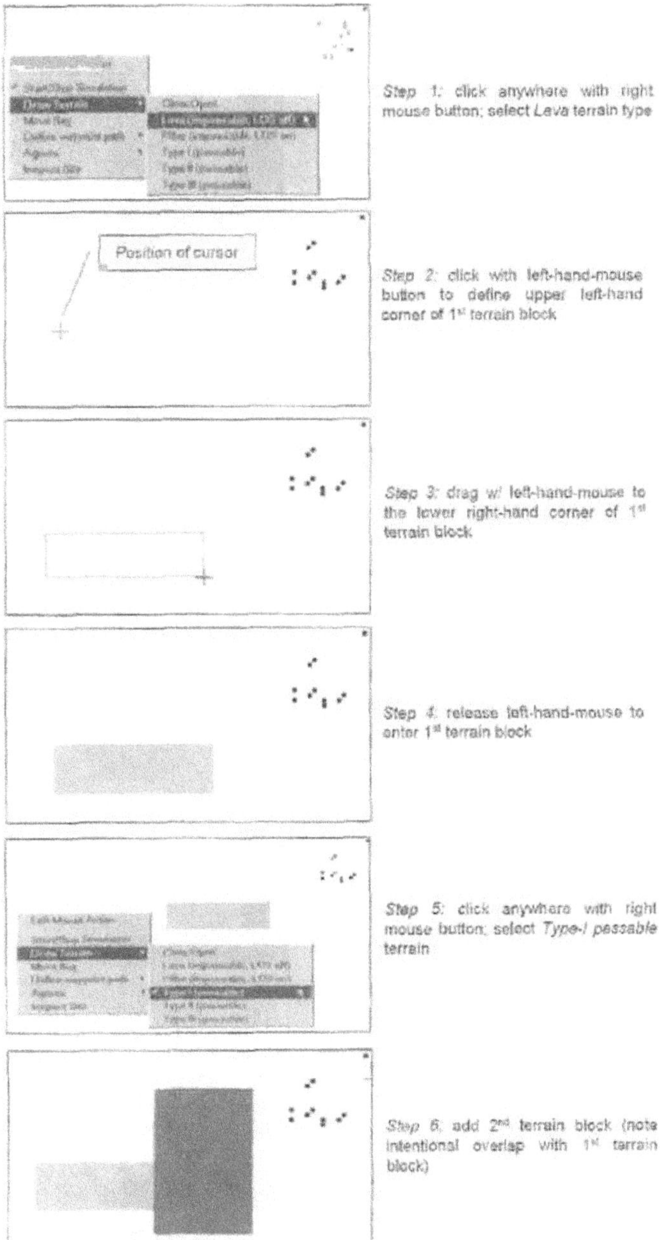

Color Plate 5. Snapshots from a sample terrain-editing session (for EINSTein versions 1.1 and newer); see page 341 in section 5.6.2.1 for details.

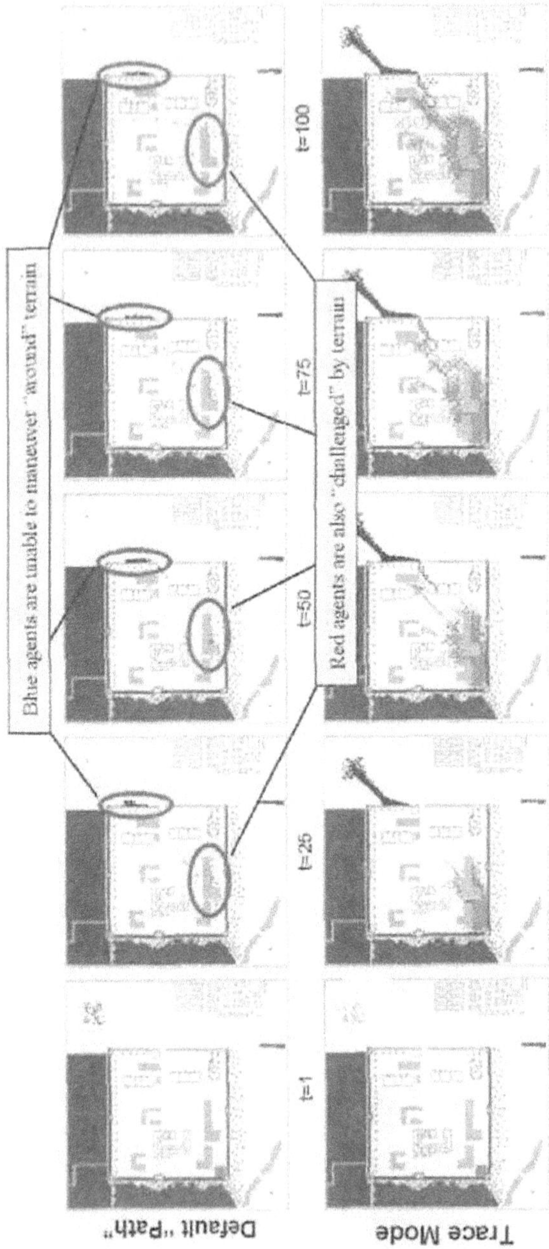

Color Plate 6. Snapshots of a typical run without using Dijkstra-optimal path data or user-defined waypoints; see discussion starting on page 358 in section 5.7.2.7 for details.

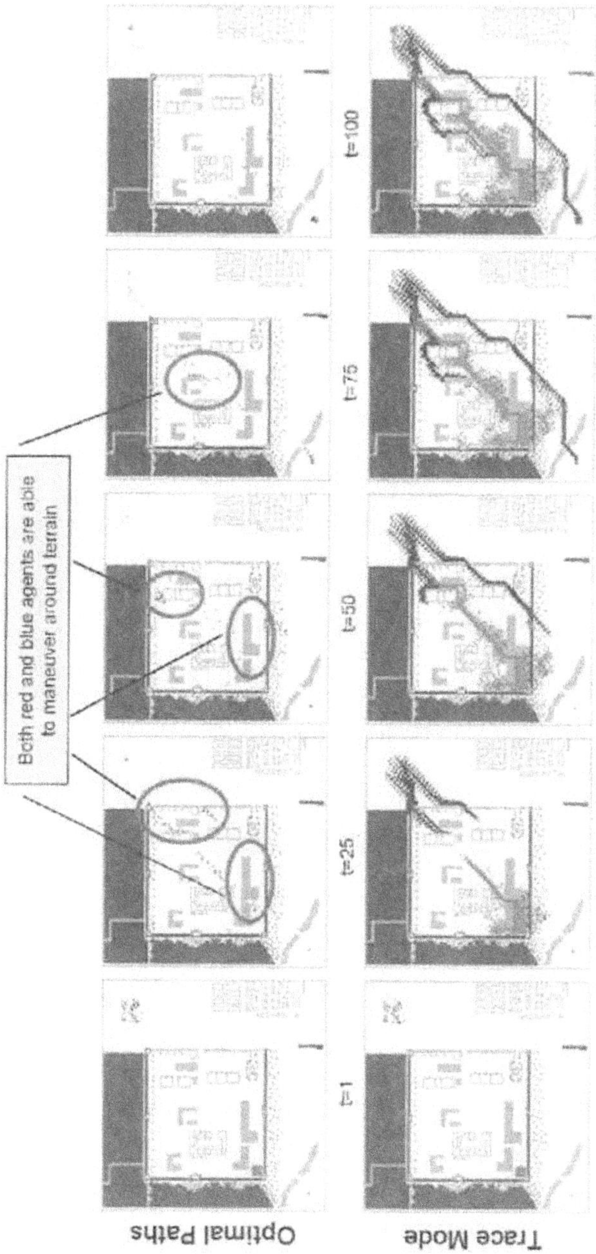

Color Plate 7. Snapshots of a typical run using Dijkstra optimal-path data; see discussion starting on page 359 in section 5.7.2.7 for details.

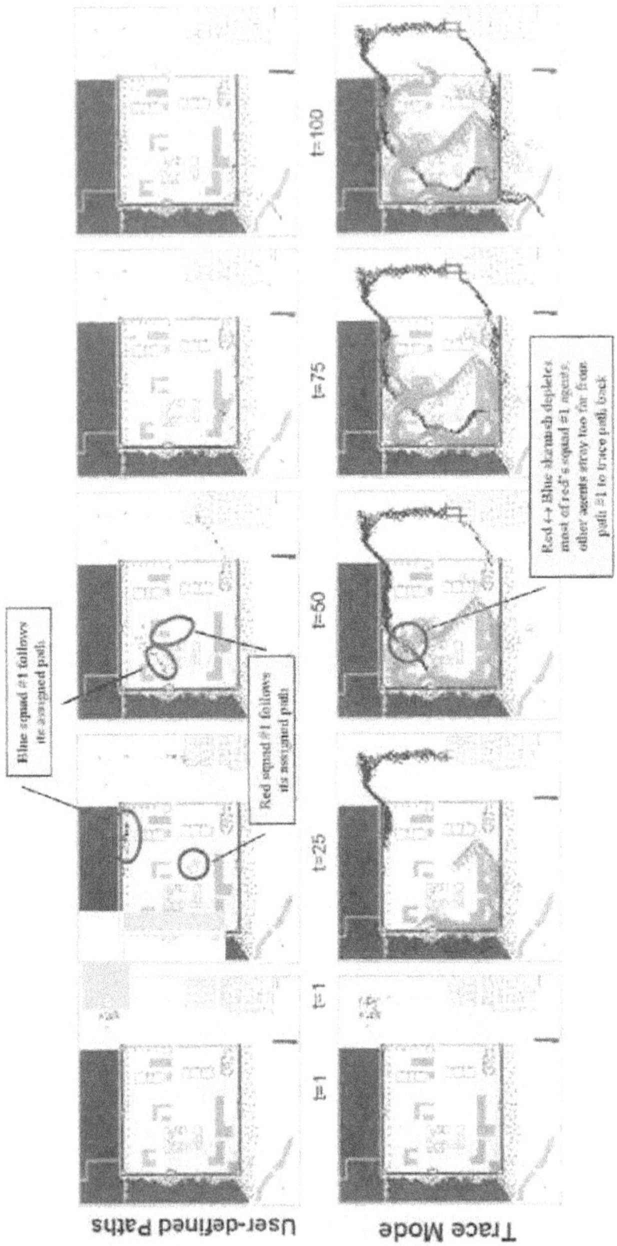

Color Plate 8. Snapshots of a typical run in which each squad (two red and two blue) is assigned a unique user-defined path; see discussion on page 359 in section 5.7.2.7 for details.

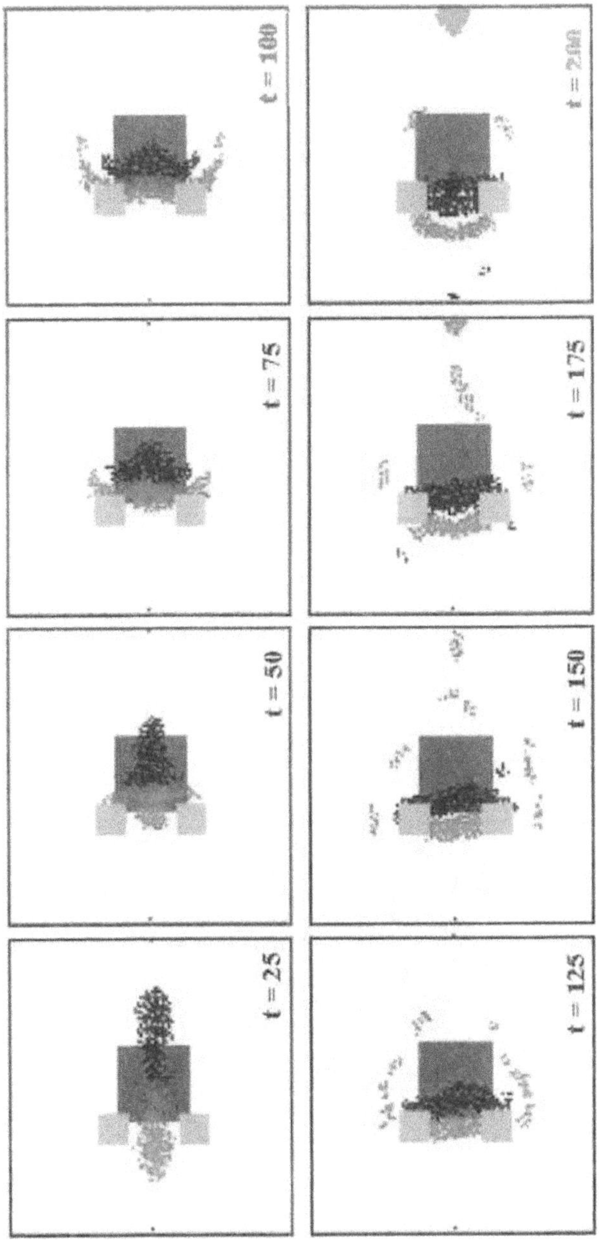

Color Plate 9. Snapshots of a run using a slightly asymmetrized form of default parameter settings defining the scenario classic fronts along with user-defined terrain elements; see discussion starting on page 450 in section 6.3.2.4 for details.

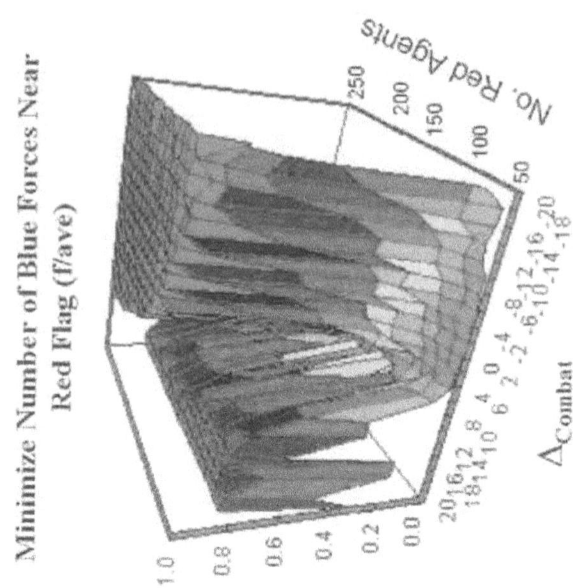

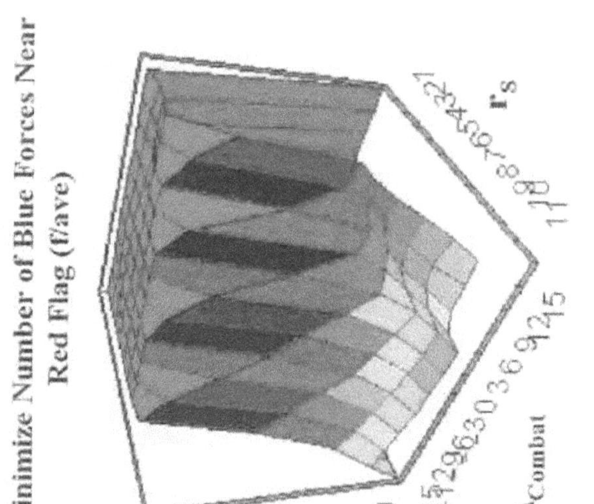

Color Plate 10. Two fitness landscapes for the *classic fronts scenario* discussed starting on page 451 in section 6.3.3.4; mission fitness = *minimize number of blue agents near red flag.*

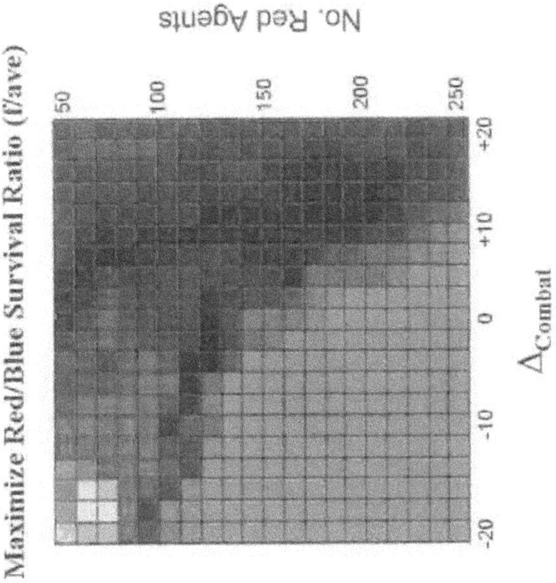

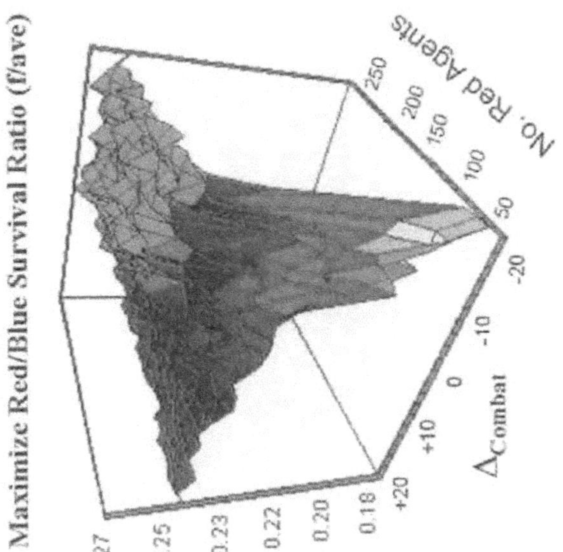

Color Plate 11. Two fitness landscapes for the *classic fronts scenario* discussed on page 451 in section 6.3.3.4; mission fitness = *maximize red/blue survival ratio.*

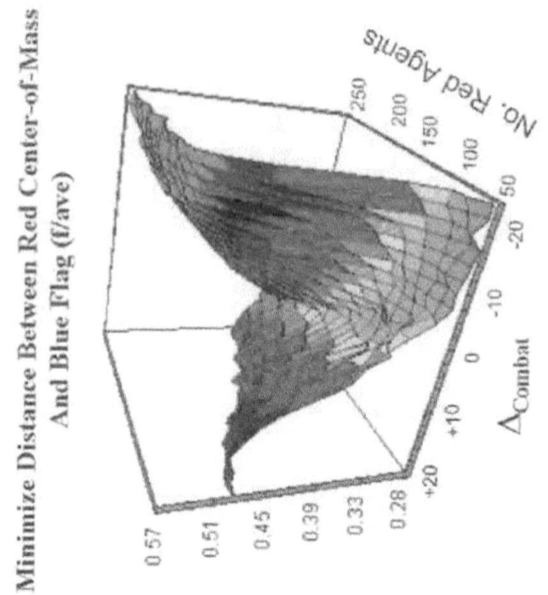

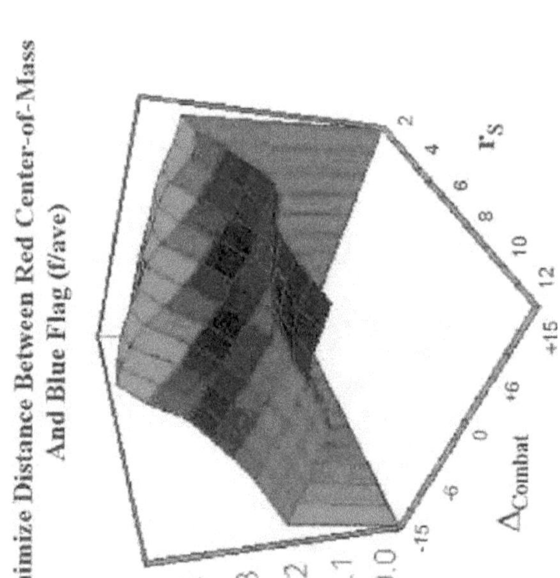

Color Plate 12. Two fitness landscapes for the *classic fronts scenario* discussed on page 451 in section 6.3.3.4; mission fitness = *minimize red center-of-mass to blue flag*.

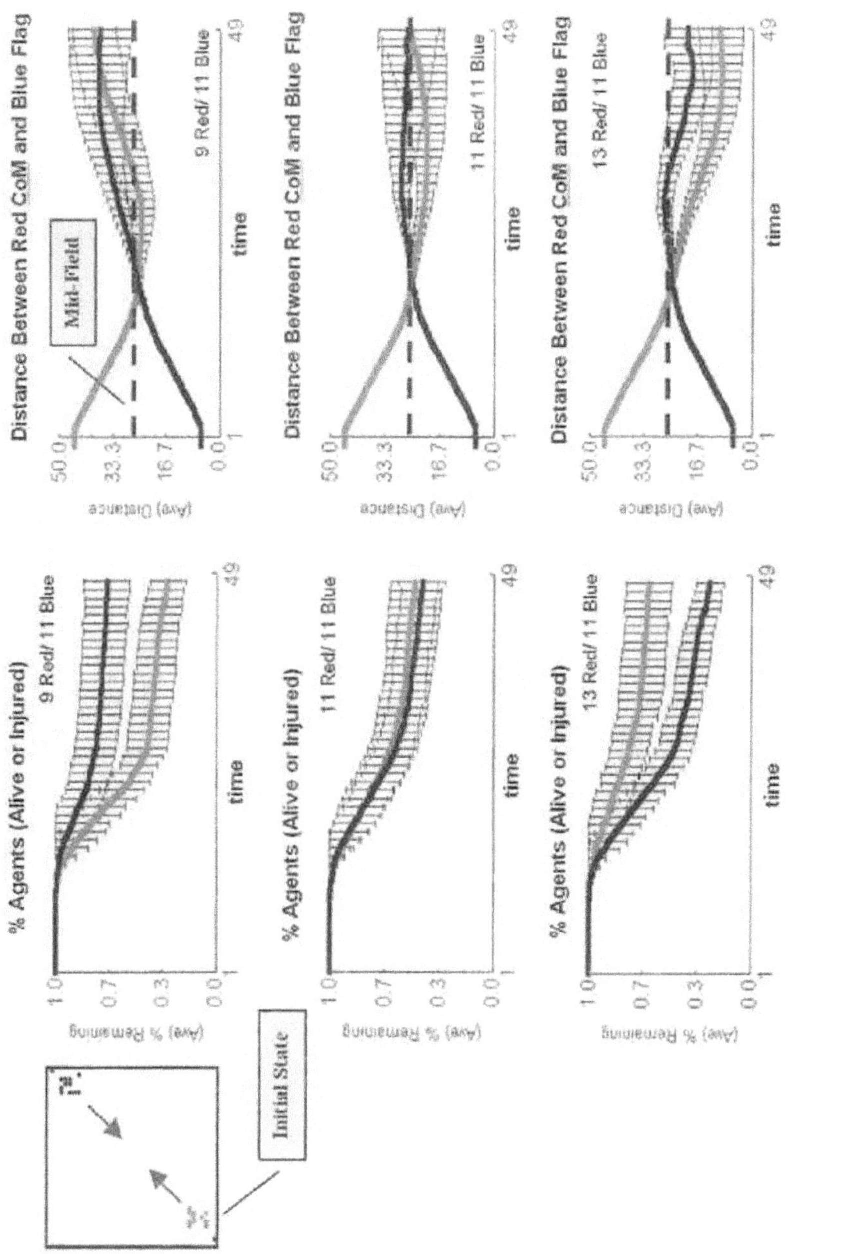

Color Plate 13. Time-series statistics for the *Squad vs. Squad* case study discussed on page 471 in section 6.5.2; plots are for (red/blue) squads = (9/11), (11/11) and (13/11).

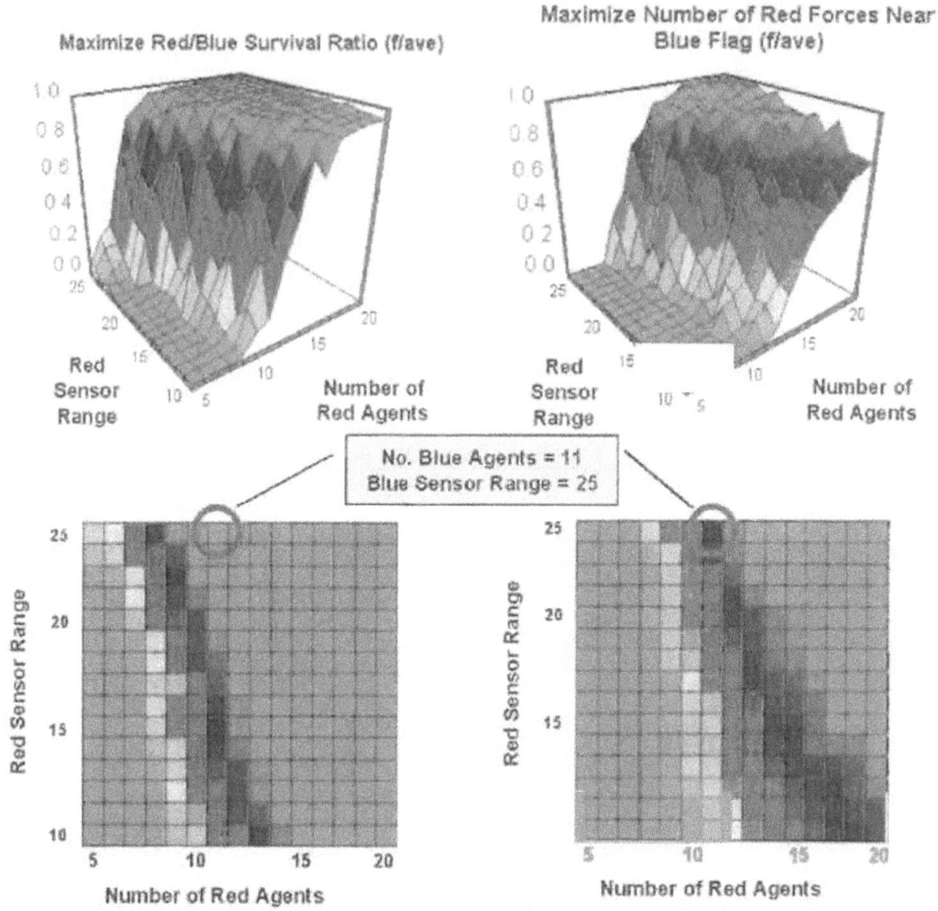

Color Plate 14. Fitness landscape plots for *Squad-vs-Squad* case study discussed on page 471 in section 6.5.2.

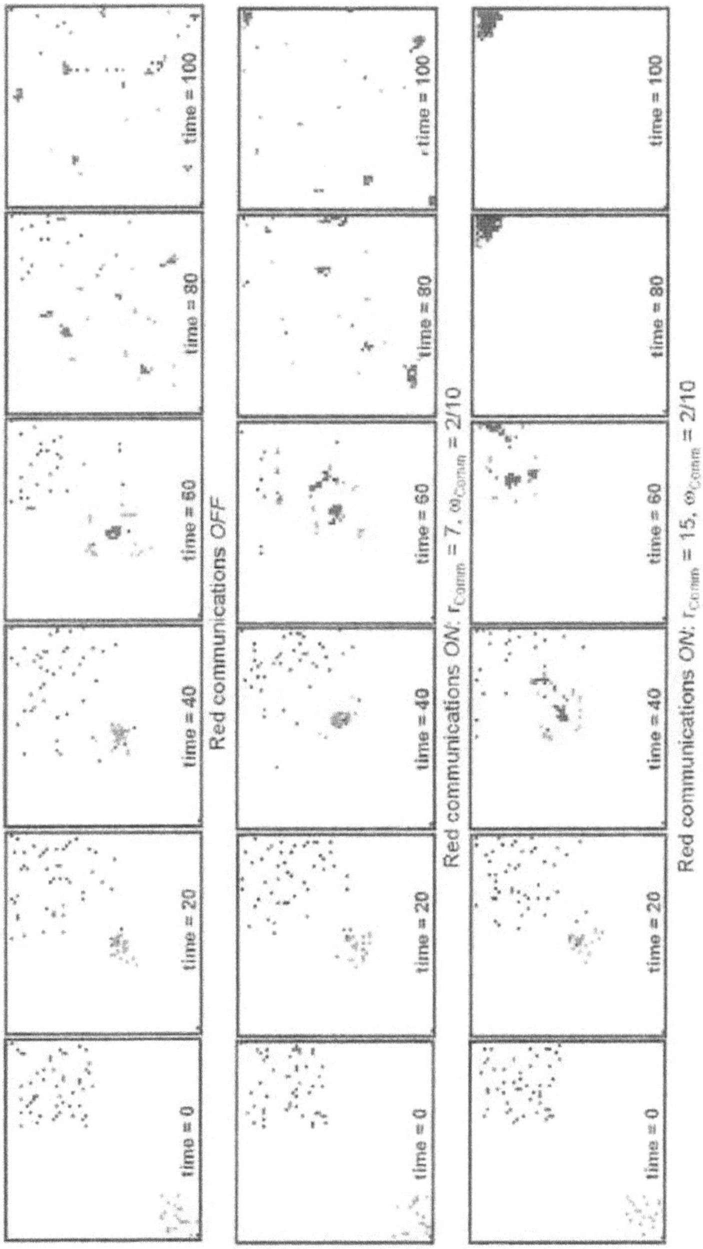

Color Plate 15. Screenshots from typical runs of the *attack scenario* discussed on page 476 in section 6.6; agent parameters are defined in table 6.5.

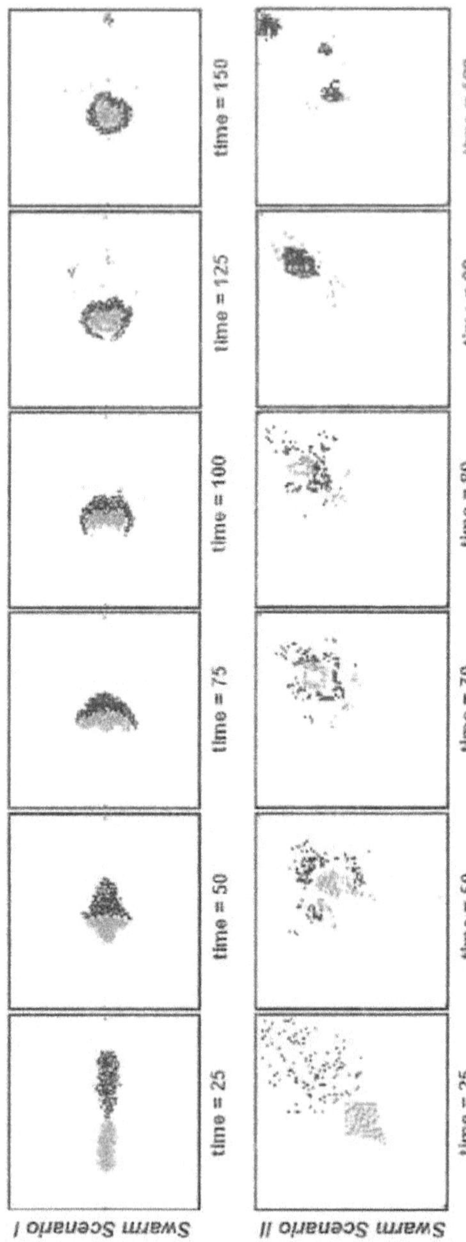

Color Plate 16. Screenshots from typical runs of the *swarm scenarios* I and II discussed on page 482 in section 6.8; agent parameters are defined in table 6.7.

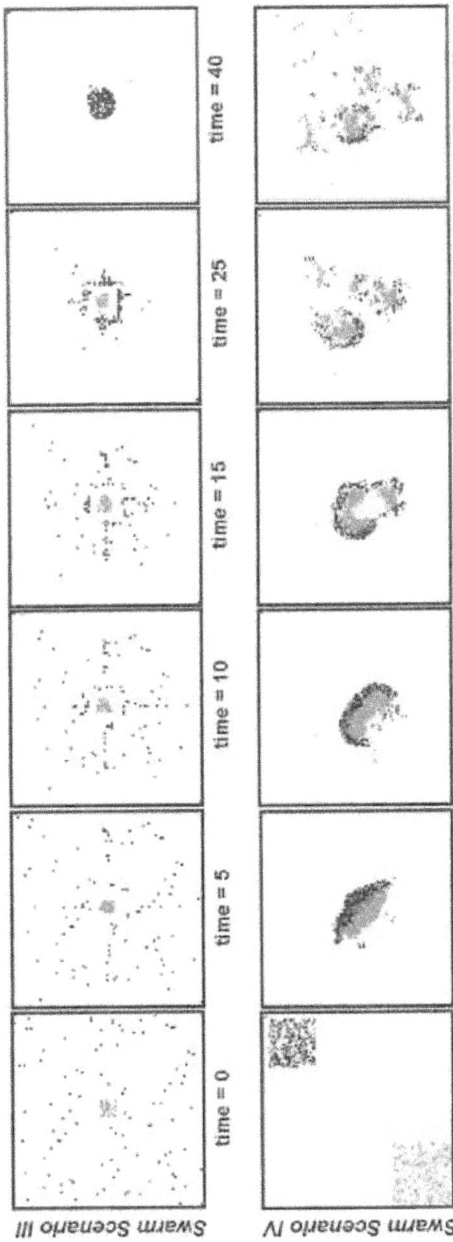

Color Plate 17. Screenshots from typical runs of the *swarm scenarios* III and IV discussed on page 482 in section 6.8; agent parameters are defined in table 6.7.

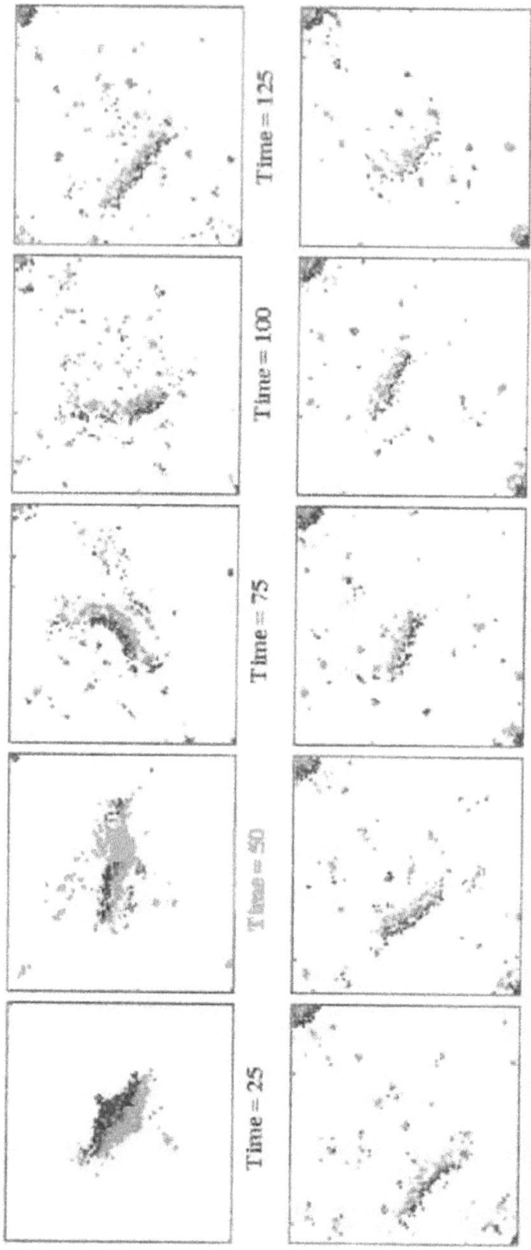

Color Plate 18. Screenshots of an interactive run of the *autopoietic skirmish scenario* discussed on page 487 in section 6.10; agent parameters are defined in table 6.9.

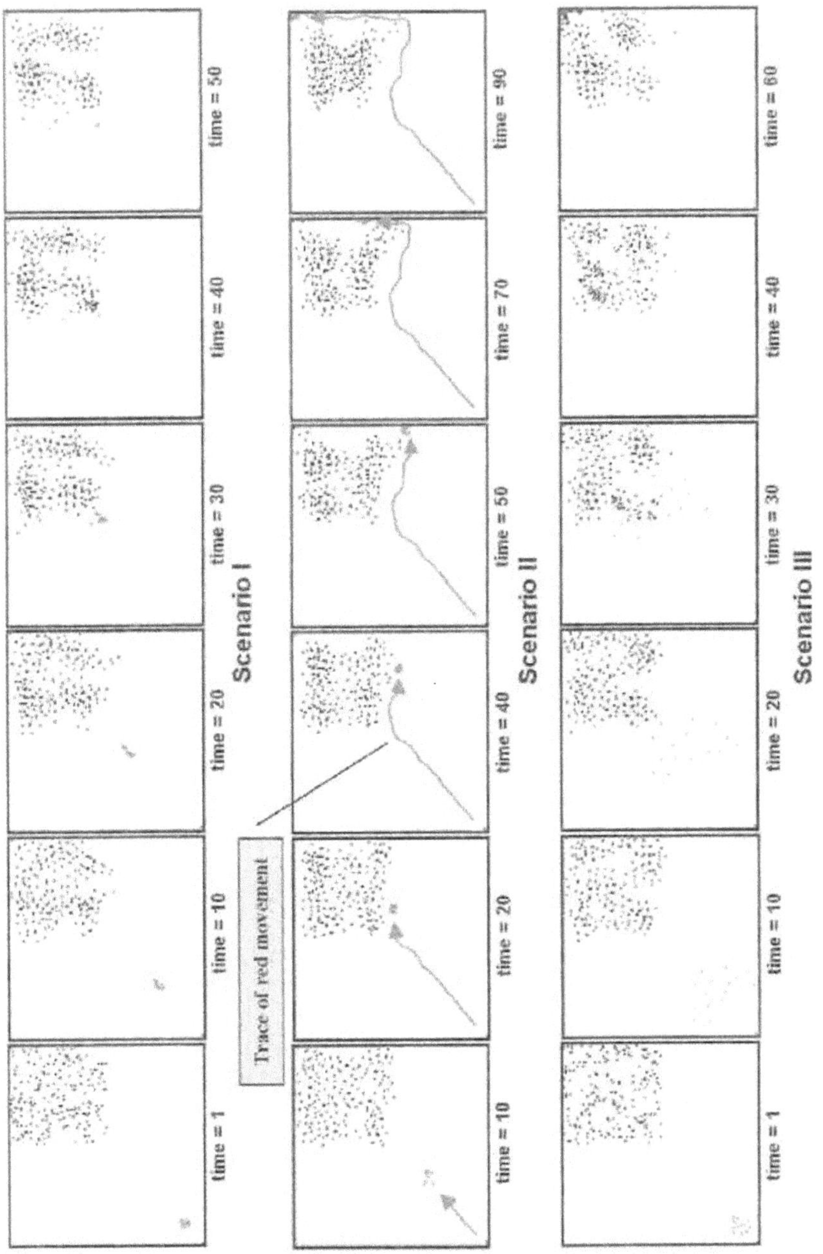

Color Plate 19. Screenshots from runs of the *small insertion scenario* discussed on page 488 in section 6.11; agent parameters for scenarios I, II and III are defined in table 6.10.

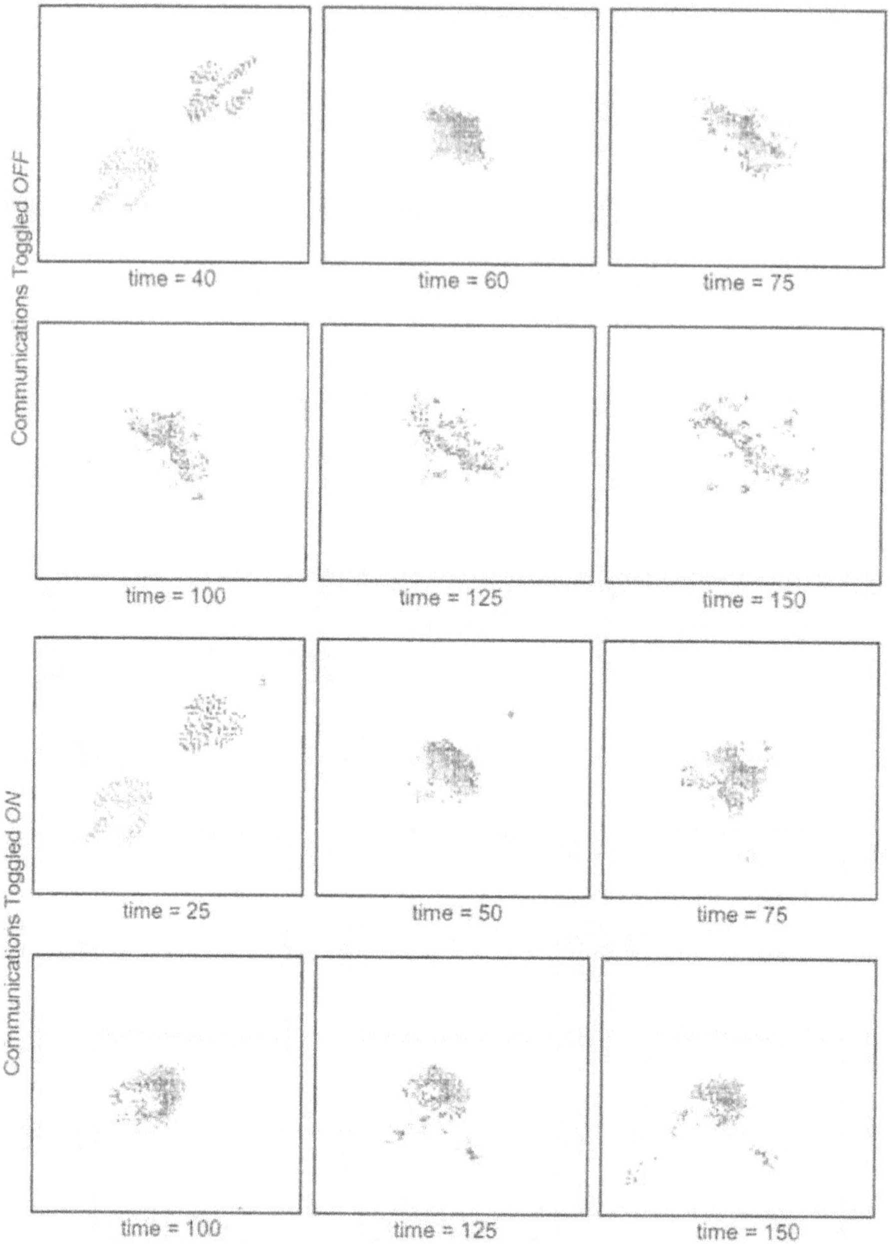

Color Plate 20. Screenshots from two runs of the *firestorms and comms scenario* discussed on page 496 in section 6.12.3 of the main text. The parameter values defining red and blue agent behaviors are the same for the two runs, except that during the second run (appearing on the last two rows of the color plate), blue agents are allowed to communicate with one another. We see that communication effectively binds agents together.

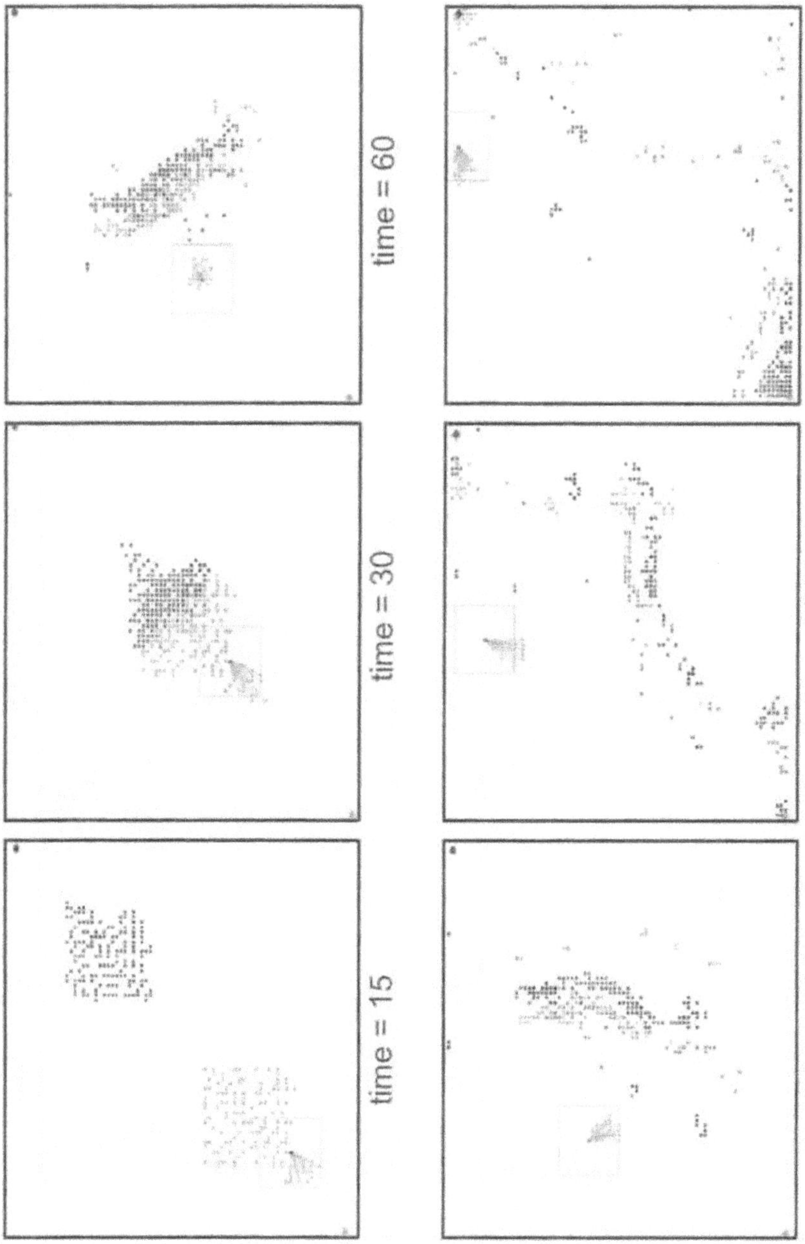

Color Plate 21. Screenshots from a run of a scenario in which one red squad is assigned a *local command agent*; the blue force remains decentralized. The scenario is discussed on page 497 in section 6.12.4 of the main text.

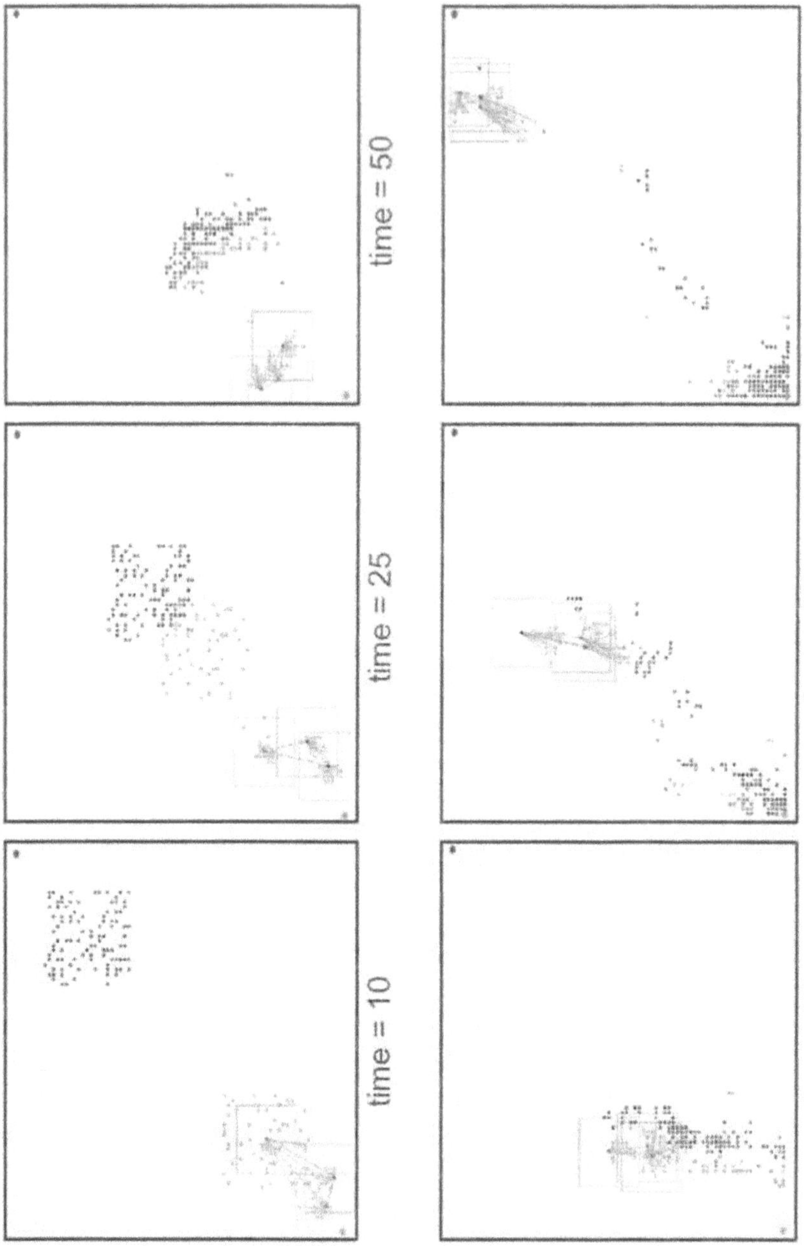

Color Plate 22. *Screenshots from a run of a scenario in which the red force contains three local command agents and one global commander; the blue force remains decentralized. The scenario is discussed on page 498 in section 6.12.5 of the main text.*

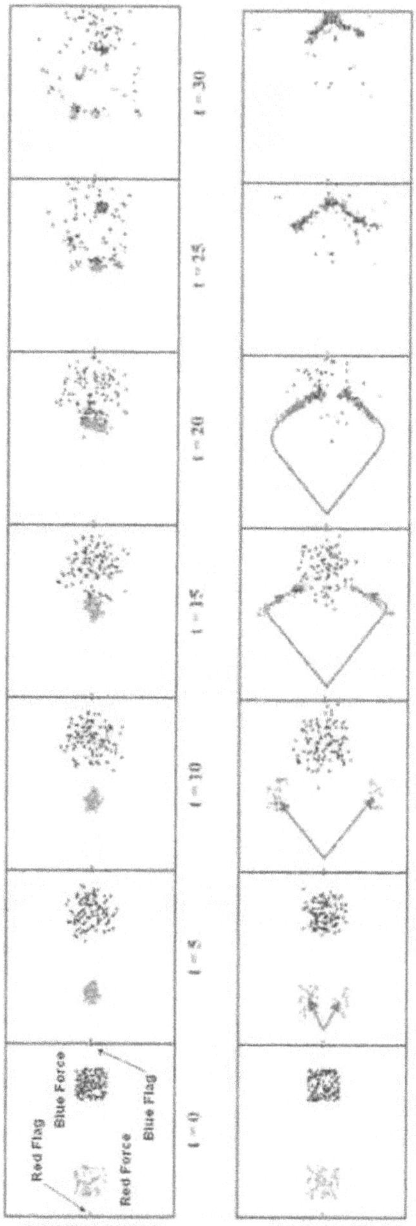

Color Plate 23. Screenshots from sample runs of GA-breeding experiment No. 2. The top row shows a trial red attacking force (consisting of typical parameter values that are not explicitly tuned for performing any specific mission); the bottom row shows screenshots from a typical run using the GA-bred red force. The mission is for red to penetrate through to the blue flag. See discussion starting on page 534 in section 7.3.2.

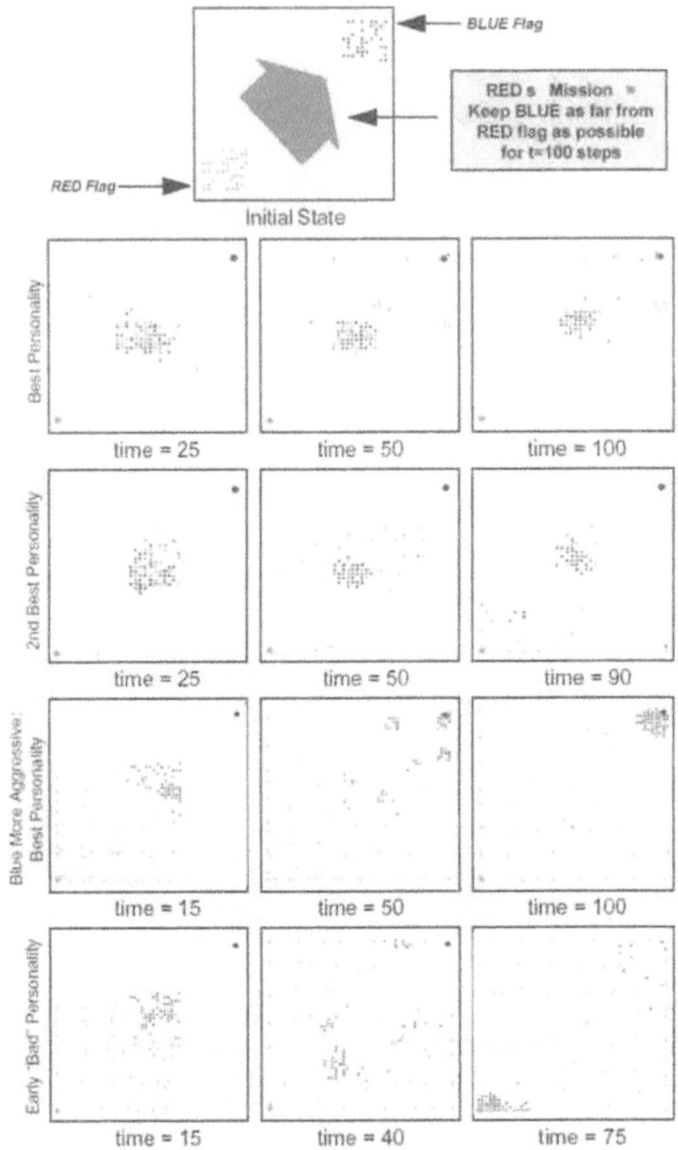

Color Plate 24. Screenshots from several sample runs of GA-bred red agents for GA "breeding" experiment *No. 3* discussed on page 537 in section 7.3.3. The top row shows a run using the highest ranked red agents after 50 generations. The second row shows the second highest ranked red force. The third row shows how the red force adapts to a more aggressive blue force. Finally, the fourth row shows an example of how a sub-optimal red force performs; the red force parameter values for this sequence were deliberately chosen from pool of agents occupying an early portion (generation 10) of the GA's learning curve.

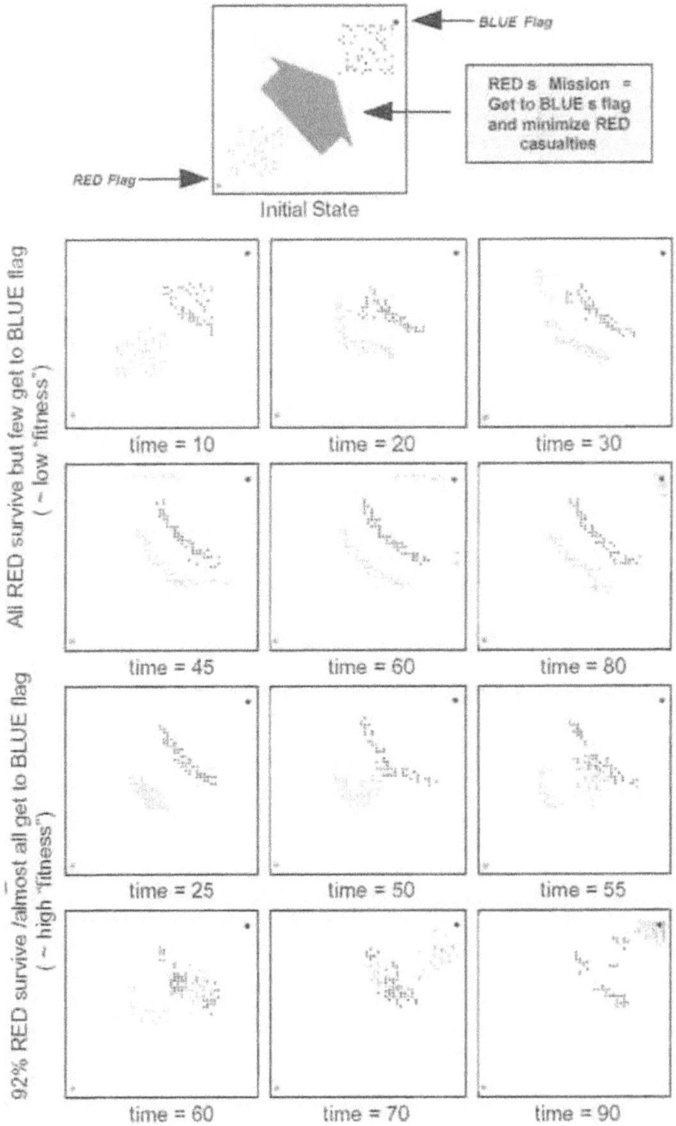

Color Plate 25. Screenshots from several sample runs of GA-bred red agents for GA "breeding" experiment *No. 4* discussed on page 539 in section 7.3.4. The red force's mission is to *get to blue flag and minimize red casualties.* The top two rows show a run using an interim, low-ranked, set of red agent parameter values (the entire red force survives but only a few agents make it to the blue flag). The third and fourth rows show snapshots of a run using the highest ranked red force (92% of the initial red force survives and almost all red agents get to the blue flag).

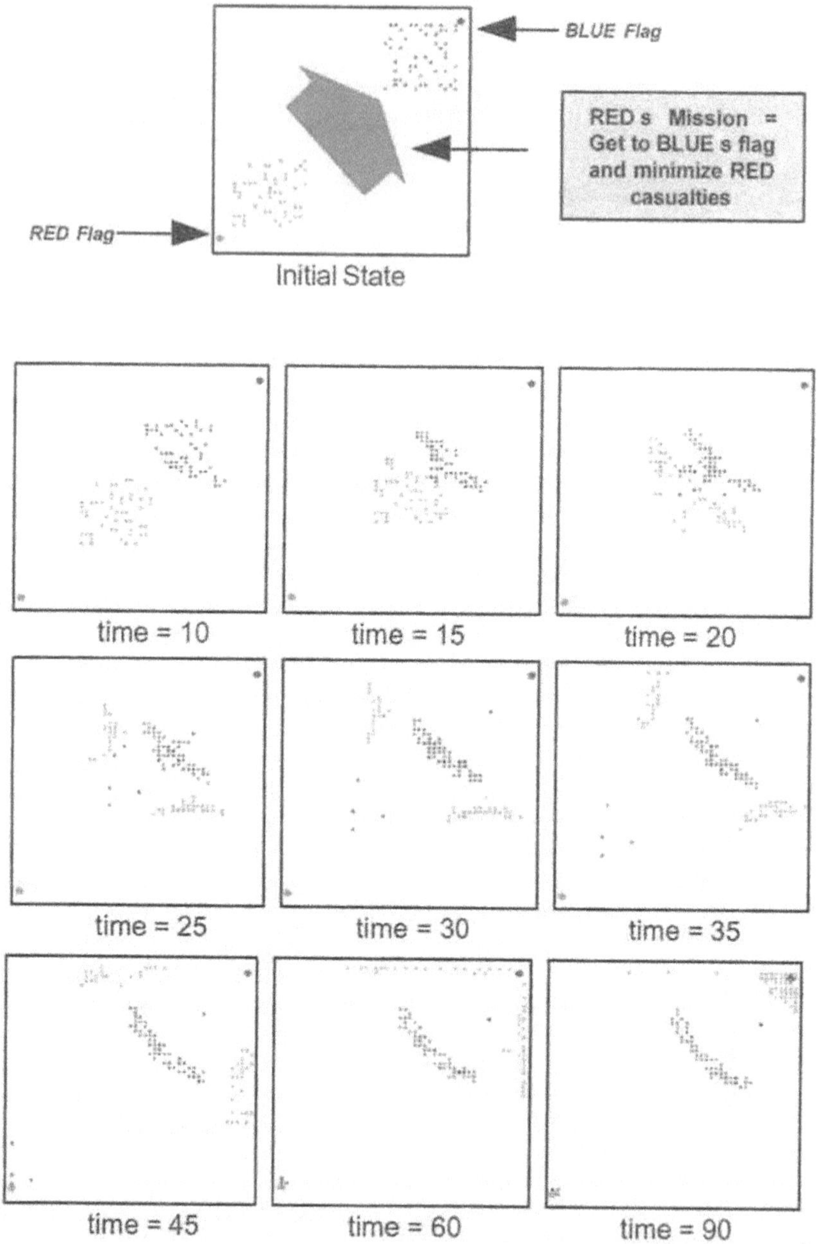

Color Plate 26. Screenshots from a sample run of GA-bred red agents for GA "breeding" experiment *No. 4* discussed on page 539 in section 7.3.4. The red force's mission is the same as for the run in the previous figure (*"Get to the blue flag and minimize red casualties"*). The GA-bred red parameter values are the *second* highest ranked after 50 generations. The emergent "tactic" appears to be, *"weaken the center of blue's defense, then maneuver around the remaining blue forces."*

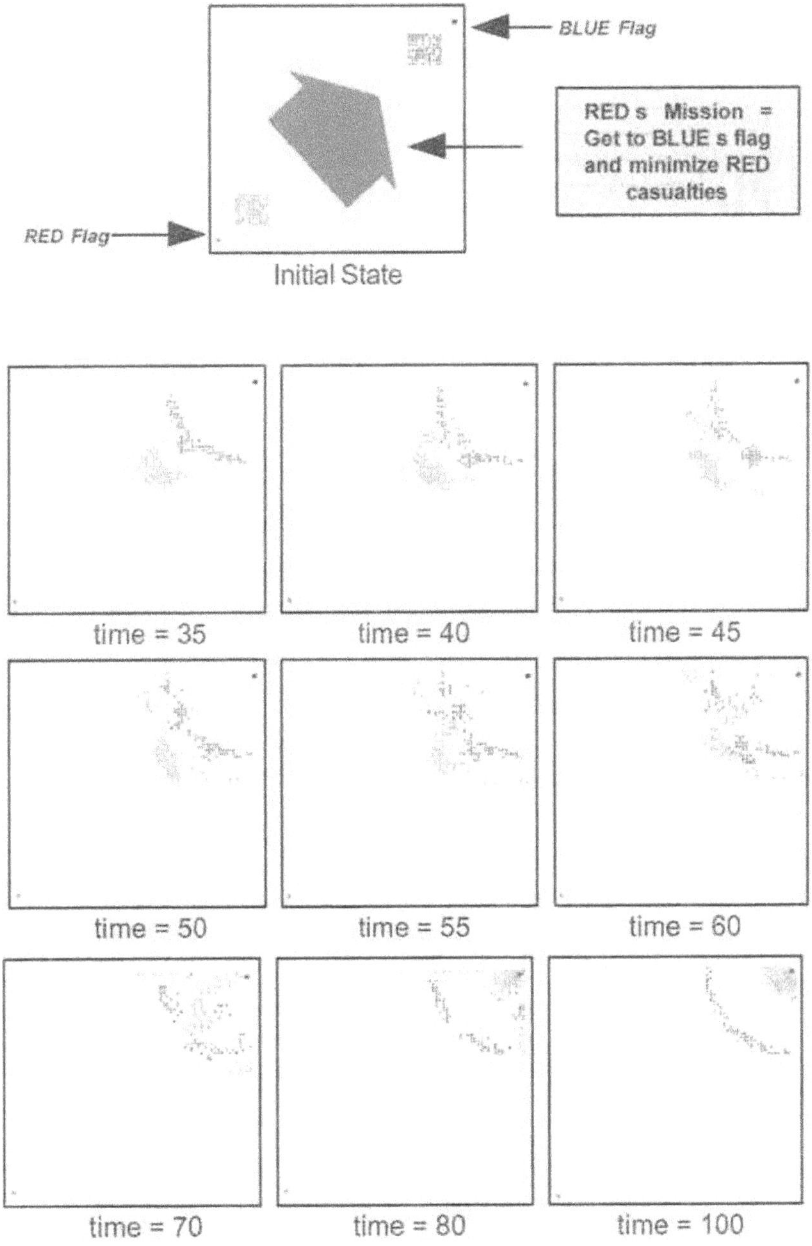

Color Plate 27. Screenshots from a sample run of GA-bred red agents for GA "breeding" experiment *No. 4* discussed on page 539 in section 7.3.4. The red force's mission is the same as for the runs appearing in the previous two color plates (*"Get to the blue flag and minimize red casualties"*). The GA-bred red parameter values are the *third* highest ranked after 50 generations. The emergent "tactic" appears to be, *"spread and weaken, then surge through the thinned blue defenses."*

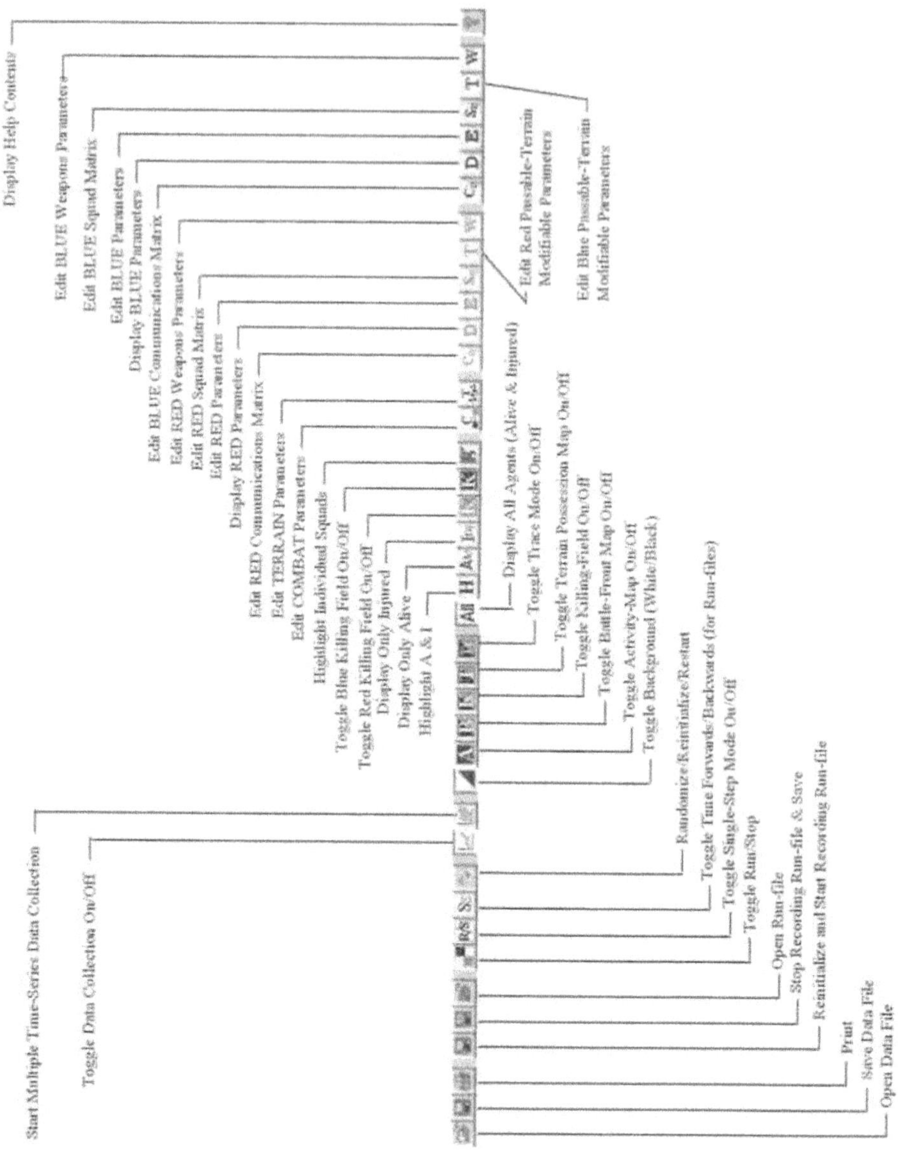

Color Plate 28. A guide to EINSTein's toolbar buttons. The screenshot shown here is captured from EINSTein version 1.0. A detailed description of the function of each of the buttons appears in *Appendix E: A Concise User's Guide to EINSTein*. *Appendix E* summarizes the differences between this toolbar and the toolbar that appears in versions 1.1 and higher.

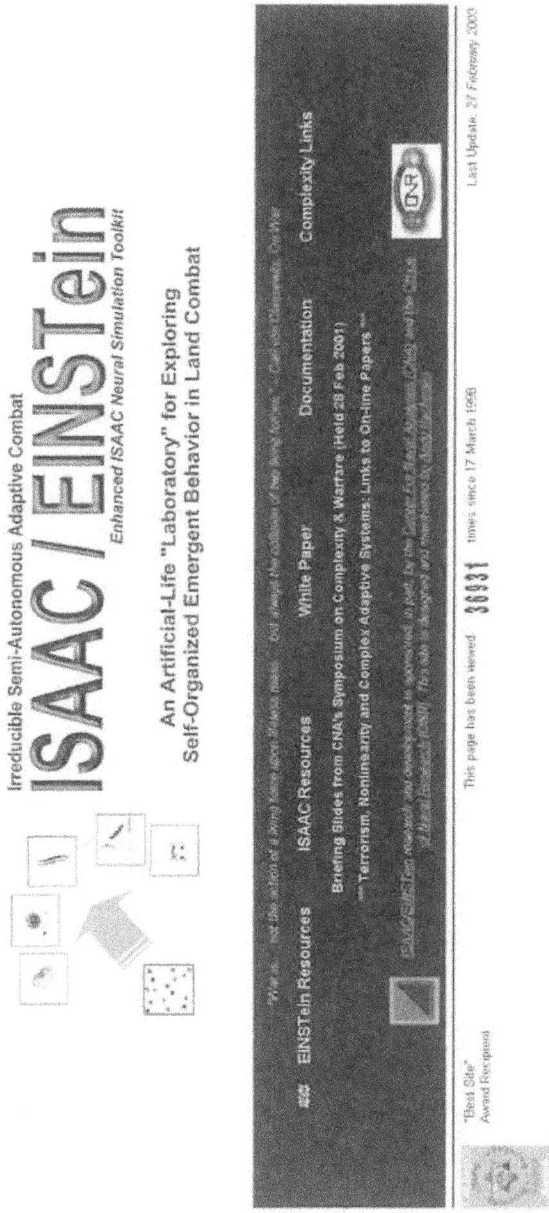

Color Plate 29. Snapshot of EINSTein's homepage. This CNA-sponsored site contains over 200 MB worth of EINSTein-related material, including program documentation, tutorials, sample screenshots and movies, help files, and briefing slides. The site also includes general resources for research in applying complex adaptive systems theory to understanding the dynamics of warfare.

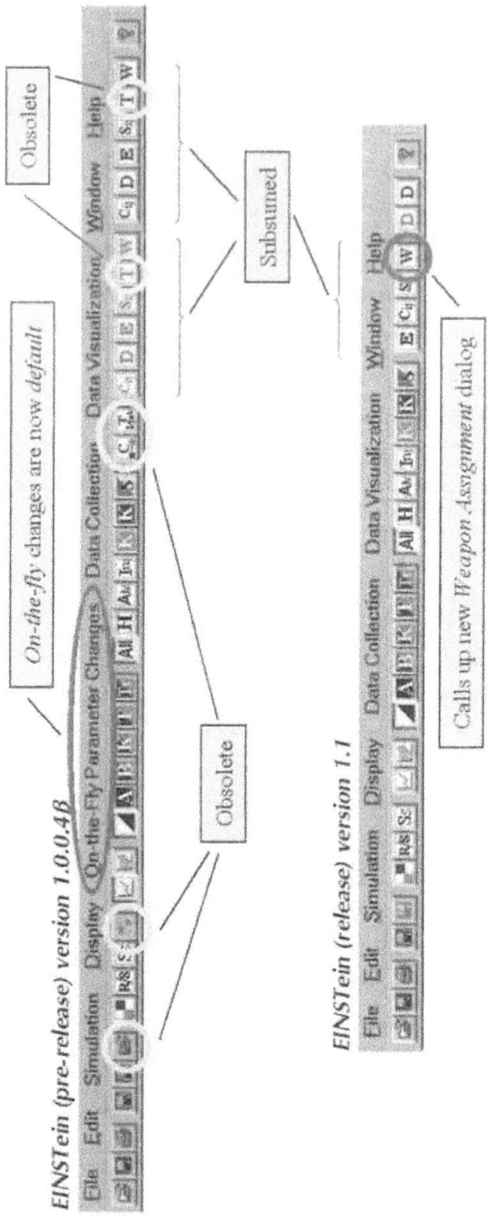

Color Plate 30. Comparison between toolbars used in EINSTein versions 1.0.0.4β (and older) and 1.1 (and newer). See Appendix F.

Chapter 5

EINSTein: *Methodology*

"Now if the estimates made in the temple before hostilities indicate victory it is because calculations show one's strength to be superior to that of his enemy; if they indicate defeat, it is because calculations show that one is inferior. With many calculations, one can win; with few calculations, one cannot. How much less chance of victory has one who makes none at all! By this means I examine the situation and the outcome will be clearly apparent."

—Sun Tzu, *The Art of War*

This chapter provides a detailed discussion of EINSTein's design. It applies the general mathematical principles of multiagent-based modeling techniques, as described in the previous chapter—and which underlie a very broad class of complex adaptive systems—to the specific problem of *simulating combat*. The discussion includes a summary of the overall program flow, introduces the concept of object-oriented program design, describes EINSTein's notional two-dimensional battlefield, combat agents and their sensor capabilities and primitive behaviors (i.e. *personalities*), defines the penalty-function-based action selection process and use of behavior-shaping meta-rules, and provides an overview of how EINSTein handles agent-to-agent communication, combat attrition, reconstitution and fratricide, terrain and path navigation using (either user-defined or automatically computed) waypoints.

5.1 Program Structure

5.1.1 *Source Code*

EINSTein is written, and compiled, using Microsoft's *Visual C++*,* uses Pinnacle Publishing Inc.'s *Graphics Server*† for displaying time-series plots and three-dimensional renderings of fitness-landscapes, and currently consists of about 150K lines of *object-oriented* (see below) source code.

* *Microsoft Visual C++*, Professional Version 6.0: http://msdn.microsoft.com/developer/.

† Graphics Server is a commercial plug-in, licensed from *Pinnacle Publishing*: http://www.graphicsserver.com.

The source code is divided into three basic parts: (1) the *combat engine*, (2) the *graphical user interface* (GUI), and (3) *data collection* and *data visualization* functions. These parts are essentially machine (i.e. CPU and/or operating system) independent and may be compiled separately. EINSTein's source code base is thus highly portable and is relatively easy to modify to suit particular problems and interests. For example, an EINSTein-based combat environment may be developed as a standalone program on a CPU platform other than the original MS Windows target machine used for EINSTein's original development. Any developer/analyst interested in porting EINSTein over to some other machine and/or operating system is tasked only with providing his own machine specific GUI as a "wrap-around" to the stand-alone combat and data-visualization engines (that may be provided as DLLs). Moreover, it is very easy to add, delete and/or change the existing source code, including making complicated changes that significantly alter how agents decide their moves.

At the heart of EINSTein lies the *combat engine* (the most important parts of which are discussed in detail below). The combat engine processes all run-time, combat-related logical decisions, and is the core script upon which multiple time-series data collection, fitness landscape sweeps over the agents' parameter space, and genetic algorithm searches all depend.

5.1.2 *Object-Oriented*

The history of object-oriented (OO) programming languages can be traced to the development of the SIMULA languages at the *Norwegian Computing Center* in the early 1960s.* This language introduced two key concepts of object-oriented programming, *objects* and *classes* (as well as *subclasses*, or the idea of *inheritance*).

All object-oriented programs share the same basic characteristics:

- Everything is an *object.*
- Every object is an *instance* of a *class.*
- Classes are repositories of the properties of, and behaviors associated with, objects.
- Computation proceeds by objects communicating with other objects by sending and receiving *messages*, which are requests made of other objects to perform specific actions, bundled with whatever information is necessary for those actions to be completed.

*Given that the subject of this book is the conceptual development of a tool for understanding combat as a complex system, it is amusing to note that the SIMULA languages were themselves created, in part, because one of their developers (Kristen Nygaard) needed tools to simulate complex man-machine systems that he came across in his work in operations research. Thus, in 1961, the idea emerged for developing a language that could be used to both describe *systems* (of individuals) and prescribe *system behavior* (as a computer program).

Inheritance is also a key concept, and refers to the rooted-tree structure into which the classes are organized. Behaviors associated with instances of a class C are automatically available to all classes that descend from C on this tree.

5.1.2.1 *Objects*

Booch [Booch91] defines *objects* as programming entities that have "state, behavior, and identity." The *state* refers to the set of properties that characterize an object, such as speed, strength, maneuverability, and so on. An object's *behavior* includes actions that the object can make, such as moving from one battlefield position to another, looking around to gather information about its environment, or engaging in combat. Finally, an object's *identity* refers to properties that label a particular instance of an object. For example, while all combat agents in EINSTein belong to one of a few squads, the program is able to distinguish one agent from another, as independent combatants, by individually assigned attributes. Another way to think of objects, from a programming point of view, is as entities that include both *data* (that define an object's state properties) and *actions* (that prescribe what an object is able to do).*

5.1.2.2 *Classes*

While objects are the primitive elements of any OO design, the basic building blocks with which actual programs are made are classes. Booch defines a class as a "set of objects that share a common structure and common behavior." A class actually constitutes a rather general set, and does not necessarily need to include a set of objects. When an object is created, it inherits the general attributes of other objects belonging to the same class. However, the state of those attributes may differ from object to object. For example, all **Terrain** objects have x and y coordinates associated with them, but the states of x and y in each individual object may be different.

There are two basic methods by which classes can be extended to build upon, and work with, each other: inheritance and composition (or layering). Inheritance refers to the derivation of one class from another, already existing, class. The new class—the derived class—includes the data members and operations of the base class. Derived classes are typically created when the developer wishes to extend the capabilities of some existing class. Inheritance is sometimes said to denote an *"is-a"* relationship between classes, as in Class *Local Commander* **is-a** (type of) Class *Combat Agent.*

*This simple, but provocative, idea is essentially identical to the concept behind John von Neuman's pioneering self-reproducing automata, which hinged on treating the "blueprint data" defining a virtual organism as *simultaneously* (i) consisting of active instructions that must be executed, and (ii) as an assemblage of information that is an otherwise passive component of the overall structure that must be copied and attached to an offspring machine; for details see Chapter 11 in [ilach01b].

Composition denotes a *"has-a"* relationship between classes, as in Class *Force* **has-a** (type of) Class *Squad*. A composition relationship exists when a class contains data members that are themselves class objects. Composition thus makes it possible to create new classes by combining existing ones. Once a class has been defined, the program can then define an instance of the class, called the class object.

EINSTein's classes structure includes public functions for:

- *Agent*
- *Battlefield*
- *Force*
- *Goal*
- *Squad*
- *Path*
- *Terrain*
- *Weapons*

An important benefit of EINSTein's OO code structure is the ability to generate a stand-alone *dynamic link library* (DLL) that includes only EINSTein's core engine. DLLs may be distributed to other researchers/developers, who can then essentially "program" EINSTein using their favorite interpretive language (Python, Perl, Tcl/Tk, etc.). This also frees users to develop their own, highly tailored, graphical user interface on alternative CPU platforms (Unix, Window, MacOS X, etc.).

5.1.3 *Program Flow*

A typical sequence of programming steps during an interactive run consists of multiple loops through the following basic steps:

1. *Initialize battlefield and agent distribution parameters*
2. *Initialize time-step counter*
3. *Adjudicate combat*
4. *Refresh battlefield graphics display*
5. *Find context-dependent personality weight vector for each red and blue agent*
6. *Compute local penalty for each of the possible moves that each red and blue agent may make from its current position*
7. *Move agents to their newly selected position (some may choose to remain at their current position)*
8. *Refresh graphics display and loop through adapt/compute-penalty/move steps*

The most important parts of this skeletal structure are contained in steps 5, 6, and 7; i.e., the parts dealing with the adjudication of combat, the adaptation of personality weights, and the decision-making process that each agent goes through in order to select its next move. Before describing the details of what each of these steps involves, we must first discuss how each agent partitions its local information.

5.2 Combat Engine

"He changes his methods and alters his plans so that people have no knowledge of what he is doing. He alters his camp-sites and marches by devious routes, and thus makes it impossible for others to anticipate his purpose.... Weigh the situation, then move."

—Sun Tzu, *The Art of War*

5.2.1 *Agents*

The basic element of EINSTein is an *agent*, which loosely represents a primitive combat unit (infantryman, tank, transport vehicle, etc.) that is equipped with the following characteristics:

- *Doctrine:* a default local-rule set specifying how to act in a generic environment
- *Mission:* goals directing behavior
- *Situational Awareness:* sensors generating an internal map of environment
- *Adaptability:* an internal mechanism to alter behavior and/or rules

Each agent exists in one of three states: *alive*, *injured*, or *killed* (later we will introduce continuous health values). Injured agents can (but are not required to) have different personalities and offensive/defensive characteristics from when they were alive. For example, the user can specify that injured agents are able to move half as far, and shoot half as accurately, as their "alive" counterparts. Up to ten distinct groups (or "squads") of personalities, of varying sizes, can be defined. The user can also how agents from one squad react to agents from other squads.

Each agent has associated with it a set of *ranges* (such as sensor range, fire range, and communications range; see below), within which it senses and assimilates simple forms of local information, and a *personality*, which determines the general manner in which it responds to its environment. A global rule set determines combat attrition, reconstitution and (in future versions) reinforcement. EINSTein also contains both local and global commanders, each with their own command radii, and obeying an evolving *command and control* (C^2) hierarchy of rules.

All decision-making rules, on all information-processing levels ranging from the lowest-level (consisting of individual combat agents) to local commanders to global commanders (to the user of the program; i.e., the *supreme* commander), consistently adhere to the same basic template: each agent senses and makes decisions based upon local information that is interpreted according to an agent's local set of values and contexts (see figure 5.1).

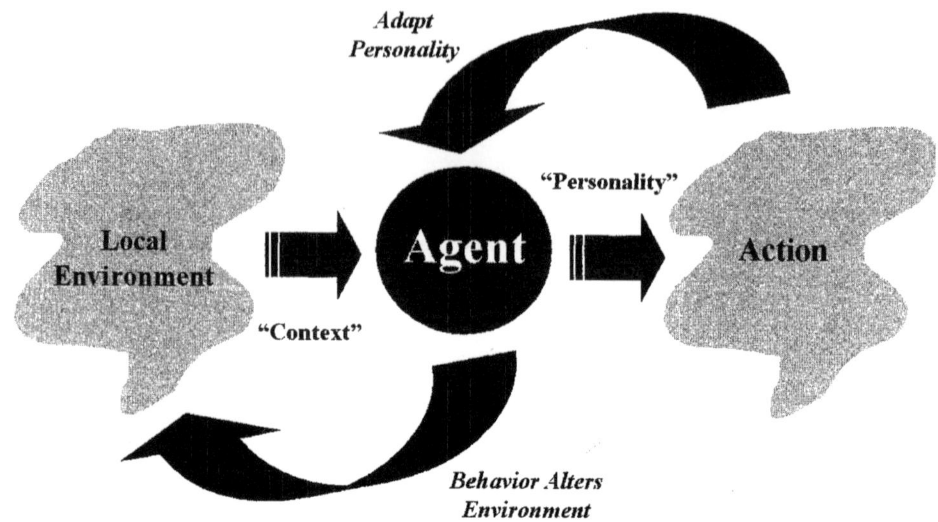

Fig. 5.1 Schematic of an agent situated in a general environment in EINSTein.

EINSTein is local because each agent senses, reacts, and adapts only to information existing within a prescribed finite sensor range. It is decentralized because there is no master *oracle* dictating the actions of each and every agent. Instead, each agent senses, assimilates, and reacts to all information individually and without guidance. It is nonlinear because of the nonlinear nature of the local decision-making process that each agent uses to choose a move. It is adaptive because each agent adaptively changes its default ("doctrinal") rules according to its local environment at each time step. There is thus a continual dynamical feedback between the local and global levels. The manner in which its rules are changed proceeds according to each agent's personality, or its intrinsic value system. Each of these points is discussed in more detail below.

EINSTein's basic approach is obviously very similar to cellular automata (CA)* but augments the conventional CA framework in two ways: (1) individual units can move through the lattice (recall that in CA, what moves is the information, not the site), and (2) evolution proceeds not according to a fixed set of rules, but to a set of rules that adaptively evolves over time. When the appropriate internal flags are set to make use of a hierarchical command and control structure, EINSTein differs from conventional CA models in one additional way: individual states of cells (or combatants) do not just respond to local information, but are capable of assimilating nonlocal information (via a notional control structure) and command hierarchy. In future versions, global rule (i.e., command) strategies will evolve in time (say, via a genetic algorithm). In this case, orders pumped down echelon will

*Cellular automata are discussed in Chapter 2 (see pages 137-148).

be based on evolved strategies played out on possibly imprecise mental maps of local and/or global commanders. Thus, EINSTein is an ideal test-bed in which to explore such questions as *"What is the tactical and/or strategic impact of information?"*

5.2.2 *Battlefield*

The putative combat battlefield is represented by a two-dimensional lattice of discrete sites (see figure 5.2). Each site of the lattice may be occupied by one of two kinds of agents: *red* or *blue.**

The initial state consists of user-specified formations of red and blue agents positioned anywhere within the battlefield. Formations may include squad-specific bounding rectangles or may be completely random. Red and blue flags are also typically (but not always) positioned in diagonally opposite corners. A typical goal, for both red and blue agents, is to reach the enemy's flag.

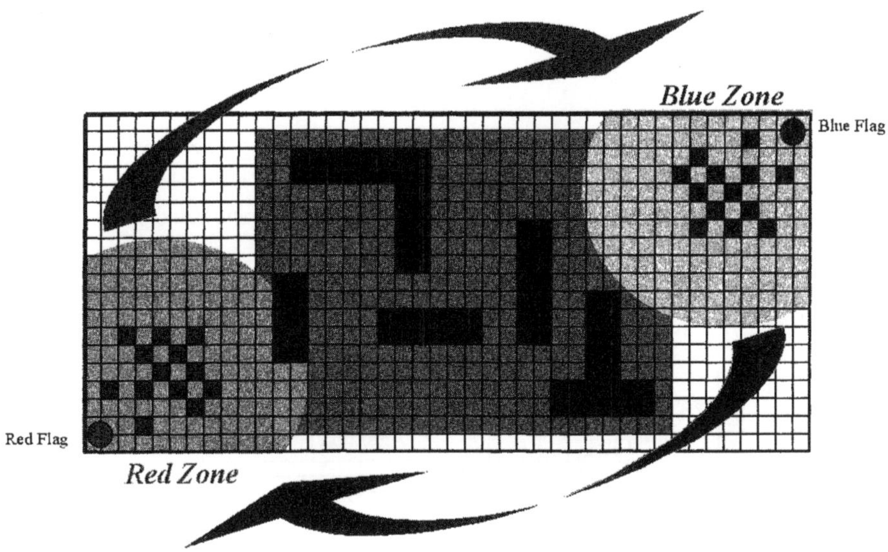

Fig. 5.2 Putative two-dimensional combat battlefield in EINSTein.

EINSTein includes an option to add notional terrain elements. Terrain can be either passable or impassable. If passable, the user can also tune an agent's behavior to a particular terrain type. For example, if an agent is positioned within "heavy brush," its movement range and visibility (from other nearby agents) may be curtailed in a specified way. Moreover, users also have the option of having EINSTein

*Note that while EINSTein nominally accommodates only two kinds of forces (red and blue), a notional *white* force can also be defined by exploiting the features of EINSTein's multi-squad option.

precompute optimal paths that agents will attempt to follow for scenarios that contain complicated terrain elements. Waypoints and paths may also be defined. These additional battlefield features are described in greater depth in section 5.7 (page 342).

5.2.3 *Agent Sensor Parameters*

Each agent can detect, and react to, information that is local to its immediate position. Figure 5.3 shows a schematic of the various kinds of user-specified ranges that surround each agent:

- *Attention range* $(= r_A)$
- *Combat (or threshold) range* $(= r_T)$
- *Communications range* $(= r_C)$
- *Fire range* $(= r_F)$
- *Movement range* $(= r_M)$
- *Sensor range* $(= r_S)$

Note that while the figure appears with the various ranges ordered according to $r_M \leq r_T \leq r_A \leq r_F \leq r_S \leq r_C$, the user is free to choose any relative ordering of magnitudes. The sole exception to this rule is that r_F is constrained to be less than or equal to r_S.

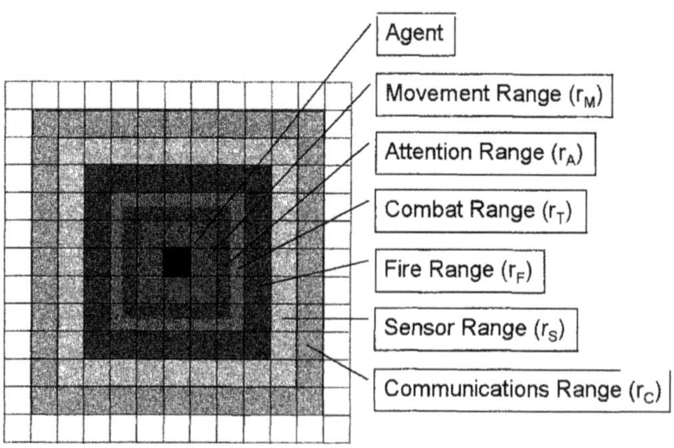

Fig. 5.3 Schematic illustrating the various kinds of sensor ranges that surround each agent; see text for details.

In all cases, distances are measured using either a *cookie-cutter* or *Euclidean* metric (the method used is at the discretion of the user). The distance between agents A and B, $d(A, B)$, is computed according to:

$$\begin{cases} d_{\text{Cookie-Cutter}}(A,B) = \text{maximum}\{x_B - x_A, y_B - y_A\}, \\ d_{\text{Euclidean}}(A,B) = \sqrt{(x_B - x_A)^2 + (y_B - y_A)^2}. \end{cases} \tag{5.1}$$

5.2.3.1 *Attention Range*

The *attention range* ($= r_A$), shown as the gray box in figure 5.3, defines the maximum area surrounding (and centered on) the yellow-colored agent, within which the agent will react to (i.e. give attention to) other agents in its neighborhood. Note that—in keeping with the overall design goal of achieving a balance between simplicity and computational speed—an agent's attention range defines a boxed area around the agent and not a circle of radius r_A.

5.2.3.2 *Combat Range*

The threshold range ($= r_T$) defines a boxed area surrounding an agent with respect to which that agent computes the numbers of friendly and enemy agents that play a role in determining what move to make on a given time step. It is also used in determining whether an agent will engage in combat with nearby enemy agents.

5.2.3.3 *Communications Range*

The communications range ($= r_C$) defines a boxed area surrounding an agent such that any friendly agent within a range r_C of that centrally located agent communicates the information content of its local sensor field back to that agent. How the centrally located agent uses that information in adjudicating its moves is discussed in a later section.

5.2.3.4 *Fire Range*

The fire range ($= r_F$) defines the boxed area surrounding an agent within which the agent can engage enemy agents in combat. Any enemy agent that is closer to a given agent than the given agent's fire range may be fired upon by the given agent.

5.2.3.5 *Movement Range*

The movement range ($= r_M$) defines a boxed area surrounding an agent that defines the region of the lattice from which the agent can select a move on a given time step. Movement ranges are typically between 1 and 4, but the maximal value for r_M is limited only by available memory. A movement range *zero* can be used to represent an agent that is permanently attached to a specific site.

5.2.3.6 *Sensor Range*

The sensor range ($= r_S$) defines the maximum range at which the agent can sense other agents in its neighborhood. Unless the attention range option is toggled ON (see above), an agent detects and reacts to all other agents (and both friendly and enemy flags) that are within a range r_S of its current position.

5.2.4 *Agent Personalities*

At the heart of the local decision-making process of every agent—be it an individual combatant, a local or global commander—lies the agent's *personality*. An agent's personality represents its internal value system as applied to the set of all possible relevant features of its environment that the agent must use to decide upon a move or strategy. It is nominally defined by a six-component *personality weight vector*:

$$\vec{\omega} = (\omega_1, \omega_2, \ldots, \omega_6), \tag{5.2}$$

where $-1 \leq \omega_i \leq +1$ and $\Sigma_i |\omega_i| = 1$. The components of $\vec{\omega}$ specify how an individual agent responds to specific kinds of local information within its sensor range.

The personality weight vector may be health dependent. That is, $\vec{\omega}_{alive}$ need not, in general, be equal to $\vec{\omega}_{injured}$. The components of $\vec{\omega}$ can also be *negative*, in which case they signify a propensity for moving away from, rather than toward, a given entity.

The default personality rule structure is defined as follows. Since there are two kinds of agents (*red* and *blue*), and each agent can exist in one of two states (*alive* and *injured*), each agent can respond to effectively four different kinds of information appearing within its sensor range r_S: (1) the number of alive friendly (i.e., like-colored) agents; (2) the number of alive enemy (i.e., different colored) agents; (3) the number of injured friendly agents; and (4) the number of injured enemy agents. Additionally, each agent can respond to how far it is from both its own (like-colored) flag and its enemy's flag. The ith component of $\vec{\omega}$ represents the relative weight afforded to moving closer to (or farther away from, if the component is negative) the ith type of information.

A personality is defined by assigning a weight to each of the six kinds of information. For example, one agent might give all its attention to like-colored agents, and effectively ignore the enemy: $\vec{\omega} = (1/2, 0, 1/2, 0, 0, 0)$. An example of a fairly aggressive personality is one whose weight vector is given by $\vec{\omega} = (1/20, 5/20, 0, 9/20, 0, 5/20)$. Such a personality is five times more "interested" in moving toward alive enemies than it is in moving toward alive friends (effectively ignoring injured friends altogether), and is more interested in moving toward injured enemies than it is even in advancing toward the enemy flag. An agent that has a personality defined by entirely *negative* weights—say, $\vec{\omega} = (-1/6, -1/6, -1/6, -1/6, -1/6, -1/6)$—wants to move away from, rather than toward, every other agent and both flags; i.e. it wants to avoid action of any kind.

Table 5.1 provides a small sampling of the many different kinds of personalities that may be defined using these six components. Considerably more complicated personalities—that are able to respond to a far greater range of environmental stimuli—may be defined by assigning nonzero values to additional measures: maintaining formation with squad mates, obey and and/or staying close to a local commander, and following a user-defined path, among others. Some of these will be discussed in the next section (see table 5.2); others will be introduced and discussed in the next chapter.

ω_1	ω_2	ω_3	ω_4	ω_5	ω_6	**Description**
1/2	0	1/2	0	0	0	ignore enemy and both flags
1/4	-1/4	1/4	-1/4	0	0	stay near friends; run away from enemies
0	1/2	0	1/2	0	0	sense and react only to enemy agents
0	0	0	0	1	0	stay near own (i.e., friendly) flag
0	0	0	0	0	1	move toward enemy flag, exclusively
1/3	-1/3	0	1/3	0	0	stay near alive friends; move away from alive enemies but toward injured enmies
1/10	0	0	9/10	0	0	stay near alive friends; ignore alive enemies; move strongly to injured enemies
1/6	1/6	1/6	1/6	1/6	1/6	give equal weight to all agents and flags
-1/4	-1/4	-1/4	-1/4	0	0	move away from all agents

Table 5.1 Sample personalities constructed using the first six components of an agent's personality weight vector.

5.2.5 *Agent Action Selection*

> *"Simple action consistently carried out will be the most certain way to reach the goal.."*
>
> —Helmuth von Moltke, *Prussian field marshall* (1800-1891)

5.2.5.1 *General Logic*

Recall, from our earlier discussion of how agents are represented in EINSTein (see figure 5.1), that the manner in which an agent chooses a specific action to take at time t is a function of the local environmental context that it is in at that time, and depends on the agent's personality (as prescribed by its personality weight vector).

Consider some basic questions that each agent must address before deciding on what specific action to take:

- *What do I see?* Answers include all possible environmental and sensory information that constitutes its local context (other agents, flags, local battle intensity, territorial possession, enemy's offensive/defensive strength, etc.) It may also include information that is communicated to it by other agents.
- *What do I act on?* Sometimes it is best to act on everything that is within an agent's sensor-field view, sometimes only a selected subset of that view.

There are two classes on information that an agent can act on:

- *Static information,* which represents discrete "snapshots" of sensed data, such as the positions of other agents, waypoints, battlefield position, proximity to flag, etc., and
- *Dynamic information,* which represents actions that are either sensed by, or performed upon, the agent, such as the number of times an agent was fired upon during last iteration step, an estimate of how dynamically "active" its local environment was on the last time step, etc.

Different parts of an agent's local environment may be more or less relevant to that agent for selecting its move in different contexts. If the agent has no support and is surrounded by enemy agents, the agent may choose to ignore all other aspects of its environment but the size of the enemy force; if the agent is in the open territory, and is still far from its goal, it may choose to include more features of its environment in its decision.

- *What do I value?* Depending on their individual value systems (i.e. their personalities), agents may give more, or less, weight to surviving, to being surrounded by a threshold number of friends, to defending their own flag (or other area), to take the enemy's flag. Agents may also distinguish between (1) *short-term goals,* which are incorporated into a local penalty function, and (2) *long-term goals,* which are incorporated into a multi-objective mission fitness function that measures the success of the overall mission.
- *Where do I want to be?* Answer include being near own flag in order to defend the area around it, near the enemy flag to attack, near closest friendly territory (as measured by territorial possession map), fight near center of field, etc.
- *Should I act alone or coordinate my actions with other agents?* While all agents are, fundamentally, autonomous entities that always act alone, they may, in the proper contexts, decide to coordinate sensor information and/or certain parts of their action-selection logic with other nearby friendly agents.

5.2.5.2 *Environmental Context*

An agent's context is an important primitive element of EINSTein's core design. It represents an agent-centric, filtered view of its immediate environment. An agent's "intelligence" is determined by how successfully an agent is able to map the space of all possible contexts to actions. A partial listing of local contexts follows:

- *Combat Intensity:* How intense is the level of combat in the agent's local environment?

- *Enemy Fire:* How many times has the agent (and nearby friends) been shot an iteration step ago? ...within two iteration steps ago?...
- *Enemy Threat:* How many enemy agents are there within whose weapon range the given agent is currently in?
- *Heath:* Is the agent in its default state, has it been shot (once, twice,...)? What is the health of nearby friends? ...of nearby squad-mates?
- *Position:* Is the agent in the open, near impassable terrain, passable terrain, near an edge of the battlefield? Are other agents positioned to the front, flank or rear of the closest battle-front?
- *Proximity to other agents:* How close are an agent's friends? Squad-mates? What is the distance to an agent's nearest friend? Nearest enemy?
- *Surrounding Force Strengths:* What is the number of friendly and enemy agents within sensor range? Within weapon range?

What an agent chooses to do, during each move-phase of a run, is a function of that agent's evolving context. A trivial agent may, for example, choose to disregard its local conditions and blindly advance toward the enemy flag. The consequences of such an action, however, while potentially interesting, will hardly be realistic. In general, agents must intelligently sift through the space of all possible environmental features, identify which features are relevant in what context, and weigh all possible moves that are consistent with those contexts, according to their internal "personality" value-system.

5.2.5.3 *Engineering Agents vs. Engineering Missions*

From a user's perspective, there is an obvious trade-off that must be made between, on the one hand, having a small enough set of primitive rules that permits desired behaviors to be tuned "by hand" (but which may not result in a desired level of realism), and, on the other hand, having a much richer set of rules that can be used to define realistic scenarios and mission objectives, but which, because of its shear size and/or complexity, is difficult (or impossible) to use without having some additional tools made available to help search for desired behaviors.

In the first case, the focus is on exploring collective behaviors: one defines specific kinds of agents, with known "personalities," and then uses EINSTein to explore the dynamical consequences of their collective interactions; i.e. *engineering agents.* In the second case, the focus is on exploring the space of possible agents: one starts from a given scenario or mission objective and uses a heuristic tool (such as a genetic algorithm*) to search for agents that yield the desired behavior (where agents are now regarded as full-blown intelligent entities that map local contexts to specific actions); i.e. *engineering missions.*

While the second focus obviously applies to any set of rules, regardless of how "simple" or "complex" that set of rules is, it can be meaningfully applied only

*See chapter 7, **Breeding Agents**, that begins on page 501.

when the rule set is sufficiently rich enough to support the emergence of the kind of behaviors the researcher is seeking.

A helpful analogy is the set of microscopic collision rules used by two-dimensional cellular automata models of fluid flow (i.e. lattice gas models): there is a well-defined minimal set of rules for which the emergent macroscopic behavior reproduces is consistent with what is predicted by the incompressible Navier-Stokes equations [Hass88].

Since EINSTein is designed as a multi-purpose tool, "sufficiently rich enough" in this case means that EINSTein's primitive rule base must be rich enough to support a wide spectrum of possible research questions, ranging from taking simple excursions away from Lanchester-equation-like descriptions of non-intelligent, stationary agents to exploring semi-realistic simulations of real-world engagements.

5.2.5.4 *Fundamental Axioms of EINSTein's Action Selection Logic*

Earlier, we defined the global state of the combat model at (discrete) time t, $\Sigma(t)$, as a formal "snapshot" of the system at t that records the identity and locations of all objects, agents, and their internal states. Of course, individual agents typically have access only to some subset of the information contained in $\Sigma(t)$.

Define the local state, as perceived by an agent $\mathcal{A}$, $\Sigma_{\mathcal{A}}(t) \subseteq \Sigma(t)$, to be the set of all features of $\mathcal{A}$'s local environment that are filtered by $\mathcal{A}$; i.e., it is the set of features that are either sensed directly by, or communicated to, $\mathcal{A}$.

The two fundamental axioms of EINSTein's action selection logic are then:

1. *All agent actions derive from time varying assessments of the relative value among features* $f \in \Sigma_{\mathcal{A}}(t)$.

(1) The local state is defined by the matrix of $\mathcal{A}$'s penalty function values: $(Z_{\mathcal{A}})_{ij}$, evaluated for all sites within a movement range, r_m, of $\mathcal{A}$ (where $i = x_{\mathcal{A}} - r_m, ..., x_{\mathcal{A}} + r_m, j = y_{\mathcal{A}} - r_m, ..., y_{\mathcal{A}} + r_m$, and $\mathcal{A}$ is at the site $\vec{x}_{\mathcal{A}} = (x_{\mathcal{A}}, y_{\mathcal{A}})$; see figure 5.4).

Assessments are functions of personality, and consist, in part, of making distinctions between what available features are, and are not, relevant to A for selecting an appropriate set of actions in a given context. While one set of features might be important to consider in one context, a different set of features might be important for another. No agent can credibly mimic being "intelligent" unless it is able to tailor its actions to specific needs, and adapt to changing contexts. Agents must therefore have some way of identifying which features are most important in a given context, and to deduce which actions are appropriate for the given features.

In EINSTein, the user specifies the features that are visible to each agent, and agents select their action, via the penalty function, $Z_{\mathcal{A}}$, by mapping a given context (i.e., a given vector of feature values visible to it) to motivations for moving toward (or away from) nearby sites. As the value of $Z_{\mathcal{A}}$, at a given site, $\vec{x}$, increases, $\mathcal{A}$'s

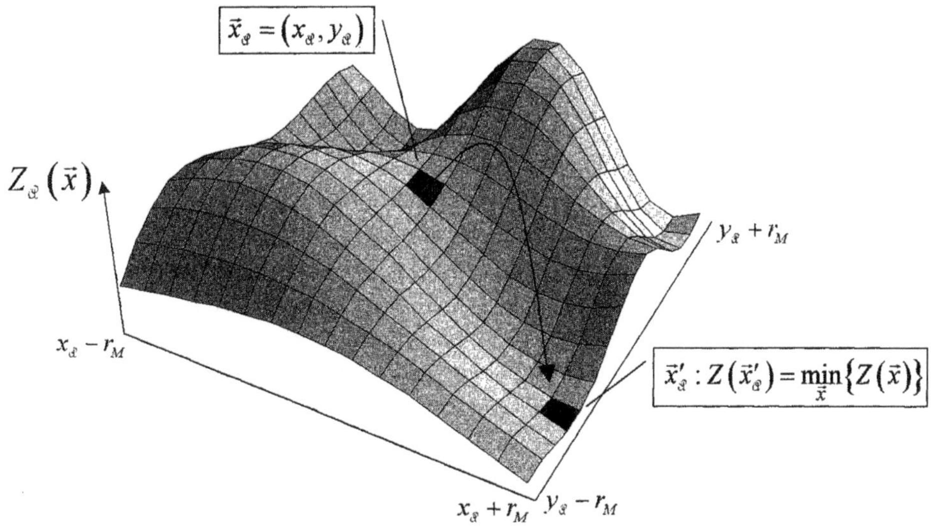

Fig. 5.4 Schematic illustration of EINSTein's action selection.

desire to move to $\vec{x}$ decreases, relative to other sites. As the value of $Z_{\mathcal{A}}$ decreases, $\mathcal{A}$'s desire to move increases. The site at which $Z_{\mathcal{A}}$ attains its minimum value ($\vec{x}'_{\mathcal{A}}$) is the site at which $\mathcal{A}$ expects to best satisfy its (personality-weight specified) objectives.*

Thus, fundamentally, $Z_{\mathcal{A}}$'s *form* implicitly embodies the filters by which $\mathcal{A}$ "sees" the world, and the matrix of $Z_{\mathcal{A}}$'s *values*, evaluated over the space of all possible moves, explicitly determines how A "reacts" to its world.

From $\mathcal{A}$'s point of view, all behavior ultimately reduces to a calculus of feature values: $\mathcal{A}$'s contexts are defined by features (i.e., by $\mathcal{A}$'s perception of the local state), $\mathcal{A}$ identifies the features that are important in its current context (which vary according to an agent's "personality"), and $\mathcal{A}$ selects an action that essentially represents $\mathcal{A}$'s "best guess" (as defined by $Z_{\mathcal{A}}$) as to which move leads to a local state in which the values of the perceived features come closest to what $\mathcal{A}$ "wants" them to be.

If $\mathcal{A}$ were the only agent occupying the battlefield, and the environment was unchanging, $\mathcal{A}$ would quickly find the one site (or sites) that best satisfies its needs and stop there. What makes the model interesting, of course, is the presence of multiple agents, all mutually interacting within a changing environment. Each agent's landscape of penalty function values is thus continuously deformed by the actions of other agents. Just as one agent moves closer to "solving" its local problem,

*The fact that $\mathcal{A}$ seeks to *minimize*, rather than maximize, the value of its penalty function is an artifact of the author's training as a physicist. In physics, one typically solves for the minimal energy states of a system.

other agents move farther away from solving theirs, and all agents face the specter of needing to tune their solutions to constantly shifting problems.

5.2.5.5 *Penalty Function*

An agent's personality weight vector is used to rank each possible move according to a *penalty function, Z*. The penalty function effectively measures the total distance that the agent will be from other agents (which includes both friendly and enemy agents) and from its own and enemy flags, each weighted according to the appropriate component of $\vec{\omega}$. An agent moves to the position that incurs the least penalty; i.e., an agent's move is the one that best satisfies it's personality-driven desire to "move closer to" or "farther away from" other agent's in given states and either of the two flags (see figure 5.5).

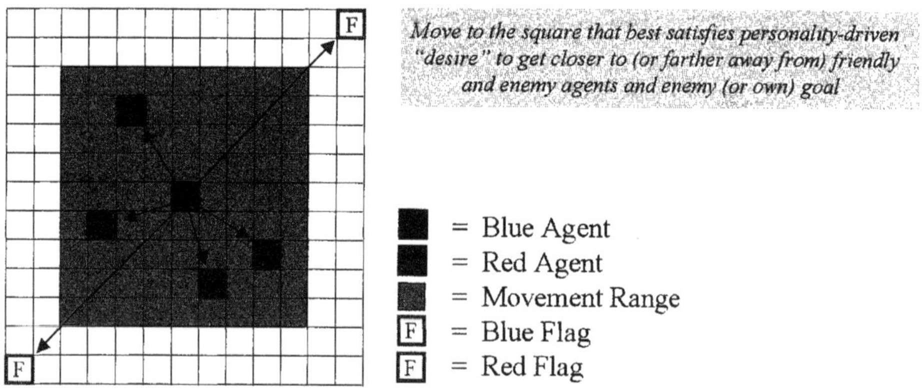

Fig. 5.5 Schematic of an agent's default move selection logic. In practice, an agent is able to respond (and adapt) to many more battlefield characteristics than shown here; see text for details.

The general form of the penalty function is given by:

$$\begin{aligned} z(B_{xy}) &= \frac{1}{\sqrt{2r_{F,s}}}\left[\frac{\omega_{AF}}{N_{AF}}\sum_{i\in AF}^{N_{AF}} D_{i,B_{xy}} + \frac{\omega_{AE}}{N_{AE}}\sum_{j\in AE}^{N_{AE}} D_{j,B_{xy}}\right] \\ &+ \frac{1}{\sqrt{2r_{E,s}}}\left[+\frac{\omega_{IF}}{N_{IF}}\sum_{k\in IF}^{N_{IF}} D_{k,B_{xy}} + \frac{\omega_{IE}}{N_{IE}}\sum_{l\in IE}^{N_{IE}} D_{l,B_{xy}}\right] \\ &+ \omega_{FF}\frac{D^{new}_{FF,B_{xy}}}{D^{old}_{FF,B_{xy}}} + \omega_{EF}\frac{D^{new}_{EF,B_{xy}}}{D^{old}_{EF,B_{xy}}}, \end{aligned} \tag{5.3}$$

where B_{xy} is the $(x,y)_{\text{th}}$ coordinate of battlefield B; AF, IF, AE and IE represent, respectively, the sets of alive friends, injured friends, alive enemies and injured enemies within the given agent's sensor range, r_S; ω_i are the components of the personality weight vector; $1/\sqrt{2r_{F,s}}$and $/\sqrt{2r_{E,s}}$ are the friendly and enemy scale factors, respectively; N_X is the total number of elements of type X within the given agent's sensor range (for example, N_{AF} number of alive friends); $D_{A,B}$ is the distance between elements A and B; FF and EF denote the friendly and enemy flags, respectively; and $D^{new}_{x,y}$and $D^{old}_{x,y}$ represent distances computed using the given agent's new (i.e., candidate move) position and old (i.e., current) position, respectively.

A penalty is computed for each possible move; that is, for each of the N possible sites to which an agent can "step" in one time step: $Z_1(B_{x,y})$, $Z_2(B_{x-1,y})$, $Z_3(B_{x+1,y})$..., $Z_N(B_{x+n,y+n})$. If the movement range $r_m = 1$, the number of possible moves is $N = 9$; if $r_m = 2$, $N = 25$. The actual move is the one that incurs the least penalty. If there is a set of moves (consisting of more than one possible move) all of whose penalties are within $\varepsilon_{Penalty}$ of the minimal penalty, an agent randomly selects the actual move from among the candidate moves making up that set. Users can also define paths near which agents must try to stay while manoeuvring toward their ultimate goal.

The penalty function shown above includes only a few relative-proximity-based weights. In practice, the penalty function is more complicated, and incorporates more terms, though its basic form is the same. Additional terms can include (see table 5.2):

- *Battlefield Boundary weight* ($= \omega_{BB}$)
- *Direction Weight* ($= \omega_{Direction}$)
- *Area Weight* ($= \omega_{Area}$)
- *Formation Weight* ($= \omega_{squad}$)
- *Inter-Squad Connectivity Weight* ($= \omega^{S}_{ij}$)
- *Intra-Squad Connectivity Weight* ($= \omega^{SS'}_{ij}$)
- *Local Command Weight* ($= \omega_{LC}$)
- *Local Command Obey Weight* ($= \omega_{Obey\ LC}$)
- *Terrain Weight* ($= \omega_{Terrain}$)

5.2.5.6 *Battlefield Boundary Weight*

ω_{BB} is the relative weight for moving toward (or away from) the boundary of battlefield. Some agents may want to "hug" the boundary to stay away from close combat in the interior, so that $\omega_{BB} > 0$. Other agents may want maneuver clear of the boundary in order to maximize readiness for combat within the interior of the battlefield; in this case $\omega_{BB} < 0$.

5.2.5.7 *Area Weight*

ω_{Area} is the relative weight for moving toward (or away from) a squad-specific fixed area A.

Weight	Meaning $\longrightarrow$ Relative Weight for
ω_{AF} $(=\omega_1)$	...moving towards/away-from alive friendly agents
ω_{IF} $(=\omega_2)$	...moving towards/away-from injured friendly agents
ω_{AE} $(=\omega_3)$	...moving towards/away-from alive enemy agents
ω_{IE} $(=\omega_4)$	...moving towards/away-from injured enemy agents
ω_{FF} $(=\omega_5)$	...moving towards/away-from friendly flag
ω_{EF} $(=\omega_6)$	...moving towards/away-from enemy flag
ω_{BB}	...moving towards/away-from the battlefield boundary
ω_{area}	...staying near some (squad-specific) area
ω_{squad}	...maintaining formation with own squad-mates
$\omega_{fire-team}$	...maintaining formation with own fireteam-mates
ω_{Comm}	..using information that is communicated to agent by friends
S_{ij}	... how agents from squad S_i react to squad S_j
$(SE)_{ij}$	... how agents from squad S_i react to enemy squad E_j
ω_{LC}	...moving towards/away-from local commander
ω_{obeyLC}	...obeying orders issued by local commander
$\omega_{terrain}$	...moving towards/away-from terrain elements
$\omega_{enemy-fire}$	...moving towards/away-from enemies that have fired on agent

Table 5.2 A Partial list of EINSTein's pritimive weight set; see text.

- If an agent is located within A and $\omega_{Area} > 0$, then ω_{Area} is temporarily set equal to zero;
- If an agent is outside A, the agent will want to move toward (or away from) the center of A with weight ω_{Area}.

If $\omega_{Area} < 0$, the agent always wants to move away from the center of ω_{Area}. By default, A is set equal to the bounding rectangle for squad S_1's initial spatial disposition, but may be repositioned to any desired battlefield location by the user at any time.

5.2.5.8 *Formation Weight*

ω_{Squad} is the relative weight relative weight that individual agents use to maintain formation with their own squad-mates. Currently, formation-dynamics are defined in terms of local *flocking*:

- If the distance between an agent and the center-of-mass of nearby (squad-mate) agents is less than R_{min}, then the agent will want to move away from the center-of-mass position with weight ω_{Squad}.
- If the distance between an agent and the center-of-mass of nearby (squad-mate) agents is greater than $R_{\max}$, then the agent will want to move toward the center-of-mass position with weight ω_{Squad}.

- If the distance between an agent X and the center-of-mass of nearby (squad-mate) agents, $d \geq R_{\min}$ **AND** $d \leq R_{\max}$ then X is assumed to be "in formation."

Note that the local center-of-mass position toward (or away from) which a given agent X will make its move is by default calculated using the positions of agents within X's sensor range. If communications are ON, the local center-of-mass position is calculated using the positions of agents within X's communication range. In both cases, all agent positions are weighed equally (i.e. no adjustment is made for communications weight).

5.2.5.9 *Inter-Squad Connectivity Weight*

The inter-squad connectivity weight ω_{ij}^S is the relative weight with which squad S_i reacts to S_j. It is a real number between -1 and +1. By default, $\omega_{ij}^S = 1$ for all i and j. If $\omega_{ij}^S = 0$ for a given pair (i, j), that means that all agents from squad S_i effectively ignore all agents from squad S_j. If $\omega_{ij}^S = 1/2$, agents from squad S_i react to agents from squad S_j by first premultiplying S_i's default personality weights ω_1 (for alive friend) and ω_3 (for injured friend) by $1/2$. Thus, ω_{ij}^S is essentially a squad-specific premultiplier factor that appears in the penalty calculation for agents from squad S_i. Intuitively, ω_{ij}^S defines how much weight an agent from S_i gives an agent from S_j relative to S_i's default personality weight vector. See figure 5.6.

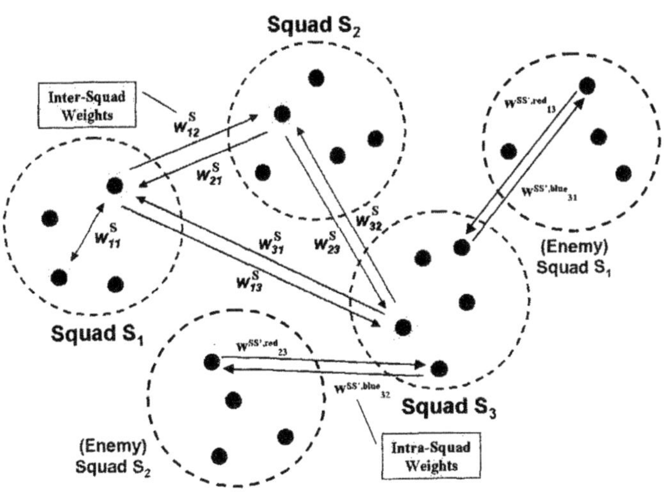

Fig. 5.6 Schematic illustration of *inter-squad* and *intra-squad* connectivity weights

Note ω_{ij}^S is not necessarily equal to ω_{ji}^S, as agents from S_j may react differently to agents from S_i than agents from S_i to S_j

5.2.5.10 *Intra-Squad Connectivity Weight*

The intra-squad connectivity weight $\omega_{ij}^{SS'}$ generalizes the personality weight vector to include enemy squads. It is the relative weight with which an agent from friendly squad S_i "reacts to" an agent from enemy squad S'_j. It is a real number between -1 and $+1$. By default, $\omega_{ij}^{SS'} = 1$ for all i and j. If $\omega_{ij}^{SS'} = 0$ for a given pair (i, j), that means that all agents from red squad S_i effectively ignore all enemy agents from blue squad S'_j. Intermediate values of $\omega_{ij}^{SS'}$ define intermediate squad-specific weights with which friendly agents from a given squad react to enemy agents from a specific enemy squad. See figure 5.6.

5.2.5.11 *Local Command Weight*

ω_{LC} is relative weight for moving toward (or away from) an agent's local commander (for scenarios that include agents that are subordinate to a local commander).*

5.2.5.12 *Local Command Obey Weight*

$\omega_{Obey\ LC}$ is relative weight for obeying orders issued by an agent's local commander (for scenarios that include agents that are subordinate to a local commander).*

5.2.5.13 *Terrain Weight*

$\omega_{Terrain}$ is the relative weight for moving toward (or away from) nearby terrain blocks. Unlike other auxiliary weights, this weight has an additional "near terrain" flag ($= f_{NT} \in \{0, 1\}$) associated with it, which determines how actual terrain elements will be used in the penalty assessment used as part of an agent's move decision. If $f_{NT} = 0$, then all nearby terrain blocks are used, site by site, to determine the local penalty function; if $f_{NT} = 1$, then the local neighborhood is first scanned for the battlefield block that contains the nearest terrain element, and the penalty function is then calculated using $\omega_{Terrain}$ with respect to the position of that nearest terrain element.

5.2.5.14 *Example*

Figure 5.7 shows a portion of the notional battlefield surrounding a red agent positioned at the center. The range of possible move options (assuming that the movement range $r_m = 1$) is shaded gray in the figure. There are three red agents (a,b and c at distances D_a, D_b and D_c from the agent in the center, respectively) and two blue agents (A and B, at distances D_A and D_B, respectively) within the given agent's sensor range. We assume that $r_{F,s} = r_{E,s} = r_s$.

The agent's move is determined by calculating the penalty $z(B_{xy})$ that would be incurred by moving to each of the nine nearest neighboring sites within the gray

*See section 5.8, **Command and Control**, on page 360.

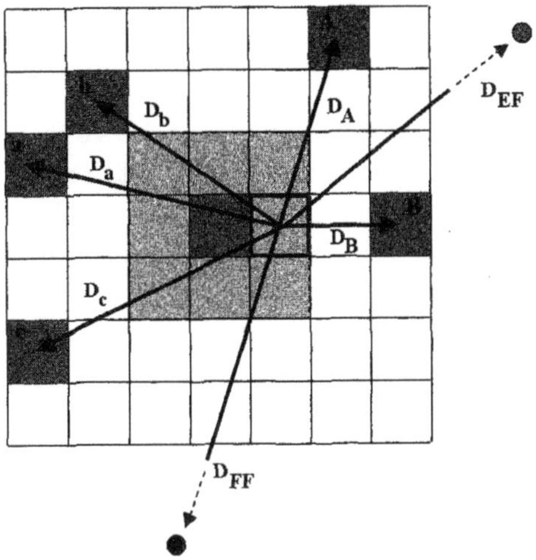

Fig. 5.7 Sample configuration for calculating penalty function defined in equation 5.4.

region (including staying at the center site), and selecting the site that incurs the least penalty. The penalty is given explicitly by:

$$z(B_{xy}) = \frac{\omega_F}{3\sqrt{2r_s}}(D_a + D_b + D_c) + \frac{\omega_E}{3\sqrt{2r_s}}(D_A + D_B) \qquad (5.4)$$

$$+ \omega_{FF}\frac{D_{FF}}{D_{0,FF}} + \omega_{EF}\frac{D_{EF}}{D_{0,EF}}. \qquad (5.5)$$

While the application of EINSTein's penalty function is straightforward, even in more complicated cases where agents rely on multiple environmental features to adjudicate their moves, *previsualizing* the consequences of specific weight vectors is not always easy. One can trivially predict that an agent with a large positive weight for moving toward alive friends will do precisely that, in the event that no enemy agents are nearby and/or all other personality weights are equal to zero. However, it is much more difficult to predict how an agent will react to different relative configurations of friends and enemies (not to mention other environmental contexts) in the more general case where a significant number of the weight vector components are nonzero. Remember that the weights specify *relative propensities, not specific actions.* Technical Appendix 2 (at the end of this chapter) introduces a graphical tool called a *movement map* as an aid to previsualizing an agent's candidate-move space. Examples in one and two dimensions are used to illustrate how movement maps may be used to develop an intuition about how primitive rules and feature-to-weight functions map onto behaviors.

5.2.6 *Move Decision Logic Flags*

5.2.6.1 *Sampling Order*

There are two ways in which candidate moves can be sampled during an EINSTein run. At the start of each run, a randomly ordered list of red and blue agents is first set up prior to the start of the actual dynamics loop. During all subsequent passes, agent moves are then determined either by (1) sequencing through the agents on this list in *fixed order*, or, for better realism, (2) in *random order*. The user can choose a fixed or random sampling order by setting a **move-sampling flag** at run-time (see EINSTein's *User's Guide* [Ilach99a]).

By default, each agent selects a move (to the site for which the penalty function, $Z_{Penalty}$, is minimum, as described above) at each time step of the simulation. While agents always have the option to remain at their current site, the decision to do so or not is made at each step. For some scenarios, however, it may be advantageous to prevent agents from deciding upon a move on each update of the battlefield. For example, restricting an agent's motion may provide the basis for more realistically modeling the relative scaling between weapon and movement ranges.

An agent's actual location during times for which it does not change its notional battlefield coordinates can in such cases be interpreted as representing fine-grained maneuvering that is not resolvable using the integer-values lattice grid. However, even when agents do not move during a given time step, combat among enemy agents is always adjudicated.

5.2.6.2 *Curtailment Flags*

There are two ways in which an agent's moves can be restricted in time: (1) *Making the likelihood of selecting a move a stochastic variable.* With this option, each agent $\mathcal{A}$ will, at each time t, calculate its penalty function to decide upon a move with a (*squad*- and *state*-specific) probability-of-move, $0 \leq P_{move} \leq 1$ the probability that $\mathcal{A}$ will not make a move at this time is therefore equal to $(1 - P_{move})$; and (2) *Allowing an agent to make a move only after a certain time has elapsed since its last move.* With this option, each agent adjudicates it first move at time $t = 1$ and every Δt time steps thereafter. This integer-valued time delay, Δt, is, like its P_{move} counterpart, squad- and state-specific.

5.2.7 *Meta-Rules*

> *"Take time to deliberate, but when the time for action has arrived, stop thinking and go in."*—Napoleon Bonaparte (1769 - 1821)

An agent's personality may be augmented by a set of μ-rules—hereafter called μ-rules—that tell it how to alter its default personality according to dynamic environmental contexts (see figure 5.8). A typical μ-rule consists of altering a few of the components of an agent's personality vector according to a set of associated local threshold constraints, measured with respect to a user-specified threshold range.

As discussed above, EINSTein has been designed to accommodate a personality-based local dynamics. This means that, despite changing local environments and conditions, each agent responds to what it "senses" round itself according to its own individual personality. The term "personality" here is of course used figuratively, as it only loosely refers to what is conventionally thought of as a human personality. However, it does accurately reflect the uniquely individual manner in which agents consistently assimilate and act upon information in their sensor fields. One way in which such a consistent, but thus far fixed, manner of responding to information can be augmented is to allow each agent's personality to adapt to changing contexts and/or evolve over time.

Conceptually, the idea is very simple. Each agent is equipped not only with a fixed default personality (as defined by its personality weight vector), but with a set of rules that tell it how to alter its default personality according to various environmental conditions. In other words, each agent is endowed with a meta-personality that tells it how to adapt its default personality. Figure 5.8 shows a schematic representation of this approach. Table 5.3 summarizes some of EINSTein's μ-rules.*

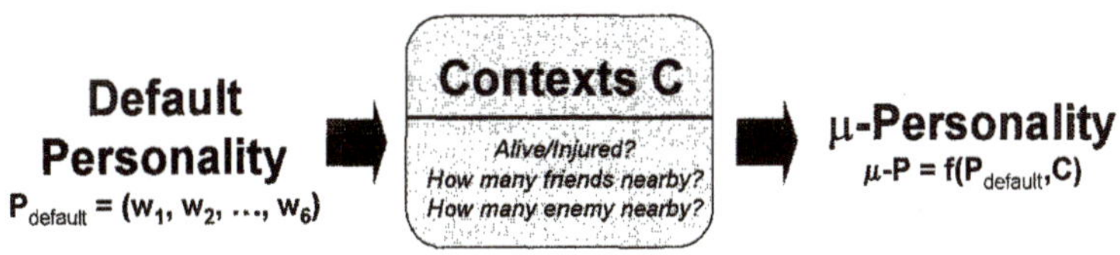

Fig. 5.8 Schematic of an agent's μ (or *meta*) personality; see text for details.

5.2.7.1 *Advance*

The *Advance* μ-rule is defined by a threshold number of friendly agents, $\tau_{Advance}$, that must be within a given agent's threshold range r_T in order for that agent to continue advancing toward the enemy flag (figure 5.9).

Recall that, of the six default components that define an agent's personality weight vector, w_6 represents the relative weight that is assigned toward "moving closer to" the enemy flag (see table 5.2). If the actual number of neighboring friendly agents is greater than or equal to the threshold value, the given agent uses the default weight $\omega_{6,default}$ to decide upon its next move. However, if the actual

*Note that threshold constraints ($\tau_{Advance}$, $\tau_{Cluster}$, Δ_{Combat}) are explicitly defined only for the first three meta rules. These meta rules are used in the sample genetic algorithm agent breeding "experiment" discussed below. In fact, each of the meta rules appearing in table 5.3 has one or more threshold constraints associated with it, and the set—as a whole—also requires additional logic to dynamically resolve ambiguities as they arise during the course of a run. A more detailed mathematical discussion of these issues than appears in this brief overview is given in the following chapter.

μ-rule	Description
Advance	Advance to enemy flag if N(friends) > $\tau_{Advance}$
Cluster	Stop seeking friends if N(friends) > $\tau_{Cluster}$
Combat	Engage enemy if the N(friends) - N(enemies) > Δ_{Combat}
Hold	Hold current position if the patch of the battlefield is occupied by friendly forces
Pursuit-I	Temporarily ignore enemy agents if there are fewer than a threshold number if nearby enemy agents
Pursuit-II	Temporarily ignore all other personality-driven motivations except for those enemy agents if there are fewer than a threshold number if nearby enemy agents
Retreat	Retreat toward own flag unless you are surrounded by a sufficient number of friendly forces
Run Away	Run away, fast, from enemy agents
Support-I	Temporarily ignore all other personality-driven motivations except for those injured friendly agents (i.e. provide support) if there are greater than a threshold number of nearby injured friendly agents
Support-II	Temporarily ignore all other personality-driven motivations except for moving toward nearby alive friendly agents (i.e. seek support) if there are greater than a threshold number of nearby injured friendly agents
Min_D-Friend	Try to maintain minimum distance from all friendly agents
Min_D-Enemy	Try to Maintain minimum distance from all enemy agents
Min_D-Flag	Try to Maintain minimum distance from friendly flag
Min_D-Terrain	Try to Maintain minimum distance from terrain
Min_D-Area	Maintain minimum distance from a fixed area on battlefield

Table 5.3 A Partial list of EINSTein's meta-rule set; see text.

number of neighboring friendly agents is less than the threshold value, the given agent decides its next move by using $-|\omega_6|$ (i.e. minus the absolute value of ω_6) to decide upon its next move. That is, it effectively attempts to "move away from" rather than "move closer to" the enemy goal.

Intuitively, the advance constraint embodies the idea that unless an agent is surrounded by a sufficient number of friendly forces (i.e. senses sufficient local "fire-support"), it will not advance toward the goal.

5.2.7.2 *Cluster*

The *Cluster* μ-rule specifies the threshold number of friendly agents, $N_{Cluster}$, that must be within a given agent's constraint range r_T beyond which that agent will no longer seek to move toward friendly agents. See figure 5.10.

If the actual number exceeds that threshold, the given agent will decide upon its next move using $\omega_1 = \omega_3 = 0$ (see table 5.2), thereby effectively ignoring (albeit temporarily) nearby friendly forces. If, upon the next time step, the agent finds itself

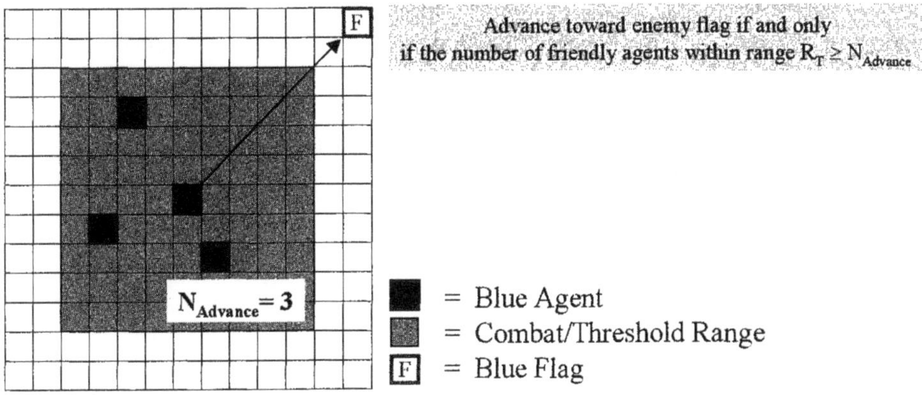

Fig. 5.9 Schematic for *Advance μ-rule* action

surrounded by less than the threshold number of friendly agents, it will immediately resume moving toward all visible friendly agents using its default weights ω_1 and ω_3.

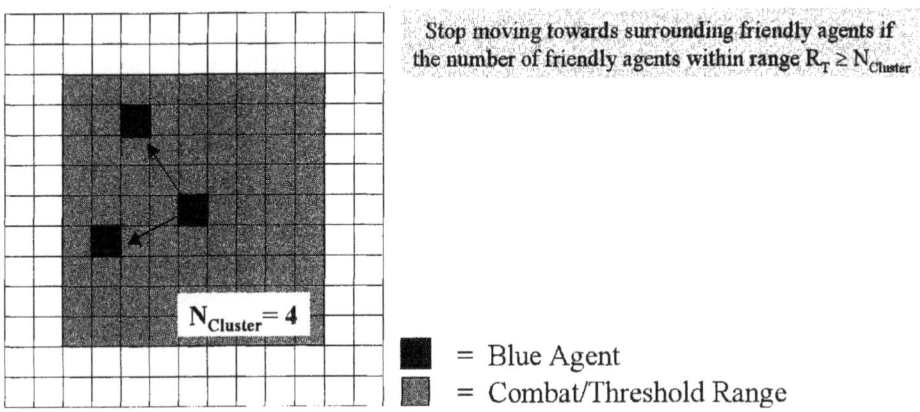

Fig. 5.10 Schematic for *Cluster μ-rule* action

Intuitively, the cluster constraint embodies the idea that once an agent is surrounded by a sufficient number of friendly forces, that agent will no longer attempt to "move closer to" friendly forces.

5.2.7.3 *Combat*

The *Combat* μ-rule specifies the local conditions for which a given agent will choose to move toward or away from possibly engaging an enemy agent. Intuitively, the idea is that if a given agent senses that it has less than a threshold advantage of surrounding forces over enemy forces, it will choose to move away from engaging enemy agents rather than moving toward (and, thereby, possibly engaging) them. See figure 5.11.

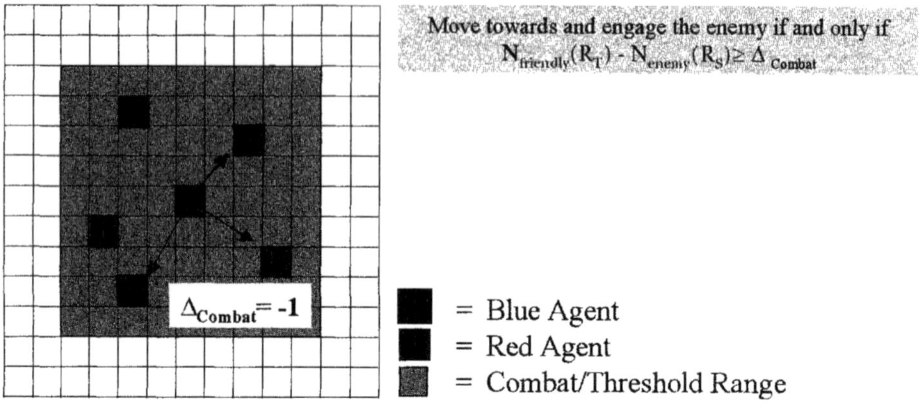

Fig. 5.11 Schematic for *Combat μ-rule* action.

More specifically, the combat constraint consists of choosing a threshold value of the difference (= Δ_{Combat}) between the number of friendly forces contained within the given agents combat/threshold range box (= $N_{friendly}(r_T)$) and the number of enemy forces contained within the given agents sensor range (= $N_{enemy}(r_S)$):

$$\Delta_{Combat} = N_{friendly}(r_T) - N_{enemy}(r_S). \tag{5.6}$$

If the actual difference, Δ_{actual}, is greater than this threshold advantage, the default weight set remains unaffected and the given agent proceeds to move toward the enemy. If Δ_{actual} is less than Δ_c, then the given agent will decide upon its next move using the weights:

$$\begin{aligned} \omega_2 &= -\left|\omega_{2,default}\right|, \\ \omega_4 &= -\left|\omega_{4,default}\right|, \end{aligned} \tag{5.7}$$

where $\omega_{2,default}$ and $\omega_{4,default}$ are the default weights for moving toward alive and injured enemy agents (see table 5.2).

A large *positive* combat threshold represents a defensive mannered agent force, since such agent's will choose to move away from rather than engage an enemy unless they have a strong advantage. A large *negative* combat threshold represents an offensive mannered agent force, since such a force will choose to move toward and possible engage an enemy even if the relative force strengths overwhelmingly favor the enemy. At the two extremes of aggressiveness are (1) $\Delta_{Combat} = -$*(total number of enemy agents)*, that defines a maximally aggressive agent that is always willing to engage nearby enemy agents in combat, and (2) Δ_{Combat} = + *(total number of friendly agents)*, that defines a minimally aggressive agent that always backs away from a fight.

5.2.7.4 *Hold Position*

The *Hold Position* μ-rule specifies the local *territorial possession* conditions for which a given agent will temporarily hold its current (x, y) position. Intuitively, the idea is that if a given agent occupies a patch of the battlefield that is locally occupied by friendly forces, that agent will temporarily set its movement range $(= r_M)$ equal to zero.

A site at (x, y) "belongs" to an agent (red or blue) according to the following logic: the number of like agents within a territoriality-distance (τ_D) is greater than or equal to territoriality-minimum $(\tau_{\min})$ and is at least territoriality-threshold (τ_T) number of agents greater than the number of enemy agents within the same territoriality-distance.

For example, if $(\tau_D, \tau_{\min}, \tau_T) = (2, 3, 2)$ then a battlefield position (x, y) is said to belong to, say, red, if there are at least 3 red agents within a distance 2 of (x, y) and the number of red agents within that distance outnumber blue agents by at least 2.

EINSTein provides a view of the current state of the battlefield using a *territorial possession map* filter in which a pixel's color represents either red or blue occupancy (see figure 5.12). This option may be selected either by pressing the button on the toolbar, or by selecting the *Territorial Possession Map* option of the *Display* main menu list of options.

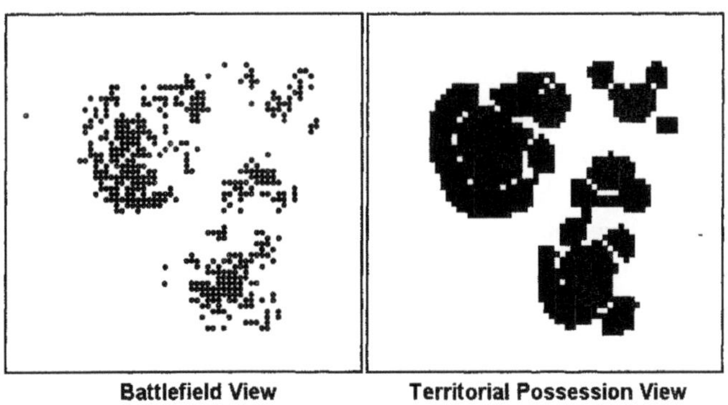

Fig. 5.12 Sample *territorial possession map* screenshot.

If an agent senses that the average number of sites $(0 < f_{color} < 1)$ within its sensor range r_S that belong to its side's color (as defined by the current territorial possession map parameters) is less than or equal to the hold threshold π_{Hold} (if

π_{Hold} is *positive* or *zero*), or greater than or equal to π_{Hold} (if π_{Hold} is *negative*), then, temporarily, $r_M = 0$ (and, thus effectively, $\omega_1 = ... = \omega_6 = \omega_{terrain} = 0$). See figure 5.13.

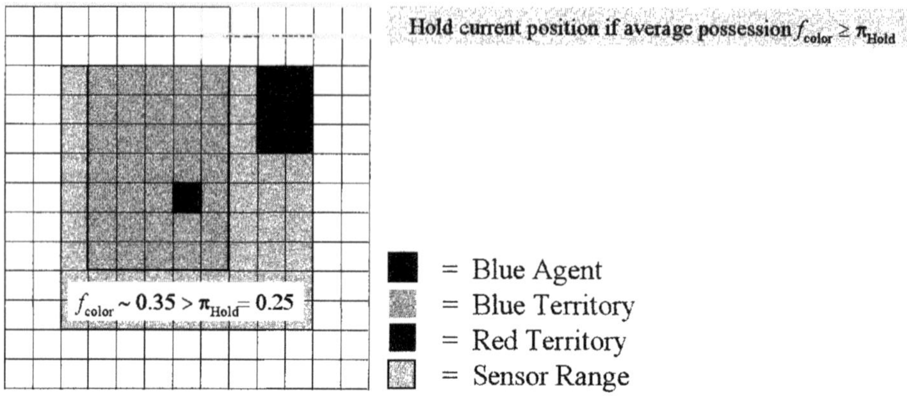

Fig. 5.13 Schematic for *Hold μ-rule* action.

See **Decision Logic** below for a discussion of the precise conditions under which the Hold μ-rule is enabled.

5.2.7.5 *Pursuit-I (Pursuit Off)*

The *Pursuit-I* μ-rule specifies the local conditions for which a given agent will choose to pursue (or ignore) nearby enemy agents. Intuitively, the idea is that if a given agent senses that there are fewer than a threshold number if nearby enemy agents, it will temporarily ignore those agents (i.e. neither moving toward nor away).

Specifically, if an agent senses that the number of enemy agents within the sensor range r_S is less than or equal to the *Pursuit-I* threshold, P_c^I (if the sign of P_c^I is negative) or greater than or equal to P_c^I (if the sign of P_c^I is positive), then, temporarily, personality weights defining an agent's relative propensity for moving towards (or away from) enemy agents is set equal to zero: $\omega_2 = \omega_4 = 0$.

Note that insofar as the *Pursuit-I* μ-rule affects only the default values of weights ω_2 and ω_4, it can be considered a refinement of the *Combat* μ-rule.

5.2.7.6 *Pursuit-II (Exclusive Pursuit On)*

The *Pursuit-II* μ-rule specifies the local conditions for which a given agent will choose to pursue nearby enemy agents, ignoring all other actions. Intuitively, the idea is that if a given agent senses that there are fewer than a threshold number if nearby enemy agents, it will temporarily ignore all other personality-driven motivations except for those enemy agents.

Specifically, if an agent senses that (1) the number of enemy agents within the sensor range r_S is less than or equal to the *Pursuit-II* threshold, P_c^{II} (if the sign of P_c^{II} is negative) or greater than or equal to P_c^{II} (if the sign of P_c^{II} is positive), and (2) that there is sufficient local fire support (i.e. that the local combat threshold condition is satisfied; see *Combat* μ-rule above), then, temporarily, a positive weight is assigned to moving towards enemy agents:

$$\begin{aligned} \omega_2 &\rightarrow +\left|\omega_{2,default}\right|, \\ \omega_4 &\rightarrow +\left|\omega_{4,default}\right|, \end{aligned} \tag{5.8}$$

where $\omega_{2,default}$ and $\omega_{4,default}$ are the default weights for moving toward alive and injured enemy agents (see table 5.2), and all personality weights other than ω_2 and ω_4 are set equal to zero: $\omega_1 = \omega_3 = \omega_5 = \omega_6 = ... = \omega_{terrain} = 0$.

Note that, like *Pursuit-I*, the *Pursuit-II* μ-rule is essentially a refinement of the *Combat* μ-rule.

5.2.7.7 *Retreat*

The *Retreat* μ-rule specifies the threshold number of friendly agents that must be within a given agent's combat/threshold range r_T in order for that agent to continue advancing toward the enemy flag. Intuitively, the *Retreat* μ-rule embodies the idea that unless an agent is surrounded by a sufficient number of friendly agents (i.e. senses sufficient local "fire-support"), it will retreat back to its own goal.

Recall that ω_6 represents the relative weight that is assigned toward moving closer to the enemy flag. If the actual number of neighboring friendly agents, $N_{friendly}(r_T)$, is greater than or equal to the threshold value, $N_{c,Retreat}$, the given agent uses the default weight $+w_6$ to decide upon its next move. However, if $N_{friendly}(r_T) < N_{c,Retreat}$, then if $\omega_{6,default} > 0$, $\omega_5 = |\omega_{6,default}|$ and $\omega_6 = 0$, else $\omega_5 = \textit{maximum value of}(\omega_1, \omega_2, \omega_3, \omega_4, \omega_5)$ and $\omega_6 = 0$. That is, the agent will retreat back to its own flag, and stay there until it is surrounded by a sufficient number of friendly agents.

5.2.7.8 *Run Away*

The *Run Away* μ-rule specifies the local conditions for which a given agent will choose to quickly move away from nearby enemy agents, ignoring all other actions. Intuitively, the idea is that if a given agent senses that it has less than a threshold advantage of surrounding forces over enemy forces, it will choose to run away from enemy agents as rapidly as possible (i.e. as allowed by the current value of its movement range).

The *Run Away* μ-rule uses the same threshold, $D_{Run-Away} = N_{friendly}(r_T) - N_{enemy}(r_S)$ as is used by the *Combat* μ-rule. If $D < D_{Run-Away}$, all of the agent's personality weights are temporarily clamped to the value zero, except for $\omega_2 = -1$ and $\omega_4 = -1$.

5.2.7.9 *Support-I (Provide Support)*

The *Support-I* μ-rule specifies the local conditions for which a given agent will choose to provide support for nearby injured friendly agents, ignoring all other actions. Intuitively, the idea is that if a given agent senses that there are greater than a threshold number of nearby injured friendly agents, it will temporarily ignore all other personality-driven motivations except for those injured friendly agents. See figure 26.

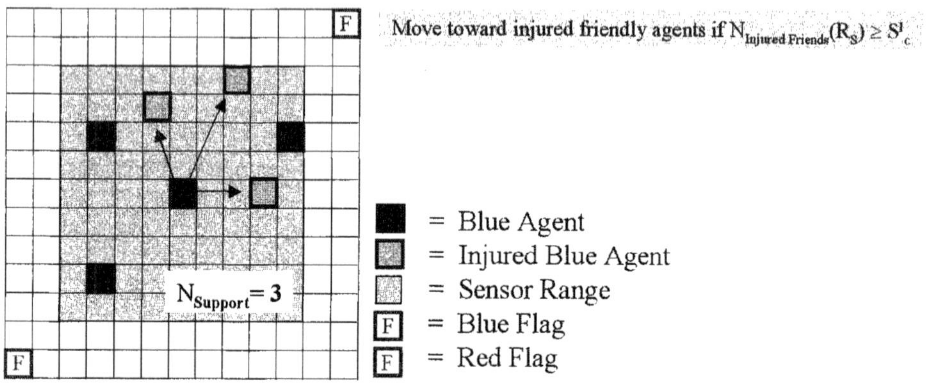

Fig. 5.14 Schematic for *Support-I μ-rule* action.

Specifically, if an agent senses that the number of injured friendly agents within the sensor range r_S, $N_{injured-friends}(r_S)$ is less than or equal to the *Support-I* threshold, S_c^I (if the sign of S_c^I is negative) or greater than or equal to S_c^I (if the sign of S_c^I is positive), then, temporarily:

$$\begin{aligned} \text{if } \omega_{3,default} &> 0 \text{ then } \omega_3 = |\omega_{3,default}|, \\ \text{else } \omega_3 &= |\text{ Maximum}(\omega_1, \omega_2, \omega_3, \omega_4, \omega_5, \omega_6)\ |, \end{aligned} \tag{5.9}$$

and all personality weights other than ω_3 are set equal to zero: $\omega_1 = \omega_2 = \omega_4 = \omega_5 = \omega_6 = ... = \omega_{terrain} = 0$. The number of injured friendly agents must be greater than zero in either case.

Additionally, if not retreating (see *Retreat* μ-rule), then $\omega_5 = 0$. (See also **Decision Logic** and **Ambiguity Resolution Between Support-I and Support-II** below).

5.2.7.10 *Support-II (Seek Support)*

The *Support-II* μ-rule specifies the local conditions for which a given agent will choose to seek support for itself, ignoring all other actions. Intuitively, the idea is that if a given agent senses that there are greater than a threshold number of enemy agents, it will temporarily ignore all other personality-driven motivations except for moving toward nearby alive friendly agents to seek their support.

Specifically, if an agent senses that the number of enemy friendly agents within the sensor range r_S, $N_{enemy}(r_S)$ is less than or equal to the *Support-II* threshold, S_c^{II} (if the sign of S_c^{II} is negative) or greater than or equal to S_c^{II} (if the sign of S_c^{II} is positive), then, temporarily:

$$\begin{aligned} \text{if } \omega_{1,default} &> 0 \text{ then } \omega_1 = |\omega_{1,default}|, \\ \text{else } \omega_1 &= |\text{ Maximum}(\omega_1, \omega_2, \omega_3, \omega_4, \omega_5, \omega_6) \text{ }|, \end{aligned} \tag{5.10}$$

and all personality weights other than w1 are set equal to zero: $\omega_2 = \omega_3 = \omega_4 = \omega_5 = \omega_6 = ... = \omega_{terrain} = 0$. The number of injured friendly agents must be greater than zero in either case. Additionally, if not retreating (see *Retreat* μ-rule), then $\omega_5 = 0$. (See also **Decision Logic** and **Ambiguity Resolution Between Support-I and Support-II** below).

5.2.7.11 *Min-D to Friendly Agents*

The *Min-D to Friendly Agents* μ-rule specifies the minimum distance that an agent will seek to maintain from other friendly agents.

If a given agent ever finds itself at a distance less than the threshold distance to another friendly agent ($= D_{friend,min}$) it will choose to move away from rather than toward that entity. For example, if the minimum distance threshold is set to 5 and a given agent finds itself at a distance 7 from a particular friendly agent, this μ-rule has no effect, and the given agent chooses its next move using the appropriate default personality weights $\omega_1 = \omega_{1,default}$ and $\omega_3 = \omega_{3,default}$. However, if the given agent finds itself at a distance 2 from another friendly agent, the μ-rule temporarily sets:

$$\begin{aligned} \omega_1 &\rightarrow -|\omega_{1,default}| < 0, \\ \omega_3 &\rightarrow -|\omega_{3,default}| < 0. \end{aligned} \tag{5.11}$$

Figure 5.15 shows screenshots of two runs to compare the effect of applying $D_{friend,min} = 5$ to the default case. The rules are the same for both cases ($\omega_{1,default} = 0.25$), with the weight assigned to moving toward the blue flag (located at the far right of the battlefield), $\omega_6 = \omega_{1,default}$.

Note that unlike other μ-rules—which determine what weights are applied to neighboring agents collectively—minimum distance μ-rules are applied to neighboring agents individually and locally. That is to say, that the decision to use either the default personality weight or its negative is made on an individual agent basis, and is made according to whether each neighboring agent is closer to or farther away from the given agent than the prescribed threshold distance. This decision is made during the calculation of the penalty function and is therefore implicit in each of the sums appearing in the previous expression for $Z_{Penalty}$.

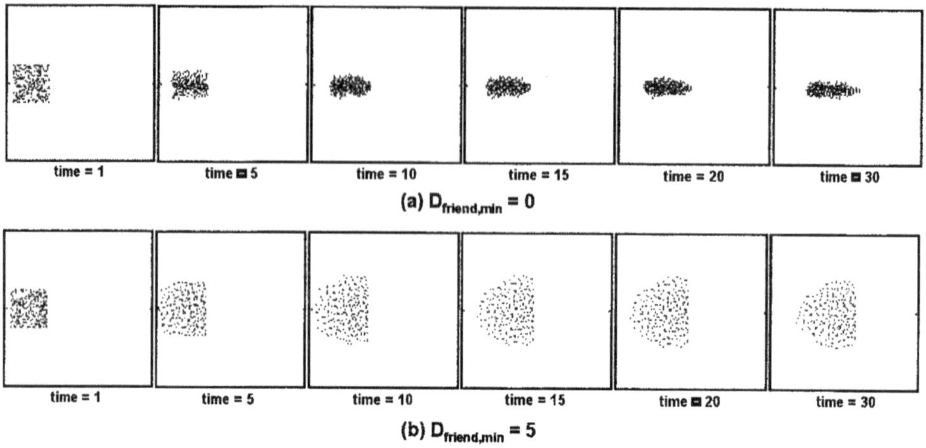

Fig. 5.15 Effect of applying *Min-D to Friendly Agents* μ-rule

5.2.7.12 *Min-D to Enemy Agents*

The *Min-D to Enemy Agents* μ specifies the minimum distance that an agent will seek to maintain from enemy agents.

If a given agent ever finds itself at a distance less than the threshold distance to an enemy agent ($= D_{enemy,min}$) it will choose to move away from rather than toward that entity. For example, if the minimum distance threshold is set to 3 and a given agent finds itself at a distance 5 from a particular enemy agent, this μ-rule has no effect, and the given agent chooses its next move using the appropriate default personality weights $\omega_2 = \omega_{2,default}$ and $\omega_4 = \omega_{4,default}$. However, if the given agent finds itself at a distance 2 from another enemy agent, the μ-rule induces the given agent, the μ-rule temporarily sets:

$$\begin{aligned} \omega_2 &\rightarrow -\left|\omega_{2,default}\right| < 0, \\ \omega_4 &\rightarrow -\left|\omega_{4,default}\right| < 0. \end{aligned} \tag{5.12}$$

As for the minimum distance to friendly agents μ-rule, and in contrast to other μ-rules, this μ-rule is applied to neighboring agents *individually* and *locally*: i.e. the decision to use either the default personality weight or its negative is made on an individual agent basis, and is made according to whether each neighboring agent is closer to or farther away from the given agent than the prescribed threshold distance. This decision is made during the calculation of the penalty function and is therefore implicit in each of the sums appearing in the previous expression for $Z_{Penalty}$.

5.2.7.13 *Min-Distance to Own Flag*

The minimum distance to own flag μ-rule specifies the minimum distance that an agent will seek to maintain from its own flag. If a given agent ever finds itself at a distance less than the threshold distance to its flag ($= D_{min,own-flag}$) it will choose to move away from rather than toward it. This μ-rule can thus be used to define simple "goal-defense" scenarios in which agents are positioned near their own flag.

For example, if the minimum distance threshold is set to 10 and a given agent finds itself at a distance = 20 from its own flag, this μ-rule has no effect, and the given agent chooses its next move using the appropriate default personality weights $w_5 = w_{5,default}$. However, if the given agent finds itself at a distance = 8 from its flag, the μ-rule induces the given agent to use $\omega_5 = -|\omega_{5,default}| < 0$. Figure ?? shows the result of applying $D_{min,own-flag} = 25$.

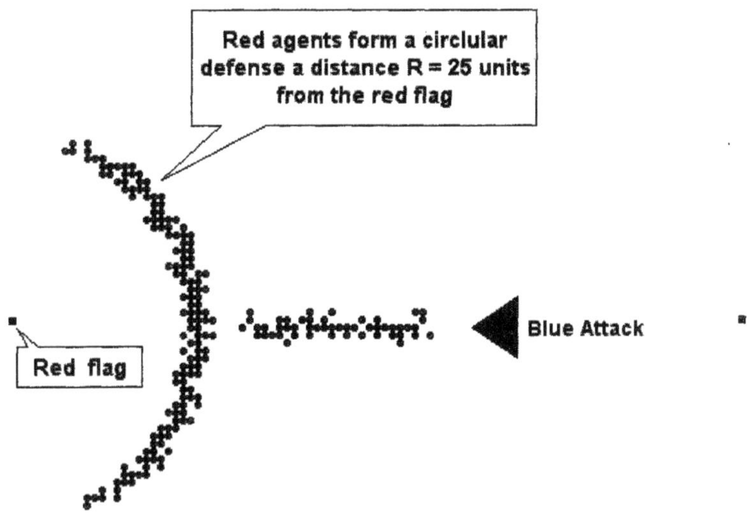

Fig. 5.16 Effect of applying *Min-Distance to Own Flag* μ-rule

Note this μ-rule can obviously be meaningfully applied only if $\omega_{5,default} > 0$, otherwise it has no effect on an agent's decision logic.

5.2.7.14 *Min-D to Nearby Terrain*

The *Min-D to Nearby Terrain* μ-rule specifies the minimum distance that an agent will seek to maintain from nearby terrain. If a given agent ever finds itself at a distance less than the threshold distance to nearby terrain it will choose to move away from rather than toward it.

For example, if the minimum distance threshold is set to 2 and a given agent finds itself at a distance = 4 from terrain, this μ-rule has no effect, and the given agent chooses its next move using the appropriate default personality weights $\omega_{terrain} =$

$\omega_{terrain,default}$. However, if the given agent finds itself at a distance $= 1$ from terrain the μ-rule induces the given agent to use $\omega_{terrain} = -|\omega_{terrain,default}| < 0$.*

5.2.7.15 *Min-D to Fixed Area*

The minimum distance to a fixed area μ-rule specifies the minimum distance that an agent will seek to maintain from a fixed user-defined area. If a given agent ever finds itself at a distance less than the threshold distance to nearby terrain it will choose to move away from rather than toward it.

For example, if the minimum distance threshold is set to 2 and a given agent finds itself at a distance $= 4$ from terrain, this μ-rule has no effect, and the given agent chooses its next move using the appropriate default personality weights $\omega_{area} = \omega_{area,default}$. However, if the given agent finds itself at a distance $= 1$ from terrain the μ-rule induces the given agent to use $\omega_{area} = -|\omega_{area,default}| < 0$.

Note this μ-rule can obviously be meaningfully applied only if $\omega_{area,default} > 0$, otherwise it has no effect on an agent's decision logic.

5.2.8 *Decision Logic*

The following μ-rule decision logic determines how an agent's personality weight vector is altered as a function of its local environment (in the order in which the logical decisions are made):

1. Only those μ-rules whose use_flags have been set are enabled (see EINSTein's *User's Guide* [Ilach99a]).† All others are ignored.
2. *Advance*, *Cluster* and *Combat* μ-rules are adjudicated without ambiguity. That is, each of the three weight vector changes can be enabled simultaneously without conflicting with other changes.
3. If the *Advance* logic results in setting $\omega_6 = 0$, the μ-rule logic tests whether a full *Retreat* is required, otherwise the a test for retreat is not performed. If the test for retreat comes back positive, then $\omega_5 = |\omega_{6,default}|$.
4. If *Support-I* and/or *Support-II* tests pass, the changes to the weights override those that may have been imposed by the *Cluster* μ-rule test. For example, if the Cluster test resulted in $\omega_1 = \omega_3 = 0$ and the *Support-I/II* μ-rule logic has determined that an agent must provide local support, $\omega_3 = |\omega_{3,default}|$, overriding the (earlier) results of the *Cluster* test. A possible conflict might arise when tests for providing and seeking support both come back positive, in which case the ambiguity is always resolved in favor of an agent seeking (rather than providing) support.

*Note this μ-rule can obviously be meaningfully applied only if (1) the **terrain_flag** is set for use (see EINSTein's *User's Guide* [Ilach99a]) and (2) $w_{terrain,default} > 0$, otherwise it has no effect on an agent's decision logic. See **Terrain**, beginning on page 337, for a discussion on how EINSTein implements terrain.

†See also **Appendix E: A Quick User's Guide to EINSTein** (page 581).

5. *Pursuit-I* and *Pursuit-II*, which are adjudicated next, are essentially refinements of the *Combat* μ-rule logic. If the *Combat* test results in changing the values of w_2 and w_4, *Pursuit-I/II* tests are both ignored; these tests are performed only if the *Combat* test does not change any weight values. A possible conflict might arise when tests for *Pursuit-I* and *Pursuit-II* both come back positive, in which case the ambiguity is resolved in a manner that is consistent with an agent's intrinsic aggressiveness.
6. If a conflict between *Pursuit-II* and either *Support-I* or *Support-II* arises, it is resolved in a manner that is again consistent with an agent's aggressiveness.

Finally, if the **use_flag** for the *Hold Position* μ-rule is set, and the test comes back positive for holding position, an agent will do so if and only if (1) the agent is not *Retreating*, (2) the *Combat* μ-rule has not changed any weights, (3) the agent is neither providing (*Support-I*) nor seeking (*Support-II*) support, and (4) the agent is not pursuing enemy agents (*Pursuit-II*).

5.2.9 *Ambiguity Resolution Logic*

While most μ-rules can be applied unambiguously (i.e. such that the logical triggers for and/or dynamical consequences of each rule do not overlap with or otherwise interfere with other rules), there are circumstances under which ambiguities can occur. In such cases, EINSTein invokes the following ambiguity resolution logic to resolve the difficulty.

5.2.9.1 *Pursuit-I vs. Pursuit-II*

If *Pursuit-I* and *Pursuit-II* μ-rules both have their **use_flags** set, local conditions around agents may arise that require resolution of conflicting constraints. Using the notation

- P_c^I = *Pursuit-I* threshold,
- P_c^{II} = *Pursuit-II* threshold,
- $sign(I)$ = sign (i.e. "+" or "−") of the *Pursuit-I* threshold,
- $sign(II)$ = sign of the *Pursuit-II* threshold,
- N_E = # of enemy agents within the agent's sensor range,

there are four possible ambiguities for adjudicating the *Pursuit-I/II* logic:

Ambiguity 1: $sign(I) = sign(II) = +,\ N_E \geq P_c^I,\ N_E \geq P_c^{II}$,
Ambiguity 2: $sign(I) = +, sign(II) = -,\ P_c^I \leq N_E \leq P_c^{II}$,
Ambiguity 3: $sign(I) = -, sign(II) = +,\ P_c^{II} \leq N_E \leq P_c^I$,
Ambiguity 4: $sign(I) = -, sign(II) = -,\ N_E < P_c^I,\ N_E < P_c^{II}$.

Ambiguities 1 and 4 are resolved simply by giving precedence to the threshold value (P_c^I or P_c^{II}) that is closest to the actual number of enemy agents (N_E). For example, for ambiguity type 1, $P_c^{II} > P_c^I$ would be resolved by using *Pursuit-II* logic and $P_c^I > P_c^{II}$ by using *Pursuit-I* logic. Note that P_c^I and P_c^{II} are assumed to be unequal.

If $P_c^I = P_c^{II}$, a random selection is made between *Pursuit-I* and *Pursuit-II*, with equal weight assigned to each.

Ambiguities 2 and 3 are resolved by using an agent's intrinsic aggressiveness (as measured by the sign of the *Combat* threshold) to decide which pursuit μ-rule option to follow:

- Positive combat thresholds (i.e. low aggressiveness) favor *Pursuit-I* logic;
- Negative combat thresholds (i.e. high aggressiveness) favor *Pursuit-II* logic.

If *sign* = 0, a random selection is made between *Pursuit-I* and *Pursuit-II*, with equal weight assigned to each.

5.2.9.2 *Support-I vs. Support-II*

An agent's priority is self-preservation. Thus an agent can provide support (i.e. enable *Support-I* logic) only when that agent does not require the support of other agents (i.e. *Support-II* logic is disabled).

5.2.9.3 *Pursuit-I vs. Support-I/II*

An ambiguity between *Pursuit-II* and either *Support-I* or *Support-II,* if it arises, is resolved by using an agent's intrinsic aggressiveness (as measured by the sign of the *Combat* threshold) to decide which pursuit μ-rule option to follow:

- Negative combat thresholds (i.e. high aggressiveness) favor *Pursuit-II* logic;
- Positive combat thresholds (i.e. low aggressiveness) favor *Support-I/II* logic.

If *sign* = 0, a random selection is made between *Pursuit* and *Support* options, with equal weight assigned to each.

5.3 Squads

EINSTein allows the user to define up to ten different personality weight vectors (both alive and injured) for ten separate squads of agents. Like almost everything else in EINSTein, squads are entirely notional entities and refer simply to collections of agents sharing the same personality. They may (or may not) be equivalent to a "real" military squad, composed of a fixed number of soldiers. Indeed, the notional definition is flexible enough to permit the user to effectively define an additional "colored" squad: say, a white squad that is technically within the "blue" force, but which behaves as though it were a separate force. Aside from enhancing the innate dynamical richness of EINSTein's general conceptual phase-space in an intuitive way, squad-specific parameters can be used to explore such basic *"What If?"* questions of the form *"What if I had a just a few more good soldiers?"*

Squad-specific parameters in the current version of EINSTein include initial *spatial disposition, sensor, fire and movement range, alive and injured personality weight vectors, notional defensive strength, alive* and *injured* μ-rules, *single-shot probability* and *maximum target number*. Moreover, although a single flag is assigned, by default, to represent the "goal" for an entire force, the user is free at any time during a run to assign individual "goals" on a squad-by-squad basis.

5.3.1 *Inter-Squad Weight Matrix*

The inter-squad weight matrix, ω_{ij}^S, defines the weight with which squad i reacts to squad j.

ω_{ij}^S is a real number between -1 and +1. By default, $\omega_{ij}^S = 1$ for all i and j. If $\omega_{ij}^S = 0$ for a given pair (i, j), that means that all agents from squad S_i effectively ignore all agents from squad S_j. If $\omega_{ij}^S = 1/2$, agents from squad S_i react to agents from squad S_j by first premultiplying S_i's default personality weights ω_1 (for alive friend) and ω_3 (for injured friend) by $1/2$. Thus, ω_{ij}^S is essentially a squad-specific premultiplier factor that appears in the penalty calculation for agents from squad S_i. Intuitively, ω_{ij}^S defines how much weight an agent from S_i gives an agent from S_j relative to S_i's default personality weight vector. See figure 5.6. (Note ω_{ij}^S is not necessarily equal to ω_{ji}^S, as j may react differently to i than i does to j.)

Having squad-specific parameters available makes it possible to effectively populate the notional battlefield with other forces; i.e., forces whose personalities do not include a motivation factor to move toward either red or blue flags, but who otherwise participate in the simulated conflict. Future versions of EINSTein will include separate white and purple force classes.

5.4 Combat

"When ten to the enemy's one, surround him...when five times his strength, attack him...if double his strength, divide him...If equally matched you may engage him...if weaker numerically, be capable of withdrawing...and if in all respects unequal, be capable of eluding him, for a small force is but booty for one more powerful...he who understands to use both large and small forces will be victorious."—Sun Tzu, *The Art of War*

The way in which EINSTein adjudicates combat depends on its release version. In all versions *prior to* version 1.1, combat is modeled in a straightforward manner that consists essentially of single "roll of a die." Versions 1.1 and higher all include an entirely new *Weapons* class of functions and an associated set of *rules of engagement* (including intelligent targeting) that is considerably more flexible and robust (that are also, to a certain degree, backwards compatible with older versions).

5.4.1 *As Implemented in Versions 1.0 and Earlier*

During the combat phase of an iteration step for the whole system, each agent X (on either side) is given an opportunity to "fire" at all enemy agents $\{Y_i\}$ that are within a fire range r_F of X's position (see figure 5.17).

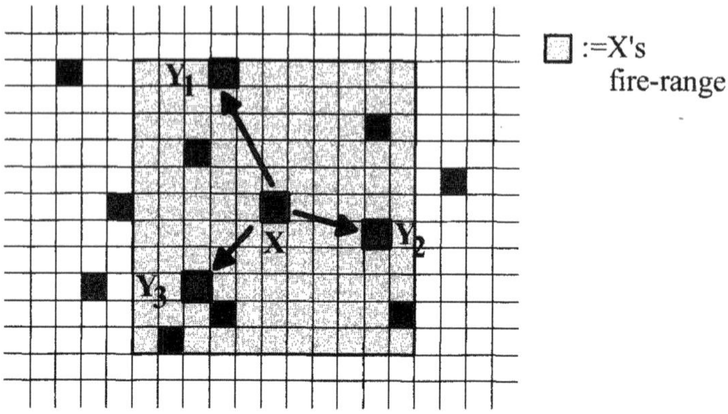

Fig. 5.17 Schematic of how notional combat is adjudicated in EINSTein (versions *prior to* 1.1).

If an agent is shot by an enemy agent, its current state is degraded either from *alive* to *injured* or from *injured* to *killed.* Once killed, an agent is permanently removed from the battlefield. The probability that a given Y_i is shot is fixed by user specified single-shot probabilities for red-by-blue ($P_{ss} = P_{RB}$) and blue-by-red ($P_{ss} = P_{BR}$). The single-shot probability for an injured agent, P^I_{ss}, is, by default, equal to one half of its single-shot probability when it is alive ($P^I_{ss} = P^I_{ss}/2$), but, like almost every other parameter value used by EINSTein during a run, can be changed at any time by the user..

By default, all enemy agents within a given agent's fire range are targeted for a possible hit. However, the user has the option of limiting the number of enemy targets that can be engaged simultaneously. If this option is selected, and the number of enemy agents within an agent's fire-range exceeds a user-defined threshold number (say N_{targets}), then N_{targets} agents are randomly chosen from among the agents in this set.

EINSTein has two different classes of weapons that may be assigned to agents: (1) *squad-specific weapons* and (2) *agent-specific weapons.* Squad-specific weapons include only point-to-point weapons and consist effectively of defining simple *probability of hit* versus *fire-range* curves for each weapon. As the class name implies, these weapons are defined for each squad, and each agent that belongs to a given squad is assigned the same set of weapons. This is an older class of weapons that is included mainly for compatibility which older source (including ISAAC source code) and is replaced completely by the class of agent-specific weapons in versions

1.1 and higher. Agent-specific weapons not only include a generalized version of squad-specific point-to-point weapons, but introduce an entirely new class of area-weapons as well. Both of these weapon classes are discussed in more detail below.

5.4.1.1 *Visualizing Combat*

Combat Intensity. Combat *intensity* is a local measure of how many enemy agents are engaged in combat. The combat intensity may be seen as a filtered view of the battlefield configuration that highlights regions in which the most intense combat is taking place; the view may be either a simple (colored) *threshold* or *greyscale* . This option may be selected either by pressing the red or blue buttons on the toolbar, or by choosing the *Battle-Front Map* option of the *Display* menu.

A site at (x, y) is grey-scaled according to the number of red and blue agents within a range R of (x, y) (i.e. within the "box" whose corners are defined by $(x \pm R, y \pm R)$ when both sets of agents simultaneously exceed a user-defined battle-front threshold Δ_B. By default $R = 2$ and $\Delta_B = 3$. Figure 5.18 shows an example of a battle-front view of the combat intensity (appearing in the right screenshot) of the agent-space, that appears to its left.

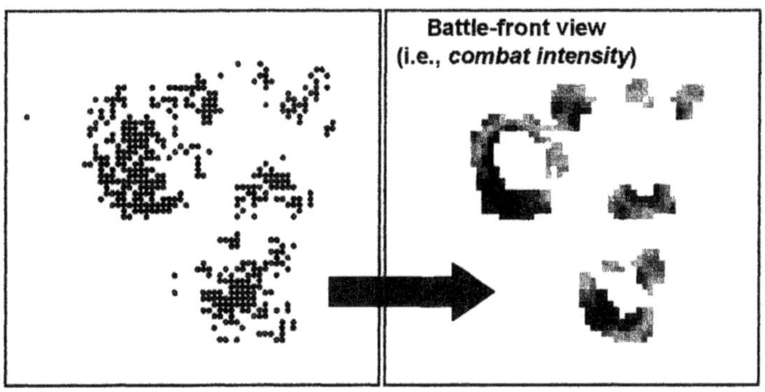

Fig. 5.18 Screenshot of the *battle-front* view of combat intensity (using parameter values $R = 2$ and $\Delta_B = 3$; see text).

Killing Field. The *killing field* marks the locations on the battlefield where agents were previously killed; i.e. agents whose state was degraded from injured to killed and who are therefore no longer taking part in combat (see figure 5.19). Locations where red agents are killed are marked with an '×' locations where blue agents are killed are marked with '·'.

The user has the option of showing *only red* kill locations (by selecting appropriate main-menu *View* option or the red-colored button of the toolbar), *only blue* kill locations (by selecting appropriate option or the blue-colored K button of the toolbar), *both red and blue* kill locations, or temporarily clearing the display of still playing agents to highlight only the (color-neutral) *kill locations* (by selecting the appropriate option or the K button of the toolbar).

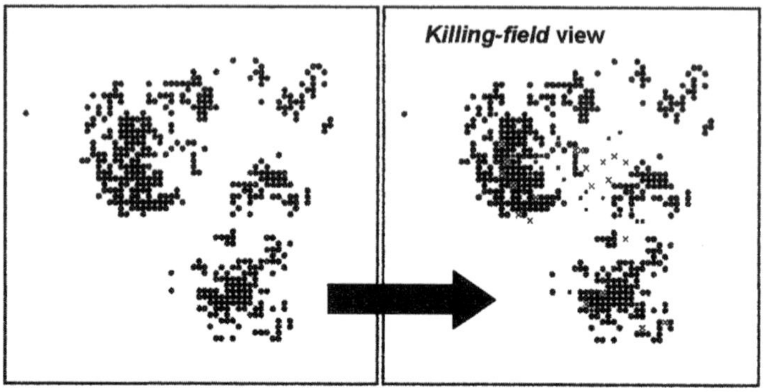

Fig. 5.19 Screenshot of the *killing field* view of the current combat state of the battlefield.

5.4.1.2 *Squad-Specific Weapons*

Squad-specific point-to-point weapons are defined by one of three possible forms of the single-shot probability-of-hit versus fire-range function (see figure 5.20):

- *Fixed*
- *Normalized*
- *User-Defined*

In all cases, eight parameters are required to define a lethality contour for each weapon:

- $P(r < r_{\min})$
- $r_{\min}$
- $r_{\max}$
- $P(r = r_{\min})$
- $P(r = r_{\max})$
- $n(=$ *falloff power*$)$
- $P(r > r_{\max})$

The meaning of each of these parameters is illustrated in figure 5.21.

The decay rate determines how fast the single-shot probability-of-hit function decays with fire-range, slow or fast. In the figure, fast = "–" and slow = "+."

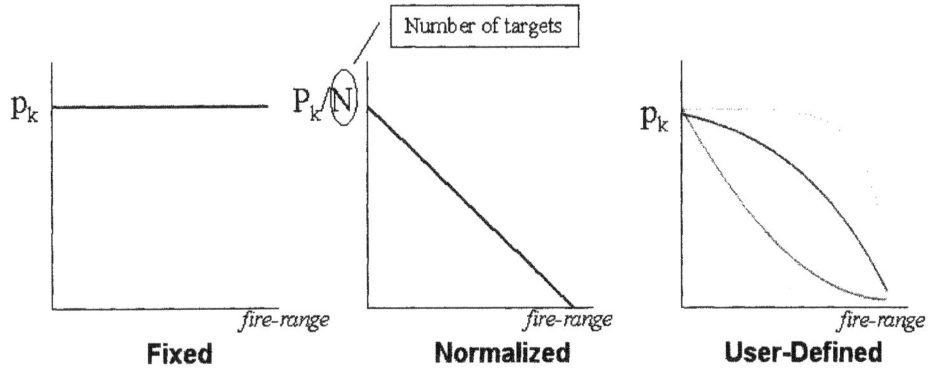

Fig. 5.20 *Fixed*, *normalized* and *user-defined* single-shot probability-of-hit (P_k) vs. fire range functions.

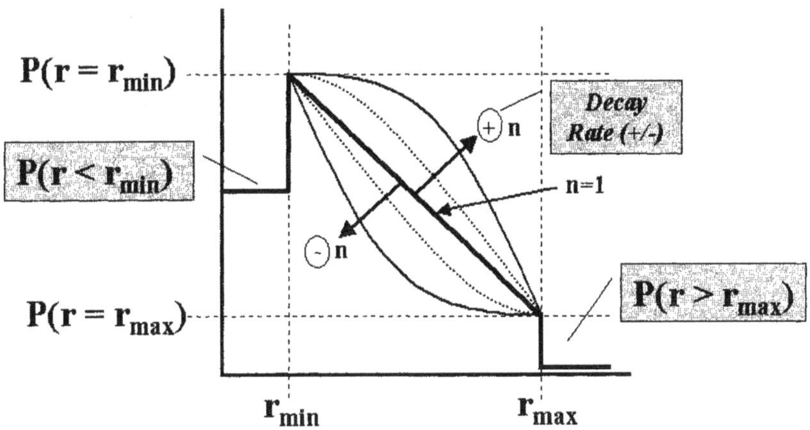

Fig. 5.21 Generic form of *user-defined* single-shot probability-of-hit (P_k) vs. fire range function.

By default, agents are initially assigned a fixed constant values of single-shot probability-of-hit. The user can define up to ten different squad-specific weapons, with user-specified lethality contours. Different value of the weapon characteristics may be defined for different agent states (alive and injured). Also, more than one squads may be assigned the same weapon.

The actual values of the probability-of-hit versus fire-range function are computed using either a simple cookie-cutter or Euclidean metrics (as defined in equation 5.1).

5.4.1.3 *Agent-Specific Weapons*

The agent-specific weapon class includes both *point-to-point* and *area-weapon* (i.e. grenade-class) weapons.

Point-to-Point Weapons. Agent-specific point-to-point weapons are simple extensions of their squad-specific counterparts. The edit dialog shown in figure 5.22 shows the parameter values that define this class of weapons. This dialog may be called up either by clicking (in succession) the main menu choices *Edit* (followed by), *Red (Blue) Data* (followed by), *Agent-Specific Weapons Parameters* (followed by), *Weapon Assignments*; or *On-the-Fly Parameter Changes* (followed by), *Red (Blue) Parameters* (followed by), *Weapon Assignments* (followed by), *Agent-Specific Weapon Assignments.*

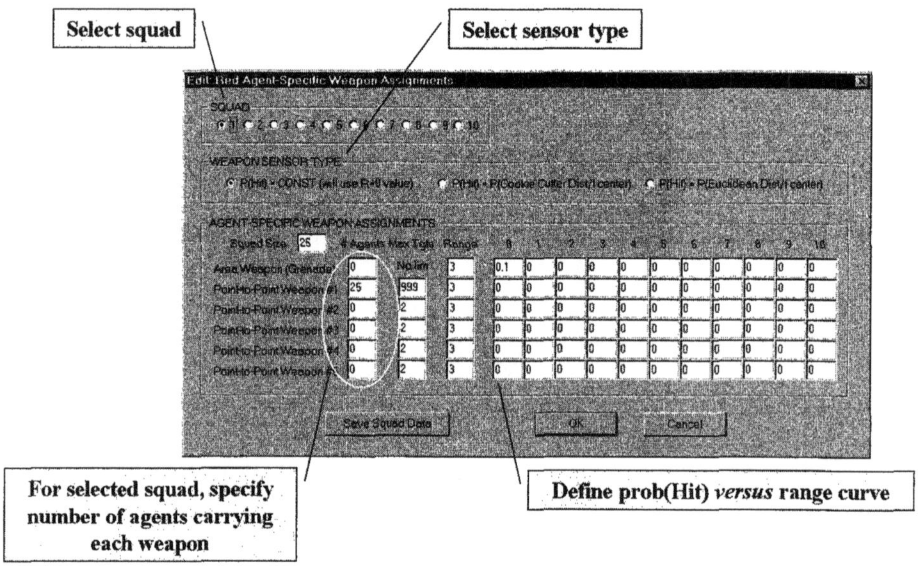

Fig. 5.22 EINSTein's agent-specific point-to-point weapon parameters. (Note that this dialog appears only in versions *prior* to 1.1; for newer versions see discussion beginning on page 323.)

The weapons dialog allows the user to arm a desired number of agents per squad with one of five different point-to-point weapons. The maximal number of simultaneously targetable enemy agents per time step and an explicit representation of a given weapon's single-shot probability of hit as a function of range from shot can also be defined.

A squad may be assigned any number of (the five possible kinds of) point-to-point weapons. The maximal number of simultaneously targetable enemy agents per time step and an explicit representation of a given weapon's single-shot probability of hit as a function of range can also be defined. (Note that the squad-size edit box appears for reference only; this value cannot be changed using this dialog.)

Area-Weapons. EINSTein includes a new class of area-weapons (i.e. *grenades*). The user selects the minimum and maximum throw ranges and the likelihood that the grenade thrown at a targeted coordinate (x_{target}, y_{target}) will "land" at that coordinate. The user must also define the probability $P_d(d = 1, 2, \ldots)$ that the grenade will land a distance d from the targeted site. See figure 5.23.

The damage done by a grenade is characterized by the grenade's blast range and its probability-of-hit versus range function ("range" is referenced from the actual landing spot). Note that, unlike the case for point-to-point weapons that either hit or miss their targets, the states of all (red and blue) agents within a grenade's blast range are degraded if hit by a grenade blast.

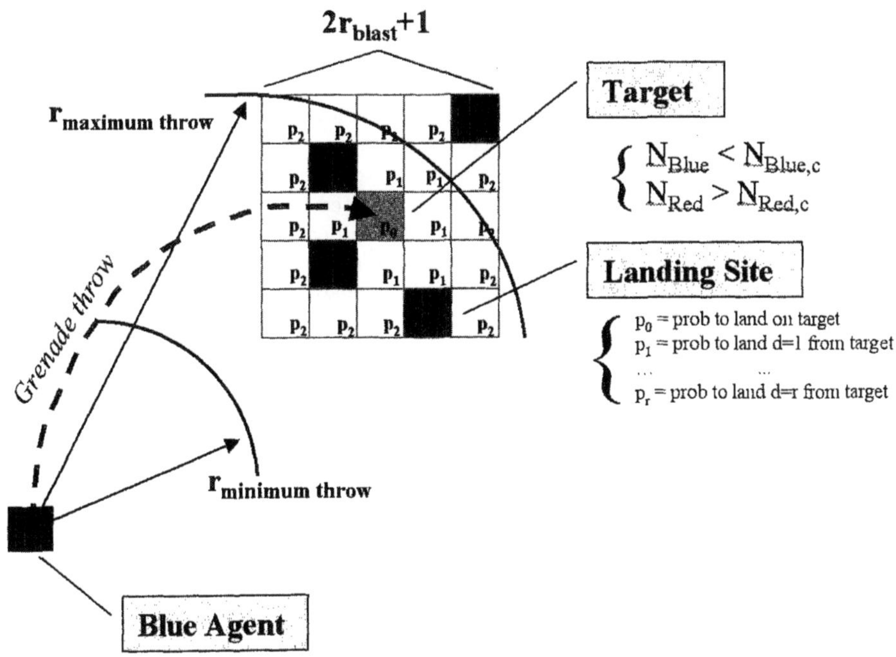

Fig. 5.23 Schematic for EINSTein's area-weapon class (i.e. *grenades*; note that this applies only to versions *prior* to 1.1; a discussion of how weapons are defined in newer versions begins on page 323.)

The penalty function used by individual agents for selecting a particular target site may be tailored by assigning two threshold requirements: (1) a maximal tolerable number of friendly agents within the targeted blast area, $N_{friend,c}$ (nominally equal to zero; i.e. zero expected fratricide), and (2) the minimal number of enemy agents within a possible target blast area that an agent will consider throwing a grenade toward, $N_{enemy,c}$ (nominally equally to one).

An agent chooses the target (x, y) (from among all possible targets that meet the threshold-criteria defined above and are located between the min/max throw range from the agent) according to *the maximal number of enemy agents within a target area A*, where A is defined as the intersection between blast area and sensor range of the throwing agent. If more than one target site shares the same penalty, the target will be chosen randomly out of that set of targets. Table 5.4 summarizes the user-defined parameters that may be used to describe the logic behind, and effects of, the area-weapons class.

Parameter	Description	Min	Max
$R_{\text{throw,min}}$	Minimum throw range	0	15
$R_{\text{throw,max}}$	Maximum throw range	1	15
R_{blast}	Area-weapon blast effects will be felt for all (x, y) positions less than or equal to a distance R_{blast} from the actual landing point	0	10
$P_{\text{landing}}(R)$	Probability that area-weapon will land at the (x, y) location to which it thrown	0	1
$N_{\text{friend,c}}$	Fratricide tolerance = maximal tolerable number of friendly agents within the targeted blast area	0	99
$N_{\text{enemy,c}}$	Enemy presence = minimal number of enemy agents within a possible target blast area that an agent will consider throwing a grenade toward	0	99
τ_{sensor}	Sensor type = probability of hit = constant (0), cookie cutter (1) or measured using Euclidean metric (2)	0	2
$P_{\text{blast}}(R)$	Probability that an agent (friend or enemy), positioned at range R from the landing location, will feel the area-weapon's blast	0	1

Table 5.4 Summary of area-weapon class of weapons.

Figure 5.24 shows a screenshot of ENSTein's area-weapon user-input dialog. It may be called up at any time during an interactive run by pressing either the red or blue toolbar button, or by selecting the *Agent-Specific Weapons Parameters* option under the *Edit::Red/Blue Data* main menu option list.

Data Collection. As described in detail in EINSTein's *User's Guide* [Ilach99a], EINSTein has an extensive set of data collection routines, including routines that collect attrition data resulting from the use of the new class of agent-specific weapons. On-line plots of a subset of that data can also be automatically displayed in a separate window during an interactive run.

Data collection is enabled by toggling data collection *on* (by checking the first toggle switch appearing under the data collection main menu option) and either checking the *Set All* option or the *Weapon Shots/Hits Toggle* switch. Once an interactive run is completed, the user can plot either snapshots of data for individual times t or data automatically totaled for all times $t < T$ (see figure 5.25). Other

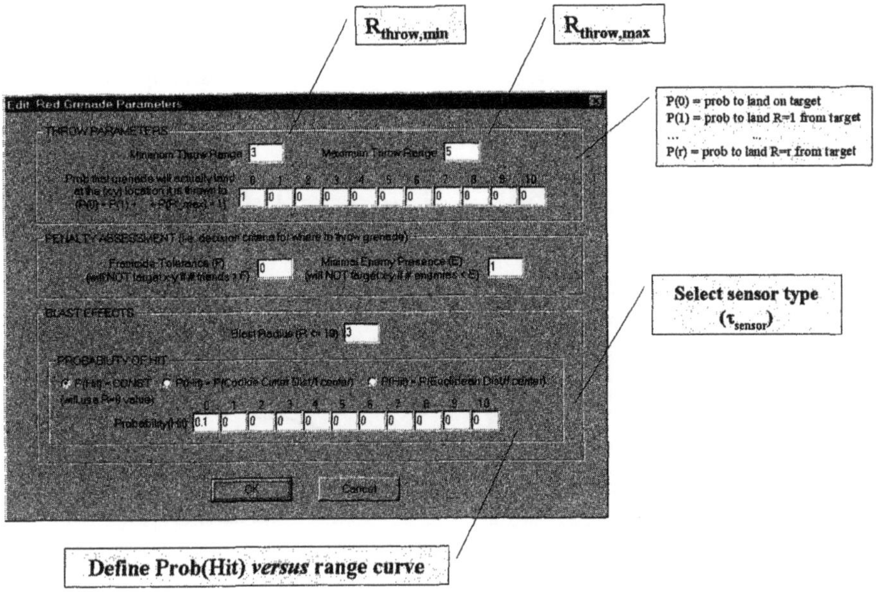

Fig. 5.24 Screenshot of EINStein's area-weapons user-input dialog. (Note that this applies only to versions *prior* to 1.1; for a discussion of how weapons are defined in newer versions begins on page 323.)

choices include whether to plot data for individual squads or all squads at once and whether to scale the data for the number of agents per squad or plot individual totals. The user can select a specific subset of the available data to display on screen.

The following attrition data collection options are available for summarizing multiple time-series runs:

- *Total number of samples run.*
- *Time per sample.*
- *Red, blue, and total (red + blue) attrition sum, average per sample, and standard deviation.*
- *Red and blue squad-specific attrition sum, average per sample, and standard deviation.*
- *Red, blue, and total (red + blue) attrition by sample.*
- *Fractional red, blue, and total (red + blue) attrition by sample.*
- *Red and blue squad-specific attrition by sample.*
- *Distribution of attrition rates for red, blue and total attrition.*
- *Distribution of red, blue and total casualties (for all runs).*
- *Distribution of red and blue squad-specific casualties (for all runs).*
- *Time to achieve a specified red, blue and total attrition (nominally, computed for 90%, 75%, 50% and 10% of initial force size), by sample.*

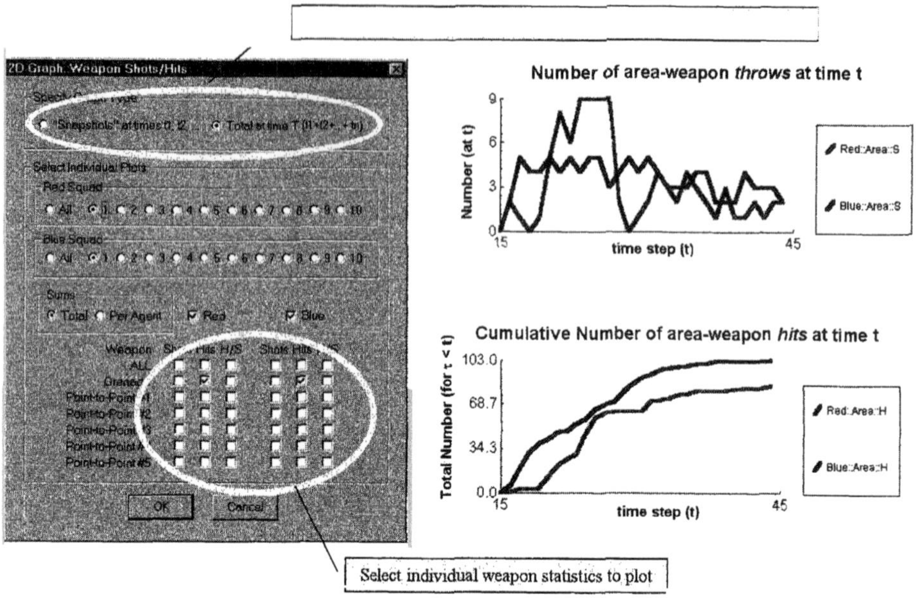

Fig. 5.25 Agent-specific weapons data options and sample plot. (Note that this applies only to versions *prior* to 1.1; for a discussion of how weapons are defined in newer versions begins on page 323.)

- *Time to achieve a specified number of red, blue and total casualties (nominally, computed for 10, 25, 50 and 75 casualties), by sample.*
- *Red, blue and total attrition rates, per sample.*

5.4.1.4 *Defense*

Each agent is endowed with a notional defensive capability (i.e., "armor") that defines the number of successful "hits" that are required to degrade an alive agent to an injured state or remove an injured agent from further play.

By default, the notional defensive strength of all (alive and injured) agents is equal to 1, meaning that a single hit is sufficient to degrade an agents state. Setting the notional defensive strength of one side equal to the total number of iteration steps desired for the entire run effectively renders that side impervious to enemy fire.

5.4.1.5 *Fratricide*

If the **fratricide_flag** is set at run time (see EINSTein's *User's Guide* [Ilach99a]), every potential engagement of an enemy agent entails the possibility of fratricide. Specifically, if an agent X targets an enemy agent Y (that is within the fire range r_F of X) but does not hit Y – a hit/miss being decided by X's single-shot probability

P_{ss}—then, with probability P_{frat}, a friendly agent X' within a fratricide range r_{frat} of Y may be hit instead (see figure 5.26).

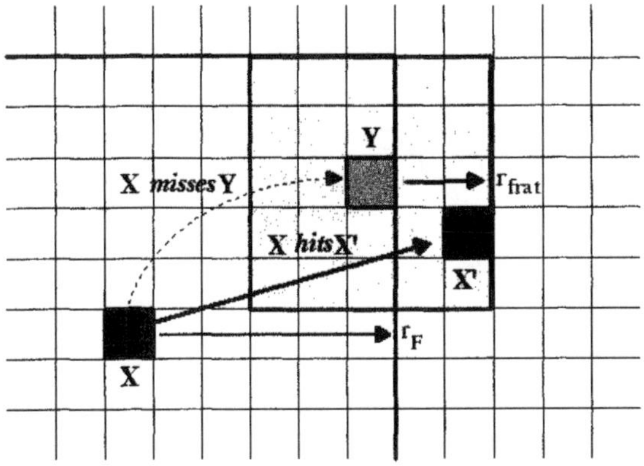

Fig. 5.26 Schematic of a fratricide "hit" of $X\prime$ by X.

5.4.1.6 *Reconstitution*

If the **reconstitution_flag** is set at run time,[*] each agent is endowed with a fixed reconstitution time t_{recon}. This adds the logic that if an agent X, after being hit by an enemy agent Y (and thereby being degraded from an alive to an injured state), is not hit during the next t_{recon} iteration steps, X is reconstituted to its alive state. Note that setting reconstitution time to $t_{recon} = 0$ is effectively equal to having an infinite notional defense, since an agent that is hit by the enemy is immediately reconstituted and can therefore be neither injured nor killed.

5.4.2 *As Implemented in Versions 1.1 and Later*

An entirely new weapons class has been developed for EINSTein versions 1.1 and higher.[†] This new weapons class subsumes the older (and separate) *point-to-point* and *area* weapons, allows users to define arbitrary weapons and their lethality characteristics, and maintains backwards compatibility with the weapons parameter definitions that appear in older **.dat* files.

In newer versions of EINSTein. all weapons are ballistic weapons, and are characterized by six parameters (the values of which may be freely set by the user at any time, prior to or during a run): power, range, firing rate, spread, deviation, and reliability (see figure 5.27).

[*]See page 593 in Appendix E and page 666 in Appendix G.

[†]EINSTein's new weapons class was implemented by physicist and programmer *extraordinaire*, Fred C. Richards

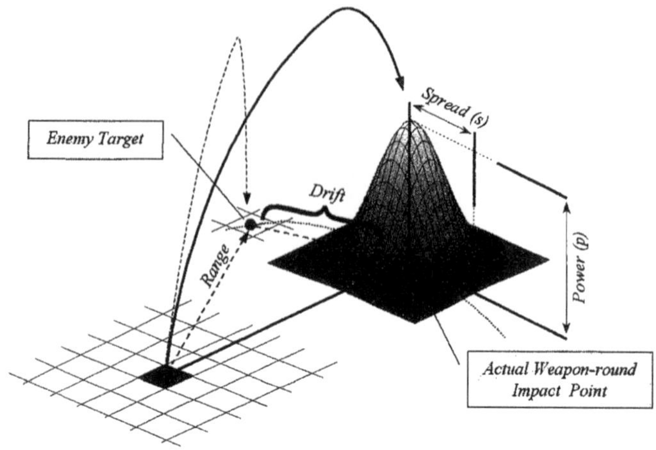

Fig. 5.27 Schematic illustration of EINSTein's weapon logic, as implemented in versions 1.1 and higher.

5.4.2.1 *Innate Power*

This is the raw, destructive power of the weapon ($= p$), and represents the destructive potential within the "kill zone" of a single round of the weapon. In practice, the amount to which an agent's health is degraded by the weapon may depend on other factors, such as the degree of *shelter** provided by the local terrain.

5.4.2.2 *Range*

This is the maximum range of the weapon, and is equivalent to the fire-range ($r_F \geq 0$) parameter used in EINSTein versions 1.0 and earlier. The weapon can target and fire at any site that is less than or equal to this distance from the owner agent. (The value of r_F is assumed to be equal to zero or positive. If it is negative, EINSTein sets the weapon's range equal to zero.)

5.4.2.3 *Firing rate*

This is the maximum number of simultaneous targets at which a weapon can be fired, and is equivalent to the **max_tgt_num** parameter used in EINSTein versions 1.0 and earlier.

A weapon's firing rate ($= \mathcal{R}$) can also indirectly influence its accuracy (see below). One attribute of an agent is how its ability to use its assigned weapon degrades with increasing numbers of targets. For a single target this factor does not come into play. However, if an agent is surrounded by multiple targets, this operator-error increases linearly with the target set size (see below).

*See discussion in section 5.6, **Terrain**, starting on page 337.

5.4.2.4 *Spread*

This defines the size of a weapon kill zone. The kill zone is the power distribution for a single round. For a weapon with *innate* power $p \geq 0$ and spread $s \geq 0$, the weapon's effective destructive power, $P(d)$, as a function of distance away from where a given round of the weapon lands, is (approximately) given by a Gaussian distribution:

$$P(d) = p \times \exp\left[-\left(\frac{2d}{s}\right)^2\right]. \tag{5.13}$$

Power is equal to zero for distances greater than the spread. If the spread is zero, then fired rounds will only inflict damage at a single point: i.e., the site on the battlefield where a weapon's round actually lands. If the spread is non-zero, then a round only inflicts damage in the area surrounding the point where a round lands. If the user defines a negative spread, EINSTein automatically sets the spread equal to zero. The degree of damage potential falls off with the square of the distance from the round's landing point.

5.4.2.5 *Deviation*

This is a rough measure of a weapon's accuracy. Deviation ($= \mathcal{D}$) is defined as the average distance between an agent (i.e., a weapon's point-of-origin) and the target that an individual fired round actually strikes. The value of deviation is assumed to be positive (or zero). If it is negative the weapon's deviation is set equal to zero.

Note that since deviation is defined at the weapon's *maximum firing range*, it is effectively a function of the weapon firing range. Thus, if the user changes the firing range of a weapon, that same weapon's deviation also changes so as to preserve the original deviation-distance relationship. For example, if a weapon's default deviation is some value d, then doubling this weapon's firing range also doubles its deviation to $2d$.

The actual distance from the target that a round strikes is determined probabilistically from a standard Gaussian distribution. This distance increases linearly with increasing distance from the firing agent to the target.

Additional firing inaccuracies may also be induced by an agent's internal state as well, via *Agent::tremor()* and *Agent::frazzle()*.

Frazzle. Frazzle ($0 \leq \mathcal{F} \leq 1$) measures the degree to which an agent's weapon firing accuracy diminishes with increasing numbers of multiple, simultaneous targets.

Nonzero value of frazzle mare invoked only when a weapon is fired at more than one target simultaneously. The greater the number of simultaneous targets the weapon is fired at, the greater the frazzle factor becomes, increasing linearly and reaching its full value at the weapon's maximum target limit. The maximum frazzle effect is to cause a weapon to hit *one standard deviation farther* from the target, on average.

Tremor. Tremor ($0 \leq \mathcal{T} \leq 1$) measures the degree to which an agent's internal state affects its assigned weapon's firing accuracy. If $\mathcal{T} = 0$, the weapon's accuracy is completely unaffected by the agent. If $\mathcal{T} = 1$, the agent adds one standard deviation to the (assigned weapon's) average distance from the target that the weapon's round is likely to land.

The distance by which a fired round misses the target due to agent-induced error is determined by multiplying an agent's *frazzle* and tremor *factors* by its *deviation.* The following code fragment from *Weapon::fire()* illustrates the method:

```
if (deviation_ == 0.0) {
    hit = t->first;// right on target
}else{
    float drift;
    drift = 1.0;// inherent to Weapon
    drift += owner_->tremor();
    if (n > 1) {
        drift += owner_->frazzle() * (n - 1)/(rate_ - 1);
    }
    drift *= deviation_;
    std::pair<float, float> offset = rng.gaussian2d(drift, drift);
    int x_hit = t->first.x + round(offset.first);
    int y_hit = t->first.y + round(offset.second);
    if (x_hit < 0 || x_hit >= battlefield.rows() ||
    y_hit < 0 || y_hit >= battlefield.columns() ){
        continue;// shot out of bounds, skip this target
    }
    hit = Coord(x_hit, y_hit);
}
```

5.4.2.6 *Reliability*

A weapon's reliability ($0 \leq W_r \leq 1$) is equal to the probability that the weapon will fire an individual round when triggered. User-defined values outside of this range are automatically clipped by the program.

To use its weapon an agent first scans for nearby agents (friend and enemy), and then passes this information to the *Weapon::target()* method which selects as many targets as its current firing rate allows. The agent then calls the *Weapon::fire()* method to inflict damage on the selected targets:

The actual combat phase is initiated by *Force::engage()*, which calls, in order *Agent::target()*, *Agent::fire()* (see figure 5.28 for code fragments), which in turn use *Weapon::fire()* (figure 5.29), and *Weapon::target()* (figure 5.30).

While the *Weapon::target()* and *Weapon::fire()* implementations are fixed, one can derive new weapon types by overriding the *Weapon::efficacy()* method, which represents the logic according to which agents select their targets.

```
Force::engage(Force& foe, const Grid<Agent*>& operating_picture)
{
    assert(this->agents <= this->agent.size());

    unsigned int i;
    for (i = 0; i < this->agents; ++i) {
        Agent* agent = this->agent[i];
        assert(agent != NULL);

        if (agent->is_dead() == false) {
            unsigned int target_count;
            target_count = agent->target(bf_);
            if (target_count > 0) {
            unsigned int total_hit;
            total_hit = agent->fire(bf_, operating_picture);
            if (this->fratricide_allowed == 1 && total_hit > 0) {
                fratricide_count_ +=
                    (total_hit - agent->foe_hit());
            }
          }
        }
    }

} // Force::engage()
```

```
unsigned int Agent::target(const Battlefield& battlefield)
{
    assert(need_to_scan_ == false);

    // Merge the detected and reported agents sets.
    std::vector<const Agent*> foe = foe_detected_;
    foe.insert(foe.end(), foe_reported_.begin(),
        foe_reported_.end());

    // Only consider nearby allies if fratricide is a concern.
    std::vector<const Agent*> allies;
    if (force_->fratricide_allowed == 1) {
        allies = allies_detected_;
        allies.insert(allies.end(), allies_reported_.begin(),
        allies_reported_.end());
    }

    need_to_target_ = false;
    return [redacted]
}
```

See figure 5.30

```
unsigned int Agent::fire(const Battlefield& battlefield,
                const Grid<Agent*>& operating_picture)
{   assert(need_to_target_ == false);

    need_to_target_ = true;

    //
    // Weapon::fire() can call this->inflict_damage()
    // which will increment foe_hit_.
    //
    foe_hit_ = 0;
    return [redacted]
}
```

See figure 5.29

Fig. 5.28 Source code fragments for EINSTein's implementation of the *Force::engage()*, *Agent::target()* and *Agent::fire()* functions; see text for details.

```
unsigned int Weapon::fire(const Grid<Agent*>& operating_picture, const Battlefield& battlefield)
{   targeted_ = false; // reset for next round
    RNG& rng = RNG::instance();
    // For each target figure out where the round actually hits and then inflict damage
    // according to the blast size and strength. Keep a tally of how many foe are struck.
    unsigned int tally = 0;
    unsigned int n = targets_.size();
    std::vector<Target>::const_iterator t;
    std::vector<Target>::const_iterator tend = targets_.end();
    for (t = targets_.begin(); t != tend; ++t) {
        if (rng.coin(reliability_) == true) {
            Coord hit;
            if (deviation_ == 0.0) {
                hit = t->first;// right on target
            } else {
                // Combine all the factors contributing to firing
                // inaccuracy into one and multiply that by the
                // Weapon's inherent inaccuracy, the deviation,
                float drift;
                drift = 1.0; // inherent to Weapon
                drift += owner_->tremor();
                if (n > 1) drift += owner_->frazzle() * (n - 1)/(rate_ - 1);
                drift *= deviation_;
                std::pair<float, float> offset = rng.gaussian2d(drift, drift);
                int x_hit = t->first.x + round(offset.first);
                int y_hit = t->first.y + round(offset.second);
                if (x_hit < 0 || x_hit >= battlefield.rows() ||
                    y_hit < 0 || y_hit >= battlefield.columns() )
                { continue; // shot out of bounds, skip this target }
                hit = Coord(x_hit, y_hit);
            }
            // Now that we know where we hit, figure out what is inside the blast zone
            // to get hurt. Agents may be protected by the Terrain they are in.
            if (spread_ == 0.0) {// Optimized for "point" Weapon.
                Agent* victim = operating_picture(hit);
                if (victim != NULL) {
                    float pscale = 1.0 - battlefield.terrain(hit).shelter();
                    owner_->inflict_damage(*victim, pscale*max_power_);
                    ++tally;
                }
            } else {// General "area" Weapon.
                std::pair<Coord, Coord> killzone;
                killzone = battlefield.clipped_region(hit, spread_+1);
                unsigned int x, y;
                for (x = killzone.first.x; x <= killzone.second.x; ++x) {
                    for (y = killzone.first.y; y <= killzone.second.y; ++y) {
                        Coord c(x, y);
                        Agent* victim = operating_picture(c);
                        if (victim != NULL) {
                            Distance& dist = Distance::instance();
                            unsigned int r = round(dist(hit, c));
                            assert(r < range_);
                            float pscale = 1.0 - battlefield.terrain(c).shelter();
                            owner_->inflict_damage(*victim, pscale*power_[r]);
                            ++tally;
                        }
                    }
                }
            }
        }
    }
    return tally;
} // Weapon::fire
```

Fig. 5.29 Source code fragment for EINSTein's *Weapon::fire()* function; see text for details.

```
unsigned int Weapon::target(const std::vector<const Agent*>& foe,
      const std::vector<const Agent*>& ally, const Battlefield& battlefield)
{   targeted_ = true;
    targets_.clear();

    if (rate_ == 0 || foe.empty() == true) return 0;

    // Consider every site within firing range and estimate
    // the benefit of firing at each.  Save all the coordinates of
    // sites with a positive value as a target.
    std::pair<Coord, Coord> fire_region;
    fire_region = battlefield.clipped_region(owner_->position(), range_);

    unsigned int i, j;
    for (i = fire_region.first.x; i <= fire_region.second.x; ++i) {
        for (j = fire_region.first.y; j <= fire_region.second.y; ++j) {
            Coord c = Coord(i, j);
            float eff = [redacted]   <-------- See figure 5.31
            if (eff > 0.0) {
            targets_.push_back(std::make_pair(c, eff));
            }
        }
    }

    // Keep only the best targets that are within our capability of
    // shooting at simultaneously.  Try to avoid systematic biases
    // when selecting between targets of equal value.
    if (rate_ < targets_.size()) {
        std::random_shuffle(targets_.begin(), targets_.end(), RNG::instance());
        std::partial_sort(targets_.begin(), targets_.begin() + rate_,
                          targets_.end(), greater_efficacy());
        targets_.resize(rate_);
    }

    assert(targets_.size() <= rate_);
    return targets_.size();

} // Weapon::target()
```

Fig. 5.30 Source code fragment for EINSTein's *Weapon::target()* function; see text for details.

```
Float Weapon::efficacy(const Coord& c, const std::vector<const Agent*>& foe,
                       const std::vector<const Agent*>& ally) const
{   Distance& dist = Distance::instance();

    // We don't want to kill the owner.
    if (dist.in_range(c, owner_->position(), spread_) == true) {
        return -1.0;
    }

    //
    // For now consider the kill zone a well defined region.
    // Eventually we need to include some measure of uncertainty,
    // i.e. treat the region within one deviation differently.
    //
    unsigned int ally_vulnerable = 0;
    unsigned int foe_vulnerable = 0;
    std::vector<const Agent*>::const_iterator i;
    std::vector<const Agent*>::const_iterator iend = ally.end();
    for (i = ally.begin(); i != iend; ++i) {
        if (dist.in_range(c, (*i)->position(), spread_) == true) {
            ++ally_vulnerable;
        }
    }

    iend = foe.end();
    for (i = foe.begin(); i != iend; ++i) {
        if (dist.in_range(c, (*i)->position(), spread_) == true) {
            ++foe_vulnerable;
        }
    }

    if (foe_vulnerable == 0 && ally_vulnerable == 0) {
        return 0.0;
    } else if (foe_vulnerable == 0) {
        return -ally_vulnerable;
    } else if (ally_vulnerable == 0) {
        return foe_vulnerable;
    } else {
        return (foe_vulnerable / (ally_vulnerable + foe_vulnerable));
    }
} // Weapon::efficacy()
```

Fig. 5.31 Source code fragment for EINSTein's *Weapon::efficacy()* function; see text for details.

5.4.2.7 *Targeting Logic*

In EINSTein versions 1.0 and older, all enemy agents within a given agent's fire range are targeted for a possible hit. Loosely speaking, the only "targeting logic" available to an agent is the option to constrain the number of simultaneously engageable enemy targets. If this option is selected, and the number of enemy agents within an agent's fire-range exceeds a user-defined threshold number (say $N_{targets}$), then $N_{targets}$ agents were randomly chosen from among the agents in this set.

For versions 1.1 and newer, the *Weapon::efficacy()* method estimates the relative benefit of firing at the given coordinate. The function returns a negative value if the weapon owner would be damaged or if only friendly agents are expected to be damaged (i.e., in the event that there are no enemy agents within sensor or fire range to target).

The function returns the value zero if no enemy is expected to be damaged. It returns a positive value (whose magnitude is less than one) in the event that both enemy and friendly agents may be damaged. *Weapon::efficacy()* returns a number greater than one, if an agent expects that only enemy agents will be damaged (i.e., fratricide is impossible in the current context).

The *Weapon::target()* function invokes *Weapon::efficacy()* for every battlefield site within firing range. However, it saves the coordinates (and efficacy) only for sites that have positive efficacy (see figure 5.31).

User-definable. The *Weapon::efficacy()* method is declared as "virtual" so that the user can, if desired, override it in a derived class and therefore change the fundamental targeting behavior of a new weapon type without affecting the underlying code that is used to target and fire weapons. (The programming-savvy user need only remember to have a derived *Weapon::efficacy()* method return a negative (or zero) value for any site that he wishes an agent not to target.)

Inflicted damage. The actual damage that is inflicted on another agent (whether a targeted enemy or, unintentionally, a friendly agent if the fratricide flag is toggled on; see below), is determined by the *Agent::inflict_damage()* method. The degree of inflicted damage is represented by a real-valued number between zero and one (values outside this range are clipped), and is a function of the victim's *armor strength*:*

```
if (impact <= 0.0 ||
      victim.health_ <= victim.damage_sustained_ ||
      (victim.force_->use_armor==true &&
      victim.armor_strength_ >= 1.0f ) ) {
          return;
}
```

*__Armor_strength__ is a real-valued replacement for the older, and *integer-valued*, **defense_strength** parameter used in EINSTein versions 1.0 and older. See page 677 in Appendix G.1.1.8.

```
if (victim.force_->use_armor == true && victim.armor_strength_ > 0.0) {
    victim.damage_sustained_ += impact * (1.0 - victim.armor_strength_);
} else {
    victim.damage_sustained_ += impact;
}
```

A victim's health does not actually change until the take_stock() method is invoked:

```
if (health_ > 0.0) {
    if (damage_sustained_ > 0.0) {
        if (damage_sustained_ > health_) {
            health_ = 0.0;
        } else {
            health_ -= damage_sustained_;
        }
        damage_sustained_ = 0.0;
        if (health_ <= 0.0) {
            operating_picture(pos_) = NULL;
        }
    } else {
        if (health_ < 1.0 && force_->allow_recovery == 1) {
            health_ += force_->recovery_rate;
            if (health_ > 1.0f) {
            health_ = 1.0f;
            }
        }
    }
}
```

Thus agents engage in battle on an essentially equal footing until *all agents have an opportunity to fire their weapons.*

Note that the older, integer-valued, *reconstitution-time* parameter (used in EINSTein versions 1.0 and older) is replaced with a real-valued, *recovery-rate*. "Recovery" refers to the gradual replenishment of an agent's health following health degradation due to weapon fire.

5.4.2.8 *Weapon selection*

Weapon objects are created, destroyed and assigned to agents by the squad. The squad tells its agents to arm themselves with a particular weapon type by invoking the *Agent::arm_with()* method. This sets the weapon's owner so that it can be targeted and fired. (Since weapon ownership is not transferred by the assignment operator, this is the only way to set a weapon's owner.)

A squad's default arsenal consists of five weapon types:

- *Bolt-action rifle*
- *Semi-automatic rifle*
- *Machine gun*
- *Grenade*
- *Mortar*

Table 5.5 lists the parameter values used to define each type of default weapon.

Weapon	**Description**	r_F	$\mathcal{R}$	p	s	$\mathcal{D}$	W_r
Bolt-action Rifle	Accurate & Reliable	7	1	0.1	0	0	1
Semi-automatic rifle	Less range; faster rate	4	5	0.1	0	0.5	1
Machine gun	Occasionally jams	5	10	0.2	0	0.5	0.8
Grenade	Harder to target	5	1	0.3	3	1.5	1
Mortar	Good range; easier to target than a grenade	6	1	0.5	3	1.0	1

Table 5.5 Summary of EINSTein default weapon arsenal (applies only for EINSTein version 1.1 and newer).

User-defined weapons may be identified by unique labels, and stored in a separate file for future use. Weapons are assigned to individual agents, and may be arbitrarily mixed within squads.

All combat-related parameters, fratricide, and reconstitution options may be set by the user via the *Force-wide Parameters* dialog, which is accessed by selecting the *Edit* main menu option (see figure 5.32).

Weapon assignments are defined either directly, by accessing the *Weapon Assignments* option on the *Edit* main menu, or indirectly, by clicking on the button that appears in the *Agent Behavior Parameters* dialog (see figure 5.33).*

5.5 Communications

Other than "communicating" their force-identity to nearby agents (i.e. providing other agents with a simple *friend* or *enemy* "tag"), agents do not normally communicate any other kind of information to one another. However, more complicated scenarios including a rudimentary form of inter-agent communication can be defined.

EINSTein provides options that allow agents to increase their effective sensor range by including battlefield data that is normally outside of their default sensor

*See **Appendix E: A Concise User's Guide to EINSTein** (page 581) for more details.

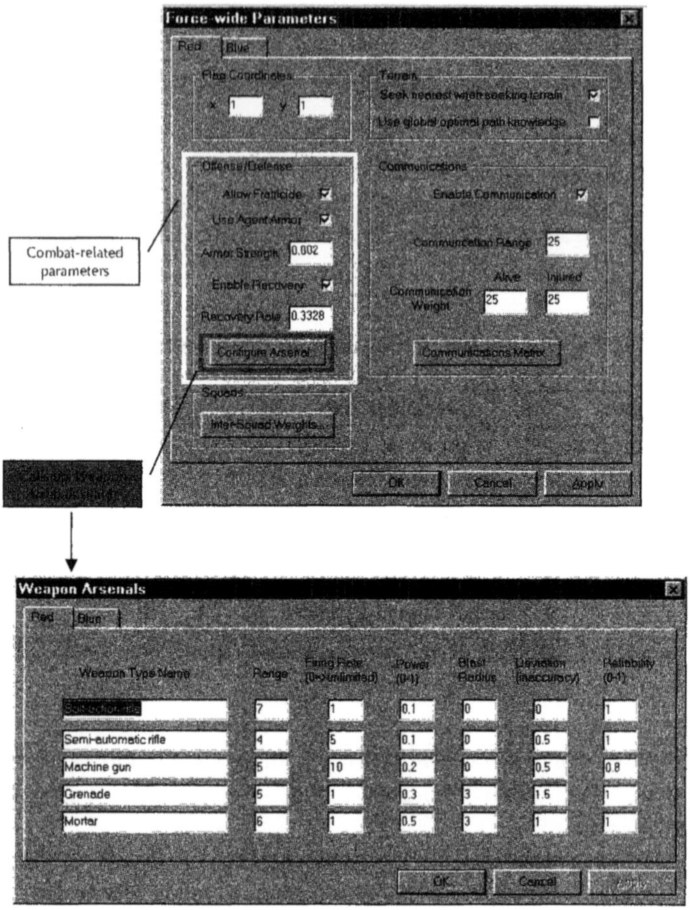

Fig. 5.32 Screenshots of EINSTein's *Force-wide Parameters* and *Weapon Arsenals* edit dialogs (valid for versions 1.1 and newer).

range in their local move-penalty calculation. This additional information about the *location* of friendly and/or enemy agents is provided via a notional communications link to nearby friendly agents.

Figure 5.34 illustrates the communications logic. All friendly agents Y within the *communications range* r_C of agent X (positioned at the center of the figure) communicate to X the information contained within their own sensor range r_S. This information consists of positions of friendly and enemy agents that are normally outside of X's sensor range. Agent X then incorporates this additional information into its penalty function by weighing all communicated information with a communication weight $\omega_{Comm} \geq 0$. The full penalty is defined by:

$$Z_{Penalty}(w_C) = Z_{Penalty}(w_C = 0) + \omega_{Comm} \cdot Z_C, \tag{5.14}$$

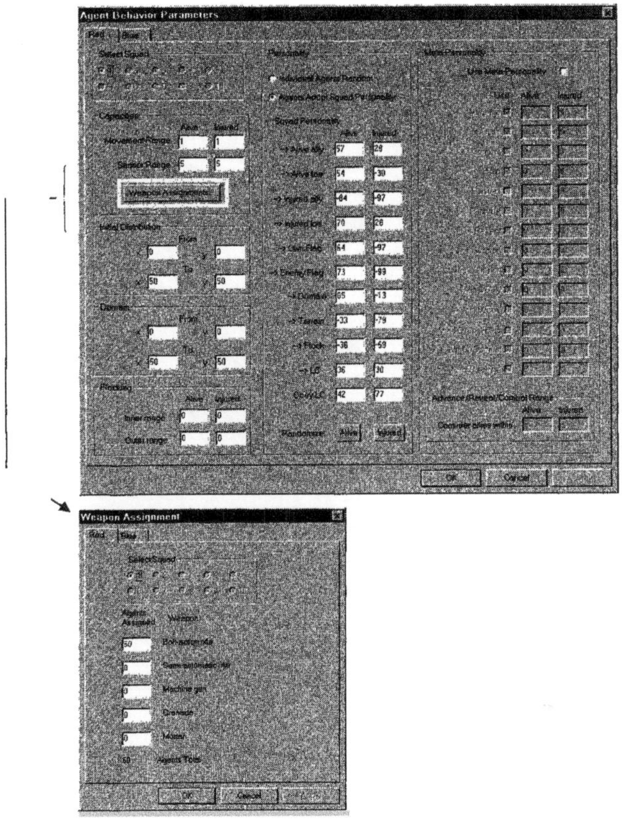

Fig. 5.33 Screenshots of EINSTein's *Agent Behavior Parameters* and *Weapon Arsenals* edit dialogs (valid for versions 1.1 and newer).

where $Z_{Penalty}(0)$ is the communications-free penalty function defined earlier (see equation 5.3), and Z_C is the same penalty function applied to communicated information.

If $\omega_{Comm} = 0$, X effectively ignores all communicated information; if $\omega_{Comm} = 1/2$, X affords all communicated information *half* the weight relative to the information contained within its own sensor field; if $\omega_{Comm} = 1$, X reacts to all communicated information with exactly the same weight as it reacts to information appearing within its own sensor range.

If the communications option is enabled, note that (1) all agents communicated with all other friendly agents within their respective communications ranges with *exactly the same weight* ($= \omega_{Comm}$), and (2) communicated information (such as information passed from Y to X in figure 5.34) *does not* include information that is passed to Y from other agents within Y's communication range; i.e. information may be communicated a maximum distance of one communication-link.

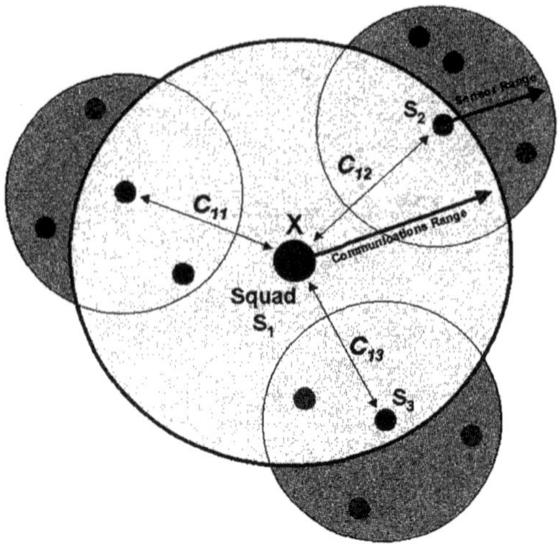

Fig. 5.34 Schematic of agent-to-agent communications logic.

5.5.1 *Inter-Squad Communication Weight Matrix*

EINSTein's notional communications logic can be enhanced by defining one- or two-way, inter-squad communication links, C_{ij}.

This enhancement allows one to specify which squads can communicate with which other squads:

$$C_{ij} = \begin{cases} 1 \text{ if and only if } S_i \text{ receives information from } S_j, \\ 0 \text{ else.} \end{cases} \tag{5.15}$$

Note that C_{ij} need not, in general, equal C_{ji}. Thus agents from squad i can receive information from squad j agents, but agents from squad j *need not* receive any information from squad i.

For example, a reconnaissance mission might include two squads S_1 and S_2, where agents from S_2 are "tasked" with scouting ahead and communicating back to agents from S_1 what they find; agents from S_1 remain near their own flag and move forward only when S_2 detects the enemy (see color plate 4, page 250).

5.6 Terrain

Just as combat logic and weapon parameters are defined and treated differently in EINSTein version 1.0 (and older) versus version 1.1 (and newer; see page 5.4), the way that terrain is handled by the program depends on which version of EINSTein is being used. Some, but not all, properties of terrain, as they are used in versions 1.0 and older, are carried over to newer versions.

5.6.1 *As Implemented in Versions 1.0 and Earlier*

Terrain may be added to a scenario either by (1) defining the sizes and positions of some (typically small number of) medium-sized *terrain blocks*, or (2) systematically building up more complicated terrain maps by individually positioning primitive (1-by-1 sized) *terrain elements.* In either case, terrain maps may always be predefined and loaded into an initially terrain-*less* scenario by loading a predefined terrain input data file. Terrain input data files have the default extension **.ter*, and must consist either of *all terrain blocks* or *all terrain elements*, but not a mixture of the two.*

5.6.1.1 *Terrain Blocks*

Terrain blocks are defined by *length*, *width*, and *center* (x, y) coordinates, along with a logic flag (i.e. an *on/off* toggle switch) indicating whether it will be actually be used during the current run. This makes it convenient to define a default set of blocks, and to then define which specific subset of these blocks will be used (while retaining the definition of all blocks in memory). A maximum of 32 separate terrain blocks can be defined for a single run.†

5.6.1.2 *Terrain Elements*

Terrain elements are essentially 1-by-1 terrain blocks. They may be added interactively, during a run, by clicking anywhere on the battlefield window with the right-hand mouse button (assuming that the user has selected the *add-terrain* option under the *Edit::Terrain* menu; see EINSTein's *User's Guide* [Ilach99a]). The number of individual terrain elements is limited only by the size of the battlefield.

EINSTein versions 1.0 and older allow six kinds of terrain elements (TEs):‡

- TE_0 = *Empty*
- TE_1 = *Impassable terrain with line-of-site off*
- TE_2 = *Impassable terrain with line-of-site on*
- TE_3 = *Passable terrain* (Type-I)
- TE_4 = *Passable terrain* (Type-II)
- TE_5 = *Passable terrain* (Type-III)

Terrain TE_1 can be thought of as a *lava pit*, across which agents can see, but through which they cannot pass. Terrain TE_2 can be thought of as an *impenetrable pillar*: agents can neither see through it nor walk through it. TE_2 is often useful for

*See page 690 in Appendix G and page 598 in Appendix E.

†For EINSTein versions 1.1 and newer, there is effectively no limit to the number of terrain elements that may be used in a given scenario (except that obviously imposed by available computer memory).

‡These six varieties apply equally to terrain blocks.

defining urban-warfare-like scenarios in which, with a little patience, quite realistic representations of buildings and streets can be designed. Figure 5.35, for example, shows two complicated terrain scenarios that include over 11,000 individual 1-by-1 pixel terrain elements.

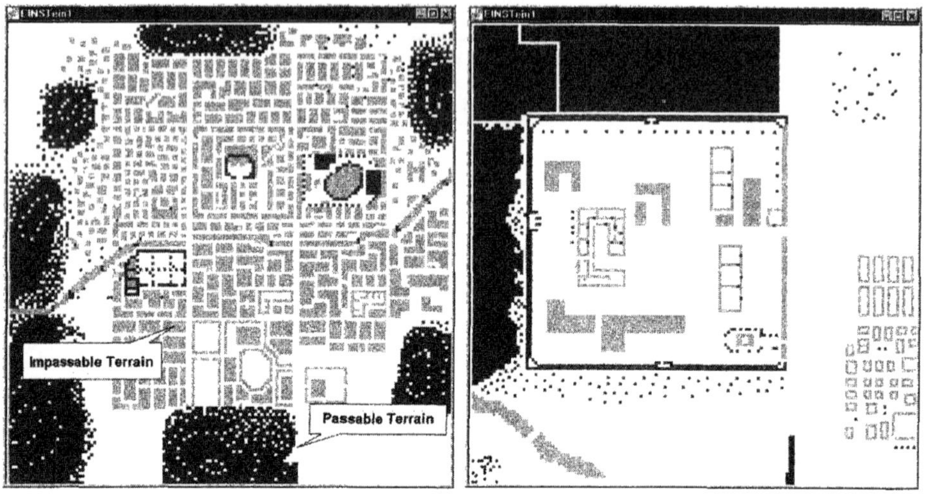

Fig. 5.35 An example of two urban-terrain-like scenarios generated using EINSTein's built-in terrain-edit facilities (as implemented in versions 1.0 and older).

Impassable terrain elements are displayed as ; passable terrain elements are displayed as .

5.6.1.3 *Agent Behavior Tailored to Terrain*

For passable terrain (TE_3, TE_4, and TE_5), certain characteristics of agents may be modified (either by adding/subtracting $(+/-\Delta)$ from, or multiplying $(*f)$, their default values) to provide a greater sense of realism. These characteristics include:

- $(-\Delta)$ *Sensor range*
- $(-\Delta)$ *Fire range*
- $(-\Delta)$ *Combat/threshold range*
- $(-\Delta)$ *Movement range*
- $(-\Delta)$ *Communications range*
- $(*f)$ *Communications weight*
- $(+\Delta)$ *Defensive strength*
- $(*f)$ *Single-shot probability of hit*
- $(-\Delta)$ *Maximum # of simultaneously targetable enemy agents*

Pseudo-realistic scenarios may thus be defined to include passable terrain that, for example, impedes an agent's motion (so that the movement range is reduced from, say, 4 units to 2), reduces its sensor and fire ranges from, say, 5 and 4 units to 3 and 2 units, respectively, and doubles their effective defensive strength.

Visibility Index. A terrain-specific parameter—the *visibility index*—may also be invoked to define the probability with which an agent $\mathcal{A}$ occupying a battlefield position (x, y) that contains a passable terrain-element of Type TE_X (where $X = 3$, 4 or 5) will be seen by another (F = *friendly* or E = *enemy*) agent, given that $\mathcal{A}$ is in F's (or E's) sensor range.

Seven of the nine passable-terrain modifiable parameters X are adjusted by adding or subtracting a user-defined delta Δ from X. These seven are identified by the symbol Δ in the bulleted list above, along with a "+" or "−" indicating whether Δ is added or subtracted from the given parameter.

Two of the nine passable-terrain modifiable parameters X are adjusted by multiplying the default value X by a user-defined factor $0 \leq f \leq 1$. These two parameters are identified by the symbol $(*f)$ in the bulleted list above.

5.6.2 *As Implemented in Versions 1.1 and Newer*

The way in which terrain is defined, edited, and used EINSTein versions 1.1 and newer differs significantly from the way these functions were handled in earlier versions. For example, EINSTein no longer distinguishes between terrain "blocks"—the lengths and widths of which had to be defined by hand, and the total number of which could not exceed 32 blocks for a given scenario—and terrain "elements" (i.e., simple 1-by-1 blocks that could be used to define more complicated terrain). EINSTein now treats "terrain" simply, and intuitively, as a modified battlefield entity. That is to say, a terrain "element" is defined (and treated) in exactly the same manner as a default battlefield site, but one that assumes nonzero values of passability and visibility:*

- *Passability:* a continuous-valued parameter that ranges from *zero* (indicating terrain that is completely impassable) to *one* (indicating terrain that does not impede movement at all).
- *Visibility:* a continuous-valued parameter that ranges from *zero* (indicating terrain that is completely opaque) to *one* (indicating terrain that does not obscure anything in or behind it).

In both cases, values between zero and one are interpreted as *percentages* of passability and visibility, respectively.

*Future versions will also include *elevation*. As of this writing (October 2003), the source code for elevated terrain is defined, but is not yet accessible from the GUI or agents' personalities.

The dynamical effects of terrain are also modeled by a new parameter, called *shelter*, that is derived from *visibility* and *passability*. Shelter crudely models a terrain element's ability to protect an agent (occupying a battlefield site "covered" by the given terrain element) from weapon fire. Shelter takes on values between *zero* and *one*, where the default terrain—i.e., the "open" battlefield—provides no shelter, and completely opaque and impassable terrain provides the most shelter:

$$shelter = (1 - \ visibility) \times (1 - \ passability) \,. \tag{5.16}$$

While the user is free to define terrain elements with arbitrary values of passability and visibility (and therefore, shelter), EINSTein defaults to the six basic terrain "types" used in earlier versions (see table 5.6).

Weapon	Description	Passability	Visibility
TE_0	Empty	1.0	1.0
TE_1	Impassable terrain with line-of-site off	0.0	0.0
TE_2	Impassable terrain with line-of-site on	0.0	1.0
TE_3	Passable terrain (Type-I)	0.25	0.1
TE_4	Passable terrain (Type-II)	0.5	0.25
TE_5	Passable terrain (Type-III)	0.75	0.5

Table 5.6 EINSTein's default terrain types (applies only for EINSTein version 1.1 and newer).

5.6.2.1 *Adding Terrain Elements to an Existing Scenario*

Terrain elements may be added interactively, at any time during a run. To do so, the user must click anywhere on an open battlefield window with the *right-hand mouse button*, and select the third option ("Draw Terrain") on the pop-dialog that appears (see figure 5.36). Doing so causes a list of existing terrain types to appear. After selecting a desired type, one can add as many terrain blocks as needed may be added by following these steps:

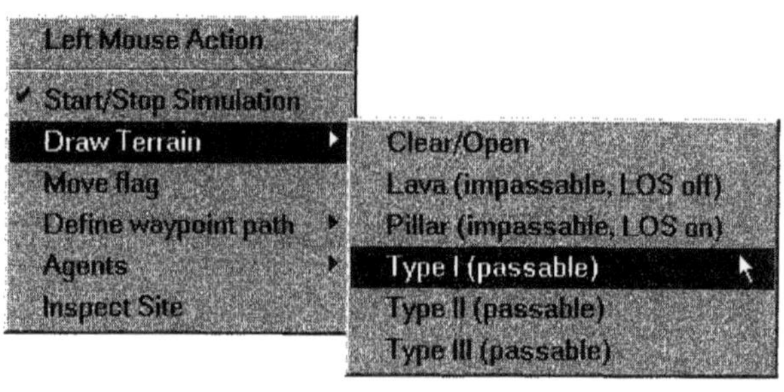

Fig. 5.36 Adding terrain elements via right-hand-mouse action in EINSTein (versions 1.1 and newer).

- *Step 1:* using the left-hand-mouse button, click anywhere on the battlefield to define the *upper left-hand corner* of the terrain block (of the chosen "type") that is to be added.
- *Step 2:* holding down the left-hand-mouse button, drag the mouse over to a site that is to become the *lower right-hand corner* of a new terrain block; if the left-hand-mouse button is simply clicked *in place*, a 1-by-1 terrain element is placed onto the battlefield at that position.
- *Step 3:* release the left-hand-mouse button to enter the new terrain block.
- *Step 4:* repeat steps 1-3 to define and place an arbitrary number of terrain blocks; use the right-hand-mouse button to call up the pop-dialog to change terrain-types, as needed.

Color plate 5 (page 251) shows several snapshots from a terrain editing session, in which two terrain blocks ("types" TE_1 and TE_3) are placed on the battlefield.

5.7 Finding and Navigating Paths

"I may not have gone where I intended to go, but I think I have ended up where I intended to be."—Douglas Adams (1952 - 2001), *The Hitchhiker's Guide to the Galaxy*

Pathfinding, in general terms, refers to the logic by which agents render a path from one point on the battlefield to another. For a human, of course, pathfinding is not usually a difficult problem, at least when the terrain is not overly complicated. In contrast, the problem of endowing agents with robust, intelligent, autonomous pathfinding and navigating abilities is highly nontrivial [Murphy00].

If there are no obstacles, and the battlefield consists only of open terrain, a simple self-initiated vectoring from a starting point to a desired end point (via a single weight component directed toward that end point) suffices to move an agent toward its goal.

But what is an agent to do if a terrain element blocks its view, and/or the straight-line-path, to its desired goal? In principle, if terrain elements were all simply convex, a trivial rule of the form *"back up, turn 45/90 deg, then move forward again"* command may suffice for most cases. However, rigid rules of this form are generally not very robust and give rise to unrealistic motion. Moreover, if a scenario includes nonconvex terrain elements (as even semirealistic scenarios are likely to do), more complex algorithms must be used to ensure that agents are able to traverse the terrain.

In addition to basic tools for generating, and editing, terrain maps, that may consist of arbitrary combinations of convex and nonconvex patterns, EINSTein (versions 1.1 and newer) provides the user with two sets of agent pathfinding logic:

- Open-field *pathfinding* using Dijkstra's optimal path algorithm.
- *Following* user-defined paths (that consist of an arbitrary number of unique waypoints).

Open-field *pathfinding* may be invoked by the user at any time, regardless of whether terrain is present or not (though, of course, if a scenario contains no terrain, the invocation of pathfinding logic is essentially superfluous). Once invoked, EINSTein pauses the run in progress to calculate the best possible route from all battlefield sites to all other accessible sites. Once the calculation is complete, and the optimal path data are stored in memory, agents have access to this information while adjudicating their moves. As we will see, the ability to use this information often has a dramatic effect on the realism displayed by agents' emergent paths, particularly for scenarios that include complicated terrain.

Path *following* logic refers to an additional set of primitive instructions that agents use to follow a series of waypoints that are placed directly (i.e., interactively, via a series of mouse-driven commands) on the battlefield to define a path. Multiple paths may be defined, with each consisting of an arbitrary number of user-defined waypoints, although only one path per squad is allowed.

Open-field pathfinding and path following logic may also be combined. For example, a user may want agents to use optimal-path data to provide "fall back" information in case they stray so far from an assigned path (for which they nominally use their assigned path following logic to traverse) that they must traverse complex terrain to "find their way" back to their assigned path.

5.7.1 *Pathfinding*

All versions of EINSTein prior to 1.0.0.3beta have included both passable and impassable terrain. However, agents have previously navigated through terrain elements in a very simpleminded manner. Except for being able to react instinctively to terrain (by effectively treating terrain elements as static battlefield entities on a par with friendly and enemy flags), agents were previously unable to walk around terrain when the terrain obstructed their view (and/or path) toward their goal.

Convex terrain blocks are particularly forgiving in this regard, because an agent can always "steer around" a block toward a more distant flag, and thereby give the appearance of having acted intelligently. An example is shown in figure 5.37.

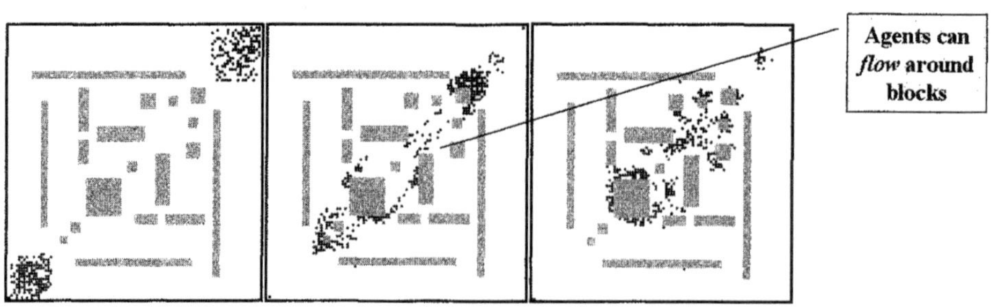

Fig. 5.37 An example of "steering around" terrain blocks (i.e. impassable terrain).

For more complicated scenarios that include bona-fide terrain obstructions, agent movement is almost always stymied. Figure 5.38, for example, shows what happens in a scenario that includes a particularly unforgiving terrain map in this regard. It is obvious from the figure that agents are easily trapped on the inside part of the "joints" between any two terrain blocks that meet at right angles.

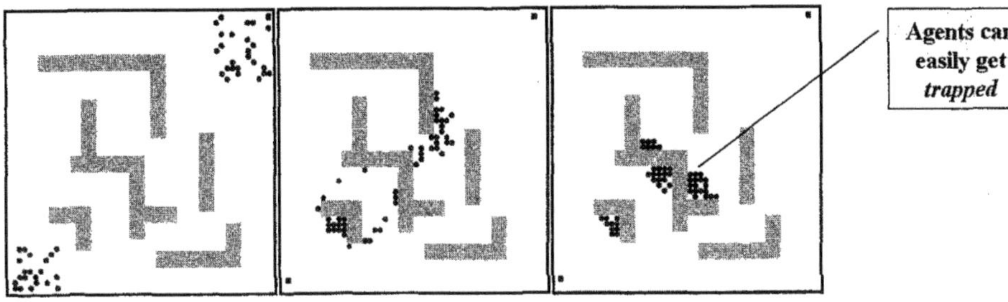

Fig. 5.38 An example of how complicated terrain maps trap agents.

The addition of semi-intelligent route planning—using a modified form of *Dijkstra's Algorithm*—partially resolves this deficiency, and allows users to define urban-warfare-like scenarios that include more complicated (and thus, more realistic) arrangements of impassable terrain elements.

5.7.1.1 *Dijkstra's algorithm*

Given a graph $G = (V, L)$, where V is the set of vertices in G and L is the set of links between vertices, the shortest path from vertex $S \in V$ to $T \in V$ is the set of links $l \in L$ that connects S to T at a minimum cost. EINSTein's battlefield lattice is a special graph in which each site (except for boundary sites) is linked to its north, south, east and west neighbors and each link incurs a "cost" (or distance) equal to one (though this may, and is, generalized to include other components such as terrain passability, elevation, etc.)

Dijkstra's algorithm is a well known "greedy" (but optimal) solution to the problem of finding the shortest path between a vertex S and all other vertices in G [Thula92]. The pseudo-code listing for Dijkstra's algorithm is shown in figure 5.39. Its computational complexity scales as $O(LV^2)$.

The algorithm works by constructing a shortest-path tree rooted at the starting vertex S and whose branches are the shortest paths from S to all other vertices. Initially, all vertices are assigned a color—say, white—and all initial shortest-path estimates are set to ∞. All vertices except S are assigned a parent node in the shortest-path tree; this parent will likely change many times as the algorithm proceeds.

From among all white vertices, select the vertex U that currently has the shortest-path estimate (initially, this is S). Color it black. Now, for each white

Step 1 Initialize by setting LABEL(S)=0, PERM(S)=1 and PATH(S)=s.
For all V ≠ S, set LABEL(V)=∞, PERM(V)=0 and PATH(V)=V.

Step 2 Set i = 0 and U = S.
(The vertex U is the last vertex that is permanently labeled in a full sweep of the all vertices of G.)

Step 3 Compute LABEL(V) and update the entries of the PATH(...) array:

```
Set i = i + 1
Do for each vertex V that has not been permanently labeled:
        Set M = min { LABEL(V), LABEL(U) + w(U,V) }
        If M < LABEL(V) then set LABEL(V) = M and PATH(V) = U.
End Do
```

Step 4 From among all vertices which have not yet been permanently labeled, identify the vertex W that has the smallest valued label. If there is more than one such vertex, choose randomly. Set PERM(W)=1 and U = W.

Step 5 If i < N - 1 (where N is the total number of vertices in G), go to step 3, otherwise STOP.

When the algorithm terminates, {V, PATH(V), PATH(PATH(V)), ..., S } are the vertices in the shortest path from S to V.

Fig. 5.39 Pseudo-code listing of *Dijkstra's algorithm.*

vertex V near U, decide whether tracing a path through U improves the shortest path computed thus far to V. This is decided by adding the distance between U and V to the shortest-path estimate for U. If this value is less than or equal to the shortest-path estimate for V, assign that value to V (as its new estimate) and assign the parent of V to U. Repeat until all vertices are colored black.

Once the shortest-path tree has been computed, the shortest path from S to any other vertex T is found by starting at T and working backwards via successive parents until S is reached. The reverse path is the shortest path from S to T.

EINSTein actually implements a variant of the basic algorithm sketched here that uses *priority queues*, which improves the computational complexity to $O(L \log V)$. A priority queue is an abstract data type (i.e., a data entity plus a set of operations on the data entity) that efficiently supports finding the node with the highest priority across a series of operations. The basic operations on a priority queue are: (1) create an empty priority queue, (2) insert an element having a certain priority to the priority queue, and (3) remove the element that has the highest priority.

5.7.1.2 *Agent-Based Pathfinding*

Semi-intelligent route planning uses Dijkstra's Algorithm to provide an array of intermediate waypoints that agents can use to navigate around terrain elements when those terrain elements obstruct their view of their own and/or enemy flags.

Interactive run-times are virtually unaffected since waypoints are computed prior to the start of a run and their use induces only a minor performance hit.

The user selects a threshold distance D from terrain at which a waypoint will be computed (as a temporary alternative to red and blue flags) using Dijkstra's algorithm. If a large threshold value is selected ($D = 10$ or $D = 15$) more (x, y) points will be used for computing shortest paths, and the computation time will therefore increase. A nominal value that proves useful in practice is the default $D = 3$.

After selecting the threshold minimum distance from terrain, the user must first save the Dijkstra's Algorithm-determined intermediate terrain waypoints to file. Note that agents will not use this information for route planning unless the user has manually loaded the appropriate file.

Figure 5.40 illustrates how the waypoint information is used for semi-intelligent route planing. If, while at coordinate (x_{agent}, y_{agent}), an agent sees the red/blue flag (x_{flag}, y_{flag}) (assuming the agent's view is not obstructed by terrain), the agent will continue moving toward (or away from) that flag according to its default movement personality.

If the agent is within a distance D of terrain (which, by default, is equal to the same D as used by Dijkstra's Algorithm above), and terrain blocks its view of the red and/or blue flags, the agent will temporarily use the red-flag and blue-flag waypoints as substitutes for the real red and/or blue flag positions to make its way around the obstructing terrain elements:

$$(x_{flag}, y_{flag}) \rightarrow (x_{waypoint}(x_{flag}, y_{flag}), y_{waypoint}(x_{flag}, y_{flag})) \,. \tag{5.17}$$

Temporary waypoint coordinates, $(x_{waypoint}, y_{waypoint})$, are functions of an agent's current position.

The virtues of using precomputed waypoints to help agents navigate through terrain include (1) *speed* (computation is fast,* since waypoints need to be computed only once, prior to an interactive run), and (2) *enhanced realism* (allowing the user to explore more realistic urban-warfare-like combat scenarios).

However, the method, as currently implemented, has two main drawbacks: (1) it can only be used for static terrain (and is essentially useless as a navigation aid for agents trying to steer around other moving agents), and (2) it does not always produce realistic pathing solutions (which, in the real world are often far from "optimal").

*For a 150-by-150 battlefield that includes moderately complicated terrain, run-times for computing waypoints (and saving them to a file) are typically 5-10 seconds for a Pentium-III/600 MHz PC, and under a second for newer Pentium IV/2+ GHz PCs. For newer processors (3+ GHz Pentium IV), the calculation time is effectively negligible. Moreover, optimal path data must be computed only *once* (at which point it is automatically stored for future use by EINSTein), prior to the start of an actual run.

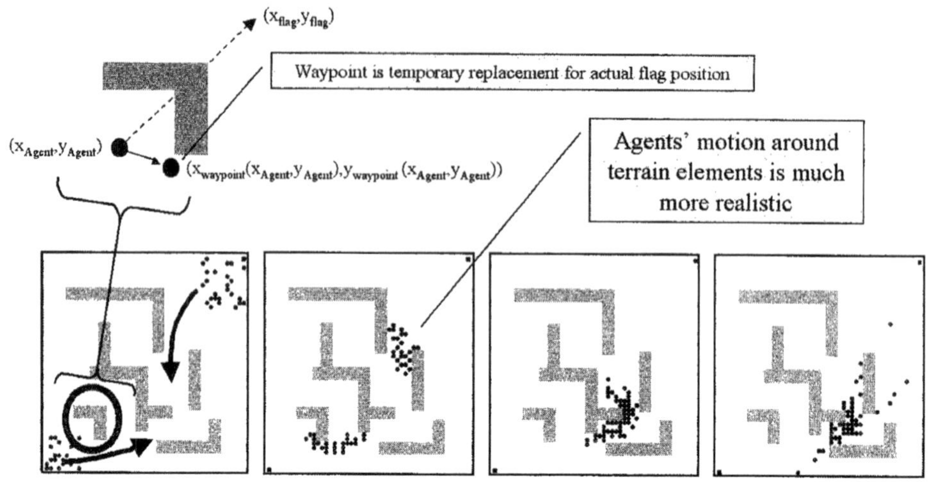

Fig. 5.40 Semi-intelligent agent path finding using waypoints as determined by EINSTein's built-in Dijkstra's algorithm.

For example, while the algorithm correctly yields optimal paths through complicated urban-terrain-like environments (such as the one depicted in the left-hand-side screenshot of figure 5.35), the paths do not faithfully reproduce real world behavior, which would tend to be more erratic and unpredictable. As a partial remedy for this, EINSTein includes the option of assigning scripted paths to squads for agents to follow during a scenario (see discussion in next section).

The user-interface for toggling the use of Dijkstra-computed global path information on and off depends on which version of EINSTein is being used. For versions 1.0 and older, the user must manually invoke the calculation of Dijkstra path data, *before a run*, and save the data in a separate **.pth* file (see Appendix G).

In versions 1.1 and newer, EINSTein automatically precomputes all global path data as it becomes necessary before, or during, a run. For example, if terrain is added during a run, via a right-button-mouse action (see discussion above, starting on page 341), global path information is automatically updated without any need for user intervention. Use of Dijkstra data is toggled on and off separately for red and blue agents (and applied on a force-wide basis) by clicking on the Edit main menu column and selecting *Force Wide Parameters*. The toggle switch—labeled "Use global optimal path knowledge"—is the second item listed under the Terrain options group on the right-hand-side of the pop-up dialog (see figure 5.41).

When the optimal path use is toggled on for the first time during the run, a pop-up dialog appears warning the user that, depending on the number and complexity of terrain blocks, computation of optimal path information may be CPU-time consuming (see figure 5.42).

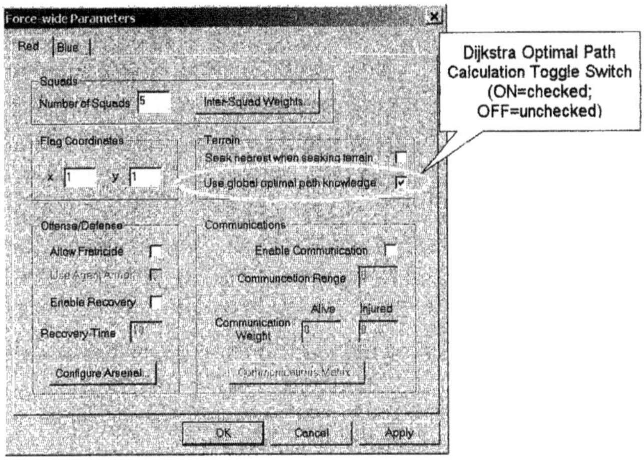

Fig. 5.41 Location of EINSTein's new Dijkstra-path toggle switch (for EINSTein *versions 1.1 and newer*).

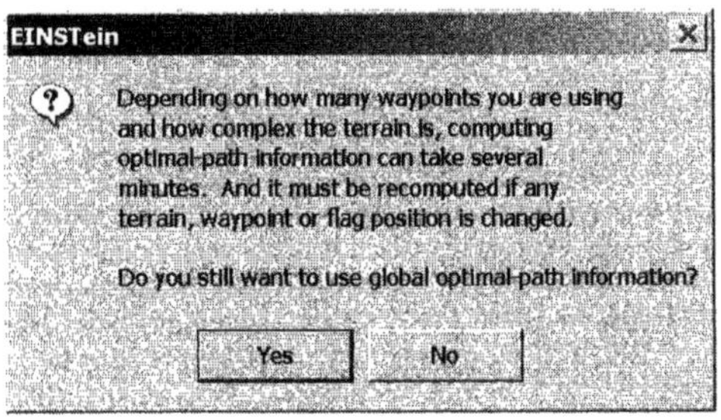

Fig. 5.42 Pop-up warning dialog that appears after toggling optimal path option "on" for the first time.

5.7.2 *Navigating User-Defined Paths*

The agent-based route planning methodology outlined above—which endows agents with just enough raw "intelligence" to successfully navigate to the flag when challenged by complicated intervening terrain elements—may be generalized to also allow agents to traverse *user-defined paths* in a semi-intelligent fashion. This is an important addition to EINSTein's built-in repertoire of behaviors because it allows the user to develop significantly more realistic scenarios.

The basic idea is to use a set of (fixed) waypoints to define a path, and to use a robust logic that is parameterized by a few intuitive control variables, and by which agents effectively "steer" their visitation of each waypoint, in turn, until the terminal waypoint of the path is reached.

5.7.2.1 *Paths and Waypoints*

Consider an agent $\mathcal{A}$ from squad S, which starts out at time $t = 0$ with a squad-assigned path $\mathcal{P}_S$, consisting of waypoints $\{p_1, p_2, ...p_N\}$. The agent is assumed to have assigned to it a (dynamically changing) *"stay on path"* personality-weight component, which the agent interprets as *"move to next waypoint on currently assigned path."* How does the agent actually move, or try to move, along $\mathcal{P}$?

Before we describe the sequence of logical steps the agent takes, we first need to introduce a few parameters and be clear about certain restrictive general assumptions regarding path logic.

5.7.2.2 *Assumptions*

Assumption #1: *If paths are to be used during a scenario the program will automatically zero out the default "move to enemy flag" and "move to friendly flag" weight components.*

Making this assumption prevents potential conflicts in which agents are assigned (by the user) to have conflicting goals. For example, an agent could be tasked with "stay near own flag" and "stay on path," where the path is intended to lead the agent away from his own flag. While an agent is free to assign a positive (or negative) weight to his own or enemy flags as the scenario unfolds and the agent deals with different contexts, his propensities for moving toward either flag are nulled, by default, at the start of a run.

The action is performed on a squad-by-squad basis. That is, squad S_1 may be assigned a path, but squad S_2 may not. In this case, the default "move to enemy flag" and "move to friendly flag" weight components will be nulled out for agents from S_1 but left alone for agents from S_2.

Assumption #2: *The positions of all waypoints of the path an agent is on are assumed known, even if they are not within an agent's sensor range.*

This is to make waypoint information consistent with the absolute knowledge that all agents possess of their own and enemy flag positions, even if either flag is beyond sensor range.

5.7.2.3 *Path-Following Parameters*

Parameter #1: Δd_{at} = *minimum waypoint attainment distance.*

If the distance, $D(\mathcal{A}, p)$, between an agent $\mathcal{A}$ and the next waypoint on its path, p, is less than or equal to Δd_{at}, $\mathcal{A}$ is assumed to have reached p. $\mathcal{A}$'s actual position does not change, of course, but immediately after having come within Δd_{at} of p, $\mathcal{A}$ must select its new waypoint (see below).

Parameter #2: Δd_{on} = *maximum "on path" distance.*

If the distance, $D(\mathcal{A}, p_{i-1})$, between agent $\mathcal{A}$ (which is currently moving toward waypoint p_i) and $\mathcal{A}$'s previous waypoint, p_{i-1}, is less than or equal to Δd_{on}, $\mathcal{A}$ is assumed to still be on the path $\mathcal{P}$. If $D(\mathcal{A}, p_{i-1}) \geq \Delta d_{on}$, $\mathcal{A}$ is assumed to be "off the path" and must select a new waypoint (i.e., p_i is no longer assumed to be the next waypoint; see below).

Parameter #3: $\Delta d_{approach}$ = *maximum "approaching next waypoint" distance.*

If the distance, $D(\mathcal{A}, p)$, between agent $\mathcal{A}$ and $\mathcal{A}$'s next waypoint, p, is less than or equal to $\Delta d_{approach}$, $\mathcal{A}$'s next waypoint assignment remains unchanged (i.e., $\mathcal{A}$ continues to move toward p).

If $D(\mathcal{A}, p_i \geq \Delta d_{approach}$, $\mathcal{A}$ is assumed to be beyond p's vicinity and must select a new waypoint (see below).

Parameter #4: $P_{StayOnPath}$ = *probability that agent $\mathcal{A}$ will stay on path $\mathcal{P}$.*

If $P_{StayOnPath} = 1$, then $\mathcal{A}$ will—with probability *one*—move toward the next waypoint on the ordered list of waypoints that define path $\mathcal{P}$. If $P_{StayOnPath} = 0$, then $\mathcal{A}$, with certainty, ignores all waypoint information (i.e., $\mathcal{A}$ acts as though its weight component for "follow path" is equal to zero). If $0 < P_{StayOnPath} < 1$, $\mathcal{A}$ first draws a random number before deciding which waypoint to use (see below).

Parameter #5: *Dijkstra*(p_i) = *Dijkstra-generated data array generalized to paths.*

Recall that the Dijkstra algorithm is a greedy (but optimal) solution to the problem of finding the shortest path between a given point on the battlefield (or any node on a graph, in general) and all other points (or nodes). EINSTein uses the Dijkstra algorithm for semi-intelligent route planning in scenarios that include terrain. Dijkstra provides an array of intermediate "goals" (not to be confused with "waypoints" as we are currently using that term in this discussion) that agents can use to navigate around terrain elements when those terrain elements obstruct their view of their own and/or enemy flags.

The Dijkstra algorithm is used to generate, prior to the start of a run-session, a set of data arrays that store intermediate-goals for all waypoints $\{p_i\}$, on all paths $\{P_j\}$, that are part of that run-session's scenario (along with the data arrays of intermediate goals for the red and blue flags, as previous versions of EINSTein have always done).

The values of Δd_{at}, Δd_{on}, $\Delta d_{approach}$, and $P_{StayOnPath}$ are all fixed prior to the start of a run, and are nominally equal for all squads, though they may be defined to be squad-specific by the user.

Armed with these assumptions, new parameters, and Dijkstra-generated data, let's resume our discussion of the steps $\mathcal{A}$ follows in moving along its assigned path, $\mathcal{P}$. Heuristically, at each time step, A needs to solve two basic problems:

1. *What waypoint should I be moving toward?*
2. *How shall I get there?*

A trivial solution is to have $\mathcal{A}$ always move from one assigned waypoint to the next, in the exact order in which waypoints appear in the user-specified path list, and use the threshold distance Δd_{at}, as defined above, to determine when an agent has reached a given waypoint.

An obvious difficulty with this solution, is that, like a blind misuse of the Dijkstra algorithm, it will almost certainly lead to highly unrealistic behavior. For example one can imagine variations of scenarios in which $\mathcal{A}$ never even makes it to the first waypoint. $\mathcal{A}$'s attention may, at the start of a run, be diverted away from the first waypoint to deal with other matters (such as moving toward retreating enemy agents, maintaining formation with squad mates, and so on) and then, only after many iterations, when the agent is perhaps already close to the enemy flag, does the agent finally "decide" to move toward the first waypoint near its own flag. An additional concern is that, in scenarios that include terrain, as $\mathcal{A}$ moves farther and farther away from an idealized "path" (i.e., from an imaginary line drawn) between two intermediate waypoints, it becomes increasingly more likely that the agent's direct (line of sight) path to the next waypoint may be obstructed by impassable terrain blocks. What is the agent to do in this case?

A better, though still not necessarily optimal, solution to both problems must include logic that allows agents to decide when, and for what reason, to shift their focus on other waypoints. An agent's action selection logic must be flexible enough to allow them to adaptively "change their mind" (depending on changing contexts) about which waypoint, on their assigned path, should be the one they must aim for.

Finer resolution questions that need to be asked, from an agent's perspective, therefore include:

- *Am I close enough to the waypoint I just reached so that I can safely say that I am still on the path to the next waypoint on the ordered list?*
- *Am I close enough to the waypoint I am moving toward to safely say that I am still on the path toward it?*
- *Am I so far from both the waypoint I last reached and the one that I was just moving toward that I have "strayed off the path?"*

5.7.2.4 *Path-Following Logic*

The logical steps that follow from obtaining answers to these questions are as follows (figure 5.43 shows a schematic of a typical trajectory followed by an agent $\mathcal{A}$ while attempting to move along a path $\mathcal{P}$):

Step #1: Has $\mathcal{A}$ attained its currently assigned (i.e., next) waypoint?

If $D(\mathcal{A}, p) \leq \Delta d_{at}$, then **YES**: select next waypoint, p (**GOTO** step 5).
If $D(\mathcal{A}, p) > \Delta d_{at}$, then $\mathcal{A}$ has not yet reached p: **GOTO** step 2.

Step #2: Has a fixed order been assigned to $\mathcal{A}$?

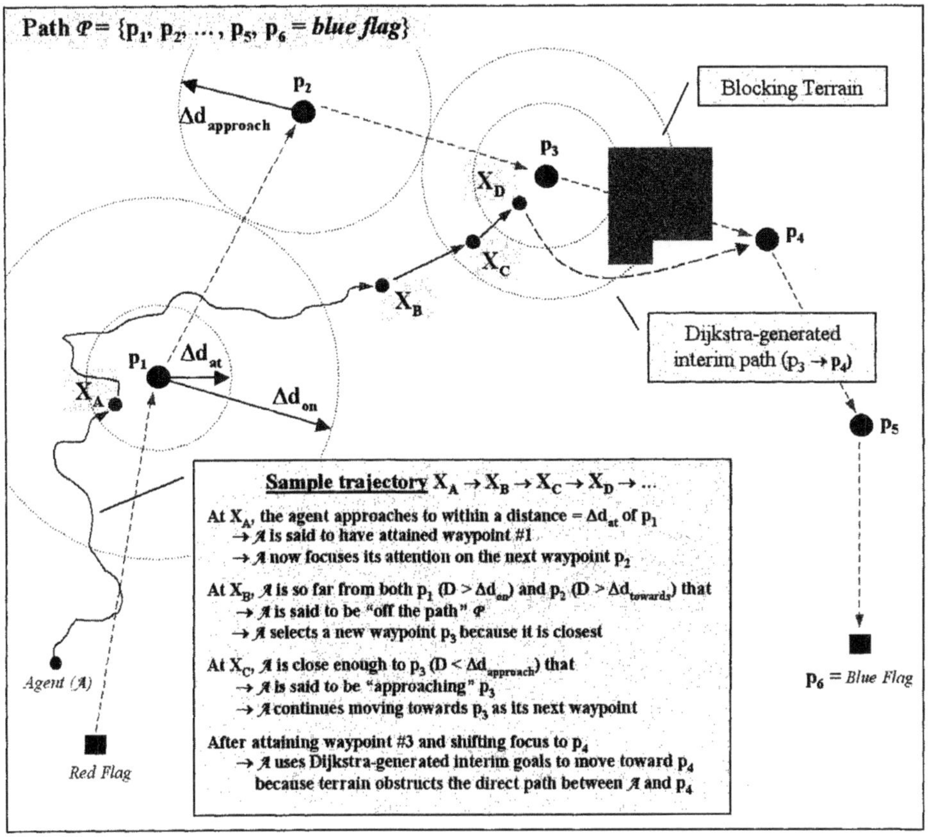

Fig. 5.43 Schematic for how agents in EINSTein navigate paths defined by a sequence of user-defined waypoints; see text for details.

If $P_{StayOnPath} = 1$, then **YES**: move to next waypoint: **GOTO** step 6. In this case, as described above, $\mathcal{A}$ always moves toward the next waypoint on the ordered list of waypoints that define path $\mathcal{P}$, regardless of where $\mathcal{A}$ is on the battlefield. For example, if $\mathcal{A}$ finds itself near p_9 while having just reached waypoint p_2, $\mathcal{A}$ ignores it and uses the next ordered waypoint, p_3, as its next waypoint (which will then be followed by p_4, by p_5, and so on).

If $P_{StayOnPath} < 1$, then **GOTO** step 3.

Step #3: Is $\mathcal{A}$ on the path toward its assigned (i.e., next) waypoint?

If $\mathcal{A}$ has already reached at least one waypoint on its path, check to see if $\mathcal{A}$ is near its previous waypoint, $p_{previous}$. (If $\mathcal{A}$ has not yet reached its first waypoint then skip this step and **GOTO** step 4.)

If $D(\mathcal{A}, p_{previous}) \leq \Delta d_{on}$, then $\mathcal{A}$ is on its path: keep moving toward p (**GOTO** step 6).

If $D(\mathcal{A}, p_{previous}) > \Delta d_{on}$, check to see if $\mathcal{A}$ is approaching p: **GOTO** step 4.

Step #4: Is $\mathcal{A}$ within maximum "approaching next waypoint" distance of p?

If $D(\mathcal{A}, p) \leq \Delta d_{approach}$, then $\mathcal{A}$ is on its path: keep moving toward p (**GOTO** step 6).

If $D(\mathcal{A}, p) > \Delta d_{approach}$, then $\mathcal{A}$ is no longer on path toward p: select next waypoint (**GOTO** step 5).

Step #5: *Select next waypoint.*

Assuming that $0 < P_{StayOnPath} < 1$, $\mathcal{A}$ rolls a random number x (between 0 and 1).

If $x < P_{StayOnPath}$, then $\mathcal{A}$ goes to the next waypoint on the ordered path list that has not yet been visited (even if this decision entails backtracking on the battlefield), else $\mathcal{A}$ moves toward the nearest (not yet visited) waypoint. Now, move to next waypoint: **GOTO** step 6. (Note: Obviously, if $P_{StayOnPath} = 0$, then $\mathcal{A}$ effectively assigns zero weight to "stay on path" at all times, and none of the steps outlined here need to be followed.)

If an agent strays "off the path" while moving toward, say, p_3, rolls a random number, and decides to direct its attention toward p_9 because p_9 is the waypoint that is currently closest, all lower ordered waypoints, p_3 through p_8, are automatically tagged as having been visited, despite the fact that none were. This prevents potential future backtracking.

Step #6: Move to next waypoint.

Use *Dijkstra*(p) to determine which "interim goal" ought to be used while attempting to move toward p. Say an agent $\mathcal{A}$ is at $(x_{\mathcal{A}}, y_{\mathcal{A}})$, and its next waypoint is p, located at (x_p, y_p). Before moving, $\mathcal{A}$ first consults its Dijkstra-generated data array, *Dijkstra*(p)), to identify the interim battlefield position, (x_D, y_D), that it should now be moving toward as it strives to "stay on the path" toward p (interim coordinates are functions of $\mathcal{A}$'s current position and next waypoint):

$$(x_p, y_p) \rightarrow (x_D(x_p, y_p), y_D(x_p, y_p)) \,. \tag{5.18}$$

During a given scenario, all agents are constrained to follow *one path at a time.* If the location, or number, of waypoints on an existing path, or entire paths, are edited during a run, the program automatically reinitializes the scenario (i.e., no on-the-fly path information changes are permitted).

Step #7: Terminate path.

The user may select one of three ways to terminate the path: (1) the last (user-defined) waypoint is linked to, and terminates at, the "enemy flag," (2) the last (user-defined) waypoint is the center of a "termination area" (defined by length/width, if the cookie-cutter metric is used, or radius if the Euclidean metric is used), that the agent is motivated to stay near after traversing the path,* or (3) the last (user-defined) waypoint is linked to the first waypoint, so that the path becomes a closed loop that the agent continues to traverse.

The waypoints used to define a path may be placed directly on the battlefield, before or during a run, by the user. The default parameter values that determine (in part) the logic by which agents will traverse a given path may be changed at any time by clicking on the *Edit* main menu column and selecting *Waypoint Path Properties.*†

This brings up the dialog shown in figure 5.44 (which also indicates which of the path-logic parameters discussed in the previous section each dialog entry refers to). Note that both *force*-specific (i.e., red or blue) and *squad*-specific parameter values may be defined.

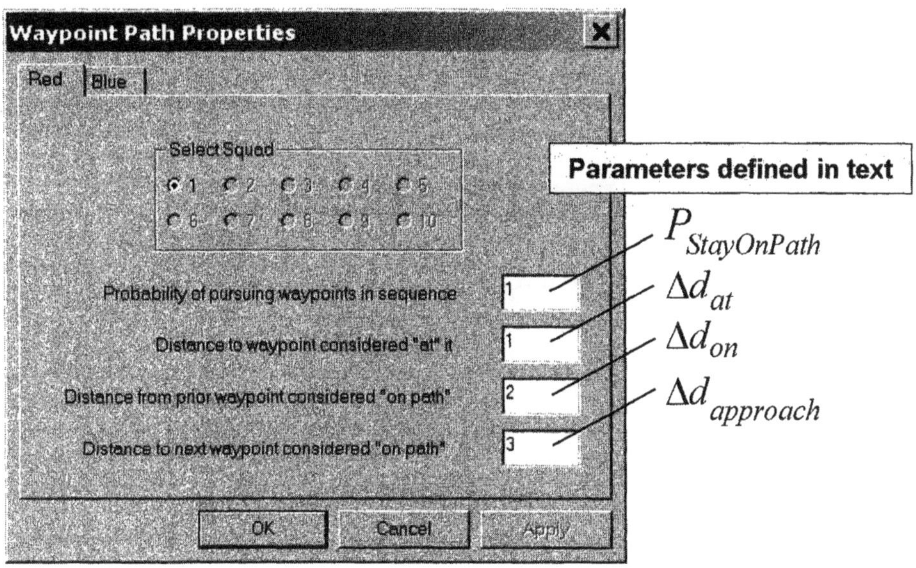

Fig. 5.44 Snapshot of the *Waypoint Path Properties* dialog. The labels refer to the symbols used to define each of the four user-editable parameters as they are defined in the previous section.

The waypoints themselves are defined, interactively, by first clicking anywhere on the battlefield with the right-mouse-button. Doing so causes a pop-up dialog to appear, the fourth option of which—labeled "Define waypoint path"—leads to

*This is defined using EINSTein's existing *patrol area* parameters [Ilach99a]

†Note that these instructions apply only to ENSTein *versions 1.1 and newer*, as older versions did not allow the user to add waypoints.

additional squad-specific red and blue waypoint path options; see figure 5.45. There will be as many red and blue squad entry options (*Squad* 1 through *Squad N*) as there are squads defined in the current scenario.

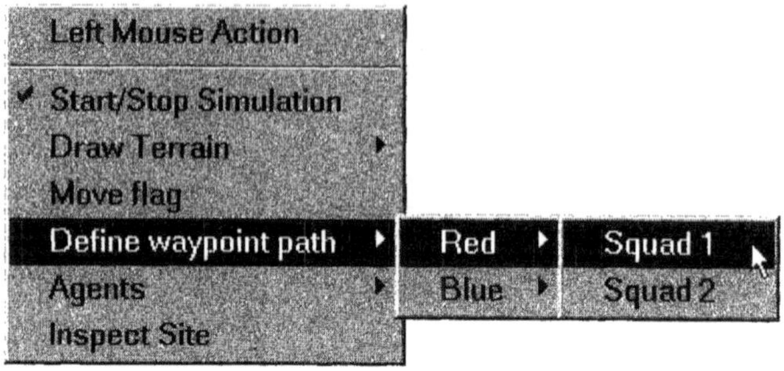

Fig. 5.45 Waypoint path definition pop-up dialog; see text for details.

When the right-mouse-button action is used to define waypoints for the *first time* during the run, a pop-up dialog appears summarizing the commands for placing, editing, and saving waypoint information (see figure 5.46).

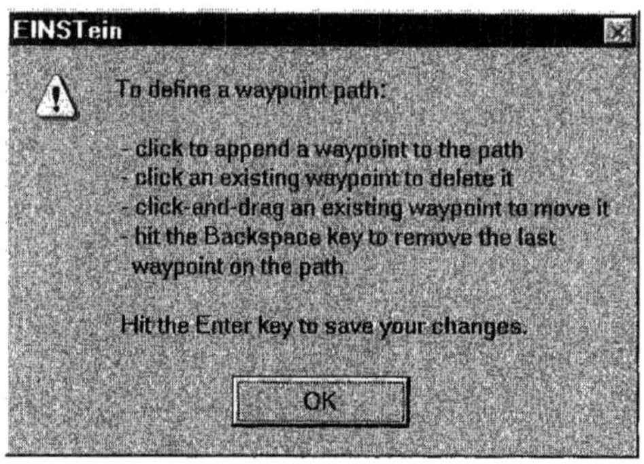

Fig. 5.46 Pop-up dialog summarizing commands for creating paths using waypoints.

There are four basic commands:

1. *Create new waypoint:* click once with the right-mouse-button to create a new waypoint and append it to the existing path.
2. *Delete waypoint:* click on any existing waypoint to delete it or hit the Backspace key to remove the last waypoint that was added to the path.
3. *Move waypoint:* click and drag any existing waypoint to move it to another location.
4. *Save path:* hit the Enter key to save all changes and store path information.

5.7.2.5 *Waypoints and Optimal Paths*

The following fact must be kept in mind at all times while experimenting with the options that determine how EINSTein uses Dijkstra optimal path data and user-defined waypoints:

> *If the Dijkstra optimal-path option is togged on prior to defining a path, a separate Dijkstra-map must be computed for each of the N waypoints that define the path.*

This fact is important for two reasons. First, it directly affects how the agents behave. And second, depending on the number of waypoints used to define a path (and on the number of paths the analyst decides to use), EINSTein may appear to "hang" while it calculates Dijkstra optimal-path for each waypoint of each path. The user must be prepared to wait for EINSTein to complete its calculations before resuming the run.

In the event that Dijkstra optimal-path data are used for user-defined paths, this means that whenever agents stray off of their assigned path, they will use Dijkstra data to "find a route" back to their path. In contrast, if Dijkstra data are switched *off*, there may be scenarios in which agents—once they lose site of their assigned paths—are unable to find a route back to their path.

5.7.2.6 *Example 1: Defining a Path*

Consider a simple scenario that consists of one red and one blue squad, to which the user desires to add a blue path. Figure 5.47 shows a few snapshots from a waypoint-editing session during which the user defines five waypoints.

The first step is to click anywhere on the open battlefield with the right-mouse-button, and select the *Define waypoint path→Blue→Squad* 1 option (Step 1 in figure 5.47). Doing so temporarily pauses the current run, and forces EINSTein to go into "input mode," in which the program is idle, awaiting the user to define and anchor the first waypoint.

This is done by clicking on the desired location with the left-mouse-button. A small blue box, centered on the selected position, indicates that EINSTein has registered the user input. The current location of the mouse cursor is indicated by a "+" symbol, which replaces the usual arrow while EINSTein is in left-mouse-button action mode (Step 2 in figure 5.47).

As the second, third, fourth, and fifth waypoints are defined, EINSTein indicates their order by drawing a line to connect successive waypoints (Steps 3-6).

When finished, the *Enter* key must be pressed to save the path; not doing so deletes all waypoint data and the path must be redefined from scratch. The scenario is reinitialized, and EINSTein is put back into run mode, by clicking with the right-mouse-button to call up the action dialog and selecting the option *Start/Stop Simulation* (Step 7). Note that the user-defined path now appears as a dotted line connecting the first waypoint and the enemy flag.

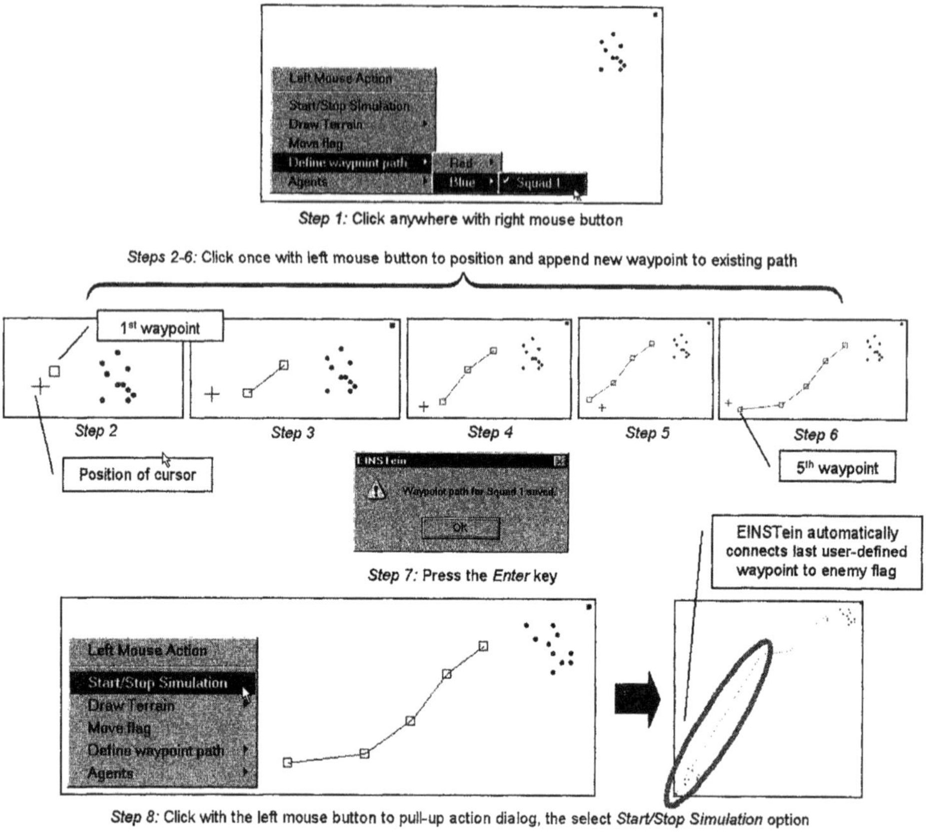

Fig. 5.47 Snapshots from a sample waypoint editing session; see text for details.

The enemy flag is (in this example) automatically appended to the fifth, and last, waypoint defined by the user (Step 8). In general, upon hitting the ENTER key, the user is prompted (by the dialog shown in figure 5.48) to specify the *path termination conditions*. The user may select to either terminate on the current (squad-assigned) goal (option #1), or to loop back to the first waypoint and repeatedly traverse the same path (option #2). The second option is useful for scenarios in which certain squads are used to patrol specific paths within larger patrol areas.

5.7.2.7 *Example 2: Comparing Default, Optimal, and Path-Following Logic*

Consider a more complicated urban-combat-like scenario that consists, in part, of two red and two blue squads, and several hundred different (combinations of passable and impassable) terrain blocks; see figure 5.49.*

*This scenario arguably represents the upper-bound on the degree of terrain complexity that is possible to achieve with EINSTein's built-in terrain editing tools.

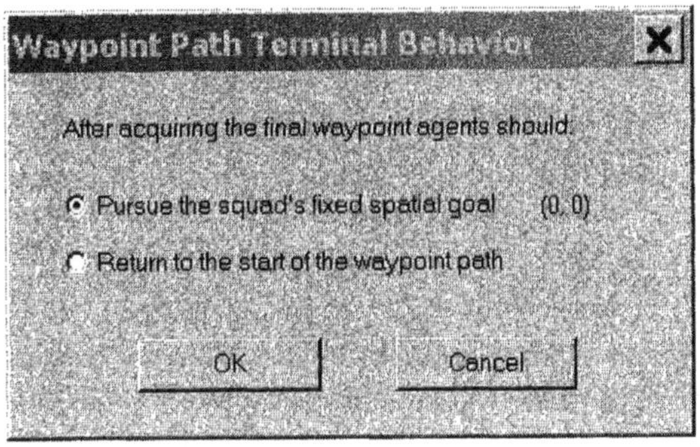

Fig. 5.48 Screenshot of the pop-up dialog, prompting the user to specify path termination conditions, that appears after the user hits the ENTER key to complete manual entry of waypoints.

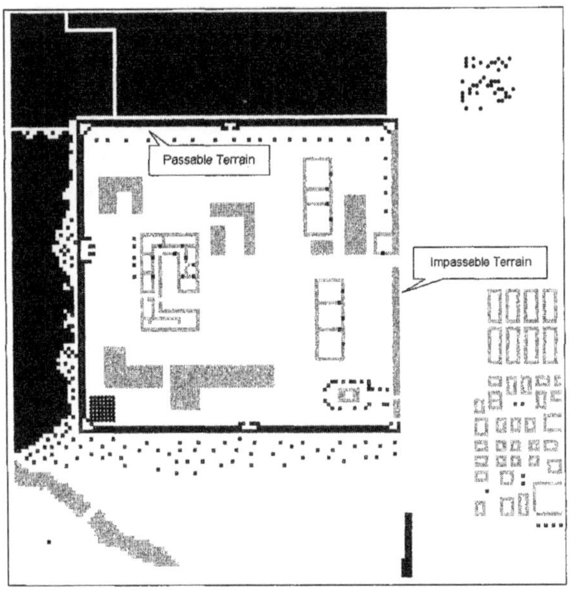

Fig. 5.49 Snapshot of battlefield for the urban-combat-like scenario used in example 2.

How do the agents' behaviors change as a function of the rules they use to traverse a terrain-laden battlefield? By default, agents navigate as best as they can locally, without relying on user-assigned waypoints or precomputed optimal path data. That is, agents are motivated only by moving toward (or away from) other agents and their behavior with respect to terrain—even if it appears, at times, to be "reasonable" or intuitive—is merely an artifact of interacting with other agents and adhering to the constraints that are imposed on their movement by the presence of terrain elements.

Color plate 6 (page 252) shows a few snapshots from a typical run in which agents use only their *non*-terrain-related personality weight components for navigation (which includes a positive-valued motivation for moving toward the enemy flag). The top row shows the normal (i.e., default) view of the scenario in which red and blue agents appear as small red and blue colored "dots," and in which the display is refreshed at each time step.

The bottom row of snapshots shows exactly the same run but with the trace-mode option toggled on (by pressing the Tr button on the main menu). While in trace-mode, EINSTein displays the cumulative map of agent-positions, in which all red and blue red agent-positions *up to and including the current time step* are displayed simultaneously. The trace-map thus provides a rough "history" of a given run, and may be used as a general visualization aid. As we expect to find in such a complicated scenario, it is difficult for both red and blue agents to maneuver around many of the terrain elements that block their line-of-site to the enemy flag.

The blue force performs very poorly in this regard. Its advance is effectively halted by the very first impassable wall that it encounters (impassable terrain elements are colored grey in the figure), which intersects the blue agents' straight-line path into red territory. The red force fares somewhat better, and is able to maneuver about half of its agents toward blue territory. It too, however, is also clearly "challenged" by the large impassable terrain bock that partially impedes the movement of red agents (near the bottom of the battlefield). Arguably, neither side's actions appear even remotely intelligent.

Color plate 7 (page 253) shows snapshots from a run of the same scenario as defined in color plate 6 (page 252), but with the Dijkstra optimal path calculation option toggled *on* (see figure 5.41). We see that when armed with (and able to adjudicate their moves partly on the basis of) global terrain information, both red and blue agents are able to effectively, and intelligently, maneuver around the same terrain elements that previously impeded their motion.

The trace-map, in particular, clearly shows the "purposeful" advance of both red and blue agents toward their respective goals. The actions of both forces are constrained by terrain, as before, but—whereas in the default case, neither side was able to use terrain to its advantage—the inclusion of Dijkstra data now permits both sides to act semi-intelligently in the presence of terrain.

Consider the four user-defined paths shown in figure 5.50. Figure 5.50 shows a snapshot of the same terrain scenario as in figure ??, but with multiple waypoints used to define unique paths for each of the two red and two blue squads.

Color plate 8 (page 254) shows snapshots from a typical run using the four user-defined paths shown in figure 5.50.*

While it is not immediately obvious from the series of default view snapshots that appear on the top row of color plate 8, the trace view (shown on the bottom

*Note that Dijkstra optimal-path data are *not used* in this example.

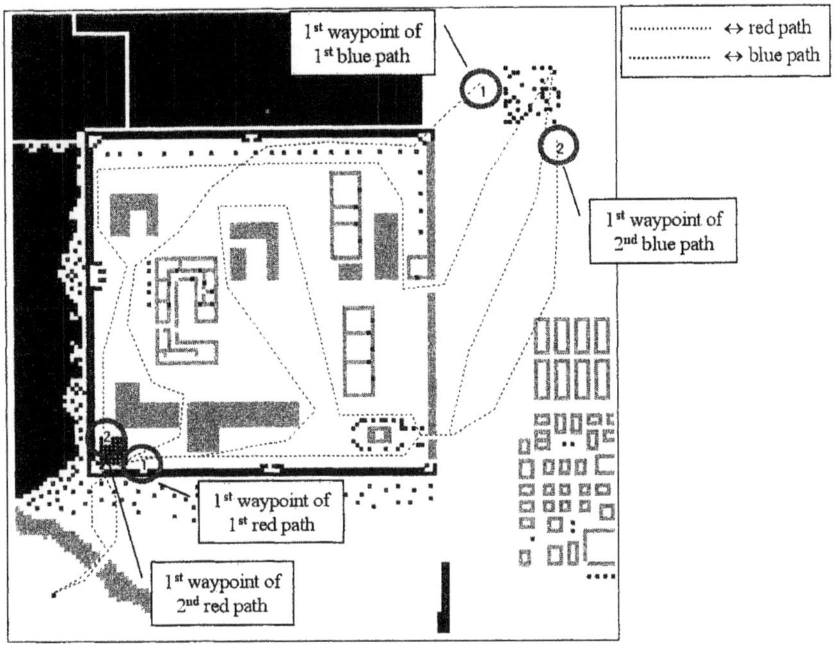

Fig. 5.50 Snapshot of battlefield for the urban-combat-like scenario used in example 2 and showing four user-defined paths.

row) shows that agents follow their assigned trails rather closely. In particular, the two blue squads split as intended from the outset, each faithfully following their respectively assigned paths.

Red agents follow suit, split along, and follow their respectively assigned paths, at least initially. A prolonged skirmish between red and blue forces, starting around time $t = 35$, depletes and/or disperses a large number of red agents belonging to squad #1. By the time the skirmish ends around time $t = 50$ (see highlighted region in the bottom row of the figure), the remaining agents lose sight of their assigned path. The few that do remain, decide to cluster with the larger group of remaining squad #2 agents and, from that time on, effectively follow in their footsteps along path #2.

5.8 Command and Control

In its simplest interactive run mode, EINSTein has only one notional squad, agents do not communicate with any other agents and all agents base their decisions on information that is strictly local to their sensor's field-of-view. While such a design is adequate for exploring the dynamical consequences of having a decentralized *command and control* (C^2) structure, any serious analysis tool of real combat must, of course, include some form of a functioning C^2 hierarchy.

To this end, the user has the option of defining a notional command and control (C2) hierarchy within EINSTein. This hierarchy consists of three kinds of agents (see figure 5.51):

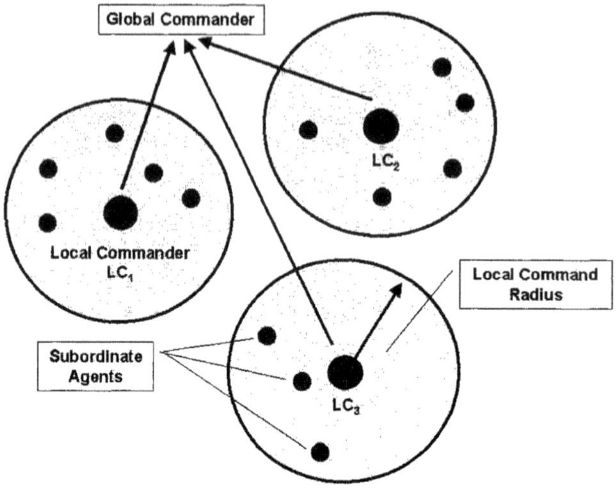

Fig. 5.51 Schematic representation of EINSTein's *command and control* (C^2) structure.

- *Elementary combatants:* these are the individual agents as described in earlier sections, but are now thought of as subordinate agents to the local commander.
- *Local commanders:* these are agents that command, and coordinate information flow among, local clusters of elementary combatants.
- *Global commanders:* these are agents that have a global view of the entire battlefield, and coordinate the actions of the local commanders under their command.

Local and global command consists, essentially, of specifying local goals that subordinate agents must try to accomplish. These goals are defined using information derived from local command areas (inn the case of local command) or the entire battlefield (in the case of global command). One way in which, say, local commanders can issue orders to the elementary combatants under their command—in a way that is also consistent with the general individual-personality-driven decision-making logic that is the basis of most of EINSTein's dynamics—is to issue intermediate "goals" that the elementary combatants must attain within certain time frames and within given blocks of sites.

The elementary combatants use exactly the same personality-driven criteria (and use the same penalty function; see page 292) to select their local moves as described before, except that their goals now no longer consist solely of getting to the enemy's flag. Goals for subordinate agents include a variety of local goals issued by their local commanders. The logic behind selecting these local goals, in turn, is driven by global information that is adjudicated by global commanders (see below).

5.8.1 *Local Command*

If the local command option is selected,* the nominal agent-based and squad-based logic of the program is augmented by adding two components to an individual agent's default six-component personality weight vector:

- Local commanders (LCs) are introduced, and are given a certain number of subordinate agents to command; these are bound to existing squads.
- Agents that are under the command of a LC are endowed with two LC-specific weights:† (1) ω_{LC}, which is the relative weight for *moving toward (or away from) an agent's local commander*, and (2) $\omega_{Obey\ LC}$, which is the relative weight for *obeying orders issued by an agent's local commander.*

5.8.1.1 *Local Command Area*

Local commanders are endowed with a surrounding command area (defined by a command radius $R_{command}$) that "follows them" as they maneuver throughout the battlefield. This command area is partitioned either into 3-by-3 or 5-by-5 blocks of smaller blocks. Figure 5.52 shows a schematic of a typical local command structure partitioned into nine sub-blocks.

5.8.1.2 *Local Goals*

The center positions of these smaller blocks represent transient local goals that a local commander can order its subordinates to "move toward" during a given move (how these orders are actually issued is discussed immediately below). The size of these smaller blocks is equal to $(2r_{block} + 1)$-by-$(2r_{block} + 1)$, where r_{block} is the effective (user-defined) "radius" of the block. The overall command area is therefore either a $3 \cdot (2r_{block} + 1)$-by-$3 \cdot (2r_{block} + 1)$ or a $5 \cdot (2r_{block} + 1)$-by-$5 \cdot (2r_{block} + 1)$ square.

The user can define up to 25 different LCs, each of which can have up to 100 subordinate agents under their command. Each LC is also endowed with a unique movement– and command–personality.

*Which is done by setting an appropriate "flag" appearing in the *Red/Blue Global Command Parameters* section of EINSTein's data-input file; see discussion in EINSTein's *User's Guide* [Ilach99a].

†See table 5.2 on page 293.

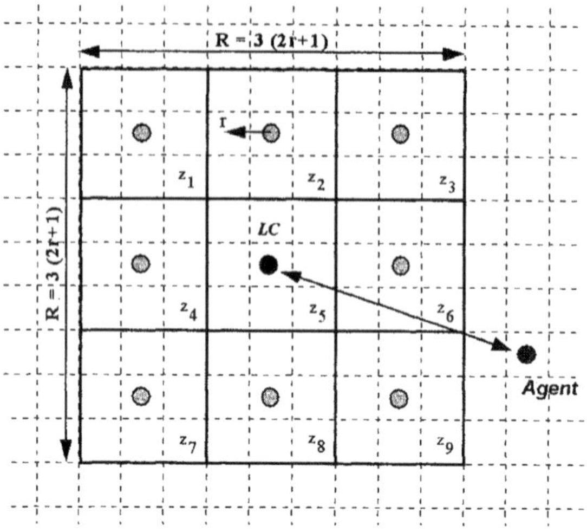

Fig. 5.52 Schematic of local command parameters.

5.8.1.3 *LC Movement Personality*

A LC's movement personality is defined by exactly the same personality weight vector described earlier for individual agents, except that it may be different from the personality weight vector assigned to its subordinate agents. For example (focusing our attention on the first six components of the weight vector), while a LC's subordinates may be defined by the personality weight vector $\vec{\omega} = (1/5, 1/5, 1/5, 1/5, 0, 1/5)$ and an *Advance* μ-rule using a threshold of $N_{friends} = 5$ friendly agents, their commander may "want" only to progress toward the enemy flag: $\vec{\omega} = (0, 0, 0, 0, 0, 1/5)$.

Making subordinate agent and LC personality weight vectors effectively independent of one another allows one to explore, in principle, the dynamical consequences of having particular combinations of temperaments. One might inquire, for example, whether certain missions are better served by matching subordinates with a certain personality with LCs with another (related?) personality? Or, how closely matched must the personalities of LCs be with that of their subordinates in order for the squad to successfully perform its mission?

If no enemy agents appear within the LC's sensor range, all components of the LC's personality weight vector are temporarily set to zero ($\omega_1 = ... = \omega_5 = 0$) except ω_6 (i.e., enemy flag).

5.8.1.4 *LC Command Personality*

The *local command personality* is defined by four weights (α_{local}, β_{local}, δ_{local} and γ_{local}) that prescribe the relative degree of importance the LC places on various measures of relative information contained in each block of sites within his command area. Specifically, the LC weighs each block of sites by a penalty weight z_i:

$$z_i = \frac{1}{F_b}[\alpha_{local}(F_{a,b} - E_{a,b}) + \beta_{local}(F_{a,b} - E_{i,b}) + \delta_{local}(F_{i,b} - E_{a,b}) + \gamma_{local}(F_{i,b} - E_{i,b})], \tag{5.19}$$

where $F_{a,b}$ and $F_{i,b}$ are the number of alive and injured friendly agents in the bth block, $E_{a,b}$ and $E_{i,b}$ are the number of alive and injured enemy agents in the bth block, $0 \leq \alpha_{local} \leq \beta_{local} \leq \delta_{local} \leq \gamma_{local} \leq 1$ and $\alpha_{local} + \beta_{local} + \delta_{local} + \gamma_{local} = 1$.

In words, an LC identifies the block of sites within his command area that contains the smallest fractional difference between friendly and enemy forces; i.e., the block B for which z_i is a minimum. All subordinate agents are then "ordered" to move toward the center of that block. In the event that more than one block yields the same minimum value, the LC chooses the one that is closest to the block chosen on the previous iteration step.

If a local commander is killed, a random agent under its command is "promoted" to LC status and assumes the previous LC's command functions.

5.8.2 *Subordinate Agents*

As mentioned above, once the local command option is enabled, the personality weight vector defining the elementary agents under the command of a LC is automatically enhanced to include two new weights:

- $0 \leq \omega_{LC} \leq 1$, that defines the relative weight afforded to *staying close to their* LC, and
- $0 \leq \omega_{Obey\ LC} \leq 1$, that defines the relative weight afforded to *obeying the orders issued by their* LC.

In the case of $\omega_{LC} > 0$, a subordinate agent will seek to move closer to its LC (or, more specifically, its LC's x and y coordinates) whenever that subordinate is outside his LC's command area. If the subordinate agent is inside his LC's command area, ω_{LC} is temporarily (i.e., during that iteration step) set to zero. Note that ω_{LC} is actually determined by a user-specified agent-LC *scale factor* α that multiplies the maximum value of an agent's personality weight vector (see EINSTein's *User's Guide* [Ilach99a]); i.e.,

$$\omega_{LC} = \alpha \times \text{ Maximum}\left(|\omega_1|, |\omega_2|, ..., |\omega_6|\right). \tag{5.20}$$

Once the LC issues a *move to block B* order, its subordinate agents respond by incorporating the (x, y) coordinates of the center of block B $(= x_B, y_B)$ by using the following penalty function for their individual move selection:

$$Z = Z_0 + \omega_{LC} \cdot [\text{move to } (x_{LC}, y_{LC})] + \omega_{Obey\ LC} \cdot [\text{move to } (x_B, y_B)], \tag{5.21}$$

where Z_0 is the penalty function used by individual agents (in the absence of a local commander; see equation 5.3).

The values of ω_{LC} and $\omega_{Obey\ LC}$ relative to the value *one* (the effective constant in front of Z_0) define the relative weights that an individual agent gives to either "staying close to" or "obeying" his LC. For example, a maximally insubordinate agent (or one that totally disregards his LC's orders) would be assigned a weight $\omega_{Obey\ LC} = 0$.

5.8.3 *Example*

Figure 5.53 shows an example of a blue LC defined by local command weights $\alpha_{local} = \beta_{local} = \delta_{local} = \gamma_{local} = 1/4$. In this example, the penalty weight for the ith block, B_i, of the command area is simply equal to the difference between the number of blue and red agents in B_i divided by the total number of red agents in the entire command area.

With the local distribution of red and blue agents as shown in figure 5.53, the LC finds that—consistent with his command personality as defined by the weights $\alpha_{local}, \beta_{local}, \delta_{local}$, and γ_{local}—block B_3 (in which a single blue agent in block B_3 is outnumbered by three red agents) is the block that is in the greatest need of local blue assistance. The LC therefore issues a *move to block* B_3 order to all subordinate agents.

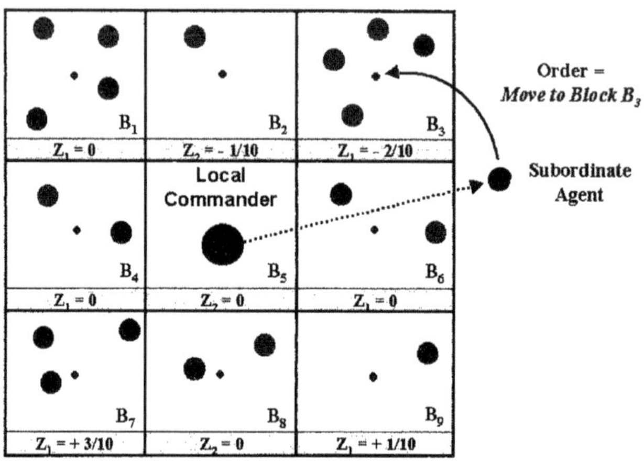

Fig. 5.53 Local command example; see text for details.

5.8.4 *Global Command*

Global commanders (GCs) issue orders to local commanders using global (i.e., battlefield-wide) information. GCs have an effectively omniscient view of the overall state of the battle at time t. GCs generally issue orders conveying two kinds of information:

1. *The conditions under which LCs may maneuver towards other LCs*, and
2. *The preferred into which LCs and their subordinates should move.*

5.8.4.1 *GC Command of LC–LC interaction*

Interaction among LCs is mediated by the GC, who effectively "decides" when to order a local commander LC_i(and therefore his subordinate agents) to "help" a nearby LC_j according to the relative health states of LC_i and LC_j.

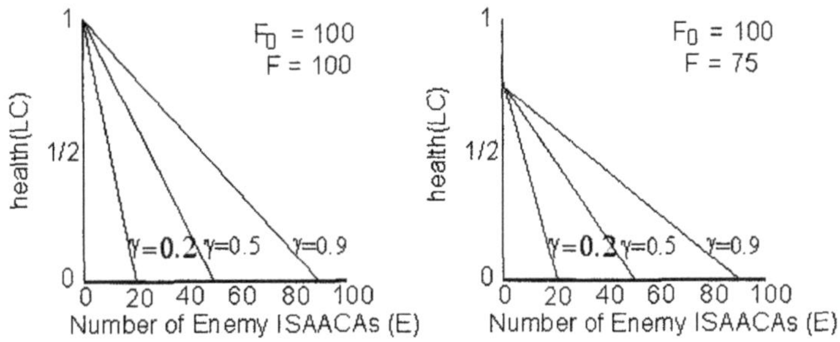

Fig. 5.54 Plot of *health*(LC) versus number of enemy agents.

Health States. The health state of the ith local commander, $0 \leq \textit{health}(\text{LC}) \leq 1$, is a simple measure of how close the overall state of that LC's command area is to its initial state. If all subordinates are present and there are no enemy agents within the command area, the health state is maximum and $\textit{health}(\text{LC}_i) = 1$. If all subordinates have been killed or the command area contains the maximum number of allowable enemy agents, the health state is minimum and $\textit{health}(\text{LC}_i) = 0$. Intuitively, as an LC's health value decreases, the LC's need for assistance increases. More specifically, $\textit{health}(\text{LC}_i)$ is defined as follows:

$$\textit{health}(LC_i) = \sigma\left(\frac{F(1+\gamma F_0 - E)}{F_0(1+\gamma F_0)}\right), \tag{5.22}$$

$\sigma(x) = x$ if $0 \leq x \leq 1$, else $\sigma(x) = 0$, F_0 is the total number of alive friendly subordinates under LC_i's command, F is the current number of subordinates within the local command area, E is the current number of enemy agents within the local command area, and $0 \leq \gamma \leq 1$ is a factor that specifies the maximum number of allowable enemy agents (expressed as a fraction of the initial number of friendly subordinates).

For example, if $\gamma = 1$, then $health(\mathrm{LC}_i) \sim 0$ when $E = F_0$ and $health(\mathrm{LC}_i)$ ~1/2 when $E = F/2$. Figure 5.54 shows plots of $health(\mathrm{LC}_i)$ as a function of E for $\gamma = 0.2$, $\gamma = 0.5$, and $\gamma = 0.9$ for the cases ($F_0 = 100$, $F = 100$) and ($F_0 = 100$, $F = 75$).

If a given LC_i is "healthy" enough—that is, if its health state exceeds a given threshold, h_{thresh}—it looks for other LC_j's within its help range R_{help} that it can maneuver toward to help. Candidate LCs to help are those for which the relative fractional health ($= \Delta_{ij}$) is greater than a health threshold ($= \Delta h_{thresh}$). LC_i moves toward the closest LC_j that requires help:

$$\mathrm{LC}_i \text{ helps } \mathrm{LC}_j \text{ if } \begin{cases} health(\mathrm{LC}_i) & \geq & h_{thresh}, \\ \Delta_{ij} \equiv health(\mathrm{LC}_i - \mathrm{LC}_j) & \geq & \Delta h_{thresh}, \\ |\mathrm{LC}_i - \mathrm{LC}_j| & \leq & R_h. \end{cases} \tag{5.23}$$

5.8.4.2 *GC Command of Autonomous LC Movement*

In addition to mediating the interaction among subordinate local commanders, the GC also determines the direction into which each of its LCs shall move. Before we discuss how a GC "decides" upon a direction, we must first introduce three ideas (see figure 5.55):

- *Battlefield sectors*,
- *Waypoints*, and
- *GC-fear index*.

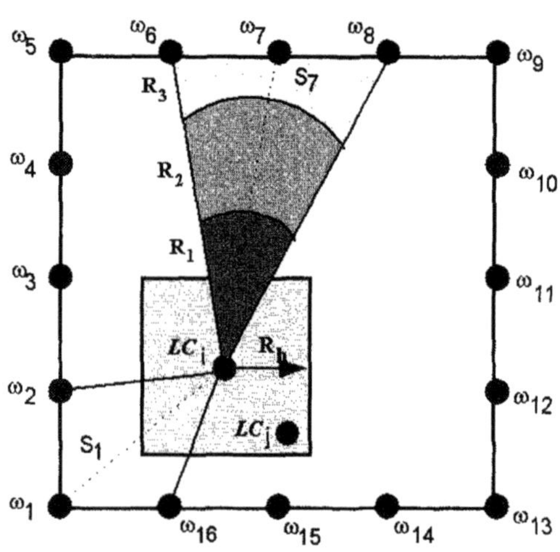

Fig. 5.55 Schematic of EINSTein's global command parameters; see text for details.

Battlefield Sectors. Consider a local commander LC_i under the command of a GC. Using the (x_i, y_i) coordinates of LC_i's position at time t, the GC partitions the entire battlefield into 16 sectors $(S_1, S_2, ...S_{16})$. The boundary of each of these sectors is set by (x_i, y_i) and the (x, y) coordinates of 16 next-nearest neighboring way-points $(w_1, w_2, ...w_{16})$, equally spaced along the edge of the battlefield. These way-points represent the possible directions into which a subordinate LC might be ordered to move. The definition of sectors S_1 and S_7 are shown in figure 5.55.

Waypoints. Each waypoint w_i is assigned a weight that represents the penalty that will be incurred if LC_i moves in that point's direction. Assume that the red and blue flags are positioned near the lower-left and upper right of the battlefield, respectively. Since the red GC wants to get to the blue flag (near w_9), the red GC way-point weight distribution is fixed by setting w_1 to the maximal possible value, *one*, and w_9 to the minimal value, *zero*; the remaining weights for $w_2 - w_8$ and $w_{10} - w_{16}$ are then assigned values between 0 and 1, with higher penalties appearing for points closer to $w_1 : w_9 = 0 \leq w_8, w_{10} \leq ... \leq w_2, w_{16} \leq w_1 = 1$. For blue GCs that want to get to the red flag near w_1, the way-point weight distribution is just the opposite: w_9 is assigned the maximal possible value, w_1 the minimal value, and $w_1 = 0 \leq w_2, w_{16} \leq ... \leq w_8, w_{10} \leq w_9 = 1$.

Figure 5.55 shows that each sector S_i is subdivided into three rings: an inner ring (that is closest to LC_i's position) R_1, a middle ring R_2, and an outer ring R_3. In guiding an individual LC's motion, the GC attaches successively less weight to the information contained in these rings, as the distance between them and given LC's position increases.

The information that the GC uses to adjudicate LC maneuvering is the *density of enemy agents within the sub-regions of a given sector*. Thus the inner-most region, consisting of all sites in the sector out to a radius R_1 from the LC_i's position, represents that area around LC_i to which the GC attaches the greatest weight. The middle area, at distances $R_1 < R < R_2$ from LC_i's position, represents an intermediate level of importance. The outer ring, at distances greater than R_2, represents an area of the battlefield to which the GC assigns the least weight.

In defining these sectors and their sub-regions, the user supplies values for R_1, and R_2 along with the numerical weights that specify the relative degree of importance that the GC will assign to the corresponding sub-regions of each sector: $0 \leq w_{R_1}, w_{R_2}, w_{R_3} \leq 1$, and $w_{R_1} + w_{R_2} + w_{R_3} = 1$.

Having defined *battlefield sectors* and *waypoints*, we are now finally in a position to describe how a GC "decides" upon a direction into which to send each of its subordinate LCs, as well as what those LCs do with such orders. In words, the GC computes a penalty value, P_i, for ordering a LC into sector S_i (spanning waypoints w_{i-1} and w_{i+1}), and orders the LC toward the sector S_i for which P_i is minimal.

Fear Index. The penalty value consists of two parts: the intrinsic penalty incurred by moving toward way-point w_i, and the penalty incurred by moving into a sector that has a given density of enemy agents. Specifically,

$$P_i = (1 - f_{GC}) \cdot w_i + f_{GC} \cdot \rho_E(S_i), \tag{5.24}$$

where $\rho_E(S_i)$ is the number of enemy agents per unit area in sector S_i (using weights w_{R_1}, w_{R_2}, and w_{R_3} for rings R_1, R_2 and R_3 in each sector; see above), and $0 \leq f_{GC} \leq 1$ is the GC *fear index.*

If $f_{GC} = 0$, the GC is effectively fearless of the enemy and the criteria by which it decides what direction to send each of his LCs into consists entirely of the intrinsic penalty value associated with each way-point; i.e., $P_i = w_i$.

If $f_{GC} = 1$, the GC wants only to keep all LCs (and their subordinates) away from harm's way and its choice of movement vector is predicated entirely upon the enemy force strength in each sector. Any value for f between these two limits represents a GC command-personality-defined trade-off between wanting to simultaneously satisfy two desires: moving LCs closer to the enemy flag and preventing them from encountering too many enemy forces while doing so.

The general rule for GC command of LC movement is summarized symbolically as follows:

$$\text{Order LC to Sector } S_i \text{ for which penalty } P_i \text{ is minimum :}$$

$$\begin{cases} P_i &= (1 - f_{GC}) \cdot w_i + f_{GC} \cdot \rho_E(S_i), \\ \rho_E(S_i) &\equiv \alpha \cdot \rho_{alive,E}(S_i) + \beta \cdot \rho_{injured,E}(S_i), \\ 0 \leq f_{GC} &\leq 1. \end{cases} \tag{5.25}$$

5.8.4.3 *LC Response to GC Commands*

Having received an "order" from its GC, a local commander must weigh several different factors before deciding on its own course of action: its sensor view of battlefield, the disposition of its subordinate agents within its command area, and the trade-off between helping other local commanders (that are, according to the GC, in need of assistance), and moving toward the enemy flag. The LC's decision is shaped by using three additional command weights:

- $0 \leq \Omega_{\text{help}} \leq 1$, that defines the relative weight assigned to moving toward and "assisting" another LC,
- $0 \leq \Omega_{\text{sector}} \leq 1$, that defines the relative weight assigned to moving into a GC-ordered battlefield sector, and
- $0 \leq \Omega_{Obey\ LC} \leq 1$, that defines the relative weight assigned to obeying GC orders.

LC Response Function. Once the GC issues orders to "move toward another LC" and/or "move toward way-point w_2,"subordinate LCs adjudicate their own moves according to the following penalty function:

$$\begin{aligned} Z \quad = \quad & Z_0 + \Omega_{Obey\ LC} \cdot [\Omega_{\text{help}} \cdot (\text{move toward LC}_i) \\ & + \Omega_{sector} \cdot (\text{move toward GC-prescribed sector})]. \end{aligned} \tag{5.26}$$

The value of $\Omega_{Obey\ LC}$ relative to the value *one* (the effective constant in front of Z_0) defines the relative weight that LC assigns to the movement vectors ordered by the GC. For example, $\Omega_{Obey\ LC} = 1$ means that the LC treats its own information and the information supplied by the GC on an equal footing; $\Omega_{Obey\ LC} = 0$ means that the LC effectively ignores the GC's orders.

Appendix 1: *Enhanced Action Selection Logic*

While EINSTein's overall architecture, graphical user interface, and most of its agent functions (on both the user-accessible and the source-code levels) are all consistent with the descriptions provided in the main text of this book—as of this writing (November 2003)—many details of EINSTein design are still under active development. This means that some functionality may change in later versions, perhaps in significant ways. This technical appendix provides a brief tour of some of the algorithms that will be incorporated into future versions, focusing on a significantly enhanced *action selection logic*. Interested readers can use the ideas presented in this appendix as the basis for their own musing about possible conceptual extensions to the art of multiagent-based modeling, in general, and combat simulation, in particular.

In the version of EINSTein described in the main text of this chapter, the focus is on achieving a simple agent logic that tailored specifically for experimenting with military *swarm* dynamics. In future versions of EINSTein, the emphasis is shifting to designing a robust, multilayered agent-logic architecture, one that can gracefully scale the *full spectrum of behaviors* from large agent-swarms (as is currently handled by EINSTein, although the new architecture includes many enhanced abilities) to more intelligent behaviors on the *squad* and *single-agent* levels.

Loosely speaking, this shift of emphasis represents a shift away from describing the mutual interactions among *many simple agents* to designing an architecture that also describes interactions among a *relatively few complex agents* (which may also be endowed with a richer—and dynamic—internal structure). Where prior versions focused on the complexity of emergent behaviors on the system level, the most recent work adds the ability to explore the complexity of emergent behaviors on the individual agent level as well. EINSTein's enhanced agent logic significantly extends the dynamic range of possible combat scenarios that can now be explored.

An agent's personality, using the enhanced action-selection logic described in this appendix, describes not only how an agent reacts to a given stimulus in a broadly defined generic context (as before), but also how the full range of agent responses themselves change as a function of changing stimuli and environments. Moreover, while EINSTein's current code provides users with a limited palette of about a dozen, hard-wired, μ-rules with which they can "tune" an agent's otherwise fixed default personality, EINSTein's enhanced logic (1) extends the palette to over 30 different primitives, (2) permits pre-programmed behaviors to be selectively activated by specific "trigger" events, and (3) allows users to define personality weight values as essentially arbitrary functions of up to three different environmental features at a time. In this way, agent actions become much more tightly coupled to their local environment than before.

EINSTein's enhanced penalty function includes many more (optional) features beyond the simple distances between agents. For example, in addition to simply weighing motivations for moving toward (or away) from other agents and flags, agents can adapt to various static and dynamic elements of their local environments such as the cost of traversing terrain, vulnerability to enemy fire, concealment from enemy sensors, accessibility to/from other sites and enemy positions, and combat intensity, as well as relative measures between themselves and other agents (for example, relative health, relative energy, relative firepower, and so on). An agent's internal features, such as fear, morale, and fatigue, are also becoming fully realized dynamic components of its action selection process. Likewise, communication logic is being generalized from allowing agents to communicate only positional information to being able to communicate any information that they can sense directly with their own sensors. Finally, a set of *primitive response activation functions* (see page 386) are defined, which—by mapping environmental features to specific weight components—provide a behavioral "basis set" that the genetic algorithm can use to more fully explore the dynamical landscape.

Overview

Figures 5.56 and 5.57 summarize the main components of EINSTein's enhanced action selection logic. Figure 5.56 provides a schematic logic flow; figure 5.57 traces the same steps more formally.

Out of the total N environmental features—$\{f_1, f_2, \ldots, f_N\}$—that are automatically kept track of, behind-the-scenes, by EINSTein's combat engine and are thus *a priori* available to agents as information to be used in assessing their moves, each agent $\mathcal{A}$ typically selects a subset of $N_{\mathcal{A}}$ features—$\tilde{f}_1, \tilde{f}_2, \ldots, \tilde{f}_{N_{\mathcal{A}}}$, $N_{\mathcal{A}} \leq N$—on which to focus its attention.

Step 1

Determine if any trigger states are in effect. $\mathcal{A}$'s first step toward deciding where to move consists of determining if any actions need to be taken immediately.

Formally, a function, $\Psi_{Trigger}$, is applied to the $N_{\mathcal{A}}$ features "visible" to $\mathcal{A}$ to determine whether a predefined trigger state, T_s, has been activated. If the answer is YES, weight values defining an appropriate set of trigger actions that correspond to the triggered state ($= \hat{\omega}[T_s]$) are assigned and $\mathcal{A}$ executes its move immediately (see Step 6). If the answer is NO, then $\mathcal{A}$'s logic proceeds to Step 2.

The nature of, and conditions for, all trigger states are explicitly defined and ranked by the user (using predefined templates), and may consist both of assigning trigger-state-specific weight values, as shown here, and temporarily altering the values of some of $\mathcal{A}$'s functional characteristics (such as movement range, sensor range, reaction range, and so on). For example, if the "suppressed from enemy fire" trigger state is activated, $\mathcal{A}$ temporarily stays in place (so that its movement range is reduced to zero), refrains from firing its weapon, and reduces its default visibility by "hunkering down." $\mathcal{A}$'s default state is restored after a suppression-state refractory period has expired.

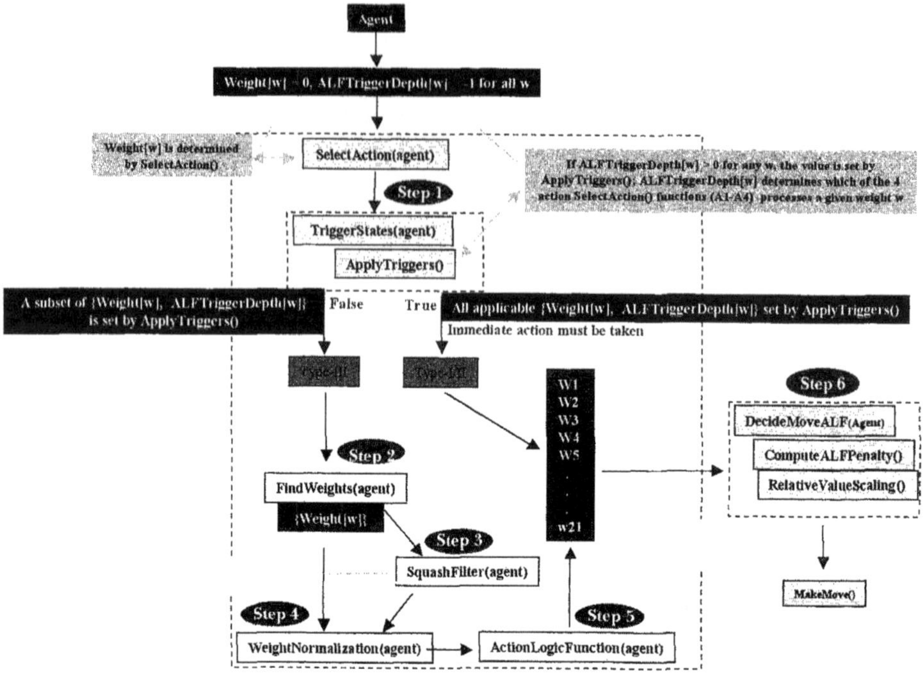

Fig. 5.56 Schematic summarizing the main components of EINSTein's enhanced *action selection algorithm*; see text for details.

If it is determined that more than one trigger state is in effect, the one with the highest rank is executed. If the ranks of two or more triggered states are all equal, the executed action is selected randomly from among the triggered state options.

Step 2

Calculate weights. The second step consists of calculating all active weight values—i.e., all weights whose values have net yet been determined via the trigger module—using a set of response activation functions (which are, themselves, functions of various environmental features) and, in cases where a weight depends on more than one feature, one of two feature summation function types.

If no trigger states have been activated during Step 1, $\mathcal{A}$'s second step toward deciding where to move consists of calculating the value of all of its active weights. Just as one aspect of $\mathcal{A}$'s personality regulates how $\mathcal{A}$ filters all the available environmental features (thus generating a manageably small set of features on which $\mathcal{A}$ focuses its full attention), another aspect of $\mathcal{A}$'s personality determines which subset of the total set of available weights $\mathcal{A}$ uses to make its move. Out of a total of M *a priori* available weights (as defined by the source code), an agent activates a subset of weights $M_A \leq M$ that it will use to adjudicate its moves throughout a scenario.

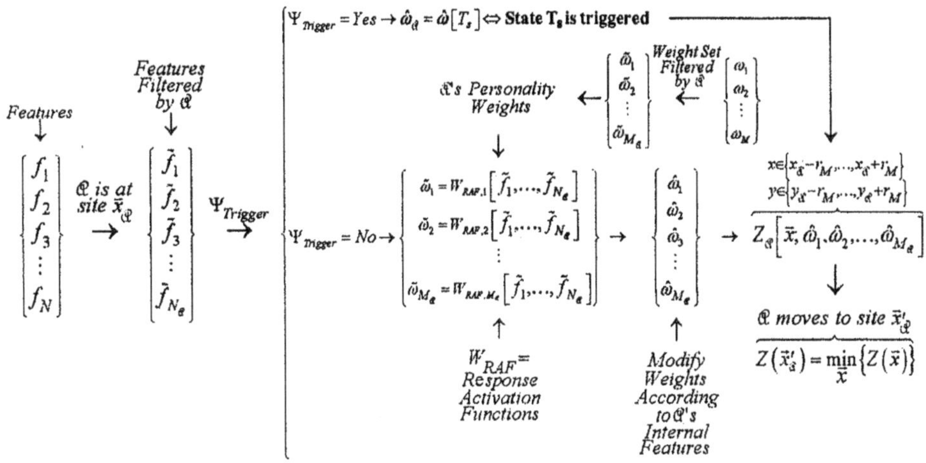

Fig. 5.57 Formal schematic of the main steps of EINSTein's *enhanced action selection logic.*

During each time step, $\mathcal{A}$ uses a set of *primitive response activation functions* ($= W_{RAF}$) to calculate the weight values that are appropriate for a given context. The W_{RAF} are the basic "building blocks" that shape $\mathcal{A}$'s behavior, and depend on $\mathcal{A}$'s filtered set of environmental features. Because of the variety of functional forms to choose from, simultaneous dependencies on different features may be combined to create robust, heavily context-dependent, agent behaviors. Examples of how W_{RAF} may be used to *engineer* behaviors appear in [Ilach02].

Step 3

Modify weights according to internal features. $\mathcal{A}$'s third step toward deciding where to move consists of modifying the value of all of its active weights according to features that describe it *internal* state, such as health, fatigue, combat-fear, morale, and obedience. (Since an agent's internal state also evolves, along with all other external elements of the battlefield, inner and outer dynamical environments are tightly coupled at all times.)

Weights are modified using *squash functions* ($= s$), that (depending on the value of a particular internal feature) either leave $\mathcal{A}$'s default weight alone (if the value of the squash function $s = 0$) or, if $s = 1$, replace the default weight ω by a limiting value, ω_∞. Squash factors interpolate between the existing weight value as determined in Step 2 and the limiting value ω_∞.

The squashed weight function is a personality-based modifier of generic weights. The limiting value ω_∞ is the desired limiting value for weight ω (independent of all factors that the weight is normally a function of). The value of ω_∞ is typically set equal to -1 (giving maximum weight to avoiding performing the action associated with the weight being squashed), 0 (which ignores all actions associated with) or $+1$ (giving maximum weight to performing the action associated with ω).

Step 4

Normalize weights. All weights are normalized according to both *strength* and *relative rank.* A weight's *strength* is equal to its absolute value and represents the strength of an agent's motivation to perform the action associated with the weight. A weight's *rank* is a measure that is assigned by the user prior to the start of a run and its value thereafter remains fixed. Rank may be used to fine-tune an agent's personality.

Step 5

Apply Action Logic Function (ALF). The ALF processes an input list of the values (and therefore strengths) of all active weights to determine which specific weights (and thus which primitive actions) will be executed. Only those weights that remain active after passing through the ALF will be used to evaluate $\mathcal{A}$'s penalty function, and therefore serve as the basis of $\mathcal{A}$'s move.

The ALF therefore effectively acts as the final "filter" through which active weights must pass to determine which weights will remain active and thus be executed by an agent. ALF is useful for discriminating between (and fine-tuning the behavior for) cases in which several weights remain active after Step 4. While the default is for the ALF to act as a "dummy"filter, letting all weight values pass through unaltered, the user has the option to tune the ALF's behavior. For example, the ALF can be adaptively tuned so that when a subset of active weight strengths exceeds some large-value threshold, all other "weaker" weights are deactivated; or the ALF can be instructed to allow only the top three ranking weights to remain nonzero. This effectively forces an agent to focus its attention on actions that are associated only with the strongest weights. Other discriminatory schemes are also possible.

Step 6

Apply penalty function. $\mathcal{A}$'s move is determined during this last step, which consists of minimizing the value of a penalty function, $Z_{\mathcal{A}}$, which is computed for all accessible sites and the components of which consist of agent-specific motivations for performing basic tasks.

For weights that involve other agents, the user can instruct the ALF to use *relative-value scaling functions* to refine the interim weight values (as computed in steps one through five) on an *agent-by-agent* basis. In this way, agents can tailor their actions to the specific characteristics of other agents. For example, an agent may be more urgently motivated to move away from a nearby enemy agent than from one that is farther away.

The relative-value scalings are functions of such factors as the distance between agents, relative health, relative fire power, and relative morale, and can be either multiplicative or additive. The availability of such scalings is critical in the context of behavior engineering, where dynamical mechanisms must often be used to counteract the appearance of counterintuitive local behaviors (explicit examples are given below).

"Old" Versus "New" Logic

While the core of EINSTein's action selection logic remains essentially the same as the logic used in prior versions, the new design entails considerably more breadth and depth. Table 5.7 summarizes the differences between EINSTein's older and enhanced action selection logic.

EINSTein's current code consists of four basic steps:

- *Scan environment.*
- *Define an agent's default weight vector* (the components of which are fixed by the user).
- *Modify the default weight vector* according to a small set of μ-rule threshold conditions (such as combat, cluster with friends, and advance toward the enemy flag).
- *Evaluate the penalty function and move.*

The current penalty function is also limited to using measures that depend only on the distance between agents and between agents and flags. In particular, agents are unable to take into account any dynamically relevant contextual information other than the distance to other agents.

The most important enhancements that are being made to these basic components include:

- The ability to predefine trigger states and the contexts under which they become active (*Step 1*).
- A robust weight vector generating logic that provides a much finer coupling between an agent's local environment and motivations (*Step 2*).
- The ability to modify an agent's motivations according to changing internal states (*Step 3*).
- The ability to fine-tune the way in which an agent interacts with other agents on an agent-by-agent basis using relative-value scaling functions within individual terms of the penalty function (*Step 6*).

Example

Figure 5.58 contains a sample set of agent personality weights, as defined and used by EINSTein's current action selection logic (versions 1.1 and older), along with three μ-rules that regulate how an agent behaves in the presence of friendly agents, enemy agents and the enemy flag in a variety of contexts. Recall, that EINSTein's current μ-rule logic allows only a limited set of thresholds to be set.

Step	Current Selection Logic	Enhanced Selection Logic
0	*Scan Environment:* Record positions and health states of all agents that are either sensed directly by the sensor or are communicated by linked friends.	*Scan Environment:* Record all pertinent environmental information that is sensed or communicated by linked friends; this information consists of a large selection of environmental and combat-related features.
1	*Select Default Weight Set:* Determine health state (*alive* or *injured*). Assign appropriate default weight set to agent: $w_{\mathbf{default}} = w_{\mathbf{alive}}$ or $w_{\mathbf{default}} = w_{\mathbf{injured}}$. Individual components of $w_{\mathbf{default}}$ are fixed throughout a scenario run.	*Parse for Trigger States:* Determine if any actions must be taken immediately. Other trigger states may temporarily reassign the values of certain agent characteristics but otherwise not impede the normal logic processing flow.
2a	*Apply Meta-Rules:* Modify default weight values using meta-weight thresholds (using small set of environmental features). Modified weight values may take on only one of three values: $w_{\mathbf{default}}$, 0, or $-\lvert w_{\mathbf{default}}\rvert$. Each component of an agent's weight vector is a function of exactly one environmental feature.	*Apply Weight Functions:* Weight values are continuously adapted to an agent's context (at each time t) by using a "basis set" of primitive response activation functions. Each component of an agent's weight vector may depend on up to three environmental features, the effects of which are combined using fuzzy-summation.
2b	*Apply Ambiguity Resolution Function.*	N/A
3	*Compute Penalty Function and Make Move:* Select site that minimizes penalty function, evaluated over all possible moves within movement range. Penalty function limited to measures only of relative proximity between agents and between agents and flags.	*Parse Effects of Agents' Internal States:* Modify selected weights according to real-valued (and co-evolving) internal features, such as health, fatigue, fear, morale and obedience.
4	N/A	*Normalize Weights According to Rank.*
5	N/A	*Apply Action Logic Filter:* Discriminate between cases in which multiple weights remain active after Step 4. By strengthening some weights and/or weakening (or deactivating) others, agents are able to selectively focus their attention on the most important actions.
6	N/A	*Apply Relative-Value Scalings to Make Move:* Select the site that minimizes the penalty function, evaluated over all possible moves within an agent's movement range. For weights that involve other agents, relative values (of such measures as distance, health, fire power, and morale) are used to refine those weights on an agent-by-agent basis. In this way, agents can tailor their actions to the specific characteristics of other agents.

Table 5.7 Summary of differences between EINSTein's *current* and (planned) *enhanced* action selection logic.

For example, an agent's motivation for moving toward friends may nominally be any nonzero value, but is temporarily assigned the value zero when an agent is surrounded by a threshold number of friendly agents. Similar thresholds may be assigned for other motivations (such as *Combat* and *Advance-to-Flag*, shown in Table 5.58).

		Friend		**Enemy**		**Friendly**	**Enemy**
		Alive	*Injured*	*Alive*	*Injured*	**Flag**	**Flag**
Agent	*Alive*	$(\omega_{AF})_{alive}$	$(\omega_{IF})_{alive}$	$(\omega_{AE})_{alive}$	$(\omega_{IE})_{alive}$	$(\omega_{FF})_{alive}$	$(\omega_{EF})_{alive}$
	Injured	$(\omega_{AF})_{injured}$	$(\omega_{IF})_{injured}$	$(\omega_{AE})_{injured}$	$(\omega_{IE})_{injured}$	$(\omega_{FF})_{injured}$	$(\omega_{EF})_{injured}$
Meta-Rules:		$N_F \geq N_{CLS}$ ↓ $(\omega_{AF})_{CLS}=0$, $(\omega_{IF})_{CLS}=0$		$N_F - N_E \leq \Delta_{Combat}$ ↓ $(\omega_{AE})_{Combat}=-\lvert\omega_{AE}\rvert$, $(\omega_{IE})_{Combat}=-\lvert\omega_{IE}\rvert$			$N_F \leq N_{ADV}$ ↓ $(\omega_{EF})_{ADV}=0$

Fig. 5.58 Sample set of agent personality weight values used by EINSTein's *action selection logic* in versions 1.1 and older.

Figure 5.59 shows, schematically, how the rules and μ-rules as they are currently defined, appear (in translated form) using EINSTein's enhanced action-selection logical primitives planned for future releases of the program. Aside from the obvious fact that the newer primitives are backwards compatible—i.e., that they allow such translations between "old" and "new" rules to be made easily in almost all cases—what we wish to emphasize is the way in which they generalize the class of existing rules.

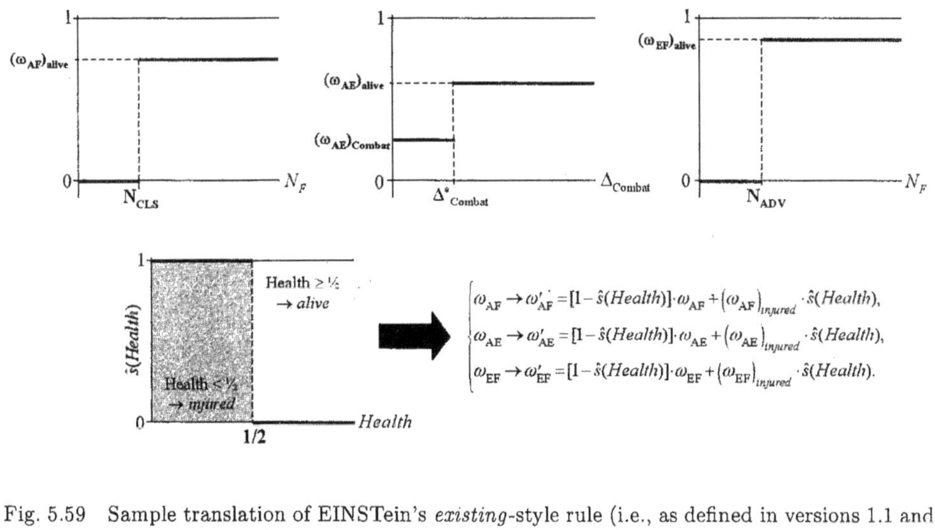

Fig. 5.59 Sample translation of EINSTein's *existing*-style rule (i.e., as defined in versions 1.1 and older), defined in figure 5.58, to the generalized graphical form planned for future versions of the program.

Where EINSTein currently allows only a single definite value to be assigned to individual weight components, and μ-rules are currently defined *only* by either changing the sign of an existing weight or temporarily setting it equal to zero, EINSTein's new logic includes these two enhancements:

- The values of individual weight components may be (essentially arbitrary) functions of up to three different contextual measures, and
- Meta-rules are more robust behavioral trigger *functions*, and may also take on a continuum of values.

For example, each of the simple step-function forms used for this particular translation (see top of figure 5.59) may be deformed (and/or generalized) to more complicated functions to accommodate a much wider range of weight-value responses for given local context. Likewise, the step-function that is used here for maintaining a backwards compatibility with EINSTein's older binary-valued health state (see bottom of figure 5.59), may also be generalized to accommodate a greater range (even a continuum) of effective health states. Other internal triggers, in addition to health, may, of course, also be defined.

Appendix 2: *Trigger State Activation*

The first step of EINSTein's enhanced *Activation Selection Logic Function* (ASLF) consists of determining whether any actions must be taken immediately. A trigger state—T_i, where $i = 1, 2. \ldots, N_T$—is any (user defined) local context in which an agent must execute a specific action (or actions).

Actions may consist either of specific values being assigned to certain components of an agent's personality weight vector and/or of temporary assignments being made to certain behavioral parameters. For example, if normally mobile agents find themselves in a "fire suppressed" trigger state, they may be temporarily assigned a movement range equal to zero (among other temporary changes) to simulate being in a "hunkered down" state.

Trigger states are analogous to—but are considerably more flexible than—the meta-rules introduced in earlier versions of EINSTein. Recall that meta-rules alter an agent's default personality according to dynamic contexts, and typically consist of altering a few of the components of an agent's personality vector according to a set of associated local threshold constraints.

For example, consider EINSTein's older *combat* meta-rule, which uses the difference between the number of friendly agents within threshold range, $N_{friendly}(R_T)$, and the number of enemy agents within sensor range, $N_{enemy}(R_S)$, $\Delta_{Combat} = N_{friendly}(R_T) - N_{enemy}(R_S)$, as a triggering mechanism:

$$\begin{cases} w_{\text{move towards enemy}} = w_{\text{move towards enemy, default}} \quad if\ \Delta_{Combat} \leq \Delta^*_{Combat}, \\ \text{else } w_{\text{move towards enemy}} = -\left| w_{\text{move towards enemy, default}} \right|, \end{cases}$$

where Δ^*_{Combat} is a fixed threshold and $w_{\text{movetowardsenemy,default}}$ is the default weight for moving toward enemy agents. Thus, in general, older meta-rule thresholds can be thought of as triggers between a "default" weight and a "triggered" weight, which is itself almost always a simple variant of the default value; i.e., the triggered value is either shifted in sign, multiplied by a constant (such as a factor of 1/2 in the case of degraded single-shot probability-of-hit if an agent is injured), or set equal to zero. Note that earlier versions of EINSTein also harbored a trivial health state trigger of the form: "If agent's health = *alive* then use weight wet w_{alive}, else use $w_{injured}$."

While meta-rules depend on (largely ad-hoc) hard-coded logic to resolve possible ambiguities between overlapping contexts*—*What happens when the local conditions are consistent with an agent both retreating and supporting a squad-mate somewhere in enemy territory?*—EINSTein's new trigger state logic includes a more robust set of dynamically allocated options. Agents now have the ability to make quick, but intelligent, "on the fly" decisions regarding the need to perform specific triggered actions. Possible conflicts are resolved gracefully according to an agent's personality.

*See *Ambiguity Resolution Logic* on page 311.

Depending on its context, for example, an agent may choose to immediately perform a specific action, to perform a scripted series of actions, and/or to have the values of some of its default activation-strengths temporarily overridden (as an adaptive response to contexts that the user has identified as trigger states), but still follow through with some (or all) of the normal steps of the ASLF. Possible trigger states include:

- *Zero state* (= default state at time $t = 0$ and in the early stages of a scenario in which no prior or current enemy agents have been either detected or their presence has been communicated to an agent by other friendly agents) $\longrightarrow$ agent is assigned a personality-specific set of actions. Some agents may be tasked simply with "staying in formation" and "follow your local commander," others to simply "march toward the enemy flag," still others to "stay near to, and defend, assigned area." The *zero state* is roughly equivalent to default state in older versions of EINSTein, though its meaning and dynamic triggers that immediately remove an agent from its zero state have obviously changed.
- *Fire suppression* (= terminally high incoming and/or nearby fire density) $\longrightarrow$ agent goes into a suppressed state in which it does not move (i.e., its movement range is temporarily set equal to zero), does not fire, has reduced visibility (including both a reduced sensor range and visibility to other agents), and does not communicate.
- *Terminally low health* $\longrightarrow$ run away from all enemy agents and, if possible, seek maximal cover and/or seek support from nearby friends.
- *Terminally high fatigue* $\longrightarrow$ mimic "exhaustion" by reducing movement range to 1 or 0 for a specified refractory period.
- *Terminally large number of enemy agents within lethality range* $\longrightarrow$ run away from enemy agents (that are within a distance of agent) and focus fire on those enemy agents.
- *Terminally large number of enemy agents within sensor range* $\longrightarrow$ run away from enemy.
- *Terminal isolation* (= agent is in enemy territory, there are no nearby friends, and the agent's fear of combat is very high) $\longrightarrow$ run away from enemy and move toward friendly territory.
- *Overwhelming local threat* $\longrightarrow$ run away from enemy and retreat.
- *One-on-one predator state* (= there is only one enemy agent within sensor range, an agent's health is maximum, and the agent is maximally aggressive) $\longrightarrow$ move toward the enemy agent exclusively (temporarily set all other penalty weights to zero).
- *Panic state* = (terminally low morale and maximal fear and isolated from friends) $\longrightarrow$ agent "panics" (and irrationally) blindly moves toward the enemy to engage in combat.

- *Shot at for first time* $\longrightarrow$ agent gives maximal weight to taking cover, temporarily relaxing motivation for advancing to flag and/or moving toward next waypoint.
- *Wildcard.* The "wildcard" trigger—defined by the user—is used when the user desires that some scripted action be performed when certain contextual cues are missing. For example, if an agent is out in the open battlefield and no other agents are present. While an agent's default personality would gracefully handle this situation (by yielding an appropriate set of weight values), the user has the option of forcing the agent into executing a specific action in this specific context (that might override the behavior resulting from a blind application of the default weight values).

The *Trigger State* function performs three tasks: (1) Determines which, if any, of the user-defined trigger states have been activated by an agent's current context; (2) Finds, and performs, all appropriate personality weight and behavior changes; and (3) Propagates all agent responses along the remaining channels of the ASLF.

While some trigger states result in a change that must be made to a single weight, other triggers entail specific values assigned to multiple weights. $W_A[T_i] = \{w_{i1}, w_{i2}, ..., w_{iN_A}\}$ is the set of personality weights associated with trigger state, T_i, and will play a role in how trigger depths are assigned (see discussion below).

Trigger State Activation

Trigger states are activated probabilistically. The user selects one or more contextual features, f_i, to define a *"probability of activating trigger state T"* function, $P_A[T; \{f_i\}]$. A random draw of a real valued number $0 \leq z \leq 1$ is then used to trigger state T: if $z \leq P_A[T; \{f_i\}]$ then T is triggered, else it is not triggered.

Trigger contexts are selected out of a master environmental feature set $\mathcal{F}_E$, and represent primitive forms of local information that agents generally react to. The function $P_A[T; f]$, for a single feature, f, is defined using four parameters: $f_{low}, f_{high}, p_{low}$ and p_{high} (i.e., using low and high threshold values for the given feature, and low and high threshold probabilities for triggering state T). It is assumed that $f_{low} \leq f_{high}$, but except for the obvious constraint, $0 \leq p_{low}, p_{high} \leq 1$, there is no implied relative ordering between p_{low} and p_{high}. Figure 5.60 illustrates their meaning.

In general, if trigger state activation depends on more than one environmental feature, then $P_A[T] = \prod_i P_A[T; f_i]$. For example, suppose the trigger state = *fire suppression*, and that it depends on two features: (1) Number of enemy shots that have landed nearby ($= N_{Shots}$), and (2) Number by which friendly agents are locally outnumbered by the enemy ($= \Delta_{Combat}$). Figure 5.61 shows the fire suppression trigger state activation probability function, $P_A[Suppression]$, assuming the forms of single-feature functions shown on the left of the figure. For the sample parameter values used here, we see that the probability of fire suppression activation is gener-

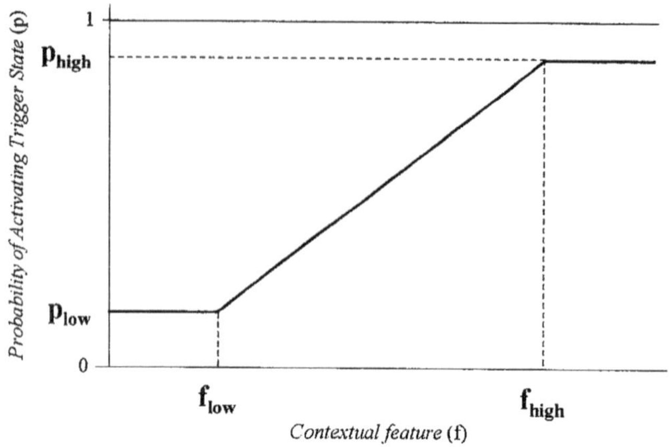

Fig. 5.60 Trigger state activation probability function; see text.

ally low unless an agent detects a large number of enemy shells falling nearby and is significantly outnumbered by the enemy. Fire suppression is *certain* to be activated if $N_{Shots} > 7$ and $\Delta_{Combat} < -7$.

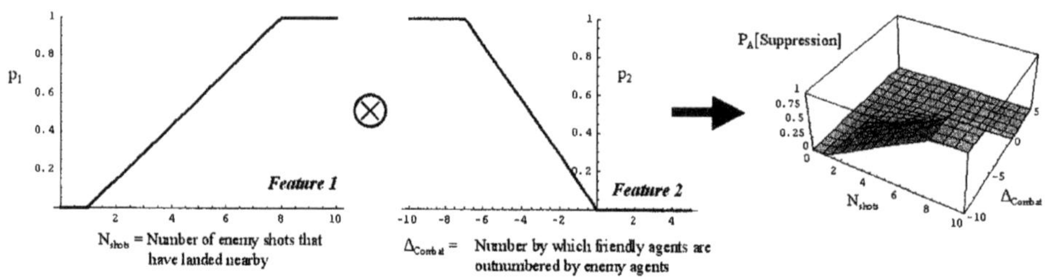

Fig. 5.61 Sample suppression state probability calculation; see text.

Trigger State Processing

How a given trigger state is processed by the ASLF depends on three properties (each of which is assigned, by the user, prior to the start of a given run): (1) *Rank*, (2) *Type*, and (3) *Depth*.

Rank. The rank of trigger state T_i, $0 \leq R_T[T_i] \leq 100$, is a simple measure of relative importance. The rank set fixes the order in which potential trigger states are probed to determine activation. A given trigger state can be activated during a run only if its rank is nonzero. If the ranks of two or more triggered states are all equal, the action that will be executed is selected randomly among the triggered state options. Since each squad can be assigned its own unique trigger ranking, rank can thus not only be used as a component of an individual agent's personality, but as a discriminant between the "personality" of squads as well.

Trigger types. All trigger states belong to one of three possible trigger type classes: $T[T_i] \in \{1, 2, 3\}$. Type 1 and Type 2 trigger states are executed immediately, bypassing all other trigger states and all other functions of the action selection logic function. If multiple Type-1 or 2 trigger states are activated simultaneously, the highest ranking trigger state is executed. Type 3 trigger states may incur temporary assignments to be made to a subset of an agent's active weight set but do not otherwise impede the normal processing flow of the ASLF.

More specifically:

- *Type-1 triggers:* The scripted action (i.e., explicit weight values) associated with the highest ranked trigger state is performed immediately. Only one Type-1 trigger may be activated at one time.
- *Type-2 triggers:* As for Type-1 trigger states, the weight associated with the highest ranked trigger state are assigned explicit values and the action is executed immediately, except that *multiple* Type-2 trigger states may be activated simultaneously.
- *Type-3 triggers:* Specific high (or low) values are explicitly assigned to selected weights (associated with their scripted triggered actions). The way in which these assigned weights are processed during subsequent steps of the action selection logic function depends on their *trigger depth* (see below). In essence, if a Type-3 state is triggered, all environmental feature dependencies are bypassed, and the user (as part of a scenario's initialization) assumes the role that is normally automatically carried out by EINSTein's automated *FindWeights* function. However, unlike the case for trigger types 1 and 2, while an agent carries out the specific triggered action as prescribed by the explicit weight values assigned by the user, the values for all other weights are still determined by the *FindWeights* function.

Depth. The depth of trigger state „ effectively determines the number of steps of the ASLF that are used to process the set of weights associated with trigger state (for those trigger states that do not automatically entail an immediate action):

- If $D_T[T_i] = -1$, no trigger action is applied with respect to weights w_j associated with trigger state T_i.
- If $D_T[T_i] = 0$, the weights will not bc used in any of the subsequent calculations of the ASLF, regardless of their relative magnitude. The trigger-state-specific weight value assigned at this step is carried through to the end of the ASLF.

- If $D_T[T_i] = +1$, the weights will be used in *Step 5*, but not in any of the preceding *Steps 2, 3*, or *4*.
- If $D_T[T_i] = +2$, the triggered-value assigned at this step will be normalized along with all other nonzero weights still active prior to the *Step 4* (i.e., *normalization*).
- If $D_T[T_i] = +3$, the triggered-value assigned at this step will be squashed along with all other nonzero weights still active prior to the *Step 3* (i.e., *squash weights* according to state of internal feature space; see page 400).

In short, $D_T[T_i] > 0$ means that all personality weights associated with T_i, $w_j \in W_A[T_i]$, have been triggered and assigned a depth $D_W[w_j \in W_A[T_i]] = D_T[T_i]$ for all w_j. For example, if $D_T[T] = 2$ and T activates weights w_2, w_3, and w_5, then $D_W[w_1] = D_W[w_2] = D_W[w3] = D_T[T] = 2$. The subsequent action selection logic for these weights bypasses the weight value function evaluation that is normally carried out in step two. $D_T[T_i] = -1$ means that weights $w_j$all pass through the *TriggerStates* functions unaffected and are treated on an equal footing with all other "active" weights by all subsequent functions of the ASLF.

There are two reasons why might be set equal to zero:

1. When the entity associated with weight w is not within sensor (or communications range), e.g., if $w =$ *"move toward squad-mates"* and there are currently no friends within sensor range of the agent. In this case, while it is possible that $S[w_i] > 0$, there is no reason to weigh its merits against other possible actions since it is effectively a "non action." It is thus assigned $D_T[T_i] = 0$ and is temporarily ignored.
2. When it is desired that certain penalty terms (for example, maintain minimum distance from enemy, cover, and concealment) remain on regardless of their activation strengths. While their minimum values may be fixed by the preliminary weight-factor calculations during *Step 2* (i.e., set $m_0 > 0$ for all factors), their execution is not assured unless $D_T[T_i] = 0$.

Multiple triggers. Suppose multiple trigger states are activated in the *same type class* (say, $\{T_1, T_2, \ldots, T_N\} \in \text{Type} - 3$), and each has more than one weight associated with it. In this case, if (1) there are two or more triggers whose depths are different (i.e., $\exists\, i,j | D_T[T_i] \neq D_T[T_j]$), and (2) their associated weight sets overlap (so that $W_A[T_i] \cap W_A[T_j] \neq \emptyset$), the trigger depth of a given weight w, $D_W[w]$, is equal to the minimum depth of all associated triggers:

$$D_W[w] = \underset{i=1,2,\ldots N_{\hat{T}}}{\text{Minimum}} \left\{ D_T[\hat{T}_i\,[w]] \right\}, \tag{5.27}$$

where $\hat{T}_i\,[w]$ is the set of $N_{\hat{T}}$ triggers associated with weight w. Note that some triggers affect only penalty weights, while other triggers affect both penalty weights and behavioral characteristics, such as an agent's movement range, sensor range, targeting logic, etc.

Appendix 3: *Find Weights*

The second step of EINSTein's enhanced action selection logic consists of using a set of context-dependent response activation functions to calculate all active weight values. By "active" we mean all weights whose values have not yet been determined via the *TriggerStates* function and whose trigger depth $D_T[T_i] = -1$.

At the heart of EINSTein's new logic lies the *FindWeights* function. *FindWeights* uses response activation functions that formally generalize EINSTein's older fixed personality-weight value set. Whereas, in previous versions, weights associated with specific agent motivations were independent of changing conditions and remained fixed throughout a given run,* the user may now tailor the components of an agent's personality weight vector to multiple environmental features. As we will see below, this not only significantly expands the spectrum of possible behaviors that a user can use to shape pseudo-realistic behaviors, but adds an important new dimension to EINSTein's already powerful genetic algorithm heuristic search tool. Response activation functions are also flexible enough to ensure a backwards compatibility with EINSTein's older logic.

Primitive Response Activation Functions

The basic component of shaping agent behaviors, via weight values as functions of environment, is a 7-parameter primitive *Response Activation Function* (RAF), $W = W(a, b, c, d;\ m, m_0, M)$, where the parameters are constrained by $a \leq b \leq c \leq d$ and $-1 \leq m,\ m_0,\ M \leq +1$.

Figure 5.62 shows the generic functional form of W and defines, schematically, the parameters a, b, c, d, m, m_0, and M. It is worth noting that EINSTein's current action selection logic, as demonstrably capable as it is at generating complex behavior, depends solely on fixed weight value components of its personality vector; i.e., the user did not previously have the option to effectively "tune" an agent's behavior to its environment.

Despite their simplicity, RAFs can be used to define rather complex agent behaviors, particularly when multiple RAFs are combined to define a single weight using different environmental features (see *Combining two or more features* below). A useful way of thinking about (and developing an intuition for) how to use RAFs to configure behaviors is to examine the range of possible functional forms, as par-

*Agents in current versions of EINSTein only gave the appearance of adapting to their environment. What is really changing is not an agent's reaction to local stimuli, but the relative configuration of agents (and other environmental features) to which the otherwise fixed-weight-based response is directed. Take, as a trivial example, an agent X that responds only to the presence of an enemy agent. Such an agent only *appears* to "adapt" its behavior once the enemy appears within sensor range. In reality, the strength of interaction with enemy agents remains fixed and emergent behavior is strictly a consequence of the number of enemy agents that X is surrounded by at time t.

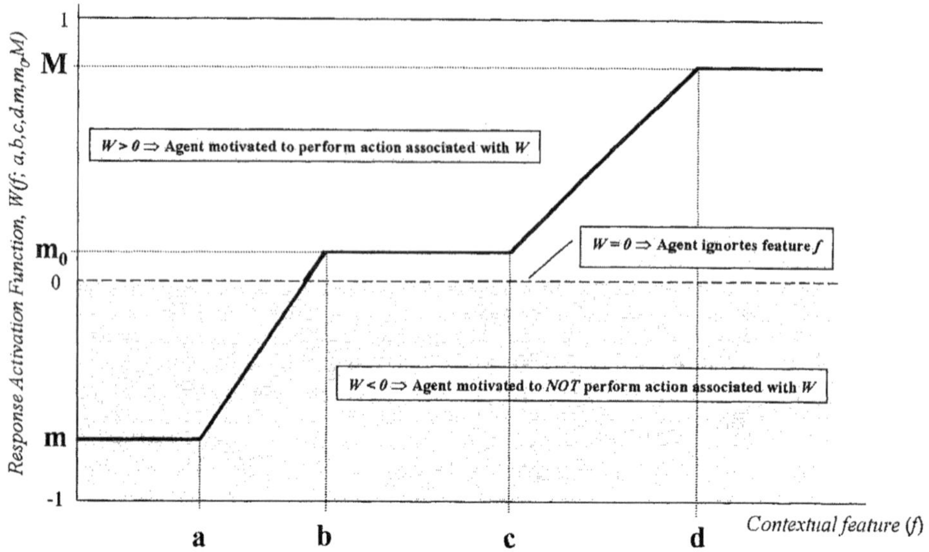

Fig. 5.62 Generic form of EINSTein's new *response activation function*, W.

titioned according to the relative values of their defining parameters. For example, consider the diversity of forms possible for (1) fixed magnitude parameters (m, m_0 and M), and (2) fixed feature thresholds (a, b, c, and d).

Fixed m, m_0 and M

For a fixed set of values of the magnitude parameters m, m_0 and M, eight basic functional forms are possible for W, depending on the relative values of a, b, c, and d (see table 5.8). Figures 5.63 and 5.64 show the primitive forms $W_0(m, m_0, M)$,... $W_7(m, m_0, M)$ for $(m, m_0, M) = (-1, 0, +1)$ and $(m, m_0, M) = (+1, -1, +1)$, respectively. Note that the 7th "step function" form of W (for which $d = c = b = a$) is roughly equivalent to EINSTein's current threshold μ-rule: if $\mu > \tau$, for some measure μ and threshold τ, then the weight $w = w_{default}$ (where $w_{default}$ is the default weight, else $w = 0$).

Typically (though not always), agents are tailored to: (1) "want to" perform some action that is associated with a given weight for one set of values of a contextual feature (so that $M > 0$ over that set), (2) "not want to" perform the action over another set of values of that same feature (so that $m < 0$ over that set), and (3) ignore the feature altogether for whatever set of feature values are left over (so that $m_0 = 0$ over this remaining set).

Thus, for forms W_0, W_2, W_3 and W_4 in figures 5.63 and 5.64, the flat "m_0 plateaus" represent regions of values of the given environmental feature within which the agent effectively ignores the feature. For example, suppose that the form W_4 is a function of feature f and is used to define weight w, associated with action

Primitive Form	a	b	c	d
W_0 (Default)	*arbitrary*	*arbitrary*	*arbitrary*	*arbitrary*
W_1	*arbitrary*	*arbitrary*	b (typically $=(a+d)/2$)	*arbitrary*
W_2	*arbitrary*	a	*arbitrary*	*arbitrary*
W_3	*arbitrary*	a	d	*arbitrary*
W_4	*arbitrary*	*arbitrary*	d	*arbitrary*
W_5	*arbitrary*	a	a	*arbitrary*
W_6	*arbitrary*	d	d	*arbitrary*
W_7	*arbitrary*	a	a	a

Table 5.8 Primitive forms of the *response activation function*, partitioned according to fixed values of m, m_0, and M.

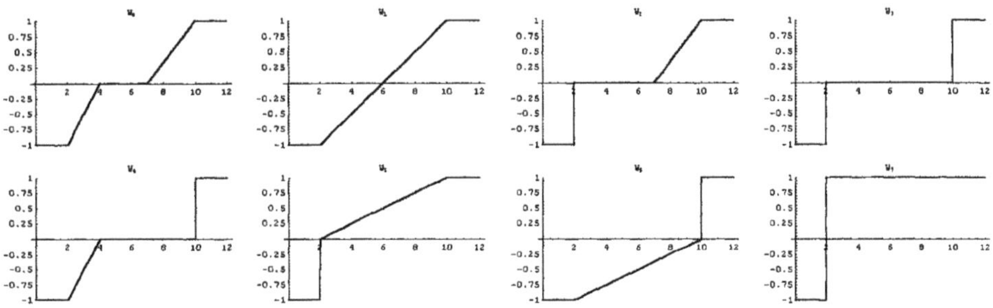

Fig. 5.63 Eight primitive forms of the RAF for $m = -1$, $m_0 = 0$, and $M = +1$ (see table 5.8).

$\mathcal{A}_w$. Its interpretation (i.e., how it is used to direct an agent's behavior) is then: (1) "If $f < 2$ then assign a maximal motivation ($= -1$) to not perform the action $\mathcal{A}_w$ associated with w," (2) "If $f > 10$ then assign a maximal motivation ($= +1$) to perform the action associated with w," and (3) "If $2 \leq f \leq 10$ ignore feature f (i.e., take no action as a consequence of f)."

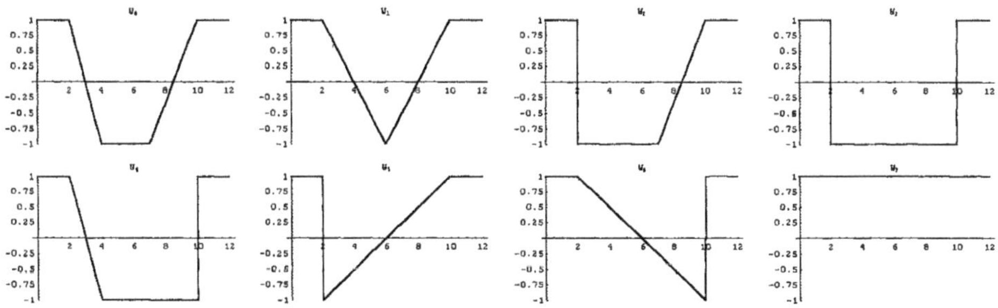

Fig. 5.64 Eight primitive forms of the RAF for $m = +1$, $m_0 = -1$, and $M = +1$ (see table 5.8).

Fixed a, b, c, and d

For fixed a, b, c, and d (but constrained by $a \leq b \leq c \leq d$), the W_i take on various primitive behavioral *basis-function* forms, $\varphi_{m,m_0,M}$, as m, m_0 and M are varied.

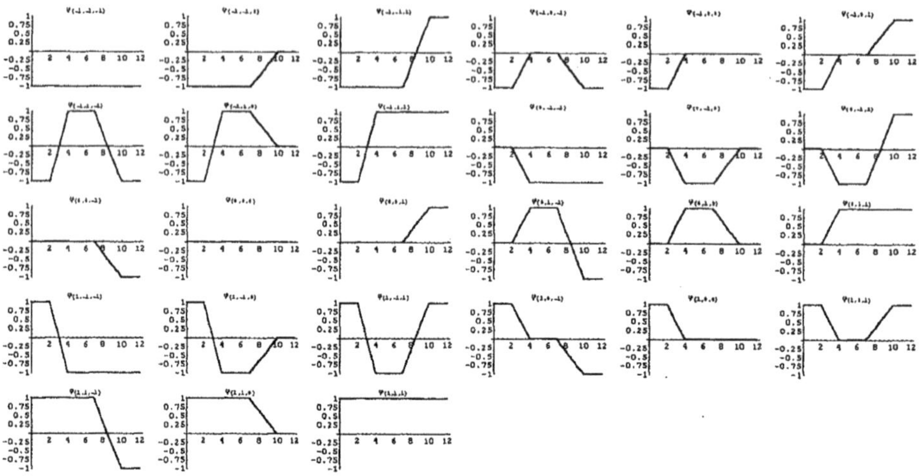

Fig. 5.65 Basis-function forms (ϕ) for the W_0.

Figures 5.65 and 5.66 show the possible forms for W_0 and W_7, respectively. We use the suggestive term "basis function" in anticipation of using the W_i (along with an associated set of strength coefficients, $0 \leq \alpha_i \leq 1$) as the basic building blocks that EINSTein's genetic algorithm can use to shape desired behaviors.

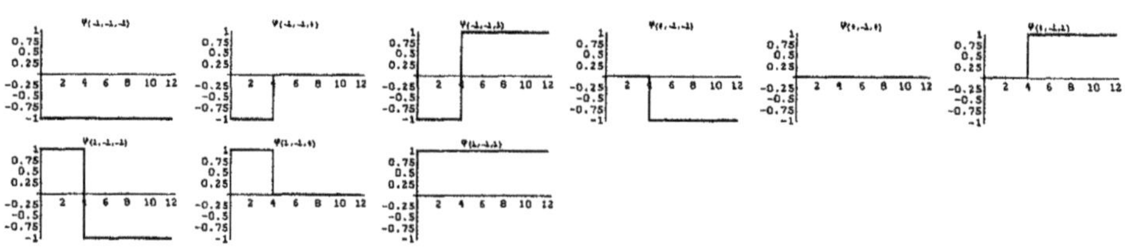

Fig. 5.66 Basis-function forms (ϕ) for W_7.

As an aid to interpreting the plots in these figures, recall that (1) $\varphi < 0$ means that the agent is motivated to not perform the associated action, (2) $\varphi > 0$ means that the agent is motivated to perform the action, and (3) $\varphi = 0$ means that the agent effectively ignores the associated action.

Combining Two or More Features

Apart from adding the general ability to use environmental features to modify an agent's personality weight vector (via the response activation functions discussed above), EINSTein's enhanced action selection logic also allows the user to shape and/or refine desired weight behaviors by combining the effects of two or more features.

This is done by using one of three basic feature combination types (two are additive, one multiplicative):

- Type-I: *Linearly weighed summation,*
- Type-II: *Weight summation as certainty-factor combination,*
- Type-III: *Multiplicative weight strength scaling.*

Type-I Combination

Type-I feature combination is simply a linearly weighed sum of a set of single-feature response activation functions. Suppose we must calculate the total weight, w, that is a function of N features, $\{f_1, f_2, \ldots, f_N\}$. Introducing the factor $0 \leq \alpha_j \leq 1$ as a measure of the relative importance of feature f_j, w is given by:

$$-1 \leq w = \sum_j \alpha_j \omega(f_j) / (\sum_j \rho_j \alpha_j) \leq 1, \tag{5.28}$$

where $\omega(f_j)$ is the *response activation function** as defined for feature f_j and:

$$\rho_j = \begin{cases} 0 & if\, \alpha_j = 0 \;\; or \;\; \omega(f_j) = 0, \\ 1 & otherwise. \end{cases} \tag{5.29}$$

As an example, suppose that feature f_1 = *number of friends within threshold range* (= N_f) and f_2 = *number of friends within threshold range* − *number of enemy agents within sensor range* (= Δ_{Combat}), and that we must compute the single-feature dependent weight functions for weight $w \sim$ *move toward friends.*

Figure 5.67 shows how the partial weights $\omega(f_1)$ (the form of which appears as the left plot) and $\omega(f_2)$ (the form of which appears as the middle plot) combine to form the total weight for the case where f_1 and f_2 are assigned equal relative importance (right-hand-side 3D plot).

Type-II Combination

Type-II feature combination borrows the technique of combining certainty factors according to evidential reasoning in fuzzy logic [Chen96].

*The user defines an appropriate set of parameters—a, b, c, and d—that are consistent with feature f_j and $\omega(f_j)$ is equal to W_X ($X = 0, 1, ..., 7$), where W_X is one of the eight *primitive response activation* functions introduced earlier (see table 5.8).

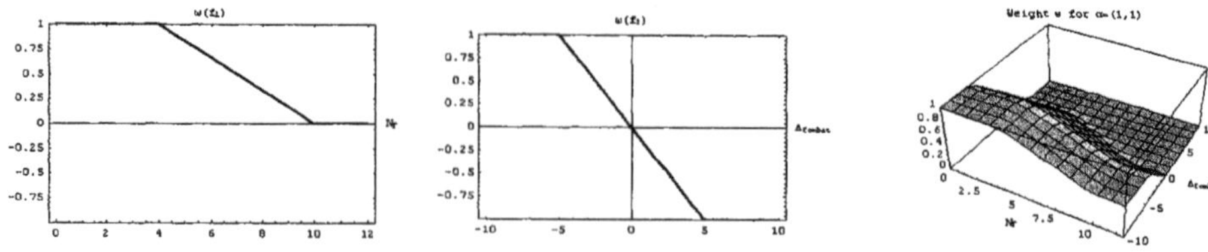

Fig. 5.67 Sample Type-I weight combination for two features (f_1, f_2); see text.

Certainty factors, C, first introduced as part of the MYCIN expert system,* refer to arbitrary (but self-consistent) measures of an expert "belief" regarding some hypothesis. The maximum value of a certainty factor is $+1$ (meaning definitely true) and the minimum value is -1 (meaning definitely false). Positive values < 1 represent relative degrees of belief, and negative values > -1 represent relative degrees of disbelief.

In expert systems using certainty factors, knowledge is typically stored as a set of *"IF <evidence> THEN <hypothesis>"* rules, and the developer is interested in establishing the certainty of the hypothesis:

C(<hypothesis>) =
belief that hypothesis is true given that evidence is true

Evidential reasoning consists of a set of rules for combining certainty factors. For example, in the case of a single antecedent rule, if one's belief in evidence is *C(<evidence>)*, the combined certainty factor *C(<evidence>, <hypothesis>)* is simply *C(<evidence>)*C(<hypothesis>)*. In the case of multiple antecedents, we have certainty factor combination rules of the form:

AND
IF <evidence1> AND <evidence1> AND ... AND<evidenceN>
THEN <hypothesis> ⟶
C(<evidence1> AND ... AND<evidenceN>, <hypothesis>)=
MinimumC(<evidence1>),..., C(<evidenceN>) * C(<hypothesis>)

OR
IF <evidence1> OR <evidence2> OR... OR<evidenceN>
THEN <hypothesis> ⟶
C(<evidence1> OR <evidence2> ...OR<evidenceN>, <hypothesis>)=
MaximumC(<evidence1>),..., C(<evidenceN>) * C(<hypothesis>)

In order to connect this small digression with how single-feature weight functions are combined in EINSTein, we interpret the ith partial weight (that depends on

*MYCIN, developed in 1975, is a fuzzy-logic-based expert system for diagnosing and suggesting therapies for blood infections and meningitis [Buch84].

feature f_i), $\alpha_i\omega(f_i)$, to mean the *degree of importance an agent assigns to the ith feature as a viable determinant of the action associated with weight w_i.*

The degree of "importance" is analogous to "confidence" (or belief). Environmental features are analogous to "evidence," and "hypothesis" in the expert system is, in EINSTein, equivalent to the total weight. Given that any of EINSTein's weights can depend in complicated ways on different features (see figures 5.65 and 5.66, for example), we are particularly interested in calculating the combined certainty factor when the same *hypothesis* is obtained as a consequence of applying two or more single-*evidence* rules. In EINSTein's parlance, we must calculate the combined certainty of two factors, $\alpha_i\omega(f_i)$ and $\alpha_j\omega(f_j)$.

Following Durkin [Durkin94], we use the following equation to combine two single-feature weights:

$$\alpha_i\omega(f_i) \oplus \alpha_j\omega(f_j) =$$

$$\begin{cases} \alpha_i\omega(f_i) + \alpha_j\omega(f_j)\left[1 - \alpha_i\omega(f_i)\right], & \text{if } f_i, f_j > 0, \\ \alpha_i\omega(f_i) + \alpha_j\omega(f_j)\left[1 + \alpha_i\omega(f_i)\right], & \text{if } f_i, f_j < 0, \\ \text{else } \left[\alpha_i\omega(f_i) + \alpha_j\omega(f_j)\right]/(1 - \text{Minimum}\left\{\left|\alpha_i\omega(f_i)\right|, \left|\alpha_j\omega(f_j)\right|\right\}), \end{cases} \tag{5.30}$$

where $|\alpha_i\omega(f_i)|$ is the absolute value of $\alpha_i\omega(f_i)$, and Minimum $\{|\alpha_i\omega(f_i)|, |\alpha_j\omega(f_j)|\}$ is the minimum of $\alpha_i\omega(f_i)$ and $\alpha_j\omega(f_j)$.

While this function may, at first, appear somewhat strange, it possesses several intuitively desirable properties. For example, apart from its simplicity, we immediately note that all certainty factors (interpreted now as EINSTein weights) are bounded between -1 and $+1$: as long as $|x| \leq 1$ and $|y| \leq 1$, $|x \oplus y| \leq 1$. Adding a zero belief to a nonzero certainty leaves the existing certainty unchanged: $x \oplus 0 = x$. Equal certainties that differ in sign combine, as expected, to yield zero effective certainty: $x \oplus (-x) = 0$. Figure 5.68 provides a few illustrative plots of the behavior of $x \oplus y$.

All three subexpressions of the Durkin-sum have very natural interpretations. For example, the Durkin-sum of two positive certainties, defined by the top-most expression appearing on the right-hand-side of equation 5.30, can be expressed in words as, *"Reduce the influence of one certainty by the remaining uncertainty of the other, and add the result to the certainty of the first."*

Likewise, the Durkin-sum of two negative certainties, given in the middle row of equation 5.30, is equivalent to taking the Durkin-sum of two positive certainties and negating the result. Finally, combining a positive and negative certainty is equal to multiplying the difference by the reciprocal of the smallest remaining uncertainty.

Nonetheless, equation 5.30 represents a purely heuristic method of combining weights. Since single-feature weight components are nothing more than, essentially arbitrary, functions, they cannot justifiably be interpreted as, say, probabilities, for which a more rigorous inference engine based on Bayesian reasoning could be used. However, despite the lack of mathematical correctness, the performance of expert

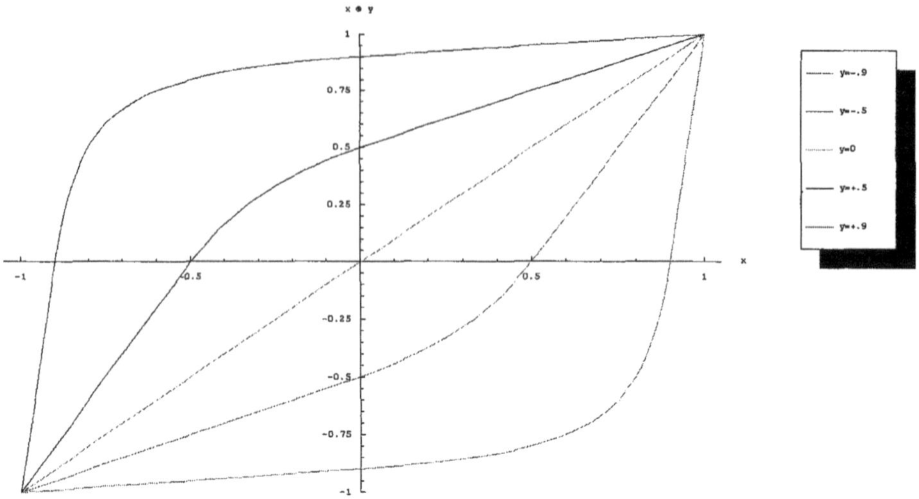

Fig. 5.68 Behavior of certainty factor summation (see equation 5.30)

systems based on certainty factors has, on occasion, *outperformed* Bayesian reasoning (at least in systems designed to mimic human diagnostic judgment [Durkin94]). At the very least, equation 5.30 provides a reasonably intuitive way of combining multiple feature dependencies that is easy to calculate (i.e., does not require many CPU cycles to compute). This is important since, in general, many such combinations must be computed to update the system on every turn.

Figure 5.69 shows how the partial weights $\omega(f_1)$ and $\omega(f_2)$ (the forms for which are shown on the left and middle plots*) yield the Type-II combined weight for the case where f_1 and f_2 are assigned equal relative importance.

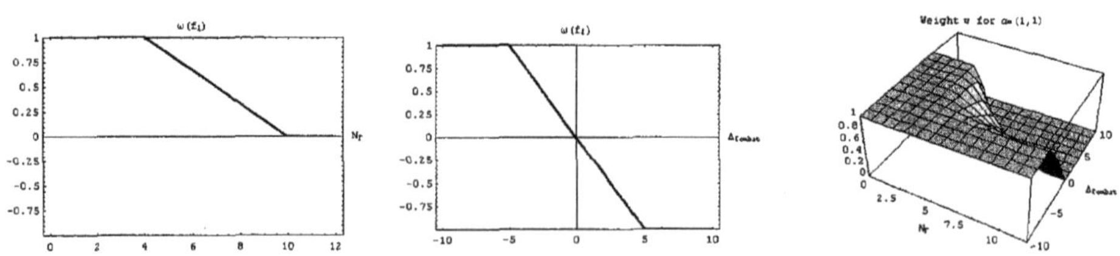

Fig. 5.69 Sample Type-II weight combination for two features (f_1, f_2).

Figure 5.70 illustrates how two partial weights, $\omega(f_1)$ and $\omega(f_2)$ (the plots of which appear in the top row), can be combined to take on a variety of forms,

*Note that $\omega(f_1)$ and $\omega(f_2)$ are the same functions as used in the sample Type-I combination shown earlier in figure 5.67.

$W = \alpha_1 \omega(f_1) \oplus \alpha_2 \omega(f_2)$. They are "shaped" into these forms by being assigned different degrees of relative importance, as embodied by the coefficients α_1 and α_2, ranging from $(\alpha_1, \alpha_2) = (1, 0)$ at the top left of the figure, to $(\alpha_1, \alpha_2) = (1, 1)$ (shown in the grey box at the center), to $(\alpha_1, \alpha_2) = (0, 1)$ at the bottom right.

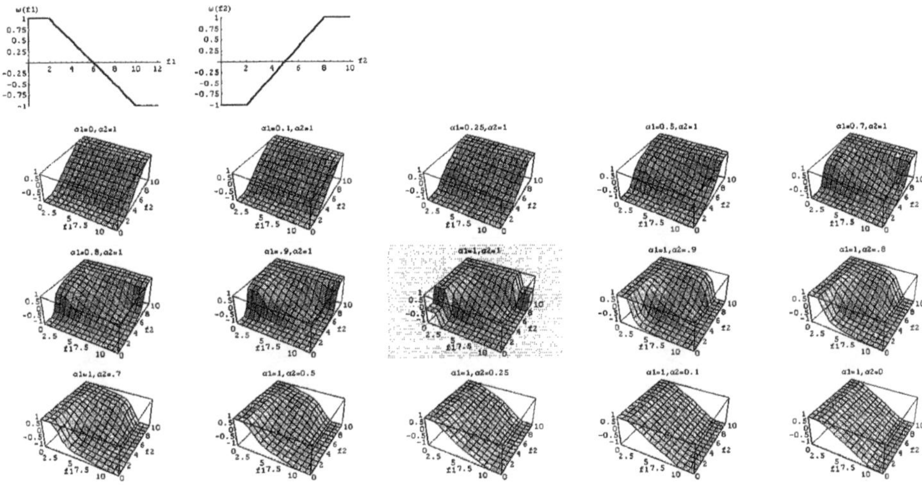

Fig. 5.70 Sample Type-II weight combination "shaping" by varying the relative degrees of importance of features f_1 and f_2.

Multiple features. *What if there are more than two features?* Suppose some weight w depends on N features, $\{f_1, f_2, ..., f_N\}$ $(= \mathcal{F})$, and, as before, $\alpha_i \omega(f_i)$ represents the ith single-feature weight component, where α_i is the relative importance of feature. Because the Durkin-sum (equation 5.30) is symmetric (i.e., $x \oplus y = y \oplus x$), so long as the signs (+ or −) of individuals terms are all equal, the order in which partial sums are evaluated is irrelevant. Thus, we can combine the single-feature weight components by first partitioning $\mathcal{F}$ into sets yielding only positive components ($\mathcal{F}_+ = \left\{\alpha_1^+ \omega(f_1^+), \alpha_2^+ \omega(f_2^+), \ldots, \alpha_{N_+}^+ \omega(f_{N_+}^+)\right\}$) and only negative components ($\mathcal{F}_- = \left\{\alpha_1^- \omega(f_1^-), \alpha_2^- \omega(f_2^-), \ldots, \alpha_{N_-}^- \omega(f_{N_-}^-)\right\}$), zero components contributing nothing, and combining the separately evaluated positive and negative partial sums:

$$\begin{aligned} \oplus_{i=1}^N \alpha_i \omega(f_i) \quad = \quad & \left\{\alpha_1^+ \omega(f_1^+) \oplus_+ \cdots \oplus_+ \alpha_{N_+}^+ \omega(f_{N_+}^+)\right\} \\ & \oplus_{+-} \left\{\alpha_1^- \omega(f_1^-) \oplus_- \cdots \oplus_- \alpha_{N_-}^- \omega(f_{N_-}^-)\right\}, \end{aligned} \tag{5.31}$$

where $\oplus_+$, $\oplus_-$, and $\oplus_{+-}$ are defined by:

$$\begin{cases} x \oplus_+ y = x + y\,[1 - x]\,, \text{ for } x, y > 0, \\ x \oplus_- y = x + y\,[1 + x]\,, \text{ for } x, y < 0, \\ (x + y)/(1 - \text{Minimum}\,\{|x|\,, |y|\})\,, \text{ for sign}(x) = -\text{sign}(y). \end{cases} \tag{5.32}$$

Figure 5.71 compares how the three partial weights $\omega(f_1)$, $\omega(f_2)$ and $\omega(f_3)$ (the forms for which are shown on the top row) combine to form Type-I ($\omega(f_1)+\omega(f_2)+\omega(f_3)$; middle row) and Type-II ($\omega(f_1) \oplus \omega(f_2) \oplus \omega(f_3)$; bottom row) total weight for the case where features f_1, f_2, and f_3 are assigned equal relative importance.

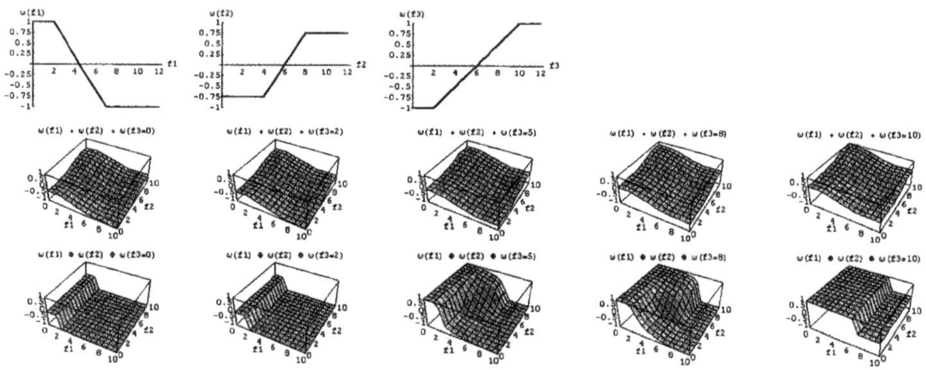

Fig. 5.71 Sample Type-I and Type-II weight combination for three features (f_1,f_2,f_3).

Note the qualitatively different functional forms that result from combining weights using *linear* (i.e., Type-I) and *Durkin* (i.e., Type-II) weight summation. Whereas Type-I summations consist largely of smooth value gradations, the Durkin-summed weights consist of discrete "plateaus," with the discrete set of values depending on position in feature-space. Neither summation type is "better" than the other, of course. How useful either is at shaping desired behaviors (both at the agent and force levels) is a function of scenario, agent characteristics, and user preferences. While it is hard to generalize across all possible weight combinations, Durkin summation generally tends to be a "sharper" rendition of linear summation; i.e., where Type-I summation yields smooth gradations of weight values, Type-II summation typically yields strong, quasidiscrete, transitions between weight value plateaus.

Type-III Combination

Type-III feature combination effectively uses the weight-factor dependence on one feature, say f, to scale, multiplicatively, a partial weight-sum, $w\left(\tilde{f}\right)$, that is a function of another feature, $\tilde{f}$. Using, as before, the factor $0 \leq \alpha_f \leq 1$ as a measure of the *relative importance* of feature f, w is given by:

$$-1 \leq w = w(\tilde{f}) \otimes \omega_{III}(f) = w(\tilde{f}) \cdot \{(1-\alpha_f) + \alpha_f \cdot \omega_{III}(f)\} \leq 1, \quad (5.33)$$

where we have used the symbol $\otimes$ to denote Type-III combination, and $0 \leq \omega_{III}(f) \leq +1$ is the non-negative multiplicative scaling factor associated with feature f. The quantity $\omega_{III}(f)$ may assume any of the generic forms of the response activation function defined earlier, but with the constraint $0 \leq m,\ m_0,\ M \leq +1$.

What if two or more partial weight factors must be combined using both Type-I/II and Type-III combination? Suppose some weight w depends on $N = N_A + N_M$ features, $\{f_1, f_2, \ldots, f_{N_A}, f_{N_A+1}, f_{N_A+2}, \ldots, f_{N_A+N_M}\}$, where $\mathcal{F}_A = \{f_1, f_2, \ldots, f_{N_A}\}$ denote the N_A features that will be used for *additive*, Type-I/II combination, and $\mathcal{F}_M = \{f_{N_A+2}, \ldots, f_{N_A+N_M}\}$ denote the N_M features that will be used for *multiplicative*, Type-III combination. If, as before, α_i represents the relative importance of the ith feature f_i, then w is given by:

$$w = \left\{ \begin{array}{c} Type-I: \dfrac{\sum_{i \in F_A} \alpha_i \omega(f_i)}{\sum_{i \in F_A} \rho_j \alpha_j} \\ \text{or} \\ Type-II: \ \oplus_{i \in F_A} \alpha_i \omega(f_i) \end{array} \right\} \otimes \overbrace{\prod_{j \in F_M} \{(1-\alpha_j) + \alpha_j \cdot \omega_{III}(f_j)\}}^{Type-III}. \quad (5.34)$$

A Type-III scaling factor may only be combined with either an existing partial weight for some other feature or with an existing Type-I or Type-II partial weight sum; it does *not* represent a standalone weight value.

To make this last point clear, we emphasize that, unlike the case for Type-I and Type-II combination, where each partial weight, $\omega(f)$, represents an *actual weight value* (for a given feature f), Type-III partial weights, denoted by $\omega_{III}(f)$, are interpreted strictly as *multiplicative scaling factors.* Thus Type-III combination is less a "combination" of partial weights than it is a *filter* for existing partial weight combinations. Its intended use is to either set otherwise nonzero weights to zero for a selected range of feature values, reduce the strength of existing weight values, and/or specify a range of feature values for which the value of an existing partial weight will be left unchanged. Indeed, Type-III feature combination has been added to EINSTein's new arsenal of behavior shaping functions, in part, because it provides an obvious way in which the effects of older rules (which rely exclusively on fixed weight values that depend on discrete states) may be reproduced using the newer code, as the following example illustrates.

Consider a typical rule that defines how an agent interacts with a friendly agent, using EINSTein's older action selection logic: an agent is assigned a weight $\omega = +1$

for moving toward an *alive* friend, another weight $\omega = -1$for moving away from an *injured* friend, and uses the meta-rule *"IF number of friends ($= N_F$) is less than or equal to* 3 *THEN"* to determine the context for which it is to temporarily ignore nearby friends.

Figure 5.72 illustrates how this current-style rule may be reproduced using EINSTein's new class of behavior shaping functions. The 3D plot on the right-hand-side of figure 30 shows the result of combining $\omega_1(N_F)$ and $\omega_2(H_F)$ in Type-III fashion: $\omega_1(N_F) \otimes \omega_2(H_F)$.

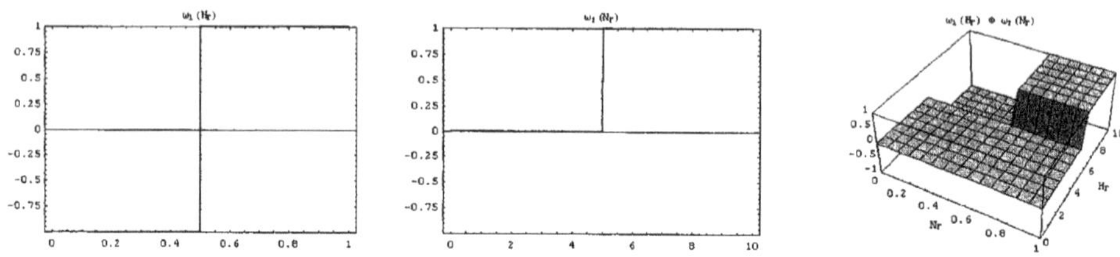

Fig. 5.72 Sample Type-III weight combination; see text.

EINSTein's current-style rule is reproduced in two steps: (1) An agent's partial weight for moving toward a friend is first determined by applying the basis-function $\omega_1(H_F) = \varphi_{-1,-1,+1}(H_F)$ (as defined for the seventh response activation function, W_7; see Table 5.8) to feature $f_1 = H_F$ (see plot on the left-hand-side of figure 5.72), and (2) $\omega_2(N_F)$ is combined with (i.e., *filtered* by) a Type-III basis function $\omega_2(N_F) = \varphi_{0,-1,+1}(N_F)$, applied to feature $f_2 = N_F$, where N_F is the number of friendly agents located within the given agent's sensor range (see center plot in figure 5.72). (Note that $\omega_1(H_F)$ effectively toggles between discrete-valued alive and injured states according to whether an agent's continuous-valued health H is *less than* or *greater than or equal to* a critical value, H^*; in this case, $H^* = 1/2$.)

Figure 5.73 helps illustrate the differences among the three different ways of combining partial weights by showing the result of combining $\omega_1(H_F)$ and $\omega_2(N_F)$ in Type-I and Type-II fashion.

From the four different contexts that an agent can be in for this example (a context being defined by the values of H_F and N_F), $(H_F, N_F) = (< 1/2, < 5)$, $(< 1/2, \geq 5)$, $(\geq 1/2, < 5)$, $(\geq 1/2, \geq 5)$, the possible Type-I, Type-II and Type-III combined weight values are, respectively:

$\underbrace{(H_F, N_F)}$	$Type-I$ ↓	$Type-II$ ↓	$Type-III$ ↓
$(< 1/2, < 5)$:	$-1/2$	-1	0
$(< 1/2, \geq 5)$:	0	0	-1
$(\geq 1/2, < 5)$:	$1/2$	$+1$	0
$(\geq 1/2, \geq 5)$:	$+1$	$+1$	$+1$

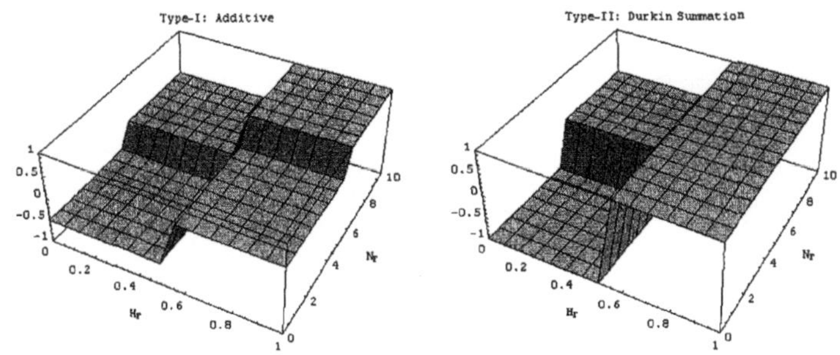

Fig. 5.73 $\omega_1(H_F)$ and $\omega_2(N_F)$ combined in Type-I and Type-II fashion; see text.

While these simple calculations suffice to show how EINSTein's enhanced logic can be used to reproduce older rules, and show the effect that the various weight combination options have on the total weight values, the enhanced code's real strength lies in its ability to gracefully shift from older-style discrete-valued state transitions to more realistic continuous-valued behavioral motivations.

For example, consider the ramp-linear generalizations of the step functional forms (shown earlier in figure 5.69) for $\omega_1(H_F)$ and $\omega_2(N_F)$, shown in figure 5.74.

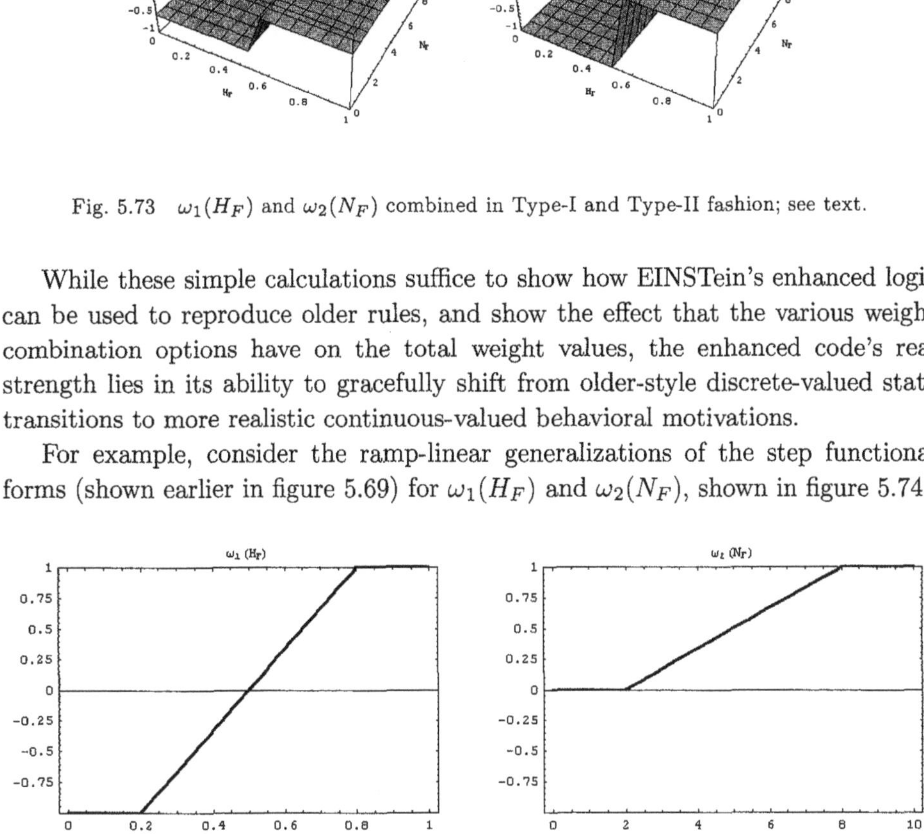

Fig. 5.74 Sample linear ramp-functional forms for $\omega_1(H_F)$ and $\omega_2(N_F)$.

Figure 5.75 shows plots of the total weight value, obtained by applying each of three summation types (and with equal relative importance assigned to the two features being summed). Whereas Type-II and Type-III combined forms span the full set of positive and negative values (between -1 and +1), Type-I combination effectively dampens the contribution of the component weights.

In general, Durkin summation may be characterized as yielding a sharper local-transitional version of Type-I combination; i.e., if, for a given range of feature values, Type-I combination yields a range $|\Delta_I \omega|$ of the total weight, a Durkin sum of the same weights for the same range of feature values, typically yields some range $|\Delta_{II} \omega|$ $> |\Delta_I \omega|$. Figuratively speaking, Durkin sum forms appear as *squeezed* (along the

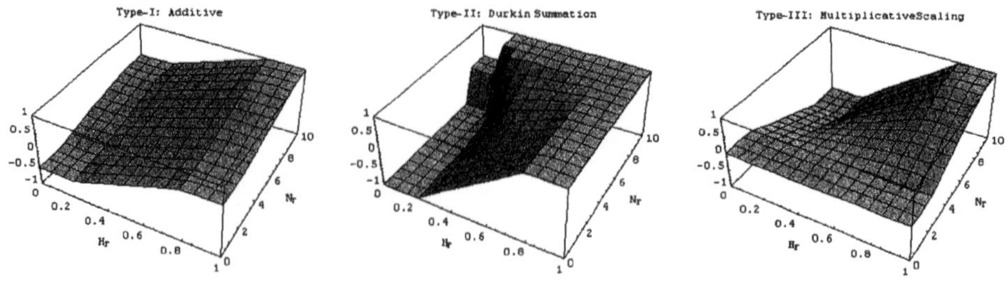

Fig. 5.75 Type-I, Type-II and Type-III total weight combinations for the functional forms for $\omega_1(H_F)$ and $\omega_2(N_F)$ shown in figure 5.74.

$x - y$ axes) and/or *pinched* (along the z axis) versions of Type-I combinations. Type-III combinations, on the other hand, as remarked earlier, are simply *filtered* versions of the actual weight value component of the combination.

We emphasize that the fact that the functional forms of the combined weight values tend to be all different, is not a flaw of the system (that the user must find a way to circumvent), but is rather a deliberately designed feature of the selection logic. There is no objectively *correct* (or *incorrect*) method of combining weights, just as a given weight has no objectively correct (or incorrect) functional dependence on a set of features.

Indeed, one can imagine many different, but equally valid, ways of combining partial weight values, and of mapping features to weights. While some weight combination methods, and some functions, inevitably prove more or less useful than others, depending on the emergent behaviors that are being sought, the particular choices are, objectively speaking, arbitrary. The simulation software is useful only to the extent that it provides a well defined palette of procedures that it is *incumbent upon the analyst* to use, judiciously and intelligently, for engineering desired behaviors.

Appendix 4: *Weight Modification via Internal Feature Space*

Thus far we have described weight value initialization (*Step 0*), trigger state processing (*Step 1*), and the preliminary stage of weight value determination (*Step 2*). Much of the discussion of the last section focused on how EINSTein's enhanced action selection logic uses the functional dependence of a set of generalized response activation functions on *environmental features* ($e_j \in F_E$) and *entity* features ($f_j \in F_F$) to effectively "shape" desired agent behaviors.

In *Step 3* of EINSTein's enhanced action selection logic, all active weights for which preliminary values were assigned during the preceding step are modified as a function of an agent's *internal* features ($i_j \in F_E$).

Squash Functions

This modification consists of shifting weight values up (toward +1) or down (toward −1) by using *squash-factor functions*, $\hat{s}(f)$, the forms of which depend on an agent's internal features (f), such as *health*, *fatigue*, *fear* (of combat), *morale*, and *obedience.*

Consider a weight, w, which we assume is "active" for some agent $\mathcal{A}$. The squashed weight value, $S(w)$, is a function of w and is parameterized by (1) *squash strength* ($= \beta$), (2) *limiting value* (w_∞), and (3) *squash factor*, ($= \hat{s}(f)$), where f represents any of $\mathcal{A}$'s internal features:

$$w \to w' = S(w; \beta, w_\infty, \hat{s}, f) = [1 - \beta \cdot \hat{s}(f)] \cdot w + w_\infty \cdot \beta \cdot \hat{s}(f), \qquad (5.35)$$

where $-1 \leq w,\ w_\infty \leq +1$ and $0 \leq \beta,\ \hat{s}(f) \leq +1$. The complete set of squashed weights, $\{S(w_1), S(w_2), \ldots, S(w_N)\}$, may be assigned, uniquely, to individual agents. The manner in which weights are modified by internal features is thus another component of an agent's overall personality.

The way to interpret each of the factors appearing in equation 5.35 is as follows:

- $-1 \leq w_\infty \leq +1$: w_∞ is the desired limiting value for weight w (i.e., a fixed value that is independent of all features that w itself is normally a function of). is typically equal to −1, in which case maximum weight is assigned to *avoiding* performing whatever action is associated with w being squashed; 0, in which case the action normally associated with w is ignored; or +1, in which case maximum weight is given to performing the action associated with w.

- $0 \leq \beta \leq 1$: the squash strength determines how strong a role the squash-weight-filter plays in the multistep process of assigning values to active weights: $\beta = 0$ means that $S(w) = w$ and w remains unchanged regardless of the calculated value of the squash factor; $\beta = 1$ means that w is maximally squashed by the amount appropriate for the calculated value of the squash factor.

- $0 \le \hat{s}(f) \le 1$: the squash factor determines the degree to which w is squashed. Since it is an explicit function of the internal feature, f (that the user associates with w as part of defining an agent's personality), it is really the only true dynamic ingredient of the squash-weight filter. If $\hat{s}(f) = 0$ then an agent's internal features have no effect on w; if $\hat{s}(f) = 1$ then (assuming $\beta = 1$) $S(w) = w_\infty$; values in-between these endpoints interpolate between the two extremes.

The squash factor depends on five parameters—high and low feature values (f_{low} and f_{high}, respectively), high and low squash factors (s_{low} and s_{high}, respectively), and a squash power (n_s)—and assumes a very simple general form (see figure 5.76):

$$\hat{s}(f_{low}, f_{high}, s_{low}, s_{high}) =$$

$$\begin{cases} s_{high} \text{ if } f \le f_{low}, \\ s_{low} \text{ if } f \ge f_{high}, \\ \text{else} \begin{cases} (s_{high} - s_{low}) \cdot \left[1 - \left(\dfrac{f - f_{low}}{f_{high} - f_{low}}\right)\right]^{n_s} + s_{low} \text{ if } n \ge 0, \\ (s_{high} - s_{low}) \cdot \left[1 - \left(\dfrac{f - f_{low}}{f_{high} - f_{low}}\right)^{-n_s}\right] + s_{low} \text{ if } n < 0. \end{cases} \end{cases} \tag{5.36}$$

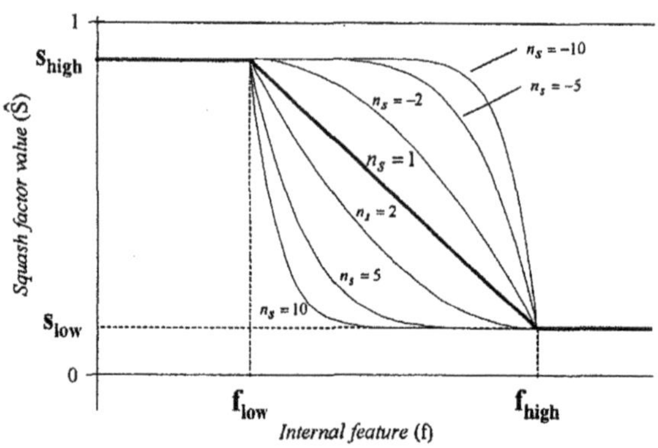

Fig. 5.76 Generic form of the *squash-factor function*, $\hat{s}(f)$; see text.

Consider the sample weight form, w, and squash factor function, $\hat{s}(f)$, using $n_s = 1$, shown in figure 5.77. Figure 5.78 shows snapshot views of the squash-filtered weight for $\beta = 0.1, 0.5$, and 1; $f = 0, 0.5$, and 1; and $w_\infty = 0.5$. Notice that w remains unchanged from its original form when $f = 1$ (since $\hat{s}(f = 1) = 0$; see bottom right of figure) and collapses to the fixed value $w_\infty = 0.5$ when the squash strength $\beta = 1$ and squashing factor attains its maximum value ($\hat{s}_{\max} = \hat{s}(f = 0) = 1$; see top left of figure). Intermediate values of β and $\hat{s}(f)$ interpolate between the nominally minimum and maximum values of w.

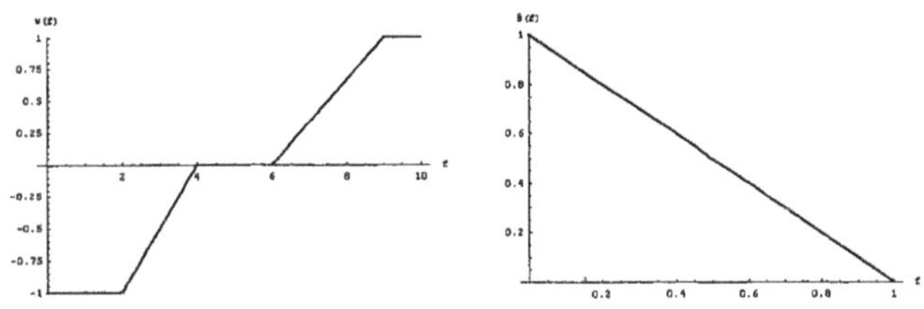

Fig. 5.77 Sample weight form and squash-factor function.

If more than one internal feature is used to modify an active weight, then, assuming that $w_{\infty,i} = w_{\infty}$ for all i (where $w_{\infty,i}$ is the limiting weight value for the ith feature), then:

$$\begin{aligned} &S_{tot}(w;\beta,w_{\infty},\hat{s}_i,f_i) = \\ &\quad S_N(S_{N-1}(\cdots S_1(w;\beta,w_{\infty},\hat{s}_1,f_1);\beta,w_{\infty},\hat{s}_{N-1},f_{N-1});\beta,w_{\infty},\hat{s}_N,f_N). \end{aligned} \tag{5.37}$$

That is, S_{tot} consists of a series of nested applications of the "operator" $S(w)$ defined in equation 5.35: one first evaluates $S_1(w)$ as though feature f_1 were the only active feature; next, one takes the modified weight as an input and evaluates $S_2(w = S_1(w))$ as though feature f_2 were the only active feature; and so on for each of the N features. So long as the limiting weight value and β are the same for all features, the evaluation order does not affect the outcome.

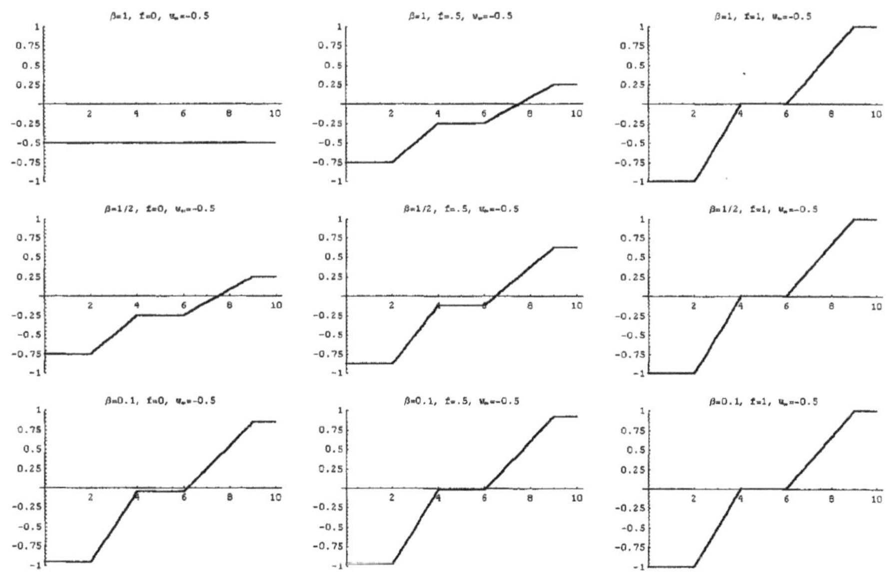

Fig. 5.78 Squashed weight forms for $\beta = 0.1, 0.5$, and 1, $f = 0, 0.5$, and 1, and $w_{\infty} = 0.5$ for the weight and squash-factor shown in figure 5.77.

Appendix 5: *Action Logic Function (ALF)*

The last step of EINSTein's enhanced action logic (see table 5.7 on page 377) is the application of the *Action Logic Function* (ALF). The ALF acts as the final "filter" through which active weights must pass to determine which weights (and therefore which primitive actions) will remain active and thus be executed by an agent. ALF is useful for discriminating between (and fine-tuning the behavior for) cases in which several weights remain active after *Step 4*. In particular, the ALF can be adaptively tuned so that when, for example, a subset of active weight strengths exceeds some large-value threshold, all other "weaker" weights are *deactivated.* This effectively forces an agent to focus its attention on actions that are associated only with the strongest weights.

For example, suppose that two active weights remain (w_1 and w_2), and consider two cases: (1) $w_1 = 0.9$ and $w_2 = 0.3$, and (2) $w_1 = 0.7$ and $w_2 = 0.5$. While both sets of values can certainly be used to select an agent's action (and would generally lead to slightly different behaviors since the two cases differ in their relative weight value assignments), the user has the option to fix an activation threshold of, say 0.8, so that, in the first case, only $w_1 = 0.9$ remains active.

The ALF depends on four quantities:

- *Weight strength,* $S[w_i] = |w_i|$.
- *Minimum top-strength,* $0 \leq s_{\text{Min-Top}} \leq 1$, which is a function of the top-weight number (N_{ALF}); see below.
- *Minimum strength,* $S_{Min} = \text{Minimum}\{S[w_i]\}$.
- *Maximum strength,* $S_{Max} = \text{Maximum}\{S[w_i]\}$.

The ALF also depends on several important user-defined parameter values and logic flags, (whose meaning will be made clear during the discussion below):*

- *Weight depth,* $D_W[w_i] \in \{-1, 0, +1, +2, +3\}$, is normally assigned to a weight w_i during *Step 1* as part of performing trigger-state related actions. means that w_i remains an active ALF component; results in w_i being ignored by ALF. If an active weight has a nonzero value but zero depth, its value remains unchanged (by ALF) and is used "as is" without further modification by the penalty function.
- *Minimum strength threshold,* $0 \leq \alpha_{\text{ALFMin}} \leq 1$.
- *Maximum strength threshold,* $0 \leq \alpha_{\text{ALFMax}} \leq 1$.
- *Strength threshold factor,* $0 \leq \Delta_S \leq 1$.
- *Top-weight number,* $1 \leq N_{\text{ALF}} \leq N_{\text{Weights}}$.
- *ALF-decision flag,* $f_{ALF} \in \{1, 2, 3, 4, 5, 6\}$.

*Note that ALF-parameters apply globally to action selection by all agents. In other words, they describe EINSTein's action selection logic, not agent personalities (which specify the way in which agents use EINSTein's otherwise fixed action selection logic to make their moves).

Using these formal definitions, we can now describe *Step 5* of EINSTein's action selection logic. It consists of two basic steps: (*Step 5a*) Use the minimal strength threshold, α_{ALFMin}, to eliminate the weakest weights:

Set $w_i \to w_i = 0$ if $S[w_i] \leq \alpha_{\text{ALFMin}}$, else leave the value of w_i unchanged, and

(*Step 5b*) Select a subset of the weights that remain active after *Step 4* according to specific logic prescribed by the ALF-decision flag; i.e., with respect to all weights w_i whose depth $D_W[w_i] \neq 0$, and depending on the (user-assigned) value of the decision flag, f_{ALF}, the ALF proceeds along one of six "logical" channels:

- *Channel 1* ($f_{ALF} = 1$): use all nonzero, active weight values in the penalty function, regardless of relative strengths.
- *Channel 2* ($f_{ALF} = 2$): if $S_{Max} \geq \alpha_{\text{ALFMax}}$, then keep only those weight values w_i such that $S[w_i] \geq \alpha_{\text{ALFMax}}$, else keep all weights such that:

$$[S_{Max} - \Delta_S \cdot (S_{Max} - S_{Min})] \leq S[w_i] \leq S_{Max}. \tag{5.38}$$

- *Channel 3* ($f_{ALF} = 3$): keep all weight values w_i for which equation 5.38 is satisfied, regardless of the value of S_{min} and S_{max}.
- *Channel 4* ($f_{ALF} = 4$): keep weight value w_i with probability $\text{P}[w_i] \propto S[w_i]$.
- *Channel 5* ($f_{ALF} = 5$): use top N_{ALF} ranking nonzero weights, regardless of their relative strengths.
- *Channel 6* ($f_{ALF} = 6$): same as for $f_{ALF} = 5$ plus keep all weight values w_i such that:

$$[S_{\text{Min-Top}} - \Delta_S \cdot (s_{\text{Min-Top}} - S_{Min})] \leq S[w_i] \leq S_{\text{Min-Top}}. \tag{5.39}$$

As an example of how the ALF processes weight values, suppose that there are nine active, nonzero weights remaining at the end of *Step 4*: $w_1 = +0.04$, $w_2 = +0.25$, $w_3 = -0.35$, $w_4 = -0.48$, $w_5 = +0.52$, $w_6 = +0.63$, $w_7 = +0.67$, $w_8 = +0.8$, and $w_9 = -0.85$. Suppose, further, that the ALF is defined by the following set of parameters: $\alpha_{\text{ALFMin}} = 0.15$, $\alpha_{\text{ALFMax}} = 0.75$, $\Delta_S = 0.5$, and $N_{\text{ALF}} = 3$.

Figure 5.79 illustrates the action of the ALF for each of the ALF's six decision-flag options ($f_{ALF} \in \{1,2,3,4,5,6\}$). In the figure, the w_i are arranged along the lefthandside axis according to their strength ($S[w_i]$), from weakest (at the bottom), to the strongest (at the top).

The weights arranged along the dashed columns to the right of the axis correspond to the six ALF-filtered set of weights, with each set being determined by assuming one of the six possible values of the ALF's decision-flag. Notice that the

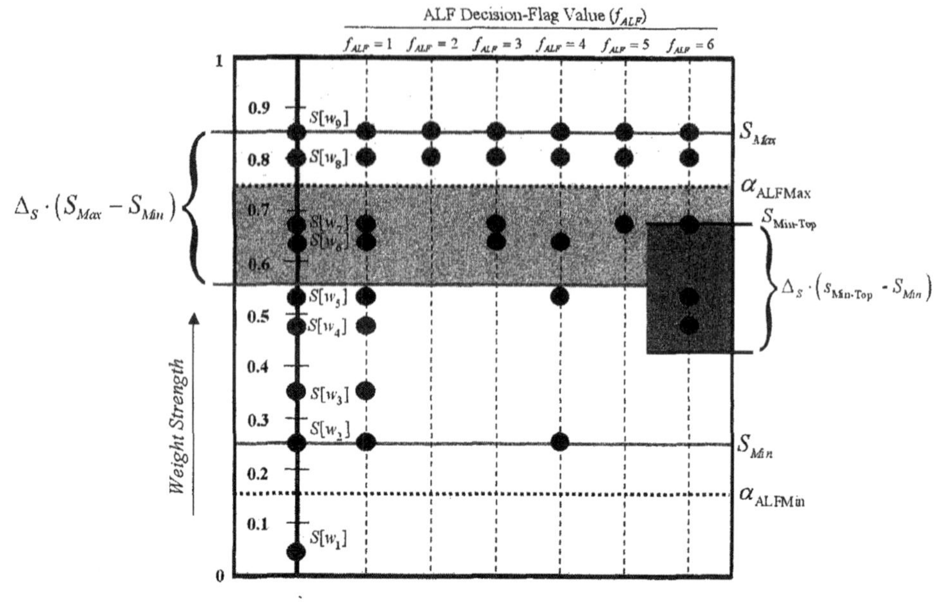

Fig. 5.79 Result of ALF applied to sample weights w_1, w_2,..., and w_9.

weakest weight (w_1), shown in blue at the bottom of the left-hand-side of the figure), does not appear in any of the filtered columns. Because of this weight's strength, $S[w_1] \leq \alpha_{\text{ALFMin}}$, it does not survive the ALF's *zero-filtering* (*Step 5a*).

The black circles appearing along the first dashed column in figure 5.79 (under the label) represent the weights that remain after passing through the ALF filter's first action channel. This channel acts essentially as an identity-filter and thus allows all weight values (that have not already been canceled out by the zero-filter) to pass through. The red circles appearing at the top of the figure represent those values in our sample weight set whose strengths exceed the maximal threshold (α_{ALFMax}). The ALF-filter's second action channel (for $f_{ALF} = 1$) removes all active weights except for these two weights. Its effect is shown along the second dashed column.

The third column shows the weights that remain by removing all weights whose strength $S[w_i] < S_{Max} - \Delta_S \cdot (S_{Max} - S_{Min})$ (i.e., by removing all weights below the dark-gray boundary). The weights appearing in column four represent *one possible result* of applying the ALF's 4th action channel. In this case, the presence (or absence) of each weight, w_i, depends on a randomly generated real number x_i (between 0 and 1). If $x_i \leq p[w_i]$ then w_i is allowed to "pass" through the filter, else w_i is *de*-activated and removed from the active-weight list. In the example shown, weights w_2, w_5, w_6, w_8, and w_9 remain.

The ALF's 5th action channel retains only the top $N_{ALF} = 3$ ranking weights, in this case being weights w_7, w_8, and w_9. Finally, the sixth and last column shows the effect of applying the ALF's 6th action channel. This channel keeps the top $N_{ALF} = 3$ ranking weights (i.e., the same as for the 5th channel) and keeps all weights $S[w_i] \geq S_{Min-Top} - \Delta_S \cdot (S_{Min-Top} - S_{Min})$, where $S_{Min-Top}$ is the minimally ranked weight out of the top $N_{ALF} = 3$ ranking weights (i.e., $S_{Min-Top} = S[w_7]$).

Penalty Function

Since agent-based models are designed to strip away many, if not all, of the detailed physics of a real system, arguably the most important remaining (albeit, likewise distilled) component of the model is the algorithm that prescribes how an agent *moves.* The previous five steps of the ALF all deal with weight-value assignments and behavioral tuning, and collectively comprise the logic by which agents determine what they must focus their attention on, and to what degree, in a given dynamical context. However, EINSTein's dynamical core resides in the last step of the ALF. Namely, in the penalty function that agents use to make their move. Indeed, one could credibly argue that agent-based models are *defined* by how agents assess penalties.

Recall, from our earlier general discussion, that agents adjudicate their moves by minimizing the value of a penalty function, Z, which is computed for all accessible sites and the components of which consist of agent-specific motivations for performing basic tasks. The general form of Z is given by:

$$Z(\vec{x}) = \sum_A \omega_A(\{f_i^A\}) \cdot \mu_A(\vec{x}), \tag{5.40}$$

where:

- $\vec{x}$ is the site at which Z is being evaluated,
- $\omega_A(\{f_i^A\})$ is a numerical weight value that represents an agent's motivation for maximizing (if $\omega_A > 0$) or minimizing (if $\omega_A < 0$) its expected gain from performing the action A,
- $\{f_i^A\}$ are the environmental features that the agent uses as a dynamical context within which to assign specific values to ω_A (the particular subset of all available features that are used is a function of action, A), and
- $\mu_A(\vec{x})$ represents a measure of how well an agent expects to perform action A in the event that it chooses to move to site.

The battlefield site to which an agent $\mathcal{A}$ moves, , is given by:

$$\begin{aligned} \vec{x}_M &= \text{Position } \vec{x} \text{ such that } Z \text{ is minimum} \\ &= \underset{\text{all } \vec{x} \text{ such that } D[\vec{x}_A,\vec{x}] \leq r_M}{\text{Minimum}} \{Z(\vec{x})\}, \end{aligned} \tag{5.41}$$

where the search for the minimum value of $Z(\vec{x})$ is conducted over all positions $\vec{x}$ whose distance from $\vec{x}_A$ (i.e., $\mathcal{A}$'s position), $D[\vec{x}_A, \vec{x}]$, is less than or equal to $\mathcal{A}$'s movement range, r_M. If there is a set of moves for which the penalties are all equal to the minimum penalty value, an agent's actual move is randomly selected from among the candidate moves making up that set.

Penalty Selector Constant

The user has the option of defining a nonzero *penalty selector constant*, $0 \leq \varepsilon_Z \leq 1$ (which is fixed for all agents, throughout a run), that determines a range of penalty values, and therefore a range of candidate sites, from which the actual move is selected. Let $X_{Candidate}(\varepsilon_Z)$ be a set of moves, $\vec{x}_A \rightarrow \vec{x}_1$, $\vec{x}_A \rightarrow \vec{x}_2$, ..., $\vec{x}_A \rightarrow \vec{x}_{N_{Candidate}}$, all of whose penalty values lie in the range:

$$Z_{\text{min}} \leq Z\left(\vec{x}_1\right), Z\left(\vec{x}_2\right), \ldots, Z\left(\vec{x}_{N_{Candidate}}\right), \leq Z_{\text{min}} + \varepsilon_Z \cdot \left(Z_{\text{max}} - Z_{\text{min}}\right), \quad (5.42)$$

where Z_{min} and Z_{max} are the minimum and maximum penalty values, respectively. Then an agent's move is randomly selected from the candidate moves in $X_{Candidate}(\varepsilon_Z)$, with the probability that the ith candidate is chosen, $Prob(\vec{x}_i \in X_{Candidate}) = N_{Candidate}^{-1}$ for all i.

Appendix 6: *Previsualizing Agent Behaviors*

"Know the enemy and know yourself; in a hundred battles you will never be in peril. When you are ignorant of the enemy but know yourself, your chances of winning or losing are equal. If ignorant both of your enemy and yourself, you are certain in every battle to be in peril."—Sun Tzu, *The Art of War*

The obvious price that must be paid for endowing agents with a more powerful and robust action selection logic (than was available to the user in previous versions of EINSTein) is a commensurate increase in difficulty in developing an intuition for how different combinations of parameter values affect an agent's behavior. This section introduces a graphical tool called a movement map as an aid in previsualizing an agent's' candidate-move space. Examples in one and two dimensions are used to illustrate how movement maps may be used to develop an intuition about how primitive rules and feature-to-weight functions map onto behaviors.

Developing an Intuition for Agent Behaviors

On the one hand, the primitive functional weight forms used to define an agent's penalty function are obviously well-defined entities: they are well-defined conceptually, well-defined mathematically, and well-defined on the programming (i.e., source-code) level. On the other hand—*before a run is executed*—there is no obvious way of deducing the set of macroscopic behaviors that will emerge from a particular set of primitive weights.

Of course, this observation is not restricted to EINSTein alone, as it reflects both the strength and weakness of most, sufficiently interesting, agent-based models.* We are interested in such models precisely because it is not easy to predict, before hand, how the collective actions of agents depend on the primitive rules that the agents obey.

Because the number of separate terms that appear in EINSTein's penalty function can be quite large, it is generally difficult to know, *a priori*, how each of these terms affects agents' moves. Indeed, developing an intuition even about the interactions between only *two, fixed-value* penalty components is nontrivial.

Where ought one to intuitively expect an agent to move, if the agent is equally motivated to move toward the enemy flag and away from an enemy agent that happens to lie exactly half-way between the agent's current position and the flag? Should the agent remain in its current position, move toward the enemy, or away from both the enemy and therefore, unavoidably, the enemy flag as well? *What if an agent's motivation for moving toward the flag is double that of its motivation for moving away from enemies?* Should we expect an agent, in this case, to approach the flag, but turn away if the enemy is positioned half as far as initially from the agent?

* "Sufficiently interesting" refers to agent-based models whose dynamical outcomes cannot, in any obvious way, be immediately traced to the set of rules that define their primitive behaviors; i.e., *sufficiently interesting* agent-based models are those that display genuinely emergent properties.

What if an agent's motivation for moving toward the flag is tripled? Should we expect the agent to now approach the flag, at all costs, and ignore all enemies that stand between it and the flag? If not, then how many times larger ought an agent's motivation for moving toward the flag be than its motivation to stay away from an enemy standing between it and the flag—*5 times, 10 times,...?*—before the agent is to decide to completely ignore the enemy?

Expected Behavior vs. Emergent Behavior

That the answers to basic questions such as these are not obvious underscores the fact that what the user *wants* an agent to do (a detailed description of which may often be given in only verbal terms) is not necessarily equivalent to what an agent *actually does.*

An agent's behavior is necessarily constrained by the assumptions underlying the built-in logic of the program, and is frequently rendered unpredictable in all but the simplest dynamical contexts because of the complications introduced via its mutual interactions with other agents. Thus, an agent's *observed repertoire of behaviors* will generally differ (often greatly) from the repertoire that a user expects an agent to have. EINSTein's output may be correctly interpreted only if the user of the program understands the difference between behaviors that are *reasonable to expect* to result from a given set of rules, and behaviors that actually emerge, but do so in some *a priori* unexpected (i.e., unscripted) fashion.

For example, it is reasonable to expect an agent that is assigned a positive weight for approaching friends, to approach a nearby squad mate in an open battlefield (i.e., in the absence of other environmental features that would otherwise vie for its "attention"). However, one ought not be surprised if that same agent, simultaneously tasked with adjudicating the effects of multiple features, "decides" to move away from that same nearby squad mate.

While the decision to move away from an agent, that a given agent $\mathcal{A}$ is nominally motivated to move toward, is always objectively "reasonable" from $\mathcal{A}$'s point of view—since $\mathcal{A}$ "knows" only how to minimize its local penalty function, its moves are therefore consistently well-defined at all times—$\mathcal{A}$'s move may nonetheless appear counterintuitive from the point of view of the user. To minimize the possibility for this kind of "apparently counterintuitive" behavior to emerge during a run, the user must become familiar with, and develop an intuition for, EINSTein's many built-in behavior-shaping functions.

The difficulty in developing a general intuition about how agents will behave during an actual run, in arbitrary dynamical contexts, not to mention the difficulty of designing agents whose behaviors conform to some set of desired measures, is only compounded by including in the penalty function other, non-positionally-related terms (such as concealment, accessibility, and combat intensity). The ability to maintain a coherent mental map of primitive rules and possible behaviors rapidly becomes intractable.

As a first step toward developing this intuition, it is essential for the user to understand the details of how agents' moves are shaped by their penalty function. The simplest way to do this, of course, is to use EINSTein itself to experiment, before the start of an actual run, with various penalty functional forms, until a penalty function that generates a desired set of behaviors is found. EINSTein is first used to play a series of *"What if?"* games to find a desired set of penalty functions, the forms of which are then fixed and the dynamical consequences of which may then be studied in earnest.

A more refined method, which is discussed in a later section, is to use a genetic algorithm to automatically search for the "best" combination of primitive weight components that satisfy a set of measures of high-level agent behaviors desired by the user. Note that, unlike force-level heuristic searches, which have always been a part of EINSTein (and date back to older ISAAC code), the new element here is the ability to use a genetic algorithm to search for *individual agents.*

An intermediate method, illustrated by the examples below, is to use a stand-alone tool, such as *Mathematica* [Math41], to help *previsualize* agents' candidate-move options, by effectively "peering into" their decision space to see how agents behave in a limited set of predefined contexts. By examining how the elements of the decision space change as a function of the components of an agent's penalty function, one develops an intuition about how primitive rules and feature-to-weight functions map onto behaviors.

As a user's intuition grows deeper through previsualization (or other techniques), so does the user's confidence in being able to design sophisticated combat agents that behave, locally, in some desired (albeit, still largely unscripted) fashion.

We illustrate the technique of developing an intuition for agent behaviors by previsualizing an agent's decision space with two detailed examples: (1) *A "simplified" one-dimensional battlefield,* and *(2) A nominal two-dimensional battlefield.*

Example 1: One Dimension

Consider a one-dimensional battlefield that is 20 (arbitrary) units in length, and in which an agent ($\mathcal{A}$), friend (F), enemy (E) and enemy flag (EF) occupy the positions shown in figure 5.80. $\mathcal{A}$ is fixed at the center site ($x_{\mathcal{A}} = 10$) and its sensor and movement ranges (r_S and r_M, respectively), are both equal to 10.

The penalty includes only terms that depend explicitly on *position.* All other measures—such as combat intensity, line-of-site, and concealment—via which the penalty may indirectly depend on positional variables, are ignored. The focus here is solely on the positions of $\mathcal{A}$, E, F, EF and $\mathcal{A}$'s candidate move, x_m.* Consider the penalty function, $Z_A(x_m)$, defined as:

*Note that one dimensional scenarios—though unrealistic—can easily be defined within EINSTein either by blocking out all but a line of sites by impassable terrain or defining a battlefield of size $= N$–by–1.

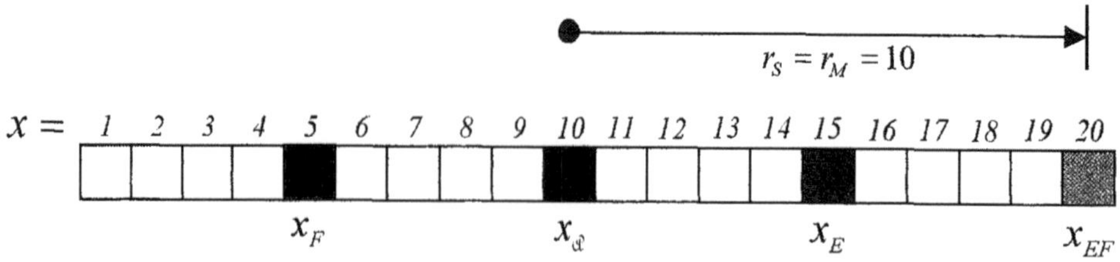

Fig. 5.80 Schematic illustration, and notation, for sample penalty calculations in one dimension.

$$
\begin{aligned}
Z_A(x_m) = {} & \overbrace{\omega_F \cdot \mu_D\left(\tfrac{|x_F - x_m|}{r_M}; n_F\right)}^{\text{move towards friend}} + \overbrace{\omega_{\text{minD}_{A\leftrightarrow F}} \cdot \mu_{\text{minD}_{A\leftrightarrow F}}\left(|x_F - x_m|\right)}^{\text{maintain minimum distance from friend}} \\
& + \overbrace{\omega_{\delta D_{mF}} \cdot \mu_{\delta D_{mF}}(\delta D_{mF}; \omega_F)}^{\substack{\text{penalty for changes} \\ \text{in distance to friend}}} + \overbrace{\omega_E \cdot \mu_D\left(\tfrac{|x_E - x_m|}{r_M}; n_E\right)}^{\text{move towards enemy}} \\
& + \overbrace{\omega_{\text{minD}_{A\leftrightarrow E}} \cdot \mu_{\text{minD}_{A\leftrightarrow E}}\left(|x_E - x_m|\right)}^{\text{maintain minimum distance from enemy}} + \overbrace{\omega_{\delta D_{mE}} \cdot \mu_{\delta D_{mE}}(\delta D_{mE}; \omega_E)}^{\substack{\text{penalty for changes} \\ \text{in distance to enemy}}} \\
& + \overbrace{\omega_m \cdot \mu_D\left(\tfrac{|x_m - x_A|}{r_M}; n_m\right)}^{\text{movement penalty}} + \overbrace{\omega_{EF} \cdot \mu_D\left(\tfrac{|x_{EF} - x_m|}{2r_M}; n_{EF}\right)}^{\text{move toward enemy flag}} \\
& + \overbrace{\omega_{\text{minD}_{A\leftrightarrow EF}} \cdot \mu_{\text{minD}_{A\leftrightarrow EF}}\left(|x_{EF} - x_m|\right)}^{\text{maintain minimum distance from enemy flag}} ,
\end{aligned}
\tag{5.43}
$$

where:

- $1 \leq x_m \leq 20$ is the position of $\mathcal{A}$'s candidate move,
- $-1 \leq \omega_E \leq +1$ and $-1 \leq \omega_{EF} \leq +1$ are the weights for moving toward (or away from) E and EF, respectively,
- $-1 \leq \omega_{\text{minD}_{A\leftrightarrow E}} \leq +1$ and $-1 \leq \omega_{\text{minD}_{A\leftrightarrow EF}} \leq +1$ are the weights for maintaining a minimum distance from E and EF,
- $-1 \leq \omega_m \leq +1$ is the weight for minimizing (or maximizing) $\mathcal{A}$'s projected move distance, $D_{Am} = |x_m - x_A|$,
- $-1 \leq \omega_{\delta D_{mF}} \leq +1$ is the weight for minimizing (or maximizing) the difference between $\mathcal{A}$'s current and projected distance from F, $\delta D_{mF} = |x_m - x_F| - |x_F - x_A|$,
- $-1 \leq \omega_{\delta D_{mE}} \leq +1$ is the weight for minimizing (or maximizing) the difference between $\mathcal{A}$'s current and projected distance from E, $\delta D_{mE} = |x_m - x_E| - |x_E - x_A|$,
- ω_m are the weights for moving toward x_m (i.e., $\mathcal{A}$'s movement penalty),
- $-1 \leq \mu_{\text{minD}_{A\leftrightarrow E}} \leq +1$ is $\mathcal{A}$'s adaptive weight for maintaining a minimum distance from E, and is a function of the distance between $\mathcal{A}$'s current position and E's position, $|x_E - x_m|$,

- $-1 \le \mu_{\text{minD}_{A \leftrightarrow EF}} \le +1$ is $\mathcal{A}$'s adaptive weight for maintaining a minimum distance from EF, and is a function of the distance between $\mathcal{A}$'s current position and the position of the enemy flag, $|x_{EF} - x_m|$,
- $-1 \le \mu_D(x; n_D) \le +1$ is a distance measure associated with weights ω_F, ω_E, and ω_{EF}, and is parameterized by the factor $-\infty \le n_D \le +\infty$,
- $\mu_{\delta D_{mF}}(\delta D_{mF}; \omega_F)$ and $\mu_{\delta D_{mE}}(\delta D_{mE}; \omega_E)$ are the relative distance penalty functions for which $\omega_{\delta D_{mF}}$ and $\omega_{\delta D_{mE}}$ act as effective strengths, respectively (see below).

Figure 5.81 shows the general functional form of the relative distance penalty component, $\omega_{\delta D_m} \cdot \mu_{\delta D_m}$. Since $\mathcal{A}$ moves to the site that minimizes total penalty, the relative distance penalty component (1) *penalizes* (i.e., adds to $\mathcal{A}$'s penalty total) sites for which the relative change in $\mathcal{A}$'s distance from the enemy increases (when $\omega_E > 0$), or decreases (when $\omega_E < 0$), and (2) *rewards* (i.e., subtracts from $\mathcal{A}$'s penalty total) sites for which the relative change in $\mathcal{A}$'s distance from the enemy decreases (when $\omega_E > 0$), or increases (when $\omega_E < 0$). For the case where $x_m = x_{\mathcal{A}}$, the relative distance component $\mu_{\delta D} = 0$.

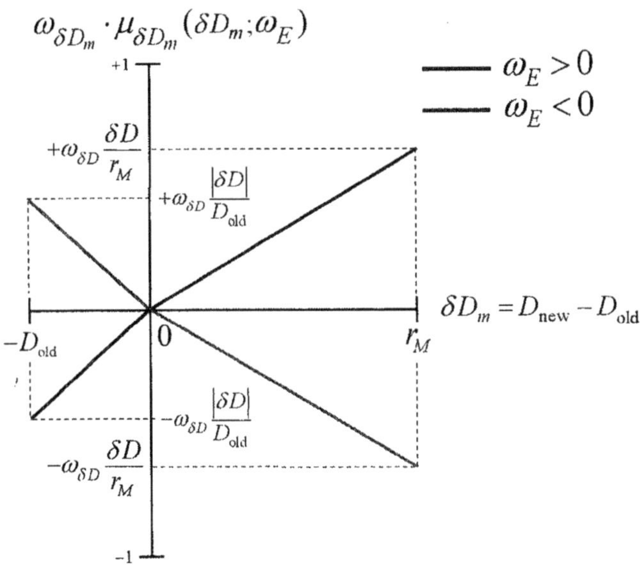

Fig. 5.81 General form of the relative distance penalty, $\omega_{\delta D} \mu_{\delta D}$.

If $\omega_E > 0$, $\mathcal{A}$ is motivated to move toward E, and is thus penalized for selecting a move that takes it *farther* from E (for which $\delta D > 0$) and rewarded for moves that take it *closer* to E (for which $\delta D < 0$). Likewise, if $\omega_E < 0$, $\mathcal{A}$ is motivated to move away from E, and is thus penalized for selecting a move that takes it *closer* to E, and rewarded for moves that take it *farther away*.

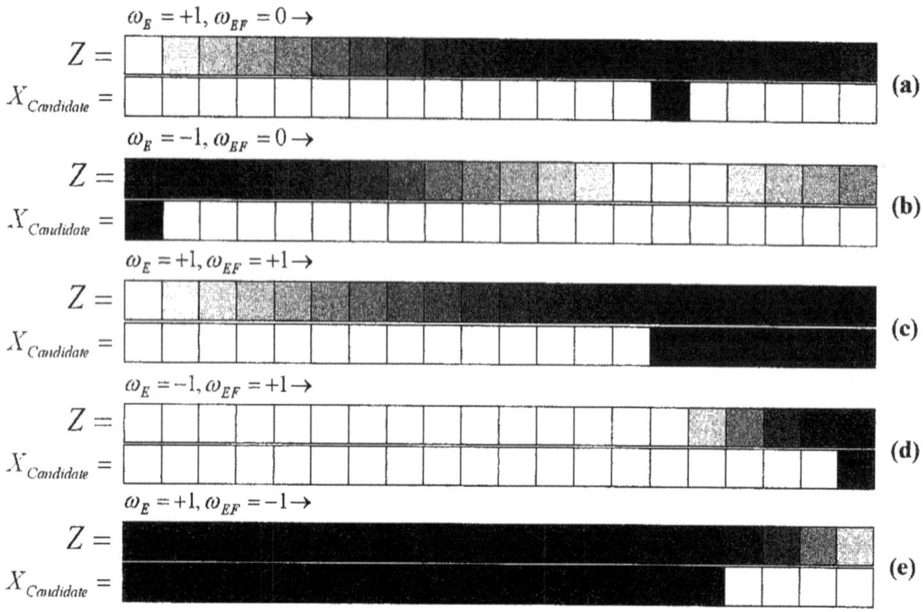

Fig. 5.82 Sample grayscale plots of penalty values and sites belonging to $X_{Candidate}(\varepsilon_Z = 0.01)$ for the one-dimensional scenario shown in figure 5.80.

Previsualizing $\mathcal{A}$'s Action Selection

There are two ways of previsualizing $\mathcal{A}$'s move, for a given configuration of nearby agents and flags:

- Use greyscale tones to indicate the penalty value that is assigned to each of the sites within $\mathcal{A}$'s movement range, and
- Color black only those sites within $\mathcal{A}$'s movement range that are members of $\mathcal{A}$'s candidate move set, $X_{Candidate}(\varepsilon_Z)$, for a given penalty selector constant, $0 \leq \varepsilon_Z \leq 1$.

The greyscale plot shows the distribution of penalty values that result from applying $\mathcal{A}$'s personality weights to $\mathcal{A}$'s current context. Darker tones represent values with lower penalty values, and lighter tones represent higher penalty values. $X_{Candidate}$ defines the set of sites from which $\mathcal{A}$ (randomly) selects its actual move.

As a first example, suppose that all weights appearing in equation 5.43 are zero except for the weights for moving toward (or away from) E and EF. Figure 5.82 shows greyscale plots of penalty values, Z, and sites that belong to for the cases $(\omega_E, \omega_{EF}) = (+1, 0)$ (figure 5.82-a), $(-1, 0)$ (figure 5.82-b), $(+1, +1)$ (figure 5.82-c), $(-1, +1)$ (figure 5.82-d), and $(+1, -1)$ (figure 5.82-e).

Figure 5.82-a shows that, as expected, when $\mathcal{A}$'s only motivation is to move closer to E, the penalty function attains its minimal value at x_E, and decays as the distance between $\mathcal{A}$'s candidate move site and x_E increases. Similarly, figure 5.82-b shows that if $\mathcal{A}$'s only motivation is to move away from E, the penalty function attains its minimal value at $x = 1$ (i.e., the site that is farthest away from x_E), and attains its maximum value precisely at x_E.

Figures 5.82-c,d,e provide the first signs of what might mistakenly be interpreted as constituting "counterintuitive" behaviors. The word "counterintuitive" is used here in the sense explained above. It refers to agent behaviors that do not appear to be consistent with the intuitive meaning of some (or all) of the component weights, despite the fact that their combined effects are well-defined by the penalty function.

For example, consider the plots of Z and $X_{Candidate}$ shown in figure 5.82-c. For this plot, $\mathcal{A}$'s motivations for moving toward E and EF are both equal to $+1$. Since $\mathcal{A}$ starts out at $x_{\mathcal{A}} < x_E < x_{EF}$, one may intuitively expect $\mathcal{A}$ to move to its right, with $x_{move} = (x_E + x_{EF})/2$ representing the "best" move (since this is the site at which $\mathcal{A}$ is as close to both sites as possible). However, as figure 5.82-c shows, and as a quick calculation using equation 43 confirms, all sites between x_E and x_{EF} yield exactly the same penalty, since the combined distance between E and EF remains the same. $\mathcal{A}$'s move thus consists of a random selection of any of these sites.

In figure 5.82-d, $\mathcal{A}$ is motivated to move toward EF ($\omega_{EF} = +1$), but is also motivated to move away from E ($\omega_E = -1$). Since E is initially closer to $\mathcal{A}$ than is EF, one might intuitively (but incorrectly) expect $\mathcal{A}$ to either stay where it is or move away from E. Figure 5.82-d shows that $\mathcal{A}$ overwhelmingly favors moving toward EF. From $\mathcal{A}$'s point of view, this is an objectively valid move because it keeps $\mathcal{A}$ the same distance from E and brings it as close as possible to EF. However, from the user's point of view, the move appears counterintuitive because in moving toward EF, $\mathcal{A}$ must pass over E—an agent that it is motivated to move away from.

Figure 5.82-e illustrates another apparently counterintuitive behavior. In this case, $\mathcal{A}$ is motivated to move toward E ($\omega_E = +1$), and away from EF ($\omega_{EF} = -1$). While one expects $\mathcal{A}$ to "want" to move toward E, the penalty incurred for moving away from E is exactly compensated for by the reward received for moving away from EF. Thus, from the point of view of $\mathcal{A}$'s total penalty function, all sites between $x = 1$ and $x = x_E$ represent equally viable moves.

Selective Behavior-Shaping

Consider again the case shown in figure 5.82-c, for which $\mathcal{A}$'s motivations for moving toward E and EF are both equal to $+1$ (remember that $\mathcal{A}$ starts out at the center of the figure, at $x_{\mathcal{A}} = 10$). The figure shows that, if $\mathcal{A}$ is limited to using only these two motivations (and no others), $\mathcal{A}$ is unable to find a "best" site to move to, as all sites between x_E and x_{EF} incur exactly the same penalty.

A natural question to ask is, *"How do additional distance-related penalty terms affect $\mathcal{A}$'s action selection?"* In particular, we would like to know how other components may be used to selectively shape $\mathcal{A}$'s behavior. In this simple example, we are exploring the consequences of assigning fixed-weight values to E and EF.

However, during an actual run, the user has access to many options for tuning an agent's behavior. For example, during the rank normalization step of the action selection logic (see *Step 4*), the user may have ranked moving toward the enemy flag sufficiently higher than reacting to enemy agents, so that, by the time $\mathcal{A}$ reaches *Step 6* and is ready to make its move, $\mathcal{A}$'s effective (i.e., normalized) motivation for moving toward E is less than its motivation for moving toward EF. The symmetry shown in figure 5.82-c is thus broken and $\mathcal{A}$ chooses to move toward EF.

Other methods for breaking the symmetry between E and EF, and thereby selectively focusing $\mathcal{A}$'s attention on a specific range of neighboring sites, include:

- Changing the value of the penalty selector constant, ε_Z, to either increase (if ε_Z is increased) or decrease (if ε_Z is decreased) the set of candidate sites from which $\mathcal{A}$ randomly selects its move.
- Adding a term that penalizes (or rewards) $\mathcal{A}$ as a function of how far $\mathcal{A}$ expects to move (but is otherwise independent of the agent or battlefield position toward which it is moving).
- Adding a term that penalizes (or rewards) moves toward (or away from) a specific agent or battlefield position, that is a function of $\mathcal{A}$'s current distance from the specific agent or position.
- Adding a term that penalizes (or rewards) moves that bring $\mathcal{A}$ closer (or farther) from a specific agent or battlefield position.
- Adding a term that penalizes (or rewards) moves according to whether $\mathcal{A}$'s expected distance from a specific agent or battlefield position is increased (or decreased) from its initial distance.

Whatever method, or methods, one wishes to use, *desired results*, if they are possible to achieve at all, can only be achieved by first previsualizing the effect that additional weight values (as well as the form of their associated action measures) have on the total penalty. Consider, for example, adding a penalty term, $\omega_m \mu_D$, that depends on $\mathcal{A}$'s projected move distance, $|x_m - x_\mathcal{A}|$, and is parametrized by a power (see figure 5.83):

$$\mu_D\left(\frac{|x_m - x_\mathcal{A}|}{r_M}; n_m\right) = \begin{cases} \left(\dfrac{|x_m - x_\mathcal{A}|}{r_M}\right)^{n_m}, & \text{if } n_m \geq 0, \\ \left[1 - \left(1 - \left(\dfrac{|x_m - x_\mathcal{A}|}{r_M}\right)\right)^{|n_m|}\right], & \text{if } n_m < 0, \end{cases} \tag{5.44}$$

where r_M is $\mathcal{A}$'s movement range. The parameter n_m defines the rate of increase in penalty (or decrease, if the weight $\omega_m < 0$) with distance. (If the internal *fatigue* feature is toggled ON, ω_m and n_m both become functions of an agent's energy level.)

Figure 5.84 shows how the additional movement penalty term, μ_m, affects greyscale plots of Z, and sites that belong to $X_{Candidate}$, for the cases $(\omega_m, n_m) = (0.1, 1)$ (figure 5.84-b), $(\omega_m, n_m) = (0.5, 1)$ (figure 5.84-c), $(\omega_m, n_m) = (1, 1)$ (figure 5.84-d),

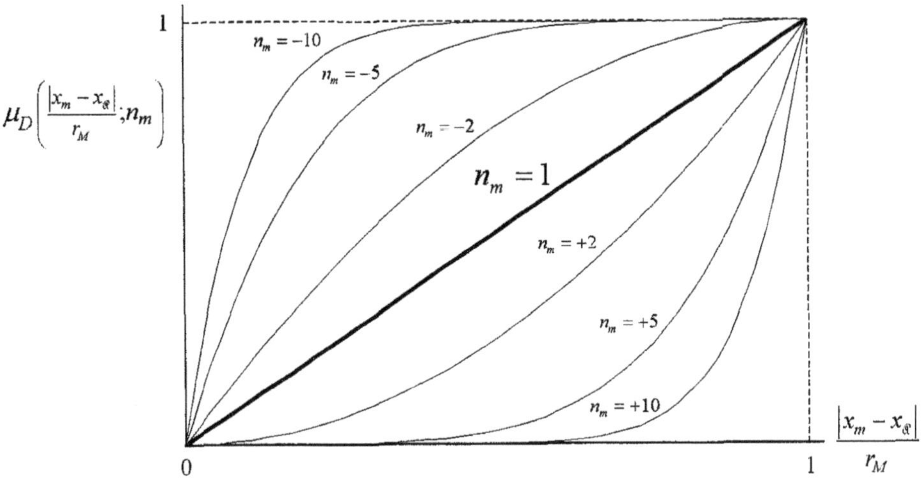

Fig. 5.83 General form of move-distance penalty function, μ_m.

and $(\omega_m, n_m) = (1, 2)$ (figure 5.84-e). (Figure 48-a reproduces the baseline case, $\omega_m = 0$, shown earlier in figure 5.82-c for comparison.)

Compared to the baseline case, figure 5.84-b shows that even a small ($\omega_m = 0.1$), linear ($n_m = 1$), movement penalty is sufficient to compel $\mathcal{A}$ to move to a site that is closer to x_E than x_{EF}. While increasing $\mathcal{A}$'s movement penalty weight to $\omega_m = +0.5$ (figure 5.84-c) forces $\mathcal{A}$ to move to x_E, figure 5.84-d shows that a further increase to ω_m effectively recreates the same range of ambiguity in selecting a "best" move as exists for the baseline case, except that now the ambiguity exists for the range of sites between $x_{\mathcal{A}}$ and x_E. By making the rate of increase in movement penalty quadratic ($n_m = 2$; figure 5.84-e), $\mathcal{A}$'s move options are again restricted to one of two sites near x_E (using the same penalty selector constant as before: $\varepsilon_Z = 0.01$).

Add a Friend

Suppose now we add the friendly agent, F, to $x_F = 5$ (see figure 5.80), and want to know how its presence is likely to affect $\mathcal{A}$'s move. Figure 5.85 shows greyscale plots of Z, and sites that belong to $X_{Candidate}$ for several combinations of values for ω_F, ω_E, and ω_{EF}.

Figure 5.85-a shows that when $\mathcal{A}$'s only motivation is to move closer to F, the penalty function attains its minimal value at x_F, and decays as the distance between $\mathcal{A}$'s candidate move site and x_E increases. Figure 5.85-b shows that (as was the case in the earlier example shown in figure 5.84-c), if $\mathcal{A}$ is equally motivated to move toward two sites—in this case, x_F and x_{EF}—all sites between x_F and x_{EF} yield exactly the same penalty. $\mathcal{A}$'s move thus consists of a random selection of any

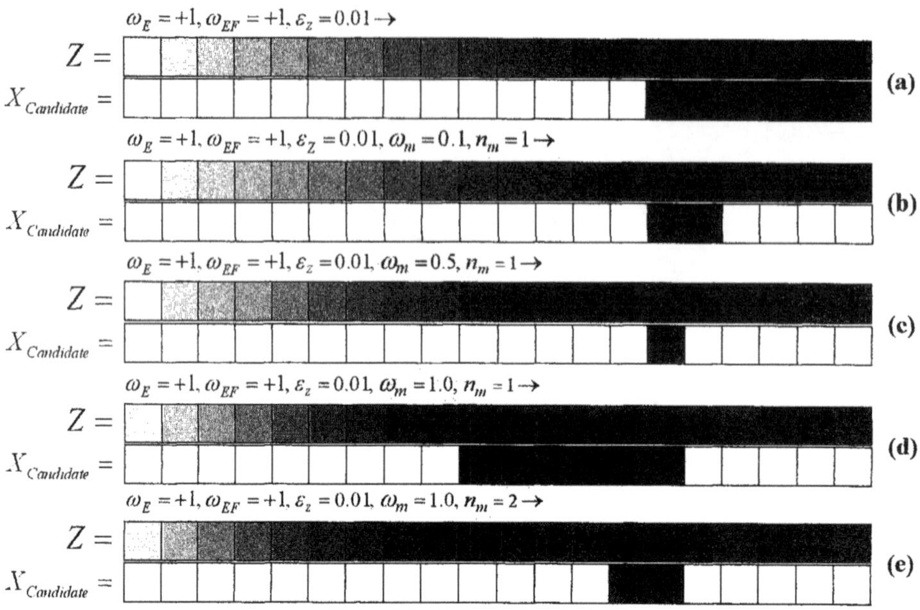

Fig. 5.84 Sample grayscale plots of penalty values and sites belonging to $X_{Candidate}$ for one-dimensional scenario shown in figure 5.80.

of the large block of black sites that define $X_{Candidate}$. A similar spread occurs for when $(\omega_F, \omega_{EF}) = (+1, +1)$, shown in figure 5.85-c.

When $\mathcal{A}$ is equally motivated to move toward all three sites—F, E, and EF—$\mathcal{A}$ is likely to either move to x_E (for $\varepsilon_Z = 0.01$; figure 5.85-d) or to a site that is near x_E (for $\varepsilon_Z = 0.1$; figure 5.85-e). Figure 5.85-f shows an example of how the set $X_{Candidate}$ may become disconnected. Typically, this occurs when an agent is simultaneously motivated to move toward some agents (or sites) and away from others, and/or is constrained in some way, such as maintaining a minimum distance from a site (an example of which we will see in the next section) or penalized for moving. In figure 5.85-f, $\mathcal{A}$ is motivated to move away from F and E, move toward EF, and is penalized by a movement penalty term that increases linearly with $\mathcal{A}$'s distance to its candidate move site, x_m (i.e., we add a term $\omega_m \mu_D(n_m)$, with $\omega_m = 1$ and $n_m = 1$). Looking at the plot for $X_{Candidate}$ in figure 5.85-f, we see that in this case (using $\varepsilon_Z = 0.1$), $\mathcal{A}$ moves either to a site near x_A or to a site that is close to x_{EF} (and, as expected, keeps its distance from x_F).

Sample Decision Maps

We conclude our discussion of an idealized one-dimensional battlefield by presenting two larger (albeit still incomplete) maps of $\mathcal{A}$'s decision space. The objective is not to provide an exhaustive list of $\mathcal{A}$'s actions for a given context; rather, our more

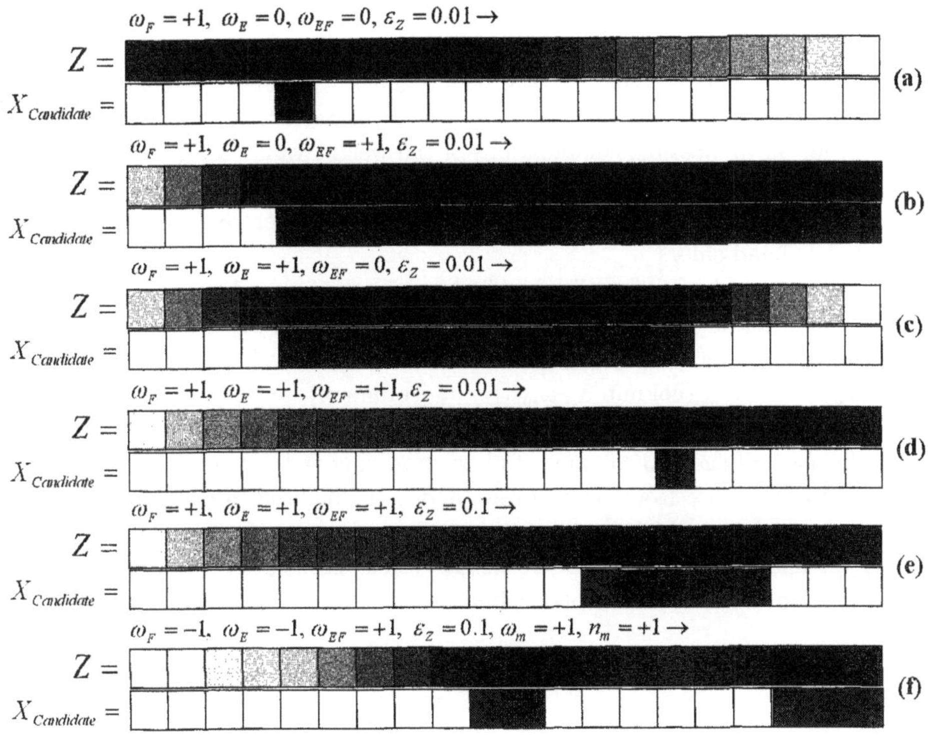

Fig. 5.85 Sample grayscale plots of penalty values and sites belonging to $X_{Candidate}$ for one-dimensional scenario shown in figure 5.80.

modest aim is to use the previsualization techniques described above to illustrate how $\mathcal{A}$'s motivations and associated penalty terms combine to generate an enormous range of possible actions.

Suppose we again restrict our attention to just three entities: two agents, $\mathcal{A}$ and E, and the enemy flag, EF (leaving out the friend at $x_F = 1$). The positions of $\mathcal{A}$ and EF are fixed at $x_{\mathcal{A}} = 10$ and $x_{EF} = 20$, respectively.

The top three rows of figure 5.88 show a series of $X_{Candidate}$ plots (using action selector parameter $\varepsilon_Z = 0.1$) for $x_E = 1$ (top row), $x_E = 15$ (middle row), and $x_E = 10$ (bottom of top three rows). Each of the nine "boxes," in each row, contain nine separate plots of the set $X_{Candidate}$ (stacked from top to bottom in each box), calculated for a given value of ω_{EF} (for a given column) and ω_E (for a given subrow of a given row). The values of the weights ω_{EF} and ω_E both range from -1 to $+1$ in steps of $\Delta\omega = 0.25$: $\omega_E, \omega_{EF} \in \{-1, -.75, -.5, -.25, 0, +.25, +.5, +.75, +1\}$.

The six rows that appear in the lower part of figure 5.88—labeled *Group A* through *Group F*—assume that E is fixed at $x_E = 15$, and show the changes to $X_{Candidate}$ that are incurred by adding one or more penalty terms: $\omega_{\delta D_m} = 1$ (*Group A*), $\omega_m = 1$ (*Group B*), $\omega_{\delta D_m} = 1$, $\omega_m = 1$ (*Group C*), $\omega_{\min D_{\mathcal{A}\leftrightarrow E}} = 1$

(Group D), $\omega_{\min D_{A \leftrightarrow EF}} = 1$ *(Group E)*, and $\omega_{\delta D_m} = 1$, $\omega_m = 1$, $\omega_{\min D_{A \leftrightarrow E}} = 1$, $\omega_{\min D_{A \leftrightarrow EF}} = 1$ *(Group F)*.

Now put the friendly agent F back on site $x_F = 10$. The first column at the top left in figure 5.89 shows plots of $X_{Candidate}$ (using action selector parameter $\varepsilon_Z = 0.1$) for all 27 possible combinations of the weight values ω_F, ω_E, and ω_{EF}, assuming that each weight assumes only one of three values: -1, 0 and $+1$.* The triplet of weight values, $(\omega_F, \omega_E, \omega_{EF})$, that is used to generate each plot is listed along the left-hand-side.

For comparison to the "baseline case" shown in the first column, each row—for a given weight value triplet, $(\omega_F, \omega_E, \omega_{EF})$—in columns two through five at the top of figure 5.89 displays $X_{Candidate}$, calculated using one additional weight value: $\omega_{\delta D_m}$ (column 2), ω_m (column 3), $\omega_{\min D_{A \leftrightarrow E}}$ (column 4), and $\omega_{\min D_{A \leftrightarrow EF}}$ (column 5). The functional forms of these weights are shown in figures 5.86 and 5.87.

Finally, each of the two columns of plots appearing at the bottom of figure 5.89 takes one baseline case from the top row (and is highlighted in green), and shows the result of applying all 27 possible combinations of the weight values, $\omega_{\min D_{A \leftrightarrow F}}$, $\omega_{\min D_{A \leftrightarrow E}}$, and ω_m. The triplet of weight values associated with each plot of $X_{Candidate}$ appears along the center column.

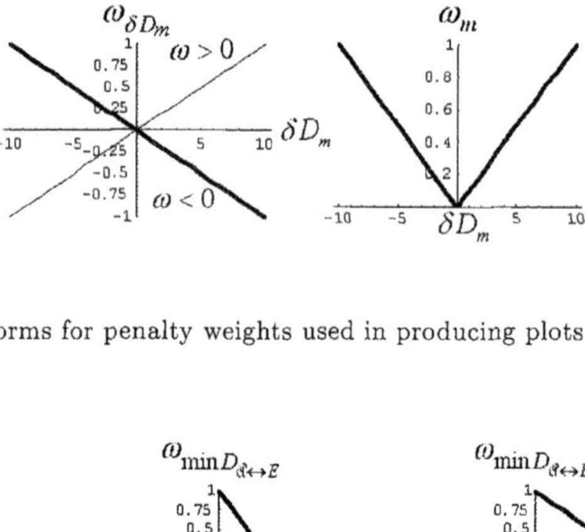

Fig. 5.86 Functional forms for penalty weights used in producing plots in figure 5.89 (*Part 1*).

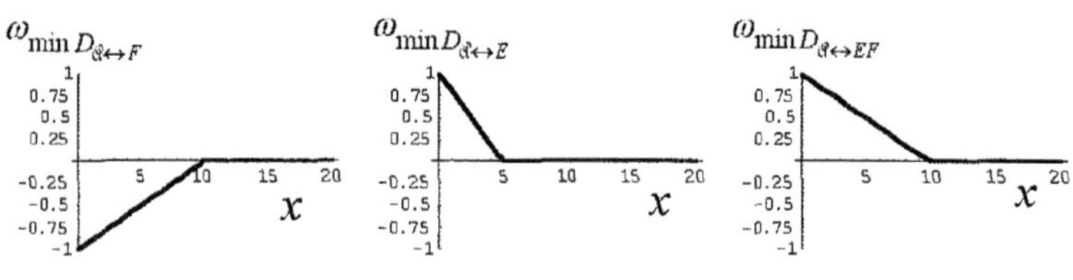

Fig. 5.87 Functional forms for penalty weights used in producing plots in figure 5.89 (*Part 2*).

*The reader is reminded that, in general, the number of possible combinations of three weights is much greater than 27, as each weight may depend on up to three different environmental features and take on any real value between -1 and $+1$. The discrete set of values used to produce the plots appearing in figures 5.88 and 5.89 are purposefully selected to represent the maximal numerical differences that may arise between individual weights during an actual run of the program.

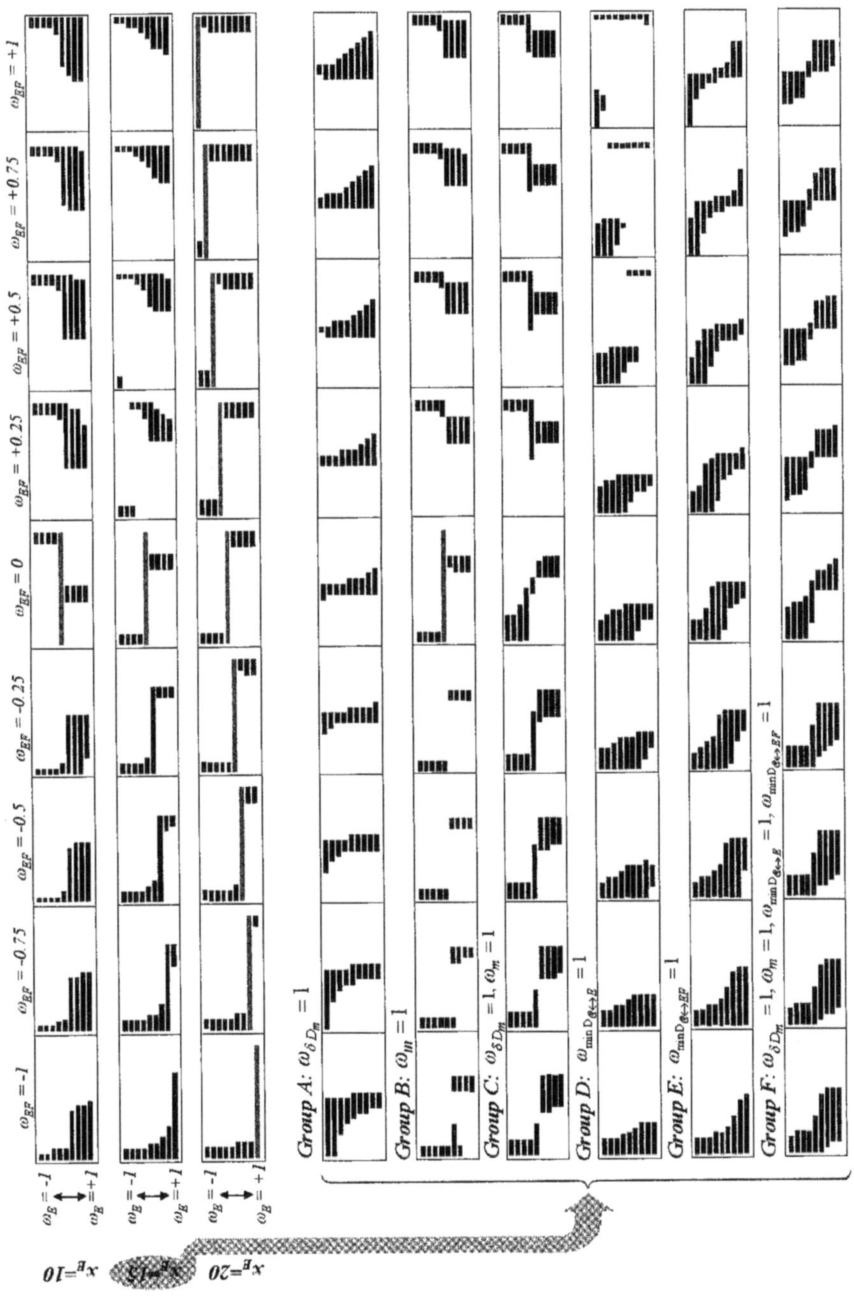

Fig. 5.88 $X_{Candidate}(\varepsilon_Z = 0.1)$ for the one-dimensional scenario shown in figure 5.80.

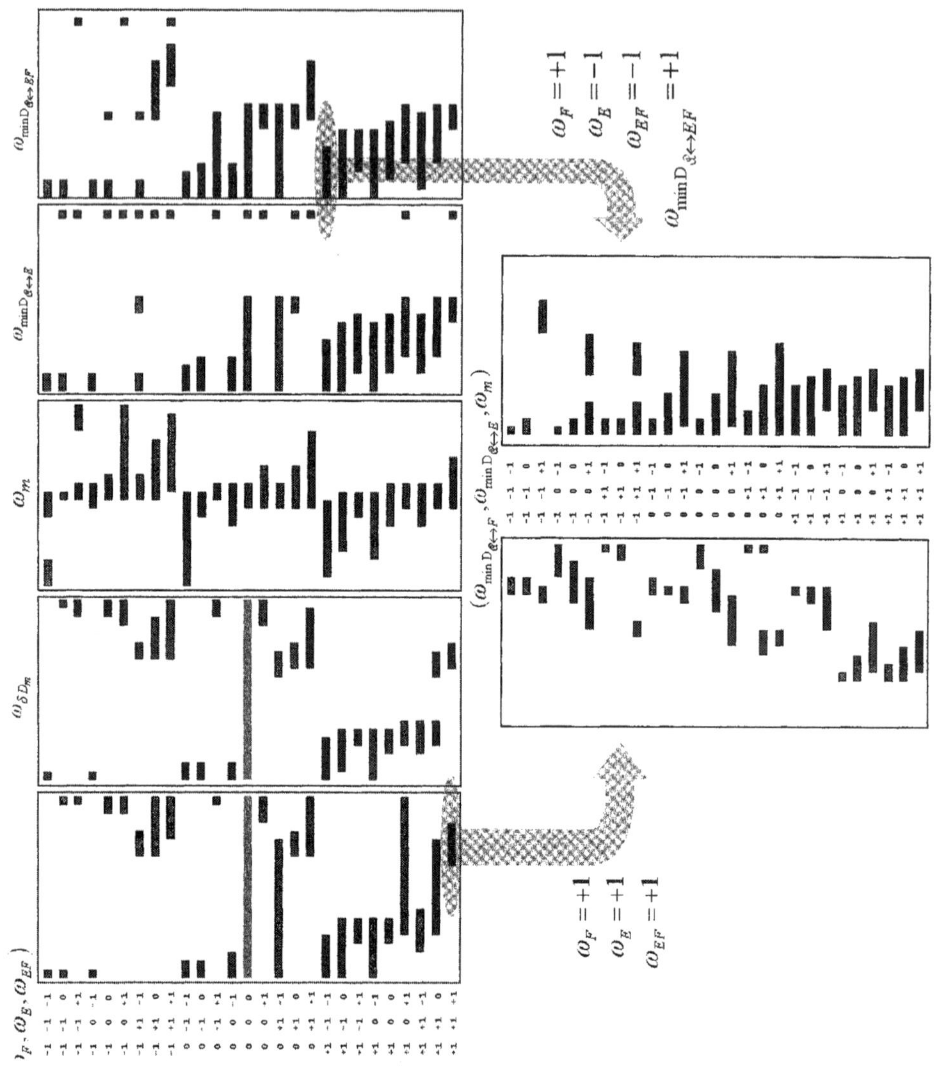

Fig. 5.89 $X_{Candidate}(\varepsilon_Z = 0.1)$ for the one-dimensional scenario shown in figure 5.80 (*Experiment #2*).

Example 2: Two Dimensions

Consider the 11-by-11 battlefield and the distribution of agents shown in figure 5.90. Agent $\mathcal{A}$ occupies the center site, $(x, y) = (5, 5)$, and is in the process of evaluating its penalty function for this turn, $Z_{\mathcal{A}}$. Within $\mathcal{A}$'s sensor range are four friendly agents (F_1, F_2, F_3, and F_4), and four enemy agents (E_1, E_2, E_3, and E_4). The blue flag is at $(x, y) = (1, 1)$, and the red flag is at $(x, y) = (11, 11)$. $\mathcal{A}$'s sensor range is $r_S = 5$ (so that $\mathcal{A}$ can, effectively, "see" the entire battlefield), and its movement range $r_M = 3$, which is highlighted in light grey (i.e., the interior are bounded on the corners by $\vec{x}_a$, $\vec{x}_b$, $\vec{x}_c$, and $\vec{x}_d$).

$\mathcal{A}$'s penalty function is a simplified form of the function defined in equation 5.43. We assume that $\omega_{A\to F}$, $\omega_{A\to E}$, $\omega_{\text{minD}_{A\leftrightarrow F}}$, and $\omega_{\text{minD}_{A\leftrightarrow E}}$, which in general may be functions of various environmental features, depend only on F and E, respectively. In particular, we assume that $\mu_D(x) = x$:

$$\begin{aligned} Z_A(\vec{x}_m) &= \frac{1}{N_{A\to F}} \sum_{i\in F}^{N_F} \omega_{A\to F}(i) \frac{D[\vec{x}_i, \vec{x}_m]}{D_F} \\ &+ \frac{1}{N_{\text{minD}_{A\leftrightarrow F}}} \sum_{i\in F}^{N_F} \omega_{\text{minD}_{A\leftrightarrow F}}(i) \mu_{\text{minD}_{A\leftrightarrow F}}(D[\vec{x}_i, \vec{x}_m]) \\ &+ \frac{1}{N_{A\to E}} \sum_{j\in E}^{N_E} \omega_{A\to E}(j) \cdot \frac{D[\vec{x}_j, \vec{x}_m]}{D_E} \\ &+ \frac{1}{N_{\text{minD}_{A\leftrightarrow E}}} \sum_{j\in E}^{N_E} \omega_{\text{minD}_{A\leftrightarrow E}}(j) \cdot \mu_{\text{minD}_{A\leftrightarrow E}}(D[\vec{x}_j, \vec{x}_m]) \\ &+ \omega_{A\to FF} \cdot \frac{D[\vec{x}_{FF}, \vec{x}_m]}{N_{FF}} + \omega_{A\to EF} \cdot \frac{D[\vec{x}_{EF}, \vec{x}_m]}{N_{EF}}. \end{aligned} \tag{5.45}$$

Visualizing the Penalty Function

What range of values does the penalty function assume for the candidate sites to which $\mathcal{A}$ can move? The answer depends on what terms we wish to include in $\mathcal{A}$'s penalty function. We begin by considering the simplest case where all weights are zero, except for $\mathcal{A}$'s motivation for moving toward friendly agents, $\omega_{A\to F}$. We use a Type-II scaling factor and Type-III normalization factor:

$$\begin{aligned} Z_A(\vec{x}_m) &= \frac{1}{(N_{A\to F})_{III} \cdot (D_F)_{II}} \cdot \\ & \left\{ \begin{array}{l} \omega_{A\to F}(F_1) D[\vec{x}_{F_1}, \vec{x}_m] + \omega_{A\to F}(F_2) D[\vec{x}_{F_2}, \vec{x}_m] \\ \quad + \omega_{A\to F}(F_3) D[\vec{x}_{F_3}, \vec{x}_m] + \omega_{A\to F}(F_4) D[\vec{x}_{F_4}, \vec{x}_m] \end{array} \right\}. \end{aligned} \tag{5.46}$$

The top row of figure 5.91 shows density plots of the values of $Z_{\mathcal{A}}$ for each of the 7-by-7 block of sites within which $\mathcal{A}$ is allowed to move for five different combinations of weight values, $\omega_1 = \omega_{A\to F}(F_1)$, $\omega_2 = \omega_{A\to F}(F_2)$, $\omega_3 = \omega_{A\to F}(F_3)$, and $\omega_4 = \omega_{A\to F}(F_4)$ (colored light grey in figure 5.91).

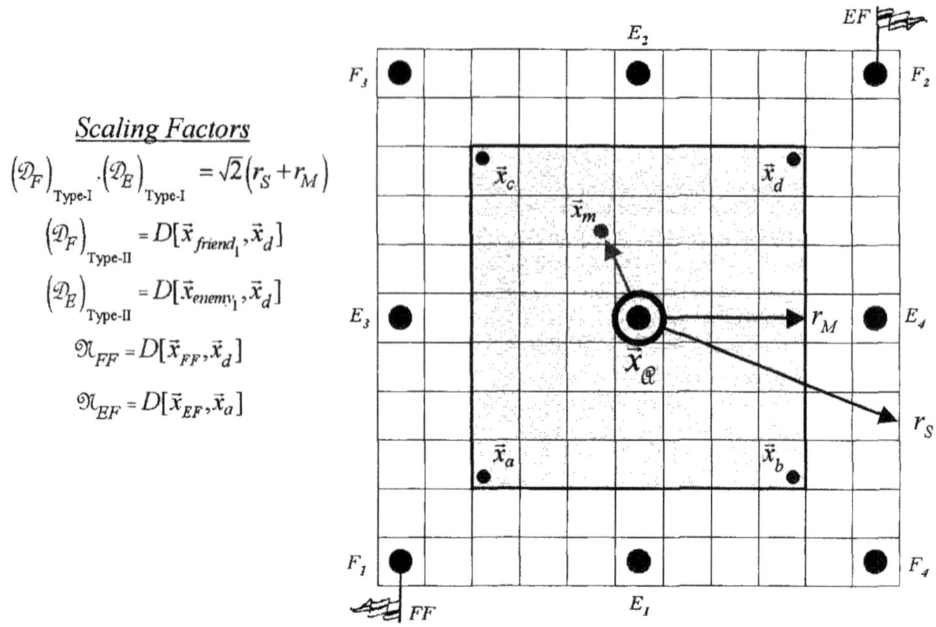

Fig. 5.90 Schematic battlefield configuration used in sample penalty calculation for example in two dimensions; see text.

Ten levels of grey appear in the figure, with the minimum value (colored black) and maximum value (colored white) for each weight combination shown at the top of each plot. The greyscales interpolate between these two extremes. The weight values combination used for each plot appears in the middle row. In each of the plots along the bottom row, the sites that belong to the candidate move set $X_{Candidate}$ (defined by $\varepsilon_Z = 0.1$) are colored black. Recall that $X_{Candidate}$ consists of all sites within $\mathcal{A}$'s movement range whose penalty is no more than 10 percent of the minimum value. $\mathcal{A}$'s move (not shown) is to a site that is randomly selected from this set.

Consider the first density plot, shown at the extreme left of figure 5.91, for $\omega_1 = \omega_2 = \omega_3 = \omega_4 = 1$. In this case, $\mathcal{A}$ balances its motivation to move toward each of four symmetrically positioned friendly agents at $\vec{x}_{F_1} = (1,1)$, $\vec{x}_{F_2} = (11,11)$, $\vec{x}_{F_3} = (1,11)$, and $\vec{x}_{F_4} = (11,1)$ by choosing to either remain in its current position (since $\underset{D[\vec{x}_A,\vec{x}] \leq r_M}{\text{Minimum}} \{Z_A(\vec{x}_m)\} = 0.625$, and occurs at $\vec{x} = (5,5) = \vec{x}_{\mathcal{A}}$) or to move no farther than one unit away.

The second column shows the density plot (and sites $(x,y) \in X_{Candidate}$) that results when $\mathcal{A}$ is motivated to move toward F_2, F_3 and F_4, but move away from F_1. In this case, $\mathcal{A}$ effectively chooses to move close to F_2, simultaneously minimizing the cumulative distance from F_2, F_3 and F_4 and maximizing its distance from F_1.

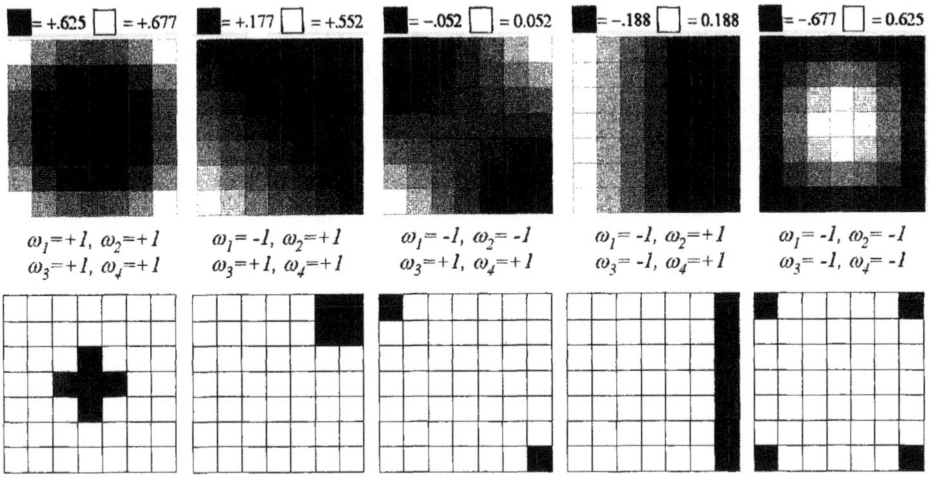

Fig. 5.91 Density plots of penalty values for several different sets of $\mathcal{A} \to F$ weight values; $\varepsilon_Z = 0.1$ is used for the plots along the bottom row.

The remaining three plots show how an agent behaves when it is motivated to move toward F_3 and F_4 and away from F_1 and F_2 (middle plot); move toward F_2 and F_4 and away from F_1 and F_3 (next-to-last plot); and away from all four friends (right-most plot).

Although we could have, of course, chosen to evaluate the penalty function for many other weight value combinations, the density plots shown in figure 5.91 suffice to highlight the basic differences in the way an agent responds to the same configuration of (in this case, friendly) agents, as a function of the weights that it assigns to those agents. The plots in figure 5.91 also highlight an apparently counterintuitive behavior, and hint at its "solution," which we discuss next.

Countering a Counterintuitive Behavior

Consider again the first density plot, shown at the extreme left in figure 5.91. Recall that for this case, $\mathcal{A}$ is motivated to move toward all four friendly agents (with weight value equal to one): F_1 at $(1,1)$, F_2 at $(11,11)$, F_3 at $(1,11)$, and F_4 at $(11,1)$. While the density plot correctly indicates that $\mathcal{A}$ chooses to stay close to its starting position, $\mathcal{A}$'s move appears to be counterintuitive. *Why does $\mathcal{A}$ confine its choice of possible moves to sites that are relatively far from any of the agents toward which it is ostensibly motivated to move closer to?*

As we had seen in our earlier analysis of the one-dimensional example (see pages 410-421), the answer is that if $\mathcal{A}$ is allowed to use only the single weight $\omega_{A\to F}$ to tune its behavior, the "best" $\mathcal{A}$ can do to simultaneously satisfy its motivation to "move closer to" all four agents that are symmetrically positioned at the corners of its sensor field, is to position itself equidistantly from each of those agents. If we rescale the 11-by-11 sensor field, so that each of its sides is assigned a dimension of one (arbitrary) unit, we see that while the penalty for occupying any of the corners is equal to $Z_{Corner} = 2 + \sqrt{2} \approx 3.41$ (the length of a side contributing twice and the main diagonal once), the penalty for the center site $Z_{Center} = 4 \times \sqrt{2}/2 \approx 2.82 < Z_{Corner}$. The center site thus represents the optimal, but somewhat counterintuitive, move for $\mathcal{A}$, as it is the one site at which $\mathcal{A}$ is closest to its neighboring friendly agents *as a group*. The center site also happens to be a site that is not particularly close to any one agent.

Notice that the situation cannot be remedied by resorting to, say, nonconstant weight functions that depend on some judiciously selected features of F_1, F_2, F_3, and F_4. As long as all of the agents' features are equal (from $\mathcal{A}$'s point of view), and as long as the agents occupy mutually symmetric positions relative to $\mathcal{A}$'s starting position, the weight functions always yield identical values, and $\mathcal{A}$ thus consistently chooses to stay near the center. In short, it is impossible to introduce an asymmetry into a symmetric configuration solely by tweaking the "move toward agent" weights ω_1, ω_2, ω_3, and ω_4. An obvious question is, *"How can we nudge $\mathcal{A}$ to move away from the center?"*

One way of doing this is to add to $\mathcal{A}$'s penalty function a component that rewards $\mathcal{A}$ whenever it moves close to an agent, and penalizes $\mathcal{A}$ whenever it moves away:

$$
\begin{aligned}
Z_A(\vec{x}_m) = & \overbrace{\frac{1}{(N_{A\to F})_{III}\cdot(D_F)_{II}}\times \left\{ \begin{array}{l} \omega_{A\to F}(F_1)D[\vec{x}_{F_1},\vec{x}_m] + \omega_{A\to F}(F_2)D[\vec{x}_{F_2},\vec{x}_m] \\ \quad + \omega_{A\to F}(F_3)D[\vec{x}_{F_3},\vec{x}_m] + \omega_{A\to F}(F_4)D[\vec{x}_{F_4},\vec{x}_m] \end{array} \right\}}^{\textit{move towards friendly agents}} \\
& + \overbrace{\left[\frac{1}{(N_{\mathrm{minD}_{A\leftrightarrow E}})_{III}}\times \left\{ \begin{array}{l} \omega_{\mathrm{minD}_{A\leftrightarrow F}}(F_1)\mu_{\mathrm{minD}_{A\leftrightarrow F}}(D[\vec{x}_{F_1},\vec{x}_m]) \\ \quad + \omega_{\mathrm{minD}_{A\leftrightarrow F}}(F_2)\mu_{\mathrm{minD}_{A\leftrightarrow F}}(D[\vec{x}_{F_2},\vec{x}_m]) \\ \quad + \omega_{\mathrm{minD}_{A\leftrightarrow F}}(F_3)\mu_{\mathrm{minD}_{A\leftrightarrow F}}(D[\vec{x}_{F_3},\vec{x}_m]) \\ \quad + \omega_{\mathrm{minD}_{A\leftrightarrow F}}(F_4)\mu_{\mathrm{minD}_{A\leftrightarrow F}}(D[\vec{x}_{F_4},\vec{x}_m]) \end{array} \right\} \right]}^{\textit{maintain minimum distance from friendly agents}},
\end{aligned}
\tag{5.47}
$$

where $\omega_{\mathrm{minD}_{A\leftrightarrow F}}(F_x)$ is $\mathcal{A}$'s weight for maintaining a minimum distance from agent F_x ($x = 1$, 2, 3, and 4), and $-1 \le \mu_{\mathrm{minD}_{A\leftrightarrow F}}(D[\vec{x}_{F_x},\vec{x}_m]) \le +1$ is the dynamically allocated penalty cost that $\mathcal{A}$ assigns to a candidate move $\vec{x}_m$, when $\vec{x}_m$ is a distance $D[\vec{x}_{F_x},\vec{x}_m]$ away from F_x.

Consider the form for $\mu_{\mathrm{minD}_{A\leftrightarrow F}}(D)$ shown in figure 5.92. The figure shows that if a candidate site is closer than two units away from a friendly agent, the value of $\mathcal{A}$'s penalty function is reduced by one unit; i.e., $\mathcal{A}$'s motivation to occupy that site is increased. The reward decreases linearly as the distance between a candidate site and a friendly agent increases to six units, beyond which increasing distance has no effect on $\mathcal{A}$'s default propensity for moving toward the agent. Heuristically, we expect that when $\mathcal{A}$'s reward for approaching a given agent is large enough to compensate for the penalty that is incurred for staying away, $\mathcal{A}$ will be motivated to move closer to one of the surrounding agents.

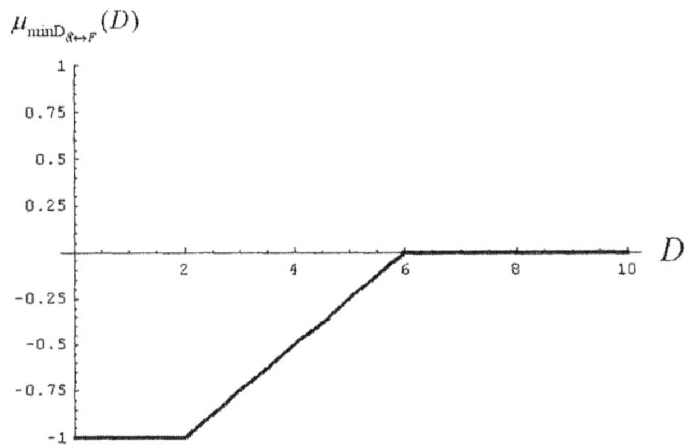

Fig. 5.92 Sample functional form for $\mu_{\text{minD}_{\mathcal{A}\leftrightarrow F}}(D)$; see text.

Figure 5.93 shows density plots of the values of $Z_{\mathcal{A}}$ defined by equation 5.45 for the same five combinations of weight values used earlier for the plots in figure 5.91. As in figure 5.91, ten levels of grey are used to display values between the minimum value (colored black) and maximum value (colored white). The black sites that appear in the bottom row of plots represent the sites that belong to the candidate move set $X_{Candidate}$ (defined by $\varepsilon_Z = 0.1$), from which $\mathcal{A}$ selects its move.

Comparing the corresponding plots in figures 5.91 and 5.93, we see that adding a penalty term for maintaining a minimum distance from agents serves its intended purpose. Namely, in each case, $\mathcal{A}$ now selects a move that is *close to one of the agents*.

In some cases, the additional term has no effect (for example, for the cases $(\omega_1, \omega_2, \omega_3, \omega_4) = (-1, -1, +1, +1)$ and $(\omega_1, \omega_2, \omega_3, \omega_4) = (-1, -1, -1, -1)$). In other cases, the additional term refines the selection that $\mathcal{A}$ makes in its absence, but does not otherwise change the character of the resulting move (for $((\omega_1, \omega_2, \omega_3, \omega_4) = (-1, +1, +1, +1)$ and $(\omega_1, \omega_2, \omega_3, \omega_4) = (-1, +1, -1, +1)$). And, in the case that previously led to what appears to be a counterintuitive move, for the case $(\omega_1, \omega_2, \omega_3, \omega_4) = (+1, +1, +1, +1)$, the additional term effectively "nudges" $\mathcal{A}$ to select the more intuitive move: where, before, $\mathcal{A}$'s candidate moves were confined to the center sites, $\mathcal{A}$ is now guaranteed to select a site that is close to one of its neighboring friends.

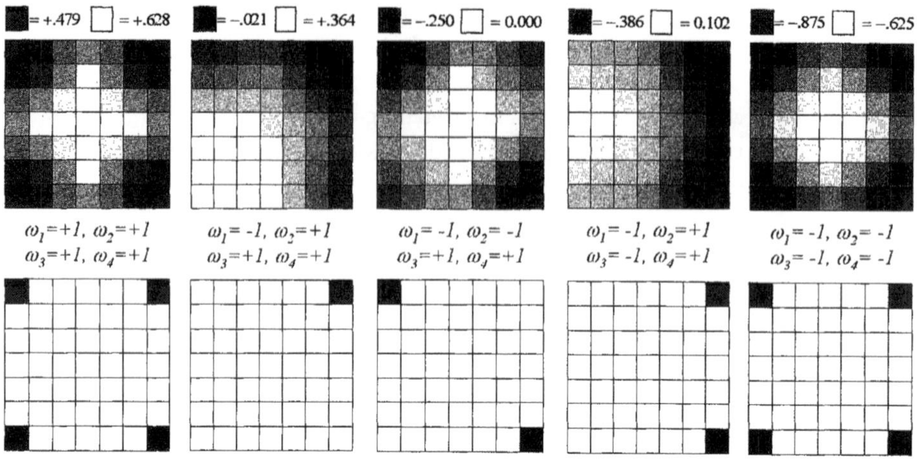

Fig. 5.93 Density plots of penalty values using both $\omega_{A \to F}$ and $\omega_{\text{minD}_{A \leftrightarrow F}}$ weight values; $\varepsilon_Z =$ 0.1is used for the bottom row

Weight Value Combinations

Figure 5.95 shows density plots of each of the six distance-related components (columns C_1-C_6). The density plot of the total penalty function, $Z_{\mathcal{A}}$ (defined by equation 5.45), is shown in right most column. Table 5.9 lists the weight value combinations that are used to generate the density plot appearing in row R_i and column C_j of figure 5.95.

	C_1	C_2	C_3	C_4	C_5	C_6
R_1	+1	+1	+1	+1	+1	+1
R_2	−1	+1	+1	+1	+1	+1
R_3	+1	−1	+1	+1	+1	+1
R_4	+1	+1	−1	+1	+1	+1
R_5	+1	+1	+1	−1	+1	+1
R_6	+1	+1	+1	+1	−1	+1
R_7	+1	+1	+1	+1	+1	−1
R_8	−1	−1	+1	+1	+1	+1
R_9	+1	+1	−1	−1	+1	+1
R_{10}	−1	−1	−1	−1	+1	+1

Table 5.9 Weight values used for density plots shown in figure 5.95.

For example, looking at table 5.9, we see that the plot located at R_4 and C_3 (in figure 5.95) is the density plot of the "move toward enemy agents" component ($\omega_{A \to E}$) of $\mathcal{A}$'s penalty function, and is calculated by assigning value -1 to each of the four enemy agents. As in the earlier figures 5.91 and 5.93, ten levels of grey are used in figure 5.95 to display penalties between the minimum value (colored black) and maximum value (colored white). The minimum and maximum values are also displayed, numerically, at the top of each plot.

Symmetric 2F-2E Scenario

Consider a scenario in which $\mathcal{A}$ is surrounded by two friendly agents, F_1 at $(1,1)$ and F_2 at $(11,11)$, and two enemy agents, E_1 at $(1,11)$ and E_2 at $(11,1)$. Figures 5.96-5.98 show density plots and the candidate move sets $X_{Candidate}$ (using $\varepsilon_Z = 0.1$ and $\varepsilon_Z = 0.25$), for all possible combinations of the values -1, 0 and $+1$ for the weights $\omega_{A\rightarrow F}$, $\omega_{\mathrm{minD}_{A\leftrightarrow F}}$, $\omega_{A\rightarrow E}$, and $\omega_{\mathrm{minD}_{A\leftrightarrow E}}$.

The combination of weight values that are used to produce the figures is indicated at the top of each plot. Figure 5.94 shows the function $\mu_{\mathrm{minD}_{A\leftrightarrow E}}(D)$used to generate figures 5.96-5.98.

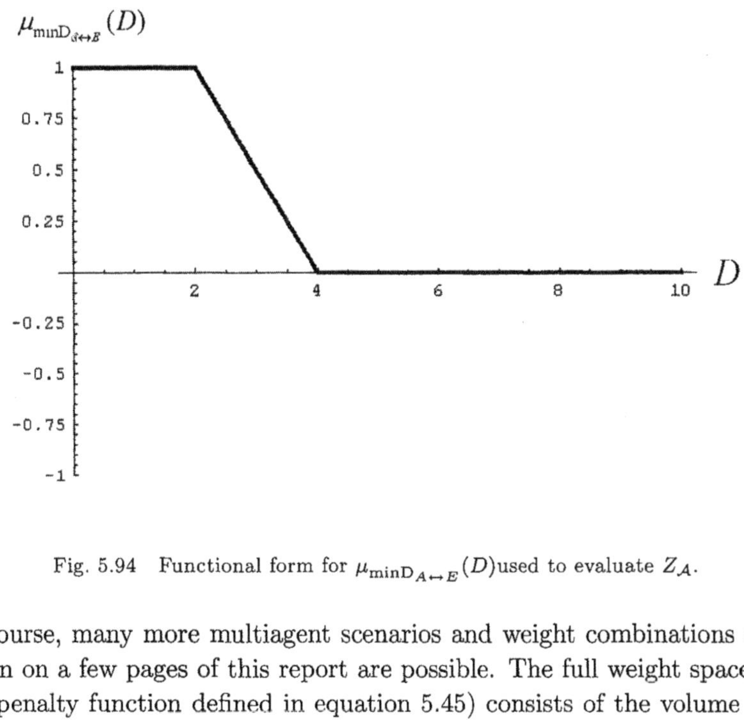

Fig. 5.94 Functional form for $\mu_{\mathrm{minD}_{A\leftrightarrow E}}(D)$used to evaluate $Z_{\mathcal{A}}$.

Of course, many more multiagent scenarios and weight combinations than can be shown on a few pages of this report are possible. The full weight space (for the sample penalty function defined in equation 5.45) consists of the volume inside of a multidimensional hypercube, each side of which spans the space of all real values between -1 and $+1$.

Figures 5.96-5.98are provided to illustrate the wide range of penalty values that arise quite naturally, even in simple scenarios, and the ways in which particular weight values affect the total penalty, and therefore, an agent's move.

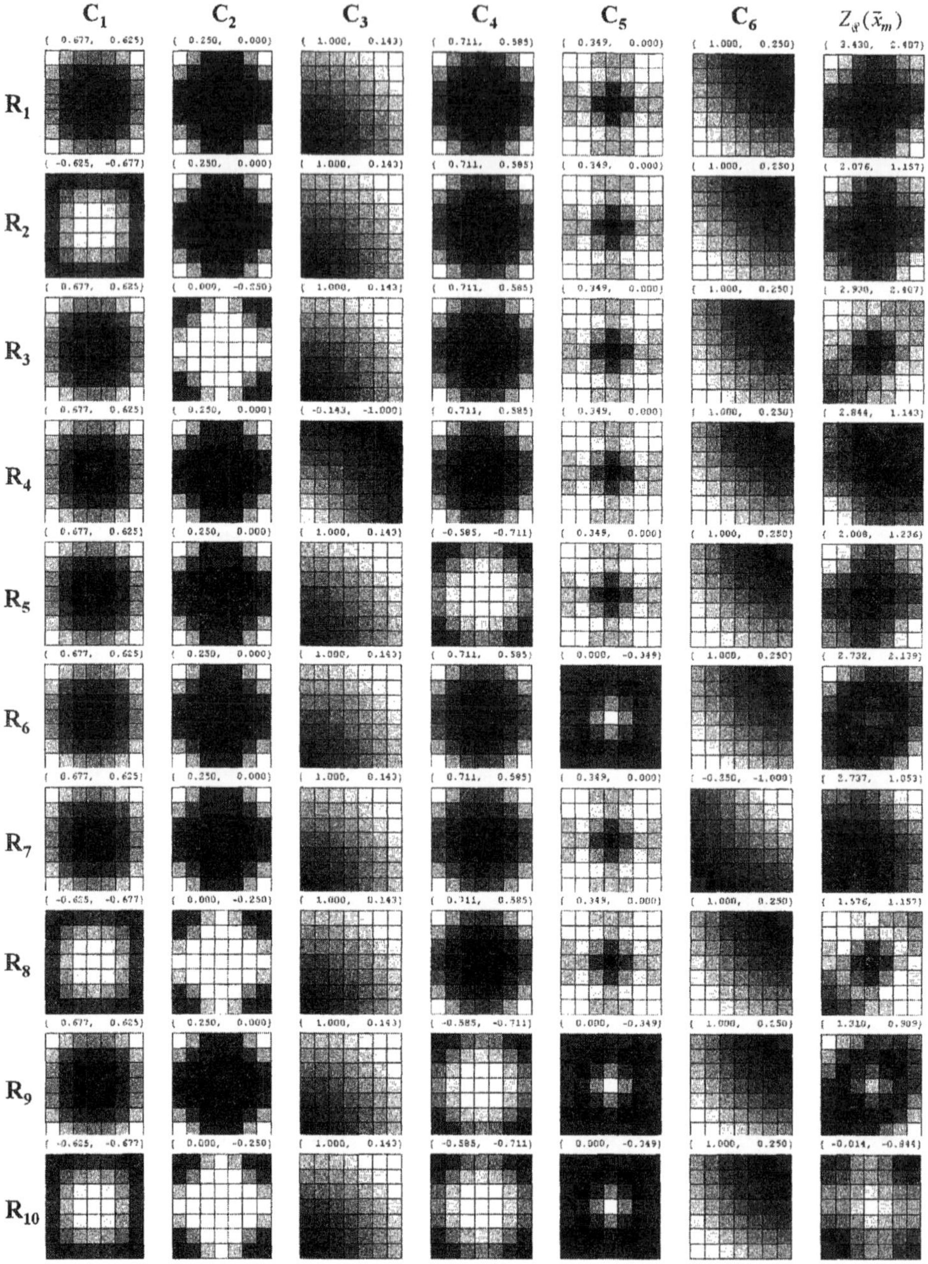

Fig. 5.95 Density plots of penalty function defined in equation 5.45; see text.

Fig. 5.96 Density plots for the 2-friendly and 2-enemy agent scenario for all possible combinations of $\{\omega_{A\rightarrow F}, \omega_{\mathrm{minD}_{A\leftrightarrow F}}, \omega_{A\rightarrow E}, \omega_{\mathrm{minD}_{A\leftrightarrow E}}\}$.

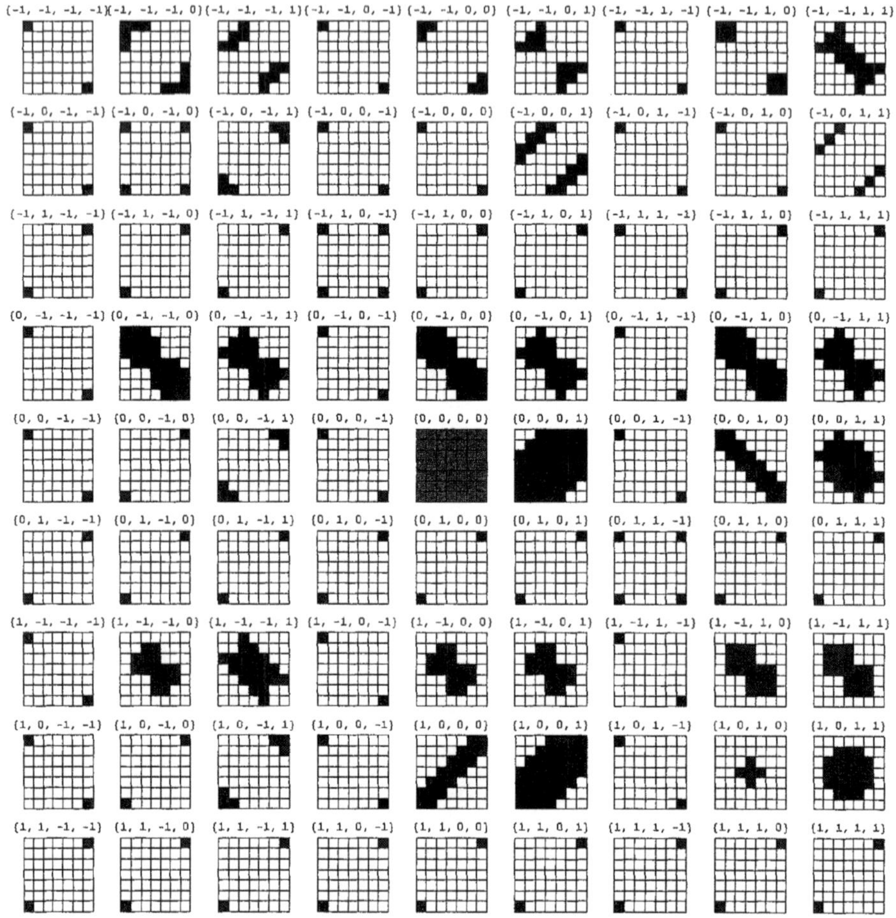

Fig. 5.97 $X_{Candidate}(\varepsilon_Z = 0.1)$ for the 2-friendly and 2-enemy scenario for all possible combinations of $\{\omega_{A \to F}, \omega_{\text{minD}_{A \leftrightarrow F}}, \omega_{A \to E}, \omega_{\text{minD}_{A \leftrightarrow E}}\}$.

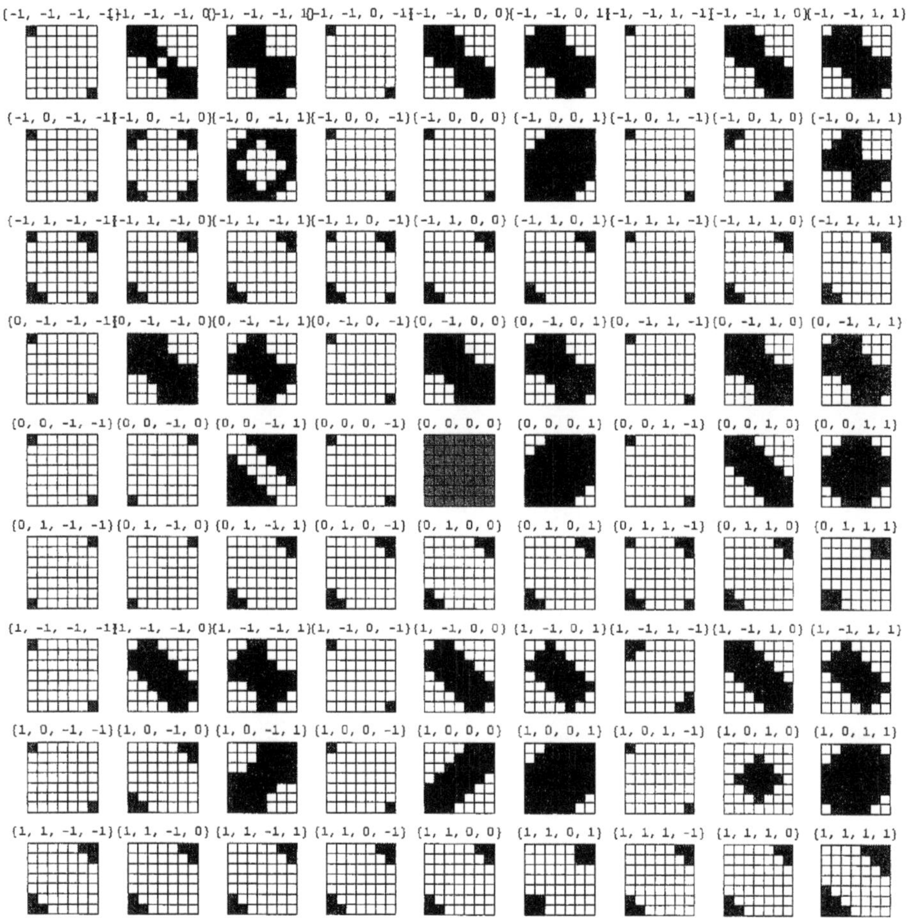

Fig. 5.98 $X_{Candidate}(\varepsilon_Z = 0.25)$ for the 2-friendly and 2-enemy scenario for all possible combinations of $\{\omega_{A\rightarrow F}, \omega_{\mathrm{minD}_{A\leftrightarrow F}}, \omega_{A\rightarrow E}, \omega_{\mathrm{minD}_{A\leftrightarrow E}}\}$.

Chapter 6

EINSTein: *Sample Behavior*

"Computer based models provide a half-way house between theory and experiment. Computer based models are not experiments in the usual sense because they do not directly manipulate the world being modeled. Nevertheless, as the model is executed, patterns and symmetries will typically show up in the ongoing action...Such emergent characteristics can suggest experimental designs for real situations."—John Holland, *Emergence* [Holl99]

6.1 Overview

First and foremost, EINSTein is a tool that allows the researcher to explore a wide range of self-organized emergent patterns of macroscopic behavior that result from the collective interactions of individual agents, fireteams, squads and entire forces; and to explore the feedback that these patterns might have on the rules governing an individual agent's behavior. A typical workflow always begins by defining a *scenario*, which consists of a specific disposition of red and blue agents (with squads assigned to "boxes" that themselves can be arranged anywhere on the battlefield) and sets of nominal values for all pertinent parameters (such as personality weights, sensor and fire ranges, μ-rule thresholds, weapon selections, terrain and/or waypath data).

While the process of setting the values of EINSTein's built-in parameters within the program is straightforward (at least once the researcher has thoroughly familiarized herself with the meaning of each parameter)—and may be further streamlined by simply modifying, at most, a few lines in one of the sample data files that are included in EINSTein's install program (by using a basic text editor)—because so many of EINSTein's parameters are interdependent, great care must be made while defining a scenario to ensure that what the researcher *wants* to model has, in fact, been correctly incorporated into the scenario.

Simple mistakes, such as wanting a squad to *"move toward the enemy flag if and only if agents in the squad are surrounded by at least five friends,"* and thereby setting the *Advance* μ-rule threshold $\tau_{Advance} = 5$ (see page 298), but neglecting to simultaneously set the *"move toward enemy flag"* component of an agent's nominal personality weight vector to a positive value ($\omega_{EF} > 0$), are easy to spot and correct.* Other mistakes may be more subtle, and not so easy to spot. For example, wanting an agent to decide to either keep moving toward the enemy flag or to engage enemies at close quarters using a threshold range of $r_T = 5$ (see page 285), but neglecting to set a sensor range $r_S \geq r_T$. In this case, agents are unable to see far enough (via their sensor range) to count the number of surrounding friends.

To minimize the chances of making such errors, and certainly before designing a scenario entirely from scratch, researchers are encouraged to first develop both an understanding of, and an intuition for, the dynamic role each primitive parameter plays in EINSTein. All parameters are defined in chapter 5. Additional references are provided in Appendices E (*A Concise User's Guide to EINSTein*; see page 581) and G (*EINSTein's Data Files*; see page 663).

Once a scenario is defined (in the form of an input data file which we call, generically, *scenario.dat*), or an existing *scenario.dat* file is altered by the user and resaved, EINSTein loads the file and is ready to be run. At this point, one is free to explore squad sizes and compositions, inter-squad interactions, terrain effects, weapons trade-offs, effects of reconnaissance missions, communications and sensor capabilities, and many other ground combat variables. Waypoints and squad-specific paths may be used to precisely tailor intended movement and/or intentionally constrain maneuver. Patrol areas may be set up and assigned on a squad-by-squad basis. In addition, EINSTein allows multiple runs, has extensive data collection capabilities, and automatically calculates various statistical *measures-of-effectiveness* (MOEs) such as force attrition, position, and dispersion.†

6.1.1 *Simulation Run Modes*

Any given work session with EINSTein currently consists of any combination of these three basic run modes:

1. *Interactive Mode*, in which EINSTein's combat engine is run interactively using a fixed set of rules. This mode, which allows the user to make *on-the-fly* changes to the values of any (or all) parameters defining a given run, is particularly well suited for quickly and easily playing simple *"What if?"* scenarios. This simulation run mode is useful for interactively searching for interesting emergent behavior.
2. *Data-Collection Mode*, in which the user can (1) generate time series of various changing quantities describing the step-by-step evolution of a battle,

*If the user intentionally, and *correctly*, defines $\tau_{Advance} = 5$ for the scenario, but mistakenly sets $\omega_{EF} < 0$, agents will *never be motivated to move toward the enemy flag*, regardless of how many friends they may be surrounded by, because the value of an agent's personality weight component takes precedence over the μ-rule threshold.

†EINSTein's *data collection*, *data analysis* and *data visualization* capabilities are fairly extensive. See sections G.1.11 (page 701), E.6 (page 628), and E.7 (page 631) for details.

(2) keep track of certain measures of how well mission objectives are met at a battle's conclusion, and (3) sample behavioral profiles on two-dimensional slices of an agent's (much larger) N-dimensional parameter phase-space.

3. *Genetic Algorithm "Breeder" Mode*, in which a genetic algorithm is used to breed a personality for one side that is "best suited" for performing some well-defined mission against a fixed personality (and force disposition) for the other.*

6.1.2 *Observations*

Fundamentally, EINSTein is a conceptual laboratory designed to provide tools for exploring the mapping between primitive *local actions*—as defined for, and performed by, individual agents—and *global behaviors*, that describe the collective, emergent activity patterns of an agent force as a whole. As such, and despite its simple local rule base, EINSTein possesses an impressive repertoire of emergent behaviors (see figure 6.1):

- *Attack posturing,*
- *Containment*
- *Flanking maneuvers*
- *Forward advance,*
- *Frontal attack,*
- *Guerrilla-like assaults,*
- *Local clustering,*
- *Penetration,* and
- *Retreat,* among many others.

Moreover, behaviors frequently arise that appear to involve some form of intelligent division of red and blue forces to deal with local firestorms and skirmishes, particularly those forces whose personalities have been bred (via a genetic algorithm) to perform a specific mission. It is important to point out that such behaviors are not hard-wired but rather appear naturally and spontaneously, as emergent consequences of a decentralized, but dynamically interdependent, swarm of agents.

Color plate 3 (page 249), which shows screen captures of spatial patterns resulting from 16 different rules, illustrates the diversity of behaviors that emerges out of a relatively simple rule base. (Note that the sample patterns shown here are for red and blue forces consisting of a *single* squad. Multi-squad scenarios, in which agents belonging to different squads obey different rules, often result in considerably more complicated emergent behaviors.) An important long-term goal is that EINSTein can be used as a more general tool (that transcends the specific notional combat

* *Genetic algorithms*—what they are, how they used by EINSTein, along with a tutorial on how to set up breeding experiments and selected case studies— are discussed in section 7.1 (**Breeding Agents**); see page 501.

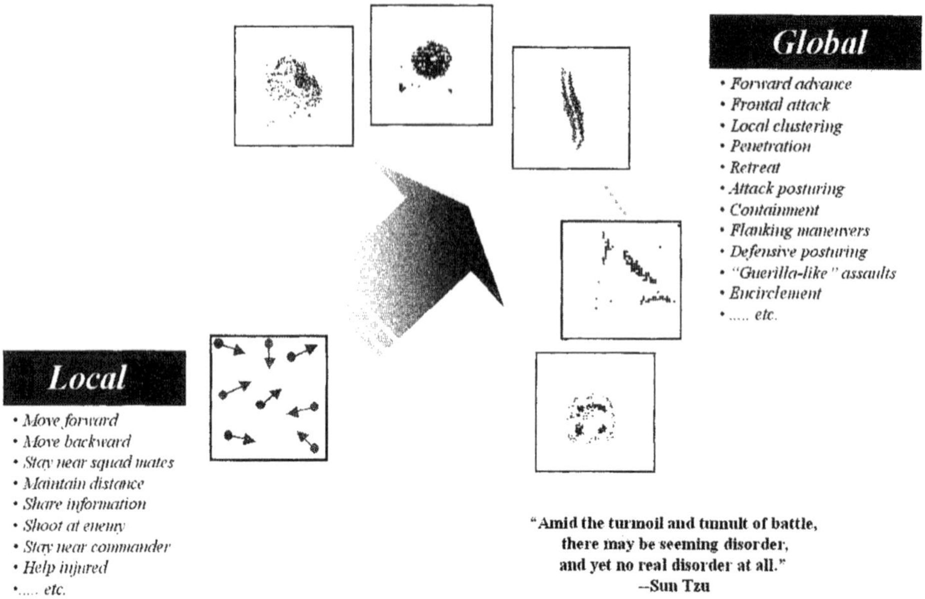

Fig. 6.1 Schematic illustrating global behaviors emerging out of mutual interactions among agents obeying local rules.

environment to which it is obviously tailored) for exploring the still only poorly understood mapping between primitive rules that define how agents interact on the *micro*-scale and self-organized behaviors that emerge on the *macro*-scale.

6.1.3 *Classes of Behavior*

Simulations run for many different scenarios and initial conditions suggest that EINSTein's collective behavior generally falls into one of six broad qualitative classes (labeled, suggestively, according to different kinds of fluid flow):

1. *Laminar flow*, which typically consists of one (or, at most, a few) well-defined "linear" battlefronts. This class is so named because it is visually suggestive of laminar fluid flow of two fluid, and is reminiscent of static trench warfare in World War I. Laminar rules can actually be divided into two types of behaviors, characterized according to a system's overall stability (i.e. according to whether the system is stable, or not stable, to initial conditions).
2. *Viscous Flow*, in which the unfolding battle typically consists of a single tight cluster (or, at most, a few clusters) of loosely interpenetrating red and blue agents. Viscous flows are characterized by both sides engaging the other (sometimes at close quarters and for prolonged times), yet simultaneously remaining cohesive fighting forces as a whole.

3. *Dispersive Flow*, in which—as soon as red and blue agents maneuver within view of the opposing side's forces—the battle unfolds as a single, explosive, dispersion of forces. Dispersive systems exhibit little, if any, of the "front-like" linear structures that form for laminar-flow rules.
4. *Turbulent Flow*, in which combat consists of either spatially distributed, but otherwise confined and/or clustered individual combat zones, or a series of close-to space-filling local firestorms. In either case, there is almost always a significant degree of local maneuvering.
5. *Autopoeitic Flow*,* in which agents self-organize into persistent dissipative structures. These formations typically maintain their integrity for long times (on the scale of individual agents entering and leaving the structure) and undergo "higher level" maneuvering, including longitudinal motion and rotation.
6. *Swarming*, in which agents self-organize into nested swarms of attacking and/or defending forces.

This taxonomy is neither complete nor well defined, in a mathematical sense. Because of the qualitative distinctions between classes, there is considerable overlap among them. Moreover, a given scenario, as it unfolds in time, usually consists of several phases of behavior during which one class predominates at one time and other classes at other times. Indeed, for such cases, which occur frequently, it is of considerable interest to understand the nature of the transition between distinct behavioral phases. For example, the initial stages of a scenario may unfold in typically laminar fashion and suddenly transition over into a turbulent phase.

A finer distinction among these six classes can be made on the basis of a more refined statistical analysis of emergent behavior. There is strong evidence to suggest, for example, that while attrition rates for certain classes of rules display smooth Gaussian statistics, other classes (overlapping with viscous flow and turbulent flow rules) display interesting fractal power-law scaling behaviors [Lauren00b]. Insofar as the "box-counting" *fractal dimension* [Krantz97] is useful for describing the degree of agent clustering on the battlefield, it can also be used as a simple discriminant between laminar and turbulent classes of behavior.† Measuring temporal correlations in the time-series of various statistical quantities describing combat is also useful in this regard.

The sample case studies presented in this section are selected to illustrate–in broad "brush-stroke" fashion—the qualitative behavioral classes described above. Figures 6.2 Table 6.1 provides a summary of the runs.

*Autopoiesis refers to dynamics within systems that are simultaneously *self-creating* and *self-maintaining* (see page 110 in chapter 2 for a brief discussion). The concept was introduced as an explanatory mechanism within biology by Maturana and Varela [Varela74]. An example of this kind of behavior in EINSTein appears in section 6.10 (see page 487).

†EINSTein contains a built-in (spatial, "box counting") fractal dimension estimator function, which is accessible under the the *Data Visualization* main menu option list.

No.	Case Study	Classes	Brief Description
1	Lanchesterian Combat	1	Approximation of conditions under which Lanchester's equations are valid
2	Classic Battle Front *(Tutorial)*	1(Types I/II)	Collision of symmetric forces with a series of *"What If?"* experiments; includes self-contained tutorial on setting up an interactive run session
3	Explosive Skirmish	3	Collision resulting in a series of widely dispersed firefights and skirmishes; the possibly fundamental role that fractal dimensions and other power-law scalings may play in turbulent phases of combat is discussed
4	Squad-vs-Squad	2	An experiment that probes the increasing/decreasing relative squad-size
5	Red Attack	2,4	Example of how attack strength may be enhanced by communications
6	Red Defense	2,4,6	Example of how defensive strength may be enhanced by communications
7	Swarming Forces	2,6	Examples of decentralized swarming
8	Non-Monotonicity	2,3,4	Example of non-monotonic scaling of mission success with agent capability
9	Autopoeitic Skirmish	5	Example of a self-organized *persistent* structure
10	Small Insertion	2,6	Small red force must penetrate through larger defending swarm to enemy flag

Table 6.1 Case study samples discussed in this chapter.

6.2 Case Study 1: Lanchesterian Combat

On the simplest level, EINSTein is an interactive, exploratory tool that allows users to take conceptual excursions away from Lanchesterian oversimplifications of real combat. It is therefore of interest to first define a Lanchesterian scenario within EINSTein that can subsequently be used as a test bed to which the outcomes of other, non-Lanchesterian, scenarios can be compared. The set of simulation parameters that are appropriate for simulating a maneuverless, Lanchester-like combat scenario in EINSTein includes a red/blue movement range of $r_m = 0$ (so that the position of all agents is fixed) and a red/ blue sensor range that is large enough so that all agents have all enemy agents within their view (for the example below, $r_S = 40$).

Figure 6.2 shows several snapshots of a typical run. Initial conditions consist of 100 red and 100 blue agents (in a tightly packed block formation, with block-centers 15 units distant on a 60-by-60 battlefield) and a red/blue single-shot probability of hit $P_{hit} = 0.005$. Note that the outcome of the battle is a function of the initial sizes of red and blue forces and P_{hit} alone, and does not depend on maneuver or any other agent, squad, or force characteristics.

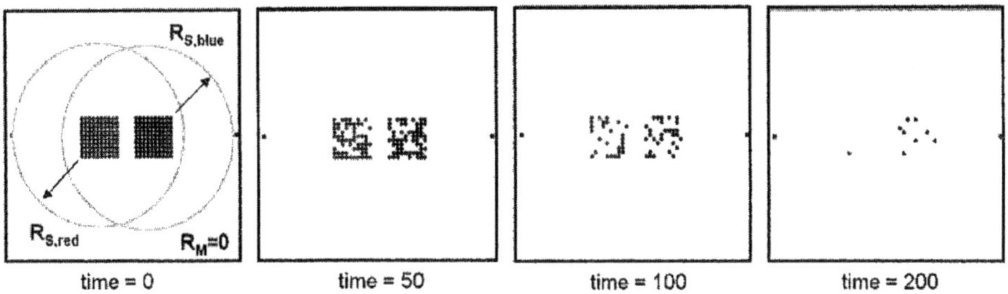

Fig. 6.2 Screenshots of a typical run using an EINSTein rule-set that approximates *Lanchester-equation-driven* combat.

While the Lanchester scenario shown here is highly unrealistic, of course, it is important to remember that most conventional military models (even those that include some form of maneuvering) adjudicate combat by effectively sweeping over a series of similarly idealized maneuver-less skirmishes until one side, or both sides, of the conflict decide to withdraw after sustaining a threshold number of casualties. Most models are still almost entirely attrition-driven. The only substantive role that is played by maneuver and adaptability is in getting the individual combatants into position to fight. Once the combatants are in place and are ready to engage in battle, they do so in the simplest "shoot out" fashion.

A typical signature of such *Lanchesterian*-like combat scenarios is a linear dependence of the *mean attrition rate*—defined as the average number of combatants lost, $\langle\alpha\rangle$, during some specified time interval, $\Delta\tau = t - t_0$—on the *single-shot kill* (or, in our case here, *single-shot hit*) probability, P_{ss}:

$$\langle\alpha\rangle = \left\langle \frac{\Delta n}{\Delta\tau} \right\rangle = \left\langle \frac{n(t_0+t) - n(t_0)}{\Delta\tau} \right\rangle = \sum_{i=1}^{N} P_{ss}(i) = NP_{ss}, \tag{6.1}$$

where N is the total number of agents, $n(t)$ is the number of agents at time t, $P_{ss}(i)$ is the single-shot hit probability of the ith agent, and we have assumed, for the final expression on the right, that $P_{ss}(i) = P_{ss}$ for all i.

Figure 6.3 shows that this is exactly what occurs for this simple example. The plot is obtained by running the Lanchesterian scenario *100* times for different values of P_{ss}; we set $(P_{ss})_{red} = (P_{ss})_{blue} = P_{ss}$ for each run. Runs are terminated as soon as 50% of the agents are killed.

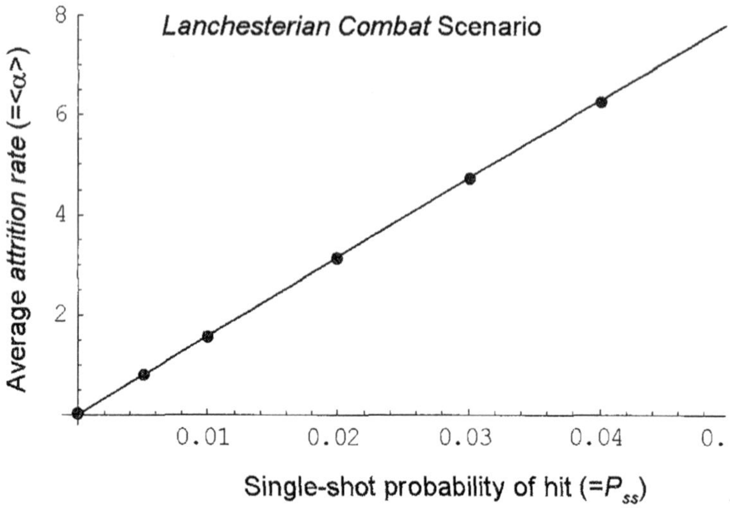

Fig. 6.3 A plot of attrition rate versus single-shot probability of hit for the *Lanchesterian* combat scenario discussed in the text.

What happens if agents are allowed to maneuver? If the maneuver is in any sense "intelligent"—i.e., if agents react reasonably intelligently to changing levels of combat intensity as a battle unfolds, intuitively we should not expect the same linear dependence between $\langle\alpha\rangle$ and P_{ss} to hold. In the extreme case of infinitely timid combatants that run away at the slightest provocation, no fighting at all will occur. In the case where one side applies sophisticated targeting algorithms to maximize enemy casualties bit minimize friendly casualties, we might expect a marked increase in that force's relative fighting ability. Lauren [Lauren00b] has used EINSTein (and other multiagent-based models of combat that explicitly include rules for maneuver; see [Lauren99]) to identify some significant differences between agent-based attrition statistics and results derived from stochastic LE-based models. By examining a large number of runs obtained by running a version of ISAAC on the Maui supercomputer [HPCS], Lauren found a higher degree of correlation and structure in the attrition data, as well as a much greater degree of intermittency in the casualties, than what is typically observed using conventional combat models. Lauren also provides strong evidence that the intensity of battles in multiagent-based models such as EINSTein obeys a fractal power-law dependence on frequency, and displays other traits characteristic of high-dimensional chaotic systems, such as fat-tailed probability distributions and intermittency.

In particular, Lauren has found that for some scenarios that include maneuver the attrition rate depends on the *cube root* of the kill probability, which stands in marked contrast to results obtained for stochastic variants of Lanchester's model, in which, as we have just seen (see figure 6.3), the attrition rate scales *linearly* with an increase in kill probability. If the agent-based model more accurately represents real combat processes, a $\sim 1/3$ power-paw scaling (or more generally, $D < 1$) implies that a relatively "weak" force, with a small kill probability, may actually constitute a much more potent force than a simple Lanchester-based approach suggests. The potency comes from the ability to maneuver (which is never explicitly modeled by Lanchester-based approaches) and to selectively concentrate fire-power while maneuvering. We will pick up this discussion of fractals and combat later on in this chapter when we explore *Case 3: Explosive Skirmish* (see page 457).

6.3 Case Study 2: Classic Battle Front (Tutorial)

The *classic fronts* scenario consists of a simple head-to-head collision between symmetric red and blue forces: red forces defend their flag on the left-hand-side of the notional battlefield and blue forces defend their flag on the right-hand-side. The behavioral characteristics of the red and blue forces are (initially) equal. Figure 6.4 provides a screenshot of how EINSTein appears at the start of an interactive run session.

The run is started by (1) selecting the run/stop toggle sub-menu choice of the *Simulation* main-menu option, (2) pressing the R/S button on the toolbar, or (3) clicking anywhere on the battlefield with the left mouse button. The status bar on the bottom of the main viewscreen shows the data file containing parameters for the current *run*, *time* (= 1), and *initial numbers* of red and blue agents (225 each). Notice that the behavioral characteristics of the red and blue agents are equal.

Combat unfolds as one might expect for two symmetric forces: battle ensues along a classic *front*, where neither side is able to dominate the other. Figure 6.5 shows snapshots summarizing the evolution at times $t = 25, 50, \ldots, 200$.

6.3.1 *Collecting Data*

Suppose you want to collect some statistical data to provide a more quantitative characterization of the run than can be obtained via interactive visual displays alone.

By default, the input file, *einstein_classic_fronts.dat* sets all data collection flags to zero.* You must thus toggle data collection ON during an interactive run. This can be done by either selecting the *Data Collection Toggle* sub-menu option of the *Data Collection* menu, or by pressing the button on the toolbar. Once data

*See entry listing in the *statistics parameters* section of EINSTein's input data file in *Appendix* G (section G.1.1.3, page 667).

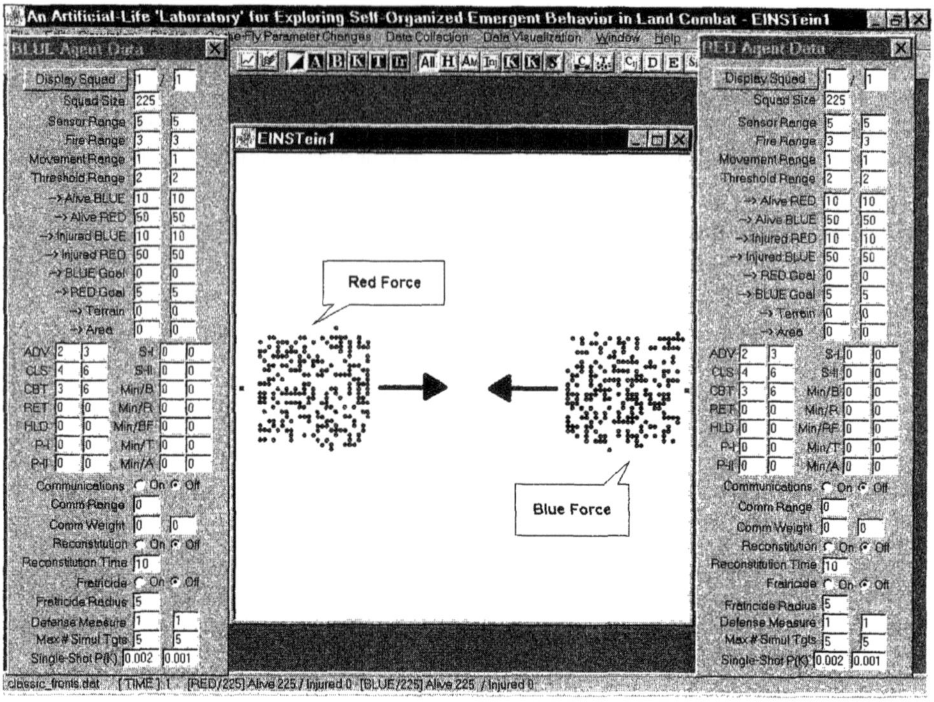

Fig. 6.4 Screenshot of the initial state of the *classic fronts* scenario.

collection is turned on, you can keep track of all available primitive data streams by checking the *Set All* option.

For this sample session, you also want to enable the *Multiple Time-Series* run-mode, which is an option under the *Simulation::Run-Mode* main-menu option. This may also be done pressing the button on the toolbar. When a dialog appears prompting you to specify the number of *initial conditions* (I) and *total run time* (T), select $I = 25$ and $T = 100$.

After the batch-run is complete (a dialog will pop-up informing you of this), go to the *Data Visualization* main-menu option list to select time-series plots of desired data primitives. Figure 6.6 shows time-series plots of *attrition*, position of *red/blue center-of-mass* (measured as distance from red flag) and *average cluster-size*.

6.3.2 *Asking "What If?" Questions*

6.3.2.1 *What If a Small Dynamic Asymmetry is Introduced?*

Suppose you are interested in exploring how combat unfolds in this scenario when a small dynamic asymmetry is introduced. For example, suppose you want to know the impact that the red agents' *sensor range* has on the battle.

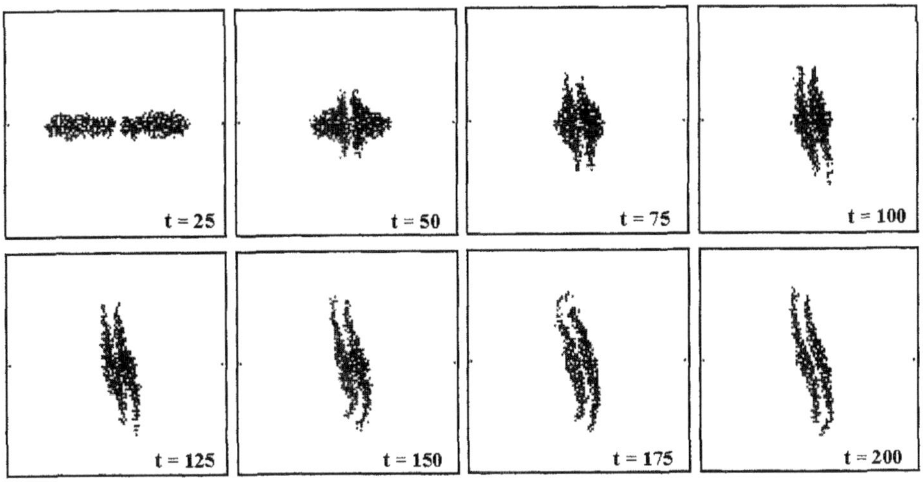

Fig. 6.5 Snapshots of a run using the parameter settings defining the scenario *classic fronts* (see data file *einstein_ classic_ fronts.dat*).

To change red's sensor range, first either select *Red Agents::Red Data* under the *Edit* main-menu option or press the red E button on the toolbar. This calls up an edit dialog that contains the user-definable parameters that define a red agent's dynamic behavior.

The alive/injured sensor range entries appear in the box labeled "RANGES" in the upper left of the dialog (see figure 6.7).

Change the default values of *five** to *seven.* Press the SAVE Squad Data button (appearing directly above the two edit boxes you just made changes in) to save the updated sensor range values. Click OK at the bottom of the dialog to exit the dialog.

EINSTein automatically reinitializes the run with red's new sensor range values, resets the timer to $t = 1$, and sits idle waiting for user input. Start the new run as before: select the run/stop toggle sub-menu choice of the *Simulation* main-menu option, press the R/S button on the toolbar, or click anywhere on the battlefield with the left mouse button.

Let EINSTein run the slightly *asymmetrized* version of *einstein_ classic_ fronts.dat* for 200 time steps. As you would expect, the symmetry of the default run degrades into a pronounced asymmetry: in this case blue effectively plows its way toward the red flag. However, notice that—somewhat counterintuitively—red's increased sensor did not enhance red's offensive capability; though the red force sustains fewer casualties. What lies at the heart of any agent-based model of combat such as EINSTein is the ability to systematically explore how certain changes to an agent's

*Defined in the sample file *einstein_ classic_ fronts.dat* (see Appendix G).

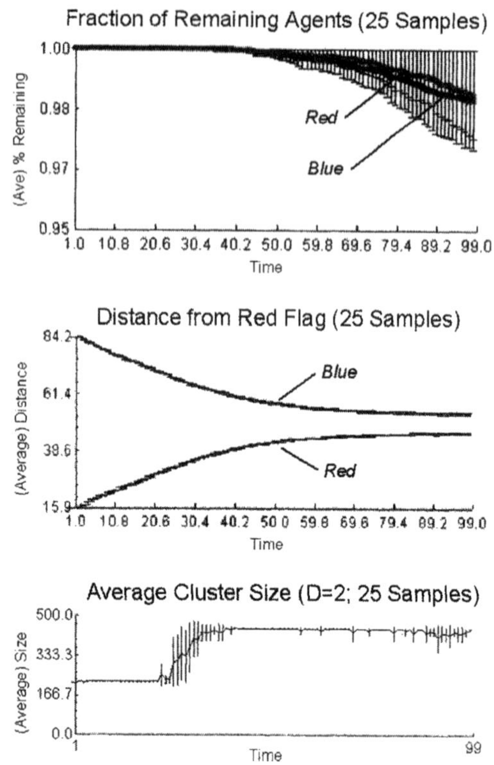

Fig. 6.6 Sample time-series plots of *attrition*, *center-of-mass* and *cluster size* for the *Classic Fronts* scenario discussed in the text.

primitive characteristics affect the emergent behavior. Figure 6.8 shows snapshots summarizing the *asymmetrized* run at times $t = 25, 50, ..., 200$.

6.3.2.2 *What if the Blue Force is More Aggressive?*

What happens if the blue force is made more aggressive? Suppose, for example, that blue's combat μ-rule threshold is decreased to $\Delta_{Combat} = -3$, meaning that blue agents will engage enemy red agents in combat even if they are, locally, *outnumbered* by 3. The values of all other parameters defining red and blue agents are equal to those appearing in the default *einstein_classic_fronts.dat* input data file.

Figure 6.9 shows snapshots of a typical run with more aggressive blue agents. While the general *Class-1* (i.e. *laminar fluid-flow*-like) pattern of behavior persists, the battle front slowly drifts toward the red flag (located at the left-hand side of the battlefield).

Figure 6.10 shows how the system responds to both an increased blue combat aggressiveness and a greater blue weight attached to moving toward the red flag ($\omega_6 = 5 \rightarrow \omega_6 = 90$).

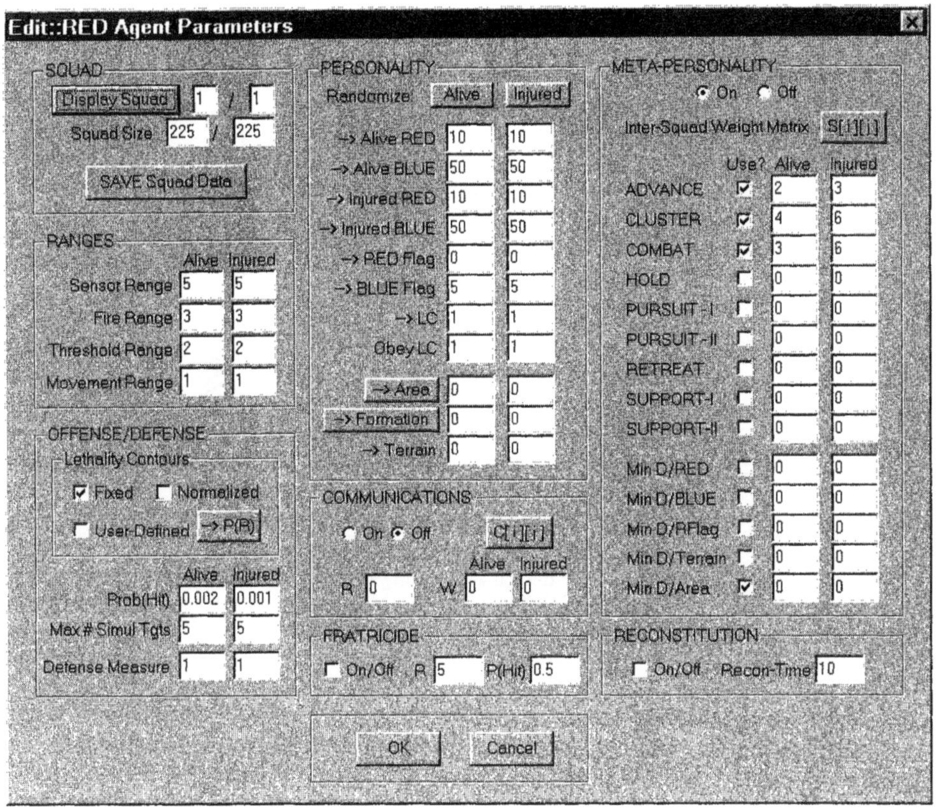

Fig. 6.7 Screenshot of EINSTein's *Edit Red Agent* dialog (versions 1.0 and older).

6.3.2.3 *What if Both Red and Blue Forces are More Maneuverable and More Aggressive?*

What happens if the red and the blue force are *both* made more aggressive and more maneuverable? Suppose, for example, that the red and blue combat μ-rule thresholds are both decreased to $\Delta_{Combat} = -3$, and that the movement range is increased from one to two. The values of all other parameters remain equal to the values that define the default *classic fronts* scenario.

Figure 6.11 shows snapshots taken of two separate runs, differing only in the initial disposition of forces. While the initial stages of both runs appear very similar, and consist of the same "linear" battle-fronts that characterize the *Class-1* rule defined by einstein_classic_fronts.dat, the latter stages of the two runs are markedly different. The battle-front for initial seed #1 breaks to the *left*; the battle-front for initial seed #2 breaks to the *right*. This occurs despite the fact that the primitive behaviors are exactly the same in both cases. The scenario thus provides a simple example of a *Type-2:Class-1* rule, in which at least one defining element (in this

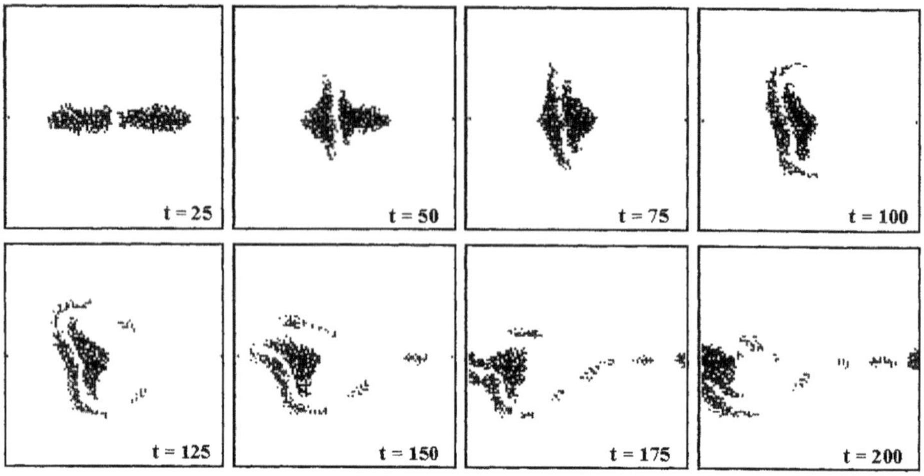

Fig. 6.8 Snapshots of a run using a slightly asymmetrized form of default parameter settings defining the scenario *classic fronts* (see data file *einstein_ classic_ fronts.dat*).

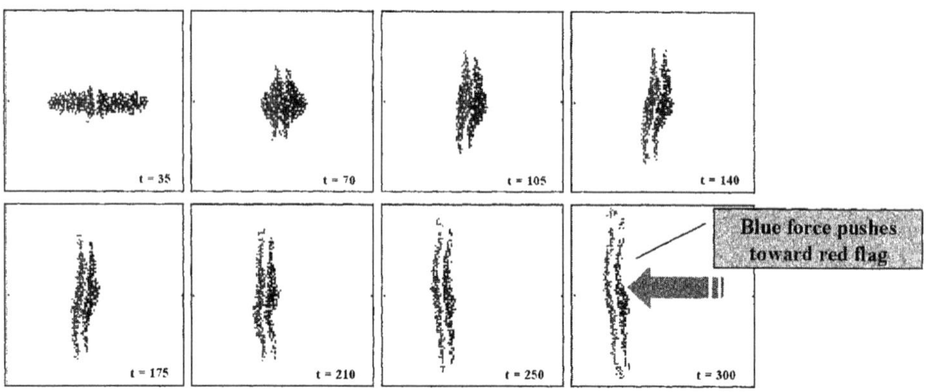

Fig. 6.9 Snapshots of a run using the default parameter settings for the scenario *classic fronts* but with more aggressive blue agents; see text for details.

case, the direction into which the main battle-front tends to first break) is unstable with respect to initial conditions. A more careful analysis would reveal the set of local conditions that are more (or less) conducive for the first break to appear either towards the left or towards the right of the main battle-front.

6.3.2.4 *What If the Basic Scenario Unfolds on Terrain?*

Suppose you are interested in exploring how combat unfolds in this scenario when terrain elements are added. In particular, suppose you want to explore ways in

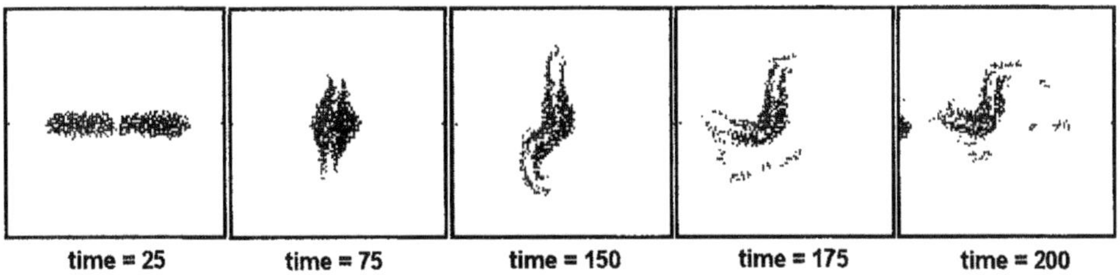

Fig. 6.10 Snapshots of a run using the default parameter settings for the scenario *classic fronts* but with blue agents that are (1) more aggressive, and (2) more eager to get to the red flag; see text for details.

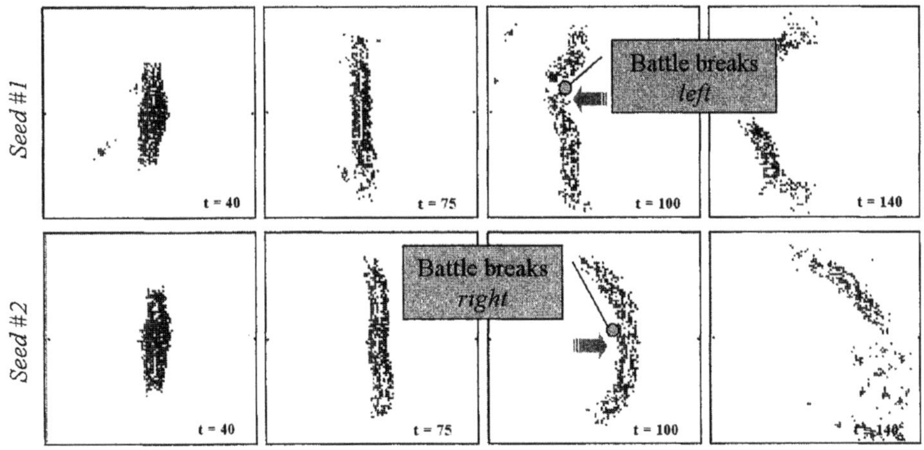

Fig. 6.11 Snapshots of a run using the default parameter settings for the scenario *classic fronts* but with red and blue movement range increased to $r_M = 2$, and combat μ-rule threshold $\Delta_{Combat} = -3$.

which terrain can be used to compensate (at least partially) for red's decline in offensive and/or defensive capability (as exhibited in the last example when red's sensor range was increased from a default value of *five* to *seven*).

To explore this possibility (using EINSTein version 1.0 and older), you will need to call up three dialogs: the *Edit-Terrain*, *Edit Red Passable-Terrain Modifiers*, and *Edit Blue Passable-Terrain Modifiers*.

Step 1. Lets start with the *Edit-Terrain* dialog. To call it up, either select *Terrain::Terrain Blocks* under the *Edit* main-menu option or press the [T] button on the toolbar. Toggle terrain on by clicking the *On* radio button at the top of the dialog. Next, check the first four check-boxes (for terrain blocks 1 - 4) and add the values shown in Table 6.2 to the corresponding edit boxes.

Terrain Block	Type	Length	Width	x	y
1	3	25	25	50	50
2	2	10	10	35	65
3	2	10	10	35	65
4	2	5	5	37	50

Table 6.2 Terrain-block definitions that augment the default classic fronts scnerio discussed in this section.

Finally, when finished, click OK at the bottom of the dialog to exit the dialog. EINSTein will automatically reinitialize the run, reset the timer to time = 1, and update the notional battlefield view so that it appears as in figure 6.12. Recall that EINSTein has five terrain types: terrain *type-2* can be thought of as an impenetrable pillar (through which agents can neither see nor walk); terrain *type-3* is a passable terrain type. Impassable terrain is displayed as ; passable terrain is displayed as .

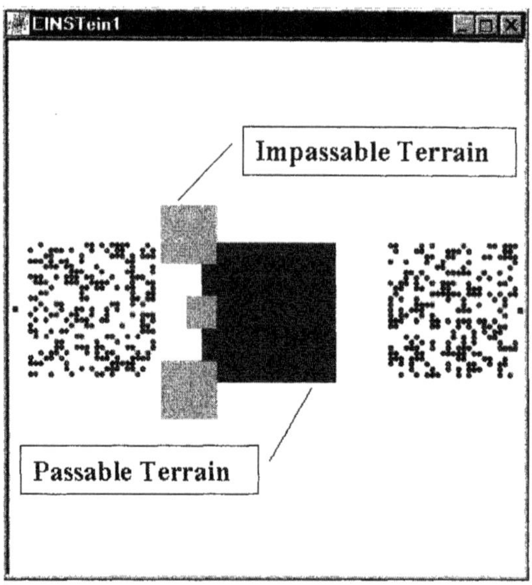

Fig. 6.12 Snapshot of the initial state of the default *classic fronts* scenario with added terrain elements; see text for details.

Step 2. You need to modify EINSTein's default values of passable-terrain modifiers for both red and blue agents. To call up the *Edit Red Passable-Terrain Modifiers* dialog, either select *Red Data::Passable Degradation Parameters* under the *Edit* main-menu option or press the red T button on the toolbar. This dialog shows user-defined entries for agent parameters that are tailored to terrain type; it will appear as shown in figure 6.13, which displays the default values.

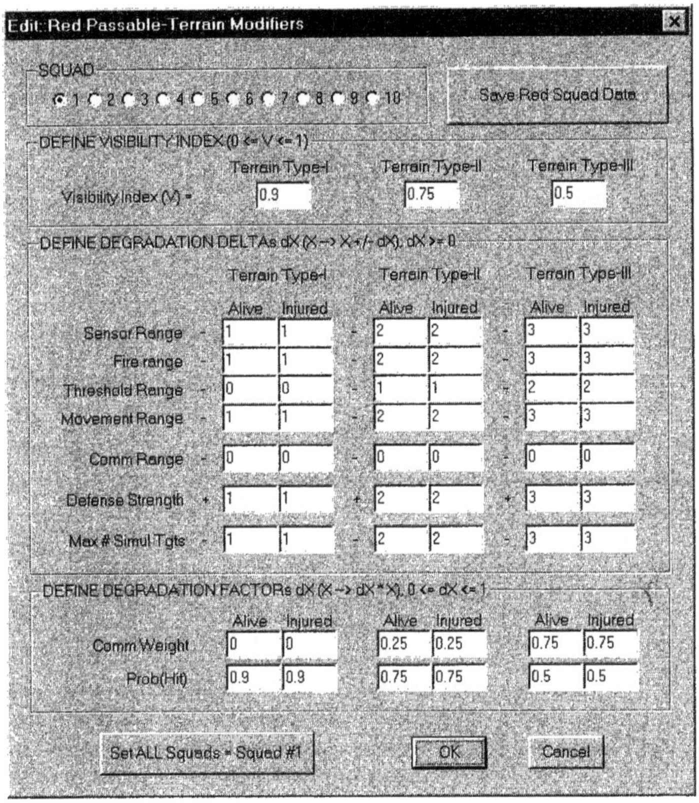

Fig. 6.13 Screenshot of the *Edit Passable-Terrain Degradation Parameters* dialog (as it appears for EINSTein versions 1.0 and older).

Notice that for passable terrain type-I (the type of terrain defined in Step 1 above), red's sensor, fire and movement ranges, as well as the number of blue agents that red agents an simultaneously target, are all degraded by *one*.*

Since the movement range of both red and blue agents is equal to *one* (in the default *classic fronts* scenario), you must specify a movement range degradation of zero to make certain that neither red nor blue agents stop moving when they encounter a passable terrain element. A movement degradation of zero ensures that both red and blue agents continue making their local move decisions based on their default movement range.

Having opened the *Edit Red Passable-Terrain Modifiers* dialog, locate the edit boxes for alive and injured movement range for type-I (passable) terrain. These edit boxes are located on the left and toward the center of the dialog. Replace the entries appearing there (both equal to *one*) with *zero*. Press the  button

*The degradation values appearing in the *Edit Blue Passable-Terrain Modifiers* dialog are the same as for their red counterparts.

(at the top right of the dialog) to save the updated movement range degradation values. Click OK at the bottom of the dialog to exit the dialog. Do the same with the *Edit Blue Passable-Terrain Modifiers* dialog, which you open by either selecting *Blue Data::Passable Degradation Parameters* under the *Edit* main-menu option or press the blue T button on the toolbar.

As in the previous examples, let EINSTein run for 200 time steps. Start the run by either selecting the run/stop toggle sub-menu choice of the *Simulation* main-menu option or pressing the R/S button on the toolbar, or click anywhere on the battlefield with the left mouse button. In this case, we see that the added terrain has a significant impact on red's ability to defend its flag area against the blue force.

In an earlier run of the *classic fronts* series (see figure 6.8), blue was able to advance toward the red flag essentially unopposed. In the current scenario, the dynamic interplay between agent behavior and terrain placement results in a significantly enhanced red defense: red is able to contain most of the blue forces throughout most of the run. Color plate 9 (page 255) shows snapshots summarizing the run at times $t = 25, 50, ..., 200$.

6.3.3 *Generating a Fitness Landscape*

Suppose you are interested in exploring how combat unfolds in the basic scenario (without terrain) over a two-dimensional subspace of the parameter space defining the dynamics of red agents. For example, suppose you want to gauge the red forces' offensive and defensive capability as a function of red's *sensor range* and *combat aggressiveness* (as parametrized by red's combat threshold).

6.3.3.1 *Step 1*

You must first enable the *two-parameter fitness-landscape* run-mode (see *Simulation Menu*). In this mode, EINSTein automatically scans, and measures a user-defined mission fitness, over a prescribed two-dimensional $x - y$ parameter space. This run-mode is enabled by selecting the *Run Mode::2-Parameter Fitness Landscape Exploration* option of the *Simulation::Run* main-menu item.

6.3.3.2 *Step 2*

Once the two-parameter fitness-landscape run-mode is enabled, you will be presented with two pop-up edit dialogs: (1) *Edit Run-Time Parameters*, (2) *Edit XY-Coordinates.*

The *Edit::Run-Time Parameters* dialog specifies the values of run-time variables such as number of initial conditions to average over, maximum run-time, and so on. For this sample session, change the default *Number of Initial Conditions* (i.e. the first entry at the top of the dialog) from 2 to 10 and change the default *Maximum Time to Enemy Flag* (the second entry) from 50 to 100 time steps. Click OK to save the changes and exit the dialog.

The *Edit::(X, Y) Coordinates* dialog specifies the x and y coordinates over which EINSTein will perform the automatic mission fitness scan. For this sample session, change the default number of x-range samples from five to ten. The edit box for this entry is the right-most entry in the box labeled **DEFINE X-RANGE** near the center of the dialog. Leave all other entries at their default values. When finished, click OK to save the changes and exit the dialog.

EINSTein is now ready to perform an automatic scan of red's mission fitness (see below) over the two-dimensional subspace spanned by:

Red Sensor Range: $r_S = 1, 2, ..., 10, 11,$
Red Combat Threshold: $\Delta_{Combat} = -15, -12, ..., 0, ..., +12, +15.$

For each combination of r_S and Δ_{Combat}, EINSTein will average over 10 initial conditions, each run over 100 time steps (as defined by the changes you made to the *Edit::Run-Time Parameters* dialog).

6.3.3.3 *Step 3*

To start the mission-fitness scan, click anywhere within the text-field in the battlefield view. EINSTein will automatically start the run, informing you of its progress via the status-bar at the lower left of the display screen. The status bar keeps track of the current *x coordinate* (labeled [x]), *y coordinate* (labeled [y]), *initial-condition* (labeled [IC]), and *time* (labeled [T]), of current run for the given initial condition. When finished, EINSTein will pop-up a dialog to inform you that the run is complete.

6.3.3.4 *Step 4*

To display a mission fitness landscape, select the *3D Graphs::Fitness Landscape* option under the data visualization main-menu item. A pop-up edit dialog will prompt you to define the actual mission-fitness function that will be plotted, the color of the plot (*color* or *greyscale*), the plot-type (*fitness average* or *absolute deviations*), and the graph type (*3D surface, interpolated over (x,y) nodes, a 2D density plot, color-coded for fitness value*, or *win-plot*; see figure 6.14).

Color plates 10-12 (pages 256- 258) show 3D surface graphs for three mission objective functions:

- *Minimize number of enemy agents (i.e. blue) near friendly (i.e. red) flag*,
- *Maximize red/blue survival ratio*, and
- *Minimize friendly center-of-mass to enemy flag.*

Color plate 10 (page 256) shows that while the red force is very successful in defending its own flag when the red agents all have a sensor range of $r_S < 4$ (with mission fitness ~ 1, meaning no blue agents are allowed to approach the red flag within a certain range), red's success diminishes rapidly as the sensor range is increased.

The maximal sensor range for which red forces can successfully defend the red flag increases with red's aggressiveness (i.e. as red's combat threshold Δ_{Combat} is

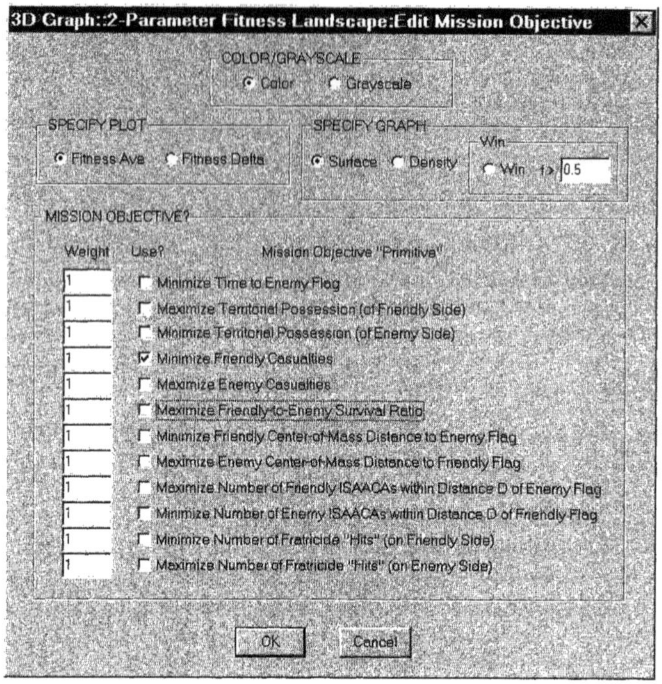

Fig. 6.14 Pop-up dialog for displaying 3D mission-fitness landscape; see text for details.

decreased). Note that this behavior is consistent with the run shown in figure 6.8, where an increase in red's sensor range obviously has a negative impact on its defensive capability.

The fitness landscape on the left-hand-side of color plate ?? suggests that red's offensive capability also tends to diminish at first with increasing sensor range, but then tends to be enhanced at greater values when the force is locally less aggressive (i.e. each red agents' combat threshold is large and positive).

Keep in mind that these somewhat counterintuitive results represent only the first step towards understanding a more complex underlying dynamics. For example, remember that mission-fitness plots assume that *all parameter values other than the* (x, y) *coordinates chosen for a specific plot remain constant.* It may seen odd that offensive and/or defensive capability diminishes with increasing sensor range; it becomes less odd when it is appreciated what that increase actually represents: more information to which each agent must respond (with the same local-penalty-driven tasks as before, such as move forward, stay away from enemy, approach goal, etc.), using exactly the same resources as before. As each agent becomes aware of a greater range of information and activity around itself, it becomes less able to optimize its decisions. The interesting question is, *"How must an agent's resources be re-allocated so as to ensure at least the same level of mission fitness?"*

6.4 Case Study 3: Explosive Skirmish

The behavior of *Class-3* (i.e. *dispersive* flow) EINSTein rules is characterized by a rapid, explosive burst of agents that then more maneuver close-in during a series of local firefights and skirmishes as the battle slowly dissipates. An example of two sets of parameter values that can lead to *Class-3* behavior is given in table 6.3. Figure 6.15 shows some snapshot views of a typical run using these values.

	Sample 1		Sample 2	
Parameter	Red	Blue	Red	Blue
Agents	250	250	100	100
r_S	5	5	5	5
r_F	3	3	3	3
r_M	2	2	1	1
ω_1	10	10	10	10
ω_2	40	40	40	25
ω_3	10	10	10	10
ω_4	40	40	40	25
ω_5	0	0	0	0
ω_6	25	25	5	50
$\tau_{Advance}$	3	3	3	3
$\tau_{Cluster}$	8	3	5	8
Δ_{Combat}	-99	-3	-10	-3

Table 6.3 Some parameter values that lead to *Class-3* Behavior.

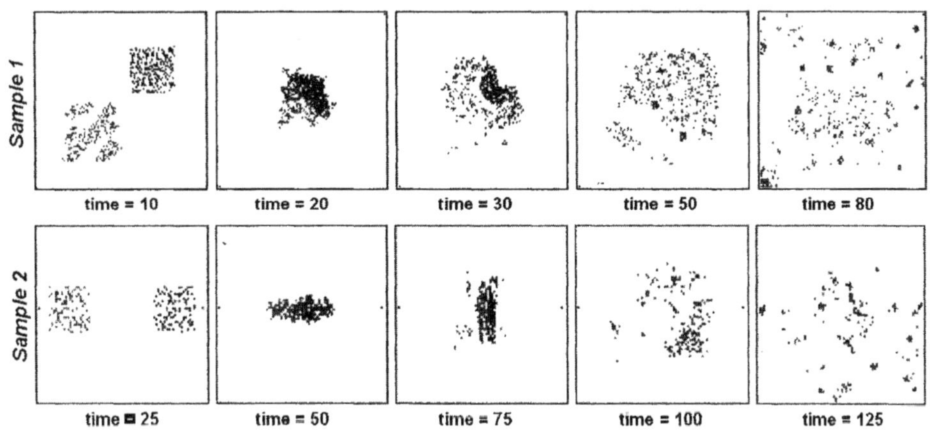

Fig. 6.15 Screenshots from typical runs using the default *explosive skirmish* scenario parameters from table 6.3.

6.4.1 *Agent-Density Plots*

Except for the simplest scenarios, such as the *Lanchesterian*-combat example discussed on page 438, it is generally difficult to convey the behavioral character of a particular scenario using words alone. Space-time plots of individual runs of a scenario, such as those shown in figure 6.15, tell part of the story of course; but because they represent no more than a single "snapshot" of what is, in principle, a finite volume of the system's available dynamic phase space, the information that such plots contain is necessarily limited. Fortunately, EINSTein contains tools that allow one to both directly explore multiple time-series runs of a particular scenario and/or to collect raw data that can be later explored (outside of EINSTein) using other data analysis and visualization tools. Appendix G summarizes EINSTein's raw-data collection facilities.

One of the simplest visualizations that can be used to summarize the overall character of how a scenario unfolds in time is the *agent-density plot.* The agent-density plot consists of exactly the same sequence of snapshots as a regular (single-run) series of space-time plots, but instead of showing color-coded (red and blue) agent positions it shows a greyscaled time-averaged density of red and blue agents over a sequence of many runs (for the same scenario); i.e., the greyscaled value of each "pixel" (or battlefield site) represents the average visitation frequency of an agent of a specified color: darker shades represent more frequent visitation, lighter shades represent less frequent visitation. Other time-averaged quantities of interest may also be displayed, of course.

Figure 6.16, for example, contains a typical agent-density plot for the *Sample-1* scenario. The top row shows greyscaled densities for the red force. The middle row shows greyscale densities for the blue force. The bottom row shows the *killing-field* density for this scenario (that is, the frequency of appearance of positions where agents, of either color, have been *killed* during the battle).*

6.4.2 *Spatial Entropy*

In order to obtain a finer characterization of behavior, a more quantitative approach must be taken. Figure 6.17 shows time-series plots of selected statistical measures that can be used to characterize the *explosive skirmish* scenario. Each plot represents an average over 50 samples, and samples differ only in the initial disposition of red and blue agents (which is randomly determined within fixed red and blue bounding boxes). In the following two sections we introduce two powerful sets of dynamic measures: (1) *Spatial entropy*, and (2) *Fractal dimensions.*

Figure 6.17-a shows a plot of the *spatial entropy* as a function of time for the *Sample-1* scenario, the relative values of which can be used as a crude, but useful, pattern recognition tool for characterizing and/or comparing runs: tight, relatively

*See page 623 (in Appendix E) for a brief description of EINSTein's built-in facility to display the *Killing Field Map* for interactive runs.

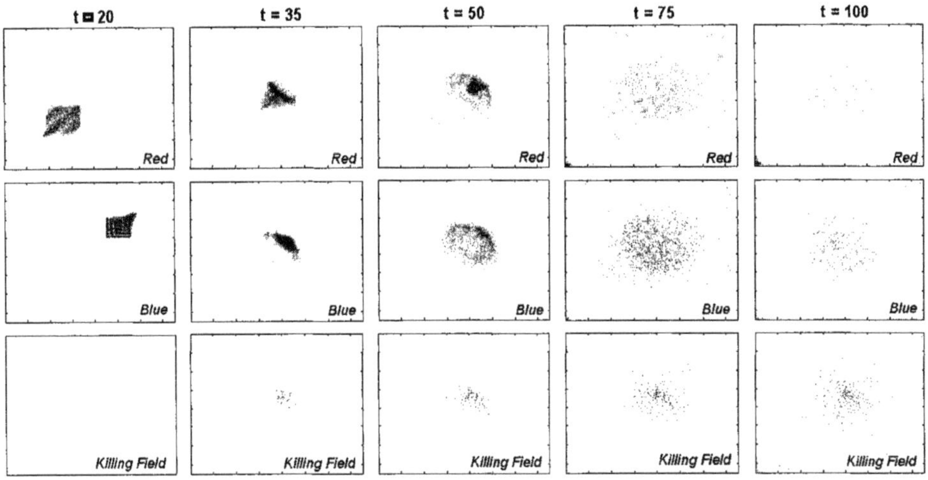

Fig. 6.16 Snapshots of a typical *agent-density plot* for the *Sample-1* scenario defined in table 6.3, averaged over 25 runs (each run starts using the same agent-parameter values but using a different random starting configuration). The top row shows greyscaled densities for the red force; the middle row shows greyscale densities for the blue force; and the bottom row shows the *killing-field* density for this scenario. In each case, darker shades represent more frequent visitation, lighter shades represent less frequent visitation.

nondispersed patterns yield low entropy; disorganized, space-filling patterns have a high entropy.

It is computed by partitioning the 80-by-80 battlefield into an 8-by-8 array of 10-by-10 sub-blocks. In general, the spatial entropy, $E = E(b)$, where b is the size of the sub-block of the (B/b)-by-(B/b) array of sub-blocks, and B is the length of the battlefield, is defined by:

$$E(b) = \frac{1}{2\log_2 b} \sum_{i=1}^{b^2} p_i\,(b) \log[p_i\,(b)], \tag{6.2}$$

where $p_i\,(b) = N_i(b)/N$, $\log_2 x$ is the logarithm base-2 of x, N is the total number of agents on the battlefield, b^2 is the number of sub-blocks into which the battlefield is partitioned, and the factor appearing before the summation sign, $(2\log_2 b)^{-1}$, is a normalization constant. Note that $p_i\,(b)$ estimates of the probability of finding an agent in the ith sub-block.

If a single sub-block contains all the points, then the spatial entropy has its minimal possible value: $E(b) = 0$. On the other hand, if the agents are all scattered throughout the battlefield in such a way that $p_i\,(b) = p = 1/b^2$ for all sub-blocks i, then E takes its maximal possible value ($= 1$). The closer the value of E is to *zero*, the "closer" the agent distribution is to one that is tightly clustered near a single sub-block. The closer the value of E is to *one*, the more scattered is

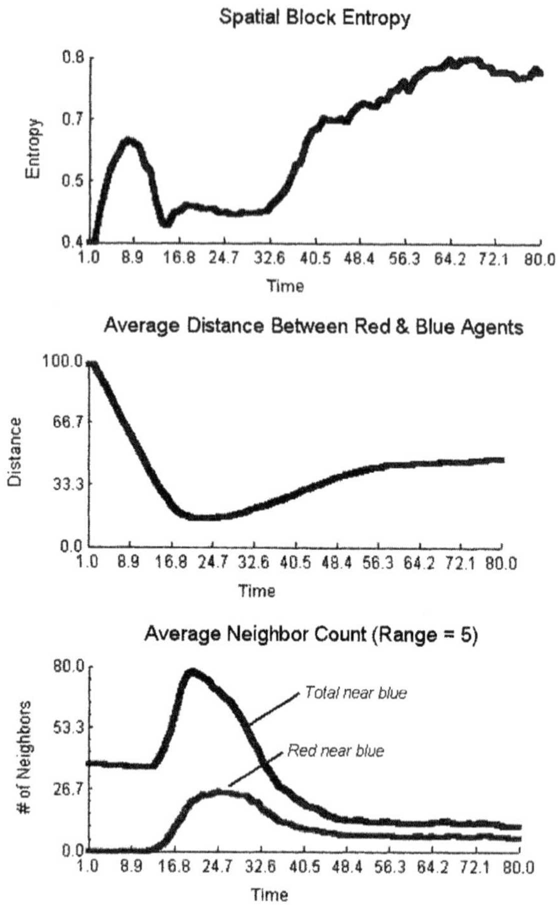

Fig. 6.17 Timeseries data from the explosive skirmish *Scenario-1* shown in figure 6.15; see text for details.

the agent distribution. A time-series plot of entropy, as its values scatter between the minimal and maximal values for a particular scenario, provides a convenient statistical snapshot of the spatiotemporal regularities (and irregularities) over the whole battle. Entropy plots may also be used to help identify natural boundaries between behavioral regimes; such as the plateau between times $t = 17$ and $t = 30$ in figure 6.17-a, during which agents undergo the most intense combat during the *Sample-1* scenario.

Figure 6.17-b shows a plot of the average distance between red and blue agents as a function of time. The curve starts out at a distance $d \sim 100$ that is equivalent to the initial separation distance between the starting boxes of the red and blue forces. As the two forces move toward their opponent's flag, and thus approach one another, the average inter-agent distance steadily diminishes—reaching a minimum as the two forces collide near the center of the battlefield—then slowly increases as the forces disperse and maneuver for position, before reaching an temporary "equilibrium" at $t \sim 60$.

Figure 6.17-c shows the average number of red (and red + blue) agents near blue agents as a function of time. Note that this average neighbor count reaches its "equilibrium" value around $t \sim 50$, which is earlier than either the time at which the spatial block entropy saturates ($t \sim 65$) or when the average inter-agent distance itself begins to level off ($t \sim 60$). This suggests that red and blue agents are able to effectively lock into a mutually "optimal" (albeit, still dynamic) relative local posture, despite the fact that whole battle area continues to expand.

6.4.3 *Fractal Dimensions and Combat*

During our discussion of the *Lanchesterian* combat scenario (see page 438), we argued that for maneuverless combatants, each of whom "sees" the enemy at all times, the time averaged attrition rate, $\langle\alpha\rangle$, ought to scale linearly with the single-shot probability of kill (or single-shot probability of hit, P_{ss}, as it is defined in EINSTein): $\langle\alpha\rangle \propto P_{ss}$ (see equation 6.1). Recall also, that our tentative answer to the question, "*What happens if agents are allowed to maneuver?*" was that there was no *a priori* reason to expect the same linear dependence between $\langle\alpha\rangle$ and P_{ss} to hold in the general case where agents are allowed to intelligently maneuver around the battlefield.

If we examine what happens during a typical explosive skirmish scenario, we find that this basic intuition appears correct. For example, figure 6.18 shows that the attrition rate versus single-shot probability of hit for the *Sample-1* scenario defined in table 6.3 appears to follow a P_{ss}^n curve, where $n \lesssim 1/2$.*

Lauren, a researcher with New Zealand's *Defence Operational Technology Support Establishment*, has used ISAAC, EINSTein and, most recently, a new EINSTein-like combat simulation called MANA,† to identify some significant differences between the attrition statistics describing the outcome of agent-based models of combat (that explicitly include rules for maneuver) and results derived from stochastic Lanchester models [Lauren99]. Specifically, for some regimes of what might loosely be called "turbulent flow," the attrition rate appears to depend on the *cube root* of the kill probability (though other nonlinear dependencies are also possible; see below). To see why this may be so, we follow Lauren [Lauren02] in making a plausibility argument that the attrition rate ought, in general, to depend not just on

*As in the earlier example (see figure 6.3 on page 440), this plot is obtained by running the *Sample-1* scenario *100* times for several different values of P_{ss}; we set $(P_{ss})_{red} = (P_{ss})_{blue} = P_{ss}$ for each run. Runs are terminated as soon as 50% of the agents are killed. Note that in calculating $\langle\alpha\rangle$, the actual ensemble over which the average is taken includes only those times during which "dispersive" combat ensues (i.e., the first 25 iterations, during which the red and blue agents simply advance forward and do not yet make contact with the enemy, are ignored).

†MANA is discussed briefly on page 56 in chapter 1.

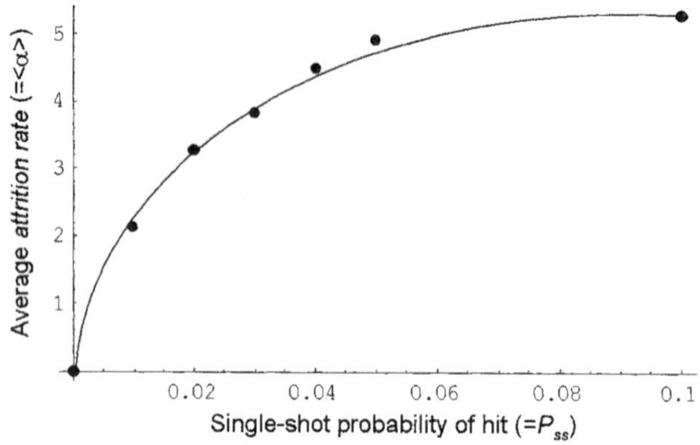

Fig. 6.18 A plot of attrition rate versus single-shot probability of hit for the turbulent phase of the *Sample-1* combat scenario defined in table 6.3; see text for details. (Compare to figure 6.3 on page 440, which is the same plot, but using data for the Lanchester scenario.)

P_{ss} alone, but on both P_{ss} and the *fractal dimension* D_F representing the spatial distribution of agents.

Before presenting the argument, let us briefly review what we mean by *fractals.* Fractal dimensions such as the *Capacity* dimension (or "Box counting" dimension; also referred to as the *Hausdorff* dimension), *Information* dimension and *Correlation* dimension, were discussed earlier in the context of nonlinear dynamical system theory.* Essentially, fractal dimensions are measures that provide useful structural and/or statistical information about a given point set. Recall that fractals are geometric objects characterized by some form of self-similarity; that is, parts of a fractal, when magnified to an appropriate scale, appear similar to the whole. Fractals are thus objects that harbor an effectively infinite amount of detail on all levels. Coastlines of islands and continents and terrain features are approximate fractals. A magnified image of a part of a leaf is similar to an image of the entire leaf. Strange attractors also typically have a fractal structure.

Loosely speaking, a fractal dimension specifies the minimum number of variables that are needed to specify an object. For a one-dimensional line, for example, say the x-axis, one piece of information, the x-variable, is needed to specify any position on the line. The fractal dimension of the x-axis is said to be equal to 1. Similarly, two coordinates are needed to specify a position on a two-dimensional plane, so that the fractal dimension of a plane is equal to 2. Genuine (i.e., "interesting") fractals are objects whose fractal dimension is *noninteger.*

How might fractals relate specifically to combat? Intuitively, since real combat consists of anything but a series of random skirmishes in which opposing sides constantly shoot at each other, we expect attrition data to contain spatiotemporal

*See discussion beginning on page 95 in section 2.1.5.

correlations. Because EINSTein includes rules for maneuver, we expect to see spatiotemporal correlations emerge as a consequence of maneuver (as we would expect to also see in other multiagent-based combat simulations that contain intelligent maneuver dynamics).

Think of the changing distributions of agents on a battlefield as nothing more than abstract points on a lattice. The degree of clustering and maneuver can then be measured by calculating a fractal dimension for the distribution in exactly the same way we had earlier calculated the fractal dimension for point sets representing various *one-* and *two*-dimensional attractors of dynamical systems. The only real difference between using the (x, y) positions of agents and points of an attractor, in practice, is that when dealing with agents we are naturally limited in the number of "data points" that we have to work with. Even large scenarios are limited to about 500 agents or so to a side. Moreover, agents are allowed to sit only on integer-valued sites, so that the set of possible (x, y)'s is also more limited. Nonetheless, the actual calculation of fractal dimensions proceeds in exactly the same manner for the two cases; and, just as for continuous dynamical systems, the measures provide an important insight into the geometry of the spatial distributions.

As a concrete example, consider the *Capacity* dimension, which is defined by:

$$D_F = \lim_{\epsilon \to 0} \frac{\ln [N(\epsilon)]}{\ln(1/\epsilon)}, \tag{6.3}$$

where $N(\epsilon)$ is the number of d-dimensional boxes of side ϵ that contain at least one agent. Alternatively, we can write that:

$$N(\varepsilon) = \varepsilon^{-D_F}, \tag{6.4}$$

and call D_F the power-law *scaling exponent.* For a solid block of maneuverless agents, such the solid red and blue blocks of agents dueling it out in the Lanchesterian scenario shown in figure 6.2 (see page 439), $D_F \sim 2$; D_F will be *less than* 2 if the agents occupy only a portion of the entire battlefield, as the whole battlefield is be used to estimate D_F.

Figure 6.19 compares single-time estimates of D_F for (1) two spatial dispositions of real-world forces (figures 6.19-a and 6.19-b, and (2) a snapshot of notional forces as arrayed during the dispersive-flow phase of the *Explosive Skirmish* scenario in EINSTein (6.19-c). The (x, y) locations of the real-world data consists of the longitudes and latitudes of Coalition ground forces during *Operation Iraqi Freedom* in 2003.* In each case, the (x, y) locations are first scaled so that (both the real

*These (scaled) geo-locations are from *Command and Control PC* software databases maintained, and kindly provided to the author, by Drs. Michael Shepko and David Mazel of *The CNA Corporation*, Alexandria, VA. Dr. Mazel was also instrumental in providing many of the fractal plots that appear in this section, and has written several stand-alone *Matlab* and *C*-code programs to further assist in data analysis and visualization. The author gratefully acknowledges all of Dr. Mazel's help.

and notional) battlefields assume the same effective "size" of 1-by-1 and the scaled battlefield is then divided into a total of $N_{total} = \varepsilon^{-2}$ boxes of length ε. Several different values of ε are chosen, and for each ε the number of boxes, $N(\varepsilon)$, that contain at least one point soldier (or agent) are counted. Since we are limited by how finely we are able to partition the battlefield (as well as by the relatively limited number of soldiers and agents that defined our set of (x, y) locations: ~ 500), the fractal dimension is estimated by the slope of a linear fit on a plot of $\log[N(\varepsilon)]$ versus $\log[1/\varepsilon]$. (Note that we are not in any way suggesting that a finite distribution of either real or notional combatants represents a genuine fractal in a *mathematically* rigorous sense. We are only suggesting that for limited domains (in battlefield size, duration of conflict and number of agents) their distribution is such that it can reasonably well be characterized by a fractal-like power-law scaling.)

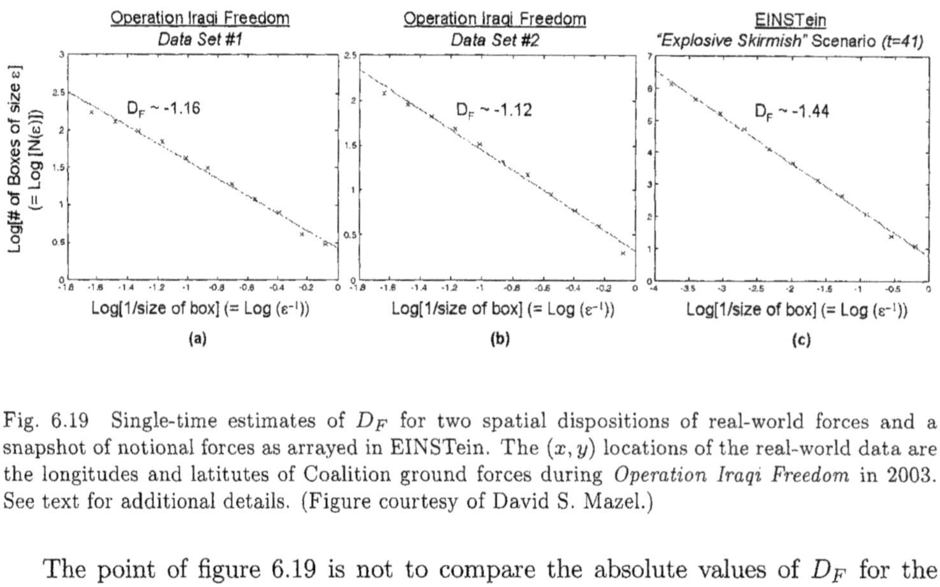

Fig. 6.19 Single-time estimates of D_F for two spatial dispositions of real-world forces and a snapshot of notional forces as arrayed in EINSTein. The (x, y) locations of the real-world data are the longitudes and latitutes of Coalition ground forces during *Operation Iraqi Freedom* in 2003. See text for additional details. (Figure courtesy of David S. Mazel.)

The point of figure 6.19 is not to compare the absolute values of D_F for the different cases—which we could have anticipated as being different, particularly since EINSTein's *Explosive Skirmish* example does not intentionally model any real-world scenario—but rather to illustrate the important fact that EINSTein is able to reproduce a spatial fractal scaling *at all* (at least for the limited spatial ranges being considered). In EINSTein, as in the real world, "intelligent maneuvering" implies an agent's (or soldier's) position, at any time t, is strongly correlated with local combat conditions. While it has for a long time been known, on the basis of empirical evidence, that real-world forces tend to arrange themselves in self-organized fractal fashion (see [Dock93b] and [RichLF60], and discussion below), no satisfactory generative explanation for why this is so has yet appeared; a deficiency that is only fueled by the fact that most conventional combat simulations still adhere to an oversimplified "line-up and shoot-it-out" model (for which fractal scaling—indeed, any correlated spatial positioning at all—is effectively rendered irrelevant).

To the same extent that EINSTein's agents mimic (not necessarily exactly reproduce) real-world adaptive maneuver, so too they are able to self-organize into correlated spatial distributions that are described, on a limited scale, by a fractal dimension. Unfortunately, a deeper understanding of the dynamic relationship between (both spatial and temporal) fractal dimensions and traditional measures of combat (such as attrition; see discussion below) remains an open problem.

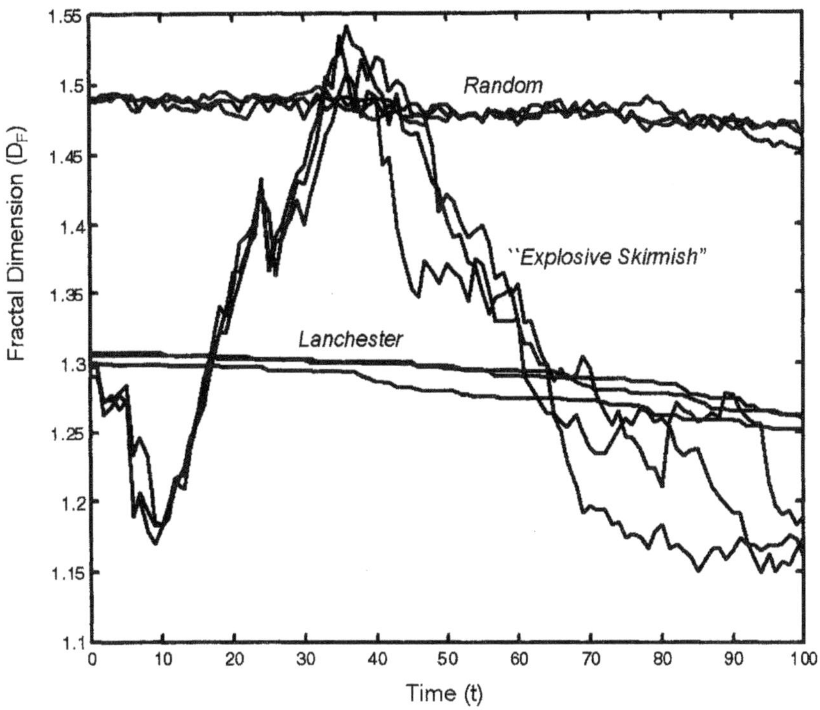

Fig. 6.20 Three sample plots each (using different initial configurations of agents) of the fractal dimension D_F (see equation 6.3) as a function of time for the *Lanchesterian* (i.e., maneuverless) scenario discussed in *Case Study #1* on page 438, a scenario in which the agents are allowed to move but do so completely *randomly* (and are also initially distributed randomly on the battlefield), and the *Sample-1 "Explosive Skirmish"* scenario defined by the parameters appearing in table 6.3. (Figure courtesy of David S. Mazel.)

How does the fractal dimension change during combat? To illustrate the kinds of spatial configurations that can arise, and evolve, in different combat scenarios—as viewed by using an estimate of the fractal dimension—consider figure 6.20. Figure 6.20 shows three plots each (using different initial configurations of agents) of D_F as a function of time for (1) the *Lanchesterian* (i.e., maneuverless) scenario, (2) a scenario in which the agents are allowed to move but do so completely randomly (and are initially distributed randomly on the battlefield), and (3) the *Sample-1* explosive-skirmish scenario defined by the parameters appearing in table 6.3.*

These three cases are defined by first using the *"Explosive Skirmish"* scenario to select a single-shot probability of hit, P_{ss}, for which the mean attrition after 100 time steps is equal to 20%. That same value is then used for the other two cases as well. Also, in order to better place the random scenario in-between the Lanchester scenario (in which all agents "see" and "fire at" all other agents at all times) and the *"Explosive Skirmish"* scenario (in which agents' sensor and fire ranges are relatively small), agents in the *Random* scenario are assigned sensor and fire ranges equal to *three times their value* for the *"Explosive Skirmish."* Because these three cases represent qualitatively different combat scenarios that range from maneuverless, all-seeing/all-shooting agents to intelligently maneuvering agents able to sense, and adapt to, only local streams of information, it is instructive to use them as a basis for comparing simulation output.

Notice that in figure 6.20, except for a small drift of values among different runs for the same scenario and/or differences in precise values at a given time for a given run, the scenarios are each characterized by the unique manner in which the fractal dimension of its associated spatial distribution evolves in time; i.e., the time-evolution of fractal dimension may be used as a kind of *behavioral signature* of a given scenario.

The fractal dimension for the *Lanchesterian* scenario, for example, remains fairly flat with minimal variability as the agent population gradually succumbs to attrition and the initial solid blocks of agents becomes ever more sparsely populated. The fractal dimension for the *Random* scenario starts at a higher value (than the *Lanchesterian* scenario) but also remains fairly flat as agents are gradually killed. Compared to the Lanchesterian scenario, there is a great deal more local variability to estimates of fractal dimension, as a result of random agent motion. In contrast to these two "generic" cases, we see that the *Explosive Skirmish* scenario—in which agents are fully endowed with an adaptive maneuver logic—yields both a consistent structure in time across all three runs, and great variability in local value at a particular time for a given run.

6.4.4 *Attrition Count*

A time series of total attrition at time t, even for a single run of a given scenario, is often revealing, as it hints at a characteristic signature of complex systems; namely, *punctuated equilibrium.* Punctuated equilibrium refers to behavior in which there are (sometimes long) periods of relative stability which are periodically punctuated by outbursts of some kind (which in our case is marked by "number of agents killed"). Figure 6.21 compares plots of total attrition number (red + blue) as a

*EINSTein (versions 1.0 and older) has a built-in function to calculate the "box counting" fractal dimension. It appears as the third option under the *Data Collection* main menu entry, and is described in *Appendix E: A Concise User's Guide* to EINSTein (see pages 628 and 633).

function of time (t) for the same three input data files that are used to generate figure 6.20 (i.e., *Lanchester*, *Random*, and the *Sample-1* "Explosive Skirmish" scenarios).

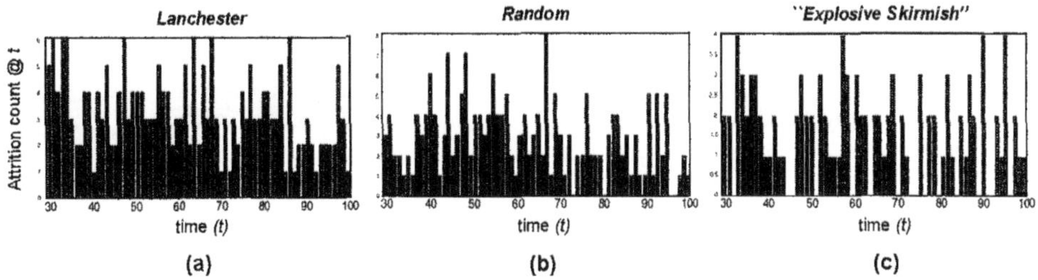

Fig. 6.21 Attrition count as a function of time for a single run each for the following three scenarios: (a) *Lanchester* scenario, (b) *Random* scenario, and (c) *Sample-1* of the "Explosive Skirmish" scenario; see text for details.

While the plots are no more than anecdotal (since they represent only a snapshot of a single run for each scenario), they nonetheless contain some useful distinguishing characteristics. For example, notice that while the attrition count for both the *Lanchester* and *Random* scenarios appears random (as expected), the first two time-series display much less of the staccato-like appearance than the time-series for the *"Explosive Skirmish"* scenario. The latter, as we see, appears to display more of an intermittent behavior, with periods of occasional stasis, punctuated by bursts of activity. A reasonable question to ask is whether there is any regularity to this behavior?

Perhaps the simplest way to look for underlying behavioral regularities is to sit back and watch for them; i.e., accumulate statistics until trends present themselves. One of the measures that is commonly used in studies of complex systems is the distribution of waiting times between meaningful "events." In this example, we define an "event," for an entire run of a given scenario, as the time it takes for the system as whole (i.e., red and blue forces) to sustain 50% casualties. Figure 6.22 shows the histograms that result after 1000 runs each of the *Lanchester* and *"Explosive Skirmish"* scenarios.

While it is impossible to draw any firm conclusions from this limited sample set, one important feature clearly emerges: the width of the distribution significantly broadens when agents are allowed to maneuver. For the *"Explosive Skirmish"* scenario, a 50% casualty loss may be sustained at times that are both *much smaller* and *much larger* than is typically the case for runs of the *Lanchester* scenario. In particular, note that there is a non-zero probability for the *"Explosive Skirmish"* scenario to take a *very long time* to reach the 50% casualty mark: one event (out of a total 1000 runs) each for $t_{Casualty \geq 50\%} = 88, 91, 96$, and 99, compared to $\left(t_{Casualty \geq 50\%}\right)_{Max} = 78$ for the *Lanchester* scenario. Moreover, since the his-

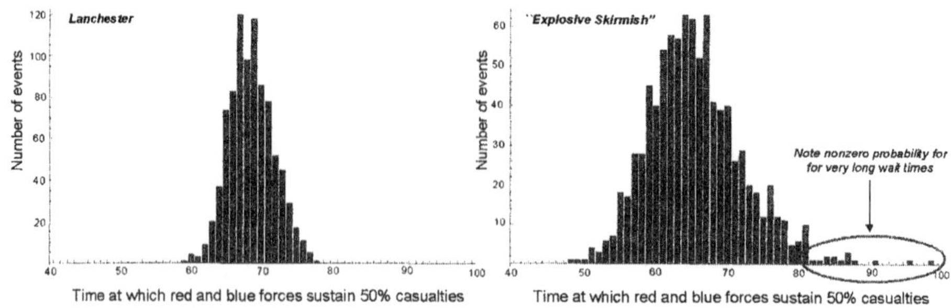

Fig. 6.22 Histograms that result after 1000 runs each of the *Lanchester* and *"Explosive Skirmish"* scenarios; see text for discussion.

togram shows counts recorded only between times 40 and 100, what does not appear in figure 6.22 are two other recorded values of $t_{Casualty \geq 50\%}$ that lie between 100 and 200. Note also, that $\Delta\tau = \left(t_{Casualty \geq 50\%}\right)_{Max} - \left(t_{Casualty \geq 50\%}\right)_{Min}$ only increases as the number of participating agents declines. For example, reducing the number of agents per side to 50 yields a distribution that lies between $\left(t_{Casualty \geq 50\%}\right)_{Min} \sim 80$ and $\left(t_{Casualty \geq 50\%}\right)_{Max} \sim 400$, with an increasing number of runs that never yield 50% casualty loss (up to 500 run-steps).*

The widening of the probability densities of $t_{Casualty \geq 50\%}$, as well as the (sometimes very) long-time "tails" that emerge, insofar as these are both statistical measures of "extreme behaviors," are consequences that are due mainly to the fact that in the *"Explosive Skirmish"* scenario agents continually adapt to their surroundings; a fact which is obviously untrue for the *Lanchester* scenario, in which all agents remain rigidly pinned to their starting positions throughout a run. This means that rather than simply "shooting it out" until one or the other side's entire force is depleted, agents only fight after they have had a chance to maneuver into positions they believe are advantageous to them. As the conditions become unfavorable, agents will once again move away rather then continue fighting.

In some cases, individual agents (or whole squads) may find it necessary to maneuver for extended periods of time before encountering locally favorable combat

*The situation is actually a bit more complicated than suggested by figure 6.22 alone. Lauren [Lauren99], for example, presents evidence that the variance of the distribution, *diverges* as a function of the number of runs used to obtain it. Since an increase in divergence can only come about as a result of the increasing number of "extreme events," this seems to imply that these extreme events may belong to different dynamical states into the system may evolve (see, for example, figure 8 in [Lauren99]); a "state" being defined as the portion of the systems's (generally much larger) attainable phase space within which all various attrition-related statistical measures are all the same. A systematic exploration of whether and/or under what conditions, EINSTein (or any other multiagent-based combat model) evolves into different dynamical states (during runs of a *given* scenario) remains an interesting, and open, problem. It is tempting to speculate, on grounds of similar behavior that has been observed in other complex systems, that a closer examination of plots such as those in figure 6.22, would reveal a Weibull or Lognormal distribution (characterized by "long" tails); see [Weiss02].

conditions. The result, heuristically, is a growing propensity for extreme events, and longer and longer waiting times between milestone events characterizing the flow of battle.

Another way to gain insight into possible temporal correlations is to map a return map of attrition. That is, to examine the probability density function of attrition $A(t+1)$ at time $t+1$, given that the attrition count at t is $A(t)$; see figure 6.23.

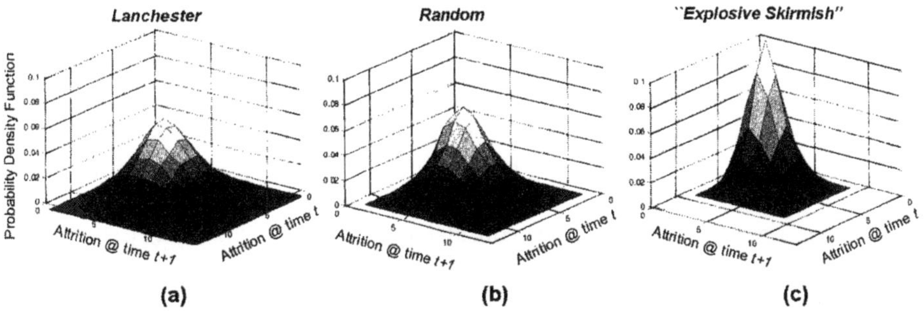

Fig. 6.23 Probability density function for atttrition count at time t+1 as a function of attrition at time t for multiple runs for the same three scenarios used for figures 6.20 and 6.21: (a) *Lanchester* scenario, (b) *Random* scenario, and (c) *Sample-1* of the "Explosive Skirmish" scenario; see text for details. (Figure courtesy of David S. Mazel.)

Figure 6.23 shows two distinct trends as we examine the behavior from left (*Lanchester* scenario; figure 6.23-(a)) to middle (*Random* scenario; figure 6.23-(b)) to right (*"Explosive Skirmish"* scenario; figure 6.23-(c)): first, the relative value of the peaks of the bell-shaped "hills" increases, and, second, the width of the hills decreases.* The figures suggest that when agents are able to maneuver (at least semi-intelligently), temporal correlations are likely to accrue: $A(t+1)$ tends to be a sharper function of attrition at the immediately preceding time step than it is for either when agents move randomly or are stationary. Although it is a bit difficult to see in the figure, it is also true that only in case (c) is there an appreciable probability of having $A(t+1) = 0$.

Intuitively, what happens in case (c) that *does not* happen in either case (a) or (b), is that agents are able to both cluster together to concentrate firepower (and to remain clustered for however many time steps elapse before the agents deem conditions unfavorable for engaging the enemy) and judiciously step away from combat when local skirmishes become too intense (so that attrition abruptly drops to zero as the two forces disengage and maneuver to more favorable positions). The result is a pronounced proclivity for correlated short-term attrition. However, achieving

*The dark toned low-lying patches that end abruptly in figure 6.23-(b) and 6.23-(c), before reaching the edge along the bottom, are rendered in this fashion to highlight the fact that there are no attrition counts to plot beyond those shown.

any deeper insights than this requires more thorough analyses to be made, particularly those that take into account higher-order correlations. Perhaps the most important problem that begs long-term study is to fully understand (and perhaps find universal traits of) the relationship between changing *spatial correlations* (as measured by fractal, information, correlation, and other fractal measures) and *temporal correlations* (as exemplified by correlations in time-series attrition data, but with one eye toward identifying and using other kinds of pertinent combat data).

6.4.5 *Attrition Rate*

Being now armed with at least some sense of the important role that fractals and power-law scalings might play in combat, we now turn to the plausibility argument we had promised earlier to make, that the attrition rate generally depends not just on P_{ss} alone (as is the case for Lanchesterian scenarios), but on both P_{ss} and the *fractal dimension* D_F of the distribution of agents.

Following Lauren [Lauren02], we consider the *mean attrition rate* $\langle \alpha \rangle$—defined as the average number of combatants lost during some specified time interval, $\Delta\tau = t - t_0$: $\langle \alpha \rangle = \langle \Delta n / \Delta\tau \rangle$, where $n(t)$ is the number of agents at time t. Suppose, instead of the block-arrayed and immobile agents that make up the Lanchesterian combat scenario we examined above (see page 439)—and for which we found that $\langle \alpha \rangle$ scales linearly with P_{ss}—we have agents that are *fully maneuverable*; i.e., we have agents that are able to react with a full complement of their personality weight components and μ-rules. Suppose further, that at any time t, their distribution is characterized by a fractal dimension D_F.

Where, in deriving equation 6.1 for Lanchesterian combat, we had naturally assumed that one side's attrition rate is proportional to the opposing side's size (and *nothing else*), we must now assume that the attrition rate must also depend on the probability that an agent actually "sees" an enemy (or cluster of enemy agents, $N_{Cluster}$) in a given period of time. To estimate the likelihood of this happening, we make use of the fact that the expected number of boxes that contain at least one agent has a power-law dependence on the size of the box.

So, where in the Lanchesterian case, $\langle \alpha \rangle$ was, in general, a function $f = f(N, P_{ss})$ of the total number of agents N and single-shot probability of hit, we now write:

$$\langle \alpha \rangle_{Dispersive} = \hat{f} = \hat{f}(\varepsilon^{-2D_F} N_{Cluster}, P_{ss}), \tag{6.5}$$

where we have replaced N by the number of boxes of side ε (which is proportional to ε multiplied by the average number of agents per box, $N_{Cluster}$). We have also added the subscript *"Dispersive"* to $\langle \alpha \rangle$ as a reminder that unlike the Lanchesterian case, in which the attrition rate is averaged over all times of a given run, in general we must be careful to ensure that the averaging is performed over an appropriate ensemble of runs. In particular, for the case being considered here, in estimating the value of $\langle \alpha \rangle$, we must be careful to include only those times during which combat is in a "dispersive-flow" phase.

For the *Sample-1* scenario, this means that the first 25 iterations, which represent a period during which the red and blue agents simply advance forward and do not yet make contact with the enemy, are effectively ignored. We are also using D_F as the fractal dimension of our *entire distribution* of red and blue agents. In general, each side's attrition rate likely depends on two separate fractal dimensions: one that characterizes the spatial distribution of *friendly forces* (which would therefore be some function of how agents use this local information to *maneuver*), and another that characterizes the spatial distribution of *enemy forces* (and which therefore contains information germane to the local adjudication of combat).

Observe that the *size* of the boxes used to cover the battlefield can also be related to *time*. An agent, as it maneuvers around the battlefield, traces out an area whose extent depends on how fast the agent is moving. The probability that an agent encounters a box that contains a cluster of enemy agents thus also depends on the agent's speed, and, thus, on t. Substituting t for ε, we can therefore also write $\langle\alpha\rangle_{Dispersive} = \hat{f}(t^{-2D_F} N_{Cluster}, P_{ss})$.

While we do not know the exact form of $\hat{f}$, of course, we can guess that:

$$\langle\alpha\rangle_{Dispersive} \sim t^{-2D_F} N_{Cluster} \cdot P_{ss}^{1-2D_F}, \tag{6.6}$$

since P_{ss} has dimensions of time and we must have a dimensionless product. Recalling that $\langle\alpha\rangle = \langle\Delta n/\Delta\tau\rangle$, we arrive at the following intriguing prediction that Lauren provocatively suggests may be the "new Lanchester equation" of the complex dynamics of combat [Lauren99]:*

$$\langle n(t_0 + t) - n(t_0)\rangle_{Dispersive} \propto t^{1-2D_F} \cdot N_{Cluster} \cdot (P_{ss})^{1-2D_F}.$$

Obviously, from a tactical point of view, a nonlinear dependence of attrition rate on P_{ss} entails rather significant consequences. If the multiagent-based model more accurately represents real combat processes than models based on some variant of the Lanchester equations, and $D_F \lesssim 1/2$, this implies that a relatively "weak" force, with a small kill probability, may actually constitute a much more potent force than a simple Lanchester-based approach suggests. The potency of the force comes from its ability to maneuver (which is never explicitly modeled by Lanchester-based approaches) and to selectively concentrate firepower on the enemy while maneuvering. This deceptively simple result has an important consequence for peacekeeping ac-

*Lauren [Lauren99] focuses on the transitional region between *laminar*-like and *turbulent*-like behaviors, and relies heavily on a suggestive analogy between this transition in EINSTein and the onset of turbulence in real fluids. Lauren observes that there are two critical factors that determine behavior: (1) *force gradients* in which agents attempt to reduce local imbalances in relative force strengths, and (2) *friction* (or *viscosity*), as measured by the degree to which agents cluster. The analogy naturally leads Lauren to speculate about the existence of some dimensionless *Reynold's Number*, that, just as it does for real fluid flow, regulates the onset of turbulent, or fractal, behavior in EINSTein (or any other multiagent-based model that includes intelligent maneuvering).

tivities in the Third World, where a strong, modern force may (and often, does) significantly underestimate the ability of ostensibly poorly trained and/or poorly armed militia to inflict damage.

The appearance of fractal power-law scalings in EINSTein (as well as in a growing number of other multiagent-based combat models) is particularly interesting in light of the fact that it has been observed before in real combat. This has been reported by Richardson [RichLF60], Dockery and Woodcock [Dock93a], and Roberts and Turcotte [Roberts88]. In particular, Dockery and Woodcock show that the number of battles that took place on the Western front during WWII in Normandy in which the number of battles for which the number of casualties ($N_{Casualties>C^*}$) exceeded some threshold value C^*, obeys a power-law distribution as a function of C^* (see figure 6.24):

$$N_{Casualties>C^*} \propto (C^*)^{-D}, \tag{6.7}$$

where $D \sim 1$ [Dock93b].

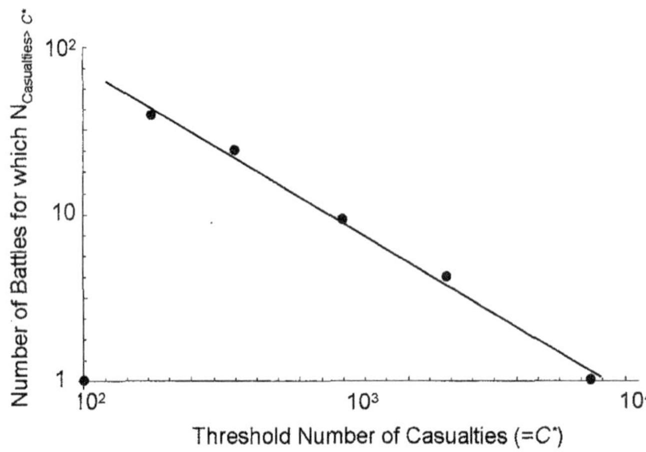

Fig. 6.24 Analysis of WWII casualty data on the western front after Normandy (after Dockery and Woodcock, [Dock93b]).

While it may be argued, intuitively, that this can only be due to the dynamic coupling between *local information processing* and *maneuver*—features that are completely ignored by Lanchesterian models—it is also true that no rigorous (or even generative) "explanation" for why fractal power-law scaling holds true in combat has heretofore existed. It is tempting to speculate that there are phases of real combat that are poised at *self organized critical* (SOC) states ([Bak96], [Jensen98], [Meisel96] and [Roberts88]).*

*See discussion on *self-organized criticality* in section 2.2.8, page 149.

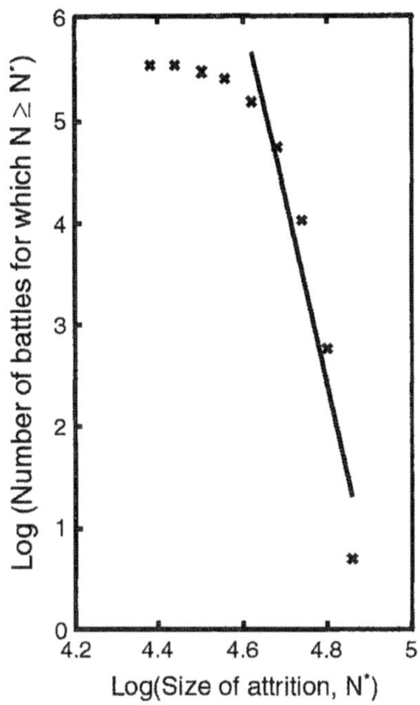

Fig. 6.25 A plot of the *log* of the number of battles for which the total attrition (N) exceeds a threshold attrition number (N^*) versus the *log* of the threshold attrition. Data consists of 250 runs of the *Sample-1* "Explosive Skirmish" scenario, defined in table 6.3. The straight-line fit is extended only over the range of N^* for which the relationship appears to be approximately linear. (Plot courtesy of David S. Mazel.)

Of course, tentative steps toward demonstrating SOC in combat have already been made, in efforts led principally by the pioneering work of Lauren (see [Lauren99]-[Lauren02]). Considering the *"Explosive Skirmish"* scenario that has been at the heart of our prolonged discussion in this section, we see that even a limited sample size of 250 runs is enough to hint at a regime of SOC-like linearity in a plot of the *log* of the number of battles for which the total attrition (N) exceeds a threshold attrition number (N^*) versus the *log* of the threshold attrition (shown in figure 6.25), although one needs to use a considerably larger sample size (along with scenarios that allow for a greater range of total attrition) to make a more definitive claim.

The fundamental problems of ascertaining the precise set of conditions under which SOC-like behavior either *does* or *does not* appear in EINSTein (or any other multiagent-based model that includes intelligent maneuver), and—even more ambitiously—of establishing a well-defined mathematical relationship between SOC-like power-law scalings and the set of primitive characteristics and rules of behavior that govern the actions of individual agents in a model, remain open. Perhaps some dedicated reader of this book will discover a heretofore undiscovered law that links the *micro* with the *macro*.

6.5 Case Study 4: Squad vs. Squad

The *Center for Naval Analyses'* recently completed *Ground Combat Study* (GCS) [TaylorD00] used EINSTein as an experimental test-bed to analyze the "optimal" size and organization of small squad (and fire team) units by exploring their associated dynamic phase space in a series of notionally recreated combat scenarios.

6.5.1 *Background*

Historically, the *United States Marine Corps* (USMC) squad-size has remained relatively stable at 13, with three homogeneous fire teams.* On the other hand, the Army squad has undergone a number of changes in both size or organization. The changes in military technology introduced immediately prior to WWI had a dramatic impact on how squads evolved, while trench warfare during WWI played a key role in why squads evolved. Toward the end of WWI, the Army used an 8-man squad with no fire teams. While American squads consisted, for a time, of 16-man sections (a size that was influenced heavily by small unit tactics developed by the French Army), between WWI and WWII the Army reorganized their squads to include three heterogeneous teams, totaling 12 men: a two-man scout team, a four-man rifle team, and a five-man maneuver and assault team. Following WWII, squad size was reduced 9 men, with no fire teams. During Korea, fire teams were again required and the size of the squad increased. Finally, in the early 80s, the Army again reduced the size of its squads to 9 men.

The USMCs experience in "small wars" in such places as Nicaragua and Shanghai in the early part of the 20th century spawned a different philosophy behind squad composition (a difference than was only fueled during WWII, during which the USMC's experience of fighting in jungle environments and general island warfare, was markedly different from the Army's). The USMC considered the automatic rifle as the central base of fire. Before WWII, a typical USMC infantry platoon consisted of a seven-man headquarters, an eight-man rifle squad, and three nine-man rifle squads. As WWII broke out, the USMC adapted its platoon and squad compositions for jungle and island fighting. The rifle squad was increased in size to 12 men, and was now composed of a squad leader, an assistant squad leader, six riflemen (with two assistants), and two automatic-rifle-men. The rifle squad was thus broken down into two six-man fire teams, each containing an automatic rifle and five semi-automatic rifles.

Taylor, *et.al.*, conclude their historical survey by listing what they found to be the four critical drivers of squad size and organization [TaylorD00]: (1) *Firepower*, which is a rough gauge of the degree of a squad's "suppression potential," as a

*By *homogeneous* fire teams we mean fire teams that have the same composition. For example, two *riflemen*, one *machine gunner*, and one *grenadier*. As a reference, a 13 man US *Marine Corps* infantry squad is composed of three fire teams (as defined above) and one squad leader.

function of the numbers and types of weapon systems carried by the squad; (2) *Resiliency*, which is the squad's ability to sustain losses without losing its identity and cohesion; (3) *Maneuverability* (or *Control*), which refers to a squad leader's ability to adaptively and dynamically control his squad's movement; and (4) *Mobility* (not to be confused with maneuverability), which measures a squad's physical ability to move towards its mission objective, particularly when under fire. While maneuverability is more a function of the squad leader's communication skills, mobility is more a function of the innate abilities of the entire squad.

6.5.2 *Scenario Definition*

Consider a simple scenario in which *one red squad* and *one blue squad*—with pairwise equal behavioral characteristics—engage in combat. We fix the blue squad size at 11, and probe the dynamic effects of having this squad engage, in succession, *equal-*, *smaller-* and *larger*-sized red squads (see Table 6.4).

Parameter	**Red**	**Blue**
Agents	13,11,9	11
r_S	25	25
r_F	25	25
r_M	1	1
ω_1	2	2
ω_2	10	10
ω_3	2	2
ω_4	10	10
ω_5	0	0
ω_6	10	10
$\tau_{Advance}$	8	8
$\tau_{Retreat}$	6	6

Table 6.4 Some parameter values for *squad-vs-squad* case study; see text for details.

This basic step is an important one to take at the outset, if for no other reason than it can be used to assure the analyst conducting the formal study that EINSTein's output generates intuitively expected results for known test cases.

For example, it is reasonable to expect that if we keep the values of all parameters *other than squad size* fixed, larger squads ought to perform better than smaller squads. "Performing better," of course, is ill-defined, as it may mean suffering fewer casualties, being able to maneuver closer to the enemy flag, killing more enemy agents, or any number of similarly obvious "missions."

Color plate 13 (page 259) provides some basic statistics derived from multiple time-series runs for scenarios in which the respective (red/blue) squad sizes are (9/11), (11/11) and (13/11). The plots on the left-hand-side of the figure show the average number of remaining red and blue agents as a function of time 't' (a number that includes all alive and all injured agents at given 't'). Plots on the right-hand-side of color plate 13 show the average distance between the center-of-mass of the red squad relative to the position of the blue flag as a function of time 't.' The blue flag is located at battlefield site $(80, 80)$. In each case, individual statistics are averaged over 100 sample runs.

The figure shows that—at least with respect to these two simple measures of mission success—the emergent behavior is intuitive: equal forces perform equally well, on average, and collisions between unequal forces typically favor the larger-sized squad (larger squads reduce total attrition and are better able to penetrate enemy territory).

Color plate 14 (page 260) shows 3D fitness landscapes for two mission objective functions: (1) *maximize red-to-blue survival ratio*, and (2) *maximize number of red forces near blue flag* (where "near" is defined as anywhere within 10 battlefield-units). Both plots sweep over *red squad size* $(5, 6, ..., 20)$ and *red sensor range* $(10, 11, ..., 25)$. The two density plots appearing at the bottom of the figure represent top-down projections of the 3D graphs. The circles identify the position at which the corresponding red squad size and sensor range matches that of the blue agents (which remains fixed throughout all runs).

The figure shows several interesting behaviors:

(1) If red's mission objective is to maneuver as many agents near the blue flag as possible (while suffering zero casualties), the red force is able to do this only when the squad size is very large (~ 20); it will be unable to do this for any squad size less than 20 if the sensor range falls to even a few units below blue's.

(2) Relative to red's ability to perform its mission for parameter values that match blue's (i.e. near the colored circles), having even a minor disadvantage in squad size leads to a significant decline in red's ability to perform its mission. Interestingly, the decline appears to become more gradual as the sensor range decreases.

(3) There are clearly defined combinations of squad-size and sensor range for which red *fails completely*.

6.5.3 *Weapon Scaling*

An issue that becomes prominent only when attempting to explicitly model "realistic" behavior within EINSTein—which, remember, contains only purely *notional* representations of real agents and their behavioral characteristics—is how to properly scale weapon characteristics and effects. In EINSTein (versions 1.0 and older), a machine gun can crudely be represented either by a high value of the single-shot probability of hit parameter, p_{ss} (see page 313), or as an agent (that is assigned this same notional machine gun) that can simultaneously shoot, say, *ten* other agents during each combat phase, with $p'_{ss} \sim p_{ss}/10$ at some long range. But what are the appropriate values to use for p_{ss} and fire range of a weapon, if the objective is to use EINSTein to model more realistic scenarios?

EINSTein has maximum and minimum limits for most of the spatially dependent variables. For example, the maximum battlefield size is 150 units and the minimum box size is 1 unit, which gives a maximum of 150^2 total units to cover the battlespace. All other ranges, such as movement range, sensor range, communication ranges, and point-to-point and area weapon ranges must all fall within these limits. Now, consider some realistic weapon parameters: (1) a point-to-point weapons range of 1000 meters for the machine gun, (2) 550 meter range for a rifle, and (3) 350 meter range for a launched grenade with a burst radius of approximately 10 meters.

Following the discussion in [TaylorD00], and using the maximum battlefield size of 150, we obtain some fundamental scaling ratios to use in designing their counterparts in EINSTein:

$$\begin{array}{c} \textit{Machine gun: } 150/1000 = 0.15; \\ \textit{Rifle: } 150/550 = 0.27; \\ \textit{Grenade: } 150/350 = 0.43. \end{array}$$

We can now scale our weapons parameters for use in scenarios using the maximum battlefield size by taking the smallest number (0.15) for our scaling parameter and dividing all the ranges. This leaves us with a set of battlefield-scaled weapons parameters $\{R\}$ defined by:

$$\{R\} = \left\{ \begin{array}{c} r_{\text{machine gun}} \\ r_{\text{rifle}} \\ r_{\text{grenade}} \\ r_{\text{burst}} \end{array} \right\} = \left\{ \begin{array}{c} 150 \\ 83 \\ 53 \\ 1.5 \end{array} \right\}.$$

One additional problem arises once the battlefield and weapons ranges are scaled. We have just defined the scaled blast radius of a launched grenade at 10 meters as effectively a single unit on the battlefield. An obvious issue that must immediately be dealt with is finding a proper associated scaling of other pertinent ranges such as movement, sensor, and communication ranges. EINSTein nominally handles these ranges on the assumption of a ladder-like organization of scale sizes:

$$\left\{ \begin{array}{c} \textit{movement range} \\ \textit{sensor range} \\ \textit{communication range} \\ \textit{fire range} \\ \textit{battlefield size} \end{array} \right\} = \left\{ \begin{array}{c} 1 \\ 10 \\ 10 - 10^2 \\ 10^2 - 10^3 \\ \gg 1 \end{array} \right\}.$$

Thus, for a scaled battlespace there may be large discrepancies among the relative values of the weapons range, the movement range, and to a lesser degree the sensor range. Without further modification, EINSTein would have agents move one to three orders of magnitude faster than they could in the real world. On the scaled battlefield, each *step* during the movement phase occurs over 10 meters and occurs as quickly as an agent is able to shoot. Assuming that a rifle can be fired every couple of seconds, then the agent that moves each time the rifle is fired must also be advancing at about 10 meters every 2 seconds (or about 10 miles per hour).

To solve this problem, EINSTein has an option to *slow down* the agents, by including a time delay so that the agents are allowed to move only after a certain number of time steps have elapsed since their last move. In this way, agents may be slowed down sufficiently so that their speed effectively matches the "real" rates of advance and also properly scales with the other battlespace parameters.

6.5.4 *3:1 Force Ratio Rule-of-Thumb*

With an eye towards exploring non-Lanchesterian scenarios (examples are provided below), consider an example that includes both simple *maneuver* and *terrain*. Figure 6.26 shows the initial state, consisting of 12 red and 12 blue agents positioned near their respective "flags" (in the lower left and upper right corners, respectively).

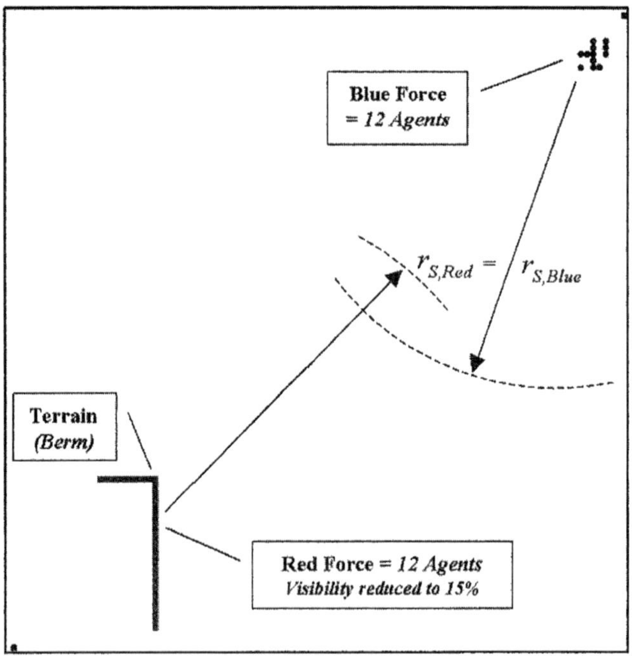

Fig. 6.26 Initial state for a simple non-Lanchesterian scenario; see text for details.

The red agents are arrayed along a berm (i.e. a permeable terrain element, which appears green in the figure), whose dynamic effect is reduce their visibility to the approaching blue enemy agents to 15% of the nominal value. As blue agents approach the red flag, red agents remain fixed at their positions (simulating a notional "hunkered-down" condition). The red and blue weapon characteristics (probability of hit and range) are equal.

Runs typically proceed as follows. Because of the stealth afforded the dug-in red agents by their berm, red agents are targeted and engaged with a much lower probability than the approaching blue force. The attrition of the attacking force (blue) is significantly higher than the attrition of the defending force (red). When the attackers are able to survive (with some of their force intact)—on some particular run of the scenario—it is because they are able to maneuver out of range (which occurs when the force strength drops below the combat effective threshold of 50% and attempts to withdraw) and red is unable to pursue. (As an aside, EINSTein's ability to prescribe retreat conditions adds a certain realism to the model. Faced with mounting attrition, real squads fall back and regroup.)

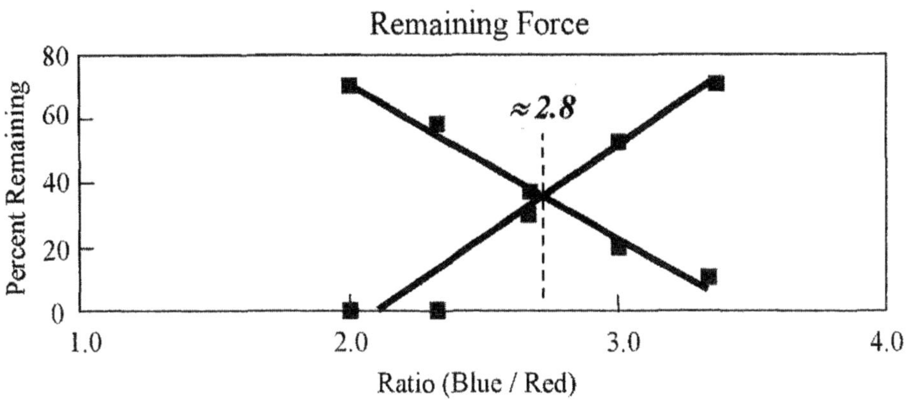

Fig. 6.27 Impact of attacker-to-defender force ratio on survival for the simple non-Lanchesterian scenario shown in the previous figure. The red (light grey) and blue (dark grey) survival curves merge at about a 2.8 to 1 ratio, which compares favorably to the well-known "rule of thumb" that attackers require a 3:1 force ratio against a defended position [TaylorD00].

The red force usually remains at full strength after the engagement (the probability of zero red casualties is about 80%). This result is intuitively satisfying, since, historically (all other factors being equal), defending forces have the advantage over an attacking force traversing open ground. An obvious question to ask, is "How large a blue force is required to overcome the advantage of the red's terrain?" Figure 6.27 plots the fraction of the initial forces that remain at the end of the engagement (150 steps) versus the attacker-to-defender force-size ratio (the lines are simple fits to the data to guide the eye).

In the runs used to generate this graph, the size of the blue force ranges from 12 to 40 agents, while the red force remains at 12. Note that the red and blue survival curves merge at roughly a 2.8:1 ratio; which is interesting in that it appears to reproduce a well-known "rule of thumb" that attackers require a 3:1 force ratio in order to successfully mount an offense against a defended position [TaylorD00].

6.6 Case Study 5: Attack

Consider a simple attack scenario that probes red's offensive capability as a function of *force size*, *combat aggressiveness* and *communications*:

Table 6.5 shows red and blue parameter values for the default scenario. The blue force consists of 50 randomly maneuvering agents that attack all intruding enemy agents within their fire range. Blue's sensor range is nominally twice that of red's and blue agents are generally very aggressive in combat.

Parameter	Red	Blue
Agents	20	50
r_S	5	10
r_F	3	7
r_M	2	2
ω_1	10	0 (10 if injured)
ω_2	40	99
ω_3	10	0 (10 if injured)
ω_4	40	99
ω_5	0	0
ω_6	25	25
$\tau_{Advance}$	3	N/A
$\tau_{Cluster}$	3	5 (if injured)
Δ_{Combat}	0	-20
Comms	no, yes ($r_{Comm} = 7, 15$)	no

Table 6.5 Default parameter values for *attack* case study; see text for details.

Color plate 15 (page 261) shows snapshots of typical run using these values for three cases: (1) default red and blue parameter values, with communications off for both sides, (2) same as (1) but with red agents able to communicate using $r_{Comm} = 7$ and $\omega_{Comm} = 0.2$, and (3) same as (2) but with $r_{Comm} = 15$.

Figure 6.28 shows time-series plots of the distance between the center-of-mass of red forces from the blue flag (located in the top right corner of the battlefield) and the number of red agents that are located within a distance $D = 5$ of the blue flag at time t). Each of these measures is plotted for cases 1 (no comms) and 3 (red comms with $r_{Comm} = 15$) and are averaged over 100 samples.

As might be expected, on intuitive grounds, we see that red's capacity to maneuver toward the blue flag (as measured by the center-of-mass plot) and/or penetrate the blue defense (as measured by the goal-count plot) is significantly enhanced when

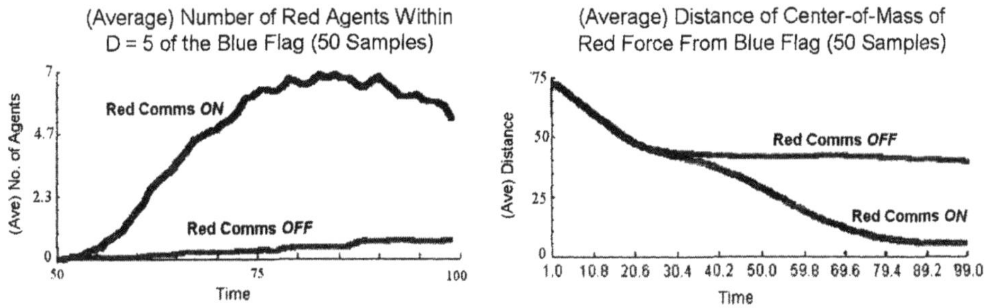

Fig. 6.28 Timeseries plots for the (*red*) *attack* scenario discussed in the text.

red agents are able to communicate with other red agents; though the middle series of snapshots in color plate 15 suggest that some threshold communications range is needed.

We can explore the dependence of red's ability to penetrate blue's defense by looking at "slices" through its fitness landscape. For example, consider the mission objective function $0 \leq f(x,y) \leq 1$ that attains its maximum value in the event that all red agents get to within ten units of the blue flag within a specified elapsed time (50 steps).

Figure 6.29 shows a three-dimensional plot of the fitness f as a function of (x,y), averaged over 50 initial states. The number of red agents ($= N_{red}$) is the x-coordinate of the two-dimensional "slice" (that ranges from 5 to 35) and the combat aggressiveness ($= \Delta_{Combat}$) as the y-coordinate (that ranges from -20 to $+20$).

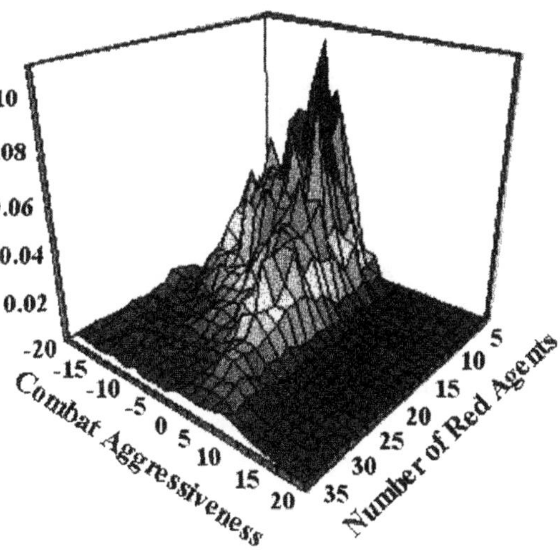

Fig. 6.29 *Attack* scenario fitness landscape for mission = *maximize number of red agents near blue flag*; see text for details.

Figure 6.29 shows that the red's ability to perform its mission is close to zero unless the red force is relatively small ($N_{red} < 20$) and the agents are fairly aggressive ($\Delta_{Combat} < 0$). Maximum mission fitness is achieved near $N_{red} \sim 10$ and $\Delta_{Combat} \sim -10$.

What happens when red agents can communicate with other red agents? Figure 6.30 shows the benefit of adding a communications capability to the red force. A region of relatively low fitness for a non-communicating medium-sized force ($N_{red} \sim 20$) can be increased to almost match that of the previous fitness maximum by allowing red force agents to communicate.

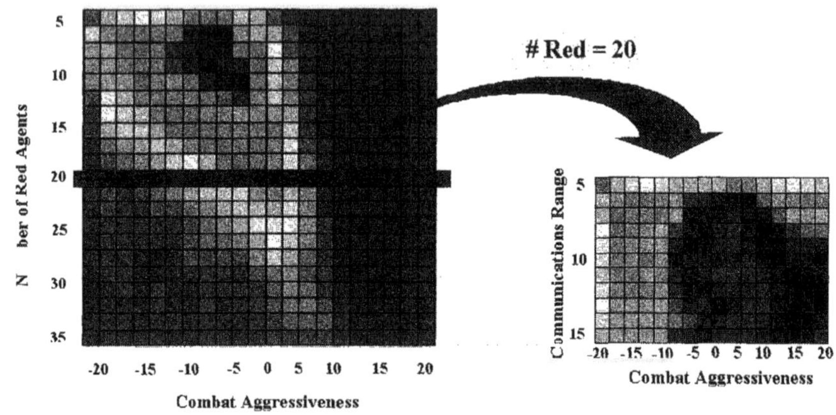

Fig. 6.30 Effect of adding *communications* to the red force in the *attack* scenario discussed in the text..

In this simple example, the dynamics are easy to understand. A force that is too large and/or too timid (i.e. with a large, positive Δ_{Combat}) will tend to disperse more and thus be less successful in seizing the blue flag. In addition, communicating agents lead to a tighter red formation that can more easily defend itself as it maneuvers toward the enemy flag. For more complex scenarios, where the number (and kinds) of local decisions that are made by each agent may be very involved, mission-fitness landscapes such as the one shown in figure 6.30 are indispensable for gaining useful insights into how all of the different parameters "fit together" to shape the overall flow of battle.

Of course, there are other possible measures of "mission success," not all of which yield "intuitively obvious" results. Figure 6.31 shows density plots for two additional mission objectives, using the same two-dimensional range of values as for the landscape appearing in figure 6.30. The red objective used to generate the left landscape is to *maximize enemy casualties*; the objective for the right landscape is to *minimize the distance between the red center-of-mass and the blue flag*. The communications option is off for both cases.

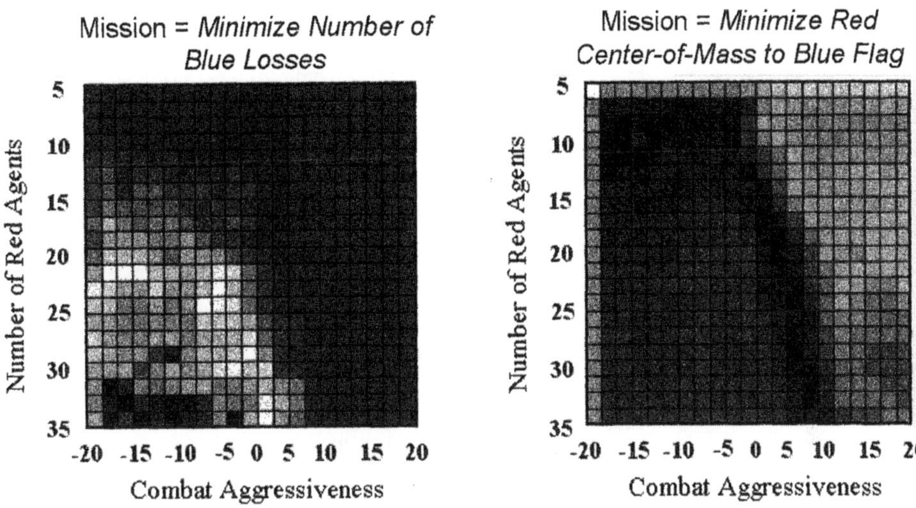

Fig. 6.31 Density plots of *attack* scenario fitness landscapes; mission #1 (left-hand-side plot) = *minimize number of blue losses*, mission #2 (right-hand-side of plot) = *minimize red center-of-mass to blue flag*.

Notice that while the "optimal" combination of red force size and combat aggressiveness is ($N_{red} \sim 10$, $\Delta_{Combat} \sim -5$) for the mission = maximize number of red agents near blue flag, it shifts to (i) ($N_{red} > 35$, $\Delta_{Combat} \sim -12$) for the mission = maximize blue losses, and (ii) ($N_{red} \sim 30$, $\Delta_{Combat} \sim -5$) for the mission = minimize red center-of-mass to blue flag. This simple example underscores the subjective nature of assigning a numerical measure of "success" to how a mission actually unfolds in time.

6.7 Case Study 6: Defense

Consider a scenario that probes red's defensive capability as a function of force size, sensor range, combat aggressiveness and comms.

Table 6.6 shows the default red and blue parameter values used throughout the runs. The blue force consists of 50 attacking agents. Red agents defends the area near their own flag (in the lower left corner of the battlefield) by attacking all intruding enemy agents within their fire range with equal weight, and are generally more aggressive in combat.

Figure 6.32 shows snapshots of the first few time steps of a typical run using these values.

As a measure of red's ability to defend its flag area, consider the mission objective function, f, that attains its maximum value in the event that the red agents prevent all blue agents from maneuvering within 10 units of the red flag within a specified

Parameter	Red	Blue
Agents	50	50
r_S	5	3
r_F	3	2
r_M	1	1
ω_1	0	10
ω_2	50	40
ω_3	0	10
ω_4	50	40
ω_5	0	0
ω_6	0	50
$\tau_{Advance}$	N/A	3
$\tau_{Cluster}$	8	3
Δ_{Combat}	-5	0

Table 6.6 Default parameter values for *defense* case study; see text for details.

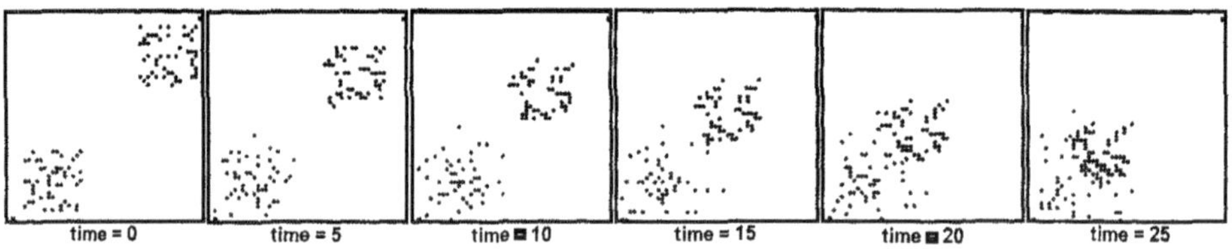

Fig. 6.32 Screenshots from a run using the default *red defense* scenario parameters from Table 6.6.

elapsed time (50 steps).

Figure 6.33 shows three-dimensional plots of f as a function of red *sensor range* ($= r_S$)—that ranges from 1 to 11—and red's *combat aggressiveness* ($= \Delta_{Combat}$)—that ranges from -15 to $+15$. The plot on the left is for the case where communications are turned off; the plot on the right is for the case where communications are on ($r_{Comms} = 15$, $\omega_{Comms} = 0.25$).

We see that, from red's perspective, it is better to be equipped with a relatively short sensor range—one that permits rapid-fire, instinct-like, reactions to encroaching blue agents—than with a long-range sensor that needlessly dilutes agents' "attention." Figure 6.33 also shows that, at least with respect to r_S and Δ_{Combat}, the red force's ability to keep blue out of its flag area is not a strong function of having its agents able to communicate with one another.

One reason why communications do not appear to make an impact—which may not be clear at first—is suggested by figure 6.34. Figure 6.34 shows landscapes for the same fitness measure as in figure 6.33 but instead sweeps over $\Delta_{Combat}$and the red force size ($= N_{red} = 5, 6, ..., 80$). Here we see that communications significantly

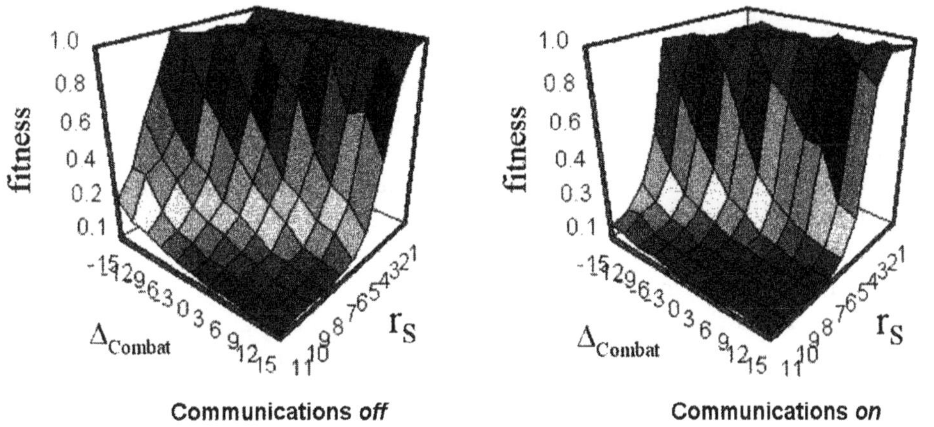

Fig. 6.33 Red defense scenario fitness landscapes (for mission = *minimize number of blue forces near red flag*) for $(x, y) = (\Delta_{Combat}, r_S)$; communications are switched *off* in left-hand-side plot, and switched *on* for the right-hand-side plot; see text for details.

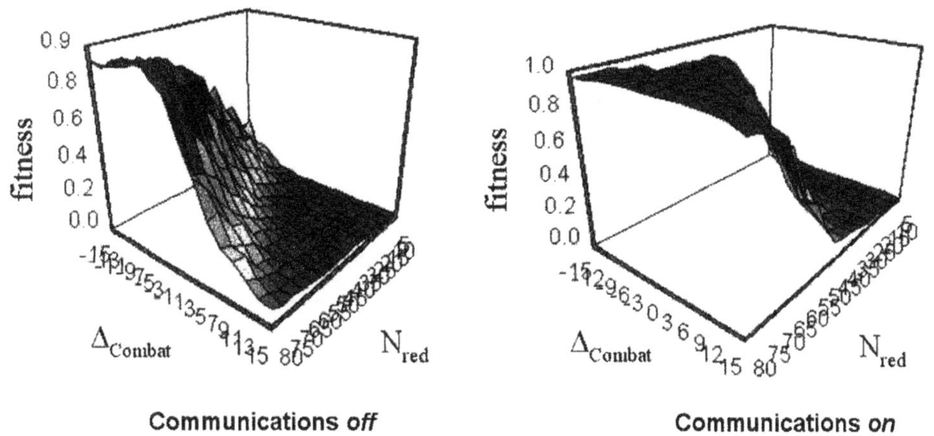

Fig. 6.34 Red defense scenario fitness landscapes (for mission = *minimize number of blue forces near red flag*) for $(x, y) = (\Delta_{Combat}, N_{red})$; communications are switched *off* in left-hand-side plot, and switched *on* for the right-hand-side plot; see text for details.

enhances the ability of the red force to perform its mission only when the red force is large enough to allow agents to take advantage of, and respond to, the information that is communicated to them.

6.8 Case Study 7: Swarms

One of the first detailed studies of swarming, as a major theme in military history, was recently conducted by Sean Edwards, as part of the *Swarming and the Future of Conflict* project at RAND [Edwards00].* Edwards' report focuses on ten carefully selected historical examples of swarming, includes a series of important lessons-learned distilled from these examples about the advantages and disadvantages of swarming, and provides some examples of successful countermeasures that have been used against swarming in the past.

Edwards notes that swarming consists of four overlapping stages: (1) *location*, (2) *convergence*, (3) *attack*, and (4) *dispersion*. Moreover, swarming forces must be capable of a sustainable *pulsing*; i.e. networks of swarming agents must be able to come together rapidly and stealthily on a target, then redisperse and finally to recombine for a new pulse:

> The swarm concept is built on the principles of complexity theory, and it assumes that blue units have to operate autonomously and adaptively according to the overall mission statement....It is important that swarm units converge and attack simultaneously. Each individual swarm unit is vulnerable on its own, but if it is united in a concerted effort with other friendly units, overall lethality can be multiplied, because the phenomenon of the swarm effect is greater than the sum of its parts. Individual units or incompletely assembled groups are vulnerable to defeat in detail against the larger enemy force with its superior fire-power and mass.

The report notes that swarming scenarios have already played a role in certain high-level wargaming exercises, such as at the *Dominating Maneuver Game*, held at the U.S. Army War College in 1997. Edwards concludes his survey by speculating about the feasibility of a future "swarming doctrine," that would consist of small, distributed, highly maneuverable units converging rapidly on specific targets:

> The concept relies on a highly complex, artificial intelligence (AI)-assisted, theater-wide C4ISR architecture to coordinate fire support, information, and logistics. Swarm tactical maneuver units use precise, organic fire, information operations, and indirect strikes to cause enemy loss of cohesion and destruction. Swarming blue units operate among red units, striking exposed flanks and critical command and control (C2), combat support (CS), and combat service support (CSS) nodes in such a way that the enemy must constantly turn to multiple new threats emerging from constantly changing axes.

Because of its decentralized rule-base and rich space of behavioral primitives, EINSTein is an ideal testbed with which to explore the nature of battlefield swarm-

*See also the proceedings of a recent conference on swarming on the battlefield [Inbody03].

ing and the efficacy of swarm-like tactics. It has already been noted that *Class-6* behavior in EINSTein consists of self-organized "swarms" of attacking or defending agents.

	Scenario I		Scenario II		Scenario III		Scenario IV	
Parameter	**Red**	**Blue**	**Red**	**Blue**	**Red**	**Blue**	**Red**	**Blue**
Agents	150	225	90	125	25	100	200	200
r_S	5	5	5	10	3	7	5	5
r_F	3	3	3	7	2	5	3	3
r_M	1	1	1	2	1	1	2	2
ω_1	25	10	10	0	5	0	10	10
ω_2	25	50	40	99	40	50	40	40
ω_3	75	0	10	0	5	0	10	10
ω_4	25	99	40	99	90	50	40	40
ω_5	0	0	0	0	0	0	0	0
ω_6	75	25	50	0	0	0	50	50
$\tau_{Advance}$	5	1	3	0	3	1	2	2
$\tau_{Cluster}$	15	3	3	12	5	5	8	3
Δ_{Combat}	5	-7	0	-15	-5	-10	-2	-3
Comms	no	no	no	yes	no	yes	no	no
r_{Comm}	0	0	0	25	0	35	0	0

Table 6.7 Default parameter values for *swarms* case study; see text for details.

Typically, but not always, one side appears to swarm the other when there is a significant mismatch in firepower, total force strength and/or maneuvering ability. While it is common to find swarm-like behavior for personalities that include large *Cluster* μ-rule thresholds, $\tau_{Cluster}$ (which increases the likelihood that agents will remain in close proximity to friendly agents), the most interesting "self-organized" examples of swarming are those for which $\tau_{Cluster}$ is, at most, a few agents.

Table 6.7 lists some of the parameter values defining three representative swarm scenarios (I-IV). In scenario I, blue *attacks* red in swarm-like fashion; in scenario-II, blue *defends.* Blue agents are more aggressive than red in both scenarios (as defined by the values of their respective combat μ-rule thresholds, Δ_{Combat}), and, in scenario II, defending blue agents are able to communicate with other blue agents.

Color plates 16 and 17 (pages 262 and 263) show snapshots of typical runs using parameters for scenarios I -IV, respectively.

6.9 Case Study 8: Non-Monotonicity

For a fixed set of force characteristics, number, type and lethality of weapon systems, and tactics, one might intuitively expect that as one side's capability is unilaterally enhanced—say, by increasing sensor range or its ability to maneuver—the other side's ability to perform its mission ought to commensurately diminish. In other words, our expectations are that mission success scales monotonically with force capability.

In fact, *non*-monotonicities abound in both real-world behavior and simulations. With respect to models and simulations, of course, one must always be on guard against the possibility that the non-monotonic scalings are artifacts of the code and therefore do not represent any real processes. As pointed out by a RAND study that addressed this issue [Dewar91], "a combat model with a single decision based on the state of the battle...can produce non-monotonic behavior in the outcomes of the model and chaotic behavior in its underlying dynamics."

Figure 6.35 shows an instructive example of genuinely non-monotonic behavior (i.e. where the non-monotonicity emerges directly out of the primitive rule set). The three rows contain snapshots of three separate runs in which red's sensor range is systematically increased in increments of two: $r_{S,red} = 5$ for the top sequence; $r_{S,red} = 7$ for the middle sequence; $r_{S,red} = 9$ for the bottom sequence. Blue's sensor range, $r_{S,blue}$, remains fixed at $r_{S,blue} = 5$ throughout all three runs. The values of other pertinent red and blue agent parameters are given in Table 6.8.

Parameter	Red	Blue
Agents	100	50
r_S	5,7,9	5
r_F	4	3
r_M	1	1
ω_1	10	10
ω_2	90	90
ω_3	10	10
ω_4	50	50
ω_5	0	0
ω_6	99	99
$\tau_{Advance}$	2	2
$\tau_{Cluster}$	4	4
Δ_{Combat}	-4	-4

Table 6.8 Default parameter values for *non-monotinicity* example; see text for details.

In each of the runs, there are 100 red and 50 blue agents. Red is also the more the aggressive force: blue will engage red in combat if the number of friendly and enemy agents is locally about even, while red will fight even if outnumbered by four enemy combatants. Both sides have the same fire range ($r_F = 4$), the same single-shot probability ($p = 0.005$) and can simultaneously engage the same maximum of three enemy targets. Note that the flags for this sample run are located near the middle of the left and right edges of the notional battlefield.

The top row of figure 6.35 shows screenshots for when red's sensor range is equal to blue's. Here the red force pushes its way through the blue defenses into blue's flag. As red advances toward blue's flag, a number of agents are "stripped" away from the central red-flag:blue-flag axis as they respond to the presence of nearby blue agents. The snapshots for the middle row of figure 6.35 show that when red's sensor range is two units greater than blue's, red is not only able to mass almost all of its forces on the blue flag (a later snapshot would reveal blue's flag completely enveloped by red forces by time $t = 100$), but to defend its own flag from all blue forces as well. In this instance, the red force knows enough about, and can respond quickly enough to enemy action such that it is able to march into enemy territory effectively unhindered by enemy forces and "scoop up" blue agents as they are encountered.

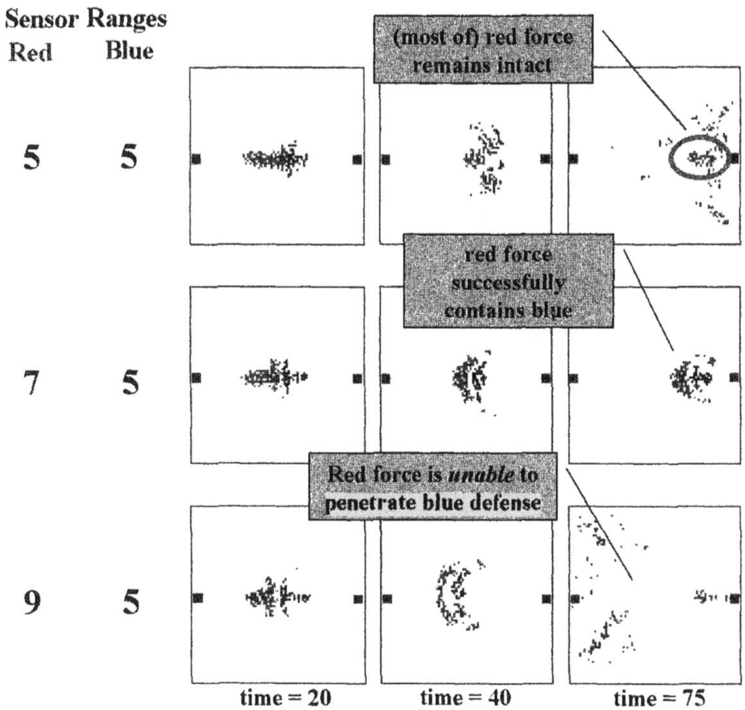

Fig. 6.35 An example of non-monotonic behavior. The three rows contain snapshots of three separate runs in which red's sensor range is increased in increments of two (from rS,red=5 on the top row to rS,red=9 on the bottom). Blue's sensor range is fixed throughout. Comparing the bottom row to the top two rows, we see that increasing red's sensor range appears to have a detrimental effect on red's overall ability to penetrate blue's defense. Parameter values for this scenario are given in table 6.8.

What happens when red's sensor range is increased still further? One might intuitively guess that red can only do at least as well; certainly no worse. However, as the snapshots for bottom row of figure 6.35 reveal, when red's sensor range is increased to $r_{S,red} = 9$, red does objectively worse than it did in any of the preceding runs. "Worse" here means that red is less effective in (a) establishing a presence near the blue flag, and (b) defending blue's advance toward the red flag.

The nonmonotonic behavior is immediately obvious from figure 6.36, which shows a 3D fitness landscape for mission objective = *maximize number of red agents near blue flag* (where "near" is defined as anywhere within 10 battlefield-units). The landscape sweeps over red sensor range ($= 1, 2, ..., 16$) and red combat μ-rule threshold Δ_{Combat} ($= -15, -14, ... + 15$). The non-monotonic behavior is also evident in each of the three landscapes (calculated for three different mission objectives) shown in figure 6.37.

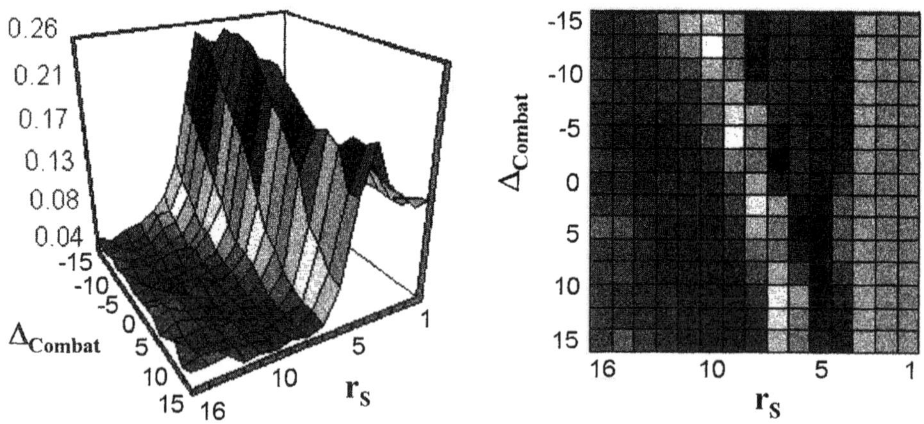

Fig. 6.36 Red defense scenario fitness landscapes (for mission = *maximize number of red agents near blue flag*) for $(x, y) = (\Delta_{Combat}, r_S)$. Higher valued fitness values translate to mean better performance. Note that (this particular fitness measure) *does not* scale monotonically with sensor range.

This example illustrates that when the resources and personalities of both sides remain fixed in a conflict, how "well" side X does over side Y does not necessarily scale monotonically with X's sensor capability. As one side is forced to assimilate more and more information (with increasing sensor range), there will inevitably come a point where the available resources will be spread too thin and the overall fighting ability will therefore be curtailed. Agent-based models such as EINSTein are well suited for providing insights into more operationally significant questions such as How must X's resources and/or tactics (i.e., personality) be altered in order to ensure at least the same level of mission performance?

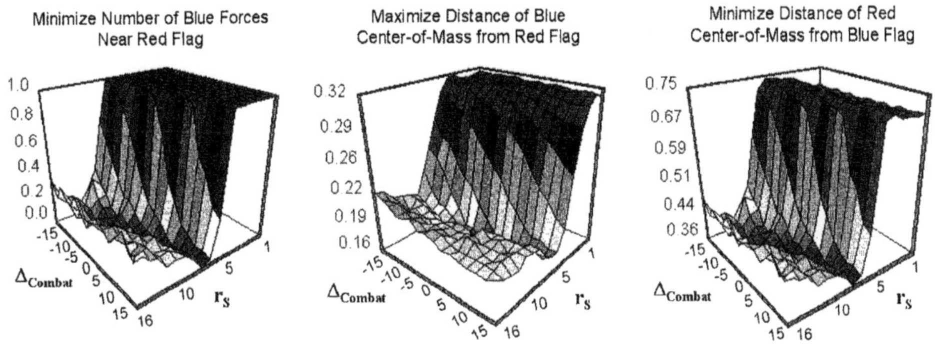

Fig. 6.37 *Red defense* scenario fitness landscapes for $(x, y) = (\Delta_{Combat}, r_S)$.

6.10 Case Study 9: Autopoietic Skirmish

Autopoeisis means, etymologically, "self-creation" (from the Greek *auto* = self and *poiesis* = creation/production) and refers to a process that defines and sustains itself. More precisely, an autopoeitic system is a network of mutually interacting processes that continuously both create, and sustain, components that regenerate the network of processes that produce them.

Originally developed as an explanatory mechanism within biology by Maturana and Varela [Varela74], autopoietic theory deals with systems that are self-reproducing and self-maintaining. A striking example is the giant "red spot" on the planet Jupiter. This enormous vortex has managed to sustain itself for centuries, or for a time that is orders of magnitude greater than the time-scales governing the molecular interactions that sustain it. Of course, arguably the most spectacular example of an autopoietic system is life itself. Given that autopoiesis typically results from the self-organized collective interactions of networked entities, it is reasonable to ask whether EINSTein's agent-based logic supports autopoeitic structures?

The answer is yes; autopoietic-like structures frequently emerge. Table 6.9 shows blue and red parameter values that result in an autopoietic-like skirmish. Notice that the two forces are essentially the same, except that (1) red tends to cluster more ($\tau_{Red,Cluster} = 8$, $\tau_{Blue,Cluster} = 3$), (2) blue is a bit more aggressive ($\Delta_{Blue,Combat} = -3$, $\Delta_{Red,Combat} = -2$; though when injured, $\Delta_{Red,Combat} = -4$), and (3) while both red and blue agents nominally move within a range of two units, blue agents slow down to a maximum of $r_{Blue,M} = 1$ when injured.

Color plate 18 (page 264) shows some snapshots from an interactive run. A cluster of red and blue agents undergoing intense combat self-organizes near the center of the battlefield and persists for a very long time despite agents continually flowing in and out of it. This cluster also appears to be driven by a higher-level (i.e. emergent) dynamics in which it first rotates counterclockwise and drifts slowly toward the red goal, comes to a stop, reverses direction and moves toward the blue

Parameter	Red	Blue
Agents	250	250
r_S	5	5
r_F	3	3
r_M	2	2 (1 when injured)
ω_1	10	10
ω_2	40	40
ω_3	10	10
ω_4	40	40
ω_5	0	25
ω_6	25	0
$\tau_{Advance}$	3	3
$\tau_{Cluster}$	3	8
Δ_{Combat}	-2 (-4 when injured)	-3

Table 6.9 Default parameter values for *autopoietic skirmish* example; see text for details.

flag, then reverses direction once again and moves back toward the red flag before finally disintegrating. This emergent behavior is easier to see using the *battlefront-map* (shown at the top of figure 6.38). The battle-front map is a filtered view of the battlefield that highlights regions in which the most intense combat is taking place.*

Interesting questions naturally suggest themselves: *What are the conditions for an such an autopoietic structure to emerge? How stable is this structure? Are there conditions under which the one structure splits into two or more autopoietic structures?*

6.11 Case Study 10: Small Insertion

Consider a scenario in which a small red force (15 agents) is tasked with penetrating a large, dispersed enemy force (200 agents). This sample case study probes red's defensive capability as a function of force size, sensor range, combat aggressiveness and communications. It also introduces the first example of agent behavior that is prescribed entirely by a genetic algorithm.†

Table 6.10 lists the values of red and blue parameters used for three *Small Insertion* scenarios. Color plate 19 (page 265) shows snapshots of typical runs using these values.

*The *battlefront-map* appears in one of five shades of gray, indicating the degree of combat intensity within a box of radius centered at each (x, y). This option may be selected either by pressing the **B** button on the toolbar, or by selecting the appropriate option of the *Display* menu. For additional details see EINSTein's *User's Guide* [Ilach99a] and Appendix G of this book.

†A detailed discussion of how the genetic algorithm is implemented in the code, as well as how EINSTein can be used to "breed" forces using a genetic algorithm, appears in the next chapter.

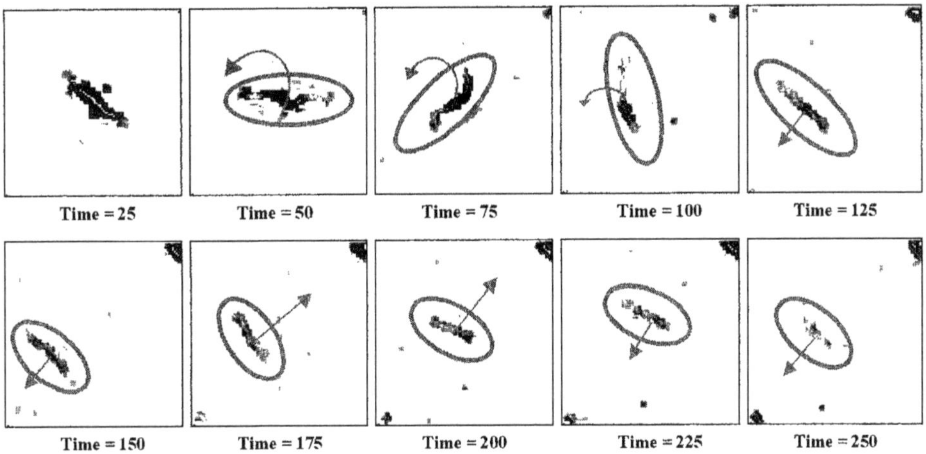

Fig. 6.38 Battlefront-map snapshots of an interactive run of the *autopoietic skirmish* scenario discussed in the text; screenshots of this run are shown in color plate 18.

Parameter	Blue	Scenario I Red	Scenario II Red	Scenario III Red
Agents	200	15	15	15
r_S	5	3	9	5
r_F	3	2	9	5
r_M	1	2	2	2
ω_1	10, 40 if injured	10	30	-36
ω_2	99	40	72	-11
ω_3	0	10	20	-10
ω_4	99	40	-8	97
ω_5	0	0	-68	-58
ω_6	0	75	40	93
$\tau_{Advance}$	N/A	3	0, 4 if injured	7, 1 if injured
$\tau_{Cluster}$	10	8	19, 7 if injured	19, 11 if injured
Δ_{Combat}	-5	-2	24, 1 if injured	-1, -23 if injured
P_{hit}	0.05 (I/II), 0.005 (III)	0.005	0.005	0.005

Table 6.10 Default parameter values for *small insertion* case study; see text for details.

The blue force consists of 200 defending agents, and is relatively slow ($r_M = 1$) but aggressive ($\Delta_{Combat} = -5$). For the first two scenarios (I & II), blue is also much more lethal than red ($P_{Blue,hit} = 10 \cdot P_{red,hit}$).

The series of screenshots for Scenario-I, shown at the top of color plate 19, suggests that, because of blues' stronger firepower, direct frontal assaults by red are unlikely to succeed in penetrating through to the blue flag. In fact, multiple runs of this same scenario show that red almost never succeeds in positioning even a single agent within 10 units of the blue flag for any time < 100 steps. *What can red do to succeed?*

The middle sequence of screenshots appearing in color plate 19 summarizes a typical run that uses genetic-algorithm-bred red agent parameter values. The red arrow shown in the figure traces the trajectory of the red force. The genetic algorithm uses a fitness function to rank interim solutions as they evolve. The function used for this example is proportional to the cumulative number of (alive or injured) agents whose location for any time < 100 falls within 10 units of the blue flag. The red parameter values appearing under the Scenario-II column in Table 6.10 represent the "best" agent found by the genetic algorithm at the end of 100 "generations" of its search; blue parameter values are not a part of the search.

The genetic algorithm has found red agents that *act as though* they are intelligently maneuvering around the defending force. Whether the red insertion force moves to the right or left of the blue agents, or repeatedly advances and retreats, as if probing for any sign of weakness, is a function of initial disposition and random factors. In all cases, however, red consistently positions itself far enough away from blue's firepower to minimize casualties and is successfully able to exploit periodic breaks in blue's defense to slowly maneuver closer to the blue flag. Figure 6.39 shows the number of red agents within 5 units of the blue flag, averaged over 100 samples.

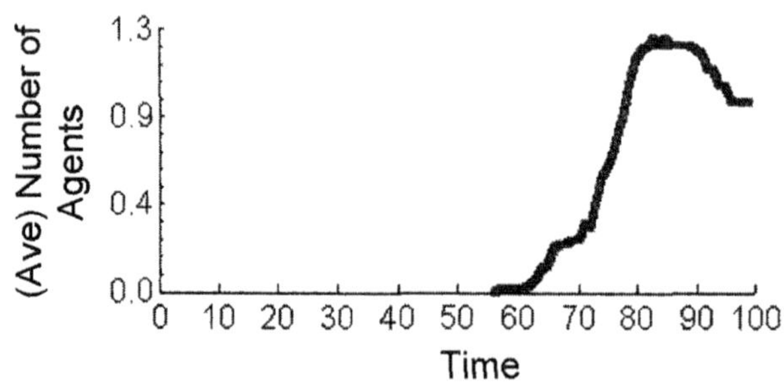

Fig. 6.39 Number of red agents near blue flag, averaged over 100 runs of the *small insertion* scenario II; agent parameters are defined in table 6.10.

The sequence of screenshots appearing on the bottom of color plate 19 shows that when blue's firepower advantage is taken away (so that $P_{Blue,hit} = P_{red,hit} = 0.005$), the genetic algorithm settles onto a very different red "personality." Now, rather than maneuvering *around* potential skirmishes and firefights, while in a tight cluster, red agents attack the enemy directly in a spread out formation. They are also more willing to engage the enemy in local fights ($\Delta_{Combat} = -1$) and are prone to help injured friends ($\omega_4 \sim 100$).

What happens as a function of red force size and aggressiveness? Figure 6.40 shows a fitness landscape, and its associated density plot, calculated for *Scenario-I* parameter values, but with blue $P_{Blue,hit} = P_{red,hit} = 0.005$. The "mission" is for red to maneuver as many agents near the blue flag as possible.

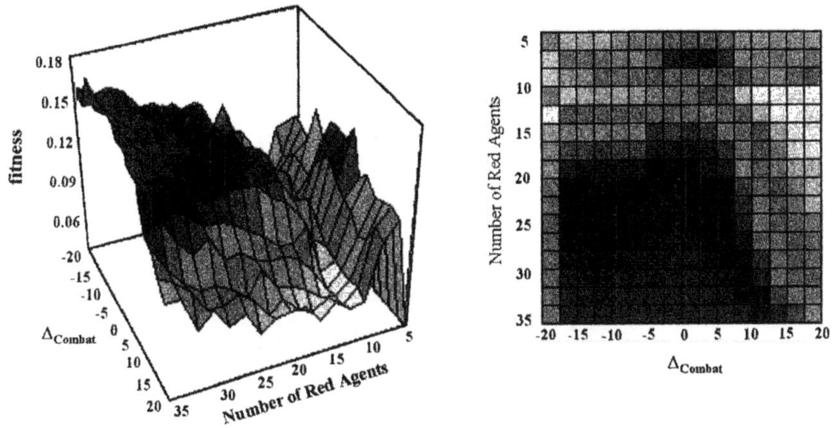

Fig. 6.40 Fitness landscape (and corresponding density plot) for mission = *maximize number of red agents near blue flag*; agent parameters are defined in table 6.10.

The interesting result is that while the red force generally performs its mission better as it gets larger, this is only true for force sizes that are greater than some critical size. For less than about 15 agents, the force actually performs better with, say *five* agents than it does with ten.

The reason for this surprising result becomes clear only after looking at multiple runs, and comparing patterns of behavior. When the number of agents is small enough, agents generally do not receive much support from other friendly agents as they advance toward the enemy flag. This is because the force consists of so few agents to begin with. Agents can thus maneuver quickly around defending agents, and advance toward the flag effectively unscathed. They are able to do so quickly, because they do not need to divert as much attention (or time, which tends to limit their efficiency) to seeking out friendly forces as they do when more friendly agents are present. As the number of agents increases a small amount, the likelihood of encountering friendly agents also increases. This, in turn, increases the likelihood of both slowing down, in their collective progress toward the enemy flag, and of encountering enemy agents, which begin to swarm around the periphery of the small advancing cluster of red agents, which only further slows down the red forces' progress. As the number of red agents increases still further, the red force finally capitalizes on its growing relative strength in numbers and is able to advance toward the blue flag with increasing efficiency.

6.12 Case Study #11: Miscellaneous Behaviors

We conclude our presentation of sample case studies in this chapter by looking at a few miscellaneous behaviors, including precession, encirclement, local firestorms (along with the effects of adding agent-to-agent communications), and some examples of embedding local and global commanders within a scenario.

6.12.1 *Precessional Maneuver*

Figure 6.41 shows a few snapshots of a run in which a self-organized cluster of red and blue agents locked in combat undergoes a slow clockwise precession.

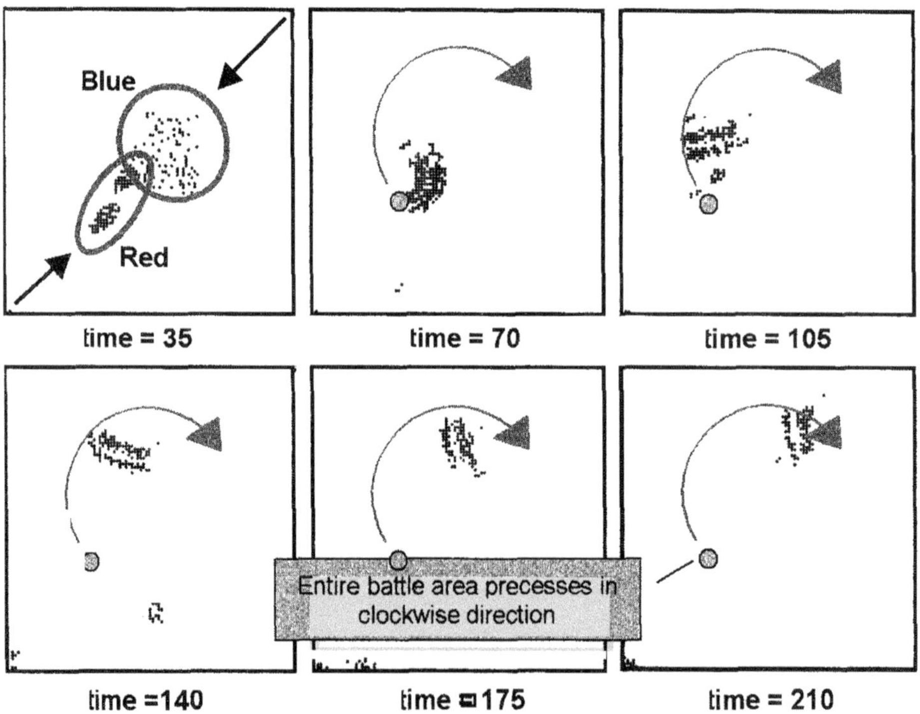

Fig. 6.41 Screenshots from a run showing a slow clockwise precession of a self-organized cluster of red and blue agents locked in combat. *Red agents want to avoid a fight almost as badly as blue agents want to start one!*

The two sides are equipped with the same sensor ($r_S = 5$) and fire ranges ($r_F = 3$), but have markedly different personalities and additional movement constraints:

$$\left\{ \begin{array}{c} \vec{\omega}_{red} = (25, 10, 75, 25, 0, 50) \\ \tau_{red,Advance} = 5, \tau_{red,Cluster} = 10, \Delta_{red,Combat} = 4, \ Min_{red,D-Friend} = 3 \\ \vec{\omega}_{blue} = (10, 35, 10, 80, 0, 50) \\ \tau_{blue,Advance} = 1, \tau_{blue,Cluster} = 3, \text{ and } \Delta_{blue,Combat} = -5 \end{array} \right\}. \tag{6.8}$$

Red agents thus strongly favor moving toward alive and injured friends over moving toward alive and injured blue forces. In contrast, blue agents are considerably more motivated to move toward red forces than toward friends. Red agents advance toward the goal only if surrounded by at least 5 friendly forces (within a threshold range $r_T = 2$), continue moving toward friendly forces until surrounded by at least 10 reds, and move to engage an enemy agent only if they sense a local numerical advantage of *four* over blue forces. Moreover, red forces wish to maintain a minimum distance of 3 from all enemy agents. In contrast, blue forces advance toward the red flag even when surrounded by a single friend within a threshold range $r_T = 3$, continue to cluster with friendly agents only until they are surrounded by at least 3 other agents, and move to engage an enemy even if they sense that they are locally outnumbered by the enemy by *five* agents. Moreover, they want to get as close to the enemy as possible (i.e., the minimum distance $Min_{blue,D-Friend} = 0$).

This stark contrast in personalities can be succinctly summarized, in words, as "*reds want to avoid a fight as badly as blues want to start one.*" And once a fight has started, and blues sense that the enemy has been injured, blue agents are motivated to "finish off" the enemy more so than they are motivated to advance towards the enemy's flag.

As in many of the previous examples, red and blue agents are initially positioned in diagonally opposite corners (i.e., near their respective flags; though this starting configuration is not shown in the figure). The first frame of figure 6.41 shows the two sides colliding near the center (at time $t = 37$). Red forces cluster into two advancing groups, while the blue forces consist of one large, and widely dispersed, cluster. What is immediately apparent in this particular sample run is the distinct manner in which these two very different personalities interact, as summarized by the last three frames of the scenario, shown for times $t = 75$, 125 and 250.

The two forces remain essentially locked together in heavy but localized combat, maneuvering slowly around the upper half of the battlefield. Except for a few stray "leakers" and small groups of blue agents that occasionally wander away from the main battle (and head toward red's flag), the firefight remains tightly confined to the one large cluster of red and blue agents, and no other scattered skirmishes, large or small, arise during the run.

Notice also that this slow precess of the cluster of agents locked in close combat evolves over a relatively long time. The single "super-cell" of red and blue agents remains well-formed even up to the very last frame shown for this run, showing the state of the battle at time $t = 250$.

We make two other observations about the precession of this super-cell: (1) it is driven first by blue's desire to engage (and finish-off) red forces coupled with red's desire to flee, and later—as the red force moves closer to the blue flag—by red's desire to get to its goal (while still being chased by blues); (2) it does not arise because of any *one particular rule* that defines an individual agents' behavior, rather it emerges as a collective confluence of the entire set of mutually interacting red and blue agents.

6.12.2 *Random Defense*

Figure 6.42 shows a few snapshots taken from a simple "goal defense" scenario in which a behavior reminiscent of a *phase-transition* takes place.

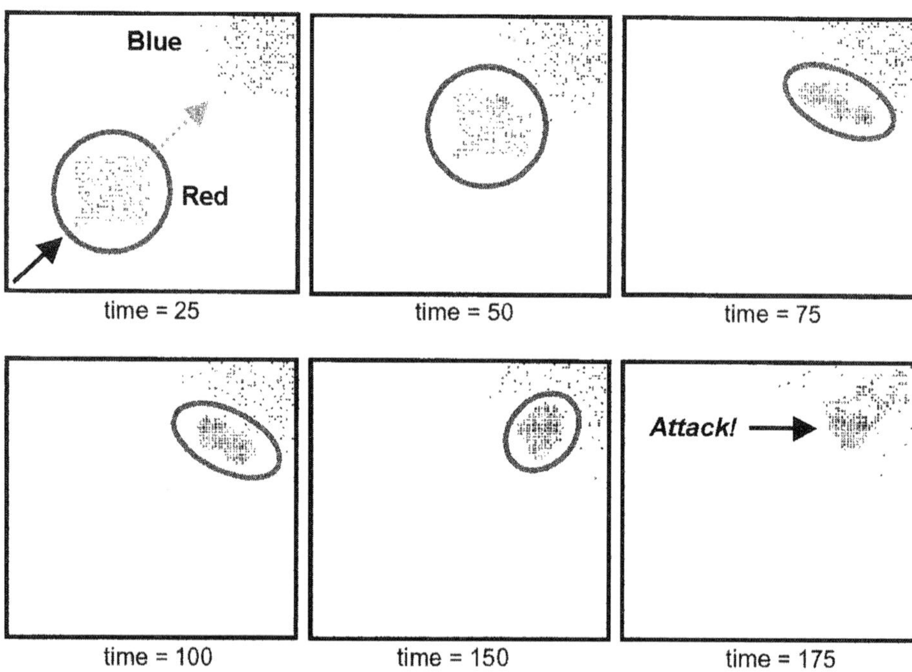

Fig. 6.42 Screenshots from a run in which blue agents defend their flag (and react only to enemy agents), and in which the suddenness of red's final "attack" (at time $t = 175$) is very reminiscent of a *phase-transition*.

In this run, blue defends its own flag against a red attack and has a very simple personality:

$$\left\{ \begin{array}{c} \vec{\omega}_{blue} = (0, \omega_{AE} = 10, 0, \omega_{IE} = 10, 0, 0) \\ \tau_{blue,Advance} = \text{N/A} \\ \tau_{blue,Cluster} = \text{N/A} \\ \Delta_{blue,Combat} = -99 \end{array} \right\}. \quad (6.9)$$

In particular, since only the second and fourth components of blue's personality weight vector are non-zero, blue "sees" only enemy agents. Since blue agents are initially only surrounded by other blue agents, and thus all possible moves incur exactly the same penalty—until red forces come within range of the blue side—all blue agents effectively execute a "random walk" around their starting positions. In contrast, the red force responds to both red and blue agents, though is "blind" to injured friends:

$$\left\{ \begin{array}{c} \vec{\omega}_{red} = (\omega_{AF} = 10, \omega_{AE} = 50, \omega_{IF} = 0, \omega_{IE} = 100, 0, \omega_{EF} = 25) \\ \tau_{red,Advance} = 1 \\ \tau_{red,Cluster} = 3 \\ \Delta_{red,Combat} = -3 \end{array} \right\}. \quad (6.10)$$

Red and blue forces are endowed with equal sensor ($r_S = 5$) and fire ranges ($r_F = 3$), equal single-shot probabilities of hit ($P_{hit} = 0.005$) and can both simultaneously engage a maximum of 3 enemy targets. There are 150 agents per side.

What is interesting about this run is the unexpected, sudden *phase-transition-like* change of behavior that occurs a relatively long time into the close-combat that ensues near the blue flag. Upon reaching the outer area of blue's defensive posture (see snapshots for times $t = 50$ and $t = 150$), red skirmishes with a few forward-positioned blue agents, but from a distance, and remains in a tightly clustered formation. Red continues fighting in this clustered mode for a relatively long time (see snapshots for times $t = 75$ through $t = 150$) until, *suddenly*, most of red's forces rapidly push outward and stream toward the blue flag.

The static snapshots shown in figure 6.42 do not do justice to the abruptness of this behavioral transition, which can be likened to turning on a lamp by a flicking a light switch. It is interesting to note that neither the clustering nor the sudden forward thrust of forces is "explained" by any of the red agent parameters. Locally, agents remain motivated to cluster with friends only until they are surrounded by at most 3 friends (i.e. $\tau_{red,Cluster} = 3$); yet, we see that as a force, reds tend to cluster to a much greater degree than one might expect to see solely as a consequence of the local clustering threshold. Also, red's local combat constraint ($\Delta_{red,Conbat} = -3$) is not, by itself, sufficient to explain the unexpected, and rapid, push towards the enemy flag. Both of these behaviors are thus emergent phenomena stemming from the confluence of multiple, simultaneous factors that are at play during the evolution. What happens if the *same input file* is used to generate other sequences of runs" While the exact *times* at which the phase-transition-like behavior occurs is certainly different from run to run (and clearly depends on how the red and blue are initially aligned relative to one another), it is also almost certain that the phase-transition-like behavior *itself*—as an emergent phenomenon–will occur at some time during a run. In other words, while low-level details of agent positioning depend on the initial conditions, the high-level *pattern of behavior remains fixed.*

6.12.3 *Communications*

Color plate 20 (page 267) shows screenshots from two runs of the same scenario. The runs are the same (i.e., the parameter values that define the agents' behaviors are the same), except that during the *second run* (appearing in the bottom two rows), the blue agents are allowed to communicate with one another.

The red and blue forces are virtually identical in this scenario: each is endowed with the same sensor ($r_S = 4$) and fire ranges ($r_F = 3$), each has the same single-shot probabilities of hit ($P_{hit} = 0.003$) and can simultaneously engage the same maximum of 3 enemy targets, and each obeys the same movement and combat constraint conditions ($\tau_{Advance} = 4$, $\tau_{Cluster} = 10$, and $\Delta_{Conbat} = -4$). Their personalities differ in that while all blue agents are assigned an identical personality weight vector ($\overrightarrow{\omega}_{blue} = (10, 40, 10, 40, 0, 50)$), each red agents obeys its own, *randomly generated*, weight vector. There are 150 agents per side.

The first two rows of color plate 20 show a run in which neither red nor blue agents communicate. The only noteworthy feature of this baseline run is the slightly disorganized overall pattern of behavior. After the collision between the two forces at time $t \sim 60$, the combat unfolds mainly as small, tightly clustered "firestorms" that arise near the center of the battlefield. Neither side appears well organized, as both red and blue agents migrate from firestorm to firestorm. The bottom two rows of color plate 20 show one example of the effects of endowing one side with an ability to communicate.

For this run, the blue agents are able to communicate with one another. In particular, blue's communications range $r_{Comms} = 6$, and blue's communications weight $\omega_{Comms} = 0.25$. This means that blue agents use not only the information that they are aware of in their own filed-of-view (out to a sensor range $r_S = 4$), but also the information that is *communicated to them* by other blue agents within a range $r_{Comms} = 6$. This additional information is assigned *one-fourth* the weight relative to information supplied by an agent's own-sensor. As in the first run, red agents *do not* communicate.

Instead of the small, tightly clustered "firestorms" that characterize the first run (and in the *absence* of blue communications), the second run is characterized by blue's ability to maintain a strong organized central presence. No blue strays too far from the area of the most intense combat, and few isolated skirmishes appear, as they had in the first run. It is interesting to note that while red undeniably "follows" blue's lead throughout the encounter—that is to say, that blue initiates an action to which red immediately responds—red also appears to be better organized than in the previous example. This, despite the fact that red *does not use communications in either example.* The rudimentary "lesson learned" is that when one side unilaterally enhances its internal organization, that action may—ironically—enhance the apparent organization of *both sides.*

6.12.4 *Local Command*

This example consists of a simple scenario in which the red force is endowed with one *local commander* (LC).* The blue force is, as in all preceding examples, strictly decentralized.

Figure 6.43 shows a fragment of the input data file used to generate this run. This fragment is used to define the parameters of the red local commanders. Figure 6.43 shows that there are three LCs (*num_RED_comdrs = 3*). Each LC has 20 subordinate agents under its command (*(1)_R_undr_cmd = 20*)† and reacts only to enemy agents (*w2:alive_B = w4:injrd_B = 35*) and the enemy flag (*w6:B_goal = 50*). The LCs in this sample run are also fairly timid, both as individuals (with a combat threshold of $\Delta_{Combat} = +25$) and as commanders (with *negative* command weights). Negative local command weights mean that the LCs tend to send their subordinates *away from* (rather than toward) areas in which the red forces are outnumbered by blue.

Individual red and blue agents are equipped with the same sensor ($r_S = 5$) and fire ranges ($r_F = 3$), but have different personalities and additional movement constraints:

$$\left\{\begin{array}{c} \vec{\omega}_{red,alive} = (10,40,10,40,0,50), \vec{\omega}_{red,alive} = (75,60,-5,99,50,0) \\ \text{alive red: } \tau_{Advance} = 3, \tau_{Cluster} = 3, \Delta_{Combat} = 0 \\ \text{injured red: } \tau_{Advance} = 4, \tau_{Cluster} = 9, \Delta_{Combat} = +6 \\ \vec{\omega}_{blue,alive} = \vec{\omega}_{blue,injured} = (10,40,10,40,0,50) \\ \text{alive blue: } \tau_{Advance} = 2, \tau_{Cluster} = 8 \text{ and } \Delta_{Combat} = +3 \\ \text{injured blue: } \tau_{Advance} = 3, \tau_{Cluster} = 12 \text{ and } \Delta_{Combat} = +5 \end{array}\right\}. \quad (6.11)$$

Color plate 21 (page 267) shows a few snapshots taken from a play-back of the run using these parameters. The position of the local command agent, his subordinates and command area can all be tracked by clicking on the associated display option under the main menu *Display* option (the selections may be found under the heading *Highlight Command Structure*; see section E.4.8 in *Appendix E: A Concise User's Guide to EINSTein*).

Color plate **??** shows that as soon as the LC encounters enemy forces at the periphery of its command area (see snapshot at $t = 30$), it moves away from them

*Local commander agents are discussed on page 362.

†The data file fragment in figure 6.43 shows only the parameters values of the first local commander. The other two local commanders are identical.

```
*****************************
* RED LOCAL COMMAND PARAMETERS
*****************************
RED_command_flag  1
num_RED_comdrs    3
R_patch_type      1
R_patch_flag      2
*
* local commander parameters
*
(1)_R_undr_cmd    20
(1)_R_cmnd_rad    2
(1)_R_SENSOR_rng  7
*
* local commander personality
*
(1)_w1:alive_R    0.000000
(1)_w2:alive_B    35.000000
(1)_w3:injrd_R    0.000000
(1)_w4:injrd_B    35.000000
(1)_w5:R_goal     0.000000
(1)_w6:B_goal     50.000000
*
* local commander constraints
*
(1)_R_ADV_range   4
(1)_ADVANCE_num   0
(1)_CLUSTER_num   0
(1)_COMBAT_num    25
*
* local command weights
*
(1)_R_w_alpha     -1.
(1)_R_w_beta      -1.
(1)_R_w_delta     -1.
(1)_R_w_gamma     -1.
*
* global command weights
*
(1)_w_obey_GC_def 1.
```

Fig. 6.43 Fragment of EINSTein's (text-based) input data file that contains local command parameter values.

(and away from the ensuing combat near the center of the battlefield), and orders its subordinates to follow. From that point on, the LC manages to stay clear of all enemy agents, and thereby steer its subordinates from harm's way. After most of the fighting near the center of the battlefield has subsided, the LC finally "sees" a clear path toward the blue flag towards which it finally maneuvers (see snapshot at $t = 155$).

6.12.5 *Global Command*

This example consists of a simple scenario in which the red force is endowed with *one global* (GC) and *three local commanders* (LC).* The blue force consists of individual agents.

Figure 6.44 shows a fragment of the input data file used to generate this run.

Individual red and blue agents are equipped with the same sensor ($r_S = 5$) and fire ranges ($r_F = 3$), but have different personalities and additional movement constraints:

*Local commander agents are discussed on page 362.

```
*****************************
* RED GLOBAL COMMAND PARAMETERS
*****************************
RED_global_flag  1
*
* direction parameters
*
GC_fear_index    1.
GC_w_alpha       1.
GC_w_beta        1.
GC_frac_R[1]     .3
GC_frac_R[2]     .6
GC_w_swath[1]    1.
GC_w_swath[2]    1.
GC_w_swath[3]    1.
*
* help parameters
*
GC_max_red_f     2.5
GC_help_radius   40
GC_h_thresh      .1
GC_rel_h_thresh  1.5
```

Fig. 6.44 Fragment of EINSTein's (text-based) input data file that contains global command parameter values.

$$\left\{ \begin{array}{c} \vec{\omega}_{red,alive} = (10,40,10,40,0,50), \vec{\omega}_{red,alive} = (75,60,-5,99,50,0) \\ \text{alive red: } \tau_{Advance} = 3, \tau_{Cluster} = 3, \Delta_{Combat} = 0 \\ \text{injured red: } \tau_{Advance} = 4, \tau_{Cluster} = 9, \Delta_{Combat} = +6 \\ \vec{\omega}_{blue,alive} = \vec{\omega}_{blue,injured} = (10,40,10,40,0,50) \\ \text{alive blue: } \tau_{Advance} = 0, \tau_{Cluster} = 5 \text{ and } \Delta_{Combat} = +3 \\ \text{injured blue: } \tau_{Advance} = 0, \tau_{Cluster} = 8 \text{ and } \Delta_{Combat} = +5 \end{array} \right\}. \quad (6.12)$$

The initial state and almost all parameters defining the red and blue forces are the same as in the previous sample run (*Local Command*). One important difference, however, is that whereas the red local commanders were all previously very timid—as exemplified by them all having negative command weights (see figure 6.43)—here the local commanders all have *positive* weights. This means that the LCs always order their subordinates *toward* (rather than away from, as in the previous sample run) the area in greatest need of red firepower.

In contrast, the GC is very timid. Figure 6.44 shows that the global commander's *GC_fear_index* is set equal to *one*, meaning that the GC vectors his local commanders toward the blue flag if and only if he finds a "sector" pointing at the blue flag that is completely free of blue agents.*

Color plate 268 shows that the GC is able to keep his local commanders (and therefore their own subordinate agents) away from harm's way until the blue force moves close to the red flag. Note that the cluster of red agents that collides with the

*Battlefield *sectors*, and how they are used by the GC to issue move-orders to its subordinate LCs, are discussed on page 368.

blue force at time $t = 25$ are not under either local or global command. Note the presence of both a command-box surrounding each local commander (representing the LC's field-of-view and area of responsibility) and a thin dark line indicating that the three LCs are implicitly tethered to one another via their command link to the GC..

Chapter 7
Breeding Agents

"Overall, then, we will view [complex adaptive systems] (CAS) as systems composed of interacting agents described in terms of rules. These agents adapt by changing their rules as experience accumulates. In CAS, a major part of the environment of any given adaptive agent consists of other adaptive agents, so that a portion of any agent's efforts at adaptation is spent adapting to other adaptive agents."

—John Holland, *Hidden Order* [Holl95]

7.1 Background

One of EINSTein's most powerful built-in features is a genetic algorithm "breeder" run-mode. *Genetic algorithms* (GAs) are a class of heuristic search methods and computational models of adaptation and evolution based on natural selection. In nature, the search for beneficial adaptations to a continually changing environment (i.e., evolution) is fostered by the cumulative evolutionary knowledge that each species possesses of its forebears. This knowledge, which is encoded in the chromosomes of each member of a species, is passed on from one generation to the next by a mating process in which the chromosomes of "parents" produce "offspring" chromosomes.

GAs mimic and exploit the genetic dynamics underlying natural evolution to search for optimal solutions of general combinatorial optimization problems. They have been applied to the traveling salesman problem, VLSI circuit layout, gas pipeline control, the parametric design of aircraft, neural net architecture, models of international security, and strategy formulation.

While their modern form is derived mainly from John Holland's work in the 1960s [Holl92a], many key ideas such as using "selection of the fittest" population-based selection schemes and using binary strings as computational analogs of biological chromosomes, actually date back to the late 1950s. More recent work is discussed by Goldberg [Goldb89], Davis [DavisL91] and Michalewicz [Michal92] and in conference proceedings edited by Forrest [Forrest91]. A comprehensive review of the current state-of-the-art in genetic algorithms is given by Mitchell [MitchM96].

The basic idea behind GAs is very simple. Given a "problem"—which can be as well-defined as maximizing a function over some specified interval or as seemingly ill-defined and open-ended as evolution itself, where there is no a-priori discernible or fixed function to either maximize or minimize—GAs provide a mechanism by which the solution space to that problem is searched for "good solutions." Possible solutions are encoded as chromosomes (or, sometimes, as sets of chromosomes), and the GA evolves one population of chromosomes into another according to their fitness by using some combination (and/ or variation) of the genetic operators of reproduction, *crossover* and *mutation.*

Although GA are undeniably powerful computational tools and have been successfully applied to an impressive variety of problems (see below), they certainly do not represent a panacea solution to all types of problems. One finds that, in practice, certain problems are more amenable to this kind of solution scheme than others, and that it is not always obvious why that is so. Indeed, the celebrated *No Free Lunch Theorem*, proven by Wolpert and Macready in 1996 [Wolp96], asserts that the performance of all search algorithms, when averaged over all possible cost functions (i.e., averaged over all possible problems), is *exactly the same.* In other words, no search algorithm is better, or worse, on average than blind guessing. Much foundational work still remains to be done in developing a complete theory of GA behaviors and capabilities.

7.1.1 *Genetic Operators*

Each chromosome is usually defined to be a bit-string, where each bit position (or *locus*) takes on one of two possible values (or *alleles*), and can be imagined as representing a single point in the *solution space.* The fitness of a chromosome effectively measures how "good" a solution that chromosome represents to the given problem. Aside from its intentional biological roots and flavoring, GAs can be thought of as parallel equivalents of more conventional serial optimization techniques: rather than testing one possible solution after another, or moving from point to point in the solution phase-space, GAs move from entire populations of points to new populations.

Figure 7.1 shows examples of the three basic genetic operations of *reproduction*, *crossover* and *mutation*, as applied to a population of 8-bit chromosomes. Reproduction makes a set of identical copies of a given chromosome, where the number of copies depends on the chromosome's fitness. The *crossover* operator exchanges subparts of two chromosomes, where the position of the crossover is randomly selected, and is thus a crude facsimile of biological sexual recombination between two single-chromosome organisms. The *mutation* operator randomly flips one or more bits in the chromosome, where the bit positions are randomly chosen. The mutation rate is usually chosen to be small.

While reproduction generally rewards high fitness, and crossover generates new chromosomes whose parts, at least, come from chromosomes with relatively high

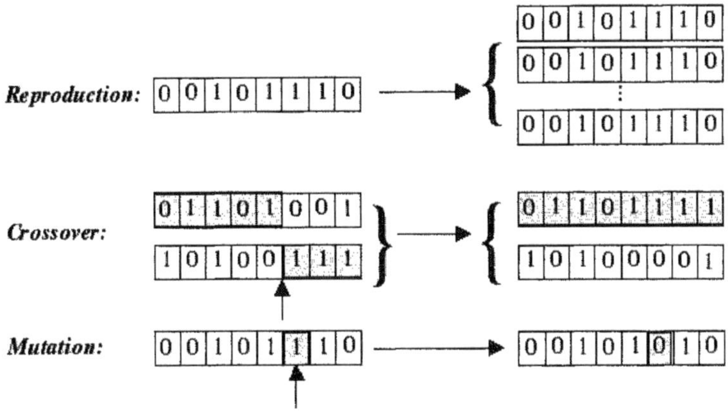

Fig. 7.1 Schematic of basic GA operations; see text for details.

fitness (this does not guarantee, of course, that the crossover-formed chromosomes will also have high fitness; see below), mutation seems necessary to prevent the loss of diversity at a given bit-position [holl92a]. For example, were it not for mutation, a population might evolve to a state where the first bit-position of each chromosome contains the value 1, with there being no chance of reproduction or crossover ever replacing it with a 0.

A solution search space together with a fitness function is called a *fitness landscape*. Eventually, after many generations, the population will, in theory, be composed only of those chromosomes whose fitness values are clustered around the global maximum of the fitness landscape.

7.1.2 *The Fitness Landscape*

As mentioned above, a solution search space, $\overrightarrow{x}$, together with a fitness function, $f(\overrightarrow{x})$, make up what is called a *fitness landscape*. The term "landscape" comes from visualizing a three-dimensional geographical landscape consisting of heights $h = f(x,y)$ of a two-dimensional location $\overrightarrow{x} = (x,y)$. Particular problems, of course, may involve an arbitrary number of dimensions, but it is still helpful to keep this simple image in mind.

The term "fitness" comes from Darwinian biology, and refers to the fitness of an individual to survive as a function either of its *phenotype* (or higher-level properties and/or behaviors) or its *genotype* (or lower-level genetic code). Biological fitness is generally very difficult to define since it is usually a complicated (and changing!) function of the interactions between an organism and other organisms and interactions between the organism and its environment. In a biological context and/or biology-based setting (such as in studies of *artificial life*), the fitness landscape is also often referred to as an *adaptive landscape*, paying homage to an idea first introduced by Wright in 1932 [Wrights32]. Other "fitness functions," which, depending on the particular problem, may be considerably easier to define than their biological cousins, include *energy* and *free-energy* landscapes from physics and chemistry, and *cost* (or *objective*) functions from combinatorial optimization problems in computer science.

As our simple geographical landscape metaphor might suggest, a variety of fitness landscapes are possible, each with their own strengths and weaknesses when it comes to "submitting" to a GA solution: completely flat landscapes, landscapes with a single isolated minimum and/or maximum, landscapes having several minima and/or maxima with equal heights, or landscapes with many unequal and irregularly spaced local minima and/or maxima.

Since GAs, like other combinatorial optimization schemes (such as simulated annealing), depend essentially on their "hill-climbing" ability to ascend (or descend) towards the desired global maximum (or minimum), how successful the climb—and hence, the approach to the solution—will be, depends on what the landscape looks like. What a given landscape looks like, in turn, depends strongly on its metric; that is, on the function $d = d(\vec{x}, \vec{y})$ that is used to measure the distance between any two points $\vec{x}$ and $\vec{y}$. Since GAs tend to keep nearby bits near each other, embedded correlations among subsets of a chromosome's genes can sometimes be exploited to produce a "natural ordering" for the given landscape [Goldb89].

Landscapes with a single smoothly increasing "bump," such as the one shown in figure 7.2-a, for example, are usually amenable to any systematic climb towards larger values. On the other hand, landscapes with a single isolated maximum that sits on an otherwise even-leveled surface may not be so easy to "solve," because at no point on the surface is there a clue as to which direction to proceed in to move towards the maximum.

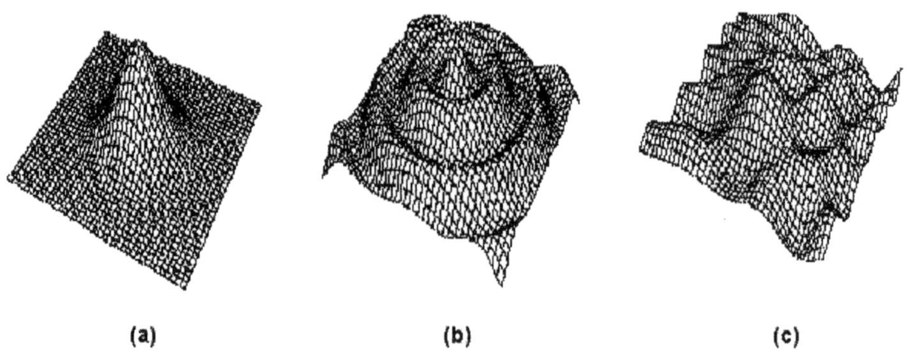

Fig. 7.2 Three sample fitness landscapes: (a) has a single smooth maximum, (b) has many equivalent local maxima and one global maximum, but is circularly symmetric; (c) has many irregularly spaced local maxima, and is a good example of a *rugged landscape*.

More "rugged" landscapes, such as those shown in figures 7.2-b and 7.2-c, with their multiple, and in the case of figure 7.2-c, irregularly spaced and sized, local maxima, may present even greater challenges to "hill-climbing" methods. An excellent review of optimization on rugged landscapes is given by Palmer [Palmerg91]. Kauffman ([Kauff92], [Kauff93]) discusses the biological implications of rugged fitness landscapes.

7.1.2.1 *N-k landscapes*

Kauffman ([Kauff89], [Kauff90]) has introduced a class of parametrizable fitness landscapes called *NK-landscapes*, that provide a formalism for studying the efficacy of GA evolution as a function of certain statistical properties of the landscape.*

Given N binary variables $x_i = \pm 1$, so that $\vec{x} = (x_1, x_2, \ldots, x_N)$ represents a vertex of an N-dimensional hypercube, an NK-landscape is defined by a fitness function, $\mathcal{F}$, of the form:

$$\mathcal{F}(\vec{x}) = \sum_{i=1}^{N} f_i(x_i, x_{i1}, x_{i2}, \ldots x_{iK}), \tag{7.1}$$

where the ith contribution, f_i, depends on x_i and K other x_{ij}'s. This functional form for $\mathcal{F}$ represents epistatic interactions between the ith bit and K other bits that are assumed to affect i's fitness contribution. The K bits associated with each locus can be either the ith bit's immediate neighbors or their positions can be completely random. The functions f_i are usually random functions of their arguments, with values chosen randomly from among the 2^{K+1} possible values. Once all the x_{ij}s and f_i's are chosen, they remain fixed and the behavior of $\mathcal{F}$ is then explored as a particular instance of a well-defined NK-landscape. The goal is to explore how the statistical properties of NK-landscapes—such as the number of local optima, the average length of an "adaptive walk" from a given point to a global maximum, and so on, and as parametrized by N and K—affect the performance of GAs.

As K increases from 0 (where $\mathcal{F}(\vec{x}) = \sum_i f_i(x_i)$) to $N - 1$ (where $\mathcal{F}$ becomes the sum of N independent random numbers), the NK-landscape goes from having a single maximum to having more and more maxima that become less and less correlated to, finally, being essentially totally random. The parameter K can therefore be used to *tune* the degree of "ruggedness" of the landscape.

Some preliminary suggestions of how NK-landscapes can be used to predict GA performance are discussed by Kauffman [Kauff89] and Manderick, de Weger and Spiessens [Mand91].

*NK-landscapes are slightly different representations of Kauffman's *Random Boolean Networks*, discussed on pages 429-436 (section 8.6) in [Ilach01].

7.1.3 *The Basic GA Recipe*

Although GAs, like cellular automata, come in many different flavors, and are usually fine-tuned in some way to reflect the nuances of a particular problem, they are all more or less variations of the following basic steps (see figure 7.3):

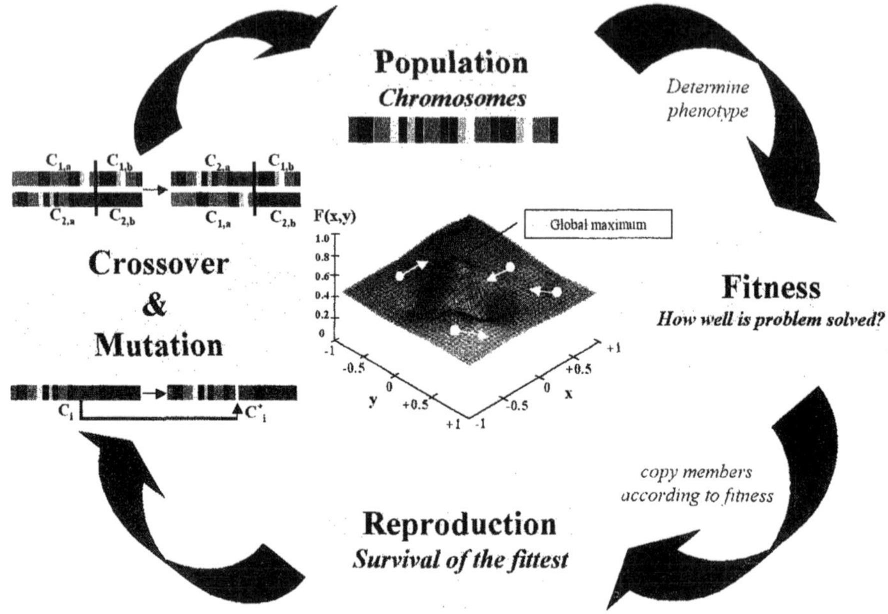

Fig. 7.3 Basic steps of a genetic algorithm.

Step 1: Begin with a randomly generated population, $\mathcal{P}_{K,N}$, of K length-N chromosome encoded "solutions" to a given problem. Let the nth chromosome $\mathcal{C}_n$ be the binary string $\mathcal{C}_n = \beta_1\beta_2\cdots\beta_N$, where $\mathcal{C}_n = \beta_1\beta_2\cdots\beta_N$.

Step 2: Calculate the fitness, f_n, of each chromosome $\mathcal{C}_n$ in the population: $f_n = f(\mathcal{C}_n)$. (See **Mission-Fitness Measures** below.)

Step 3: Generate a new size-K population of chromosomes from the old population using *fitness-scaled* genetic reproduction. That is, copy each chromosome $\mathcal{C}_n$ a number of times, τ_n, that is proportional to its fitness divided by the average fitness of the entire population: $\tau_n \propto f_n/\sum_i f_i$.

Step 4: Randomly pairing up the chromosomes in the new population, apply the genetic crossover operator to each pair. That is, randomly select a bit-position, say

k, for each pair of chromosomes, say $\mathcal{C}_{n_1}$ and $\mathcal{C}_{n_2}$, and replace this pair with two new pairs—$\mathcal{C}'_{n_1}$ and $\mathcal{C}'_{n_2}$—constructed via genetic crossover: $\mathcal{C}'_{n_1}$ consists of the first k bits of $\mathcal{C}_{n_1}$ and the last $(N-k)$ bits of $\mathcal{C}_{n_2}$; and $\mathcal{C}'_{n_2}$ consists of the first k bits of $\mathcal{C}_{n_2}$ and the last $(N-k)$ bits of $\mathcal{C}_{n_1}$.

Step 5: Loop through each bit of each chromosome in the population and perform genetic mutation; i.e. flip the bit-value ($0 \to 1$ and $1 \to 0$) at each locus with some (typically small; see below) probability, p_m. (In practice, this step is combined with **Step 4**.)

Step 6: Goto **Step 2** and repeat ***Steps 2-6*** until desired level of "fitness" is achieved.

This basic six step algorithm will be adapted to simple "mission-specific" combat scenarios in the next section.

7.1.3.1 *A Simple Example*

As a concrete example, suppose our problem is to maximize the fitness function $f(x) = x^2$, using a size $K = 6$ population of 6-bit chromosomes of the form $\mathcal{C} = (\beta_i\beta_2 \cdots \beta_6)$, where $\beta_i \in \{0,1\}$, $i = 1, 2 \ldots, 6$. $\mathcal{C}$'s fitness is determined by first converting its binary representation into a base-10 equivalent value and squaring: $f(\mathcal{C}) = (\sum_{i=1}^{6} 2^{i-1}\beta_{7-i})^2$.

$\mathcal{P}$	$f(\mathcal{P})$	τ_n	$\mathcal{P}'$	Crossover	Mutation	f_{new}
(101101)	2025	1.4→1	(101101)	$(1\underline{3}4) \to (101001)$	(101001)	1681
(010110)	484	0.3→0	(111001)	$(2\underline{2}6) \to (111101)$	(111101)	3481
(111001)	3249	2.2→3	(111001)	$(3\underline{5}5) \to (111001)$	(111001)	3249
(101011)	1849	1.3→1	(111001)	$(4\underline{3}1) \to (111101)$	$(1111\underline{1}1)$	3969
(010001)	289	0.2→0	(101011)	$(5\underline{5}3) \to (101011)$	$(10101\underline{0})$	1764
(011101)	841	0.6→1	(011101)	$(6\underline{2}2) \to (011001)$	(011001)	625

Table 7.1 One pass (read left to right) through the steps of a basic genetic algorithm scheme to maximize the fitness function $f(x) = x^2$ using a population of six 6-bit chromosomes. The crossover notation $(\alpha_1\underline{n}\alpha_2)$ means that chromosomes $\mathcal{C}_{\alpha_1}$ and $\mathcal{C}_{\alpha_2}$ exchange bits beyond the nth bit. The underlined bits in the "Mutation Operation" column are the only ones that have undergone random mutation. See text for other details.

Table 7.1 shows the intermediate steps of the first pass through the above six steps of the basic GA recipe. Step 1 is to construct six random bit-strings representing our original population:

$$\begin{cases} C_1 &= (101101) \\ C_2 &= (010110) \\ C_3 &= (111001) \\ C_4 &= (101011) \\ C_5 &= (010001) \\ C_6 &= (011101) \end{cases} \quad (7.2)$$

These chromosomes have fitness values of 2025, 484, 3249, 1849, 289 and 841, respectively. The average fitness is 1456. By luck of the *fitness-scaled* draw, where the number of copies of a given chromosome is determined according to its fitness, scaled by the average fitness of the entire population, three copies of C_3 are made for the next population (owing to its relatively high fitness), one copy each for chromosomes C_1, C_4 and C_6 and none for the remaining chromosomes. These copies form the mating population.

Next, we randomly pair up the new chromosomes, and perform the genetic crossover operation at randomly selected bit-positions—chromosomes C_1 and C_4 exchange their last three bits, C_2 and C_6 exchange their last four bits, and C_3 and C_5 exchange their last bit:

$$\begin{cases} C_1 \times C_4 \text{ at bit } 3 &= (101^{\downarrow}101) \times (101^{\downarrow}011) \to (101001) \\ C_2 \times C_6 \text{ at bit } 2 &= (01^{\downarrow}0110) \times (01^{\downarrow}1101) \to (111101) \\ C_3 \times C_5 \text{ at bit } 5 &= (11100^{\downarrow}1) \times (01000^{\downarrow}1) \to (111001) \\ C_4 \times C_1 \text{ at bit } 3 &= (101^{\downarrow}011) \times (101^{\downarrow}101) \to (111101) \\ C_5 \times C_3 \text{ at bit } 5 &= (01000^{\downarrow}1) \times (11100^{\downarrow}1) \to (101011) \\ C_6 \times C_2 \text{ at bit } 2 &= (01^{\downarrow}1101) \times (01^{\downarrow}0110) \to (011001) \end{cases} \quad (7.3)$$

Finally, we mutate each bit of the resulting chromosomes with some small probability—say $p_m = 0.05$. In our example we find that values of the *fifth* bit in C_4 and *sixth* bit in C_5 are flipped. The resulting strings make up our 2nd generation chromosome population. By chance, the first loop through the algorithm has successfully turned up the *most-fit* chromosome—C_4 =(111111)→ $f(C_4) = 63^2 = 3969$—but in general the entire procedure would have to be repeated many times to approach the "desired" solution.

7.1.4 *How Do GAs Work?*

While GAs are very simple to describe and implement on a computer, their behavior can be quite complex: complex in its unpredictability, complex to understand, and often exhibiting a complex-system-like emergent behavior [Forrest90]. There are a number of fundamental questions concerning how GAs work, not all of which have been completely answered. The first, and obvious, question is how do they manage to work at all? Given the vast number of possible genotypes of a size-N "solution" ($= 2^N$), it is not immediately clear why *any* finite search-strategy—be it serial, parallel, hill-climbing or whatever—should ever consistently come close to the desired solution in a reasonable time, particularly for large N. Since the efficacy of an optimization scheme depends strongly on the fitness landscape, one would also like to characterize the kinds of fitness landscapes that are most amenable to a GA solution. It is also important to explore ways in which GAs differ from more traditional hill-climbing methods like gradient-ascent. Are all such methods, GAs included, equally adept at "solving" the same sorts of problems? Or are different methods best suited for specific kinds of problems? If so, how are these problems, and presumably their fitness landscapes, different from one another? While it would take us too far afield to explore these and other important questions in any great depth, we will briefly discuss a notion that most formal studies of the theory behind GAs begin with: the *building-block hypothesis.*

7.1.4.1 *The Building-Block Hypothesis*

An heuristic explanation of why GA work—called the *building-block hypothesis* ([Goldb89], [Holl92a])—is based on the idea that good solutions tend to be formed out of sets of good building-blocks (or *schemas*). GAs discover these solutions by assigning higher fitness-levels to—and therefore tending to retain, over the course of successive generations—sets of strings containing good schemas.

By schema, we mean templates, or forms for particular kinds of strings. For example, the schema $\mathcal{S} = (1****0)$, where $*$ is a "wildcard" that stands for either bit-value 0 or 1, represents the template for all length-6 chromosomes whose first bit $\beta_1 = 1$ and last bit $\beta_6 = 1$. In this case, since the schema contains one fixed bit and the distance between the outer most fixed bits is 5, $\mathcal{S}$ is said to be an *order*-1 schema with *defining length* $\delta = 5$. The above example, in which we used length-6 chromosomes to maximize the function $f(x) = x^2$, illustrates why schema can be thought of as simple building-blocks of "fit" genes. In that example, any chromosome of the form $(1*****)$ is obviously more fit than $(0*****)$, and thus forms a basic building block out of which the best "solutions" must be constructed.

Now, to be sure, not every possible subset of the solution-space can be described as a schema. Simple counting shows that a length-N chromosome can have 2^N possible configurations, and therefore 2^{2^N} possible subsets, but only 3^N different schemas. Nonetheless, it is a central axiom of the building-block hypothesis that it is precisely the set of schemas that are effectively being processed by GAs.

The schema population can be estimated using a simple mean-field-like argument. Let $\mathcal{S}$ represent a schema in a size-K population $\mathcal{P}(t)$ at time t, and $Z(\mathcal{P},t)$ instances of the schema at time t. Let $f(s)$ be the fitness of the string s, $\bar{f}_{\mathcal{S}}$ be the average fitness of instances of $\mathcal{S}$ at time t, and $\bar{f} = K^{-1}\sum_i f_i$ be the average fitness of the population. Then the expected number of instances of $\mathcal{S}$ at time $t+1$, $Z(\mathcal{P},t+1)$, is equal to:

$$Z(\mathcal{P},t+1) = \sum_{s\in\mathcal{S}} \frac{f(s)}{\bar{f}} = \frac{\sum_{s\in\mathcal{S}} f(s)}{\bar{f}} = \frac{\bar{f}_{\mathcal{S}}}{\bar{f}} Z(\mathcal{P},t), \tag{7.4}$$

since, by definition, $\bar{f}_{\mathcal{S}} = \sum_{s \in \mathcal{S}} f(s)/Z(\mathcal{P}, t)$.

This basic difference equation—known as the *Schema Theorem* [Holl92a]—expresse the fact that the sample representation of schemas whose average fitness remains above average relative to the whole population increases exponentially over time. As it stands, however, this equation addresses only the reproduction operator, and ignores effects of both crossover and mutation.

A lower bound on the overall effect of crossover, which can both create and destroy instances of a given schema, can be estimated by calculating the probability, $p_C(\mathcal{S})$, that crossover leaves a schema $\mathcal{S}$ unaltered. Let p_c be the probability that the crossover operation will be applied to a string. Since a schema $\mathcal{S}$ will be destroyed by crossover if the operation is applied anywhere within its defining length, the probability that $\mathcal{S}$ will be destroyed is equal to $p_c \times \delta(\mathcal{S})/(K-1)$, where $\delta(\mathcal{S})$ is the defining length of $\mathcal{S}$. Hence, the probability of survival $p_{\mathcal{S}} = 1 - p_c\delta(\mathcal{S})/(K-1)$, and equation 7.4takes the updated form:

$$Z(\mathcal{P}, t+1) \geq \frac{\bar{f}_{\mathcal{S}}}{\bar{f}} \left(1 - p_c \frac{\delta(\mathcal{S})}{K-1}\right) Z(\mathcal{P}, t). \tag{7.5}$$

Finally, in order to also take into account the mutation operator, we note that the probability that a schema $\mathcal{S}$ survives under mutation is given by $p_M(\mathcal{S}) = (1 - p_m)^{\mathcal{O}(\mathcal{S})}$, where p_m is the single-bit mutation probability and $\mathcal{O}(\mathcal{S})$ is the number of fixed-bits (i.e. the order) or $\mathcal{S}$. With this we can now express the *Schema Theorem* that (partially) respects the operations of reproduction, crossover and mutation:

$$Z(\mathcal{P}, t+1) \geq \frac{\bar{f}_{\mathcal{S}}}{\bar{f}} \left(1 - p_c \frac{\delta(\mathcal{S})}{K-1}\right) \left\{(1 - p_m)^{\mathcal{O}(\mathcal{S})}\right\} Z(\mathcal{P}, t). \tag{7.6}$$

We conclude from this basic theorem that the sample representation of low-order schemas with above average fitness relative to the fitness of the population increases exponentially over time.*

7.2 GAs Adapted to EINSTein

Figure 7.4 illustrates how GAs are used in EINSTein. Chromosomes define individual agents. Alleles encode the components of the personality weight vector, sensor range, fire range, μ-rule thresholds, etc. The initial GA population consists of a set of randomly generated chromosomes. The fitness function represents a user-specified mission "fitness" (see below).

*The fact that we have ignored possible crossover and/or mutation induced creations of previously nonexisting instances of schemas means only that the right hand side of the above equation represents a lower bound; the conclusion remains generally valid, as it stands.

The target of the GA search is always the red force. The parameter values defining the blue force, once they are defined at the start of a search, are held fixed.

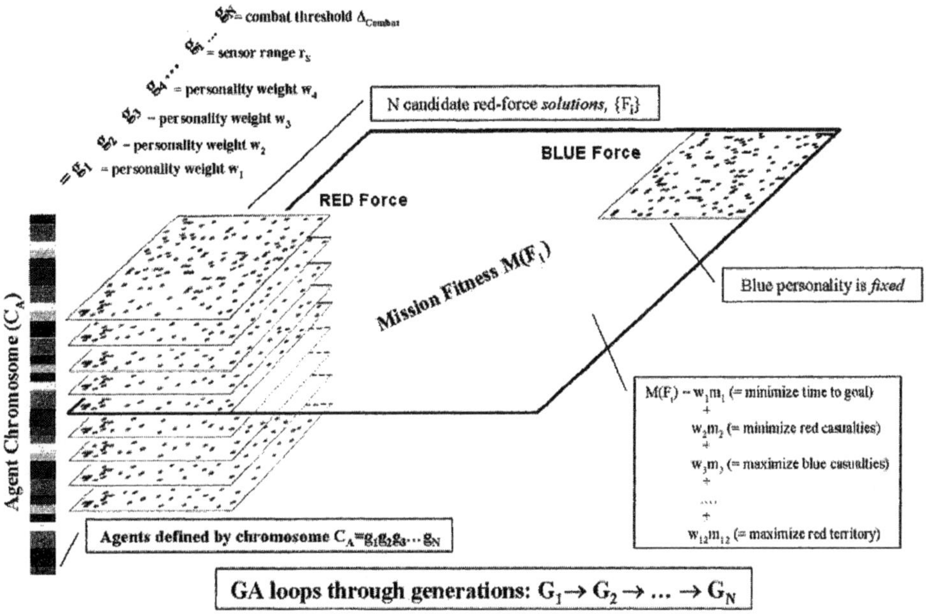

Fig. 7.4 Schematic of EINSTein's built-in genetic algorithm. The blue (dark grey) force and mission fitness (MF) are both fixed by user input. The GA encodes components of the agents' personality weight vector, sensor range, fire range, μ-rule thresholds, etc. and breeds the "best" red (light grey) force using populations of N red force "candidate" solutions; see text for details.

EINSTein currently uses up to 80 genes to conduct a GA search, although this set of genes neither spans the entire set of EINSTein primitives nor is necessarily used in its entirety during a given search. Some genes are integer valued (such as the agent-to-agent communication links), while others are real valued. All appropriate translations to integer values and or binary toggles (on/off) are performed automatically by the program. For the most part, each gene encodes the value of a basic parameter defining the red force. For example, g_1 encodes red's sensor range when an agent is in the alive state, g_3 encodes red's alive-state fire range, and so on. Some special genes encode the sign (+ or −) of an associated parametric gene. Thus, the actual value of each of the components of red's personality weight vector, for example, is actually encoded by two genes; one gene specifying the component's absolute value, the other defining its sign.

7.2.1 *Mission Fitness Measures*

The *mission fitness* (MF) is a measure of how well agents perform a user-defined mission. Typical missions might be to get to blue flag as quickly as possible, minimize red casualties, maximize the ratio of blue to red casualties, and so on, or some combination of these. MFs are always defined from red's perspective. The user assigns up to twelve weights:

$$0 \le w_1, w_2, w_3, ... w_{12} \le 1, \tag{7.7}$$

to represent the relative degree of importance of each mission fitness primitive, m_i (see table 7.2). While the mission primitives are relatively few in number and simple, they can be combined to define more complicated multi-objective functions.

GA Weight	Primitive	Description
w_1	m_1	minimize time to goal
w_2	m_2	minimize friendly casualties
w_3	m_3	maximize enemy casualties
w_4	m_4	maximize friendly-to-enemy survival ratio
w_5	m_5	minimize friendly center-of-mass distance to enemy flag
w_6	m_6	maximize enemy center-of-mass distance to friendly flag
w_7	m_7	maximize number of friendly agents within distance D_F of enemy flag
w_8	m_8	minimize number of enemies within distance D_E of friendly flag
w_9	m_9	minimize number of friendly fratricide hits
w_{10}	m_{10}	maximize number of enemy fratricide hits
w_{11}	m_{11}	maximize friendly territorial possession
w_{12}	m_{12}	minimize enemy territorial possession

Table 7.2 EINSTein's genetic algorithm mission fitness primitives.

The MF function, M, used by the GA, is a weighted sum of mission primitives:

$$M = w_1 m_1 + w_2 m_2 + ... + w_{12} m_{12}. \tag{7.8}$$

A simple mission objective might be to *"get to the blue flag as quickly as possible,"* in which case $w_1 = 1$ and $M = m_1$. If, in addition, you wish to *"minimize red losses"* (defined by primitive m_2), but care more about minimizing the time it takes red to get to the blue flag than about casualties, you might set w_1 equal to 3/4 and $w_2 = 1 - w_1 = 1/4$. The total mission fitness in this case is then given by $M = (3/4) \cdot m_1 + (1/4) \cdot m_2$. A still more complicated mission objective might be to simultaneously satisfy several mission primitives:

- *Maneuver as many red agents within a certain range of the blue flag as possible* (m_7),

- *Keep blue forces as far from red flag as possible* (m_6),
- *Minimize red casualties* (m_2),
- *Maximize red to blue losses* (m_4),
- *Minimize red fratricide* (m_9),

so that, if each of these primitives is afforded equal weight, the composite mission objective is in this case given by $M = 1/5 \cdot (m_2 + m_4 + m_6 + m_7 + m_9)$. Of course, not all such composite missions make sense, or lead to red force personalities that are able to perform them to a desired fitness level. It is the analyst's task to ensure that mission objectives are both logically consistent and amenable to a "solution." Since GA searches are usually time consuming, it is helpful, in practice, to first use EINSTein to map out a few fitness-landscapes, over parameter subspaces of interest. In this way, one can get an idea of how rugged the landscape will be, and thus of where to better target the GA search.

Future versions of EINSTein will include a richer set of mission-fitness primitives, including:

- *Locate and kill enemy squad leaders,*
- *Stay close to friends,*
- *Stay away from enemies,*
- *Combat efficiency (as measured by cumulative number of hits on enemy),*
- *Clear specified area of enemy agents,*
- *Occupy area for specified period of time, and*
- *Take the enemy flag under specific conditions (for example, the user is asked to specify the number of agents that must occupy a given area around the enemy flag for a given length of time).*

7.2.2 *Fitness Function*

Note that half of the GA weights refer to mission primitives that involve functions whose values (as described above) must be minimized (m_1, m_2, m_5, m_8, m_9, and m_{12}) and half refer to primitives that involve functions whose values must be maximized ($m_3, m_4, m_6, m_7, m_{10}$ and m_{11}). In fact, all mission primitives are internally represented by a function that takes values between zero (corresponding to zero fitness) and one (corresponding to maximum fitness) and that the GA always attempts to maximize. The result is that while it may be intuitive to refer to some mission primitives (such as m_1 = *minimize time to goal*) in terms of a quantity that must be minimized, in fact, all primitives are actually defined inside of the program in such a way that the GA consistently tries to *maximize their fitness.*

The general template for how each primitive is treated internally by the program is as follows. First, for each primitive m_i, the minimal ($= x_{min}$) and maximal ($= x_{max}$) possible values for the pertinent parameter x is identified. For example, for m1 = minimize time to goal the pertinent variable is x = *time to goal*; for m_2 =

minimize red casualties, the pertinent variable is x = *number of red casualties*, and so on. Next, and without loss of generality, a simple function $f = f(x)$ is defined that takes on values between *zero* and *one* so that $f(x_{min}) = 0$ corresponds to minimal fitness and $f(x_{max}) = 1$ corresponds to maximal fitness:

$$f(x) = \left(1 - \frac{x_{max} - x}{x_{max} - x_{min}}\right)^n, \tag{7.9}$$

where the (user-defined) power n determines how rapidly $f(x)$ falls off from its maximal to minimal fitness.* In general, the closer the value of $f(x)$ is to the value 1, the better the red agents are said to have performed the particular mission primitive that $f(x)$ is the fitness function for; see figure 7.5.

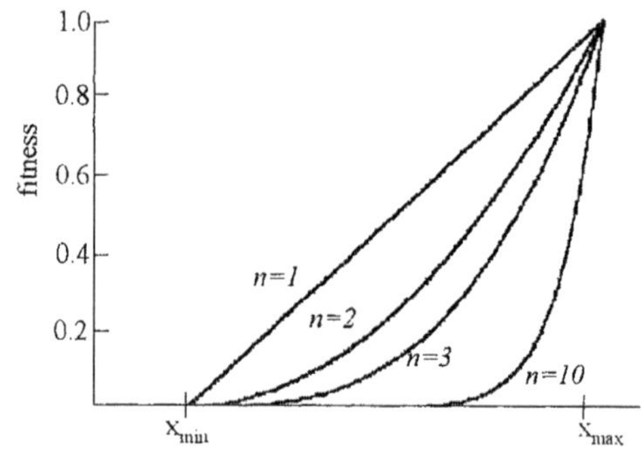

Fig. 7.5 The generic form of EINSTein's normalized mission fitness function (equation 7.9).

We now introduce each of the twelve mission primitives and their corresponding fitness functions.

7.2.2.1 *Mission primitive* m_1

The first mission primitive consists of minimizing the time to goal. You can define an auxiliary condition triggering the red-at-goal flag by requiring that a certain number of red agents must be within a range R of the blue flag.

The pertinent parameter for m_1 is t_G = *time to goal*. The minimal possible value of t_G, $t_{G,min}$, is determined by computing how much time it would take an agent that is closest to the blue flag to get to the flag if there were no other agents on the battlefield. The maximum value, $t_{G,max}$, is set by the user.

The fitness function for m_1 is given by:

$$f_1 = \left[\frac{t_{G,max} - t_G}{t_{G,max} - t_{G,min}}\right]^n. \tag{7.10}$$

*The power n is called **penalty_power** in EINSTein's iunput data file; see *Appendix E: A Concise User's Guide to EINSTein* (page E).

Notice that if the red agents reach the blue flag only at the maximum allotted time, their mission fitness is zero. Conversely, if they reach the flag in the minimal possible time, their fitness is one.

7.2.2.2 *Mission primitive* m_2

The second mission primitive consists of minimizing the total number of red casualties. The pertinent parameter for m_2 is R_t = *number of red agents at time* t. Note that no distinction is made between alive or injured agents. The minimal possible value of R_t, R_{min}, is equal to zero, while the maximum possible value is $R_{max} = R_0$, or the total number of red agents at time $t = 0$.

The fitness function for m_2 is given by:

$$f_2 = \left(\frac{R_T}{R_0}\right)^n, \tag{7.11}$$

where T is the termination time for the run (which can vary depending on the selected termination condition). Notice that if red suffers no losses at all, so that $R_T = R_0$, then $f_2 = 1$. Conversely, if all red agents are lost, then their mission fitness for this primitive is zero.

7.2.2.3 *Mission primitive* m_3

The third mission primitive consists of maximizing the total number of blue casualties. The pertinent parameter for m_3 is B_t = *number of blue agents at time* t. Note that no distinction is made between alive or injured agents. The minimal possible value of B_t, B_{min}, is equal to zero, while the maximum possible value is $B_{max} = B_0$, or the total number of blue agents at time $t = 0$.

The fitness function for m_3 is given by:

$$f_3 = \left(1 - \frac{B_T}{B_0}\right)^n, \tag{7.12}$$

where T is the termination time for the run (which can vary depending on the selected termination condition). Notice that if blue suffers no losses at all, so that $B_T = B_0$, then, from red's point of view, the mission fitness is minimal, and $f3 = 0$. Conversely, if the red agents have successfully killed all blue agents—so that $B_T = 0$—then their mission fitness is maximal, and $f_3 = 1$.

7.2.2.4 *Mission primitive* m_4

The fourth mission primitive consists of maximizing the ratio between red and blue casualties. There are two pertinent parameters for m_4: R_t = *number of red agents at time* t and B_t = *number of blue agents at time* t. Note that no distinction is made between alive or injured agents. The minimal possible values of R_t and B_t, are equal to zero, while the maximum possible values are $R_{max} = B_0$ and $B_{max} = B_0$, or the total number of red and blue agents at time $t = 0$.

The fitness function for m_4 is given by:

$$f_4 = f_4(R_T, B_T) = \left(\frac{R_T/R_0}{B_T/B_0}\right) \left[(\frac{B_0 - 2}{B_0 - 1})(\frac{R_T/R_0}{B_T/B_0}) + \frac{B_0}{B_0 - 1} \right]^{-n}, \tag{7.13}$$

where T is the termination time for the run (which can vary depending on the selected termination condition). This fitness function is defined to give intuitively reasonable values for some extremal values. For example, $f_4(R_T = 0, B_T) = 0$ for any value of B_T, reflecting the intuition that if the entire red side is killed, the mission fitness is minimal, regardless of the number of remaining blue forces. If the fraction of remaining forces is equal on both sides, so that, say, $R_T/R_0 = B_T/B_0 = \rho$, then $f_4(\rho R_0, \rho B_0) = 1/2$, reflecting the intuition that if red only keeps pace with blue casualties (but that, perhaps, both sides have suffered some casualties), the mission fitness lies somewhere halfway between its minimal and maximal values. Finally, if the number of red agents at time $t = T$ is equal to the initial number of red agents while the number of blue agents has been reduced to one, the mission fitness approaches its maximal possible value: $f_4(R_T = 0, B_T = 1) \to 0$. Intermediate values of R and B_T yield values for f_4 between zero and one.

7.2.2.5 *Mission primitive* m_5

The fifth mission primitive consists of minimizing the average red center-of-mass distance to the blue flag. The pertinent parameter for m_5 is d = *distance between the center-of-mass* (CM) of the red force and the position of the blue flag at time t. The $x_{red,CM}$ and $y_{red,CM}$ coordinates of the red center-of-mass are defined by:

$$x_{red,CM}(t) = \frac{1}{R_t} \sum_{i=1}^{R_t} x_{red,i}(t), \quad y_{red,CM}(t) = \frac{1}{R_t} \sum_{i=1}^{R_t} y_{red,i}(t), \tag{7.14}$$

where $x_{red,i}(t)$ and $y_{red,i}(t)$ are the x and y positions of the ith red agent at time t, respectively, and R_t is the number of red agents at time t.

The fitness function for m_5 is given by:

$$f_5 = \left(\frac{d_{max} - d_{red,ave}}{d_{max}}\right)^n, \tag{7.15}$$

where $d_{max} = \sqrt{2} \cdot$ *battlefield_size* and $d_{red,ave}$ is the average red center-of-mass distance to the blue flag:

$$d_{red,ave} = \frac{1}{T} \left[(x_{\text{blue-flag}} - x_{red,CM}(t))^2 + (y_{\text{blue-flag}} - y_{red,CM}(t))^2 \right]^{1/2}, \tag{7.16}$$

where T is the termination time for the run (which can vary depending on the selected termination condition). Notice that if the red force is close to the blue flag at all times (so that $d_{red,ave} \sim 0$), then $f5 \sim 1$. Conversely, if the red agents spend most of their time far from the blue goal (so that $d_{red,ave} \sim d_{max}$), then $f_5 \sim 0$.

7.2.2.6 *Mission primitive m_6*

The sixth mission primitive consists of maximizing the average blue center-of-mass distance to the red flag. The pertinent parameter for m_6 is d = *distance between the center-of-mass* (CM) of the blue force and the position of the red flag at time t. The $x_{blue,CM}$ and $y_{blue,CM}$ coordinates of the red center-of-mass are defined by:

$$x_{blue,CM}(t) = \frac{1}{B_t}\sum_{i=1}^{B_t} x_{blue,i}(t), \quad y_{blue,CM}(t) = \frac{1}{B_t}\sum_{i=1}^{B_t} y_{blue,i}(t), \tag{7.17}$$

where $x_{blue,i}(t)$ and $y_{blue,i}(t)$ are the x and y positions of the ith blue agent at time t, respectively, and B_t is the number of blue agents at time t.

The fitness function for m_6 is given by:

$$f_6 = \left(\frac{d_{blue,ave}}{d_{max}}\right)^n, \tag{7.18}$$

where $d_{max} = \sqrt{2}\cdot$ *battlefield_size* and $d_{blue,ave}$ is the average blue center-of-mass distance to the blue flag:

$$d_{blue,ave} = \frac{1}{T}\left[\left(x_{\text{red-flag}} - x_{blue,CM}(t)\right)^2 + \left(y_{\text{red-flag}} - y_{blue,CM}(t)\right)^2\right]^{1/2}, \tag{7.19}$$

where T is the termination time for the run (which can vary depending on the selected termination condition). Notice that if the blue force is close to the red flag at all times (so that $d_{blue,ave} \sim 0$), then $f_6 \sim 0$. Conversely, if the blue agents spend most of their time far from the red flag (so that $d_{blue,ave} \sim d_{max}$), then $f_6 \sim 1$.

7.2.2.7 *Mission primitive m_7*

The seventh mission primitive consists of maximizing the number of red agents within a user-defined distance of the blue flag. The pertinent parameter for m_7 is $R_t(D)$ = *number of red agents within a distance D of the blue flag at time t*, where D is a user-specified parameter. Note that no distinction is made between alive or injured agents. The minimal possible value of $R_t(D)$ is equal to zero, while the maximum possible value, R_{max}, clearly depends on D and is internally calculated by the program.

The fitness function for m_7 ($= f_7$) is given by a time average of $(R_t(D)/R_{max})^n$, averaged between t_{min} (corresponding to the earliest possible time that a red agent could move to within a distance D of the blue flag) and $t_{max} = T$ is the termination time for the run (which can vary depending on the selected termination condition):

$$f_7 = \frac{1}{T - t_{\min}} \sum_{t=t_{\min}}^{T} \left(\frac{R_t(D)}{R_{max}} \right)^n . \tag{7.20}$$

Notice that if red is completely unable to penetrate blue's territory for the duration of the run, so that $R_t(D) = 0$ for times t, then $f_7 = 0$. Conversely, if red is able to maintain a constant presence within a distance D of blue's flag (which is likely only in the event that there are few or no blue forces defending the flag), then their mission fitness for this primitive approaches the value one.

7.2.2.8 *Mission primitive m_8*

The eighth mission primitive consists of minimizing the number of blue agents within a user-defined distance of the red flag. The pertinent parameter for m_8 is $B_t(D)$ = *number of blue agents within a distance D of the red flag at time t*, where D is a user-specified parameter. Note that no distinction is made between alive or injured agents. The minimal possible value of $B_t(D)$ is equal to zero, while the maximum possible value, B_{max}, clearly depends on D and is internally calculated by the program.

The fitness function for m_8 ($= f_8$) is given by a time average of $(1 - B_t(D)/B_{max})^n$, averaged between t_{min} (corresponding to the earliest possible time that a blue agent could move to within a distance D of the red flag) and $t_{max} = T$ is the termination time for the run (which can vary depending on the selected termination condition):

$$f_8 = \frac{1}{D - t_{\min}} \sum_{t=t_{\min}}^{T} \left(1 - \frac{B_t(D)}{B_{max}} \right)^n . \tag{7.21}$$

If blue is completely unable to penetrate red's territory for the duration of the run, so that $B_t(D) = 0$ for times t, then red may be said to have "succeeded in keeping blue away from its own flag" and $f_8 = 1$. Conversely, if blue is able to maintain a constant presence within a distance D of red's flag (which is likely only in the event that there are few or no red forces available to defend the flag), $B_t(D) \sim B_{max}$ and red's mission fitness for this primitive approaches zero.

7.2.2.9 *Mission primitive m_9*

The ninth mission primitive consists of minimizing the total number of red fratricide hits. This primitive is viable only if the *red_frat_flag* logical toggle switch is set equal to *one* in EINSTein's input data file, so that the red fratricide option during a run is enabled.*

*See page 666 in Appendix G.

The pertinent parameter for m_9 is F_{red} = *total number of red fratricide hits during the run.* The minimal possible value of F_{red} is obviously zero, while the maximum possible value is arbitrarily clamped at $F_{red,max} = R_0$, or the total number of red agents at time $_{t=0}$. If the actual value F_{red} exceeds $F_{red,max}$, F_{red} is internally redefined to equal $F_{red,max}$.

The fitness function for m_9 is given by:

$$f_9 = \left(1 - \frac{F_{red}}{R_0}\right)^n . \tag{7.22}$$

If red suffers no fratricide hits at all, so that $F_{red} = 0$, then $f_9 = 1$. Conversely, if red agents are hit by friendly forces at least R_0 times, then red's overall mission fitness for this primitive is zero.

7.2.2.10 *Mission primitive* m_{10}

The tenth mission primitive consists of maximizing the total number of blue fratricide hits. This primitive is viable only if the *blue_frat_flag* logical toggle switch is set equal to *one* in EINSTein's input data file, so that the blue fratricide option during a run is enabled.*

The pertinent parameter for m_{10} is F_{blue} = *total number of blue fratricide hits during the run.* The minimal possible value of F_{blue} is obviously zero, while the maximum possible value is arbitrarily clamped at $F_{blue,max} = B_0$, or the total number of blue agents at time $t = 0$. If the actual value F_{blue} exceeds $F_{blue,max}$, F_{blue} is internally redefined to equal $F_{blue,max}$.

The fitness function for m_{10} is given by:

$$f_{10} = \left(\frac{F_{blue}}{B_0}\right)^n . \tag{7.23}$$

If blue suffers no fratricide hits at all, so that $F_{blue} = 0$, then $f_{10} = 0$. Conversely, if blue agents are hit by other blue forces at least B_0 times, then red's overall mission fitness for this primitive is one (i.e. red has successfully induced maximum blue fratricide).

7.2.2.11 *Mission primitive* m_{11}

The 11th mission primitive consists of maximizing red's *territorial possession.* Recall that any site at (x, y) "belongs" to an agent (red or blue) according to the following logic: the number of like agents within a territoriality-distance (τ_D) is greater than or equal to territoriality-minimum (τ_{min}) and is at least territoriality-threshold (τ_T) number of agents greater than the number of enemy agents within the same territoriality-distance. For example, if $(\tau_D, \tau_{min}, \tau_T) = (2, 3, 2)$ then a battlefield position (x, y) is said to belong to, say, red, if there are at least 3 red

*See page 666 in Appendix G.

agents within a distance 2 of (x, y) and the number of red agents within that distance outnumber blue agents by at least 2.

The area for which territorial possession will be calculated is defined by the user by specifying the corners of a bounding box, B.

The pertinent parameter for m_{11} is R_T = *average fraction of sites within bounding box B that belong to red.* The minimal possible value of R_T, R_{min}, is equal to zero, while the maximum possible value is $R_{max} = 1$, attained if all sites in B belong to the red force. The fitness function for m11 is given by $f_{11} = (R_T)^n$.

7.2.2.12 *Mission primitive* m_{12}

The 12th mission primitive consists of minimizing blue's territorial possession (see above). As for the red counterpart just discussed, the pertinent parameter for m_{12} is B_T = *average fraction of sites within bounding box B that belong to blue.* The minimal possible value of B_T, B_{min}, is equal to zero, while the maximum possible value is $B_{max} = 1$, attained if all sites in B belong to the blue force. The fitness function for m_{12} is given by:

$$f_{12} = (1 - B_T)^n \,. \tag{7.24}$$

7.2.3 *EINSTein's GA Recipe*

The GA uses EINSTein's combat engine to conduct its searches, although, typically, a given GA search uses only a subset of the total available set of parameters that define individual agents. In pseudocode, the main components of EINSTein GA recipe are as follows:

for generation=1,$G_{\mathbf{max}}$
for personality=1,$P_{\mathbf{max}}$
    decode chromosome
    for initial_ condition IC=1 to $IC_{\mathbf{max}}$
    run combat engine
    calculate fitness (for given IC)
    next initial_ condition
    calculate mission fitness
next personality
find the best personality
select survivors from population
perform (single-point) crossover operation
perform mutation operation
update progress/status
next generation
write best personality to file

In words, the GA uses a randomized pool of chromosomes to define the first generation of red personalities. For each such red personality, and for each of IC_{max} initial spatial configurations of red and blue forces,* the program then runs EINSTein's combat engine to determine the mission fitness.

After looping through all personalities and initial conditions, the GA first sorts and ranks the personalities according to their mission fitness values, then selects some to be eliminated from the pool and others to breed. The GA then performs the basic operations of crossover and mutation. Finally, after defining a new generation of red personalities, the entire process is repeated until either the user interactively interrupts the evolution or the maximum generation number has been reached.

Table 7.3 lists the typical minimum and maximum values of GA run-time parameters.

Parameter	Minimum	Typical	Maximum
Population Size ($= P_{max}$)	5	50	250
Number of initial conditions ($= \mathrm{IC}_{\mathrm{max}}$)	1	10	100
Run-time/sample (depends on scenario)	1	75	250
Penalty power factor	1	2	10
Number of Generations ($= G_{max}$)	1	50	500
Mutation Probability	0	0.10	1
Crossover Probability	0	0.75	1

Table 7.3 The values of some GA run-time parameters used by EINSTein.

A short primer on how to set up a GA search is provided in *Agent "Breeding" Experiment #1* below (see page 525). A more detailed discussion of how to use the GUI to initiate, interact with and terminate GA searches appears in Appendix E (see also EINSTein's *User's Guide* [Ilach99a]).

7.2.4 *EINSTein's GA Search Spaces*

The user has the option to conduct any one of five kinds of GA searches:

- *Single-Squad Personality:* GA searches over the personality-space defining a single squad.
- *Multiple-Squad Personality:* GA searches over the personality-space defining multiple squads. The number of squads and the size of each squad remains fixed throughout this GA run mode.
- *Squad Composition:* GA searches over squad composition space. The personality parameters defining squads 1 through 10 are fixed according to the values defined in the default input data file used to start the interactive run.

*The boxed areas within which red and blue forces are initially placed are kept fixed throughout the GA search; the individual agent positions within those areas are randomized at the start of each sample run.

The GA searches over the space defined by the number of squads (1-10) and size of each squad (constrained by the total number of agents as defined by the data file).

- *Inter-Squad Communications Connectivity:* GA searches over the zero-one entries defining the communications matrix. The number of squads and the number of agents per squad is kept fixed at the values defined in the default input data file used to start the interactive run.
- *Inter-Squad Weight Connectivity:* GA searches over (real-valued) entries defining the squad interconnectivity matrix. The number of squads and the number of agents per squad is kept fixed at the values defined in the default input data file.

7.2.4.1 *Single-Squad Search Space*

The personality, $P_i(G)$, of the ith red agent in the personality pool for generation G, is defined by a unique agent chromosome, $C_i(G)$, defined by:

$$C_i(G) = g_1^{(i)} g_2^{(i)} g_3^{(i)} ... g_N^{(i)}, \tag{7.25}$$

where $g_j^{(i)}$ is the jth gene. EINSTein currently uses $N = 63$ genes for conducting GA searches over the single-squad search space, although this set of genes neither spans the entire set of EINSTein primitives nor is necessarily always used in its entirety during a given GA search. Table 7.4 describes the function of the single-squad GA search space genome.

Note that, unlike some common textbook GA examples, the chromosome is not a binary-valued string that consists only *zeroes* and *ones*. Instead, each gene is *real valued*, and any appropriate translations to integer values and or binary toggles (on/off) are performed automatically by the program.

For the most part, each gene encodes the value of a basic parameter defining the red force. For example, g_1 encodes red's sensor range when an agent is in the alive state, g_3 encodes red's alive-state fire range, and so on. Some genes—for example, the even numbered genes between g_{10} and g_{32}—encode the sign (+ or −) of the immediately preceding gene, but not the actual value. Thus, the actual value of each of the components of red's personality weight vector, for example, is actually encoded by two genes; one gene specifying the component's *absolute value*, the other gene defining its *sign*.

7.2.4.2 *Multiple-Squad Search Space*

The chromosome for multiple-squad searches consists of the same 63 genes as the single-squad genome, except that it is squad-specific. That is, the GA search is conducted over an effective total of $63 \cdot N_{squads}$ genes; one 63-gene-long chromosome for each squad composing the whole force. Squad size and number are both kept fixed throughout the search.

Gene	Function	Min	Max	Gene	Function	Min	Max
1	$(r_{Sensor})_{\text{alive}}$	0	15	33	$(\tau_{Advance})_{\text{alive}}$	0	25
2	$(r_{Sensor})_{\text{injured}}$	0	15	34	$(\tau_{Advance})_{\text{injured}}$	0	25
3	$(r_{Fire})_{\text{alive}}$	0	15	35	$(\tau_{Cluster})_{\text{alive}}$	0	25
4	$(r_{Fire})_{\text{injured}}$	0	15	36	$(\tau_{Cluster})_{\text{injured}}$	0	25
5	$(r_{Threshold})_{\text{alive}}$	0	10	37	$(\Delta_{Ccombat})_{\text{alive}}$	0	25
6	$(r_{Threshold})_{\text{injured}}$	0	10	38	sign (+ or -) of g_{37}	0	1
7	$(r_{Movement})_{\text{alive}}$	0	5	39	$(\Delta_{Ccombat})_{\text{injured}}$	0	25
8	$(r_{Movement})_{\text{injured}}$	0	4	40	sign (+ or -) of g_{39}	0	1
9	$(\omega_{AF})_{\text{alive}}$	0	100	41	$D_{\text{min}}(FF)$	0	10
10	sign (+ or -) of g_9	0	1	42	$(Min_{\text{D,red}})_{\text{alive}}$	0	10
11	$(\omega_{IF})_{\text{alive}}$	0	100	43	$(Min_{\text{D,red}})_{\text{injured}}$	0	10
12	sign (+ or -) of g_{11}	0	1	44	$(Min_{\text{D,blue}})_{\text{alive}}$	0	10
13	$(\omega_{AE})_{\text{alive}}$	0	100	45	$(Min_{\text{D,blue}})_{\text{injured}}$	0	10
14	sign (+ or -) of g_{13}	0	1	46	$(Min_{\text{D,RF}})_{\text{alive}}$	0	10
15	$(\omega_{IE})_{\text{alive}}$	0	100	47	$(Min_{\text{D,RF}})_{\text{injured}}$	0	10
16	sign (+ or -) of g_{15}	0	1	48	$(P_{\text{hit}})_{\text{alive}}$	0	1
17	$(\omega_{FF})_{\text{alive}}$	0	100	49	$(P_{\text{hit}})_{\text{injured}}$	0	1
18	sign (+ or -) of g_{17}	0	1	50	$(Max_{\text{tgts}})_{\text{alive}}$	0	25
19	$(\omega_{EF})_{\text{alive}}$	0	100	51	$(Max_{\text{tgts}})_{\text{injured}}$	0	25
20	sign (+ or -) of g_{19}	0	1	52	$Defense_{\text{alive}}$	0	10
21	$(\omega_{AF})_{\text{injured}}$	0	100	53	$Defense_{\text{injured}}$	0	10
22	sign (+ or -) of g_{21}	0	1	54	R_{Comms}	0	50
23	$(\omega_{IF})_{\text{injured}}$	0	100	55	$(\omega_{\text{Comm}})_{\text{alive}}$	0	1
24	sign (+ or -) of g_{23}	0	1	56	$(\omega_{\text{Comm}})_{\text{injured}}$	0	1
25	$(\omega_{AE})_{\text{injured}}$	0	100	57	$\tau_{\text{reconstitution}}$	0	15
26	sign (+ or -) of g_{25}	0	1	58	$r_{\text{fratricide}}$	0	15
27	$(\omega_{IE})_{\text{injured}}$	0	100	59	$Prob_{\text{fratricide}}$	0	0.25
28	sign (+ or -) of g_{27}	0	1	60	$(B_0)_{\text{width}}$	1	50
29	$(\omega_{FF})_{\text{injured}}$	0	100	61	$(B_0)_{\text{length}}$	1	50
30	sign (+ or -) of g_{29}	0	1	62	$(B_0)_{x-\text{coordinate}}$	1	100
31	$(\omega_{EF})_{\text{injured}}$	0	100	63	$(B_0)_{y-\text{coordinate}}$	1	100
32	sign (+ or -) of g_{31}	0	1				

Table 7.4 EINSTein's *single-squad* genome.

7.2.4.3 *Squad Composition Search Space*

A GA squad composition search consists of searching over the space defined by the number of squads (up to a maximum of eight squads), size of squad, and the components of the inter-squad connectivity matrix.

Personality parameters defining squads one through ten remain fixed according to the values defined in the default input data file. The maximum size of each squad is also constrained by the total number of agents specified in the input data file. Table 7.5 describes the function of the squad-composition GA search space genome.

Gene	Function	Type	Min	Max
1	number of squads: Bit 1 of 3	Binary	0	1
2	number of squads: Bit 2 of 3	Binary	0	1
3	number of squads: Bit 3 of 3	Binary	0	1
4	size of squad 1	Integer	0	50
5	size of squad 2	Integer	0	50
6	size of squad 3	Integer	0	50
7	size of squad 4	Integer	0	50
8	size of squad 5	Integer	0	50
9	size of squad 6	Integer	0	50
10	size of squad 7	Integer	0	50
11	size of squad 8	Integer	0	50
12	Inter-squad connectivity matrix weight ω_{11}	real	-1	1
13	Inter-squad connectivity matrix weight ω_{21}	real	-1	1
14	Inter-squad connectivity matrix weight ω_{31}	real	-1	1
...	...		...	
N	Inter-squad connectivity matrix weight ω_{ij}	real	-1	1
..	...		...	
73	Inter-squad connectivity matrix weight ω_{68}	real	-1	1
74	Inter-squad connectivity matrix weight ω_{78}	real	-1	1
75	Inter-squad connectivity matrix weight ω_{88}	real	-1	1

Table 7.5 EINSTein's *squad-composition* genome.

Gene	Function	Type	Min	Max
1	Inter-squad connectivity matrix component C_{11}	Binary	0	1
2	Inter-squad connectivity matrix component C_{21}	Binary	0	1
3	Inter-squad connectivity matrix component C_{31}	Binary	0	1
...	...		...	
N	Inter-squad connectivity matrix component C_{ij}	Binary	0	1
...	...	Binary	0	1
62	Inter-squad connectivity matrix component C_{68}	Binary	0	1
63	Inter-squad connectivity matrix component C_{78}	Binary	0	1
64	Inter-squad connectivity matrix component C_{88}	Binary	0	1

Table 7.6 EINSTein's *inter-squad communications* genome.

7.2.4.4 *Inter-Squad Communications Connectivity Search*

A GA communications search consists of searching over the space defined by the components of the inter-squad communication matrix elements. Table 7.6 describes the function of the genome used to define the search.

7.2.4.5 *Inter-Squad Weight Connectivity*

A GA inter-squad search consists of searching over the space defined by the components of the inter-squad weight matrix elements. The chromosome consists of the 64 genes, labeled 12 through 75, in table 7.4.

7.3 GA Breeding Experiments

In this section we present a few illustrative sample "breeding" experiments using EINSTein's built-in genetic algorithm. The first such example also includes a self-contained *tutorial* on how to set up, interact with, and extract data from, a typical run.

7.3.1 *Agent "Breeding" Experiment #1 (Tutorial)*

Suppose you are interested in using a genetic algorithm to automatically search over an agent's personality space; i.e. to search over the N-dimensional space that defines an individual agent's dynamical behavior. For example, suppose you want to find the "best" (or, what in practice will generally amount to being a "good") red force that is able to penetrate the defense of a superior blue force and reach the blue flag within a prescribed time.

To see how this is done, first load the *ga_search_sample.dat* input data file to define the scenario.[*] Click either the red or blue D buttons to display an on-screen summary of the associated agent parameter values. Notice that the red force consists of four squads (with sizes 12, 12, 12 and 14, respectively)–each with a different personality–and that the single-shot probability of hit of each blue agent is ten times that of any red agent of any squad ($p_{hit,blue} = 0.05$; $p_{hit,red} = 0.005$). The blue force consists of a single squad.

Figure 7.6, which shows a few snapshots from a typical run of 50 total time steps, gives an idea of the strength of the defending blue force. At time $t = 1$ (not shown), the red force is confined to the lower left region of the battlefield (near the red flag) and the blue force is confined in the upper right region, near its own flag. Observe that, in the sample run shown, *not a single red agent is able to reach the blue flag.* From red's point of view, getting to the blue flag is a challenge.

[*] All sample files, tutorials, and other EINSTein-related documentation may be downloaded from URL address http://www.cna.org/isaac.

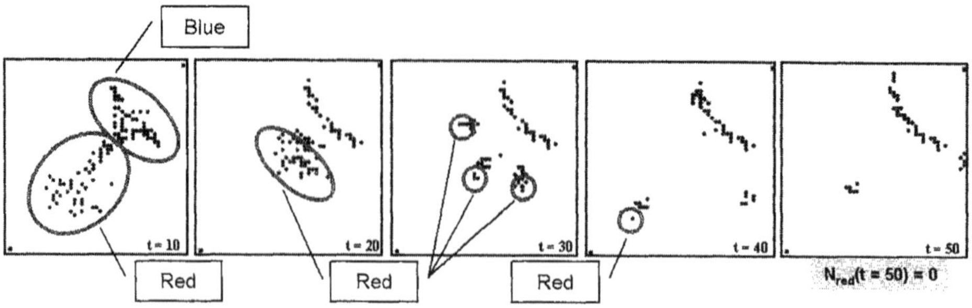

Fig. 7.6 Snapshots of a run using the default GA-breeding scenario #1 (as defined in input data file *ga_ search_ sample.dat*); see text for details.

7.3.1.1 *Setting Up the Run*

Looking at the sample run shown in figure 7.6, it is tempting to ask, *"Can a genetic algorithm find the right mix of red-squad personalities so that at least a few red agents are able to consistently penetrate to within a certain distance of the blue flag within 50 time steps?"* Steps 1 through 6 illustrate how to go about answering this question using EINSTein.

Step 1. Select the *multiple-squad* search option of the *one-sided genetic algorithm* run-mode. It is the second option of the eight listed options. In this mode, EINSTein automatically conducts a genetic algorithm search over the four-squad personality space defined in the *ga_ search_ sample.dat* input data file. While the number of squads and the number of agents per squad will remain fixed throughout the search, the genetic algorithm is otherwise free to explore essentially the entire agent-parameter space.

Once the one-sided genetic algorithm run-mode is enabled, you will be presented with four successive pop-up edit dialogs: (1) *Edit Run-Time Parameters*, (2) *Edit Mission Objective*, (3) *Agent Chromosome*, and (4) *Agent Gene Minimum/Maximum Values.*

Step 2. The *Edit::Run-Time Parameters* dialog specifies the values of run-time variables such as number of initial conditions to average over, maximum run-time, and so on (see figure 7.7). For this sample session, change the default values of *Population Size* (i.e. the first entry at the top of the dialog) from 15 to 75, *Number of Generations* from 50 to 150, and *Number of Initial Conditions* from 2 to 5. Keep all other parameters at their default values. Click [OK] to save the changes and exit the dialog.

Step 3. The *Edit::Mission Objectives Parameters* dialog defines the fitness measure used to rank individual population members during the genetic algorithm run (see figure 7.8). For this sample session, use the left-hand mouse button to uncheck the

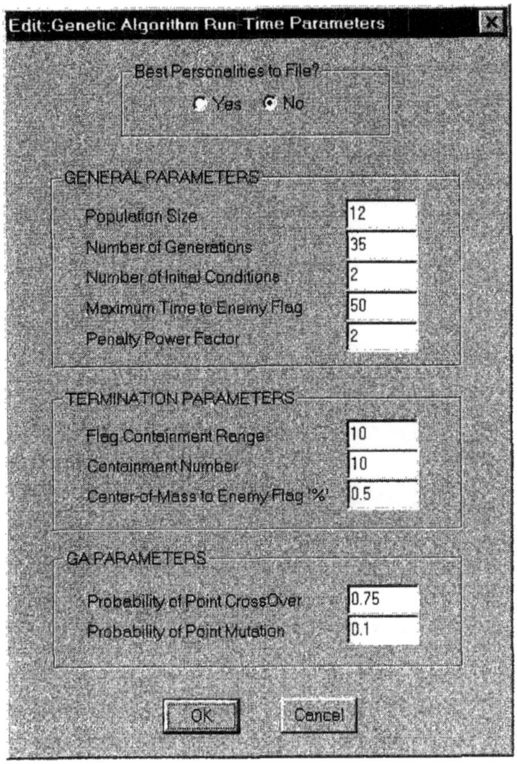

Fig. 7.7 A screenshot of EINSTein's genetic algorithm *run-time parameters* dialog.

entry that is by default checked (*Maximize Enemy Casualties*). Put a check next to the seventh mission primitive = *Maximize Number of Friendly Agents Within Distance D of Enemy Flag*. Also, replace the '0' that appears in the edit box to the left of the check you just set with the value '1'. Keep all other parameters at their default values. Click  to save the changes and exit the dialog. This change tells the genetic algorithm that you want find a red force that will successfully penetrate blue's defense, *without explicit regard for casualties that the red force might suffer in attempting to do so.*

Note that the distance D that is part of the mission primitive specification was actually defined implicitly in the previous step. The value of D is equal to the value of the parameter labeled *Flag Containment Range* appearing near the center of the *Edit::Run-Time Parameters* dialog. The default value, which you left unchanged, is equal to 10. The value of the parameter *Containment Number* (that appears immediately below *Flag Containment Range*) defines the threshold value of red agents N such that if the red force succeeds in positioning at least N red agents within a distance D of the blue flag the mission objective will be maximally fulfilled (i.e. fitness $f \sim 1$).

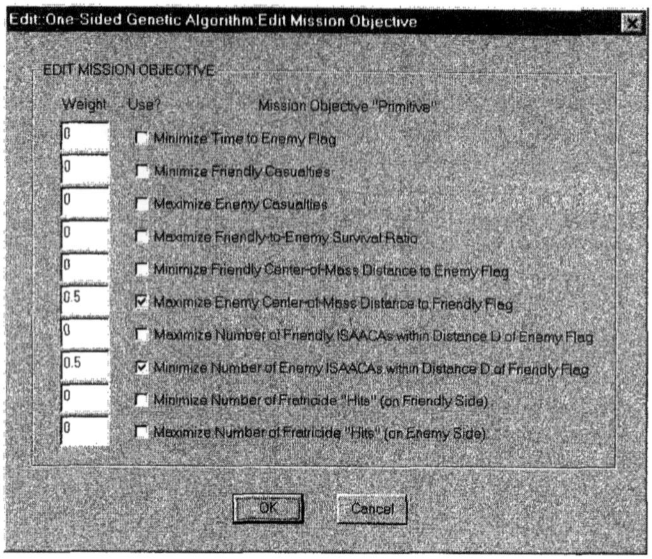

Fig. 7.8 A screenshot of EINSTein's genetic algorithm *mission objectives* dialog.

Step 4. The *Edit::Agent Chromosome Parameters* dialog defines the set of alleles that will be used during the genetic algorithm search; see figure 7.9. For this example, keep the default set of alleles as defined. Click  to define the alleles and exit the dialog.

Step 5. The *Edit::Agent Gene Minimum/Maximum Values* dialog defines the minimum and maximum values of each of the alleles used during the genetic algorithm search; see figure 7.10. For this example, keep the default set of minimum and maximum values as defined. Click  to exit the dialog.

Once this last dialog is closed, EINSTein is ready to perform a genetic algorithm search over a four-squad red agent parameter space. EINSTein replaces its battlefield view of red and blue agents with a simple text-message as shown in figure 7.11, indicating that it is ready to start the run.

Step 6. To start the genetic algorithm search, click anywhere within the text-field in the battlefield view. EINSTein will automatically start the run, informing you of its progress via the status-bar at the lower left of the display screen. The status bar keeps track of the *current generation* [G], *personality* [P], *initial-condition* [IC], *time* [T] of current test-run, and the *best fitness* [F] (x/10000) found thus far (see figure 7.12). When finished, EINSTein will display a dialog to inform you that the run is complete.

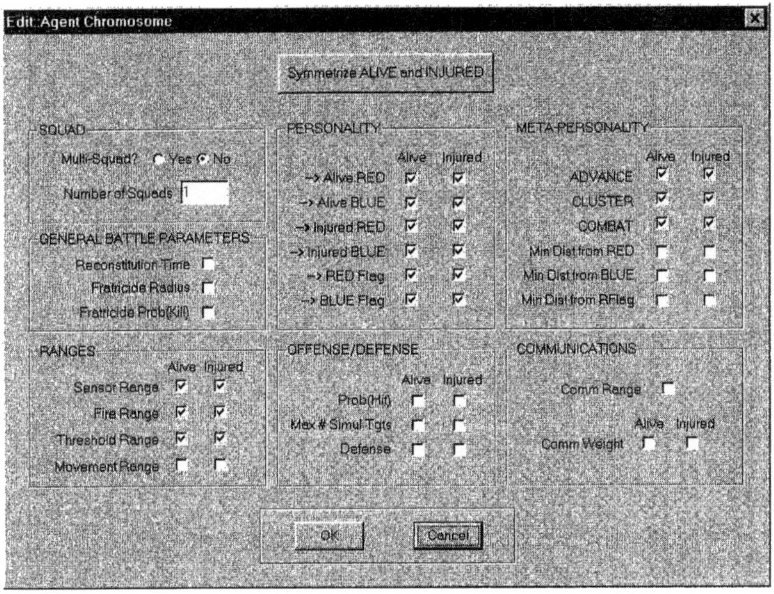

Fig. 7.9 A screenshot of EINSTein's genetic algorithm *agent chromosome* dialog.

7.3.1.2 *Interrupting the Run*

While the full run (over 150 generations), using the run-time settings as defined in the previous section, takes about three hours to complete on a Pentium III 1 GHz CPU, it can be temporarily interrupted at any time to allow EINSTein to perform any of the following functions:

- *Display Statistical Summary of Current Run:* provides a statistical summary of the progress made thus far by the genetic algorithm.
- *Display Current Chromosome:* displays the parameter values defining the red force currently being sampled.
- *Display Best Chromosome:* displays the parameter values defining the best red force that has been thus far found.
- *Display Time-Series:* displays a time-series of fitness values to track the progress of the overall genetic algorithm search.

The first three functions are accessed via the three options appearing at the bottom of the *Display::Data* menu options list. The last function is accessed via the *Genetic Algorithm Progress* option of the *Data Visualization* main menu item.

Display Statistical Summary. Select the option labeled *1-Sided Genetic Algorithm Summary* under the main-menu *Display::Data* options list. This pops up a dialog that summarizes the run; see figure 7.13.

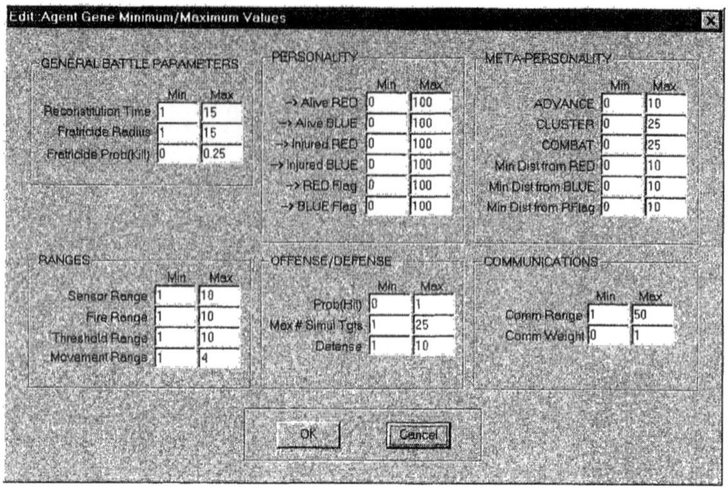

Fig. 7.10 A screenshot of EINSTein's genetic algorithm *agent gene minimum/maximum* dialog.

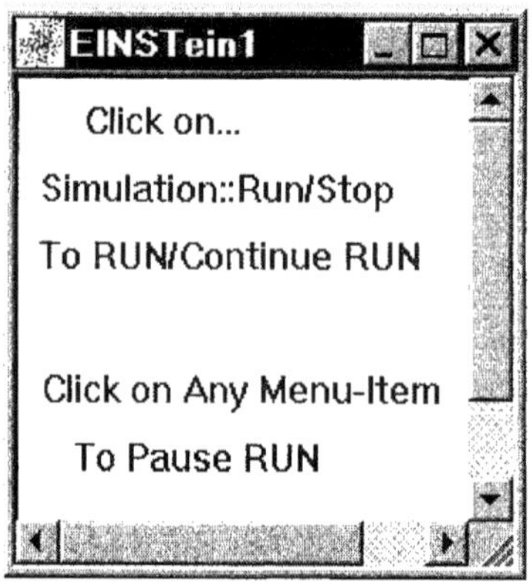

Fig. 7.11 Text dialog that appears after the user has completed setting up a genetic algorithm run in EINSTein; see text for details.

Display Current Chromosome. Select the option labeled 1-Sided Genetic Algorithm Current Chromosome under the main-menu Display::Data options list. This pops up a dialog that shows the parameter values defining the red force currently being sampled in the population. These values (along with the active blue force parameter values) can be saved to an EINSTein input data file (that can later be retrieved/opened in the normal fashion) by pressing the 

key.

Display Best Chromosome. Select the option labeled *1-Sided Genetic Algorithm Best Chromosome* under the main-menu Display::Data options list. This pops up a

Fig. 7.12 A screenshot of EINSTein's status bar (appearing along the bottom of the window in which the program is running) when in *genetic algorithm search* run mode.

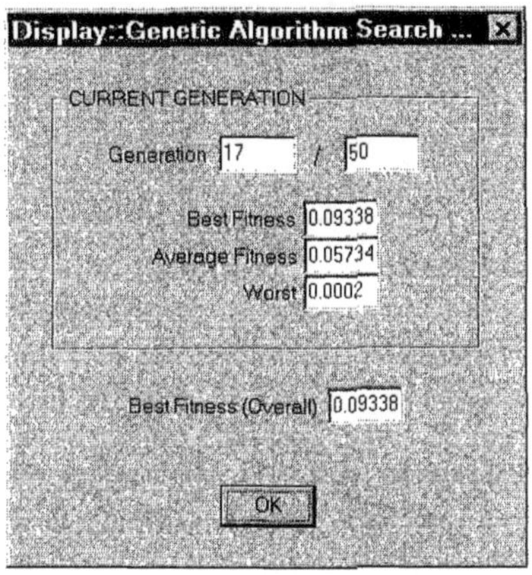

Fig. 7.13 Screenshot of EINSTein's *1-Sided Genetic Algorithm Summary* dialog

dialog that shows the parameter values that define the best red force that has been found up until the current generation by the genetic algorithm. These values (along with the active blue force parameter values) can be saved to an EINSTein input data file (that can later be retrieved/opened in the normal fashion) by pressing the 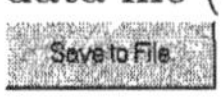

key.

Display Time-Series. Select the option labeled *Mission Fitness* (*Time-Series*) option of the main-menu *Data Visualization::Genetic Algorithm Progress* options list; see figure 7.14. This pops up a dialog prompting you to select the type of plot desired. You can plot the time-series for any, or all, of the following four quantities:

- *Best fitness for each generation,*
- *Worst fitness for each generation,*
- *Best overall fitness, and*
- *Average fitness.*

7.3.1.3 *Displaying Results*

Figure 7.15 shows a sample *learning curve* obtained after 150 generations for the scenario defined in input data file *ga_search_sample.dat* with genetic algorithm run-time parameter settings as defined in the previous section.

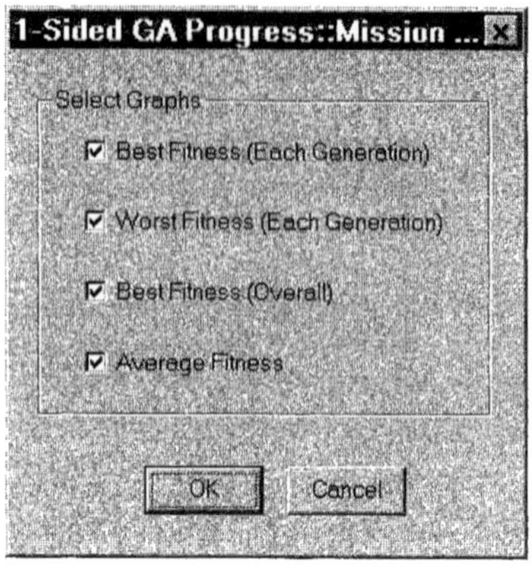

Fig. 7.14 Screenshot of ENSTein's genetic algorithm *Mission Fitness* (*Time-Series*) dialog.

While learning curves will, of course, be different for different runs, some basic features are common to most curves. For example, because all runs begin with a random population of personalities, the initial gene pool tends to be relatively poor at performing whatever mission has been specified for a given run. The mission fitness at $t = 1$ will therefore be typically low. As the GA sorts the personalities according to their fitness values, and evolves this pool, the mission fitness generally rises; quickly at first, then eventually saturating at a value that represents the effective fitness maximum for a given mission objective. Since not all objectives are equally as amenable to a GA "solution"—in fact, some may not be "solvable" at all given the parameter space available to the GA—the value of the mission fitness at which any given curve saturates may not be as close to the value one as the user intuitively expects (or desires).

In this particular example, we see that while the red force initially does very poorly (starting out with a fitness $f \sim 0$), its performance steadily improves until, after about generation 70, it reaches a peak of $f \sim 0.3$.

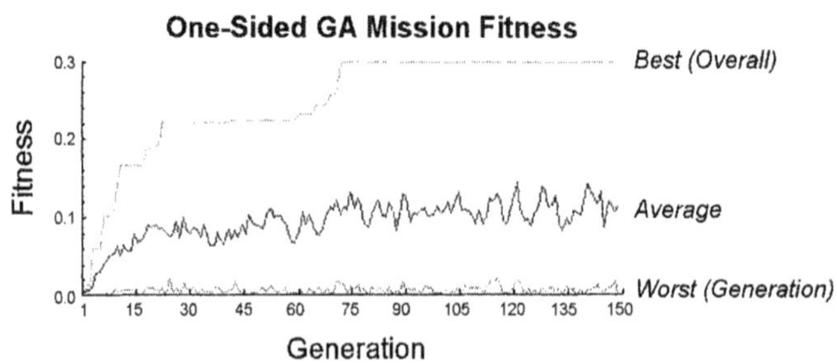

Fig. 7.15 Sample *learning curve* for GA agent "breeding" experiment *No. 1*, after 150 generations; see text for details.

Assuming that you had opted to display the best chromosome on screen at any point during the run after generation 70, and had also saved that chromosome to a file (called, say, *ga_search_results.dat*), you can inspect how well the genetic-algorithm-bred red force actually does against the blue defense by opening *ga_search_results.dat* when EINSTein is back in interactive run-mode.

Figure 7.16 shows snapshots of a typical run. Notice how much better red performs the given mission—*get as many red agents near the blue flag as possible*—than it did in the generic run shown earlier (figure 7.6). In contrast to the earlier run, in which the entire red force is annihilated before $t = 50$, the genetic-algorithm-bred red force is able to both remain almost entirely intact (suffering relatively few casualties), and to successfully penetrate toward the blue flag. Note that the parameters defining the blue force—in particular, the blue force's high single-shot probability of hit relative to the red forces"—are exactly the same for the two runs shown in figures 7.6 and 7.16.

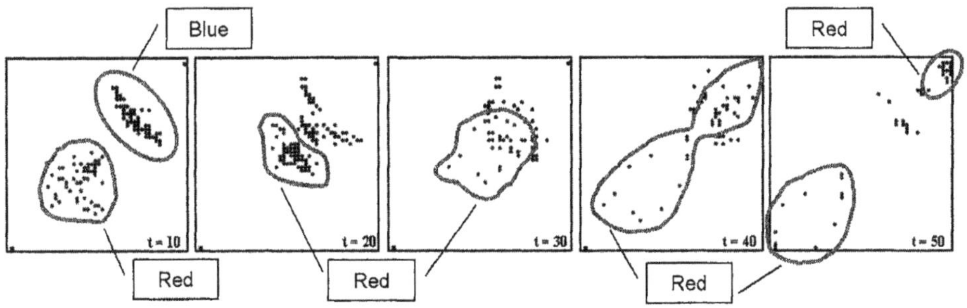

Fig. 7.16 Snapshots of a run using the default GA-breeding scenario #1 (as defined in input data file *ga_search_sample.dat*), but with the four-squad red force agent parameters defined by values found by a genetic algorithm after 150 generations.

How effective is the genetic-algorithm bred red force at surviving? Figures 7.17-a and 7.17-b, respectively, show time-series plots of the fraction of remaining red and blue agents for the default scenario (as defined by parameter values appearing in *ga_search_sample.dat*) and for the genetic algorithm bred red forces. In both cases, attrition is averaged over 25 initial conditions.

Figure 7.17-a suggests that the total annihilation of the red force shown illustratively for a single run in figure 7.16 is actually a typical outcome for the red and blue agent personalities defined for this scenario. On average, only 10% of the red force remains cither alive or injured by the end of the run.

Figure 7.17-b shows that while the mission does not explicitly demand the survival of the red force (recall that the objective is simply to get as many red agents near the blue flag as possible), the survival of the red force emerges as an implicit requirement for successfully achieving the goal.

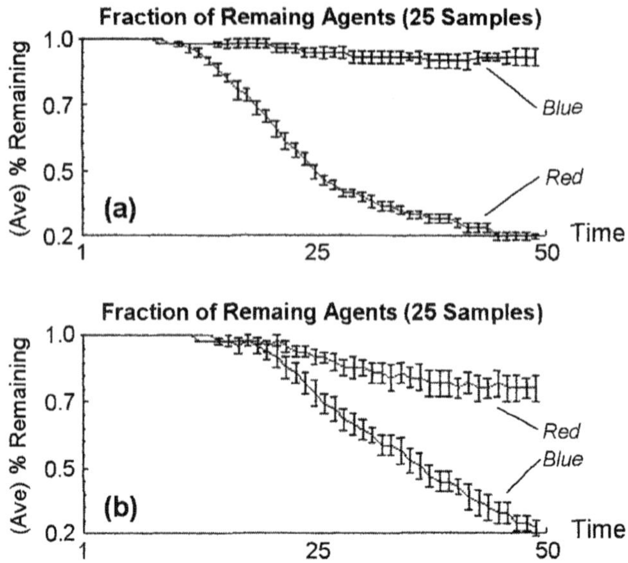

Fig. 7.17 Time-series plots of the fraction of remaining red and blue agents: (a) default GA-breeding scenario #1 (as defined in input data file *ga_search_sample.dat*), (b) four-squad, GA-bred, red force agent parameters (defined by values found by a genetic algorithm after 150 generations).

The genetic algorithm has found a red-force personality that, while explicitly satisfying the mission objective as stated, in part achieves that goal by implicitly exploiting markedly improved odds for the survival of the red force (that, together with a highly efficient emergent collective dynamics of four red squads). The GA-bred red force almost succeeds in annihilating blue!

7.3.2 *Agent "Breeding" Experiment #2*

Consider a scenario in which the blue force defends its flag against a smaller attacking red force. The GA is used to find a red force that is able to penetrate the blue defense. Table 7.7 lists some pertinent parameter values defining the two forces. The middle row of the table (i.e. red *trial* values) lists baseline red force parameter values used to test the scenario. The bottom row (i.e. GA-bred values) lists the GA bred red force "solution." Notice that, in both cases, the number of agents is the same and is fixed (with blue outnumbering red, 100 to 50 in all runs). The numbers in parentheses appearing for GA-bred parameters refer to GA-bred values for injured agents.

Figure 7.18 shows screenshots from a typical run using the red-trial values. Red agents attack, unsuccessfully, in a tight cluster. The larger blue force (whose agents initially move about randomly until a red agent comes within their sensor range)

Parameter	Blue	Red Trial	Red GA-bred
N_{Agents}	100	50	50
r_{Sensor}	5	5	8 (5)
r_{Fire}	3	3	8 (5)
r_{Move}	2	2	2 (2)
w_{AF}	0	10	3 (-22)
w_{AE}	100	40	40 (95)
w_{IF}	0	10	46 (-86)
w_{IE}	100	40	38 (-14)
w_{FF}	0	0	-70 (14)
w_{EF}	0	25	65 (31)
$\tau_{Advance}$	0	3	3 (1)
$\tau_{Cluster}$	5	10	13 (17)
Δ_{Combat}	-20	0	-19 (20)

Table 7.7 Red and blue agent parameters for sample genetic algorithm breeding experiment.

dispels the red force rather easily (within the 30 time steps shown here).

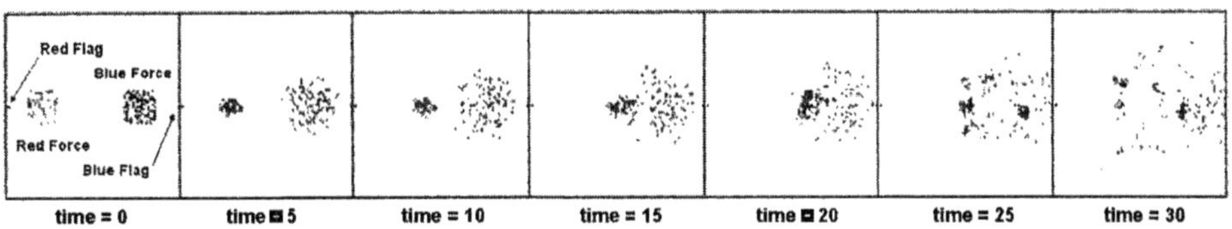

Fig. 7.18 *Trial* red (light grey) attacking force (consisting of typical parameter values that *are not* explicitly tuned for performing any specific mission). Red performance is used simply as a reference for interpreting the output of the sample GA breeding experiment discussed in the text. (A color plate that includes this figure appears on page ??.)

The GA-bred parameters listed along the bottom row in table 7.7 define the highest ranked red force that EINSTein's GA is able to find (after 30 generations) with respect to performing the mission = *maximize the number of red agents able to penetrate within a distance* $d = 7$ *units of the blue flag within* 40 *time steps.* A population size of 75 was used (i.e. each generation of the GA search consists of 75 red force candidate "solutions") and mission fitness, for a given candidate solution, is averaged over 10 initial spatial dispositions of red and blue forces.

7.3.2.1 *Learning Curve*

Figure 7.19 shows a typical learning curve, where the "Best" curve plots the fitness of the highest ranking candidate solution and "Average" curve plots the average fitness among all candidate solutions per generation. The fitness equals *one* if a candidate solution performs the specified mission in the best conceivable manner (i.e. if the red force sustains zero casualties and all agents remain within $d = 7$ of the blue flag starting from the minimal possible time at which they move to within that distance, for all ten initial states) and equals zero if a candidate solution fails to place a single red agent within $d = 7$ of the blue flag for all ten initial states (within the allotted time). Run times are generally fast for Pentium-III/IV class computers. The 30 generation GA-run described here requires between one and two hours to complete.

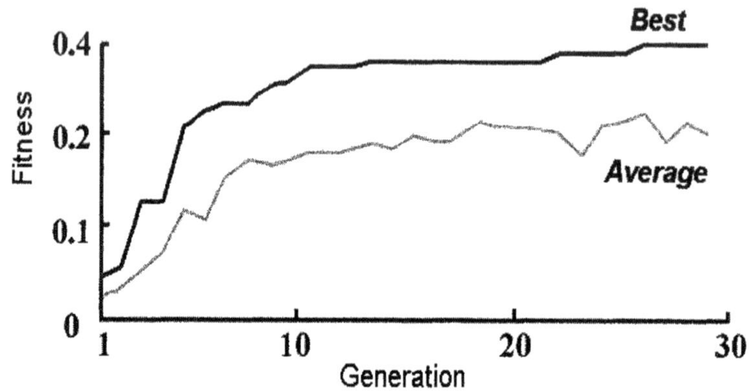

Fig. 7.19 GA learning curve for GA breeding experiment *No. 2* discussed in the text.

Figure 7.20 shows screenshots from a typical run using the GA-bred red force values.* (The green arrows are drawn as visual aids, and simply trace the motion of the red agent clusters.) Comparing this sequence of steps to those in the trial run shown in top row of the figure, it is obvious that the two "attack strategies" are very different. Indeed, the GA has found just the right mix of agent-agent proximity weights and μ-rules to define a red force that effectively exploits a relative weakness in the randomly maneuvering blue defenders.

The emergent "tactic" is to *separate into two roughly equal-sized units, regroup beyond enemy sensor range, and then simultaneously strike, as a pincer, into the heart of the enemy cluster.* Apart from the anecdotal evidence supplied by screenshots of this particular run, the efficacy of this simple GA-bred tactic is illustrated by comparing graphs of the number of agents near the blue flag (averaged over 50 runs) as a function of time for the red-*trial* and GA-*bred* cases.

Figure 7.21 shows that whereas fewer than three red-trial agents, on average, penetrate close to the blue flag (figure 7.21-a), almost 80% of the entire GA-bred red force is able to do so (figure 7.21-b); and begins penetrating at an earlier time. Other (well performing) tactics are possible, of course.

*A color plate that includes figures 7.18 and 7.20 appears on page 270.

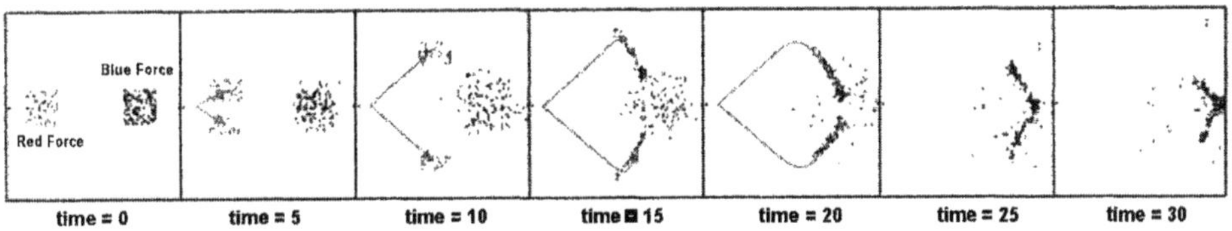

Fig. 7.20 Screenshots from a typiucal run using the GA-bred red (light grey) force for the sample GA breeding experiment discussed in the text. Red agents are defined by parameter values that are the highest ranked (after 30 generations) with respect to performing the mission = "*maximize the number of red agents able to penetrate within a distance d* = 7 *units of the blue flag within* 40 *time steps.*" (A color plate that includes this figure appears on page ??.)

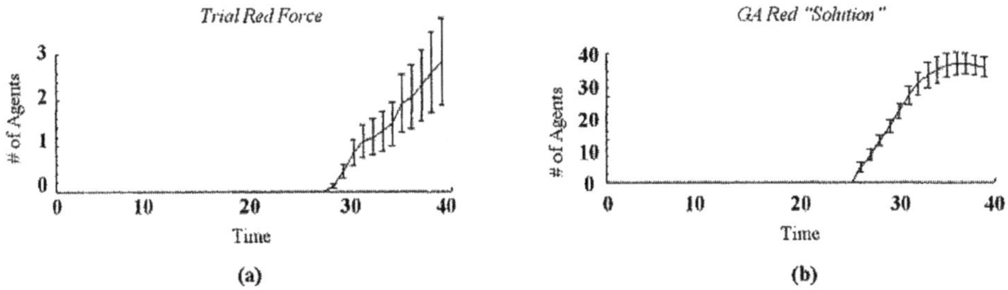

Fig. 7.21 A comparison between the average number of red (light grey) agents that approach within a distance $d = 7$ of the blue (dark grey) flag for (a) *trial*, and (b) *GA-bred* red (light grey) forces (aberaged over 50 runs). We see that the GA_bred force typically performs this mission an order of magnitude more successfully than the trial force.

A representative sampling is generally provided by looking at the behaviors of some of the higher ranking red forces remaining at the end of a GA search. It is particularly interesting to run a series of GA runs to systematically probe how red forces might adapt to different blue personalities. As the behavior of the blue agents changes, various—often dramatically different—GA-bred red personalities emerge to exploit any new weaknesses in the blue's defensive posture.

7.3.3 *Agent "Breeding" Experiment #3*

Consider the (red force) mission, *"Keep blue agents as far away from the red flag as possible, for as long as possible (up to a maximum 100 iteration steps)."* This means that the mission fitness f will be close to its maximal value *one* only if red is able to keep all blue agents pinned near their own flag (at a point farthest from the red flag) for the entire duration of the run, and f will be near its minimal value *zero* if red allows blue agents to advance completely unhindered toward the red flag.

Table 7.8 shows the user input to this GA agent-breeding experiment. Combat unfolds on a 40-by-40 battlefield, with 35 agents per side. The GA is run using a pool of 50 red personalities for 50 generations, and each personality is averaged over 25 initial spatial configurations.

Parameter	Blue
Number of generations	50
Number of initial conditions	25
Maximum time to goal	100
penalty_power	2
GA weights $w_1 - w_5$, w_6, $w_9 - w_{12}$	0
GA weights w_6, w_8	1
Flag containment range ($= D_E$)	12

Table 7.8 User input for GA agent breeding experiment *No. 3*. The two nonzero GA weights are w_6 = *maximize enemy center-of-mass distance to friendly flag* and w_8 = *minimize number of enemy agents within distance D_E of enemy flag*; see text for details.

Screenshots from a typical run using the highest ranked red personality that the GA is able to find for this mission (taken at times t = 25, 50 and 100), are shown along the top row of color plate 24 (page 270). They show that red is very successful at keeping blue forces away from its own flag; the closest that red permits blue agents from approaching the red flag—during the entire allotted run time of 100 iteration steps—is some point roughly near midfield. In words, the "tactic" here seems to be—from red's perspective—*"fight all enemy agents within sensor range, and move toward the enemy flag slowly enough to drive the enemy along."* This tactic is fairly robust, in the sense that if the battle is initialized with a different spatial disposition of red and blue forces (while keeping all personality parameters fixed), red typically performs this particular mission about as well suggested by these screenshots.

Screenshots from a typical run using the *second* highest ranked red personality (taken at times t = 25, 50 and 90), are shown along the second row of color plate 24. These show a slightly less successful, but nonetheless innovative, alternative tactic. Initially, red agents move away from their own goal to meet the advancing blue forces, just as in the first case (see t = 25). Once combat ensues, however, any red agents that find themselves locally isolated now "double back" toward their own flag (positioned in the lower left corner of the battlefield) to "regroup" with other friendly agents. The red force thus, effectively, forms an impromptu secondary defense against possible blue leakers. Because a few blue agents do manage to fight their way near the red flag at later times (at least in the particular run these screenshots have been taken from; see snapshot for t = 90), the red agent parameter values underlying this emergent tactic are not as highly ranked as the parameter values underlying the run shown in the top row.

The series of screenshots appearing in the third row of color plate 24 show the emergent tactic used by the highest ranked red personality found by the GA after the blue force is made a bit more *aggressive*. For this case, prior to initializing the

GA search, blue's personality weight-vector components for moving toward red (i.e., $\omega_{AE} = \omega_3$, and $\omega_{IE} = \omega_4$) are first increased by 50%. We see that EINSTein's GA effectively finds an entirely different (and more effective!) "tactic" to use. Here, the red force quickly "spreads out" to cover as much territory as possible and individual agents attack the enemy as soon as they come within view. As red agents' local territorial coverage is thinned—either through attrition or gradual advance toward the blue flag—other red agents (namely, agents that had previously been positioned near the periphery of the battlefield) move closer to the center of the battlefield, thus filling emerging voids. This tactic succeeds in not only preventing any blue agents from reaching the red flag, but manages to push most of the surviving blue force back toward its own flag (near the top right corner of the battlefield)! As is true of the other cases in this experiment, this tactic is also fairly robust, and is not a strong function of the initial spatial disposition of red and blue forces.

The last row of plots in color plate 24 contains snapshots from a run using interim red agent parameter values, before the GA has had a chance to evaluate a large number of candidate solutions (i.e. sampled from a generation appearing early on in the GA's learning curve; see figures 7.15 or 7.19). This example is included merely to illustrate how an obviously *sub*-optimal pool of agents behaves differently from their optimized counterparts. The mission parameters and blue-force agent personalities are the same as in the case represented by the screenshots in the third row. We see that, initially at least, there does not seem to be much difference in the optimal and sub-optimal behaviors; red agents quickly disperse outward to cover a large area. However, because the GA has not yet had the time to "fine tune" all of red's genes, the red force is in this instance unable to prevent blue agents from penetrating deeply into its territory. The defensive tactic, however it may be characterized, is obviously ineffective.

7.3.4 *Agent "Breeding" Experiment #4*

Color plates 25-27 (pages 271– 274) show a few GA-bred "tactics" for the mission, *"Get to the blue flag as quickly as possible while minimizing red casualties."* The user-input parameter values for setting up the GA run are identical to what appear in table 7.8, except that the only nonzero GA mission weights are those associated with *minimizing time to goal* ($w_1 = 1$) and *maximizing the number of red agents near enemy flag* ($w_7 = 1$). As in the previous breeding experiment, the GA is run using a pool of 50 red personalities for 50 generations, and each personality is averaged over 25 initial configurations.

Color plate ?? shows snapshots of the evolution of two early red "attack tactics." Red's first tactic is to station its forces out of reach of blue's fire power, and then—after opening a hole blue's right flank by slowly drawing out a few enemy agents—to maneuver a small section of friendly agents toward and around that opening. Despite the fact that, in the end, the entire red force survives, the overall *mission* has not been a particularly successful one, because only a relatively few red agents have actually advanced far enough into enemy territory to be counted as being "near the blue flag."

Red's second tactic (illustrated by the sequence of snapshots appearing in the bottom two rows of color plate 25) proves to be more successful. Here, the red force again advances toward blue's defensive position, and temporarily takes up station at a far enough range so as to avoid blue's fire power (see snapshot for $t = 25$). Then, after a relatively long period of time during which there is considerable random "posturing" on both sides, red suddenly "strikes" as it senses a weakening in blue's forces (near the center region of blue's defensive position), sending most of its force through the blue defenses and toward the enemy flag. As blue agents counterattack and surround the penetrating red force, a second squad of red agents penetrates through a newly created "hole" in blue's defense. 92% of red's initial force successfully penetrates through to the blue flag.

Color plate 26 shows snapshots of a *third* tactic that emerges for the red force for the same mission as above. The tactic exploits (or *sacrifices!*) a few red agents positioned at the front of the advancing red force. The snapshots for times $t = 15$ and $t = 20$ show that as most of the force splits into two groups and moves off toward blue's left and right flanks, a few red agents (those that are originally near the center of the split) proceed to maneuver forward and penetrate blue's defense. By enticing blue to counterattack red's penetration (by sending forces toward the middle), red effectively dilutes blue's strength along the outer edges of its defensive station. This, in turn, creates "openings" on both sides of blue's defense through which the two separate groups into which red had earlier split can now move virtually unopposed. The snapshot for $t = 90$ shows that red has successfully penetrated through to the blue flag well before the maximum allotted time for this run has expired ($t_{max} = 100$).

Snapshots of the fourth, and final, sample red tactic for this mission is shown in color plate 27. Red's tactic here is again, as in the previous example, to exploit a few red agents at the front of the advancing red force. This time, however, red does not "sacrifice" these agents. Instead, red uses them to split apart blue's forces in order to temporarily "weaken" the center region of blue's defense. As soon as this center region is sufficiently weakened, red quickly penetrates through to the blue flag. What is surprising is the robustness of red's personality with respect to this tactic. Red is more often than not able to successfully employ the same general tactic against an *arbitrary* blue initial force disposition.

What is most surprising about these runs is that the red force *appears to task different agents with different missions,* despite the fact that each agent is actually endowed with exactly the same personality! It is important to point out that the tactic—*"Use the two forward positioned agents to weaken the enemy's center"*—is scripted neither by the user nor by EINSTein's weights or μ-rules; it emerges, naturally, as a high-level consequence of the collective interactions of identical low-level decision rules: i.e., it is an example (as is but one of many, as the reader can easily verify by playing with the program) of an apparently centralized order induced totally by decentralized local dynamics.

Chapter 8

Concluding Remarks & Speculations

> *"The musical notes are only five in number but their melodies are so numerous that one cannot hear them all.*
>
> *The primary colors are only five in number but their combinations are so infinite that one cannot visualize them all.*
>
> *The flavors are only five in number but their blends are so various that one cannot taste them all.*
>
> *In battle there are only the normal and extraordinary forces, but their combinations are limitless; none can comprehend them all.*
>
> *For these two forces are mutually reproductive; their mutual ineraction as endless as that of interlocked rings. Who can determine where one ends and the other begins?"*
>
> —Sun Tzu, *The Art of War*

Sun Tzu's poetic metaphors about how the complexity of warfare arises from the ineffably infinite combinations of otherwise simple elements offer a remarkably precise and prescient view of one of the central tenets of modern complex adaptive systems theory. Namely, that *surface complexity can emerge out of a deep simplicity.* Complex systems theory teaches us that what at first appears to be complicated behavior—particularly when viewed from a "'birds-eye" perspective, from which the behavior of the whole system may be observed all at once—in fact may actually stem from a much simpler set of underlying dynamic rules. The reverse is also often true, of course. *Surface simplicity can emerge out of a deep complexity:* enormously complicated systems that *a priori* have very many degrees-of-freedom and therefore are expected to display "complicated" behavior, can, either by self-organizing, or via a selective "tuning" by a set of external control parameters, behave as though they were really low-dimensional systems exhibiting much simpler behavior. We have seen many examples of both kinds of behavior throughout this book. Arguably, the most interesting systems—systems that are, not surprisingly, also usually the most difficult to understand—are those that simultaneously harbor both extremes of behavior. Combat is a wonderful example of just such a system.

What is surprising is that the deeper one probes the nature, and dynamic origins, of any complex adaptive system's (CAS's) typically diverse repertoire of behaviors, the more one comes to appreciate that "complexity" (used here as a generic descriptor of observed high-level behavior) may be at least as strong a function of our *perception*, and of our subjective choices—as independent researchers—of how to dissect a system into manageably small pieces, as it is of an objective reality. To be sure, the degree to which a complex system *appears* "complex" depends, in part, on the primitive elements by which it is irreducibly defined. However, a system's perceived "complexity" also strongly depends *on how we choose to observe and/or study it.* As we cautioned during our heuristic discussion of models and simulations in chapter 1 (see page 32), before building a model of anything, a developer must first develop a deep respect for the fact that what we observe—either directly by our senses, or indirectly, via the output of our models—is not the reality, but the reality as it is exposed to our method of questioning.

And what of combat, in particular? Assuming one accepts our earlier argument that combat is a CAS (see table 1.3 on page 12), and therefore also agrees that combat may be usefully studied in the same manner as are other accepted CASs (such as natural ecologies, social systems, or the human brain), a natural question to ask is, *"How must combat be studied so that its integrity as a complex adaptive system is not compromised?"*

We have seen how the Lanchesterian-based approach to combat so oversimplifies its primitive elements that it effectively strips away all but the crudest features of its behavior as a "system." In contrast, the EINSTein simulation described in this book is, first and foremost, an interactive exploratory tool that is designed to allow researchers to understand combat along the lines suggested in the above quote by Sun Tzu. Rather than trying to "solve for" the outcome of a battle (as in: *"Who won?"*) by using oversimplified differential equations to describe a homogenous battlefield, strewn with an infinite number of identical "all knowing" and "all seeing" combatants—as all models based on the Lanchester equations of combat essentially do—EINSTein instead provides control over only the *raw ingredients* of combat, such as the primitive rules that determine how individual combatants (i.e., agents) behave in the context of their changing local environment. Answers to questions like *"How does the whole force behave?"* and *"What are all the possible outcomes of a series of battles?"* emerge naturally, and are unscripted, dynamic consequences of the myriad combinations of agent characteristics, behaviors and interactions.

In the same way as, for Sun Tzu, rainbows, melodies and fine cuisine are all natural outcomes of combining musical notes, primary colors and basic flavors, so too EINSTein may be viewed as an "engine" that converts a primitive grammar—i.e., a grammar composed of the basic notes, colors and flavors of combat—into the limitless symphonic patterns and possibilities of war. The researcher chooses and/or tunes primitive, low-level rules; and EINSTein provides the dynamic arena within which these rules interact and spawn high-level patterns and behaviors.

8.1 EINSTein

Because EINSTein is still being actively developed, no interim report on its state-of-progress—such as this book, or any other document, that has been produced as part of CNA's multiyear complexity-project (see [Ilach96a] through [Ilach03b])—can hope to be more than a "snapshot" of an ongoing process. As such, and despite its length, this book is neither complete, nor all-encompassing. However, it is a detailed, and essentially self-contained, summary of the most important aspects of EINSTein's evolving architecture at the time of this writing (December 2003).

Expanding somewhat on the more poetic description of EINSTein as a grammar parsing/processing "engine" given above, we state three main reasons for developing EINSTein:

1. To demonstrate the efficacy of agent-based simulation alternatives to more traditional Lanchester-equation–based models of combat [TaylorG80].
2. As a general prototype artificial-life model/toolkit that can be used as a testbed for exploring self-organized emergent behavior in complex adaptive systems (CASs).
3. To provide the military operations research community with an easy-to-use, intuitive CAS-based combat-simulation laboratory that—by respecting both the principles of real-world combat and the dynamics of complex adaptive systems—may lead researchers one step closer to a fundamental theory of combat.

To better appreciate how each of these motivations has contributed to EINSTein's (still evolving) architecture, consider the conceptual map of its design, as illustrated schematically in figure 8.1. On the bottom level of the figure—or *genotype* level—lies the set of primitive characteristics of individual agents and primitive rules governing their behavior. It is on this level that all consequent emergent behaviors are ultimately grounded; for it is the set of behavioral genotypes that contain the raw information that drives the complex adaptive system as a whole.

EINSTein provides a powerful dynamical "engine" with which to explore how self-organized patterns emerge out of a set of primitive local rules of combat, both on the individual agent level—via interactions among internal motivations (see the *Phenotype-I* level, that appears as the middle level in figure 8.1)—and squad and force levels (labeled *Phenotype-II* in figure 8.1, and which appears as the top-most level in the figure)—via mutual interactions among many agents in a changing environment.

Of course, a deeper understanding of phenomena governing behaviors on the top-most level can only be achieved by developing a suite of appropriate pattern recognition tools (the need for which is indicated symbolically at the top of figure 8.1 by a matrix of 3D plots). Although a number of interesting, and highly suggestive, high-level patterns have already been discovered, there is much that still remains to be done. Consider, for example the seemingly ubiquitous appearance of various

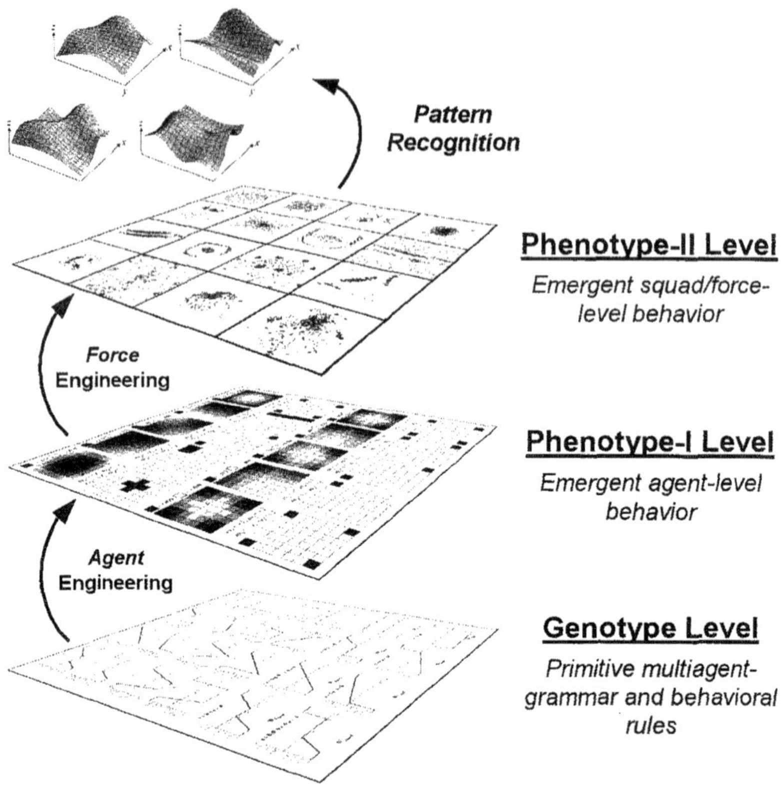

Fig. 8.1 Schematic illustration of the hierarchical tier of levels governing the meta-context for using EINSTein.

power-law scalings and fractal dimensions describing space-time patterns, attrition rates and possibly other emergent features. The existence of power-law scalings, in particular, strongly suggests that a self-organized-critical-like dynamical mechanism might govern turbulent-like phases of combat (see discussion in sections 2.2.8 and 6.4.3). But the data collection and analysis necessary to rigorously establish the nature of these findings (as well as to establish a mathematically precise set of conditions under which power-law scalings either *do* or *do not* occur) has only just started.

With the introduction of *Primitive Response-Activation Functions* (RAFs; see page 374 in chapter 5) and an ontological architecture that assigns specific meaning to the symbolic relationship between *environment* and *action*, EINSTein—for the first time—can also be used to take a preliminary step toward addressing the complementary problem of *reverse-behavior-engineering*. "Reverse engineering" refers to the problem of finding an appropriate set of primitives (characteristics and rules) that lead to empirically observed macroscopic patterns of combat (i.e., finding ways of going from either phenotype level to the genotype level).

As a consequence of its inherent difficulty, the reverse-engineering problem remains essentially unsolved. However, the basic tools for addressing it are already in place. The grammar for defining the basic relationships between environment and internal motivations to act is prescribed on the genotype level. While the behavioral consequences of specific genomes must remain hidden (until revealed directly by simulation)—even on an individual agent-level if an agent has a complex internal architecture—an intuition about what behaviors may be expected to appear under what general circumstances may be developed by using the behavior-previsualization tools described in technical Appendix 6 (to chapter 5; see page 408) to explore the emergent agent behavior (on the phenotype-I level).

To further illustrate the conceptual difference between the bottom-most genotype level and phenotype-I/II levels shown in figure 8.1, note that, when the system-queries and system-responses appropriate to each of these levels are expressed in natural language, each level provides—and may therefore be distinguished by—recognizably different forms for system-queries and system-responses:

1. *Typical system-query/system-response on the genotype level.* System-query: "What are the rules governing how agents behave in given contexts?" System-response: "Rules are weighted combinations of motivations to perform basic acts; motivations are arbitrary functions of environmental features. Example: survive at all costs, and if sufficiently healthy, and surrounded by a sufficient level of fire-support, advance toward the enemy flag, keeping out of harms way as much as possible."
2. *Typical system-query/system-response on phenotype level I.* System-query: "What does an agent do in a given context?" System-response: "A wide variety of possible behaviors is possible, depending on internal and external conditions defining the agent. An agent always seeks to minimize its local penalty function, and whose preferred actions may be previsualized using density plots."
3. *Typical system-query/system-response on phenotype level II.* System-query: "How does a given squad. and/or a multi-squad force, behave as a whole?" System-response: "Depending on initial conditions and system-wide constraints, a variety of spatial and temporal patterns are possible. These may take the form of swarms, fronts, transient clusters, firestorms (among others) for individual runs, and regularities in statistical measures that characterize multiple runs."

8.2 What Have We Learned?

The central point of this book is that if combat—on a real battlefield—is viewed from a "birds-eye" perspective, so that the motions of individual soldiers are indistinguishably blurred and only the overall dynamic patterns of behavior are observed, in gestalt-like fashion, then...

> *...a wide range of these patterns may be shown to be self-organized collective phenomena that emerge from the mutual interactions of a set of heterogenously distributed semi-autonomous agents obeying simple local rules.*

When combat is viewed in this light, it is obvious that a multiagent-based description of combat as a "complex adaptive system" provides a natural description. Let us review some of the main results of using EINSTein. EINSTein is fundamentally different from most conventional models of combat because it represents the first systematic attempt, within the military operations research community, to simulate combat—on a small to medium scale—by using autonomous agents to model *individual behaviors and personalities* rather than specific weapons. EINSTein is the first analytical tool of its kind to have gained widespread use in the military operations research community that focuses its attention on exploring *emergent patterns and behaviors* (that are mapped over entire scenario spaces) rather than on much simpler, and unrealistically myopic, force-on-force attrition statistics. In addition to introducing this idea of synthesizing high-level behaviors, from the ground up, using low-level agent↔agent interaction rules, EINSTein also takes the important next step of using a genetic algorithm to essentially *breed entire combat forces* that optimize some set of desirable warfighting characteristics. Finally, on a more conceptual level, EINSTein may be viewed as a prototypical model of future combat simulations that will care less about which side "wins" and more about exploring the regularities (and possibly *universalities*) of the fundamental processes of war.

Despite its simple local rule base, the simulation possesses a large repertoire of emergent behaviors, including *attack posturing, containment, flanking maneuvers, forward advance, frontal attack, Guerrilla-like assaults, local clustering, penetration,* and *retreat.* Moreover, behaviors frequently arise that appear to involve some form of intelligent division of red and blue forces to deal with local firestorms and skirmishes, particularly those forces whose personalities have been bred, via EINSTein's built-in genetic algorithm, to perform a specific mission. What is particularly striking about these behaviors is that they are not hard-wired in, but rather appear spontaneously, as naturally emergent consequences of a decentralized, but highly interdependent, swarm of agents.

Numerous simulations that have been run using EINSTein suggest that emergent collective behavior generally falls into one of six broad qualitative classes (labeled, suggestively, according to different kinds of fluid flow):

- *Class-1—Laminar fluid flow*, which typically consists of one (or, at most, a few) well-defined "linear" battlefronts, and is so named because the behavior is visually suggestive of the laminar fluid flow of physical fluids; and is also reminiscent of static trench warfare in World War I. Some Class-1 systems appear stable with respect to initial conditions, while others are not. For example, in runs made with Class-1/Type-1 rules, one side almost always "wins," and if the entire battle-front tends to "break to the right" for a given starting configuration, it will almost always do so for other starting configurations; i.e., the overall behavior is usually not a strong function of the initial conditions. Certain qualitative features of the evolutions of Class-1/Type-2 systems, on the other hand, are typically unstable with respect to minor perturbations. For example, the battlefront of a Class-1/Type-2 rule may break right or left, depending on how a battle actually unfolds during an individual run.

- *Class-2—Viscous fluid flow*, in which a single tight cluster (or, at most, a few clusters) of interpenetrating red and blue agents appears and dominates the evolution.
- *Class-3—Dispersive flow*, in which, as soon as red and blue agents maneuver within view of the opposing side's forces, the battle then unfolds as a single explosive (and often rapid) dispersion of forces. Class-3 systems exhibit little, if any, of the "front-like" linear structures that form for Class-1 rules.
- *Class-4—Turbulent flow*, in which either spatially distributed, but otherwise confined and/or clustered individual combat zones, or a series of close-to space-filling local firestorms dominate the evolution. In either case, there is almost always a significant degree of accompanying local maneuvering.
- *Class-5—Autopoeitic flow*, in which agents self-organize into persistent dissipative structures. These formations typically persist for long times (compared to the time scale on which individual agents enter and leave a given structure) and undergo their own "higher level" maneuvering, including longitudinal motion and rotation.
- *Class-6—Swarming*, in which agents assemble into decentralized, but self-organized, swarms of attacking and/or defending forces; responding, as needed to changing local (and semi-local; i.e. out of sensor range of individual agents making up a swarm but within communications range of friendly agents and or squad-mates) conditions.

As the verbal descriptions given above suggest, it is relatively easy to make qualitative distinctions among behaviors belonging to different classes—for specific scenarios—on the basis of direct visual examination. However, much work remains to be done to establish well-defined quantitative measures that characterize the behavior within a given class (the use of mutual information is one logical candidate).

For example, while there is strong evidence to suggest that fractal power-law scalings may be used to describe attrition rates (among other combat measures) under certain conditions (see discussion on pages 453-468 in chapter 6 and [Lauren00a]), the relationship between power-law scalings and the underlying agent characteristics and/or behavioral rules remains unclear. Moreover, the ubiquity (or lack, thereof) of power-law scalings in the broader context of all possible agent-combat environments has also not yet been established. Likewise, the nature of the transition between two or more behavioral classes—such as the transition between laminar (*Class-2*) and turbulent (*Class-4*) behavior—remains essentially unexplored. Finally, new visualization tools must be developed to help chart larger volumes of EINSTein's n-dimensional phase space of possible behaviors.

Other important related questions include: *"Do other characteristic traits of high-dimensional chaotic systems also characterize emergent combat behavior?"* and *"Are there other, heretofore unidentified, or otherwise 'unconventional,' measures of combat that may provide insight into the dynamics of real world conflict?"*

8.3 Payoffs

The most important immediate payoff to using EINSTein is that—compared to more traditional models and simulations—it offers a radically new way to look at fundamental issues of combat. However, as has been stressed throughout this book, multiagent-based models are intentionally distillations of the real system they are designed to model, and are thus best used to enhance *understanding;* not to predict specific outcomes. Among many other possible applications, EINSTein may be used to:

- Help analysts understand how all of the different elements of combat fit together in an overall combat phase space: *"Are there regions that are sensitive to small perturbations, and, if so, might there be a way to exploit this in combat (as in selectively driving an opponent into more sensitive regions of phase space)?"*
- Assess the true operational value of information: *"How can blue agents exploit what they 'know' the red force does not know about them?"*
- Explore trade-offs between centralized and decentralized command-and-control (C2) structures: *"Are some C2 topologies more conducive to information flow and attainment of mission objectives than others?" "What do emergent forms of a self-organized C2 topology look like?"*
- Provide a natural arena in which to explore consequences of the qualitative characteristics of combat, such as unit cohesion, morale, and leadership.
- Explore emergent properties and/or other "novel" behaviors arising from low-level rules (even combat doctrine if it is well encoded): *"Are there universal patterns of combat behavior?"*
- Provide clues about how near-real-time tactical decision aids may eventually be developed using evolutionary programming techniques.
- Address questions such as *"How do two sides of a conflict coevolve with one another?"* and *"Can one side exploit what it knows of this coevolutionary process to compel the other side to remain out of equilibrium?"*

EINSTein's source code contains a hardwired set of basic command and control (C^2) functions, so that the dynamics of a given C^2 structure can easily be explored. However, a more compelling question is, *"What is the best C^2 topology for dealing with a specific threat, or set of threats?"* One can imagine using a genetic algorithm, or some other heuristic search tool to aid in exploring potentially very large fitness landscapes and to search for alternative C^2 structures. What forms should local and global command take, and what is the optimal communication connectivity pattern among individual combatants, squads and their local and global commanders?

An even deeper issue has to do with identifying the primitive forms of information that are relevant on the battlefield. Traditionally, the role of the combat operations research analyst has been to assimilate, and provide useful insights from, certain conventional streams of battlefield data: attrition rate, posture profiles, available and depleted resources, logistics, rate of reinforcement, FEBA location, morale, etc. While all of these measures are obviously important, and will remain so, the availability of an agent-based simulation permits one to ask the following provocative question: *"Are there any other forms of primitive information—perhaps derived from measures commonly used to describe the behavior of nonlinear and complex dynamical systems—that might provide a more thorough understanding of the fundamental dynamical processes of combat?"* We have seen that the intensity of battles appears to obey a fractal power-law dependence on frequency, and displays other traits characteristic of high-dimensional chaotic systems. Are there other, similar but heretofore unexamined, measures that may provide insight into the dynamics of combat?

The strength of multiagent-based models lies not just in their providing a powerful new general approach to simulation, but also in their natural propensity to prod researchers into continually asking interesting new questions. Observations of individual runs invariably lead to a series of *"What if?"* speculations, which in turn lead to further explorations and further questions, followed by a dedicated series of multiple time-series runs, data collection, assimilation and more questions. Rather than focusing on a single scenario, and estimating the values of simple attrition-based measures of single outcomes (that, in more traditional settings, more often than not end with a final tally of total number killed and a declaration of which side has *"won"* the battle), users of multiagent-based simulations of combat typically walk away from an interactive session with an enhanced intuition of what the overall combat fitness landscape looks like. Users are also given an opportunity to construct a conceptual context for understanding their own conjectures about the dynamics of combat and emergent behavior on the real battlefield. The multiagent-based simulation is therefore most accurately described, and is best used, as a medium in which questions and insights continually feed off of one another.

8.4 Validation

Recall, from our discussion of multiagent-based modeling in chapter 1 (see pages 44-59), that before *any* combat model (whether it is multiagent-based or not) is deemed as genuinely useful to the military operations researcher, it must pass *two* important tests: (1) it must provide insight into the specific set of problems or issues the researcher is interested in studying, on its own, in a well-defined and self-contained conceptual context (this is an obvious requirement of even the most basic mathematical model; see pages 29-39), and (2) it must be consistent with behavior that is either accepted to be true or has otherwise been observed to occur in the real-world. In other words, a successful model of combat must respect the critical interplay between real-world *experience* (or *data*) and simulation *outcome* (or *theory*). This is what in chapter 1 we called the interplay between the *forward*-problem of using the model to predict behaviors and identify patterns, and the *inverse*-problem of using experience and real-world data to add to, change and/or refine the rules and behaviors that define the model (see figure 8.2). In short, if a model is to be accepted and its output trusted, at some point it must be *validated.*

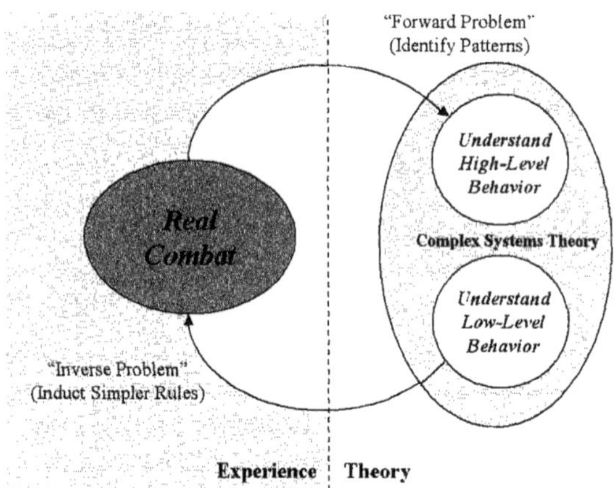

Fig. 8.2 Schematic of the interplay between experience and theory in the *forward*- and *inverse*-problems of simulating combat.

Since EINSTein was conceived primarily as a *conceptual* model—or as only a pseudo-realistic model for exploring qualitative tradeoffs between purely notional combat parameters—validation is less of an issue than it might be for more ostensibly realistic models. As long as EINSTein's outcomes are intuitive and its inputs are easy to generalize (or translate) for use by more realistic models, EINSTein will remain useful for many different kinds of exploratory analyses (a fact that is underscored by both the scope and depth of, as well as the number of research papers generated by, studies that have thus far been conducted using EINSTein; see table

1.5 on page 20). Nonetheless, we mention the issue here both because of its basic importance, and also because—if EINSTein is ever to evolve to a point where it is powerful enough to simulate realistic real-world scenarios (as current plans call for future versions of EINSTein to do)—EINSTein's output must at some point in its future be validated in some fashion.

Preliminary steps toward this end have already been taken. For example, recall that when EINSTein was used as an experimental test-bed to analyze the "optimal" size and organization of small squad (and fire team) units, the first step of the process was to "validate" expected outcomes for simple scenarios (see discussion of *Case Study #4* that starts on page 470).

Before they started to seriously use EINSTein for their exploratory work, the CNA analysts performing the study first numerically scaled EINSTein's notional agent and weapon characteristics to more closely match their real-world counterparts called for by the study, and closely monitored EINSTein's output for a selected series of "test" scenarios. It was only after they had satisfied themselves that EINSTein's output was both expected and intuitive, and the dynamic consequences of making simple changes to some of EINSTein's basic parameter values could be reliably predicted, did the analysts embark on their real work in earnest. The relative ease with which EINSTein reproduced the well-known "rule of thumb" that attackers require a 3:1 force ratio in order to successfully mount an offense against a defended position [TaylorD00], was also a welcome sign that EINSTein indeed does seem to capture some critical dynamical drivers of real combat.

8.4.1 *EINSTein and JANUS*

More recently, an attempt to validate EINSTein (version 1.0.0.0β) by comparing its outputs to those of another well-known (and well-established) combat simulation model, called JANUS,* was undertaken at the United States West Point Military Academy's *Operations Research Center for Excellence* by Klingaman and Carlton [Kling02].

The study endeavored to establish the combat effectiveness of EINSTein agents executing a *National Training Center* (NTC)-type scenario. The scenario replicates (to the extent possible, within EINSTein) a single armored company of 14 "friendly" tanks versus a similar size force of 14 "enemy" main battle tanks. One set of "friendly" agents is allowed to gain knowledge (or "learn") by using EINSTein's built-in genetic algorithm agent "breeder" function (see chapter 7). Another set of friendly agents is not allowed to learn. In both cases, EINSTein's combat results for all agent actions are recorded. These *observed actions* are then programmed into JANUS (EINSTein's automatic record of center-of-mass positions are used to define the routes in JANUS), and, for each case, the combat effectiveness resulting from JANUS is compared to the outcome in EINSTein. The "validation" test consists of

*Janus is mentioned briefly on page 42 in chapter 1.

verifying the reasonable expectation that the knowledgeable agents exhibit noticeably different (and, hopefully, improved) behavior and have a significantly better loss-exchange ratio (LER) in both EINSTein and JANUS.†

Using a general linear model analysis of two factors (agent type and model) with two levels each (default/GA-bred and EINSTein/JANUS), the study found that although the LER was different for the two models, the LER data in both models follow similar trends. The standard deviations of the mean LER also decrease from the default agents to GA-bred agents in both models. Overall, the study found that EINSTein's agents may be used to portray similarities of combat vehicles reasonably well, and that "learning" as portrayed in EINSTein can be transferred into another combat model. Citing various limitations due to model-specific constraints on translating agent (and environmental) characteristics from one model to the other, as well as unavoidable conceptual differences between the two models,* Klingaman and Carlton conclude their report by offering a number of useful suggestions: (1) that multiagent-based models (ABMs) need increased fidelity in terms of terrain and weapons performance, (2) traditional models, such as JANUS, ought to incorporate ABM-like personality traits and decision making algorithms to allow for more realistic combatant actions, and (3) traditional models ought to incorporate some mechanism to allow for adaptive "learning."

8.4.2 *Alignment of Computational models*

One other important suggestion that belongs on Klingaman's and Carlton's list of general recommendations is due to Axtell, *et.al.* [Axtel96] (see also [Axel97b]), who argue for the need to *align simulation models*. "Alignment" (or "docking") refers to the process of testing to see whether two models can produce the same results. In other words, alignment consists of finding ways of using one model to "check" the output of another, but in a more general and systematic manner than was used in the one-time EINSTein↔JANUS comparison discussed above. The idea is similar to a common practice among technical researchers to use not one, but *two or more* mathematical packages (such as *Mathematica* and *Maple*) to help check their calculations.

The authors illustrate this concept by using, as their test-bed simulations, a

†LER was selected as the comparison measure because (1) it is a commonly used metric in combat models, and (2) it is calculated, and used internally, by both EINSTein and JANUS.

*Among the modeling issues cited for EINSTein were the lack of a terrain elevation feature (resulting in unrealistic sceranio transfers to JANUS), an inability to model roads and trails (a limitation which, by the way, is no longer an issue since newer versions now allow users to define squad-specific paths using an arbitrary number of waypoints), EINSTein's maximum 150-by-150 battlefield size and relative 1-by-1 agent "size" not corresponding to vehicles in JANUS, and the fact that EINSTein's agents are able to "see" everything within a 360 deg circle (which is not the case in JANUS). JANUS-specific issues include an inability to allow agents to make real-time decisions based on the local state of combat, no facility to allow for agent↔agent information sharing, a lack of scripted mission primitive objectives to drive agent actions and an absence of any embedded heuristic "learning."

model of cultural transmission designed by Axelrod [Axel97c] and the *Sugarscape* multiagent-based simulation of evolution that takes place on a notional "sugar" field, developed by Epstein and Axtell [Epstein96]. Since the models differ in many ways (and have been designed with quite different goals in mind), the comparison was not an especially easy one to make. Nonetheless, the authors report that the benefits of the sometimes arduous process of "alignment" far outweighed the hardships. In the end, the user communities of *both models* benefitted from the alignment process by gaining a deeper understanding of how each program works, of their similarities and differences, and of how the inputs and outputs of each program must be modified before a fair comparison of what "really happens in either model" can be made.

Although there was at least one rudimentary cellular-automata-based model of combat that existed before ISAAC,* it is the EINSTein simulation that has arguably pioneered the serious application of multiagent-based simulation techniques to combat modeling. Both ISAAC and EINSTein are now used for basic exploratory analyses by a growing world-wide community of military, academic and commercial researchers. As the list of applications grows, the already diverse set of interests broadens, and as more researchers become familiar with multiagent-based simulation tools, more EINSTein-like programs—beyond those that have already appeared, such as CROCADILE, MANA, SEM, Socrates, and SWarrior (see pages 55-59 in chapter 1)—will undoubtedly emerge. While each of these programs will likely be designed with a specific problem or set of operational issues in mind, and be developed with only a limited community of users in mind, if the research community as a whole is to benefit from the development of new simulations, there will arise a critical need for their "alignment," in the sense defined by Axtell, *et.al.*[Axtel96].

Finally, because all multiagent-based models are based on the fundamental precept of generating emergent phenomena *from the bottom up*, prospective researchers entering the field must address the important issue of what constitutes an "explanation" of an observed and/or emergent phenomenon (see discussion on page 53). Epstein and Axtell have strongly advocated that, with the advent of newer and more sophisticated multiagent-based modeling techniques, the modeling community ought to reexamine—and perhaps *redefine*—the scientific process as a whole, asserting that multiagent-based modeling "...may change the way we think about explanation in the social sciences. What constitutes an explanation of an observed social phenomenon? Perhaps one day people will interpret the question, 'Can you explain it?' as asking 'Can you grow it?'."[Epstein96]

8.5 Future Work

Most of the basic ingredients of the bottom three tiers of EINSTein's hierarchy (i.e. the *genotype* and *phenotype-I/II* levels in figure 8.1) are already in place, though not

*See our discussion of an early effort by Woodcock, Cobb and Dockery in 1988 [Woodc88] (and a follow-on to that work by Olanders [Olanders96]) on page 56 in chapter 1.

all aspects of EINSTein's enhanced action selection logic have yet been integrated into the source code. Undoubtedly, as problems and issues inevitably arise, changes will be made to the code as it is developed. However, up-to-date documentation will be included within all future versions of the source code to facilitate modifications to the code that may be made by other interested researchers.

Particular attention is being given to enriching the space of possible primitive contexts that individual agents can react to: (1) the set of local environmental contexts will include more realistic terrain, along with local estimates of cover and concealment, user-defined or command-agent prescribed waypoints and paths, and local combat intensity, (2) agents will be endowed with an enhanced space of internal, dynamically changing, characteristics, including measures for combat suppression, fear, morale, energy, obedience, and a more robust real-valued health state (which is currently limited to alive and injured), and (3) a new set of relational measures between agents is being added, which can be used to refine and/or tailor, actions to the relative states (such as health, firepower, and vulnerability between two or more agents. Other additions include a class of more realistic offensive and defensive capabilities (including a more intelligent targeting logic), an enhanced internal "value-system," and endowing individual agents with both a memory of, and a facility to learn from, their past actions (using both neural-network and reinforcement learning techniques).

The next major, and challenging, stage of EINSTein's evolution will consist of enhancements made to the top-most tier of the hierarchy illustrated in figure 8.1; i.e., enhancements that focus on identifying, recognizing and understanding high-level emergent patterns of behavior. Toward this end, careful thought must be given to designing and developing an appropriate suite of data-collection and data-visualization routines—beyond the basic suite already included in EINSTein. In particular, attention will be given to developing novel ways of representing and displaying multidimensional forms of information [Card99].

One approach is to generalize EINSTein's *activity map* (see page 621). Currently, an activity map is merely a filtered view of the battlefield in which individual pixels represent grey-scaled approximations of the local activity level. However, "activity" is currently defined simply by the fraction of sites (within some user-defined box of size R) for which an agent has moved, and five grey-scales are used to represent an actual "level" of activity at a given site. The activity map has, from the start, been used more as a "place holder" than a bona-fide dynamical measure; and its real utility and purpose had to await the development of a more sophisticated internal agent architecture. Future activity maps will use more refined measures of an agent's actual decision process—and exist not in a (notionally) "physical" space but rather in an abstract "decision" space that represents all possible actions accessible to an agent at a given instant in time. This generalized activity map will hence provide insight into how an agent's *internal dynamics* (i.e., an agent ability to "adapt" to changing contexts) affects the spatial patterns as they emerge on the macroscale.

Figure 8.3 is a schematic illustration of a typical pattern recognition "problem" in EINSTein. Suppose one is interested in a particular operational *measure of effectiveness* (MOE). The MOE can be a function of the casualty rate (both sustained and/or inflicted upon the enemy), the amount of enemy territory that has been "captured," or some other objective criteria by which a win or lose end-state may be well defined. Let ∂ represent the boundary between two (in general, multidimensional) areas: a *red-wins* area, and a *blue-wins* area. Then, in abstract terms, a typical problem might be of finding the functional relationship between ∂ and a set of associated phenotype-level patterns (labeled π in figure 8.3).

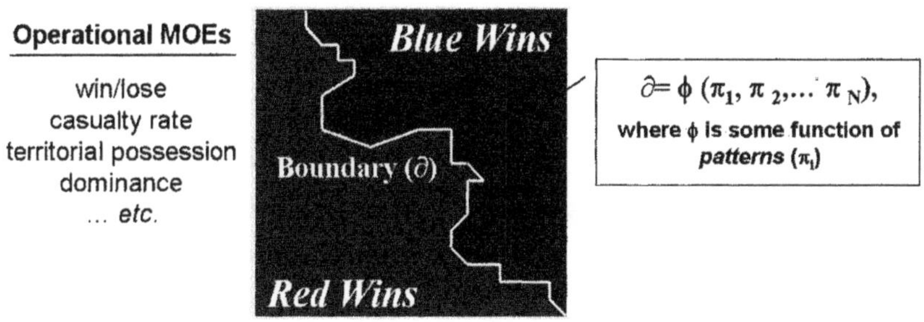

Fig. 8.3 Schematic overview of a typical "pattern-recognition problem" in EINSTein.

Finally, what lies at the heart of an artificial-life approach to simulating combat, is the hope of discovering a fundamental relationship between the set of higher-level emergent processes (penetration, flanking maneuvers, containment, etc.) and the set of low-level primitive actions (movement, communication, firing at an enemy, etc.). Wolfram [Wolfram84a] has conjectured that the macro-level emergent behavior of all cellular automata (CA) rules falls into one of only four universality classes, despite the huge number of possible local rules (see discussion on page 137). While EINSTein's rules are obviously considerably more complicated than those of their elementary CA brethren, it is nonetheless tempting to speculate about whether there exists—and, if so, what the properties are, of—a *universal grammar of combat.*

As discussed briefly in the *Preface* and at the start of chapter 1, the motivation for developing EINSTein has, from the start, included showing how the basic precepts of complex adaptive systems may be used to achieve a considerably broader applicability of the multiagent-based simulation paradigm that embodies those precepts than the purely combat-centric context in which EINSTein was developed. In particular, because the important aspects of emergent behavior depends more on the abstract set of interrelationships among information-sensing and information-processing primitive entities than it does on the details of how those entities are explicitly defined in a given simulation (such as EINSTein), EINSTein may be viewed as an exemplar of a much more general programming architecture for developing multiagent-based simulations.

In principle, any physical system that may be objectively decomposed into various interrelated and mutually coevolving parts that receive, interpret, locally process, communicate and/or transform information, is amenable to being simulated by using the conceptual architecture that underlies EINSTein. In addition to the already-cited example of how EINSTein has been used to design an ostensibly "different" noncombat-related multiagent-based boardgame (i.e., SCUDHunt), examples of applications that are amenable to the same treatment given SCUDHunt include border patrol for illegal aliens, the dynamics of integrated air-defense systems, base realignment and closure option considerations, and the command and control of distributed robot swarms and unmanned aerial vehicles.

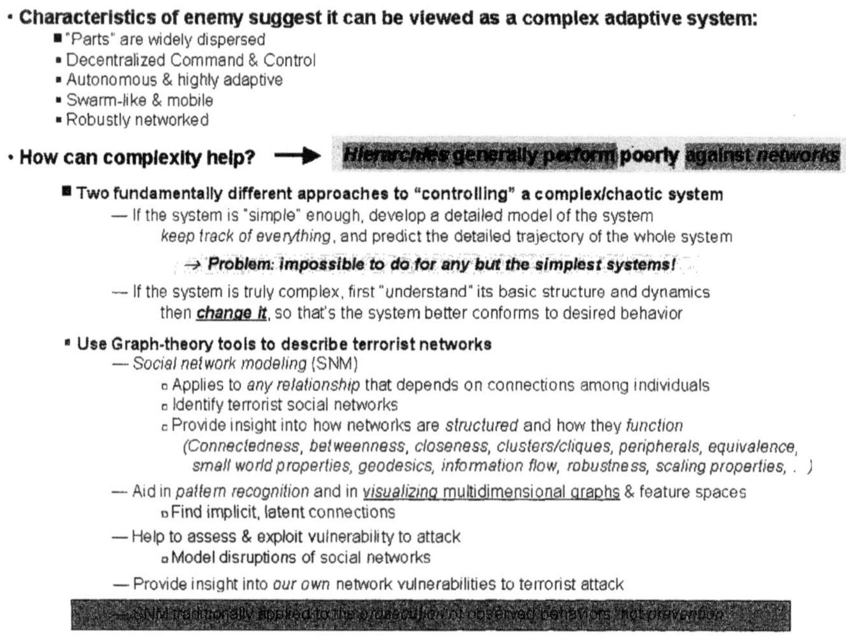

Fig. 8.4 Application of complexity-based research to the study and combat of terrorism; *slide one.*

As far as military matters are concerned, the most far-reaching application of complexity theory in general—and EINSTein in particular—is to the understanding of the dynamics of terrorism and terrorist cells (see figures 8.4 and 8.5). In light of the tragic events of 9/11, the timing (as noted by Gen Paul van Riper in his *Preface* to this book*) could not have been more fortuitous. The challenging times that lie immediately before us will require novel approaches and innovative solutions.

Complexity theory immediately stands out as the strongest candidate for har-

*See page x

boring precisely the right set of conceptual and modeling tools for understanding the new form of enemy as terrorist. Indeed, even if one looks at only the most basic dynamic characteristics of the emerging threat, it is obvious that terrorist networks constitute a perfect "textbook" example of a complex adaptive system (even more so, in many ways, than the more "conventional" forms of combat discussed at length in this book): they consist of widely dispersed, autonomous cells that obey a decentralized command and control structure, are highly adaptive and compartmentalized, are structurally robust and largely impervious to local attack, and typically function in a localized, mobile, intensely swarm-like fashion. This strongly suggests that insights into the operation of terrorist networks—as well as ways of intruding into them and/or disrupting their effectiveness—may be gleaned by studying patterns and behaviors that emerge from a multiagent-based simulation of their dynamics.

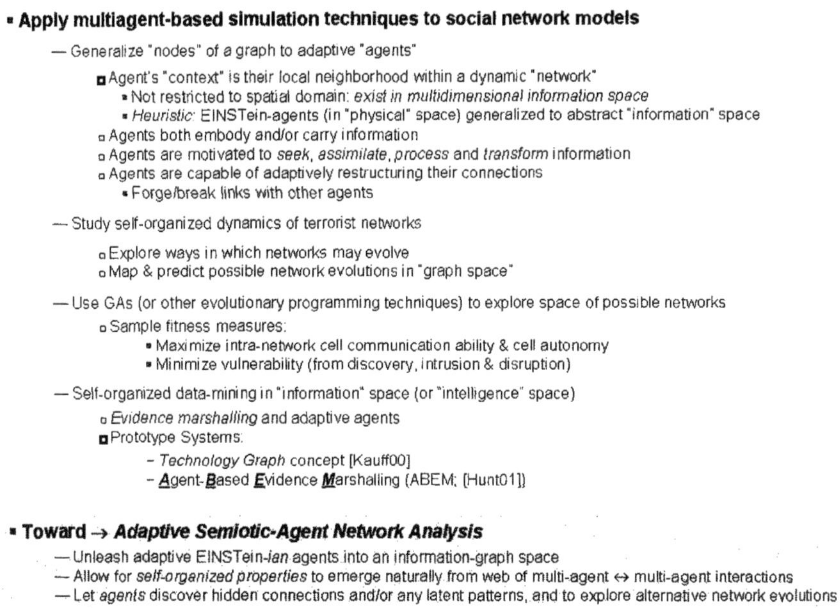

Fig. 8.5 Application of complexity-based research to the study and combat of terrorism; *slide two*.

The mathematical theory (and computer explorations) of the topology and dynamics of networks and graphs, as well as a better developed mathematical theory of the fundamental role that information plays on the new terrorist-defined battlefield (a "battlefield" that now necessarily encompasses both physical dimensions as well as the multiple virtual dimensions of cyberspace), are likely to emerge as the critical conceptual and technological drivers behind understanding the new enemy.* It is hard to overemphasize the critical need that now exists for developing new complex systems theory inspired analytical tools and models for understanding the dynamics of the terrorist threat, and for providing needed insights into how to combat it. If ever there was a time for complexity theory to come into its own *within the military operations research community*—much in the same way as mathematical search theory did in WWII when the need arose for finding and employing novel strategies to search for German U-boats—that time is now.

8.6 Final Comment

The last decade has witnessed the development of an entirely new and powerful modeling and simulation paradigm based on the distributed intelligence of swarms of autonomous, but mutually interacting, agents. First applied to natural systems such as ecologies and insect colonies, later to population dynamics and artificial intelligence, and then to social, economic and cultural evolution, this paradigm has recently finally entered the mainstream consciousness of military operations research.

Despite the fact that many of these ideas and tools are still in their infancy, and the success of multiagent-based modeling depends strongly on developing and nurturing a close-knit but interdisciplinary research community, I am convinced that the role they will play in helping us understand the fundamental processes of warfare *will eventually far exceed that of any other mathematical tools heretofore brought to bear on this problem.* The even more far-reaching possibilities of using complex adaptive system theory to discover new fundamental laws of self-organized emergent behavior in the universe at large, are limitless!

*A number of papers and books discussing the dynamics of networks have appeared in recent years. Some of the better ones, written on a popular level, are by Barabasi [Bara02] and Watts [WattsD03]. Watts also earlier authored a pioneering monograph in the field, called *Small Worlds* [WattsD99]. An excellent technical review of network theory is the one by Newman [Newm03].

Appendix A
Additional Resources

This appendix lists sources of information (sorted by subject, and that are all available on the world wide web as of this writing) that pertain to combat, complexity, nonlinear dynamics, and multiagent-based modeling and simulation. These resources include papers, simulation and modeling tools, visualization aids, pointers to other research groups, and additional links. Additional resources may also be found at the author's website at the *Center for Naval Analyses* (and EINSTein's homepage): *http://www.cna.org/ isaac.*

A.1 General Sources

Santa Fe Institute:
http://www.santafe.edu/
Computer science bibliographies:
ftp://ftp.cs.umanitoba.ca/pub/bibliographies/index.html
Bibliography of measures of complexity:
http://www.fmb.mmu.ac.uk/~bruce/combib
Principia Cybernetica:
http://pespmc1.vub.ac.be/
Complexity & Artificial Life Research Concept for Self-Organizing Systems:
http://www.calresco.org/
New England Complex Systems Institute (NECSI):
http://necsi.org/
The Stony Brook Algorithm Repository:
http://www.cs.sunysb.edu/~algorith/

A.2 Adaptive Systems

Complex adaptive systems research resources:
http://www.casresearch.com/

Evolutionary and Adaptive Systems at Sussex:
http://www.cogs.susx.ac.uk/easy/index.html

A.3 Agents

Agent construction tools:
http://www.agentbuilder.com/AgentTools/index.html
Boids (by Craig Reynolds):
http://www.red3d.com/cwr/boids/
Complexity of Cooperation (archive; by Robert Axelrod):
http://pscs.physics.lsa.umich.edu/Software/ComplexCoop.html
Multiagent Modeling Language:
http://www.maml.hu/
Multiagent Systems Lab (UMass):
http://dis.cs.umass.edu/
Multiagent Systems (news and information):
http://www.multiagent.com/
UMBC AgentWeb:
http://agents.umbc.edu/

A.4 Artificial Intelligence

About AI (resources):
http://www.aboutai.net/DesktopDefault.aspx
AI Depot (resources):
http://ai-depot.com/Main.html
Artificial intelligence resources:
http://www.cs.berkeley.edu/~russell/ai.html
Generation5 (resources):
http://www.generation5.org/
Journal of Artificial Intelligence Research:
http://www.cs.washington.edu/research/jair/home.html
Bibliographies on artificial intelligence:
http://liinwww.ira.uka.de/bibliography/Ai/index.html
Navy Center for Applied Research in Artificial Intelligence:
ftp://ftp.aic.nrl.navy.mil/pub/papers/

A.5 Artificial Life

Artificial life database:
http://www.aridolan.com/ad/adb/adib.html

Avida (digital life laboratory; Cal Tech):
http://dllab.caltech.edu/avida/
A Semi-annotated artificial life bibliography:
http://www.cogs.susx.ac.uk/users/ezequiel/alife-page/ alife.html
Artificial life on-line resources:
http://www.insead.fr/CALT/Encyclopedia/ComputerSciences/AI/aLife.htm
Artificial life resources:
http://www.cs.ucl.ac.uk/staff/t.quick/alife.html
Floys: Social, Territorial Artificial-Life Creatures (Java applets; by Ariel Dolan):
http://www.aridolan.com/JavaFloys.html
Framsticks (3D artificial life):
http://www.frams.poznan.pl/
Lotus artificial life:
http://alife.co.uk/index.html\

A.6 Cellular Automata

3D Life (by Konstantin Bashevoy):
http://sungraph.jinr.dubna.su/life3dinside/
CAPOW (continuous-valued cellular automata for WIndows-based PCs):
http://www.cs.sjsu.edu/faculty/rucker/capow/
Cellular automata links:
http://psoup.math.wisc.edu/mcell/ca_links.html
CellLab (by Rudy Rucker and John Walker):
http://www.fourmilab.ch/cellab/
Conway's 2D life-rule:
http://hensel.lifepatterns.net/
Conway's 2D Life-rule resources:
http://www.radicaleye.com/lifepage/
Discrete Dynamics Lab (by Andrew Wuensche):
http://www.ddlab.com/
Life32 (for Windows):
http://www.engr.iupui.edu/~eberhart/web/PSObook.html
MCell (1D and 2D cellular automata explorer by Mirek Wojtowicz):
http://www.mirwoj.opus.chelm.pl/ca/
Stephen Wolfram's on-line collection of cellular automata papers:
http://www.wolfram.com/s.wolfram/articles/indices/ca.html

A.7 Chaos

Applied Chaos Laboratory at Georgia Tech:
http://www.neuro.gatech.edu/acl/

Chaos e-Print Archive at Los Alamos:
http://xxx.lanl.gov/archive/chao-dyn/
Chaos Group at the University of Maryland at College Park:
http://www-chaos.umd.edu/
Nonlinear dynamics and chaos resources:
http://www.mec.utt.ro/~petrisor/dynsyst.html
Visualization of complex dynamical systems:
http://www.cg.tuwien.ac.at/research/vis/dynsys/

A.8 Complexity

Complexity Digest (weekly summary of articles and news; by G. Mayer-Kress);
http://www.comdig.org/
Complexity International (an on-line refereed journal);
http://journal-ci.csse.monash.edu.au/?ci.html
Complexity concept map (by Yaneer Bar-Yam of the *New England Complex Systems Institute*):
http://necsi.org/guide/concepts/
Hypertext bibliography of measures of complexity (by Bruce Edmonds):
http://bruce.edmonds.name/combib/

A.9 Conflict & War

Defense Modeling and Simulation Office:
https://www.dmso.mil/public/
Information warfare resources:
http://www.fas.org/irp/wwwinfo.html
War, Chaos and Business:
http://www.belisarius.com/
Military Theory and Theorists:
http://www.au.af.mil/au/awc/awcgate/awc-thry.htm
Military Operations Research Society:
http://www.mors.org/
MOVES Institute (Navy Post Graduate School):
http://www.movesinstitute.org/Projects/MOVESresearchcenter.html
Clausewitz and Complexity:
http://www.clausewitz.com/CWZHOME/Complex/CWZcomplx.htm
Terrorism, Nonlinearity and Complex Systems:
http://www.cna.org/isaac/terrorism_and_cas.htm
The Art of War (trtansation by Lionel Giles of Sun Tzu's classic):
http://classics.mit.edu/Tzu/artwar.html

Game Theory:
http://www.gametheory.net/

A.10 Fuzzy Logic

Fuzzy logic archive of resources:
http://www.austinlinks.com/Fuzzy/
Fuzzy logic Frequently Asked Questions (FAQ):
http://www-2.cs.cmu.edu/Groups/AI/html/faqs/ai/fuzzy/part1/faq.html
Fuzzy logic resources:
http://www.abo.fi/~rfuller/fuzs.html

A.11 Game Programming

AIForge (extensive list of AI/game-programming related links):
http://tpga.virtualave.net/game-links.htm
AIWisdom (a comprehensive database of gaming AI):
http://www.aiwisdom.com/
Gamasutra (gaming journal and resources):
http://www.gamasutra.com/
Game AI (resources maintained by Steve Woodcock):
http://www.gameai.com/

A.12 Genetic Algorithms

European Network of Excellence in Evolutionary Computing (*EvoWeb*):
http://evonet.dcs.napier.ac.uk/
Genetic algorithms archive (at Naval Research Labs):
http://www.aic.nrl.navy.mil/galist/
Genetic algorithm resources:
http://www.geneticprogramming.com/
Genetic algorithm search engine:
http://www.optiwater.com/GAsearch/
Illinois Genetic Algorithm Repository:
http://gal4.ge.uiuc.edu/

A.13 Information Visualization

GGobi Data Visualization System:
http://www.ggobi.org/

Resources (by Gary Ng):
http://www.cs.man.ac.uk/~ngg/InfoViz/
Information Applications and Techniques:
http://www.ils.unc.edu/~geisg/info/infovis/paper.html
Information Visualization Resources on the Web (by Tamara Munzner):
http://graphics.stanford.edu/courses/cs348c-96-fall/resources.html
Olive (On-line Library of Information Visualization Environments):
http://otal.umd.edu/Olive/
Scientific visualization sites:
http://www.nas.nasa.gov/Groups/VisTech/visWeblets.html
WEBSOM (Self-organizing maps):
http://websom.hut.fi/websom/

A.14 Machine Learning

Machine learning in games:
http://satirist.org/learn-game/
Reinforcement learning (archive maintained by Rich Sutton):
http://www-anw.cs.umass.edu/~rich/sutton.html
Reinforcement learning resources (edited by Andrés Perez-Uribe):
http://www.geocities.com/fastiland/rlrobots.html#reinfo

A.15 Newsgroups

Cellular automata:
comp.theory.cell-auto
Artificial intelligence:
comp.ai
Artificial life:
comp.ai.alife
Genetic algorithms:
comp.ai.genetic

A.16 Philosophical

Autopoiesis bibliography:
http://www.informatik.umu.se/%7Erwhit/Bib.html
Biosemiotics (edited by Alexei Sharov and Jesper Hoffmeyer):
http://www.ento.vt.edu/~sharov/biosem/
Digital Physics (by Ed Fredkin):
http://digitalphilosophy.org/

Semiosis resources:
http://www.library.utoronto.ca/see/

A.17 Robotics

Autonomous Robotics Research Group (NASA):
http://ic-www.arc.nasa.gov/section.php?sec=14
Braitenberg Vehicles:
http://people.cs.uchicago.edu/~wiseman/vehicles/
Lego Mindstorms:
http://www.crynwr.com/lego-robotics/
RoboCup:
http://www.robocup.org/
Robotics research resources:
http://www.robots.net/
Stanford robotics laboratory:
http://robotics.stanford.edu/

A.18 Simulation Systems

Evaluation of Software Tools (by Julie Dugdale, GRIC-IRIT, France):
http://www.irit.fr/COSI/training/evaluationoftools/Evaluation-Of-Simulation-Tools.htm
Ascape (Brookings Institute):
http://www.brook.edu/dybdocroot/es/dynamics/models/ascape/
Complexity in Social Science:
http://www.irit.fr/COSI/
Computer simulation of societies resources:
http://www.soc.surrey.ac.uk/research/simsoc/
Journal of Artificial Societies and Social Simulation:
http://jasss.soc.surrey.ac.uk/JASSS.html
Legion (agent-based pedestrian traffic simulation; developed by Keither Still):
http://www.crowddynamics.com/Egress/legion.html
MITSimLab:
http://mit.edu/its/mitsimlab.html
Multiagent Modeling Language:
http://www.maml.hu/
Myriad (agent-based crowd dynamics simulation):
http://www.crowddynamics.com/Myriad/Intro.htm
NetLogo (Northwestern University):
http://ccl.northwestern.edu/netlogo/
NetVis (dynamic visualization of social networks):

http://www.netvis.org/
RePast (University of Chicago; JAVA):
http://repast.sourceforge.net/
Self-organized networks (Univ. Notre Dame):
http://www.nd.edu/~networks/
SOAR (University of Michigan):
http://sitemaker.umich.edu/soar
StarLogo (MIT):
http://education.mit.edu/starlogo/
Sugarscape:
http://www.brookings.edu/es/dynamics/sugarscape/default.htm
Swarm:
http://www.swarm.org/intro.html
Transim (agent-based traffic simulation; Los Alamos):
http://www-transims.tsasa.lanl.gov/

A.19 Swarm Intelligence

Ant-colony optimization resources:
http://iridia.ulb.ac.be/~mdorigo/ACO/ACO.html
Evolving ant-colony optimization (seminal paper by Botee and Bonabeau):
http://www.santafe.edu/sfi/publications/wpabstract/199901009
Resources:
http://dsp.jpl.nasa.gov/members/payman/swarm/

A.20 Time Series Analysis

Nonlinear dynamics and topological time series analysis archive:
http://www.drchaos.net/drchaos/intro.html

Appendix B

EINSTein Homepage

An important long-term objective of the EINSTein project is to develop a platform independent, easily modifiable, toolkit that can be used freely by the academic and military operations research communities. Much of that objective has been accomplished in recent years, as updates to EINSTein have been made available for download on a CNA-sponsored web page. Tables 1.4 (on page 20) and 1.5 (on page 20) list affiliations of registered users and summarize some of the EINSTein-related research that has thus far been conducted outside of CNA.

Indeed, almost all of the EINSTein project work that has been conducted, first, under the sponsorship of the *Marine Corps Combat Development Command*, and, more recently, the *Office of Naval Research*—including research papers, briefing slides, and a *Microsoft* Windows (95-through-XP, NT, and 2000) executable form of EINSTein (as well as a DOS executable of the older "proof of concept" combat simulation, ISAAC, along with all of its support files, including a phase-space "mapper" program and genertic algorith "breeder")—is available on-line on the WWW at EINSTein's homepage (see Color Plate 29 on page 275 and figures B.1, B.2, and B.3):

http://www.cna.org/isaac.

B.1 Links

EINSTein's homepage includes additional resources related to nonlinear dynamics, complex adaptive systems, multiagent-based modeling and combat, including:

- A "short list" of WWW URL links:

  http://www.cna.org/isaac/complexs.htm.

- A "long list" of WWW URL links:

  http://www.cna.org/isaac/on-line-papers.htm.

- A list of resources that focus on terrorism, nonlinearity and terrorism:

http://www.cna.org/isaac/terrorism_and_cas.htm.

- Links to additional EINSTein-related resources, including sample screenshots, sample AVI movies, briefing slides, and an on-line user's guide:

http://www.cna.org/isaac/einstein_page.htm.

- EINSTein download page:

http://www.cna.org/isaac/einstein_install.htm.

- Additional papers and briefs:

http://www.cna.org/isaac/complexity_conference.htm.

This last page contains links to papers that were presented at CNA's Feb 2001 symposium, *Complexity: An Important New Framework for Understanding Warfare.* Speakers at this conference included Stuart Kauffman (of the *Santa Fe Institute* and *BiosGroup*, Inc.), Joshua Epsteain (from the *Brookings Institute*), Ken DeJong (of the *Krasnow Institute* at *George Mason University*), Michael Lauren (from New Zealand's *Defence Operational Technology Support Establishment*), and John Hiles (formally from Thinking Tools and now an instructor at the *Naval Postgraduate School* in Monterey, California). The keynote speaker was Lieutenant General (Retired) Paul K. van Riper.

B.2 Screenshots

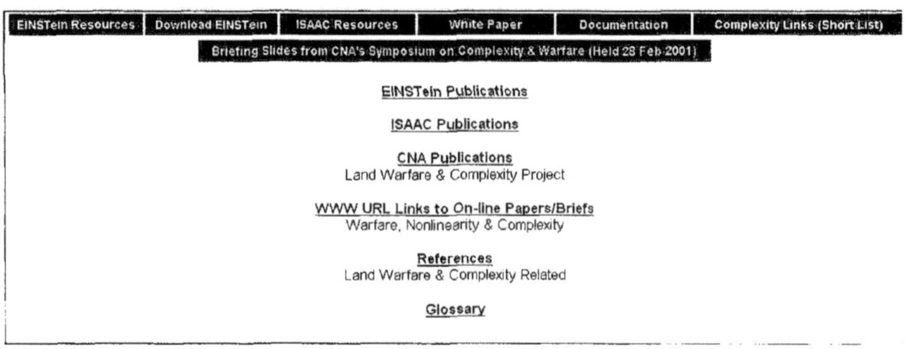

Fig. B.1 Snapshot of EINSTein's *Documentation* page (http://www.cna.org/isaac/downref.htm).

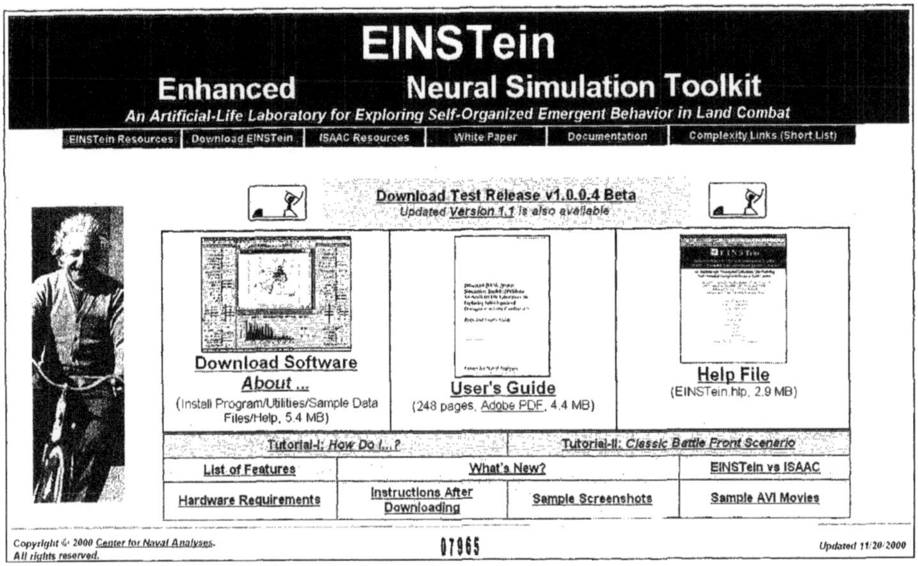

Fig. B.2 Snapshot of EINSTein's *Download* page (www.cna.org/isaac/einstein_test_version.htm).

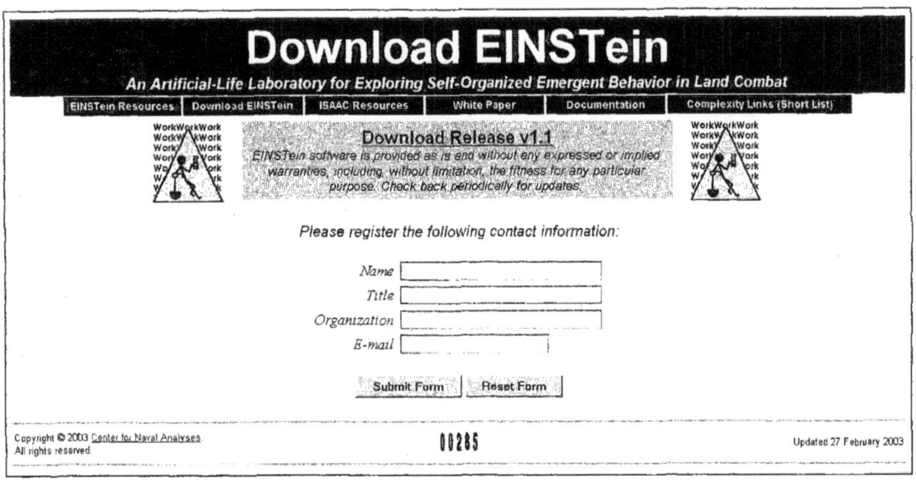

Fig. B.3 Snapshot of EINSTein's *Registration* page (www.cna.org/isaac/einstein_setup11.htm).

Appendix C

EINSTein Development Tools

EINSTein was written and compiled using Microsoft *Visual C++* version 6.0 and *Developer Visual Studio* version 6.0:

http://msdn.microsoft.com/developer/.

Version control and archiving services were performed by the open-source program called CVS (*Concurrent Version System*), version 1.2:

http://www.cvshome.org.

EINSTein's on-line data visualization functions use Pinnacle's *Graphics Server Toolkit* for Windows:

http://www.graphicsserver.com/.

EINSTein's on-line help was authored using HSG Software Solution's *HelpMATIC Pro* Version 1.22:

http://members.aol.com/harbsg/hmpro.html.

Screenshots were made using TechSmith's screen capture program *SnagIt* version 6.2:

http://www.techsmith.com.

EINSTein's setup files were created using TG BYTE's Software's *Setup Specialist* version 2.1:

http://www.setupspecialist.com/.

Miscellaneous off-line calculations and experiments in visualization were performed using Wolfram Research's *Mathematica*, version 4.1:

http://www.wri.com/products/mathematica/index.html.

Appendix D

Installing EINSTein

D.1 Versions

There are two main versions of EINSTein (three, if one includes EINSTein's DOS-based predecessor program, called ISAAC*): (1) Version 1.0.0.0β and *older*, and (2) Version 1.0 and *newer*. Differences between these two versions—both cosmetic and substantive—are outlined in Appendix F (page 651).

D.2 System Requirements

- An IBM-compatible Pentium class CPU. For best performance, a Pentium III/IV or higher class CPU with 1 GHz clockspeed or higher is recommended.
- Microsoft Windows-Me/XP or Windows 2000.
- A minimum of 128 MB RAM. 256+ MB RAM is preferred.
- Approximately 15 MB Hard Disk space, with 30+ MB recommended for storing various data, run and output files.

Note: Dialogs will appear incomplete and/or otherwise truncated if run in screen resolutions $<$ 1024-by-768 with *large* fonts.

D.3 Installing EINSTein

The installation steps outlined here assume the user is installing EINSTein version 1.0.0.4β. Except for certain files and the appearance of the programs opening About screen, the installation procedure for both versions is the same. Version 1.0.0.4β may be downloaded from internet at URL address

*See page 14. ISAAC is still available, and may be downloaded at URL address **http://www.cna.org/isaac/downsoft.htm**.

http://www.cna.org/isaac/einstein_test_version.htm .

The latest release version of EINSTein (version 1.1 at the time of this writing[*]) is available on this page:

http://www.cna.org/isaac/einstein_install.htm .

EINSTein is installed by running the setup program *EINSTein_beta_setup.exe* (we assume that the program is being installed on a PC running Microsoft's Windows XP). The setup program automatically installs all necessary components, including the main executable, DLLs, on-line help, sample data and sample run files. It also includes a *einstein_readme.txt* file that the user is urged to consult for any instructions and/or other documentation not included in this user's manual.

To start the installation process, double-click the *My Computer* icon, then double-click the folder that holds the EINSTein setup program. Double-click on the file *EINSTein_beta_setup.exe* to begin the installation. Then, follow the instructions on the screen.

Setup automatically creates an EINSTein folder and places an EINSTein icon shortcut on the desktop. The EINSTein folder contains 39 files (see table D.1).[†]

D.4 Running EINSTein

The setup procedure automatically creates an EINSTein shortcut on the desktop. Double-click on the  icon to start the program. The program will first open a dialog prompting you to select a data file to open from the default working directory you selected during the installation process (figure D.1).

Select a file with extension **.dat* from the list shown in the dialog (or from any other folder that you have stored EINSTein input data files) and press the *Open* button. EINSTein will display an opening splash screen (figure D.2) for a few seconds, then the main interactive display screen (figure D.3). Note that you may click with the left-hand mouse button anywhere within the borders of the splash screen at any time to remove it from view.

EINSTein's display screen consists of four parts:

(1) *Main menu*, at the top of the screen,
(2) *Toolbar*, directly beneath the main menu,
(3) *Battlefield viewscreen*, and
(4) *Status bar*, at the bottom of the window.

The main menu consists of nine menu options:

[*] November 2003.

[†] Adobe's *Acrobat Reader* for Windows is required to view EINSTein's *User's Guide*. This software can be downloaded from **http://www.adobe.com/products/acrobat/readermain.html**.

Type	Files
Executable	*EINSTein.exe* (this is the main executable), *Gsw32.exe* (graphics server for data visualization)
Data	*agent_data_test.agt* (sample agent position data), *dynamic_front.run*, (fast play-back sample run), *einstein_5squads.dat* (5 squad sample data file), *einstein_disperse.dat* (sample data file), *einstein_disperse.run*, (sample play-back run), *einstein_disperse_with_blue_comms.run* (sample run file), *einstein_classic_fronts.dat* (sample data file), *einstein_classic_fronts.run* (sample play-back run), *einstein_gc.dat* (sample global commander data file), *einstein_lc.dat* (sample local commander data file), *fitness_landscape_parameters.fl* (sample fitness landscape data file), *ga_parameters.ga1* (sample genetic algorithm data file), *passable_ terrain_sample.dat* (sample passable terrain data file), *sample_ terrain_data.ter* (sample impassable terrain data file), *terrain_modified_agent_data_sample.tma* (sample terrain-modified agent data file), *weapons.wp* (sample weapons data file)
DLLs	*Comcat.dll* (for 32 bit ActiveX Control), *Gsjpg32.dll* (grahics server support DLL), *Gspng32.dll* (grahics server support DLL), *Gsprop32.dll* (grahics server 32 bit property DLL), *Gswag32.dll* (grahics server support DLL), *Gswdll32.dll* (grahics server support DLL), *Mfc42.dll* (for 32 bit ActiveX Control), *Msvcirt.dll* (for 32 bit ActiveX Control), *Msvcrt.dll* (for 32 bit ActiveX Control)
Help	*EINSTein.hlp* (EINSTein help file), *EINSTein.cnt* (EINSTein help file contents), *Graphppd.hlp* (graphics server help file), *Graphppd.cnt* (graphics server help file contents)
Icon	EINSTein.ico (EINSTein's desktop icon)
Misc	*Graphs32.dep*, *Graphs32.ocx* (32 bit ActiveX Control), *default.gsp* (default graphics server graphic element)
Text	*einstein_readme.txt*, *license.txt*, *readme.txt*
User's Guide	*einstein_users_guide.pdf* (Adobe pdf version of EINSTein's user guide, portions of which are included in this appendix

Table D.1 A list of the 39 files that will be found in the default (or user specified) EINSTein folder after version 1.0.0.4β of the program has been installed.

- **File.** Provides data file load/save and print options.
- **Edit.** Provides dialogs to edit agent, terrain and various run-time parameter values.
- **Simulation.** Provides various run options.
- **Display.** Provides options for manipulating the battlefield display screen.
- **On-the-Fly Parameter Changes.** Provides dialogs to make on-the-fly parameter changes to various agent parameters.
- **Data Collection.** Toggles data collection on/off and sets individual data collection flags.
- **Data Visualization.** Provides dialogs for displaying time-series, mission-fitness landscape and genetic algorithm progress plots for collected data.

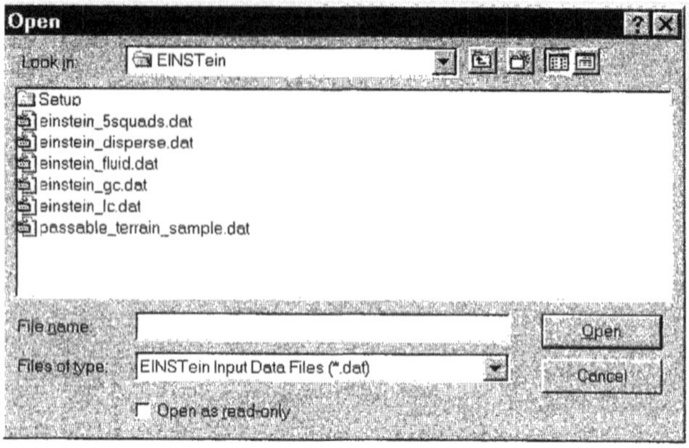

Fig. D.1 EINSTein's opening dialog prompting you to select an input data file

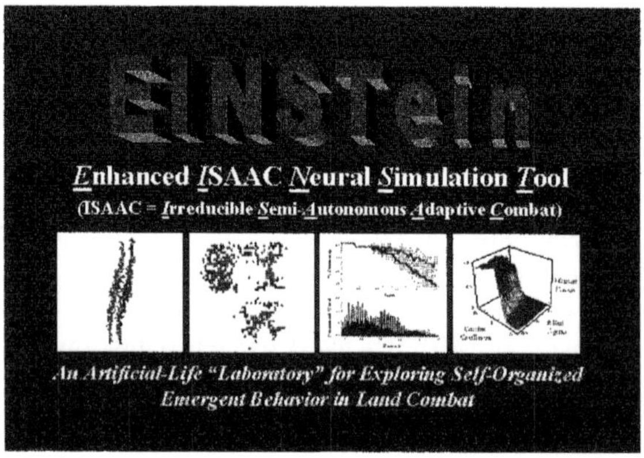

Fig. D.2 EINSTein's opening splash screen

- **Window.** Provides basic window display options.
- **Help.** Provides on-line help screens.

Each of these menu options will be described in detail in the following sections. The toolbar consists of 40 shortcuts to common operations (see **Appendix** []: **Short User's Guide** for details), including

- 6 file I/O commands
- 4 simulation options
- 13 display options
- 14 edit parameters
- 2 data collection options

The status-bar at the bottom of the screen contains basic information summa-

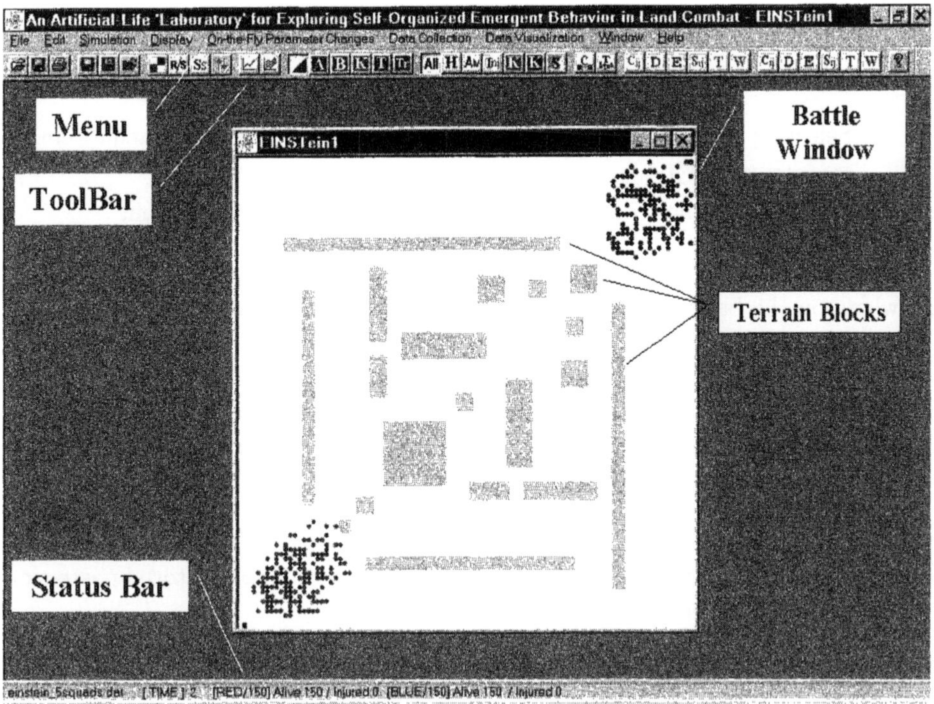

Fig. D.3 EINSTein's main battlefield viewscreen

rizing the current state of a running scenario. Its content changes depending on the context. If you opened EINSTein by selecting the *einstein_ 5squads.dat* sample input file, for example, the status bar would appear as shown in figure D.4.

Fig. D.4 EINSTein's main *status bar*, located on the bottom of the main battlefield view window.

In the figure, *[TIME]* labels the scenario's current time, *[RED/150] Alive 150/ Injured 0* denotes the fact that there initially 150 red agents, all of whom are in the alive state, and *[BLUE/150] Alive 150/ Injured 0* denotes the fact that there initially 150 blue agents, all of whom are also in the alive state. As agents are injured and/or killed, these status bar entries will change to reflect the current conditions as they unfold in time.

The simulation can be *started* in three ways:

- Selecting the Run/Stop toggle sub-menu choice of the Simulation main-menu item
- Pressing the  button on the Toolbar

- Clicking anywhere on the battlefield with the left mouse button.

Once the simulation is running, it may be *stopped* at any time in three ways:

- Selecting the Pause sub-menu choice of the Simulation main-menu item
- Pressing the  button on the Toolbar
- Clicking anywhere on the battlefield with the left mouse button.

If the user toggles Single-Step Execution Mode (see Display Menu), clicking anywhere on the battlefield with the left mouse button advances the run a single iteration step before pausing.

By default, the simulation runs in *Interactive Mode*, meaning that the user can pause, edit parameters on-the-fly, collect time-series data, and so on interactively. (Other run-modes are available as options under the *Simulation::Run-Mode* menu item.) Specific functions that can be performed in this mode include

- Using various "filters" (or *maps*) by which to observe a battle as it unfolds in time; maps include the activity map, battle-front map, territorial possession map, and killing-field map.
- Adding terrain and/or altering how agents behave on terrain .
- Editing agent parameter values as defined in the input data file.
- Displaying current parameter values on-screen as the simulation continues to run.
- Collecting and displaying data.

See **Appendix E: A User's Guide to EINSTein** for more details.

Appendix E

A Concise User's Guide to EINSTein

The main menu (see top of figure D.3) consists of nine menu options:

- **File.** Provides data file load/save and print options.
- **Edit.** Provides dialogs to edit agent, terrain and various run-time parameter values
- **Simulation.** Provides various run options.
- **Display.** Provides options for manipulating the battlefield display screen.
- **On-the-Fly Parameter Changes.** Provides dialogs to make on-the-fly parameter changes to various agent parameters.
- **Data Collection.** Toggles data collection on/off and sets individual data collection flags.
- **Data Visualization.** Provides dialogs for displaying time-series, mission-fitness landscape and genetic algorithm progress plots for collected data.
- **Window.** Provides basic window display options.
- **Help.** Provides on-line help screens.

The selections available under each of these menu options are described in detail below.

E.1 *File* Menu

The *File Menu* contains basic file input/output options. See figure E.1.

E.1.1 *Load...*

E.1.1.1 *Load EINSTein Input Data File*

Loads EINSTein's Input Data File, and initializes EINSTein's Core Engine for an interactive run.

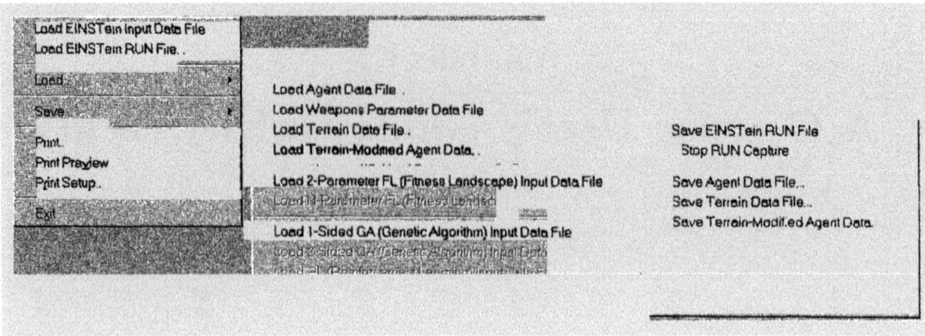

Fig. E.1 EINSTein's main-menu *File* options (for versions 1.0 and older).

E.1.1.2 *Load EINSTein RUN-file*

Loads a RUN-File (i.e., a previously stored interactive run; see *Simulation Menu::Run Modes*) for fast playback. This option can also be selected by pressing the button on the toolbar.

E.1.1.3 *Load Agent Data File*

Loads EINSTein's *Combat Agent Input Data File.* The agent file defines the initial spatial disposition of red and blue agents, and overrides the definition of initial agent-block placements as defined in EINSTein's main input data file.

E.1.1.4 *Load Weapons Parameter Data File*

Loads EINSTein's *Weapon Data File.*

E.1.1.5 *Load Terrain Data File*

Loads EINSTein's Terrain Data File.

E.1.1.6 *Load Terrain-Modified Agent Data*

Loads EINSTein's *Terrain-Modified Agent Data File.* The terrain-modified agent parameters input data file defines how an agent's parameters will be modified whenever an agent is positioned on one of three kinds of passable terrain.

E.1.1.7 *Load Fitness Landscape (FL) Input Data File*

Loads the *Two-Parameter Fitness Landscape Input Data File*, and automatically steps the user though two prompt screens to verify that default parameter values are correct. The fitness landscape run actually starts only when the user resumes the run (by selecting the run/stop toggle selection of the simulation menu).

E.1.1.8 *Load One-Sided Genetic Algorithm (GA) Input Data File*

Loads *One-Sided Genetic Algorithm Input Data File*, and automatically steps the user though a series of five prompt screens to verify that default parameter values are correct. The GA run actually starts only when the user resumes the run (by selecting the run/stop toggle selection of the simulation menu).

E.1.2 *Save...*

E.1.2.1 *Save EINSTein Input Data File*

Saves the current set of parameter values to a file (with default extension **.dat*) that can later be loaded for an interactive run.

E.1.2.2 *Save EINSTein RUN-file*

Reinitializes the battlefield with the current set of parameter values, and (after the user starts the run by selecting the run/stop option of the simulation menu, or 

button of the toolbar) keeps track of time-data that will be stored to a RUN-file when the run is terminated. A RUN-file must be terminated by either selecting the *...Stop Run Capture* option of the file menu or pressing the  button of the *Toolbar.*

E.1.2.3 *...Stop Run Capture*

Stops a RUN-file capture in progress and saves current data to a RUN-file (with default extension **.run*). A previously stored RUN-file can be loaded into memory for fast-playback.

E.1.2.4 *Save Agent Data File*

Saves current red and blue agent positions to EINSTein's *Combat Agent Input Data File.*

E.1.2.5 *Save Weapons Parameter Data File*

Saves current red and blue weapons parameters to EINSTein's *Weapon Data File.*

E.1.2.6 *Save Terrain Data File*

Saves current terrain elements to EINSTein's *Terrain Data File.*

E.1.2.7 *Save Terrain-Modified Agent Data*

Saves the current red and blue terrain-modified agent parameters to EINSTein's *Terrain-Modified Agent Data File.*

E.1.2.8 *Save Current (1-Sided) Chromosome*

Saves the current best agent chromosome to file as an input data file.

E.1.3 *Exit*

Exits the program.

E.2 *Edit* Menu

The Edit Menu contains options for editing various parameter values: combat parameters, terrain parameters, territorial possession parameters, red agent parameters, blue agent parameters, multiple time-series run parameters, fitness landscape run parameters, genetic algorithm run parameters. See figure E.2.

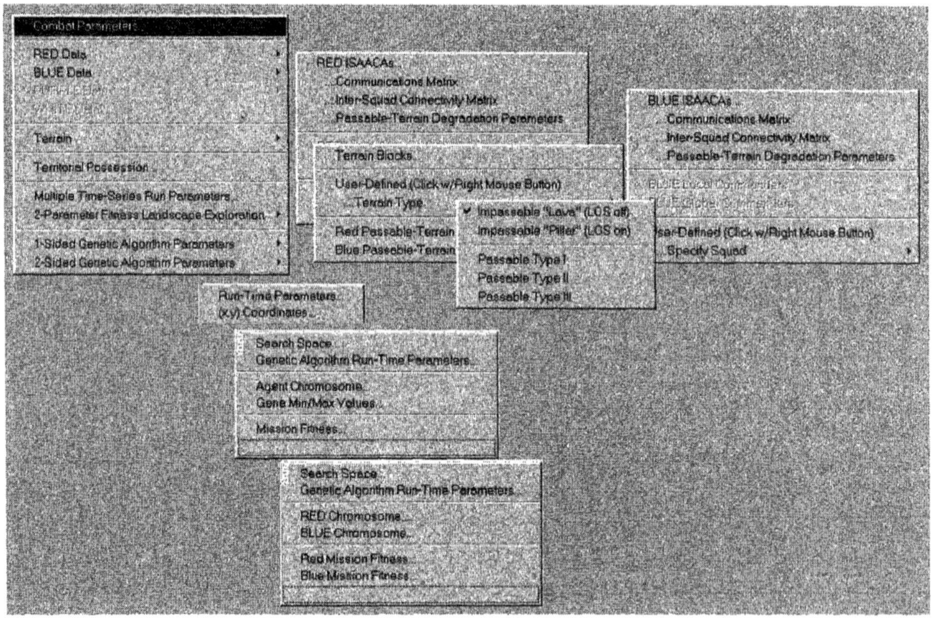

Fig. E.2 EINSTein's main-menu *Edit* options (for versions 1.0 and older).

E.2.1 *Combat Parameters...*

This is the main dialog from which almost all general combat parameter values can be set (see figure E.3). This dialog can also be displayed by pressing the button on the toolbar.

At top of the dialog, the user can define the size of the battlefield, specify whether

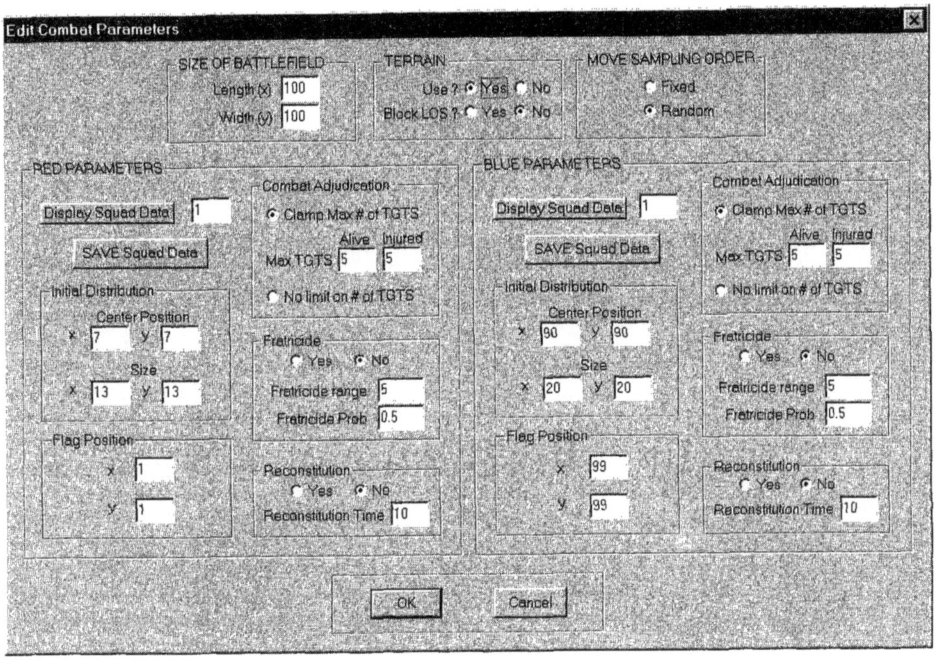

Fig. E.3 Screenshot of EINSTein's *Combat Dialog* (valid for versions 1.0 and older).

terrain blocks are to be used, and the move sampling order to be used at runtime. (EINSTein defaults to randomizing the order in which agents are sampled for their move at each time step; the user has the option to compare this default behavior to a sampling order that is randomly selected at time $t = 0$ and thereafter fixed throughout a run).

The remainder of the edit combat dialog is split into red combat parameters (on the left) and blue parameters (on the right).

Note that the dialog displays the current values for one squad only. The number of that squad is indicated immediately to the right of the *Display Squad Data* button. The button on the left hand side is for the red force; the button on the right is for the blue force. If you wish to display the parameter values for another squad (the default squad number is always 1), you must replace the displayed value with the desired squad number and click on the *Display Squad Data* button with the mouse. The parameter values will be instantly updated.

Once any changes are made to various parameters for a given squad, the user must press the *Save Squad Data* button to actually redefine the squad parameters.

If you click on the *Cancel* button at the bottom of the dialog, no changes to current combat parameter values will be made. If you click on the OK button, the changes you have made to any (or all) of the displayed values will be recorded. EINSTein will reinitialize and restart the run with the updated values.

E.2.2 *Red Data*

E.2.2.1 *Red Agents*

Prompts the user with a pop-up dialog containing all user adjustable red parameters (see figure E.4). This dialog can also be displayed by pressing the red **E** button on the toolbar.

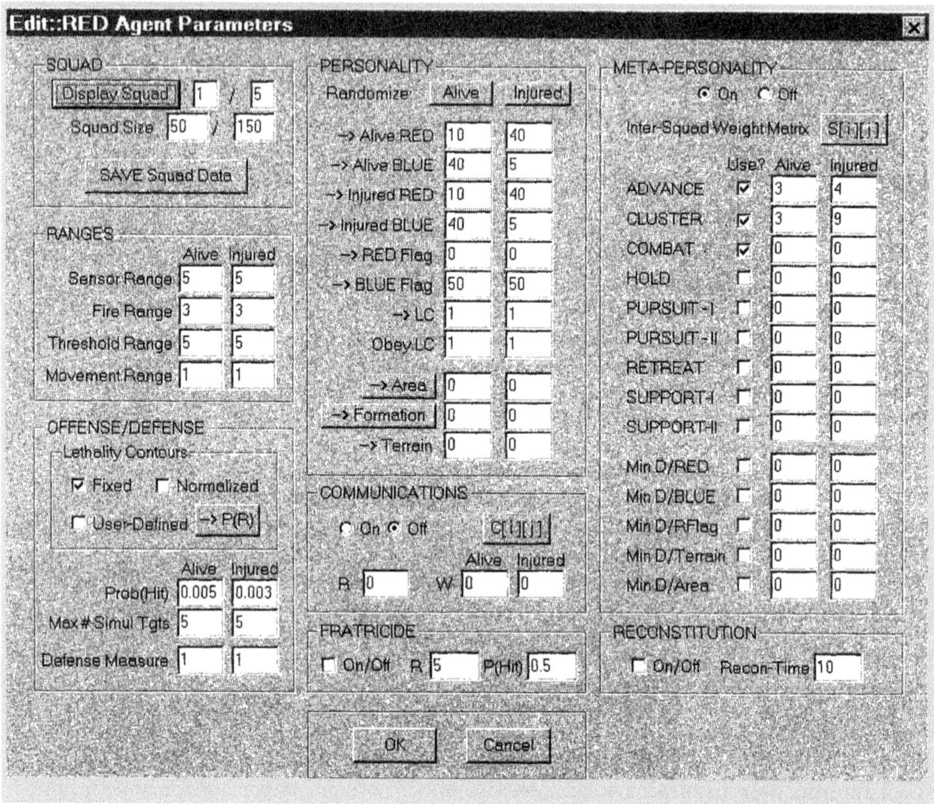

Fig. E.4 Screenshot of EINSTein's *Edit Red Agent Parameter Values* dialog (valid for versions 1.0 and older).

The *Edit Red Agents* dialog is broken up into eight sections:

- Squad
- Ranges
- Personality
- Meta-Personality
- Offense/Defense
- Communications
- Fratricide/Reconstitution

Squad. The dialog displays the current values for one squad only. The number of that squad is indicated immediately to the right of the Display Squad button.

If you wish to display the parameter values for another squad (the default squad number is always 1), you must replace the displayed value with the desired number and click on the *Display Squad* button with the mouse. The parameter values will be instantly updated. Once all desired changes are made to the red parameters for a given squad, the Save Squad Data button must be pressed to actually redefine the squad parameters.

Ranges. In this section you define an agent's sensor range, fire range, threshold range and movement range. The first column defines ranges for alive agents; the second column defines ranges for injured agents.

Personality. In this section of the dialog (top, center), you define the red agents' core personality weights. The two columns—alive and injured, respectively—refer to the value of the weight shown on the left-hand-side when an agent is either in the alive or injured state. Individual entries can range from -100 to $+100$. See page 286 of main text for discussion.

Pressing the *Alive* or *Injured* buttons at the top of this section will randomize red's entire alive and injured personality weight vector. These buttons may be pressed repeatedly. Each of the entries may be overwritten manually, as is the case for all parameter values displayed in this dialog.

More complicated scenarios may be defined that augment the nominal 6-component personality vector by any (or all) of the following five weights:

- ω_{LC} = relative weight for moving toward (or away from) an agent's local commander (for scenarios that include agents that are subordinate to a local commander).
- $\omega_{Obey-LC}$ = relative weight for obeying orders issued by an agent's local commander (for scenarios that include agents that are subordinate to a local commander).
- $\omega_{Terrain}$ = relative weight for moving toward (or away from) terrain blocks.
- ω_{Area} = relative weight for moving toward (or away from) a squad-specific fixed area A. If an agent is located within A and $\omega_{Area} > 0$, then ω_{Area} is temporarily set equal to zero; if an agent is outside A, the agent will want to move toward (or away from) the center of A with weight ω_{Area}. If $\omega_{Area} < 0$, the agent always wants to move away from the center of ω_{Area}. By default, A is set equal to the bounding rectangle for squad #1's initial spatial disposition, but may be re-defined by the user at any time during a run.
- $\omega_{Formation}$ = relative weight relative weight that individual agents use to maintain formation with their own squad-mates. Currently, formation-dynamics are defined in terms of local flocking: if the distance between an agent and the center-of-mass of nearby (squad-mate) agents is less than

R_{min}, then the agent will want to move away from the center-of-mass position with weight $\omega_{Formation}$; if the distance between an agent and the center-of-mass of nearby (squad-mate) agents is greater than R_{max}, then the agent will want to move toward the center-of-mass position with weight $\omega_{Formation}$. If the distance between an agent X and the center-of-mass of nearby (squad-mate) agents, $d \geq R_{min}$ AND $d \leq R_{max}$, then X is assumed to be in formation. Note that the local center-of-mass position toward (or away from) which a given agent X will make its move is by default calculated using the positions of agents within X's sensor range. If communications are *on*, the local center-of-mass position is calculated using the positions of agents within X's communication range. In both cases, all agent positions are weighed equally (i.e., no adjustment is made for communications weight).

Pressing the 

button calls up a dialog prompting the user to define a squad-specific area–center (x, y) coordinates and range in x and y directions–that will used in the penalty calculation (see figure E.5).

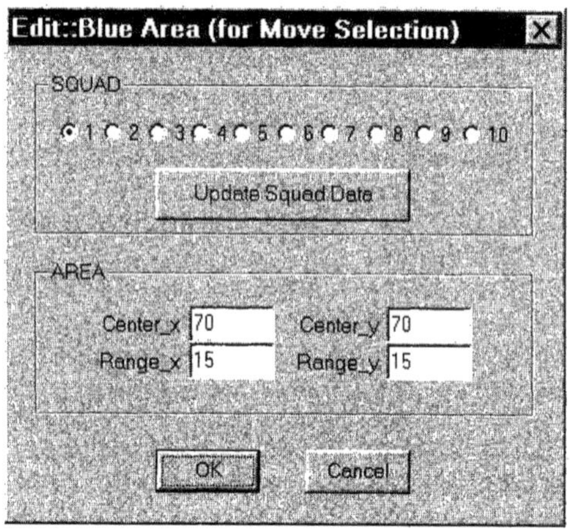

Fig. E.5 Screenshot of EINSTein's *Edit Blue Area* dialog (for weight calculation); valid for versions 1.0 and older.

Pressing the calls up a dialog that prompts the user to specify the values of the inner and outer rings defining the red agent's primitive stay-in-formation weight, $\omega_{Formation}$ (= R_{min} and R_{max}, respectively). (see figure E.6).

Meta-Personality. In this section of the Edit Red Agent Parameter dialog, you define an agent's *meta*-personality. Meta-personality rules tailor an agent's behavior to changing local contexts. A typical meta-rule consists of altering a few of the components of the default personality weight vector according to associated local threshold constraints, measured with respect to a user-specified threshold range.

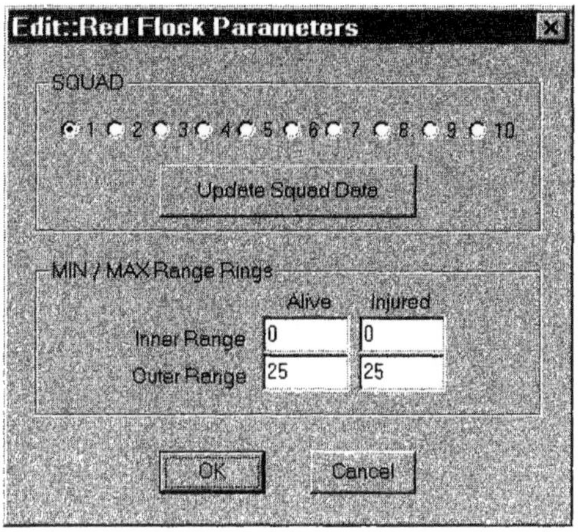

Fig. E.6 Screenshot of EINSTein's *Edit Blue Flock Parameters* dialog (for weight calculation); valid for versions 1.0 and older.

The use of meta-rules is toggled on/off by the *movement_flag* in EINSTein's input data file.

EINSTein (version 1.0 and older) supports 14 meta-rules, each of which can be individually enabled/disabled by setting its own associated *use_flag* by checking the corresponding check-box (for details, see discussion on page 298):

- *Advance to Enemy Flag:* specifies the threshold number of friendly agents, $\tau_{Advance}$, that must be within a given agent's threshold range r_T in order for that agent to continue advancing toward the enemy flag. Intuitively, the advance constraint embodies the idea that unless an agent is surrounded by a sufficient number of friendly forces (i.e., senses sufficient local fire-support), it will not advance toward the goal.
- *Cluster with Friendly Agents:* specifies the threshold number of friendly agents, $\tau_{Cluster}$, that must be within a given agent's constraint range r_T beyond which that agent will no longer seek to move toward friendly agents. Intuitively, the cluster constraint embodies the idea that once an agent is surrounded by a sufficient number of friendly forces, that agent will no longer attempt to "maneuver closer to" friendly forces.
- *Combat:* specifies the local conditions for which a given agent will choose to move toward or away from possibly engaging an enemy agent. Intuitively, the idea is that if a given agent senses that it has less than a threshold advantage of surrounding forces over enemy forces (Δ_{Combat}), it will choose to move away from engaging enemy agents rather than moving toward (and, thereby, possibly engaging) them.
- *Hold Position:* specifies the local territorial possession conditions for which a given agent will temporarily hold its current (x, y) position. Intuitively,

the idea is that if a given agent occupies a patch of the battlefield that is locally occupied by friendly forces, that agent will temporarily set its movement range ($= r_M$) equal to zero.

- *Pursuit-I (Turn Pursuit Off):* specifies the local conditions for which a given agent will choose to pursue (or ignore) nearby enemy agents. Intuitively, the idea is that if a given agent senses that there are fewer than a threshold number if nearby enemy agents, it will temporarily ignore those agents (i.e., neither moving toward nor away).
- *Pursuit-II (Turn Exclusive Pursuit On):* specifies the local conditions for which a given agent will choose to pursue nearby enemy agents, ignoring all other actions. Intuitively, the idea is that if a given agent senses that there are fewer than a threshold number if nearby enemy agents, it will temporarily ignore all other personality-driven motivations except for those enemy agents.
- *Retreat:* specifies the threshold number of friendly agents that must be within a given agent's threshold range r_T in order for that agent to continue advancing toward the enemy flag. Intuitively, the retreat meta-rule embodies the idea that unless a combatant is surrounded by a sufficient number of friendly forces (i.e., senses sufficient local "fire-support"), he will retreat back to his own goal.
- *Support-I (Provide Support):* specifies the local conditions for which a given agent will choose to provide support for nearby injured friendly agents, ignoring all other actions. Intuitively, the idea is that if a given agent senses that there are greater than a threshold number of nearby injured friendly agents, it will temporarily ignore all other personality-driven motivations except for those injured friendly agents.
- *Support-II (Seek Support)*: specifies the local conditions for which a given agent will choose to seek support for itself, ignoring all other actions. Intuitively, the idea is that if a given agent senses that there are greater than a threshold number of enemy agents, it will temporarily ignore all other personality-driven motivations except for moving toward nearby alive friendly agents to seek their support.
- *Minimum Distance to Friendly Agents:* specifies the minimum distance that an agent will seek to maintain from other friendly agents.
- *Minimum Distance to Enemy Agents:* specifies the minimum distance that an agent will seek to maintain from enemy agents.
- *Minimum Distance to Own Flag:* specifies the minimum distance that an agent will seek to maintain from its own flag. This meta-rule can thus be used to define simple "goal-defense" scenarios in which agents are positioned near their own flag.
- *Minimum Distance to Nearby Terrain:* specifies the minimum distance that an agent will seek to maintain from nearby terrain.

- *Minimum Distance to Fixed Area:* specifies the minimum distance that an agent will seek to maintain from a fixed user-defined area.

Inter-Squad Weight Matrix. The inter-squad weight matrix, which may be edited by pressing the button labeled $S[i][j]$ in the meta-personality section of the *Edit Red Agent Parameters* dialog (see figure E.4), defines the weight with which squad i "reacts to" squad j. Figure E.7 shows a sample screenshot.

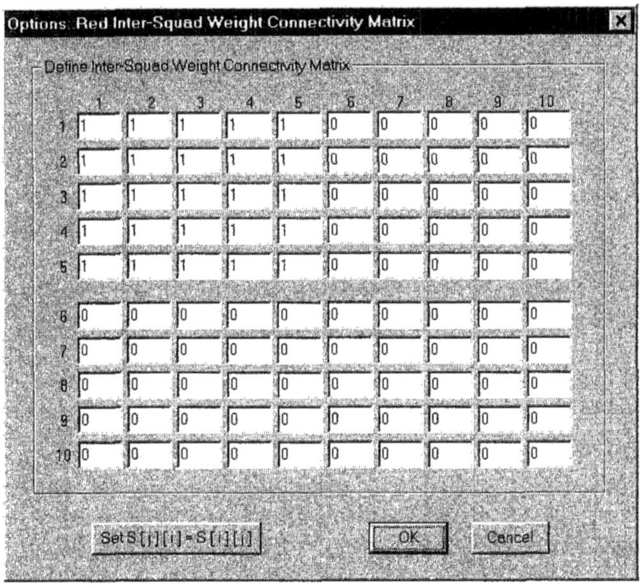

Fig. E.7 Screenshot of EINSTein's (version 1.0 and older) *Edit Red Inter-squad Weight Matrix* dialog.

S_{ij} are real numbers between 0 and 1, and can be negative or positive. By default, $S_{ij} = 1$ for all i and j. If $S_{ij} = 0$ for a given pair (i, j), that means that agent i effectively ignores agent j. If $S_{ij} = 1/2$, agent i reacts to agent j by first premultiplying i's default personality weights ω_1 (for *alive* friend) and ω_3 (for *injured* friend) by $1/2$. Thus, S_{ij} is essentially a squad-specific premultiplier factor that appears in i's penalty calculation. Intuitively, S_{ij} defines how much weight an agent from squad i gives an agent from squad j, relative to i's default personality weight vector.

Note S_{ij} is not necessarily equal to S_{ji} , as j may react differently to i than i does to j.

Offense/Defense. In the *Lethality Contours* group of the Offense/Defense section of the dialog (bottom, left), you must choose one of three possible forms of the single-shot hit-probability vs. fire range function (see figure E.8):

- *Fixed* (which is always selected by default)
- *Normalized*
- *User-Defined*

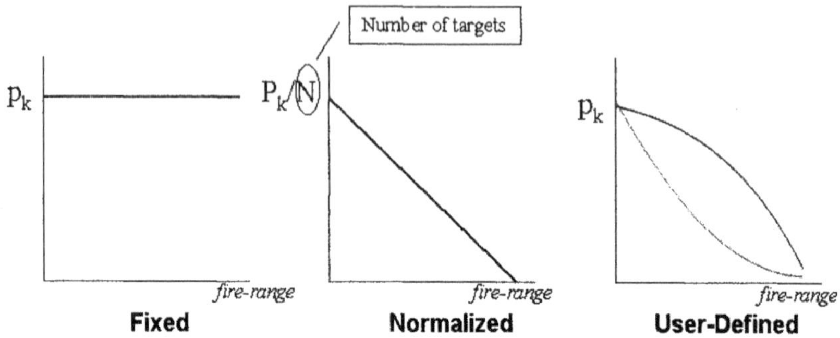

Fig. E.8 *Fixed*, *normalized* and *user-defined* single-shot probability-of-hit (P_k) vs. fire range functions.

The default flag is for the agent to use fixed constant alive and injured values of single-shot probability-of-hit (shown in the bottom half of this section). Checking User Defined box forces the agent to use the user-defined single-shot probability-of-hit function, the default form of which may be changed by pressing the *Define P(R)* button and calling up the *Single-Shot HIT Probability vs. Fire Range* edit dialog.

Single-Shot HIT Probability vs. Fire Range Edit Dialog. The button labeled $\longrightarrow P(R)$ (appearing in the *Lethality Contours* group of the *Offense/Defense* section of the *Edit Red Agent Parameters dialog*; see figure E.4) pops up a dialog prompting the user to define red's single-shot probability of hitting a targeted enemy agent as a function of red's fire range.

Communications. In this section you toggle red communications *on/off.* If communications are enabled (i.e., the "on" radio button is clicked), you must define the communications range and *alive* and *injured* communications weights in the edit boxes shown in figure E.4.

The button labeled *Define Comm Matrix* $C[i][j]$ appearing in the *Communications* box (bottom, center) pops up a dialog that prompts you to define red's communication connectivity matrix (figure E.9). This dialog can also be displayed by pressing the Cij button on the toolbar. This allows you to specify which squads can communicate with what other squads, by placing a check in the box corresponding to the appropriate connection: $C_{ij} = 1$ if and only if i receives information from j, else $C_{ij} = 0$. Note that C_{ij} need not, in general, equal C_{ji}. Thus agents from squad i can receive information from squad j agents, but agents from squad j need not receive any information from squad i.

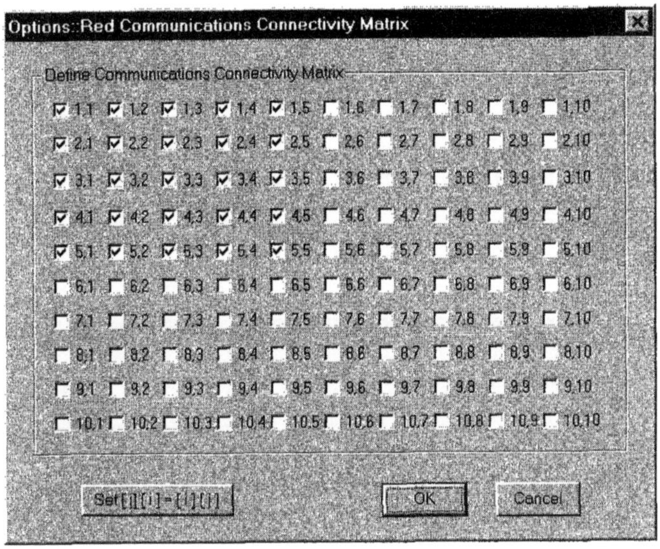

Fig. E.9 Screenshot of EINSTein's (version 1.0 and older) *Edit Red Communications Matrix* dialog.

Fratricide. Toggles red fratricide *on/off.* If fratricide is enabled, red agents will be able to accidentally target friendly red agents, otherwise no fratricide will take place.

Radius defines the range around a targeted enemy agent such that, if fratricide is enabled, all red agents located within the box defined by this range become potential victims of fratricide. *Prob(Kill)* defines the probability that a red (i.e., friendly) agent will be inadvertently hit by a shot that was intended to hit a nearby enemy (i.e., blue) agent.

Reconstitution. Toggles reconstitution option *on/off.* If reconstitution is toggled *on*, then *Reconstitution Time* defines the number of iteration steps following a "hit" (either by blue or, if fratricide is toggled on, red agents) such that if during that time interval a given red agent is not hit again, that agent's state is reconstituted back to alive.

E.2.2.2 ...*Communications Matrix*

Pops up a dialog that prompts you to define red's communication connectivity matrix (figure E.9). This dialog can also be displayed by pressing the C_{ij} button on the toolbar.

E.2.2.3 ...*Inter-squad Connectivity Matrix*

Pops up a dialog that prompts you to define red's inter-squad connectivity matrix S_{ij} (see figure E.4).

E.2.2.4 ...*Passable-Terrain Degradation Parameters*

Pops up a dialog that prompts you to define red's passable-terrain degradation parameters (see figure E.10).

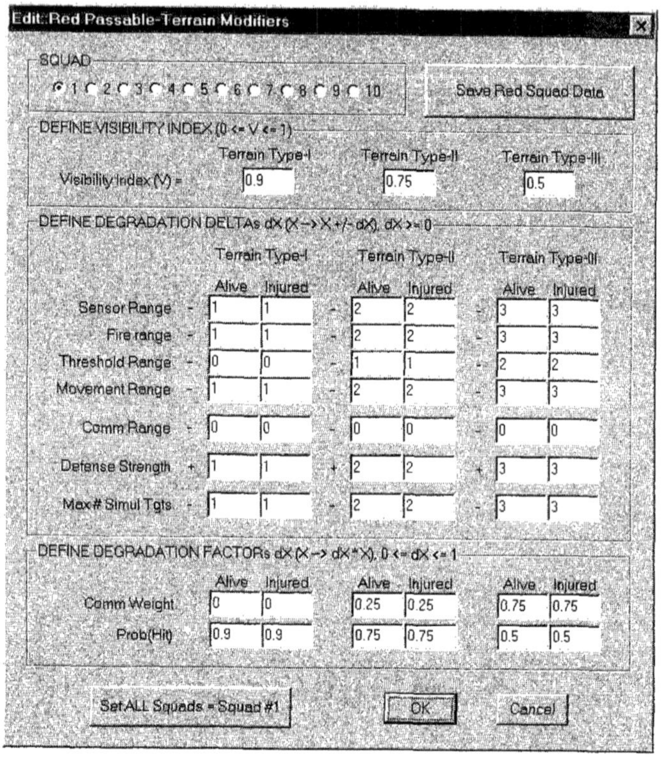

Fig. E.10 Screenshot of EINSTein's (version 1.0 and older) *Edit Passable-Terrain Degradation Parameters* dialog.

For passable terrain (Types I-III), certain characteristics of agents may be modified (either by adding/subtracting ($\pm D$) from, or multiplying ($\times f$), their default values) to provide a greater sense of realism. These characteristics include:

- ($-D$) Sensor Range
- ($-D$) Fire Range
- ($-D$) Threshold (i.e., Constraint) Range
- ($-D$) Movement Range

- $(-D)$ Communications Range
- $(\times f)$ Communications Weight
- $(+D)$ Defensive Strength
- $(\times f)$ Single-Shot Probability of Hit
- $(-D)$ Maximum # of Simultaneously Targetable Enemy Agents

In addition, the *visibility index* may also be invoked to define the probability with which an agent A occupying a battlefield position (x, y) that contains a passable terrain-element of Type-X (where $X = I, II$ or III) will be seen by another (F = friendly or E = enemy) agent, given that $\mathcal{A}$ is in F's (or E's) sensor range.

Seven of the nine passable-terrain modifiable parameters X are adjusted by adding or subtracting a user-defined delta D from X. These seven are identified by the symbol D in the bulleted list above, along with a "+" or "−" indicating whether D is added or subtracted from the given parameter.

Two of the nine passable-terrain modifiable parameters X are adjusted by multiplying the default value X by a user-defined factor $0 \leq f \leq 1$. These two parameters are identified by the symbol "$\times f$" in the bulleted list above.

E.2.2.5 *...Squad-Specific Weapons Parameters*

Pops up a dialog that prompts you to define red's *squad-specific* weapon parameters (see figure E.11). The user can define up to ten different squad-specific weapons, with user-specified lethality contours; weapon characteristics for alive and injured agents can be different from one another.

The *Edit Red Prob(Hit) vs. Fire Range* dialog contains seven buttons and five main sections.

- **Sections** (*Squad, Sensor Type, Weapon, Function, Updated Prob(Hit)/Range Array), and*
- **Buttons** (*Update Squad-Weapon Data, Symmetrize A/I (In Function section), Symmetrize Alive/Injured (in Updated Prob(Hit)/Range Array section), Generate Array, Show Function, OK, Cancel).*

Squad Section. Select the squad $(1 - 10)$ for which to display/update weapon parameters by clicking the appropriate radio button in this group.

Sensor-Type Section. Lethality Contours are used internally by an agent in two ways: (1) *Cookie-Cutter*, or (2) *Euclidean Distance.* (See equation 5.1 on page 284.)

Weapon Section. Each squad is assigned a unique weapon, which is selected by clicking on the appropriate radio button in this group. Multiple squads can be assigned the same weapon. Each weapon has separate alive and injured sets of defining parameters.

Function Section. Eight parameters are required to define a lethality contour for each weapon, one value each for alive and injured agents:

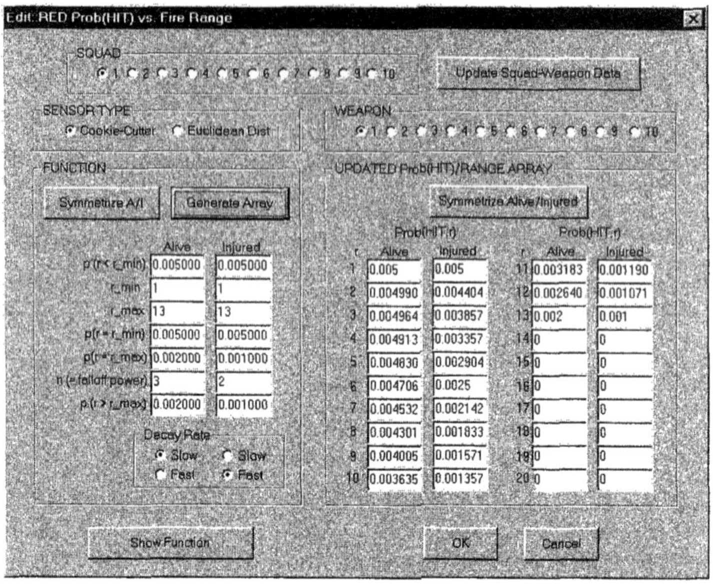

Fig. E.11 Screenshot of EINSTein's (version 1.0 and older) *Edit Prob(Hit) vs. Fire Range* dialog.

- $P(r < r_{\text{min}})$
- r_{min}
- r_{max}
- $P(r = r_{\text{min}})$
- $P(r = r_{\text{max}})$
- n (= *falloff power*)
- $P(r > r_{\text{max}})$

The meaning of each of these parameters is illustrated in figure E.12.

The decay rate determines how fast the single-shot probability-of-hit function decays with fire-range, slow or fast. In the figure, fast = "− "and slow = "+."

After defining each of these eight parameters, press the *Generate Array* button to compute a discretized array of the single-shot probability-of-hit values for fire-ranges $r = 1, 2, ..., 20$ (shown at the bottom right of the dialog under *Update Prob(HIT)/Range Array* section).

Update Squad-Weapon Data Button. Pressing this button updates the currently displayed weapons parameters and squad-specific weapon selections to memory for the current interactive run. Until this button is pressed, no actual changes are made; i.e., changing parameter values and not pressing the *Update Squad-Weapon Data* button is equivalent to pressing the *Cancel* button.

Symmetrize A/I Button. Pressing this button automatically sets the injured function parameters equal to the set of alive values.

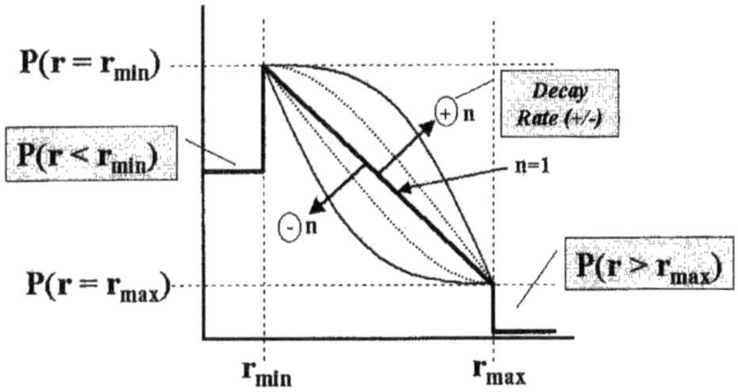

Fig. E.12 Generic form of user-defined Prob(Hit) vs. Fire Range function (used in EINSTein versions 1.0 and older).

Generate Array Button. Pressing this button automatically computes and displays a discretized array of the single-shot probability-of-hit values for fire-ranges $r = 1, 2, ..., 20$ (shown at the bottom right of the dialog under *Update Prob(HIT)/Range Array* section).

Update Prob(HIT)/Range Array Section. This group displays the current values of the discretized array of the single-shot probability-of-hit Function for fire-ranges $r = 1, 2, ..., 20$. This array is essentially the "look-up" table that an agent will use internally to determine whether a targeted enemy agent has been successfully "hit" in the case that its sensor type is cookie-cutter.

Symmetrize Alive/Injured Button. Pressing this button automatically sets the injured discretized array of the single-shot probability-of-hit values equal to the set of alive values.

Show Function Button. Pressing this button displays a graph of the currently defined single-shot probability-of-hit function.

E.2.2.6 *...Agent-Specific Weapons Parameters*

Allows the user to define and/or edit parameter values the define grenade characteristics and agent-specific weapon assignments; see figures E.13 and E.14. The various quantities that appear in these two dialogs are defined in section 5.4.1 (see discussion that begins on page 319 of the main text).

E.2.2.7 *User-Defined (Click w/Right Mouse Button)*

Toggles interactive (i.e., mouse-driven) placement of red agents on the notional battlefield. You may make as many right-hand mouse button clicks as needed to define the desired number of red agents. Clicking with the right-hand mouse button on an existing agent removes that agent from the battlefield.

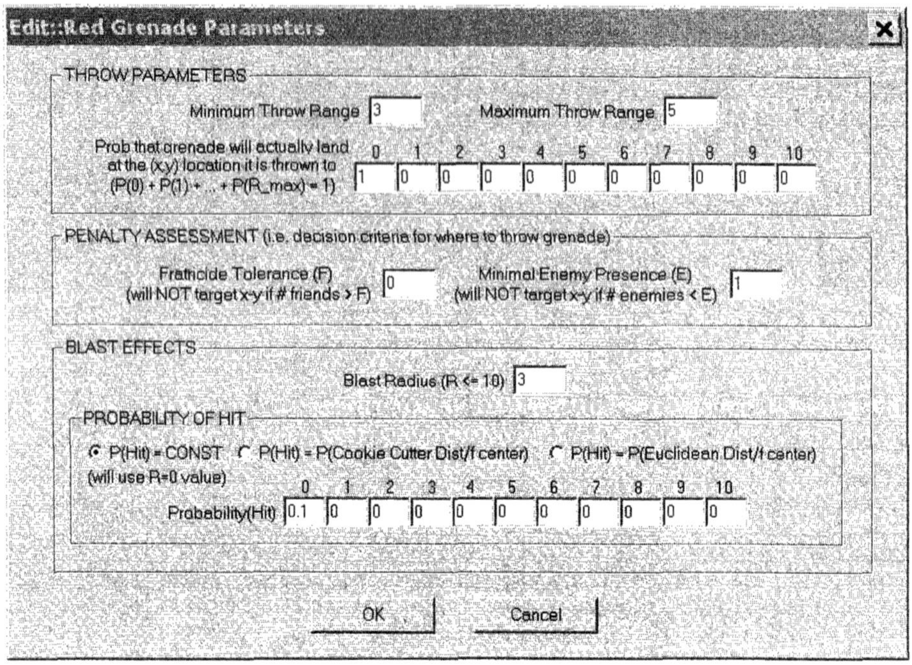

Fig. E.13 Screenshot of EINStein's area-weapons (i.e., *grenade*) user-input dialog. (Note that this applies only to versions *prior* to 1.1; for a discussion of how weapons are defined in newer versions begins on page 323.)

E.2.2.8 ...*Specify Squad*

Specifies the squad (from a list of available squads for the current scenario) to which the agent placed on the battlefield interactively with a right-hand mouse click will be attached.

E.2.3 *Terrain*

E.2.3.1 *Terrain Blocks...*

Brings up a pop-up Terrain Dialog that prompts you to define up to 32 separate terrain blocks, and—at the top of the dialog—toggle the use of these terrain blocks (figure E.15). This dialog can also be displayed by pressing the  button on the toolbar.

Each terrain block is defined by the its length, width, center (x, y) corrdinates and a flag indicating whether it will be actually be used during the current simulation. This makes it convenient to define a default set of blocks, and to then define which specific subset of these blocks will be used (while retaining the definition of all blocks in memory).

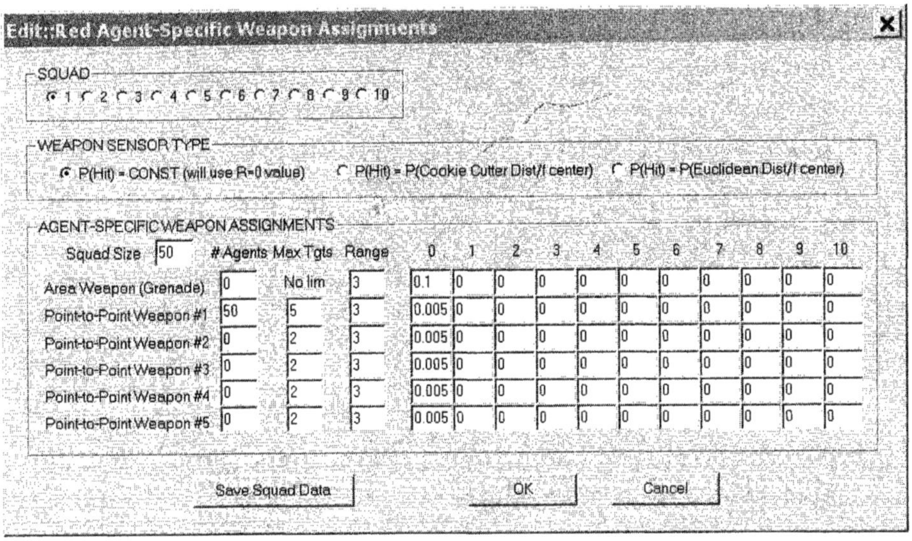

Fig. E.14 EINSTein's agent-specific *point-to-point* weapon parameters. (Note that this dialog appears only in versions *prior* to 1.1; for newer versions see discussion in section 5.4.2 that begins on page 323.)

EINSTein versions 1.0 and older allow six kinds of terrain elements (TEs):

- TE_0 = *Empty*
- TE_1 = *Impassable terrain with line-of-site off*
- TE_2 = *Impassable terrain with line-of-site on*
- TE_3 = *Passable terrain* (Type-I)
- TE_4 = *Passable terrain* (Type-II)
- TE_5 = *Passable terrain* (Type-III)

Terrain TE_1 can be thought of as a *lava pit*, across which agents can see, but through which they cannot pass. Terrain TE_2 can be thought of as an *impenetrable pillar*: agents can neither see through it nor walk through it. TE_2 is often useful for defining urban-warfare-like scenarios in which, with a little patience, quite realistic representations of buildings and streets can be designed.

Impassable terrain elements are displayed as ▒; passable terrain elements are displayed as ■.

E.2.3.2 *User-Defined (Click w/Right Mouse Button)*

Toggles interactive (i.e., mouse-driven) placement of individual (i.e., size 1–by–1) terrain elements by clicking anywhere on the battlefield window with the right-hand mouse button. You may specify any of the five terrain element types (see above) for each given (x, y) position. As many right-hand mouse button clicks may be

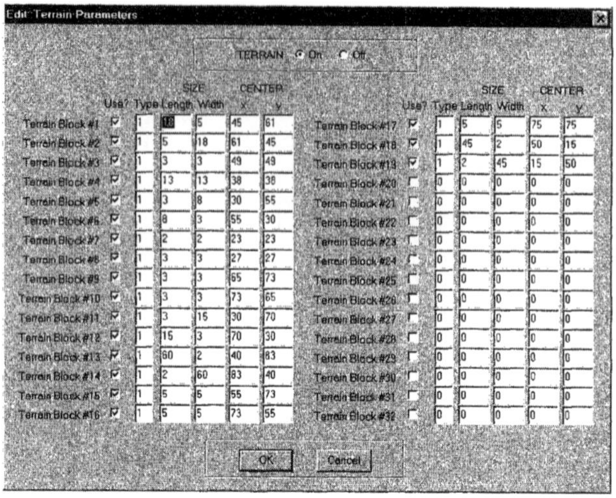

Fig. E.15 Screenshot of EINSTein's (version 1.0 and older) *Edit Terrain* dialog.

made as needed to define the desired number of terrain elements. Clicking with the right-hand mouse button on an existing terrain element removes that element from the battlefield.

E.2.3.3 *...Terrain Type*

Specifies the terrain element type ($TE_1 - TE_5$) that will be placed at (x, y) position marked by the cursor using the right-hand mouse button in interactive terrain placement mode.

E.2.3.4 *Red Passable-Terrain Degradation Parameters*

Pops up a dialog that prompts you to define red's passable-terrain degradation parameters (see figure E.10).

E.2.3.5 *Blue Passable-Terrain Degradation Parameters*

Pops up a dialog that prompts you to define blue's passable-terrain degradation parameters (see figure E.10).

E.2.4 *Territorial Possession*

Pops up a dialog prompting you to specify the parameters that EINSTein will use to define *territorial possession* (figure E.16).*

*See discussion on page 303.

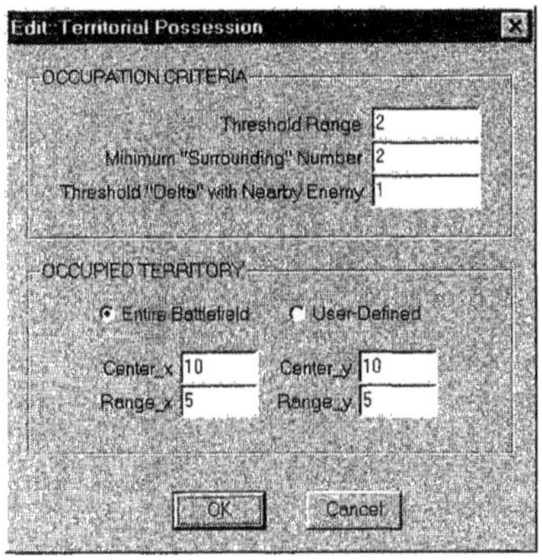

Fig. E.16 Screenshot of EINSTein's (version 1.0 and older) *Edit Territorial Possession* dialog

A site at (x, y) "belongs" to an agent (red or blue) according to the following logic: the number of like agents within a territoriality-distance (τ_D) is greater than or equal to territoriality-minimum ($\tau_{\min}$) and is at least territoriality-threshold (τ_T) number of agents greater than the number of enemy agents within the same territoriality-distance. For example, if $(\tau_D, \tau_{\min}, \tau_T) = (2, 3, 2)$ then a battlefield position (x, y) is said to belong to, say, red, if there are at least 3 red agents within a distance 2 of (x, y) and the number of red agents within that distance outnumber blue agents by at least 2.

E.2.5 *Multiple Time-Series Run Parameters*

Pops up the multiple time-series dialog, prompting you to define the number of initial conditions (i.e., samples) over which to average the data you will be collecting and the number of time steps you wish to step through for each sample (figure E.17).

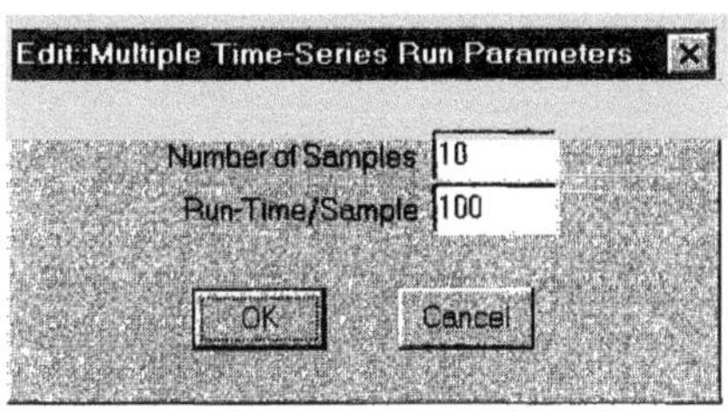

Fig. E.17 Screenshot of EINSTein's *Multiple Time-Series* dialog

In multiple time-series run mode, EINSTein re-runs the same scenario a user-specified number of times. Each run lasts for a certain fixed number of iteration steps, and differs from other runs of the same scenario only in the initial spatial disposition of red and blue agents. See **Simulation::Multiple Time-Series Run-Mode**.

E.2.6 *2-Parameter Fitness Landscape Exploration*

For a more detailed discussion of EINSTein's *2-Parameter Fitness Landscape Run Mode*, see **Simulation::Run-Modes::2-Parameter Phase Space Exploration** below.

E.2.6.1 *Run-Time Parameters*

Calls up the Edit Run-Time Parameters dialog that specifies the values of run-time variables such as number of initial conditions to average over, maximum run-time, and so on. You can change, or keep, any of the default values indicated in the edit boxes of the dialog.

E.2.6.2 *(x,y) Coordinates*

Calls up the *Edit (X, Y) Coordinates* dialog that specifies the x and y coordinates over which EINSTein will perform an automatic mission fitness scan. You can also change the default values of minimum and maximum values of these coordinates, along with the desired number of samples over which to scan.

E.2.7 *1-Sided Genetic Algorithm Parameters*

For a more detailed discussion of EINSTein's *1-Sided Genetic Algorithm Parameters Run Mode*, see **Simulation::Run-Modes::1-Sided Genetic Algorithm Parameters** below.

E.2.7.1 *Search Space*

Calls up the *Search-Space* dialog that defines the particular search that the genetic algorithm will be used to perform. The default is a simple single-squad search using a basic 63-allele agent chromosome.

E.2.7.2 *Run-Time Parameters*

Calls up the *Run-Time Parameter* dialog that defines the values of run-time variables such as population size, number of generations, number of initial conditions to average over, mutation probability, and so on.

E.2.7.3 *Agent Chromosome*

Calls up the *Agent Chromosome* dialog that specifies (via mouse-clicked "checks") which alleles will be used during the GA run. Pressing the [Symmetrize ALIVE and INJURED] button at the top symmetrizes between alive and injured parameters.

E.2.7.4 *Gene Min/Max Values*

Calls up the *Gene Min/Max* dialog that specifies the minimum and maximum values of each of the alleles used during the current GA run.

E.2.7.5 *Mission Fitness*

Calls up the *Mission Fitness* dialog that defines the fitness measure used to rank individual population members during the current GA run.

E.3 *Simulation* Menu

The *Simulation Menu* provides commands to define the run: run mode, display clear, simulation run/stop toggle, step-execute mode, reseed random number generator, restart simulation, and simulation terminate. See figure E.18.

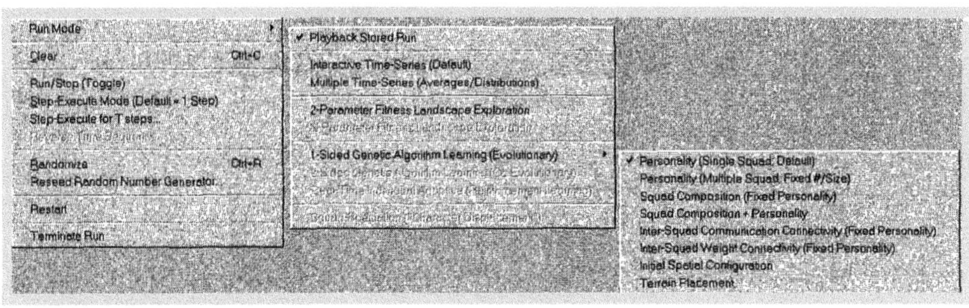

Fig. E.18 EINSTein's main-menu *Simulation* options (for versions 1.0 and older).

E.3.1 *Interactive Run Mode*

Interactive run mode is EINSTein's default run mode. In this mode, the user can run, restart, change initial conditions, alter various parameter settings and collect and display data. Upon opening an input data file, EINSTein initializes for a run and Pauses, waiting for the user to press the R/S button on the *Toolbar* (or to select the run/stop toggle option of the simulation menu) to start. The list below summarizes some of the actions the user can take during an interactive run:

- *Pause Run*
- *Step-Execute Mode*
- *Toggle Background Color*

- *Display All agents*
- *Display All agents (Highlight Injured)*
- *Display Alive agents Alone*
- *Display Injured agents Alone*
- *Toggle Trace Mode*
- *Display Activity Map*
- *Display Killing Field*
- *Highlight Individual Squads*
- *Toggle Data Collection*
- *On-line time-series plots of collected data*
- *On-the-Fly Parameter Changes*

E.3.2 *Play-Back Run Mode*

RUN-files are regular input data files, augmented by temporal data summarizing a previous run. The user can start to capture a RUN-file by pressing the  button on the toolbar. The current run is saved when the  button is pressed.

Once loaded (by pressing the  button on the toolbar), RUN-files can be played back at significantly higher speeds (typically, three to five times faster on older PCs) than interactive runs. The user can return to interactive mode by selecting the Interactive Time Series suboption of the RUN-Mode choice under the simulation menu option.

During a playback of a RUN-file, the user can select to go either forward or backward in time either by right-clicking with the mouse anywhere on the battlefield, or pressing the  button on the *Toolbar*.

E.3.3 *Multiple Time-Series Run Mode*

In *Multiple Time-Series run* mode, EINSTein re-runs the same scenario a user-specified number of times. Each run lasts for a certain fixed number of iteration steps, and differs from other runs of the same scenario only in the initial spatial disposition of red and blue agents.

This mode is designed to be used with *Data Collection* routines enabled. Once a time-series run is completed, sample-averaged plots of each of the data primitives that are enabled for a given scenario can be displayed using the options of the *Data Visualization* menu. The difference between the plots as they are displayed after a time-series run and the same plots as they are displayed after an interactive run, is that in the time-series run case each data point represents an average over the number of run-samples, along with error-bar displays of the average absolute deviation.

E.3.3.1 *Starting a Multiple Time-Series Run*

You start a run by first selecting whatever data collection options you wish to use, and then either

- Selecting the *Multiple Time-Series (Averages/Deviations)* option under the Simulation::Run Mode menu option, or
- Pressing the associated *Toolbar* Button.

The multiple time-series dialog will pop up, prompting you to define the number of initial conditions (i.e., samples) over which to average the data you will be collecting and the number of time steps you wish to step through for each sample (figure E.17).

E.3.3.2 *Monitoring a Multiple Time-Series Run in Progress*

A multiple time-series run in progress may be monitored by watching the status-bar (figure E.19). The status-bar displays the name of the input data file along with the sample number and the time-step of the current sample.

Fig. E.19 Screenshot of the status bar that appears when EINSTein is put into the multiple time-series run mode; the status bar is displayed along the bottom of the main window.

E.3.3.3 *Stopping a Run*

A multiple time-series run will terminate automatically after sweeping through the user-defined number of samples by displaying a termination box (figure E.20). At this point, the user can go to the Data Visualization menu to select various graph options.

Fig. E.20 Multiple time-series termination message box.

E.3.3.4 *Saving Raw Data*

The user has the option of saving the raw data collected. Once a specific graph has been selected for viewing on-screen, a pop-up dialog (figure E.21) appears prompting the user about save-raw-file options.

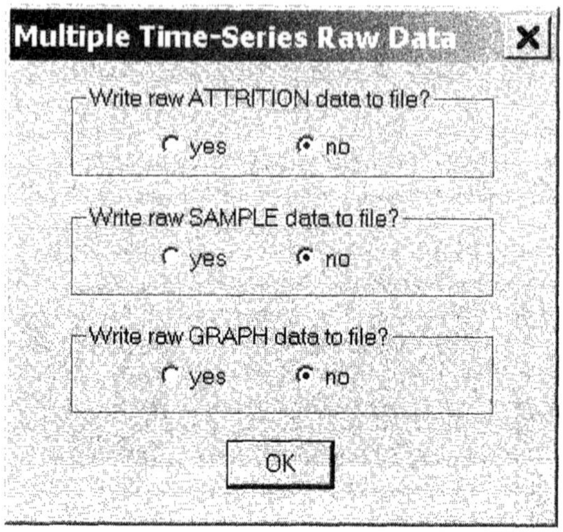

Fig. E.21 Multiple time-series *Save Raw-Data* dialog.

Part of the raw attrition data that EINSTein automatically keeps track of includes the number of iterations (for each run of a given scenrio *.dat file) that it takes either side to reach a specified attrition level or before a fixed number of agents have neem either injured or killed. By default, EINSTein computes these quantities for 90%, 75%, 50% and 10% attrition (or 10, 25, 50 or 75 injured or killed). If the user chooses to save raw attrition data to file (i.e. clicks "yes" in the top row of figure E.21), then a second dialog immediately pops up to allow the user to edit the default parameters that EINSTein otherwise will use to compute attrition statistics (see figure E.22).

E.3.3.5 *Visualizing the Data*

Once the multiple time-series run has terminated—EINSTein will display a termination box (figure E.20)—the user can immediately go to the *Data Visualization* menu to select various graph options. Each plot will show a time-series graph of the average value of the selected data-primitive, along with error bars designating the average absolute deviation of each point. Figure E.23 shows a sample plot of the average neighbor count for the total number of agents within a range $R = 3$ of red and blue, sampled over 25 initial conditions.

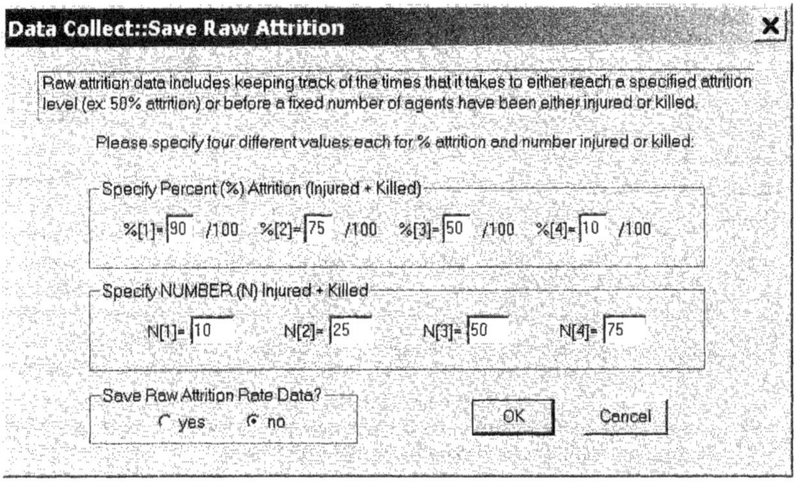

Fig. E.22

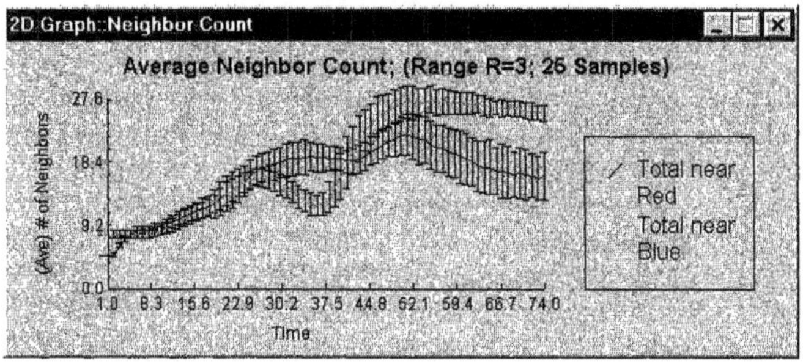

Fig. E.23 Multiple time-series sample graph of *average neighbor count* versus *time*.

E.3.4 *2-Parameter Phase Space Exploration*

In the two-parameter fitness landscape mode, EINSTein takes two-dimensional slices of the full N-dimensional parameter space. The blue force, by default, is fixed throughout a given run. That is to say, once the blue personality and combat parameters have all been defined—except for initial force disposition, which is always randomized at the beginning of a sample run—the blue side is clamped, and remains unaltered throughout a run. The actual "slice" is taken through the *red forces'* parameter space.

To this end, the user defines red's personality and combat parameters in the usual way, except that two special parameters (of the user's choosing)—x and y—are identified to be the (x, y) coordinates over which the system's behavior will be sampled. To each (x, y) combination of variable parameters (all other red parameters remaining constant), the program associates a quantitative measure of how well the red agents have performed a user-defined mission, and averages this measure over a desired number of initial conditions (for both red and blue initial force disposition). A measure of how well the red force performs a given mission is provided by a well-defined mission fitness.

E.3.4.1 *How to Initiate a Fitness Landscape Run*

Choosing the *Run Mode::2-Parameter Fitness Landscape Exploration* option of the *Simulation::Run* menu puts EINSTein into fitness-landscape mode. In this mode, EINSTein automatically scans, and measures the mission fitness, over a user defined two-dimensional $x - y$ parameter space.

The status-bar at the lower left of the display screen keeps track of the current x coordinate [x], y coordinate [y], initial-condition [IC], and time [T] of current run (see figure E.24). The mission fitnesses thus far scanned over may be displayed at any time by selecting the *3D Graphs::Fitness Landscape* option of the *Data Visualization* menu.

Fig. E.24 A screenshot of the status bar that appears along the bottom of the main window when EINSTein is put into two-parameter mission fitness mode.

E.3.4.2 *What do I do After a Run is Complete?*

After the full sweep is completed, two pop-up dialogs appear: (1) an edit-box that defines the mission-fitness weights and the desired graph, and (2) a query-box asking whether the user wants to store the raw mission-fitness data to a file.

E.3.4.3 *Edit Run-Time Parameters*

Calls up the *Run-Time Parameters* dialog that specifies the values of run-time variables such as number of initial conditions to average over, maximum run-time, and so on (figure E.25). You can change, or keep, any of the default values indicated in the edit boxes of the dialog.

E.3.4.4 *Edit XY-Coordinates*

Calls up the *Edit::(X, Y) Coordinates* dialog that specifies the x and y coordinates over which EINSTein will perform an automatic mission fitness scan (figure E.26). You can also change the default values of minimum and maximum values of these coordinates, along with the desired number of samples over which to scan.

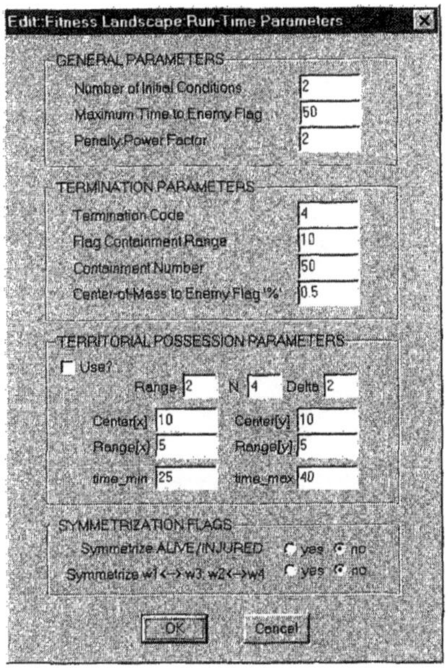

Fig. E.25 Screenshot of EINSTein's two-parameter mission *Fitness Landscape Run-Time Parameters* dialog.

E.3.4.5 *Display Fitness Landscape*

Select the *3D Graphs::Fitness Landscape* option of the *Data Visualization* menu to display either a 3D graph of the mission-fitness $f(x, y)$ or a 2D density plot.

E.3.5 ***One-Sided Genetic Algorithm Run Mode***

Choose the One-Sided Genetic Algorithm option of the Simulation::Run menu to put EINSTein into GA-mode. In this mode, EINSTein searches over a user selected search space to find the "best" red force for performing a specified mission. The status-bar at the lower left of the display screen keeps track of the current generation [G], personality [P], initial-condition [IC], time [T] of current test-run, and the best fitness [F] (x/10000) found thus far; see figure E.27.

A GA search may be interrupted at any time by clicking the mouse anywhere within the menu area. The user may look at the chromosome with the highest fitness at any time by selecting the *Display::Data::1-Sided Genetic Algorithm BEST Chromosome* option of the *Display* menu. The best chromosome may be saved to an EINSTein **.dat* file from the pop-up dialog by pressing the *Save to File* button; see tutorial beginning on page 525.

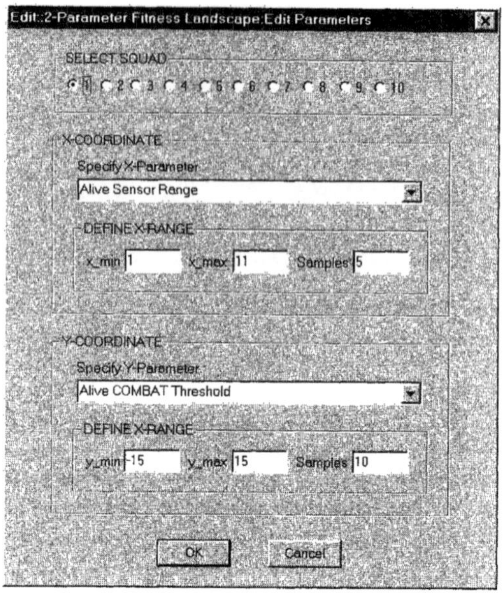

Fig. E.26 Screenshot of EINSTein's *Edit Two-Parameter Mission Fitness Landscape X-Y Paramaters* dialog.

Fig. E.27 A screenshot of the status bar that appears along the bottom of the main window when EINSTein is put into its *one-sided genetic algorithm seach-space* run mode.

E.3.5.1 *Search Space*

Calls up the Search-Space Dialog that defines the particular search that the genetic algorithm will be used to perform (figure E.28). The default is a simple single-squad search using a basic 63-allele agent chromosome.

EINSTein (version 1.0 and older) is configured to perform GA searches over five of the eight search spaces shown in the search-space dialog:

- *Single-Squad Personality:* GA searches over the personality-space defining a single squad.
- *Multiple-Squad Personality:* GA searches over the personality-space defining multiple squads. The number of squads and the size of each squad remains fixed throughout this GA run mode.
- *Squad Composition:* GA searches over squad composition space. The personality parameters defining squads 1 through 10 are fixed according to the values defined in the default input data file used to start the interactive run. The GA searches over the space defined by the number of squads (1-10) and

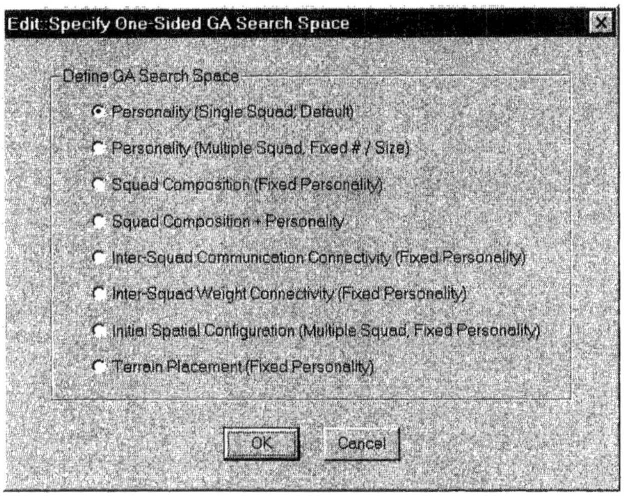

Fig. E.28 EINSTein's *One-Sided Genetic Algorithm Search-Space* dialog.

size of each squad (constrained by the total number of agents as defined by the data file).

- *Inter-Squad Communications Connectivity:* GA searches over the zero-one entries defining the communications matrix. The number of squads and the number of agents per squad is kept fixed at the values defined in the default input data file used to start the interactive run.
- *Inter-Squad Weight Connectivity:* GA searches over (real-valued) entries defining the squad interconnectivity matrix. The number of squads and the number of agents per squad is kept fixed at the values defined in the default input data file.

E.3.5.2 *Genetic Algorithm Run-Time Parameters*

Calls up the *Run-Time Parameter* dialog that specifies the values of run-time variables such as population size, number of generations, number of initial conditions to average over, mutation probability, and so on; see figure E.29. The user can change, or keep, any of the default values indicated in the edit boxes of the dialog.

E.3.5.3 *Agent Chromosome*

Calls up the *Agent Chromosome* dialog that specifies which alleles will be used during the GA run; see figure E.30. Pressing the 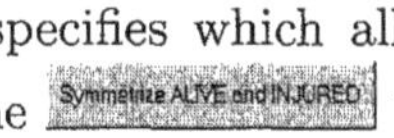

button at the top symmetrizes between alive and injured parameters.

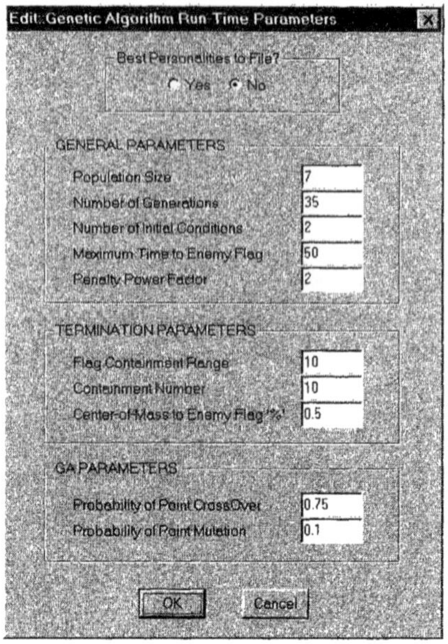

Fig. E.29 EINSTein's *One-Sided Genetic Algorithm Run-Time Parameters* dialog.

E.3.5.4 *Gene Min/Max Values*

Calls up the *Gene Min/Max* dialog that specifies the minimum and maximum values of each of the alleles used during the current GA run (figure E.31).

E.3.5.5 *Mission Fitness*

Calls up the *Mission Fitness* dialog that defines the fitness measure used to rank individual population members during the current GA run (figure E.32).

E.3.5.6 *Track Genetic Algorithm Progress*

To track the progress of the genetic algorithm, or to view a time-series of mission fitness measures, select the *Genetic Algorithm Progress::Mission Fitness (Time Series)* option of the *Mission Fitness (Time Series)* dialog.

E.3.6 ***Clear***

Clears the display of active window.

E.3.7 ***Run/Stop Toggle***

Toggles the current run *on/off*. Active in both interactive and play-back run modes. Can also be accessed by the or button of the toolbar.

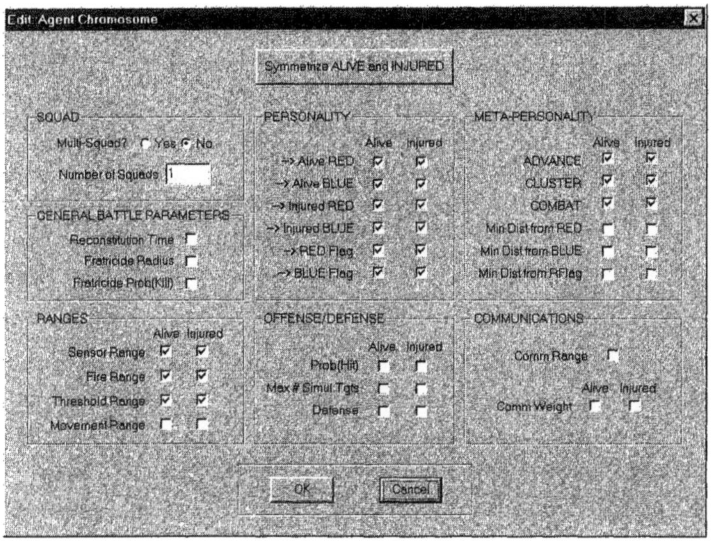

Fig. E.30 EINSTein's *One-Sided Genetic Algorithm Agent Chromosome* dialog.

E.3.8 *Step-Execute Mode*

Toggles step-execute mode *on/off*. If enabled, the current run is updated the number of time steps defined by *Step Execute for T Steps...* dialog (see below).

E.3.9 *Step Execute for T Steps...*

Calls up a dialog prompting you to enter the number of steps you would like EINSTein to update the current run before pausing (figure E.33).

E.3.10 *Randomize*

Restarts the scenario using currently defined agent, terrain, and weapon-parameter values but with a random initial condition. Can also be accessed via the  button on the toolbar.

E.3.11 *Reseed Random Number Generator*

Prompts the user, via a pop-up dialog, to specify a new seed for the random number generator (figure E.34). Enter a large negative integer.

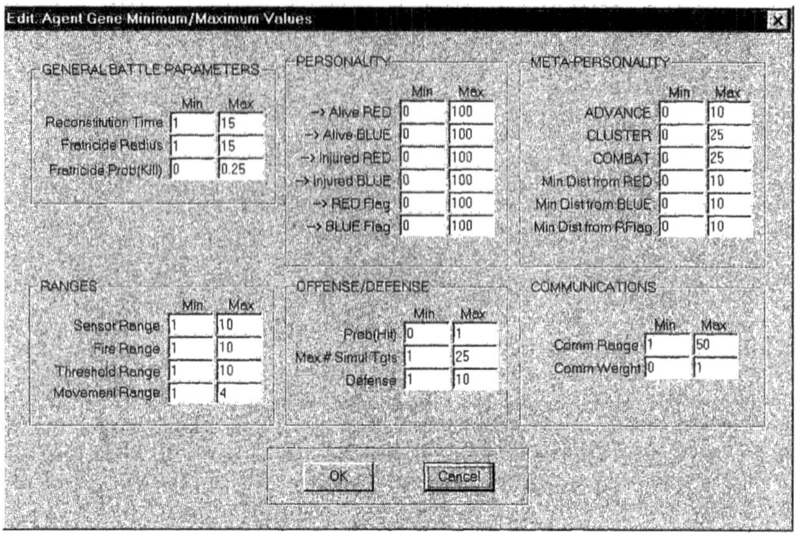

Fig. E.31 EINSTein's *One-Sided Genetic Algorithm Gene Min/Max* dialog.

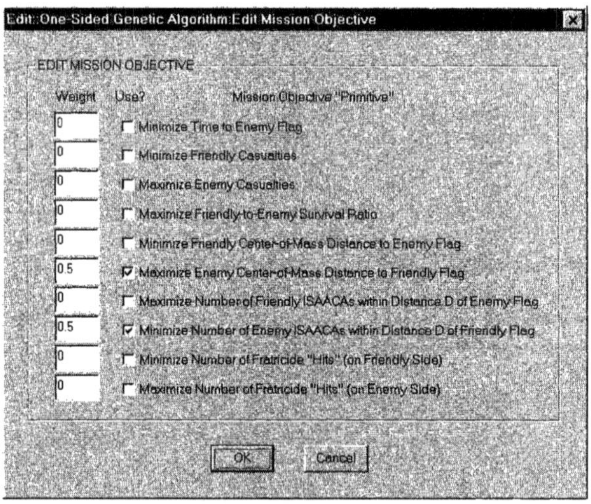

Fig. E.32 EINSTein's *One-Sided Genetic Algorithm Mission-Fitness* dialog.

E.3.12 *Restart...*

E.3.12.1 *Go...*

Reinitialize and restart the scenario. Unlike the *Randomize* option (see above) *Restart::Go...* does not randomize initial positions.

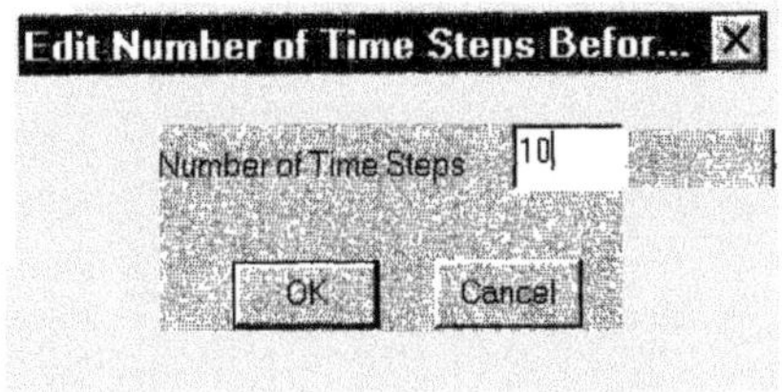

Fig. E.33 *Step Execute for T Steps* dialog.

Fig. E.34 EINSTein's *Reseed Random Number Generator* dialog

E.3.12.2 *Use (x,y) Block Data Defined in EINSTein's Input Data File*

Restarts run using initial agent positions as defined in EINSTein's input data file.

E.3.12.3 *Use Agent (*.agt) Data File*

Retstarts run using initial agent positions as defined in EINSTein's agent input data file.

E.3.13 *Terminate Run*

Terminates current run, then prompts you to open an EINSTein input data file (see figure D.1).

E.4 *Display* Menu

The Display Menu contains various controls to adjust what is displayed on the battlefield: Red Data and Blue Data, Toggle Background Color (White/Black), Highlight Squad, Command Structure, Territorial Possession Map, Activity Map, Killing Field, and Zoom. See figure E.35.

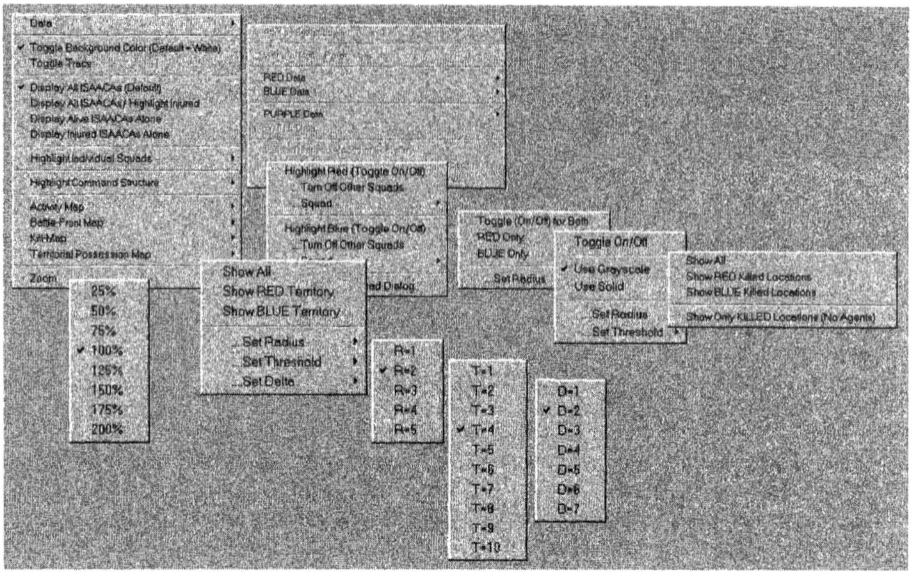

Fig. E.35 EINSTein's main-menu *Display* options (for versions 1.0 and older).

E.4.1 *Data*

E.4.1.1 *Red Data*

Displays an inert pop-up modeless dialog that summarizes the current red force parameters. This dialog can also be displayed by pressing the (red colored) D button on the toolbar. Note that unlike the full edit dialogs (see *Edit Menu*), this dialog only displays currently active parameter values; *it does not permit any changes to be made to those values* (see figure E.36). You can drag the dialog to any position on EINSTein's main viewscreen and keep it open on screen while an interactive or play-back run is being executed.

Data is initially shown for the first squad only. For scenarios containing more than one squad, data for squad S may be displayed at any time by entering S at the top of the dialog and clicking with the left-mouse button on the Display Squad button. As in edit dialogs, wherever there are two columns, the first column refers to parameter values in effect when the agent is in the alive state; the second column refers to parameter values in effect when the agent is in the injured state.

Most entries appearing in this dialog are self-explanatory: *squad size*, *sensor range*, *fire range*, etc. The entries labeling the four columns near the center of the dialog refer to the following agent meta-personality parameters:

- *ADV = Advance to Enemy Flag*
- *CLS = Cluster with Friendly Agents*

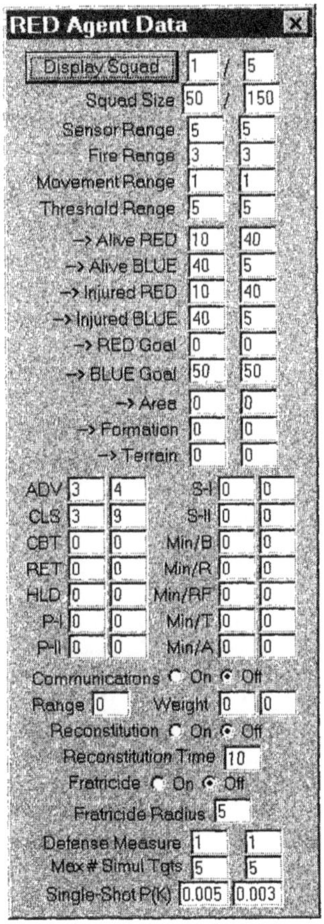

Fig. E.36 Sample modeless dialog showing red data.

- *CBT = Combat*
- *RET = Retreat*
- *HLD = Hold Position*
- *P-I = Pursuit-I (Turn Pursuit Off)*
- *P-II = Pursuit-II (Turn Exclusive Pursuit On)*
- *S-I = Support-I (Provide Support)*
- *S-II = Support-II (Seek Support)*
- *Min/B = Minimum Distance to Friendly (i.e., Blue) Agents*
- *Min/R = Minimum Distance to Enemy (i.e., Red) Agents*
- *Min/RF = Minimum Distance to Own Flag*
- *Min/T = Minimum Distance to Nearby Terrain*
- *Min/A = Minimum Distance to Fixed Area*

E.4.1.2 *Blue Data*

Displays an inert pop-up modeless dialog that summarizes the current blue force parameters. This dialog can also be displayed by pressing the (blue colored)  button on the toolbar.

You can drag the dialog to any position on EINSTein's main viewscreen and keep it open on screen while an interactive or play-back run is being executed.

E.4.2 *Toggle Background Color*

The default battlefield background color is white. This sub-menu item toggles between white and black. Can also be displayed by pressing the  button on the toolbar.

E.4.3 *Trace Map*

By default, EINSTein refreshes the battlefield after each time step to show the natural movement of all combatants. It is sometimes convenient to gauge the overall flow of events to have an on-screen reminder of past states. When the trace mode is enabled, the battlefield is no longer refreshed and shows previous time steps. Figure E.37 shows a sample screenshot.

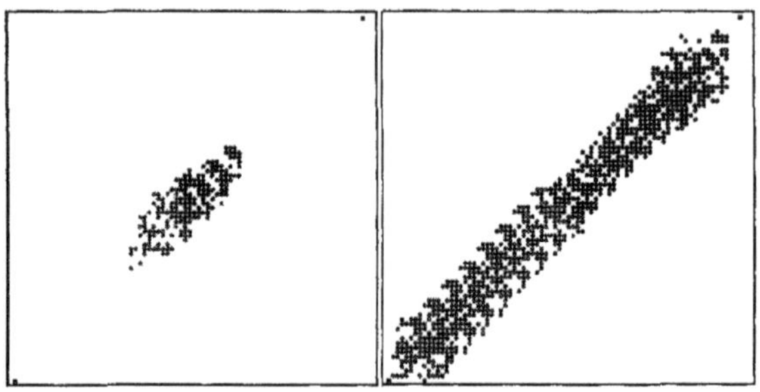

Fig. E.37 Sample *trace map* screenshot.

This option can also be selected by pressing the  button on the toolbar.

E.4.4 *Display All Agents (Default)*

By default, EINSTein displays all agents, using red for all red (whether alive or injured) and blue for blue (whether alive or injured). Can also be displayed by pressing the  button on the toolbar.

E.4.5 *Display All Agents (Highlight Injured)*

Displays all agents, but chooses a different hue for injured red and blue agents to distinguish them from their alive counterparts. Can also be displayed by pressing the **H** button on the toolbar.

E.4.6 *Display Alive Agents Alone*

Displays red and blue agents only when they are alive. Injured combatants are not displayed. Can also be displayed by pressing the AM button on the toolbar.

E.4.7 *Display Injured Agents Alone*

Displays red and blue agents only when they are injured. Alive combatants are not displayed. Can also be displayed by pressing the Inj button on the toolbar.

E.4.8 *Highlight Individual Squad*

This sub-menu selection displays a pop-up dialog (figure E.38) prompting the user to specify which squads (one red and one blue), to highlight by using a different hue.

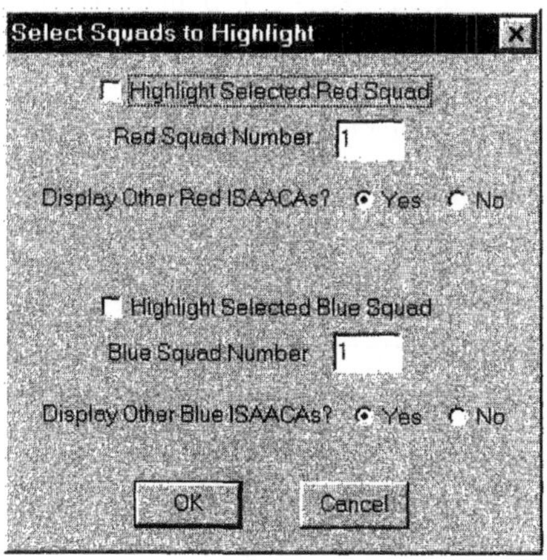

Fig. E.38 *Highlight Individual Squads* dialog.

The user has the option to turn off the display of all squads other than the one squad selected to be highlighted (on either side). The dialog can also be displayed by pressing the **S** button on the toolbar. Figure E.39 shows a sample screenshot where one red and one blue squad are highlighted.

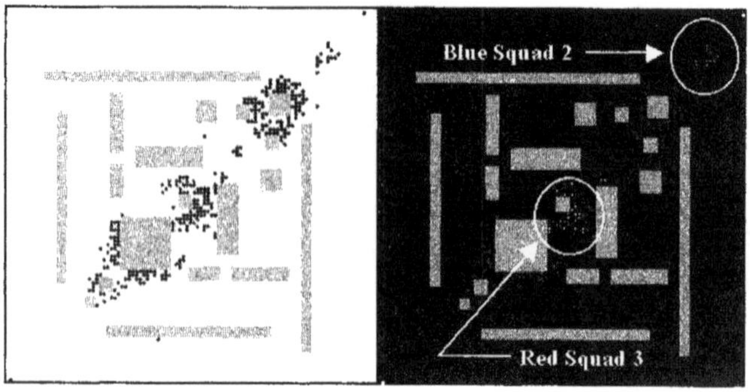

Fig. E.39 Sample *highlight individual squad* screenshot.

E.4.9 *Highlight Command Structure*

E.4.9.1 *Location of Red Local Commanders*

Highlights the location of red local commanders. If a global-commander is defined for the scenario, the highlighted red commanders will also be connected by a narrow gray tether. See figure E.40.

E.4.9.2 *Red Local Command Area*

Highlights the red local command areas of responsibility. Area is shown as a colored box. See figure E.40.

E.4.9.3 *Red Local Command Subordinates*

Highlights the red local command unit by highlighting the location of each red local commander and linking him with his subordinate agents. See figure E.40.

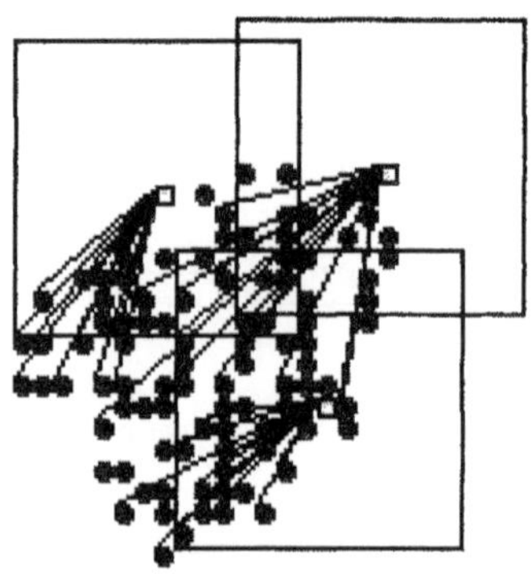

Fig. E.40 Sample screenshot showing *local-command highlights*.

E.4.9.4 *Location of Blue Local Commanders*

Highlights the location of red local commanders.

E.4.9.5 *Blue Local Command Area*

Highlights the red local command areas of responsibility. Area is shown as a colored box.

E.4.9.6 *Blue Local Command Subordinates*

Highlights the red local command unit by highlighting the location of each red local commander and linking him with his subordinate agents.

E.4.10 *Activity Map*

An *Activity-Map* is a filtered view of the battlefield in which individual pixels represent gray-scaled approximations of the local activity-level (see figure E.41) . Currently, this activity level is defined simply by the fraction of sites within a user-defined box (of range R) for which an agent has moved. There are five gray-scales, ranging from black (meaning that no, or very little, motion has taken place) to white (meaning that a large fraction of the possible motion within the box has taken place). Future activity-maps will include views of the agents' patterns of local decision-making (i.e., adaptation), and will act as a first-step towards visualizing emergent patterns in a meta decision-space.

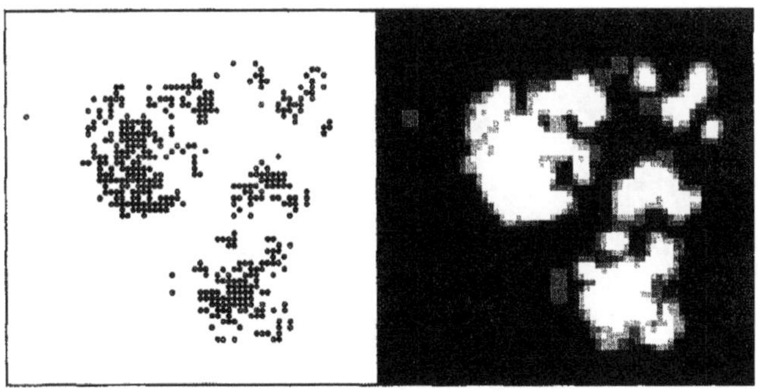

Fig. E.41 Sample *activity map* screenshot.

This option may be selected either by pressing the A button on the toolbar, or by selecting the *Activity-Map* option of the *Display* menu.

E.4.10.1 *Toggle On/Off for Both*

Displays activity map for both red and blue agents simultaneously.

E.4.10.2 *Red Only*

Displays activity map for red agents only. Effectively ignores all blue agent location and/or movement information.

E.4.10.3 *Blue Only*

Displays activity map for blue agents only. Effectively ignores all red agent location and/or movement information.

E.4.10.4 *...Set Radius*

Sets the radius, R, that defines the box around a given pixel (i, j) within which the activity-level is measured for displaying the activity map. The box is a $(2R + 1)$–by–$(2R+1)$ area centered on the pixel (i, j). The user has the option of selecting $R = 0$, $R = 1$,..., $R = 5$.

E.4.11 *Battle-Front Map*

A *Battle-Front Map* is a filtered view of the battlefield that highlights regions in which the most intense combat is taking place (see figure E.42). The view may be either a simple threshold or greyscale (see blow).

This option may be selected either by pressing the B button on the toolbar, or by selecting the *Battle-Front Map* option of the *Display* Menu.

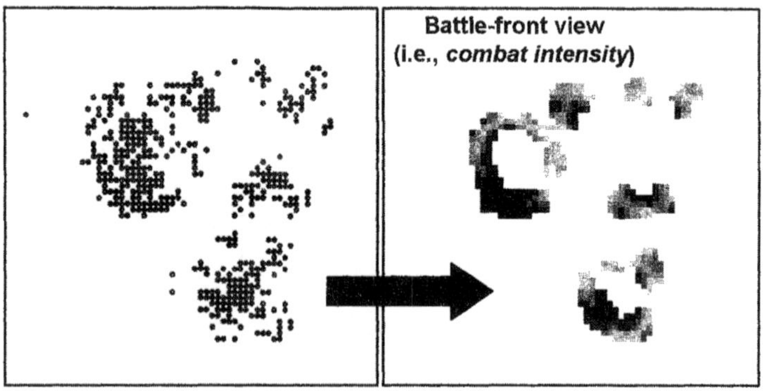

Fig. E.42 Sample *Battle-Front Map* screenshot.

E.4.11.1 *Toggle On/Off*

Toggles the display of the battle-front map.

E.4.11.2 *Use Greyscale*

Displays the battle-front map in solid mode. In this mode, the user selects range R (as for the solid display mode; see below), and EINSTein automatically applies one of five shades of gray indicating the degree of combat intensity within a "box" of radius centered at each (x, y).

E.4.11.3 *Use Solid*

Displays the battle-front map in *greyscale* mode. In this mode, a site at (x, y) is highlighted (i.e. colored either white or black on a black or white background, respectively) if the number of red and blue agents within a range R of (x, y) (i.e. within the "box" whose corners are defined by $(x \pm R, y \pm R)$ both exceed a user-defined battle-front threshold Δ_B. By default $R = 2$ and $T = 3$.

E.4.11.4 *Set Radius*

Sets the radius R used in defining solid or grayscale display codes of the battle-front map.

E.4.11.5 *Set Threshold*

Sets the battle-front threshold Δ_B used in defining solid or grayscale display codes of the battle-front map.

E.4.12 *Killing Field Map*

The *Killing Field Map* marks the locations on the battlefield where agents were previously killed; i.e. agents whose state was degraded from injured to dead and who are therefore no longer "playing" during a current run (see figure E.43). Locations where red agents are killed are marked with an "×" locations where blue agents are killed are marked with "·."

The user has the option of showing only *red kill locations* (by selecting appropriate option or the red-colored K button of the toolbar), only *blue kill locations* (by selecting appropriate option or the blue-colored K button of the toolbar), *both* red and blue kill locations, and temporarily clearing the display of still playing agents to highlight only the *kill locations* (by selecting appropriate option or the red and blue colored K button of the toolbar).

E.4.12.1 *Show All*

Shows locations where either red or blue agents have been killed at any time prior to the current iteration time of a given run.

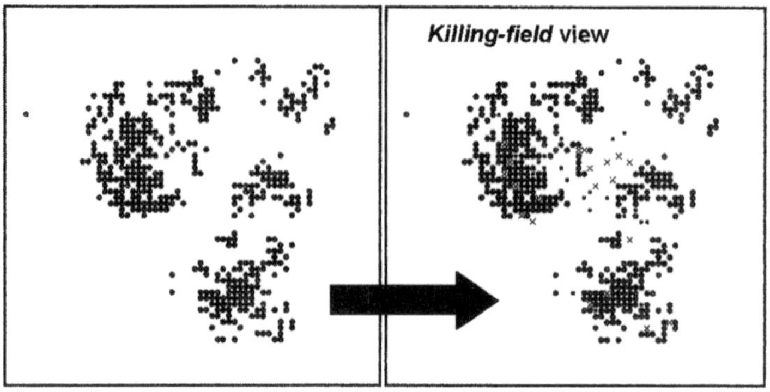

Fig. E.43 Sample *Killing Field Map* screenshot.

E.4.12.2 *Show Red Killed Locations*

Shows locations where red agents have been killed at any time prior to the current iteration time of a given run.

E.4.12.3 *Show Blue Killed Locations*

Shows locations where blue agents have been killed at any time prior to the current iteration time of a given run.

E.4.12.4 *Show Only Killed Locations (No Agents)*

Shows locations where either red or blue agents have been killed at any time prior to the current iteration time of a given run and *excludes from view* the locations of all currently active (i.e. alive or injured) agents.

E.4.13 *Territorial Possession Map*

A *Territorial Possession Map* is a filtered view of the battlefield in which a pixel's color represents either red or blue occupancy (see figure E.44).

A site at (x, y) "belongs" to an agent (red or blue) according to the following logic: the number of like agents within a territoriality-distance (τ_D) is greater than or equal to territoriality-minimum ($\tau_{\min}$) and is at least territoriality-threshold (τ_T) number of agents greater than the number of enemy agents within the same territoriality-distance. For example, if $(\tau_D, \tau_{\min}, \tau_T) = (2, 3, 2)$ then a battlefield position (x, y) is said to belong to, say, red, if there are at least 3 red agents within a distance 2 of (x, y) and the number of red agents within that distance outnumber blue agents by at least 2.

This option may be selected either by pressing the  button on the toolbar, or by selecting the *Territorial Possession Map* option of the *Display* main menu list of options.

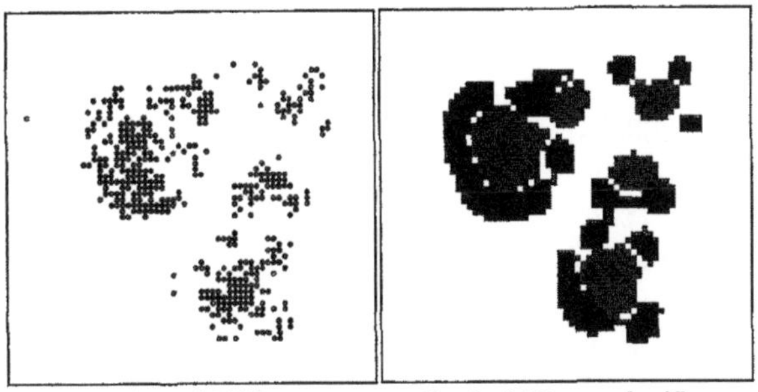

Fig. E.44 Sample *Territorial Possession Map* screenshot.

E.4.13.1 *Show All*

Displays *both red or blue territory* as defined by the current values of territoriality-distance (τ_D), territoriality-minimum ($\tau_{\min}$) and territoriality-threshold (τ_T). Individual agent locations are suppressed.

E.4.13.2 *Show Red Territory*

Displays locations of red territory as defined by the current values of territoriality-distance (τ_D), territoriality-minimum ($\tau_{\min}$) and territoriality-threshold (τ_T). Individual agent and blue territory locations are suppressed.

E.4.13.3 *Show Blue Territory*

Displays locations of blue territory as defined by the current values of territoriality-distance (τ_D), territoriality-minimum ($\tau_{\min}$) and territoriality-threshold (τ_T). Individual agent and red territory locations are suppressed.

E.4.13.4 *...Set Radius*

Defines the territoriality-distance (τ_D) used in calculating the territorial possession map; see above.

E.4.13.5 *...Set Threshold*

Defines the territoriality-minimum ($\tau_{\min}$) used in calculating the territorial possession map; see above.

E.4.13.6 *...Set Delta*

Defines the territoriality-threshold (τ_T) used in calculating the territorial possession map; see above.

E.4.14 *Zoom*

Either enlarges or reduces the display window. Choices are 25%, 50%, 75%, 100%, 125%, 150%, 175% or 200% of normal view.

E.5 *On-the-Fly Parameter Changes* Menu

The *On-the-Fly Parameter Changes* menu contains dialogs that prompt the user to make on-the-fly parameter changes to essentially all of the parameters appearing in the Edit Menu dialogs. See figure E.45.

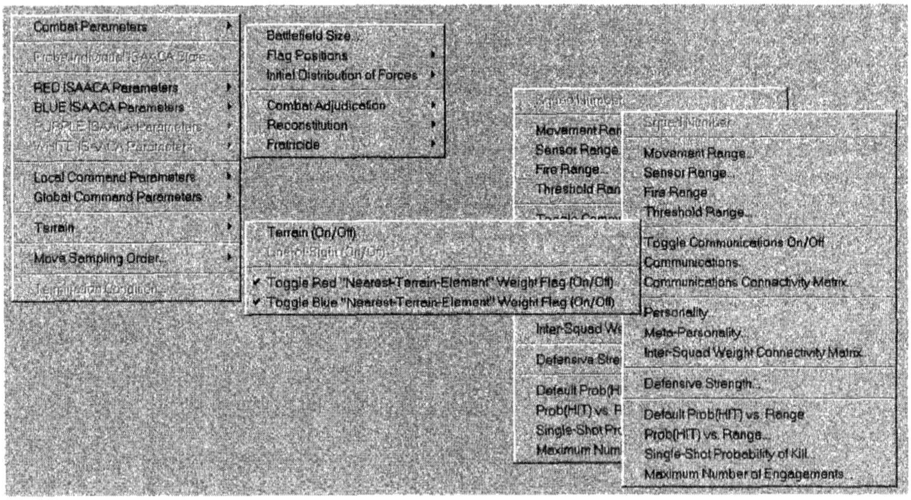

Fig. E.45 EINSTein's main-menu *On-theFly Parameter Changes* options (for versions 1.0 and older).

Unlike changes made to the values of parameters appearing in the edit dialogs (see *Edit* Menu; page 584), after which EINSTein automatically reinitializes the run, changes made to any values using the on-the-fly parameter changes menu dialogs take effect immediately, without resetting the run. You can thus easily experiment with various *"What if I give red a better sensor range at this point of the battle?"* scenarios.

Note that on-the-fly changes can only be made when EINSTein is in interactive run mode (see *Simulation* Menu; page 603).

For example, selecting *Personality* under the *Red Agents Parameters* menu option calls up the dialog shown in figure E.46. By default, parameter values are shown for the first squad. If there is more than one squad defined for the current scenario, clicking with the left-hand mouse button on radio button N $(= 1, 2, ..., 10)$ displays values for that squad. When you have completed editing the displayed parameter values, press the 

button to record the changes. The simulation will pick up at the time it was interrupted and continue to run using the updated blue agent personality.

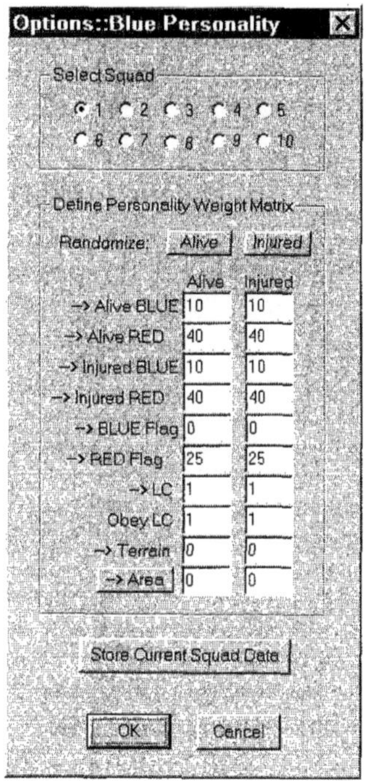

Fig. E.46 *On-the-Fly Parameter Changes* dialog for blue agents (for EINSTein versions 1.0 and older).

E.5.1 *EINSTein's On-the-Fly Parameter Changes Menu Options*

Parameters that can be edited on-the-fly include:

- *Combat parameters* (battlefield size, flag positions, initial distribution of forces, combat adjudication, reconstitution, and fratricide),
- *Individual red/blue agent parameters* (movement range, sensor range, fire range, threshold range, toggle communications (*on/off*), communications range/weight, communications connectivity matrix, personality, meta-personality thresholds, inter-squad weight connectivity matrix, defensive strength, default Prob(HIT) vs. range function, Prob(HIT) vs. range function, single-shot probability of kill, and maximum number of engagements),
- *Terrain elements*, and
- *Move sampling order.*

E.6 *Data Collection* Menu

The *Data Collection Menu* provides options for defining EINSTein's interactive data collection routines. See figure E.47.

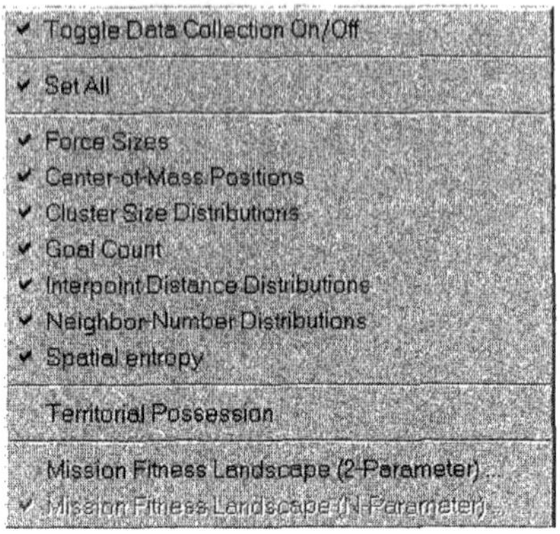

Fig. E.47 EINSTein's main-menu *Data Collection* main-menu options (for versions 1.0 and older).

Data collection is enabled by setting the *stat_flag* variable appearing in EINSTein's input data file equal to 1, toggling data collection directly (by clicking on the first sub-menu choice of the *Data Collection* main-menu item), or pressing the button on the toolbar. The user also has the option of saving raw data from *Multiple-Time Series* runs to a file by pressing the toolbar button.

E.6.1 *Toggle Data Collection On/Off*

Toggles data collection routines on/off. By default, and regardless of what other data collection options are set, EINSTein computes basic attrition data.

E.6.2 *Set All*

When data collection has been enabled, this option sets the flags for all primitive data elements simultaneously.

E.6.3 *Capacity Dimension*

This sets the flag for automatic calculation of the *Hausdorff* (i.e. "box counting") fractal dimension, discussed on page 95 in chapter 2. The fractal dimension is computed for sets of (x, y) positions occupied by *red*, *blue* and the *total* force.

E.6.4 *Force Sizes*

This sets the flag for basic attrition data. This flag is enabled by default.

Attrition data consists of basic red and blue agent force strengths, measured as the remaining fractions of the original force size. Separate measures are provided for alive red, alive blue, injured red, injured blue and total red and total blue forces. The *Carvalho-Rodrigues Combat-Entropy* is also computed (see *Data Visualization*). Note that this flag is the only flag that is set by default, and force size data is kept track of even if the overall data collection is toggled *off*.

E.6.5 *Center-of-Mass Positions*

Enables the center-of-mass data flag. This class of data consists of keeping track of the (x, y) coordinates of the center-of-mass position of the red, blue and total (i.e., red + blue) force, as well as the distances between the red and blue forces and both flags.

E.6.6 *Cluster-Size Distributions*

Enables the cluster-size distribution data flag. This class of data consists of keeping track of the averages and distributions of the sizes of clusters of agents, using inter-cluster distance criteria of $D = 1$ and $D = 2$. (An inter-cluster distance criteria of $D = d$ means that two agents that are within a distance d of each other are defined to belong to the same cluster.) Because this class of data provides an insight into the gross structural appearance of the entire battlefield, it can be thought of as a crude pattern recognition measure. Another such measure is provided by spatial entropy (see below). *Appendix G* of [Ilach97a] contains a heuristic description of the *Hoshen-Kopelman* algorithm used to calculate the cluster distribution.

E.6.7 *Goal Count*

Enables the goal-count data flag. This class of data keeps track of the number of agents that are within a given distance ($D = 1, 2, ..., 7$) of either the red or blue flag.

E.6.8 *Interpoint Distance Distributions*

Enables the interpoint-distance data flag. This class of data consists of keeping track of the averages and distributions of the number of neighbors that red and blue agents have that are within a range $R = 1, 2, ..., 5$ of them. Separate measures are provided for red, blue and all (either red or blue) agents near red agents, red, blue and all (either red or blue) agents near blue agents, and red and blue agents near both red and blue flags.

E.6.9 *Neighbor-Number Distributions*

Enables the neighbor-number data flag. This class of data consists of keeping track of the averages and distributions of the number of neighbors that red and blue agents have that are within a range $R = 1, 2, ..., 5$ of them. Separate measures are provided for red, blue and all (either red or blue) agents near red agents, red, blue and all (either red or blue) agents near blue agents, and red and blue agents near both red and blue flags.

E.6.10 *Spatial Entropy*

Enables the spatial-entropy data flag. This class of data consists of keeping track of the spatial entropy of the configuration of the red, blue and total (i.e., red + blue) force.

Spatial entropy provides a measure of the degree of disorder of a battlefield state. For example, a large group of tightly clustered agents is relatively highly "organized" and therefore has low entropy. In contrast, a battlefield that consists of many and widely dispersed small groups of agents is relatively "disorganized" and thus has a high entropy. (See page 454.)

E.6.11 *Territorial Possession*

Enables the territorial-possession data flag. This class of data consists of keeping track of the territorial possession of red and blue forces. The territory of red (or blue) is defined as the fraction of the battlefield that "belongs" to each color. Parameters may be edited by selecting the territorial possession dialog of the Edit menu. The user has the option of specifying whether occupancy will be calculated for the entire battlefield or only for some bounding rectangular area. In the latter case, the user will be prompted for the center coordinates and size of the bounding rectangle.

EINSTein provides two measures of territorial possession:

- *Raw possession*, which is the raw fraction of the entire battlefield (or user-defined bounding area) that "belongs" to each color, and
- *Normalized possession*, which is the normalized fraction of the entire battlefield (or user-defined bounding area), defined as raw possession divided by the area that would be occupied if no enemy agents existed. In other words, normalized possession measures how much territory a given side would currently be occupying if there were no enemy.

E.6.12 *Mission-Fitness Landscape (2-Parameter)...*

Selecting this option puts EINSTein into the *2-parameter mission-fitness landscape run-mode*. The user will be prompted for various data-collection and run-time parameters (see *Run-Modes* in *Simulation* Menu; page 603).

In the two-parameter fitness landscape mode, EINSTein takes two-dimensional slices of the full N-dimensional parameter space. The blue force, by default, is fixed throughout a given run. That is to say, once the blue personality and combat parameters have all been defined—except for initial force disposition, which is always randomized at the beginning of a sample run—the blue side is clamped, and remains unaltered throughout a run. The actual "slice" is taken through the red forces' parameter space.

To this end, the user defines red's personality and combat parameters in the usual way, except that two special parameters (of the user's choosing)—x and y—are identified to be the (x, y) coordinates over which the system's behavior will be sampled. To each (x, y) combination of variable parameters (all other red parameters remaining constant), the program associates a quantitative measure of "how well" the red agents have performed a user-defined mission, and averages this measure over a desired number of initial conditions (for both red and blue initial force disposition). A measure of "how well" the red force performs a given mission is provided by a well-defined mission fitness (see *GA Fitness function*, page 513).

E.6.13 *Calculate Capacity Dimension (Snapshot at time t)*

Selecting this option a run, temporarily pauses the run and calls up a dialog prompting the user to supply an output data file name (with default extension **.cdm*) that, once saved, contains the raw capacity dimension data for point sets consisting of *red*, *blue* and the *total* force, as calculated at time t. This raw data consists of box size (= *length*) ε, box count of the given point set for the given $N(\varepsilon)$, $N(\varepsilon)$, $log[1/\varepsilon]$ and $log[N(\varepsilon)]$. The estimated capacity dimension, $D_C = log[N(\varepsilon)]/log[1/\varepsilon]$ is also provided.

E.7 *Data Visualization* Menu

The Data Visualization menu contains dialogs prompting the user to select on-screen plots for data that has been collected thus far for the current simulation (see figure E.48). The plot options that are available are directly tied to the primitive data collected (see *Data Collection*, *Genetic Algorithm Run-Mode* and *Fitness Landscape Run-Mode*).

In each case, right-clicking on a displayed graph calls up a pop-up dialog (figure E.49) providing various options to alter the graph's appearance, including x and y axis ranges, labels, colors, statistical fits, and (in the case of 3D graphs) orientation in space.

If EINSTein is in multiple time-series run-mode, each of the on-screen plot options described below automatically uses data collected from the multiple runs. (See *Neighbor Count* below for sample output.)

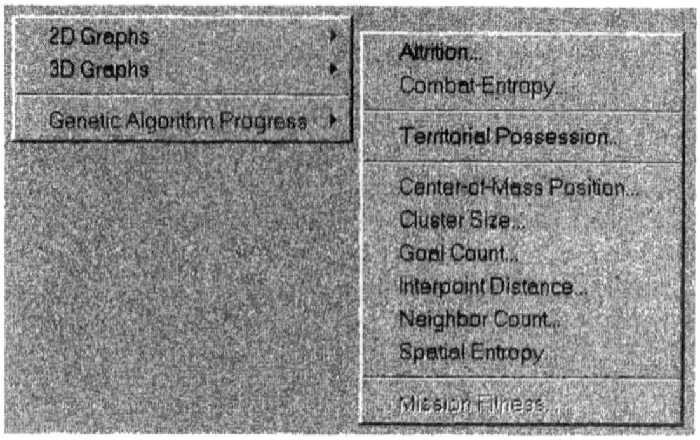

Fig. E.48 EINSTein's main-menu *Data Visualization* main-menu options (for versions 1.0 and older).

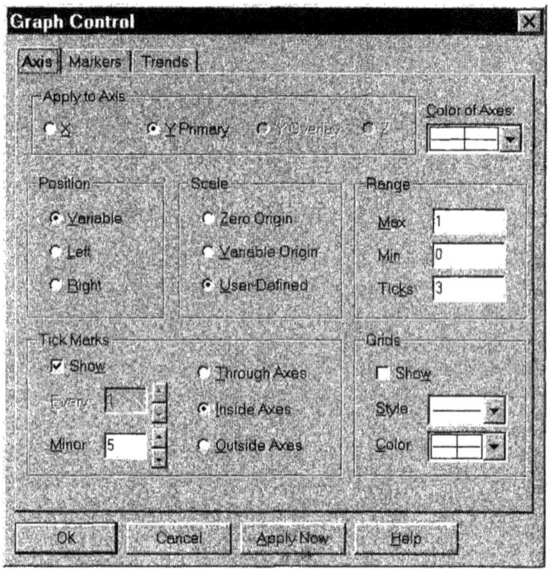

Fig. E.49 Pop-up dialog for altering 2D graph appearance

E.7.1 *2D Graphs*

E.7.1.1 *Attrition*

Calls up a dialog that contains editable parameters defining time-series graphs of attrition statistics (figure E.50).You can plot any, or all, of seven basic measures:

- *% remaining red + blue*
- *% remaining alive red*

- *% remaining injured red*
- *% remaining (alive + injured) red*
- *% remaining alive blue*
- *% remaining injured blue*
- *% remaining (alive + injured) blue*

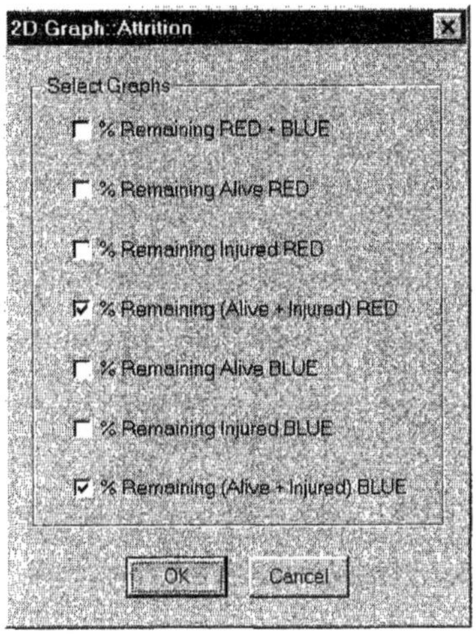

Fig. E.50 Screenshot of the *Attrition Graph* dialog

Figure E.51 shows a sample attrition graph.

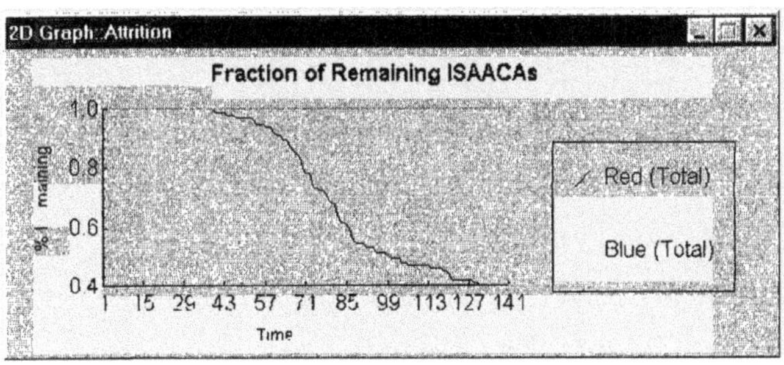

Fig. E.51 Sample *Attrition Graph* plot

E.7.1.2 *Capacity Dimension*

Calls up a dialog (see figure E.52) that contains editable parameters defining time-series graphs of the *Hausdorff* (i.e. "box counting") fractal dimension, discussed on page 95 in chapter 2. The fractal dimension is estimated for sets of (x, y) positions occupied by *red*, *blue* and the *total* force for all times $1 \leq t \leq T_{pause}$, where T_{pause} is the time at which the run was paused to generate the graph.

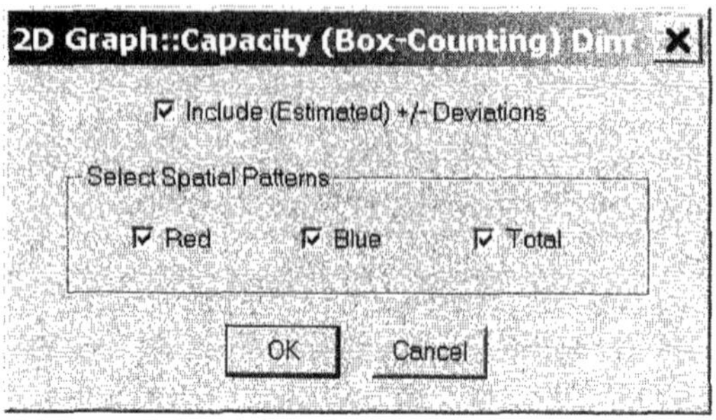

Fig. E.52 Screenshot of the *Capacity Dimension* dialog.

Figure E.53 shows a sample time-series graph of the capacity dimension.

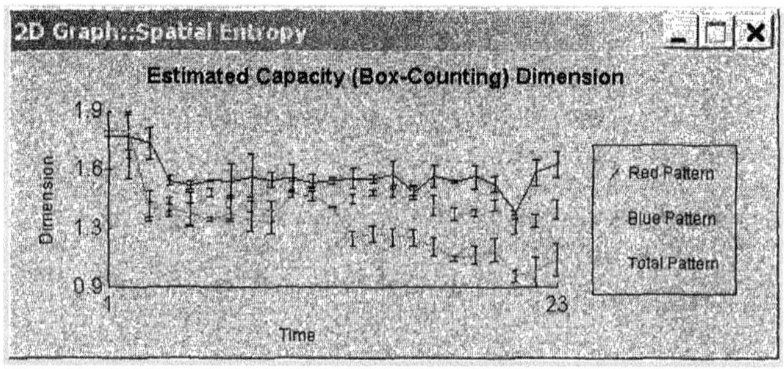

Fig. E.53 Sample *Capacity Dimension* time-series graph

E.7.1.3 *Center-of-Mass Position*

Calls up a dialog (figure E.54) that contains editable parameters defining time-series graphs of center-of-mass position.

You can plot the center-of-mass positions of red, blue or total agent populations. One of four kinds of graphs can be selected:

- *Distance from Red Flag*
- *Distance from Blue Flag*
- $x - y$ *plot (looking down on battlefield)*
- $x - y +$ *time plot, in which the* z*-axis* $=$ *time*

Figure E.55 shows a sample Center-of-Mass $x - y$ graph.

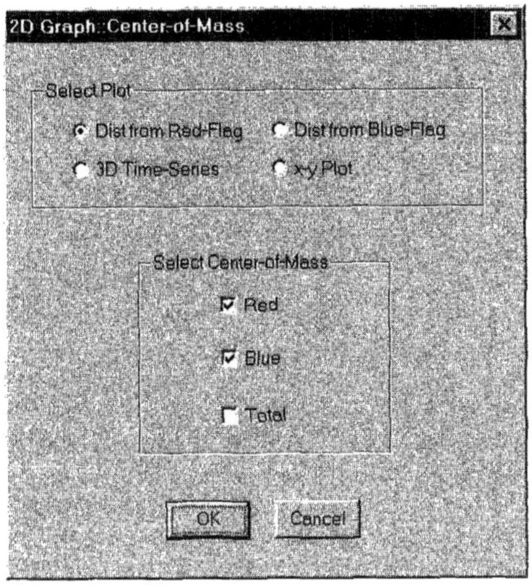

Fig. E.54 Screenshot of the *Center-of-Mass Graph* dialog

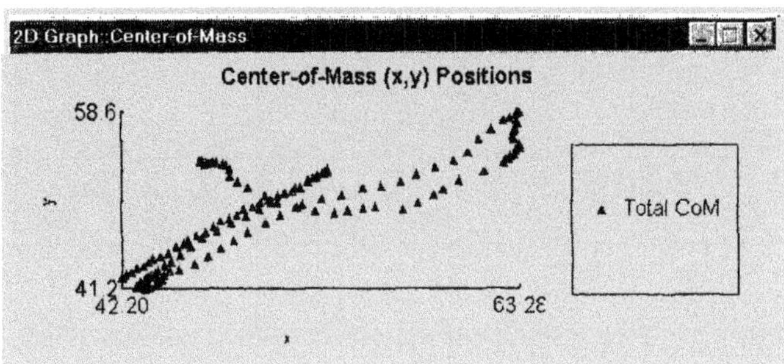

Fig. E.55 Sample *Center-of-Mass Graph* plot.

E.7.1.4 *Cluster Size*

Calls up a dialog (figure E.56) that contains editable parameters defining graphs of cluster-size. You can plot either a time-series average or histogram distribution of cluster sizes, using an inter-cluster distance criterion of either $D = 1$ or $D = 2$.

Figure E.57 shows a sample graph of cluster-size versus time. Figure E.58 shows a sample plot of the distribution of cluster-size for a selected snapshot in time.

E.7.1.5 *Combat Entropy*

Calls up a dialog that contains editable parameters defining graphs of combat entropy (figure E.59) . You can plot either an $x - y$ plot or x-y+time plot of the *Carvalho-Rodriques Combat Entropy.*

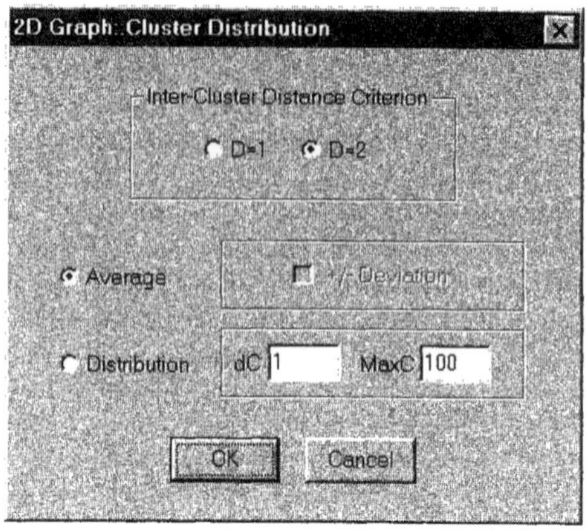

Fig. E.56 Screenshot of the *Cluster Size* dialog.

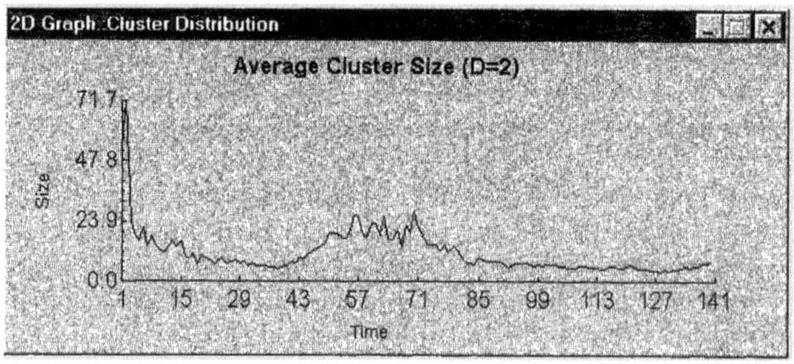

Fig. E.57 Screenshot of a sample *Cluster Size* time-series graph

Carvalho-Rodriques [Carv89] has suggested using entropy, as computed from casualty reports, as a predictor of combat outcomes. Whether or not combat can be described as a complex adaptive system, it may still be possible to describe it as a dissipative dynamical system. As such, it is not unreasonable to expect entropy, and/or entropy production, to act as a predictor of combat evolution. Carvalho-Rodriques defines his casualty-based entropy E by

$$E(i) = \left(\frac{c_i}{N_i}\right) \log \left(\frac{c_i}{N_i}\right),$$

where c_i represents the casualty count (in absolute numbers) and N_i represents the force strength of the ith adversary (either red or blue). It is understood that both c_i and N_i can be functions of time.

Figure E.60 shows graph of combat-entropy.

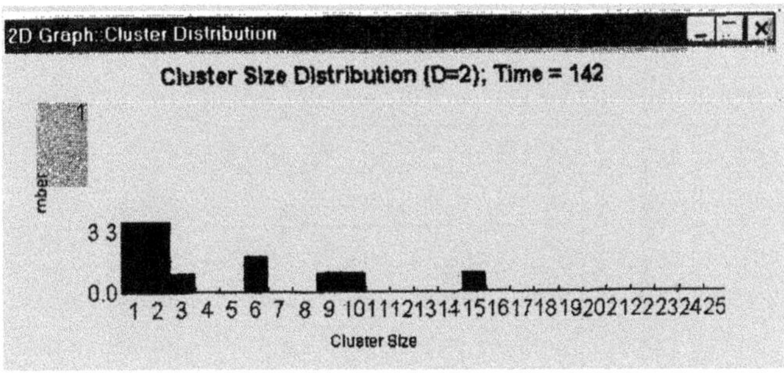

Fig. E.58 Screenshot of a sample *Cluster Size* histogram distribution graph

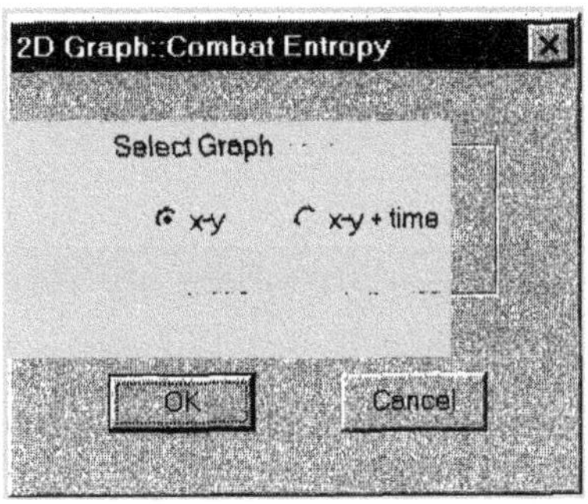

Fig. E.59 Screenshot of the *Combat Entropy* dialog

E.7.1.6 *Goal Count*

Calls up a dialog that contains editable parameters defining time-series graphs of goal-count statistics (figure E.61).

You can plot a time series of the number of agents within a user-specified distance ($D = 1, 2, ..., 7$) from either the red or blue flag:

- *Red agents near red flag*
- *Red agents near blue*
- *Blue agents near red flag*
- *Blue agents near blue flag*

Figure E.62 shows a sample graph of goal-count versus time.

E.7.1.7 *Interpoint Distance*

Calls up a dialog that contains editable parameters defining time-series graphs of interpoint-distance statistics (figure E.63).

You can plot a time-series of the total number of neighbors that are within a

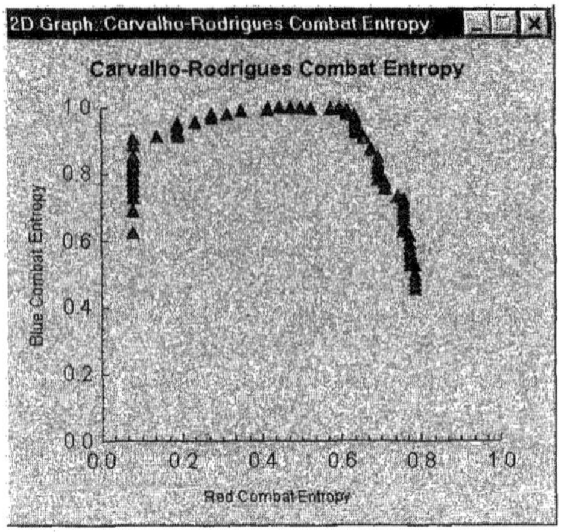

Fig. E.60 Screenshot of a sample *Carvalho-Rodrigues Combat Entropy* graph.

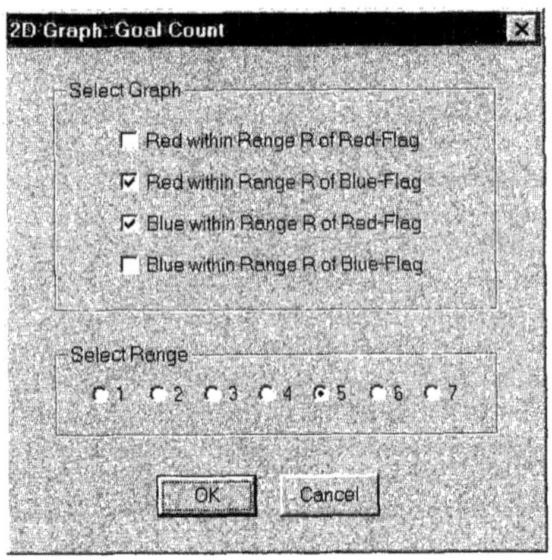

Fig. E.61 Screenshot of the *Goal Count* dialog.

user-specified distance ($D = 1, 2, ..., 7$) from either red or blue agents. Up to six different graphs can be selected:

- *Total Number of agents near Red*
- *Total Number of agents near Blue*
- *Red Number of agents near Red*
- *Red Number of agents near Blue*
- *Blue Number of agents near Red*
- *Blue Number of agents near Blue*

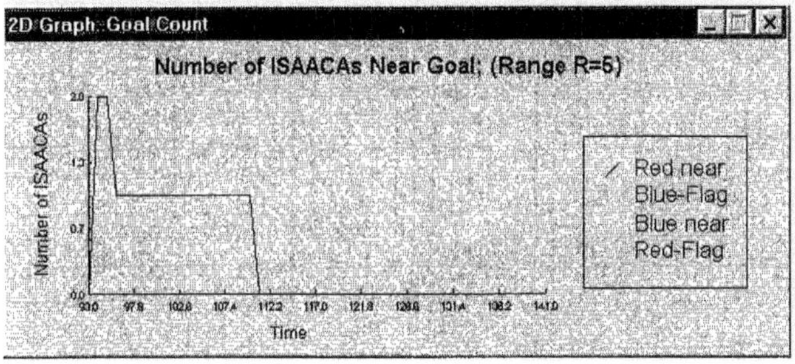

Fig. E.62 Screenshot of a sample *Goal Count* graph

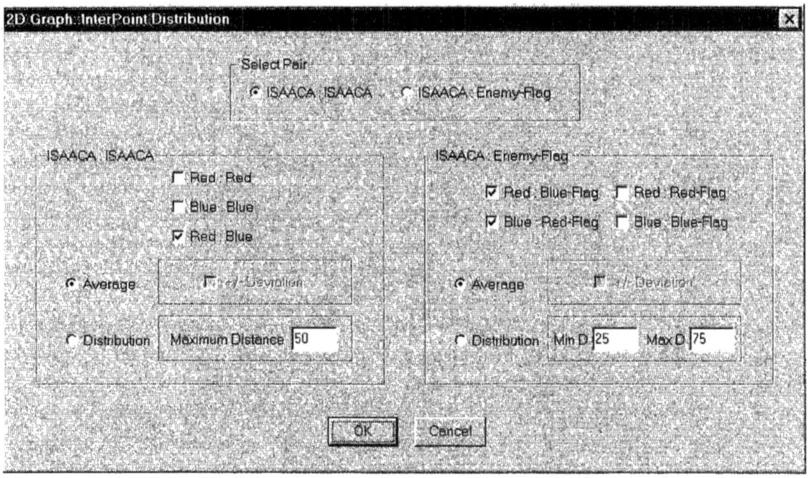

Fig. E.63 Screenshot of the *Interpoint Distance* dialog

Figure E.64 shows a sample plot of the distribution of agent:agent interpoint-distances for a selected snapshot in time.

E.7.1.8 *Neighbor Count*

Calls up a dialog that contains editable parameters defining time-series graphs of neighbor count statistics (figure E.65). You can plot a time-series of the total number of neighbors that are within a user-specified distance ($D = 1, 2, \ldots, 7$) from either red or blue agents.

Up to six different graphs can be selected:

- *Total Number of agents near Red*
- *Total Number of agents near Blue*

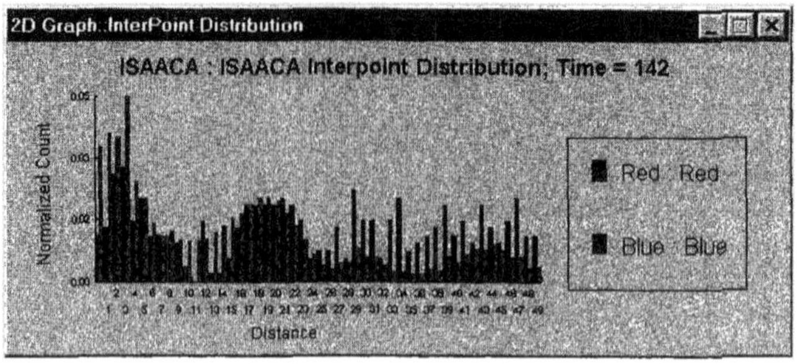

Fig. E.64 Screenshot of a sample *Interpoint Distance* distribution plot; the distribution is taken at time $t = 142$ during this run.

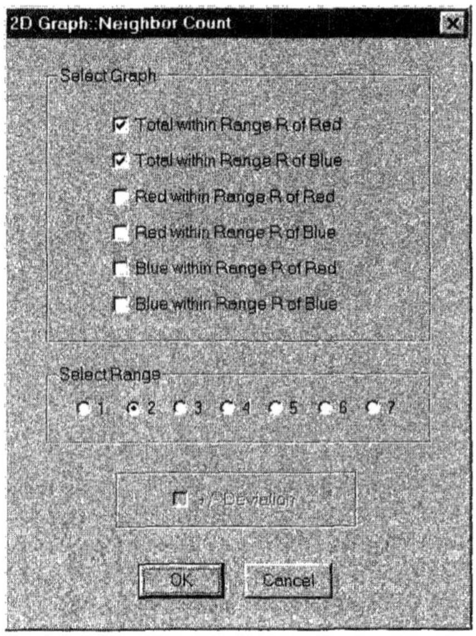

Fig. E.65 Screenshot of the *Neighbor Count* dialog.

- *Red Number of agents near Red*
- *Red Number of agents near Blue*
- *Blue Number of agents near Red*
- *Blue Number of agents near Blue*

Figure E.66 shows a sample graph of neighbor-count versus time. If the neighbor-count option is selected after a multiple time-series run is completed (see run-mode in *Simulation Menu*; page 603), EINSTein automatically graphs the average neighbor count, along with bars indicating the mean absolute deviation for each time (see figure E.23 on page 606).

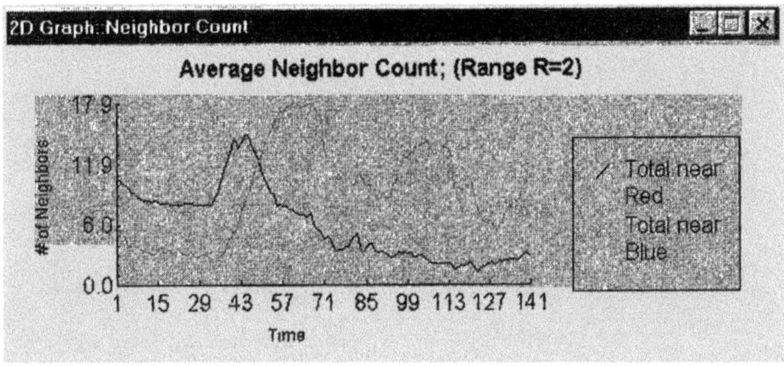

Fig. E.66 Screenshot of a sample *Neighbor Count* plot; the number of neighbors in this example is counted within a box of "radius" $R = 2$.

E.7.1.9 *Spatial Entropy*

Calls up a dialog that contains editable parameters defining time-series graphs of spatial entropy (figure E.67).

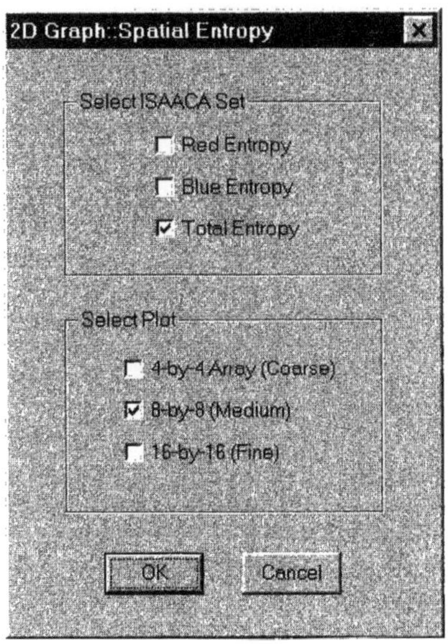

Fig. E.67 Screenshot of the *Spatial Entropy* dialog.

You can plot a time-series of the spatial entropy of either red, blue or total agent population sets. The can select to use either a 4–by–4 array (i.e. coarse) decomposition, an 8–by–8 array (i.e. medium), or a 16–by–16 (i.e. fine) decomposition of the battlefield. Figure E.68 shows a sample graph of spatial-entropy versus time.

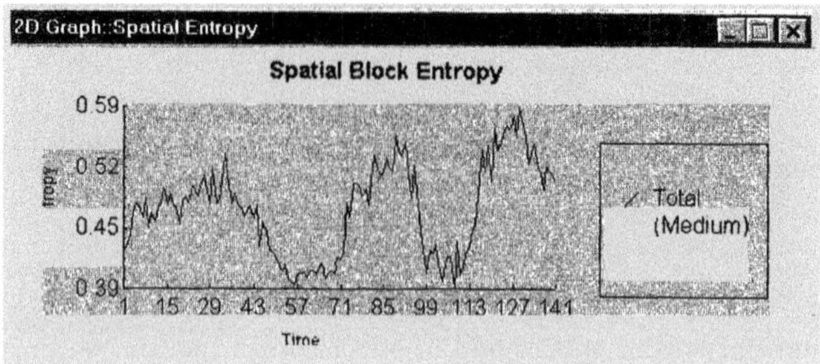

Fig. E.68 Screenshot of a sample *Spatial Entropy* plot.

E.7.1.10 *Territorial Possession*

Calls up a dialog that contains editable parameters defining time-series graphs of territorial possession (figure E.69). You can plot a time-series of the territorial possession of red and/or blue agents. The territory of red (or blue) is defined as the fraction of the battlefield that "belongs" to each color.

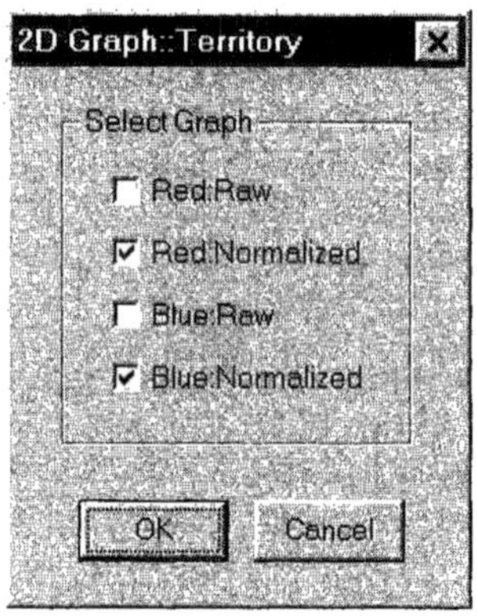

Fig. E.69 Screenshot of the *Territorial Possession* dialog.

Up to four kinds of graphs can be selected:

- *Red raw possession*
- *Blue raw possession*
- *Red normalized possession*
- *Blue normalized possession*

Raw possession is the raw fraction of the entire battlefield (or user-defined bounding area) that "belongs" to each color. Normalized possession is the normalized fraction of the entire battlefield (or user-defined bounding area), defined as raw possession divided by the area that would be occupied if no enemy agents existed. In other words, normalized possession measures how much territory a given side would currently be occupying if there were no enemy.

Figure E.70 shows a sample graph of territorial-possession versus time.

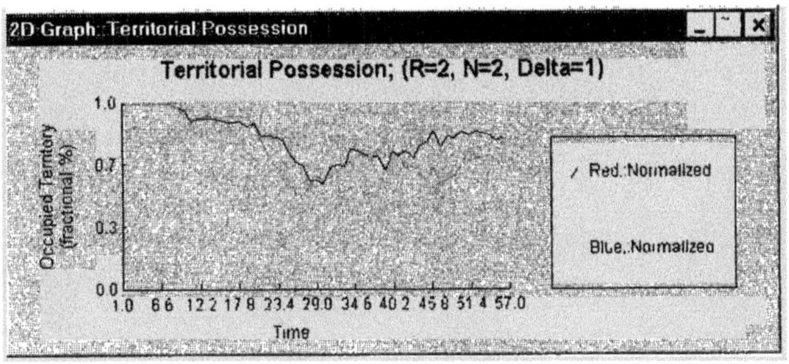

Fig. E.70 Screenshot of a sample *Territorial Possession* plot.

E.7.2 *3D Graphs*

E.7.2.1 *Fitness Landscape*

Calls up a dialog that contains editable parameters defining 3D graphs of mission-fitness (see figure 6.14 on page 451 of the main text). You can assign arbitrary weights ($0 \leq w \leq 1$) to 12 pre-defined mission primitives (which are calculated and stored internally during a fitness-landscape data run) in order to define a mission objective function to plot. You have three options to choose from (for a total of six kinds of graphs):

- *Color* (either color or greyscale)
- *Plot-type* (either fitness average or absolute deviations, for each x, y parameter pair)
- *Graph-type* (either 3D surface, interpolated over (x, y) nodes, 2D density plot, color-coded for fitness value, or a Win-graph). If the Win-graph option is selected, the user can define a threshold value of mission fitness f_C such that $f(x, y) \geq f_C$ defines the winning condition. The associated density plot consists of two colors: red for (x, y) regions where the winning condition is satisfied; black for (x, y) regions where the winning conditions is not satisfied.

Absolute deviations are averaged over the number of initial conditions entered in the fitness landscape run-time dialog. Right-clicking on the displayed graph calls up a pop-up dialog that provides options for altering the graph's appearance, labels, colors, and orientation in space (figure E.71).

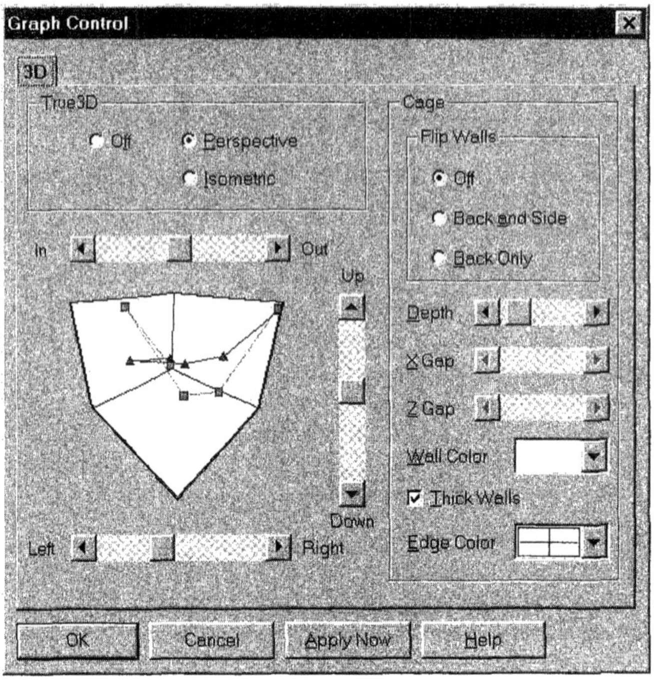

Fig. E.71 Pop-up dialog for changing a 3D-plot's appearance.

The average absolute deviation, *ADev*, of a sequence of values $S = \{x_1, x_2, ..., x_N\}$ is defined by:

$$ADev\,(x_1, x_2, ..., x_N) = \frac{1}{N}\left\{|x_1 - x_{ave}| + \;\; ... \;\; + |x_N - x_{ave}|\right\},$$

where x_{ave} is the average of S, and $|x|$ is the absolute value of x. *ADev* provides a robust estimate of the width of the distribution of a given sample of values.

Figures E.72— E.74 show a sample 3D mission-fitness landscape, a sample density plot of the same function, and a sample Win-graph for $f(x, y) \geq f_C = 0.08$, respectively.

E.7.2.2 *Genetic Algorithm Progress*

Calls up a dialog that contains editable parameters for tracking the progress of an on-going genetic-algorithm evolution (see figure 7.14 on page 531). You can plot any (or all) of four graphs simultaneously: best and worst fitness (current generation), best fitness (overall), and average fitness (see figure 7.15 on page 533).

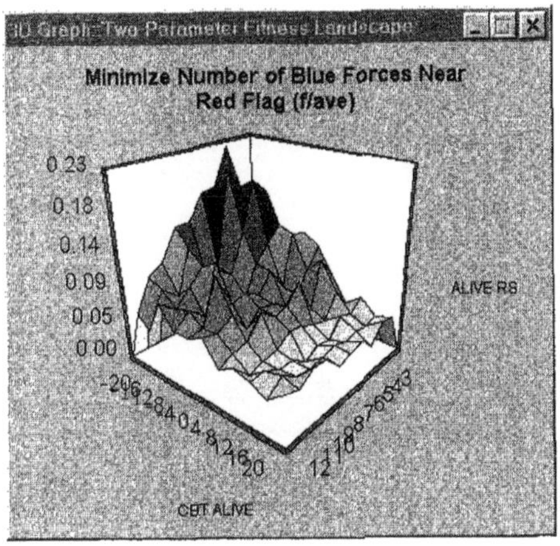

Fig. E.72 Sample fitness landscape surface graph.

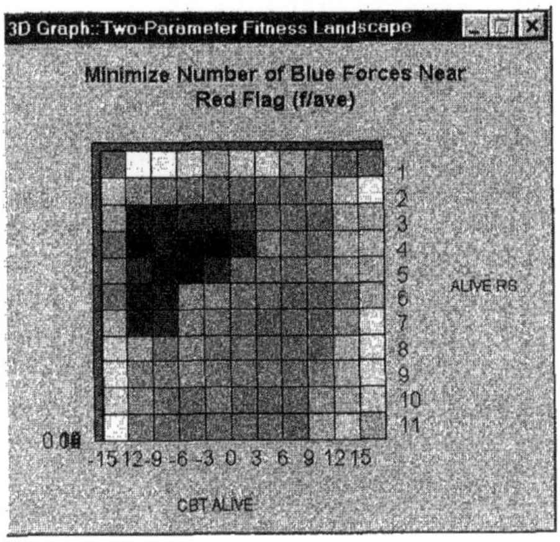

Fig. E.73 Sample fitness landscape density graph.

E.8 *Help* Menu

E.8.1 *Help Topics*

Calls up EINSTein's on-line help (figure E.75). EINSTein's help includes over 150 individual hyperlinked help topics as well as extensive background material, a self-contained on-line paper, a glossary of terms, over 400 complex systems theory and nonlinear dynamics related references, and over 40 URL links. This printed version of EINSTein's user's guide represents a subset of EINSTein's full on-line help.

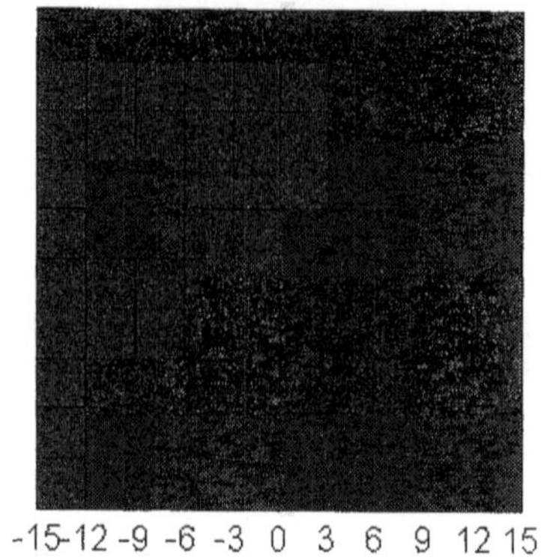

Fig. E.74 Sample win-graph

Fig. E.75 Contents page of EINSTein's on-line help file

E.8.2 *About EINSTein...*

Calls up a dialog that contains a basic copyright statement, current release version number and build date, and a pointer to EINSTein's homepage from which the latest version can be downloaded (figure E.76).

Fig. E.76 EINSTein's *"About..."* page.

E.9 Toolbar

The toolbar contains shortcut buttons that provide a convenient access to commands and/or dialog boxes. A brief description of each button's function may be obtained at any time by holding the mouse cursor over a given button.

Table E.1 shows the various groupings of toolbar icons and their associated function types. Color plate 28 (page 274) provides an overview (in color) of each button.

Button Group	Function Type
	File Input/Output
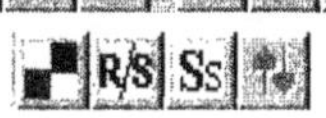	Simulation Options
	Display Options
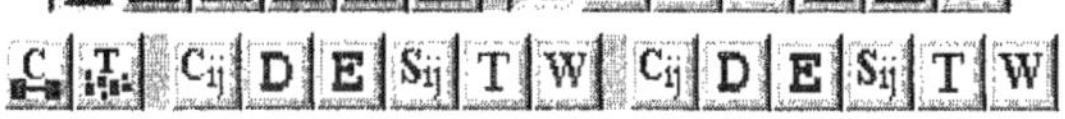	Edit Parameters
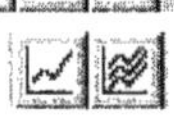	Data Collection
	Help

Table E.1 EINSTein's toolbar button groups (for versions 1.0 and older)

E.9.1 *Toolbar Reference*

The complete functional listing of each of EINSTein's 40 toolbar shortcuts is provided below, in the order in which they appear under the main menu:

- Open EINSTein input data file
- Save current set of parameter values as input data file
- Print current window
- Start RUN-file capture
- Stop RUN-file capture
- Load RUN-file
- Run/Stop toggle
- Enable single-step option
- Forward/backward (in time) toggle
- Restart run using randomized initial condition
- Toggle background between white/black
- Toggle activity-map on/off
- Display only locations where agents have been killed
- Display territorial possession map
- Display battle-front map
- Toggle trace mode (on/off)
- Display all agents
- Display all agents, highlighting injured with a different color
- Display only alive agents
- Display only injured agents
- Display locations where *red* (if button has red background) or *blue* (if blue background) agents have been killed
- Highlight individual squad
- Open edit combat parameters dialog
- Open edit terrain parameters dialog
- Open edit *red* (if text is colored red) or *blue* (if text is colored blue) communications matrix dialog
- Display *red* (if text is colored red) or *blue* (if text is colored blue) agent parameter values
- Open edit *red* (if text is colored red) or *blue* (if text is colored blue) agent parameters dialog
- Open edit *red* (if text is colored red) or *blue* (if text is colored blue) inter-squad connectivity matrix dialog

-  Open edit *red* (if text is colored red) or *blue* (if text is colored blue) passable-terrain degradation parameters
-  Open *red* (if text is colored red) or *blue* (if text is colored blue) weapons parameter dialog
-  Toggle data collection (on/off)
-  Enable multiple time-series data collection
-  Access on-line help

Appendix F

Differences Between EINSTein Versions 1.0 (and older) and 1.1 (and newer)

This appendix provides a visual summary (mainly in the form of screen captures) of some of the major changes that have been made to EINSTein's graphical user interface and main edit dialogs between versions 1.0 (and *older*) and 1.1 (and *newer*).

F.1 Toolbar and Main Menu

Color plate 30 (page 276) shows that the changes that have been made to EINSTein's toolbar and main menu are mostly cosmetic.

A few buttons—those marked *obsolete*—that are no longer relevant and/or whose functionality has been subsumed by pop-up dialogs activated by other buttons, have been removed. The older *On-the-fly Parameters Changes* main menu option has been eliminated as well, since almost all changes to any battlefield or agent parameter values made by the user during a run are now assumed to be "on the fly." (If the values of those few parameters that do require that a scenario be first reinitialized before resuming a run are changed by the user, a warning prompt appears advising the user of this fact prior to displaying the edit dialog and recording the changes.

The major change is that since all of EINSTein's dialogs that contain agent-specific data are now tabbed (i.e. possess separate red and blue "tabbed" pages for data entry on a single over-arching edit dialog; see below), there is no longer any need to maintain separate red and blue toolbar buttons. Thus the older red and blue agent edit dialogs have been subsumed by a single group of neural-colored buttons in version 1.1. Individual red and blue *Data Display* buttons have been retained, and are now the last two buttons (apart from the Help button) to appear on the extreme right of the toolbar.

F.2 Main Menu *Edit* Options and Dialogs

Figure F.1 compares EINSTein's older and new main menu *Edit* option lists. Most of EINSTein's new and/or redesigned edit dialogs appear on this list, and are shown in the figures that follow (see figures F.1 through F.9).

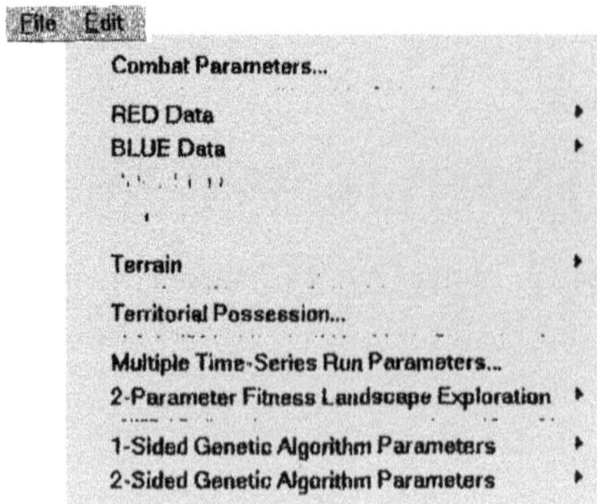

EINSTein (pre-release) version 1.0.0.4β

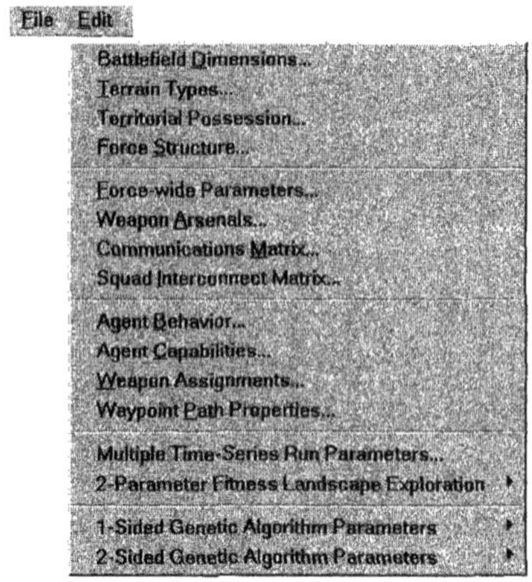

EINSTein (release) version 1.1

Fig. F.1 Comparison between EINSTein's older (version 1.0.0.4β and below) and newer (version 1.1 and above) main menu *Edit* options.

F.2.1 *Agent Parameters*

Figure F.2 compares EINSTein's older (version 1.0.0.4β and below) and newer (version 1.1 and above) *agent-behavior parameter* edit dialogs. The older dialog was called *Edit::Agent Parameters*, and was invoked by selecting *Edit→Red Data→Red Agents* (for red agents) or *Edit→Blue Data→Blue Agents* (for blue agents). The newer dialog is called *Agent Behavior Parameters* and is invoked by selecting *Edit→Agent Behavior*. Red and blue agent parameter values may be changed on separate pages, accessed via red/blue tabs located at the top left corner of the dialog.

Aside from having tabbed dialogs, the major differences are as follows:

- The older, and cumbersome, *Save Squad Data* button located in the SQUAD box (at the top left)—which users had to remember to press to save any parameter value changes—has been replaced by the more intuitive *Apply* button located beside Windows' usual OK and Cancel button along the bottom row of the dialog.
- All of the parameter values in the older *Offense/Defense* group (lower left hand corner of the top screenshot in figure F.2), along with those appearing in the Fratricide group (along the bottom), have been removed from the dialog and may be accessed (along with new features and options) by pressing the *Weapon Assignments...* dialog button appearing the new *Capacities* group (which replaces the older *Ranges* options).

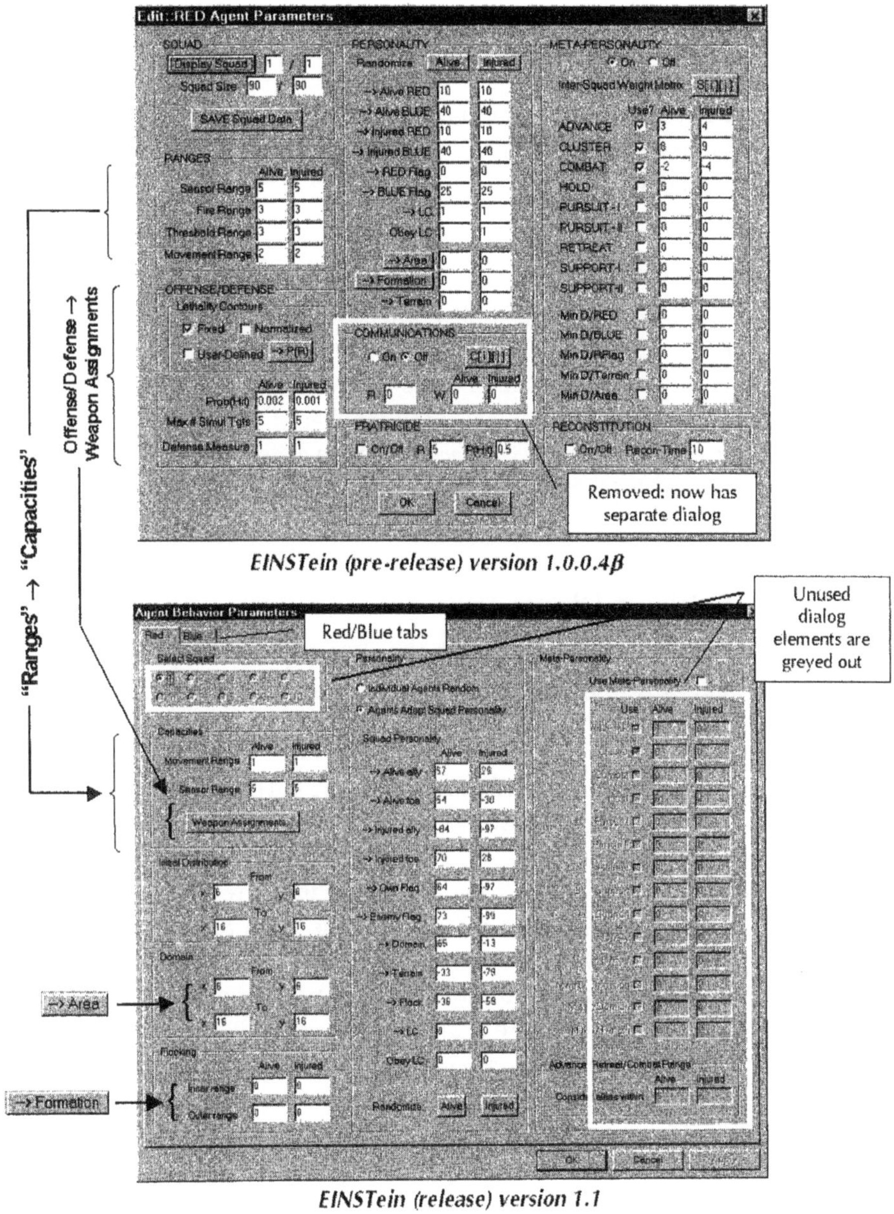

Fig. F.2 Comparison between EINSTein's older (version 1.0.0.4β and below) and newer (version 1.1 and above) *agent-behavior parameter* edit dialogs.

- The separate pages of parameter values for each squad are clearly identified by an associated squad-number dialog button appearing the *Select Squad* group (top left of lower screenshot in figure F.2). Squads that are not defined for the given scenario are greyed out, as are all unused meta-personality elements.
- The older *Area* and *Formation* buttons appearing in the Personality group, now appear as separate *Domain* and *Flocking* groups in the lower left corner of the new dialog.

F.2.2 *Edit Terrain Type*

Terrain elements are now defined as arbitrary battlefield sites that assume nonzero values of *passability* and *visibility*. While six default types of terrain (open terrain, two impassable types, and four passable types) are always available, the user is free to define, and provide a label for, an arbitrary number of other terrain types.

The terrain type edit dialog is the second option listed under the main menu edit choices (see figure F.1). Selecting this option calls up the dialogs shown in figure F.3.

F.2.3 *Combat-Related Dialogs*

Figure F.4 shows EINSTein's older *Edit::Combat Parameters* dialog (version 1.0.0.4β and older), and indicates the parts that have been subsumed and/or replaced by newer dialogs:

- The *Size of Battlefield* (top left corner in figure F.4) is replaced by a separate dialog that may be invoked by selecting the main Edit option and clicking on *Battlefield Dimensions.*
- The *Move Sampling Order* (top right corner in figure F.4) is replaced by a separate dialog that is called by selecting the main Simulation option and clicking on *Move Sampling Order.*
- The *Initial Distribution* parameters are now specified on the *Agent Behavior Parameters* dialog (see figure F.2).
- *Terrain*, *Combat Adjudication*, *Fratricide*, *Reconstitution* options and *Flag Position* have all been moved to a separate *Force-wide Parameters* dialog (see figure F.5 below).

F.2.3.1 *Weapon Selection*

In versions 1.1 and newer, weapons may be assigned to agents by the squad. A squad's default arsenal consists of five weapon types (see figure F.6):

- *Bolt-action rifle*

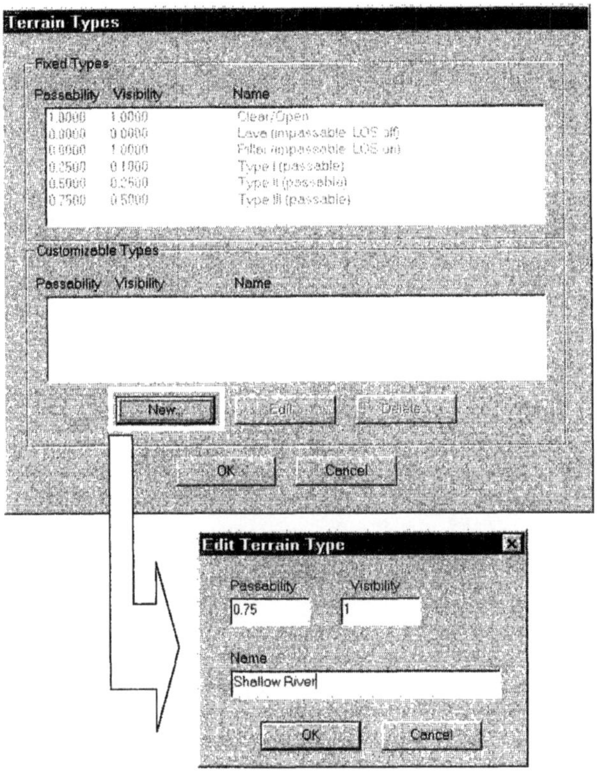

Fig. F.3 EINSTein's (version 1.1 and newer) *Terrain Type* edit dialog

- *Semi-automatic rifle*
- *Machine gun*
- *Grenade*
- *Mortar*

Table 5.5 (page 334) lists the parameter values used to define each type of default weapon.

F.2.3.2 *Weapon Assignment*

Weapons are assigned to individual agents, and may be arbitrarily mixed within squads (see figure F.7).

F.2.4 *Main Menu Simulation Pptions/Dialogs*

Figure F.10 compares EINSTein's main menu *Simulation* option lists as they appear in versions 1.0 (and older) and 1.1 (and newer).

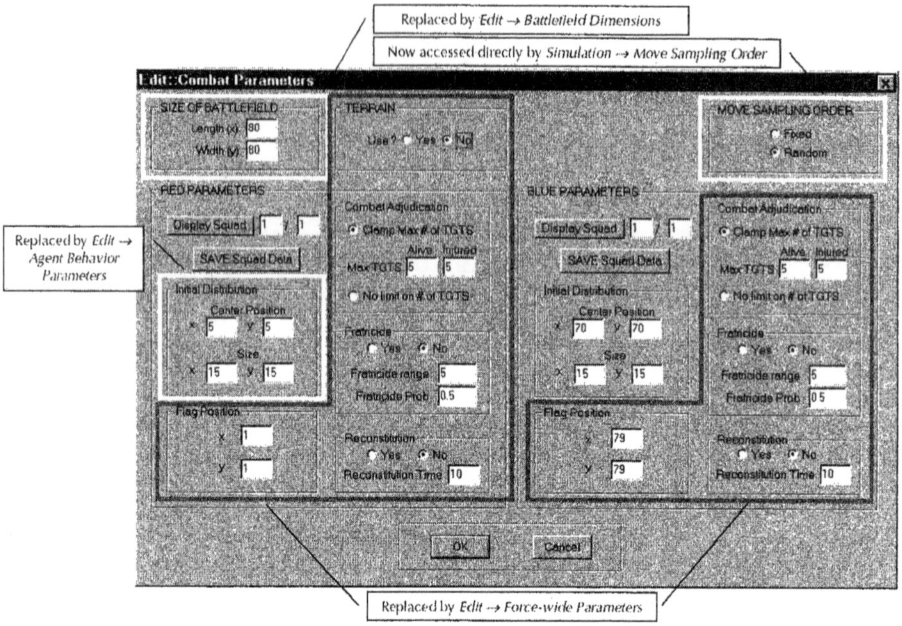

Fig. F.4 EINSTein's older (version 1.0.0.4β and below) *Combat* edit dialog.

F.2.5 *Main Menu Display Options*

Figure F.11 compares EINSTein's older and new main menu Display option lists. The only substantive change is the addition of a Display Waypoint Paths option, that provides an on/off toggle switch for displaying user-defined waypoints and paths. (The option has no effect, of course, unless waypoints have been already been defined via the right-hand-mouse action.)

F.2.6 *Right-Hand Mouse Action*

EINSTein version 1.1 includes a versatile new right hand mouse button pop-up action dialog. Clicking with the right-hand-mouse button, anywhere in an open battlefield window, pauses the run and displays a list of options—shown in figure F.12—to appear.

The user may use the left mouse button to:

- *Draw new (and/or edit old) terrain,*
- *Move the red and blue flags to new locations,*
- *Define waypoints to draw red and blue paths (which may be squad-specific),*
- *Add or delete agents,*
- *Inspect the properties of a given battlefield site.*

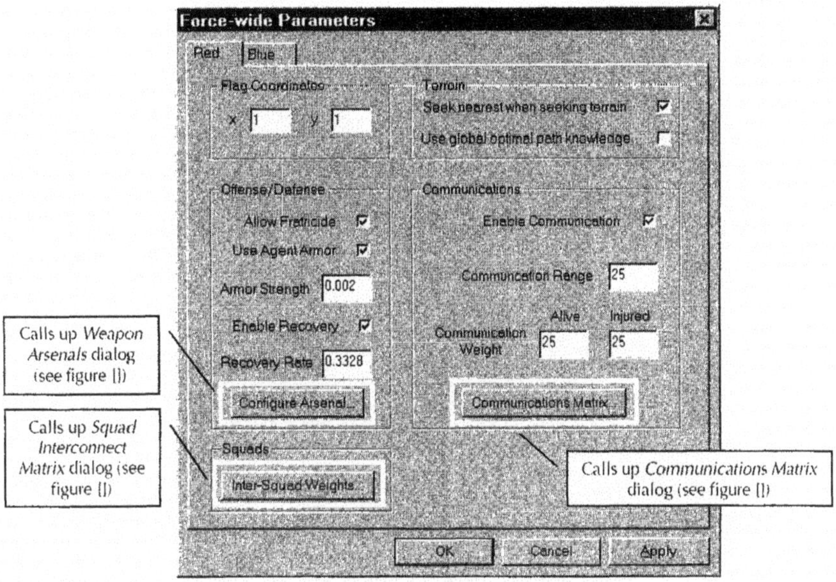

Fig. F.5 EINSTein's (version 1.1 and newer) *Force-Wide Parameters* dialog

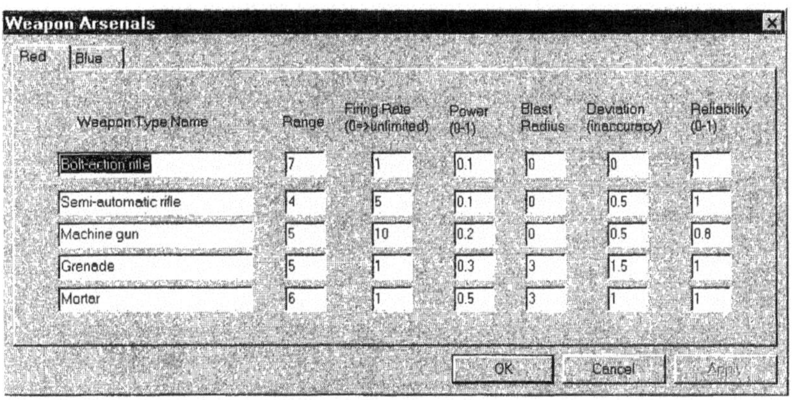

Fig. F.6 EINSTein's (version 1.1 and newer) *Weapon Arsenals* dialog

Examples of using the terrain and waypoint/path editing functions are provided in the main text in chapter 5 section *Pathfinding* (see page 343).

Figure F.13 shows sample screenshots from applying the *inspect site* function to sites occupied by terrain and a blue agent.

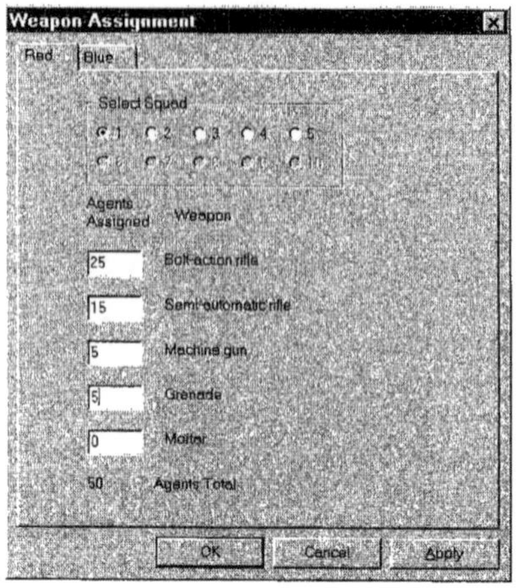

Fig. F.7 EINSTein's (version 1.1 and newer) *Weapon Assignment* dialog

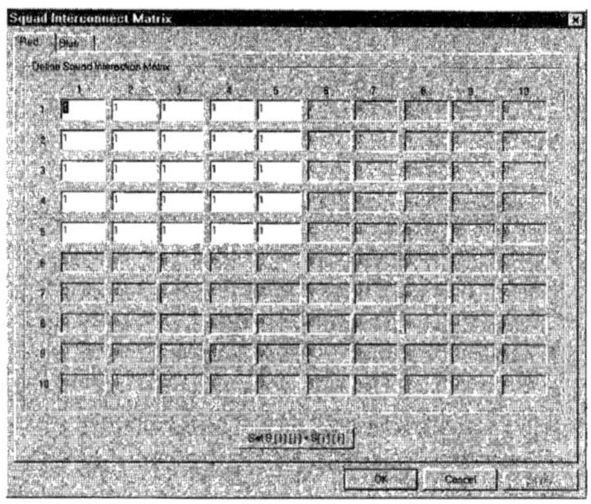

Fig. F.8 EINSTein's (version 1.1 and newer) *Squad Interconnect Matrix* dialog

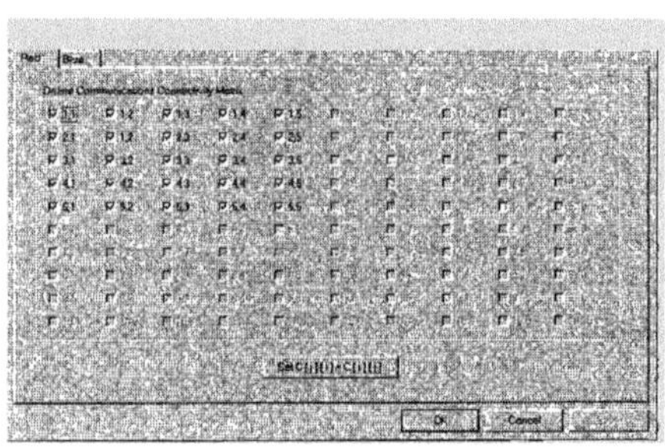

Fig. F.9 EINSTein's (version 1.1 and newer) *Squad Communications Matrix* dialog.

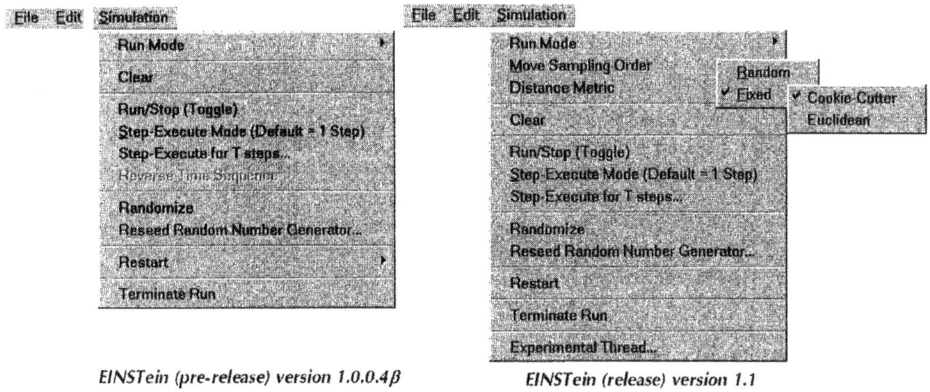

Fig. F.10 Comparison between EINSTein's older (version 1.0.0.4β and below) and newer (version 1.1 and above) main menu *Simulation* options.

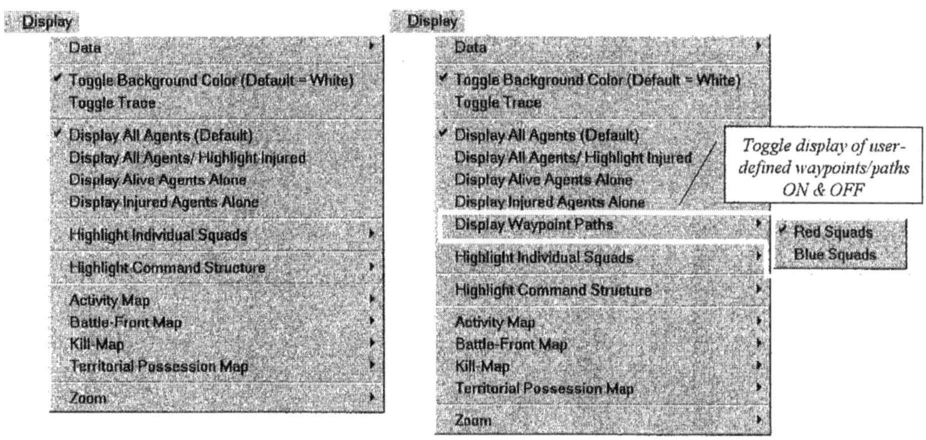

Fig. F.11 Comparison between EINSTein's older (version 1.0.0.4β and below) and newer (version 1.1 and above) main menu *Display* options.

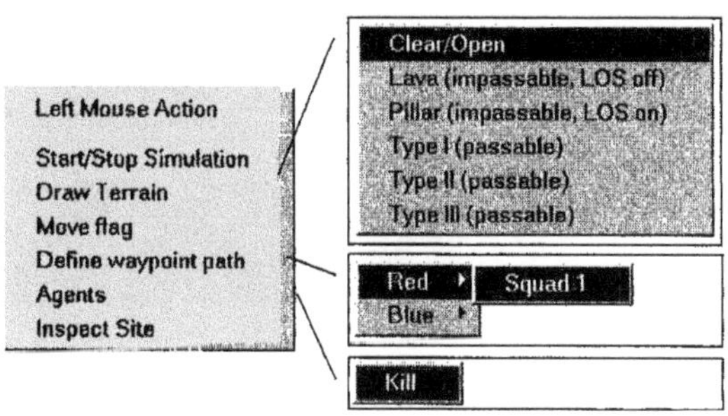

Fig. F.12 EINSTein's new *right-hand-mouse* action pop-up dialog

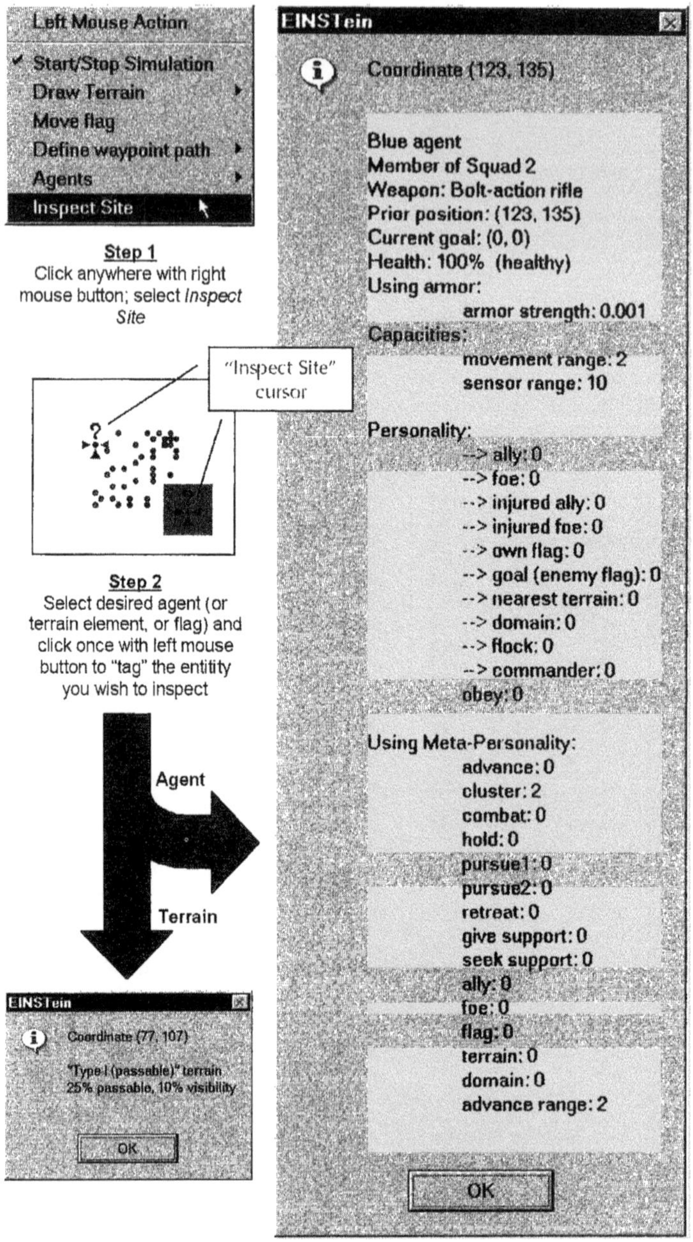

Fig. F.13 Screenshots showing a sample use of EINSTein's new *inspect site* right-hand-mouse button action

Appendix G

EINSTein's Data Files

EINSTein is configured to read/write several different data files. The types and contents of the data files depends on the version of the program: *versions 1.0* (and older) rely on ASCII-text data files; *versions 1.1* (and newer) use *eXtensible Markup Language* (XML) formatting, but are otherwise backwards compatible with the older files. Both are described in this appendix.

G.1 Versions 1.0 and Earlier

A typical data file is nothing more than text-based listing of labeled parameter values. It is usually partitioned into several self-contained sections. There are eight different kinds of input data files:

- *Input Data for Interactive Runs*; the default extension is **.dat.*
- *Combat Agent Input Data File*; the default extension is **.agt.*
- *Input Data for playback of Run-files*; the default extension is **.run.* Run-files are identical to EINSTein's default input data file for interactive runs, except that actual run-time data (in the form of agent states and positions for times '*t*') is appended to the file. This file is not normally edited by the user but contains useful information that summarizes the gross statistics of multiple runs of the same scenario (a scenario being defined by the parameter values appearing in the main **.dat* file).
- *Terrain Data*; the default extension is **.ter.*
- *Input Data for Passable-Terrain-Modified Agent Parameters*; the default extension is **.tma.*
- *Weapon Data*; the default extension is **.wpn.*
- *Two-Parameter Mission-Fitness Landscape Data*; the default extension is **.f1.*
- *One-Sided Genetic Algorithm Data*; the default extension is **.ga1.*

In addition, there are several different kinds of output files, consisting of data generated during multiple time-series, fitness-landscape runs and genetic-algorithm evolutions:

- *Raw Attrition Time-Series Sample Data*, the default extension is **.att.*
- *Raw Multiple Time-Series Sample Data*; the default extension is **.mts.*
- *Raw Multiple Time-Series Graph Data*; the default extension is **.mtg.*
- *Raw Multiple Time-Series Weapon Data; the default extension is *.rwd.*
- *Raw Two-Parameter Fitness Landscape Data*; the default extension is **.fit.*

G.1.1 *Input Data File*

A typical EINSTein input data file is nothing more than a lengthy listing of labeled parameter values partitioned into several self-contained sections (the default extension is **.dat*):

- *Run-time Parameters*
- *General Battle Parameters*
- *Statistics Parameters*
- *Global Command Parameters*
- *Local Command Parameters*
- *Agent Parameters*
- *Terrain Parameters*

Note that most sections are further subdivided into one or more subsections containing clusters of related variables. Not all sections contain values that are used in all scenarios, however. Also, some sections, such as those for defining local command parameters and terrain are variable in length. Once loaded, however, almost all of the parameter values appearing in the input data file can be changed interactively during the run.

G.1.1.1 *Run-Time parameters*

data_version: data_version takes on integer values defining which version of EINSTein is needed to run the file:

- *3 = version 0.9.9.9 Alpha and above*
- *2 = version 0.9.9.6 Alpha and above*
- *1 = versions prior to 0.9.9.6 Alpha*

G.1.1.2 *General battle Parameters*

battle_size: The first entry is battle_size, which defines the length of one of the sides of the two-dimensional square lattice on which the run is to take place. The user can specify any integer number between 10 and 150.

init_dist_flag: init_dist_flag can take on one of three integer values: 1, 2 or 3. If init_dist_flag = 1, the user defines the actual spatial distribution of red and blue agents (see next few parameter entries); if init_dist_flag = 2, red and blue agents initially consist of random formations near the lower-left and upper-right corners of the notional battlefield; if init_dist_flag = 3, red and blue agents are initially randomly placed within a square box at the center of the battlefield.

R_box_(l,w): This defines the (length, width) of the "box" containing the initial distribution of red agents for each of ten squads. Note that EINSTein assumes that all ten fields will be filled in even if there are fewer than ten red squads.

RED_cen_(x, y): The (x, y) coordinates of the center of the box containing the initial distribution of red agents for each of ten squads: $0 < x, y <$ battle_size. Note that EINSTein assumes that all ten fields will be filled in even if there are fewer than ten red squads. x and y are constrained to lie between 1 and battle_size.

B_box_(l,w): This defines the (length, width) of the "box" containing the initial distribution of blue agents for each of ten squads. Note that EINSTein assumes that all ten fields will be filled in even if there are fewer than ten red squads.

BLUE_cen_(x, y): The (x, y) coordinates of the center of the "box" containing the initial distribution of blue agents for each of ten squads: $0 < x, y <$ battle_size. Note that EINSTein assumes that all ten fields will be filled in even if there are fewer than ten red squads. x and y are constrained to lie between 1 and *battle_size.*

B_flag_(x, y): The (x, y) coordinates of the blue flag:$0 < x, y <$ battle_size.

R_flag_(x, y): The (x, y) coordinates of the red flag: $0 < x, y <$ battle_size.

termination?: This parameter flag specifies the termination condition that will be used during this run: if termination is set equal to 1 then the run is terminated whenever any agent (red or blue) reaches the opposing color's flag for the first time; if it is set to 2, the run continues until the run is terminated by the user.

move_order?: There are two ways in which moves can be sampled during an EINSTein run. If move_order = 1, then, at the start of each run, a randomly ordered list of red and blue agents is first set up prior to the start of the actual dynamics loop. During all subsequent passes, agent moves are then determined either by sequencing through the agents on this list in fixed order. If move_order = 2, this sequencing occurs in random order.

combat_flag?: If combat_flag = 0 then there is no limit to the max number of possible simultaneous engagements: all enemy agents within a given agent's fire range will be automatically targeted for engagement. If combat_flag = 1, each side simultaneously targets a maximum number of enemy agents per iteration step.

terrain_flag?: The software flag terrain_flag controls the use of notional terrain and takes on one of three values:

- *0 = terrain will not be used,*
- *1 = terrain blocks will be used,*
- *2 = terrain elements (i.e. 1-by-1 blocks) will be used.*

LOS_flag?: Toggles the use of line-of-sight. If line-of-sight is turned *off*, think of the terrain blocks as lava pits: agents can see across them but cannot pass through them. If line-of-sight is turned *on*, think of the terrain blocks as impenetrable pillars: agents can neither see through them nor walk through them.

red_frat_flag?: The software flag red_frat_flag controls the use of fratricide on the red side and takes on one of two values: 0 or 1. If red_frat_flag = 1 then red agents will be able to accidentally target friendly red agents; if red_frat_flag = 0 then fratricide will not be possible.

blue_frat_flag?: The software flag blue_frat_flag controls the use of fratricide on the red side and takes on one of two values: 0 or 1. If blue_frat_flag = 1 then red agents will be able to accidentally target friendly blue agents; if blue_frat_flag = 0 then fratricide will not be possible.

red_frat_rad: This parameter defines the radius around a targeted enemy agent such that, if the red_frat_flag=1 (so that fratricide is possible on the red side), all red agents located within the box defined by this radius become potential victims of fratricide.

blue_frat_rad: This parameter defines the radius around a targeted enemy agent such that, if the blue_frat_flag=1 (so that fratricide is possible on the blue side), all blue agents located within the box defined by this radius become potential victims of fratricide.

red_frat_prob: The probability that a red (i.e., friendly) agent is inadvertently hit by a shot that was intended to hit a nearby enemy (i.e., blue) agent.

blue_frat_prob: The probability that a blue (i.e., friendly) agent is inadvertently hit by a shot that was intended to hit a nearby enemy (i.e., red) agent.

reconst_flag?: The software flag reconst_flag toggles the reconstitution option. If reconst_flag = 1 then reconstitution will be used; if reconst_flag = 0 then reconstitution will not be used.

RED_recon_time: If the reconstitution flag reconst_flag is set equal to 1, then RED_recon_time defines the number of iteration steps following a hit(either by blue or, if the fratricide flag red_frat_flag is enabled, red agents) such that if during that time interval a given red agent is not hit again, that agent's state is reconstituted back to alive.

BLUE_recon_time: If the reconstitution flag reconst_flag is set equal to 1, then BLUE_recon_time defines the number of iteration steps following a hit(either by red or, if the fratricide flag blue_frat_flag is enabled, blue agents) such that if during that time interval a given blue agent is not hit again, that agent's state is reconstituted back to alive.

G.1.1.3 *Statistics Parameters*

stat_flag?: If stat_flag is set to 1 then statistics will be calculated for this run, otherwise no.

goal_stat_flag?: Assuming that stat_flag is set to 1 (so that statistics calculations are enabled for this run), EINSTein will calculate various proximity-to-goal statistics if goal_stat_flag = 1, otherwise no. Goal statistics include the number of red and blue agents within range $R = 1, 2, ..., 5$ of the red and blue flags.

center_mass_flag?: Assuming that stat_flag is set to 1 (so that statistics calculations are enabled for this run), EINSTein will calculate various center-of-mass statistics if center_mass_flag = 1, otherwise no. Center-of-mass statistics include keeping track of the (x, y) coordinates of the center-of-mass of all red agents, all blue agents and all combined forces, as well as distances between the center-of-mass of red and blue agents and enemy flag.

interpoint_flag?: Assuming that stat_flag is set to 1 (so that statistics calculations are enabled for this run), EINSTein will calculate various interpoint distance statistics if interpoint_flag = 1, otherwise no. Interpoint distance statistics include keeping track of the distribution of distances between red and red agents, blue and blue agents, red and blue agents, red agents and blue flag, and blue agents and red flag.

entropy_flag?: Assuming that stat_flag is set to 1 (so that statistics calculations are enabled for this run), EINSTein will keep track of the approximate spatial entropy of the entire force disposition if entropy_flag = 1, otherwise no. Red, blue and total spatial entropy is calculated using 16 blocks of 20–by–20 sub-blocks, 64 blocks of 10–by–10 sub-blocks and 256 5–by–5 sub-blocks.

cluster_1_flag?: Assuming that stat_flag is set to 1 (so that statistics calculations are enabled for this run), EINSTein will calculate the cluster-size distribution (including ave +/- deviation) at each iteration step assuming an inter-cluster distance criteria of $D = 1$, otherwise no.

cluster_2_flag?: Assuming that stat_flag is set to 1 (so that statistics calculations are enabled for this run), EINSTein will calculate the cluster-size distribution (including ave +/- deviation) at each iteration step assuming an inter-cluster distance criteria of $D = 2$, otherwise no.

neighbors_flag?: Assuming that stat_flag is set to 1 (so that statistics calculations are enabled for this run), EINSTein will calculate various neighboring agent statistics, otherwise no. Neighboring agent statistics include averages and deviations for the number of friendly, enemy and total agents $\leq$ range $R = 1, 2, ..., r_S$ (including red in red, red in blue, blue in blue, blue in red, all in red and all in blue).

G.1.1.4 *Global Command Parameters*

BLUE_global_flag?: If blue_global_flag is set to 1 then a global commander will be used for the blue agents during this run, otherwise there will be no global commander (even if the other variables in this input section have valid entries).

GC_fear_index: The GC's fear index, which is a number between 0 and 1, represents a GC personality-defined tradeoff between wanting to simultaneously satisfy two desires: moving LCs closer to the enemy flag and preventing them from encountering too many enemy forces while doing so. If GC_fear_index = 0, the GC is effectively fearless of the enemy; if GC_fear_index = 1, the GC is maximally fearful of the enemy and wishes only to keep LCs and their subordinate agents away from the enemy.

GC_w_alpha: This is relative weight that the global commander assigns to the density of alive enemy agents located within each of the three annular subregions of the battlefield sectors. It is a number between 0 and 1.

GC_w_beta: This is relative weight that the global commander assigns to the density of injured enemy agents located within each of the three annular subregions of the battlefield sectors. It is a number between 0 and 1.

GC_frac_R[1]: This defines the size of the first of the three annular subregions of the battlefield sectors as the fraction (between 0 and 1) of the distance between the (x, y) coordinates of a given local commander and the way-point corresponding to a given sector.

GC_frac_R[2]: This defines the size of the second of the three annular subregions of the battlefield sectors as the fraction (between 0 and 1) of the distance between the (x, y) coordinates of a given local commander and the way-point corresponding to a given sector. Note that EINSTein automatically sets GC_frac_R[3] = 1-GC_frac_R[1] - GC_frac_R[2].

GC_w_swath[1]: This is relative weight that the global commander assigns to the first of the three annular subregions of the battlefield sectors; i.e., the sector that is closest to the (x, y) coordinates of a given local commander. It is a number between 0 and 1.

GC_w_swath[2]: This is relative weight that the global commander assigns to the second of the three annular subregions of the battlefield sectors. It is a number between 0 and 1.

GC_w_swath[3]: This is relative weight that the global commander assigns to the third of the three annular subregions of the battlefield sectors. It is a number between 0 and 1.

GC_max_red_f: This defines the maximum number of allowable enemy agents (as a fraction of the initial number of friendly subordinates) within the local command area.

GC_help_radius: Defines the size of the box around a given subordinate local commander within which that local commander can possibly assist other local commanders.

GC_h_thresh: Defines the threshold health state for a local commander such that if that local commander's actual health is greater than or equal to GC_h_thresh, that local commander can then be ordered to assist(i.e., move toward) another nearby local commander. It is a number between 0 and 1.

GC_rel_h_thresh: Defines the relative fractional health threshold ($=\Delta h_{thresh}$) between the health states of local commanders LC_i and LC_j such that if the actual relative fractional health, LC_i can be ordered by the GC to move toward (i.e., assist) LC_j.

G.1.1.5 *Red Global Command Parameters*

The Red Global Command Parameters section of the input data file consists of flags and variables defining the red agent force's global command personality. Except for the fact that they obviously refer to red rather than blue parameters, all entries in this section of the data input file have exactly the same meaning as their blue counterparts, defined above.

G.1.1.6 *Blue Local Command Parameters*

BLUE_local_flag: If blue_local_flag is set to 1 then the local commander option will be used for the blue agents during this run; If blue_local_flag = 0, there will be no local commanders. An important point to remember is that if this flag is set to 0 then all other entries in this section of data input file must be removed.

num_BLUE_cmdrs: This defines the number of blue local commanders (between 1 and 10). Note that all entries in this section that follow the subheading local commander parameters and begin with (1)________ (i.e., (1)_B_undr_cmd, (1)_B_cmnd_rad, etc.) refer to parameter entries for the 1st local commander. If num_BLUE_cmdrs > 1, then this entire cluster of parameters beginning with (1)________ must be repeated, in the same order, and with appropriate values, for each of the num_BLUE_cmdrs local commanders. That is, the start of the parameter cluster for the 2nd local commander (i.e., the entry (2)_B_undr_cmd) must immediately follow the last entry for the 1st local commander ((1)_w_help_LC_def; see below). The first value for the parameter cluster for the 3rd local commander follows the last value for the parameter cluster for the 2nd local commander, and so on.

B_patch_type: Recall that a local commander's command area may be partitioned into either 3–by–3 or 5–by–5 blocks of smaller blocks. B_patch_type = 1 partitions this area into 3–by–3 sub-blocks; B_patch_type = 2 partitions this area into 5–by–5 sub-blocks.

B_patch_flag: A flag that regulates how a local commander breaks a tie between two or more sub-blocks that he calculates will incur the same penalty if he orders his subordinate agents to move toward them. If B_patch_flag = 1, the LC chooses a random sub-block out of this same-penalty set. If B_patch_flag = 2, the sub-block that is chosen is the one nearest the sub-block that was previously chosen.

(n)_B_undr_cmd: This parameter specifies the number of blue agents under the command of the nth blue local commander. In the current version of EINSTein, the maximum number of subordinate agents for one local commander is 100.

(n)_B_cmnd_rad: This defines the radius of one of the sub-blocks that the nth blue local commander's local command area is subdivided into. This area is subdivided either into 3–by–3 subblocks (if B_patch_type = 1; see above) or 5–by–5 blocks (if B_patch_type = 2).

(n)_B_SENSOR_rng: This defines the nth blue local commander's sensor range. As such, it can be different from the sensor range of the local commander's subordinate agents.

(n)_w1:alive_B: This defines the 1st component of the nth blue local commander's personality weight vector. This first component represents the relative weight afforded to moving toward alive blue (i.e., friendly) agents. It is a number between 0 and 100.

(n)_w2:alive_R: This defines the 2nd component of the nth blue local commander's personality weight vector. This 2nd represents the relative weight afforded to moving toward alive red (i.e., enemy) agents. It is a number between 0 and 100.

(n)_w3:injrd_B: This defines the 3rd component of the nth blue local commander-der's personality weight vector. This third component represents the relative weight afforded to moving toward injured blue (i.e., friendly) agents. It is a number between 0 and 100.

(n)_w4:injrd_R: This defines the 4th component of the nth blue local commander's personality weight vector. This fourth component represents the relative weight afforded to moving toward injured red (i.e., enemy) agents. It is a number between 0 and 100.

(n)_w5:B_goal: This defines the 5th component of the nth blue local commander's personality weight vector. This fifth component represents the relative weight afforded to moving toward the blue (i.e., friendly) goal. It is a number between 0 and 100.

(n)_w6:R_goal: This defines the 6th component of the nth blue local commander's personality weight vector. This sixth component represents the relative weight afforded to moving toward the red (i.e., enemy) goal. It is a number between 0 and 100.

(n)_w_terrain: This defines the relative weight afforded by n^{th} blue local commander to moving toward a terrain element. It is a number between 0 and 100.

(n)_B_THRS_range: This defines the nth blue local commander's threshold range. The threshold range defines a boxed area surrounding the LC with respect to which that LC computes the numbers of friendly and enemy agents that play a role in determining what move to make on a given time step.

(n)_ADVANCE_num: This defines the nth blue local commander's advance threshold number, which represents the minimal number of friendly agents that must be within the threshold range (= (n)_B _THRS_range) for which the LC will continue moving toward the enemy flag (if it has a nonzero weight to do so).

(n)_CLUSTER_num: This defines the nth blue local commander's cluster threshold number, which represents a friendly cluster ceiling such that if the LC senses a greater number of friendly forces located within its threshold range (= (n)_B _THRS_range), it will temporarily set its personality weights for moving toward friendly agents (=(n)_w1:alive_B and (n)_w3:injrd_B) to zero.

(n)_COMBAT_num: This defines the nth blue local commander's combat threshold number, which fixes the local conditions for which the LC will choose to move toward or away from possibly engaging an enemy agent. Intuitively, the idea is that if the LC senses that it has less than a threshold advantage of surrounding forces over enemy forces, it will choose to move away from engaging enemy agents rather than moving toward (and, thereby, possibly engaging) them.

(n)_B_w_alpha: This defines the 1st of four local command weights that prescribe the relative degree of importance the LC places on various measures of relative information contained in each block of sites within his command area. This first component represents the relative weight afforded to the fractional difference between alive friendly and alive enemy agents relative to the total number of friendly agents in each sub-block.

(n)_B_w_beta: This defines the 2nd of four local command weights that prescribe the relative degree of importance the LC places on various measures of relative information contained in each block of sites within his command area. This second component represents the relative weight afforded to the fractional difference between alive friendly and injured enemy agents relative to the total number of friendly agents in each sub-block.

(n)_B_w_delta: This defines the 3rd of four local command weights that prescribe the relative degree of importance the LC places on various measures of relative information contained in each block of sites within his command area. This third component represents the relative weight afforded to the fractional difference between injured friendly and alive enemy agents relative to the total number of friendly agents in each sub-block.

(n)_B_w_gamma: This defines the 4th of four local command weights that prescribe the relative degree of importance the LC places on various measures of relative information contained in each block of sites within his command area. This fourth component represents the relative weight afforded to the fractional difference between injured friendly and injured enemy agents relative to the total number of friendly agents in each sub-block.

(n)_w_obey_GC_def: This defines the nth blue local commander's relative weight afforded to obeying his GC's orders. It is a number between 0 and 1.

(n)_w_help_LC_def: This defines the nth blue local commander's relative weight afforded to moving toward and assisting another LC. It is a number between 0 and 1.

G.1.1.7 *Red Local Command Parameters*

The Red Local Command Parameters section of the input data file consists of flags and variables defining the red agent force's local command personality. Except for the fact that they obviously refer to red rather than blue parameters, all entries in this section of the data input file have exactly the same meaning as their blue counterparts, defined above.

G.1.1.8 *Blue Agent Parameters*

num_blues: This defines the total number of blue agents. Version 1.0 (and older) of EINSTein limits this number to 400 or less.

squads: This defines the total number of blue squads. This is a number between 1 and a maximum of 10.

num_per_squad: This defines the number of blue agents per squad for each of the 10 possible squads. Note that all 10 entries must appear in the input file, even if there are less than 10 squads (as defined by the squads parameter above). There is an internal check on the sum of the squad sizes that is performed by EINSTein to prevent possible overflow conditions.

A:M_range: Alive Movement Range. This defines the movement range, r_M, for each of the 10 possible blue agent squads for alive agents. Note that all 10 entries must appear in the input file, even if there are less than 10 squads (as defined by the squads parameter above). In the current version of EINSTein, r_M can either be set to equal 1 (meaning that agents choose there move from within a 3–by–3 box surrounding their current position), 2 (meaning that agents choose there move from within a 5–by–5 box surrounding their current position), 3 or 4. Can edit using main Edit or On-the-Fly dialogs.

I:M_range: Injured Movement Range. This defines the movement range, r_M, for each of the 10 possible blue agent squads for injured agents. Note that all 10 entries must appear in the input file, even if there are less than 10 squads (as defined by the squads parameter above). In the current version of EINSTein, r_M can either be set to equal 1 (meaning that agents choose there move from within a 3–by–3 box surrounding their current position), 2 (meaning that agents choose there move from within a 5–by–5 box surrounding their current position), 3 or 4.

personality: This software flag specifies how the blue agent's personality weight vector will be determined. If personality = 1, then the components of are defined explicitly by the appropriate parameter entries that appear below (see entries w1_a:B_alive_B through w6_i:B_R_goal). If personality = 2, then the components of are randomly assigned. In this case, each blue agent is assigned a different random weight vector.

near_terrain_flag: If terrain_flag is *on*, the value of this flag determines how an agent's relative weight for moving towards (or away from) nearby terrain is computed. If near_terrain_flag = 0, then all nearby terrain blocks are used, site by site, to determine the local penalty function; if near_terrain_flag = 1, then the local neighborhood is first scanned for the battlefield block that contains the nearest terrain element, and the penalty function is calculated using w_terrain_alive (or w_terrain_injured) with respect to the position of the nearest terrain element.

w1_a:B_alive_B: This defines the 1st component of the alive blue agent's personality weight vector. This first component represents the relative weight afforded by alive blue agents to moving toward alive blue (i.e., friendly) agents. It is a number between 0 and 100. (Recall that only the relative values among all six components matter here: the set $\{1, 2, 3, 4, 5, 6\}$ represents exactly the same set of weights as $\{10, 20, 30, 40, 50, 60\}$, as far as EINSTein is concerned.) Note that all 10 entries must appear in the input file, even if there are less than 10 squads (as defined by the squads parameter above).

w2_a:B_alive_R: This defines the 2nd component of the alive blue agent's personality weight vector. This second component represents the relative weight afforded by alive blue agents to moving toward alive red (i.e., enemy) agents. It is a number between 0 and 100. (Recall that only the relative values among all six components matter here: the set $\{1, 2, 3, 4, 5, 6\}$ represents exactly the same set of weights as $\{10, 20, 30, 40, 50, 60\}$, as far as EINSTein is concerned.) Note that all 10 entries must appear in the input file, even if there are less than 10 squads (as defined by the squads parameter above).

w3_a:B_injrd_B: This defines the 3rd component of the alive blue agent's personality weight vector. This third component represents the relative weight afforded by alive blue agents to moving toward injured blue (i.e., friendly) agents. It is a number between 0 and 100. (Recall that only the relative values among all six components matter here: the set $\{1, 2, 3, 4, 5, 6\}$ represents exactly the same set of weights as $\{10, 20, 30, 40, 50, 60\}$, as far as EINSTein is concerned.) Note that all 10 entries must appear in the input file, even if there are less than 10 squads (as defined by the squads parameter above).

w4_a:B_injrd_R: This defines the 4th component of the alive blue agent's personality weight vector. This fourth component represents the relative weight afforded by alive blue agents to moving toward injured red (i.e., enemy) agents. It is a number between 0 and 100. (Recall that only the relative values among all six components matter here: the set $\{1, 2, 3, 4, 5, 6\}$ represents exactly the same set of weights as $\{10, 20, 30, 40, 50, 60\}$, as far as EINSTein is concerned.) Note that all 10 entries must appear in the input file, even if there are less than 10 squads (as defined by the squads parameter above).

w5_a:B_B_goal: This defines the 5th component of the alive blue agent's personality weight vector. This fifth component represents the relative weight afforded by alive blue agents to moving toward the blue (i.e., friendly) goal. It is a number between 0 and 100. (Recall that only the relative values among all six components matter here: the set $\{1, 2, 3, 4, 5, 6\}$ represents exactly the same set of weights as $\{10, 20, 30, 40, 50, 60\}$, as far as EINSTein is concerned.) Note that all 10 entries must appear in the input file, even if there are less than 10 squads (as defined by the squads parameter above).

w6_a:B_R_goal: This defines the 6th component of the alive blue agent's personality weight vector. This sixth component represents the relative weight afforded by alive blue agents to moving toward the red (i.e., enemy) goal. It is a number between 0 and 100. (Recall that only the relative values among all six components matter here: the set $\{1,2,3,4,5,6\}$ represents exactly the same set of weights as $\{10,20,30,40,50,60\}$, as far as EINSTein is concerned.) Note that all 10 entries must appear in the input file, even if there are less than 10 squads (as defined by the squads parameter above).

w_terrain_alive: This defines the relative weight afforded by alive blue agents to moving toward a terrain element. It is a number between 0 and 100. (Recall that only the relative values among all six components matter here: the set $\{1,2,3,4,5,6\}$ represents exactly the same set of weights as $\{10,20,30,40,50,60\}$, as far as EINSTein is concerned.) Note that all 10 entries must appear in the input file, even if there are less than 10 squads (as defined by the squads parameter above).

w_area_alive: This defines the relative weight afforded by alive blue agents to staying near a fixed rectangular area. It is a number between 0 and 100. (Recall that only the relative values among all six components matter here: the set $\{1,2,3,4,5,6\}$ represents exactly the same set of weights as $\{10,20,30,40,50,60\}$, as far as EINSTein is concerned.) Note that all 10 entries must appear in the input file, even if there are less than 10 squads (as defined by the squads parameter above).

w_flock_alive: This defines the relative weight afforded by alive blue agents to staying near their own squad-mates. It is a number between 0 and 100. (Recall that only the relative values among all six components matter here: the set $\{1,2,3,4,5,6\}$ represents exactly the same set of weights as $\{10,20,30,40,50,60\}$, as far as ISAAC is concerned.) Note that all 10 entries must appear in the input file, even if there are less than 10 squads (as defined by the squads parameter above).

w1_i:B_alive_B: This defines the 1st component of the injured blue agent's personality weight vector. This first component represents the relative weight afforded by injured blue agents to moving toward alive blue (i.e., friendly) agents. It is a number between 0 and 100. (Recall that only the relative values among all six components matter here: the set $\{1,2,3,4,5,6\}$ represents exactly the same set of weights as $\{10,20,30,40,50,60\}$, as far as EINSTein is concerned.) Note that all 10 entries must appear in the input file, even if there are less than 10 squads as defined by the squads parameter above).

w2_i:B_alive_R: This defines the 2nd component of the injured blue agent's personality weight vector. This second component represents the relative weight afforded by injured blue agents to moving toward alive red (i.e., enemy) agents. It is a number between 0 and 100. (Recall that only the relative values among all six components matter here: the set $\{1,2,3,4,5,6\}$ represents exactly the same set of weights as $\{10,20,30,40,50,60\}$, as far as EINSTein is concerned.) Note that all 10 entries must appear in the input file, even if there are less than 10 squads (as defined by the squads parameter above).

w3_i:B_injrd_B: This defines the 3rd component of the injured blue agent's personality weight vector. This third component represents the relative weight afforded by injured blue agents to moving toward injured blue (i.e., friendly) agents. It is a number between 0 and 100. (Recall that only the relative values among all six components matter here: the set $\{1,2,3,4,5,6\}$ represents exactly the same set of weights as $\{10,20,30,40,50,60\}$, as far as EINSTein is concerned.) Note that all 10 entries must appear in the input file, even if there are less than 10 squads (as defined by the squads parameter above).

w4_i:B_injrd_R: This defines the 4th component of the injured blue agent's personality weight vector. This fourth component represents the relative weight afforded by injured blue agents to moving toward injured red (i.e., enemy) agents. It is a number between 0 and 100. (Recall that only the relative values among all six components matter here: the set $\{1,2,3,4,5,6\}$ represents exactly the same set of weights as $\{10,20,30,40,50,60\}$, as far as EINSTein is concerned.) Note that all 10 entries must appear in the input file, even if there are less than 10 squads (as defined by the squads parameter above).

w5_i:B_B_goal: This defines the 5th component of the injured blue agent's personality weight vector. This fifth component represents the relative weight afforded by injured blue agents to moving toward the blue (i.e., friendly) goal. It is a number between 0 and 100. (Recall that only the relative values among all six components matter here: the set $\{1,2,3,4,5,6\}$ represents exactly the same set of weights as $\{10,20,30,40,50,60\}$, as far as EINSTein is concerned.) Note that all 10 entries must appear in the input file, even if there are less than 10 squads (as defined by the squads parameter above).

w6_i:B_R_goal: This defines the 6th component of the injured blue agent's personality weight vector. This sixth component represents the relative weight afforded by injured blue agents to moving toward the red (i.e., enemy) goal. It is a number between 0 and 100. (Recall that only the relative values among all six components matter here: the set $\{1,2,3,4,5,6\}$ represents exactly the same set of weights as $\{10,20,30,40,50,60\}$, as far as EINSTein is concerned.) Note that all 10 entries must appear in the input file, even if there are less than 10 squads (as defined by the squads parameter above).

w_terrain_injured: This defines the relative weight afforded by injured blue agents to moving toward a terrain element. It is a number between 0 and 100.

(Recall that only the relative values among all six components matter here: the set $\{1,2,3,4,5,6\}$ represents exactly the same set of weights as $\{10,20,30,40,50,60\}$, as far as EINSTein is concerned.) Note that all 10 entries must appear in the input file, even if there are less than 10 squads (as defined by the squads parameter above).

w_area_injured: This defines the relative weight afforded by injured blue agents to staying near a fixed rectangular area. It is a number between 0 and 100. (Recall that only the relative values among all six components matter here: the set $\{1,2,3,4,5,6\}$ represents exactly the same set of weights as $\{10,20,30,40,50,60\}$, as far as EINSTein is concerned.) Note that all 10 entries must appear in the input file, even if there are less than 10 squads (as defined by the squads parameter above).

w_flock_injured: This defines the relative weight afforded by injured blue Agents to staying near their own squad-mates. It is a number between 0 and 100. (Recall that only the relative values among all six components matter here: the set $\{1,2,3,4,5,6\}$ represents exactly the same set of weights as $\{10,20,30,40,50,60\}$, as far as ISAAC is concerned.) Note that all 10 entries must appear in the input file, even if there are less than 10 squads (as defined by the squads parameter above).

w7:B_loc_comdr: If the blue local command option is enabled (i.e., if the parameter blue_local_flag is set equal to 1), and a given blue agent is under the command of blue local commander, w7:B_loc_comdr effectively acts as the 7th component of that blue agent's personality weight vector. This seventh component defines the relative weight afforded by a subordinate blue agent to staying close to its local commander. It is a number between 0 and 1.

w8:B_loc_goal: If the blue local command option is enabled (i.e., if the parameter blue_local_flag is set equal to 1), and a given blue agent is under the command of blue local commander, w8:B_loc_goal effectively acts as the 8th component of that blue agent's personality weight vector. This seventh component defines the relative weight afforded by a subordinate blue agent to obeying the orders issued by its local commander. It is a number between 0 and 1.

defense_flag: A software flag that regulates the notional defense option. If defense_flag = 1, the defense option is enabled (and defined by the parameters alive_strength and injured_strength below); if defense_flag = 0, the defense option is disabled.

alive_strength: If the notional defense option is enabled (i.e., if defense_flag = 1), then alive_strength defines the defensive strength of alive blue agents. The value of this parameter equals the number of hits(either by enemy or, if the fratricide option is enabled by setting blue_frat_flag = 1, friendly fire) that it takes to degrade an alive blue agent to an injured state. The minimal (and default) value is 1. Setting alive_strength to a large positive number effectively renders blue agents impervious to fire. Note that all 10 entries must appear in the input file, even if there are less than 10 squads (as defined by the squads parameter above).

injured strength: If the notional defense option is enabled (i.e., if defense_flag = 1), then injured_strength defines the defensive strength of injured blue agents. The value of this parameter equals the number of hits(either by enemy or, if the fratricide option is enabled by setting blue_frat_flag = 1, friendly fire) that it takes to kill an already injured blue agent. The minimal (and default) value is 1. Setting alive_strength to a large positive number effectively renders injured blue agents impervious to fire. Note that all 10 entries must appear in the input file, even if there are less than 10 squads (as defined by the squads parameter above).

A:S_range: Alive Sensor Range. This defines the sensor range, r_S, for each of the 10 possible blue agent squads for alive agents. Note that all 10 entries must appear in the input file, even if there are less than 10 squads (as defined by the squads parameter above). S_range can take on the value zero (in which case the agent senses nothing around itself) and any positive integer value.

I:S_range: Injured Sensor Range. This defines the sensor range, r_S, for each of the 10 possible blue agent squads for injured agents. Note that all 10 entries must appear in the input file, even if there are less than 10 squads (as defined by the squads parameter above). S_range can take on the value zero (in which case the agent senses nothing around itself) and any positive integer value.

A: F_range: Alive Fire Range. This defines the fire range, r_F, for each of the 10 possible blue agent squads for alive agents. Note that all 10 entries must appear in the input file, even if there are less than 10 squads (as defined by the squads parameter above). F_range can take on the value zero (in which case the agent is unable to shoot at anything) and any positive integer value.

I: F_range: Injured Fire Range. This defines the fire range, r_F, for each of the 10 possible blue agent squads for injured agents. Note that all 10 entries must appear in the input file, even if there are less than 10 squads (as defined by the squads parameter above). F_range can take on the value zero (in which case the agent is unable to shoot at anything) and any positive integer value.

COMM_flag: This software flag regulates the communications option for blue agents. If COMM_flag = 1, the communications option is enabled (and defined by the parameters COMM_range and COMM_weight below); if COMM_flag = 0, the communications option is disabled.

COMM_range: If the communications option is enabled (i.e., if COMM_flag = 1), then COMM_range defines the range of blue agent communications.

A:COMM_weight: Alive Communications Weight. If the communications option is enabled (i.e., if COMM_flag = 1), then A:COMM_weight defines the relative weight afforded by blue agents to using information communicated to them by other blue agents (within a communications range COMM_range of their position) in calculating their move selection penalty function. COMM_weight is typically assigned a real value between 0 and 1, though values greater than 1 can also be used to prescribe scenarios where blue agents give greater weight to communicated information then to information existing within their own sensor field.

I:COMM_weight: Injured Communications Weight. If the communications option is enabled (i.e., if COMM_flag = 1), then A:COMM_weight defines the relative weight afforded by blue agents to using information communicated to them by other blue agents (within a communications range COMM_range of their position) in calculating their move selection penalty function. COMM_weight is typically assigned a real value between 0 and 1, though values greater than 1 can also be used to prescribe scenarios where blue agents give greater weight to communicated information then to information existing within their own sensor field.

movement_flag: This software flag controls the use of μ-rule constraint thresholds (see Meta-Personality Dynamics). If movement_flag = 1, then μ-rules whose use_flags are set equal to one (see next 13 entries) will be used. If movement_flag = 0, μ-rules will not be used.

ADVANCE_flag: If the movement_flag is set, setting this flag equal to 1 enables the Advance to Enemy Flag μ-rule.

CLUSTER_flag: If the movement_flag is set, setting this flag equal to 1 enables the Cluster with Friendly Agents μ-rule.

COMBAT_flag: If the movement_flag is set, setting this flag equal to 1 enables the Combat μ-rule.

HOLD_flag: If the movement_flag is set, setting this flag equal to 1 enables the Hold Position μ-rule.

PURSUIT1_flag: If the movement_flag is set, setting this flag equal to 1 enables the Pursuit-I μ-rule.

PURSUIT2_flag: If the movement_flag is set, setting this flag equal to 1 enables the Pursuit-II μ-rule.

RETREAT_flag: If the movement_flag is set, setting this flag equal to 1 enables the Retreat μ-rule.

SUPPORT1_flag: If the movement_flag is set, setting this flag equal to 1 enables the Provide Support (Support-I) μ-rule.

SUPPORT2_flag: If the movement_flag is set, setting this flag equal to 1 enables the Seek Support (Support-II) μ-rule.

R_R_min_dist_flag: If the movement_flag is set, setting this flag equal to 1 enables the Minimum Distance to Friendly Agents μ-rule.

R_B_min_dist_flag: If the movement_flag is set, setting this flag equal to 1 enables the Minimum Distance to Enemy Agents μ-rule.

R_R_goal_min_flag: If the movement_flag is set, setting this flag equal to 1 enables the Minimum Distance to Own Flag μ-rule.

R_terrain_min_flag: If the movement_flag is set, setting this flag equal to 1 enables the Minimum Distance to nearby Terrain μ-rule.

R_area_min_flag: If the movement_flag is set, setting this flag equal to 1 enables the Minimum Distance to Fixed Area μ-rule.

T_range: This defines the blue agent's threshold range, r_T; it can be assigned any positive integer value. The threshold range defines a boxed area surrounding the agent with respect to which that agent computes the numbers of friendly and enemy agents that play a role in determining what move to make on a given time step. This local decision-making process is described in Meta-Rule Dynamics.

A:ADVANCE_num: This defines the alive blue agent's advance threshold number, which represents the minimal number of friendly agents that must be within the threshold range ($= r_T$) for which the blue agent will continue moving toward the enemy flag (if it has a nonzero default weight to do so). Note that all 10 entries must appear in the input file, even if there are less than 10 squads (as defined by the squads parameter above).

A:CLUSTER_num: This defines the alive blue agent's cluster threshold number, which represents a friendly cluster ceiling such that if the blue agent senses a greater number of friendly forces located within its threshold range ($= r_T$), it will temporarily set its personality weights for moving toward friendly agents (w1_a:B_alive_B and w3_a:B_injrd_B if the blue agent is alive, and w1_i:B_alive_B and w3_i:B_injrd_B if the blue agent is injured) to zero. Note that all 10 entries must appear in the input file, even if there are less than 10 squads (as defined by the squads parameter above).

A:COMBAT_num: This defines the alive blue agent's combat threshold number, which fixes the local conditions for which the blue agent will choose to move toward or away from possibly engaging an enemy agent. Intuitively, the idea is that if the blue agent senses that it has less than a threshold advantage of surrounding forces over enemy forces, it will choose to move away from engaging enemy agents rather than moving toward (and, thereby, possibly engaging) them. The value of A:COMBAT_num must be a (positive or negative) integer. Note that all 10 entries must appear in the input file, even if there are less than 10 squads (as defined by the squads parameter above).

A:HOLD_f: This defines the threshold fraction of sites within an agent's sensor range that must belong to its side's color (as defined by the current territorial possession map parameters) in order for the agent to hold his position (i.e. temporarily set his movement range to zero). Intuitively, the idea is that if a given agent occupies a patch of the battlefield that is locally occupied by friendly forces, that agent will temporarily set its movement range equal to zero.

A:PURSUIT1_num: This defines the threshold number of nearby enemy agents that must be within an agent's sensor range for the agent to pursue (or ignore) nearby enemy agents. Intuitively, the idea is that if a given agent senses that there are fewer than a threshold number if nearby enemy agents, it will temporarily ignore those agents (i.e. neither moving toward nor away). See Pursuit use_flag and Pursuit-I (Turn Pursuit Off) μ-rule logic for details.

A:PURSUIT2_num: This defines the threshold number of nearby enemy agents that must be within an agent's sensor range for the agent to pursue enemy agents exclusively. Intuitively, the idea is that if a given agent senses that there are fewer than a threshold number if nearby enemy agents, it will temporarily ignore all other personality-driven motivations except for those enemy agents. See Pursuit use_flag and Pursuit-II (Turn Exclusive Pursuit On) μ-rule logic for details.

A:RETREAT_num: The Retreat μ-rule consists of specifying a threshold number of friendly agents that must be within a given agent's constraint range r_C in order for that agent to continue advancing toward the enemy flag. See Advance. Intuitively, the retreat μ-rule embodies the idea that unless a combatant is surrounded by a sufficient number of friendly forces (i.e. senses sufficient local fire-support), he will retreat back to his own goal. See Retreat use_flag and Retreat μ-rule logic for details.

A:SUPPORT1_num: The Provide Support (Support-I) μ-rule consists of specifying the local conditions for which a given agent will choose to provide support for nearby injured friendly agents, ignoring all other actions. Intuitively, the idea is that if a given agent senses that there are greater than a threshold number of nearby injured friendly agents, it will temporarily ignore all other personality-driven motivations except for those injured friendly agents. See Support-I use_flag and Support-I (Provide Support) μ-rule logic for details.

A:SUPPORT2_num: The Seek Support (Support-II) μ-rule consists of specifying the local conditions for which a given agent will choose to seek support for itself, ignoring all other actions. Intuitively, the idea is that if a given agent senses that there are greater than a threshold number of enemy agents, it will temporarily ignore all other personality-driven motivations except for moving toward nearby alive friendly agents to seek their support. See Support-II use_flag and Support-II (Seek Support) μ-rule logic for details.

I:ADVANCE_num: This defines the injured blue agent's advance threshold number, which represents the minimal number of friendly agents that must be within the threshold range ($= r_T$) for which the blue agent will continue moving toward the enemy flag (if it has a nonzero default weight to do so). Note that all 10 entries must appear in the input file, even if there are less than 10 squads (as defined by the squads parameter above).

I:CLUSTER_num: This defines the injured blue agent's cluster threshold number, which represents a friendly cluster ceiling such that if the blue agent senses a greater number of friendly forces located within its threshold range ($= r_T$), it will temporarily set its personality weights for moving toward friendly agents (w1_a:B_alive_B and w3_a:B_injrd_B if the blue agent is alive, and w1_i:B_alive_B and w3_i:B_injrd_B if the blue agent is injured) to zero. Note that all 10 entries must appear in the input file, even if there are less than 10 squads (as defined by the squads parameter above).

I:COMBAT_num: This defines the injured blue agent's combat threshold number, which fixes the local conditions for which the blue agent will choose to move toward or away from possibly engaging an enemy agent. Intuitively, the idea is that if the blue agent senses that it has less than a threshold advantage of surrounding forces over enemy forces, it will choose to move away from engaging enemy agents rather than moving toward (and, thereby, possibly engaging) them. The value of A:COMBAT_num must be a (positive or negative) integer. Note that all 10 entries must appear in the input file, even if there are less than 10 squads (as defined by the squads parameter above).

I:HOLD_f: This defines the threshold fraction of sites within an agent's sensor range that must belong to its side's color (as defined by the current territorial possession map parameters) in order for the agent to hold his position (i.e. temporarily set his movement range to zero). Intuitively, the idea is that if a given agent occupies a patch of the battlefield that is locally occupied by friendly forces, that agent will temporarily set its movement range equal to zero. See Hold Position use_flag and Hold Position μ-rule logic for details.

I:PURSUIT1_num: This defines the threshold number of nearby enemy agents that must be within an agent's sensor range for the agent to pursue (or ignore) nearby enemy agents. Intuitively, the idea is that if a given agent senses that there are fewer than a threshold number if nearby enemy agents, it will temporarily ignore those agents (i.e. neither moving toward nor away). See Pursuit use_flag and Pursuit-I (Turn Pursuit Off) μ-rule logic for details.

I:PURSUIT2_num: This defines the threshold number of nearby enemy agents that must be within an agent's sensor range for the agent to pursue enemy agents exclusively. Intuitively, the idea is that if a given agent senses that there are fewer than a threshold number if nearby enemy agents, it will temporarily ignore all other personality-driven motivations except for those enemy agents. See Pursuit use_flag and Pursuit-II (Turn Exclusive Pursuit On) μ-rule logic for details.

I:RETREAT_num: The Retreat μ-rule consists of specifying a threshold number of friendly agents that must be within a given agent's constraint range r_C in order for that agent to continue advancing toward the enemy flag. See Advance. Intuitively, the retreat μ-rule embodies the idea that unless a combatant is surrounded by a sufficient number of friendly forces (i.e. senses sufficient local fire-support), he will retreat back to his own goal. See Retreat use_flag and Retreat μ-rule logic for details.

I:SUPPORT1_num: The Provide Support (Support-I) μ-rule consists of specifying the local conditions for which a given agent will choose to provide support for nearby injured friendly agents, ignoring all other actions. Intuitively, the idea is that if a given agent senses that there are greater than a threshold number of nearby injured friendly agents, it will temporarily ignore all other personality-driven motivations except for those injured friendly agents. See Support-I use_flag and Support-I (Provide Support) μ-rule logic for details.

I:SUPPORT2_num: The Seek Support (Support-II) μ-rule consists of specifying the local conditions for which a given agent will choose to seek support for itself, ignoring all other actions. Intuitively, the idea is that if a given agent senses that there are greater than a threshold number of enemy agents, it will temporarily ignore all other personality-driven motivations except for moving toward nearby alive friendly agents to seek their support. See Support-II use_flag and Support-II (Seek Support) μ-rule logic for details.

T_RANGE_(m,M): These two values (m, M) define the lower $(= m)$ and upper $(= M)$ limits of the interval of values within which the blue agent's threshold range, r_T, will be assigned a random positive integer value. These parameter settings are used only if (1) the personality flag personality is set equal to one (so that the blue agents are assigned random personality weight vectors), and (2) the movement flag movement_flag is set equal to 2 (so that blue agent personalities are augmented by additional constraints). The threshold range defines a boxed area surrounding the agent with respect to which that agent computes the numbers of friendly and enemy agents that play a role in determining what move to make on a given time step.

A:ADV_(m,M): These two values (m, M) define the lower $(= m)$ and upper $(= M)$ limits of the interval of values within which the alive blue agent's advance threshold number will be assigned a random positive integer value. These parameter settings are used only if (1) the personality flag personality is set equal to one (so that the blue agents are assigned random personality weight vectors), and (2) the movement flag movement_flag is set equal to 2 (so that blue agent personalities are augmented by additional constraints). The advance threshold number represents the minimal number of friendly agents that must be within the threshold range $(= r_T)$ for which the blue agent will continue moving toward the enemy flag (if it has a nonzero default weight to do so).

A:CLUS_(m,M): These two values (m, M) define the lower $(= m)$ and upper $(= M)$ limits of the interval of values within which the alive blue agent's cluster threshold number will be assigned a random positive integer value. These parameter settings are used only if (1) the personality flag personality is set equal to one (so that the blue agents are assigned random personality weight vectors), and (2) the movement flag movement_flag is set equal to 2 (so that blue agent personalities are augmented by additional constraints). The cluster threshold number represents a friendly cluster ceiling such that if the blue agent senses a greater number of friendly forces located within its threshold range $(= r_T)$, it will temporarily set its personality weights for moving toward friendly agents (w1_a:B_alive_B and w3_a:B_injrd_B if the blue agent is alive, and w1_i:B_alive_B and w3_i:B_injrd_B if the blue agent is injured) to zero.

A:COMB_(m,M): These two values (m, M) define the lower $(= m)$ and upper $(= M)$ limits of the interval of values within which the alive blue agent's combat threshold number will be assigned a random integer value. These parameter settings are used only if (1) the personality flag personality is set equal to one (so that the blue agents are assigned random personality weight vectors), and (2) the movement flag movement_flag is set equal to 2 (so that blue agent personalities are augmented by additional constraints). , which fixes the local conditions for which the blue agent will choose to move toward or away from possibly engaging an enemy agent. Intuitively, the idea is that if the blue agent senses that it has less than a threshold advantage of surrounding forces over enemy forces, it will choose to move away from engaging enemy agents rather than moving toward (and, thereby, possibly engaging) them. The values of 'm' and 'M' must be a (positive or negative) integers.

I:ADV_(m,M): These two values (m, M) define the lower $(= m)$ and upper $(= M)$ limits of the interval of values within which the injured blue agent's advance threshold number will be assigned a random positive integer value. These parameter settings are used only if (1) the personality flag personality is set equal to one (so that the blue agents are assigned random personality weight vectors), and (2) the movement flag movement_flag is set equal to 2 (so that blue agent personalities are augmented by additional constraints). The advance threshold number represents the minimal number of friendly agents that must be within the threshold range (= r_T) for which the blue agent will continue moving toward the enemy flag (if it has a nonzero default weight to do so).

I:CLUS_(m,M): These two values (m, M) define the lower (= m) and upper (= M) limits of the interval of values within which the injured blue agent's cluster threshold number will be assigned a random positive integer value. These parameter settings are used only if (1) the personality flag personality is set equal to one (so that the blue agents are assigned random personality weight vectors), and (2) the movement flag movement_flag is set equal to 2 (so that blue agent personalities are augmented by additional constraints). The cluster threshold number represents a friendly cluster ceiling such that if the blue agent senses a greater number of friendly forces located within its threshold range (= r_T), it will temporarily set its personality weights for moving toward friendly agents (w1_a:B_alive_B and w3_a:B_injrd_B if the blue agent is alive, and w1_i:B_alive_B and w3_i:B_injrd_B if the blue agent is injured) to zero.

I:COMB_(m,M): These two values (m, M) define the lower (= m) and upper (= M) limits of the interval of values within which the injured blue agent's combat threshold number will be assigned a random integer value. These parameter settings are used only if (1) the personality flag personality is set equal to one (so that the blue agents are assigned random personality weight vectors), and (2) the movement flag movement_flag is set equal to 2 (so that blue agent personalities are augmented by additional constraints). , which fixes the local conditions for which the blue agent will choose to move toward or away from possibly engaging an enemy agent. Intuitively, the idea is that if the blue agent senses that it has less than a threshold advantage of surrounding forces over enemy forces, it will choose to move away from engaging enemy agents rather than moving toward (and, thereby, possibly engaging) them. The values of 'm' and 'M' must be a (positive or negative) integers.

A:B_B_min_dist: This defines the alive blue agent's blue-blue minimum distance constraint, which represents the minimal distance that an alive blue agent wants to maintain away from each blue (i.e., friendly) agent in its sensor field. A:B_B_min_dist must be set equal to either zero (for no constraint) or to some positive integer value. Note that all 10 entries must appear in the input file, even if there are less than 10 squads (as defined by the squads parameter above).

A:B_R_min_dist: This defines the alive blue agent's blue-red minimum distance constraint, which represents the minimal distance that an alive blue agent wants to maintain away from each red (i.e., enemy) agent in its sensor field. A:B_R_min_dist must be set equal to either zero (for no constraint) or to some positive integer value. Note that all 10 entries must appear in the input file, even if there are less than 10 squads (as defined by the squads parameter above).

A:B_B_goal_min: This defines the alive blue agent's blue/blue-goal minimum distance constraint, which represents the minimal distance that an alive blue agent wants to maintain away from the blue (i.e., friendly) goal. A:B_B_goal_min must be set equal to either zero (for no constraint) or to some positive integer value. Note that all 10 entries must appear in the input file, even if there are less than 10 squads (as defined by the squads parameter above).

A:R_terrain_min: This defines the alive blue agent's blue/terrain minimum distance constraint, which represents the minimal distance that an alive blue agent wants to maintain away from any nearby terrain elements. A:B_B_terrain_min must be set equal to either zero (for no constraint) or to some positive integer value. Note that all 10 entries must appear in the input file, even if there are less than 10 squads (as defined by the squads parameter above).

A:R_area_min: This defines the alive blue agent's fixed-area minimum distance constraint, which represents the minimal distance that an alive blue agent wants to maintain away from a user-defined fixed area. A:B_B_area_min must be set equal to either zero (for no constraint) or to some positive integer value. Note that all 10 entries must appear in the input file, even if there are less than 10 squads (as defined by the squads parameter above).

A:R_flock_min: This defines the alive blue agent's flocking minimum distance constraint: If the distance between an agent and the center-of-mass of nearby (squad-mate) agents is less than A:R_flock_min, then the agent will want to move away from the center-of-mass position with weight w_flock_alive. Note that all 10 entries must appear in the input file, even if there are less than 10 squads (as defined by the squads parameter above).

A:R_flock_max: This defines the alive blue agent's flocking maximum distance constraint: If the distance between an agent and the center-of-mass of nearby (squad-mate) agents is greater than A:R_flock_max, then the agent will want to move toward the center-of-mass position with weight w_flock_alive. Note that all 10 entries must appear in the input file, even if there are less than 10 squads (as defined by the squads parameter above).

I:B_B_min_dist: This defines the injured blue agent's blue-blue minimum distance constraint, which represents the minimal distance that an alive blue agent wants to maintain away from each blue (i.e., friendly) agent in its sensor field. I:B_B_min_dist must be set equal to either zero (for no constraint) or to some positive integer value. Note that all 10 entries must appear in the input file, even if there are less than 10 squads (as defined by the squads parameter above).

I:B_R_min_dist: This defines the injured blue agent's blue-red minimum distance constraint, which represents the minimal distance that an alive blue agent wants to maintain away from each red (i.e., enemy) agent in its sensor field. I:B_R_ min_dist must be set equal to either zero (for no constraint) or to some positive integer value. Note that all 10 entries must appear in the input file, even if there are less than 10 squads (as defined by the squads parameter above).

I:B_B_goal_min: This defines the injured blue agent's blue/blue-goal minimum distance constraint, which represents the minimal distance that an alive blue agent wants to maintain away from the blue (i.e., friendly) goal. I:B_B_goal_min must be set equal to either zero (for no constraint) or to some positive integer value. Note that all 10 entries must appear in the input file, even if there are less than 10 squads (as defined by the squads parameter above).

I:R_terrain_min: This defines the injured blue agent's blue/terrain minimum distance constraint, which represents the minimal distance that an alive blue agent wants to maintain away from any nearby terrain elements. I:B_B_terrain_min must be set equal to either zero (for no constraint) or to some positive integer value. Note that all 10 entries must appear in the input file, even if there are less than 10 squads (as defined by the squads parameter above).

I:R_area_min: This defines the injured blue agent's fixed-area minimum distance constraint, which represents the minimal distance that an injured blue agent wants to maintain away from a user-defined fixed area. A:B_B_area_min must be set equal to either zero (for no constraint) or to some positive integer value. Note that all 10 entries must appear in the input file, even if there are less than 10 squads (as defined by the squads parameter above).

I:R_flock_min: This defines the injured blue agent's flocking minimum distance constraint: If the distance between an agent and the center-of-mass of nearby (squad-mate) agents is less than I:R_flock_min, then the agent will want to move away from the center-of-mass position with weight w_flock_injured. Note that all 10 entries must appear in the input file, even if there are less than 10 squads (as defined by the squads parameter above).

I:R_flock_max: This defines the injured blue agent's flocking maximum distance constraint: If the distance between an agent and the center-of-mass of nearby (squad-mate) agents is greater than I:R_flock_max, then the agent will want to move toward the center-of-mass position with weight w_flock_injured. Note that all 10 entries must appear in the input file, even if there are less than 10 squads (as defined by the squads parameter above).

A:shot_prob: Alive Single-Shot Probability. This defines the blue agent's single-shot probability, p_{ss}, which represents the probability that a targeted enemy agent is hit for an alive agent. It is a number between 0 and 1. Note that all 10 entries must appear in the input file, even if there are less than 10 squads (as defined by the squads parameter above).

I:shot_prob: Injured Single-Shot Probability. This defines the blue agent's single-shot probability, p_{ss}, which represents the probability that a targeted enemy agent is hit for an injured agent. It is a number between 0 and 1. Note that all 10 entries must appear in the input file, even if there are less than 10 squads (as defined by the squads parameter above).

A:B_max_eng_num: Alive Maximum Number of Targets. This defines the maximum number of simultaneously targetable red (i.e., enemy) agents by a blue agent. If the number of targetable enemy agents within a blue agent's sensor field is less than B_max_eng_num, the value of B_max_eng_num has no effect. If there are a greater number of targetable enemy agents within a blue agent's sensor field than B_max_eng_num, then B_max_eng_num of them will be randomly targeted. Note that all 10 entries must appear in the input file, even if there are less than 10 squads (as defined by the squads parameter above).

I:B_max_eng_num: Injured Maximum Number of Targets. This defines the maximum number of simultaneously targetable red (i.e., enemy) agents by a blue agent. If the number of targetable enemy agents within a blue agent's sensor field is less than B_max_eng_num, the value of B_max_eng_num has no effect. If there are a greater number of targetable enemy agents within a blue agent's sensor field than B_max_eng_num, then B_max_eng_num of them will be randomly targeted. Note that all 10 entries must appear in the input file, even if there are less than 10 squads (as defined by the squads parameter above).

G.1.1.9 *Red Agent Parameters*

The Red Agent Parameters section of the input data file consists of flags and variables defining red agents. Except for the fact that they obviously refer to red rather than blue parameters, all entries in this section of the data input file have exactly the same meaning as their blue counterparts, defined in Blue Agent Parameters section above.

G.1.1.10 *Terrain-Block Parameters*

terrain_blocks: Total number of terrain blocks that will be used for the run.

type(n): Defines terrain block type:

- *1 = impassable terrain with line-of-site (LOS) off (i.e. lava)*
- *2 = impassable terrain with line-of-site (LOS) on (i.e. pillar)*
- *3 = Type-I passable terrain*
- *4 = Type-II passable terrain*
- *5 = Type-III passable terrain*

terrain_l_w_(n): This defines the length and width of the nth terrain block. terrain_l_w_(n) can be assigned any positive integer values.

terrain_x_y_(n): This defines the (x, y)-coordinate of the center of the nth terrain block (x=1 defines the extreme left-hand-side of the notional battlefield, y=1 defines the bottom edge of the notional battlefield). terrain_x_y_(n) can be assigned any positive integer values.

G.1.2 *Combat Agent Input Data File*

EINStein's *Combat Agent Input Data File* defines the initial spatial disposition of red and blue agents (and overrides the definition of initial agent-block placements as defined in EINSTein's main input data file). It is broken into two parts: the first defines red agent positions, the second defines blue agent positions. Combat agent input data files have the default extension **.agt*. The actual parameter values are as follows:

Line [1]: number of red agents (R)
Line [2]: status[1], squad[1], x-coor[1], y-coor[1]
Line [3]: status[2], squad[2], x-coor[2], y-coor[2]
...
Line [R+1]: status[R], squad[R], x-coor[R], y-coor[R]
Line [R+2]: number of blue agents (B)
Line [R+3]: status[1], squad[1], x-coor[1], y-coor[1]
...
Line [R+B+2]: status[B], squad[B], x-coor[B], y-coor[B]

Agent data may be saved by selecting the *Save Agent Data File...* option of the *File* menu. Predefined terrain data files may be loaded by selecting the *Load Agent Data File...* option of the *File* menu.

number of red agents (R): The number of red agents for which the given combat agent input data file contains positional data.

number of blue agents (R): The number of blue agents for which the given combat agent input data file contains positional data.

status[i]: Defines the status of the ith agent:

- *status = 0: killed*
- *status = 1: injured*
- *status = 2: alive*

squad[i]: Specifies the squad $(1, 2, ..., 10)$ to which the ith agent belongs. If squad[i] > number of red squads in the current scenario, all squad values that exceed the actual number are redefined to equal the maximal squad number.

x-coor[i]: The x coordinate of the ith agent: $0 < x <$ battle_size.

y-coor[i]: The y coordinate of the ith agent: $0 < y <$ battle_size.

G.1.3 *Run-File*

Run-files (with default extension **.run*) are identical to EINSTein's default input data file for interactive runs, except that actual run-time data (in the form of agent states and positions for times '*t*') is appended to the file. This file is not normally edited by the user but contains useful information that summarizes the gross statistics of multiple runs of the same scenario (a scenario being defined by the parameter values appearing in the main **.dat* file). See page 604 in Appendix E for a brief tutorial for *recording* and *displaying* previously stored run-files. The appended data takes the following template form:

[Red Agent Block]
[Sample #1 Data Block]
time agent state(=alive(2)/injured(1)/killed(0)) x-coordinate y-coordinate
[Sample #2 Data Block]
time agent state(=alive(2)/injured(1)/killed(0)) x-coordinate y-coordinate
...
[Sample #N Data Block]
time agent state(=alive(2)/injured(1)/killed(0)) x-coordinate y-coordinate
[Blue Agent Block]
[Sample #1 Data Block]
time agent state(=alive(2)/injured(1)/killed(0)) x-coordinate y-coordinate
[Sample #2 Data Block]
time agent state(=alive(2)/injured(1)/killed(0)) x-coordinate y-coordinate
...
[Sample #N Data Block]
time agent state(=alive(2)/injured(1)/killed(0)) x-coordinate y-coordinate

G.1.4 *Terrain Input Data File*

The first two entries of EINStein's *Terrain Input Data File* (with default extension **.ter*) specify (1) the battlefield size of the scenario for which the given terrain data file is defined, and (2) the number of terrain elements defined in the given file, followed by a succession of as many two-line parameter-value sets of the following form as there are terrain elements:

Line [n]: [x] [y]
Line [n+1]: [occupation code] [terrain type]

For example, if the scenario for which the terrain data was saved has battlefield size battle_size = 100, the number of terrain elements is 5, there are three sites – $(x, y) = (25, 25)$, $(25, 26)$ and $(25, 27)$ – containing terrain of type 1, and there are two sites – $(x, y) = (50, 50)$ and $(50, 51)$ – containing terrain of type 2, the stored terrain data file appears as follows:

100
5
25 25
2 1
25 26
2 1
25 27
2 1
50 50
2 2
50 51
2 2

Terrain data may be saved by selecting the *Save Terrain Data File...* option of the File menu. Predefined terrain data files may be loaded by selecting the *Load Terrain Data File...* option of the File menu.

[x]: The x coordinate of the given battlefield (x, y) position: $0 < x <$ battle_size.

[y]: The y coordinate of the given battlefield (x, y) position: $0 < y <$ battle_size.

[occupation code]: Temporary placeholder for future use. Currently is equal to 0 (meaning (x, y) is empty, or 2 (meaning (x, y) contains a terrain element).

[terrain type]: Defines terrain element type at site (x, y):

- *1 = impassable terrain with line-of-site (LOS) off (i.e. "lava")*
- *2 = impassable terrain with line-of-site (LOS) on (i.e. "pillar")*
- *3 = Type-I passable terrain*
- *4 = Type-II passable terrain*
- *5 = Type-III passable terrain*

G.1.5 *Terrain-Modified Agent Parameters Input Data File*

EINSTein's *Terrain-Modified Agent Parameters* input data file defines how an agent's parameters will be modified whenever an agent is positioned on one of three kinds of passable terrain.

The values appearing in this data file over-ride the default values that are defined at the start of a run. The default extension is **.tma*. The file consists of six separate blocks of various parameter modifications defined for squads 1 through 10 (columns

1-10); note that, except for *visibility*,* entries for all agent parameters refer not to the absolute value that those parameters will take when an agent is on a corresponding passable terrain element, but to the *relative modification that will be made to those parameters*:

** Red:Passable-Terrain Type-I*
visibility 1 1 1 1 1 1 1 1 1 1
A:comm_range 5 5 5 5 5 5 5 5 5 5
I:comm_range 5 5 5 5 5 5 5 5 5 5
A:comm_weight 1 1 1 1 1 1 1 1 1 1
I:comm_weight 1 1 1 1 1 1 1 1 1 1
A:threshold_range 0 0 0 0 0 0 0 0 0 0
I:threshold_range 0 0 0 0 0 0 0 0 0 0
A:sensor_range 1 1 1 1 1 1 1 1 1 1
I:sensor_range 1 1 1 1 1 1 1 1 1 1
A:fire_range 1 1 1 1 1 1 1 1 1 1
I:fire_range 1 1 1 1 1 1 1 1 1 1
A:movement_range 1 1 1 1 1 1 1 1 1 1
I:movement_range 1 1 1 1 1 1 1 1 1 1
A:defense_alive 1 1 1 1 1 1 1 1 1 1
I:defense_alive 1 1 1 1 1 1 1 1 1 1
A:max_tgts_alive 1 1 1 1 1 1 1 1 1 1
I:max_tgts_alive 1 1 1 1 1 1 1 1 1 1
A:pk_alive v1 1 1 1 1 1 1 1 1 1
I:pk_alive 1 1 1 1 1 1 1 1 1 1
** Red:Passable-Terrain Type-I...*
** Blue:Passable-Terrain Type-III...*

G.1.6 *Weapons Input Data File*

EINSTein's *Weapons* input data file defines an agent's weapon parameters. You can define up to ten different squad-specific weapons, with user-specified lethality contours. Weapon characteristics for alive and injured agents can also be different from one another. The default extension is **.wp*.

The file consists of two main blocks (red & blue weapons) that are each divided into six separate sub-blocks of various parameters:

- *Assign Weapons to Squad*
- *ALIVE General Function Parameters*
- *ALIVE Function Array*

*The visibility index defines the probability with which an agent A occupying a battlefield position (x, y) that contains a passable terrain-element of Type-X (where $X = I, II$ or III) will be "seen" by another (F = *friendly* or E = *enemy*) agent, given that A is in F's (or E's) sensor range.

- *INJURED General Function Parameters*
- *INJURED Function Array*

function_type: Value zero = default alive and injured values of the single-shot probability-of-hit; Value one = user-defined single-shot probability-of-hit function.

sensor_type: Value zero = Cookie-Cutter distance calculations; Value one = Euclidean Distance calculations.

weapon_squad: Columns 1-10 specify which weapon ($w = 1, 2, ..., 10$) is to be assigned to which corresponding squad (squad = column).

plow_alive, plow_injured: User-defined single-shot probability-of-hit parameter. See figure 5.21 (on page 317) for definition. In the figure, plow = p(r < r_min).

phigh_alive, phigh_injured: User-defined single-shot probability-of-hit parameter. See figure 5.21 (on page 317) for definition. In the figure, $p_{high} = p(r > r_{min})$.

pmin_alive, pmin_injured: User-defined single-shot probability-of-hit parameter. See figure 5.21 (on page 317) for definition. In the figure, $p_{min} = p(r = r_{min})$.

pmax_alive, pmax_injured: User-defined single-shot probability-of-hit parameter. See figure 5.21 (on page 317) for definition. In the figure, $p_{max} = p(r = r_{max})$.

rmin_alive, rmin_injured: User-defined single-shot probability-of-hit parameter. See figure 5.21 (on page 317) for definition. In the figure, $r_{min} = r\_min$.

rmax_alive, rmax_injured: User-defined single-shot probability-of-hit parameter. See figure 5.21 (on page 317) for definition. In the figure, $r_{max} = r\_max$.

power_alive, power_injured: User-defined single-shot probability-of-hit parameter. See figure 5.21 (on page 317) for definition. In the figure, *power* = n (= *falloff power*).

decay_alive, decay_injured: User-defined single-shot probability-of-hit parameter. See figure 5.21 (on page 317) for definition. In the figure, *decay* = *Decay Rate.*

A:p_r[n], I:p_r[n]: Specifies the alive (A) and injured (I) single-shot probability-of-hit for fire-range $r = n$.

G.1.7 *Two-Parameter Fitness Landscape Input Data File*

EINSTein's *Two-Parameter Fitness Landscape* input data file defines the run-time parameters required for the two-parameter mission-fitness landscape run-mode. The default extension is **.fl*. The file consists of five separate blocks of various parameters:

- *FL Run Parameters*
- *territorial possession Parameters*
- *(x-y) sample space*
- *graph parameters*
- *mission primitive weights (1-100)*

alive_inj_symmetrization_flag: If this flag is set equal to 1, EINSTein automatically symmetrizes alive and injured parameter values during the initialization phase of each run.

w13_w24_symmetrization_flag: If this flag is set equal to 1, EINSTein automatically symmetrizes weights w3 & w1 and weights w4 & w2 during the initialization phase of each run.

num_initial_conds: This is the total number of randomized initial spatial configurations of red and blue agents that will be averaged over in calculating a mission fitness for a given personality.

max_time_to_goal: This variable sets a limit on the maximum number of iteration steps allowable per each run of the scan. Depending on the termination condition (see termination_code?), a given run may end prior to the time specified in max_time_to_goal. Typical values for battlefield sizes of ~80-by-80 are between 100-150 iteration steps.

power: This variable refers to the power n used in defining the fitness function, f, for each of the ten mission primitives. The value of penalty_power effectively determines how rapidly f falls off from its maximal to minimal value ($n = 1$ yields a linear fall-off, $n = 2$ yields a quadratic fall-off, and so on).

termination_code?: This software flag controls how a run will terminate. It can be assigned one of four integer values: 1, 2, 3 or 4. If termination_code? = 1, a run will terminate when the first red agent reaches the blue flag. If termination_code? = 2, a run will terminate when the number of red agents within a range R = flag_containment_range (see below) exceeds the threshold N = containment_number (see below). If termination_code? = 3, a run will terminate when the position of the red force's center-of-mass is closer to the blue flag than a threshold distance (defined by red_CM_to_BF_frac; see below). If termination_code? = 4, a run will terminate when the number of iterations t = max_time_to_goal.

flag_containment_range: This variable sets a range around either the red or blue flags (depending on the values of other variables) which is used to count the number of agents near a flag. For example, if the relative weight for maximizing the number of red agents near the blue flag is nonzero (see Mission Objective), the value of flag_containment_range sets the pertinent range from the blue flag.

containment_number: If the termination flag is set for terminating a run when the number of red agents within a range R (= flag_containment_range) exceeds a certain threshold N—i.e., if termination_code? = 2; see above—N is specified by the variable containment_number.

red_CM_to_BF_frac: If the termination flag is set for terminating a run when the position of the red force's center-of-mass is closer to the blue flag than a threshold distance D—i.e., if termination_code? = 3; see above—D is specified by the variable red_CM_to_BF_frac.

territorial_possession_flag: If this flag is set equal to 1, EINSTein will include territorial possession calculations in its internal data collection for the two-parameter fitness landscape sweep. Territorial possession parameters are defined by the following nine entries appearing in the Two-Parameter Fitness Landscape input data file.

territory_possession_max_time: A site (x, y) belongs to an agent (red or blue) according to the following logic: the number of like-colored agents within a territoriality-range (t_D) is greater than or equal to territoriality-minimum (t_M) and is at least territoriality-threshold (t_T) number of agents greater than the number of enemy agents within the same territoriality-distance. For example, if (t_D, t_M, t_T) = (2, 3, 2) then a battlefield position (x, y) is said to belong to, say, red, if there are at least 3 red agents within a distance 2 of (x, y) and the number of red agents within that distance outnumber blue agents by at least 2.

territorial_range: This defines the range around each (x, y) battlefield coordinate to which the territorial possession logic will be calculated.

territorial_minimum_threshold: This defines the minimum number of like-colored agents that must be within territorial_range of (x, y) in order for the (x, y) battlefield coordinate to "belong" to the color of these agents. See territorial possession for the complete set of conditions that must be satisfied for (x, y) to be registered as belonging to color X.

territorial_red_blue_delta: This defines the number by which like-colored agents must exceed that of agents of the other color within territorial_range of (x, y) in order for the (x, y) battlefield coordinate to "belong" to the color of these agents. See territorial possession for the complete set of conditions that must be satisfied for (x, y) to be registered as belonging to color X.

territorial_possession_area_cen_x: Defines the center x-coordinate of the area within which territorial possession calculations will be performed. The total area will be the bounding box defined by corner coordinates [cen_x - range_x, cen_y + range_y]–by–[cen_x + range_x, cen_y - range_y].

territorial_possession_area_range_x: Defines the x-range around the center x-coordinate of the area within which territorial possession calculations will be performed. The total area will be the bounding "box" defined by corner coordinates [cen_x - range_x, cen_y + range_y]–by–[cen_x + range_x, cen_y - range_y].

territorial_possession_area_cen_y: Defines the center y-coordinate of the area within which territorial possession calculations will be performed. The total area will be the bounding "box" defined by corner coordinates [cen_x - range_x, cen_y + range_y]–by–[cen_x + range_x, cen_y - range_y].

territorial_possession_area_range_y: Defines the y-range around the center y-coordinate of the area within which territorial possession calculations will be performed. The total area will be the bounding "box" defined by corner coordinates [cen_x - range_x, cen_y + range_y]–by–[cen_x + range_x, cen_y - range_y].

territory_possession_min_time: Defines the minimum time for which territorial possession calculations will be performed.

territory_possession_max_time: Defines the maximum time for which territorial possession calculations will be performed. If this maximum time > max_time_to_goal, then maximum time will be redefined to equal max_time_to_goal.

squad: Specifies the (red) squad number for which the scan will take place.

x_label: Labels the x-coordinate over which EINSTein will perform a mission fitness scan.

x_parameter_min: Specifies the minimum value of the x-coordinate (see x_label).

x_parameter_max: Specifies the maximum value of the x-coordinate (see x_label).

x_parameter_samples: Specifies the number of samples of the x-coordinate (see x_label).

y_label: Labels the y-coordinate over which EINSTein will perform a mission fitness scan.

y_parameter_min: Specifies the minimum value of the y-coordinate (see y_label).

y_parameter_max: Specifies the maximum value of the y-coordinate (see y_label).

y_parameter_samples: Specifies the number of samples of the y-coordinate (see y_label).

plot_type: If plot_type=1, then EINSTein will display fitness averages (averaged over num_initial_conds number of initial conditions per (x, y) pair); if plot_type=2, EINSTein will display absolute deviations.

graph_type: If graph_type=1, EINSTein will display a 3D surface graph; if graph_type=2, EINSTein will display a 2D density graph.

color_flag: If color_flag=1, the graph will be displayed using a 128-color palette, ranging from red (for fitness ~ 0) to dark blue (for fitness ~ 1); if color_flag=2, the graph will be displayed using 128 greyscales, ranging from black (for fitness ~ 0) to white (for fitness ~ 1).

G.1.8 *One-Sided Genetic Algorithm Input Data File*

EINSTein's *One-Sided Genetic Algorithm* input data file defines the run-time parameters required for the one-sided genetic algorithm run-mode. The default extension is **.ga1*. The file consists of five separate blocks of various parameters:

- *GA run parameters*
- *Penalty weights*
- *Define chromosome*

one_sided_ga_search_space: This effectively defines the "sub-space" of the EINSTein's full N-dimensional parameter space that the genetic algorithm will search over. The currently only possible choice is a search over the personality space for a single-squad. Future versions will include options to search over multiple squads, squad composition, inter-squad communications capability, and terrain placement.

population_size: This is the total population size of chromosomes. It remains constant from generation to generation.

num_generations: This is the total number of generations that the user wants to run. A single generation consists of running EINSTein's core engine for each initial condition (see num_initial_conds) and each personality.

num_initial_conds: This is the total number of randomized initial spatial configurations of red and blue agents that will be averaged over in calculating a mission fitness for a given personality.

max_time_to_goal: This variable sets a limit on the maximum number of iteration steps allowable per each run of the evolution. Depending on the termination condition (see termination_code?), a given run may end prior to the time specified in max_time_to_goal. Typical values for battlefield sizes of ~80–by–80 are between 100-150 iteration steps.

penalty_power: This variable refers to the power n used in defining the fitness function, f, for each of the ten mission primitives. The value of penalty_power effectively determines how rapidly f falls off from its maximal to minimal value ($n = 1$ yields a linear fall-off, $n = 2$ yields a quadratic fall-off, and so on).

best_personalities_to_file?: This software flag determines whether the program will automatically keep track of the best current personality (i.e., chromosome) during the evolution. If best_personalities_to_file? = 1, a user-specified file will contain a running tally of the best chromosomes for the entire run. In particular, whenever, after the first generation, the program finds a personality whose mission fitness exceeds that of the previously recorded personality it appends the appropriate data file with the better chromosome. Since the computational cost needed to perform this function is minimal, the user is encouraged to keep it always set equal to 1. If best_personalities_to_file? = 0, no updates of best personalities is made.

min_dist_genes_flag: This software flag controls the use of genes g36 through g42, that define red's minimal distance constraints. If min_dist_genes_flag = 1 these genes will be used in defining the red personalities, else they will not. Keep in mind that even if min_dist_genes_flag = 1, the program may itself determine that it would be "better" not to use any minimal distance constraints by finding an appropriate value of g36 = min_dist_flag.

initial_condition_genes_flag: This software flag controls the use of genes g43 through g45, that define the size and x,y coordinates of red's initial spatial configuration. If initial_condition_genes_flag = 1 these genes will be used in defining red's initial condition, else they will not.

w1_time_to_goal: This variable defines the relative weight afforded to the 1st mission primitive, that consists of minimizing the time to goal.

w2_friendly_loss: This variable defines the relative weight afforded to the 2nd mission primitive, that consists of minimizing the total number of red casualties.

w3_enemy_loss: This variable defines the relative weight afforded to the 3rd mission primitive, that consists of maximizing the total number of blue casualties.

w4_red_to_blue_survival_ratio: This variable defines the relative weight afforded to the 4th mission primitive, that consists of maximizing the ratio between red and blue casualties.

w5_friendly_CM_to_enemy_flag: This variable defines the relative weight afforded to the 5th mission primitive, that consists of minimizing the cumulative distance between the center-of-mass of the red agents and the blue flag.

w6_enemy_CM_to_friendly_flag: This variable defines the relative weight afforded to the 6th mission primitive, that consists of maximizing the cumulative distance between the center-of-mass of the blue agents and the red flag.

w7_friendly_near_enemy_flag: This variable defines the relative weight afforded to the 7th mission primitive, that consists of maximizing the total number of red agents that are within a user-defined distance D (see flag_containment_range) of the blue flag.

w8_enemy_near_friendly_flag: This variable defines the relative weight afforded to the 8th mission primitive, that consists of minimizing the total number of blue agents that are within a user-defined distance D (see flag_containment_range) of the red flag.

w9_red_fratricide_hits: This variable defines the relative weight afforded to the 9th mission primitive, that consists of minimizing the total number of red fratricide hits.

w10_blue_fratricide_hits: This variable defines the relative weight afforded to the 10th mission primitive, that consists of maximizing the total number of blue fratricide hits.

termination_code?: This software flag controls how a run (for a given personality) will terminate. It can be assigned one of four integer values: 1, 2, 3 or 4. If termination_code? = 1, a run will terminate when the first red agent reaches the blue flag. If termination_code? = 2, a run will terminate when the number of red agents within a range R = flag_containment_range (see below) exceeds the threshold N = containment_number. If termination_code? = 3, a run will terminate when the position of the red force's center-of-mass is closer to the blue flag than a threshold distance (defined by red_CM_to_BF_frac). If termination_code? = 4, a run will terminate when the number of iterations t = max_time_to_goal.

flag_containment_range: This variable sets a range around either the red or blue flags (depending on the values of other variables) which is used to count the number of agents near a flag. For example, if the relative weight for maximizing the number of red agents near the blue flag is nonzero (i.e., if the value of the variable w7_friendly_near_enemy_flag > 0), the value of flag_containment_range sets the pertinent range from the blue flag.

containment_number: If the termination flag is set for terminating a run when the number of red agents within a range R (= flag_containment_range) exceeds a certain threshold N—i.e., if termination_code? = 2; see above—N is specified by the variable containment_number.

red_CM_to_BF_frac: If the termination flag is set for terminating a run when the position of the red force's center-of-mass is closer to the blue flag than a threshold distance D—i.e., if termination_code? = 3; see above—D is specified by the variable red_CM_to_BF_frac.

G.1.8.1 *Agent Chromosome Entries: gene[i]*

The remaining entries—gene[1] through gene[63]—define not the values of the individual genes of a red personality chromosome but the minimum and maximum values that those genes are actually allowed to take in the program. The first entry in the 3-tuple sets an internal flag that indicates that the ith gene will be used for the genetic algorithm search; the ith gene will not be used if this flag equals zero.

For example, the first entry,

gene[1]:alive_sensor_range   1   1   10

means that the first gene, corresponding to red's alive sensor range, can only take on values between 1 and 10. Note that the minimum and maximum entries for genes that correspond to the signs (+ or −) of other variables (such as gene[10]:alive_alive_red_sign) are 0 and 1, respectively. Either of these values can actually be set equal to any real value between 0 and 1. The sign is determined internally by generating a random number between 0 and 1, comparing this number to the gene "value" (also between 0 and 1), and choosing the "+" sign if the random number > gene value, else choosing the "−" sign. A greater or lesser likelihood of choosing "+" versus "−" can therefore be regulated by selecting appropriate minimum and maximum entries for a given sign gene.

G.1.9 *Communications Matrix Input Data File*

EINSTein's *Communications Matrix* input data file defines red and blue communications matrix values, C_{ij} : $C_{ij} = 1$ if and only if i receives information from to j, else $C_{ij} = 0$. The default extension is *.cmw. The file consists of two blocks of individual matrix value entries: *red agent matrix values*, followed by *blue agent matrix values*.The format is as follows:

```
*************************************
 Red Communications Matrix Weights
*************************************
C[1][1] C[1][2] ... C[1][10]
C[2][1] C[2][2] ... C[2][10]
. . ... .
C[10][1] C[10][2] ... C[10][10]
```

****

Blue Communications Matrix Weights

****

C[1][1] C[1][2] ... C[1][10]
C[2][1] C[2][2] ... C[2][10]
. . ... .
C[10][1] C[10][2] ... C[10][10]

G.1.10 *Squad Interconnectivity Matrix Input Data File*

EINSTein's *Squad Interconnectivity Matrix* input data file defines red and blue communications matrix values, $-1 \leq S_{ij} \leq 1$, where S_{ij} defines the weight with which squad i reacts to squad j and is a real number between 0 and 1. The default extension is **.smw*. The file consists of two blocks of individual matrix value entries: *red agent matrix*, followed by values *blue agent matrix values*. The format is as follows:

****

Red Squad Matrix Weights

****

S[1][1] S[1][2] ... S[1][10]
S[2][1] S[2][2] ... S[2][10]
. . ... .
S[10][1] S[10][2] ... S[10][10]

****

Blue Squad Matrix Weights

****

S[1][1] S[1][2] ... S[1][10]
S[2][1] S[2][2] ... S[2][10]
. . ... .
S[10][1] S[10][2] ... S[10][10]

G.1.11 *Output Data Files*

EINSTein (version 1.0 and older) supports several different kinds of output data files for storing raw data:

- *Raw Attrition Time-Series Sample Data*
- *Raw Multiple Time-Series Sample Data*
- *Raw Multiple Time-Series Graph Data*
- *Raw Two-Parameter Fitness Landscape Data*
- *Best One-Sided Genetic Algorithm Chromosome*

The user is prompted with context-sensitive dialogs that appear after a multi time-series data-clloection run has been completed (see page 606 in Appendix E).

G.1.11.1 *Raw Attrition Time-Series Sample Data*

The *Raw Attrition Time-Series Sample Data* output file (default extension **.att*) contains the raw attrition data that summarizes a series of multiple runs (or samples) for a given input scenario **.dat* file. The format (as for all of the input and output files for EINSTein versions 1.0 and older)* is ASCII text and broken up into the following blocks of data:

```
*****************
 Raw Attrition Data
*****************
Samples Time/Sample
Red Attrition Ave Abs Dev Std Dev Var
Blue Attrition Ave Abs Dev Std Dev Var
Total Attrition Ave Abs Dev Std Dev Var

=== (Total) Attrition: Sample # [Red Inj+Killed] [Blue Inj+Killed] [Total Inj+Killed]
=== Distribution of Red Attrition Rates ===
=== Min Time  Max Time
=== Format: [Attrition Rate] [PDF]
=== Distribution of Blue Attrition Rates ===
=== Min Time  Max Time
=== Format: [Attrition Rate] [PDF]
=== Distribution of Total (Red + Blue) Attrition Rates ===
=== Min Time  Max Time
=== Format: [Attrition Rate] [PDF]
=== Distribution of Red Casualties ==
=== Format: [Casualty Number] [PDF]
=== Distribution of Blue Casualties ==
=== Format: [Casualty Number] [PDF]
=== Distribution of Total (Red + Blue) Casualties ==
=== Format: [Casualty Number] [PDF]
=== (Fractional) Attrition: Sample #  [Red %(I+K)] [Blue %(I+K)] [Total %(I+K)]
=== Red Squad-specific Attrition: [Squad 1] [Squad 2] [Squad 10]; ===
Average: [Squad 1] [Squad 2] [Squad 10]
Absolute Dev: [Squad 1] [Squad 2] [Squad 10]
Standard Dev: [Squad 1] [Squad 2] [Squad 10]
Variance: [Squad 1] [Squad 2] [Squad 10]
```

*EINSTein versions 1.1 and newer all use *Apache Software*'s open-source *Xerces* XML (eXtensible Markup Language) parser in C++ to provide XML I/O functionality; see page 707.

=== Blue Squad-specific Attrition: [Squad 1] [Squad 2] [Squad 10]; ===
Average: [Squad 1] [Squad 2] [Squad 10]
Absolute Dev: [Squad 1] [Squad 2] [Squad 10]
Standard Dev: [Squad 1] [Squad 2] [Squad 10]
Variance: [Squad 1] [Squad 2] [Squad 10]
=== Red Squad-specific Attrition: Sample # [Squad 1] [Squad 2] [Squad 10]
=== Blue Squad-specific Attrition: Sample # [Squad 1] [Squad 2] [Squad 10]
=== Distribution of Red Squad-Specific Casualties ===
=== Format: [Casualty Number] [Squad 1 PDF] ... [Squad 10 PDF]
=== Distribution of Red Squad-Specific Casualties ===
=== Format: [Casualty Number] [Squad 1 PDF] ... [Squad 10 PDF]
=== Probability Density Function (PDF)
=== red_bin:center pdf_red blue_bin:center pdf_blue tot_bin:center pdf_tot
Number of Bins
Red Bin Width Blue Bin Width (R+B) Bin Width
=== Time to achieve a specified percentage attrition
%[1]= 0.90000 %[2]= 0.75000 %[3]= 0.50000 %[4]= 0.10000
Format: R[%1] ... R[%4] B[%1] ... B[%4] Total[%1] ... Total[%4]
If given attrition level not achieved within (a fixed) run time = 10 then the entry = -1
=== Time to achieve a specified number of injured+killed agents
N[1]= 10.000 N[2]= 25.000 N[3]= 50.000 N[4]= 75.000
Format: R[N1] ... R[N4] B[N1] ... B[N4] Total[N1] ... Total[N4]
If given attrition level not achieved within (a fixed) run time = 10 then the entry = -1
=== (Single-Step) Attrition ===
=== = Number either injured or killed at time t for first 25 samples===
Format: t #Red[1][t] #Blue[1][t] #Total[1][t] ... #Total[25][t]

G.1.11.2 *Raw Multiple Time-Series Sample Data*

The *Raw Multiple Time-Series Sample Data* output file (default extension **.mts*) contains the raw data EINSTein uses to generate on-screen multiple time-series graphs and from which EINSTein generates sample statistics. This file is written when the *squad-specific* weapons are used in versions 1.0 and older (see page 314 in section 5.4.1 of the main text and page 595 in Appendix E.2.2.5). The prompt for saving this raw data is displayed immediately after the user has selected a specific graph to display on-screen.

The file contains entries for each kind of data (labeled, generically, as *Block N* in the fragment below) the user has flagged for collection under the *Data Collection* main menu option.

The format of the file is as follows:

[Label of Data Block 1: example=Attrition Red Alive]
time sample[1][time] sample[2][time] ... sample[25][time]

...

[Label of Data Block 2: example=Attrition Red Injured]

time sample[1][time] sample[2][time] ... sample[25][time]

...

[Label of Data Block n: example=Cluster Count]

time sample[1][time] sample[2][time] ... sample[25][time]

G.1.11.3 *Raw Multiple Time-Series Graph Data*

The *Raw Multiple Time-Series Graph Data* output file (default extension **.mtg*) contains the actual data EINSTein uses to display on-screen multiple time-series graphs. The prompt for saving this raw data is displayed immediately after the user has selected a specific graph to display on-screen.

The format of the file is as follows:

time data_ave[time] data_absolute_deviation[time]

In the event that a particular graph contains more than one plot—for example, the *Attrition Dialog* plot may contain up to seven individual plots—the raw data output file contains separate blocks of data for each plot, and each plot is appropriately labeled for reference.

G.1.11.4 *Raw Multiple Time-Series Weapon Data*

The *Raw Multiple Time-Series Weapon Data* output file (default extension **.rwd*) contains the *shots-taken* (S) and *hit-by* (H) weapon data for *agent-specific area* and *point-to-point* weapon assignments (used in versions 1.0 and older (see page 318 in section 5.4.1.3 of the main text and page 597 in Appendix E.2.2.6). The format of the file is as follows:

```
* red squads
* red agents per squad
* grenades per squad
* pt-to-pt #1 per squad
* pt-to-pt #2 per squad
* pt-to-pt #3 per squad
* pt-to-pt #4 per squad
* pt-to-pt #5 per squad
*
* blue squads
* blue agents per squad
* grenades per squad
* pt-to-pt #1 per squad
* pt-to-pt #2 per squad
```

```
* pt-to-pt #3 per squad
* pt-to-pt #4 per squad
* pt-to-pt #5 per squad
*
* time RED BLUE
* time GS GH P1S P1H - P5S P5H GS GH P1S P1H - P5S P5H
* [red squad 1] ... [red squad max] [blue squad 1] ... [blue squad max]
[Data Block for Sample 1]
[Data Block for Sample 2]
...
[Data Block for Sample N]
```

G.1.11.5 *Raw Two-Parameter Fitness Landscape Data*

This file contains the raw mission-fitness data summarizing the output of a *Two-Parameter Fitness Landscape* run. It consists of three sections (*Sections I, II,* and *III*). The default extension is **.fit.*

Section I. Section I lists the x and y coordinates that were chosen for the completed run, along with the list of mission-primitive weights that define the actual mission. A typical listing appears as follows:

```
**********************************************************
RAW TWO_PARAMETER-FITNESS DATA
**********************************************************
x_parameter: ALIVE RS
y_parameter: CBT ALIVE
Minimize Time to Goal: 0.00000
Minimize Number of Red Losses: 0.00000
Minimize Number of Blue Losses: 0.00000
Maximize Red/Blue Survival Ratio: 0.50000
Minimize Dist between Red-CoM and Blue-Flag: 0.00000
Maximize Dist Between Blue-CoM and Red-Flag: 0.00000
Maximize Number of Red Forces Near Blue Flag: 0.50000
Minimize Number of Bluc Forces Near Red Flag: 0.00000
Minimize Total Number of Red Fratricide Hits: 0.00000
Maximize Number of Blue Fratricide Hits: 0.00000
Maximize Red territorial possession: 0.00000
Minimize Blue territorial possession: 0.00000
```

Section II. Section II contains a complete listing of the raw mission-primitive values, computed for each (x, y) combination for the x and y parameter values defined in Section I, and using the default linear fitness function (i.e. power = 1). A typical listing (for two initial conditions) appears as follows:

****

IC t_G R_loss B_loss Surv RCM/BF BCM/RF R/BF B/RF RFr BFr

****

x = 1.0000

y = -15.000

1 0.00000 1.0000 0.00000 0.50000 0.0047415 0.012572 1.0000 1.0000 0.00000 0.00000

2 0.00000 0.96000 0.00000 0.48959 0.0048889 0.013189 1.0000 1.0000 0.00000 0.00000

AVE: 0.0 0.98000 0.00000 0.49480 0.0048152 0.012880 1.0000 1.0000 0.00000 0.00000

...

x = 11.000

y = 15.000

1 0.00000 1.0000 0.00000 0.50000 0.0031730 0.013397 1.0000 1.0000 0.00000 0.00000

2 0.00000 1.0000 0.00000 0.50000 0.0037431 0.013589 1.0000 1.0000 0.00000 0.00000

AVE: 0.00000 1.0000 0.00000 0.50000 0.0034581 0.013493 1.0000 1.0000 0.00000 0.00000

The format codes on the second line are defined by:

- *IC = initial condition*
- *t_G = minimize time to goal*
- *R_loss = minimize Red loss*
- *B_loss = maximize Blue loss*
- *Surv = maximize Survival Ratio*
- *RCM/BF = maximize Red center-of-mass to blue flag*
- *BCM/RF = minimize Blue center-of-mass to red flag*
- *R/BF = maximize Red agents near blue flag*
- *B/RF = minimize Blue agents near red flag*
- *RFr = Minimize red fratricide*
- *BFr = Maximize blue fratricide*
- *RTr = Maximize red territorial possession*
- *BTr = Minimize blue territorial possession*
- *AVE = averages the given mission primitive over the number of initial conditions*

Section III. Section III contains a complete listing of the raw mission values used by EINSTein for 3D display (as defined using the mission fitness dialog that appears after the two-parameter fitness landscape run is completed). The format is as follows:

x_sample :: y_sample :: fitness :: mean_absolute_deviation

A typical listing appears as follows:

****

RAW TWO_PARAMETER-FITNESS DATA (for selected mission)

FORMAT:
x_sample::y_sample::fitness::mean_absolute_deviation
****

1.0000 -15.000 0.24485 0.0051498
1.0000 -9.0000 0.24487 0.00000
1.0000 -3.0000 0.24485 0.0051498
...
11.000 3.0000 0.24744 0.0025630
11.000 9.0000 0.25000 0.00000
11.000 15.000 0.25000 0.00000

G.2 Versions 1.1 and Newer

Starting with versions 1.1 (and newer), EINSTein uses *Apache Software*'s open-source *Xerces* XML (eXtensible Markup Language) parser in C++ to provide XML I/O functionality.* XML is essentially a text-based language that defines the grammar of documents (and thus separates a document's structure from its content). XML is rapidly an industry standard for data description and exchange. Some of the main benefits of using XML include:

- *Editable text files*,
- *Compatibility with old (and future) parsers* (a fact that derives from the self-describing nature of XML file formats: one can read new file types with older parsers because they can ignore unrecognized parameters, and one can read old files with newer parsers because necessary default values can easily be defined as part of the file format), and
- *Widespread availability of free XML tools* and libraries for constructing, parsing and validating files (thus users can use their favorite XML-editing tools to assist them in composing their own parameter files; e.g., for batch-mode runs).

Note that compatibility with EINSTein's older **.dat* file format (see page 664) has been retained in the form of *import/export* functions that appear under the *Load* and *Save* options of the main *File* menu (labeled "Import EINSTein 1.0 file" and "Export EINSTein 1.0 file," respectively). The new XML-formatted data files may be loaded and saved using their associated options labeled "EINSTein Battlefield Configuration."

The following are fragments of a prototypical EINSTein data file in XML format:

**Xerces C++ Parser* version 2.3 is used. It is available at URL address http://xml.apache.org/xerces-c/index.html.

```
<?xml version="1.0" encoding="UTF-8" standalone="no" ?>
- <test xmlns="http://www.cna.org/einstein"
xmlns:xsi="http://www.w3.org/2001/XMLSchema-instance"
xsi:schemaLocation="http://www.cna.org/einstein ../schema/test.xsd">
- <battlefield>
    <rows>20</rows>
    <columns>30</columns>
  - <terrain-map>
    - <types>
    - <terrain>
        <passability>1</passability>
        <visibility>0.5</visibility>
        <name>Fog</name>
      </terrain>
    - <terrain>
        <passability>0</passability>
        <visibility>0</visibility>
        <name>Pillar</name>
      </terrain>
    </types>
    <map>0 0 0 0 0 0 0 0 0 0 0 0 0 0 0 0 0 0 ...
    0 0 0 0 0 0 0 0 1 1 1 1 1 1 1 0 0 0 0 0 ...
    .......................
    0 0 0 0 0 0 0 0 0 0 0 0 0 0 0 0 0 0 0 0 0 0</map>
    </terrain-map>
  </battlefield>
</test>
```



```
<?xml version="1.0" encoding="UTF-8" ?>
- <personality xmlns="http://www.cna.org/einstein"
    xmlns:xsi="http://www.w3.org/2001/XMLSchema-instance"
    xsi:schemaLocation="http://www.cna.org/einstein ../schema/personality.xsd">
    <ally>10.0</ally>
    <foe>100.0</foe>
    <injured-ally>-10.0</injured-ally>
    <injured-foe>-100.0</injured-foe>
    <goal>50.0</goal>
    <domain>0.0</domain>
    <flock>10.0</flock>
    <commander>-10.0</commander>
    <obey>-10.0</obey>
</personality>
```

```
<?xml version="1.0" encoding="UTF-8" ?>
- <metapersonality xmlns="http://www.cna.org/einstein"
    xmlns:xsi="http://www.w3.org/2001/XMLSchema-instance"
    xsi:schemaLocation="http://www.cna.org/einstein ../schema/meta.xsd">
    <advance>0</advance>
    <cluster>0</cluster>
    <combat>0</combat>
    <hold>0</hold>
    <pursue1>0</pursue1>
    <pursue2>0</pursue2>
    <retreat>0</retreat>
    <give-support>0</give-support>
    <seek-support>0</seek-support>
    <ally>0</ally>
    <foe>0</foe>
    <flag>0</flag>
    <terrain>0</terrain>
    <domain>0</domain>
    <advance-range>0</advance-range>
</metapersonality>

<?xml version="1.0" encoding="UTF-8" ?>
- <arsenal xmlns="http://www.cna.org/einstein"
    xmlns:xsi="http://www.w3.org/2001/XMLSchema-instance"
    xsi:schemaLocation="http://www.cna.org/einstein ../schema/arsenal.xsd">
  - <weapon>
      <name>Single-shot rifle</name>
      <range>5</range>
      <firing-rate>1</firing-rate>
      <spread>0</spread>
      <power>1.0</power>
      <deviation>0</deviation>
      <reliability>1.0</reliability>
    </weapon>
</arsenal>

<?xml version="1.0" encoding="UTF-8" ?>
- <capacity xmlns="http://www.cna.org/einstein"
    xmlns:xsi="http://www.w3.org/2001/XMLSchema-instance"
    xsi:schemaLocation="http://www.cna.org/einstein ../schema/capacity.xsd">
    <sensor-range>2</sensor-range>
    <move-range>5</move-range>
    <tremor>0.0</tremor>
```

```
        <frazzle>0.0</frazzle>
        <armor-strength>0.0</armor-strength>
        <camouflage>0.1</camouflage>
        <recovery-rate>0.5</recovery-rate>
        <mass>0.3</mass>
        <stamina>0.3</stamina>
        <memory>0.25</memory>
    </capacity>

<?xml version="1.0" encoding="UTF-8" ?>
- <einstein xmlns="http://www.cna.org/einstein"
      xmlns:xsi="http://www.w3.org/2001/XMLSchema-instance"
      xsi:schemaLocation="http://www.cna.org/einstein ../schema/engine.xsd">
      <description>This is a test file.</description>
    - <force color="red">
          <flag>0 0</flag>
    - <squad>
          <population>25</population>
          <weapon-assignments>25</weapon-assignments>
        - <initial-distribution>
              <coord>0 0</coord>
              <coord>10 15</coord>
          </initial-distribution>
        - <waypath>
            - <path-parameters>
                  <ordinality>1.0</ordinality>
                  <at>1.0</at>
                  <on>2.0</on>
                  <approaching>3.0</approaching>
                  <loop>false</loop>
              </path-parameters>
            - <path>
                  <coord>1 0</coord>
                  <coord>10 15</coord>
                  <coord>18 22</coord>
              </path>
          </waypath>
    ............
 </einstein>
```

Bibliography

[Abar96] Abarbanel, H. D. I., *Analysis of Observed Chaotic Data*, Springer-Verlag, 1996.

[Abou96] Aboufadel, A., "A Mathematician Catches a Baseball," *American Mathematical Monthly*, December 1996.

[Abu95] Abu-Mostafa, Yaser S., "Machines that learn from hints," *Scientific American*, Volume 272, No. 4, 64-71, April 1995.

[Adami98] Adami, C., *Introduction to Artificial Life*, Springer-Verlag, 1998.

[Adami98b] Adami, C., Richard K. Belew, Hiroaki Kitano, and Charles E. Taylor, *Artificial Life VI: Proceedings of the Sixth International Conference on Artificial Life*, MIT Press, 1998.

[Adams00] Adams, Thomas K., "The Real Military Revolution," *Parameters*, pages 54-65, Autumn 2000.

[Alam96] Alamgir, M., Jeon Kwon Cheon, and Dean J. Longo, *Chaotic Arms Control: Decision Making in the Post Cold War*, Maxwell AFB, AL: Air University, 1996.

[Albert] *Project Albert Consortium*: http://www.mcwl.usmc.mil/divisions/albert/index.

[Alberts97] Alberts, D. S. and T. Czerwinski, *Complexity, Global Politics and National Security*, National Defense University, 1997.

[Allen92] Allen, P., Situational Force Scoring: Accounting for Combined Arms Effects in Aggregate Combat Models, RAND, N-3423-NA, 1992.

[AmH94] *American Heritage CD-ROM Electronic Dictionary*, 3rd edition, Softkey International, 1994.

[Ancker92] Ancker, C. J., and A.V. Gafarian, *Modern Combat Models: A Critique of Their Foundations*, Operations Research Society of America, 1992.

[Ancker95] Ancker, C. J., "A Proposed Foundation for a Theory of Combat," *Naval Research Logistics*, Volume 42, No. 3, 311-344, April 1995.

[AnderJA88] Anderson, J. A. and E. Rosenfeld, editors, *Neurocomputing: Foundations of Research*, MIT Press, 1988.

[AnderLB95a] Anderson, L. B., "Attrition Formulas for Deterministic Models of Large-Scale Combats," *Naval Research Logistics*, Volume 42, No. 3, 345-374, April 1995.

[AnderLB95b] Anderson, L. B. and F. A. Miercort, "On Weapons Scores and Force Strengths," *Naval Research Logistics*, Volume 42, No. 3, 375-396, April 1995.

[AnderPW98] Anderson, P.W., K. J. Arrow and D. Pines, editors, *The Economy as an Evolving Complex System*, Addison-Wesley, 1988.

[AnderPW91] Anderson, P.W., "Is complexity physics? Is it science? What is it?," *Physics Today*, Volume 44, 9-10, 1991.

[AnderPW92] Anderson, P.W., "Complexity II: The Santa Fe Institute," *Physics Today*,

Volume 45, 9-10, 1992.

[Aragon01] Aragon, A.R, *Agent-Based Simulation of a Marine Infantry Squad in an Urban Environment*, Masters Thesis, Naval Postgraduate School, Monterey, California, September 2001.

[Arbib66] Arbib, M.A., "A simple self-reproducing universal automaton," *Infor. and Cont.*, Volume 9, 1966.

[Arkin98] Arkin, R.C., *Behavior-Based Robotics*, MIT Press, 1998.

[ArmyMS] *Army Model And Simulation Office*: http://www.amso.army.mil.

[Arquilla93] Arquilla, J. and D. Ronfeldt, "Cyberwar is coming!", *Comparative Strategy*, Volume 12, 141, 1993.

[ASCAPE] *ASCAPEProject*, Brooking Institute, http://www.brook.edu/dybdocroot/es/dynamics/models/ascape/.

[Ash00] Ash, D.W. and V.G. Dabija, *Planning for Real Time Event Response Management*, Prentice Hall, 2000.

[Athans83] Athans, M., "System theoretic challenges in military C3 systems," *Naval Research Reviews*, Volume XXXV, 18-28, 2/1983.

[Atkin74] Atkin, R. H., *Mathematical Structure in Human Affairs*, Crane, Russak and Company, 1974.

[Atman93] Atmanspacher, H., and G. J. Dalenoort, editors, *Inside versus Outside*, Springer-Verlag, 1993.

[Auyang98] Auyang, Sunny Y., *Foundations of Complex-system Theories: In Economics, Evolutionary Biology, and Statistical Physics*, Cambridge University Press, 1998.

[Axel97] Axelrod,R., "Advancing the Art of Simulation in the Social Sciences," pages 21-40 in *Simulating Social Phenomena*, edited by Conte, R., R. Hegselmann and P. Terna, Springer-Verlag, 1997.

[Axel97b] Axelrod,R., *The Complexity of Cooperation: Agent-Based Models of Competition and Cooperation*, Princeton University Press, 1997.

[Axel97c] Axelrod,R., "The dissemination of culture: a model with global polarization," *Journal of Conflict Resolution*, Volume 41, 1997.

[Axel99] Axelrod,R. and M.D. Cohen, *Harnessing Complexity: Organizational Implications of a Scientific Frontier*, The Free Press, 1999.

[Axtel96] Axtell, R., R.Axelrod, J.Epstein, and M.D.Cohen, "Aligning simulations models: a case study and results," *Computational and Mathematical Organization Theory*, Volume 1, 1996.

[Axtel00] Axtell, R., "Why Agents? On the Varied Motivations for Agent Computing in the Social Sciences." CSED Working Paper, No. 17, *Brookings Institute*, 2000.

[Axtel01a] Axtell, R., "Zipf Distribution of U.S. Firm Sizes," *Science*, Volume 293, September 2001.

[Axtel01b] Axtell, R., "Emergent Cities: A Microeconomic Explanation for Zipf's Law," *Computing in Economics and Finance*, Volume 154, 2001.

[Baas93] Baas, N.A., "Emergence, hierarchies, hyperstructures, and self-organization," *Proceedings of ISSS Conference*, International Society for the Systems Sciences, Louisville, Kentucky, July 1993.

[Baas94] Baas, N.A., "Emergence, hierarchies, and hyperstructures," pages 515-537 in [Lang94].

[Back93] Back, T. and Hans-Paul Schwefel, "An Overview of evolutionary algorithms for parameter optimization," *Evolutionary Computation*, Volume 1, No. 1,, 1-24 Spring 1993.

[Badii97] Badii, R. and A. Politi, *Complexity: Hierarchical Structures and Scaling in Physics*, Cambridge University Press, 1997.

[Bai84] Bai-lin, Hao, ed., *Chaos*, World Scientific, 1984.

[Bai87] Bai-lin, Hao, ed., *Directions in Chaos: Volume I*, World Scientific, 1987.

[Bai88] Bai-lin, Hao, ed., *Directions in Chaos: Volume II*, World Scientific, 1988.

[Baigent00] D. L. Baigent and M.K. Lauren, *Exploring the Recce-Counter Recce Scenario with ISAAC, Defense Operational technology Support Establishment*, DOTSE Report 171, NR 1349, July 2000.

[Bak87] Bak, P., C.Tang and K.Wiesenfeld, "Self-organized criticality: an explanation of 1/f noise," *Physical Review Letters*, Volume 59, 1987.

[Bak88] Bak, P., C.Tang and K.Wiesenfeld, "Self-organized criticality," *Physical Review A*, Volume 38, 1988.

[Bak89] Bak, P., K.Chen and M.Cruetz, "Self-organized criticality in the 'Game of Life'," *Nature*, Volume 342, 1989.

[Bak90] Bak, P., K.Chen and C.Tang, "A forest-fire model and some thoughts on turbulence," *Physics Letters*, Volume 147, 1990, 297-300.

[Bak91] Bak, P. and K. Chen, "Self-Organized Criticality," *Scientific American*, Volume 26, 46-53, January 1991.

[Bak93] Bak, P. and M. Paczuski, "Why nature is complex," *Physics World*, Volume 6, No. 12, 39-43, December 1993.

[Bak96] Bak, P., *How Nature Works: The Science of Self-Organized Criticality*, Springer-Verlag, 1996.

[Banks98] Banks, J., editor, *Handbook of Simulation: Principles, Methodology, Advances, Applications, and Practice*, Interscience, 1998.

[Bankes93] Bankes, S., "Exploratory modeling for policy analysis," *Operations Research*, Volume 41, No. 3, May-June 1993, 435-449.

[Bankes94a] Bankes, S. and James Gillogly, "Validation of Exploratory Modeling," *Proceedings of the Conference on High Performance Computing*, edited by Adrian M. Tentner and Rick L. Stevens, San Diego, CA: The Society for Computer Simulation, 1994.

[Bankes94b] Bankes, S., "On the Edge: Statistics and Computing," *Chance*, Winter, 1994.

[Bara02] Barabasi, Albert-Laszlo, *Linked: How Everything Is Connected to Everything Else and What It Means*, Perseus Publishing, 2002

[Barlow02] M. Barlow and A. Easton, "Crocodile: An Open Extensible Agent-Based Distillation Engine," *Information & Security*, Volume 8, Number 1, 2002.

[Barn88a] Barnsley, M. F. and A. Sloan, "A better way to compress images," Byte, January 1988, 215-223.

[Barn88b] Barnsley, M. F., *Fractals Everywhere*, Academic Press, 1988.

[Barr96] Barr, D.R. and E. Todd Sherill, "Entropy Modeling," pages 114-139 in [Woodc96].

[Barrett97] Barrett, C., "Simulation Science as it Relates to Data/Information Fusion and C2 Systems," Los Alamos, Briefing Slides, 1997.

[BarY00] Bar-Yam, Y., editor, *Unifying Themes in Complex Systems*, New England Complex Systems Institute Series on Complexity, Perseus Books, 2000.

[Bass94] Bassford, C., *Clausewitz In English: The Reception of Clausewitz in Britain and America 1815-1945,* New York: Oxford University Press, 1994.

[Bass95] Bassford, C. and Edward J.Villacres, "Reclaiming the Clausewitzean Trinity," *Parameters*, Autumn, 1995.

[Bass98] Bassford, C., "Nonlinearity in Marine Corps Doctrine," in F.G. Hoffman and Gary Horne, eds., *Maneuver Warfare Science*, United States Marine Corps Combat Development Command, 1998.

[Bates80] Bateson, Gregory, *Mind and Nature: A Necessary Unity*, Bantam Books, 1980 (reissued by Hampton Press, 2002)..

[Beau94] Beaumont, R., *War, Chaos, and History*, Wesport, Connecticut: Praeger, 1994.
[Beck99] Beckerman, Linda P., "The Non-Linear Dynamics of War," *Science Applications International Corporation*, 1999.
[Beckers94] Beckers, R., E. Holland and J. L. Deneubourg, "From local actions to global tasks: stigmergy and collective robotics," pages 181-189 in *Artificial Life IV: Proceedings of the Fourth International Workshop on the Synthesis and Simulation of Living Systems*, edited by R. Brooks and P. Maes, MIT Press, 1994.
[Bedau00] Bedau, M., John S. McCaskill, Norman H. Packard, and Steen Rasmussen, *Artificial Life VII: Proceedings of the Seventh International Conference on Artificial Life*, MIT Press, 2000.
[Belew91] Belew, R. K. and L.Booker, editors, *Genetic Algorithms in Search, Optimization, and Machine Learning: Proceedings of the Fourth International Conference on Genetic Algorithms*, Morgan Kauffman, San Francisco, 1991.
[Belew96] Belew, R. K. and M. Mitchell, editors, *Adaptive Individuals in Evolving Populations: Models and Algorithms*, Addison-Wesley, 1996.
[Bender00] Bender, E. A., *An Introduction to Mathematical Modeling*, Dover Publications, 2000.
[Benett76] Benettin, G., L. Galgani and J. M. Strelcyn, "Kolmogorov entropy and numerical experiments," Physical Review A, Volume 14, 2338, 1976.
[Benn86] Bennett, C.H.,"On the nature and origin of complexity in discrete, homogeneous, locally interacting systems," *Foundations of Physics*, Volume 16, 1986.
[Benn90] Bennett, C.H.,"Undecidable dynamics," *Nature*, Volume 346, 1990.
[Bent01] Bent, N., *Socrates User Manual* , Emergent Information Technologies Inc., 2001.
[Bentley02] Bentley, P.J. and D.W. Corne, editors, *Creative Evolutionary Systems*, Academic Press, 2002.
[Benzi81] Benzi, A. Sutera and A. Vulpiani, "The mechanism of Stochastic Resonance," *J. Phys. A: Math. Gen.*, Volume 453, 1981.
[Berk82] Berkelamp, E.R., J.H. Conway, and R.K. Guy, *Winning Ways for Your Mathematical Plays*, Volume 2, Academic Press, 1982, Chapter 25.
[Bert68] Bertalanffy, Ludwig von, *General System Theory: Foundations, Development, Applications*, Braziller, New York, 1968.
[Best95] Best, Lloyd A. and R. D. Sanders, "Using genetics-based learning methods to improve simulation model fidelity," *John Hopkins APL Technical Digest*, Volume 16, No. 2, 123-135, 1995.
[Beyer92] Beyerchen, A., "Clausewitz, Nonlinearity, and the Unpredictability of War," *International Security*, Volume 17, No. 3, Winter 1992/93, 59-90.
[Beyer97] Beyerchen, A., "Clausewitz, Nonlinearity, and the Importance of Imagery," in Alberts, David S. and Thomas J. Czerwinski, eds., *Complexity,Global Politics and National Security,* Washington, DC: National Defense University, June 1997.
[Bezd92] Bezdek, J. C. and S. K. Pal, editors, *Fuzzy Models for Pattern Recognition: Methods that Search for Structures in Data*, IEEE Press, 1992.
[Bianco90] Bianco and Read, 1990, US patent number 5,048,086.
[Bloom95] Bloom, H., *The Lucifer Principle*, The Atlantic Monthly Press, 1995.
[Bocc93] Boccara, N., E. Goles, S. Martinez, and P. Picco, editors, *Cellular Automata and Cooperative Systems, Conference Proceedings, Les Houches, France, June 22 - July 2, 1992*, NATO ASI Series Volume 396, Kluwer Academic Publishers, 1993.
[Bocc94] Boccara, N., O. Roblin and M. Roger, "Automata network predator-prey model with pursuit and evasion," *Physical Review E*, Volume 50, No. 6, 4531-4541, 1994.
[Bohm80] Bohm, D., *Wholeness and the Implicate Order*, Routledge and Kegan Paul, 1980.
[Bohm93] Bohm, D. and B.J.Hiley, *The Undivided Universe: An Ontological Interpretation*

of Quantum Theory, Routledge and Kegan Paul, 1993.

[Boll79] Bollobas, B., *Graph Theory*, Springer-Verlag, 1979.

[Bona99] Bonabeau, E., *Swarm Intelligence: From Natural to Artificial Systems, Santa Fe Institute Studies on the Sciences of Complexity*, Oxford University Press, 1999.

[Booch91] Booch, G., *Object Oriented Design*, Benjamin/Cummings Publishing Company, Inc., 1991.

[Bower95a] Bower, B., "Return of the group: people may have evolved to further collective as well as individual interests," *Science News*, Volume 148, 328-329, November 18, 1995.

[Bower95b] Bower, B., "Ultrasocial Darwinism: cultural groups may call the evolutionary shots in modern societies," *Science News*, Volume 148, 366-367, November 25, 1995.

[Bowm01] Bowman, M., Antonio M. Gheorghe Tecuci, "Ontology Development for Military Applications," paper presented at the *39th Annual ACM Southeast Conference*, March 2001: http://webster.cs.uga.edu/~jam/acm-se/review/referee/ michael. bowman. doc.

[Boyd87] Boyd, J., USAF (Ret.), *A Discourse on Winning and Losing*, August 1987. Many of Col Boyd's briefings are available on-line at: http://www.belisarius.com/.

[Braim95] Braiman, Y., J. F. Lindner and W. L. Ditto, *Nature*, 30 Nov 1995, 465.

[Brait84] Braitenberg, V., *Vehicles: Experiments in Synthetic Psychology*, MIT Press, 1984.

[Brand01] Brandstein, A., et. al., "High Performance Computing Support for Analysis of Entity-Based Simulations of Land Combat," in 2001 Application Briefs, Maui High Performance Computing Center, 2001: http://www.mhpcc.edu/research/appbriefs/ 2001/2001MHPCCAppBriefs.pdf.

[Brill56] Brillouin, L., *Science and Information Theory*, Academic Press, 1956.

[Brooks94] Brooks, R., "Elephants don't play chess," pages 3-15 in *Designing Autonomous Agents*, edited by P. Maes, MIT Press, 1994.

[Brooks99] Brooks, R., *Cambrian Intelligence: The Early History of the New AI*, MIT Press, 1999.

[Brown00] Brown, L.P., *Agent-Based Simulation as an Exploratory Tool in the Study of the Human Dimension of Combat*, Masters Thesis, Naval Postgraduate School, Monterey, California, March 2000.

[BrownM00] Brown, M., A. May and M.Slater, *Defeat Mechanisms: Military Organizations as Complex, Adaptive, Nonlinear Systems*, Science Applications International Center, SAIC-00-6960+SAC, March 10, 2000.

[Buch84] Buchanan, B.G. and E.H. Shorti, *Rule-Based Expert Systems: The MYCIN Experiments of the Stanford Heuristic Programming Project*, Addison-Wesley, 1984.

[Buck68] Buckley, W., editor, *Modern Systems Research for the Behavioral Scientist*, Aldine Publishing Company, 1968.

[Buls96] Bulsara, A. R. and Gammaitoni, L. "Tuning in to Noise," *Physics Today*, Volume 49 March 1996.

[Burks70] Burks, A.W., editor, *Essays on Cellular Automata*, University of Illinois Press, 1970.

[Byl89] Byl, John, "Self-reproduction in small cellular automata," *Physica D*, Volume 34, 1989.

[Caian87] Caianiello, E. R. and M. A. Aizerman, editors, *Topics in the General Theory of Structures*, D. Reidel Publishing Company, 1987.

[Camaz01] Camazine, S., J.-L. Deneubourg, N.R. Franks, J. Sneyd, G. Theraulaz and E. Bonabeau, *Self-Organization in Biological Systems*, Princeton University Press, 2001.

[Camp90] Campaigning, U. S. Marine Corps FMFM 1-1, January 1990.

[Capra86] Capra, F., "The concept of paradigm and paradigm shift," *ReVision*, Volume 9, 1986.

[Capra97] Capra, F., *The Web of Life: A New Understanding of Living Systems*, Doubleday, 1997.

[Card99] Card, S., et.al., *Information Visualization*, Morgan Kauffman, 1999.

[Carian92] Cariani, P., "Emergence and artificial life," pages 775-797 in [Lang92].

[Carl90] Carlson, J., J.Chayes, E.Grannan and G.Swindle, "Self-Organized criticality in sandpiles: nature of the critical phenomenon," *Phys. Rev. A*, Volume 42, 1990.

[Caroll93] Caroll, Thomas L. and L. M. Pecora, "Communicating with Chaos," Naval Research Reviews, Volume XLV, 4-11, March/1993.

[Carter93] Carter, M. E., C. Dean, C. Pollatz, A. Brink, D. Canody, P. Barry, T. Wallace, J. Dockery, and D. Littman, "Architecture for intelligent virtual agents that employ multiple learning strategies: or smart tanks avoid black holes," pages 263-270 in *Proceedings of the 3rd Conference on Computer Generated Forces and Behavioral Representation*, March 17-19, 1993, Orlando, Florida, Institute for Simulation and Training, Technical Report IST-TR-93-07, 1993.

[Carv89] Carvalho-Rodrigues, F., "A proposed entropy measure for assessing combat degradation," *Jour. Opl. Res. Soc.* (UK), Volume 40, No. 8, 1989, 789-793.

[Casd89] Casdagli, M., "Nonlinear prediction of chaotic time series," *Physica D*, Volume 35, 1989.

[Casd92] Casdagli, M., "Nonlinear forecasting, chaos and statistics," pages 131-152 in *Modeling Complex Phenomena*, edited by Lui Lam and V. Naroditsky, Springer-Verlag, 1992

[CAST] CASTFOREM, US Army TRADOC Analysis Center, Technical Operations Directorate, Ft. Leavenworth, KS, http://www.msrr.army.mil/.

[Casti79] Casti, J., *Connectivity, Complexity and Catastrophe in Large Scale Systems*, John Wiley and Sons, 1979.

[Casti88] Casti, J., *Alternate Realities: Mathematical Models of Nature and Man*, John Wiley and Sons, 1988.

[Casti92] Casti, J., *Reality Rules, Volumes I and II*, John Wiley and Sons, 1992.

[Casti94] Casti, J., *Complexification: Explaining a Paradoxical World Through the Science of Surprise*, HarperCollins, 1994.

[Casti95] Casti, J. and A. Karlqvist, editors, *Cooperation and Conflict in General Evolutionary Processes*, John Wiley and Sons, Inc., 1995.

[Casti96] Casti, J., *Would-Be Worlds: How Simulation is Changing the Frontiers of Science*, John Wiley & Sons, 1996.

[Cay57] Cayley, A, "On the theory of analytical forms called trees," *Phil. Mag.*, Volume 13, 1857.

[Cec88] Cecatto, H.A. and B.A.Huberman, "The complexity of hierarchical systems," *Physica Scripta*, Volume 37, 1988.

[Chait75] Chaitin, G.J., "Randomness and mathematical proof," *Scientific American*, Volume 232, 1975.

[Chait87] Chaitin, G.J., *Information, Randomness and Incompleteness*, World Scientific, 1987.

[Chal94] Chaliand, G., editor, *The Art of War in World History: From Antiquity to the Nuclear Age*, University of California Press, 1994.

[Chamb95] Chambers, L., editor, *Practical Handbook of Genetic Algorithms: Applications*, CRC Press, 1995.

[Chand74]Chandler, David G., *The Art of Warfare on Land*, Penguin Books, 1974.

[Chand98]Chandler, David G., *Atlas of Military Strategy: The Art, Theory and Practice of War, 1618-1878*, Arms and Armour, 1998.

[Chase02] Chase, J. V., "A Mathematical Investigation of the Effect of Superiority in Combats Upon the Sea," 1902 (Reprinted in Fiske, B.A., *The Navy as a Fighting Machine*, Annapolis, MD: U.S. Naval Institute Press, 1994).

[Chen96] Chen, C. H., editor, *Fuzzy Logic and Neural Network Handbook*, McGraw-Hill, 1996.

[ChenG98] Chen, G. and X. Dong, *From Chaos to Order: Methodologies, Perspectives and Applications*, World Scientific, 1998.

[Ching02] Ching, W.S., *An Exploratory Analysis on the Effects of Human Factors on Combat Outcomes*, Masters Thesis, Naval Postgraduate School, Monterey, California, March 2002.

[Cliff94] Cliff , D., Philip Husbands, Jean-Arcady Meyer, and Stewart W. Wilson, *From Animals to Animats 3: Proceedings of the Third International Conference on Simulation of Adpative Behavior*, MIT Press, 1994.

[Codd70] Codd, E.F., *Cellular Automata*, University of Illinois Press, 1970.

[Combs99] Combs, W.E., *The Fuzzy Systems Handbook*, Academic Press, 1999.

[Comm89] *Communications*, U. S. Marine Corps FMFM 3-30, April 1989.

[Con88] Conolly, B. and J. G. Pierce, *Information Mechanics: Transformation of Information in Management, Command, Control and Communications*, Ellis Horwood Limited, 1988.

[Conte97] Conte, R., R. Hegselmann and P. Terna, editors, *Simulating Social Phenomena*, Springer-Verlag, 1997.

[CoopC93] Cooper, C., "Complexity in C3I systems," in *Complex Systems: From Biology to Computation*, edited by D. G. Green and T. J. Bossomaier, Amsterdam: IOS Press, 1993.

[CoopJ95] Cooper, J., "Dominant battlespace awareness and future warfare," pages 103-120 in *Dominant Battlespace Knowledge: The Winning Edge*, edited by S. Johnson and M. Libicki, National Defense University Press, 1995.

[Cov95] Coveney, P. and R. Highfield, *Frontiers of Complexity: The Search for Order in a Chaotic World*, Fawcett Columbine, 1995.

[Cowan94] Cowan, G.A., D.Pines and D.Meltzer, *Complexity: Metaphors, Models and Reality*, Addison-Wesley, 1994.

[Cox02] Cox, G., *EINSTein visits the Persian Gulf (via Monterey, CA): A naval requirements war "gamelet" held at the Naval Postgraduate School, 11-15 Feb, 2002*, Center for Naval Analyses, Annotated Brief, March 2002.

[Crich02] Crichton, Michael, *Prey*, HarperCollins, 2002.

[Crow94] Crowston, K., "Evolving novel organizational forms, pages 19-38 in *Computational Organization Theory*, edited by K. M. Carley and M. J. Prietula, Lawrence Erlbaum: Hinsdale, N. J., 1994.

[Crutch87] Crutchfield, J. P., J. D. Farmer, N. H. Packard, and R. S. Shaw, "Chaos," *Scientific American*, 46-57, 1987.

[Cvit84] Cvitanovic, P., editor, *Universality in Chaos*, Adam Hilger, 1984.

[Czer96] Czerwinski, T., "Command and Control at the Crossroads," *Parameters*, Autumn 1996.

[Czer98] Czerwinski, T., *Coping With the Bounds: Speculations on Nonlinearity in Military Affairs*, National Defense University, 1998.

[DavisL91] Davis, L., editor, *Handbook of Genetic Algorithms*, von Nostrand Reinhold, 1991.

[DavisM83] Davis, M.D. and E.J. Weynker, *Computability, Complexity, and Languages*,

Academic Press, 1983.

[DavisP95a] Davis, P. K., "Distributed interactive simulation in the evaluation of DoD warfare modeling and simulation," *Proceedings of the IEEE*, Volume 83, No. 8, 1138-1155, August 1995.

[DavisP95b] Davis, P. K., *Applying Artificial Intelligence Techniques to Strategic-Level Gaming and Simulation*, Santa Monica, CA- Rand, 1988.

[DavisP95b] Davis, P. K., *Aggregation, Disaggregation, and the 3:1 Rule in Ground Combat*, RAND, MR-638-AF/A/OSD, 1995.

[Deal92] Deal, Jr., F.C., "Using conditional entropy to evaluate a correlator/tracker," *John Hopkins APL Technical Digest*, Volume 13, No. 2, 286-290, 1992.

[DeAng92] DeAngelis, D. L. and L. J. Gross, editors, *Individual-based Models and Approaches in Ecology: Populations, Communities and Ecosystems*, Chapman and Hall, 1992.

[Deco01] Deco, G. and B. Schurmann, *Information Dynamics: Foundations and Applications*, Springer-Verlag, 2001.

[Deitch62] Deitchman, S. J., "A Lanchester model of guerrilla warfare," *Operations Research*, Volume 10, 818-827, November/December 1962.

[DeLanda91] De Landa, M., *War in the Age of Intelligent Machines*, New York: Zone Books, 1991.

[DennE82] Denning, E., *Cryptography and Data Security*, Addison-Wesley, 1982

[DennP90] Denning, P. J., "Modeling Reality," *American Scientist*, November-December 1990, 495-498.

[Dent02] Dent, Eric B. & Cameron G. Holt., 11CAS in War, Bureaucratic Machine in Peace: The US Air Force Example," *Emergence*, Vol.3, No.3, 2002.

[Deut97] Deutsch, David, *The Fabric of Reality*, Penguin, 1997

[Devaney89] Devaney, R., *An Introduction to Chaotic Dynamical Systems*, Addison-Wesley, 1989.

[Dewar91] Dewar, J. A., J. J. Gillogly and M. L. Juncosa, "Non-Monoticity, Chaos, and Combat Models," RAND , R-3995-RC, 1991.

[Dewd89] Dewdney, A.K., "Computer recreations: Two dimensional Turing machines and turmites make tracks on a plane," *Scientific American*, September, 1989.

[DHum86] d'Humieres, D. and P.Lallemand, "Lattice gas automata for fluid mechanics," *Physica*, Volume 140A, 1986, 326-335.

[Ditto93] Ditto, William L. and Louis M. Pecora, "Mastering Chaos," *Scientific American*, August 1993.

[Dock79] Dockery, J. T., "The Use of Fuzzy Sets in the Analysis of Military Command," pages 355-394 in *Decision Information*, edited by C. P. Tsokos and R. M. Thrall, Academic Press, 1979.

[Dock88] Dockery, J. T. and R. S. Santoro, "Lanchester Revisited: Progress in Modeling C2 in Combat," *Signal*, July, 1988, 41-50.

[Dock93a] Dockery, J. T. and A. E. R. Woodcock, "No New Mathematics! No New C2 Theory!," pages 63-96 in *Towards a Science of Command, Control, and Communications*, edited by C. Jones, American Institute of Aeronautics and Astronautics, Inc., 1993.

[Dock93b] Dockery, J. T. and A. E. R. Woodcock, *The Military Landscape: Mathematical Models of Combat*, Cambridge, England: Woodhead Publishing Limited, 1993.

[DoD95] Department of Defense, *Modeling and Simulation Master Plan*, October 1995; available on-line at http://www.dmso.mil/briefs/msdocs/policy/msmp.pdf.

[Dorigo98] Dorigo, M. and M. Colombetti, *Robot Shaping: An Experiment in Behavior Engineering*, MIT Press, 1998.

[Dotter92] Dotterway, Kristen Ann,. *Systematic Analysis of Complex Dynamic Systems: The Case of the USS Vincennes*, Monterey, CA: Naval Postgraduate School, 1992.

[Dres74] Dresden, M., "Reflections on fundamentality and complexity," in *Physical Reality and Mathematical Description*, edited by Enz and Mehra, D.Reidel Publishing Company, Dordrecht-Holland, 1974.

[Dunn82] Dunnigan, J. F., *How to Make War: A Comprehensive Guide to Modern Warfare*, William Morrow and Company, Inc., 1982.

[Dunn92] Dunnigan, J. F., *The Complete Wargames Handbook*, Quill William Morrow, 1992.

[Dup85] Dupuy, T. N., *Numbers, Predictions, and War: Using History to Evaluate Combat Factors and Predict The Outcome of Battles*, Fairfax Virginia: Hero Books, 1985.

[Dup87] Dupuy, T. N., *Understanding War: History and Theory of Combat*, Paragon House Publishers, 1987.

[Dup90] Dupuy, T. N., *Attrition: Forecasting Battle Casualties and Equipment Loses in Modern War*, Fairfax Virginia: Hero Books, 1990.

[Durh97] Durham, Maj Susan E., *Chaos Theory for the Practical Military Mind*, Air Command and Staff College, March 1997.

[Durkin94] Durkin, *Expert Systems: Design and Development*, Prentice Hall, 1994.

[Eche95] Echevarria, Antulio, J., "Clausewitz: toward a theory of applied strategy," *Defense Analysis*, Volume 11, No. 3, 229-240, 1995.

[Eche97a] Echevarria, Antulio, J., "Optimizing Chaos on the Nonlinear Battlefield," *Military Review*, September-October 1997.

[Eche97b] Echevarria, Antulio, J., "Dynamic Inter-Dimensionality: A Revolution in Military Theory," *Joint ForceQuarterly*, Spring 1997.

[ECHO] ECHO, Santa Fe Institute, http://www.santafe.edu/projects/echo/echo.html.

[Edmonds97] Edmonds, B., *Hypertext Bibliography of Measures of Complexity*, URL address http://bruce.edmonds.name/combib/, last updated 1997.

[Edwards00] Edwards, S. J. A., *Swarming on the Battlefield: Past, Present, and Future*, RAND Corporation, National Security Research Division, MR-1100-OSD, 2000.

[ELAN] ELAN, TRADOC Analysis Center-White Sands Missile Range.

[Emmeche91] Emmeche, C. and J. Hoffmeyer, "From language to nature: the semiotic metaphor in biology," Semiotica, Volume 84, No. 1/2, 1991, 1-42.

[Emmeche94] Emmeche, C., *The Garden in the Machine: The Emerging Science of Artificial Life*, Princeton University Press, 1994.

[Epstein92a] Epstein, J. M., "On the mathematical biology of arms races, wars, and revolutions," pages 425-436 in *1991 Lectures in Complex Systems*, edited by L. Nadel and D. Stein, Addison-Wesley, 1992.

[Epstein92b] Epstein, J. M., "The adaptive dynamic model of combat," pages 437-459 in *1991 Lectures in Complex Systems*, edited by L. Nadel and D. Stein, Addison-Wesley, 1992.

[Epstein96] Epstein, J. M. and R. Axtell, *Growing Artificial Societies: Social Science From the Bottom Up*, MIT Press, 1996.

[Epstein97] Epstein, J. M., *Nonlinear Dynamics, Mathematical Biology, and Social Science*, Perseus Publishing, 1997.

[Epstein99] Epstein, J. M., "Agent-Based Computational Models and Generative Social Science," *Complexity*, Volume 4, No. 5, June 1999, 41-60.

[Epstein00] Epstein, J. M., "Agent-Based Computational Models and Generative Social Science," *Slides,* 2000: http://www2.kke.co.jp/event/gas/files/EPSTEIN.pdf.

[Epstein01] Epstein, J. M., J.D. Steinbruner, and M.T. Parker, "Modeling Civil Violence: An Agent-Based Computational Approach," Working Paper Number 20, *Center on*

Social and Economic Dynamics, Brookings Institute, 2001.

[Ercetin01] Ercetin, A., *Operational-Level Naval Planning Using Agent-Based Simulation*, Masters Thesis, Naval Postgraduate School, Monterey, California, March 2001.

[Eub89] Eubank, S. and D. Farmer, "An introduction to chaos and randomness," pages 75-190 in *1989 Lectures in Complex Systems: The Proceedings of the 1989 Complex Systems Summer School, Santa Fe, New Mexico, June 1989*, edited by E. Jen, Addison-Wesley, 1990.

[Fain75] Fain, J., "The Lanchester Equations and Historical Warfare: An Analysis of Sixty World War II Land Engagements," in *Proceedings of the 34th Military Operations Research Symposium*, Alexandria, Virginia: Military Operations Research Society, 1975.

[Farmer84] Farmer, J. D., T. Toffoli, and S. Wolfram, eds., *Cellular Automata*, North-Holland, 1984.

[Farmer88] Farmer, J. D. and J. J. Sidorowich, "Predicting chaotic dynamics," pages 265-292 in *Dynamic Paterns in Complex Systems*, edited by J. A. S. Kelso, A. J. Mandell and M. F. Shlesinger, World Scientific, 1988.

[Feig78] Feigenbaum, M.J., "Quantitative universality for a class of nonlinear transformations," *Jour. Stat. Phy.*, Volume 19, 1978.

[Feig79] Feigenbaum, M.J., "The universal metric properties of nonlinear transformations," *Jour. Stat. Phy.*, Volume 21, 1979.

[Feig80] Feigenbaum, M.J., "Universal behavior in nonlinear systems," *Los Alamos Science*, Volume 1, 1980.

[Ferber99] Ferber, J., *Multi-Agent Systems: An Introduction to Distributed Artificial Intelligence*, Addison-Wesley, 1999.

[Flake98] Flake, G.W., *The Computational Beauty of Nature: Computer Explorations of Fractals, Chaos, Complex Systems, and Adaptation*, MIT Press, 1998.

[Flood88] Flood, Robert L. and Ewart R. Carson, *Dealing With Complexity: An Introduction to the Theory and Application of Systems Science*, New York: Plenum, 1988.

[Fogel93] Fogel, D.B., "Evolving behaviors in the iterated prisoner's dilemma," *Evolutionary Computation*, Volume 1, No. 1, 77-97, Spring 1993.

[Forrest90] Forrest , S., editor, *Emergent Computation: Self-Organizing, Collective, and Cooperative Phenomena in Natural and Artificial Computing Networks*, MIT Press, Cambridge, Massachusetts, 1990.

[Forrest91] Forrest , S. and G. Mayer-Kress, "Genetic algorithms, nonlinear systems, and models of international security," pages 166-185 in *Handbook of Genetic Algorithms*, edited by L. Davis, von Nostrand Reinhold, 1991.

[Fran92] Franceschetti, D.R., B.W.Campbell, J.W. Hamneken, "Hamming nets, Ising sets, cellular automata, neural nets and random walks," *American Journal of Physics*, Volume 61, 1992, 50-53.

[Fraw92] Frawley, William J., Gregory Piatetsky-Shapiro, and Christopher J. Matheus, Knowledge Discovery in Databases: An Overview, *AAAI*, 57-70, Fall 1992.

[Fried92] Friedrich, R. and A. Wunderlin, editors, *Evolution of Dynamical Structures in Complex Systems*, Springer-Verlag, 1992.

[Gadd94] Gaddis, John L., "Chaos, Complexity, and Contemporary History," *Think Piece Series No. 30*, Athens, OH: Contemporary History Institute, May 1994.

[Gall94] Gallagher, J. J., *Combat Leader's Field Guide*, 11th Edition, Stackpole Books, 1994.

[GardJ70] Gardner, James N. "Mastering Chaos At History's Frontier: The Geopolitics of Complexity," *Complexity*, Vol. 3, No. 2, 1997.

[Gard70] Gardner, M., "Mathematical Games: The Fantastic Combinations of John Conway's New Solitaire Game Life," *Scientific American*, Volume 223, No. 4, 120-123, 1970.

[Garey79] Garey, M. and D. S. Johnson, *Computers and Intractability: A Guide to the Theory of NP-Completeness*, W. H. Freeman and Company, 1979.

[Garre99] Garreau, J., "Point Men For A Revolution: Can the Marines Survive a Shift From Hierarchies to Networks?," *Washington Post*, March 6, 1999.

[Garri93] Garrido, M. S. and R.V.Mendes, editors, *Complexity in Physics and Technology*, World Scientific, 1993.

[GellM88] Gell-Mann, M., "Simplicity and complexity in the description of nature," *Engineering and Science*, Volume 3, 1988.

[GellM94] Gell-Mann, M., *The Quark and the Jaguar: Adventures in the Simple and the Complex*, W.H.Freeman and Company, 1994.

[GellM97] Gell-Mann, M., "The Simple and the Complex," in Alberts, David S. and Thomas J. Czerwinski, eds., *Complexity, Global Politics and National Security,* Washington, DC: National Defense University, June 1997.

[Gerber97] Gerber, David K., *Adaptive Command and Control of Theater Air Power*, Maxwell AFB, AL: School of Advanced Airpower Studies, 1997.

[Gerh89] Gerhardt, M. and H. Schuster, "A cellular automaton describing the formation of spatially ordered structures in chemical systems," *Physica*, Volume 36D, 1989, 209-221.

[Gilb95] Gilbert, N. and R. Conte, editors, *Artificial Societies: The Computer Simulation of Social Life*, UCL Press, 1995.

[Gilb99] Gilbert, N. and K. G. Troitzsch, *Simulation for the Social Scientist*, Open University Press, 1999.

[Gill01] Gill, A., *Impact of Reconnaissance on Mission Success*, Briefing, Defense Science and Technology Organization, Australia, 2001.

[Gilm81] Gilmore, R., *Catastrophe Theory for Scientists and Engineers*, John Wiley and Sons, 1981.

[Gleick87] Gleick, J., *Chaos: Making a New Science*, Viking Penguin, Inc., 1987.

[Glenn96] James, Maj Glenn E, *Chaos Theory: The Essentials for Military Applications*, Naval War College: Newport Paper Number Ten, October 1996.

[Godel31] Godel, Kurt, "Uber formal unentscheidbare Satze der Principia Mathematica und verwandter Systeme," *Monats. Math. Phy.*, Volume 38, 1931.

[Goldb89] Goldberg, D. E., *Genetic Algorithms in Search, Optimization, and Machine Learning*, Addison-Wesley, 1989.

[Gong95] Gongora, T., M. Fortmann and S. Lefebvre, "Modern land warfare doctrines and non-offensive defense: an interesting idea," Defense Analysis, Volume 11, No. 1, 47-64, April 1995.

[Gord99] Gordan, D., Ants at Work: How An Insect Society Is Organized, Free Press, 1999.

[Gore96] Gore, J., Chaos, *Complexity, and the Military,* Washington, DC: National War College, 1996 (available at http://www.ndu.edu/library/n1/96-E-61.pdf).

[Gorm00] Gorman, G. Scott, *Endgame in the Pacific Complexity, Strategy, and the B-29*, Fairchild Paper, Air University Press, Maxwell Air Force Base, Alabama, 2000: https://research.au.af.mil/papers/special_collection/Fairchild/Gorman.pdf.

[Grand00] Grand, S., *Creation: Life and How to Make it*, Weidenfeld & Nicolson, London, 2000.

[Grass83] Grassberger, P. and I.Procaccia, "Measuring the strangeness of strange attractors," *Physica D*, Volume 9, 1983.

[Grass86] Grassberger, P., "Toward a quantitative theory of self-generated complexity,"

Int. Jour. of Theo. Phy., Volume 25, 1986.

[Green90] Green, D. G., "Syntactic modelling and simulation," *Simulation*, Volume 56, No. 6, 1990, 281-286.

[Grefen91] Grefenstette, J. J., "Strategy acquisition with genetic algorithms," pages 186-201 in *Handbook of Genetic Algorithms*, edited by L. Davis, von Nostrand Reinhold, 1991.

[Gross89] Grossman, S. and G. Mayer-Kress, "The Role of Chaotic Dynamics in Arms Race Models," *Nature*, 337, 701-704, 1989.

[Gruber93] Gruber, T. R., "A translation approach to portable ontology specifications," *Knowledge Acquisition*, Volume 5, No. 2, 1993.

[Gumer69] Gumerman, G.J. and T. A Kohler, "Creating alternative cultural histories in the prehistoric southwest: agent-based modeling in archaeology," *Santa Fe Institute*, 96-03-007, 1996.

[Gupta93] Gupta, R., *Defense Positioning and Geometry: Rules for a World with Low Force Levels*, The Brookings Institute, 1993.

[Guth95] Guthrie, Samuel A., *Knowledge-Based Operations: The "So What" of Information Warfare,* Fort Leavenworth, KS: U.S. Army Command and General Staff College, School of Advanced Military Studies, 1995.

[Guto90] Gutowitz, H. A., editor, *Cellular Automata: Theory and Experiment*, Elsevier Science Publishers, 1990.

[Guto93] Gutowitz, H. A., "Cryptography with dynamical systems," pages 237-274 in *Cellular Automata and Cooperative Systems*, edited by N. Boccara, E. Goles, S. Martinez, and P. Picco, NATO ASI Series Volume 396, Kluwer Academic Publishers, 1993.

[Haken83] Haken, H., *Advanced Synergetics: Instability Hierarchies of Self-Organizing Systems and Devices,* Springer-Verlag, 1983.

[Hall01] Hallam, B., Dario Floreano, John Hallam, Gillian Hayes, and Jean-Arcady Meyer, *From Animals to Animats 7: Proceedings of the Seventh International Conference on Simulation of Adaptive Behavior*, MIT Press, 2002.

[Hamm01] Hammond, G.T., *The Mind of War: John Boyd and American Security*, Smithsonian Institution Press, 2001.

[Hand01] Handel, M.I., *Masters of War: Classical Strategic Thought*, Third Edition, Frank Class Publishers, 2001.

[Har69] Harary, F., *Graph Theory*, Addison-Wesley, 1969.

[Harned95] Harned, Glenn M., *The Complexity of War: The Application of Nonlinear Science to Military Science,* Quantico, VA: Marine Corps War College, 1995.

[Hart91] Hart, B. H. Liddell, *Strategy*, Second revised edition, Meridian, 1991

[Hartley95] Hartley III, R.S. and R. L. Helmbold, "Validating Lanchester's square law and other attrition models," Naval Research Logistics, Volume 42, May, 609-633, 1995.

[Hart67] Hartman, R. S., *The Structure of Value: Foundations of Scientific Axiology*, Southern Illinois University Press, 1967.

[Harvey94] Harvey, D. L. and M. H. Reed, "The evolution of dissipative social systems," *Journal of Social and Evolutionary Systems*, Volume 17, No. 4, 371-411, 1994.

[Hass88] Hasslacher, B., "Discrete Fluids," *Los Alamos Science*, Volume 15, 1988.

[Hedge93] Hedgepeth, W. O., "The Science of Complexity for Military Operations Research," *Phalanx,* Volume 26, No. 1, 1993, 25-26.

[Helm65] Helmbold, R. L., "A modification of Lanchester's equations," *Operations Research*, Volume 13, 857-859, September/October 1965.

[Hencke98] Hencke, Richard B., *An Agent-Based Approach to Analyzing Information and Coordination in Combat, Thesis*, Naval Postgraduate School, Monterey, California,

September 1998.

[Hend85] Henderson, D., *Cohesion: The Human Element in Combat*, National Defense University Press, 1985.

[Henry98] Henry, R. and C. Edward Peartree, "Military Theory and Information Warfare," *Parameters*, Autumn 1998.

[Hent83] Hentschel, H.G.E. and I.Procaccia, "The infinite number of generalized dimensions of fractals and strange attractors," *Physica D*, Volume 8, 1983.

[Hertz91] Hertz, J., A. Krogh and R. G. Palmer, *Introduction to the theory of neural computation*, Addison-Wesley, 1991.

[Hilb94] Hilborn, R. C., *Chaos and Nonlinear Dynamics: An Introduction for Scientists and Engineers*, Oxford University Press, 1994.

[Hill03] Hill, R., G.A. McIntyre, T.R.Tighe, and R.K.Bullock, "Some experiments with agent-based combat models," *Military Operations Research*, Volume 8, No. 3, 2003.

[Hilleb94] Hillebrand, E. and J. Stender, editors, *Many-Agent Simulation and Artificial Life*, IOS Press, 1994.

[Hilles93a] Hillestad, R. J. and M. L. Juncosa, "Cutting Some Trees to See the Forest: On Aggregation and Disaggregation in Combat Models," RAND, MR-189-ARPA, 1993.

[Hilles93b] Hillestad, R. J., J. G. Owen and D. Blumenthal, "Experiments in Variable-Resolution Combat Modeling," RAND, N-3631-DARPA, 1993.

[Hillis90] Hillis, W. D., "Co-evolving parasites improve simulated evolution as an optimization procedure," *Physica D*, Volume 42, 1990, 228-234.

[Hoeber81] Hoeber, F. P., *Military Applications of Modeling: Selected Case Studies*, Gordon and Breach Science Publishers, 1981.

[Hofb88] Hofbauer, J. and K. Sigmund, *Evolutionary Games and Population Dynamics*, Cambridge University Press, 1988.

[Hoff98] Hoffman, F. G. and G. Horne, editors, *Maneuver Warfare Science*, United States Marine Corps, Marine Corps Combat Development Command, Qunatico, VA, 1998.

[Holl89] Holland, John H., Lashon B. Booker, and David E. Goldberg, "Classifier systems and genetic algorithms," *Artificial Intelligence*, 40:235–282, 1989.

[Holl92a] Holland, John H., *Adaptation in Natural and Artificial Systems: An Introductory Analysis with Applications to Biology, Control and Artificial Intelligence*, Second Edition, MIT Press, 1992.

[Holl92b] Holland, John H., "Genetic Algorithms," *Scientific American*, Volume 278, No. 1, 66-72, July, 1992.

[Holl95] Holland, John H., *Hidden Order: How Adaptation Builds Complexity*, Addison-Wesley Publishing Company, 1995.

[Holl99] Holland, John H., *Emergence: From Chaos to Order*, Helix Books, 1999.

[Hooker93] Hooker Jr., Richard D., editor, *Maneuver Warfare: An Anthology*, Presidio, 1993.

[Hopc79] Hopcroft, J. E. and J. D. Ullman, *Introduction to Automata Theory, Language, and Computation*, Addison-Wesley, 1979.

[Hass88] Hasslacher, B., "Discrete Fluids," *Los Alamos Science*, Volume 15, 1988.

[HPCS] *High Performance Computer Support For Analysis Of Entity-Based Simulations Of Land Combat*, Maui High Performance Super Computer: http://pipeline.mhpcc.edu/.

[Huber75] Huber, Reiner K., L. F. Jones and E. Reine, *Military Strategy and Tactics: Computer Modeling of Land Warfare Problems*, Plenum Press, 1975.

[HuberB85] Huberman, B.A. and T. Hogg, "Attractors on finite sets: the dissipative dynamics of computing structures," *Phy. Rev. A*, Volume 32, 1985.

[HuberB85b] Huberman, B.A., "Dynamics of computing structures," *Physica Scripta*, Volume T9, 1985.

[HuberB86] Huberman, B.A. and T. Hogg, "Complexity and adaptation," *Physica D*, Volume 22, 1986.

[Hubler92] Hubler, A., "Modeling and control of complex systems: paradigms and applications," pages 5-65 in *Modeling Complex Phenomena*, edited by L. Lam and V. Naroditsky, Springer-Verlag, 1992.

[Hughes84] Hughes Jr., W. P., editor, *Military Modeling*, The Military Operations Research Society, 1984.

[Hughes94] Hughes Jr., W. P., "Uncertainty in Combat," *Military Operations Research*, Summer 1994.

[Hunt88] Hunt, Carl W., "Uncertainty Factor Drives New Approach to Building Simulations," *Signal*, October 1998.

[Hunt01] Hunt, Carl W., *Agent-Based Evidence Marshalling: Agent-Based Creative Processes for Discovering and Forming Emergent Scenarios and Hypotheses*, Ph.D. Thesis,George Mason University, 2001.

[HunWar] *Marine Corps News Release 567*, Division of Public Affairs, United States Marine Corps, Washington, DC; available on line at: http://www.fas.org/irp/ news/1997 /usmc_970822c.htm

[Ilach96a] Ilachinski, A., *Land Warfare and Complexity, Part I: Mathematical Background and Technical Sourcebook*, Center for Naval Analyses Information Manual CIM-461, March 1996; can be downloaded from the WWW at URL address http://www.cna.org / isaac/lw1.pdf..

[Ilach96b] Ilachinski, A., *Land Warfare and Complexity, Part II: An Assessment of the Applicability of Nonlinear Dynamics and Complex Systems Theory to the Study of Land Warfare*, CNA, CRM-68, 1996; can be downloaded from the WWW at URL address http://www.cna.org/isaac/lwpart2.pdf..

[Ilach96c] Ilachinski, A., *A Mobile Cellular Automata Approach to Land Combat*, Center for Naval Analyses Information Manual CIM-482, 1996.

[Ilach97a] Ilachinski, A., *Irreducible Semi-Autonomous Adaptive Combat (ISAAC): An Artificial Life Approach to Land Warfare*, CNA Research Memorandum CRM 97-61, 1997; can be downloaded from the WWW at URL address http://www.cna.org/isaac /crm9761.htm.

[Ilach97b] Ilachinski, A., "An Artificial Life Approach to Land Warfare," paper presented at Ernst and Young's *Embracing Complexity Conference* held in Boston, MA, September 1997: http://www.cbi.cgey.com/events/pubconf/1997-04-5/proceedings/ irreduciblesemi.pdf.

[Ilach99a] Ilachinski, A., *Enhanced ISAAC Neural Simulation Toolkit (EINSTein), User's Guide*, CNA Information Memorandum CIM 610.10, November, 1999; available online, in Adobe's Acrobat format, at WWW URL address http://www.cna.org/isaac/ einstein_users_guide_beta.pdf.

[Ilach99b] Ilachinski, A., "Case Study in "Experimental Complexity": An Artificial-Life Approach to Modeling Warfare," banquet talk at the *5th Experimental Chaos Conference*, held in Orlando, Florida, edited by Mingzhou Ding, William L Ditto, Louis M Pecora and Mark L Spano, World Scientific Press, 1999.

[Ilach00a] Ilachinski, A., *EINSTein: An Artificial Life Laboratory for Exploring Self Organized Emergence in Land Combat*, CNA Research Memorandum CRM D239.A1, September 2000.

[Ilach00b] Ilachinski, A., "Irreducible Semi-Autonomous Adaptive Combat (ISAAC): An Artificial-Life Approach to Land Warfare," *Military Operations Research*, Volume 5, Number 3, 2000.

[Ilach01a] Ilachinski, A., *EINSTein: Version 1.0.0.4β*, Center for Naval Analyses, Multimedia CD-ROM, D0003394.A1, February 2001.

[Ilach01b] Ilachinski, A., *Cellular Automata: A Discrete Universe*, World Scientific Press, September 2001.

[Ilach02] Ilachinski, A., *Multi-Agent-Based Synthetic Warfare: Towards Developing A General Axiological Ontology of Complex Adaptive Systems*, Center for Naval Analyses Research Memorandum CRM D0007376.A1, 2002.

[Ilach03a] Ilachinski, A., *EINSTein: Release Version 1.1*, Center for Naval Analyses, Multimedia CD-ROM, D0007498.A1, February 2003.

[Ilach03b] Ilachinski, A., "Exploring Self-Organized Emergence in an Agent-Based Synthetic Warfare Lab," *Artificial-Life Software Special Issue, Kybernetes Journal*, January 2003.

[Inbody03] Inbody, CAPT Donald, C. Chartier, D.DiPippa, B. McDonald, editors, *Swarming: Network Enabled C4ISR, 13-14 January 2003, Conference Proceedings*, Joint C4ISR Decision Support Center, 2003 (available on-line at URL address http://www.dodccrp.org/Publications/pdf/Swarming_Conf_Pro.pdf).

[Infantry93] *Infantry Division Operations: Tactics, Techniques, and Procedures*, Department of the Army FM 71-100-2, August 1993.

[Ingber91a] Ingber, L., H. Fujio, and M. F. Wehner, "Mathematical Comparison of Combat Computer Models to Exercise Data," *Mathematical Computer Modeling*, Volume 15, No. 1, 65-90, 1991.

[Ingber91b] Ingber, L., "Statistical Mechanics of Combat With Human Factors," *Mathematical Computer Modeling*, Volume 15, No. 11, 99-127, 1991.

[Ingber93] Ingber, L., "Statistical Mechanics of Combat and Extensions," pages 117-149 in *Towards a Science of Command, Control, and Communications*, edited by C. Jones, American Institute of Aeronautics and Astronautics, Inc., 1993.

[Iooss83] Iooss, G., R.H.G. Helleman and R. Stora, editors, *Chaotic Behavior of Deterministic Systems*, North-Holland, 1983.

[Iwasaki96] Iwasaki, Yumi, Adam Farquhar, and Richard Fikes, "A web-based compositional modeling system for the sharing of physical knowledge," *Knowledge Systems Laboratory*, Department of Computer Science, 1996.

[Jackson89] Jackson, E.A., *Perspectives of Nonlinear Dynamics*, Volumes 1 and 2, Cambridge University Press, 1989.

[Jacobs93] Jacobs, E. W. and R. D. Boss, "Attractors of iterated systems and their application to image compression," Naval Research Reviews, Volume XLV, 49-61, March, 1993.

[Jacyna01] Jacyna, G., *Diagnostic and Analysis Tools for Agent based Combat Simulation Models*, Briefing Slides, Mitre Corporation: http://www.mitre.org/ technology/tech01/briefings/modeling_simulation/jacyna_presentation/.

[James95] James, Glenn E., Major, USAF, *Chaos Theory: The Essentials for Military Applications*, Naval War College, Newport, R. I., 1995.

[Jantsch80] Jantsch, E., *The Self-Organizing Universe: Scientific and Human Implications of the Emerging Paradigm of Evolution*, Pergamon Press, 1980.

[JANUS] JANUS, TRADOC Analysis Center-White Sands Missile Range, http://www-leav.army.mil/nsc/famsim/janus/index.htm.

[Jen90] Jen, E., editor, *1989 Lectures in Complex Systems: The Proceedings of the 1989 Complex Systems Summer School, Santa Fe, New Mexico, June 1989*, Addison-Wesley, 1990.

[Jensen98] Jensen, H. J., *Self-Organized Criticality: Emergent Complex Behavior in Physical and Biological Systems*, Cambridge University Press, 1998.

[Jervis97] Jervis, R., *System Effects: Complexity in Political and Social Life,* Princeton

University Press, 1997.

[JMASS] JMASS Program Office homepage: http://www.jmass.wpafb.af.mil.

[JohnJ95] Johnson, J., "A language of structure in the science of complexity," *Complexity*, Volume 1, No. 3, 22-29, 1995.

[JohnS95] Johnson, S., *Emergence: The Connected Lives of Ants, Brains, Cities, and Software*, Scribner, 2002.

[JonesC93] Jones, Carl, editor, *Toward a Science of Command, Control, and Communications*, American Institute of Aeronautics and Astronautics, Inc., 1993.

[JonesT96] Jones, Teresa M., "A Non-Linear Interpretation of Clausewitz and Intelligence," Washington, DC: National War College, October 25, 1996.

[Joseph93] Josephson, J., B. Chandrasekaran, and D. Moberg, "Synthetic purposive agents: generic tasks and abstract data types," pages 429-435 in *Proceedings of the 3rd Conference on Computer Generated Forces and Behavioral Representation, March 17-19, 1993, Orlando, Florida, Institute for Simulation and Training*, Technical Report IST-TR-93-07, 1993.

[JSim99] *Joint Simulation System Operational Requirements Document*, Version 3.0, USACOM Joint Warfighting Center, Fort Monroe, VA, 23 June 1999.

[Jumarie75] Jumarie, G., "A relativistic information theory model for general systems Lorentz transformation of organizability and structural entropy," *International Journal of Systems Science*, Volume 6, 1975, 865-886.

[JWARS98] Joint Warfare System (JWARS), *Operational Requirements Document*, 27 August 1998, available on-line at http://www.dtic.mil/jwars/library.html.

[Kafa90] Kafatos, M. and R.Nadeau, *The Conscious Universe: Part and Whole in Modern Physical Theory*, Springer-Verlag, 1990.

[Kampis91] Kampis, G., *Self-Modifying Systems in Biology and Cognitive Science: A New Framework for Dynamics, Information and Complexity*, Pergamon Press, Oxford, 1991.

[Kaneko89] Kaneko, K., "Spatiotemporal chaos in one- and two-dimensional coupled map lattices," *Physica D*, Volume 37, 60-82, 1989.

[Kaneko93] Kaneko, K., editor, *Theory and Applications of Coupled Map Lattices*, John Wiley and Sons, 1993.

[Kantz97] Kantz, H. and T. Schreiber, *Nonlinear Time Series Analysis*, Cambridge University Press, 1997.

[Karr81] Karr, A. F., *Lanchester Attrition Processes and Theater-Level Combat Models*, Institute for Defense Analyses, P-1528, September 1981.

[Kauff89] Kauffman, S., "Adaptation on rugged fitness landscapes," pages 527-618 in [Stein89].

[Kauff90] Kauffman, S., "Requirements for evolvability in complex systems: orderly dynamics and frozen components," *Physica*, 42D, 135-152, 1990.

[Kauff91] Kauffman, S. and S.Johnsen, "Coevolution to the edge of chaos: coupled fitness landscapes, poised states, and coevolutionary avalanches," Jour. Theor. Biol., Volume 149, 1991.

[Kauff92] Kauffman, S., and S.Johnsen, "Coevolution to the edge of chaos: coupled fitness landscapes, poised states, and coevolutionary avalanches," pages 325-370 in [Lang92].

[Kauff93] Kauffman, S., *Origins of Order: Self-Organization and Selection in Evolution*, Oxford University Press, 1993.

[Kauff95a] Kauffman, S., *At Home in the Universe: The Search for Laws of Self Organization and Complexity*, Oxford University Press, 1995.

[Kauff95b] Kauffman, S. and W. Mcready, "Technological evolution and adaptive organizations," *Complexity*, Volume 1, No. 2, 26-43, 1995.

[Kauff00] Kauffman, S., *Investigations*, Oxford University Press, 2000.

[Kelly94] Kelly, K., *Out of Control: The Rise of Neo-Biological Civilization*, Addison-Wesley, 1994.

[Kelso88] Kelso, J. A. S., A. J. Mandell and M. F. Shlesinger, editors, *Dynamic Patterns in Complex Systems*, World Scientific, 1988.

[Kelso95] Kelso, J. A. S., *Dynamic Patterns: The Self-Organization of Brain and Behavior*, MIT Press, 1995.

[Kenn01] Kennedy, J. and R.C. Eberhart, *Swarm Intelligence*, Morgan Kauffman Publishers, 2001.

[Kess90] Kessler, D.A., H.Levine and W.N.Reynolds, "Coupled-map lattice model for crystal growth," *Phys. Rev.*, Volume 42A, 1990, 6125.

[Kewley01] Kewley (Major), R.H., *Combat Operations Support System for Adaptive Command and Control*, United States Military Academy, Briefing Slides, February 2001.

[Kiel93] Kiel, L. D., "Nonlinear dynamical analysis: assessing systems concepts in a government agency," *Public Administration Review*, Volume 53, No. 2, 142-153, March/April 1993.

[King95] King, James A., "Intelligent agents: bringing good things to life," *AI Expert*, February 1995, 17-19.

[Kitano98] Kitano, H., editor, *RoboCup-97: Robot Soccer World Cup I*, Springer-Verlag, 1998.

[Klein90] Klein, J. T., *Interdisciplinarity: History, Theory and Practice*, Wayne State University: Detroit, 1990.

[Kling02] Klingaman, Randall R. and William B. Carlton, *EINSTein Model Validation*, Military Academy, West Point New York, Department of System Engineering, Operations Research Center of Excellence Technical Report DSE-TR-02-03, August 2002.

[Koest83] Koestler, Arthur, Janus: A Summing Up, Pan Macmillan Press, 1983.

[Kohon90] Kohonen, T., "Self-organizing map," *Proceedings IEEE*, Volume 78, 1464-1480, 1990.

[Kolen03] Kolenda, Christopher D., "Transforming How We Fight: A Conceptual Approach," *Naval War College Review*, Vol. LVI, No. 2, Spring 2003.

[Kolm65] Kolmogorov, A.N., "Three approaches to the quantitative definition of information," *Prob. Peredach. Inform.*, Volume 1, 1965.

[Koop80] Koopman, B.O., *Search and Screening*, Pergamon, 1980.

[Koza93] Koza, J. R., *Genetic Programming: On the Programming of Computers by Means of Natural Selection*, MIT Press, 1993.

[Krantz97] Krantz, H. and T. Schreiber, *Nonlinear Time Analysis*, Cambridge University Press, 1997.

[Krueger92] Krueger, J. L., "Pitfalls in Combat Simulations," *Military Review*, 20-25, June, 1992.

[Kuck03] Kuck, I., *Warfare Simulation: Status and Issues for Space, Parts 1-5*, Air Force Research Laboratory, Directed Energy Directorate, Air Force Materiel Command, Kirtland Air Force Base, NM, Report AFRL-DE-TR-2003-1037, 2003.

[Kupp93] Kuppers, G., "Social order: from individual activity to functional cooperation," pages 127-137 in *Interdisciplinary Approaches to Nonlinear Complex Systems*, edited by H. Haken, and A. Mikhailov, Springer-Verlag, 1993.

[Lakoff80] Lakoff, G., and M. Johnson, *Metaphors we Live By*, University of Chicago Press, 1980.

[Lam92] Lam, Lui and V. Naroditsky, editors, *Modeling Complex Phenomena*, Springer-Verlag, 1992.

[Lanch95] Lanchester, F. W., *Aircraft in Warfare*, Lanchester Press, 1995 (Originally published in 1916 by Constable & Co, London, England).

[Lane95] Lane, D. and R. Maxfield, "Foresight, Complexity, and Strategy," *Santa Fe Institute*, 95-12-106, 1995.

[Lang86] Langton, C. G., "Studying artificial life with cellular automata," *Physica D*, Volume 22, 1986, 120-149.

[Lang89] Langton, C. G., editor, *Artificial Life: The Proceedings of an Interdisciplinary Workshop on the Synthesis and Simulation of Living Systems Held September, 1987 in Los Alamos, New Mexico*, Addison-Wesley, 1989.

[Lang90] Langton, C. G., "Computation at the edge of chaos: phase transitions and emergent computation," *Physica D*, Volume 42, 1990, 12-37.

[Lang92] Langton, C. G., C. Taylor, J. Doyne Farmer and S. Rasmussen, editors, *Artificial Life II: The Proceedings of the Workshop on Artificial Life Held February, 1990 in Santa Fe, New Mexico*, Addison-Wesley, 1992.

[Lang94] Langton, C. G., editor, *Artificial Life III: The Proceedings of the Workshop on Artificial Life Held February, 1992 in Santa Fe, New Mexico*, Addison-Wesley, 1994.

[Lang95] Langton, C. G., editor, *Artificial Life: An Overview*, MIT Press, 1995.

[Lauren99] Lauren, M. K., "Characterizing the Difference Between Complex Adaptive and Conventional Combat Models," *Defense Operational technology Support Establishment*, DOTSE Report 169, NR 1345, November, 1999.

[Lauren99b] Lauren, M. K., "Modeling Combat Using Fractals and the Statistics of Scaling Systems," *Defense Operational technology Support Establishment*, 1999.

[Lauren00a] Lauren, M. K. and D. L. Baigent, *Exploring the Recce-Counter Recce Scenario with ISAAC, Defense Operational technology Support Establishment*, DOTSE Report 171, NR 1349, July 2000.

[Lauren00b] Lauren, M. K., "Firepower Concentration in Cellular Automata Models: An Alternative to the Lanchester Approach," *Defense Operational technology Support Establishment*, DOTSE Report 177, NR 1358, November, 2000.

[Lauren00c] Lauren, M. K. and R.T.Stephen, "Modeling Patrol Survivability in a Generic Peacekeeping Setting Using ISAAC," *Defense Operational technology Support Establishment*, DOTSE Report 172, NR 1350, June, 2000.

[Lauren01] Lauren, M. K., R. T. Stephen, and M. A. Anderson, *MANA Users Manual*, DTA Technical note 01/4, NR 1365, ISSN 1175-6608. Defence Technology Agency, New Zealand, 2001.

[Lauren02] Lauren, M. K. and R. Stephen, "Fractals and combat modeling: Using MANA to explore the role of entropy in complexity science," *Fractals*, Vol. 10, No. 4, 2002.

[Laszlo96] Laszlo, Ervin, *The Systems View of the World: A Holistic Vision for Our Time*, Hampton Press, 1996.

[Leon91] Leonhard, R., *The Art of Maneuver: Maneuver-Warfare Theory and AirLand Battle*, Presidio, 1991.

[Leping87] Lepingwell, J. W. R., "The Laws of Combat? Lanchester Reexamined," *Int. Sec.*, Volume 12, No. 1, 89-134, 1987.

[Leping90] Lepingwell, J. W. R., "Lanchester Revived? A Critique of Lanchester Modeling in U.S. Army Guard and Reserve: Rhetoric, Realities, Risks," *Defense Analysis*, Volume 6, No. 4, 399-404, December 1990.

[Lewontin74] Lewontin, R.C., *The Genetic Basis of Evolutionary Change*, Columbia University Press, 1974.

[Lesser95] Lesser, V., editor, *Proceedings of the First International Conference on Multi-Agent Systems*, MIT Press, 1995.

[Levis93] Levis, Alexander H., "Colored Petri Net model of command and control nodes," pages 181-192 in *Toward a Science of Command, Control, and Communications*, edited by Carl Jones, American Institute of Aeronautics and Astronautics, Inc., 1993.

[Levy92] Levy, S., *Artificial Life: How Computers are Transforming Our Understanding of Evolution and the Future of Life*, New York: Pantheon Books, 1992.

[Lewin92] Lewin, R., *Complexity: Life at the Edge of Chaos*, Macmillan Publishing Company, 1992.

[Libicki95] Libicki, M., "Mesh and the net: speculations on armed conflicts in an age of free silicon," McNair Paper 28, *National Defense University*, 1995.

[Linde89] Lindemayer, A. and P. Prusinkiewicz, "Developmental models of multicellular organisms: a computer graphics perspective," pages 221-249 in [Lang89].

[Liotta98] Liotta, P. H. "A Strategy of Chaos," *Strategic Review*, Spring 1998.

[Little86] Littlebury, F. E. and D. K. Praeger, *Invisible Combat: C3CM, A Guide for the Tactical Commander*, AFCEA International Press, 1986.

Liu, J., Autonomous Agents and Multiagent Systems: Explorations in Learning, Self-Organization and Adaptive Computation, World Scientific, 2001.

[Lloyd88] Lloyd, S. and H.Pagels, "Complexity as thermodynamic depth," *Annals of Physics*, Volume 188, 1988.

[Lloyd90] Lloyd, S., "Physical measures of complexity," pages 67-73 in *1989 Lectures in Complex Systems: The Proceedings of the 1989 Complex Systems Summer School, Santa Fe, New Mexico, June 1989*, edited by E. Jen, Addison-Wesley, 1990.

[Lough] Loughran, J., *Island of Complexity Models and Adaptive Agent Simulations*, on-line review, Simulation Interoperability Standards Organization: http://www.sisostds.org/webletter/siso/iss_39/art_156.htm.

[Louis98] Louisell, Chuck. "A Systems Dynamics Model for National Power Applied to Achieve Dominance," *Secretary of Defense Strategic Studies Group*, 1998.

[Love79] Lovelock, J.E., *Gaia: A New Look at Life on Earth*, Oxford University Press, 1979.

[Maes90] Maes, P., editor, *Designing Autonomous Agents: Theory and Practice from Biology to Engineering and Back*, MIT Press, 1990.

[Maes93] Maes, P., "Behavior-based artificial intelligence," pages 2-10 in *From Animals to Animats 2: Proceedings of the Second International Conference on Simulation of Adaptive Behavior*, edited by Jean-Arcady Meyer, H. L. Roitblat and Stewart W. Wilson, MIT Press, 1993.

[Maes94] Maes, P., "Modeling Adaptive Autonomous Agents," *Artificial Life*, Volume 1, No. 1, 135-162, 1994.

[Maes96] Maes, P., Maja J. Mataric, Jean-Arcady Meyer, Jordan Pollack, and Stewart W. Wilson, *From Animals to Animats 4: Proceedings of the Fourth International Conference on Simulation of Adaptive Behavior*, MIT Press, 1996.

[Main94] Mainzer, K., *Thinking in Complexity*, Springer-Verlag, 1994.

[Mand91] Manderick, B., M. de weger and P.Spiessense, "The genetic algorithm and the structure of the fitness landscape," in [Belew91].

[MandB82] Mandlebrot, B., *The Fractal Geometry of Nature*, W.H. Freeman, 1982.

[Mann92] Mann, Steven R., "Chaos theory and strategic thought," *Parameters*, Volume 22, 54-68, 1992.

[Manuca95] Manuca, Radu and R. Savit, "Model misspecification tests, model building and predictability in complex systems," *Santa Fe Institute*, 95-09-075.

[Mata94] Mataric, M., *Interaction and Intelligent Behaviors*, Ph.D. Dissertation, Dept. of Electrical Engineering And Computer Science, MIT, 1994.

[Mata95] Mataric, Maja J., "Designing and understanding adaptive group behavior,"

Adaptive Behavior, Volume 4, No. 1, December 1995.

[Math41] *Mathematica: A System for Doing Mathematics*, Version 4.1, Wolfram Research: http://www.wri.com.

[May76] May, R. M., "Simple mathematical models with very complicated dynamics," *Nature*, Volume 261, 459-467, 1976.

[MayerK92] Mayer-Kress, G., "Nonlinear Dynamics and Chaos in Arms Race Models," pages 153-183 in *Modeling Complex Phenomena, Proceedings of the Third Woodward Conference, San Jose State University, April 12-13, 1991*, edited by Lui Lam and Vladimir Naroditsky, Springer-Verlag, 1992.

[McBeath95] McBeath M., M. Kaiser, and D. Shaffer, "How Baseball Outfielders Determine Where to Run to catch Fly Balls," *Science*, 1995.

[McCue02] McCue, Brian, *Wotan's Workshop: Military Experiments Before the Second World War*, Center for Naval Analyses, Occassional Paper, October 2002.

[McNam90] McNamara, B. and K.Wiessenfeld, "Self organized critical vector avalanche automata," *Physical Review A*, Volume 41, 1990.

[Mcneil01] McNeilly, M., *Sun Tzu and the Art of Modern Warfare*, Oxford University Press, 2001.

[McQuie88] McQuie, R., *Historical Characteristics of Combat for Wargames (Benchmarks)*, US Army Concepts Analysis Agency Research Paper CAA-RP-87-2, 1988.

[Meisel96] Meisel, L.V. and M.A.Johnson, "Fractal Scaling in Cellular Automata Simulations of Dissipative Dynamical Systems," *US Army Armament Research Development and Engineering Center*, Watrervliet, New York, Technical Report ARCCB-TR-96021, July 1996.

[Mert01] Mert, E. and E.W. Jilson, *Modeling Conventional Land Combat in a Multi-Agent System Using Generalization of the Different Combat Entities and Combat Operations*, Masters Thesis, Naval Postgraduate School, Monterey, California, March 2001.

[Metro73] Metropolis, N., M.L.Stein and P.R.Stein, "On finite limit sets for transformations on the unit interval," *Journal Combinatorial Theory*, Volume 15, 1973.

[Meyer91] Meyer, Jean-Arcady and Stewart W. Wilson, editors, *From Animals to Animats: Proceedings of the First International Conference on Simulation of Adaptive Behavior*, MIT Press, 1991.

[Meyer93] Meyer, Jean-Arcady, H. L. Roitblat and Stewart W. Wilson, editors, *From Animals to Animats 2: Proceedings of the Second International Conference on Simulation of Adaptive Behavior*, MIT Press, 1993.

[Meyer00] Meyer, Jean-Arcady, Alain Berthoz, Dario Floreano, Herbert L. Roitblat, and Stewart W. Wilson, *From Animals to Animats 6: Proceedings of the Sixth International Conference on Simulation of Adaptive Behavior*, MIT Press, 2000.

[Meystel02] Meystel, A.M. and J.S. Albus, *Intelligent Systems: Architecture, Design and Control*, John Wiley and Sons, 2002.

[Michal92] Michalewicz, Z., *Genetic Algorithms + Data Structures = Evolution Programs*, Springer-Verlag, 1992.

[MillerJ96] Miller, J. H., "Active nonlinear tests (ANTs) of complex simulation models," 5 Feb, 1996 (electronic postscript copy downloaded from http://www.zia.hss.cmu.edu.)

[MillerL93] Miller, L. D., M. F. Sulcoski, *Foreign Physics Research with Military Significance: Military Implications of Research on Complex Adaptive Systems*, Defense S&T Intelligence Study, DST-1820S-440-93, December 1993.

[MillerL95] L. D. Miller, M. F. Sulcoski, *Foreign Physics Research with Military Significance: Applying Nonlinear Science to Military Programs*, Defense Intelligence Reference Document, NGIC-1823-614-95, March 1995.

[Miram93] Miramontes, O., R. V. Sole, and B. Goodwin, "Collective behavior of random-activated mobile cellular automata," *Physica D*, Volume 63, 145-160, 1993.

[MitchM93a] Mitchell, M., P. T. Hraber and J. P. Crutchfield, "Revisiting the edge of chaos: evolving cellular automata to perform computations," *Complex Systems*, Volume7, No. 2, 89-130, April 1993.

[MitchM93b] Mitchell, M., "Genetic algorithms," pages 3-87 in *1992 Lectures in Complex Systems*, edited by L. Nadel and D. Stein, Addison-Wesley, 1993.

[MitchM96] Mitchell, M., *An Introduction to Genetic Algorithms*, MIT Press, 1996.

[MOAB] Model of Animal Behavior (MOAB), US Geological Survey, http://www.usgs.gov/tech-transfer/factsheets/FS-056-97.htm.

[ModSAF] ModSAF: http://www.stricom.army.mil/STRICOM/E-DIR/ES/MODSAF/.

[ModSim96] *Modeling and Simulation: Linking Entertainment and Defense*, Commission on Physical Sciences, Mathematics, and Applications, National Research Council, National Academy Press, 1997; available on-line at http://www.nap.edu/html/ modeling/.

[ModSimR] *Modeling and Simulation Resource Repository*: http://www.msrr.dmso.mil/.

[Modrick79] Modrick, J. A., "Decision Support in a Battlefield Environment," pages 457-472 in *Decision Information*, edited by C. P. Tsokos and R. M. Thrall, Academic Press, 1979.

[Moff02] Moffat, J. and Susan Witty, "Phase changes in Meta-modelling using the Fractal Dimension," *Information and Security*, Volume 8, Number 1, 2002.

[Morris94] Morris, Peter, *Introduction to Game Theory*, Springer-Verlag, 1994.

[Morse51] Morse, P. M. and G. E. Kimball, *Methods of Operations Research*, MIT Press, 1951.

[Moss95] Moss, F. and K. Weisenfeld, *Nature*, Volume 373, 1995, 33-36.

[Mowsh68] Mowshowitz, A., "Entropy and the complexity of graphs: I. An index of the relative complexity of a graph," *Bull. Math. Bio.*, Volume 30, 1968.

[MSC++] Microscoft, *Visual C++*, Professional Version 6.0: http://msdn.microsoft.com/developer.

[Mueller90] Mueller, Theodore H., "Chaos Theory: The Mayaguez Crisis." *U.S. Army War College*, Military Studies Program, Carlisle Barracks, PA, March 15, 1990.

[Murphy00] Murphy, R.R., *Introduction to AI Robotics*, MIT Press, 2000.

[Murray93] Murray, J. D., *Mathematical Biology*, Second Edition, Springer-Verlag, 1993.

[Nadel91] Nadel, L. and D. Stein, editors, *1990 Lectures in Complex Systems*, Addison-Wesley, 1991.

[Nadel92] Nadel, L. and D. Stein, editors, *1991 Lectures in Complex Systems*, Addison-Wesley, 1992.

[Nadel93] Nadel, L. and D. Stein, editors, *1992 Lectures in Complex Systems*, Addison-Wesley, 1993.

[Nadel94] Nadel, L. and D. Stein, editors, *1993 Lectures in Complex Systems*, Addison-Wesley, 1995.

[Newm03] Newman, M.A.J., "The structure and function of complex networks," *SIAM Review*, Volume 45, 2003.

[NewTech02] *New Techniques: A Better Understanding of Their Application to Analysis*, MORS, held November 19-21, 2002 at John Hopkins University, Maryland: http://www.mors.org/meetings/new_techniques/new_tech_final.htm.

[Nich94] Nicholls, D. and T. D. Tagarev, "What Does Chaos Theory Mean for Warfare?," *Airpower*, Volume 8, No. 3, 48-57, 1994.

[Nicol95] Nicolis, G., *Introduction to Nonlinear Science*, Cambridge University Press, 1995.

[NicolJ86] Nicolis, J.S., *Dynamics of Hierarchical Systems*, Springer-Verlag, 1986.

[NIMA] *National Imagery and Mapping Agency*, URL address: http://164.214.2.59/ index.html.

[Nitz97] Nitzschke, Stephen G., Major, United States Marine Corps, *Vietnam: A Complex Adaptive Perspective*, Thesis, 1997.

[OHare96] O'Hare,M., "Chaos pitch," *New Scientist*, 8 June 1996, 24-28.

[Olanders96] Olanders, K. A., *Re-Engineering Of A Cellular Automata Combat Modeling Tool*, Report GMU/C3I-175-TH, C3I Center, Fairfax, Virginia, George Mason University, 1996.

[Oper93] *Operations*, Department of the Army FM 100-5, June 1993.

[Oster03] Ostergaard, E. H. and H. H. Lund, "Co-evolving complex robot behavior," in *Proceedings of ICES2003 in Trondheim, Norway*, March 2003.

[Ortony93] Ortony, A., editor, *Metaphor and Thought*, Second Edition, Cambridge University Press, 1993.

[Osipov95] Osipov, M., translated by R. L. Helmbold and A. S. Rehm, "The Influence of the Numerical Strength of Engaged Forces in Their Casualties," *Naval Research Logistics*, Volume 42, No. 3, April, 435-490, 1995.

[Ott90] Ott, E., C. Grebogi and J. A. Yorke, "Controlling chaos," *Physical Review Letters*, Volume 64, 1196, 1990.

[Ott94] Ott, E., T. Sauer and J. A. Yorke, editors, *Coping with Chaos: Analysis of Chaotic Data and the Exploitation of Chaotic Systems*, John Wiley and Sons, 1994.

[Pack88] Packard, N. H., "Adaptation toward the edge of chaos," pages 293-301 in *Dynamic Patterns in Complex Systems*, edited by J. A. S. Kelso, A. J. Mandell and M. F. Shlesinger, World Scientific, 1988.

[Pack90] Packard, N. H., "A genetic learning algorithm for the analysis of complex data," *Complex Systems*, Volume 4, No. 5, 1990.

[Palmer85] Palmer, E. M., *Graphical Evolution: An Introduction to the Theory of Random Graphs*, John-Wiley and Sons,1985.

[Palmerg91] Palmer, R.G., "Optimization on rugged landscapes," pages 3-25 in *Molecular Evolution on Rugged Landscapes: Proteins, RNA, and the Immune System*, edited by A.S. Perelson and S.A.Kauffman, Volume IX of the Santa Fe Institute Proceedings Volumes, Addison-Wesley, 1991.

[Palus95a] Palus, M., "Detecting nonlinearity in multivariate time series," *Santa Fe Institute*, 95-07-059, 1995.

[Palus95b] Palus, M., L. Pecen and D, Pivka, "Estimating predictability: redundancy and surrogate data method," *Santa Fe Institute*, 95-07-060, 1995.

[Paret86] Paret, Peter, editor, *Makers of Modern Strategy From Machiavelli to the Nuclear Age*, Princeton University Press, 1986.

[Pat73] Pattee, H.H., *Hierarchy Theory: The Challenge of Complex Systems*, George Braziller, 1973.

[Pawl01] Pawloski, J.S., *Modeling Tactical Level Combat Using a Multi-Agent System Design Paradigm*, Masters Thesis, Naval Postgraduate School, Monterey, California, March 2001.

[Pecora90] Pecora, L. M. and T. L. Carroll, "Synchronization in chaotic systems," *Physical Review Letters*, Volume 64, 1990, 821-824.

[Peitgen92] Peitgen, Heintz-Otto, H.Jurgens and D.Saupe, *Chaos and Fractals: New Frontiers of Science*, Springer-Verlag, 1992.

[Pell95] Pellegrini, Robert P., *The Links Between Science and Philosophy and Military Theory: Understanding the Past: Implications For the Future,* Maxwell AFB, AL: School of Advanced Airpower Studies, Air University, June 1995.

[Pent93] Pentland, Pat A., *Center of Gravity Analysis and Chaos Theory, or How Societies*

Form, Function, and Fail, Maxwell AFB, AL: School of Advanced Airpower Studies, 1993-94.

[Perla90] Perla, Peter P., *The Art of Wargaming: A Guide for Professionals and Hobbyists*, United States Naval Institute Press, 1990.

[Perla02] Perla, Peter P., A. Ilachinski, C.M.Hawk, M.C.Markowitz, and C.A. Weuve, *Using Gaming and Agent Technology to Explore Joint Command and Control Issues*, Center for Naval Analyses Research Memorandum, CRM D0007164, October 2002.

[Perry92] Perry, James J., "Computer war games in the 21st century," pages 103-112 in *Visions of the Future: Art, Technology and Computing in the Twenty-First Century*, edited by C. Pickover, St. Martins Press, 1992.

[Peschel86] Peschel, Manfred and W. Mende, *The Predator-Prey Model: Do We Live in a Volterra World?*, Springer-Verlag, 1986.

[Pew98] Pew, R. W. and A. S. Mavor, editors, *Modeling human and Organizational Behavior: Application to Military Simulations*, National Academy Press, 1998.

[Pfeif98] Pfeifer, R., Bruce Blumberg, Jean-Arcady Meyer, and Stewart W. Wilson, *From Animals to Animats 5: Proceedings of the Fifth International Conference on Simulation of Adaptive Behavior*, MIT Press, 1998.

[Phip92] Phipps, M.J., "From local to global: the lesson of cellular automata," pages 165-187 in *Individual-Based Models and Approaches in Ecology: Populations, Communities and Ecosystems*, edited by Deangelis, D.L. and L.J.Gross, Chapman and Hall, 1992.

[Piatetsky91] Piatetsky-Shapiro, G. and W. J. Frawley, editors, *Knowledge Discovery in Databases*, MIT Press, 1991.

[Picard97] Picard, R.W., *Affective Computing*, MIT Press, 1997.

[Pinn] Pinnacle Publishing Inc., *Graphics Server*, Version 5.5: http://www.graphicsserver.com.

[Priet88] Prietula, M.J., K.M.Carley and L.Gasser, editors, *Simulating Organizations: Computer Models of Institutions and Groups*, MIT Press, 1988.

[Protop89] Protopopescu, V., R. T. Santoro, J. Dockery, "Combat Modeling with Partial Differential Equations," *Eur. J. Oper. Res.* 38, 178, 1989.

[Pound85] Poundstone, W., *The Recursive Universe: Cosmic Complexity and the Limits of Scientific Knowledge*, Contemporary Books, Inc., 1985.

[Pres93] Prescott, Tony J. and J. E. W. Mayhew, "Building long-range cognitive maps using local landmarks," pages 233-242 in *From Animals to Animats 2: Proceedings of the Second International Conference on Simulation of Adaptive Behavior*, edited by Jean-Arcady Meyer, H. L. Roitblat and Stewart W. Wilson, MIT Press, 1993.

[Prest84] Preston, K. and M. Duff, eds., *Modern Cellular Automata, Theory and Applications*, Plenum Press, 1984.

[Prig80] Prigogine, I., *From Being to Becoming: Time and Complexity in the Physical Sciences*, Freeman and Company, 1980.

[Proc93] *Proceedings of the 3rd Conference on Computer Generated Forces and Behavioral Representation*, March 17-19, 1993, Orlando, Florida, Institute for Simulation and Training, Technical Report IST-TR-93-07, 1993.

[Proc94] *Proceedings of the 4th Conference on Computer Generated Forces and Behavioral Representation*, May 4-6, 1994, Orlando, Florida, Institute for Simulation and Training, Technical Report IST-TR-94-12, 1994.

[Prop94] Prop, J., "Further Antics," in Mathematical Entertainments, edited by D.Gale, *The Mathematical Intelligencer*, Volume 16, Winter 1994, 37-42.

[Przem94] Przemieniecki, J. S., *Mathematical Methods in Defense Analyses*, Second Edition, American Institute of Aeronautics and Astronautics, Inc.,1994.

[Quar95] Quaranta, Therese F., "Fuzzy systems for simulating human-like reasoning and control," *John Hopkins APL Technical Digest*, Volume 16, No. 1, 43-58, 1995.

[Rasb90] Rasband, S.N., *Chaotic Dynamics of Nonlinear Systems*, John Wiley, 1990.

[Rash55] Rashevsky, N., "Life, information theory, and topology," *Mathematical Biophysics*, Volume 17, 1955.

[RayT93] Ray, Thomas S., "Evolution, Ecology and Optimization of Digital Organisms," *Santa Fe Institute* working paper 92-08-042, 1992; available on-line at URL address http://www.his.atr.co.jp/~ray/pubs/tierra/.

[RayW93] Ray, W. J. "EEG and chaos: Explorations in using dimensional estimation to estimate psychological state", in *Biobehavioral Self-Regulation in the East and West*, edited by Kikuchi, Springer-Verlag, Tokyo, 1993.

[Repast] Repast, University of Chicago's Social Science Research Computing Laboratory, http://repast.sourceforge.net/

[Rey87] Reynolds,C., "Flocks, herds, and schools: a distributed behavioral model," *Computer Graphics*, Volume 21, 25, July, 1987.

[RichFC90] Richards, F. C., T. P. Meyer and N. H. Packard, "Extracting cellular automata rules directly from experimental data," *Physica D*, Volume 45, 1990, 189-202.

[RichK90] Richardson, Kurt A., Graham Mathieson, and Paul Cilliers, "The Theory and Practice of Complexity Science: Epistemological Considerations for Military Operational Analysis," *SysteMexico*, 2000: available at http://www.concentric.net/ ~kurtar/Berty2/Comp/milcomplexity.pdf.

[RichLF60] L. F. Richardson, *Statistics of Deadly Quarrels*, Pittsburgh, PA: Boxwood, 1960.

[Rinaldi95] Rinaldi, Steven M., Major, USAF, *Beyond the Industrial Web: Economic Synergies and Targeting Methodologies*, Air University Press, Maxwell Air Force Base, Alabama, 1995.

[Rinaldi97] Rinaldi, Steven M., "Complexity Theory and Air Power," in Alberts, David S. and Thomas J. Czerwinski, eds., *Complexity,Global Politics and National Security,* Washington, DC: National Defense University, June 1997.

[Roberts88] Roberts, D. C., and D. L. Turcotte, "Fracticality and Self-Organized Criticality of Wars," *Fractals*, Vol. 6(4), 351-357, 1988.

[Roddy00] Roddy, K.A. and M.R. Dickson, *Modeling Human and Organizational Behavior Using a Relation-Centric Multi-Agent System Design Paradigm*, Naval Post Graduate School Masters Thesis, September 2000.

[Rome92] Romeiras, F., C. Grebogi, E. Ott and W. P. Dayawansa, "Controlling chaotic dynamical systems," *Physica D*, Volume 58, 165, 1992.

[Rose97] Rosenau, James N., "Many Damn Things Simultaneously: Complexity Theory and World Affairs," in Alberts, David S. and Thomas J. Czerwinski, eds., *Complexity,Global Politics and National Security,* Washington, DC: National Defense University, June 1997.

[Ross01] Ross, S., *Simulation*, Academic Press, 2001.

[Rough96] Roughgarden, J., A. Bergman, S. Shafir and C. Taylor, "Adaptive computation in ecology and evolution: a guide for future research," Chapter 2 in *Adaptive Individuals in Evolving Populations: Models and Algorithms*, edited by R. K. Belew and M. Mitchell, Addison-Wesley, 1996.

[Ruelle80] Ruelle, D., "Strange Attractors," *The Mathematical Intelligencer*, Volume 2, 1980, 126-37.

[Salt85] Salthe, S.N., *Evolving Hierarchical Systems*, Columbia University Press, 1985.

[Sand98] Sanders, T. Irene, *Strategic Thinking and the New Sciences: Planning in the Midst of Chaos, Complexity, and Change*, The Free Press, 1998.

[Sand03] Sanders, T. Irene and J.A.McCabe, *The Use of Complexity Science: A Survey of Federal Departments and Agencies, Private Foundations, Universities, and Independent Education and Research Centers*, Washington Center for Complexity & Public Policy, 2003: http://www.complexsys.org/pdf/ComplexityScienceSurvey.pdf

[Saper84] Saperstein, A., "Chaos – a Model for the Outbreak of War," *Nature*, 309, 303-305, 1984.

[Saper95] Saperstein, A., "War and Chaos," *American Scientist*, Volume 83, 548-557, November-December, 1995.

[Saper99] Saperstein, A., *Dynamical Modeling of the Onset of War*, World Scientific, 1999.

[Sauer92] Sauer, T., "Time series prediction by using delay coordinate embedding," pages 175-193 in *Nonlinear Modeling and Forecasting: Proceedings of the Workshop on Nonlinear Modeling and Forecasting Held September, 1990 in Santa Fe, New Mexico*, edited by M. Casdagli, and S. Eubank, Addison-Wesley, 1992.

[Schmitt95a] Schmitt, J. F., "How We Decide," *Marine Corps Gazette*, October 1995.

[Schmitt95b] Schmitt, J. F., Chaos, *Complexity and War: What the New Nonlinear Dynamical Sciences May Tell us About Armed Conflict,* Draft, 4 September 1995.

[Schmitt96] Schmitt, J. F. and Gary A. Klein, "Fighting in the Fog: Dealing with Battlefield Uncertainty," *Marine Corps Gazette*, August 1996.

[Schmitt97] Schmitt, J. F., "Command and (Out Of) Control: The Military Implications of Complexity Theory," in Alberts, David S. and Thomas J. Czerwinski, eds., *Complexity, Global Politics and National Security,* Washington, DC: National Defense University, June 1997: 219-246; available on the WWW at URL address http://www.dodccrp.org/comch09.html.

[Schroeder91] Schroeder, M., *Fractals, Chaos, Power Laws: Minutes from an Infinite Paradise*, W. H. Freeman and Company, 1991.

[Schus88] Schuster, Heintz G., *Deterministic Chaos: An Introduction*, Second Edition, VCH Publishers, 1988.

[Segel95] Segel, L. A., "Grappling with complexity," *Complexity*, Volume 1, No. 2, 18-25, 1995.

[Segel99] Segel, L. A., "Immunology viewed as the study of an autonomous decentralized system," pages 65-88 in *Artificial Immune Systems and Their Applications*, edited by D. Dasgupta, Springer-Verlag, 1999.

[Senge90] Senge, P., *The Fifth Discipline: The Art and Practice of the Learning Organization*, Currency Doubleday, 1990.

[Shann49] Shannon, C.E. and W.Weaver, *The Mathematical Theory of Communication*, University of Illinois Press, Urbana, Illinois, 11949.

[Sherm97] Shermer, Michael., "The Crooked Timber of History," *Complexity*, Vol. 2, No. 6, 1997.

[Shin92] Shinbrot, T., W. Ditto, C. Grebogi, E. Ott, M Spano and J. A. Yorke, "Using the sensitive dependence of chaos (the "Butterfly Effect") to direct trajectories in an experimental chaotic system," *Physical Review Letters*, Volume 68, 2863, 1992.

[Shles93] Shlesinger,Michael F., "Applications of Chaos and Fractals," *Naval Research Reviews*, Volume XLV, 2-3, March, 1993.

[Simon62] Simon, H., "The architecture of complexity," *Proc. Am. Phil. Soc.*, Volume 106, 1962.

[Simon90] Simon, H. A., "Prediction and Prescription in Systems Modeling," *Operations Research*, Volume 38, No. 1, 7-14.

[Smith56a] Smith, N. M., "A calculus for ethics: a theory of the structure of value. Part I," *Behavioral Science*, Volume 1, No. 2, April, 1956, 111-142, January/February 1990.

[Smith56b] Smith, N. M., "A calculus for ethics: a theory of the structure of value. Part II," *Behavioral Science*, Volume 1, No. 3, July, 1956, 186-211.

[Smull80] Smullyan, R., *This Book Needs No Title: A Budget of Living Paradoxes*, Prentice-Hall, 1980.

[Snyder93] Snyder, Jack and Robert Jervis, eds., *Coping with Complexity in the International System,* Westview Press, 1993.

[Soar] Soar Intelligent FORces (IFOR) project. This is a collaborative effort between researchers at the Carnegie Mellon University School of Computer Science, the University of Michigan's Artificial Intelligence Laboratory, and the University of Southern California's Information Sciences Institute; the website for this project is http://www.isi.edu/soar/soar-ifor-project.html.

[Sole91] Sole, R.V. and J.Valls, "Order and chaos in a 2D Lottka-Voltera coupled map lattice," *Phys. Lett.*, Volume 153, 330, 1991.

[Sole93] Sole, R.V., O. Miramontes, and B. C. Goodwin, "Emergent behavior in insect societies: global oscillations, chaos and computation," pages 77-88 in *Interdisciplinary Approaches to Nonlinear Complex Systems*, edited by H. Haken, and A. Mikhailov, Springer-Verlag, 1993.

[Solo64] Solomonov, R.J., "A formal theory of inductive inference," *Information Control*, Volume 7, 1964.

[Somm95] Sommerer, J. C., "The end of classical determinism," *John Hopkins APL Technical Digest*, Volume 16, No. 4, 333-347, October-December 1995.

[Spano93] Spano, Mark L. and W. L. Ditto, "Controlling Chaos," *Naval Research Reviews*, Volume XLV, 12-21, March, 1993.

[Stand03] Standish, R., Mark A. Bedau, and Hussein A. Abbass, *Artificial Life VIII: Proceedings of the Eighth International Conference on Artificial Life*, MIT Press, 2003.

[Starlogo] Starlogo, *MIT*: http://education.mit.edu/starlogo/

[Stein89] Stein, D.L., editor, *Lectures in the Sciences of Complexity: The Proceedings of the 1988 Complex Systems Summer School in Sante Fe, New Mexico*, Addison-Wesley, 1989.

[Stone00] Stone, P., Layered Learning in Multiagent Systems: A Winning Approach to Robotic Soccer, MIT Press, 2000.

[STOW] STOW, *Synthetic Theater of War*, DOD Advanced Concept Technology Demonstration, DARPA: http://web-ext2.darpa.mil/iso/stow/.

[Steels95] Steels, L. and R. Brooks, editors, *The Artificial Life Route to Artificial Intelligence: Building Embodied, Situated Agents*, Lawrence Erlbaum Associates, Publishers: Hillsdale, New Jersey, 1995.

[Stein89] Stein, D.L., ed., *Lectures in the Sciences of Complexity: The Proceedings of the 1988 Complex Systems Summer School in Sante Fe, New Mexico*, Addison-Wesley, 1989.

[Stine00] Stine, J.L., *Representing Tactical Land Navigation Expertise*, Masters Thesis, Naval Postgraduate School, Monterey, California, September 2000. (Available on web at URL address http://movesinstitute.org/Theses/JasonStine.pdf.)

[Subr98] Subrata, D., A. Caglayan and PaulGonsalves, ""Increasing Agent Autonomy in Dynamic Environments," in Sycara Katia, P., Wooldridge Michael, editors, *Proceedings of the Second International Conference in Autonomous Agents*, ACM Press, 1998.

[Sunv99] Sunvold, Daniel D., *Concept of Operations for a Self-Organizing Theater Ballistic Missile Defense Network*, Masters Thesis, Naval Postgraduate School, Monterey, California, March 1999.

[Suth94] Sutherland, B. R. and A. E. Jacobs, "Self-organization and scaling in a lattice predator-prey model," Complex Systems, Volume 8, 385-405, 1994.

[Sutton98] Sutton, R.S. and A.G. Barto, *Reinforcement Learning: An Introduction*, MIT Press, 1998.

[SWARM] SWARM Project, http://www.swarm.org/.

[SWarrior] SWARM Marine Infantry Combat Model (SWarrior), SAIC: http://sac.saic.com /am/docs/Agent_Based_Modeling_Paper/agent_based_modeling.htm.

[Tactics91] *Tactics*, U. S. Marine Corps FMFM 1-3, June 1991.

[Tabor89] Tabor, M., *Chaos and Integrability in Nonlinear Dynamics*, John Wiley and Sons, 1989.

[Tagarev94] Tagarev, T., M. Dolgov, D. Nicholls, R. C. Franklin and P. Axup, *Chaos in War: Is it Present and What Does it Mean?*, Submitted to the Air Command and Staff College in fulfillment of the requirement of the AY94 Research Program, June 1994.

[Tagarev96] Tagarev, T. and D. Nicholls, "Identification of Chaotic Behavior" in *Warfare, Nonlinear Dynamics in Human Behavior*, edited by W. Sulis and A. Combs, World Scientific, 126-143, 1996.

[TaylorD00] Taylor, D., C. Schmal and A. Hashim, *Ground Combat Study: Summary of Analysis*, CNA CRM D2706, 2000.

[TaylorG80] James G. Taylor, *Force-On-Force Attrition Modeling*, Operations Research Society of America, 1980.

[TaylorG83] James G. Taylor, *Lanchester Models of Warfare,* Volumes I and II, Operations Research Society of America, 1983.

[TaylorT00] Taylor, Theodore C., "Principles of modern tactics: the n-square law and beyond," *Defense Analysis*, Volume 6, No. 3, 277-288, September 1990.

[Tech97] *Technology for the United States Navy and Marine Corps, 2000-2035: Becoming a 21st-Century Force*, Naval Studies Board, National Research Council, National Academy Press, 1997. (The complete text of Volume 9:Modeling and Simulation, is available on-line: http://www.nap.edu/html/tech_21st/msindex.htm.)

[That62] Thatcher, J. "Universality in the von Neumann cellular model," pages 132-186 in [Burks70].

[Thibault84] Thibault, George E., editor, *The Art and Practice of Military Strategy*, National Defense University Press, 1984.

[THOR] Project THOR, Kritsina Olanders, C3I Center, George Mason University, http://viking.gmu.edu/http/projects/thor/content.htm.

[Thula92] Thulasiraman, K. and M. Swami, *Graphs: Theory and Algorithms*, John Wiley and Sons, 1992.

[Tidm84] Tidman, Keith R., *The Operations Evaluation Group: A History of Naval Operations Analysis*, Naval Institute Press, 1984.

[Tighe99] Tighe (Maj), T.R., *Strategic Effects of Airpower and Complex Adaptive Agents*, Air Force Institute of Technology: https://research.au.af.mil/papers/ay1999/afit/tighe_tr.pdf.

[Todd93] Todd, Peter M. and S. W. Wilson, "Environment structure and adaptive behavior from the ground up," pages 11-20 in *From Animals to Animats 2: Proceedings of the Second International Conference on Simulation of Adaptive Behavior*, edited by Jean-Arcady Meyer, H. L. Roitblat and Stewart W. Wilson, MIT Press, 1993.

[Toffoli77] Toffoli,, T., *Cellular Automata Mechanics*, Technical Report 208, Comp. Comm. Sci. Dept., The University of Michigan, 1977.

[Toffoli87] Toffoli,, T. and N. Margolus, *Cellular Automata Machines: a New Environment for Modeling*, MIT Press, 1987.

[Tooke95] Tooke, L.r, and Ralph Allen, "Strategic Intuition and the Art of War," *Military Review*, March-April 1995.

[Tsokos79] Tsokos, C. P. and R. M. Thrall, editors, *Decision Information*, Academic Press, 1979.

[Turing36] Turing, A.M., "On computable numbers with an application to the Entscheidungsproblem," *Proc. London Math. Soc. Ser.*, Volume 42, 1936, 230-265.

[Twist91] Twist, Mark van and L. Schaap, "Introduction to autopoiesis theory and autopoietic steering," in *Autopoiesis and Configuration Theory: New Approaches to Societal Steering*, edited by R. J. Reid, L. Schaap, C. J. A. M. Termeer and M. van Twist, Kluwer Academic Publishers, Dordrecht, 1991.

[Tyson76] Tyson, J.J., *The Belousov-Zhabotinski Reaction*, Lecture Notes in Biomathematics, Volume 10, Springer-Verlag, 1976.

[Tzu91] Tzu, Sun, *The Art of War*, translated by Thomas Cleary, Shambala, 1991.

[Ulam52] Ulam, S., "Random processes and transformations," *Proc. Int. Con. Math.*, Volume 2, 1952.

[Ulam62] Ulam, S., "On some mathematical problems connected with patterns of growth of figures," *Proceedings of Symposia in Applied Mathematics*, Volume 14, 1962, 215-224.

[Unrath00] Unrath, C.S., *Dynamic Exploration of Helicopter Reconnaissance Through Agent-Based Modeling*, Naval Post Graduate School Masters Thesis, March 2000.

[Uesaka01] Uesaka, Y., P. Kanerva and H. Asoh, editors, *Foundations of Real-World Intelligence*, CSLI Publications, 2001.

[vanP96] van Riper, Paul K., "Corps Competence: How the Marines Simulate the Chaos of War," lecture delivered at *Embracing Complexity Conference*, sponsored by Ernst and Young, San Francisco, CA, July 17-19, 1996.

[vanP97a] Van Riper, Paul K., "Strategy and the Formulation of National Security Policy: The Military Content," *1997 Topical Symposium: Strategy and the Formulation of National Security Policy*, Institute for National Strategic Studies, National Defense University, October 7-8, 1997.

[vanP97b] Van Riper, Paul K., "Information Superiority," *Marine Corps Gazette*, June 1997 (Statement to subcommittees of the House National Security Committee on 20, March 1997).

[vanP97c] Van Riper, Paul K. and Robert Scales, "Preparing for War in the 21st Century," *Strategic Review*, Summer 1997.

[vanP98] Van Riper, Paul K. and F.G. Hoffman, "Pursuing the Real Revolution in Military Affairs: Exploiting Knowledge-Based Warfare," *National Security Studies Quarterly*, Summer 1998.

[Varela74] Varela, F. J., Humberto R. Maturana, and R. Uribe, "Autopoiesis: The Organization of Living systems, its Characterization and a Model," *Biosystems*, Vol. 5, 187-196, 1974.

[Varela79] Varela, F. J., *Principles of Biological Autonomy*, New York: Elsevier, North Holland, 1979.

[Varela92] Varela, F. J. and P. Bourgine, editors, *Toward A Practice of Autonomous Systems: Proceedings of the 1st European Conference on Artificial Life*, MIT Press, 1992.

[Vast86] Vastano, J. A. and E. J. Kostelich, "Comparison of algorithms for determining Lyapunov exponents from experimental data," pages 100-107 in *Dimensions and Entropies in Chaotic Systems*, edited by G. Mayer-Kress, Springer-Verlag, 1986.

[Virr93] Virr, L. E., A. Fairley and F. Yates, "Tactical application of genetic algorithms," *J. N. S.*, Volume 19, No. 3, 159-169, 1993.

[vonN51] Von Neumann, J., "The general and logical theory of automata," in *Cerebral Mechanisms in Behavior*, L.A. Jeffress, ed., Wiley (1951) 1-32.

[vonN66] Von Neumann, J., *Theory of Self-Reproducing Automata*, University of Illinois Press, 1966.

[Wald92] Waldrop, M., Complexity: The Emerging Science at the Edge of Order and Chaos, New York: Simon and Schuster, 1992.

[Warf89] *Warfighting*, U. S. Marine Corps FMFM 1, March 1989.

[Watan85] Watanabe, S., *Knowing and Guessing: A Quantitative Study of Inference and Information*, John Wiley and Sons, 1985.

[Watts96] Watts, Barry D., *Clausewitzean Friction in Future War,* McNair Paper 52, Washington DC: Institute for National Strategic Studies, National Defense University, 1996.

[WattsD99] Watts, D., *Small Worlds*, Princeton Unversity Press, 1999.

[WattsD03] Watts, D., *Six Degrees: The Science of a Connected Age*, W.W.Norton and Company, 2003.

[Weeks01] Weeks, Michael R., "Chaos, Complexity and Conflict," *Air and Space Power Chronicles*, July 2001.

[Weigend94] Weigend, Andreas S. and N. A. Gershenfeld, editors, *Time Series Prediction: Forecasting the Future and Understanding the Past*, Addison-Wesley, 1994.

[Wein75] Weinberg, Gerald M., *An Introduction to General Systems Thinking*, John Wiley and Sons, 1975.

[WeissG99] Weiss, G. editor, *Multiagent Systems: A Modern Approach to Distributed Artificial Intelligence*, MIT Press, 1999.

[Weisb91] Weisbuch, G., *Complex Systems Dynamics*, Addison-Wesley, 1991.

[WeissH57] Weiss, H. K., "Lanchester-type models of warfare," *Proceedings of 1st Conference on Operations Research*, Operations Research Society of America, 82-99, 1957.

[West99] West (Major), Michael B., USMC, *From Metaphors to Models: Broadening the Lens of the Hunter Warrior Experiment with a Complex Adaptive System Tool*, Thesis, AY 98-99, Marine Corps Combat Development Command, Quantico, VA.

[Wheat92] Wheatley, Margaret J., *Leadership and the New Science: Learning about Organization from an Orderly Universe*, Berrett-Koehler Publishers, Inc., 1992.

[Weiss02] Weisstein, Eric W., *CRC Concise Encyclopedia of Mathematics*, Second Edition, CRC Press, 2002.

[Wiesen89] Wiesenfeld, Kurt, Chao Tang and Per Bak, "A Physicist's sandbox," *Jour. Stat Phy.*, Volume 54, 1989.

[Wigner60] Wigner, E., "On the Unreasonable Effectiveness of Mathematics in the Natural Sciences," *Comm. Pure. Appl. Math.*, Volume 13, 1-14, 1960.

[Wilh98] Wilhelm, Karen S., "Linear Thinkers in a Nonlinear World: Is There a Way Out?," Washington, DC: *National War College*, November 1998.

[Wilh99] Wilhelm, Karen S., *Toward a Nonlinear Theory of War*, Washington, DC: *National War College*, 1999: http://www.ndu.edu/library/n1/99-ASE-03.pdf.

[Wing95] Lt. Col. I. G. R. Wing, "Chaos theory and intelligence analysis," *Australian Defence Force Journal*, Volume 115, Nov/Dec 1995, 22-26.

[Wolfram83] Wolfram, S., "Statistical mechanics of cellular automata," *Rev. Mod. Phy.*, Volume 55, 1983, 601-644.

[Wolfram84a] Wolfram, S., "Universality and complexity in cellular automata," *Physica 10D*, 1-35, 1984.

[Wolfram84b] Wolfram, S., "Random sequence generation by cellular automata," *Advances in Applied Mathematics*, Volume 7, 1984, 123.

[Wolfram85] Wolfram, S., "Undecidability and intractability in theoretical physics," *Phy.*

Rev. Lett., Volume 55, 1985, 735-738.

[Wolfram86] Wolfram, S., editor, *Theory and Applications of Cellular Automata*, World Scientific, 1986.

[Wolfram94] Wolfram, S., *Cellular Automata and Complexity: Collected Papers*, Addison-Wesley, 1994.

[Wolfram02] Wolfram, S., *A New Kind of Science*, Wolfram Media, Inc., 2002.

[Wolp96] Wolpert, D. and W. Macready, "No free lunch theorems for optimization," *IEEE Transactions on Evolutionary Computation*, 1996.

[WolpL97] Wolpert, L., *Principles of Development*, Oxford University Press, 1997.

[Womack95] Womack, Scott Ellis., *Chaos,Clausewitz and Combat: A Critical Analysis of Operational Planning in the Vietnam War,* Monterey, CA: Navy Postgraduate School, December 1995.

[Wooda00] Woodaman, R.F.A., *Agent-Based Simulation of Military Operations Other Than War, Small Unit Combat*, Masters Thesis, Naval Postgraduate School, Monterey, California, September 2000.

[Woodc88] Woodcock, A. E. R., L. Cobb and J.T. Dockery, "Cellular Automata: A New Method for Battlefield Simulation," *Signal*, January, 41-50, 1988.

[Woodc96] Woodcock, A. E. R. and D. Davis, editors, *Analytic Approaches to the Study of Future Conflict*, The Canadian Peacekeeping Press, 1996.

[Woodc00] Woodcock, A. E. R. and L. Cobb, "Societal Dynamics Conflict Models and the Deployable Exercise Support (DEXES) System: http://www.dodccrp.org/ Proceedings/ DOCS/wcd00000/wcd0007a.htm; see also DEXES homepage: http://www. aetheling. com/models/MOOTW/DEXES.html.

[Wool02] Woolman, M., *Digital Information Graphics*, Watson-Guptill Publications, 2002.

[Wrang88] Wrangham, Richard W., "War in evolutionary perspective," pages 77-83 in *Emerging Syntheses in Science*, edited by D. Pines, Addison-Wesley, 1988.

[Wrights32] Wright, S., "The roles of mutation, inbreeding, crossbreeding and selection in evolution," pages 356-366 in *Proceedings of the Sixth International Congress on Genetics*, 1932.

[Wright89] Wright, W., *SimCity* (computer game), Orinda, California: Maxis Corporation, 1989.

[Yates87] Yates, F. Eugene, A. Garfinkel, D. Walter, and G. Yates, editors, *Self-Organizing Systems: The Emergence of Order*, Plenum Press, 1987.

[Youss95] Youssefmir, M. and B. A. Huberman, "Clustered volatility in multiagent dynamics," *Santa Fe Institute*, 95-05-051, 1995.

[Zieg00] Ziegler, B.P., H. Praehofer and T.G. Kim, *Theory of Modeling and Simulation: Integrating Discrete Event and Continuous Complex Dynamic Systems*, Second Edition, Academic Press, 2000.

[Zurek89] Zurek, W.H., "Algorithmic randomness and physical entropy," *Physical Review A*, Volume 40, 1989.

[Zurek90] Zurek, W. H., editor, *Complexity, entropy, and the physics of information: The Proceedings of the 1988 workshop on Complexity, Entropy and the Physics of Information, held May-June, 1989 in Santa Fe, New Mexico*, Addison-Wesley, Reading, MA, 1990.

[Zuse69] Zuse, K., *Rechnender Raum*, Vieweg, Braunschweig, 1969, translated as *Calculating Space*, Tech. Trans. AZT-70-164-GEMIT, MIT Project MAC, 1970.

Index

Lightning Source UK Ltd.
Milton Keynes UK
UKHW030642270919
350533UK00002B/27/P

9 789812 388346